Q
641.5636
S

A Worldwide Vegetarian Journey to Discover the Foods That Nourish America's Immigrant Soul

Judith Ader Spinzia

VOLUME I

Virtualbookworm Publishing   College Station, Texas

2015

"A Worldwide Vegetarian Journey to Discover the Foods That Nourish America's Immigrant Soul: Volume 1," by Judith Ader Spinzia ISBN 978-1-62137-731-3.

Library of Congress Control Number on file with Publisher.

Published 2015 by Virtualbookworm.com Publishing Inc., P.O. Box 9949, College Station, TX 77842, US.
© 2015 Judith Ader Spinzia. All rights reserved. No part of this publication may be reproduced, stored in a retrieval system, or transmitted in any form or by any means, electronic, mechanical, recording or otherwise, without the prior written permission of Raymond E. or Judith Ader Spinzia.

Manufactured in the United States of America

Table of Contents

Volume I

Acknowledgment and Dedication.	iv
Introduction .	v
Europe	1-462
Middle East	463-582
Caucasus	583-620
Central Asia	621-634
South Asia	635-707
Index (includes references to recipes in volumes I and II)	708

An individual table of contents precedes each section.

Volume II

Africa

Asia

Oceania

The Americas

Appendix of Basic Recipes

Index (includes references to recipes in volumes I and II)

I am sincerely grateful to my husband Raymond

for his never-ending support,

his ever-receptive palate for the new and unusual,

and for the considerable time and effort

needed to create the maps which accompany each section.

These two volumes are dedicated to the explorers who enabled this story

by carrying the foods of the Western Hemisphere around the globe

and to the generations of women who adopted these foods

and carried them back to the Western Hemisphere – our ethnic heritage.

introduction

Whether it was an apple or a tomato, whether it was *khintzor* (Armenian), *iabloki* (Russian), or *maca* (Portuguese); *pomodoro* (Italian), *paradicsom* (Hungarian), *domata* (Greek), it was recognizable in the New World. An abundance and variety of dishes exists because of this recognition. "Foods from home" could be prepared here and we are all the richer. The comings and goings on this continent throughout history have brought us a richness of culture and cuisine which we simply take for granted. So many foods came from the Western Hemisphere, the New World, making their way back to the Old World where they became a part of cuisines so diverse as to be truly remarkable. As these foods returned to America in the "receipt" boxes and handwritten notebooks of immigrants, we became the benefactors of the exploration of the Western Hemisphere all those centuries ago when we were not even a gleam in the ancestral eye.

As a "melting pot" we accept our collective "stew" and call it cuisine, generally, without any thought to its ingredients or origin. There is a complex and fascinating matrix upon which to build which offers us an opportunity to catapult our taste buds into a globe-spanning mindset, as yet, unrealized. Demand for spices, vegetables, and fruits by ethnic populations enrich us all as do those who write about their native cuisines in magazines and cookbooks. So too are we enriched by reconsideration of our native foods. It is this unique and most remarkable collective "mind" that is America; it is the America we must treasure and preserve, and pass on to future generations. For those of us who chose to eat neither meat nor fish there is a world of culinary inspiration and opportunity out there, and deep inside us.

What passes for "American cooking" is not, in our opinion representative of the rich, multi-layered cuisine that fills the kitchens of our country. It is presented by restaurants devoid of any interest or depth and it is rarely satisfying, although filling. This is not what Americans have received from their forebearers; this is not what Americans cook at home. The "pinches of this and that" added in the home kitchens of America can usually be traced through a family. We are seen as a young, often obstreperous, but forward-looking nation. Americans are always "the kids on the block" who try everything new, "teching" our way into the future, making new traditions that fit into new lifestyles, and using the phases "old-fashioned" and "get with it," perhaps too often. If we, indeed, are as forward-looking as we are reputed to be, then let us look forward into this century in terms of the food supply and the world's population potential. Does the "with it" world really have a handle on the future?

Our mothers and their generation were thrilled with canned and, then, frozen foods. They began to cut back on home gardening and their own preserving. The "Green Giant," cookie elves, friendly, efficient food economists, and generic chefs smiling out at us from packaging, became part of our family. We went to college and ate "mystery meat" and "gray chow mein" and soft white bread. We ate canned peach cobbler and frozen strawberry shortcakes in sponge cake cups, and artificially-flavored and artificially-colored everything.

introduction

We were doomed but we were too enthusiastic about the promises for the "World of Tomorrow" to comprehend what was happening.

After the institutional food experience anything tasted great. We began to accept the loss of taste and variety. The phenomenal success of "fast foods" during those years just reinforced our diminished expectations. We are at a crossroads in America today at which we can lose our culinary heritage to prepared foods and restaurant cooking. Two career families, busy schedules, and the readily-available prepared food products make people less and less willing to make the effort to learn to cook and to invest time in planning meals. The more that we accept the homogenized, packaged cuisine presented to us by the food industry, the more we lose the joy that cooking can be and the heritage we all can find inside ourselves if we scratch the surface a little. Families dispersed across our country do not hand down the technique of food preparation or the family recipes in the multi-generational kitchens of yesteryear. The dependence upon commercial products has been dramatically, and sadly, reflected in the success of a cookbook which collected "favorite" recipes from the side panels of boxed products. It is also clear when the term "from scratch" has come to mean nothing more than adding an egg and water to a mix!

This homogenization also seriously threatens us with a loss of variety and this, in turn, threatens the stability of the earth's food supply. The automated food industry demands uniformity. High yield and "hybrid vigor" have become the operational phrases. Unless you grow your own vegetables or live, as we do now, in a rural area where heirloom seeds may still be planted, the variety in greengrocers and grocery chain stores is increasingly limited to crop varieties which return a high profit and have a long and stable shelf-life. The loss of potato varieties is about as outrightly stupid as any society can possibly get, most especially a society which includes descendants of the approximately one million Irish who immigrated to the United States between 1815 and 1845 because of the crop failures, a period now generally known as the "Great Potato Famine." By 1855 one million of the Irish who remained behind had died due to starvation or sickness. Between 1855 and 1920, three million more emigrated from Ireland to the United States. It is in no way stretching a point to speculate that these too were victims of the crop failures. The following excerpted verse from Irish folk literature found in Oscar Handlin's 1968 book, *Boston Immigrants: A Study in Acculturation,* p. 144, illustrates: */the blackening of the potatoes / that drove us over the sea / to earn our pay in Baltimore/.*

Photographs of despondent Long Island farmers watching their dry, lifeless land being auctioned off to developers eerily remind us of the "dust bowl" tragedy in our Great Plains in the 1930s. The loss of the potato industry on Long Island in the 1940s and 1950s as a result of the Golden Nematode is not ancient history and to those farmers the "Great Potato Famine" was recent history. It is, however, clearly a senseless repeating of an agricultural tragedy by a society so arrogant as not to learn from history, and to those on Long Island and throughout the country who continued to plant the same potato variety since the 1940s.

A recent article stated that as few as four varieties of potato are grown commercially in the United States. A blight or the reemergence of the Golden Nematode or another voracious resistant mutation of the devastating potato beetle or some other unforeseen six-legged sabotage artist and its larvae, could, effectively,

introduction

destroy our potato growing-capability in a single season with catastrophic human and economic consequences. The same lack of biodiversity is true of many food crops including corn. Think of the ramifications of a total failure of the corn crop in the United States. Its consequences are almost unfathomable. Explore your local area and find out just how many different kinds of corn are being grown both as animal feed crops and for human consumption. Then ask how many of those corn hybrids set viable seeds which can be saved by the farmer for the subsequent year's crop. You may be quite shocked. Have you ever seen Bolivian red corn? Can you imagine a field of such beauty maturing in the July sun? Can you imagine a dish prepared with this dramatic corn? Blue corn varieties have found a niche and are available as wonderfully earthy-tasting products, albeit highly processed, such as corn chips but have you tried the ground blue corn meal instead of white or yellow corn meal or in combination?

"Seed and crop banks," such as the native Peruvian potato preservation projects and other projects which preserve and cultivate native American and non-hybridized varieties, including Seeds of Change (Santa Fe, New Mexico), Native Seeds/SEARCH (Tucson, Arizona), Hudson's Ethnobotanical Catalog of Seeds (Redwood City, California), Seed Savers Exchange (Decorah, Iowa), and Companion Plants (Athens, Ohio), offer us more hope than most of us truly comprehend but they can not store seeds in quantities sufficient to save a starving planet. Dramatic words? Perhaps, but the possibility can not be ignored. Alarmingly, it is estimated that some twenty-seven thousand flora and fauna species become extinct annually, an astounding acceleration from what would be considered a "natural rate" of species extinction. This is an average of over seventy species per day, so it would seem that the alarm has been sounded! The problem is, however, that extinction is such a silent alarm.

Tomatoes are a perfect example, but clearly a flawed result, of hybridizing for the commercial market. Occasionally, a letter to a food editor or garden column bemoans the loss of the tasty tomato and asks for sources from which to purchase seeds. The same person may order lettuce and tomato on a sandwich and accept the fact that they ate a slice of tomato whether it tasted like one or not; it was round and pink (never red anymore), and had seeds . . . . Can we truly afford to accept this destruction of that which makes our three-times-a-day eating habit enjoyable?

The threads of DNA are the links from the past to the present. These can be threads of diversity, threads of change, and, devastatingly, threads of extinction. When the patterns of diversity encoded in the genetic material are lost, so too is life. Variety is not just important as inspiration to the cook; it is vital to the survival and vitality of a species.

Historic crops such as amaranth, a relative of pigweed cultivated by the Aztecs, and quinoa, a relative of the common weed lamb's-quarters cultivated by the Incas, with their magnificent protein profiles are making a comeback and this is hopeful.

Beans, grains, and other seeds have survived a bit better in that the variety available is more extensive, but still a fraction of what was and what could be. Biodiversity continually shrinks as demand decreases. Have you tried Egyptian red (or pink) lentils, Borlotti beans, Adzuki beans, cranberry beans, or Roman beans?

introduction

Do you use buckwheat groats, grits, or flour in your baking? How many kinds of rice are included in your larder? Are glutinous or sweet rice, black, Asian soft Jasmine, Italian *Arborio*, and Indian *Basmati* varieties among them? How many varieties of wheat flour do you use in your cooking and baking? Decorative displays of legumes are sold in import and decorating stores. Granted they are destined for kitchen counters as decoration but we see these displays as a reminder that beans and pulses are beautiful and that there is unimagined diversity. Perhaps these small "life machines in seed coats" will awaken and sustain the survival mentality in those kitchens.

How many times have you heard someone tell you, "You can't solve all the world's problems; it's beyond your reach." Keep reaching. The amount of our annual grain harvest dedicated to the production of beer and liquor could sustain twenty million people for a year. (*Laurel's Kitchen*, p. 52.) Doesn't that make you want to keep reaching out no matter how short your reach? We now grow crops for biofuel production thus decreasing the supply dedicated to feeding the world and greatly increasing the cost of feed and food while using fossil fuels to produce the biofuel. Who are we fooling; how blind can we be?

We all know that most ruminant livestock, who are not allowed to graze freely but who instead spend most of their lives in feedlots, consume large quantities of grains and soybean byproducts that could feed human beings. Ruminants, such a beef cattle, are very efficient "four-stomach-machines" when they are allowed to graze freely or are fed silage. Grains and legumes, which could go directly to the feeding of the earth's human population, are consumed by monogastric livestock such as hogs and poultry to the exclusion of almost all other feed. This is especially true in the United States where these animals are fed almost exclusively with grains and soybean byproducts. Beef cattle are generally fed forage materials until the animals reach a weight of about 800-900 pounds. Grain-to-meat conversion ratio estimates for beef range widely and depend on several factors but it can be accurately said that about eight to ten pounds of grain is fed to feedlot animals to produce just one pound of meat. This is, in my view, an extremely inefficient system of protein management to address the nutritional needs of the world's hungry considering the fact that grazing animals convert only about six percent of the grasses on which they feed into weight. Grains are, on the other hand, completely edible by humans while only two-thirds of a butchered animal is eaten. Another factor to be considered when one accesses the "cost" of meat products in terms of resources is the water footprint, a concept developed in 2003. An estimate of about 1,800-2,000 gallons of water is required to produce one pound of beef, 576 gallons to produce one pound of pork, 468 gallons to produce one pound of chicken while the water footprint for soybeans is 206 gallons per pound; for wheat, 138 gallons per pound; and for corn, 108 gallons per pound.

Why not start with a small herb garden? Herbs give you beauty, fragrance, and excellent flavor in a single garden. Many herbs are meccas to pollinating insects and the larval or caterpillar stages of butterfly life cycles. Planning companion plantings and the inclusion of herbs and edible flowers which repel insect pests, attract insects that will do pest control for you, or attract pollinators, can become second only to the anticipation of the harvest as impetus. Leaves and seeds can easily be dried for culinary use throughout the

introduction

winter. Since there are herb varieties with first-class taste, a *small* herb garden can offer an unexpectedly large bonus to simple food preparations!

The annual herb may be in the greatest danger. If we do not take the time and effort to plant annual herbs and save their seeds, the demand for the seeds and plants decreases until they are no longer available. Sweet marjoram, summer savory, borage, dillweed, rosemary, chamomile, fennel, chervil, parsleys including fresh coriander or *cilantro*, a wide variety of basils including the red varieties, lemon verbena, tender salvias (sages), nasturtiums, and calendulas (or true marigolds) are all annuals that can contribute remarkable flavor nuances to our foods.

Mesclún, which has become unbelievably trendy, offers variety and we applaud its success. Cutting small, young leaf crops as you need them is ultimately practical, as well. It amazes us that stores still sell piles and piles of iceberg lettuce. A couple of rows of lettuces and related greens in your herb garden will provide a summer's fresh greens for your family—tiny little leaves of fresh spinach in the spring and hardy varieties in the fall and on into the winter, tiny beet greens, arugula, purslane, mache (lamb's lettuce or corn salad), mustards, miner's lettuce *(Claytonia montia)*, dandelions, sorrels; red and green leaf lettuces such as black-seeded Simpson, soft bibb or Boston, limestone, or butterhead varieties, curly and royal oakleaf lettuces, speckle and merlot, cress and *tatsoi*; summer heat resistant baby beet greens, deertongue, apollo, buttercrunch, old-fashioned French *kinemontpas*, and red lettuces such as a ruby red and red riding hood, cob or Romaine lettuce grown for just the small early leaves, curly endive, chicory, or *frisée*, as the tender young leaves are now designated. Even in a very small garden, such variety insures supply throughout the summer. If any member of this "lettuce committee" fails because of drought or too much rain or hungry deer or caterpillars, etc., another variety will be ready to feed. The kitchen garden represents on a small, very visible scale the larger and more dramatic need for biodiversity at a level which must ultimately be worldwide. It is, in essence, a microcosm of the challenge.

It is said that as much as seventy-five percent of the world eats "vegetarian" on any given day, generally not by choice but, instead, by necessity. What do these people eat? From what do they obtain their protein needs? It is far simpler than most people imagine. Our lifestyle fascinates our meat-eating friends but they always ask the same question, "How do you get enough protein?" We are and have been lacto-ovo vegetarians for more than forty years. Although we complement our proteins and eat vegan often and for extended periods, eggs and dairy products offer us more creative options. It is a comfortable ethical, nutritional, and culinary choice for us.

The concern over protein is unnecessary. Most people in the United States eat too much protein and, often in the same mouthful, too much fat. Meat-eating as a symbol of affluence is a worldwide phenomenon. A well-educated and well-traveled Muscovite, whom we met while visiting the former Soviet Union, admonished us on our meatless lifestyle saying that our daughter, then sixteen years old, needed meat. We were in her words, starving our child to death. She frequently quoted an article in *Pravda* that said that the person who ate meat three-times-a-day would be healthy. By the end of our visit, she admitted that we were

introduction

not suffering, we had plenty of energy, and we were thinner than she, so she was going to try a few meatless meals. Even in Asian countries where vegetables have a glorious role, the biggest and best piece of meat is removed from a dish by the host and presented to honored guests. Killing the fatted calf, the new lamb, or the best chicken to honor and celebrate, are traditions that die hard.

We have searched and experimented for years and we present to you an introduction to the world, if you will. The menu ideas included here are offered just to start you down a road of dinnertime adventure that need never end. We do not travel as much as we once did; we still travel and you too can travel as we do. Our destinations today are to our dining table to sample what makes America unique in this world, our collective heritage. Searching the old and new cookbooks and e-postings of other cooks I have seen the clues to supply and demand; to poverty and plenty; to agricultural practices, good and bad; to personal and national identity; and to seasonal joy. I have seen the evolution of my own family's eating habits as a result of World War II and as a result of health awareness. This vision I share with you.

Please note that in the menus and recipes that follow, you will see that we do not eschew carbohydrates, we maintain a low-fat life-style, and we try diligently to eat no more than our share of the earth's protein. You will also see that in our low-fat focus we have also chosen, for health reasons, to limit our exposure to Salmonella by using fat-free pasteurized eggs. The often banquet-sized menus that have been included in this work are presented to give you choice. It is very much like the perennial Thanksgiving question, "What do you eat, if you don't eat turkey?" There are plenty of options . . .

To make menu planning easy, food values accompany each recipe. It should be noted that these values are not the result of laboratory analysis and are, therefore, only approximate.

I give you my thoughts, my recipe ideas, and my own very personal style of recipe notation, albeit unorthodox, which has served me well for decades, and as complex and useful an index as possible but the rest is very much up to you. Adapt, adjust, modify, and enjoy the enormous variety of foods that you will encounter as you search.

Judith Ader Spinzia

Europe

Europe

Albania	3	Macedonia	261
Andorra	14	Malta	271
Austria	22	Moldova	280
Belarus	32	Montenegro	292
Belgium	43	The Netherlands	298
Bosnia and Herzegovina.	58	Norway	308
Bulgaria	69	Poland	319
Croatia	81	Portugal	328
Czech Republic	89	Romania	339
Denmark	99	Russia	349
Estonia	110	Serbia	362
Finland	119	Slovakia	371
France	130	Slovenia	381
Germany	141	Spain	391
Greece	155	Sweden	398
Hungary	172	Switzerland	405
Iceland	187	Ukraine	422
Ireland (Republic of)	192	United Kingdom / England	432
Italy	204	United Kingdom / Scotland	448
Latvia	229	United Kingdom / Wales	456
Liechtenstein	238		
Lithuania	244		
Luxembourg	252		

Europe–**Albania**

Albania

Paleolithic artifacts recovered in Xarrë in Albania, near the capital of Tirana, show a remarkable resemblance to those found at Paleolithic sites in Montenegro and in northwestern Greece suggesting the possibility of related, migratory peoples. Bronze Age artifacts also show this relationship. Greco–Roman historical records reference an area called Illyria, a region from which modern Albania emerged during the Middle Ages as the Principality of Arbër and the Sicilian dependency commonly referred to as the Kingdom of Albania. These two elements were merged into the Bulgarian Empire in the ninth century. Subsequently conquered and ruled by the Serbian Empire, Albania found itself under the rule of the Ottoman Empire by the fifteenth century, a rule that continued until 1912. In 1914 Prince William of Wied, a nephew of Queen Elisabeth of Romania, was chosen by the Great Powers to be the sovereign of the newly independent nation of Albania. He arrived in March and fled Albania in September with the outbreak of World War I, leaving the nation divided among religious and tribal loyalties. Muslims looked to Turkey for support while others felt that Italy and Serbia could better represent their interests. Later that same year Greece moved into southern Albania. Serbia and Montenegro occupied northern Albania until displaced by the Central Powers which led to the occupation of about two-thirds of the country by Austro–Hungarian and Bulgarian armies. In addition, areas of land including Valona were promised to Italy in the 1915 Treaty of London, as an inducement to Italy to enter the war against Austria–Hungary. Through all of the post-war partitions and struggles for control, Albania technically remained a monarchy until 1925 because William had never abdicated although he had chosen to leave this throne to return to Germany where he joined the German Army and fought on the Eastern Front. The First Albanian Republic, declared in 1924, survived only until 1928 when King Zogu (subsequently known as King Zog I) declared the republic again a monarchy. This monarchy survived until 1939 when Albania was absorbed into Fascist Italy. After the defeat of the Axis Powers, Albania declared itself the Socialist People's Republic of Albania. The communist regime in Albania ended in the 1990s after the collapse of the Soviet Union and Albania along with many other nations in the former Eastern Bloc began the difficult process of reorganizing their government along democratic principles. Stabilization of these emergent economies has been particularly difficult for these nations caught in the ripple effect of a worldwide financial recession. This instability has led to a large scale emigration from Albania to Italy, Greece, Switzerland, Germany, Canada, and to the United States.

Albania remained quite isolated for decades prior to the 1990s, leaving us a clear picture of its preserved historical contacts and the influences of these contacts that can be seen in its culture and cuisine as it emerges into the twenty-first century. Although Albania is categorized as a Balkan country, which clearly ties Albania to Europe, evidence of the Moslem traditions of the Middle East allow us to trace the fascinating history that created a culture quite unique in the modern world. Street vendors sell *byrek*, the crisp, baked *phyllo* triangles filled with cheese, spinach or meat that one also finds in the Middle East. *Baklava, kadaif, hallvë, dolmas* of all types, and *meze* platters also demonstrate the enduring debt that is owed to those from the East who conquered and ruled this country. Italian and Greek influences also abound in the Albanian cuisine.

Albania remains a nation that retains a seasonal approach to the foods eaten. Although you will see great variation from area to area, these traditional variations are all based on the availability of locally grown produce. Many authors are concerned that the importation of new foods and new dishes will cause the traditional respect for seasonality in the cuisine to be lost and the regional differences in cuisine to become less distinct. Food ideas are changing due in some part to the return of expatriates, the increase in tourism, and the now more open policy of foreign travel and foreign investment.

Europe–Albania

Individual Omelets with Cheese
Vezë me Feta

Meze Platter:
Brined Cheeses
Olives
Roasted Red Peppers
and
Stuffed Grape Leaves
Japrak

Linguine with *Feta* Cheese, Butter, and Black Pepper
Julka

Buttermilk
Dhalle

~

Vegetable Soup with Cabbage
Supë me Perimesh

Rice Soup with Eggs and Lemon
Supë Orizi me Vezë dhe Limon

~

Vegetable Salad
Sallat Grek

Potato Salad
Sallate me Patate

~~~~~~~~~~~~~~~~~~~~

Soy Meatballs with Garlic and Yogurt Curd
Qofte me Kos

Baked Leeks
Tave me Presh

~~~~~~~~~~

Spinach Pie
Byrek me Spinaq

Steamed and Sautéed Whole Carrots

~~~~~~~~~~

White Beans in Tomato Sauce
Jani me Fasul

Rice *Croquettes*
Qofte me Oriz

with Fried Tomato Slices
Domate Jahni

~~~~~~~~~~~~~~~~~~~~

Farina Pudding with Honey
Hashure

Egg Sponge Cake with Sugar Syrup
Pandispanjë

Fig Tarts
Byrek me Gliko me Fiq të Egër

Fig Pudding
Hoshaf me Fiq të Thatë

Goat Cheese and Pomegranates

Fruit Compote composed of a mixture of the following: Cherries, Peaches, Pears, Melon Balls, Fig Slices, Grapes, Apricots, or Apple Chunks with Ground Walnut Garnish

Europe–**Albania**

INDIVIDUAL OMELETS WITH CHEESE
Vezë me Feta
TPT - 12 minutes

Individual omelets make welcome and nutritious first-course offerings or light lunches. We have found that cooks in restaurants all over the world are always willing to accommodate the lacto-ovo vegetarian with an omelet, stuffed with vegetables and/or cheese. In Albania the cheeses most often found are a fresh white cheese, similar to queso blanco or mozzarella, and a briny feta.

Per serving:
1 large egg
1 teaspoon water

Freshly ground mixed peppercorns—red, black, and white— to taste

2 tablespoons *finely* **chopped** *part-skimmed milk mozzarella* **or** **Italian** *fontina* **cheese, as preferred**
About 1 tablespoonful *feta* **cheese**

Preheat oven to 200 degrees F. Place an oven-proof plate in the oven.

In a small dish or measuring cup, combine egg and water. Using a fork, mix well. Season with ground mixed peppercorns.

Turn into a 7-inch preheated non-stick-coated skillet. Allow egg to set on the bottom.

In the upper right-hand quarter of the omelet, pile *mozzarella* and *feta* cheese. Fold the bottom half of the omelet up over the top half of the omelet and cheese. Fold the left side over the right side forming a 90-degree wedge. Slide out with the help of a spatula onto the preheated plate in the oven. Return to the oven to allow the cheese to melt.

Repeat as many times as necessary.

Serve onto heated salad plates when cheese as melted.

Yields 1 serving

1 SERVING – PROTEIN = 12.3 g.; FAT = 11.2 g.; CARBOHYDRATE = 1.0 g.;
CALORIES = 149; CALORIES FROM FAT = 68%

ALBANIAN VEGETABLE SOUP WITH CABBAGE
Supë me Perimesh
TPT - about 55 minutes

Albanian food influences are not exclusively from the Mediterranean as this popular soup shows. The call for cream in this recipe is clear evidence that other influences are at work. Every winter evening soups similar to this show up on tables in the countries where German, Austrian, and Hungarian influences were left behind or to which these recipes were carried by émigrés. Albanians too have adopted and adapted recipes from the many cuisines to the North. This soup, no doubt, owes homage to borsht.

1 tablespoon butter
1/2 large onion—*finely slivered*

1 medium carrot—pared or scraped and diced
1/2 cup diced celery

2 teaspoons unbleached white flour
1/4 cup VEGETARIAN BROWN STOCK *[see index]* or VEGETABLE STOCK FROM SOUP *[see index]*
1/4 cup canned, *crushed* tomatoes *or* tomato purée

2 1/2 cups VEGETARIAN BROWN STOCK *[see index]* or VEGETABLE STOCK FROM SOUP *[see index]*
1 cup *finely* shredded cabbage

1 tablespoon red wine vinegar

1 medium potato—peeled and diced
1 medium beet—peeled and diced
Salt, to taste
Freshly ground black pepper, to taste

6 tablespoons light cream *or* half and half, for garnish

In a large kettle set over *MEDIUM* heat, melt butter. Add slivered onion and sauté just until onion softens, *being careful not to allow onion to brown.*

Add diced carrots and celery. Sauté for several minutes.

ALBANIAN VEGETABLE SOUP WITH CABBAGE (cont'd)

Add flour and cook, stirring constantly for a minute or two. *Gradually*, while stirring constantly, add the 1/4 cupful of stock and the crushed tomatoes to the ingredients in the kettle.

When the flour has been thoroughly integrated and a thick sauce has formed, *gradually* add the remaining 1 1/2 cupfuls stock and the shredded cabbage, stirring constantly while adding.

Add vinegar and cook, stirring frequently, for 15-20 minutes.

Add diced potatoes, diced beets, salt, and black pepper. Cook, stirring frequently, for about 20 minutes, or until vegetables are *crisp-tender*. Taste and correct seasoning if necessary.

Turn into a heated soup tureen. Serve into heated soup plates. Add 1 tablespoonful of cream to each serving.

Yields about 6 cupfuls

Note: This recipe can be doubled, when required.

1/6 SERVING – PROTEIN = 1.5 g.; FAT = 3.4 g.; CARBOHYDRATE = 5.2 g.;
CALORIES = 56; CALORIES FROM FAT = 55%

ALBANIAN RICE SOUP WITH EGGS AND LEMON
Supë Orizi me Vezë dhe Limon
TPT - 28 minutes

Undoubtedly Greek egg and lemon soup, avgolemono súpa, was introduced to the Albanians long before the modern era. Greeks often prefer to use orzo macaroni but Albanians, although fond of pasta to which they were introduced during periods of Greek and Italian occupation, omit the orzo and use rice.

7 cups VEGETARIAN WHITE STOCK [see index] **or VEGETABLE STOCK FROM SOUP** [see index]
1/3 cup dry converted rice
1/8 teaspoon *very finely* **and freshly grated** *organic* **lemon zest**

3 tablespoons freshly squeezed lemon juice
1/2 cup *fat-free* **pasteurized eggs (the equivalent of 2 eggs)****

Salt, to taste
Freshly ground *white* **pepper, to taste**

6 thin lemon slices, for garnish
1 1/2 tablespoon chopped fresh parsley, for garnish

In a kettle set over *MEDIUM* heat, bring stock to the boil. Add rice and grated lemon zest. Boil for about 30 minutes. Remove from heat.

In a mixing bowl, using a wire whisk, beat pasteurized eggs into lemon juice until light in color. While beating, add 2 tablespoonfuls hot soup stock. Continue adding hot stock—*tablespoonful by tablespoonful*—until about one-half of stock has been added. While stirring the remaining warm stock with a wooden spoon, add egg–lemon–stock mixture. Set over *LOW* heat and blend thoroughly while heating through. *Do not allow soup to come to the boil again as the egg may curdle.*

Taste and season with salt and *white* pepper, as necessary. Pour into a heated soup tureen.

Serve at once into heated soup cups. Float a thin slice of lemon, sprinkled with chopped parsley, on each serving.

Yields six 1-cup servings

Notes: *Because raw eggs present the danger of *Salmonella* poisoning, commercially-available pasteurized eggs are recommended for use in preparing this dish.

When required, this recipe may be doubled or tripled with ease.

1/6 SERVING – PROTEIN = 2.5 g.; FAT = 0.1 g.; CARBOHYDRATE = 4.1 g.;
CALORIES = 28; CALORIES FROM FAT = 3%

Europe–**Albania**

ALBANIAN VEGETABLE SALAD
Sallat Grek

TPT - 30 minutes;
  20 minutes = artichoke cooling period

If you think this salad is somehow familiar, you surely must have eaten a salad found in all Greek-American diners. This salad suggests a clear thread to the cuisines of the eastern Mediterranean, specifically to that Greek salad, horiatiki salata, but, unlike the Greek version, it is rarely served with a dressing other than a drizzle of olive oil.

2 teaspoons *extra virgin* olive oil
1/2 cup *frozen* artichoke hearts—*defrosted*

2 tomatoes—well-washed and chopped
1 cucumber—peeled, if not organic, halved, and sliced
1 small onion—*thinly* sliced
1/2 green pepper—thinly cut into strips
3 tablespoons *pitted Kalamata* olives—sliced

1 tablespoon *extra virgin* olive oil
Freshly ground black pepper, to taste
1/2 cup chopped *feta* cheese

In a skillet set over *MEDIUM* heat, heat the 2 teaspoonfuls olive oil. Add defrosted artichoke hearts. Sauté just until the artichokes begin to brown. Transfer to a mixing bowl. Refrigerate for 20 minutes to cool.

To the artichoke hearts, add chopped tomato, cucumber and onion slices, green pepper strips, and sliced olives. Toss to mix. Turn onto a platter.

Drizzle remaining tablespoonful of olive oil over. Grind black pepper over. Scatter *feta* cheese over.

Serve chilled.

Yields 6 servings
adequate for 4 people

Note: This recipe can be halved or doubled, when required.

1/6 SERVING – PROTEIN = 4.0 g.; FAT = 7.8 g.; CARBOHYDRATE = 5.4 g.;
CALORIES = 107; CALORIES FROM FAT = 69%

POTATO SALAD
Sallate me Patate

TPT - 1 hour and 46 minutes;
  10 minutes = potato cooling period;
  1 hour = salad refrigeration period

Although quite different from the potato salads made by my family, one step is consistent with that which was noted in the recipe book of my great-grandmother. Onions, vinegar, salt, and pepper are added to the potatoes while the potatoes are hot. Even in my mother's potato salad with mayonnaise, the onions, vinegar, salt, and pepper are added to the hot potatoes before chilling and then adding the remaining ingredients, a procedure taught to her by my German grandmothers.

4 quarts *boiling* water
4 long *narrow, not round,* russet potatoes—well-scrubbed

1/2 cup *finely* chopped onion
2 tablespoons GARLIC–BASIL VINEGAR *[see index] or* other vinegar of choice
Salt, to taste
Freshly ground black pepper, to taste
2 tablespoons *extra virgin* olive oil

2 tablespoons *finely* chopped fresh parsley

In a large kettle set over *MEDIUM-HIGH* heat, combine *boiling* water and potatoes. Boil for about 25 minutes, or until cooked but still firm. Remove to cutting board. Allow potatoes to cool for about 10 minutes. Peel and pat dry. Slice potatoes into even, 1/4-inch slices. Place slices attractively on a serving platter.

Sprinkle *finely* chopped onion over the potatoes. Sprinkle vinegar evenly over warm potatoes. Sprinkle salt and black pepper over potatoes. Drizzle olive oil over potatoes. Refrigerate for at least 1 hour to allow for flavor development.

POTATO SALAD (cont'd)

Sprinkle parsley over before serving. Serve chilled or at room temperature, as preferred.

Yields 6 servings
adequate for 4 people

Note: This recipe can be halved or doubled, when required.

1/6 SERVING – PROTEIN = 1.5 g.; FAT = 3.8 g.; CARBOHYDRATE = 15.3 g.;
CALORIES = 102; CALORIES FROM FAT = 34%

SOY MEATBALLS WITH GARLIC AND YOGURT CURD
Qofte me Kos
TPT - 12 minutes

Meatballs are most often made from ground lamb meat in Albania but "sham" meatballs, as they are called by one travel author, are also widely consumed. These sham meatballs are also bathed in all kinds of sauces and served in homes and in restaurants in Albania making it possible for a vegetarian to enjoy the seasoning that is so uniquely Albanian. Isolated for decades, Albania has preserved its cuisine but fast food restaurants are opening in all the cities. Believe it or not, if you can't find a vegetarian dish in a local restaurant, you most likely will have the alternative of pizza just down the block.

In this version the yogurt is allowed to curdle giving this dish a very different texture and allowing the diner to scoop up the garlicky milk solids with each forkful of meatball.

1 1/2 cups PLAIN YOGURT *[see index]* **or**
commercially-available plain yogurt
2 tablespoons GARLIC OIL *[see index]*

18 small vegetarian "meatballs"

In a small bowl, combine yogurt and garlic oil. Using a small wire whisk, combine thoroughly. Turn into a non-stick-coated skillet set over *MEDIUM* heat.

Add meatballs. Cook, stirring frequently, until meatballs are heated through and the yogurt has curdled. Pour through a sieve, discarding the liquid extruded. Turn the meatballs and the yogurt curds into a heated serving dish.

Serve at once.

Yields 6 servings
adequate for 4 people

Note: This recipe can be halved, when required.

1/6 SERVING (i. e., 3 meatballs with sauce) –
PROTEIN = 10.5 g.; FAT = 7.1 g.; CARBOHYDRATE = 10.9 g.;
CALORIES = 142; CALORIES FROM FAT = 45%

ALBANIAN BAKED LEEKS
Jave me Presh
TPT - 1 hour and 20 minutes

Leeks are often included in our menus. I have found over the years that sautéed leeks are good but sautéed and baked leeks are truly wonderful. This recipe from Albania transforms the leeks into a soft and sweet side dish that is so good that I never have leftovers no matter how many leeks I prepare. Albanians often add ground meat to this dish but we are more than satisfied with this recipe.

ALBANIAN BAKED LEEKS (cont'd)

3 large leeks—trimmed of green portion, well-washed, and cut into diagonal slices

2 tablespoons *extra virgin* olive oil

1/2 cup *finely* chopped onion

3 tablespoons tomato purée
2 tablespoons water
Salt, to taste
Freshly ground mixed peppercorns—black, red, and white—to taste

Preheat the oven to 300 degrees F. Prepare a 1-quart soufflé dish or other oven-to-table baking dish by coating with non-stick lecithin spray coating.

Place leeks slices in a salad spinner. Rinse and spin and drain until all the sand has been removed. Spin dry.

In a large skillet set over *LOW-MEDIUM* heat, heat oil. Add *finely* chopped onion and leeks and sauté until soft and translucent, *being careful not to allow vegetables to brown*. Remove from heat.

Add tomato purée, water, salt, and ground mixed peppercorns. Mix well. Turn into prepared baking dish. Cover tightly with aluminum foil. Bake in preheated 300 degree F. oven for 1 hour.

Serve hot.

Yields 6 servings
adequate for 4 people

Notes: This recipe can be halved or doubled, when required.

Leftovers can be frozen, if desired.

1/6 SERVING – PROTEIN = 0.6 g.; FAT = 3.8 g.; CARBOHYDRATE = 3.7 g.;
CALORIES = 50; CALORIES FROM FAT = 68%

ALBANIAN SPINACH PIE
Byrek me Spinaq
TPT - 1 hour and 3 minutes

This is not spanakopita, the spinach pie so often badly made and over salted that one finds in Greek-American delis and diners. It is a delicate, not soggy, and easily made main course or appetizer. By baking it on a cookie sheet, instead of in a baking pan or pie plate, the bottom remains dry and crisp.

5 ounces baby spinach leaves—trimmed of petioles and well-rinsed*

1/2 cup diced *feta* cheese
1/2 cup *finely* chopped onion *or* scallions, if preferred
1/2 cup *fat-free* pasteurized eggs (the equivalent of 2 eggs)

10 full sheets *frozen phyllo* pastry—*defrosted*
2 tablespoons safflower *or* sunflower oil
2 tablespoons grated *pecorino Romano* cheese**

Preheat oven to 350 degrees F. Prepare a 9 x 15-inch baking sheet by lining it with culinary parchment paper and by coating the parchment with non-stick lecithin spray coating.

Put spinach leaves into a large saucepan set over *LOW-MEDIUM* heat. Do not add water; the water adhering to the leaves from rinsing should be sufficient. Cover and steam until spinach is wilted. Using a fork, remove spinach to paper toweling and pat dry to remove as much residual moisture as possible. Turn into a mixing bowl.

Add diced *feta*, *finely* chopped onion, and pasteurized eggs. Mix well. Set aside briefly.

Place one sheet of *phyllo* pastry on prepared baking sheet. Brush with oil and sprinkle grated cheese around the edge of the pastry sheet. Repeat until you have five sheets of *phyllo* in place.

Spoon spinach–*feta* mixture across the stacked *phyllo* leaves, being sure to spread it evenly. Allow a margin all the way around of at least 1/2 inch.

Place one sheet of *phyllo* pastry on top of the spinach mixture. Brush with oil and sprinkle grated cheese around the edge just as you did with the base layers. Repeat until you have the remaining five sheets of *phyllo* in place.

Using a sharp knife, score the spinach pie to delineate six pieces.

Bake in preheated 350 degree F. oven for about 35 minutes, or until crisp and browned.

Europe–**Albania**

ALBANIAN SPINACH PIE (cont'd)

Cut on scored lines to make six servings. *Serve hot.*

Yields 6 servings
adequate for 4 people

Notes: *Do not substitute canned or frozen spinach.

**Grated cheese between the layers of *phyllo* helps to hold the layers together.

This recipe can be halved, when required.

1/6 SERVING – PROTEIN = 7.4 g.; FAT = 9.2 g.; CARBOHYDRATE = 12.8 g.;
CALORIES = 167; CALORIES FROM FAT = 50%

ALBANIAN WHITE BEANS IN TOMATO SAUCE
Jani me Fasul

TPT - 33 minutes

Although Albanian cooks go to great trouble to make this dish using dried white beans, canned cannellini beans can get this dish to the table in very short order.

1 can (15.5 ounces) *cannellini* **beans**

1/2 cup water

1 tablespoon *extra virgin* **olive oil**
1/2 cup *finely* **chopped onion**

3 tablespoons canned, *crushed* **tomatoes** *or* **thick tomato purée**
1/2 teaspoon salt
1/2 teaspoon chili powder

2 tablespoons chopped parsley
1 tablespoon chopped fresh mint *or* **1 teaspoon crushed, dried mint**

Drain *cannellini* beans, reserving canning liquid. Set beans aside until required.

In a measuring cup combine 1/2 cupful of reserved canning liquid and 1/2 cupful water. Mix to combine. Set aside until required.

In a saucepan set over *LOW-MEDIUM* heat, heat the 1 tablespoonful of oil. Add *finely* chopped onions and sauté until onions are soft and translucent, *being careful not to allow onions to brown.*

Add crushed tomatoes, canning liquid–water, salt, and chili powder. Cook, stirring frequently, until quite thick.

Add chopped parsley and mint, and drained beans. Cook, stirring frequently, until hot. Turn into a heated serving bowl.

Serve hot.

Yields 6 servings
adequate for 4 people

Notes: This recipe can be doubled, when required.

Cooked, dried beans can be used in this recipe. However, the bean cooking water does not give the same thick consistency to the sauce.

1/6 SERVING – PROTEIN = 3.1 g.; FAT = 2.2 g.; CARBOHYDRATE = 12.1 g.;
CALORIES = 82; CALORIES FROM FAT = 24%

Europe–**Albania**

ALBANIAN RICE *CROQUETTES*
Qofte me Oriz

TPT - 1 hour and 28 minutes;
1 hour = refrigeration period

When you first become a vegetarian, you do "think protein" a bit too much and if your new lifestyle effects a child, the world "talks protein" way too much. I remember well the excessive concern for our sixteen-year-old daughter's health expressed by our guide in Russia. She even quoted an article in Pravda that extolled meat-eating and warned against vegetarianism. As we have traveled the world we have often encountered the question as to why would one choose not to eat meat if one had the money to buy meat. The Albanian recipes that I have collected over the years seem to reflect the philosophy that a dish made with meat could always profit from the addition of another kind of meat, eggs, and/or cheese. I knew that beneath this bravado of protein plenty there must be another repertoire of recipes such as this recipe which was touted as "rice meatballs" by one author. They are delicious and quite delicate.

1 1/2 cups *chilled, cooked,* **short grain rice**
1/4 cup *fat-free* **pasteurized eggs (the equivalent of 1 egg)**
1 teaspoon *crushed, dried* **mint leaves**
Freshly ground black pepper, to taste

High-heat **safflower** *or* **sunflower oil**

In a mixing bowl, combine *cooked, cold* rice, pasteurized eggs, crushed, dried mint, and black pepper. Mix well. Refrigerate for 1 hour.

Pour oil into a deep skillet to a depth of 1/2-inch. Set over *MEDIUM* heat.

Using two soup spoons, create a *croquette* by packing a portion of the rice mixture firmly. Slide it into the hot oil. Form several more and add them to the skillet. Allow to fry until lightly browned on the bottom. Carefully turn each over and brown on the remaining side. Remove to paper toweling to drain while you continue to form and fry the remaining *croquettes*.

Place drained *croquettes* on a heated serving platter.

Serve hot.

Yields about 12 *croquettes*

Note: This recipe can be halved or doubled, when required

1/12 SERVING (i. e., per *croquette*) –
PROTEIN = 1.0 g.; FAT = 1.7 g.; CARBOHYDRATE = 6.1 g.;
CALORIES = 39; CALORIES FROM FAT = 39%

ALBANIAN EGG SPONGE CAKE WITH SUGAR SYRUP
Pandispanjë

TPT - 1 hour and 36 minutes;
1 hour = syrup soaking period

This recipe, usually made with whole eggs, can be made with fat-free pasteurized eggs. It is still a rich-tasting dessert but it then becomes a treat that allows for a second helping without guilt. I also make a light sugar syrup rather than the heavier syrup popular among Albanian cooks.

1 1/4 cups *fat-free* **pasteurized eggs (the equivalent of 5 eggs)**
5 tablespoons sugar
1 1/2 teaspoons pure vanilla extract

5 tablespoons unbleached white flour

SIMPLE SYRUP:
    1 cup sugar
    2 cups water

Preheat oven to 350 degrees F. Prepare an 8-inch square or 6 x 10-inch baking pan by coating with non-stick lecithin spray coating for baking.

In the bowl of the electric mixer, combine pasteurized eggs, 5 tablespoonfuls sugar, and vanilla extract. Mix at LOW speed until the mixture is thick.

Add flour. Mix until integrated. Turn into prepared baking pan. Bake in preheated 350 degree F. oven for 25 minutes, or until golden brown.

ALBANIAN EGG SPONGE CAKE WITH SUGAR SYRUP (cont'd)

While cake is baking, PREPARE SIMPLE SYRUP by placing the 1 cupful sugar and 2 cupfuls water in a deep saucepan set over *MEDIUM* heat. Boil until syrup reaches 200 degrees on a candy thermometer. At this point you should have a syrup that drips slowly from a spoon. Pour the syrup over the cake. Set aside for about 1 hour to allow the syrup to penetrate.

Cut into squares to serve. Remove to a serving plate using a small spatula or *lasagne* serving spoon.

Yields 8 servings
adequate for 6 people

Note: This recipe can be doubled and baked in a 13 x 9 x 2-inch baking pan, if required.

1/6 SERVING – PROTEIN = 4.2 g.; FAT = 0.04 g.; CARBOHYDRATE = 42.2 g.;
CALORIES = 185; CALORIES FROM FAT = <1%

ALBANIAN FIG TARTS
Byrek me Gliko me Fiq të Egër
TPT - 53 minutes

Since Albanians still observe the seasonality of the food supply, much as my family did when I was growing up, preservation of harvested fruits and vegetables for winter use is an important task of each homemaker. As a consequence one finds many recipes that employ dried fruits such as prunes and figs. These tarts are so simple and yet dramatic when presented as "another dessert" after a holiday meal. You can make your own fig conserve or jam. These are usually dense and more flavorful than are the commercially-available products. Failing this, specialty shops and well-stocked grocery stores often carry fig jams.

6 sheets *frozen phyllo* pastry—*defrosted*
2 tablespoons *melted* butter

4 tablespoons fig preserve

Preheat oven to 375 degrees F.

Place one sheet of *phyllo* pastry on a work surface. Brush with butter. Divide in half. Fold one of the halves in half again. Brush with butter. Fold in half again. Press the square of buttered *phyllo* into a muffin/cupcake tin.

Continue in the same manner with the remaining half-a-sheet and then proceed to do the same to the remaining five sheets of *phyllo*.

Bake in preheated 375 degree F. oven for about 13 minutes. Remove from muffin tin to a serving plate.

Spoon a teaspoonful of fig preserve in the center of each baked *phyllo* tart.

Serve at room temperature.

Yields 12 servings

Note: This recipe can be halved or doubled, when required.

1/12 SERVING (i. e., per pastry) –
PROTEIN = 0.4 g.; FAT = 2.0 g.; CARBOHYDRATE = 8.0 g.;
CALORIES = 47; CALORIES FROM FAT = 38%

Europe–Albania

ALBANIAN FIG PUDDING
Hoshaf me Fiq të Thatë

TPT - 41 minutes

I go out of my way to find figs that have not been preserved with chemicals but the shelf-life of natural dried figs is much shorter than those that have infused with sulfites and benzoates. Often, too often, dried figs, bought in the fall, become hard as rocks by mid-winter. I used to stew them until I stumbled across this Albanian recipe and now I sort of hope that there will be a forgotten bag of figs in the downstairs refrigerator.

12 *hard, dried* figs—well-brushed and rinsed
3 cups *boiling* water

1 quart *two-percent* milk
3/4 cup sugar

Ground cinnamon

Place dried figs in a bowl. Add *boiling* water. Allow to stand for about 5 minutes to soften slightly. Remove and drain. Cut figs in half.

Put figs into the work bowl of the food processor fitted with steel knife and process until finely chopped.

In a saucepan, preferably non-stick-coated, set over *MEDIUM* heat, combine milk and sugar. Cook, stirring frequently, until sugar is dissolved.

Add chopped figs. Cook, stirring frequently, until mixture boils and thickens. Remove from heat and divide among six small dessert dishes.

Sprinkle each serving with cinnamon. Refrigerate to cool or allow to cool to room temperature, if preferred.

Yields 6 individual servings

Note: This recipe can be halved or doubled, when required.

1/6 SERVING – PROTEIN = 6.2 g.; FAT = 3.5 g.; CARBOHYDRATE = 55.2 g.;
CALORIES = 265; CALORIES FROM FAT = 12%

Andorra

As I finished my chapter on Spain, I was disappointed not to be able to include more of the unique cuisine of Catalonia. It deserved a chapter of its own so I decided to explore the cuisine of Andorra, an isolated principality where the Catalan language is spoken and where the Catalan cuisine is preserved.

Formed in 1278, Andorra is a tiny principality in the Pyrenees that borders France and Spain. It is the fourth smallest nation in Europe. With a land mass of only 181 square miles Andorra is about the size of San Jose, California, or the combined land mass of the New York City Boroughs of Queens and Brooklyn. Andorra's population is about 78,000 while San Jose's population is about 946,000 and Queens and Brooklyn together are home to close to five million people.

Andorra's parliamentary principality is actually a co-principality in which the President of France and the Spanish bishop of Urgell function as a joint suzerainty. This unusual co-governing structure has existed since 1278. Prior to that it was a territory created in the 800s AD through a charter granted by Charlemagne with the intention of creating a buffer between the Moors and the French. With Charlemagne's death in 814, the territory was inherited by his son. The territory was within the diocese of Urgell, a diocese that had become infamous as the seat of a heretic bishop known as Felix, Bishop of Urgell, whose teachings were declared adoptianist in 794 by the Council of Frankfurt. Proclaimed a heretic, Felix was exiled from Urgell, dying twenty-four years later in Lyon. Through Charlemagne's son and his family, the scandal of the former bishop notwithstanding, the territory passed to the Bishop of La Seu d'Urgall, who, to this day, retains a governing position due to the fact that during the eleventh century the bishop's office and lands became a protectorate of the Lord of Caboet. Subsequently, through intermarriage, the French Count of Foix became heir to the territory initiating a dispute between the French count and the Catalan bishop. In 1278 the unusual governance plan resolved the dispute.

Andorran's reputation as a tax haven, banking center, and tariff-free commerce center have brought it from relative obscurity into the mainstream of European commerce in recent decades. Tourism is now Andorra's most important industry due to its spectacular mountainous terrain which provides for both winter and summer activities. They host an estimated 10.2 million visitors annually.

The demand for diversity in restaurant cuisine has greatly impacted a cuisine that for centuries has been insolated from other European cuisines. Nevertheless, traditional Catalan dishes and local dishes can still be found. A case-in-point are *calçots*, passionately consumed by those who enjoy Catalan cuisine. Yes, they are green onions but not your run-of-the-mill scallions. They, I have found, can be grown in the kitchen garden. Buy large Spanish onions in September and cut the tops off about one inch down. Set them into a trench about eight inches deep. When they begin to sprout, pile dirt around the new growth to blanch it as you would for celery. Many *calçots* will grow from a single onion surface. In January or February harvest, wash thoroughly, grill, and wrap the onions in newspapers to steam. The outer leaves are then peeled off, the white portion is dipped in Romesco sauce, and you throw your head back and unceremoniously slurp down the onion. I have planted them and eaten them and am convinced that no Vidalia salad onion can be sweeter.

Europe–Andorra

Goat Cheese on Toast

~

Warm Spinach Salad with Mushrooms and Garlic
Espinacas Calent amb Bolets

Wilted Dandelion Salad
Diente de Leòn Marchitada

~

Savory Apple Soup
Consomé de Pomes

~~~~~~~~~~~~~~~~~~~~~~

Mixed Grilled Vegetables
Escalivada

with

Sweet and Sour Onion Relish with Olives
Amanida de Cebas

and

Allioli Sauce with Eggs
Allioli amb Ous

Mushroom Fritters   and   Lima Beans
Bunyols de Ciurenys

~~~~~~~~~~

Savory Bread with Vegetables and Sausage
Coca amb Recapte

Baked Tomato Halves with Parsley and Pine Nuts

~~~~~~~~~~~~~~~~~~~~~

Sliced Pears with Ice Cream and Fresh Strawberry Sauce
Peras y Gelat de Canyella amb Culis de Maduixes

Warm Cream Cheese with Honey
Mel i Matò

ANDORRAN WARM SPINACH SALAD WITH MUSHROOMS AND GARLIC
Espinacas Calent amb Bolets

TPT - 1 hour and 23 minutes;
1 hour = raisin soaking period

Americans tend to consider a dish like this a vegetable and not a salad but I can't tell you how many times I have been served such a dish in Europe as a salad course. I have a friend to whom a salad is a specific assortment of cold, coarsely chopped, raw vegetables and lettuce to which one adds bottled dressing; it never varies. She might even say that we can't have a salad tonight because we don't have a red pepper. Salads can take many forms; my files overflow with ideas. Some traditional warm salads have survived such as wilted lettuce and roasted root vegetable salads, both of which are still traditional in my family.

ANDORRAN WARM SPINACH SALAD WITH MUSHROOMS AND GARLIC (cont'd)

3 tablespoons *preservative-free dark* raisins
1 cup *boiling* water

2 tablespoons *extra virgin* olive oil
10 ounces mushrooms—trimmed, rinsed, cleaned well with a brush, and chopped*

2 garlic cloves—*thinly* sliced

3 tablespoons white wine

10 ounces baby spinach—trimmed, well-washed, and dried

Salt, to taste
Freshly ground black pepper, to taste
2 tablespoons slivered, *preservative-free* almonds

In a small bowl, combine raisins and *boiling* water. Cover and allow the raisins to plump for at least 1 hour. Drain thoroughly.

In a non-stick-coated skillet set over *LOW-MEDIUM* heat, heat oil. Add chopped mushrooms. Cook, stirring frequently, until mushrooms are dry and lightly browned.

Add garlic slices and continue sautéing until garlic is soft, *being careful not to allow the garlic to brown.*

Add wine and cook, stirring constantly, to deglaze the skillet. Remove skillet from heat.

Add spinach and raisins. Stir until spinach is wilted.

Season with salt and pepper. Toss to mix well. Add almond slivers. Toss. Turn into a serving bowl.

Serve while still warm.

Yields 6 servings
adequate for 4 people

Notes: *Shaggy mane or pom pom mushrooms are my favorite mushrooms to use in this salad, although others will do.

This recipe can be doubled when required.

1/6 SERVING – PROTEIN = 3.3 g.; FAT = 5.3 g.; CARBOHYDRATE = 9.7 g.;
CALORIES = 97; CALORIES FROM FAT = 49%

WILTED DANDELION SALAD
Diente de León Marchitada
TPT - 10 minutes

I remember the many times I saw elderly ladies gathering dandelion greens along the parkways on Long Island. Neither a safe nor healthy adventure, thought I, and bought dandelion greens from an organic greengrocer instead. As long as I can remember, nature's spring tonic has appeared as a feature of spring menus. My mother eschewed such foraging but everybody else I knew loved the bitter greens either drenched in a sweet vinaigrette or wilted as in this recipe. I have even been served dandelion greens with a mayonnaise dressing. These bitter greens are usually dressed with a warm bacon vinaigrette in Andorra; I have substituted coarsely grated Romano or Parmesan cheese.

40 dandelion leaves (4 1/2 cups)—trimmed, well-washed, and dried
2 scallions *or calçots*, if you have grown them —*thinly* sliced
4 teaspoons sugar
Freshly ground black pepper, to taste

6 tablespoons vegetable oil
2 garlic cloves—smashed
6 tablespoons apple cider vinegar

4 teaspoons *coarsely* grated *pecorino Romano or* Parmesan cheese

Break leaves into bite-sized pieces, discarding tough vein areas. Turn into warmed serving bowl. Add scallion slices, sugar, and black pepper. Toss thoroughly.

In a small skillet or saucepan set over *MEDIUM-HIGH* heat, heat oil and smashed garlic clove. Sauté clove in oil for about 3 minutes. Remove clove and discard. Add cider vinegar and continue heating. When *very hot*, pour over dandelion mixture and toss until wilted.

Sprinkle grated cheese over. Toss.

Europe–**Andorra**

WILTED DANDELION SALAD (cont'd)

Serve at once using a large slotted spoon and large meat fork as utensils. *(1/2 cupful of oil-cider vinegar dressing should be residual in the serving dish.)*

Yields 6 servings
adequate for 4 people

Note: Dandelions, like spinach or lettuce, wilt down significantly. You may wish to double this recipe if you have six or more diners.

1/6 SERVING – PROTEIN = 1.5 g.; FAT = 8.9 g.; CARBOHYDRATE = 6.7 g.;
CALORIES = 109; CALORIES FROM FAT = 73%

SAVORY APPLE SOUP
Consomé de Pomes

TPT - 23 minutes

A beautiful consommé was most definitely still a first course option in the 1960s and 1970s. I even made my own chicken and beef stock. The slow sipping of a clear soup did take the edge off the appetite. Few people today would even think of consommé for a family meal. Times do change. Andorrans still enjoy clear soups and I have put rather a twist on this delightful soup by making it with vegetable stock.

6 cups VEGETABLE STOCK FROM SOUP
[see index] **or other vegetarian stock of choice**
5 Gala *or* **Golden Delicious apples—peeled, cored, and chopped**

Salt, to taste
Freshly ground black pepper, to taste

1 Gala *or* **Golden Delicious apple—peeled, cored, and chopped—for garnish**

Line a fine sieve with a cotton tea towel and set it over a saucepan.

In another saucepan set over *MEDIUM* heat, combine vegetable stock and the five chopped apples. Allow to come to the boil. Reduce heat to *LOW-MEDIUM* and allow the soup to simmer until the apples are mushy. Remove from heat.

Using the electric blender, purée the soup in batches until totally liquefied. Pour through the towel-lined sieve. Place the saucepan with the sieved consommé over *LOW-MEDIUM* heat and allow it to heat through. Taste and season with salt and black pepper, if necessary. Turn into a heated tureen.

Serve into heated soup plates. Garnish each serving with the reserved, chopped apple.

Yields 6 cupfuls

Note: This recipe can be halved or doubled, when required.

1/6 SERVING (i. e., per cupful) –
PROTEIN = 0.2 g.*; FAT = 0.3 g.*; CARBOHYDRATE = 12.4 g.*;
CALORIES = 55*; CALORIES FROM FAT = 1%*

*Vegetable stocks offer nutrition but calculating homemade stocks is just guesswork. Therefore, no values have been included in the soup's nutritional calculation.

Europe–**Andorra**

CATALAN – STYLE MIXED GRILLED VEGETABLES
Escalivada

TPT - 1 hour and 44 minutes

"Escalivada" derives from the Spanish verb "escalivar" which means to cook in hot ashes. In parts of Spain this is called "Ensalada murciana" since the grilled or roasted vegetables are served cold, dressed with oil, lemon, salt, and pepper. The vegetables can be grilled on an outdoor barbecue, prepared on an indoor grill or grill pan, or baked in the oven. When we were in Italy, we found that a similar cold salad of vegetables is available in most restaurants for the noon meal. Accompanied with piece of fresh mozzarella, a crusty loaf of bread, and a glass of wine, it is a good lunch and a treasured memory.

2 tablespoons *extra virgin* olive oil
1 garlic clove—smashed
1 bay leaf—halved

2 small eggplants—sliced lengthwise
1 small Italian red onion—peeled and sliced into thick slices
1 small Spanish onion—peeled and sliced into thick slices
2 medium all-purpose potatoes—peeled and cut into thick slices

1 tablespoon *extra virgin* olive oil
2 red bell peppers—well-washed
2 green bell peppers—well-washed
6 large garlic cloves—*unpeeled*

Salt, to taste
Freshly ground black pepper, to taste
Lemon wedges

In a skillet set over *MEDIUM* heat, combine 2 tablespoons olive oil, smashed garlic, and bay leaf pieces. Heat until hot.

In a jelly roll pan or cookie sheet with sides, arrange eggplant, onion, and potato slices. Pour hot oil over. Turn frequently to coat vegetables with seasoned oil.

Meanwhile, preheat oven to 350 degrees F. Prepare an 8 x 11 x 2-inch baking pan, preferably non-stick coated, by drizzling 1 tablespoon olive oil over pan surface.

Add red and green peppers with garlic cloves. Toss and stir to coat peppers and garlic with oil.

Bake in preheated 350 degree F. oven for about 40-45 minutes, *turn frequently* to encourage even roasting. The outer surfaces of the peppers will become charred and the garlic will become crisp and browned on the outside but soft on the inside.*

Remove from oven. Place garlic cloves on heated serving platters set on warming tray. Place peppers in a heavy brown paper bag in dry sink. Roll the top of the bag down and allow to steam for about 15 minutes.

While peppers are steaming, heat GRILL PAN over *MEDIUM-HIGH* heat.**

Drain bay-seasoned oil from eggplant, onion and potato slices.

Grill eggplant, onion, and potato slices, *in batches,* until marked and tender. Transfer to heated platter.

Peel, core, quarter, and remove membranes of peppers. Place on heated platter with other vegetables. Season with salt, black pepper, and a squeeze or two of lemon juice.

Serve at once, encouraging diners to squeeze the soft garlic pulp over the grilled vegetables.***

Yields 8 servings
adequate for 4-6 people

Notes: *Small whole potatoes can be oven-roasted with the garlic and peppers. Whole tomatoes can be roasted during the last 20-25 minutes of the baking period.

**If preferred, the eggplant, onion and potato slices can be grilled over a charcoal fire.

***Escalivada* may be chilled and served as a cold vegetable course.

This recipe may be halved or doubled, when required.

1/8 SERVING – PROTEIN = 2.3 g.; FAT = 4.4 g.; CARBOHYDRATE = 14.4 g.;
CALORIES = 104; CALORIES FROM FAT = 38%

Europe–Andorra

ANDORRAN SWEET AND SOUR ONION RELISH WITH OLIVES
Amaneda de Cebas

TPT - 2 hours and 5 minutes;
2 hours = flavor development period

This sweet/sour relish is wonderful with grilled vegetables and fried potatoes. I make a big crock of it and it comes out frequently to add to sandwiches.

1 large sweet onion—Vidalia, Walla Walla, or Mayan or Texas Sweet—*very finely* and uniformly chopped
1 tablespoon honey
2 teaspoons *extra virgin* olive oil
1 teaspoon GARLIC OIL [see index]
1 tablespoon red wine vinegar
Pinch salt
Freshly ground black pepper, to taste

10 ripe black olives—*finely* chopped

In a plastic container with cover, combine *very finely* chopped onion, honey, olive oil, garlic oil, red wine vinegar, salt, and black pepper. Stir to coat the onion with flavoring ingredients. Cover tightly and shake gently. Refrigerate for at least 2 hours, shaking occasionally to insure uniform marination. Turn into a crock.

Add *finely* chopped olives. Stir to combine.

Serve directly from the crock using a small slotted spoon. Tightly cover crock and refrigerate leftovers.

Yields 1 3/4 cupfuls

Note: This recipe can be doubled, when required.

1/28 SERVING (i. e., per tablespoonful) –
PROTEIN = 0.2 g.; FAT = 0.9 g.; CARBOHYDRATE = 1.4 g.;
CALORIES = 13; CALORIES FROM FAT = 62%

ALLIOLI SAUCE WITH EGGS
Allioli amb Ous

TPT - 11 minutes

It could well be that mayonnaise really owes it origins to Catalan cuisine. Allioli is the garlic and oil emulsion so passionately loved by the people in this part of the world that it has become a sacred part of their heritage. It is always served with grilled meats and also with some fish dishes. I prefer to make it with eggs since the emulsion holds longer and it can be made in a food processor. Also, the garlic impact, traditionally far more than one would find in the average garlic mayonnaise, is somewhat modified allowing it to be used with grilled vegetables without completely overwhelming the taste of the vegetables.

4 garlic cloves, or more to taste
1/4 teaspoon salt

1/3 cup *fat-free* pasteurized eggs*
3/4 cup *light* olive oil

Place garlic cloves on a bread board and chop *very finely*. Add salt and continue chopping until garlic forms a paste. Turn into work bowl of the food processor fitted with steel knife.

Add pasteurized eggs. Pulse the machine a couple of times. While the machine is still running, take the feed tube cover off. Gradually add the olive oil in a thin stream until the creamy emulsion forms. Turn into a small serving dish.

*Serve at once. Refrigerate leftovers.***

Yields about 1 cup

Notes: *If preferred you can substitute an egg yolk and a whole egg for the pasteurized eggs. Be sure you used organic eggs since this uncooked sauce could easily become contaminated with *Salmonella* bacteria.

**Leftovers that have separated can be resurrected by whisking with a small wire whisk.

1/16 SERVING (per tablespoonful) –
PROTEIN = 0.6 g.; FAT = 8.3 g.; CARBOHYDRATE = 0.5 g.;
CALORIES = 80; CALORIES FROM FAT = 93%

Europe–Andorra

ANDORRAN MUSHROOM FRITTERS
Bunyols de Cirenys
TPT - 32 minutes

In Andorra, the 181-square-mile co-principality that borders Catalonia and France; Catalonia, the 1200-square-mile, most northeastern region of Spain; Roussillon/French Catalonia, once one of the historical counties of Catalonia which is now French; and literally wherever Catalans live and cook you will find fried croquettes and fritters. They are a passion as are the freshest mushrooms. In this recipe we find both passions well satisfied. We serve them as a side dish but they are often served as an appetizer in the tapas style. Try any wild mushrooms that you can obtain: we use crimini, sliced shaggy mane mushrooms, large pieces of oyster mushrooms, and French cèpes, when available.

1 teaspoon active dry yeast
1 1/2 tablespoons *warm* **water**

3/4 cup unbleached white flour
1/8 teaspoon salt
1/8 teaspoon freshly ground black pepper
1/2 cup *skimmed* **milk—***brought to room temperature*
1 egg—lightly beaten
1 1/2 teaspoons olive oil
1 garlic clove—*very finely* **chopped**
1 tablespoon *finely* **chopped fresh parsley**
2 teaspoons *finely* **chopped fresh marjoram**

1/2 pound small mushrooms—trimmed and well-rinsed

Oil for deep-frying

Heat oil for deep-frying to 365 degrees F. Cover a surface with several layers of paper toweling.

In a small bowl, combine yeast and warm water. Allow yeast to proof while combining remainder of fritter batter.

In a mixing bowl, combine white flour, salt, black pepper, milk, beaten egg, olive oil, *very finely* chopped garlic, and *finely* chopped parsley and marjoram. Combine thoroughly.

Add yeast emulsion. Stir well.

Preheat oven to 250 degrees F.

Using spoons, roll several mushrooms in the batter and slide carefully into the hot oil. Using a long-handled spoon, turn mushrooms so that they fry evenly. When evenly browned, transfer to paper toweling to drain.

When all mushrooms have been fried. Place on baking sheet in a 250 degree F. oven to maintain crispness before serving.

Turn onto a serving platter. Serve with mayonnaise or *alloili* sauce.

Yields 6 servings
adequate for 4 people

Note: This recipe can be doubled or halved, when required.

1/6 SERVING – PROTEIN = 3.4 g.; FAT = 5.9 g.; CARBOHYDRATE = 6.4 g.;
CALORIES = 90; CALORIES FROM FAT = 59%

ANDORRAN SAVORY BREAD
WITH VEGETABLES AND SAUSAGE
Coco amb Recapte
TPT - 30 minutes

Savory and sweet" coques" (singular" coca") are breads that can not really be compared to any other flatbreads. They resemble Italian focaccio or pizzas and, instead of baking the flatbread base from scratch, I have often availed myself of a loaf of Indian nan that I might have on hand. Savory versions can be topped with nothing more than the seeds of the piñon pine, piñions, or they can be piled high with sautéed vegetables and sausage slices. They make a wonderful, casual open-faced sandwich-styled entrée. The sweet ones are baked for saints' days and for the Christmas holidays. They are usually filled with the famed Catalan crème, dried fruits, and pine nuts. Their form and ingredients depends very much on local or familial tradition or also what is in the larder. Botifarro, a white pork sausage, is customarily used but vegetarian chorizo sausages do nicely.

ANDORRAN SAVORY BREAD
WITH VEGETABLES AND SAUSAGE (cont'd)

2 loaves *nan**
Extra virgin olive oil

1 tablespoon *extra virgin* olive oil
2 plum tomatoes—seeded and chopped
1 small zucchini squash—trimmed, well-washed, and *very thinly* sliced
1 small yellow summer squash—peeled, trimmed, and *very thinly* sliced
1 medium onion—peeled and *very thinly* sliced
6 red, orange, and yellow baby peppers—well-washed, cored, and sliced into thin rounds

2 vegetarian *chorizo (chouriço)* sausages—*thinly* sliced

Preheat oven to 250 degrees F.

Brush *nan* loaves with olive oil and place on a cookie sheet.

In a skillet set over *MEDIUM* heat, heat the 1 tablespoonful of olive oil. Add chopped tomato, zucchini, yellow squash, onion, and pepper slices. Sauté for about 5 minutes. Pour into a sieve and drain. Scatter vegetables evenly over the two loaves of bread.

Place slices of *chorizo (chouriço)* on top of the vegetables. Bake in preheated 250 degree F. oven for about 15 minutes, or until vegetables begin to brown. Allow to cool for about 3 minutes.

Cut each loaf crosswise into four sections to serve.

Yields 8 servings
adequate for 4-6 people

Notes: *Indian *nan* is available, usually two loaves to a package, in the bakery section of most grocery stores.

This recipe can be halved or doubled, when required.

1/8 SERVING – PROTEIN = 6.4 g.; FAT = 5.4 g.; CARBOHYDRATE = 20.7 g.;
CALORIES = 148; CALORIES FROM FAT = 33%

ANDORRAN SLICED PEARS WITH ICE CREAM AND FRESH STRAWBERRY SAUCE
Peras y Gelat de Canyella amb Culis de Maduixes
TPT - 30 minutes

This dessert is popular in Catalonia and the small principalities in which Catalan cuisine has been preserved. Granted it is not an unusual dessert and is, in fact, a dessert that anyone might concoct if they had ripe pears, fresh strawberries, and vanilla ice cream on hand. I think you will find this combination to be a very enjoyable end to a meal.

12 large, fresh, ripe strawberries—well-washed, trimmed, and chopped

2 tablespoons sugar

3 ripe Bosc pears—peeled, cored, and sliced
1 1/2 cups vanilla ice cream
Ground cinnamon

Set a fine sieve over a small bowl.

Using an electric blender, purée the strawberries until liquefied.

Add sugar and again blend until no bits of strawberry are apparent. Pour into sieve and allow the *coulis* to drain through. Discard debris in sieve. Clean the sieve and place over a clean bowl. Pour the puréed strawberry mixture through again. Discard any residual debris. *There should be no strawberry seeds visible in the sauce.* Pour sauce into a small pitcher. Refrigerate until ready to serve.

Divide pear slices on six dessert plates or in shallow soup plates. Spread each portion into a fan. Pour prepared strawberry *coulis* over pears. Put a 1/4-cup scoop of vanilla ice cream on top. Sprinkle with ground cinnamon.

Serve at once.

Yields 6 individual servings

Note: This recipe can be halved, when required.

1/6 SERVING – PROTEIN = 2.0 g.; FAT = 1.7 g.; CARBOHYDRATE = 21.8 g.;
CALORIES = 108; CALORIES FROM FAT = 14%

Austria

The name Austria is generally accepted as a Latinized distortion of *Ostrarrichi*, Old German for "Eastern Territory" and documented from an official document dated 996 BC. The area was settled in ancient times by Celtic tribes and conquered by the Romans in 15 BC, becoming the Roman province of Noricum and remaining so until it was conquered by Charlemagne in 788 AD. In the period beginning with the defeat of Rudolf I of Germany in 1278, the story of Austria is the story of the Hapsburgs who ruled for almost seven hundred and fifty years. Under the Hapsburg dynasty Austria because a commanding influence in Europe, expanding its territory to the Iberian Peninsula. In 1867, as a consequence of the Compromise of 1867, the *Ausgleich*, the House of Hapsburg and the Kingdom of Hungary agreed to share power. The land holdings of the former Austrian Empire were divided between them. The Austro–Hungarian Empire, or Dual Monarchy as it was also known, survived for fifty-one years, collapsing in 1918 after its military defeat in World War I. Subsequently, a republican form of government succeeded with the creation of the First Austrian Republic. Austria was occupied by Nazi Germany in 1938 and its sovereignty was not restored until 1945.

Visited by many invading and occupying peoples, Austria has benefited from each and every influence to a greater or lesser degree. Cuisine is no exception. Cuisines throughout the former Austro–Hungarian Empire, such as those of the Hungarians, Bohemians, Czechs, Jews, Italians, and French together with the magnificent matrix of the Balkan cuisines, have been integrated in one way or another. Creative integration of these cuisines with the ingredients and cooking techniques learned from the Turks and Bavarians enabled a richly diverse, magnificent cuisine that is, on the one hand, uniquely Austrian and, on the other hand, very transcultural. Spanish and Italian influences via the intermarriages of the Habsburgs have also contributed to this complex richness.

A cookbook, given to me when we were first married, emphasized a meat-based, almost Imperial cuisine that was "of another age," so to speak. I had then assumed that a vegetarian would have difficulty eating in Austria and I thought visiting Vienna might just involve eating pastry and drinking coffee. Oh, was I wrong. If you by-pass the meats and meat-based foods, side-step the ubiquitous bacon and sausages, and skip the fish course, the vegetable dishes are just as imperial. One advantage of a vegetarian's exploration of Austria is that there is much more room for pastry! The divinely extravagant and rich pastries, for which Austria is known, are generally left to the *patisserie* and for that reason I have not chosen to include a *sachertorte* or a *linzertorte*, divine as they may be, and have instead included a simple apricot tart and an equally simple nut roll. The latter clearly shows that coffee was not the only food influence that traveled to Vienna with the invading armies of the Middle Eastern empires. After the Battle of Vienna, supplies of coffee left behind by the retreating Turks were discovered. This sparked the opening of the first coffeehouse in Austria in 1683 and Austrians adopted coffee with enthusiasm as they did so many other foods introduced to them by the Turks.

Europe – Austria

Tomato Soup with Brown Rice
Tomatensuppe mit Reis

Creamy Potato and Mushroom Soup
Kartoffelsuppe

~

Red Beet and Cheese Salad
Rote – Ruben ünd Käsesalat

~ ~

Noodles with Nuts and Cheese
Nussnudeln

Sautéed Asparagus with Hazelnuts
Spargel mit Hasenüssen

Pickled Onions with Sage Vinegar
Marinierte Zwiebeln

— — — — — — — — — — — — — —

Puffed Pastry Roll with Dried Fruits and Chocolate
Schnecken

Apricot Tart
Tarte aux Apricots

AUSTRIAN TOMATO SOUP WITH BROWN RICE
Tomatensuppe mit Reis

TPT - 1 hour and 33 minutes

Since brown rice is far and away the better nutritional buy, I do like to use it but I find that people are so accustomed to white rice they tend to reference the 1970s when brown rice appears on the menu. I have two Austrian tomato–rice soups in my files; one is a clear tomato broth with rice, popular in the 1950s, and the other is this one, a recipe that I have had for many years but I could not remember where I found it. Since I have been unable to find it any of my cookbooks, I was surprised when someone posted a similar version online. I do wish I could have contacted them to find out where they had found it. The reason I especially like my version of this soup is that its smooth, substantial texture hosts the brown rice beautifully and the complex flavoring penetrates the parboiled rice, discouraging the 1970s referencing.

1/3 dry long grain brown rice
2/3 cup *boiling* water

2 tablespoons butter
1 medium carrot—peeled or scraped and chopped
1 medium onion—chopped
1 large celery stalk—trimmed and chopped
2 cups canned, *diced* tomatoes in purée

1 tablespoon whole wheat flour

1 quart VEGETABLE STOCK FROM SOUP [see index] *or* VEGETARIAN BROWN STOCK [see index]
1/4 teaspoon *finely* grated *organic* lemon zest
1 1/2 teaspoons freshly squeezed lemon juice
1 large bay leaf—*broken in half**
1/2 teaspoon crushed, dried marjoram
1/2 teaspoon crushed, dried thyme
Freshly ground black pepper, to taste

AUSTRIAN TOMATO SOUP WITH BROWN RICE (cont'd)

In a saucepan set over *LOW* heat, cook brown rice in *boiling* water for just 10 minutes. Remove from heat, drain, and turn into a bowl of *cold* water to stop further cooking. Set aside until required.

In a kettle set over *LOW-MEDIUM* heat, melt butter. Add chopped carrot, onion, and celery, and diced tomatoes with the purée in which they were canned. Sauté until vegetables soften, *being careful not to allow the vegetables to brown.*

While stirring, add flour and cook for about a minute.

While stirring, *tablespoonful by tablespoonful*, add about 1/2 cupful of stock. Stir until *roux* formed by flour and butter has been integrated into the liquid. Add remainder of stock, *finely* grated lemon zest, lemon juice, crushed, dried marjoram and thyme, and black pepper. Increase heat to *MEDIUM* and allow to come to the simmer. Reduce heat to *LOW* and cook, stirring occasionally, for about 35-40 minutes. Remove from heat and allow to cool for a few minutes. Remove and discard bay leaf pieces.

Purée the soup in batches using the food processor, fitted with steel knife, or the electric blender. Purée thoroughly until *very smooth.*** Turn into a clean kettle or large saucepan set over *LOW-MEDIUM* heat. Add the parboiled rice and cook for about 12-15 minutes more, or until rice is tender. Turn into a heated soup tureen.

Serve into heated soup plates.

Yields 7 cupfuls

Notes: *The bay leaf pieces are most easily recovered if secured inside a tea ball during the simmering process.

**Conveniently for entertaining, the puréed base of this soup can be frozen. Defrost, reheat, and then add parboiled rice.

This recipe can be halved or doubled, when required.

1/7 SERVING (i. e., per cupful) –
PROTEIN = 1.7 g.; FAT = 3.3 g.; CARBOHYDRATE = 14.0 g.;
CALORIES = 88; CALORIES FROM FAT = 34%

AUSTRIAN CREAMY POTATO AND MUSHROOM SOUP
Kartoffelsuppe
TPT - 1 hour and 17 minutes

For some bizarre reason I remember learning how to say potato soup in German as a very small child. It could be that my great-grandfather, whom I do remember well, taught me bits of German as he guided me through his garden, transmitting to me, I now understand, the importance of the kitchen garden, the survival garden. The Austrian word is the same as that in German but the soup is very different. The addition of mushrooms is strictly Austrian and we did not flavor our soup with marjoram.

2 tablespoons butter
2 pounds Idaho baking potatoes—peeled and coarsely chopped to yield about 4 1/2 cups
1/2 cup chopped shallots

6 cups VEGETARIAN WHITE STOCK [see index] **or other vegetarian stock of choice**
1/2 cup *finely* chopped celery
1 tablespoon *finely* chopped fresh marjoram *or* 1 1/2 teaspoons dried, crushed marjoram*
1 tablespoon *finely* chopped fresh lovage *or* 1 1/2 teaspoons dried, crushed lovage**
1/2 teaspoon whole caraway seeds
1 large bay leaf—broken in half

1/4 cup light cream *or* half and half

2 teaspoons white wine vinegar
1/2 teaspoon salt, or to taste
Freshly ground *white* pepper, to taste

1 tablespoon butter
8 ounces mushrooms—white field *(Agaricus)*, shiitake, porcini, and/or crimini—trimmed, rinsed, cleaned well with a brush, and sliced

2 tablespoons light cream *or* half and half
Freshly ground black pepper, to taste

In a large kettle set over *MEDIUM-HIGH* heat, melt 1 tablespoonful butter. Add chopped potatoes and shallots. Sauté until shallot are tender, *being careful not to allow shallots to brown or potatoes to stick to the bottom of the kettle.*

AUSTRIAN CREAMY POTATO AND MUSHROOM SOUP (cont'd)

Add the 6 cupfuls stock, *finely* chopped celery, marjoram, and lovage, caraway seeds, and the bay leaf pieces. Allow to come to the boil. *Immediately* reduce heat to *LOW* and simmer until potatoes are *very tender* —about 30 minutes. Stir occasionally. Remove from heat.

Add the 1/4 cupful cream. Stir to combine.

Using the food processor, fitted with steel knife, or the electric blender, purée the soup base until smooth. Pour back into the kettle. Return *to LOW-MEDIUM* heat. Add vinegar and thin with additional stock until the soup is thinned to your satisfaction. Season with salt and *white* pepper.***

In a non-stick-coated skillet set over *MEDIUM* heat, melt the remaining 1 tablespoonful butter. Add sliced mushrooms and cook until mushrooms are tender—about 5 minutes. Stir frequently.

Add cream and season with black pepper. Stir for several minutes more. Turn creamed mushrooms into a small, heated serving bowl.

Turn heated, puréed potato soup into heated soup tureen.

Serve at once into heated soup bowls, topping each serving with a portion of the creamed mushrooms.

Yields about 9 cupfuls

Notes: *Marjoram *(Marjorana hortensis* - formerly *Origanum majorana)* is an annual herb much under-used by American cooks, who generally opt for the more assertive, perennial oregano varieties in their cooking. Italian cooks of southern Italy also seem to prefer oregano, but marjoram is used extensively in Northern Italy and other regions of Europe, including Austria. The British historically have referred to oregano as wild marjoram and tend to use the distinctly more subtle marjoram. Marjoram has a more perfumed scent and taste than does oregano. Drying intensifies its flavor and that is why we have chosen to use the dried form to flavor this dish.

**Lovage *(Levisticum officinale)* is an old-fashioned herb that you will find to be a useful addition to your herb repertoire. Lovage is easily cultivated in Zones 3-8 and long lived; our plant has been moved three times and is part of a plant originally planted by my great-grandfather in the late 1800s. Celery requires a long, cool growing season but lovage is not such a fussy plant, thriving in full sun and in partial shade. The dark green leaves with their celery flavor can enhance soups, stews, sauces, and salads. When dried, the leaves loose a great deal of the clean celery flavor but can still be added to winter soups, stews, and vegetable stocks. Dried lovage seeds are an excellent replacement for celery seeds. If you do not have fresh lovage leaves in your herb garden for this soup but do have celery leaves on hand, do substitute them.

***The soup can be prepared to this point a day or two ahead or frozen, if convenient.

This recipe can be halved or doubled, when required.

1/9 SERVING (i. e., per cupful) –
PROTEIN = 2.6 g.; FAT = 4.8 g.; CARBOHYDRATE = 16.4 g.;
CALORIES = 117; CALORIES FROM FAT = 37%

Europe–Austria

AUSTRIAN RED BEET AND CHEESE SALAD
Rote – Ruben und Käsesalat
TPT - 7 minutes

This recipe has been in our repertoire since the very early 1970s. It is a protein bonanza which we often serve with baked or roasted potatoes and a mixed vegetable combination or with a grain dish.

1 cup chopped celery
1 cup chopped, *cooked* beets* *or* well-drained canned beets, if necessary
1 1/2 tablespoons *calorie-reduced or light* mayonnaise
Freshly ground black pepper, to taste

4 large lettuce leaves

3/4 cup coarsely shredded (about 3 ounces) *Emmentaler*, Swiss *Gruyère*, or *Jarlsberg* cheese, as preferred
1 hard-cooked egg, cut into 6 wedges—for garnish

In a mixing bowl, combine chopped celery and beets with mayonnaise. Season to taste with black pepper. Combine thoroughly.

Arrange lettuce leaves in a serving bowl or in individual salad bowls, if preferred. Pile vegetable mixture in the middle. Sprinkle shredded cheese evenly over and garnish with hard-cooked egg wedges.

Cover with plastic wrap and refrigerate until ready to serve.

Yields 6 servings
adequate for 4 people

Notes: *To cook fresh beets: Cut off greens leaving 1 inch of petioles attached. (Reserve greens for other uses.) Scrub well. *Do not detach root portion.*
Either,
cook in gently simmering water until tender to the touch—about 30 to 45 minutes;
or,
bake on a cookie sheet in a preheated 375 degree F. oven for about 50 minutes, or until tender.

Slip skins from cooked beets under running water and allow to cool.

This recipe may be halved or doubled, when required.

1/6 SERVING – PROTEIN = 5.7 g.; FAT = 6.7 g.; CARBOHYDRATE = 4.2 g;
CALORIES = 98; CALORIES FROM FAT = 62%.

AUSTRIAN NOODLES WITH NUTS AND CHEESE
Nussnudeln
TPT - 22 minutes

Both hazelnuts and walnuts are used extensively in Austrian cooking and, as you see here, not just for desserts. "Nussnudeln" literally translates to nut noodles but it is the combination of browned breadcrumbs, grated cheese, and nuts that magically transforms plain old buttered macaroni into something amazingly delicious. It is one of those recipes for which you always have the ingredients and to which you turn when a beautiful fresh vegetable dish needs a not-too-assertive companion. Teutonic peoples revered hazelnuts ("Corylus avellana") as both the source of lightning and, if kept on the windowsill, a way of protecting themselves from the wrath of Thor as he flung his thunderbolts. They also connected hazelnuts with immortality and fertility. Ironically, the thunderbolts, from Thor, were welcomed in the spring to bring fertility to the soil and we now know the creative power of heat generated by lightning, as much as 54,000 degrees F., and its powerful electromagnetic field. The ancients were not wrong.

1/2 cup breadcrumbs

1/4 *finely* chopped, *preservative-free* hazelnuts

1/4 cup butter

4 cups dry, wide egg noodles

3 quarts *boiling* water

1/4 cup grated Parmesan cheese

AUSTRIAN NOODLES WITH NUTS AND CHEESE (cont'd)

In a non-stick-coated skillet set over *LOW* heat, toast breadcrumbs while stirring constantly. Be careful that breadcrumbs do not burn.

Add *finely* chopped hazelnuts and continue stirring until hazelnuts are lightly browned.

Add butter and allow the butter to melt. *Remove from heat briefly.*

In a large kettle set over *MEDIUM-HIGH* heat, cook egg noodles in *boiling* water according to package directions.

Just before the noodles have completed their cooking period, return the breadcrumb–hazelnut–butter mixture to *MEDIUM* heat to reheat. Add grated cheese. Stir frequently.

Drain cooked egg noodles and turn into a heated serving bowl. Pour the hot nut sauce mixture over the noodles. Toss gently.

Serve at once.

Yields 8 servings
adequate for 6 people

Note: This recipe can be halved or doubled, when required.

1/8 SERVING – PROTEIN = 16.0 g.; FAT = 10.2 g.; CARBOHYDRATE = 43.7 g.;
CALORIES = 335; CALORIES FROM FAT = 27%

AUSTRIAN SAUTÉED ASPARAGUS WITH HAZELNUTS
Spargel mit Hasenüssen
TPT - 12 minutes

Hazelnuts were considered a symbol of fertility and immortality by the Teutonic peoples of Austria and Germany, as previously noted. Whether it is the unique double flowering or the fact that this crop sustains or the complex mythological association with lightning and the god Thor, it is a small leap to spring and the fulfillment of renewal in the first flush of asparagus in the garden as a confirmation of immortality, of resurrection. It is all together fitting in my mind that asparagus should be paired with hazelnuts as they are in the Austrian recipe.

24 asparagus spears (about 2 pounds)—well-rinsed and trimmed

2 tablespoons butter
1/3 cup chopped, *preservative-free* hazelnuts

2 teaspoons freshly squeezed lemon juice
1 teaspoon *preservative-free* hazelnut meal*

Break asparagus spears so that the spears are about five inches, tip to base.

In a non-stick-coated skillet set over *MEDIUM* heat, melt butter. Add asparagus spears and chopped hazelnuts. Sauté until asparagus is *crisp-tender* and nuts are lightly browned and aromatic. Transfer to a heat serving platter with all the flower ends of the asparagus pointing in the same direction. Pour any butter remaining in the skillet over the asparagus.

Sprinkle with lemon juice. Sprinkle the hazelnut meal over the flower ends of the asparagus.

Serve at once.

Yields 6 servings
adequate for 4 people

Notes: *The food processor is useful for preparing nutmeals. Having almond, walnut, and hazelnut meal in the freezer is an enormous convenience when you need "just a sprinkling."

This recipe can be halved or doubled, when required.

1/6 SERVING – PROTEIN = 7.8 g.; FAT = 4.9 g.; CARBOHYDRATE = 6.2 g.;
CALORIES = 114; CALORIES FROM FAT = 39%

Europe–Austria

AUSTRIAN PICKLED ONIONS WITH SAGE VINEGAR
Marinierte Zwiebeln

TPT - 24 hours and 40 minutes;
24 hours = minimum flavor development period

Pickled vegetables, including pickled whole baby onions, are often enjoyed with meals in Austria as they are in Germany. These sweet and sour raw onion slices are more often found as an appetizer or with a sandwich. Personally I like to eat them with a thick slice of rye bread spread with butter or "liptauer" cheese spread.

1 cup SAGE VINEGAR *[see recipe which follows]* **or** apple cider vinegar plus two small dried sage leaves
1 cup sugar
3/4 teaspoon salt
20 whole, black peppercorns
12 whole allspice berries
1 garlic clove—cut in half
1 small bay leaf—broken in half

1 large red onion—peeled, halved, and *thinly* sliced

Prepare two one-pint canning jars by sterilizing. Also sterilize lids and rings.

In a saucepan set over *MEDIUM* heat, combine vinegar, sugar, salt, whole peppercorns and allspice berries, garlic, and bay leaf pieces. Allow to come to the boil.

Add onion slices. Allow to come to the boil again. Remove from heat. Remove and discard bay leaf pieces. Divide between sterilized jars. Be careful to include a garlic half and a sage leaf in each jar. Wipe rim of jars and seal. Allow to stand at room temperature for 24 hours before serving. *The jars will seal. If a jar does not seal, refrigerate it and use it up promptly.*

Once opened, refrigerate.

Yields 3 1/2 cupfuls

Note: This recipe can not be doubled.

1/19 SERVING (about 3 tablespoonfuls) –
PROTEIN = 0.2 g.; FAT = 0.0 g.; CARBOHYDRATE = 12.9 g.;
CALORIES = 51; CALORIES FROM FAT = 0%

SAGE VINEGAR
TPT - 3 weeks and 20 minutes;
3 weeks = flavor development period

I tend to choose this vinegar most often in the fall. The cider vinegar and sage seem to compliment my autumnal menu thinking since this is a bit more assertive than the light herb vinegars we use in the summer.

1 quart apple cider vinegar

2 cups sage leaves—freshly picked and *well-washed**
1 teaspoon mustard seeds
1 teaspoon dillweed seeds

Sage sprigs, well-washed, for garnish

Sterilize a one-quart canning jar, lid, and ring.

In a saucepan set over *MEDIUM* heat, heat apple cider vinegar to just below the boiling point. *Do not heat the vinegar quickly* and *do not allow it to boil.*

SAGE VINEGAR (cont'd)

Meanwhile, pack *well-washed* sage leaves into the sterilized canning jar. Add mustard and dillweed seeds.

Pour hot vinegar over sage leaves. Using a chopstick, stir sage leaves for about 30 seconds to start the infusion. Seal the jar and place in a cool, dark place for 3 weeks.

Sterilize a clear, condiment bottle, or several if you are planning to give the vinegar as gifts.

Place a fine sieve over a one-quart measuring cup or mixing bowl. Strain the vinegar, discarding the sage leaves and seeds recovered.

Pour vinegar into sterilized condiment bottle or bottles. Insert a sprig of sage, for garnish. Cap and label.

Store at cool room temperature for up to six months.

Yields 3 cupfuls

Notes: *Sage *(Salvia officinalis)* is an assertive and aromatic herb, rarely used in vegetarian dishes. It is, however, a delicious addition to herb breads and pasta dishes. Used judiciously, it also compliments both eggs and cheeses. Of the many varieties of this hardy and easily-grown perennial, the common garden sage or a variety called 'Berggarten' would be our choices for preparing this vinegar. *Salvia officinalis* 'Purpurea,' purple sage, is a poor choice for this vinegar since the anthocyanin pigments in the purple sage combine with the apple cider vinegar color to produce a rather strange vinegar color. The vinegar tastes the same and is interesting to some, but not to all! If you plan to grow your own sage, rosemary, lavender, and thyme are good companion plantings and the close proximity of this combination seems to keep insect pests away. Dried sage can not be substituted in this recipe.

Insects often lay their eggs on the underside of leaves so be careful to wash herb leaves well.

This recipe can also be used to prepare vinegar using fresh winter savory or a mixture of sage and savory, if preferred.

1/48 SERVING (i. e., per tablespoonful) –
PROTEIN = 0.0 g.; FAT = 0.0 g.; CARBOHYDRATE = 0.8 g.;
CALORIES = 2; CALORIES FROM FAT = 0%

PUFFED PASTRY NUT ROLL WITH DRIED FRUITS AND CHOCOLATE
Schnecken

TPT - 3 hours;
1 hour = fruit soaking period;
30 minutes = pastry rising period

Somewhere in my childhood I could still hear the word schnecken. It did not seem to come from a kitchen or bakery setting; it seemed to keep taking me to my great-grandfather's garden and, much as I tried, I just could not understand until I translated it and realized that grandpa had probably been teaching me about how to control snails/slugs in the garden as we took one of our walks together. Schnecken, which means snails in German, is also the name for a dessert in both Germany and Austria but the image evoked by the name is where the similarity ends. German schnecken, also very popular here in the United States, are sticky rolls, available in any bakery from New York to California. Austrian schnecken are the slices cut from a baked puffed pastry roll which is stuffed with nuts and fruit and rolled tightly like a strudel. When the baked roll is cut, the rolled snail structure is revealed. Most people are not aware of the chocolate in this dessert. It is a very subtle, elegant nuance.

PUFFED PASTRY NUT ROLL
WITH DRIED FRUITS AND CHOCOLATE (cont'd)

1/2 cup mixed, *preservative-free* candied fruits
   or mixed candied citrus peel
1/2 cup *preservative-free dark* raisins
1/4 cup *warm* water
1 teaspoon pure vanilla extract

1/2 cup *ground, preservative-free* walnuts
2 tablespoons sugar
2 tablespoons *grated* chocolate

1 tablespoon *melted* butter

1 sheet *frozen* puff pastry—*defrosted,* but
   still cool
1 teaspoon *melted* butter

In a small bowl, combine mixed candied fruits or citrus peel and raisins. Pour warm water, and vanilla extract over the fruits. Toss to mix thoroughly. Set aside for 1 hour to allow the fruit to soften and absorb the flavoring liquids. Drain.

In a mixing bowl, combine drained fruits, *ground* walnuts, sugar, and grated chocolate. Mix well.

Add the 1 tablespoonful melted butter. Toss to mix well.

Preheat oven to 400 degrees F. Prepare a cookie sheet by lining with parchment paper.

On a cool surface, roll the puff pastry to double its size. Fold in half and roll again. Turn and roll the pastry again to double its size and then fold in half again. About *one inch* in from one of longest edges of the rolled pastry sheet spoon the fruit and nut mixture so that it is distributed from one end of the pastry to the other. Spread the fruit–nut mixture across the pastry, *leaving one inch all the way around.* Turn the left and right side margins toward the center. Press gently. Take the pastry edge nearest to you and roll it *tightly* over the fruit. Continue rolling until you have a tight roll. Moisten the edge and ends and secure. Place sealed-side-down on prepared baking sheet.

Brush the remaining butter over the nut roll. Allow the pastry to rise at room temperature for 30 minutes.

Bake in preheated 400 degree F. oven for about 35-40 minutes, or until golden brown. Remove from baking sheet to a serving platter or cutting board. Allow to cool to room temperature.

Using a sharp knife, slice.

                              Yields 16 slices

Note: This can be halved, using a half-sheet of puff pastry, if required.

1/16 SERVING (i. e., per slice) –
PROTEIN = 2.6 g.; FAT = 10.2 g.; CARBOHYDRATE = 21.1 g.;
CALORIES = 183; CALORIES FROM FAT = 50%

Europe–**Austria**

APRICOT TART
Tarte aux Apricots

TPT - 1 hour and 50 minutes;
20 minutes = pastry cooling period;
1 hour = tart chilling period

This fabulously delicious and drop-dead simple tart was evolved from one which my mother had jotted down from a television cook show in the early 1960s. It is equally as pleasant when made with peach halves and apricot or currant jelly may be used instead of crabapple. Although whipped cream is the perfect garnish, we have often enjoyed it without the cream. It is a great dessert to take when you are asked to bring a dessert. Just take your chilled whipped cream and decorating bag along and pipe on your whipped cream garnish in a quiet corner.

1/2 cup butter—*softened to room temperature*
1/3 cup confectioners' sugar
1 cup sifted unbleached white flour
1 cup sifted whole wheat flour

1/2 cup freshly squeezed orange juice
1 tablespoon corn starch
1/2 cup crabapple jelly—preferably homemade
Dash ground mace*

3 cans (1 pound each) juice-packed apricots
—drained, pitted, and halved— *or* equivalent
in fresh apricots, if in season

1 cup heavy whipping cream—*stiffly* whipped

Preheat oven to 350 degrees F. Prepare a 12-inch tart pan by coating with non-stick lecithin spray coating.

Using the food processor fitted with steel knife or an electric mixer, cream *softened* butter with confectioners' sugar. Add white and whole wheat flours, and blend well. If too dry, add a couple of drops of orange juice. Gather into a ball. Press pastry evenly into prepared tart pan.

Bake in preheated 350 degree F. oven for 20 minutes until *lightly browned.* Remove to a wire rack and allow to cool for 20 minutes.

Meanwhile, in a saucepan, combine orange juice and corn starch. Using a wire whisk, combine thoroughly. When corn starch is completely in suspension, stir in crabapple jelly and mace. Set over *MEDIUM* heat, and cook, stirring constantly, until jelly is completely dissolved and sauce is smooth and thickened. Keep warm until ready to glaze.

Arrange *thoroughly* drained and pitted apricot halves attractively on *cooled* pastry. Pour glaze evenly over apricot halves and pastry.

Refrigerate for at least 1 hour before serving.

Pipe whipped heavy cream decoratively over tart or pass separately, if preferred.

Yields 8-10 servings
adequate for 6-8 people

Note: *Freshly grated nutmeg may be substituted for ground mace, if necessary.

1/10 SERVING – PROTEIN = 4.3 g.; FAT = 17.7 g.; CARBOHYDRATE = 55.4 g.;
CALORIES = 390; CALORIES FROM FAT = 41%

Belarus

The mountains and fertile river valleys of Belarus, an area slightly smaller than our state of Kansas, have hosted human settlements since the Stone Age, attested to by Paleolithic sites in the regions of Kalinkovichi, Cechersk, Mogilev, Grodno, and even in the region now occupied by the capitol, Minsk. By the fifth century the Baltic tribes, who had established settlements here in the third century, were assimilated into the culture of the Slavic tribes who had spread throughout the region by then. The powerful Grand Duchy of Lithuania, Rus, and Samogotia controlled the area in the Middle Ages as part of an expansive state which included Belarus, Lithuania, the Kiev, Chernigov and Volyn areas of the Ukraine, and Western Russia from the Baltic Sea to the Black Sea. In 1386, as the result of a politically-motivated marriage, the Grand Duchy of Lithuania and the Kingdom of Poland united to form the Polish–Lithuanian Commonwealth. Ivan III of Russia, known as Ivan the Great, set his sights on the lands now occupied by Belarus and the Ukraine in the late 1400s but it was not until 1795, under Catherine II, that the dissolution of the union between Lithuania and Poland brought Belarus under the rule of Czarist Russia. The Belarus Soviet Socialist Republic was formed in 1919 after the Bolshevik Revolution transformed Russia and after the withdrawal of Germany troops from Belarus in accord with the Treaty of Versailles at the end of World War I. Soviet Russia sought to recover the lands that had been held by the former Russian Empire and in 1922 Belarus became a part of the Soviet Union. By 1941 Belarus was again occupied by German troops and remained under the heel of Germany until 1945 when it was returned to the U.S.S.R.

In 1991, with the breakup of the Soviet Union, Belarus once again declared itself independent, forming a "Soviet-style" republic in which most of the economy remains state-controlled.

Approximately forty percent of Belarus' land mass is forested and it is in these forests that Belarusian families gather the mushrooms so treasured by Central Europeans. They are brushed clean and dried for winter dishes but the passion for freshly picked mushrooms is also satisfied as favorite dishes appear on the table. You will see in the menu below that we too treasure that *unami* taste. However, soil contamination from the 1986 Chernobyl nuclear reactor disaster in the Ukraine has brought into question the safety of not only the foraged mushrooms but the Belarusian-grown food supply in general.

Although eighty percent of the population are ethnic Belarusians, the food of Belarus clearly reflects its history. The potato, native to the western hemisphere, is popular in Lithuania, Poland, and Russia, but the Belarusians have a fondness for potatoes and a culinary creativity with potatoes matched only by the Germans, from whom they appeared to have borrowed literally hundreds of potato dishes that can regularly be found on Belarusian menus. There are even special potato restaurants where you can sample nothing but potato dishes including *kalduny*, boiled dumplings very similar to Russian *pelmeni*, Italian *ravioli*, or Polish *pierogi*. *Kalduny* were originally made from wheat flour but the cold, wet climate of Belarus limits wheat production in favor of barley, oatmeal, and buckwheat and today the dumplings are generally made from grated potatoes; the filling mixtures of vegetables and meats are simple unlike the exotic fillings favored in the days of privileged classes. The foods eaten before the Soviet period were replaced by an orchestrated cuisine that was thrust upon the Belarusians during the Stalinist era. There is now a concerted effort to erase identification with the Soviet era and the effort has started with the daunting task of resurrecting the national cuisine by searching out the dishes of the past.

Europe–Belarus

Egg Roll Appetizers with Potatoes
Brakat Amliety z Smažny Bulba

Sautéed Mushrooms with Onions and Sour Cream   **Wilted Cucumber Salad with Honey**
                                                    Ahurok z Miod

Cabbage Salad

Sour Rye Bread

~

Tomato Salad with Garlic and Cheese
Salata z Pamidorau i Syr

Beetroot Salad with Eggs
Salata z Buraki i Jajki

~

Mushroom Soup with Roasted Millet   **Quick, Chilled *Borsch* from Belarus**
Krupienia   *Khaladnik*

~~~~~~~~~~~~~~~~~~~~

Shredded Potato Casserole
Babka

Harvard Beets

~~~~~~~~~~

Stewed Carrots and Barley
Tušanaje Miasa z Morkoui Jacmien

Soy Sausages or Burgers

Boiled or Baked Potatoes   with   **Sour Cream Sauce with Horseradish**
                                  Sous z Smiatana i Chren

~~~~~~~~~~

Potato, Mushroom, and Onion Omelet
Tirybok

Sautéed Cabbage with Caraway Seeds

Butter-Sautéed Apple Slices

~~~~~~~~~~~~~~~~~~~~

Apple – Oatmeal Porridge
Kasa ad Ausianka i Jablki

Rehydrated Dried Fruits with Honey   Strawberries with Softly Whipped Cream

Rice Pudding with Honey
Kutya

Europe–**Belarus**

BELARUSIAN EGG ROLL APPETIZERS WITH POTATOES
Brakat Amliety z Smaźny Bulba
TPT - 35 minutes

Back in the 1970s, when entertaining for brunch was a somewhat new phenomenon, I remember making individual omelets that were stacked with hash-browned potatoes between the layers. Encountering a very large, entrée-sized version of a similar dish while studying the cuisine of Belarus, I mused as to what a perfectly lovely appetizer you could create with individual omelets. Served with a fruit salsa garnish, it could be positively elegant.

1 tablespoon butter
4 medium potatoes—peeled and shredded
Salt, to taste
Freshly ground black pepper, to taste

6 eggs
2 tablespoons *whole* **milk**

1 1/2 tablespoons grated *pecorino Romano* **cheese**

2 tablespoons snipped chives
1/4 cup *melted* **butter**

Preheat oven to 200 degrees F. Place an oven-proof serving platter in the oven.

In a skillet set over *LOW-MEDIUM* heat, melt butter. Add shredded potato, salt, and black pepper. Cook, turning frequently, until potatoes are browned. Remove from heat. Using a sharp knife cut potatoes into strips.

In a small dish or measuring cup, combine 1 egg and 1 teaspoon milk. Using a fork, mix well.

Turn into a 7-inch preheated non-stick-coated skillet. Allow egg to set on the bottom. Slide out onto a plate. Spoon *one-sixth* of the fried potatoes at one edge of the omelet. Roll the omelet to contain the potatoes. Place it on the plate in the oven.

Repeat until six egg rolls with potato have been prepared.

Sprinkle about 1/2 teaspoonful of the grated cheese over each egg roll. Return to the oven and cook until heated through and the cheese has melted. Serve onto heated salad plates.

Garnish each egg roll with about a teaspoonful of snipped chives. Pour a small pool of *melted* butter onto each plate.

Serve at once.

Yields 6 individual appetizer servings

Notes: This recipe can be doubled, when required.

Two egg rolls make a very nice serving for a breakfast or lunch, or for a light supper.

1/6 SERVING – PROTEIN = 12.1 g.; FAT = 15.7 g.; CARBOHYDRATE = 14.5 g.;
CALORIES = 235; CALORIES FROM FAT = 60%

BELARUSIAN WILTED CUCUMBER SALAD WITH HONEY
Ahurok z Miod
TPT - 4 hours and 17 minutes;
4 hours = cucumber wilting period

Cucumbers with honey . . . an intriguing notation I found in a Russian novel stayed with me for years. I never tried it until I began to explore the cuisine of Belarus and I really wish I had tried it when I first encountered it because I could have enjoying it all these years. It may well be Byzantine Greek in origin but appreciation of it has spread across Europe. It is a wonderful way to disguise the taste of a bitter cucumber.

2 large *organic* **cucumbers—peeled**
3/4 teaspoon salt

Freshly ground black pepper, to taste

2 tablespoons *wildflower* **honey**

Sprigs of fresh dillweed, for garnish

Europe–**Belarus**

BELARUSIAN WILTED CUCUMBER SALAD WITH HONEY (cont'd)

Score each peeled cucumber with the tines of a fork. Slice each *very thinly*. Place a layer in a colander or fine sieve. Sprinkle generously with salt. Continue layering and sprinkling with salt until all cucumber slices are layered. Place in the sink. Place a plate on top and place a weight of about 2 pounds on top of the plate. Allow to drain for at least 4 hours.* Rinse cucumber slices under running water *very thoroughly*. Pat dry. Turn into a large shallow bowl.

Season with black pepper, to taste.

Drizzle honey over cucumber slices.

Garnish with dillweed sprigs.

Serve at once.

Yields 6 servings
adequate for 4 people

Note: This recipe can be halved or doubled, when required.

1/6 SERVING – PROTEIN = 0.4 g.; FAT = 0.1 g.; CARBOHYDRATE = 7.6 g.;
CALORIES = 30; CALORIES FROM FAT = 3%

BELARUSIAN TOMATO SALAD WITH GARLIC AND CHEESE
Salata z Pamidorau i Syr
TPT - 11 minutes

Did you ever stand over the sink and bite into a perfectly-ripened tomato? As the juice dripped down your chin from that remarkable first bite, have you then added a slathering of homemade mayonnaise? It is one of the really special experiences so, I suppose, a tomato salad with mayonnaise might not be considered particularly unusual. However, the taste of this salad is not ho-hum and I can see why Belarusians look forward to the tomato harvest.

5 firm, ripe medium tomatoes—well-rinsed and sliced
Salt, to taste
2 large garlic cloves—crushed and *very finely* chopped
1 cup shredded *part-skimmed milk mozzarella* cheese

1/2 cup *calorie-reduced or light* mayonnaise *or* BLENDER MAYONNAISE *[see index]*
Freshly ground black pepper, to taste

On a large plate or platter, arrange tomato slices leaving an empty circle in the center. Sprinkle with salt. Scatter *very finely* chopped garlic evenly over the tomatoes. Scatter shredded cheese evenly over.

Spoon mayonnaise into the center. Grind black pepper over. Refrigerate until ready to serve.

Yields 6 servings
adequate for 4 people

Note: This recipe can be halved, when required.

1/6 SERVING – PROTEIN = 6.0 g.; FAT = 10.3 g.; CARBOHYDRATE = 5.7 g.;
CALORIES = 143; CALORIES FROM FAT = 65%

BELARUSIAN BEETROOT SALAD WITH EGGS
Salata z Buraki i Jajki
TPT - 9 minutes

Today we expect the produce department of our grocery stores to provide us with the vegetables we want to eat both in and out of season. In fact, I suspect that at least one and perhaps two generations now shop without any concept of growing seasons—corn-on-the-cob in the middle of the winter; asparagus throughout the summer, fall, and winter; apples in the summer; summer squashes and melons in the winter, if you want it, you can buy it. Global markets and shelf-life techniques have changed the way we eat food and they have changed the way we harvest and store for the leaner months. The taste is not the same but people have been worn down and no longer expect the sweetness of a summer melon or the drop-dead delicious taste of a garden-ripened tomato. Case in point, when I want to make this salad, I do not always wait for the fall harvest or go down into the root cellar; I buy a jar of canned, baby beets. In Belarus the availability of root vegetables still depends on your diligence in the fall.

BELARUSIAN BEETROOT SALAD WITH EGGS (cont'd)

DRESSING:
    1/4 cup *finely* chopped onion
    1/4 cup *reduced calorie or light* mayonnaise
    1/8 teaspoon MUSTARD SAUCE *[see index]*
    1/2 teaspoon *finely* chopped fresh parsley
    1/2 teaspoon *finely* snipped fresh dillweed

1 jar (15 ounces) baby beets—drained and quartered

2 *hard-cooked* eggs—shelled and cut into six wedges each

In a mixing bowl, combine *finely* chopped onion, mayonnaise, mustard, *finely* chopped parsley, and *finely* snipped fresh dillweed. Combine thoroughly.

Add quartered baby beets. Fold gently to coat the beets with the dressing. Turn into shallow serving bowl or onto a small platter. Refrigerate until ready to serving.

Arrange egg wedges decoratively on top at the last minute.

Yields 6 servings
adequate for 4 people

Notes: This recipe can be halved, when required.

Cooked carrots and potatoes can be added, if desired. The vegetable combination with the addition of dried herring, which I first sampled on a trip to the Soviet Union, is a salad still popular in the former republics of the Soviet Union.

1/6 SERVING – PROTEIN = 5.2 g.; FAT = 2.0 g.; CARBOHYDRATE = 21.9 g.;
CALORIES = 129; CALORIES FROM FAT = 14%

BELARUSIAN MUSHROOM SOUP WITH ROASTED MILLET
Krupienia

TPT - 1 hour and 45 minutes

An assortment of fresh or dried mushrooms, as called for in this recipe, can give a nuanced flavor that greatly enhances a soup like this. Belarusians hunt the treasured boletus mushrooms. Harvested mushroom treasures are dried to be used in such soups as this. The mushroom stock, required for this recipe, can be prepared while rehydrating the dried mushrooms.

3 tablespoons dry millet

1 cup water

2 ounces dried mushrooms—soaked in hot water to rehydrate— *or* 1/2 pound fresh mushrooms —trimmed and very well-rinsed

3 cups VEGETABLE STOCK FROM SOUP *[see index]* or other vegetarian stock of choice
3 cups MUSHROOM STOCK *[see index]*

1 tablespoon butter
1 medium carrot—peeled and *finely* chopped
1/2 cup *finely* chopped onion

2 tablespoons unbleached white flour

1 teaspoon crushed, dried oregano

1/4 cup *fat-free* dairy sour cream
Salt, to taste
Freshly ground black pepper, to taste

In a kettle set over *LOW* heat, dry-roast the millet until lightly browned. *Monitor carefully because the grain can brown easily.*

Add water. Increase heat to *LOW-MEDIUM*. Cover and allow to cook for about 30-35 minutes, or until the grains are soft. *Do not drain.*

Chop mushrooms finely. Add to millet.

Add vegetable stock and mushroom stock. Allow to come to a gentle simmer.

In a skillet set over *LOW-MEDIUM* heat, melt butter. Add *finely* chopped carrot and onion. Sauté until onion is soft and translucent, *being careful not to allow onion to brown.*

Add flour. Cook, stirring constantly, until a *roux* is formed. Ladle some of the soup stock into the skillet and cook, stirring constantly, until it thickens. Turn contents of skillet into kettle with soup stock. Stir to integrate.

**BELARUSIAN MUSHROOM SOUP
WITH ROASTED MILLET** (cont'd)

Add crushed oregano. Cook, stirring frequently, until soup thickens somewhat.

Stir in sour cream. Season with salt and pepper. Turn into a heated soup tureen.

Serve into heated soup plates.

Yields 7 cupfuls

Note: This recipe can be doubled, when required.

1/7 SERVING – PROTEIN = 3.6 g.; FAT = 2.2 g.; CARBOHYDRATE = 10.1 g.;
CALORIES = 76; CALORIES FROM FAT = 26%

QUICK, CHILLED *BORSCH* FROM BELARUS
Khaladnik

TPT - 1 hour and 39 minutes;
1 hour = refrigeration period

All over Russia and the former Eastern Bloc republics the quality of a cook's borsch (borsht) is important to his or her reputation. This is a simple summer version that makes cooking on a hot summer day seem positively cool.

1 hard-cooked egg

1 medium cucumber

2 jars (16 ounces each) baby beets

2 cups *boiling* water
1/2 teaspoon red wine vinegar
1 teaspoon sugar
Salt, to taste

1/2 cup *finely* chopped onion

6 tablespoons *fat-free* dairy sour cream *or* PLAIN YOGURT *[see index]*, if preferred

2 teaspoons chopped fresh dillweed

Chop hard-cooked egg. Turn into a small bowl, cover with plastic wrap, and refrigerate until ready to serve.

Peel, seed, and chop cucumber. Turn into a small bowl, cover with plastic wrap, and refrigerate until ready to serve.

Set a sieve over a small kettle. Pour beets into the sieve and allow to drain. Chop beets and add to canning liquid in kettle. Add *boiling* water, vinegar, sugar, and salt. Set over *MEDIUM* heat and allow to come to the boil. Reduce heat to *LOW-MEDIUM* and simmer for about 10 minutes.

Stir in *finely* chopped onion. Refrigerate for about 1 hour, until cold.

Add sour cream or yogurt, as preferred. Stir until the sour cream is thoroughly integrated. Turn into a chilled soup tureen. Garnish with fresh dillweed.

Place a spoonful of chopped eggs and a spoonful of chopped cucumber into each soup plate before ladling in the cold soup.

Yields 6 servings

Note: This recipe can be halved or doubled, when required

1/6 SERVING – PROTEIN = 4.6 g.; FAT = 1.1 g.; CARBOHYDRATE = 20.4 g.;
CALORIES = 104; CALORIES FROM FAT = 10%

Europe–**Belarus**

BELARUSIAN SHREDDED POTATO CASSEROLE
Babka

TPT - 48 minutes

The encounter, exchange, and adaptation of potato dishes in Central Europe is a fascinating study. For example, draniki are potato pancakes not unlike bulbe latkes, the potato pancakes associated with and carried by East European Jews to South and North America. Babka, like draniki, are made from shredded potatoes. Both are examples of dishes most probably borrowed from the German cuisine. This version of the classic Belarusian casserole is a satisfying vegetarian entrée.

1 tablespoon butter
1 cup *finely* **chopped onion**

4 medium potatoes—peeled, coarsely grated and squeezed dry
3/4 cup *fat-free* **pasteurized eggs (the equivalent of 3 eggs)**
1 tablespoon unbleached white flour
1/2 teaspoon salt
Freshly ground black pepper, to taste

3 tablespoons dry breadcrumbs

Fat-free **dairy sour cream, to taste***

Preheat oven to 350 degrees F. Prepare n 1 1/2-quart soufflé dish or other oven-to-table baking dish by coating with non-stick lecithin spray coating.

In a skillet set over *LOW-MEDIUM* heat, melt butter. Add *finely* chopped onions and sauté until soft and translucent, *being careful not to allow onions to brown.* Turn into a mixing bowl.

Add grated potatoes, pasteurized eggs, flour, salt, and black pepper. Turn into prepared baking dish.

Sprinkle breadcrumbs evenly over the top. Bake in preheated 350 degree F. oven for about 30-35 minutes, or until breadcrumbs are golden brown.

Serve at once with sour cream.

Yields 6 servings
adequate for 4 people

Notes: *Some cooks omit the breadcrumbs and spread the sour cream on top of the potato mixture. They bake it until the sour cream forms a brown crust. I prefer the non-dairy breadcrumb topping but it can be prepared either way.

This recipe can be halved or doubled, when required.

1/6 SERVING (exclusive of sour cream) –
PROTEIN = 5.2 g.; FAT = 2.0 g.; CARBOHYDRATE = 21.9 g.;
CALORIES = 129; CALORIES FROM FAT = 14%

HARVARD BEETS

TPT - 43 minutes;
30 minutes = flavor development period

Belarusians love sweet and sour beets as did my grandmother and great-grandmother, as do I, which made me often suspect that what we had always called Harvard beets was originally a sweet and sour beet recipe brought to the United States from Germany by my great-grandmother. The recipe I obtained from a Belarusian cook is exactly the recipe I wrote down in my grandmother's kitchen. Now that gives one pause, does it not? Mom often served Harvard beets and I remember loving them then. Beets were a much more important vegetable in the '30s, '40s and '50s since they could be stored successfully in the root cellar well into the winter. When commercially-canned beets became widely available, the season could then be extended. Fresh produce was literally unavailable in "the dead of winter" in upstate New York. When the ground was still snow-covered, pickled vegetables and the beet offered versatility for side dishes and salads.

1 1/2 teaspoons corn starch
1 tablespoon sugar
3 tablespoons apple cider vinegar *or* **distilled white vinegar, if preferred**
1/4 cup juice drained from beets

1 1/2 cups well-drained, sliced canned beets *or* **halved, canned baby beets—preferably home-canned without salt**

2 teaspoons butter

Europe–**Belarus**

HARVARD BEETS (cont'd)

In a saucepan set over *MEDIUM* heat, combine corn starch and sugar, blending well. Stir in vinegar and beet juice. Cook, stirring constantly, until thickened.

Add beets, stirring gently to coat with sauce. Remove from heat and allow to chill in the refrigerator for about 30 minutes.

When ready to serve, cook over *MEDIUM* heat, stirring frequently, until heated through. Add butter and toss gently until butter is melted.

Turn into a heated serving bowl.

Notes: This recipe is easily doubled, when required.

1/4 teaspoonful of freshly grated orange zest is a most complimentary addition, if desired.

If the vinegar is replaced with 2 tablespoonfuls orange juice and 1 teaspoonful lemon juice, both freshly squeezed of course, you have a very respectable version of YALE BEETS. Reduce the sugar to 1 teaspoonful for this version.

Yields 5 servings
adequate for 3-4 people

HARVARD BEETS – 1/5 SERVING – PROTEIN = 0.9 g.; FAT = 1.5 g.; CARBOHYDRATE = 11.4 g.;
CALORIES = 62; CALORIES FROM FAT = 22%

YALE BEETS – 1/5 SERVING – PROTEIN = 0.9 g.; FAT = 1.5 g.; CARBOHYDRATE = 9.6 g.;
CALORIES = 56; CALORIES FROM FAT = 24%

BELARUSIAN STEWED CARROTS AND BARLEY

Tutanaje Miasa z Markaui Jaemien

TPT - 1 hour and 23 minutes

Carrot slices have acquired a significance other than the fact that they are good sources of vitamin A and that they are a magnificent tool for demonstrating hair root development to a biology class. They have for centuries represented prosperity because they look like gold coins. That is probably why this dish is also known in Belarus as "ztimmes," a Yiddish word most probably introduced by those who provided food and lodging to travelers. It is served over boiled or stewed meat dishes; we serve it with sautéed soy meatballs, fried soy sausages, or grilled soy patties.

3/4 cup VEGETARIAN STOCK FROM SOUP
  [see index] **or other vegetarian stock of choice**

4 large carrots—scraped or pared and sliced into coins
1 rib celery with leaves—*finely* **chopped**
2 tablespoons dry barley
3 tablespoons butter
Pinch sugar
Pinch rosemary powder
Freshly ground black pepper, to taste

In a small kettle set over *MEDIUM* heat, heat vegetable stock until it begins to boil. Reduced heat to *LOW*.

Add carrots slices, *finely* chopped celery, barley, butter, sugar, rosemary powder, and pepper. Cover and allow to cook for about 1 1/4 hours, or until carrots and barley are tender. *Add a tablespoon or two of water if necessary to prevent vegetables from sticking to pan.* Turn into a heated serving bowl. Keep warm on warming tray until ready to serve.

Serve hot.

Yields 6 servings
adequate for 4 people

Note: This recipe can be halved or doubled, when required.

1/6 SERVING – PROTEIN = 0.8 g.; FAT = 5.8 g.; CARBOHYDRATE = 7.3 g.;
CALORIES = 97; CALORIES FROM FAT = 54%

Europe–Belarus

SOUR CREAM SAUCE WITH HORSERADISH
Sous z Smiatana i Chren

TPT - 4 minutes

I remember the huge, brown horseradish roots being shredded and placed into salt and vinegar. Horseradish was definitely a part of the cuisine that my great-grandparents brought from Germany as it is in the central valleys of Pennsylvania where many Germans settled. Shortly after we moved here, my husband noted a root vegetable in the produce department of our local grocery and asked what it was. Thinking it might be a cassava or one of the more exotic tropic roots, he was surprised to find out that it was the humble horseradish. Up to that point, I think, he had only seen preserved horseradish in a deli jar. A sauce similar to this was served to us on several occasions when we visited the Soviet Union so it is no surprise to learn that it is a popular condiment in Belarus.

This recipe sat in the inactive part of my sauce files for many years because the combination of mayonnaise and sour cream was an overwhelming fat load for our diet. The availability of fat-free sour cream made this an option. If I choose not to make my own mayonnaise, commercial mayonnaises with lowered fat can take the fat content of this sauce down even further.

1/2 cup *fat-free* dairy sour cream
1/2 cup *calorie-reduced or light* mayonnaise
1/4 cup *preserved* horseradish
1 teaspoon sugar
1/2 teaspoon coarse-grained mustard*

Salt, to taste**

Notes: *I use a *Dijon* country-style, coarse-grained mustard for this recipe.

**The amount of salt added to preserved horseradish can vary. Be sure to taste before adding more salt.

In a small bowl, combine sour cream, horseradish, and sugar. Mix well.

Season with salt. Turn into serving dish. Chill until ready to serve.

Yields 6 servings
adequate for 4 people

1/6 SERVING – PROTEIN = 1.4 g.; FAT = 3.3 g.; CARBOHYDRATE = 5.7 g.;
CALORIES = 59; CALORIES FROM FAT = 50%

BELARUSIAN POTATO, MUSHROOM, AND ONION OMELET
Tirybok

TPT - 53 minutes

It had been dark, especially in the winter, by the time I would start walking the several miles to my apartment from my University of Michigan research job and although I was hungry, tired usually won and dinner was never anything to write down; when I was in graduate school, it was worse. When we married, my recipe collection was very limited. I started collecting recipes like mad because suddenly there were two of us, hungry, tired from teaching and night graduate courses, with lessons and tests to ready before sleep. The recipe for an oven omelet with those frightful canned mushrooms was torn from a 1960s "woman's" magazine. It was very similar to a Belarusian specialty I was to learn, albeit with freshly-gathered mushrooms, of course. Belarusians enjoy omelets, and not just oven omelets. If you have ever made a frittata then you have made a "tirybok." Frittatas or tirybok are really omelets with the filling incorporated into the egg mixture instead of being put on top to be folded into the omelet center for serving. These are wonderful vehicles for leftover vegetables.

Europe–Belarus

BELARUSIAN POTATO, MUSHROOM, AND ONION OMELET (cont'd)

4 large eggs
2 tablespoons light cream *or* half and half
Freshly ground black pepper, to taste

1 quart *boiling* water
1 medium potato—peeled and diced

1 tablespoon butter
1 tablespoon *extra virgin* olive oil
8 ounces assorted wild mushrooms—well-rinsed, trimmed, if necessary, and sliced

1/2 cup *thinly* sliced Italian red onion

1 tablespoon *finely* chopped fresh parsley leaves
1 tablespoon finely chopped fresh dillweed

Fat-free dairy sour cream

In a small bowl or measuring cup, combine eggs, cream, and black pepper. Using a fork or a small wire whisk, beat well. Set aside until required.

In a saucepan set over *MEDIUM* heat, combine *boiling* water and diced potatoes. Cook for 8 minutes. Drain well.

Preheat broiler to about 350 degrees F.

In a 10-inch skillet set over *MEDIUM* heat, heat butter and olive oil.* Add sliced mushrooms. Sauté until liquid extruded from mushrooms evaporates and mushrooms begin to brown. *Reduce heat to LOW-MEDIUM.*

Add onion slices and continue to sauté until onions are soft and translucent, *being careful not to allow onions to brown.*

Add par-boiled, diced potatoes and beaten egg mixture. Stir to mix. Spread over pan surface. Cook undisturbed until the bottom begins to set. Wrap pan handle with aluminum foil, if necessary, to protect it from burning. Place under preheated broiler until *lightly browned.* *Be careful not to scorch eggs.*

Slide out of skillet onto a heated round serving platter or, if preferred, serve directly from skillet. Garnish with *finely* chopped parsley and dillweed.

Serve at once, cut into wedges and garnished with sour cream, if desired.

Yields 6 servings
adequate for 4 people

Notes: *We use a non-stick-coated skillet which we further coat with a non-stick lecithin spray coating to facilitate the release of the *frittata* for serving.

If you boil the potato and sauté the mushrooms early in the day, this omelet can be on the table in very short order.

1/6 SERVING (exclusive of sour cream) –
PROTEIN = 6.1 g.; FAT = 8.1 g.; CARBOHYDRATE = 7.1 g.;
CALORIES = 126; CALORIES FROM FAT = 58%

APPLE – OATMEAL PORRIDGE
Kaša ad Ausianka i Jablki
TPT - 44 minutes

When we go out to lunch, we are often not hungry for a multi-course meal at dinnertime. Instead of snacking on crackers and cheese, I will often cook hot breakfast cereal. Buckwheat, millet, wheat, rice, and barley are used to make sweet porridges but my favorite Belarusian porridge dessert is made with oatmeal.

3 cups *one-percent* milk
1 1/4 cups quick oatmeal (*not instant*)

2 cups stewed apples—*well-drained**

Light cream *or* half and half

APPLE – OATMEAL PORRIDGE (cont'd)

In a non-stick-coated saucepan set over *MEDIUM* heat, combine milk, oatmeal, and sugar. Cook, stirring frequently until porridge thickens. Thin with more milk, if necessary. Refrigerate until cooled—about 30 minutes.

Fold *well-drained* stewed apples into oatmeal. Turn into a serving bowl. Refrigerate until ready to serve.

Serve into small dessert dishes with cream on the side.

Yields 6 servings
adequate for 4 people

Notes: *If you can apples in the fall, they will be the perfect texture for this dessert.

When required, this recipe can be halved or doubled.

1/6 SERVING (exclusive of cream) –
PROTEIN = 7.5 g.; FAT = 3.4 g.; CARBOHYDRATE = 47.1 g.;
CALORIES = 243; CALORIES FROM FAT = 13%

RICE PUDDING WITH HONEY IN THE BELARUSIAN STYLE
Kutya
TPT - 48 minutes

Honey is the sweetener of choice more often than not in Belarus. I had never sweetened my rice pudding with honey but once I tasted this, I found I was reaching for honey more often when making desserts. If you do not eat honey in your vegetarian or vegan regime, agave nectar can be substituted.

1 cup dry converted rice
1 cup water
1 cup *two-percent* **milk**

1/2 cup *preservative-free dark* **raisins**

1/2 cup honey, of choice
1/2 teaspoon pure vanilla extract

Light cream *or* **half and half**

In a large saucepan set over *MEDIUM* heat, combine rice, water, and milk. Allow to come to the boil. *Reduce heat to LOW.* Cover and allow to cook for 15 minutes.

Add raisins. Cover again and allow to cook for 5-7 minutes more. Remove from heat. Allow to stand for 15 minutes.

Add honey and vanilla extract. Stir to combine thoroughly. Turn into a warm serving bowl.

Serve warm with cream.

Yields 8 servings
adequate for 4-6 people

Note: This recipe can be halved, when required.

1/6 SERVING (exclusive of cream) –
PROTEIN = 3.3 g.; FAT = 0.8 g.; CARBOHYDRATE = 53.8 g.;
CALORIES = 257; CALORIES FROM FAT = 3%

Belgium

When the Romans invaded this northern part of Gaul in 100 BC, they found small villages of Celtic and Germanic peoples known as the *Belgae*. The name of this country can be traced directly to the name given this province of the Roman Empire, *Gallia Belgica*. During the fifth century AD the Germanic tribes collectively known as the Franks began to establish in the Low Countries. Many of the fiefdoms, which had been established after the Treaty of Verdun in 843 AD, were united into the Burgundian Netherlands in the fourteenth and fifteenth centuries. The Eighty Years' War (1568-1648) ended with the division of the Low Countries into two distinct provinces – the northern United Provinces or *Belgica Foederata*, "Federated Netherlands," and the Southern Provinces or *Belgica Regia*, "Royal Netherlands," which comprised most of modern-day Belgium and was ruled by the Spanish and Austrian Hapsburgs and then by the French. After the defeat of Napoleon in 1815, the First French Empire was dissolved and the Low Countries reunited as the United Kingdom of the Netherlands. In 1830 Belgium seceded from the Netherlands and established a constitutional democracy under a hereditary monarchy headed by Leopold of Saxe-Coburg and Gotha who became Leopold I, King of the Belgians, and from whom all Belgian monarchs must have a provable descendancy.

Germany invaded Belgium in 1914 and much of the fighting in the German attempt to invade and defeat France was fought on Belgian soil. In 1940 Germany again invaded and occupied Belgium until 1944. King Leopold III was popularly perceived as having collaborated with the Germans and was forced to abdicate in 1951 after a series of general strikes.

In 1951 the Benelux Customs Union, an economic union formed by Belgium, The Netherlands, and Luxembourg, joined with West Germany, France, and Italy to form the European Coal and Steel Community which became known as the Benelux Economic Union and is today known as the Benelux Union. Established to insure the unfettered movement of workers, capital, services, and goods in the region, it is considered by most to be the earliest version of what is today called the European Union.

Belgium is a densely populated country about the size of Maryland with a population of about 10.5 million. When analyzing European population density, one finds that only The Netherlands has more population per square mile. Some writers simply emphasize only the Flemish and Walloon differences in Belgian. Having won the independence of its southern provinces from Holland in 1830, one would expect a detectable Dutch influence but, further, one sees French, German, Celtic, Spanish, and Austrian influences at all levels. Clear evidence of continued influence is the fact that Dutch, French, and German are all considered official languages, which incidentally makes signage a costly government responsibility. In addition, a review of Belgian culinary traditions illustrates how the cuisine is beholden to many of its neighbors and conquerors. This can be observed in the food grown and in the preparation of that food. Creativity with this plethora of influences is what make Belgian food so very, very good. Today a large immigrant population from the Middle East and North Africa is introducing its culture and cuisine. Belgium has always incorporated foreign influences and although it is assumed that at its core Belgian cuisine is a cuisine that is based on the foods grown and eaten here since the Middle Ages, it will be fascinating to see how the food preparations of these Moslem immigrants enhance the Belgian cuisine.

Europe – Belgium

Baked "Fries" with Garlic Mayonnaise
Frites

Botterhammen:

Homemade White Soft Cheese with Crusty Bread and Sliced Radishes
Fromage Blanc

~

Asparagus Spears with Lemon Mayonnaise
Salades de Asperges

Sliced Tomatoes   or   Sliced, Cooked Beetroot
with **Belgian Cold Watercress Sauce**
Crème de Cresson

Chilled Whole Carrots and Mayonnaise–Mustard Sauce with Capers
Salade de Carottes aux Sauce Mayonnaise

~

Cream of Endive Soup   **Cream of White Asparagus Soup from Mechelen**
Brabantse Witloofroomsoep   *Veloute aux Asperges de Malines*

~~~~~~~~~~~~~~~~~~~~~~

Flemish Vegetable Stew with Beer
Carbonnades Flamandes

New Potatoes with Chervil
Pommes de Terre Nouvelles au Cerfeuil

~~~~~~~~~~

Baked Eggs
Gratin de Oeufs

Pearl Onions in Cream *au Gratin* with *Gruyère* Cheese
Gratin d'Oignons

Baby Carrots in the Flemish Style
Carottes Petit a la Flamande

~~~~~~~~~~~~~~~~~~~~~

Cherry Compote from the Ardennes   **Baked Bosc Pears**
Compote des Ardennes   *Poires au Four*

Rice Pudding with Saffron
Rystpap

Fruit Cream – Fresh and Uncooked   over   **Belgian Waffles**
La Creame du Fruits Frais   *Gaufres de Brussels*

Europe–**Belgium**

BAKED "FRIES"
Frites

TPT - 49 minutes

Belgians are very fond of fried potatoes, or "fries" as we refer to them. When served as a first course or appetizer, mayonnaise-based sauces are provided for dipping. Certainly, these are not French fries in either the historical or technical sense, but they are good and, oh the bonus, they are much lower in fat.

2 large waxy all-purpose potatoes—*do not use baking potatoes*—**peeled and cut into thick fries**
2 quarts *boiling* **water**

2 tablespoons potato starch (potato flour)*

2 tablespoons light oil—*sunflower oil is our preference*

Boil potato fry-cuts in *boiling* water for 10 minutes. Drain well. Pat dry.

Preheat oven to 400 degrees F.

In a plastic bag, combine drained potato fry-cuts and potato starch. Shake *gently* to coat potato slices.

In a *second* plastic bag, combine flour-dredged potato fry-cuts and oil. Shake *gently* to coat potato slices.

Spread the starch-coated potato slices out on a preheated, non-stick-coated cookie sheet. Bake in preheated 400 degree F. oven for 30 minutes, or until *golden brown*. Using tongs or two spatulas, turn "fries" occasionally to encourage even browning.

Turn onto a heated platter and *serve at once*.

Yields 4 servings
adequate for 4 people

Notes: *Potato starch (potato flour) is available in most grocery stores in the baking section or in the kosher foods section. If not available, unbleached white flour may be substituted, but the potato flavor will be somewhat compromised.

This recipe may be halved or doubled, when required.

1/4 SERVING – PROTEIN = 3.8 g.; FAT = 7.3 g.; CARBOHYDRATE = 36.0 g.;
CALORIES = 220; CALORIES FROM FAT = 30%

BELGIAN HOMEMADE WHITE SOFT CHEESE
Fromage Blanc

TPT - 36-60 hours and 9 minutes;
24-48 hours = curdling period;
12 hours = draining period

The idea of making my own cheese is a step toward self-sufficiency that just beckons me. I do not care if it is a simple Indian paneer or a cottage cheese, such as this, the fact that I made it myself just makes me feel so good. Your own bread, your own cheese, your own gingerale, and fruit from a neighboring tree . . . what a lunch!

1 quart *two-percent* **milk**
1 cup *cultured* **buttermilk**

In a glass mixing bowl, combine milk and buttermilk. Cover the bowl tightly with plastic wrap. Leave at room temperature (70-80 degrees F.) until the mixture curdles and thickens—as little as 24 hours or as much as 48 hours.*

Line a sieve with a double layer of culinary cheesecloth. Set the sieve over a mixing bowl. Turn the thickened milk into the cheesecloth-lined sieve. Refrigerate and allow to drain for about 12 hours, or longer if you want a thicker cheese.**

Reserve and freeze the whey for use in bread baking. Remove the cheese to a small bowl, cover tightly, and refrigerate until ready to use.

BELGIAN HOMEMADE WHITE SOFT CHEESE (cont'd)

If tightly covered and refrigerated, the fresh cheese will keep for 3-4 days. Use as you would use cottage or farmers' cheeses.

Yields about 1 1/2 cupfuls

Notes: *If there is no evidence of curdling by 48 hours, sprinkle a few drops of lemon juice over the milk mixture. The acid will encourage the curdling process to begin quite quickly.

**I prefer a thicker consistency than the Belgian recipe yields. At this point I gather the corners of the cheesecloth and tie the cheese into a ball which I hang for about 6 hours more in the refrigerator.

Season the cheese with *finely* chopped garlic, onion, and herbs, of choice, and accompany with breads and *crudités* for an appetizer course or a light lunch. Blend with cream or cream cheese for a richer version.

This recipe *can not* be halved or doubled successfully.

1/24 SERVING (i. e., per tablespoonful) –
PROTEIN = 1.7 g.; FAT = 0.8 g.; CARBOHYDRATE = 2.4 g.;
CALORIES = 24; CALORIES FROM FAT = 30%

BELGIAN COLD WATERCRESS SAUCE
Crème de Cresson
TPT - 17 minutes

A hotel restaurant in Buçaco, Portugal, had a distinctly French menu. Our concierge Antonio inquired as to whether we really liked "all those heavy cream sauces." We were disappointed that the menu was not Portuguese but we managed to muddle through the cream soups and the hot cream sauces for several days. When a delicate piece of white fish smothered in a heavy white sauce but, of course, with the obligatory parsley was presented, we knew that Antonio's warning had merit. If this cold, fresh-tasting Belgian cream sauce, much more appropriate to a menu for a hot summer's evening in July, had been served, we would have a fonder memory of those dinners.

The bright celery taste of lovage is a good compliment to the watercress and cream in this recipe. If you are preparing this sauce in the winter, replace the lovage with celery leaves but do plan to make it again in the spring or summer using lovage. Dried lovage is really not an asset to this sauce.

1 1/2 tablespoons sweet *(unsalted)* butter
1 large shallot—*finely* chopped
4 ounces watercress—thick stems discarded
 —well-washed and chopped
3 fresh lovage leaves—coarsely chopped *or*
 celery leaves

1 cup light cream *or* half and half, as preferred

1 1/2 teaspoons freshly squeezed lemon juice
1 tablespoon chopped fresh chives

Salt, to taste
Freshly ground black pepper, to taste

Europe – Belgium

BELGIAN COLD WATERCRESS SAUCE (cont'd)

In a large saucepan set over *LOW-MEDIUM* heat, melt sweet (*unsalted*) butter. Add the *finely* chopped shallot and chopped watercress and lovage leaves. Cook, stirring frequently, for about 8 minutes, or until softened. *Do not allow vegetables to brown.*

In the work bowl of the food processor or in the container of the electric blender, combine the softened vegetables and cream. Process until the mixture is smoothly puréed.

Turn into a bowl. Stir in lemon juice and chopped chives. Season, to taste, with salt and black pepper.

Keep refrigerated until ready to serve. The sauce will keep well in the refrigerator for 2-3 days.

Yields about 1 3/4 cupfuls

Note: This recipe may be halved, when required.

1/28 SERVING (i. e., per tablespoonful) –
PROTEIN = 0.3 g.; FAT = 1.4 g.; CARBOHYDRATE = 0.8 g.;
CALORIES = 16; CALORIES FROM FAT = 79%

CHILLED WHOLE CARROTS AND MAYONNAISE – MUSTARD SAUCE WITH CAPERS

Salade de Carottes aux Sauce Mayonnaise

TPT - 1 hour and 5 minutes

In our grocery stores, and probably in your grocery stores, there is a frozen vegetable mixture that has always baffled me. I can not understand why anyone would buy frozen peas with diced carrots. It is even offered as a vegetable choice in restaurants here in the Mid-Atlantic states. Those little orange cubes have no taste whatsoever to me ... the logic of the combination just escapes me. Steaming whole carrots seems to release the nuances of flavors that a carrot contains; flavors that are not as pronounced when carrots are boiled or eaten raw. Steamed carrots are also irresistibly sweet. A platter piled with steamed, chilled carrots and a bowl of the mayonnaise-mustard sauce on the side is a perfect buffet offering.

MAYONNAISE – MUSTARD SAUCE WITH CAPERS:

    1 cup *calorie-reduced or light* mayonnaise
    1 1/2 tablespoons *Dijon* mustard with wine
    1 tablespoon *extra virgin* olive oil

    2 teaspoons marinated capers—rinsed,
      well-drained and coarsely chopped

**12 small-medium carrots—trimmed and scraped
  or pared, if necessary**

In a small bowl, combine mayonnaise, mustard, and olive oil. Using a small wire whisk, combine until a smooth, rich dressing results.

Add chopped capers and, using a spoon, stir them into the dressing. Refrigerate the dressing until required.

Set up a steamer sufficiently large enough to hold all 12 carrots.* Steam carrots for about 20 minutes until *crisp-tender*. Carefully lift carrots and place on a platter in the refrigerator to cool for at least 30 minutes.

Arrange two chilled carrots on each of six elongated salad-sized plates, individual *au gratin* dishes, or *sushi* plates. Attractively arrange a dollop of the prepared caper mayonnaise over each serving.

Serve chilled or at room temperature as a salad.

Yields 6 individual servings

Notes: *A stackable bamboo steamer works best for this steaming task.

This recipe can be halved, when required.

1/6 SERVING – PROTEIN = 0.7 g.; FAT = 15.3 g.; CARBOHYDRATE = 4.2 g.;
CALORIES = 181; CALORIES FROM FAT = 76%

Europe–**Belgium**

BELGIAN CREAM OF ENDIVE SOUP
Witloofroomsoep

TPT - 53 minutes;
10 minutes = cooling period

Endive (Chichorium endivia) is a bitter vegetable closely related to escarole and curly endive, or chicory. It was discovered in Brussels by Jan Lammers in 1830. Upon returning from the Belgian War for Independence, Lammers discovered that the chicory roots that he had stored in his dark, damp cellar and which he expected to grind for coffee had sprouted curly white leaves. In truth, an entire industry was born that year and by 1872 the vegetable was being produced in such quantity it was introduced in Paris where it was an instant sensation. Annual production worldwide exceeds half a million tons today. This soup is so elegant that it seems that it must be difficult to prepare and, therefore, is an item for an elegant restaurant menu. It is not at all difficult to prepare this lovely, velvety smooth soup from Belgium.

2 tablespoons butter
1 cup *finely* chopped onion
1 medium leek—*white and very pale green sections only*—sliced into rounds and *very well-rinsed*
2 small ribs of celery—trimmed, well-washed, and *finely* chopped
4 large Belgian endives—trimmed, well-rinsed, cored, and coarsely chopped

2 tablespoons unbleached white flour

5 cups VEGETARIAN WHITE STOCK *[see index]* *or* a light-colored vegetarian stock of choice

1/8 teaspoon freshly grated nutmeg
Salt, to taste
Freshly ground *white* pepper, to taste

1/2 cup heavy cream

In a large saucepan or small kettle set over *MEDIUM* heat, melt butter. Add *finely* chopped onion, leek slices, *finely* chopped celery, and chopped endive. Cook, stirring frequently, until vegetables are wilted and onion is soft and translucent, *being careful not to allow vegetables to brown.*

Sprinkle flour over. Stir flour into vegetables. Cook, stirring constantly, for another minute or two.

Add vegetable stock and simmer, stirring frequently, until vegetables are tender—about 30 minutes. *Remove from heat and allow to cool for 10 minutes.*

Add grated nutmeg, salt, and white pepper. Using an electric blender or food processor fitted with a steel knife, purée the soup in batches until very smooth.* Place a sieve over a clean saucepan. Pour purée through the sieve; discard residue.

If you plan to serve it at once, return the purée to a clean saucepan set over *LOW* heat. Add heavy cream and cook, stirring frequently, with a wire whisk until heated through. *Do not allow the soup to boil once the cream as been added.* Check seasoning and adjust, if necessary. Turn into a heated soup tureen.

Serve into heated cream soup cups or soup plates, if preferred.

Yields 7 cupfuls

Notes: *The soup can be made ahead to this point and refrigerated as much as two days before it is served.

This can be halved to serve two.

1/7 SERVING – PROTEIN = 2.0 g.; FAT = 2.6 g.; CARBOHYDRATE = 7.8 g.;
CALORIES = 116; CALORIES FROM FAT = 20%

BELGIAN CREAM OF WHITE ASPARAGUS SOUP FROM MECHELEN
Velouté aux Asperges de Malines

TPT - 1 hour and 8 minutes

Belgians have a passion for velvety, white soups and they have a passion for the bleached white vegetables that make these soups possible. Here, white asparagus is the base for such a soup. Although onion is added to the previous recipe which features endive, no onions are added to this asparagus soup so as not to overwhelm the delicate flavor of this unique variety of asparagus, a specialty of the region around Mechelen which is between Brussels and Antwerp. White asparagus is becoming more and more readily available from greengrocers and is often available in well-stocked grocery stores.

Europe – **Belgium**

BELGIAN CREAM OF WHITE ASPARAGUS SOUP FROM MECHELEN (cont'd)

1 1/2 pounds white asparagus—well-washed, trimmed of hard bases, and peeled with a vegetable peeler, if necessary

1 cup *boiling* water

1 tablespoon butter

2 cups VEGETARIAN WHITE STOCK *[see index]* or a light-colored vegetarian stock of choice

2 tablespoons butter
3 tablespoons unbleached white flour

4 cups VEGETARIAN WHITE STOCK *[see index]* or a light-colored vegetarian stock of choice

1/2 cup heavy cream
3 tablespoons *fat-free* pasteurized eggs

Salt, to taste
Freshly ground *white* pepper, to taste

2 tablespoons *finely* chopped fresh chervil or fresh parsley, if necessary, for garnish

Cut asparagus tips from the stalks and reserve. In a small bowl combine asparagus tips and *boiling* water. Allow tips to "cook" in the *boiling* water for 3 minutes. Drain thoroughly and set aside until required.

Chop remaining stalks into 1/2-inch slices. Turn into a large saucepan or small kettle set over *MEDIUM* heat.

Add the 1 tablespoonful butter. Sauté for about 5 minutes. *Reduce heat to LOW-MEDIUM.*

Add the 2 cupfuls stock. Cover and allow to simmer for about 20 minutes. Using an electric blender or food processor fitted with steel knife, purée the asparagus until very smooth with no bits of asparagus remaining. Set aside briefly.

In a clean kettle set over *LOW-MEDIUM* heat, melt remaining 2 tablespoonfuls butter. Remove from heat and, using a wire whisk, make a *roux* by beating in flour. Return to heat and, stirring constantly, cook for 2 minutes, *being careful not to burn or overbrown the roux.* Remove from heat and, using a wire whisk, gradually beat in remaining 4 cupfuls vegetable stock. Return saucepan to heat and cook, stirring constantly, until thickened.

Add asparagus purée. Stir to combine.

In a measuring cup, combine heavy cream and pasteurized eggs. Gradually, while stirring, add heavy cream–egg mixture. Season with salt and white pepper. Continue cooking and stirring with a wire whisk until thickened. *Do not allow the soup to boil once the cream has been added.* Turn into a heated soup tureen. Float the reserved asparagus tips on top.

Serve into heated soup plates. Garnish each serving with a pinch of *finely* chopped chervil or parsley.

Yields 8 cupfuls

Note: This recipe can be halved or doubled, when required.

1/8 SERVING (i. e., 1 cupful) –
PROTEIN = 2.4 g.; FAT = 9.3 g.; CARBOHYDRATE = 5.2 g.;
CALORIES = 99; CALORIES FROM FAT = 85%

FLEMISH VEGETABLE STEW WITH BEER
Carbonnades Flamandes

TPT - 2 hours and 48 minutes;
[slow cooker: 2 hours and 30 minutes on HIGH]

Beer is brewed and drunk in Belgium to the extent that would greatly amaze an American. Eleven hundred varieties of beer are available to Belgian consumers but few of those find their way to the beverage distributors here in the United States. One often has to go out of their way to find the dark, rich beer loved by the Belgians and the Dutch. Left with bottles of beer in the basement bought for a guest who turned out to drink only O'Dooles, I decided to "vegetarianize" a classic Flemish stew. Slow cooking seemed a worthwhile, time-saving plan since we were slogging away on a manuscript at the time. Dinner is always welcome in the evening after we write or research all day but having to make dinner is not always a welcome thought.

Europe–Belgium

FLEMISH VEGETABLE STEW WITH BEER (cont'd)

1 teaspoon *extra virgin* olive oil
1 teaspoon butter
3/4 pound *crimini* mushrooms—stems removed, rinsed, cleaned well with a brush, and *thickly* sliced

12 ounces brown ale or dark beer

1 tablespoon KNEADED FLOUR FOR THICKENING *(Buerre Manie)* [see index]

8 ounces *frozen* soy nuggets or strips *or tempeh*—cut into 1-inch cubes
1/2 cup chopped onion
3 medium carrots—peeled and cut into 1/2-inch chunks
1 garlic clove—peeled and *finely* chopped
1 1/2 teaspoons country-style course *Dijon* mustard
1/2 teaspoon caraway seeds
Freshly ground black pepper, to taste
2 large bay leaves—broken in pieces and secured in a tea ball

18 thin, whole green beans—well-washed and trimmed

Preheat slow cooker to HIGH. Coat the inside of the bowl with non-stick lecithin spray coating.

In the bowl of the slow cooker, allow oil and butter to heat. Add mushroom slices, cover, and allow to cook, stirring frequently, until they have given off most of their liquid.

Add beer. Cook, stirring constantly, until the foaming stops.

Add the *buerre manie*. Stir to begin the thickening process.

Add soy or *tempeh* pieces, chopped onion, carrot chunks, *finely* chopped garlic, mustard, caraway seeds, pepper, and bay leaf pieces. Stir to combine. Cover and allow to cook for about 2 hours until vegetables are tender. Stir occasionally to prevent sticking. Add a couple of tablespoons of water if evaporation is excessive and vegetables begin to stick.

Remove tea ball and discard bay leaf pieces. Turn into a heated serving bowl and keep warm on a warming tray until ready to serve. It can be served over rice or as stew with a good bread, as you prefer.

Yields 8 servings
adequate for 4-6 people

Notes: We prefer this freshly made but have squirreled leftovers in the freezer for a future lunch with great success.

This recipe can be doubled, when required.

1/8 SERVING – PROTEIN = 9.6 g.; FAT = 3.1 g.; CARBOHYDRATE = 8.8 g.;
CALORIES = 102; CALORIES FROM FAT = 27%

BELGIAN NEW POTATOES WITH CHERVIL
Pommes de Terre Nouvelles au Cerfeuil
TPT - 29 minutes

Planting the herb beds in our Pennsylvania gardens took several years and one bed became an experimental garden, a sick bay, and a place to heel-in plants for other beds-in-progress. I decided to plant sprouted potatoes from my root cellar, cutting them just as Grandma had taught me as a child. I scratched the tiny potatoes out from under the potato plants, cleaned them well, and cooked them immediately for dinner. The taste was so phenomenal, so earthy, I could not believe the incredible difference from those that I had been buying at the farmers' market. My potatoes were really "new."

2 pounds new potatoes well-washed and *carefully brushed**
2 quarts *cold* water

3 tablespoons butter—softened *to room temperature*
1/2 cup *finely* chopped fresh chervil leaves**

In a large saucepan set over *MEDIUM-HIGH* heat, combine *cold* water and prepared new potatoes. *Be sure that water covers the potatoes.* Bring water to the boil. *Reduce heat to MEDIUM.* Cook for about 15 minutes, or until potatoes are *crisp-tender. Do not allow potatoes to overcook.* Turn into a colander and allow to drain.

BELGIAN NEW POTATOES WITH CHERVIL (cont'd)

Turn potatoes into a heated serving bowl. Add *softened* butter and *finely* chopped fresh chervil. Stir gently until butter is melted.

Serve at once.

Yields 6 serving
adequate for 4 people

Notes: *True *new* potatoes are, in truth, baby potatoes and are often available in specialty greengrocers or farmers' markets in the early spring. These tiny, marble-sized potatoes do not keep well and should not be refrigerated since the taste is altered irrevocably below 50 degrees F. when the starch converts to sugar. *Do not scrub them hard when cleaning or the skins will peel off.* Small salad potatoes, often sold as new potatoes, do not have the delicate quality of the true new potato.

**Chervil *(Anthriscus cerefolium)* is best used fresh and since it is an easily cultivated annual in Zones 3-7, most gardeners can enjoy a patch of this herb. Essential to the French herb mixture know as *fines herbes*, it has a very light celery taste. Chervil reseeds itself if some of the flowers, born in umbels, are allowed to mature. It greatly prefers partial shade and a rich, moist soil bed, but seems to survive in full sun as long as it has some tall neighbors to provide a little shade.

When required, this recipe may be halved or doubled.

This recipe may be followed to make BELGIAN PARSLEYED NEW POTATOES *(Pommes de Terre Nouvelles au Persil)*. Just substitute finely chopped parsley for the chervil.

1/6 SERVING – PROTEIN = 2.7 g.; FAT = 5.8 g.; CARBOHYDRATE = 21.2 g.;
CALORIES = 146; CALORIES FROM FAT = 36%

BELGIAN BAKED EGGS
Gratin de Oeufs
TPT - 28 minutes

During World War II many foods were unavailable or in short supply but we always had plenty of fresh eggs which my grandfather brought to us from a friend's farm each week. My mom often made an egg dish similar to this to make the rationed food supply stretch a bit. I had just about forgotten that dish until I found this Belgian version. It makes a very fine, almost elegant, first course.

1 tablespoon butter
1 1/2 tablespoons whole wheat flour
1 1/2 cups skimmed milk

2 tablespoons country-style *Dijon* mustard
Freshly ground black pepper, to taste
2 tablespoons chopped Italian flat-leafed parsley

6 hard-cooked large eggs—shelled

1/4 cup shredded Swiss *Emmentaler* cheese
2 tablespoons dry whole wheat breadcrumbs

Preheat broiler to about 350 degrees F. Prepare an *au gratin* dish or other shallow baking dish, just large enough to hold the egg halves, by coating with non-stick lecithin spray coating.*

In a saucepan set over *LOW* heat, melt butter. Remove from heat and, using a wire whisk, make a *roux* by beating in flour. Return to heat and, stirring constantly, cook for 2 minutes, *being careful not to burn or overbrown the roux.* Remove from heat and gradually beat in milk. Return saucepan to heat and cook, stirring constantly, until thickened.

Stir in the mustard and black pepper, to taste. Stir in chopped parsley.

Spoon half of sauce into the bottom of the baking dish. Spread to cover surface evenly. Cut hard-cooked eggs in halves lengthwise. Arrange egg halves, cut-side-up, on the sauce. Spoon the remaining sauce over the egg halves.

In a small bowl, combine shredded cheese with breadcrumbs. Sprinkle evenly over the egg halves.

Broil under preheated broiler until the top is *lightly browned* and the sauce is bubbling.

Serve at once, allowing two egg halves per serving.

Yields 6 servings
adequate for 4-6 people

Notes: *This dish makes a most attractive presentation if prepared in individual *au gratin* dishes. Duchess potatoes may, if desired, be piped around the eggs before broiling.

Europe – **Belgium**

BELGIAN BAKED EGGS (cont'd)

When required, this recipe is easily halved or doubled.

1/6 SERVING – PROTEIN = 9.6 g.; FAT = 9.4 g.; CARBOHYDRATE = 4.9 g.;
CALORIES = 139; CALORIES FROM FAT = 61%

BELGIAN PEARL ONIONS IN CREAM *AU GRATIN* WITH *GRUYÈRE* CHEESE
Gratin d'Oignons
TPT - 35 minutes

Creamed pearl onions often appear on holiday menus in America, probably because pearl onions make their appearance in the greengrocers and at the farmers' markets in the late fall. Try this, for a change; it is worthy of a holiday table.

3 quarts *boiling* **water**
1 pound pearl onions—well-washed, but *unpeeled*****

1/3 cup light cream *or* **half and half**
Freshly ground black pepper, to taste
Freshly grated nutmeg, to taste

1/2 cup shredded natural *Gruyère* **cheese**

Preheat broiler to about 375 degrees F. Prepare a shallow *au gratin* dish, just large enough to hold the onions in a single layer, or other shallow oven-to-table baking dish by coating with non-stick lecithin spray coating.

Place a kettle of *boiling* water over *MEDIUM* heat. Add *unpeeled* pearl onions into the *boiling* water. Cook for about 15 minutes, or until tender. Drain and place under *cold, running* water.

As soon as onions can be handled, peel each and cut an **X** in the root end to prevent the onions from falling apart. Place peeled onions in the prepared *au gratin* dish.

Add cream. Season with *white* pepper and nutmeg. Stir to distribute ingredients evenly.**

Scatter the shredded *Gruyère* cheese *evenly* over the onions.

Broil under preheated 375 degree F. boiler until cheese is melted and *lightly browned.*

Serve at once, directly from *au gratin* dish.

Yields 6 servings
adequate for 4 people

Notes: *If pearl onions are not available, small white boiling onions can be substituted.

**This dish may be prepared in advance to this point, covered and refrigerated. To protect your baking dish, *bring to room temperature before sliding under the broiler.*

This recipe may be halved or doubled, when required.

1/6 SERVING – PROTEIN = 4.1 g.; FAT = 4.3 g.; CARBOHYDRATE = 6.7 g.;
CALORIES = 79; CALORIES FROM FAT = 49%

BELGIAN BABY CARROTS IN THE FLEMISH STYLE
Carottes Petit a la Flamande
TPT - 34 minutes

This version of a classic vegetable recipe from the Belgian provinces north of Brussels, the area often referred to as the Flemish North, is much less rich than the original which would contain heavy cream and egg yolks and a great deal more butter.

BELGIAN BABY CARROTS IN THE FLEMISH STYLE (cont'd)

36 Belgian baby carrots—trimmed and scraped*
1 quart *boiling* **water**

1/2 cup water
1 tablespoon butter
1 teaspoon sugar
Freshly ground *white* **pepper, to taste**

1/4 cup *fat-free* **pasteurized eggs (the equivalent of 1 egg)**
1/2 cup light cream *or* **half and half, as preferred**
2 tablespoons freshly squeezed lemon juice

2 tablespoons *finely* **chopped parsley, for garnish**

In a saucepan set over *MEDIUM-HIGH* heat, parboil the baby carrots in the 1 quart *boiling* water for 10 minutes. Drain well.

Turn drained baby carrots back into the emptied saucepan. Add the 1/2 cupful water, butter, sugar, and *white* pepper. Allow to come to just below the boiling point.

Reduce heat to LOW.

Cook, covered, for about 10 minutes, or until carrots are *crisp-tender*. Shake the pan or gently stir occasionally. *If necessary,* add a tablespoonful or two more of water to prevent carrots from sticking to the bottom of the pan. Remove pan from heat. Using a slotted spoon, remove carrots to a small bowl. Set aside briefly.

In a small bowl or measuring cup, combine pasteurized eggs, cream, and lemon juice. Using a wire whisk, combine thoroughly. *Gradually—tablespoonful by tablespoonful*—whisk the egg—cream mixture into the liquid remaining in the saucepan. *Mix very well.* Return pan to *LOW* heat. Cook, stirring constantly, until heated through and the sauce has thickened slightly. *Do not allow sauce to boil once the cream has been added.* Add reserved carrots to cream sauce and allow to heat through.

Turn into a heated serving bowl and garnish with *finely* chopped fresh parsley. Keep warm on a warming tray, if necessary, until ready to serve.

Yields 6 servings
adequate for 4 people

Notes: *Baby carrots, formerly marketed as Belgian baby carrots, are increasingly available in the produce sections of grocery stores. If not available in yours, cut about 8 medium carrots—scraped or pared—into large sticks and proceed as directed above.

When required, this recipe may be halved or doubled.

1/6 SERVING – PROTEIN = 1.5 g.; FAT = 3.9 g.; CARBOHYDRATE = 6.3 g.;
CALORIES = 65; CALORIES FROM FAT = 54%

BELGIAN CHERRY COMPOTE FROM THE ARDENNES
Compôte des Ardennes

TPT - 8 hours and 11 minutes;
8 hours = flavor development period

Because we make this with our own canned cherries, this is not just a summer dessert. And, because we make it with the syrup drained from our canned cherries, instead of wine which is traditional, it is not just an "adult dessert."

1 lemon—*well-washed*

2 jars *or* **cans (16 ounces each) dark,** *sweet* **cherries—home-canned and in light syrup, if possible**
1/2 cup red currant jelly
1/4 teaspoon ground cinnamon

Using a vegetable peeler, peel the zest from the lemon in the longest strips possible. Scrape any of the bitter, white flesh from the zest strips.

In a saucepan set over *LOW-MEDIUM* heat, combine *sweet* cherries and the syrup in which they have been canned, red currant jelly, ground cinnamon, and the strips of lemon zest. Cook, stirring frequently, until the jelly has melted. Remove from heat.

Chill, covered, in the refrigerator for at least 8 hours, or overnight if more convenient. Remove and discard lemon zest strips. Turn into a serving bowl.

Europe–**Belgium**

BELGIAN CHERRY COMPOTE FROM THE ARDENNES (cont'd)

Serve into sherbet glasses, large wine glasses, or dessert dishes.

Yields 6 servings
adequate for 4 people

Note: This recipe is easily halved or doubled, as required.

1/6 SERVING – PROTEIN = 0.7 g.; FAT = 0.0 g.; CARBOHYDRATE = 15.2 g.; CALORIES = 82; CALORIES FROM FAT = 0%

BELGIAN BAKED BOSC PEARS
Poires au Four

TPT - 73 hours and 37 minutes;
72 hours (3 days) = vanilla sugar preparation;
30 minutes = cooling period

The secret of this rather sumptuous pear dessert is the "perfuming" of the sugar. Vanilla sugar is not only divine, it is a practical item to have on-hand in your pantry. We prepare it with confectioners' sugar, as for this dish, or with granulated sugar.

VANILLA SUGAR:
    1/3 cup confectioners' sugar

    1 vanilla bean—cut into halves lengthwise

6 large, ripe Bosc pears—*well-washed and well-dried*
3 tablespoons butter—*softened to room temperature*

Light cream *or* **dessert sauce, of choice, such as ENGLISH CUSTARD SAUCE** *(Crème Anglaise)* *[see index],* **if desired**

Sift confectioners' sugar into a bowl. Pour sifted sugar into a one-pint canning jar or other airtight container with lid. Add vanilla bean halves. Secure lid and shake jar gently to distribute the pieces and seeds of the vanilla bean.

Allow to stand for at least 3 days, turning the container several times a day to evenly "perfume" the sugar.

Preheat oven to 275 degrees F.

Rub the pears with the *softened* butter. Place the pears in a non-stick-coated baking pan or on a non-stick-coated cookie sheet.

Bake in preheated 275 degree F. oven for about 1 hour, or until softened.

Using two large spoons, transfer the baked pears to a platter or into individual soup plates.

Turn prepared VANILLA SUGAR into a fine sieve. Sift sugar generously over each pear. Allow to cool to room temperature for at least 30 minutes, or chill, if preferred.

Serve, accompanied, if desired, with cream or sauce, of choice.

Yields 6 servings
adequate for 6 people

Note: This recipe may be increased or decreased proportionately, when required.

1/6 SERVING (without cream or sauce) –
PROTEIN = 0.5 g.; FAT = 5.8 g.; CARBOHYDRATE = 19.4 g.;
CALORIES = 132; CALORIES FROM FAT = 40%

Europe–**Belgium**

BELGIAN GOLDEN RICE PUDDING WITH SAFFRON
Rystpap

TPT - 2 hours and 46 minutes;
2 hours = cooling period

A similar pudding is made in Ireland but the Irish version calls for far less saffron and incorporates eggs to form a custard. The Flemish believe that if you are going to use the most expensive seasoning in the world, use it generously! White plates are a very good choice on which to serve this pudding since the saffron yellow color is well-shown against the white plate. This pudding is topped with brown sugar by most Belgians but we prefer the pudding to be less sweet so that the nuances of the subtle flavorings come through.

2 cups water
1 cup dry long grain white rice—*do not use converted rice*
1 1/4 teaspoons saffron

1/2 cup light cream *or* **half and half**
5 tablespoons white sugar
1 cinnamon quill
1/2 vanilla bean—split lengthwise

2 tablespoons heavy cream

Light **brown sugar, if desired**

In a saucepan set over *LOW* heat, bring the 2 cupfuls water to the boil.

Stir in rice and saffron. Cover and cook, *undisturbed*, over *LOW* heat for about 25 minutes.

When rice is cooked and water has been absorbed, stir in light cream or half and half, white sugar, cinnamon quill, and vanilla bean. Cook, stirring frequently, until sugar is dissolved and cream has been absorbed. Milk rice will thicken. Remove cinnamon quill and vanilla bean.

Stir in heavy cream.

Apportion the rice into six soup plates. Allow the pudding to come to room temperature—about 2 hours.

Pass a bowl of brown sugar and encourage guests to sprinkle brown sugar, as much or as little as they prefer, over the rice pudding.

Yields 6 individual servings

Note: This recipe may be halved or doubled, when required. When doubling, the pudding may be attractively presented in a wide, shallow crystal bowl or on a large round, preferably white, platter.

1/6 SERVING – PROTEIN = 1.4 g.; FAT = 3.5 g.; CARBOHYDRATE = 20.5 g.;
CALORIES = 120; CALORIES FROM FAT = 26%

BELGIAN FRUIT CREAM — FRESH AND UNCOOKED
La Creame du Fruits Frais

TPT - 35 minutes;
30 minutes = chilling period

Similar to Italian "frullatas" and "smoothies," which are drunk as beverages, this uniquely Belgian puréed fruit dessert is eaten with a spoon. It is a very refreshing end to a meal.

1 large orange—well-peeled, seeded, and chopped
1 large apple—peeled, seeded, cored, and chopped
1 cup chopped, fresh pineapple
1/4 cup light cream *or* **half and half**
1 tablespoon sugar
1/2 teaspoon pure vanilla extract

Sprigs of lemon balm, for garnish, if available*

In the work bowl of the food processor or in the container of the electric blender, combine chopped orange, apple, and pineapple pieces with cream, sugar, and vanilla extract. Process for several minutes until *very smooth*.

Apportion among four wine glasses. Refrigerate for about 30 minutes to chill thoroughly. Hang a sprig of lemon balm, if in season, over the edge of each glass as a garnish.

Europe–Belgium

BELGIAN FRUIT CREAM — FRESH AND UNCOOKED (cont'd)

Serve with iced tea spoons.

Yields 4 individual servings

Notes: *Lemon balm *(Melissa officinalis)* is an asset to any herb gardener. Its lemony mint fragrance attracts bees into the garden and its culinary uses in teas, salads, and fruit-based desserts and beverages is so extensive that we would not be without it. Although it is a member of the mint family, do not confuse it with the so-called lemon mint often seen in garden centers. The lemon fragrance and flavor of lemon balm is much more assertive. This very attractive perennial (Zones 4-9) grows well in full sun but does prefer a bit of afternoon shade. It grows best in well-drained soil and does not appreciate being over-watered or over-fertilized. A plant which naturally repels most insect pests, it is itself occasionally susceptible to spider mites during hot, humid summers.

Other seasonal fruits may be substituted, if desired. Peaches, apricots, mangoes, tangerines, clementines, bananas, and berries are all possibilities. If berries are your choice, purée the berries first and pass the purée through a fine sieve to remove seeds before adding to the other ingredients in the food processor or blender.

Since food processors and blenders have a limited capacity, prepare two batches instead of trying to double.

1/4 SERVING – PROTEIN = 0.7 g.; FAT = 1.2 g.; CARBOHYDRATE = 13.3 g.;
CALORIES = 62; CALORIES FROM FAT = 17%

BELGIAN WAFFLES
Gaufres de Brussels

TPT - 1 hour;
30 minutes = batter resting period

Let's see, how many years has it been since I first tasted this wonder? The year before we were married, the New York World's Fair came to Flushing Meadow in Queens, New York. Every time we went to the fair for the next two years, breakfast was a strawberry waffle at one of the Belgian waffle stands; as I remember there were several but the one in the central food court was our first destination. They were thick, yet crisp, and the sweetened fruit and whipped cream were piled high. My mom and dad just loved them too. Sometimes Dad would stop just before we left for the day to have another. All through these intervening years I have tried one or another version, hoping to evolve a less extravagantly caloric, more healthful version but I found each of my attempts lacking. A Belgian waffle iron has been available through mail order catalogs for several years but certainly is not a standard appliance in every household and, through this recipe, I wanted to share the taste, the pleasure, and, perhaps, the memory so I kept trying to create a recipe that can be used in a conventional waffle iron.

6 tablespoons sweet (*unsalted*) butter

1/3 cup sugar

2 large egg yolks

1/3 cup buttermilk pancake and waffle mix*
1/3 cup whole wheat pancake and waffle mix*
5 tablespoons skimmed milk
1/2 teaspoon pure vanilla extract

2 large egg whites

Using an electric mixer or food processor fitted with steel knife, cream butter until light and fluffy. Add sugar and continue to cream until again light and fluffy. Add egg yolks one at a time, beating well after each addition.

Beat in mixes alternately with milk and vanilla extract.

Set batter aside for about 30 minutes to rest.

BELGIAN WAFFLES (cont'd)

Preheat waffle iron.

Using a electric mixer fitted with *grease-free* beaters or by hand using a *grease-free* wire whisk, beat egg whites in a *grease-free* bowl until *stiff*, but *not dry*. Whisk-fold beaten egg whites into prepared batter.

Using preheated waffle iron, prepare crisp waffles. Keep warm on a warming tray—*uncovered*—until served with butter and a sprinkling of sugar. Ice cream, a fruit sauce of choice, or whipped cream make nice toppings, if preferred.

> Yields eight 3 1/2-inch square waffles
> adequate for 4 people

Notes: *The commercial pancake and waffle mixes can be replaced using 2/3 cupful of my PANCAKE, QUICK BREAD, AND WAFFLE MIX *[see index]*.

This recipe is easily halved or doubled, when required.

Although authentic Belgian waffles require a special waffle iron which produces unique waffle about twice as thick as those usually served in the United States, these are crisp and flavorful reminders of those in Belgium.

Cold, these make an interesting lunch box item.

> 1/8 SERVING (i. e., per 3 1/2-inch square waffle exclusive of topping) –
> PROTEIN = 2.2 g.; FAT = 9.3 g.; CARBOHYDRATE = 18.3 g.;
> CALORIES = 165; CALORIES FROM FAT = 51%

Bosnia and Herzegovina

Americans growing up in the 1990s knew friends and family who fought in Bosnia and experienced the military and sectarian horrors of that decade after the breakup of Yugoslavia, in much the same way my generation references the years of the "police action" we have come to know as the Korean War. The Korean War has not officially ended and the problems in Bosnia still haunt its efforts of statehood as they try to rebuild their country both physically and ideologically while simultaneously trying to establish a mentality for a market economy after decades of socialism.

Conquered by the Romans in the second and third centuries BC, the area that is now the Republic of Bosnia and Herzegovina was settled first by several Illyrian civilizations, and known as Illyricum, and then by the Celts. Through the sixth to the ninth centuries AD Slavic tribes moved into the area and during that period Bosnia was split between the nations of Serbia and Croatia. By the eleventh and into the twelfth century Bosnia was under the rule of Hungary after which it became the first independent banate in the region, the Banate of Bosnia. The Kingdom of Bosnia, as it was called by the fifteenth century, was conquered by the Ottoman Turks in 1463. The cuisine today clearly reflects the influences of this period.

From 1878 to World War I, Bosnia came under the rule of the Austro–Hungarian Empire. In 1914, while on a visit to Sarajevo, the capital of Bosnia, Archduke Franz Ferdinand of Austria–Este, the presumptive heir to the Austro-Hungarian throne, and his wife Sophie, Duchess of Hohenberg, were assassinated. This was the spark that ignited the hostilities that led to war, a war presumably to be "a war to end all wars" but which would later be known as World War I. Austria–Hungary responded to the assassination by declaring war against Serbia which resulted in mutual declarations of war by the Central Powers and the Allies, the nations allied with Serbia. After the war, with the collapse of the Austro–Hungarian Empire, the kingdom of Serbs, Croats, and Slovenes was created, later to be known as Yugoslavia. Bosnia was a part of that Versailles state. In 1945, after World War II, Bosnia and Herzegovina became a republic in the Yugoslav Socialist Federation governed by Josip Broz Tito and which included the Socialist Republics of Bosnia and Herzegovina, Croatia, Macedonia, Montenegro, Slovenia, and Serbia including the Socialist Autonomous Provinces of Kosovo and Vojvodina. Although Marshal Tito died in 1980, this union struggled on until Yugoslavia began to dissolve when Croatia and Slovenia declared independence in June 1991.

Bosnia–Herzegovina declared their combined statehood in March 1992. The nation occupies 19,741 square miles, about the size of the states of New Hampshire and Vermont combined, and is populated by about four million people.

Foods of both the East and the West all live side by side, beautifully spiced dishes and desserts drenched in honey and nuts suggesting the days of the Ottoman Empire and dishes reminiscent of the years of the Austrian rule with basic elements familiar to the Central European palate. These result in a complex and interesting juxtaposition of flavors. Meat is favored and added to any dish that a cook thinks will profit from the addition. Rarely is there a meatless dish on a restaurant menu so a vegetarian can often spend the better part of the day trying to find a meal.

Europe–Bosnia and Herzegovina

Fried Yogurt Fingers
Peksimeti
with
Mustard – Sour Cream Dipping Sauce
Umak od Kisela Paulaka i Senf

Platter of Sliced Tomatoes, Cucumbers, Onions, Hard-Cooked Eggs,
Feta Cheese, and Assorted Olives

~

Potato Milk Soup
Krompir Sopa

Tomato Soup with Herbs and Coddled Eggs

~

Baby Pepper Salad
Kiseli Paprike

~~~~~~~~~~~~~~~~~~~~~~

Bosnian Beans
Prebranac

| Grilled tomatoes | or | **Onions in Tomato Sauce** |
| on Bed of Onions Sautéed in Walnut Oil | | *Paradajas Beogradske* |

~~~~~~~~~~~

Meatballs and Green Beans in Yogurt Sauce
Pljeskavice

| Noodles with Sour Cream and *Feta* Cheese | Braised Sweet and Sour Red Cabbage |
| *Flekice* | *Varza Calita* |

~~~~~~~~~~~

Baked Acorn Squash with Rice and Cheese Stuffing
Dolma

Steamed Whole Carrots with Parsley

~~~~~~~~~~~

Baked Eggplant with Mushrooms and Cream

Steamed Spinach   Baked Potato Halves with Sour Cream

~~~~~~~~~~~~~~~~~~~~~

| **Cake with Lemon Syrup** | **Chocolate "Chemistry Class" Cake** |
| *Bosnanski Sevidzan* | *Cockoladni Torta* |

Baklava

Grilled Peaches and Plums
with
Angel Food Cookies
Nagli Fatme

Europe–Bosnia and Herzegovina

HERZEGOVINAN FRIED YOGURT FRITTERS
Peksimeti

TPT - 29 minutes

Instead of the standard appetizer dippers like chips, these fritters, wildly popular in Bosnia–Herzegovina provide a wallop of protein with that crispy fried crust you are craving. Even a little bit of leftover sauce that was frozen, because there was just too much to throw away but too little for another meal, can be the beginning of a really impressive appetizer. We often serve these with spicy salsas and an assortment of cheeses.

Oil for deep-frying

1 cup unbleached white flour
Pinch salt
Pinch baking powder

1/2 cup YOGURT CRÈME [see index] **or thick Greek-style yogurt**
2 tablespoons *fat-free* **pasteurized eggs (the equivalent of 1 egg)**
1/4 teaspoon dried yeast

1/2 cup water

In a deep skillet set over *MEDIUM* heat, pour oil in a depth of one-half inch. Allow to heat.

In a mixing bowl, combine flour, salt, and baking powder. Stir well.

Add yogurt, pasteurized eggs, and dried yeast. Stir well to combine.

Gradually, while stirring, add water until you have a thick, but still sticky, dough. Turn out onto a floured surface. Sprinkle more flour on top. Shape into a 4 x 8 x 1/2-inch rectangle. Cut crosswise into ten fingers.

Fry in hot oil until browned and crispy, turning once. Transfer to several thicknesses of paper toweling to absorb excess oil. Transfer to a heated serving platter.

Serve warm with any sauce or *salsa* you enjoy.

Yields 10 fritters
adequate for 6 people

Note: This recipe can be doubled, when required.

1/6 SERVING – PROTEIN = 4.9 g.; FAT = 0.5 g.; CARBOHYDRATE = 13.8 g.;
CALORIES = 89; CALORIES FROM FAT = 5%

MUSTARD – SOUR CREAM DIPPING SAUCE
Umak od Kisela Pavlaka i Senf

TPT - 3 minutes

The cuisine of Bosnia and Herzegovina has been influenced, as I have mentioned, from that introduced by the Ottoman Empire, exemplified by the many recipes that can be traced to Turkey. There is also a pronounced influence from the North, exemplified by their expansive repertoire of potato recipes. The use of sauces can also be attributed to northern influences. This recipe, simple as it may be, is a useful culinary tool and it too owes it origins to the cuisines of Austria and Germany.

2/3 cup *fat-free* **dairy sour cream**
1 tablespoon MUSTARD SAUCE [see index], **or more to taste**
1/2 teaspoon freshly squeezed lemon juice

1-2 tablespoons *whole* **milk**

In a small bowl, combine sour cream, mustard, and lemon juice. Mix thoroughly.

Gradually, teaspoonful by teaspoonful, beat in milk until sauce is of desired consistency. Turn into a dipping bowl or sauceboat. Refrigerate until ready to serve.

Serve chilled or at room temperature, as preferred.

Yields about 3/4 cupful

Note: This recipe can be halved or doubled, when required.

1/12 SERVING (i. e., per tablespoonful) –
PROTEIN = 2.0 g.; FAT = 0.2 g.; CARBOHYDRATE = 7.1 g.;
CALORIES = 45; CALORIES FROM FAT = 5%

Europe–**Bosnia and Herzegovina**

BOSNIAN POTATO MILK SOUP
Krampir Sapa

TPT - 1 hour and 5 minutes

Traveling in Europe, we tasted many potato soups but unlike most potato soups we encountered, the potatoes for this soup are simmered in milk. The richer the milk, the richer the soup. I use skimmed milk and then stir in sour cream to thicken and enrich. It's a body warming soup on a cold day.

1 quart skimmed milk
3 large *waxy*, **all purpose potatoes—peeled and diced**

2 tablespoons safflower *or* **sunflower oil**
1 medium onion—*finely* **chopped**

2 tablespoons unbleached white flour
3/4 teaspoon paprika

Salt, to taste
Freshly ground black pepper, to taste

1/4 cup *fat-free* **dairy sour cream**
1 tablespoon chopped fresh parsley

In a kettle set over *LOW-MEDIUM* heat, bring milk to just below the boil. Add diced potatoes. Simmer for 25 minutes, or until potatoes are tender.

Meanwhile, in a non-stick-coated skillet set over *MEDIUM* heat, heat oil. Add onion and sauté until onion is soft and translucent, *being careful not to allow onion to brown.*

Add flour and paprika. Stir to integrate thoroughly. Transfer several ladlefuls of the milk from the potato kettle into the skillet. Stir constantly until the milk has been thickened by the onion–flour mixture. Turn into kettle and cook, stirring frequently, until the soup thickens slightly.

Season with salt and pepper.

Add sour cream and parsley. Stir. Turn into a heated soup tureen.

Serve at once into heated soup bowls. Reheat leftovers *gently* to preserve potato texture.

Yields 6 cupfuls

Note: This recipe can be halved or doubled.

1/6 SERVING (i. e. per cupful) –
PROTEIN = 8.1 g.; FAT = 4.8 g.; CARBOHYDRATE = 29.8 g.;
CALORIES = 195; CALORIES FROM FAT = 22%

BABY PEPPER SALAD IN THE STYLE OF BOSNIA
Kiseli Paprike

TPT - 2 hours and 10 minutes;
2 hours = marination period

Pickling peppers is a way of preserving a harvest that those who have grown peppers know can be often overwhelming. Preserved peppers appear on Bosnian tables as an appetizer or as a salad in the winter. Since sweet bell peppers of all colors are available year round here in the United States, few would go to the trouble to pickle peppers. The following recipe is what might be called a quick pickle. It provides a sweet, sour taste that clears the palate and stimulates the appetite.

9 baby red, yellow, orange, and/or green bell peppers—trimmed, halved, and seeded with membranes removed
2 tablespoons red wine vinegar
1/2 teaspoon sugar
1/4 teaspoon salt
Freshly ground mixed peppercorns—red, white, and black—to taste

2 teaspoons *extra virgin* **olive oil**

In a plastic container with lid, combine pepper halves, vinegar, sugar, salt and ground mixed peppercorns. Tightly seal. Slosh gently to coat the peppers with the marination liquid. Refrigerate for 2 hours to allow for flavor development. Slosh occasionally to insure uniform contact with the marination liquid. Turn peppers and liquid into a fine sieve and allow to drain.

Europe – Bosnia and Herzegovina

BABY PEPPER SALAD IN THE STYLE OF BOSNIA (cont'd)

Turn drained peppers into a serving bowl. Add oil. Toss to coat the peppers with the oil. Refrigerate until ready to serve.

Serve chilled.

Yields 12 servings
adequate for 6 people

Note: This recipe can be halved or doubled, when required.

1/12 SERVING (i. e., allowing two pepper halves per serving) –
PROTEIN = 0.7 g.; FAT = 1.3 g.; CARBOHYDRATE = 4.2 g.;
CALORIES = 29; CALORIES FROM FAT = 40%

BOSNIAN BEANS
Prebranac

TPT - 44 minutes (hot) or 2 hours and 44 minutes (cold)

Whenever possible, I do prepare this dish using dried beans but not everybody has the time to cook beans from scratch and not everybody has a slow cooker which can do the job efficiently for a cook on a busy day. This recipe utilizes readily-available and quickly-prepared canned cannellini beans. Served either hot or cold, it is a marvelous legume dish for a summer menu.

1 tablespoon safflower *or* sunflower oil
1 medium onion—*finely* **chopped**

3/4 cup water
1 medium carrot—**scraped or pared and** *very*
  thinly **sliced into rounds**
1 teaspoon paprika
2 bay leaves—broken in half

1 can (15.5 ounces) *cannellini or* **white kidney**
  beans—*undrained*
Freshly ground black pepper, to taste

In a non-stick-coated skillet set over *LOW-MEDIUM* heat, heat oil. Add *finely* chopped onion and sauté until onions are soft and translucent, *being careful not to allow onions to brown.*

Add water, *very thinly* sliced carrot, paprika, and bay leaf pieces. Cook, stirring frequently, until carrot slices are tender—about 15 minutes. *Remove and discard bay leaf pieces.*

Add *undrained cannellini* beans. Stir to combine well. Season with black pepper to taste. Cook, stirring frequently, for about 15 minutes, or until heated through. Turn into a heated serving bowl.

Serve hot or refrigerate for at least 2 hours and serve cold.

Yields 6 servings
adequate for 4 people

Notes: This recipe is easily doubled, when required.

If you prefer to use cooked, dry beans, taste and add salt.

1/6 SERVING – PROTEIN = 3.2 g.; FAT = 2.1 g.; CARBOHYDRATE = 12.3 g.;
CALORIES = 83; CALORIES FROM FAT = 22%

Europe–**Bosnia and Herzegovina**

ONIONS IN TOMATO SAUCE
Paradajas Beogradske
TPT - 29 minutes

Some cooks in Bosnia–Herzegovina make this with onion slices and some prefer to cut small onions into wedges but I like to use frozen, small white boiling onions. It is an uncomplicated dish that rounds out a menu beautifully.

1 tablespoon butter
1 tablespoon *extra virgin* **olive oil**
1 pound *frozen*, **whole, white boiling onions**

1 cup canned, *diced* **tomatoes**
1 teaspoon crushed, dried marjoram
1/2 teaspoon sugar
1/4 teaspoon freshly ground mixed peppercorns
   —red, black, and white—or to taste
Salt, to taste

In a large skillet set over LOW-MEDIUM heat, heat oil and butter. Add onions. Sauté gently for several minutes.

Add tomatoes, crushed marjoram, sugar, ground mixed peppercorns, and salt. Stir. Cover and cook, stirring occasionally, for about 20 minutes. *Sauce should be thick.* Turn into a serving bowl.

Serve at once.

Yields 6 servings
adequate for 4 people

Note: This recipe can be halved or doubled, when required.

1/6 SERVING – PROTEIN = 1.4 g.; FAT = 3.9 g.; CARBOHYDRATE = 8.0 g.
CALORIES = 69; CALORIES FROM FAT = 50%

BOSNIAN MEATBALLS AND GREEN BEANS IN YOGURT SAUCE
Pljeskavice
TPT - 20 minutes

If you use meat analogue products, this adaptation of a classic Bosnian recipe will certainly be welcomed into your repertoire. It will remind you of a stroganov; perhaps it was inspired by dishes such as stroganov and rouladin encountered by Bosnians in their historical confrontations with Germany, Austria, Hungary, and Russia. We like to serve this over boiled potatoes.

1/2 cup *fat-free* **pasteurized eggs (the equivalent**
   of 2 eggs)
2 cups PLAIN YOGURT *[see index]* **or**
   commercially-available plain yogurt

1 tablespoon *finely* **chopped fresh dillweed**
Salt, to taste
Freshly ground black pepper, to taste

1 teaspoon caraway seeds

1 package (9 ounces) vegetarian "meatballs"
1/2 pound whole green beans—trimmed

In a mixing bowl, combine eggs and yogurt. Using a wire whisk, combine thoroughly. Turn into a non-stick-coated skillet set over LOW-MEDIUM heat.

Add *finely* chopped dillweed, salt, and pepper. Cook, stirring frequently, until thickened. *Be careful to keep the temperature controlled so that the mixture does not curdle.*

Meanwhile, grind caraway seeds in a mortar. Add to skillet with meatballs and green beans. Cook, stirring almost constantly, until meatballs are heated through. Turn into a heated serving bowl.

Serve at once.

Yields 6 servings
adequate for 4 people

Note: This recipe can be halved, when required.

1/6 SERVING – PROTEIN = 13.5 g.; FAT = 2.7 g.; CARBOHYDRATE = 11.2 g.;
CALORIES = 114; CALORIES FROM FAT = 21%

Europe–**Bosnia and Herzegovina**

NOODLES WITH SOUR CREAM AND *FETA* CHEESE
Flekice

TPT - 17 minutes

A college friend, who moved to Europe, married an Italian, and raised her family in northern Italy, came for lunch during a visit home to Long Island. The cheese enchilada and broccoli menu I served did not appeal to her three daughters so she said, "Give them pasta with butter and cheese; they'll be happy." Noodles not only comfort Italian children, they are a comfort food all over Europe. The cheese may change and a little this or that might be added but since the discovery that wheat could be cultivated and not only made into bread but into noodles, men, women, and children have settled into a plate of noodles with ease. This protein-rich noodle dish is very satisfying.

6 ounces broad, curly egg noodles
4 quarts *boiling* water

1/4 cup *fat-free* dairy sour cream
3 tablespoons heavy whipping cream
Freshly ground black pepper, to taste

1/4 cup crumbled *feta* cheese

In a kettle set over *MEDIUM-HIGH* heat, combine egg noodles and *boiling* water. Allow to boil, stirring occasionally to prevent sticking, according to package directions. Drain. Pour into a large skillet set over *LOW-MEDIUM* heat.

Add sour cream and heavy cream. Grind black pepper over. Cook, stirring constantly, until heated through. Turn out onto a large platter or into a serving bowl.

Sprinkle *feta* over.

Serve at once.

Yields 6 servings
adequate for 4 people

Note: This recipe can be halved, when required.

1/6 SERVING – PROTEIN = 6.8 g.; FAT = 7.0 g.; CARBOHYDRATE = 24.6 g.;
CALORIES = 180; CALORIES FROM FAT = 35%

BOSNIAN BAKED ACORN SQUASH WITH RICE- AND CHEESE-STUFFING
Dolma

TPT - 1 hour and 51 minutes

I remember well a visit to my aunt and uncle's home and how happy I was to see that she was serving baked acorn squash, her "for-a-crowd" vegetable stand-by. If you grew up, as I did, thinking that acorn squash was just a yellow vegetable choice that wintered well and not a potential main-course vehicle, a dolma, then you have a wonderful and pleasurable experience in store.

3 medium acorn squashes—well-scrubbed,
  halved, and seeded
Water

FILLING:
  1/2 cup dry converted white *or* long grain
    brown rice, as preferred
  1 cup *boiling* water

  1/4 cup dry breadcrumbs
  1/4 cup crumbled *feta* cheese
  1/4 cup *finely* chopped onion
  1/4 cup *finely* chopped fresh parsley
  1/4 cup *fat-free* pasteurized eggs (the
    equivalent of 1 egg)
  Freshly ground black pepper, to taste

1/4 cup crumbled *feta* cheese
1 tablespoon pine nuts (*pignoli*)
2 teaspoons crushed, dried basil

Preheat oven to 350 degrees F.

Place squash halves **cut-side-down** in a large baking pan or on a baking sheet with raised sides. Pour water into pan to a depth of about 1/2 inch. Bake in preheated 350 degree F. oven for 30 minutes. Remove from oven. Turn squash halves **cut-side-up**. Holding a squash half in one hand, carefully scoop our squash flesh with a spoon. *Leave at least 1/2 inch of squash flesh in shell and be careful not to pierce shells.* Turn extracted squash flesh into a mixing bowl. Set squash halves, **cut-side-up** in a dry baking pan.

In a saucepan set over *LOW* heat, combine rice and *boiling* water in a saucepan. Cover. Cook rice according to package directions. When tender, turn into a sieve to drain.

Using a potato masher, mash the squash you removed from the squash halves.

BOSNIAN BAKED ACORN SQUASH WITH RICE- AND CHEESE-STUFFING (cont'd)

Add cooked rice and using a wooden spoon, mix rice into squash.

Add breadcrumbs, 1/4 cupful crumbled *feta* cheese, *finely* chopped onion and parsley, pasteurized eggs, and a generous amount of ground black pepper. Mix well. Spoon into squash halves, dividing the filling evenly among the hollowed out squash halves. Bake in oven for about 30 minutes. Transfer to a large platter.

Garnish each serving with crumbled *feta* cheese, pine nuts (*pignoli*), and a sprinkling of crushed, dried basil.

Serve at once.

Yields 6 servings
adequate for 4 people

Notes: This recipe can be halved, when required.

You can save considerable time by baking the squash and cooking the rice ahead of time.

1/6 SERVING – PROTEIN = 6.6 g.; FAT = 4.8 g.; CARBOHYDRATE = 20.4 g.;
CALORIES = 145; CALORIES FROM FAT = 30%

BOSNIAN BAKED EGGPLANT WITH MUSHROOMS AND CREAM
TPT - 2 hours and 5 minutes;
1 hour = eggplant draining period

Occasionally this very buttery, rich eggplant dish from Bosnia–Herzegovina is a change from the southern European dishes that came to me from my husband's family. It is rich and quite reminiscent of an eggplant dish popular in the American South, although the southern version is, to my knowledge, never made with mushrooms. Baking the eggplant reduces the amount of butter or oil absorbed somewhat, considering the fact that eggplant's propensity for absorption can raise the fat level and calories of a dish considerably. A combination of oil and butter increases the complexity of this version.

1 large, narrow eggplant *or* two Asian eggplants—washed, trimmed, and sliced into 1/4-inch crosswise slices
Coarse or kosher salt

2 tablespoons butter
1 pound mixed wild mushrooms—stems removed, rinsed, and cleaned well with a brush

High-heat safflower *or* sunflower oil to coat baking pan

2 tablespoons *melted* butter
2 tablespoons GARLIC OIL *[see index]*

3/4 cup light cream *or* half and half
1/4 cup *fat-free* dairy sour cream
Freshly ground *white* pepper, to taste

Salt eggplant slices generously and place them in a sieve or colander set in the sink. Place a plate on top and a weight—a large can or a tea kettle filled with water—on top of the plate. Allow to stand for 1 hour. Rinse each slice of eggplant well to remove excess salt. Pat dry with paper toweling.

While eggplant is draining, in a large non-stick-coated skillet set over *LOW-MEDIUM* heat, melt butter. Add mushrooms and sauté until most of the water has been extruded from the mushrooms and they are beginning to brown. Remove from the heat and set aside until required.

Line a large non-stick-coated cookie sheet with aluminum foil. Brush it lightly with *high-heat* safflower or sunflower oil. Place cookie sheet in oven to heat. Preheat oven to 350 degrees F.

Add the garlic oil to the 2 tablespoonfuls *melted* butter.

Remove preheated baking sheet from oven. Arrange eggplant slices on the prepared baking sheet. Brush each slice, both sides, with *melted* butter–olive oil mixture. Bake in preheated 350 degree oven for 10 minutes. Rotate baking sheet. Continue baking for an additional 10 minutes. Remove baking sheet from oven. Turn each eggplant slice. Baste with remaining butter garlic oil mixture. Return to oven for about 10 minutes more, or until each slice is crisp and well-browned. Drain eggplant slices *thoroughly* on several thicknesses of paper toweling.

Put eggplant slices into a large non-stick coated skillet set over *LOW-MEDIUM* heat. Spoon sautéed mushrooms over. Pour cream over. Season with white pepper. Allow to heat through. Transfer eggplant slices and mushrooms to a large platter. Pour cream sauce over.

Serve at once.

Yields 8 servings
adequate for 4-6 people

Note: This recipe can be halved, when required.

BOSNIAN BAKED EGGPLANT WITH MUSHROOMS AND CREAM (cont'd)

1/8 SERVING – PROTEIN = 4.8 g.; FAT = 14.4 g.; CARBOHYDRATE = 12.1 g.;
CALORIES = 196; CALORIES FROM FAT = 66%

BOSNIAN CAKE WITH LEMON SYRUP
Bosnanski Sevidzan

TPT - 2 hours and 2 minutes;
1 hour = cooling period

Cakes are a favorite dessert in the Balkans. In Bosnia–Herzegovina I found many cakes, and even cookies, soaked with sugar syrup, as in the case of this unusual dessert. The syrup used here is flavored with lemon. Although this is a technique I also encountered in French cooking, the prevailing influence here in the Balkans is undoubtedly attributable to the Ottoman Empire.

4 egg whites

3/4 cup heavy whipping cream

4 egg yolks*
1 cup confectioners' sugar

1/4 cup butter—*melted*
1/4 cup semolina, farina, *or* Cream of Wheat cereal
1 tablespoon freshly grated organic lemon zest

LEMON SYRUP:
    1 1/2 cups granulated sugar
    2 tablespoons freshly squeezed lemon juice
    1 cup minus 2 tablespoons water
    1 vanilla bean—split open

Preheat oven to 325 degrees F. Prepare a 9 x 9-inch square, non-stick-coated baking pan by lining it with culinary parchment and then spraying that parchment with non-stick lecithin baking spray.

Using an electric mixer fitted with *grease-free* beaters or by hand, using a *grease-free* wire whisk, beat egg whites in a *grease-free* bowl until *stiff*, but *not dry*. Turn into a small bowl. Set aside briefly.

Using the electric mixer fitted with *chilled* beaters or by hand using a *chilled* wire whisk, beat heavy cream in a *clean, chilled* bowl until stiff peaks form. Turn into a small bowl. Set aside briefly.

In the electric mixer bowl, combine egg yolks and confectioners' sugar. Beat until the mixture has formed a thick foam.

Gradually, while mixer is running, add *melted* butter, semolina, and grated lemon zest. When thoroughly integrated, *replace whip attachment with paddle. At LOW speed* fold in beaten egg whites and beaten heavy cream. Turn batter into prepared baking pan. Bake in preheated 325 degree F. oven for 15-18 minutes, or until a cake tester inserted in the center comes out clean. Remove to a wire rack while preparing the syrup.

In a deep saucepan set over *MEDIUM-HIGH* heat, combine granulated sugar, lemon juice, water, and split vanilla bean. Attach a candy thermometer. Stir until sugar is dissolved. Then, boil until syrup temperature is about 220-225 degrees F. and syrup has thickened. Remove vanilla bean. Remove syrup from heat and pour over cake. Allow to cool in pan for at least 1 hour.

Slice and serve with a spatula. *Turn each slice over as you plate it.*

Refrigerate leftovers.

Yields 16 servings
adequate for 8-10 people

Notes: *If you prefer not to use egg yolks, you can substitute 3/4 cupful fat-free pasteurized eggs for the egg yolks.

This recipe can be halved and baked in a 9 x 5 x 3-inch loaf pan with great success.

1/16 SERVING – PROTEIN = 2.2 g.; FAT = 8.0 g.; CARBOHYDRATE = 32.4 g.;
CALORIES = 208; CALORIES FROM FAT = 34%

Europe–Bosnia and Herzegovina

CHOCOLATE "CHEMISTRY CLASS" CAKE
Cockoladni Torta

TPT - 1 hour and 10 minutes;
30 minutes = minimal cooling period

I remember the year that they eliminated home economics from the school district. Our friend, Dottie retired after a career of teaching and they as much as said, "Your discipline was irrelevant." Home economics departments of gas and electric companies, who answered a myriad of questions for me when I was a young homemaker and offered courses which my mother took when she was first married, have gone the same way. The chemistry of cooking was once taught; it now requires some searching to find the reasons for techniques and ingredient combinations. This cake recipe, which I first encountered as "cocoa cake," and which is also known a "wacky cake" or "three-hole cake," seems to date from the period of World War II when we were, by necessity, creative. Eggs were rationed since the need to dehydrate eggs for our troops was of uppermost importance. Although we had access to fresh eggs because a friend of my grandfather kept chickens, they were usually served at breakfast and dinner.

Bosnians love cakes and a cake very similar to this can be found in Bosnian homes and even in Bosnian bakeries.

1 1/2 cups cake flour*
3/4 cup sugar
1/4 cup *unsweetened, dark* cocoa powder
3/4 teaspoon baking soda
Pinch salt

5 tablespoons safflower oil

1 tablespoon distilled white vinegar

1 teaspoon pure vanilla extract

1 cup *cold* water

Confectioners' sugar *or* sweetened whipped cream, either or both, if desired

Preheat oven to 350 degrees F. Prepare an 8-inch-square baking pan, preferably non-stick-coated, by coating with non-stick lecithin spray coating.

In a mixing bowl, combine flour, sugar, cocoa powder, baking soda, and a pinch of salt. Using a wire whisk, mix dry ingredients. Turn into prepared baking pan.

Using the back of a spoon, make one large and two small craters in the dry ingredients:

~ Pour oil into the large crater.

~ Pour vinegar into one of the small craters.

~ Pour vanilla extract into the remaining small crater.

~ Finally, pour cold coffee and honey mixture evenly over the ingredients in the pan.

Using a rubber spatula or wooden spoon, stir until only a few streaks of white flour remain.

Using a rubber spatula or wooden spoon, stir until only a few streaks of white flour remain.

Immediately, place in preheated 350 degree F. oven and bake for 30 minutes, or until a cake tester inserted in the center comes out clean. Transfer to a wire rack and allow to cool for at least 30 minutes.

Dust with confectioners' sugar, if desired.** Serve, cut into squares, directly from pan and top each serving with a dollop of whipped cream, if desired.

Leftovers will keep well at room temperature for 3-4 days, if tightly covered and well-hidden from snackers.

Yields 8 servings
adequate for 6 people

Notes: *Unbleached or all-purpose white flour was used by World War II and Depression era cooks but the over-all cake texture improves with the unique texture of cake flour, in my opinion.

**Although we do not think a frosting is necessary, chocolate, mocha, vanilla, or even peppermint buttercream frosting can be used to frost this cake after it has cooled completely.

Modern, conventional mixing techniques are really not an improvement for this bizarre recipe.

CHOCOLATE "CHEMISTRY CLASS" CAKE (cont'd)

1/8 SERVING – PROTEIN = 2.3 g.; FAT = 9.1 g.; CARBOHYDRATE = 37.5 g.;
CALORIES = 240; CALORIES FROM FAT = 34%

BOSNIAN ANGEL FOOD COOKIES
Nazli Fatme

TPT - 1 hour and 14 minutes;
20 minutes = dough resting period

At first encounter one expects a recipe labeled as angel food to produce a light, airy cookie or a cake just loaded with egg whites. Well, that is not the case here and it certainly proves that appraisal of foods that might be eaten by angelic beings varies from culture to culture. Perhaps "nectar of the gods" would be more appropriate to lead you to envision this sweet, rich cookie which probably came to Bosnia–Herzegovina from Turkey. The technique of pouring syrup over a sweet is common in the Middle East.

1/2 cup butter—*softened to room temperature*
2 tablespoons sugar

1 3/4 cups unbleached white flour
1/4 cup *fat-free* pasteurized eggs (the equivalent of 1 egg)

BOSNIAN HONEY–LEMON SYRUP:
    1/2 cup sugar
    2 tablespoons water

    1 tablespoon honey
    2 tablespoons freshly squeezed lemon juice

Preheat oven to 350 degrees F. Prepare two cookie sheets by lining them with culinary parchment. Spread a large piece of waxed paper on the counter top Set up 1 large or 2 small wire racks on top of the waxed paper.

Using the electric mixer fitted with paddle, cream *softened* butter and the 2 tablespoonfuls sugar until light and fluffy.

Add flour and pasteurized eggs. Beat until a dough forms. Remove to a bread board or pastry cloth. Knead until smooth. Allow dough to rest for 20 minutes.

Roll dough out to a thickness of about 1/8 inch. Using a round cookie or biscuit cutter, cut out about 20 cookies. Place on culinary-lined cookie sheets. Bake in preheated 350 degrees F. oven for about 25 minutes, or until very lightly browned. Transfer to the wire racks.

While the cookies are baking, prepare a thick syrup by combining the sugar and water over *MEDIUM* heat. Remove from heat.

Add honey and lemon juice. Stir to integrate. Pour the honey–lemon syrup over the cookies while they are still hot. The syrup will soak into the cookies as they cool.

Store in a single layer in an air-tight tin.

                               Yields about 20 cookies

Note: This recipe can be doubled, when required.

1/20 SERVING (i. e., per cookie) –
PROTEIN = 1.4 g.; FAT = 4.6 g.; CARBOHYDRATE = 15.6 g.;
CALORIES = 109; CALORIES FROM FAT = 38%

Bulgaria

Since the seventh century, with the formation of the First Bulgarian Empire in 681 AD after a peace treaty with Byzantium, there has been an ethnicity and a language known as Bulgarian. The first empire survived for 337 years, until 1018. A Second Bulgarian Empire came into being in 1185 during which Albania, Epirus, Macedonia, and Thrace came under Bulgarian rule during the reign of Czar Ivan Asen II. In 1257 this progressive dynasty ended and the years that followed saw internal unrest, conflicts, and invasions by Byzantia and Hungary. By the end of the thirteenth century the areas of the empire came under the rule of the Ottoman Turks, under which they remained for five centuries until the Russo–Turkish War. By the Treaty of San Stefano in 1878 and the subsequent Treaty of Berlin, in the same year, Bulgaria became an autonomous principality. Bulgaria went on a campaign of militarization which earned it the nickname "The Prussia of the Balkans." Courted by the Central Powers during World War I and the Axis Powers during World War II, Bulgaria found itself on the losing side during both conflicts. Following both world wars Bulgaria's economic situation was dismal. In 1944 Bulgaria established a relatively successful planned economy as a people's republic styled after the Soviet Communist system. It was not until 1989 that the Bulgarian Communist Party gave up its political monopoly and Bulgaria began a transition to parliamentary democracy.

Here, as in many countries in this region of the world, the soured milk product we call yogurt or yoghurt is an important part of the daily diet. *Kiselo mleko (mlyako)*, as it is known in Bulgaria, has been consumed in the region as far back as 3,000 BC, from the period when the land was inhabited by the people known as Thracians who occupied areas of Greece, Bulgaria, and Turkey. Pliny the Elder (Caius Plinius Secundus), the Roman naturalist who lived from 12-79 AD, noted that there were nomadic tribal peoples who knew how to thicken milk to create the acidic, cultured dairy product we prize today for taste and health, suggesting that yogurt had indeed reached Rome. In Bulgaria yogurt is generally made from cows' milk but yogurt made from ewes' milk and buffalo-cows' milk is also readily available. When I first made yogurt, I went out of my way to obtain a Bulgarian starter culture of *Lactobacillus bulgaricus*. It was not as easy to find the bacterial starter then.

The pairing of spices and herbs in soups, stews, vegetable dishes, sauces, and salads evidence the exchange and adaptation of cuisine ideas and agricultural information through the centuries – from the North, from the East, from the West, and from the South. Salads are eaten at almost every meal and my collection of Bulgarian salads alone reveals the influences that have marched through the Balkans and through Bulgaria specifically, Romans, Goths, Huns, Bulgars, and Turks, who all added detectable nuances to the Bulgarian table. Vegetarian dishes and wonderful dairy products invite the non-meat eater to explore and, in our exploration of food, my husband and I have found Bulgarian food a very comfortable compromise between the cooking with which I grew up, brought to the United States from the British Isles and Germany by my ancestors, and the Italian cooking of his family.

Europe – **Bulgaria**

Roasted Eggplant and Green Pepper Appetizer Spread
Kiopoolu
served with salt, pepper, oil, and vinegar

***Feta* Baked in Foil**
Sirene
and / or
Goat Cheese
Assorted Crackers

Puff Pastry Appetizers with Bulgarian Black Olive Purée and *Hummus*
Meze ot Kasha ot Cherni Maslini n Hummus

Bulgarian Black Olive Purée
Kasha ot Cerni Maslini

Cheese-Stuffed Frying Peppers
Purgheni Chushki s Sirene

~

Chilled Cucumber and Yogurt Summer Soup
Tarator

~~~~~~~~~~~~~~~~~~~~

Root Vegetables with Bulgarian Yogurt – Dill Sauce
Guivetch s Podloochvane

Dried Wild Mushrooms with *Feta* Cheese
Guby Sirene

Onions with Tomato
Luchena Kasha

~~~~~~~~~

Baked Cheese with Eggs
Podlucheny Yaytsa s Sirene

Steamed Whole Carrots

~~~~~~~~~~~~~~~~~~~~

Semolina Dessert with Walnuts
Gris Halva

Stewed Prunes
Compot ot Siny Slivy

| **Yogurt Cake** | **Sultan's Slices** |
| *Topta cu Kisselo Mleko* | *Purgheni Filyi* |

Europe–**Bulgaria**

BULGARIAN ROASTED EGGPLANT AND GREEN PEPPER APPETIZER SPREAD
Kiapoolu

TPT - 1 hour and 15 minutes;
15 minutes = pepper steaming period

I first tasted this appetizer at a friend's house. Her husband was of Romanian descent and claimed it for Romania. Research, exhaustive I might add, places this appetizer in the cuisine of Bulgaria with nothing similar turning up in any Romanian sources. Of course, a dish like this does hint at the Ottoman period . . . and both countries are, to put it mildly, "addicted" to peppers . . . so who knows for sure . . .

1 large, sweet green bell peppers—perfect, unblemished, and well-washed

1 small eggplant—about 3/4 pound—well-washed
1/4 cup canned, *diced* **tomatoes**
1 large garlic clove—chopped
2 tablespoons chopped, fresh Italian flat-leafed parsley

1 ripe plum tomato—sliced into wedges—for garnish

Salt
Freshly ground black pepper
Extra virgin **olive oil**
Red wine vinegar *or* **GARLIC–BASIL VINEGAR** *[see index]*

Assorted of breads, crackers or toasts, and *crudités*, **of choice**

Preheat oven to 350 degrees F.

Place peppers on a cookie sheet. Roast in preheated oven for about 40 minutes, *turning frequently*.

Remove from oven and place in a heavy brown paper bag in dry sink. Roll the top of the bag down and allow to steam for about 15 minutes.

Remove stems, seeds, and membranes, and peel. Using the food processor fitted with steel knife, purée roasted green peppers. Set aside briefly.

Change the oven setting to *BROIL* and set the oven rack about 8 inches from the heat source.* Pierce the eggplant several times with a sharp knife, place it on a broiler pan so that the eggplant is about 4 inches below the heat source. Broil the eggplant for a total of about 20 minutes, *turning the eggplant with tongs frequently during the broiling period* so that the skin chars evenly. Wrap the eggplant in a dampened cotton tea towel for 5 minutes to steam. Remove the towel and peel off and discard the skin. Coarsely chop the eggplant and add to the puréed green peppers, diced tomato, chopped garlic, and chopped parsley. Process again until of uniform consistency.

Turn into a serving bowl. Garnish the top by arranging the wedges of plum tomato in the center. Refrigerate until ready to serve.

Provide salad plates and butter spreaders for each diner. Serve with condiments: salt in a salt dish with a salt spoon, if possible; black pepper in a pepper mill; and cruets of olive oil and vinegar. Encourage diners to stir these condiments into a serving of the eggplant and pepper spread to their own taste before spreading on the breads, crackers, or raw vegetables provided.

Yields about 2 cupfuls

Notes: *If preferred, the eggplant can be grilled over a charcoal fire. It does give the eggplant a superb taste. A grill pan, a gas grill, or a gas burner can also be used.

Since this spread keeps well for a week, in the refrigerator, there is really no need to halve the recipe. It, of course, may be doubled, when required.

1/32 SERVING (i. e., per tablespoonful, exclusive of crackers and garniture) –
PROTEIN = 0.2 g.; FAT = 0.03 g; CARBOHYDRATE = 0.7 g.;
CALORIES = 4; CALORIES FROM FAT = 1%

Europe–**Bulgaria**

BULGARIAN *FETA* BAKED IN FOIL
Sirene
TPT - 30 minutes

Today, some Bulgarians wrap the cheese in waxed paper and some prefer to bake the feta cheese in aluminum foil but whichever you come to prefer you will be revisiting an ancient way of preparing cheese. Not only is it a very traditional recipe, it is a remarkable recipe in that there is an indescribable transformation in the taste of the feta cheese. Spread on a piece of toast or tucked into a warm roll or just allowed to melt onto cooked vegetables, it is something you do not expect and something you will never want to forget.

8 ounces plain *feta* cheese—one large chunk

2 tablespoons soft, butter spread
1/4 teaspoon freshly ground black pepper
1/4 teaspoon HOMEMADE PAPRIKA *[see index] or* commercially-available Hungarian sweet paprika

6 small scallions—trimmed and well-rinsed

Preheat oven to 350 degrees F.

Spread two pieces of aluminum foil, each about 18 inches long, on a baking sheet, one piece of foil on top of the other. Curl the edges up to form a "tray."

Cut the chunk of *feta* cheese in half down the middle. Cut each half into six thick squares. Place the squares on the aluminum foil, leaving a space between pieces.

Spread a bit of butter on each piece of cheese and sprinkle each with black pepper and paprika. Spread two more pieces of aluminum foil, each about 18 inches long on the counter top, one piece of foil on top of the other. Place on top of the cheese-filled aluminum "tray" and gently squeeze the aluminum edges together to seal the package but be careful to keep a foil dome over the cheese. Bake in preheated 350 degree F. oven for 15 minutes. Transfer the entire aluminum foil package to a large heated platter or to a heat resistant tray. Remove the top pieces of foil or tear them back, if necessary.

Garnish with the scallions.

Serve at once.

Yields 12 servings
adequate for 6 people

Note: This recipe can be halved.

1/12 SERVING – PROTEIN = 5.4 g.; FAT = 9.2 g.; CARBOHYDRATE = 1.9 g.;
CALORIES = 114; CALORIES FROM FAT = 73%

PUFF PASTRY APPETIZERS WITH BULGARIAN BLACK OLIVE PURÉE AND *HUMMUS*
Meze ot Kasha ot Cherni Maslini n Hummus
TPT - 38 minutes

Although Bulgarian "kasha ot cherni maslini" is great as a spread for crackers and toasts, when combined with a little "hummus" and spread on puffed pastry rounds, a lovely, more formal first course is created. Here the culinary influences of those who came and went from Bulgaria over the centuries is very much in evidence.

1 sheet *frozen* puff pastry—brought to room temperature

3 tablespoons TURKISH CHICK PEA DIP (*Hummus*) *[see index] or* commercially-available *hummus*—brought to room temperature
12 tablespoons (3/4 cup) BULGARIAN BLACK OLIVE PURÉE (*Kasha ot Cherni Maslini*) *[see recipe which follows]*

Preheat oven to 400 degrees F. Prepare a baking sheet by lining with culinary parchment paper.

Spread the puff pastry sheet out on a board. Cut the sheet into twelve 3-inch rounds. Place the pastry rounds on the parchment-lined baking sheet. Prick pastry with a fork.

Spread about 1/2 teaspoonful of *hummus* over each pastry circle. Scatter 1 tablespoonful of the olive purée on each pastry round. Bake in preheated 400 degree oven for about 18-20 minutes, or until the pastry has browned on the bottom and on the sides. Remove from oven and transfer two of the baked appetizers to each of six heated individual salad plates.

Europe–**Bulgaria**

**PUFF PASTRY APPETIZERS WITH
BULGARIAN BLACK OLIVE PURÉE AND *HUMMUS*** (cont'd)

Serve at once.

Yields 6 individual servings

Note: This recipe can easily be halved or doubled, when required.

1/12 SERVING (i. e., per appetizer tartlet) –
PROTEIN = 3.0 g.; FAT = 9.4 g.; CARBOHYDRATE = 9.1 g.;
CALORIES = 133; CALORIES FROM FAT = 64%

BULGARIAN BLACK OLIVE PURÉE
Kasha ot Cerni Maslini

TPT - 45 minutes;
30 minutes = flavor development period

Bulgarians relish the pure taste of olive in this olive spread and do not combine it with any other flavor except lemon, which seems to enhance the olive richness. This is a totally different taste experience when compared with the Portuguese olive and garlic spread. Usually served with buttered bread or as a relish, it is a beautiful taste experience.

12 ounces pitted *Kalamata* olives—well-drained

1 tablespoon freshly squeezed lemon juice, or more if necessary to create a spreadable purée

Freshly ground black pepper, to taste

Spread several layers of paper toweling out on the counter top. Scatter well-drained olives on top of the paper. Place several layers of paper toweling on top of the olives and roll the paper toweling into a long tube, pressing as you go to extract as much liquid as possible. Unroll the toweling and turn the olives into the work bowl of the food processor.

Add lemon juice and process until smooth.

Season with black pepper and purée again. Scrape from work bowl into a small serving bowl, pressing it into a conical mound. Cover and refrigerate for at least 30 minutes before serving.

Yields about 18 servings
adequate for 8-9 people

Note: This recipe can be halved or doubled, when required.

1/18 SERVING – PROTEIN = 1.2 g.; FAT = 1.9 g.; CARBOHYDRATE = 1.3 g.;
CALORIES = 25; CALORIES FROM FAT = 68%

BULGARIAN CHEESE – STUFFED FRYING PEPPERS
Purzheni Chushki s Sirene

TPT - 1 hour 20 minutes;
20 minutes = pepper roasting period;
30 minutes = breading setting period

Small "finger" peppers, prepared in this manner, are often served, either whole or sliced as appetizers in Bulgaria. Although we generally avoid fried foods, every once in a while we succumb and enjoy these as a main course.

**12 *small* Italian *frying* peppers—about
2 pounds total**

6 ounces Greek *feta* cheese—rinsed and well-drained*
4 ounces farmers' cheese
[see next page]

VOLUME I - 73

Europe–**Bulgaria**

BULGARIAN CHEESE – STUFFED FRYING PEPPERS (cont'd)

1/2 cup unbleached white flour

1/2 cup *fat-free* pasteurized eggs (the equivalent of 2 eggs)

3 cups soft, fresh breadcrumbs made from a homemade wheat bread such as MAPLE OATMEAL BREAD *[see index]*, a buttermilk loaf, *or* other firm white bread
1 tablespoon grated *pecorino Romano* cheese
Freshly ground black pepper, to taste

Oil for deep-frying to the depth of about 3 inches, heated to 375 degrees F.

Preheat oven to 350 degrees F.

Place peppers on a cookie sheet. Roast in preheated oven for about 20 minutes, *turning several times.*

Remove from oven and place in a heavy brown paper bag in dry sink. Roll the top of the bag down and allow to steam for about 15 minutes.

Peel skins from peppers, remove stems and cores, and *carefully* scoop out the seeds, *leaving the peppers whole.* Set aside.

In a mixing bowl, combine *feta* and farmers' cheeses. Using a fork, mash cheese together well. Using a pastry bag, fitted with a plain tip, or a long-handled, narrow spoon, fill each of the *roasted* peppers with about 3 tablespoonfuls of cheese mixture.

Put flour in a pie plate.

Pour pasteurized eggs into a second pie plate.

Put breadcrumbs, grated *Romano* cheese, and black pepper into a third pie plate. Stir to combine.

Set oil for deep-frying over *LOW* heat.

Dredge cheese-stuffed peppers in flour, shaking off excess. Coat with eggs by rolling each in the eggs. Finally, roll each in breadcrumb mixture until thoroughly covered with crumbs. Transfer to a plate and place in the refrigerator for at least 30 minutes, to allow breading to set.***

Using a deep-frying or candy thermometer, be sure oil is heated to 375 degrees F. before frying.

Carefully fry the stuffed peppers in the hot oil, *two at a time,* turning with a slotted spoon to insure that the breading is uniformly browned. Remove from oil and drain well on paper toweling.

Transfer to a heated platter and keep warm on a warming tray or in a warm oven. Serve as soon as possible.

Yields 12 servings
adequate for 6 people

Notes: **Brynza* cheese, which would be used in this recipe, is rarely available in the United States. *Feta* cheese is an adequate substitute.

**Because raw eggs present the danger of *Salmonella* poisoning, commercially-available pasteurized eggs are recommended for use in preparing this dish since the method of cooking, employed here, does not insure sufficient cooking for safety.

***Peppers may be prepared to this point several hours before serving and refrigerated until dinner time.

This recipe may be halved or doubled, when required.

1/12 SERVING – PROTEIN = 16.9 g; FAT = 5.6 g; CARBOHYDRATE = 31.3 g;
CALORIES = 266; CALORIES FROM FAT = 19%

PURÉED BULGARIAN CHILLED CUCUMBER AND YOGURT SUMMER SOUP

Tarator

TPT - 1 hour and 25 minutes;
15 minutes = draining period;
1 hour = chilling period

This chilled cucumber and yogurt soup became one of our favorite summer soups and it is probably the most popular summer soup in Bulgaria. The availability of the electric blender, and now the food processor, have been greeted with as much enthusiasm in Bulgaria as they were in Spain where the making of gazpacho became dramatically simplified. This puréed version makes quite an impression when served in wine glasses.

VOLUME I - 74

PURÉED BULGARIAN CHILLED CUCUMBER AND YOGURT SUMMER SOUP (cont'd)

1 medium cucumber—peeled, halved and seeded
1/2 teaspoon salt

2 cups PLAIN YOGURT *[see index]* or commercially-available plain yogurt
1/4 cup chopped, *preservative-free* walnuts
2 tablespoons chopped fresh dillweed
1 tablespoon chopped fresh mint
2 garlic cloves—chopped
Freshly ground *white* pepper, to taste

1 tablespoon safflower *or* sunflower oil*

2 tablespoons crushed ice

Chopped fresh dillweed, for garnish

Dice halved and seeded cucumbers into about a 1/4-inch dice. Place in a small bowl and sprinkle salt over. Allow to stand at room temperature for about 15 minutes, stirring occasionally. Turn into a sieve and rinse *thoroughly* under cold, running water. Drain well and pat dry, using paper towels.

In a the work bowl of the food processor, fitted with steel knife, or in the container of the electric blender, combine diced cucumbers, yogurt, chopped walnuts, chopped dillweed and mint, chopped garlic, and *white* pepper. Process until smooth.

Add oil. Again process.

Apportion soup among six wine glasses, being careful not to spill the soup down the glass. Wipe any spills from the glasses. Refrigerate for at least 1 hour, or until thoroughly chilled.

Spoon a teaspoonful of crushed ice into each glass and garnish with a sprinkling of chopped dillweed.

Yields 6 servings

Notes: *Although olive oil can be used in this recipe, Bulgarians prefer to use sunflower oil.

This recipe may be halved or doubled, when required.

1/6 SERVING – PROTEIN = 5.2 g.; FAT = 4.9 g.; CARBOHYDRATE = 6.6 g.; CALORIES = 121; CALORIES FROM FAT = 36%

ROOT VEGETABLES WITH BULGARIAN YOGURT – DILL SAUCE
Guivetch s Padlaachvane
TPT - 40 minutes

Bulgaria is well-known for givetsch, an array of vegetable casseroles that changes with the seasons and with the whims of the cook, but many vegetable casseroles are popular in the Balkans. This Bulgarian dish is strikingly similar to a popular casserole served in Albania, albeit without the distinctively Bulgarian sauce. The sauce which accompanies the steamed root vegetables in this recipe is usually served with fried vegetables in Bulgaria, unlike similar sauces common to Turkish cuisine. We feel that there are no limits on how useful this sauce can be in menu planning. Not only do we choose it as a sauce for steamed and boiled vegetables, but also for roasted vegetables and as a dip for crudités. Leftovers make a terrific salad dressing.

BULGARIAN YOGURT – DILL SAUCE:
  2 large garlic cloves—*very finely* chopped
  2 tablespoons chopped fresh dillweed
  Pinch salt

  1 cup PLAIN YOGURT *[see index]* or commercially-available plain yogurt
    —*brought to room temperature*
  1 1/2 teaspoons HOMEMADE PAPRIKA *[see index]* or commercially-available Hungarian sweet paprika
  Freshly ground black pepper, to taste

2 small parsnips—peeled and cut into 2-inch lengths
12 tiny new potatoes—well-scrubbed
12 baby carrots—scraped or pared

Set up a steamer.

On a chopping board, combine *finely* chopped garlic cloves, chopped dillweed, and salt. Using the side of a chef's knife, crush the garlic and dillweed. Then, chop until *very, very finely chopped*. Again, crush and chop the ingredients together until you have a fine mixture.

In a small bowl, combine prepared garlic paste, yogurt, paprika, and black pepper. Stir to combine well. Refrigerate until ready to serve.*

Steam parsnips, potatoes, and carrots until *crisp-tender*. Transfer to a heated serving bowl and place on a warming tray.

ROOT VEGETABLES WITH BULGARIAN YOGURT – DILL SAUCE (cont'd)

Serve the sauce chilled or at room temperature as an accompaniment to the steamed vegetables.

Yields 6 servings
adequate for 4-6 people

Notes: The sauce can be prepared ahead of time and is greatly improved if it is refrigerated for an hour or two before serving.

When required, this recipe can be halved or doubled.

1/6 SERVING – PROTEIN = 5.3 g.; FAT = 1.0 g.; CARBOHYDRATE = 20.8 g.;
CALORIES = 99; CALORIES FROM FAT = 9%

BULGARIAN DRIED WILD MUSHROOMS WITH *FETA* CHEESE
Guby Sirene

TPT - 2 hours and 23 minutes;
2 hours = mushroom soaking period

Unusual and interesting fresh mushroom varietals have become easier and easier to find at grocery stores, especially in Pennsylvania which it is said grows close to sixty-percent of the nation's mushrooms, but the price of a dish, such as this, becomes seriously elevated. We dry mushrooms ourselves and buy dried mushrooms in bulk from organic growers so that dishes that appeal to our "unami," the little-recognized taste for the earthy, fleshy flavor, like this can be weekday events when our herb garden is forthcoming. Bulgarians are known for two very distinct cheeses. Kaskaval is a yellow, hard cheese that is occasionally available in cheese shops but the salty curd cheese which is scattered over dishes by the handfuls is, alas, not available here so plain feta is what we use. This same mixture can be used to fill a savory strudel too.

2 cups mixture of *dried* mushrooms—*porcini, crimini*, lobster, *chanterelles*, morels, *shiitake*, oyster, black trumpet mushrooms, and/or any others of choice—*well-rinsed and brushed to remove any foreign matter*

1 quart *boiling* water

1/4 cup butter
1/2 cup *finely* chopped onion
1 large garlic clove—*very finely* chopped

1 tablespoon chopped fresh parsley
1 tablespoon chopped fresh chives
1 tablespoon chopped fresh rosemary
1 tablespoon chopped fresh sage
Freshly ground black pepper, to taste

1/2 cup crumbled, plain *feta* cheese

In a mixing bowl, combine dried mushrooms mixture, which have been *well-rinsed and brushed to remove any foreign material*. Add *boiling* water. Allow mushrooms to soak for at least 2 hours, or until softened. Press mushrooms down into the soaking liquid occasionally to insure even reconstitution.

Using a slotted spoon, remove mushrooms from mushroom broth to a small bowl. Set aside until required. Reserve WILD MUSHROOM STOCK for future recipes.**

In a large skillet set over *MEDIUM* heat, melt butter. Add *finely* chopped onion and *very finely* chopped garlic. Sauté until onion is soft and translucent, *being careful to allow neither the onion nor the garlic to brown*. Reduce heat to *LOW*.

Add rehydrated mushrooms. Cook, stirring frequently, until mushrooms just begin to brown.

Add chopped parsley, chives, rosemary, and sage, and black pepper. Transfer to a heated serving bowl.

Scatter crumbled *feta* cheese over.

Serve at once.

Yields 6 servings
adequate for 4 people

Europe–**Bulgaria**

BULGARIAN DRIED WILD MUSHROOMS WITH *FETA* CHEESE (cont'd)

Notes: *Drying sliced, cultivated mushrooms using one of the inexpensive dehydrators available, is a very simple process. By drying mushrooms yourself you can be assured that they are *well-cleaned, well-trimmed, and flawless*.

**Porcini* (also known as *Cèpes Secjes, Boletes,* and *Steinpilze*), morels *(Morchella esculenta),* chanterelle (*Cantharellus cibarius*), and lobster (*Hypomyces lactifluorum*) mushrooms, with their seafood-like taste, lend a superbly rich and complex flavor to any dish. Although expensive and scarce in the past, these wonderful mushrooms are now widely available in the dried form. Dried Chinese black, *shiitake* mushrooms *(Lentinus edodes)* are available in Asian markets and food specialty stores. Once soaked, the hard stems of the *shiitake* should be removed before cooking.

***Save any extra WILD MUSHROOM STOCK to use to prepare vegetable stocks or to flavor soups, stews, and sauces. When frozen in cubes in the ice cube tray, this broth can become a very useful addition to many dishes that just need "a little something extra."

This recipe may be halved or doubled, when required.

1/6 SERVING – PROTEIN = 4.3 g.; FAT = 11.6 g.; CARBOHYDRATE = 2.6 g.;
CALORIES = 127, CALORIES FROM FAT = 82%

BULGARIAN ONIONS WITH TOMATO
Luchena Kasha

TPT - 54 minutes;
10 minutes = off–heat steaming period

Such simple peasant dishes as this are often overlooked, but everyday food preparations can be interesting side dishes. An amazing amount of protein is the outcome of the interesting combination of tiny whole onions and diced onions in the same skillet.

3/4 pound *very* small, white boiling onions
—*peeled*
2 quarts *boiling* water

2 tablespoons olive oil
1/4 cup water
1 1/2 pounds yellow onions— diced

2 large tomatoes—peeled, seeded and diced
2 large garlic cloves—*finely* chopped
1 teaspoon HOMEMADE PAPRIKA *[see index]*
   or   commercially-available Hungarian sweet paprika
Several dashes Hungarian *hot* paprika

Cut an X in the root end of each peeled onion to prevent the onions from falling apart.

Place kettle of *boiling* water over *MEDIUM* heat. Drop *peeled* onions into the *boiling* water. Cook for about 15 minutes, or until tender. Drain.

In a large skillet set over *MEDIUM* heat, heat oil and water. Add diced yellow onions. Sauté for about 5 minutes, or until onions are soft and transparent, *being careful not to allow onions to brown.*

Add diced tomato, *finely* chopped garlic, and both *sweet* and *hot* paprika. Sauté for an additional 10 minutes.

Add *boiled* whole onions. Sauté *gently* for additional 5 minutes.

Remove from heat. Cover and allow to steam, *off heat,* for 10 minutes.

Turn into a heated serving bowl to serve.

Yields 6 servings
adequate for 4 people

Note: This recipe can be halved or doubled, when required.

1/6 SERVING – PROTEIN = 2.7 g.; FAT = 4.0 g.; CARBOHYDRATE = 15.1 g.;
CALORIES = 102; CALORIES FROM FAT = 35%

Europe–**Bulgaria**

BULGARIAN BAKED CHEESE WITH EGGS
Podlucheny Yaytsa s Sirene
TPT - 25 minutes

Described in English as Bulgarian cheese and eggs, I fully expected something along the line of Turkish "yumurta peynirli." Was I surprised. I am told that this shirred egg dish is a popular luncheon dish served at lunch counters or prepared at home for a quick, nutritious noonday meal.

Per serving:
  1 1/2 teaspoons butter

  2 tablespoons canned, *crushed* **tomatoes**
  Freshly ground black pepper, to taste
  HOMEMADE PAPRIKA [see index] **or**
    commercially-available Hungarian sweet paprika, to taste

  1/2 ounce slice plain *feta* **cheese**
  2 slices tomato
  4 thin, ring-shaped slices red *or* **green bell pepper**

  1 large *organic* **egg***

Set an ovenproof soup bowl, such as an onion soup crock, on a warming tray set at HIGH to preheat.

In a small saucepan or Turkish coffee pot set over *LOW* heat, melt butter. Add tomatoes, black pepper, and paprika.

Coat the soup crock with lecithin non-stick coating spray. Place *feta* cheese slice in crock. Spoon the warm, spiced tomato mixture over. Top with tomato slices and then with pepper slices.

Break egg into a small bowl and slip the egg carefully into the crock so that the yolk is sitting on top of the vegetables. Place in oven. Turn oven on at 325 degrees F. and allow the contents of the soup crock to cook until the cheese is melting and the egg white has set. Remove from oven.

Serve at once.

Yields 1 individual serving**

Notes: *A shirred egg is not cooked sufficiently to kill *Salmonella* bacteria which might be present. We strongly recommend using organic eggs for this dish.

**Of course, this recipe can be increased to serve as many as necessary as long as you have a sufficient number of ovenproof soup bowls.

1 SERVING – PROTEIN = 11.5 g.; FAT = 17.6 g.; CARBOHYDRATE = 6.6 g.;
CALORIES = 230; CALORIES FROM FAT = 69%

BULGARIAN SEMOLINA DESSERT WITH WALNUTS
Gris Halva
TPT - 1 hour and 45 minutes;
1 hour = cooling period

We have long enjoyed a dessert made from farina and milk. It too is golden and is garnished with nuts and cinnamon. This classic Bulgarian dessert, so reflective of culinary influences of five hundred years of Turkish rule, becomes one of our choices when our vegan cousins come. We can all enjoy it.

1/3 cup *soft* **butter** *or* **margarine product**
1 cup farina*

1/2 cup sugar
1 1/4 cups water

1/2 cup ground, *preservative-free* **walnuts** *or*
  walnut meal**
1/2 teaspoon ground cinnamon

In a large saucepan set over *MEDIUM-LOW* heat, melt butter. Add farina and simmer, stirring frequently, for about 10-15 minutes, or until *golden brown*.

While farina is simmering, in another large saucepan set over *MEDIUM-HIGH* heat, combine sugar and water. Bring to the boil and allow to boil for about 8 minutes, or until it forms a slightly thickened syrup. *Remove from heat.*

Stir sugar syrup into sautéed farina. Mix well.

BULGARIAN SEMOLINA DESSERT WITH WALNUTS (cont'd)

Cover the pan with a thick towel and place a lid on top of the towel. Allow to sit *off heat* for 15-20 minutes. Stir with a fork and *cover again. Allow to cool completely*—about 1 hour.

Mix crushed walnuts and ground cinnamon. Set aside until required.

When farina has cooled to room temperature, turn into a serving bowl. Sprinkle walnut–cinnamon mixture over.

Serve at room temperature. Refrigerate any leftovers.

Notes: *Semolina, the hard wheat from which good quality *pasta* is made, is available in most grocery stores and natural food stores. It is also available from mail order firms. This would be the more traditional grain with which to make this dessert but we are more apt to have farina on hand.

**A *mezza-luna* is useful in preparing the walnuts, if you have one.

This recipe can be halved, if required.

Yields 8 servings
adequate for 6 people

1/6 SERVING – PROTEIN = 5.9 g.; FAT = 17.8 g.; CARBOHYDRATE = 35.8 g.;
CALORIES = 328; CALORIES FROM FAT = 49%

BULGARIAN STEWED PRUNES
Compot ot Siny Sliny

TPT - 7 hours and 36 minutes;
6 hours = soaking period;
1 hour = chilling period

Fans of Johann Stauss II's delightful "Die Fledermaus," among whom we count ourselves, certainly never think of the turnkey's favorite beverage as prune juice but if you do not make "slivovice" from fresh plums, you can always dry them. The prunes can then be prepared in the following way to be enjoyed as a winter dessert.

1/2 pound pitted, *preservative-free* prunes
1 quart *cold* water

2 cups *boiling* water

1/2 cup sugar
2 tablespoons freshly squeezed lemon juice

Light cream *or* half and half

In a bowl, combine the 1 quartful *cold* water and the pitted, dried prunes. Allow to soak for about 6 hours. Drain thoroughly.

In a saucepan set over *MEDIUM* heat, combine the 2 cupfuls *boiling* water and the soaked, drained prunes. Attach a candy thermometer to the side of the saucepan. Allow to simmer for 20 minutes.

Add sugar and lemon juice. Stir to dissolve sugar. Boil for about 8 minutes or until syrup begins to thicken, and the temperature on the thermometer reaches 230 degrees F. *Remove from heat.*

Turn into a heat-proof bowl and refrigerate for at least 1 hour, or until cold. Spoon prunes into a serving bowl. Ladle some of the syrup over.

Serve the prunes cold into dessert dishes, with a bit of syrup spooned over and a dash of cream.

Yields 6 servings
adequate for 4-6 people

Note: When required, this recipe can be halved or doubled.

1/6 SERVING (with 2 teaspoonfuls cream) –
PROTEIN = 1.2 g; FAT = 0.9 g.; CARBOHYDRATE = 43.5 g.;
CALORIES = 184; CALORIES FROM FAT = 4%

Europe–**Bulgaria**

BULGARIAN YOGURT CAKE
Topta cu Kisselo Mleko

TPT - 1 hour and 4 minutes;
10 minutes = cooling period

Bulgarians are passionate about yogurt; our grandson was passionate about yogurt by the time he was just two years old; even our cat Charlie is a yogurt lover. The moistness and protein level of this cake should be presented as delicious evidence to convince the yogurt-dubious among us.

2 cups unbleached white flour
2 teaspoons baking powder
1/2 teaspoon baking soda

1/2 cup (1 stick) butter—*softened to room temperature*
2/3 cup sugar

1/2 cup *fat-free* pasteurized eggs (the equivalent of 2 eggs)
1 tablespoon freshly grated lemon zest
2 teaspoons freshly squeezed lemon juice

1 cup PLAIN YOGURT *[see index] or* commercially-available plain yogurt

Confectioners' sugar

Preheat oven to 350 degrees F. Prepare a 9-inch round or square cake pan by coating with non-stick lecithin spray coating. Line the coated pan with a piece of parchment paper, cut to size. Coat the parchment paper with the non-stick spray coating with flour designed for baking surfaces.

Into a mixing bowl, sift white flour, baking powder, and baking soda. Set aside.

Using the electric mixer or food processor fitted with steel knife, cream butter until light and fluffy. Add sugar and continue beating until again light and fluffy.

Add pasteurized eggs, lemon zest, and lemon juice. Beat until thoroughly combined.

Alternately beat in sifted dry ingredients and yogurt, beating well after each addition until cake batter is smooth. Turn into prepared baking pan.

Bake in preheated 350 degree F. oven for about 35 minutes, or until a cake tester inserted in the center comes out clean.

Cool in pan for about 10 minutes before removing cake from baking pan to cake plate. Sieve confectioners' sugar over cake or use a cake pattern or a paper lace doily to create a decorative pattern on top of cake.

Serve warm.

Yields 10 servings
adequate for 8-10 people

1/10 SERVING – PROTEIN = 4.8 g.; FAT = 9.7 g.; CARBOHYDRATE = 34.2 g.;
CALORIES = 243; CALORIES FROM FAT = 36%

BULGARIAN SULTAN'S SLICES
Pargheni Filyi

TPT - 21 minutes

This is a unique version of what we might call French toast which makes a satisfying dessert. I especially like to use slices of Portuguese rolls for this. The bread can be dipped in eggs as one would for French toast or eggy bread, but I have become very fond of this version.

1/4 cup butter
4 Portuguese rolls *or* French bread—*sliced into 3/4-inch slices**

1/4 cup honey
Ground cinnamon, to taste

In a large skillet set over *MEDIUM* heat, melt butter. Add bread slices and fry until browned on one side. Using a spatula, turn and brown on the remaining side. Transfer to a heated serving platter.

Drizzle honey over the bread. Sprinkle with cinnamon.

Serve at once. Provide extra honey and cinnamon-sugar to accommodate individual tastes.

Yields 6 servings

Notes: *Allow about three slices per serving.

This recipe can be halved when required.

1/6 SERVING – PROTEIN = 1.7 g.; FAT = 7.7 g.; CARBOHYDRATE = 21.3 g.;
CALORIES = 158; CALORIES FROM FAT = 44%

Croatia

In the seventh century AD the Croats settled in this land that had been inhabited throughout the prehistoric period. The rivers Drava, Danube, and Sava border the Pannonian Plains, providing a large, arable area for agriculture in a country where one-third of the country is forested and a significant portion is a barren region in the Dinaric Alps. In 9 AD Croatia became the Roman province of Pannonia and was part of the Roman Empire until the last Roman emperor Julius Nepos was killed in 480 AD. Nepos ruled from the palace built by Emperor Diocletian in the Dalmatian city of Split, in present day Croatia. Subsequently almost all the Roman towns in Croatia were destroyed by the invading Avars in the seventh century. The surviving Romans fled to the mountains and to the coast; the city of Dubrovnik was settled by the survivors of the Avar invasion. From 925 AD until the end of World War I the Kingdom of Croatia existed albeit ruled by the Kingdom of Hungary, by the scions of the Hapsburg dynasty, by the Ottoman Empire, and, later, by the Austro–Hungarian Empire for many of those years.

In 1929 Croatia, together with Serbia, Slovenia, Macedonia, Bosnia and Herzegovina, and Montenegro were combined to form Yugoslavia. These were the nation states which had been combined to form the "Kingdom of the Serbs, Croats, and Slovenes" in 1918 after World War I and were then ruled by King Peter I, a Serbian. The establishment of a Serbian ruling class was a friction point from the very beginning and their authority was constantly challenged, especially by Croatian nationalists. In March 1941 a military *coup d'etat* deposed the pro-Axis Yugoslav government but this was very short-lived as Yugoslavia was invaded in April 1941 by the combined forces of Germany, Hungary, Bulgaria, and Italy with the result that Serbia and Croatia became satellites of Nazi Germany and the remaining states were divided among the other Axis nations. A civil war led to the rise to power of Marshall Josip Broz Tito's in 1943 and the creation of a communist state.

In 1991, after the dismantling of Yugoslavia, Croatia finally stood as an independent state again. At first only recognized by Iceland, Croatia gained official recognition by the European Union in 1992 and then by the United Nations. Rediscovering a national identity was for Croatia, as it was for the other countries newly reborn, an important national project in 1991 but Croatia had been down that road before having been fearful of first Hungarian and then Austrian assimilation. In 1813 Bishop Zagreb Maksimilijan Vrhovac called for the collection of "national treasures" and by the early 1830s the Illyrian movement was founded. It sought national renewal and unity of all South Slavs calling for the marginalization of the Hungarian language and the establishment of a standard language. Croatian literature was encouraged. By 1847 Croatian became the official language. Some twenty-two percent of the coastal Dalmatian population spoke Italian and they too came to recognize the importance of a national identity, a national culture, and the very outward symbol of national identity reflected in the speaking of one language.

Croatia is only about the size of the state of West Virginia, but the distribution of its land mass is entirely different. In a crescent or horseshoe shape, Croatia swings from a long coastal region inland to the Dinaric Alps and in so doing separates Slovenia from Bosnia–Herzegovina. It shares borders with Serbia, Montenegro, and Hungary as well and is just across the Adriatic Sea from northern Italy. The cuisine of this country, not surprisingly, varies from region to region and borrows from its neighbors. There is preference for fish and seafood along the coast and the influences of Italian and Greek food and food preparation techniques are clearly obvious. As you move east the influence of Hungary and Austria are more in evidence.

Europe–Croatia

Creamy Radish Appetizer
Umak od Rotkvica

Roasted Cubanella, Sweet Frying Pepper Salad
Salata od Pečenith Paprika

Cheese Spread
Kajmak

Crackers
Small Toasts

~

Puréed Celeriac and Leek Soup
Juha od Celera

or

**Angel Hair *Pasta* with Caper and Olive Sauce
in the Style of Croatian Mariners**
Jadranska Pasta Marinara

~~~~~~~~~~~~~~~~~~~~~~~

Baked Cauliflower in Casserole with Sour Cream
Cvjetača s Kiselim Vrhnjem

Steamed Asparagus with Butter and Grated Cheese	Sautéed Artichoke Hearts and Peas
Špargle sa Sirom	*Artičoke i Grašak*

~~~~~~~~~~

Slow Cooker Main Course Vegetable Soup with Beans and Barley
Ričet

Chunks of Rustic or Multigrain Bread

~~~~~~~~~~~~~~~~~~~~~

Puffed Pastry Pillows with Poppy Seed Filling
Jastuci od Maka

Figs, dried or fresh, if in season

CREAMY CROATIAN RADISH APPETIZER
Umak od Rotkvica
TPT - 6 minutes

Anyone who grows radishes knows that when the radishes are ready to pull in the early spring, there are always too many radishes. When I was young we knew when my grandfather's radishes had been harvested because every night for weeks there was a relish dish filled with the beautiful red radishes from Grandpa's garden. The salt shaker sat right next to them. Relish dishes are collector items today and we do not even put the salt shaker on our table anymore. This unusual appetizer salad is amazingly refreshing and a good way to use some of that harvest. It can also be used as a dip for crudités, small toasts, and crackers.

Europe – Croatia

CREAMY CROATIAN RADISH APPETIZER (cont'd)

1/4 cup *fat-free* dairy sour cream
2 tablespoons *reduced-calorie or light* mayonnaise
1 teaspoon *extra virgin* olive oil
Freshly ground black pepper, to taste

1 1/2 cups shredded red radishes

In a mixing bowl, combine sour cream, mayonnaise, olive oil, and black pepper. Whisk to combine thoroughly.

Add shredded radishes. Fold them into the dressing. Turn into a serving dish and refrigerate until ready to serve.

Serve chilled. Refrigerate leftovers.

Yields 6-8 servings
adequate for 4-6 people

Note: This recipe can be halved or doubled, when required.

1/8 SERVING – PROTEIN = 1.5 g.; FAT = 1.8 g.; CARBOHYDRATE = 5.1 g.;
CALORIES = 41; CALORIES FROM FAT = 40%

ROASTED CUBANELLA, SWEET FRYING PEPPER SALAD
Salata od Pčenith Paprika

TPT - 2 hours and 9 minutes;
1 hour = flavor development period

I was introduced to Italian frying peppers by my mother-in-law, since my family only cooked with bell peppers. I grew to love these long twisted peppers and used them in many dishes; I was quite bored with green bell peppers and really preferred red bell peppers to green ones anyway. Suddenly I could not find Italian frying peppers in the produce departments of my grocery stores nor were they offered for sale at the farmers' market except during a few weeks in the fall. Preparing Italian fried peppers and eggs, a family favorite, was still an option because the peppers could be frozen but this Croatian salad was reserved as an autumn harvest treat because it required fresh long, green frying peppers. Then, suddenly frying peppers reappeared labeled cubanella peppers or" long yellow peppers." Just in case you wondered what ever happened to Italian frying peppers . . .

10 long, green, sweet cubanella (alternately, cubanel) or Italian frying peppers

Salt to taste
2 medium garlic cloves—*very finely* chopped
2 tablespoons *finely* chopped fresh parsley
Drizzle of *extra virgin* olive oil
Drizzle of GARLIC–BASIL VINEGAR [see index]
or other vinegar of choice

Preheat oven to 350 degrees F.

Place peppers on a cookie sheet. Roast in preheated oven for about 40 minutes, *turning frequently*.

Remove from oven and place in a heavy brown paper bag in dry sink. Roll the top of the bag down and allow to steam for about 15 minutes.

Remove stems, seeds, and membranes, peel, keeping the peppers in large pieces. Place in a shallow serving bowl or on a platter.

Sprinkle with salt. Scatter *very finely* chopped garlic over. Scatter *finely* chopped parsley over. Drizzle a bit of oil over and then drizzle a bit of vinegar over. Refrigerate for about 1 hour to allow for flavor development.

Serve slightly chilled or at room temperature.

Yields 6-8 servings
adequate for 4-6 people

Note: This recipe can be halved or doubled, when required.

1/8 SERVING – PROTEIN = 1.1 g.; FAT = 0.6 g.; CARBOHYDRATE = 4.7 g.;
CALORIES = 31; CALORIES FROM FAT = 17%

Europe–Croatia

CROATIAN CHEESE SPREAD
Kajmak
TPT - 8 minutes

Authentic Croatian "kajmak" is made by boiling whole milk and heavy cream. It is high fat, high salt, and it takes more that thirty hours to prepare. Enter low-fat or even fat-free cream cheese or, as in this recipe, whipped low-fat cream cheese and you have the potential for a spread with much less fat which takes about ten minutes to prepare. It is a superb spread for bagels and toast—butter and a "smear" all in one knifeful. At room temperature it has the consistency of clotted cream.

1/4 cup lightly salted butter—*softened to room temperature*
5 teaspoons *whipped* cream cheese—*brought to room temperature*

In a mixing bowl, combine soften butter and cream cheese. Using a wooden paddle, work the butter and cream cheese together until smooth and completely integrated. Using a rubber spatula, scrape it from the bowl into a small serving bowl or crock. Refrigerate until required.

Remove from the refrigerator at least 20 minutes before serving.

Yields 9 tablespoonfuls servings

Note: This recipe can be halved or doubled, when required.

1/27 SERVING (i. e., per teaspoonful) –
PROTEIN = 0.2 g.; FAT = 2.2 g.; CARBOHYDRATE = 0.2 g.;
CALORIES = 23; CALORIES FROM FAT = 86%

CROATIAN PURÉED CELERIAC AND LEEK SOUP
Juha od Celera
TPT - 44 minutes

Since I was small, I have loved the refreshing sensation of celery. I clearly remember plucking two leaves from a lovage plant as I walked with my great-grandfather in his garden. We then went into the house and took two leaves from a celery stalk in the refrigerator and sat down together at the kitchen table to taste and compare. He then said, "Now, kleine, do you understand why we refer to lovage as celery plant?" Celery is to my family as fennel is to my husband's family. My mother and grandmother often made cream of celery soup with a combination of celery and lovage. This soup, of Croatian origin, incorporates another "celery plant." The soup is not only refreshing and satisfying in and of itself but it also functions well as appetizer soups are meant to do in stimulating the appetite.

2 tablespoons butter
2 medium knob celery (celeriac)—peeled and diced
1 cup VEGETARIAN WHITE STOCK *[see index]*

6 cups VEGETARIAN WHITE STOCK *[see index]*
1 bay leaf—broken in half
1/2 teaspoon crushed dried thyme
1/8 teaspoon HOMEMADE PAPRIKA *[see index]* or commercially-available Hungarian sweet paprika
1/8 teaspoon chili powder

2 medium leeks—trimmed and sliced

1 tablespoon *extra virgin* olive oil
3 tablespoons ground, *preservative-free* almonds or almond meal
2 garlic cloves—*very finely* chopped
Salt, to taste
Freshly ground *white* pepper, to taste

2 tablespoons *fat-free* dairy sour cream
1/4 cup chopped fresh parsley

2 tablespoons grated *pecorino Romano* cheese, for garnish

CROATIAN PURÉED CELERIAC AND LEEK SOUP (cont'd)

In a kettle set over *LOW-MEDIUM* heat, melt butter. Add diced knob celery (celeriac) and 1 cupful vegetable stock. Cook, stirring frequently, until *softened* and *golden in color*—about 15 minutes.

Add vegetable stock, bay leaf pieces, crushed thyme, paprika, and chili powder. Allow to heat while preparing leeks.

Place leek slices in a mixing bowl filled with water. Swish them back and forth to release any sand that might be caught between the leaves. Transfer the leek slices to a sieve and allow to drain.

In a skillet set over *MEDIUM* heat, heat oil. Add leek slices, ground almonds, and *very finely* chopped garlic. Sauté until leeks are soft and translucent, *allowing neither the onions nor the garlic to brown.* Add to ingredients in kettle.

Add sour cream and parsley. Stir to integrate.

Remove and discard bay leaf pieces.

Purée two or three ladlefuls at a time in the electric blender, or in the food processor fitted with steel knife, until very smooth. Turn into a large saucepan. Season with salt and *white* pepper, to taste. Cook over *LOW-MEDIUM* heat until hot.

Turn into a heated soup tureen and serve into heated soup plates. Garnish each serving with a teaspoonful of grated cheese.*

Yields 8 cupfuls

Notes: *Some people enjoy a more sour taste and for that reason I always put a small dish of sour cream on the table to accommodate others.

When required, this recipe may be doubled or tripled.

This soup freeze well.

1/8 SERVING (i. e., 1 cupful) –
PROTEIN = 4.0 g.; FAT = 7.9 g.; CARBOHYDRATE = 4.0 g.;
CALORIES = 97; CALORIES FROM FAT = 7%

ANGEL HAIR *PASTA* WITH CAPER AND OLIVE SAUCE IN THE STYLE OF CROATIAN MARINERS
Jadranska Pasta Marinara
TPT - 45 minutes

Fascination with the Adriatic Sea that rolls up on the beaches of the long coastline of Croatia and the 1,185 Croatian-claimed islands not only encouraged men to become fishermen, it called them to be mariners and mariners from this small country have traveled the world for centuries. Croatians sailed with Columbus to the New World and are also said to have been part of crews that explored with both Sebastian Cabot and Jacques Cartier. The influence of Italy on Croatia is evidenced in many ways but there is a most pronounced homage to Croatia's years as part of the Roman Empire in the cuisine. Pastas are consumed with gusto as are artichokes, often served as they are in Sicily, and minestrones, called "maneštras" in Croatian. The sauce for this dish derives from sauces made by Croatia mariners and although it differs considerably from my Italian marinara sauce, it is a marinara sauce and its roots are clearly Italian. We like to serve this sauce with the very thin spaghetti," spaghettini" or with nests of angel hair pasta, "capelli d'angelo."

CROATION CAPER AND OLIVE SAUCE:
 1 tablespoon *extra virgin* olive oil

 1 can (28 ounces) *whole* tomatoes canned in purée

 1/2 cup canned, *crushed* tomatoes

[see next page]

ANGEL HAIR PASTA WITH CAPER AND OLIVE SAUCE IN THE STYLE OF CROATIAN MARINERS (cont'd)

2 tablespoons preserved non-pareil capers
—soaked in cold water to remove excess salt and well-drained
15 pitted *Kalamata* olives—sliced
2 large garlic cloves—*very finely* chopped
1/4 cup chopped *fresh* basil
1/4 cup chopped *fresh* parsley
1/4 cup chopped *fresh* oregano
2 tablespoons chopped fresh thyme
2 tablespoons *finely* chopped *fresh* rosemary needles
Freshly ground black pepper, to taste

6 dry angel hair *pasta (capelli d'angelo* or, sometimes, *capellini)* nests
Boiling water

Grated *pecorino Romano or* Parmesan cheese, as preferred

In a large saucepan set over *LOW-MEDIUM* heat, heat oil.

Chop whole tomatoes in half and add to the saucepan with the purée in which they were canned and the crushed tomatoes. Allow to come to the boil.

Add capers, olives slices, *very finely* chopped garlic, chopped fresh basil, parsley, oregano, and thyme, *finely* chopped rosemary needles, and black pepper. Cook, stirring frequently, for about 20 minutes.

Fill a large, deep skillet, set over *MEDIUM* heat, with *boiling* water. Slip the angel hair nests into the water and allow to simmer according to package directions, or until *pasta* is *al dente*. Using a wide, slotted spatula or Chinese skimmer, remove the nests one a time. Allow them to drain over the sink and slip each nest into a heated soup plate. Repeat until all nests have been plated. Drizzle a spoonful of the prepared sauce over each.

Turn the sauce into a heated serving bowl.

Serve at once. Pass the sauce and grated cheese.

Yields 6 individual servings

Notes: This recipe may be halved or doubled, when required.

Leftover sauce can be frozen.

1/6 SERVING – PROTEIN = 5.2 g.; FAT = 7.3 g.; CARBOHYDRATE = 27.2 g.;
CALORIES = 176; CALORIES FROM FAT = 37%

CROATIAN BAKED CAULIFLOWER IN CASSEROLE WITH SOUR CREAM
Cvjetača s Kiselim Vrhnjem
TPT - 42 minutes

When the snowy white and golden orange cauliflowers finally come to market it is a time for celebration in our home. All summer expensive cauliflower, from who knows where, can tempt but we have to hold our ground, waiting for fresh, local cauliflower. Cauliflower salads and baked whole cauliflowers are finally on the menu again. This recipe can not, or at least should not, be made with frozen cauliflower so do wait until the fall harvest. We prefer to use the orange cauliflower, hybridized at Cornell University to improve the vitamin A content of this healthful Brassica and first grown in the cool valleys of New York and Pennsylvania. The color makes this casserole even more welcome at our autumn table and that extra vitamin A is welcome too.

1 medium cauliflower—about 10 ounces trimmed—separated into florets, trimmed, and well-rinsed

3 tablespoons butter—*melted*
1/4 cup *fat-free* dairy sour cream—whisked until smooth
Freshly ground black pepper, to taste
1/4 cup breadcrumbs

Set up steamer. Preheat oven to 325 degrees F. Prepare a 2-quart soufflé dish or other oven-to-table baking dish by coating with non-stick-lecithin spray coating.

Steam cauliflower florets until *crisp-tender*—about 12 minutes. *Be careful not to overcook.* Drain. Turn into prepared baking dish, *floret surface up.*

Pour the *melted* butter over the cauliflower. Pour the sour cream over. Grind black pepper over and sprinkle breadcrumbs evenly over the top. Bake in preheated 325 degree F. oven for about 20 minutes or until lightly browned.

**CROATIAN BAKED CAULIFLOWER IN CASSEROLE
WITH SOUR CREAM** (cont'd)

Serve at once.

Yields 6 servings
adequate for 4 people

Note: This recipe can be halved or doubled, when required.

1/6 SERVING – PROTEIN = 2.9 g.; FAT = 5.8 g.; CARBOHYDRATE = 9.9 g.;
CALORIES = 101; CALORIES FROM FAT = 52%

SLOW COOKER MAIN COURSE VEGETABLE SOUP WITH BEANS AND BARLEY IN THE STYLE OF CROATIA

Ričet

TPT - 15 hours and 22 minutes;
8 hours = bean soaking period;
1 hour = barley soaking period
[slow cooker: 4 hours at HIGH; 3 hours at LOW]

Although this might be considered by some to be a winter soup, a bowl of this barley–bean soup with a salad is appropriate for any cool evening at our latitude—fall, winter, or spring. Since I prefer to make it in the slow cooker, the kitchen does not heat up. The addition of kohlrabi is clearly a seasonal addition and I always add it when I can because it is a vegetable that evokes a very personal and very treasured memory to me. My maternal great-grandfather grew kohlrabi in the garden in his backyard. As I walked with him one day through his garden, he took out his pocket knife, pulled a kohlrabi, artfully peeled it, and sliced it for us to munch on. Then, as was his way, he guided me to the compost pile to deposit the trimmings. This soup, which is thick in the Croatian way, is chuck full of vegetable goodness. Croatians make this with smoked meats and to provide just a hint of that smoky taste, I add a couple of pieces of soy bacon.

1/2 cup dry red kidney beans—well-rinsed
3 cups water

3/4 cup dry pearl barley
2 cups water

6 cups *boiling* water
1 slice soy bacon—*cut in half*

1 large carrot—scraped or pared and sliced into rounds
1 parsley root, if available, *or* a small parsnip
—trimmed, well-washed, and sliced into rounds
1 celery stalk—trimmed and sliced
1 small leek—*white and light green portions*
—trimmed, well-rinsed, and sliced
1/4 cup onion—diced
1 red bell pepper—diced
3 canned, *whole* tomatoes--diced *or* fresh tomatoes
—peeled and diced
1 small kohlrabi, if available—peeled and diced
1 cup chopped savoy cabbage—well-rinsed
1 bay leaf—broken in half
Freshly ground black pepper, to taste
1/2 teaspoon salt, or to taste

2 medium potatoes—peeled and diced

In a mixing bowl, combine dry beans and 3 cupfuls water. Place a plate on top of the mixing bowl and allow the beans to soak overnight. Drain well in the morning.

In a mixing bowl, combine barley and the 2 cupfuls water. Allow to soak for 1 hour. Drain.

Turn slow cooker setting to HIGH.

In the bowl of the slow cooker, combine presoaked beans and barley. Add the 6 cupfuls *boiling* water and soy bacon pieces. Allow to cook for 4 hours.

Add sliced carrots, parsley, celery root, and leek, diced onion, pepper, tomatoes, and kohlrabi, chopped cabbage, bay leaf pieces, pepper, and salt. *Reduce slow cooker setting to LOW* and allow to cook, covered, for another 2 hours. Stir occasionally. Add more water, only if necessary.

Add diced potatoes and cook for an additional 1 hour.

SLOW COOKER MAIN COURSE VEGETABLE SOUP WITH BEANS AND BARLEY IN THE STYLE OF CROATIA (cont'd)

Remove and discard bacon and bay leaf pieces. Turn into a heated soup tureen.

Serve into heated soup bowls.

Yields about 9 cupfuls

Notes: Leftovers can be frozen quite successfully. Defrost completely before reheating to preserve texture of vegetables.

If preferred, this can, of course, be cooked on the stove over *VERY LOW* heat but it must be stirred frequently. Over direct heat it will take less time to cook.

1/9 SERVING (i. e., per cupful) –
PROTEIN = 7.6 g.; FAT = 0.9 g.; CARBOHYDRATE = 48.2 g.;
CALORIES = 227; CALORIES FROM FAT = 4%

CROATIAN POPPY SEED PILLOWS
Jastuci od Maka
TPT - 40 minutes

A Croatian poppy seed pillow, like a Croatian poppy seed strudel, "makovnjača", is made with a rich pastry not with phyllo pastry. Puffed pastry is, therefore, an adequate substitute. Since puff pastry is readily available with other dessert items in the freezer sections of most grocery stores, poppy seed pillows need not be put aside as a "dessert to try some day." This version takes just minutes to prepare and bakes in fifteen minutes. Do keep in mind that ingested poppy seeds can give a false positive if the person is tested for drug use within twenty-four hours so schedule this dessert carefully if necessary.

1 sheet *frozen* puff pasty—brought to room temperature and *not unrolled*

8 tablespoons sweetened, canned poppy seed cake and pastry filling*
3 drops pure almond extract

Preheat oven to 400 degrees. F. Prepare a large cookie sheet by lining with culinary parchment paper.

Leaving the puff pastry sheet still rolled as it comes from the box, slice it cross-wise into 12 equal sections. On a cool surface, such as the counter top or a baking or cheese marble, roll a section out with a rolling pin to about 2 x 4 inches.

In a small dish, combine poppy seed filling and almond extract. Stir to distribute the almond flavoring evenly. Place 2 teaspoonfuls of the poppy seed filling to one side of the rolled-out pastry. Fold the other side over and seal the three remaining edges by pinching securely. Place on the parchment-lined cookie sheet. Repeat until all twelve pillows have been formed. Bake in preheated 400 degree F. oven for 15 minutes, or until puffed and golden. Transfer from baking sheet to a serving dish. Set aside and allow to cool.

Serve at room temperature.

Yields 12 servings
adequate for 6 people

Notes: *Poppy seed filling is sold in 12.5-ounce cans in the baking aisle of most well-stocked grocery stores.

This recipe can be increased or decreased quite easily, as needed.

1/12 SERVING (i. e., per pillow) –
PROTEIN = 2.2 g.; FAT = 6.8 g.; CARBOHYDRATE = 13. 7 g;
CALORIES = 125; CALORIES FROM FAT = 49%

Czech Republic

The "Velvet Revolution" in 1989 eventually led to the dissolution of Czechoslovakia into the constituent states, the Czech Republic and Slovakia, the states that had been combined in 1918 after World War I after the collapse of the Austro–Hungarian Empire. Most of us have known only the combined nation of Czechoslovakia. The Czech state, then known as Bohemia, was formed in the ninth century AD under the Přemyslid dynasty, a dynastic power in Central Europe that persisted until the last of the line was murdered in 1306. The House of Luxembourg eventually became the ruling dynasty in Bohemia succeeded by the Hapsburg dynasty after 1526. The revolt against the Hapsburgs began in 1618 precipitating the war that spread through Europe known as the Thirty Years' War. Bohemia emerged late in the eighteenth century as part of the Austrian Empire and this period of history is reflected in the rich pastries that Czechs enjoy.

After the fall of the Austro–Hungarian Empire at the end of World War I, the independent Republic of Czechoslovakia was formed. In the 1930s Germany took advantage of the unrest among the minority populations within Czechoslovakia and, with the help of the Sudeten German Party and through the 1938 Munich Agreement, annexed the largely German-speaking Sudetenland giving Germany its valuable border fortifications. In 1939 Slovakia seceded from the republic to ally itself with Germany. The Czech resistance to Nazi occupation is notable. A government-in-exile was established, a government that was recognized by the Allied nations, and Czech citizens who found themselves outside of the country at the time of occupation and those that managed to flee fought with the Allied forces in Russia, North Africa, and the Middle East. Those who remained in Czechoslovakia suffered under Germany's heel. 345,000 Czechs were killed or executed during World War II and hundreds of thousands were imprisoned or sent to concentration camps and used as forced labor. The elections which followed World War II saw an increasingly larger and larger portion of the population drawn to Soviet-style Communist candidates giving way to a *coup d'etat* in 1948. For forty-one years Czechoslovakia remained a Communist state within the Eastern Bloc. In 1989 Czechoslovakia experienced the so–called "Velvet Revolution" and returned to a liberal democracy. In 1993 the countries of the Czech Republic and Slovakia peacefully emerged from their union as independent nations.

Czechoslovakia profoundly influenced my life. Although I never lived there, I never had the chance to visit, and I have known few people of Czech descent in my life, one Czechoslovakian, whom I never met, influenced the major academic path I was to take. Gregor Johann Mendel was a Silesian-born, Augustinian monk who experimented with garden peas in the mid-nineteenth century. Through his experimental crosses and observations he has become known as "the father of genetics" although the bulk of his published works actually related to meteorology. The handful of physical characteristics, the phenotype, that he watched play out in the gardens of his monastery and from which he formulated his principals of heredity, were the first simple lessons in genetics for those of us who chose to enter that very new and ever-fascinating branch of science. He, of course, would never know what he had begun but to honor our guide into the understanding of ourselves and ever-evolving world, I suggest that green peas, smooth not wrinkled, accompany the following menu.

Europe–Czech Republic

Steamed Cheese Pudding
Syrovy Pudink

~

Cream of Celery Root Soup
Celer Polevka

Mushroom Soup
Houbova Polevka Myslivecka

~

Boston Lettuce Salad with Onion and Sour Cream Dressing
Hlavkovy Cibulovy Salat s Kyselous Smetanou

Onion Salad
Cibulovy Salat

~~~~~~~~~~~~~~~~~~~~

Potato and Mushroom Casserole
Brambory Zapekane s Houbami

Kohlrabi with Butter and Breadcrumbs
Brukev Vařná

Steamed and Buttered Green Peas

~~~~~~~~~~

Mixed Vegetable Salad
with White Beans, Root Celery, Kohlrabi and Potatoes
Michany Salát

Sautéed Noodles with Spinach
Nudle se Špenátem

~~~~~~~~~~~~~~~~~~~~

Thin Pancakes
Palačinky
with

Poppy Seed Filling for Pancakes   or   **Peach Jam** *[see index]*
Maková Nadivka

and

Sour Cream
Kyselou Smetanou

Farina Omelet
Krupicovy Trhanec

Europe–Czech Republic

CZECH STEAMED CHEESE PUDDING
Syrový Pudink
TPT - 45 minutes

Although this recipe can be doubled to serve six, we make this smaller portion and serve it as a first course or as a main course with a vegetable and a salad. Granted, the designation as a pudding congers up a different image to those of us in the United States or in Great Britain, for that matter. You will find this savory soufflé to be useful in meal planning. Be aware that soufflés like this do not like to be reheated so leftovers are disappointing.

1/2 cup unbleached white flour
1/2 cup *fat-free* dairy sour cream
1/4 cup *two-percent* milk
2 large *organic* egg yolks*

2 large *organic* egg whites*

1/2 cup grated *pecorino Romano* or Parmesan cheese

Set up a steamer. Prepare 1-quart soufflé dish by coating generously with butter. Prepare a large piece of aluminum foil by coating the center of one side with butter. Set aside.

In a mixing bowl, combine flour, sour cream, milk, and egg yolks. Using a wire whisk, combine thoroughly.

Using an electric mixer fitted with *grease-free* beaters or by hand, using a *grease-free* wire whisk, beat egg whites in a *grease-free* bowl until *stiff*, but *not dry*. Add stiffly beaten egg whites to batter and *gently* fold the egg whites into the batter.

Add the grated cheese and again *gently* fold the cheese into the batter. Turn into prepared baking dish. Place in steamer. Cover with aluminum foil, butter-side-down. Cover steamer and steam over boiling water for 30 minutes, or until center is set.

Serve at once. Like any soufflé, this pudding does not wait for stragglers.

Yields 4 servings
adequate for 3 people

Note: *Because raw eggs present the danger of *Salmonella* poisoning, do be sure to select organic eggs for this dish.

1/4 SERVING – PROTEIN = 12.5 g.; FAT = 6.0 g.; CARBOHYDRATE = 23.5 g.;
CALORIES = 201; CALORIES FROM FAT = 27%

CZECH CREAM OF CELERY ROOT SOUP
Celer Polevka
TPT - 52 minutes

Whenever my mother made a cream soup, she would have one of us climb up to the top shelf of the cupboard where she kept her "good" dishes and hand down the cream soup cups with their charming handles. When we bought a second set of "good" dishes, I sought out an English set that had cream soup cups. It still seems like a special occasion when I climb up to get my cream soup cups down. This is a rich, filling soup, as are so many of those you will find in the Czech Republic but it can be convenient winter soup if you make a large batch of the base, i. e., without the cream, and freeze it. As soon as the celery roots come into the market, I make a double or triple batch.

2 small celery roots (knob celery or celeriac)
  —peeled and chopped
2 quarts *boiling* water

1 tablespoon butter
1/4 cup chopped fresh parsley
Freshly ground *white* pepper to taste

2 tablespoons butter

2 1/3 tablespoons unbleached white flour

5 cups VEGETARIAN WHITE STOCK *[see index]*

1/4 cup heavy whipping cream
1/4 cup light cream *or* half and half

VOLUME I - 91

CZECH CREAM OF CELERY ROOT SOUP (cont'd)

In a large saucepan set over *MEDIUM-HIGH* heat, blanch the chopped celery roots in *boiling* water for 5 minutes.

In a large skillet set over *LOW-MEDIUM* heat, melt 1 tablespoonful butter. Add diced celery root (knob celery or celeriac) and parsley. Season with *white* pepper. Cook, stirring frequently, until softened and golden in color—about 12 minutes.

In a small kettle, set over *LOW* heat, melt remaining 2 tablespoonfuls butter. Remove from heat and, using a wire whisk, make a *roux* by beating in flour. Return to heat and, stirring constantly, cook for 2 minutes, *being careful not to burn or overbrown the roux.* Remove from heat and gradually beat in the vegetable stock. Return saucepan to heat and cook, stirring constantly, until thickened.

Add cooked celery root–parsley mixture. Purée two or three ladlefuls at a time in the electric blender, or in the food processor fitted with steel knife, or mash finely and press through a fine sieve or a FOOD MILL.* Turn into a clean saucepan. Cook over *LOW-MEDIUM* heat until hot.

Gradually, using a wire whisk, stir heavy cream and half and half into the puréed mixture. Allow to heat through for several minutes. *Do not allow to boil once you have added the cream.*

Turn into a heated soup tureen and serve into heated cream soup cups.

Yields six 1-cup servings
adequate for 4 people

Notes: *The puréed base can be frozen at this point.

When required, this recipe may be doubled or tripled.

This soup freeze well.

1/6 SERVING – PROTEIN = 1.3 g.; FAT = 10.0 g.; CARBOHYDRATE = 5.2 g.;
CALORIES = 115; CALORIES FROM FAT = 78%

CZECH MUSHROOM SOUP
Houbova Polevka Myslivecka
TPT - 28 minutes

Gathering mushrooms is a family project in the Czech Republic as it is in many countries in Central Europe. After a rainy spring or summer period, mushrooms hunters head out to find the proliferation of edible fungi. Families closely guard the location of their most productive hunting grounds. Freshly gathered, wild mushrooms give this traditional soup the nuances of flavor that make it the treasure it is. Gathering mushrooms in the wild is not every family's thing and if you are uniformed, it can be a pretty dangerous family activity but foraging in grocery stores can turn up some interesting mushrooms. Granted, we now live in Pennsylvania which is famed for its mushroom production, but I can usually find a hen-of-the-woods (maitake) or a cauliflower, a pom pom (lion's mane) or a satyr's beard (bearded tooth or bear's head), some shiitake, portobello, and a stalk of fresh oyster mushrooms. Failing enough variety, I retrieve dried mushrooms from my larder. Lobster, morels, porcini, chanterelles, black trumpets (black chanterelle), cloud ears, shiitake, and wood ears are all available dried and add their own complex flavors. To this I add crimini, which are readily available in most grocery stores. It certainly is a different kind of mushroom hunting but this soup is worth the foraging.

1 tablespoon *extra virgin* olive oil
2 tablespoons butter
1 slice soy bacon—*finely* chopped
1 pound mixed mushrooms—hard stems removed, rinsed, cleaned well with a brush, and sliced*
1 small onion—chopped

3 1/2 cups VEGETARIAN BROWN STOCK *[see index]* or VEGETABLE STOCK FROM SOUP *[see index]*
1 cup WILD MUSHROOM STOCK *[see index]*

3 or 4 lumps of KNEADED FLOUR FOR THICKENING *(Buerre Manie)* *[see index]*

1/4 cup light cream *or* half and half
Freshly ground black pepper, to taste

CZECH MUSHROOM SOUP (cont'd)

In a large non-stick-coated skillet set over *LOW-MEDIUM* heat, heat oil and butter. Add *finely* chopped soy bacon, sliced mushrooms, and chopped onion. Cook, stirring frequently, until onion is soft and translucent and mushrooms are tender. *Be careful not to allow the onions to burn.* Turn cooked mushroom mixture into a small kettle.

Add vegetable and mushroom stock. Allow to come to the boil, stirring frequently.

Add several lumps of *buerre manie.* Cook, stirring constantly, until soup is thickened to your liking. Add more *buerre manie* as needed. *Reduce heat to LOW.***

Add cream. Stir to integrate. Season with black pepper. Turn into a heated soup tureen.

Serve at once into heated soup plates.

Yields 6 cupfuls

Notes: *Dried mushrooms, if you chose to use them, must be well-rinsed and soaked in hot water for at least an hour. The liquid in which they are soaked can be added to the soup in place of a portion of the vegetable stock.

**A couple of tablespoonfuls of white wine adds another layer of complexity and can be added at this point.

This recipe can be halved, when required, but since it reheats well, if not boiled, it can be a planned leftover for lunch.

1/6 SERVING – PROTEIN = 3.0 g.; FAT = 7.6 g.; CARBOHYDRATE = 4.8 g.;
CALORIES = 97; CALORIES FROM FAT = 70%

BOSTON LETTUCE SALAD AND ONION WITH SOUR CREAM DRESSING
Hlavkovy Cibulovy Salat s Kyselous Smetanou

TPT - 5 minutes

Boston lettuce is a soft-leafed lettuce that is especially receptive to this simple sour cream dressing.

2 small heads Boston lettuce—well washed, torn into pieces, and well-dried
1/4 cup chopped onion

CZECH SOUR CREAM DRESSING:
    3 tablespoons *fat-free* dairy sour cream
    2 teaspoons light cream *or* half and half
    1/4 teaspoon sugar
    1 teaspoon distilled white vinegar

Put washed and well-dried lettuce pieces into a salad bowl. Sprinkle chopped onion over the top.

In a small bowl, combine sour cream, cream, sugar, and vinegar. Using a small wire whisk, combine thoroughly.

When ready to serve, pour the dressing over the lettuce and toss.

Yields 6 servings
adequate for 4 people

Note: This recipe can be halved or doubled, when required.

1/6 SERVING – PROTEIN = 1.4 g.; FAT = 0.09 g.; CARBOHYDRATE = 4.8 g.;
CALORIES = 28; CALORIES FROM FAT = <1%

Europe–Czech Republic

CZECH ONION SALAD
Cibulový Salát

TPT - 1 hour and 11 minutes;
1 hour = marination period

This Czech salad is simple, unusual, and a very, very good winter salad.

1 cup water
1/2 cup apple cider vinegar
1 pound onions—sliced into rings

2 tablespoons CLASSIC FRENCH DRESSING
   (***Vinaigrette***) *[see index]*
1/2 teaspoon sugar

In a large saucepan set over *MEDIUM-HIGH* heat, bring water and vinegar to the boil. Add onion rings and allow to come back to the boil again. Remove immediately from heat and drain thoroughly.

In a plastic container with tightly fitting lid, combine CLASSIC FRENCH DRESSING and sugar. Stir well to combine. Add drained onion rings, close tightly, and shake to coat onion rings with salad dressing.

Refrigerate for at least 1 hour, turning container occasionally to insure even marination.

Before serving, drain well in a strainer set over the sink or use a salad spinner.

Yields 6 servings
adequate for 4 people

Note: This recipe may be halved or doubled, when required. When halved, it is advisable to use the same amount of water and vinegar for the blanching procedure.

1/6 SERVING – PROTEIN = 1.0 g.; FAT = 1.4 g.; CARBOHYDRATE = 10.6 g.;
CALORIES = 55; CALORIES FROM FAT = 23%

CZECH POTATO AND MUSHROOM CASSEROLE
Brambory Zapékané s Houbami

TPT - 2 hours and 5 minutes;
1 hour = potato chilling period

We have enjoyed this dish for decades. I, however, have had to make one change as I share this with you. The card in my files attributes this recipe to Czechoslovakia; it is now the Czech Republic. The casserole is simple, family fare and there are times, in our busy, sophisticated world, when perhaps we should all sit down to a simple meal like this and give thanks for the mushrooms gathered.

3 quarts *boiling* water
2 pounds medium all-purpose potatoes—well-scrubbed

1 medium onion—chopped
1/3 cup butter

20 ounces fresh mushrooms—trimmed, rinsed, cleaned well with a brush, and sliced*
1/2 teaspoon caraway seeds
1/4 teaspoon freshly ground black pepper, or more to taste

1 1/2 cups skimmed milk
3/4 cup *fat-free* pasteurized eggs (the equivalent of 3 eggs)

In a large kettle set over *MEDIUM-HIGH* heat, add potatoes to *boiling* water. Boil for about 25 minutes, or until potatoes are tender but still firm. Refrigerate for at least 1 hour before attempting to slice potatoes.

Prepare a 2-quart soufflé dish or other oven-to-table casserole by coating with non-stick lecithin spray coating. Preheat oven to 350 degrees F.

In a skillet set over *LOW-MEDIUM* heat, combine chopped onion with butter. Sauté until onion is soft and translucent, *being careful not to allow onion to brown.*

Add mushroom slices and caraway seeds. Sauté gently until most of moisture has been extruded from mushrooms. Grind black pepper over.

VOLUME I - 94

CZECH POTATO AND MUSHROOM CASSEROLE (cont'd)

Peel chilled potatoes and slice. Alternate layers of potatoes and sautéed mushroom–onion–caraway mixture with liquid, ending with potato slices.

In a mixing bowl, using a wire whisk, beat milk and eggs together. Pour over layered vegetables.

Bake in preheated 350 degree F. oven for 20-25 minutes, or until custard is set.

Serve at once.

Notes: *The earthier the mushrooms, the better. A mixture of *crimini*, *porcini*, hens-of-the-woods, oyster, and lobster mushrooms gives real depth to this casserole.

This recipe may be halved, when required.

Leftovers can not be successfully reheated.

Yields 6 servings
adequate for 4 people

1/6 SERVING – PROTEIN = 7.9 g.; FAT = 10.3 g.; CARBOHYDRATE = 30.6 g.;
CALORIES = 271; CALORIES FROM FAT = 34%

KOHLRABI WITH BUTTER AND BREADCRUMBS
Brukev Vařná

TPT - 36 minutes

Kohlrabi is one of the most neglected vegetables and as a Brassica, it is so good for you. People will eat and enjoy broccoli but kohlrabi, which has the texture of and tastes very much like broccoli, is bypassed. It can be eaten raw, sautéed, boiled, baked, and steamed and the leaves can be cooked just like spinach. It was a favorite snack for me as little girl. When I first introduced it to my husband, whose mother's southern European cooking did not include kohlrabi, his response was, "This is good."

4 kohlrabi—peeled and diced
2 cups *boiling* water

2 tablespoons butter—*melted*
2 tablespoons breadcrumbs

Preheat oven to 250 degrees F. Prepare an oven-to table platter by coating with butter.

In a saucepan set over *MEDIUM* heat, combine diced kohlrabi and *boiling* water. Allow to cook for 15 minutes. Drain. Turn onto prepared platter.

Pour *melted* butter over. Sprinkle with breadcrumbs. Bake in preheated 250 degree F. oven for about 15 minutes more, or until breadcrumbs are lightly browned.

Serve at once.

Yields 6 servings
adequate for 4 people

Note: This recipe can be halved or doubled, when required.

1/6 SERVING – PROTEIN = 1.8 g.; FAT = 3.9 g.; CARBOHYDRATE = 7.4 g.;
CALORIES = 67; CALORIES FROM FAT = 52%

CZECH MIXED VEGETABLE SALAD WITH WHITE BEANS, ROOT CELERY, KOHLRABI, AND POTATOES
Michany Salát
TPT - 30 minutes

Czech meals tend to be heavy on meat and starches and even when you eliminate the meat, a menu can become too much for the Western appetite. In the late summer, when the celeriac and kohlrabi come to market again, this salad is a perfect main course for a light meal. The vegetables are uniformly diced, except for the carrot, much as you prepare them for a Moscow salad. The beans need grain complementation if this is to be the centerpiece of a menu so I often serve it with noodles and spinach sautéed in the Czech style.

DRESSING:
    1/4 cup *light or reduced calorie* mayonnaise with olive oil
    1 tablespoon *fat-free* dairy sour cream
    2 teaspoons MUSTARD SAUCE *[see index]*
    1 tablespoon white wine vinegar
    Freshly ground black pepper, to taste

1 quart *boiling* water
1 fresh bay leaf or dried bay leaf, if you must —halved
1 large potato—peeled and diced

1/2 cup diced root celery (knob celery or celeriac)
1 kohlrabi root—peeled and diced

1 can (15.5 ounces) *cannellini* beans *or* Roman beans—well-drained
1/2 cup diced sweet onion—Walla Walla, Vidalia, *or* Texas or Mayan Sweet
1 large dill pickle—diced
1 small carrot—scraped or pared and coarsely grated

2 tablespoons chopped fresh dillweed

In a small bowl, combine mayonnaise, sour cream, mustard, vinegar, and black pepper. Using a small wire whisk, beat until smooth. Set aside.

Combine *boiling* water, bay leaf pieces, and diced potato in a large saucepan set over *MEDIUM* heat. Cook until potatoes are *crisp-tender*—about 12 minutes. Using a slotted spoon or skimmer remove potato pieces to a pan of cold water to stop further cooking. Return bay leaf pieces to the water.

Add diced root celery and kohlrabi to the cooking water and cook these vegetables also until *crisp tender*—about 7 minutes. Drain and transfer vegetables to cold water with potatoes. Discard bay leaf pieces or add to vegetable stock bag in freezer. When vegetables have cooled sufficiently, drain thoroughly. Turn into a mixing bowl.

Add well-drained beans, diced onion and dill pickle, and grated carrot. *Gently* mix vegetables.

Add prepared salad dressing. *Gently* fold the dressing into the vegetables. Turn into a serving bowl. Refrigerate, covered, until ready to serve.

Serve chilled, garnished with chopped, fresh dillweed.

Yields 6 servings
adequate for 4 people

Note: This recipe can be doubled, when required.

1/6 SERVING – PROTEIN = 3.6 g.; FAT = 4.1 g.; CARBOHYDRATE = 17.0 g.; CALORIES = 94; CALORIES FROM FAT = 39%

SAUTÉED NOODLES WITH SPINACH
Nudle se Špenátem
TPT - 25 minutes

This is certainly not a complicated dish and it is certainly not exclusive to the Czech cuisine but it is soul-satisfying. Fresh spinach has an intense flavor that plays off noodles and pasta, a flavor that frozen spinach can not match.

SAUTÉED NOODLES WITH SPINACH (cont'd)

3 quarts *boiling* water
1/2 pound twisted egg noodles

2 tablespoons butter
8 ounces fresh, baby spinach—well-washed and trimmed

Freshly ground black pepper, to taste

In a large saucepan set over *MEDIUM-HIGH* heat, combine *boiling* water, and noodles. Allow noodles to cook according to package directions. Drain thoroughly.

In a large skillet set over *MEDIUM* heat, melt butter. Add noodles and spinach. Cook, stirring frequently, until spinach is wilted.

Season with black pepper. Turn into a heated serving bowl.

Serve at once.

Yields 6 servings
adequate for 4 people

Note: This recipe can be halved, when required.

1/6 SERVING – PROTEIN = 5.9 g.; FAT = 5.4 g.; CARBOHYDRATE = 21.0 g.;
CALORIES = 154; CALORIES FROM FAT = 32 %

POPPY SEED FILLING FOR PANCAKES
Maková Nádivka
TPT - 2 minutes

You can make pancakes from scratch or you can make them using a mix but for Czech "palačinky" they should be very thin, almost crêpe-like, so that they can be easily folded.

6 tablespoons sweetened poppy seed filling*
2 tablespoons heavy cream
1/4 teaspoon pure vanilla extract
3 or 4 drops freshly squeezed lemon juice
Several dashes ground cloves

In a small bowl, combine poppy seed filling, heavy cream, vanilla extract, lemon juice, and ground cloves. Mix well. Refrigerate until required but bring to room temperature before filling pancakes.

Spread on *palačinky* and fold each.

Adequate to fill six pancakes

Notes: *Canned poppy seed filling can be found in the baking aisle.

This recipe can be doubled or tripled, as needed.

1/6 SERVING – PROTEIN = 1.1 g.; FAT = 3.6 g.; CARBOHYDRATE = 10.2 g.;
CALORIES = 76; CALORIES FROM FAT = 43%

Europe–Czech Republic

CZECH SWEET FARINA OMELET
Krupicovy Trhanec

TPT - 1 hour and 50 minutes;
1 hour = farina soaking period

Oven-baked omelets can present the same menu versatility as do French omelets but they have a texture so entirely different that the versatility quota goes up a notch or two. They too can be sweet or savory. This is one of those "I-have-everything-in-the-house" winter dessert recipes that cooks love. Since I found this Czech dessert many years ago, I have yet to find a fruit sauce that isn't compatible. It is a different choice for a holiday breakfast or brunch. You may want to serve it, as we do, with a fruit compote and our Christmas stöllen.

4 large egg yolks
6 tablespoons sugar
1 cup skimmed milk
1 cup farina *or* **Cream of Wheat cereal**

1 cup skimmed milk

4 large egg whites

1/4 cup butter—*melted*

1 tablespoon cinnamon–sugar, if preferred

In a mixing bowl, combine egg yolks, 1/4 cupful sugar, 1 cupful milk, and farina. Using a wire whisk, mix well. Cover mixing bowl with a plate and set aside for 1 hour.

Add second cupful of milk and mix well.

Preheat oven to 300 degrees F.

Using an electric mixer fitted with *grease-free* beaters or by hand, using a *grease-free* wire whisk, beat egg whites in a *grease-free* bowl until *stiff*, but *not dry*. *Whisk-fold* beaten egg whites *gently*, but *thoroughly*, into farina batter.

Pour melted butter into an 8 x 8-inch-square baking pan. Tip to coat the bottom of the pan well. Pour the farina batter into the pan. Bake in preheated 300 degree F. oven for 40 minutes. Remove from oven. Using a sharp knife, cut into squares. Using two spatulas remove squares to serving platter.

Sprinkle with cinnamon–sugar.

Serve at once, with a fruit sauce, if desired.

Yields 9 servings
adequate for 6 people

Note: For a dessert for two or three, you can halve this recipe and bake it in a loaf pan.

1/9 SERVING – PROTEIN = 5.4 g.; FAT = 8.6 g.; CARBOHYDRATE = 32.3 g.;
CALORIES = 228; CALORIES FROM FAT = 34%

Denmark

Copenhagen, the beautiful, cultured city on the Baltic Sea at the entrance to the Oresund Channel, is reason enough to visit Denmark, but it is only the tip of an island among many islands. The remarkable city of Copenhagen aside, the Kingdom of Denmark still resembles in many ways the land known as *Jylland* (Jutland) which was a well-established agricultural culture by the end of the eighth century A.D. When you ride out of the city, the change to a rural, farm culture is as dramatic as it is here in Pennsylvania. You know right then why the food is so very, very good in Denmark. I have never tasted better butter or cheese anywhere in the world nor have I ever tasted such wonderful oats. I actually learned to eat rolled oats in a whole new way in Denmark—uncoooked with cream and sugar. We have been eating them that way ever since our visit but we have never found a brand to equal that which we ate every morning during our stay in Denmark.

Situated as they are with the Baltic and North Seas at their doorstep, it is not surprising that the people we know today as the Danes sailed forth in the Viking era to trade and raid from the ninth to the eleventh centuries. Although descended from Norsemen, the DNA of present-day Danes bears witness to the Prussians and Austrians who invaded Denmark in 1864 in an effort at German unification, and to those French who escaped the French crown and settled. Danes are, nonetheless, still strongly rooted in a past that dominates their way of life and makes them uniquely Scandinavian, an indefinable constant. Even foods that are borrowed from other countries never say "borrowed" but always become "Danish."

Denmark did colonize but not on the grand scale as did other European countries and divested itself of its holdings after World War II. Greenland's status became that of a territory in 1953; Iceland, which had been part of Denmark since 1830, was granted independence in 1948; and the Faroe Islands achieved home rule in 1948, after 118 years of Danish rule.

Danes have a philosophical approach to dining that is unique in the world. Referred to as *hygge*, it is an encompassing view of the whole of a dining experience and means good food, good company, wine, comfortable furniture, music, laughter, and good lighting. Meals in Denmark are generally taken in the home and those who visit during the Christmas holidays often, as did we, find restaurants shuttered. In our case, the tourist agency took pity on the stranded few and bused us to Elsinore for a private tour of "Hamlet's castle," after which we enjoyed a lavish *kolde bord* Christmas lunch in Helsingor at the northern tip of *Sjaeland* (Zealand) where the Oresund Channel meets the Kattegat Channel. Since Sweden and Demark are in very close proximity, at this point, hundreds of Swedes had ferried over for Christmas lunch. I knew, after that meal, what *hygge* really meant. There also I tasted cheeses that I have never found in cheese shops in the United States, such as blue *brie*, blue cream, and Danablu. Drizzle jam over an extra-creamy imported Danish blue cheese and maybe then you will understand. I tasted wonderful creamed potato dishes and the unique sugar-browned potatoes, so much a part of Danish cuisine and part of that cuisine only since 1720 when the French Huguenots, who settled in Frederika, introduced the potato to the Danes, the potato that was brought to the Old World from the New World in the 1600s. The Danes made the potato their own too.

Europe–Denmark

Danish Blue Cheese
with Strawberry, Peach, or Pear Preserves

~

Mixed Greens with Sugar and Lemon
Hovedsalat

Shredded Onion and Vegetable Salad
Løg Salat af Grøntsager Skaret i Fine Strimler

~~~~~~~~~~~~~~~~~~~~

Sweet Browned Cabbage with Sausages
Brunkaal

Scandinavian Mustard Sauce
Sennepsaus

Sugar – Browned Potatoes
Brunede Kartofler

Parsley Sauce

Pickled Baby Beets
Syltede Rødbeder

Beer Biscuits
Øllebrød

~~~~~~~~~~

Danish Open-Faced Sandwiches
Smørrebrød

Macaroni Salad
Makaronisalat

~~~~~~~~~~~~~~~~~~~~

St. Martin's Day Apple Pudding
Gammeldags Aeblekage

Ice Cream

with

Toasted Hazelnut – Rum Hard Sauce
Hasselnødsauce

Europe–Denmark

DANISH MIXED GREENS WITH SUGAR AND LEMON
Hovedsalat

TPT - 4 minutes

The first time we tasted this salad, we were hooked. How could such a perfect way to grace a salad; such a simple, civilized way to bring out the flavor of fresh greens, have taken us so long to find?

4 cups mixed fresh greens, of choice—well-washed and well-drained
1/2 cup loosely-packed fresh herbs, of choice —salad burnet, marjoram, lovage, chervil, dillweed, fresh coriander *(cilantro)*, basil, parsley, chives, lemon balm, nasturtium leaves, sweet cicely, and even a bit of thyme or oregano, if desired

2 teaspoons sugar
2 teaspoons freshly squeezed lemon juice

In a large salad bowl, combine salad greens and herbs. Toss well.

Sprinkle sugar over. Toss. Sprinkle lemon juice over. Toss.

Serve at once.

Yields 4 servings
adequate for 4 people

Note: This recipe is easily halved or doubled, when required.

1/4 SERVING – PROTEIN = 0.2 g.; FAT = 0.03 g.; CARBOHYDRATE = 3.0 g.;
CALORIES = 14; CALORIES FROM FAT = 2%

DANISH SHREDDED ONION AND VEGETABLE SALAD
Løg Salat af Grøntsager i Fine Strimler

TPT - 10 minutes

We found Danish salads to be so fresh and "alive," and our visit was in December! One can only dream about their spring and summer salads. This is wonderful example of that fresh simplicity. Since leftovers become watery, do prepare only what will be eaten at a single meal.

2 medium onions—peeled and ends trimmed
4 large *red* radishes—trimmed
2 large carrots—scraped or pared

2 cups *knife-shredded red* Romaine *or* Simpson lettuce
1 cup fresh coriander *(cilantro)* leaves

1 teaspoon sugar
2 tablespoons freshly squeezed lemon juice

1 medium tomato—chopped—for garnish*

Using the food processor fitted with the coarse shredding disk or by hand using a box grater, shred onions, radishes, and carrots. Turn into a salad bowl. Toss to mix thoroughly, removing any large, unshredded pieces of vegetable.

Add *knife-shredded* lettuce and fresh coriander leaves. Toss well.

When ready to serve, sprinkle sugar and lemon juice over. Again, toss well.

Serve at once, garnished with chopped tomato.**

Yields 6 servings
adequate for 4 people

Notes: *Quartered grape tomatoes can be used for garnish, if preferred. They add fresh, firm sweet bites to the salad.

**This salad does not "sit well" so plan to assemble it just before you serve it.

When required, this recipe may be halved or doubled.

1/6 SERVING – PROTEIN = 1.4 g.; FAT = 0.02 g.; CARBOHYDRATE = 7.7 g.;
CALORIES = 41; CALORIES FROM FAT = < 1%

Europe–Denmark

DANISH SWEET BROWNED CABBAGE WITH SAUSAGES
Brunkaal

TPT - 1 hour and 10 minutes

I first saw this dish at a cold table buffet but the addition of pork had kept me from tasting it. Pork ribs or pork sausages are usually added to the fried cabbage to create what many Danes consider one of the ultimate comfort foods. My great-grandmother and grandmother made a similar dish of German origin but instead of using fresh cabbage, they used sauerkraut and created a dish somewhat like an Alsacienne "choucroute." This sweet fried cabbage is a perfect foil for soy sausages, as in this recipe, but it can also be prepared as a simple vegetable side dish without the sausages.

1/2 head white cabbage—trimmed of outer leaves

2 tablespoons butter
3 tablespoons sugar

Freshly ground black pepper, to taste

12 *frozen* soy sausages

SCANDINAVIAN MUSTARD SAUCE (*Sennepsaus*)
 [see recipe which follows]

Cut the cabbage into wedges and then *coarsely* shred each wedge. Put shredded cabbage into a large bowl and rinse thoroughly. Turn into a colander and allow to drain until required.

In a large non-stick-coated skillet set over *LOW* heat, melt butter. Add sugar. Stir until sugar is dissolved.

Add well-drained shredded cabbage, a handful at a time. While stirring, allow cabbage to wilt and brown before adding the next handful. Cover and allow cabbage to steam over *LOW* heat for about 30-35 minutes. Stir occasionally. Add a tablespoonful or two of water if cabbage begins to stick to the bottom of the pan.

Add black pepper, to taste. Stir to distribute the pepper.

Nestle soy sausages into the cabbage, cover, and cook for an additional 10 minutes. Stir occasionally. Turn into a heated serving bowl.

Serve at once accompanied by SCANDINAVIAN MUSTARD SAUCE.

Yields 6 servings
adequate for 4 people

Notes: When doubling this recipe, use a Dutch oven or heavy-bottomed kettle.

If preferred, this dish can be baked in a 250 degree F. oven. The oven-sweating technique takes a bit longer.

1/6 SERVING – PROTEIN = 9.4 g.; FAT = 6.8 g.; CARBOHYDRATE = 11.4 g.;
CALORIES = 148; CALORIES FROM FAT = 41%

SCANDINAVIAN MUSTARD SAUCE
Sennepsaus

TPT - 2 hours and 3 minutes;
2 hours = chilling period

Although traditionally served with salmon, this mustard sauce is equally complimentary to hard-cooked eggs and cheeses. We managed to find a way to enjoy this sauce almost every day during our 1985 Christmas holiday stay in Copenhagen. Upon returning home, we have made it a part of our Christmas each and every year since as a way to remember that wonderful holiday.

4 1/2 tablespoons safflower *or* sunflower oil
1 1/2 tablespoons distilled white vinegar
4 teaspoons country-style *Dijon* mustard
1/8 teaspoon freshly ground *white* pepper
1 teaspoon sugar
Pinch ground cardamom

SCANDINAVIAN MUSTARD SAUCE (cont'd)

In the container of the electric blender, combine all ingredients. Blend thoroughly.

Refrigerate in blender container for at least 2 hours, or overnight if more convenient.

Again, blend before serving.

> Yields 1/2 cupful
> adequate for about
> 6 hard-cooked eggs
> (or 1 pound smoked salmon)

Note: This recipe is easily doubled or tripled, when required.

> 1/8 SERVING (i. e., per tablespoonful) –
> PROTEIN = 0.0 g.; FAT = 6.5 g.; CARBOHYDRATE = 0.8 g.;
> CALORIES = 62; CALORIES FROM FAT = 94%

DANISH SUGAR – BROWNED POTATOES
Brunede Kartofler

TPT - about 1 hour;
15 minutes = cooling period

This recipe always takes me back to Helsingor, Denmark, and Christmas Day 1985. It was a Christmas dinner we will never forget with the most extensive "koldt bord" that we had ever seen. Christmas greetings and expressions of satisfaction could be heard in every language as we passed back and forth on our many trips to the buffet tables. The "osteanretning" or cheese board offered so many varieties of cheese that we could hardly choose. The meatless offerings on the side table of hot dishes were "rodkaal" and these magnificent, traditional potatoes, both traditionally served on Christmas Day in Denmark. By the time we ladled out a portion of the traditional Christmas rice pudding and topped it with cherry sauce we were full beyond belief. It was a wonderful meal.

12 small, new potatoes—well-scrubbed and unpeeled

1/4 cup sugar
2 tablespoons sweet *(unsalted)* butter—*melted*

Bring 2 quarts water to the boil. Add potatoes and cook for about 15 minutes, or until they can easily be pierced with the tip of a sharp knife. Drain and allow to cool for about 15 minutes. Peel and set aside.

In a large, non-stick-coated skillet set over *LOW* heat, melt sugar. Cook, stirring constantly with a wooden spoon, until sugar turns a light brown and begins to caramelize. *Watch very carefully* from this point on, *allowing the sugar to brown but not allowing it to become dark brown and bitter.*

Add *melted, unsalted* butter. Stir to combine.

Add peeled potatoes. Shake the pan constantly to roll the potatoes and coat them with the caramel. When thoroughly coated and heated through, transfer to a heated serving dish.

Serve at once.

> Yields 6 servings
> adequate for 4 people

Note: This recipe is easily doubled although the caramelizing of the potatoes may have to be done in two batches. Keep the first batch warm in a serving dish on a warming tray.

> 1/6 SERVING – PROTEIN = 4.0 g.; FAT = 7.7 g.; CARBOHYDRATE = 51.2 g.;
> CALORIES = 293; CALORIES FROM FAT = 14%

Europe–Denmark

DANISH PICKLED BABY BEETS
Syltede Rødbeder

TPT - 49 hours and 43 minutes;
       24 hours = flavor development period;
       24 hours = cooling period

When a windfall of tiny beets turns up, we "put up" pickled beets. The sweet and sour, gently spiced beets accent so many meals and remind me of the winter "salads" of my childhood. These delicious beet-filled jars that sat on shelves in the fruits cellars of my mother and my grandmother too. Ray had never tasted them until we married. I could not imagine living twenty-four years without pickled beets anymore than he could imagine anyone living twenty-four years without having tasted stuffed artichokes.... I have adapted a family recipe to a Danish specialty that is seasoned with caraway, bay leaves, and cloves, unlike our family recipe, of German origin, which employs allspice, cloves, and a substantial amount of cinnamon to season the beets. This is different from both recipes in that I use jarred baby beets for this version, eliminating the beet preparation that might deter a reader from trying this wonderful recipe.

2 cups water
1 cup distilled white vinegar
1 cup apple cider vinegar
2 cups sugar
2 teaspoons caraway seeds
1 bay leaf—broken in half
6 whole cloves
1/2 cinnamon quill

5 jars canned baby beets—well-drained

In a saucepan set over *MEDIUM* heat, combine the 2 cupfuls water, both vinegars, sugar, caraway seeds, bay leaf pieces, cloves, and cinnamon quill. Stir well. Bring to the boil over *MEDIUM* heat, stirring frequently to dissolve the sugar. Boil for a full 10 minutes. Turn into a large mixing bowl and allow to cool to room temperature.

Add well-drained baby beets. Cover bowl and refrigerate for 24 hours.

Sterilize five 1-pint canning jars. Also sterilize lids and rings for jars.

Using a slotted spoon, remove beets from the bowl to a clean bowl. Set aside briefly. *Discard any caraway seeds or bay leaf pieces that may be transferred with the beets.* Set a sieve over a large saucepan and strain the liquid in which the beets were marinated. Discard the recovered caraway seeds, bay leaf pieces, cloves, and the cinnamon quill. Set over *MEDIUM* heat and allow to come to the boil.

Using a slotted spoon, divide beets among five hot, sterilized pint jars. Fill jars with strained liquid to about 1/2 inch from top. Carefully wipe rims of jars. Seal with hot, sterilized lids and rings. Process in hot-water-bath canner for 30 minutes, *timing from the moment the water reaches a full rolling boil.* Remove to surface covered with thick towels or newspapers. Allow to cool for 24 hours *undisturbed*. Check to be sure jars are sealed before labeling and storing in a dark, cool, dry place.* Loosen or remove rings before storing.

                      Yields five 1-pint jarfuls

Note: *Any jars that do not seal can be stored in the refrigerator for several months or resealed using a *new lid*.

1/20 SERVING (i. e., 4 servings per pint) –
PROTEIN = 0.9 g.; FAT = 0.1 g.; CARBOHYDRATE = 21.7 g.;
CALORIES = 126**; CALORIES FROM FAT = <1%

    **If liquid is discarded, food values will be considerably different. This value is unfortunately difficult to determine without chemical analysis.

Europe–Denmark

DANISH – STYLE BEER BISCUITS
Øllebrød
TPT - 29 minutes

Danish beer bread, øllebrød, was the inspiration for these quick biscuits and my whole wheat biscuit mix was the vehicle. They are good, substantial, but light. The beer contributes extra leavening and a sweet earthy flavor.

3 cups WHEATEN BISCUIT MIX *[see index]*
  or **commercially-available baking mix like Bisquick**
5-6 ounces beer

Preheat oven to 400 degrees F.

Turn biscuit mix into a mixing bowl. Make a well in the center, pour 1/3 cupful beer into the well and stir until mixture forms a soft dough and pulls from the sides of the bowl. Add more beer, a little at a time, *only if necessary*. (*You do not want a sticky dough.*)

Turn dough out onto a *generously* floured surface. Lightly flour your hands and knead dough for only about 30 seconds. Pat or roll dough to an even 1/2-inch thickness. Cut with a floured 3-inch biscuit cutter. Using a spatula, transfer biscuit rounds to an *ungreased* baking sheet or a baking sheet lined with parchment paper, spacing them at least 1 inch apart to allow for expansion and even browning.

Bake in preheated 400 degree F. oven for 15-17 minutes, or until *golden brown*.

Serve hot, with butter and honey.

Yields 10 biscuits

Note: When necessary, this recipe may be doubled.

1/10 SERVING – PROTEIN = 3.2 g.; FAT = 9.9 g.; CARBOHYDRATE = 23.9 g.;
CALORIES = 200; CALORIES FROM FAT = 45%

Europe–Denmark

DANISH OPEN–FACED SANDWICHES
Smørrebrød

Smørrebrød, which mundanely translates to "buttered bread," is one of the most delightful phenomenon in the culinary world. I was always cognizant of its meaning but I do remember the day that I really came to understand the true scope of this word. We were walking across a bridge in Copenhagen, in December in the late morning sunshine, when right in front of us were the windows of a smørrebrød shop filled with the most beautiful luncheon selections imaginable. This extraordinary knife and fork sandwich is created with all artistic senses at attention.

EGG selections:

Butter
   Chilled cream cheese scrambled eggs
      garnish = small lettuce leaf and radish rose

Sour cream
   Thin raw onion slices
     Hard-cooked egg slices
      garnish = thin scallion slices

Butter
   Thin tomato slices
     Chilled scrambled eggs
      Crisp-cooked asparagus tips
       garnish = ripe black olive slices

Butter
   Cooked artichoke heart
     Poached egg
      Hollandaise sauce

Butter
   Raw spinach leaf
     Hard-cooked egg slices
      Creamy horseradish sauce
       Thin tomato slices

Butter
   Fried egg
     Deep-fried onion rings
      Sweet and sour red cabbage
       garnish = parsley sprigs

Cold, buttered *toast*
   Hot scrambled eggs
     Creamed, reconstituted, dried wild mushrooms
      garnish = dill sprig

Butter
   Green pepper rings
     Chopped or sliced hard-cooked eggs
      Orange mayonnaise
       garnish = small Boston lettuce leaf and shredded carrot

CHEESE selections:

Mustard butter
   Thin slices of cheese, of choice
      garnish = radish slices or slivers

Butter
   Jarlsberg or Swiss cheese slices
     Iceberg lettuce leaf
      Diced beet, celery, and mayonnaise salad
       garnish = shredded *Jarlsberg* or Swiss cheese

Cream cheese
   Green stuffed olive slices
      garnish = watercress sprigs

Butter
   Danish blue cheese slice
     Raw onion ring
      Raw egg yolk (optional, but traditional)
       garnish = paper-thin radish slices

Cream cheese
   Banana slices
      garnish = several *toasted* almond slivers

Cream cheese
   Cinnamon apple rings
      garnish = dollop of applesauce

Butter
   Well-drained pear slices
     Crumbled Danish blue cheese

SALAD selections:

Tomato aspic slice
   Curried mayonnaise
      garnish = twisted lemon slice

Mayonnaise
   Curly endive (chicory) leaf
     Mayonnaise-dressed chopped vegetable salad
      garnish = thin tomato slices

Europe–Denmark

DANISH OPEN–FACED SANDWICHES (cont'd)

more SALAD selections:

Butter
  Beet slices
    Orange slices
      Raw onion rings
        Russian dressing
          garnish = twisted cucumber slice
            and radish sprouts

Butter
  Butter-fried apple slices
    Sweet and sour red cabbage
      garnish = parsley sprigs

Cold, cooked potato slices
  Curried mayonnaise
    Italian red onion rings
      garnish = parsley sprigs

Sour cream
  Thin cucumber slices
    Sour cream
      Diced raw onion
        garnish = cherry or grape tomato halves

We have found that these sandwiches can be the centerpiece of a unique party. The preceding list of "*paalaelg*" (i. .e., "something laid on") to top your buttered bread, of choice, is offered just as starter.

Select fillings and, if you wish, type them up as a menu for your guests, choosing those which will provide well-balanced salad, protein, and vegetable "courses." Six alternatives should be sufficient variety for a party of six.

Provide assorted thinly sliced, firm whole grain bread and whipped sweet butter. Mustard butter or herbed varieties may be offered as well. Several bread boards with a butter crock at each will greatly ease the crush if you have many guests.

Arrange ample quantities of required ingredients together, keeping cold things cold and hot things hot. Do provide all prepared ingredients or you will have to designate your refrigerator and kitchen as disaster areas afterward.

If you so choose, allow your guests to cook their own eggs or "short-order" them yourself using a warming tray for convenience.

Instruct your guests to spread each bread slice with about 1 teaspoonful of butter or other spread specified. Ingredients can then be arranged in specified order as artistically as possible. Provide extra plates and silver for return trips.

DANISH MACARONI SALAD
Makronisalat

TPT - 54 minutes;
    30 minutes = macaroni cooling period

Some find it hard to think that macaroni might be used in a very Danish dish. The same people may also not accept that macaroni and cheese is very British, but if you consider the travelings of the Romans, it really is not all that surprising. This macaroni salad bears no resemblance to the American delicatessen or picnic macaroni salad most of us know. As with all Danish foods, freshness of ingredients is paramount—fresh cream, fresh sour cream, fresh eggs, homemade macaroni, and dillweed that is wet with dew.

3 quarts *boiling* water
1 tablespoon freshly squeezed lemon juice
1 3-inch strip lemon zest
2 cups (about 1/2 pound) high protein, whole wheat, *or* Jerusalem artichoke macaroni
  —combinations of elbows, shells, bow ties, and radiatore add interest

4 hard-cooked eggs—peeled and halved

2 teaspoons MUSTARD SAUCE *[see index]*
1 tablespoon prepared horseradish, or to taste
1/4 teaspoon salt
1/2 cup *fat-free* dairy sour cream
2 tablespoons light cream *or* half and half

4 cups baby spinach leaves—petioles trimmed, well-washed, and well-dried

6 fresh dillweed sprigs, for garnish

DANISH MACARONI SALAD (cont'd)

In a large kettle set over *HIGH* heat, add lemon juice and lemon zest to *boiling* water. Add macaroni and cook, stirring occasionally, over *HIGH* heat according to package directions. Drain thoroughly, discarding lemon zest. Rinse in *cold* water. Drain again, thoroughly. Chill in refrigerator for about 30 minutes.

Transfer the yolks from two hard-cooked egg halves to a small mixing bowl. Using a fork, mash the egg yolk well. Add mustard sauce, prepared horseradish, and salt. Combine well. Add sour cream and mix well. Beat in cream, *a little at a time,* until the desired consistency is achieved. Set aside.

Discard remaining egg yolks. Coarsely chop hard-cooked egg whites. In a large mixing bowl, combine chopped egg whites with well-drained, chilled macaroni. Add sour cream dressing. Toss to combine well. Chill in the refrigerator until ready to serve.

Arrange spinach leaves in a shallow serving bowl. Spoon macaroni salad over. Garnish with dill sprigs before serving. Accompany each serving with a sprig of dillweed.

Yields 6 servings
adequate for 4 people

Note: This recipe may be halved or doubled, when required.

1/6 SERVING – PROTEIN = 11.9 g.; FAT = 2.4 g.; CARBOHYDRATE = 37.2 g.;
CALORIES = 205; CALORIES FROM FAT = 10%

DANISH ST. MARTIN'S DAY APPLE PUDDING WITH BREADCRUMBS
Gammeldags Aeblekage
TPT - 40 minutes

This is not really an apple "cake," although the Danish name most definitely leads one to expect a cake. It is instead a layered pudding dessert that is worthy of every family's recipe collection. November 11th, St. Martin's Day, may be a good day to try it for the first time but once a year would be a crime. When the breadcrumb collection in the freezer, the ultimate final resting place of stale bread, is sufficient, this recipe is a really good choice to clean out the freezer. If I do not have apples in the house, I use the apples I canned the previous autumn to which I add cinnamon, nutmeg, allspice, and cloves.

A friend told me that it is also known as "bondepige med slør," which translated roughly to "peasant girl in a veil." She also said that its humbleness is probably why I did not find it on menus in Denmark.

**2 pounds tart eating apples, such as Cortland, Gala, or Mackintosh (about 8 medium apples)
—peeled, cored and sliced into thick slices
1 cup *boiling* water
1/3 cup sugar
1/2 teaspoon ground cinnamon
1/4 teaspoon ground nutmeg
1/4 teaspoon ground allspice
1/8 teaspoon ground cloves**

**3 tablespoons butter
2 1/2 cups *white* breadcrumbs
1/4 cup *light* brown sugar**

3 tablespoons light cream *or* half and half

**1 1/4 cups heavy whipping cream
1 1/2 teaspoons confectioners' sugar
1/2 teaspoons pure vanilla extract**

In a non-stick-coated skillet or a saucepan set over *LOW* heat, combine apple slices, *boiling* water, sugar, and ground cinnamon, nutmeg, allspice, and cloves. Stir to combine. Cover and allow to cook for about 20 minutes, or until apples are soft, but *not mushy*. Stir occasionally. Remove from heat and allow apples to cool to room temperature.

In a skillet set over *LOW-MEDIUM* heat, melt butter. Add breadcrumbs and brown sugar. Cook, stirring constantly, until breadcrumbs are lightly browned. Remove from heat.

Using the electric mixer fitted with *chilled* beaters or by hand using a *chilled* wire whisk, beat heavy cream in a *chilled* bowl until soft peaks form. While continuing to beat, add confectioners' sugar. Beat until stiff peaks form, adding the drops of vanilla extract as you beat.

DANISH ST. MARTIN'S DAY APPLE PUDDING WITH BREADCRUMBS (cont'd)

Using a trifle bowl or other glass serving bowl or, if preferred, individual sherbet glasses or sundae dishes, spoon a layer of breadcrumbs into the bottom of the serving dish(es). Pour the cream over the breadcrumb layer. Layer apples on top of the cream-soaked breadcrumbs. Spoon some of whipped cream over the apples. Repeat the layers until all ingredients are layered into the dish(es). Top with whipped cream.

Refrigerate until required. Refrigerate leftovers.

Notes: If you can apples, you can use them in this dish. You do not need to cook the canned apples. Just drain them, season them, and proceed with the assembly.

This recipe can be halved, when required.

Yields 8 servings
adequate for 6 people

1/8 SERVING – PROTEIN = 6.4 g.; FAT = 17.9 g.; CARBOHYDRATE = 59.0 g.;
CALORIES = 411; CALORIES FROM FAT = 39%

DANISH TOASTED HAZELNUT – RUM HARD SAUCE
Hasselnødsauce

TPT - 2 hours and 3 minutes;
2 hours = refrigeration period

Having had my fill of "julerisengrød," the ubiquitous dessert of the Christmas season, I chose a homemade ice cream sampler that was so interesting that I scrambled to get the three ice creams and three sauces recorded in my journal. This sauce, when chilled, is very much like a conventional hard sauce but when brought to room temperature, softens into a more conventional dessert sauce. It is simply made in much the same way one would make a cake icing except that neither butter nor milk are required making it acceptably vegan, albeit for a vegan who fancies rum. We often serve this with small cakes as an icing-sauce, if you will, and with ice cream, maybe not vegan but conducive to the revival of memories of that luncheon in Copenhagen.

1 cup confectioners' sugar
3 tablespoons rum

2 teaspoons water

1/2 cup chopped, *toasted, preservative-free* **hazelnuts**

In a small bowl, combine confectioners' sugar and rum. Stir with a spoon until thoroughly mixed.

Gradually add water, stirring after each addition, until the consistency is *soft*, but *not runny*.

Add chopped, *toasted* hazelnuts. Stir to combine well. Cover and refrigerate for at least 2 hours.*

Yields 1 1/4 cupfuls

Note: *The rum taste mellows with overnight refrigeration.

1/10 SERVING (i. e., about 2 tablespoonfuls) –
PROTEIN = 4.2 g.; FAT = 0.7 g.; CARBOHYDRATE = 16.0 g.;
CALORIES = 105; CALORIES FROM FAT = 6%

Estonia

Habitation by early humans can be traced to the retreat of the last glacial advance, 11,000 to 13,000 years ago, a fact applicable to most of this region of Europe. A settlement on the banks of the Pärnu River has been dated to the early ninth millennium BC. Bronze Age and early Iron Age people settled and began to farm but from this point forward there never seems to be a time in ancient history when these people were not being challenged for their fertile farming land and their ports. Baltic tribes invaded from the South but were displaced by the Swedes and then by the Danes. By the middle of the 1300s AD the Danes had sold their holdings in northern Estonia to the German Teutonic Knights. This was joined with southern areas of the country which had been conquered by the Livonian Brothers of the Swords. The oppressed, feudal Estonian life under the power of the German lords was relieved with the invasion of the Swedes in 1526. Sweden's holdings were given to Russia under the provisions of The Peace of Nystad in 1721 and the Estonians then endured both suppression from the German land-owners, the Balt, and, once again, from the czarist administrators.

In 1816 serfdom was finally abolished. Perhaps the most important element of this point in history was that the population could be educated, creating, as it did, a nationalistic movement. In the closing months of World War I Estonia achieved independence only to be again occupied by Russia and incorporated into the U.S.S.R. in 1940. The following year, and until 1944, Estonia was occupied by Germany. Soviet Russia reclaimed its Estonian Republic after World War II. Estonia's annexation by the Soviets had not been recognized by many countries who then gave refuge to Estonian diplomats and consuls who were outside of the country at the time of the annexation and who continued to function as an "Estonian government in exile." In 1989, in a demonstration unique in civilized history called the "Singing Revolution," Lithuanians, Latvians, and Estonians joined hands in protest against Soviet occupation. An estimated two million people stretched hand-to-hand across the three nations. Estonia officially declared independence from the Soviet Union in March 1990, a declaration not recognized by the U.S.S.R. It took recognition of independence by the rest of the world for the Soviets to finally back down. In 1991 the Soviet Union acknowledged Estonia to be a fully independent nation.

Estonian dishes were carried to other lands as generations of Estonians emigrated from this troubled region of Europe. There, these national dishes were often reserved for holidays or amalgamated into the cuisine of the land to which they fled. Estonians, in their attempt to recover their past, have tried to reconstruct a cuisine but influences from the many who occupied this country, adaptations due to food shortages, and the modern invasion of ethnic and fast food restaurants are making that a difficult task. Many recipes, brought to America by Estonian immigrants, can no longer be found in Estonia. In past centuries a "cold table" was a traditional first course in Estonia, much as one would experience in Denmark or Sweden. Herring and meat dishes were accompanied by beet, mushroom, and potato salads. Icy cold vodka, the traditional beverage, was served. Elaborate "cold tables" are less often encountered in Estonia today so I have chosen to include a favorite salad as a first course homage to the "cold table."

Europe – Estonia

Deviled Beet, Potato, Apple, and Egg Salad
Rossolye

~

Vegetable Soup with Barley
Talupojasupp

~~~~~~~~~~~~~~~~~~~~~~~

***Phyllo* Pastry Turnovers with Mushroom and Onion Filling**
Lihtne Lehetainas ehk Seenetäidis

Whole Cauliflower with Cheese and Breadcrumbs
Hautatud Lillkapsas

Sweet and Sour Red Cabbage with Sour Cream
Punane Kapsas Hapukoore

or

Sauerkraut
Hapukapsad

Oven-Roasted Potatoes
Pruunid Pannidartulid

Honey Barley Bread
Yachmenny Khleb

or

Black Rye Bread
Rukkileib

~~~~~~~~~~~~~~~~~~~~~~~

Farina Cream Dessert with Cranberry Sauce
Roosamanna

Rhubarb *Streusel* Coffeecake
Rabarberikook Pähklitega

***Halva* with Almond Butter**
Halva

ESTONIAN DEVILED BEET, POTATO, APPLE, AND EGG SALAD
Rossolye

TPT - 55 minutes;
30 minutes = chilling period

When I decide to visit the "leftover meat" salads of my youth, I turned to "Rossolye." This salad is found on every menu in Estonia and every cook has his or her own version. Our version, which substitutes a meat analogue product for the picked herring or cooked beef or pork and "schmaltz," is a delicious choice for a first course, a light meal, or as a buffet offering or "zakuska" table.

Europe–Estonia

ESTONIAN DEVILED BEET, POTATO, APPLE, AND EGG SALAD (cont'd)

DRESSING:
    1/3 cup heavy whipping cream

    3 tablespoons *fat-free* dairy sour cream
    1 tablespoon MUSTARD SAUCE *[see index]*
       or *Dijon* mustard with wine

3 ounces *frozen* soy strips or nuggets—defrosted and *shredded*

3 large boiled *or* baked beets—peeled and chopped into cubes— *or* jarred baby beets —chopped into cubes
1 *tart* apple—cored, peeled, and chopped into cubes
3 large waxy potatoes—boiled, peeled, and chopped into cubes
1 medium deli-style dill pickle—diced
3 tablespoons *finely* chopped onion

3 hard-cooked eggs—peeled

Freshly ground black pepper, to taste

Boston lettuce leaves, if desired

Using the electric mixer fitted with *chilled* beaters or by hand using a *chilled* wire whisk, beat heavy cream in a *chilled* bowl until stiff peaks form.

In a small bowl, combine sour cream and mustard. Using a wire whisk, combine thoroughly. Add sour cream–mustard mixture to whipped cream. Using the wire whisk, *whisk-fold* the mixture together. Refrigerate until required.

In a non-stick-coated skillet, further coated with non-stick lecithin spray coating and set over *LOW* heat, sauté meat analogue shreds until lightly browned. Remove from heat and allow to cool to room temperature.

In a large mixing bowl, combine the chopped beets, apple, potatoes, diced pickle, and *finely* chopped onion. Mix *gently* to combine.

Halve two hard-cooked eggs. Remove and discard yolks from the hard-cooked egg halves. Chop the egg whites and add to the vegetable mixture. Toss *gently* to combine. Using an EGG SLICER, slice remaining egg and reserve for garnish.

Add the *cooled* soymeat shreds and the prepared dressing. Fold the dressing *gently* into the salad mixture.

Season with black pepper, to taste. Again, mix *gently*.

A square plate is traditional.* Line the plate with lettuce leaves first, if desired, or just turn salad mixture onto the serving plate. Refrigerate for at least 30 minutes.

Garnish with reserved egg slices just before serving. *Serve chilled.*

                         Yields 6 servings
                       adequate for 4 people

Notes: *If preferred, individual salad plates may be lined with lettuce leaves and salad apportioned for individual servings.

This recipe can be doubled, when required.

1/6 SERVING – PROTEIN = 9.3 g.; FAT = 8.5 g.; CARBOHYDRATE =10.5 g.;
CALORIES = 155; CALORIES FROM FAT = 49%

ESTONIAN VEGETABLE SOUP WITH BARLEY
Talupojasupp

TPT - 2 hours;
            30 minutes = barley soaking period

Archaeological findings near the Sea of Galilee suggest that wild barley had become important to human nutrition about 8500 BC. The domestication and cultivation of barley is said to have first begun in the Near East, becoming extremely important to the survival of early civilizations, evidenced by findings that Neolithic humans used the barley seeds to brew beer and dried the stalks for weaving and thatching. Not surprisingly, barley became an important item in trade. Barley, unlike other grasses such as wheat, contains all eight essential amino acids and requires no complementation. It also helps to regulate blood glucose for up to ten hours after it has been consumed.

When I was a toddler, I am told, barley-vegetable soup was one of my favorites. Some version of this soup is familiar to every family, if your ancestors came from Europe.

Europe–**Estonia**

ESTONIAN VEGETABLE SOUP WITH BARLEY (cont'd)

1/4 cup dry pearl barley
1/4 cup *cold* water

1 tablespoon butter
1 tablespoon *extra virgin* olive oil
1 medium onion—chopped
1 cup chopped green cabbage—well-rinsed

6 cups VEGETARIAN BROWN STOCK *[see index]*, VEGETABLE STOCK FROM SOUP *[see index]*, *or* other vegetarian stock of choice

2 cups diced rutabaga
1 cup diced waxy, all purpose potato (*do not use Idaho potatoes*)
1/2 cup diced carrot
1 teaspoon *finely crushed* dried sage
1/2 teaspoon *finely crushed* dried marjoram
1/4 teaspoon salt, or to taste
1/4 teaspoon freshly ground black pepper, or to taste

2 tablespoons chopped fresh parsley

In a small bowl, combine barley and *cold* water. Allow to soak for 30 minutes. Drain.

In a large, heavy kettle set over *MEDIUM* heat, heat butter and oil. Add chopped onion and sauté until soft and translucent, *being careful not to allow the onions to brown*. Add chopped cabbage and sauté for several minutes more, allowing the cabbage to wilt.

Add stock and barley. Allow to come to the boil. Reduce to *LOW-MEDIUM* and simmer for 30 minutes.

Add diced rutabaga, potato, and carrot, *finely* crushed dried sage and marjoram, salt, and pepper. Allow to simmer for 40 minutes more. Turn into a heated soup tureen. Serve into heated soup bowls. Garnish with chopped fresh parsley.

Yields 8 servings
adequate for 6 people

Note: This recipe can be halved, when required.

1/8 SERVING – PROTEIN = 1.7 g.; FAT = 3.0 g.; CARBOHYDRATE = 13.6 g.;
CALORIES = 84; CALORIES FROM FAT = 32%

PHYLLO PASTRY TURNOVERS WITH MUSHROOM AND ONION FILLING
Lihtne Lehetainas ehk Seenetäidis

TPT - 55 minutes

Estonians are fond of turnovers filled with all manner of fillings. They are often served as first courses or as luncheon offerings but we find them to be interesting entrée dishes. This simple turnover at once shows their passion for mushrooms and reflects some influences one would probably not expect this far north in Europe. Phyllo pastry is a convenient substitute for strudel pastry and probably represents the dream of every in-home baker when it comes to flakiness. My grandmother told me when I was very young that I would probably not have the patience to roll out the pastry to paper-thin state that was required. She suggested that I go to a bakery and buy it. Today phyllo pastry and puffed pastry are so conveniently available in the freezer section of most grocery stores that my grandmother would, I am sure, be amazed.

3 tablespoons butter
2 tablespoons safflower *or* sunflower oil
1 medium onion—*finely* chopped
2 pounds fresh *crimini* mushrooms—well-washed, well-trimmed, and sliced
Pinch salt
Freshly ground black pepper, to taste

18 sheets (9 x 13) *phyllo* pastry—*defrosted*
2 tablespoons dry breadcrumbs

2 tablespoons *trans-fat-free soft* butter spread *or* whipped butter—*brought to room temperature*

2 tablespoons *fat-free* dairy sour cream

Preheat oven to 400 degrees F. Prepare a baking sheet by lining it with culinary parchment.

In a large skillet set over *LOW-MEDIUM* heat, heat butter. Add *finely* chopped onion and sliced mushrooms. Sauté until onions are soft and translucent and mushrooms have extruded all their water and are browned. *Be careful to allow neither the onions nor the mushrooms to brown*. Season with salt and pepper.

Europe – **Estonia**

***PHYLLO* PASTRY TURNOVERS
WITH MUSHROOM AND ONION FILLING** (cont'd)

Unroll *phyllo* pastry onto a clean, dry surface, cut each sheet in half, and cover with a dampened cotton towel. Take one of the half-sheets of *phyllo* and place it on a dry work surface. Using a pastry brush, lightly brush the sheet with the soft butter spread. Take a pinch of the breadcrumbs and sprinkle them over the pastry surface. Take two more half-sheets of *phyllo*, butter them, and place them on top of the first sheet. Take *one-sixth* of the mushroom filling and put it into center of the pastry square. Fold the sides in over the mushrooms and then roll the ends over, forming a square turnover. Seal with a brush of melted butter. Place cut-side-down on the prepared baking sheet. Continue until you have made six mushroom-filled bundles. Bake in preheated 400 degree F. oven for 15 minutes, or until the pastry is crisp and browned.

Serve at once with a dollop of sour cream on the side.

Yields 6 individual servings

Note: This recipe can be halved or doubled, when required.

1/6 SERVING – PROTEIN = 7.4 g.; FAT = 15.7 g.; CARBOHYDRATE = 27.1 g.;
CALORIES = 278; CALORIES FROM FAT = 51%

WHOLE CAULIFLOWER WITH CHEESE AND BREADCRUMBS
Hautatud Lillkapsas

TPT - about 33 minutes

During the years when we lived on Long Island we would travel Out East every October to get the great big beautiful, fresh-from-the-field cauliflowers that were deemed too big to go to market. We paid as little as fifty cents a head. The whole cauliflower presentation was dramatically beautiful. As the years have passed, and there are generally only the two of us enjoying one of the autumn's most beautiful flowers, we buy smaller cauliflower heads and serve it as a casserole by cooling the cooked cauliflower and slicing it into large slices which we place in an au gratin dish, top with cheese, sauce, and breadcrumbs, and heat through in a 250 degree F. oven.

Years later I found that South Africans prepare cauliflower in much the same way. Although Estonians do not use a cheese sauce when they braise whole cauliflowers, we press shredded cheese into the boiled cauliflower ostensibly as an anchor for the breadcrumbs but the extra bit of flavor is divine.

**2 quarts *boiling* water
1 medium head cauliflower—leaves removed and thoroughly washed**

**1/2 cup whole wheat breadcrumbs
2 tablespoons butter
1 tablespoon *finely* crushed dried parsley
Freshly ground black pepper, to taste**

1/2 cup shredded (about 2 ounces) *sharp* Cheddar cheese

Chopped fresh parsley, for garnish

Pour *boiling* water into a large saucepan or kettle. Add whole cauliflower and boil for 25 minutes, or until tender. *Drain thoroughly.*

Meanwhile in a skillet set over *LOW-MEDIUM* heat, combine breadcrumbs, 2 teaspoonfuls butter, crushed parsley, and black pepper. Sauté until butter has been absorbed by crumbs. Set aside until cauliflower is cooked and drained.

Preheat oven to 350 degrees F.

Place hot, cooked, and well-drained cauliflower in the center of a ceramic quiche dish or decorative, ovenproof pie plate, which has been coated with non-stick lecithin spray coating. Pat shredded cheese evenly over top surface of cauliflower. Pat buttered breadcrumbs firmly into cheese.

Bake in preheated 350 degree F. oven until cheese is melted and crumbs are *browned and crispy*—about 5 minutes.

WHOLE CAULIFLOWER WITH CHEESE AND BREADCRUMBS (cont'd)

Garnish cauliflower with chopped fresh parsley before serving. Slice cauliflower into wedges to serve.

Serve at once, slicing the cauliflower into wedges to serve.

Yields 6 servings
adequate for 4 people

1/6 SERVING – PROTEIN = 5.5 g.; FAT = 7.0 g.; CARBOHYDRATE = 7.5 g.; CALORIES =109; CALORIES FROM FAT = 57%

ESTONIAN SWEET AND SOUR RED CABBAGE WITH SOUR CREAM
Punane Kapsas Hapukoore

TPT - 8 minutes

Growing up in a family that pickled all sorts of vegetables each fall, I was used to pickled beets, corn relish, chow chow, green tomato mincemeat, and sweet and sour red cabbage. I always had pickles in the house as a vegetable option but I had married into a family from southern Europe where women do not gather together to pickle for their winter larders. In the fall, they made sauce, they made wine, they roasted red peppers but they did not make pickles and they were not accustomed to the sweet and sour taste so common to the meals of my ancestors. By draining off the sweet and sour liquid from a jar of sweet and sour red cabbage and adding sour cream, the well-flavored vegetable emerges and the pickle fades from sight.

1 jar (16 ounces) sweet and sour red cabbage

1/4 cup *fat-free* dairy sour cream
1 1/2 teaspoons butter
Freshly ground black pepper, to taste

In a saucepan set over *MEDIUM* heat, heat sweet and sour red cabbage until the liquid is bubbling. Turn into a sieve and drain the liquid from the cabbage. Return it to the saucepan. Return the saucepan to the stove and reduce the heat to *LOW*.

Add sour cream, butter, and black pepper. Stir. Cook for several minutes, stirring frequently. Turn into a heated serving bowl.

Serve at once.

Yields 6 servings
adequate for 4 people

Note: This recipe can be halved or doubled, when required.

1/6 SERVING – PROTEIN = 2.0 g.; FAT = 0.9 g.; CARBOHYDRATE = 20.0 g.; CALORIES = 113; CALORIES FROM FAT = 8%

ESTONIAN HONEY BARLEY BREAD
Yachmenny Khleb

TPT - 4 hours and 31 minutes;
1 hour and 50 minutes = automated machine preparation period*
1 hour = cooling period

Although low in gluten, barley flour can be combined with higher gluten bread flours to produce an interesting and healthful bread. This bread is similar to traditional Celtic barley breads and those often found in Scandinavian cuisines. It has a firm, beautiful texture and a good crumb. Also it can be sliced quite thinly. In Estonia it is traditionally served with butter and honey or butter and lingonberry preserves.

I prefer to start this recipe using the dough/manual setting on my bread machine. This loaf can, of course, be made without a bread machine. Allow two risings of forty-five minutes each.

Europe–Estonia

ESTONIAN HONEY BARLEY BREAD (cont'd)

3/4 cup skimmed milk
1/3 cup honey
1 tablespoon vegetable oil
1/4 cup *fat-free* pasteurized eggs (equivalent of 1 egg)

2 1/2 cups *wheat* bread flour**
6 tablespoons *fine* barley flour
1/2 teaspoon salt

1 tablespoon (1 envelope) *preservative-free* active dried yeast***

Prepare a 9 x 5 x 3-inch non-stick-coated loaf pan by coating with non-stick lecithin spray coating.

Bring all ingredients to room temperature.

Put milk, honey, oil, and pasteurized eggs into the BREAD MACHINE pan.

Add bread flour, barley flour, and salt spreading the ingredients over the liquid as you add them. *Do not stir.*

Using a spoon, create a depression in the dry ingredients, being very careful not to press down into the liquid layer below. Pour yeast into the depression.

Select DOUGH or MANUAL SETTING and push START.

Turn bread out onto a floured surface and knead until there is no trace of stickiness. Form dough into a loaf. Place in prepared loaf pan. Cover with a cotton tea towel. Allow bread to rise in a warm, draft-free kitchen until doubled in volume—about 45 minutes.

Bake in preheated 350 degree F. oven for about 40-45 minutes. Turn out of baking pan and cool completely, at least 1 hour, on a wire rack before slicing and serving.

Yields 1 loaf
of about 20 slices

Notes: *Preparation time depends, of course, on the brand of bread machine which you are using.

**Bread flour mixtures, to which whole wheat flour has been added, are available in grocery stores. They are usually labeled "wheat bread flour."

***Some packaged dried yeast available in grocery stores contain a preservative. Natural food stores carry an additive-free dried yeast. In addition, *do not use so–called fast action yeasts.* The results will not please you.

1/20 SERVING (i. e., per slice) –
PROTEIN = 2.5 g; FAT = 0.1 g; CARBOHYDRATE = 17.1 g;
CALORIES = 79; CALORIES FROM FAT = 1%

FARINA CREAM DESSERT WITH CRANBERRY SAUCE
Roosamanna

TPT - 1 hour and 20 minutes;
1 hour = cooling period

I evolved this not-too-sweet dessert one March evening in 1996 to provide a different grain complementation for a legume-based soup or stew. We love those vegan meals but something beside bread seemed in order; maybe a treat would sweep away the "winter blahs." The humble breakfast cereal rose to the occasion. I later discovered that Estonians make this dessert, often using cranberry juice to cook the farina. I give you my version of this dessert accompanied by a cranberry sauce with the thought that a cook in Estonia was also making this dessert on that March evening.

ESTONIAN CRANBERRY SAUCE:
    1/4 cup *unsweetened, organic* cranberry juice
    1 tablespoon corn starch

    3/4 cup *unsweetened, organic* cranberry juice
    2 tablespoons sugar

1 1/2 cups skimmed milk
3 3/4 tablespoons enriched quick-cooking farina or Cream of Wheat cereal—*not instant*
2 tablespoons sugar

6 tablespoons heavy whipping cream

3/4 teaspoon pure vanilla extract

FARINA CREAM DESSERT WITH CRANBERRY SAUCE (cont'd)

In a small dish combine the 1/4 cup cranberry juice with corn starch. Stir vigorously until the corn starch is in suspension. Set aside briefly.

In a saucepan set over *MEDIUM* heat, heat remaining 3/4 cupful cranberry juice and 1 tablespoon sugar until it boils. Using a wire whisk, stir vigorously while adding the corn starch suspension. Cook, stirring constantly, until the sauce thickens. Turn into a serving dish. Refrigerate until required.

In a saucepan set over *LOW-MEDIUM* heat, heat milk *just to the boiling point*. Add farina and the remaining 2 tablespoonfuls of sugar. Cook, stirring constantly, until thickened. Turn into a bowl and refrigerate for 1 hour.

Using the electric mixer fitted with *chilled* beaters or by hand, using a *chilled* wire whisk, beat heavy cream in a *chilled* mixing bowl until stiff peaks form. Set aside.

Add vanilla extract to *chilled, cooked* cereal. Using the electric mixer, beat cereal at *HIGH* speed until light and fluffy—about 3-4 minutes. Fold in stiffly beaten cream.

Divide among six individual dessert dishes. Refrigerate for no more than 30 minutes before serving with chilled cranberry sauce.

Yields 6 individual servings

Note: This recipe may be halved or doubled, when required.

1/6 SERVING – PROTEIN = 2.1 g.; FAT – 5.5 g.; CARBOHYDRATE – 15.6 g., CALORIES – 132, CALORIES FROM FAT = 38%

RHUBARB *STREUSEL* COFFEECAKE
Rabarberikook Pähklitega

TPT - 2 hours and 18 minutes;
1 hour = cooling period

My mom is renowned for her wonderful sour cream streusel coffeecakes. Well into her nineties she was still baking about twenty-four each December for gifts. They are rich with whole eggs, full-fat sour cream, and lots and lots of walnuts. Since we can not afford all that richness, some changes had to be made in Mom's very special cake. At the same time we "healthied up" the cakes by adding whole wheat and soy flours and by reducing the amount of sugar. Using this very healthy cake as a model, I evolved a rhubarb cake much like those beloved by Estonians. These cakes freeze beautifully providing a healthful convenience for drop-in company or weekend breakfasts.

Be sure to select thin, young rhubarb stalks for this recipe.

1 cup chopped, *preservative-free* pecans *or* walnuts
1/4 cup firmly packed *light* brown sugar
1/4 cup *toasted* wheat germ
1 tablespoon freshly grated orange zest
2 teaspoons ground cinnamon
1/2 teaspoon freshly grated nutmeg

3/4 cup sugar
2 tablespoons corn starch
6-10 thin, young rhubarb stalks—diced to yield about 6 cupfuls

2 3/4 cups whole wheat flour
1 cup unbleached white flour
2 tablespoons soy flour
1 tablespoon baking powder
2 teaspoons baking soda

1/2 cup (1 stick) butter
1 1/4 cups white sugar
1/2 cup *fat-free* pasteurized eggs (the equivalent of 2 eggs)
2 large egg whites—slightly beaten
2 teaspoons pure vanilla extract
2 cups PLAIN YOGURT [see index] *or* commercially-available plain yogurt*

Preheat oven to 350 degrees F. Prepare two 8 1/2-inch angel food cake pans by coating with non-stick lecithin spray coating. Dust with flour.

Prepare *streusel* topping by combining chopped nuts, 1/4 cupful brown sugar, *toasted* wheat germ, grated orange zest, ground cinnamon, and nutmeg. Set aside until required.

In a saucepan set over *MEDIUM* heat, combine the 3/4 cupful sugar, corn starch, and diced rhubarb. Cook, stirring constantly, until the rhubarb softens and the mixture comes to the boil and thickens. Set aside to cool.

Europe–Estonia

RHUBARB *STREUSEL* COFFEECAKE (cont'd)

Into a large mixing bowl, sift whole wheat, white, and soy flours with baking powder and baking soda. Set aside.

Using an electric mixer, cream butter until light and fluffy. Add 1 1/4 cupfuls sugar and cream until again light and fluffy. Add pasteurized eggs, egg whites, and vanilla extract. Again, beat until thoroughly combined.

While continuing to beat, add yogurt alternately with flour mixture. Continue to beat until a smooth batter forms.

Pour *one-fourth* of batter into one of prepared pans. Spoon *one-half* of the rhubarb filling on top of the filling, pressing it into pockets. Sprinkle *one-fourth* of *streusel* topping over it. Pour *one-third* of remaining batter over and sprinkle with *one-third* of remaining topping mixture over. Prepare second cake by alternating remaining ingredients in the same manner.

Bake in preheated 350 degree F. oven for about 40 minutes, or until a cake tester inserted comes out clean. *Cool completely,* for at least 1 hour, on a wire rack before removing from pan and serving.

Yields two 8 1/2-inch cakes
of about 16 servings each

Note: *Sour cream may be substituted if increased calories and fat levels can be tolerated.

1/32 SERVING (i. e., per slice) –
PROTEIN = 4.6 g.; FAT = 6.8 g.; CARBOHYDRATE = 30.8 g.;
CALORIES = 200; CALORIES FROM FAT = 31%

ESTONIAN *HALVA* WITH ALMOND BUTTER

Halva

TPT - 8 hours and 40 minutes;
20 minutes = first refrigeration period;
8 hours = second refrigeration period

Colorful tins have traveled across the acres to our nearest neighbors since they first moved in with just one son. He would trudge across the fields with cookies on the Saturday before Christmas and I would disappear into our pantry room to emerge with a tin of cookies and candies for him and his parents. Matthew grew up but the tins still traveled across the field for several years because the joyful exchange continued with his much younger brother and sister who would also race over here in their snow jackets on the Saturday before Christmas. Although this Estonian confection is traditionally made with a peanut butter/sesame seed combination, the almond butter version is a good confection for those allergic to peanut butter.

1/4 cup butter (1/2 stick)—*softened to room temperature*
1/2 cup almond butter*
1/2 cup honey
1 teaspoon pure vanilla extract

1 cup *instant* non-fat dry milk powder

Prepare a cookie sheet by lining with waxed paper.

Using the electric mixer or food processor fitted with steel knife cream softened butter and almond butter together until light and fluffy. Add honey and vanilla extract and continue beating until very well-blended.

Add *instant* non-fat dry milk. Beat until thoroughly combined. Scrape down sides of bowl as needed. Refrigerate the bowl containing the *halva* mixture for 20 minutes to make the mixture easier to handle.

Form dough into balls about 1/2 inch in diameter by rolling between your palms. Place on a prepared cookie sheet and chill in the refrigerator for about 8 hours, or overnight. Cover loosely with a piece of waxed paper.

When ready to serve or give, place each confection into a paper candy wrapper. Layer in a cake pan and store in refrigerator until required.

Yields about 30 confections

Notes: *Old-fashioned, freshly ground (if possible), smooth, *unsalted* peanut butter can be substituted, if preferred. Both the almond butter and the peanut butter should be available in your natural foods store.

This recipe can be doubled, when required.

1/30 SERVING (i. e., per confection) –
PROTEIN = 1.2 g.; FAT = 2.6 g.; CARBOHYDRATE = 6.5 g.;
CALORIES = 62; CALORIES FROM FAT = 38%

Europe–**Finland**

Finland

It is not surprising that Finns migrated to the United States and settled in areas of Minnesota, Michigan, and the Finger Lakes region of New York State, places that felt like home. No doubt, memories of Finland's lakes and deep forests influenced the choices of New World settlement as did the distinct four seasons of the north of our country. Finland, warmed by the Gulf Stream, also has four seasons but the extreme northern latitude of Finland means that summer daylight can be as long as fifteen hours, an advantage to the farmer who copes with a dramatically short growing season but a confusing experience for the bio-clock of the average tourist who is only used to a one-hour adjustment for daylight savings time. On the other hand, the bizarre darkness during our late December morning arrival in Helsinki and our midday departure, still in darkness, seemed almost other-worldly.

As the great ice sheet began to retreat, humans began to settle along its southernmost edge at sites fed by the glacial melt streams. Evidence of fishing populations date to about 8000 BC in present day Finland. The influence of the migration of people from the Ural Mountains, the people generally credited with introducing the basis for the present Finnish language, began in about 500 BC, at the end of the Bronze Age and extended well into the Iron Age. By 1249 AD Swedish monarchs ruled Finland. With this, Swedish became the dominant language of the upper classes and of administration and is still spoken in Finland today. Wars between Russia and Sweden in the 1700s led to occupation of Finland by Russia. In 1809, following the conquest by the armies of Alexander I of Russia, Finland was declared a Grand Duchy in the Russian Empire. Following the Bolshevik Revolution in 1917, Finland fought the Soviet Union, emerging briefly as a monarchy and then as a presidential republic. During World War II Finland found itself at war with both the Soviets and the Germans. Peace accords with the Soviets resulted in territorial losses of about ten percent of its land area, twenty percent of its industrial capacity, and two major ports including the ice-free port of Linnakhamari. Today, a population of about 5.4 million, now mostly urban, enjoys relative economic prosperity, having emerged from a deep recession in the early 1990s.

Older Finnish cookbooks emphasize foods that can winter-over, be preserved, or be hunted. As a result root vegetables, dried and salted fish, and meat dominate these older books. They seem to be guiding cooks through a survival cuisine. Since those books were written, greenhouse food production has been introduced and provides for the year-round availability of fresh produce. Nevertheless, recipes featuring cellared root vegetables, dried fish, and rich meat dishes still fill the pages of contemporary Finnish cookbooks. The lessons of how to survive in difficult times are passed from generation to generation. Tradition strongly binds Finns and is an important element of their national identity. Foods are still eaten in season and what can be dried, canned, and frozen is "put down" for the winter, which can last for as long as seven months in the North and six months in the South. With about twenty-five percent of Finland's territory located north of the Arctic Circle, agriculture is limited. Snow covers the ground in the North from October to May and true summer weather can be expected for only two or three months. In addition there is little arable land with seventy-five percent of Finland covered by forests. Grain can be grown only in the southernmost regions of the country.

Europe – Finland

Vegetables most often appear on the Finnish table in salads and I have enclosed two favorites from which to choose. We serve both of the salads below regularly on our holiday cold table.

Quark Cheese with Pepper
Pipitomrm Rahkajuusto

Strawberry – Rhubarb Juice
Heldima Mehu

Finnish Whole Grain Bread
Teraeysleipa

~

Cream of Carrot and Celeriac Soup
Porkkanakeitto

with

Finnish – Style Flatbread

~

Mushroom Salad	Red Cabbage and Black Currant Slaw
Sienisalaatti	*Punakaalisalaatti*

~~~~~~~~~~~~~~~~~~~~~~

Rutabaga and Potato Casserole	Barley and Carrot Pudding
Lanttuloora	*Porkkanalaatikko*

Baby Onions with Blue Cheese Sauce
Sinihomejuustosipulit

~~~~~~~~~~~~~~~~~~~~~~

Whipped Dessert Porridge with Farina	Custard Dessert Pancake
Vispipuuro	*Kropsua*

"Parson's" Dessert
Pappilan Hätavara

FINNISH *QUARK* CHEESE WITH PEPPER
Pippurinen Rahkajuusto

TPT - 24 hours and 4 minutes;
24 hours = draining period

I have always combined yogurt and sour cream for salad dressings and for desserts but was surprised to find this variation, which can be served as a spread in place of cheese. Quark (maitorahka) is more sour than is our yogurt. If you make your own yogurt, you can do as I do. When your homemade yogurt becomes quite tart, the clue that you need a new starter, drain that yogurt to make yogurt crème or yogurt cheese. It approximates the quark found in Europe.

FINNISH *QUARK* CHEESE WITH PEPPER (cont'd)

1 cup *tart* **PLAIN YOGURT** *[see index]* **or commercially-available plain yogurt**
1 cup *fat-free* **dairy sour cream** *or* **MEXICAN HOMEMADE THICKENED CREAM** *(Crema Espeso) [see index]*
1 tablespoon *finely* **chopped fresh chervil, parsley,** *or* **salad burnet, as preferred**
1/2 teaspoon freshly ground mixed peppercorns —white, black, and red
1/2 teaspoon salt

In a mixing bowl, combine yogurt, sour cream, *finely* chopped chervil, parsley or salad burnet, ground mixed peppercorns, and salt. Mix well.

Set two automatic drip coffeemaker filters into a sieve over a medium-sized bowl or a yogurt filter over a 2-cup measuring cup. Pour the yogurt–sour cream mixture into the filters. Place a piece of plastic wrap on top of yogurt mixture and place a weight such as a jar of water set on a saucer on top. Allow to drain in the refrigerator for about 8 hours, or until you can easily mold it. Turn out on a piece of waxed paper and proceed to mold the yogurt cheese into a cone shape or a rectangular block, similar to commercial cream cheese. Turn onto a flat serving plate. Refrigerate until required.

Serve with a spreading knife as a communal first course with Finnish hard flatbread, crackers, dry toasts, cucumber slices, and celery. Refrigerate leftovers.

Yields 1 1/2 cupfuls

1/24 SERVING (i. e., per tablespoonful) –
PROTEIN = 1.2 g.; FAT = 0.2 g.; CARBOHYDRATE = 2.6 g.;
CALORIES = 17; CALORIES FROM FAT = 11%

FINNISH STRAWBERRY – RHUBARB JUICE
Heldlmä Mehu
TPT - 35 minutes

The fruit syrups which result from canning fruits in season have always given us a non-commercial source of juice for agar gelled desserts and salads. They are also a far better sweet pick-me up with a cookie or a rusk for children and adults than are sodas and most commercial fruit drinks. To this day, I enjoy a bit of cream in the juice drained from our canned blue plums, just as I was taught by my grandmother. Finnish homemakers push this to another level, stewing the fruit and canning the juice for winter consumption. This particular combination is popular, just as it is our Midwest where pies and puddings make good use of the simultaneous bounty in the spring. Preserving the light, sweet liquid gives Finns a real head start on filling the juice shelves in their fruit cellars for the next winter. As the summer progresses berries of all kinds and crabapples are used to make juice and, then, as the apples, pears, and grapes ripen in the fall, they are combined with residual berries such as cranberries.

2 pounds young rhubarb stalks—trimmed, well-washed, and chopped
2 pints fresh strawberries—well-washed, hulled, and halved
4 quarts water

1 cup sugar

Place a jelly bag or clean cotton tea towel in a sieve and set the sieve over a mixing bowl.

In a large stainless steel kettle set over *MEDIUM* heat, combine chopped rhubarb, strawberry halves, and water. Allow to come to the boil and boil, stirring occasionally, for 15 minutes.

Add the 1 cupful sugar and stir until dissolved. Remove from heat. Pour fruit and juice into the lined sieve and allow the juice to drip through into the bowl.* Transfer the juice to a pitcher or decanters and chill before serving.**

FINNISH STRAWBERRY – RHUBARB JUICE (cont'd)

Additional sugar, honey, *or agave* nectar can be added if a sweeter beverage is desired.

Yields about 3 1/2 quarts

Notes: *Use the strained fruit to make a dessert or pudding by adding a bit more sweetener and whipped cream.

**This juice can be canned in a hot-water-bath canner or frozen, as preferred. Ladle juice into hot, sterilized 1/2-pint canning jars. Carefully wipe lips of jars. Seal with hot, sterilized lids and rings. Process in hot-water-bath canner for 10 minutes, *timing from the moment the water reaches a full rolling boil.* Remove to surface covered with thick towels or newspapers. Allow to cool for 24 hours *undisturbed.* Check to be sure jars are sealed before labeling and storing in a dark, cool, dry place. Loosen or remove rings before storing.

***In calculating food values for this beverage we have "assumed" that two tablespoonfuls each of rhubarb and the strawberry will be transferred. The food values listed below, therefore, are only approximate.

1/37 SERVING (i. e., 1/2 cup) –
PROTEIN = 0.005 g.; FAT = 0.003 g.; CARBOHYDRATE = 6.2 g.;
CALORIES = 24; CALORIES FROM FAT = <1%***

FINNISH WHOLE GRAIN BREAD

Teraeysleipa

TPT - about 4 hours;
   1 and 30 minutes = first bread rising period;
   1 hour = second bread rising period

In the 1970s, this might have been referred to as a "health bread" right along side the famous Cornell loaf and, indeed, it is but it is more. It reflects the strength and heartiness of a people who, in our opinion, challenge the limits of nature to live in one of the most beautiful parts of our planet. Although I have evolved a bread machine version of this loaf, I return often to the hands-on involvement of kneading. It evokes to us the memory of the coarse grain bread and the hearty meals which this bread accompanies. So proud are the Finns of their "good food," we were served such a bread with wonderful vegetarian meals on Finnair.

2 tablespoons honey
1/4 cup warm water (105-115 degrees F.)
1 tablespoon (1 envelope) *preservative-free*, active dried yeast*

2 cups *unsalted*, cultured buttermilk
1 1/4 cups rye flour
1 1/4 cups whole wheat flour
1/4 cup wheat germ—toasted or raw, as preferred
2 cups unbleached white flour

About 1 1/2 cups additional unbleached white flour

1/4 cup wheat germ—toasted or raw, as preferred

Prepare a baking sheet by oiling generously. Prepare a large mixing bowl by oiling.

Dissolve honey in warm water in a large mixing bowl. Sprinkle yeast over and allow to proof for about 5 minutes. Stir in buttermilk, rye and whole wheat flours, and 1/4 cupful wheat germ. Stir until well-blended. Gradually work in 2 cupfuls white flour until too stiff to handle.

Turn out onto floured surface and knead, working in additional white flour until smooth and elastic with no trace of stickiness—about 15-20 minutes.** Place in an oiled bowl, turn to coat, and cover bowl with plastic wrap and a cotton tea towel. Allow to rise in a warm (75-80 degrees F.), draft-free place until doubled in bulk—about 1 1/2 hours.***

FINNISH WHOLE GRAIN BREAD (cont'd)

Punch dough down and divide into 2 equal pieces. Take one piece and turn out onto floured surface, knead for 2 or 3 minutes, and shape into a round 6-inch cake. Brush with water and press top into remaining 1/4 cupful wheat germ. Place crease-side-down on prepared baking sheet. Repeat with second half of dough. Cover each with a cotton tea towel and allow to rise in a warm (75-80 degrees F.), draft-free place until doubled in bulk—about 1 hour. Slash a crisscross or "tic-tac-toe" pattern across the top of each with a sharp knife.

Preheat oven to 375 degrees F.

Bake loaves in preheated oven for 30 minutes, or until they "thump hollow" when tapped with your knuckles. *Cool completely* on a wire rack. Store in tightly closed plastic bags in refrigerator or freeze, if preferred.****

Yields 2 round loaves
of about 18 slices each*****

Notes: *Some packaged dried yeast available in grocery stores contain a preservative. Natural food stores carry an additive-free dried yeast.

**Thorough kneading is essential for a good "crumb!" If more convenient, the dough may be divided and *machine-kneaded* using a food processor fitted with steel knife. This greatly reduces the kneading time and effort.

***Bread rises well when placed in a closed, unheated oven or on a heating pad set at *LOW*.

****Although this freezes well, there is evidence that freezing causes loss of vitamin E and with all the vitamin E in this loaf, it would be a shame to lose any. Why not give a second loaf to a friend if you do not anticipate its consumption in a week's time?

*****Allow three full slices from each "end." The middle slices are more manageable if halved.

1/36 SERVING (i. e., per slice) –
PROTEIN = 3.1 g.; FAT = 0.5 g.; CARBOHYDRATE = 17.6 g.;
CALORIES = 79; CALORIES FROM FAT = 6%

FINNISH CREAM OF CARROT AND CELERIAC SOUP
Porkkanakeitto

TPT - 40 minutes

Unlike my Irish cream of carrot soup, this Finnish version is not thickened with potato, but instead with "buerre manie." Also it does not contain a flavorful stock base or much seasoning of consequence. However, I cook the carrots in a vegetable stock and do add a whisper of seasoning with a bouquet garni and a pinch of thyme. It is an appropriate first course for a Finnish menu which we serve with multigrain or oat Finnish flatbread or with hot baking powder biscuits.

Bouquet garni:
   2 sprigs fresh thyme
   2 sprigs fresh parsley—coarsely chopped
   1 bay leaf—halved

4 large carrots—scraped or pared and coarsely chopped
1/2 cup chopped celery root (celeriac)
1 1/2 cups VEGETABLE STOCK FROM SOUP
   [see index] **or other vegetarian stock of choice**
Pinch crushed, dried thyme

1 1/2 cups *whole* milk

2 teaspoons KNEADED FLOUR FOR THICKENING (Buerre Manie) [see index]

1 tablespoon sugar
Salt, to taste
Freshly ground *white* pepper, to taste

Chopped fresh parsley, for garnish

In a tea ball or in a cheesecloth *bouquet garni* bag, prepare a *bouquet garni* of fresh thyme and parsley sprigs and bay leaf pieces.

In a large saucepan set over *MEDIUM* heat, combine *bouquet garni*, chopped carrots, chopped celery root, stock, and crushed, dried thyme. Bring to the boil. Cook, stirring occasionally, until vegetables are tender —about 25 minutes. Turn cooked vegetables into a colander set over a bowl and allow stock to drain off. Reserve drained stock for a future recipe or freeze and add to a stock pot. Remove and discard *bouquet garni*.

Turn vegetables into the work bowl of the food processor or into the container of the electric blender. Process until vegetables are smoothly puréed. Add the *whole* milk. Process until smooth. Turn into clean saucepan and reheat over *LOW-MEDIUM* heat.

Europe – **Finland**

FINNISH CREAM OF CARROT AND CELERIAC SOUP (cont'd)

While stirring, add balls of *buerre manie*. Stir until thickened.

Add sugar, salt, and *white* pepper. Cook until heated through. *Do not allow soup to boil.*

Turn into a heated soup tureen and serve into heated soup bowls. Garnish each serving with chopped parsley.

Notes: Leftovers can not be successfully frozen, but can be reheated over *LOW* heat or in a double boiler.

This recipe may be halved or doubled, when required.

Yields 6 servings
adequate for 4 people

1/6 SERVING – PROTEIN = 2.3 g.; FAT = 2.4 g.; CARBOHYDRATE = 8.9 g.;
CALORIES = 78; CALORIES FROM FAT = 27%

FINNISH – STYLE MUSHROOM SALAD
Sienisalaati
TPT - 23 minutes

Our visit to Denmark in December 1985 introduced us to the diversity and freshness of the wonderful Scandinavian feast known as the "cold table." Each Scandinavian cuisine is now represented on our holiday "cold table" — a tradition we established because of the joyous holiday and never-to-be-forgotten food of that 1985 holiday. Several Finnish dishes, including this salad, give added dimension to our "feast of freshness."

8 ounces fresh white *(Agaricus)* mushrooms

6 large *shiitake* mushrooms

1 medium *portobello* mushroom

2 cups *boiling* water
1 tablespoon freshly squeezed lemon juice
2 tablespoons light cream *or* half and half
2 tablespoons YOGURT *CRÈME* [see index]
1 tablespoon *finely* grated onion
1/4 teaspoon sugar
1/8 teaspoon freshly ground *white* pepper

Lettuce leaves
Snipped chives, for garnish, if desired

Trim all mushrooms, rinse, and clean each with a brush. Slice mushrooms and stems into 1/8-inch slices. The *portobello* mushroom slices may have to be halved to produce a uniform mixture. Combine mushroom slices in a large mixing bowl.*

Pour *boiling* water and fresh lemon juice over mushrooms. Allow to stand for 2 minutes. *Using a wooden spoon, press mushrooms down into hot water.* Pour into a sieve and allow to drain thoroughly. Spread mushroom slices out on paper toweling and pat dry.

In a mixing bowl, combine cream, yogurt *crème*, grated onion, sugar, and white pepper. Using a wire whisk, combine thoroughly.

Just before you are ready to serve, add mushroom slices to prepared sauce and, using a large spoon, *carefully* toss mushroom slices to coat evenly.

Serve at once over lettuce leaves. Sprinkle with chives, to garnish, if desired.

Yields 6 servings
adequate for 4 people

Notes: *Remember to use ceramic, glass, enamel, or stainless steel bowls and saucepans when preparing mushrooms as aluminum tends to discolor them.

This recipe may be halved or doubled, when required.

1/6 SERVING – PROTEIN = 3.3 g.; FAT = 0.9 g.; CARBOHYDRATE = 5.4 g.;
CALORIES = 43; CALORIES FROM FAT = 19%

Europe–Finland

FINNISH RED CABBAGE AND BLACK CURRANT SLAW
Punakallisalaati

TPT - 2 hours and 5 minutes;
2 hours = flavor development period

Cabbages arrive in the market throughout the fall but I rarely settle for grocery store cabbage. I am careful to locate a couple of cabbages that has been picked after the first frost and have not been stripped of their outer leaves. Refrigerated, they will provide that crisp, fresh taste straight through the winter. In a way, it is no different than the cold cellar storage that my mother, grandmother, and great-grandmother used in upstate New York. Because of the lack of fresh greens in northern climates, cabbage has always been important to winter menus. We just peel off the outer, protective leaves when a fresh vegetable is needed. The sweet berry jam transforms the taste of this simple cabbage slaw and makes it a Christmas specialty.

4 cups *finely* **shredded red cabbage**

2 tablespoons *calorie-reduced or light* **mayonnaise**
4 tablespoons black currant jelly

Place shredded cabbage on a clean cotton tea towel. Press out as much liquid as possible. Turn into mixing bowl.

In a small bowl combine mayonnaise and black currant jelly. Break up the jelly and stir mixture to combine well. Add to shredded cabbage and toss to mix well. Refrigerate for at least 2 hours to allow for flavor development.

Turn into a serving bowl and serve with a slotted spoon.

Yields 6 servings
adequate for 4 people

Note: This recipe may be halved or doubled, when required.

1/6 SERVING – PROTEIN = 1.3 g.; FAT = 3.9 g.; CARBOHYDRATE = 14.0 g.;
CALORIES = 91; CALORIES FROM FAT = 39%

FINNISH RUTABAGA AND POTATO CASSEROLE
Lanttulaara

TPT - 10 hours and 40 minutes;
8 hours = overnight "sweetening" period;
10 minutes = breadcrumb soaking period

Rutabagas, also known as swedes or yellow turnips, are actually genetically related to both the cabbage and the turnip. They are said to have been eaten by humans since prehistoric times. I guess my family was not too fond of rutabagas; I can not really remember eating them as a child. However, I do remember my mother, when asked, identifying a root vegetable in the market as a "Canadian turnip" and that was that. We did not scoop it up for an experiment but my mother was my mother and I am me. Many years later a Portuguese recipe introduced me to this vegetable that can be a useful winter vegetable, not to mention a good source of beta carotene. It has always been an important vegetable in Finland and many dishes now made with potatoes were made with turnips and rutabagas before the introduction of and the agricultural success of the potato.

The following recipe employs the traditional overnight technique which is said to "sweeten" the dish. When I make this, I do double it and bake it in several small dishes which can be frozen.

FINNISH RUTABAGA AND POTATO CASSEROLE (cont'd)

2 quarts *boiling* water
3/4 pound rutabaga—peeled and chopped*

2 quarts *boiling* water
1 large potato—peeled and chopped

1/4 cup unbleached white flour

3/4 cup skimmed milk
1/3 cup breadcrumbs

1/4 cup light cream *or* half and half
2 tablespoons corn syrup
6 tablespoons *fat-free* pasteurized eggs
1/4 teaspoon salt
1/4 teaspoon ground allspice
Pinch ground nutmeg
Pinch ground ginger
Freshly ground black pepper, to taste

1 1/2 tablespoons butter—*melted*

Boil both the chopped rutabaga and chopped potatoes separately in *boiling* water until tender. Drain, *reserving the cooking liquid.*

In a mixing bowl, combine the cooked rutabaga and potato pieces. Add 1/2 cupful of the drained cooking liquid. Mash until well combined.

Add flour. Stir to combine well. Cover with plastic wrap and allow to sit on the counter top for 8 hours.

Preheat oven to 275 degrees F. Prepare a 1 1/2-quart baking dish or two small oven-to-table baking dishes by coating with non-stick lecithin spray coating.

In a small bowl, combine milk and breadcrumbs. Allow to soak for about 10 minutes. Add to mashed vegetables which had been allowed to ferment. Stir to combine.

Add cream, corn syrup, pasteurized eggs, salt, ground allspice, nutmeg, and ginger, and black pepper. Mix well. Turn into baking dish(es). Press it down into the dish(es) with the back of a spoon, if necessary.

Bake in preheated 275 degree F. oven for 1 hour. Remove from oven and brush the top surface with the *melted* butter. Return to the oven for an additional 1 hour. The casserole should be golden brown and pulling *slightly* from the sides of the baking dish.

Serve at once or cool completely and freeze, *well wrapped.*

Yields 6 servings
adequate for 4 people

Notes: *Most rutabagas, available in our markets are from Canada and have been waxed to increase "shelf life." The protective wax coating makes them a good winter storage candidate for your root cellar or a deep cold frame, should you choose to have one. Be sure to peel all the wax from the rutabaga before proceeding with a recipe.

This recipe can be doubled and since it can be successfully frozen, doubling is an economical use of your time.

1/6 SERVING – PROTEIN = 4.1 g.; FAT = 3.4 g.; CARBOHYDRATE = 20.4 g.;
CALORIES = 127; CALORIES FROM FAT = 24%

FINNISH BARLEY AND CARROT PUDDING
Porkkanalaatikko
TPT - 1 hour and 5 minutes

Barley, one of the most ancient grains cultivated by human beings, is a sadly neglected grain in the United States. Even the barley and vegetable baby food stew, available when our daughter was a toddler, is no longer available. I do not think I have ever seen barley offered on a restaurant menu. More than half of that produced here is used to feed animals but it has remained an important food in the cuisines of Scotland and Finland and in many other northern countries. Like soy, the amino acids in barley fully complement each other, making barley another useful tool for vegetarians. Porridges, such as this, were and are popular in many countries. These puddings are, in a word, sustenance.

FINNISH BARLEY AND CARROT PUDDING (cont'd)

1 cup *boiling* water
1/2 cup dry pearl barley

1 cup *two-percent* milk

4 medium carrots—pared or peeled and coarsely grated
1/4 teaspoon salt
1 teaspoon sugar
1/4 teaspoon ground allspice
1/4 cup *fat-free* pasteurized eggs (the equivalent of 1 egg)

1 tablespoon *cold* butter—chopped
3 tablespoons breadcrumbs

Preheat oven to 375 degrees F. Prepare a 1 quart soufflé dish or other oven-to-table baking dish by coating with non-stick lecithin spray coating.

In a saucepan set over *MEDIUM* heat, combine *boiling* water and barley. Cook, stirring frequently, until the water has been absorbed.

Add milk and cook until the milk is almost completely absorbed. The barley should be tender, *but still firm*. Add more milk if the barley is not done. *There should be at least two tablespoonfuls of milk left in the bottom of the pan.* Remove from heat.

Add grated carrot, salt, sugar, ground allspice, and pasteurized eggs. Stir to combine thoroughly. Turn into prepared baking dish.

Scatter chopped butter over. Sprinkle breadcrumbs over.

Bake in preheated 375 degree F. oven for about 40 minutes, or until lightly browned.

Serve at once.

Yields 6 servings
adequate for 4 people

Note: This recipe can be halved, when required.

1/6 SERVING – PROTEIN = 4.3 g.; FAT = 2.9 g.; CARBOHYDRATE = 21.1 g.;
CALORIES = 126; CALORIES FROM FAT = 2%

BABY ONIONS WITH BLUE CHEESE SAUCE IN THE STYLE OF FINLAND
Sinihomejuustosipulit
TPT - 30 minutes

Blue-veined cheeses are enjoyed all over Scandinavia and can bring a very distinct and exciting flavor to something as mundane as an onion. The tiny onions now available frozen are definitely a convenience to be appreciated if you have ever spent hours blanching and peeling pearl onions, a holiday ritual for some of us. They make this dish a very quick and easy vegetable side dish.

1/2 cup VEGETABLE STOCK FROM SOUP
  [see index] *or* other vegetarian stock of choice
1 bay leaf—broken in half
1/2 teaspoon crushed, dried thyme
24 *frozen* white boiling onions—about 1/2 pound

1/2 cup light cream *or* half and half
2 ounces blue cheese—*crumbled*

Sprig of thyme, for garnish

In a saucepan set over *MEDIUM* heat, combine vegetable stock, broken bay leaf, crushed thyme, and frozen baby onions. Allow to come to the boil. Reduce heat to *LOW*. Allow to simmer for about 10 minutes. Drain thoroughly.

In a non-stick-coated skillet set over *LOW* heat, combine cream and crumbled blue cheese. Allow to cook until cheese melts.

Add onions. Cover and allow onions to simmer for about 10 minutes more. Stir occasionally. Turn into a heated serving bowl.

Keep warm on warming tray until ready to serve. Garnish with the sprig of thyme before serving.

Yields 6 servings
adequate for 4 people

Note: This recipe can be halved, when required.

1/6 SERVING – PROTEIN = 3.1 g.; FAT = 4.8 g.; CARBOHYDRATE = 4.0 g.;
CALORIES = 71; CALORIES FROM FAT = 61%

Europe–Finland

FINNISH WHIPPED DESSERT PORRIDGE WITH FARINA
Vispipuuro

TPT - 1 hour and 40 minutes;
1 hour = chilling period

Watching the electric mixer whip the mixture into voluminous mounds is such fun for children, and easily amused adults too. It reminds me of watching my mother whip cream or egg whites when I was a kid. A fingerful of this dessert mixture, however, is sweet, and brings a satisfied smile, unlike the first taste of unsweetened whipped cream or those disappointing beaten egg whites. Although the sweetened cranberry juice cocktail products available in our supermarkets are a poor substitute for the flavorful berry juices, such as lingonberry, which the Finnish cook would use in this dish, they are usually all that is available to us.

1 cup strawberries—fresh *or* frozen, but *thawed*

1 cup *sweetened* cranberry–raspberry juice cocktail*
2 tablespoons sugar
1/4 cup uncooked farina *or regular* Cream of Wheat cereal—*not instant*

Lingonberry preserves, for garnish
Whipped heavy cream, for garnish, if desired

Using the electric mixer or food processor fitted with steel knife, beat strawberries until they form a purée. Press through a fine sieve to remove most of seeds. Turn purée into a 2-cup measuring cup. Add cranberry–raspberry juice to a level of 1 1/2 cupfuls.

In a saucepan set over *MEDIUM* heat, combine purée-juice mixture, sugar, and uncooked farina. Bring to the boil, stirring constantly. Reduce heat to *LOW* and cook, stirring constantly, for about 10 minutes, or until thickened.

Pour the mixture into a mixer bowl and, using the electric mixer, beat at *high* speed for about 20 minutes, or until the mixture is a light pink in color. The volume of the porridge should have increased about four-fold.

Divide evenly among four sherbet glasses or dessert dishes and refrigerate for at least 1 hour, *but not more than 3 hours.*

Garnish with lingonberry preserves and serve with whipped cream, if desired.

Yields 4 servings

Notes: *If using fresh, unsweetened berry juice, increase sugar to taste.

This recipe may be doubled, when required.

1/4 SERVING (with 2 tablespoonfuls whipped cream) –
PROTEIN = 2.2 g.; FAT = 5.3 g.; CARBOHYDRATE = 30.7 g.;
CALORIES = 177; CALORIES FROM FAT = 27%

FINNISH CUSTARD DESSERT PANCAKE
Krepsua

TPT - 45 minutes

Made in a manner similar to that in which a German apple pancake is prepared, this most satisfying dessert is often served with fresh fruits or fresh fruit sauces when available. Most of the year, however, such luxuries must only be anticipated in the frozen North so wonderful preserves are served.

1/2 cup *fat-free* pasteurized eggs (the equivalent of 2 eggs)
1 1/2 tablespoons sugar
1 cup skimmed milk
1/2 teaspoon pure vanilla extract
1/2 teaspoon ground cardamom
1/4 cup whole wheat flour
1/4 cup unbleached white flour

2 teaspoons confectioners' sugar

Lingonberry preserves* *or* all-fruit jam, of choice

Prepare a 7-inch non-stick-coated skillet by wrapping the handle well with several layers of aluminum foil. Coat with non-stick lecithin spray coating.

Preheat oven to 375 degrees F.

FINNISH CUSTARD DESSERT PANCAKE (cont'd)

Using the electric mixer, beat pasteurized eggs and sugar until thick and lemony. Add milk, vanilla extract, and cardamom. Continue mixing. Add whole wheat and white flours. Continue mixing until thoroughly combined.

Place prepared skillet in preheated oven for 5 minutes. Using an oven mitt, remove skillet from oven. Add batter. Return to oven and bake for about 22 minutes, or until *puffed and golden*.

Remove to wire rack to cool slightly—*no more than 10 minutes*. Sprinkle with sieved confectioners' sugar just before serving. Pass lingonberry preserves or jam separately.

Notes: *Lingonberry preserves are available in many food specialty stores.

This recipe may be easily doubled, using a 9-inch skillet.

Yields 4 servings
adequate for 4 people

1/4 SERVING (with 2 teaspoonfuls jam) –
PROTEIN = 6.6 g.; FAT = 0.3 g.; CARBOHYDRATE = 31.6 g.;
CALORIES = 147; CALORIES FROM FAT = 2%

FINNISH "PARSON'S" DESSERT
Pappilan Hätävara
TPT - 6 minutes

Encountered first as "the just-in-case-we-need-a-dessert dessert" and then as" the parson's dessert," I was anxious to find out the origin of the name. It seemed a pretty good bet that there was a story behind this dessert. Supposedly the trifle-like concoction dates from the era when ministers often made visits to the homes of parishioners. The one room in my grandmother's house in which grandchildren could not play was the front parlor, with its fine furniture and Oriental rug. It was reserved for special occasions like the visit of our parish minister and could be accessed without the prominent visitor having to see the rest of the house. A dessert or cookies (tea biscuits) were often served with the tea offered to the guest. In Finland, it appears, things were much the same. The ingredients for this quickly assembled dessert were kept on hand for such emergency entertaining. This dessert is, we think, surprisingly good and a wonderful recipe to teach a grandchild who wants to learn how to cook.

Per serving:
    3 Maria biscuits* *or* British digestives
    2 tablespoons light cream *or* half and half

    2 Maria biscuits *or* British digestives
    2 tablespoons light cream *or* half and half

    1/2 cup *whipped* and *sweetened* heavy cream
    1 tablespoon homemade jam—*our favorites are strawberry and peach*

In the center of a soup plate, arrange three Maria biscuits. Pour two tablespoonfuls cream over the biscuits and allow it to soak in.

Place the remaining two Maria biscuits on top of the three biscuits already absorbing the cream. Pour the remaining two tablespoonfuls of cream over.

Spoon whipped cream over. Top with jam.

Serve at once.

Yields 1 serving

Note: *Maria biscuits are available in the United States under the Goya label. Any vanilla cookie or plain rusk can be substituted.

1 SERVING – PROTEIN = 3.7 g.; FAT = 14.6 g.; CARBOHYDRATE = 42.0 g.;
CALORIES = 315; CALORIES FROM FAT = 41 %

France

"The French and Indian War," said the child, "must have been a war between the French and the Indians. How did the Indians get to France?" It is no wonder; twenty-seven percent of the adult Americans surveyed in 2010 did not know that the Fourth of July celebrates our independence from Great Britain but thought it might have been from Mexico, China, Japan, France, or just did not know. How frustrating it is to look at a history book today and see just a few paragraphs about a war that had such a profound effect on the places I lived. Growing up along the southern shore of Lake Ontario, traveling in Quebec, and living in central Pennsylvania, not far from the site where George Washington won his first military victory as a colonial officer under the British in the French and Indian War, I am perhaps more aware of an era in our history than are many. France was an ambitious colonial power and they too entered the fight for the vast territory and resources of the North American continent.

Romanized and known as Gaul, France only began to emerge as a state after the Treaty of Verdun in 843 A.D. It then became a monarchy until the declaration of the First Republic in September 1792, sixteen years after our republic was born. The First Republic, which was to be short-lived, had been preceded by the French Revolution and the largely symbolic storming of the Bastille on July 14, 1789. In 1799 power was seized by Napolèon Bonaparte, who declared himself First Consul and, later, Emperor. The First Empire which lasted from 1804 to 1814 is also the period of France's quest for European territory. The Napoleonic Wars ended with Napolèon's final defeat in 1815 at the Battle of Waterloo and thus began a second brief period of monarchy. It was followed by a short-lived Second Republic which ended in 1851, after a *coup d'etat* led by Louis-Napolèon Bonaparte. Thus began a period called the Second Empire. The Third Republic, which followed the French defeat in the Franco-Prussian War of 1870, found France's colonial ambitions again at their height but this was interrupted by World War II. During the post-war Fourth Republic, France tried to retain a colonial empire. In an attempt to regain French Indochina, France precipitated the First Indochina War and was defeated and driven from the area after defeat at the Battle of Dien Bien Phu in 1954. Their defeat and departure was to be followed by the entrance of United States forces who fought for almost twenty years in the costly, unpopular war known in the United States as the Vietnam War and in Vietnam as the Resistance War Against America. In 1958 France declared a Fifth Republic under the presidency of Charles de Gaulle and another colonial war came to an end. With a peace signed in 1962, a civil war was avoided as a response to France's attempt to maintain control of Algeria. The colonial history of France can be seen reflected in the diversity of its population which has absorbed many colonial citizens. The influence of its own periods of occupation can be seen in the Italian and Germany influence in its cuisine.

Growing up in the 1950s we were exposed to rich French food that was heavily sauced. Even our beloved Julia Child, to whom many of us owe our culinary courage, presented a cuisine that no longer appeals to the average young homemaker in America. Classic French cooking gradually gave way to bistro cooking. How clearly I remember the interpretation of French cuisine in a fine hotel in Portugal. It was so disappointing; everything was drowned in heavy cream sauces. At that moment I decided to really explore French cooking. If it has influenced so many other cuisines in this world, it had to have a complexity that could take me to the people and the soil from which it sprang. If we took off our white gloves and pillbox hats, we can surely get rid of the superficial sauces and the parsley sprigs. I did find a very different cuisine beneath the surface.

The lentil dish included here originated in the Auvergne region, one of the least populated regions in Europe. The potato recipe is from the mountainous Rouergue region; the mustard omelet is from Bearne. My ratatouille is from Provence and nothing like the steamed and sliced, knife-and-fork versions that appear on restaurant menus today. You lift a spoonful to your mouth and are consumed and satisfied with complex flavors.

Brie Almond *Pâté*   or   Unbaked Walnut and Bean *Pâté* with Vegetable Filling
Pâté au Brie   *Pâté au Haricot Blanc et Noix*

Assorted *Crudités* and Crackers

~

Individual Mustard Omelet
Omelette a la Moutarde

~

Vegetable Stew in the Style of Provence   *Ratatouille* with Puff Pastry "Pillows"
Ratatouille Parmesan   *Ratatouille aux Pâté Feuilletées*

~

Vegetarian *Niçoise* Salad
Salad Niçoise Vegetarien

French Country Herb Seasoning Mixture
Herbes de Provence

~~~~~~~~~~~~~~~~~~~~

Lentils and Shallots in Red Wine and Tomato Sauce
Lentilles et Escalotes en Vin Rouge au Sauce Tomate

Mashed Potatoes with Cheese and Garlic
Aligot

Celeriac with Creamy Mustard Sauce
Celeri – Raves aux Sauce Moutarge a la Yogourt

~~~~~~~~~~~~~~~~~~~~

Coffee Custards
Petits Pots de Crème au Café

Europe–**France**

BRIE ALMOND *PÂTÉ*
Pâté au Brie

TPT - 3 hours and 36 minutes;
3 hours = flavor development period;
30 minutes = pre-serving temperature and texture adjustment

Turning a perfectly ripened wedge of Brie into a pâté like this can offend the purist but, trust me, a very good piece of Brie makes a very good Brie pâté.

8 ounces ripe French *Brie* cheese—*brought to room temperature*
1/2 cup butter—*softened to room temperature*
1/2 cup unblanched, slivered *preservative-free* almonds—*lightly toasted*
1 tablespoon *Fino* dry sherry
1/8 teaspoon dried thyme leaves—crushed
1/8 teaspoon onion powder

Trim and discard rind of *Brie*.

Using an electric mixer or a food processor, fitted with steel knife, process all ingredients together until *very smooth*.

Spoon into a cheese crock. Cover tightly with plastic wrap and then with cheese crock cover. Refrigerate for at least 3 hours, or overnight, to let flavor develop.

Bring to room temperature—about 30 minutes—before serving with *crudités*, crackers, or lightly toasted French bread croutons.

Refrigerate any leftover *pâté*.

Yields about 1 3/4 cupfuls

Note: This recipe is easily halved or doubled, when required.

1/28 SERVING (i. e., per tablespoonful) –
PROTEIN = 1.9 g.; FAT = 6.6 g.; CARBOHYDRATE = 0.5 g.;
CALORIES = 70; CALORIES FROM FAT = 85%

UNBAKED WALNUT AND BEAN *PÂTÉ* WITH VEGETABLE FILLING
Pâté au Haricot Blanc et Noix

TPT - 24 hours and 19 minutes;
24 hours = weighted refrigeration period

A grocery chain in our area carries a colorful, layered vegetable pâté that makes a lovely presentation as a cocktail table appetizer. My walnut and bean pate was, truth be known, delicious but the lack of color made it more appropriate for a sandwich spread. When I placed a layer of colorful vegetables in the middle and pressed it in a pâté terrine overnight, I was amazed at the response. Instead of taking a knifeful to spread on a cracker or toast, people took slices. Little had changed but the presentation.

1 cup *toasted, preservative-free* walnut pieces
1 15.5-ounce can (about 2 cups) *cannellini* beans —well-rinsed and well-drained
2 tablespoons *semi-condensed* cream of mushroom soup
1 garlic clove—*finely* chopped
1 tablespoon lemon juice
1 teaspoon *extra virgin* olive oil

1/4 cup grated carrot
1/4 teaspoon dried parsley—crushed
1/4 teaspoon dried mint—crushed

1/2 cup *finely* chopped ROASTED RED PEPPERS (*Peperoni Arrosto*) [see index]

Prepare a 2-cup *pâté* terrine placing in the refrigerator to chill thoroughly.*

In the work bowl of the food processor, combine *toasted* walnuts, *cannellini* beans, mushroom soup, *finely* chopped garlic, lemon juice, and olive oil. Process until *very smooth*.

Line the chilled *pâté* terrine with a tea towel, fitting the towel tightly into the terrine but allowing the edges to hand over the sides of the dish. Further line the towel-lined terrine with strips of waxed paper to allow for easy removal of the *pâté*.

Spoon half of the walnut–bean mixture into the lined terrine and spread to the edges.

Combine the grated carrot, crushed, dried parsley, and crushed, dried mint. Stir to combine uniformly. Spread across the layer already in the terrine.

VOLUME I - 132

UNBAKED WALNUT AND BEAN PÂTÉ WITH VEGETABLE FILLING (cont'd)

Scatter the *finely* chopped roasted red pepper evenly over the grated carrot layer.

Spoon the rest of the walnut–bean mixture over the red pepper layer, carefully spreading it to the edges of the terrine. Place a strip of waxed paper on top of the last layer. Press the top of the *pâté* firmly using a meat mallet or wooden garlic crusher. Place a weight on top, if you have such a weight.** Refrigerate for at least 24 hours.***

Remove weight and top piece of waxed paper. Using the edges of the towel, lift the *pâté* from the terrine and invert it onto a rectangular serving dish. *Carefully* peel the waxed paper off. Refrigerate until required.

Serve with crackers or toasts. Provide a sharp knife and a cheese or pie server to facilitate the transfer of slices to a salad plate.

Notes: *I prefer a porcelain terrine to a metal one but either will do quite nicely. Metal ones with sides that drop away for easy removal have an advantage too.

**A scrap piece of wood, cut to fit the terrine is a perfect weight.

***If *pâté* feels too moist, remove it, replace the tea towel with a dry one, and refrigerate for an additional 24 hours.

This *pâté* makes a wonderful sandwich spread.

Yields 20 servings
adequate for 10 people

1/20 SERVING – PROTEIN = 2.7 g.; FAT = 5.4 g.; CARBOHYDRATE = 5.5 g.;
CALORIES = 79; CALORIES FROM FAT = 62%

INDIVIDUAL FRENCH MUSTARD OMELET
Omelette a la Moutarde
TPT - 20 minutes

Bearne is in southwestern France, in the region which was once part of Aquitania under the Romans. This unusual mustard omelet is a specialty in that region and nothing could be more simple. Since this is a soft, moist, creamy omelet, an "omelette baveuse" as the French say, Salmonella–negative egg products are safer choices than are fresh eggs.

Per serving:
    4 teaspoons *Salmonella*–negative pasteurized egg white powder (the equivalent of 2 egg whites)*
    1/4 cup *warm* water

    1/3 cup *fat-free* pasteurized eggs (the equivalent of 2 egg yolks)*
    2 teaspoons country-style *Dijon* mustard

Preheat broiler to 350 degrees F.

In the *grease-free* mixer bowl of the electric mixer, combine egg white powder and *warm* water. Stir gently for several minutes until completely dissolved. Using the electric mixer fitted with *grease-free* beaters or by hand using a *grease-free* wire whisk, beat egg whites until stiff peaks form. Set aside briefly.

In a mixing bowl, combine pasteurized eggs and *Dijon* mustard. Using a wire whisk, combine thoroughly.

Add beaten egg whites. *Whisk-fold* egg whites *gently*, but *thoroughly*, into egg–mustard mixture.

Coat a 7-inch non-stick-coated omelet pan or skillet with non-stick lecithin spray coating. Set over *MEDIUM* heat. Add egg mixture, spreading it evenly across pan. Cook, *undisturbed*, for 1-2 minutes, or until set.

Wrap pan handle with aluminum foil, if necessary to protect it from burning. Place under preheated broiler until nicely browned. *Be careful not to scorch eggs!*

Slide out onto a heated serving plate.

Serve at once.

Yields 1 serving

Notes: *Salmonella*–negative pasteurized egg white powder is available in food specialty stores, in some grocery stores, and from mail order firms.

INDIVIDUAL FRENCH MUSTARD OMELET (cont'd)

**Because raw eggs present the danger of *Salmonella* poisoning, commercially-available pasteurized eggs are recommended for use in preparing this dish.

If you are preparing *several* omelets, it is most efficient to use *several* 7-inch skillets simultaneously since the omelets must be served immediately or they will deflate.

1 SERVING – PROTEIN = 18.6 g.; FAT = 0.8 g.; CARBOHYDRATE = 6.6 g.; CALORIES = 112; CALORIES FROM FAT = 6%

FRENCH VEGETABLE STEW IN THE STYLE OF PROVENCE
Ratatouille Parmesan

TPT - 1 hour and 20 minutes

Ratatouille appears on the menu of every chic bistro these days but it is, we believe an intensely personal concoction—a family dish and a picnic favorite, hot or cold. I love to make a double batch in a great kettle given to me by my grandmother. As I stand there carefully turning the vegetables over and over, I am connected to all of the great kettles and wooden spoons of the past and to the kitchen gardens of all my grandmothers.

2 tablespoons *extra virgin* olive oil
3 garlic cloves—*finely* chopped
2 medium onions—*thinly* sliced into rings

2 small *unpeeled* zucchini—cut into bite-sized chunks
1 small yellow summer squash, if available —*peeled* and cut into bite-sized chunks
2 medium eggplants—cut into bite-sized chunks
1/2 cup dry white wine*

2 medium green peppers—cut into strips
1 can (28 ounces) Italian-style *whole* plum tomatoes—*undrained***
3 tablespoons chopped, fresh Italian flat-leafed parsley
1 teaspoon dried basil—crushed
1/4 teaspoon dried thyme—crushed
1/2 teaspoon freshly ground black pepper, or to taste
1 small bay leaf—broken***

3/4 pound fresh mushrooms—trimmed, rinsed, cleaned well with a brush, and sliced

1/4 cup *thinly* sliced ripe, black olives, for garnish, if desired

Grated Parmesan *or pecorino Romano* cheese, as preferred

In a large kettle with cover, set over *MEDIUM* heat, heat olive oil. *Add finely* chopped garlic and onion rings. Sauté until onion is soft and translucent, *allowing neither the onion nor the garlic to brown.*

Add zucchini, yellow squash, and eggplant chunks. Sprinkle white wine over and toss *gently*, but *thoroughly.*

Add green pepper strips, *undrained* canned plum tomatoes, chopped fresh parsley, crushed basil and thyme, black pepper, and bay leaf pieces.*** Simmer over *LOW-MEDIUM* heat, covered, for 30 minutes. Remove cover and continue simmering for an additional 30 minutes, or until slightly thickened. Stir occasionally during the cooking period. Remove and discard bay leaf pieces.

Add mushroom slices and continue cooking for just a few minutes until the mushrooms are just heated through.

Garnish with sliced black olives before serving, if desired. Pass grated cheese to accommodate individual tastes.

Yields 10 servings
adequate for 6-8 people

Notes: *Sprinkling wine over the squash and eggplant generally keeps these vegetables firmer during the cooking process. Vinegar may also be used, if preferred, but 1/4 cupful white vinegar is sufficient.

FRENCH VEGETABLE STEW IN THE STYLE OF PROVENCE (cont'd)

**The equivalent in peeled, seeded, and chopped fresh tomatoes may be substituted, if desired, but this changes the texture and richness of the resultant sauce.

***The bay leaf pieces are most easily recovered if secured inside a tea ball during the simmering process.

If possible, prepare *ratatouille* several hours or even a day ahead since the taste actually improves. Store in an airtight container in the refrigerator, if not served immediately.

Although a bit unwieldy, this recipe may be doubled and since it freezes well, we find this to be a great convenience for menu planning. Vegetable textures do vary with freezing, but the result is still very good.

Served chilled, this is most pleasant on a stifling hot evening or when a chilled vegetable first course is in order.

Leftovers make a most complimentary sauce for an omelet.

1/10 SERVING (with olives and 2 teaspoonfuls Parmesan cheese) –
PROTEIN = 4.4 g.; FAT = 4.3 g.; CARBOHYDRATE = 12.1 g.;
CALORIES = 98; CALORIES FROM FAT = 39%

1/10 SERVING (without olives and grated cheese) –
PROTEIN = 3.2 g.; FAT = 2.7 g.; CARBOHYDRATE = 11.9 g.;
CALORIES = 80; CALORIES FROM FAT = 30%

RATATOUILLE WITH PUFF PASTRY "PILLOWS"
Ratatouille aux Pâté Feuilletée

TPT - 26 minutes

The freezer began to die during the hottest July week one could envision. There we were with a potential costly mess on our hands. I knew that the puff pastry in the freezer would not make it so it and a container of my ratatouille came out of the freezer and this was the result . . . and there were two less things in the freezer to worry about. The experiment that evening was very, very successful and we found another way to enjoy the ratatouille that we freeze each fall.

3 cups FRENCH VEGETABLE STEW IN THE STYLE OF PROVENCE (*Ratatouille Parmesan*) exclusive of the Parmesan topping —*defrosted* [see recipe which precedes]

1 sheet of *frozen* puff pastry—*defrosted*

1 tablespoon grated Parmesan cheese

Preheat oven to 400 degrees F. Prepare a cookie sheet by lining with culinary parchment paper.

Turn *ratatouille* into a saucepan set over *LOW-MEDIUM* heat. Allow to heat through, *stirring frequently to prevent the vegetables from sticking to the pan*. When heated through, set on a warming tray to keep warm. Also set a soup plate for each diner on the warming tray.

Unroll *puff* pastry onto a clean, dry surface, cut each sheet into three sections along fold lines. Cut each section crosswise into twelve 2- x 3 1/2-inch "pillows." Transfer to parchment-lined baking sheet. Bake in preheated 400 degree oven for 15 minutes, or until puffed and lightly browned. Remove to a serving plate.

Put a puffed pastry "pillow" into each heated soup plate. Ladle about 1/2 cupful *ratatouille* into the soup plate beside the pastry. Place another pastry "pillow" on top of the *ratatouille*.

Sprinkle 1/2 teaspoonful grated Parmesan cheese over each serving.

Serve at once. Pass additional grated cheese to accommodate individual tastes.

Yields 6 first-course servings
or 4 main-course offerings

Notes: *Although freshly prepared *ratatouille* can be served in this manner, I prefer the texture that results from freezing.

This recipe can be halved or doubled, when required.

Europe–France

RATATOUILLE WITH PUFF PASTRY "PILLOWS" (cont'd)

1/6 SERVING (with 1/2 teaspoonful grated cheese) –
PROTEIN = 5.1 g.; FAT = 12.7 g.; CARBOHYDRATE = 20.0 g.;
CALORIES = 216; CALORIES FROM FAT = 53%

VEGETARIAN NIÇOISE SALAD
Salade Niçoise Vegetarien

TPT - 41 minutes;
30 minutes = olive and potato flavoring period

The exciting fresh taste of the classic composed salad of Provence suffers not a bit when tuna and anchovies are omitted. After all it is the garlic and tomatoes which actually make it "niçoise."

3 tablespoons *extra virgin* olive oil

3 tablespoons MIXED FLOWER VINEGAR
   WITH OREGANO *[see index] or* other
   vinegar of choice
1 1/2 tablespoons freshly squeezed lemon juice
1/8 teaspoon freshly ground black pepper

20 pitted ripe, black olives
6 small new, unpeeled potatoes—cooked, *chilled*,
   and cut into 8 pieces each

1 small head Boston lettuce—well-washed and
   dried—torn into bite-sized pieces
2 cups whole small green beans—trimmed,
   crisp-cooked, and *chilled*
2 large tomatoes—cut into large pieces
1 medium onion—*thinly* sliced
1 small clove garlic—*very finely* chopped

4 hard-cooked eggs—*chilled*, peeled, and
   quartered
FRENCH COUNTRY HERB SEASONING
   MIXTURE *(Herbes de Provence) [see recipe
   which follows]*, **to taste**

In a cruet or bottle, combine oil, lemon juice, vinegar, and black pepper. Shake vigorously.

In a plastic container with a tight fitting lid, combine black olives and potato chunks. Pour prepared *vinaigrette* over. Seal tightly. Set aside for about 30 minutes, turning the container every 5 minutes to insure uniform marination.

Set a sieve over a measuring cup. Pour olives, potatoes, and the *vinaigrette* into the sieve. Allow to drain thoroughly. Pour drained *vinaigrette* into a cruet.

When ready to serve, combine lettuce, *chilled*, whole green beans, chopped tomato, onion slices, and *very finely* chopped garlic in a large salad bowl. Toss gently. Add olives and potatoes. Toss again.

Garnish with hard-cooked eggs wedges and a sprinkling of *herbes de Provence,* rubbed between your palms.

Serve at once into individual salad bowls or onto salad plates. Pass the cruet of *vinaigrette* for those who might wish to add more.

Yields 6 servings
adequate for 4-6 people

Notes: Leftovers do not keep well.

This recipe may be halved or doubled, when required.

1/6 SERVING (without added *vinaigrette*) –
PROTEIN = 6.9 g.; FAT = 14.1 g.; CARBOHYDRATE = 16.5 g.;
CALORIES = 219; CALORIES FROM FAT = 58%

FRENCH COUNTRY HERB SEASONING MIXTURE
Herbes de Provence

TPT - 2 minutes

The very special taste of Provence is an assertive blending of herbs that are used in both Italy and France. As if the border-crossing combination is not enough to confuse the palate, lavender blossoms are added to create that very special taste that doesn't say France; that doesn't say Italy; but does say Provence. If your dried herbs have been grown in your own herb garden, all the better!

FRENCH COUNTRY HERB SEASONING MIXTURE (cont'd)

1/2 teaspoon dried basil leaves—crushed
1/2 teaspoon dried marjoram leaves—crushed
1/2 teaspoon dried French tarragon leaves
  —crushed*
1/2 teaspoon dried thyme leaves—crushed**

1/4 teaspoon dried rosemary needles
1/4 teaspoon dried winter savory needles
1/4 teaspoon fennel seeds

1 teaspoon dried French lavender blossoms
  —crushed

In a small jelly jar or spice jar, combine crushed basil, marjoram, tarragon, and thyme.

In a SPICE and COFFEE GRINDER, or in a mortar, combine rosemary and winter savory needles with fennel seeds. Grind herbs into small pieces of uniform size.

Add dried lavender blossoms and grind to a uniform, but *not too fine*, mixture. Add to crushed herbs in spice jar.

Cover tightly and shake to mix thoroughly. Store in a cool, dark place.

Yields about 1 tablespoonful

Notes: *Use only French tarragon since the tarragon often labeled Russian tarragon and, unfortunately, sold in garden centers as tarragon, is exceedingly weak in flavor,

**We always include *a bit* of lemon thyme *(Thymus x citriodora)* in this mixture.

This recipe can be doubled, when required, but since the flavor dissipates considerably due to the release of the volatile oils with crushing, it is advisable to replace the seasoning combination after about 6 months.

FOOD VALUES for such herb mixtures are almost negligible.

FRENCH LENTILS AND SHALLOTS IN RED WINE AND TOMATO SAUCE
Lentilles et Éscalotes en Vin Rouge au Sauce Tomate

TPT - 2 hours;
1 hour = lentil soaking period
[slow cooker: 3-4 hours at LOW]

Early in our marriage I had a French recipe for lentils in red wine but over the years as typewritten recipes were put into the various computers we came to own, translated into the various computer programs of each, that old recipe was lost. This recipe from Auvergne, which unlike that which was lost has a tomato sauce base, is good and the addition of butter, also different from the original, gives it a smoothness that is compatible with so many other dishes. My mother-in-law had a rule against using butter with red wine but I do think she may have liked this dish.

I set this up in the slow cooker one day when I knew that I would be out for three or four hours. The aroma that greeted me as I came in the door was incredible. We made a salad, sliced the bread, and sat down to dinner.

3/4 cup dried, brown (*or* green) lentils
3 cups *boiling* water

2 teaspoons butter
2 teaspoons *extra virgin* olive oil
2 shallots—*finely* chopped
1/2 medium onion—*finely* chopped

6 tablespoons red wine

1/2 cup tomato sauce *or* tomato purée
3/4 cup VEGETABLE STOCK FROM SOUP
  [*see index*], VEGETARIAN BROWN STOCK
  [*see index*], *or* WILD MUSHROOM STOCK
  [*see index*]
1/2 teaspoon dried thyme—*crushed*
1/4 teaspoon freshly ground black pepper
1 large bay leaf—broken in half

2 teaspoons butter

Europe–**France**

**FRENCH LENTILS AND SHALLOTS
IN RED WINE AND TOMATO SAUCE** (cont'd)

Pick over lentils and discard any of poor quality. Rinse thoroughly. Drain. Pour into a mixing bowl and add the *boiling* water. Set aside at room temperature for 1 hour. Drain.

In a large *non-aluminum** kettle set over MEDIUM heat, combine the 2 teaspoonfuls each of butter and oil. Add *finely* chopped shallots and onion. Sauté until soft and transparent, *being careful not to allow either to brown.*

Add red wine and cook, stirring frequently, until most of wine has evaporated.

Add soaked and drained lentils, tomato sauce, vegetable stock, crushed thyme, black pepper, and broken bay leaf. Allow to come to the boil. *Reduce heat to LOW,* cover, and allow to simmer for 40 minutes, stirring occasionally. Remove cover. *Increase heat to MEDIUM* and continue cooking until most of liquid has evaporated. *Stir frequently to prevent the lentils from sticking to the bottom of the pan.*

Retrieve and discard bay leaf pieces.

Add the remaining 2 teaspoonfuls butter. Stir to integrate.

Turn into a heated serving bowl.

Serve hot.

Yields 6 servings
adequate for 4-6 people

Notes: *Since aluminum discolors lentils rather unpleasantly, avoid using aluminum cookware or serving bowls in this case.

This recipe can be doubled, when required.

1/6 SERVING – PROTEIN = 7.5 g.; FAT = 3.5 g.; CARBOHYDRATE = 19.2 g.;
CALORIES = 140; CALORIES FROM FAT = 23%

MASHED POTATOES WITH CHEESE AND GARLIC IN THE FRENCH STYLE

Aligot

TPT - 32 minutes

The first forkful of these potatoes is far from anybody's expectation when you describe them as mashed potatoes, even if you identify the dish more specifically as French-style mashed potatoes. This dish follows no rules you have learned about how to handle potatoes. These mashed potatoes are not made the same way, they do not plate the same way, and they do not taste the same. The result is divine, divine, divine, rich, rich, rich; the reason for this divinity is all in the chemistry.

When we Americans teach the preparation of mashed potatoes, we admonish that potatoes are mashed or riced, never beaten, and that the electric mixer and the food processor are to be avoided at all costs. Beating or whipping potatoes causes the release of the sticky starch amylose, which makes for pretty gruesome mashed potatoes and is the reason that ricing potatoes is preferable to the brutality of mashing. In the case of this French version the sticky, gooey amylose combined with uncoiling protein molecules of the sticky, runny mozzarella cheese is just what a cook in the Rouergue region of France is trying to achieve. Tomme fraîche de Cantal (Tome d'Aligot) is the mild, young cheese generally used for this dish. Mozzarella is the best substitute that I have found, a choice which also allows for the use of a low-fat cheese.

**3 quarts *boiling* water
2 pounds Yukon gold potatoes—peeled and
 diced**

**1/2 cup *hot two-percent* milk
3 tablespoons butter
2 garlic cloves—crushed and *finely* chopped**

**Salt, to taste
Freshly ground black pepper, to taste
1/2 pound *low-moisture, part-skimmed milk
 mozzarella* cheese—*shredded*
1/4 pound *Gruyère* cheese—*shredded***

Europe–**France**

**MASHED POTATOES WITH CHEESE AND GARLIC
IN THE FRENCH STYLE** (cont'd)

In a kettle set over *MEDIUM-HIGH* heat, cook potatoes in *boiling* water for about 20 minutes, or until tender. Drain. Turn into the work bowl of the food processor fitted with steel knife.

Add *hot* milk, butter, and *finely* chopped garlic. Process until smooth. Turn into a heavy saucepan set over *LOW-MEDIUM* heat. Using a wooden spoon, *stir vigorously* for several minutes.

Add salt and pepper, to taste, and *shredded* cheeses. Continue stirring *vigorously* until the mixture forms long stringy threads as it drops from the spoon. Add a bit more *hot* milk if the *aligot* is too stiff to handle. Turn into a heated serving bowl.

Serve at once with two serving spoons for ease.

Yields 10 servings
adequate for 6 people

Notes: When necessary, this recipe can be halved. Doubling creates too large a mixture for efficient spoon-stirring.

Leftovers can be refrigerated and reheated. Heat a little milk in a pan and then gradually beat the solidified potato mixture into the hot milk until the potatoes are heated through and the stringy consistency returns. Turn into a heated serving bowl and serve at once.

1/10 SERVING – PROTEIN = 17.6 g.; FAT = 15.0 g.; CARBOHYDRATE = 15.0 g.;
CALORIES = 264; CALORIES FROM FAT = 51%

FRENCH CELERIAC WITH CREAMY MUSTARD SAUCE
Celeri – Raves aux Sauce Moutarge a la Yogourt
TPT 26 minutes

Celeriac, also called knob celery or just plain celery root, is a big, ugly black root that looks rather intimidating the first time you adventure to purchase it. It looks like a big turnip root but has an intense celery taste with a firm, crisp root texture. When peeled and cooked this way, it is one of the best tasting vegetables in the world.

1 1/2 pounds celeriac (knob celery root)
  —2 medium—well-scrubbed, peeled to remove all dark portions, and cut into 1-inch cubes
1 tablespoon freshly squeezed lemon juice

2 tablespoons *calorie-reduced or light* **mayonnaise**
2 tablespoons PLAIN YOGURT *[see index]* **or commercially-available plain yogurt**
1 tablespoon *Dijon* **mustard***
Freshly ground *white* **pepper, to taste**

Cut well-scrubbed and peeled celeriac into 1-inch chunks and place in a saucepan. Cover with water and add lemon juice. Set over *MEDIUM-HIGH* heat and bring to the boil. Reduce heat to maintain a gentle simmer and cook, covered, for 15 minutes, or until tender. Drain.

In a small bowl, using a wire whisk, combine mayonnaise, yogurt, mustard, and *white* pepper.

Europe–**France**

FRENCH CELERIAC WITH CREAMY MUSTARD SAUCE (cont'd)

Put cooked knob celery into a clean saucepan set over *LOW* heat. Add prepared mustard–yogurt sauce and *gently*, but *thoroughly*, fold the sauce into the celeriac to coat evenly. Cook, stirring constantly, only until heated through. Turn into a heated serving bowl.

Serve at once.

Yields 6 servings
adequate for 4 people

Notes: *Use any variety of *Dijon* mustard you prefer, except country-style. The texture of country-style is too coarse for this sauce.

This recipe may be halved or doubled, when required.

1/6 SERVING – PROTEIN = 1.0 g.; FAT = 1.8 g.; CARBOHYDRATE = 4.9 g.;
CALORIES = 37; CALORIES FROM FAT = 44%

COFFEE CUSTARDS
Petits Pots de Crème au Café

TPT - 2 hours;
1 hour = chilling period

Such stove-top or baked custards are often offered in cafes and restaurants to end a meal, here and in France, and can be very, very rich. This version, sans cream and egg yolks, makes these petit treasures everyday fare. If desired, a drop or two of hazelnut flavoring, sold to flavor coffees, can be added to enhance.

1 1/2 cups *whole* milk
4 teaspoons freeze-dried coffee granules
1/4 cup sugar

3/4 cup *fat-free* pasteurized eggs (the equivalent of 3 eggs)
1/2 teaspoon pure vanilla extract

Whipped heavy cream, for garnish, if desired
Grated semi-sweet chocolate, for garnish, if desired

Preheat oven to 300 degrees F. Prepare four 3-inch oven-proof ramekins or French *crème* pots, if available, by coating with non-stick lecithin spray coating.

In a saucepan set over *LOW* heat, combine milk, coffee granules, and sugar. While stirring frequently with a wire whisk, heat until bubbles form at the edge.

Meanwhile, in a mixing bowl, using a wire whisk, combine pasteurized eggs and vanilla extract. Mix well. *Gradually*—tablespoonful by tablespoonful—whisk hot milk mixture into beaten eggs.

Apportion egg–milk mixture among the four oven-proof ramekins or French *crème* pots. Skim all bubbles from surface. Cover each with a small piece of aluminum foil.

Set in a baking pan in which a 1-inch water bath has been prepared. Bake in preheated 300 degree F. oven for about 45 minutes, or until a knife inserted into the center comes out clean. *Do not allow water bath to simmer or boil,* by adding cold water or ice cubes, if necessary.

Refrigerate for at least 1 hour.

Serve garnished with whipped cream and grated chocolate, if desired.

Yields 4 individual servings

Note: This recipe is easily doubled or halved, when required.

1/4 SERVING (without garnish of whipped cream or grated chocolate) –
PROTEIN = 7.1 g.; FAT = 2.9 g.; CARBOHYDRATE = 20.0 g.;
CALORIES = 137; CALORIES FROM FAT = 19%

Europe–**Germany**

Germany

The name Germany evolved from the Latin word Germania, the name which came into used as early as 100 AD to designate the peoples east of the Rhine all the way to the Ural Mountains. It is believed that tribes, now referenced as Germanic, occupied this area during the Nordic Bronze Age, having spread from the North to the region occupied by the Celtic tribes of Gaul in the first century AD. A German king was crowned Holy Roman Emperor in 962, during the period of the reign of the Ottonian emperors (919-1024). Northern Italy and Burgundy were absorbed into the Holy Roman Empire during the reign of the Salian emperors (1024-1125). The German princes increased their influence under the Hohensaufen emperors (1138-1254), expanding south and east into Slavic regions. By the fifteenth century the Hapsburg dynasty of Austria had gained strong political control. With the Protestant Reformation, led by the monk Martin Luther, and the subsequent religious conflicts which led to the Thirty Years' War, beginning in 1618, Germany was a very changed country. German lands had been devastated, the population was diminished by one-third, and the empire had been reduced to independent principalities. The Kingdom of Prussia and the Austrian monarchy dominated from about 1740 to 1806, until the Napoleonic Wars. With the fall of Napoléon Bonaparte, a German Confederation, *Deutscher Bund*, was formed by the Congress of Vienna but it was not until 1871, at the end of the Franco–Prussian War, that German lands, with the exception of Austria, were reunified to form the German Empire, the precursor of the modern nation of Germany.

Germany's imperialism continued as they too entered the race to colonize Africa, creating German East Africa which included what is now Burundi, Rwanda, and Tanganyika, the mainland portion of present-day Tanzania; German South-West Africa which became Namibia; Kamaroon which became Cameroon; and Togoland which is now the Volta Region District of Ghana. Defeated in World War I as the leader of the Central Powers in 1919 and in World War II as the leader of the Axis Powers in 1945, Germany found the Fatherland again divided, partitioned this time by the Allies into four military occupation zones. The western sectors controlled by France, the United Kingdom, and the United States merged in 1949 to form the Federal Republic of Germany, or West Germany; the Soviet Zone became the socialist German Democratic Republic, or East Germany.

As a result, East German cuisine in the 1950s and 1960s began to more strongly reflect the influences of Russia, Hungary, and Bulgaria to the East. The lack of food supplies and the cost of what might be considered German staples during the period of the divided Germany led to the development of recipes that almost could not be recognized as German. In the summer of 1989, with the fall of the Berlin Wall, built in 1961 and a symbol of the Cold War, Germany reunified and the flow of culture and prosperity has almost completely obliterated the "East German Cuisine" of the Cold War period.

My German-born maternal grandmother adapted that which she had been taught by her Berlin-born mother and father to the tastes and traditions of my grandfather who was of English, Irish, and Scottish descent. My paternal grandfather's Munchen-born mother remarried a man of English descent and grandpa married my grandmother who was second generation Irish. The German food traditions were very hard to find as my family joined the American melting pot. Living in upstate New York, with the long winters, did, however, preserve the shared dependence on root crops, dried legumes, noodles, dumplings, hearty breads and *kuchens*, preserved meats, pickles, and cheeses.

Europe – **Germany**

Celery, Celeriac, and Radish Salad
Selleriesalat aus Rettich

~

Cream of Asparagus Soup
Spargelsuppe

Cream of Mushroom Soup with Dumplings
Champignonsuppe

~

Mom's German Potato Salad
Kartoffelsalat

Hot German Potato Salad
Warmer Kartoffelsalat

**Wilted Red Lettuce Salad with Strawberries
and Smoked Gouda Cheese**
Veraeklter Kopfsalat mit Erdbeere und Kase

~~~~~~~~~~~~~~~~~~~~

Baked Lentils with Cheese
Linsen mit Kase

Breaded Forest Mushrooms
Steinpilze Forsterinart

German Carrots with Ginger, Lemon, and Dill
Mohrruben mit Ingwer

or

Steamed and Buttered Red Cabbage Wedges

Raisin Pumpernickel Bread
Schwarzbrot

~~~~~~~~~~~~~~~~~~~~

Eggnog Bavarian
Bayerische Crème

Stewed Rhubarb with Farina
Rhabarbergriess

Blue Plum Streusel Tart	**German Christmas Bread**
Zwetschgenkuchen	*Stollen*

VOLUME I - 142

Europe–**Germany**

CELERY, CELERIAC, AND RADISH SALAD
Selleriesalat aus Rettich

TPT - 6 minutes

In the winter, absent fresh greens from the garden, I find refreshing vegetable combinations like this really do not say winter salad even if it is January. This salad, served as a salad or as an appetizer in Germany, seems to delight the taste buds and it goes with just about every menu. Although any vinegar could be used to the make the vinaigrette, I do choose from the variety of herb vinegars that were made during our last gardening season to give just another layer of flavor; my grandmother and mother would prefer apple cider vinegar.

Germans are far more fond of the ugly knob celery known as celeriac or celery root than are those of us on this side of the Atlantic. Even in highly German areas of Pennsylvania it is often difficult to find. Delicious in salads and soup, it is worth seeking out.

2 tablespoons safflower *or* sunflower oil
2 tablespoons **LOVAGE–CHIVE VINEGAR** *[see index]*,* **GARLIC–BASIL VINEGAR** *[see index]*, **MIXED FLOWER VINEGAR WITH OREGANO** *[see index]*, *or* other herb vinegar of choice
1/2 teaspoon **MUSTARD SAUCE** *[see index]*
Tiny pinch celery seeds
Freshly ground black pepper, to taste

2 large inner ribs of celery—*very thinly* cut into *half-moon* slices
1/2 of a medium sized celeriac (celery root)—peeled and sliced into *matchstick* pieces
3 large radishes—well-scrubbed, trimmed, sliced into thin round slices, and then cut into *matchstick* pieces
3 tablespoons chopped fresh celery leaves—well-washed and well-dried
1 1/2 teaspoons chopped fresh dillweed

In a cruet, combine oil, vinegar, mustard, celery seeds, and black pepper. Shake vigorously and set aside briefly.

When ready to serve, combine celery half-moon slices with celeriac and radish matchsticks in a serving bowl. Pour *vinaigrette* over and toss to coat vegetables.

Garnish with chopped celery leaves and dillweed

Serve at once.

Yields 6 servings
adequate for 4 people

Notes: *Choosing **LOVAGE–CHIVE VINEGAR** for this salad gives another layer of celery taste to a complex celery mélange.

This recipe can be halved or doubled, when required.

1/6 SERVING – PROTEIN = 0.5 g.; FAT = 4.5 g.; CARBOHYDRATE = 1.9 g.;
CALORIES = 50; CALORIES FROM FAT = 81%

GERMAN CREAM OF ASPARAGUS SOUP
Spargelsuppe

TPT - about 2 hours

Having several fields of asparagus was a great advantage to a man who had several daughters since a field of asparagus was so valued in ancient times that it could be come part of a woman's dowry. Germans love asparagus especially the white, bleached variety but this soup is most beautiful when green asparagus is used. To intensify the color I add some fresh spinach. I figure if I am going to the trouble to make a batch of soup, I might just as well make a big one. The base for this soup can be easily frozen which is a great convenience for holiday meals or when we just say to friends, "Come over for supper. I just made a kettle of soup." The trimmings from the asparagus go into the freezer in the soup stock bag and add flavor to the next batch . . . waste not, want not.

Excavations in Germany have proven that hazelnuts have been a part of the cuisine for at least 10,000 years. Since hazelnuts do compliment the taste of asparagus, I toast a few hazelnuts and chop them in my spice and coffee grinder to garnish this really beautiful soup.

Europe–**Germany**

GERMAN CREAM OF ASPARAGUS SOUP (cont'd)

About 1 pound fresh asparagus spears, to yield about 6 cupfuls when trimmed and coarsely chopped

1/4 cup chopped fresh spinach
2 large shallot cloves—coarsely chopped
6 cups water
1/2 teaspoon salt
1/2 teaspoon freshly ground black pepper

1 quart *boiling* water
3 medium potatoes—peeled and diced

1 tablespoon butter
1 cup light cream *or* half and half

Chopped, *toasted, preservative-free* hazelnuts, for garnish
6 asparagus spear tips with flowers—well-washed—for garnish

Break the ends from each asparagus spear and place both the spear and tough trimmed base in a sinkful of cold water. Slosh the asparagus spears around moving your fingers up and down the spears to release any sand that may be trapped. Rinse the trimmed bases of the asparagus, drain them well, and freeze them in your stock bag. Rinse the spears one more time in a fresh sinkful of water. Drain. Chop the asparagus spears to yield about 6 cupfuls. Transfer to a kettle set over *MEDIUM-HIGH* heat.

Add chopped fresh spinach and shallots, 6 cupfuls water, salt, and black pepper. Bring to the boil. Reduce heat to *LOW-MEDIUM* and cook for 1 hour, stirring occasionally. Set aside to cool.

In a large saucepan, cook diced potato in the 1 quart *boiling* water for 20 minutes, or until soft. Drain.

Using the electric blender or the food processor fitted with steel knife, purée broccoli mixture with cooked potatoes in small batches. Turn into a sieve, a *chinoise* sieve if available, and press through.* Discard residue or reserve for stock pot.

In a large saucepan set over *LOW-MEDIUM* heat, heat asparagus–potato purée. Add butter. Gradually whisk in cream. Taste and adjust seasoning, if necessary. Cook, stirring frequently, until heated through. Turn into a heated soup tureen.

Serve into heated soup plates. Garnish with a sprinkling of hazelnut meal and an asparagus tip.

Yields about 6 cupfuls

Notes: *This purée may be frozen in batches convenient to your menu plans at this point. Defrost completely before proceeding.

This recipe can be halved or doubled, when required.

1/8 SERVING (i. e., per cupful) –
PROTEIN = 3.4 g.; FAT = 5.8 g.; CARBOHYDRATE = 14.8 g.;
CALORIES = 123; CALORIES FROM FAT = 42%

GERMAN CREAM OF MUSHROOM SOUP
Champignonsuppe

TPT - 3 hours and 21 minutes;
2 hours rehydration period

My paternal great-grandmother, who emigrated to the United States in her teens and whom I unfortunately never knew, was born in Munchen, Germany, just a four-hour drive today from one of the most incredible sources of mushrooms in the world, the Black Forest region of Germany. Hunting and gathering chanterelle mushrooms in the Black Forest region of Germany is a family event but seeking out fresh chanterelles today takes more that hunter-gather skills. I have found only one grocery, some thirty-five miles from our home that occasionally has a supply. Chanterelles are expensive and highly perishable and since I can never bet on an available supply when I want to make this soup, I more often than not use dried chanterelles. No other mushroom gives the intense, perfect flavor I want in this soup.

1 cup *dried chanterelle* mushrooms—rinsed well*
1 cup *dried crimini or* portobello mushrooms —well-rinsed
1 quart *boiling* water

2 tablespoons butter
1 tablespoon GARLIC OIL *[see index]*
1 medium onion—chopped
2 large shallot cloves—chopped

2 tablespoons unbleached white flour
[see next page]

Europe–Germany

GERMAN CREAM OF MUSHROOM SOUP (cont'd)

5 cups VEGETARIAN DARK STOCK *[see index]*
   or **VEGETABLE STOCK FROM SOUP** *[see index]*
1/2 cup WILD MUSHROOM STOCK *[see index]*

1 bay leaf—broken
1/4 teaspoon salt
1/4 teaspoon freshly ground black pepper
Pinch freshly grated nutmeg

1 cup light cream *or* **half and half**
1 teaspoon freshly squeezed lemon juice

Put well-rinsed, dried mushrooms into a mixing bowl. Pour *boiling* water over. Place a saucer on top to weigh down the mushrooms and keep them in contact with the water. Allow to rehydrate for about 2 hours. Drain, *but reserve mushroom stock.***

In a kettle set over *MEDIUM* heat, melt butter. Add garlic oil, chopped onion, and chopped shallots. Sauté until soft and translucent, *being careful not to allow onions to brown.*

Add flour and, using a wooden spoon, make a *roux* by beating flour into the onion–shallot mixture in the kettle. Cook for 2 minutes, stirring constantly. *Be careful not to burn or overbrown the roux.* Remove from heat and gradually beat in the 5 1/2 cupfuls of stock. Return saucepan to heat.

Add rehydrated mushrooms, bay leaf pieces, salt, black pepper, and grated nutmeg. Cook, stirring frequently, for about 40 minutes. Remove and discard bay leaf pieces.

Using the electric blender or the food processor fitted with steel knife, purée mushroom mixture with cooked potatoes in small batches. Turn into sieve, a *chinoise* sieve if available, and press through. Discard residue or reserve for stock pot. Pour puréed soup into a large saucepan. Set over *LOW-MEDIUM* heat.

Add cream and lemon juice. Heat, stirring frequently with a wire whisk, until soup is heated through. Turn into a heated tureen.

Serve into heated soup plates.

Yields about 6 cupfuls

Notes: *If fresh *chanterelles* come to hand, combine them with fresh *crimini* mushrooms to make this soup.

**Freeze leftover mushroom soaking water and use in soups and stews.

This recipe can be halved, when required.

1/6 SERVING (i. e., per cupful) –
PROTEIN = 1.7 g.; FAT = 9.4 g.; CARBOHYDRATE = 4.1 g.;
CALORIES = 109; CALORIES FROM FAT = 76%

MOM'S GERMAN POTATO SALAD
Kartoffelsalat

TPT -   2 hours and 40 minutes;
         2 hours = marination and cooling period

This is my mom's version of the "family potato salad," no doubt derived from that brought to America in the 1880s by my German great-grandmother. I never saw her recipe box, so I do not know for sure, but I do remember seeing the bones of this recipe in a ledger book in which my grandmother kept recipes and clippings of recipes she intended to try. It is still my favorite potato salad recipe and the memories it evokes may be part of the reason it remains the favorite — still, it just tastes good and sprinkling apple cider vinegar, salt, and pepper on the hot potato chunks is the secret!! My addition to it is the edible garnish of dillweed flowers.

6 medium all-purpose potatoes *(not Idaho)*
   —preferably Red Bliss, if available—
   well-scrubbed, but *unpeeled*
3 quarts *boiling* **water**

2 tablespoons apple cider vinegar
Salt, to taste
Freshly ground black pepper, to taste

1 large celery rib—diced
1 medium dill pickle—diced
3 medium red radishes—sliced
3 tablespoon chopped Italian red onion
2 tablespoons *calorie-reduced or light* **mayonnaise**

6 large red lettuce leaves

1 hard-cooked egg—sliced crosswise
Paprika, for garnish
6 fresh, *well-rinsed* **dillweed flowers, if in season, for garnish**

MOM'S GERMAN POTATO SALAD (cont'd)

Cook whole potatoes in *boiling* water until *firm-tender* —about 20-25 minutes. *(They will yield to a fork, but not crumble.)* Remove skins while still hot. Cut into chunks and place in a large mixing bowl.

Sprinkle *hot* potato chunks with cider vinegar, salt, and black pepper. Toss *very gently*. Refrigerate for 2 hours. Turn potatoes occasionally to insure uniform distribution of the vinegar.

Add diced celery and pickle, sliced red radish, and chopped onion. Toss *very gently*. Fold in mayonnaise, again *very gently*.

Line serving bowl with lettuce leaves. Spoon potato salad into the center. Garnish with egg slices, paprika, and dillweed blossoms before serving.

Yields 6 servings
adequate for 4 people

Note: This recipe may be doubled or tripled, when required.

1/6 SERVING – PROTEIN = 3.4 g.; FAT = 1.9 g.; CARBOHYDRATE = 25.6 g.;
CALORIES = 132; CALORIES FROM FAT = 13%

HOT GERMAN POTATO SALAD
Warmer Kartoffelsalat
TPT - about 56 minutes

Remembering the taste of hot German potato salad as a child, but naturally not wanting the bacon and the bacon "drippings" with which is was always made, I was determined to recreate the relative taste in a vegetarian version without resorting to soy bacon bits with all their dubious additives. This is the result.

5 medium all-purpose potatoes *(not Idaho)*
—well-scrubbed, but *unpeeled*
3 quarts *boiling* **water**

2 tablespoons safflower oil *or* **other light vegetable oil**
1/4 cup chopped onion

1 tablespoon whole wheat flour
1 teaspoon sugar
1/2 teaspoon freshly ground black pepper
1/4 teaspoon celery seed
1/8 teaspoon dry mustard
5 tablespoons water
3 tablespoons red wine vinegar

1 tablespoon chopped fresh chives
1 tablespoon chopped fresh parsley

Cook whole potatoes in *boiling* water until *firm-tender* —about 20-25 minutes. (They will yield to a fork but not crumble.) Remove skins while still hot. Slice crosswise. Place slices in a serving dish, skillet, or even a *paella* pan and keep warm either on a warming tray or in a warm oven.

Meanwhile, in a skillet set over *LOW-MEDIUM* heat, heat oil with chopped onion. Sauté, stirring constantly, until onion is soft and translucent, *being careful not to allow onion to brown.*

Add flour, sugar, black pepper, celery seed, and dry mustard. Stir to combine well. Cook, again stirring constantly, for a minute or two until a *roux* forms. Gradually add water and vinegar. Continue stirring until sauce boils and thickens. Adjust consistency with a bit more water, if necessary. Spoon sauce evenly over warm potato slices.

Garnish with chopped chives and parsley.

Serve at once.

Yields 6 servings
adequate for 4 people

Notes: This recipe may be doubled or tripled, when required.

Hard-cooked egg wedges may be used for garnish if appropriate to your menu.

1/6 SERVING – PROTEIN = 1.6 g.; FAT = 3.8 g.; CARBOHYDRATE = 16.9 g.;
CALORIES = 109; CALORIES FROM FAT = 31%

Europe–Germany

WILTED RED LETTUCE SALAD WITH STRAWBERRIES AND SMOKED *GOUDA* CHEESE
Verwelkter Kopfsalat mit Erdbeere und Käse
TPT - 10 minutes

Because my vegetarian wilted lettuce salad, evolved from that of my great-grandmother, grandmother, and mother, lacks the smoky taste that bacon gives classic German wilted lettuce salads, I began to play with the idea that smoked Gouda cheese might add that certain touch. This recipe is the result of that experimentation. It is unusual and very good indeed.

15-20 large red–tipped lettuce leaves—well-washed and dried
1 cup halved fresh strawberries—about 16 large— well-washed and dried before hulling
2 teaspoons sugar
Freshly ground black pepper, to taste

3 tablespoons sunflower oil *or* **other light vegetable oil**
1 garlic clove—smashed
3 tablespoons apple cider vinegar

1 ounce *smoked Gouda* **cheese—cut into julienned slices**

Break leaves into bite-sized pieces, discarding tough vein areas. Turn into warmed serving bowl. Add halved strawberries, sugar, and black pepper. Toss thoroughly.

In a small skillet or saucepan set over *MEDIUM-HIGH* heat, heat oil and smashed garlic clove. Sauté clove in oil for about 3 minutes. Remove clove and discard. Add vinegar and continue heating. When *very hot,* pour over lettuce mixture and toss until wilted.

Sprinkle julienned cheese over.

Serve at once, using a large slotted spoon and large meat fork as utensils. *(1/4 cupful of oil–cider vinegar dressing should be residual in serving dish.)*

Yields 6 servings
adequate for 4 people

1/6 SERVING – PROTEIN = 1.6 g.; FAT = 4.1 g.; CARBOHYDRATE = 3.5 g.;
CALORIES = 56; CALORIES FROM FAT = 66%

GERMAN BAKED LENTILS WITH CHEESE
Linsen mit Käse
TPT - about 2 hours

This wonderfully convenient, versatile, nutrition-packed casserole is a great menu maker when you have out-of-town guests. It can be prepared the night before or early in the day and baked, perhaps with some biscuits, while you are preparing the salad and dessert. If your guests are vegan, the cheese can be omitted or served as a table garnish.

2/3 cup dry, brown (*or* **green) lentils**
3 cups VEGETARIAN BROWN STOCK *[see index]* **or other vegetarian stock of choice**
1 bay leaf—halved*

1 tablespoon safflower *or* **sunflower oil**
1 large onion—*finely* **chopped**
1 garlic clove—*finely* **chopped**

1 large carrot—*thinly* **sliced**
1/4 cup *thinly* **sliced celery**
1/4 cup chopped green pepper
1 cup canned, *diced* **tomatoes—well-drained— or 1 large tomato—peeled, seeded, and chopped**
1 tablespoon tomato paste
1/4 teaspoon freshly ground black pepper
1/8 teaspoon dried thyme—crushed
1/8 teaspoon ground sage
Pinch ground marjoram

1 cup shredded (about 4 ounces) *sharp* **Cheddar cheese**

GERMAN BAKED LENTILS WITH CHEESE (cont'd)

Prepare a 9-inch ceramic quiche dish, pie plate, or shallow non-aluminum baking pan by coating with non-stick lecithin spray coating.**

Sort lentils and discard those of poor quality. Rinse thoroughly.

In a non-aluminum saucepan** set over *MEDIUM* heat, combine lentils, stock, and bay leaf pieces. Bring to the boil. Reduce heat to *LOW*, cover tightly, and simmer for about 30 minutes, or until lentils are tender. Drain, reserving liquid for soup stock and discarding bay leaf pieces.

In a skillet set over *LOW-MEDIUM* heat, combine oil, *finely* chopped onion and garlic. Sauté until soft and translucent, *allowing neither the onion nor the garlic to brown.*

Preheat oven to 325 degrees F.

Add sautéed onion and garlic to cooked lentils with sliced carrot and celery, chopped green pepper and tomatoes, tomato paste, black pepper, crushed thyme, and ground sage and marjoram. Mix *gently*, but *thoroughly*.

Turn into prepared baking dish. Cover tightly with aluminum foil.*** Bake in preheated 325 degree F. oven for 50 minutes, or until vegetables are tender.

Remove from oven and uncover. Sprinkle shredded cheese evenly over baked lentils. Return to oven and bake until cheese melts and *just begins to brown*—about 5-8 minutes.

Serve at once, directly from baking dish.

Yields 6 servings
adequate for 4 people

Notes: *The bay leaf pieces are most easily recovered if secured inside a tea ball during the simmering process.

**Since aluminum discolors lentils rather unpleasantly, avoid the use of aluminum cookware or serving bowls in this case.

***This dish may be prepared in advance to this point and refrigerated until about an hour before serving time.

This recipe may be doubled or tripled with ease. Bake in a large *au gratin* or baking dish. In such quantity, this makes a fine buffet table presentation. It is also easily halved, when required.

1/6 SERVING – PROTEIN = 12.3 g.; FAT = 8.3 g.; CARBOHYDRATE = 22.5 g.;
CALORIES = 208; CALORIES FROM FAT = 36%

BREADED FOREST MUSHROOMS IN THE GERMAN STYLE
Steinpilze Försterinart
TPT - 18 minutes

My great-grandmother and grandmother taught my mother and me how to choose among the puffball fungi that would from time to time appear in our unsprayed backyard. We would slice and fry them in butter and smile at each other with every delicious mouthful. Puffballs are not poisonous and do not have any poisonous look-alikes so, other than sprays and fertilizers that might be present, teaching an eight-year-old how to gather puffballs is a pretty safe lesson. My dad, however, never learned to trust the "puffball harvesters," having saved his whole family during a meal in which poisonous mushrooms were consumed by everyone except himself. German cooks search for the perfect puffballs and remember an area where they have seen collapsed puffballs, knowing that the spores that were dispersed will produce another harvest with the next extended wet period. They also treasure "Laetiporus sulphureus," know as chicken-of-the-woods. When you can find a very young, spongy specimen of it in the woods, it is a joy, but unfortunately you usually find hard, dry brackets that are of little culinary value. Puffball slices can provide the large meaty slices that would suggest more closely the traditional German preparation of chicken-of-the-woods and can also be prepared using the following recipe.

Since chicken-of-the-woods mushrooms are not sold in stores and I can not really encourage the gathering of mushrooms to the novice without concern, I have adapted the German breading to be used with other mushrooms, which are readily available in grocery stores. You may have to search to find the large clumps or trees of oyster mushroom or for a large "hen-of-the-woods" or maitake, which is not a bracket fungus but instead a polypore mushroom valued in Asia for its medicinal properties, but it is worth the search. They make a beautiful and conversation provoking presentation.

BREADED FOREST MUSHROOMS IN THE GERMAN STYLE (cont'd)

3 tablespoons unbleached white flour

2 egg whites—*beaten*

1/2 cup *fresh* breadcrumbs
1/8 teaspoon freshly ground black pepper, or to taste

Oil for deep-frying

2 large "oyster mushroom trees" *or* 2 or 3 large "hen-of the woods" *or* maitake mushrooms
—well-rinsed to remove any residual dirt

12 *toasted, preservative-free* walnut halves, for garnish
Garlic chive blades, if available, for garnish

Garlic mayonnaise

Arrange three soup plates in a row. In one, put flour; in a second, put *beaten* egg whites; in a third, combine breadcrumbs and black pepper.

Pour oil into a deep saucepan to a depth of about 2 inches. Attach a candy/deep-fry thermometer. Place over *MEDIUM-HIGH* heat and allow to come to about 375 degrees F.

When oil has reached frying temperature, roll the mushroom clumps/trees in flour, then in the beaten egg whites, and then in breadcrumbs. Put mushrooms into the hot oil and fry, *carefully* turning with a large meat fork to insure that all sides of the breaded mushroom is crisp and browned. Transfer to paper toweling to drain *briefly*. Transfer to a serving plate.

Garnish with *toasted* walnut halves and a few garlic chive blades.

Serve hot with garlic mayonnaise.

Yields 6 servings
adequate for four people

Note: This recipe can be halved or doubled, when required.

1/6 SERVING – PROTEIN = 2.5 g.; FAT = 6.2 g.; CARBOHYDRATE = 5.8 g.;
CALORIES = 90; CALORIES FROM FAT = 62%

GERMAN CARROTS WITH GINGER, LEMON, AND DILL
Mohrrüben mit Ingwer
TPT - 18 minutes

Ground ginger and sugar would more often be used to prepare this classic dish. Ginger preserves, however, lend texture and a beautiful glaze in addition to the sweet spice taste.

1 tablespoon butter
1 tablespoon freshly squeezed lemon juice
1 tablespoon water
30 Belgian baby carrots (approximately 3 cups), all about the same size—pared or scraped*

2 tablespoons ginger preserves**
Freshly ground black pepper, to taste

1 teaspoon chopped fresh dillweed

In a skillet set over *LOW-MEDIUM* heat, melt butter. Add lemon juice, water, and carrots. Cover and cook carrots until *crisp-tender*—about 12 minutes. Stir frequently.

Add ginger preserves and black pepper. Cook, stirring frequently, for 3-4 minutes, or until preserves are melted and carrots are glazed.

Turn into a heated serving bowl. Spoon ginger sauce over carrots.

Serve at once, garnished with chopped dillweed.

Yields 5 servings

Notes: *If you find that Belgian baby carrots are unavailable in your market, carve substitutes from large carrots. Reserve trimmings for soup stock.

GERMAN CARROTS WITH GINGER, LEMON, AND DILL (cont'd)

**Excellent ginger preserves, made from fresh gingerroot and not simply flavored with ginger, can be found in food specialty stores, gift shops, and gourmet sections of many grocery stores.

This recipe is easily halved or doubled, when required.

1/5 SERVING – PROTEIN = 1.3 g.; FAT = 2.5 g.; CARBOHYDRATE = 15.7 g.; CALORIES = 71; CALORIES FROM FAT = 32%

(BREAD MACHINE) GERMAN RAISIN PUMPERNICKEL BREAD
Schwarzbrot

TPT - 3 hours;
  2 hours = automated machine preparation period;
  50 minutes = loaf rising period

... subtlety flavored with molasses, cocoa, and coffee, but even if you are not into subtle flavoring, this is very, very satisfying. The Westphalian origins of "Schwarzbrot" are all but forgotten by Americans who have taken this German black bread to their hearts and called it their own. The pumpernickel expert in our family, for whom this was evolved, said he liked the caraway variation best.

1/2 cup *preservative-free dark* raisins
1/2 cup *boiling* water

1 cup plus 2 tablespoons water
1 1/2 tablespoons *unsulfured* molasses
1 1/2 tablespoons apple cider vinegar
2 tablespoons butter
2 tablespoons Dutch-processed *unsweetened* cocoa powder
1 tablespoon freeze-dried coffee granules

1 tablespoon (1 envelope) *preservative-free* active dried yeast*
1 tablespoon sugar
1 1/2 cups bread flour
1 1/2 cups medium rye flour
1/3 cup medium ground corn meal
1/2 teaspoon salt

In a small bowl, combine raisins and *boiling* water. Set aside and allow raisins to rehydrate.

Bring remaining ingredients to room temperature.

In a saucepan set over *LOW* heat, combine water, molasses, vinegar, butter, *unsweetened* cocoa powder, and coffee granules. Cook, stirring frequently, until chocolate and butter melt and the temperature of the liquid is 105 degrees F.

In the BREAD MACHINE pan, combine yeast, sugar, bread and rye flours, corn meal, and salt. Add liquid ingredients at 105 degrees F.

Select MANUAL SETTING and push START.

Drain rehydrated raisins *well*. Set aside.

After 2 hours, when the automated preparation period is over, remove dough to a floured surface, add rehydrated raisins, and knead until smooth and all trace of stickiness is gone. Form into one round loaf. Place on a cookie sheet or baking tile and cover with a cotton tea towel. Allow to rise in a warm, draft-free kitchen until doubled in volume—about 50 minutes.

Preheat oven to 350 degrees F.

Bake in preheated oven for about 40-45 minutes. Allow to cool completely on a wire rack before slicing and serving.

Yields 1 round loaf

Notes: *Some packaged dried yeast available in grocery stores contain a preservative. Natural food stores carry an additive-free dried yeast. In addition, *do not use so-called fast action yeasts*. The results will not please you.

Two teaspoonfuls caraway seeds can be substituted for raisins. (BREAD MACHINE) GERMAN PUMPERNICKEL BREAD WITH CARAWAY SEEDS is also excellent, although less moist and less sweet.

This bread freezes well.

1/16 SERVING (i. e., per slice) –
PROTEIN = 3.1 g.; FAT = 1.9 g.; CARBOHYDRATE = 26.2 g.;
CALORIES = 134; CALORIES FROM FAT = 13%

Europe–Germany

EGGNOG BAVARIAN
Bayerische Crème

TPT - 9 hours;
30 minutes = first gelling period;
8 hours = final setting period

My first "Eggnog Bavarian" was made back in the early 1970s from egg yolks and a mountainous egg white meringue gently stiffened with gelatin. Actually, I do remember the very first test of the recipe because the mixture was "too gently" stiffened and, when unmolded, gradually gave way and spread unceremoniously across the serving plate. My dad went to the refrigerator often that Christmas Day with a spoon and kept reassuring me that it tasted good, despite the unsightly appearance. We did not make this recipe for many years because of the increasing concern about Salmonella poisoning, raw eggs being a principle source. The recipe was finally reworked using pasteurized eggs and whipped cream. It is served every Christmas in our house.

1 cup *fat-free* pasteurized eggs (the equivalent of 4 eggs)*
5 tablespoons sugar
2 teaspoons pure vanilla extract
3 cups skimmed milk

1 cup *cold* skimmed milk
4 tablespoons (4 envelopes) unflavored gelatin**

1 cup heavy whipping cream

Freshly grated nutmeg, for garnish
Semi-sweet chocolate, for garnish

Prepare a 2-quart mold by lightly oiling. Place in the freezer until required.

In a large mixing bowl, combine pasteurized eggs, sugar, and vanilla extract. Using a wire whisk, combine thoroughly. Gradually beat in the 3 cupfuls milk. Set aside at room temperature.

Put the 1 cupful *cold* milk into a saucepan. Sprinkle gelatin over and allow to soften for 5 minutes. Set over *LOW* heat and, stirring constantly, continue cooking until gelatin is completely dissolved. Set aside to cool slightly.

Gradually stir dissolved gelatin mixture into prepared, room temperature eggnog. Refrigerate until it just begins to thicken about 20-30 minutes. Remove from refrigerator and set on counter top.

Using an electric mixer fitted with *chilled* beaters or by hand using a *chilled* wire whisk, beat heavy cream in a *chilled* bowl until stiff.

Using a wire whisk, *whisk fold* whipped heavy cream into eggnog mixture.

Wipe excess oil from prepared mold. Turn mixture into mold and refrigerate for at least 8 hours.

Unmold onto chilled serving dish. Grate fresh nutmeg over and further garnish with grated chocolate or chocolate curls. Refrigerate until ready to serve. Refrigerate any leftovers immediately.

Yields 8-10 servings
adequate for 6-8 people

Notes: *Because raw eggs present the danger of *Salmonella* poisoning, commercially-available pasteurized eggs are recommended for use in preparing this dish.

**Agar-agar (*Gelidium* flakes), at natural food stores, or kosher gelatin may be substituted for plain gelatin, if preferred. Since preparation procedures differ for these products, be sure to follow package directions.

This is also beautifully presented as a soufflé or as individual soufflés, if preferred. Prepare a 1 1/2-quart soufflé dish or individual ramekins by attaching a 3-inch aluminum foil collar. Tie collar securely in place before spooning in bavarian mixture. *Chill thoroughly* before carefully removing collars prior to garnishing and serving.

Preservative-free dried holiday fruits also make attractive garnishes, if preferred.

1/10 SERVING – PROTEIN = 9.1 g.; FAT = 8.0 g.; CARBOHYDRATE = 13.1 g.;
CALORIES = 161; CALORIES FROM FAT = 45%

Europe–Germany

GERMAN STEWED RHUBARB WITH FARINA
Rhabarbergriess

TPT - 1 hour and 15 minutes;
1 hour = chilling period

In most of Germany, rhubarb, the vegetable that "would be a fruit," is sweetened and thickened with tapioca. In central Germany, farina is the preferred thickening agent and it is always served with cold milk, cream, or, on special occasions, a superb vanilla sauce. It makes a very special spring or summer breakfast dish and a very nice family dessert.

1/2 cup water

2 pounds young rhubarb—cut into 3/4-inch pieces to yield about 4 cupfuls
2/3 cup sugar
Thin lemon slice
1 cinnamon quill

1/2 cup quick–cooking farina *(not instant)* or Cream of Wheat cereal
1/2 cup light cream *or* half and half
1/2 teaspoon pure vanilla extract

Whole milk *or* light cream
Sugar

Pour water into a large kettle, with cover, set over *MEDIUM* heat. Add chopped rhubarb, sugar, lemon slice, and cinnamon quill. Stir to combine ingredients. Bring to the boil. *Reduce heat to LOW-MEDIUM* and simmer, *tightly covered,* for about 5 minutes, or until just *tender*, but *not mushy*. Stir occasionally. Remove and rinse cinnamon quill. Put it aside to dry for reuse. Remove and discard lemon slice.

Add farina and cook for about 5 minutes more, stirring frequently.

Add the 1/2 cupful light cream and vanilla extract. Stir well to integrate. Refrigerate until completely cooled, at least 1 hour.

Turn into serving dish or into individual sherbet glasses. Serve with milk or cream and sugar, to accommodate individual tastes.

Yields about 5 cupfuls
adequate for 4-6 people

Notes: Rhubarb freezes so easily that we secret a store throughout the spring and early summer. Simply remove and discard leaves, which incidentally are poisonous, and any tough strands or "strings." Wash and dry stems thoroughly. Chop into 3/4-inch pieces. Bag in freezer bags, label, and freeze.

This recipe is easily increased or decreased proportionately, when required.

1/6 SERVING (i. e., 1/2 cupful) –
PROTEIN = 2.9 g.; FAT = 2.1 g.; CARBOHYDRATE = 41.6 g.;
CALORIES = 196; CALORIES FROM FAT = 10%

GERMAN BLUE PLUM *STREUSEL* TART
Zwetschgenkuchen

TPT - 1 hour and 38 minutes;
30 minutes = cooling period

My grandmother had a German blue plum tree in the garden, a garden planted by my great-grandfather. When it became too difficult for her to climb a ladder to harvest the plums, grandchildren and great-grandchildren harvested the plums. There was, of course, always a scramble to climb the tree. The last time I climbed that tree for Grandma my daughter, then four years old, Mom, and Grandma stood at the bottom of the tree "to catch me." I suspect that tree has fond memories for others too. Grandma made the most wonderful kuchens with the harvested plums, often making half-plum and half-apple kuchens to send home with family members where there might be a preference for one over the other. This streusel tart is quite different from Grandma's kuchen but I think she might have liked mine as much as I liked hers.

GERMAN BLUE PLUM *STREUSEL* TART (cont'd)

TART CRUST AND *STREUSEL* TOPPING:
    1 cup rolled oats—old-fashioned *or* quick-cooking, *but not instant*
    1 cup unbleached white flour
    1/2 cup whole wheat flour
    1/3 cup sugar
    1 teaspoon ground cinnamon
    1 teaspoon baking powder

    3/4 cup butter—*softened to room temperature*
    3/4 teaspoon pure almond extract

Preheat oven to 375 degrees F. Prepare a 9-inch pie plate or two-piece, 13 x 4 x 1-inch tart pan by coating with non-stick lecithin spray coating.

Using an electric mixer or food processor, fitted with steel knife, prepare crust and *streusel* mixture by combining rolled oats, white and whole wheat flours, 1/3 cupful sugar, and baking powder. Mix well.

Add *softened* butter and almond extract. Mix until a crumbly dough forms.

Reserve 1 cupful of mixture to use as streusel topping.

Press remaining oat mixture into bottom and up sides of prepared pie plate or tart pan evenly to form a crust.

Bake in preheated 375 degree F. oven for 15 minutes.

FILLING:
    1/3 cup all-fruit seedless raspberry preserves
    1 tablespoon unbleached white flour
    2 tablespoons water
    2 cups (about 12 plums) sliced Italian blue prune plums*
    1 tablespoon sugar

While crust is baking, in a saucepan set over *MEDIUM* heat, combine raspberry preserves, 1 tablespoonful white flour, and water. Cook, stirring constantly, until preserves are melted and a smooth sauce results.

Arrange plum slices in concentric circles on baked, 9-inch oat crust or in tight rows if tart pan is used. Sprinkle 1 tablespoonful sugar over plums. Spoon raspberry mixture evenly over plums. Crumble reserved oat *streusel* topping mixture over fruit mixture.

Return to 375 degree F. oven and bake for an additional 30 minutes, or until *golden brown*. Transfer to a wire rack and allow to *cool completely*—about 30 minutes.

Using a sharp knife, serve in wedges, as for a pie.

                          Yields 10 servings
                         adequate for 6-8 people

Notes: *German blue plums are rarely available in the United States, unless you have the good fortune to have your own private tree source. If you do have a source of German blue plums, you will need only about 6-8, since they are about twice the size of the Italian variety. They are also available in September.

For variety, this recipe may be prepared in an 8 x 8-inch baking pan and cut into cookie bars for a tea table.

1/10 SERVING – PROTEIN = 3.8 g.; FAT = 14.6 g.; CARBOHYDRATE = 38.7 g.;
CALORIES = 301; CALORIES FROM FAT = 44%

GERMAN CHRISTMAS BREAD
Stollen

TPT - 13 hours and 45 minutes;
       1 hour and 30 minutes = first bread rising period;
       10 hours = second bread rising period;
       45-60 minutes = third bread rising period

On Christmas morning the stollen, which was prepared the evening before and rose during the night, is very much anticipated by our family. It is baked in the morning, filling the house with the most wonderful aroma, and is borne to our table with a sense of pride of heritage.

1 tablespoon (1 envelope) *preservative-free* active dried yeast*
3/4 cup warm water (105-115 degrees F.)

1/2 cup sugar
3/4 cup *fat-free* pasteurized eggs (the equivalent of 3 eggs)
1 large egg yolk (egg white reserved)
1/2 cup butter—*softened to room temperature*
2 cups unbleached white flour
[see next page]

Europe–Germany

GERMAN CHRISTMAS BREAD (cont'd)

1 1/2 cups whole wheat flour
1/2 cup chopped, blanched, *preservative-free* almonds
1/4 cup chopped *preservative-free* citron**
1/4 cup *preservative-free dark* raisins
1 tablespoon freshly grated lemon zest

2 tablespoons butter—*softened to room temperature*

1 large egg white—well-beaten

1 1/2 cups confectioners' sugar
1 1/2 tablespoons skimmed milk

Slivered, *preservative-free* almond slices, for garnish

In a large mixing bowl, sprinkle yeast over warm water and allow to proof for about 5 minutes.

Add sugar, pasteurized eggs, egg yolk, 1/2 cupful *softened* butter, and white flour. Using an electric mixer, beat at *MEDIUM* speed for 10 minutes. Scrape down sides of bowl frequently with a rubber spatula.

Using a wooden spoon, stir in whole wheat flour, nuts, citron, raisins, and lemon zest. Scrape batter from sides of bowl. Cover with plastic wrap and a cotton tea towel. Allow to rise in a warm (75-80 degrees F.), draft-free place until doubled in bulk—about 1 1/2 hours.

Stir down batter by beating with a wooden spoon. Again scrape batter from sides of bowl. Cover tightly with plastic wrap and refrigerate for 10 hours, or overnight.

Prepare a cookie sheet by coating with non-stick lecithin spray coating or by buttering.

Turn dough out onto a well-floured surface. Divide dough in half and form each half into a ball.*** Press each ball into an 8 x 4-inch oval. Spread each oval with 1 tablespoonful *softened* butter. Fold in half the long way. *Press only the folded edge firmly.* Place on a prepared cookie sheet; one at each end.

Combine well-beaten egg white with 1 tablespoonful water. Beat well. Brush egg white wash over each loaf.

Set aside in warm kitchen and allow to rise until doubled in bulk again—about 45-60 minutes.

Preheat oven to 350 degrees F.

Bake *stollen* for 30-35 minutes, or until *golden brown.* Remove from oven and allow to cool slightly on wire racks which have been set over waxed paper.

Into a small bowl, sift confectioners' sugar. Using a fork, gradually stir in milk until smooth.

While loaves are still *warm*, but *not hot*, drizzle prepared icing across loaves. (Icing which runs down the side will be caught on the waxed paper and is, therefore, easily cleaned up.)

Decorate by pressing slivered almond slices into the iced areas to simulate flowers.

Serve while still slightly warm or at room temperature.

Yields 2 medium loaves****
of about 12 slices each

Notes: *Some packaged dried yeast available in grocery stores contain a preservative. Natural food stores carry an additive-free dried yeast.

**Preservative-free citron is often available in natural food stores and specialty food stores at Christmas time. If not, it can be ordered from baking supply firms *or* chopped, dried, preservative-free apples make a good textural substitute.

***At this point, the dough may be tightly wrapped in plastic wrap and frozen successfully. Defrost completely in the refrigerator before proceeding. This is a great help to the busy holiday cook.

****This recipe may be halved, if desired, but we always make two and give the second as a Christmas morning gift. If you are expecting a large crowd for Christmas brunch, make one large loaf pressing the risen dough into a 12 x 8-inch oval before forming the loaf. It is dramatic!

Leftover *stollen*, if there is any, is delicious when lightly toasted.

This bread does not freeze well. It is best baked the morning on which it is to be served.

If preferred, the icing may be eliminated reducing the calories to 162 calories per serving.

1/24 SERVING (i. e., per slice with icing) –
PROTEIN = 3.7 g.; FAT = 6.4 g.; CARBOHYDRATE = 30.4 g.;
CALORIES = 196; CALORIES FROM FAT = 29%

1/24 SERVING (i. e., per slice without icing) –
PROTEIN = 3.7 g.; FAT = 6.4 g.; CARBOHYDRATE = 22.1 g.;
CALORIES = 162; CALORIES FROM FAT = 36%

Greece

I first "visited" ancient and classical Greece through the literature, mythology, and ancient art in my beloved old set of the Book of Knowledge. The splendid photographs of artifacts were compelling to the small child to whom the distance of time and history were not understood; she wondered, "Who were these people?"

The Minoan civilization in Crete, the Mycenaean civilization on the Greek mainland, and the Cycladic civilization on the islands in the Aegean Sea attest to Neolithic occupation dating to 3000-2800 BC while Paleolithic habitation in the area around the present city of Attica has been confirmed to perhaps as early as 30,000 BC. Ancient Greece grew and prospered but the rise of the Roman Empire, which established rule over Greek lands in 146 BC interrupted the cosmic rise of Greek thinking and culture. At this point, many Greeks migrated to cities in Asia and Africa, cities founded as a result of the conquests of Alexander the Great. Greek culture and learning were carried to these lands just as it was to be carried to Europe centuries later.

Western philosophical and political thought, literature, drama, political science, historiography, and many of the principles of science and mathematics have their roots in Greece. It is doubtful that the Renaissance would have been the incredible change in human development without Greek influence. The artists, philosophers, writers, and political thinkers who emigrated from Greece as the Ottoman Turks surged forward in the Eastern Mediterranean in the fifteenth century, brought the knowledge of centuries that became the basis from which the Renaissance blossomed. For a thousand years the Byzantine Empire had existed through times of unbelievable cultural growth and productivity and survived the setbacks to the empire during wars that repeatedly changed the map of Europe and the Middle East. A series of wars between the Byzantine and Ottoman empires resulted in the loss of Byzantine territory and the eventual fall of Constantinople to the forces of Sultan Mohammad II in 1453, foreseen perhaps by those who had emigrated to find opportunity in Europe.

The modern Greek state was established in 1830 following the Greek War for Independence but the assassination of the first governor of the new republic the following year resulted in the installation of a monarchy under Otto, of the Bavarian House of Wittelsbach, an authoritarian monarchy that was replaced a year later. Under the direction of the European monarchs another attempt to establish a Greek monarchy proceeded with the installation of King George, formerly Prince Wilhelm of Denmark. The friction between monarchs and the prime ministers through the period of two world wars and beyond eventually led to a *coup de'etat* in the wake of King Constantine II's dismissal of George Papandreou's centrist government in 1965. A counter-*coup* established Dimitrios Ionnidis as dictator. Turkey invaded the island of Cyrus in 1974 precipitating the collapse of the Ionnidis regime which allowed for the formation of the Third Hellenic Republic, a unitary parliamentary republic with a president and prime minister, a representative parliament, and a multi-party political structure.

Eighty percent of Greece is mountainous with only small areas of arable land mainly in Thessaly, Central Macedonia, and Thrace. Add the centuries of overgrazing by goat and sheep herds to the limiting geographic factors and you can see the dilemma faced by the country of over eleven million. Historically Greece has always struggled with the ratio between arable land and population growth. Despite the limitations on agriculture dictated by topography, Greek cuisine developed into a primary cuisine which has influenced not only the cuisines of other nations in the Eastern Mediterranean but the food preparation in nations throughout the western world. The Greeks who emigrated over the centuries not only carried their learning, they carried their recipes.

Europe–Greece

Meze
Meze Sausages with Lemon
Loukanika

Coffee Eggs
Avgha Vrasta

Feta – Olive Appetizer
Feta meh Ladi kai Elyies

Marinated Mushrooms
Manitaria Ladolemono

Baked Feta Cheese with Honey
Feta meh Meli

Baked Ricotta and Feta Pudding Appetizer with Fresh Fennel
Myzithropita Kalavryton

Aromatic Greek Seasoning Mix
Baharika kai Aromatika

Salads
Greek Village Tossed Salad
Horiatiki Salata

Beet and Garlic Salad
Patsarosalata

Apple Salad with Onion and Feta
Milo Salata

Melon, Tomato, and Olive Salad
Peponi Salata

Egg and Lemon Soup
Avgolemono Súpa

Chilled Chick Pea Soup with Roasted Red Peppers and Garlic
Súpa Revithia me Kokkinos Pipperies ke Skordha

~~~~~~~~~~~~~~~~~~~~~

Vegetable Kebabs
Souvlakia me Salatica

~~~~~~~~~~~

Eggplant Byzantine
Melitzanes Vizantious

~~~~~~~~~~~

Macaroni and "Meat" Casserole
Pastitso

~~~~~~~~~~~

Tomato Omelet
Omeletta me Domatoes

~~~~~~~~~~~~~~~~~~~~~

Shredded Wheat Dessert
Pseftiko Kataifi

Farina Custard
Poutika

Assorted Nuts

Europe–Greece

MEZE options

MEZE SAUSAGES WITH LEMON IN THE GREEK STYLE
Loukanika

TPT - 8 minutes

Now, soy sausages can give the vegetarian a taste of this classic, but very simple, Greek preparation found often among the offerings of a "meze" table.

1 package (about 11 ounces) Mediterranean-seasoned soy sausages—cut into 2-inch lengths

2 lemons—well-washed, *thinly* sliced, and pips removed

Prepare a non-stick-coated skillet by coating with non-stick lecithin spray coating or brush on a *light* coating of *extra virgin* olive oil.

Over *MEDIUM* heat, brown sausage links on all sides.

Turn onto a heated platter. Cover with lemon slices.

Serve at once, as a *hor d'hoeuvre* or *meze* table offering or accompany with other dishes and serve as a main course.

Yields 16 two-inch sausages
adequate for 6-8 people
as an appetizer offering
or
adequate for 4 people
as a main course offering

Note: This recipe may be increased or decreased proportionately, as required.

1/16 SERVING (i. e., per small sausage link) –
PROTEIN = 2.6 g.; FAT =1.0 g.; CARBOHYDRATE = 3.2 g.;
CALORIES = 32; CALORIES FROM FAT = 29%

GREEK COFFEE EGGS
Avgha Vrasta

TPT - 3 hours and 35 minutes;
3 hours = egg marination period;
30 minutes = chilling period

Hard-cooked eggs, in many forms, are served in the "taverna" and coffee houses and on the "meze" tables of Greece and those of neighboring countries. If you start with brown eggs, the color is even more dramatic.

3 cups strong coffee
1/4 cup olive oil*
Skins from 1 large onion—well-washed
6 *whole* eggs in shells

Calorie-reduced or light **mayonnaise *or* BLENDER MAYONNAISE** *[see index]*, **as preferred**

In a saucepan set over *MEDIUM* heat, combine coffee, olive oil, and the onion skins. Add eggs. *Add more coffee if the eggs are not covered.* Bring to the boil. Reduce heat to *LOW* and simmer for 15 minutes. Using a slotted spoon, remove eggs from coffee mixture and plunge them into ice water.

When cool enough to handle, roll eggs on the counter top until each is *thoroughly cracked*. Return cracked hard-cooked eggs to *warm* coffee marinated liquid. Allow to stand at room temperature for 3 hours. Drain and pat excess marinating liquid from eggs with paper toweling. Shell.

Refrigerate for at least 30 minutes.

Serve whole as an appetizer or part of a salad plate, allowing each diner to shell their own eggs if preferred. Accompany with mayonnaise.**

Yields 6 eggs
adequate for 6 people

GREEK COFFEE EGGS (cont'd)

Notes: *An insignificant amount of olive oil is transferred to the egg shells, which are removed before eating. The oil is necessary to fix the color and the flavoring.

**Glass or pure white plates offer the best contrast for presentation.

This recipe may be halved or doubled, when required. Be careful to choose the appropriately smaller or larger saucepan in each case to insure that the eggs will be completely covered by the marinating mixture.

1/6 SERVING (with 2 teaspoonfuls mayonnaise) –
PROTEIN = 6.4 g.; FAT = 9.0 g.; CARBOHYDRATE = 0.7 g.;
CALORIES = 111; CALORIES FROM FAT = 73%

GREEK *FETA* – OLIVE APPETIZER
Feta meh Ladi kai Elyies

TPT -   48 hours and 16 minutes;
48 hours = *feta* marination period

Marinated feta cheese, packed in oil with herbs and spices, is shipped to the United States and is often found, refrigerated, in trademark hexagonal jars in the cheese department. This product is well worth scouting out because marinating feta cheese to Greek standards can and should take several days. But, just in case you are unable to find the convenience product, I am gladly sharing my recipe for Greek marinated feta as part of this appetizer recipe. Be sure to use the very best-tasting olive oil.

10 ounces *feta* cheese—cut into cubes
4-inch sprig of fresh rosemary—well-washed
Zest of 1 *organic* lemon—*thinly* slivered
1 teaspoon freshly squeezed lemon juice
1/2 teaspoon crushed, dried oregano
1/2 teaspoon mixed whole peppercorns—black, white, and red
1 cup *extra virgin* olive oil

5 rosemary needles

1/2 jar (about 5 ounce ounces) pitted *Kalamata* ripe olives—well-drained and sliced
Freshly ground black pepper, to taste

Several long, curled strips of *organic* lemon zest

Whole grain crackers

Sterilize a quart canning jar. Also sterilize a lid and a sealing ring.

Put the *feta* cheese cubes into the jar. Add rosemary sprig, the *thinly* slivered lemon zest, lemon juice, crushed oregano, and whole black, white, and red peppercorns. Pour olive oil into jar, adding more if necessary to cover the cheese cubes. Seal tightly. Gently roll the jar to distribute the seasoning elements and the olive oil. Refrigerate for at least 48 hours. Roll the jar periodically to insure even flavoring.*

When ready to proceed with this appetizer, drain the cheese through a sieve. Remove and discard rosemary sprig and peppercorns. *Reserve the olive oil to use in salad dressings or to drizzle over appetizers or cheese or to start another batch of marinated cheese.*

Using a SPICE and COFFEE GRINDER, chop the rosemary needles quite finely.

In a small serving bowl, combine the well-drained marinated *feta* cheese cubes, olive slices, and black pepper. Toss gently. Add *finely* chopped rosemary needles. Toss again. Refrigerate until required.

Garnish with the long, curled lemon zest strips. Place the small serving bowl on a large plate, surround it with crackers, and serve. Allow diners to scoop the appetizer mixture with a slotted spoon onto a cracker.

Yields 12 servings
adequate for-6 people

Notes: *Refrigerated, this will keep for several weeks.

A well-drained 10.5-ounce jar of marinated *feta* cheese can be substituted if you do not have the time to marinate the *feta* yourself.

This recipe can be halved or doubled, when required.

1/12 SERVING – PROTEIN = 3.3 g.; FAT = 3.5 g.; CARBOHYDRATE = 0.8 g.;
CALORIES = 157; CALORIES FROM FAT = 20%

Europe–Greece

GREEK MARINATED MUSHROOMS
Manitaria Ladolemono

TPT - about 12 hours and 26 minutes;
12 hours = marination period

The hour or so before dinner, corresponding to our cocktail hour, is an important part of the Greek day. It is a time of letting go of the day and socializing before dinner. Ouzo or one of the fascinating Greek wines is sipped while "mezethakia" or "orektika," that is, little things to encourage your appetite, are served. These marinated mushrooms, served with feta cheese and Kalamata olives, make a perfect presentation for meze or as a salad.

12 ounces small, whole, fresh mushrooms
 —trimmed, rinsed, and cleaned well with a brush
1 quart *boiling* water
1 teaspoon freshly squeezed lemon juice

1/2 cup *extra virgin* olive oil
1/4 cup red wine vinegar
1/2 teaspoon paprika
1/4 teaspoon dried oregano—crushed
1/4 teaspoon dried thyme—crushed
1/8 teaspoon ground cumin

10 watercress sprigs, for garnish
1 lemon—cut into thin wedges—for garnish

Trim ends from mushroom stems. Wash *gently*, but *thoroughly*, and place in a large bowl. Pour *boiling* water over mushrooms, add lemon juice, and allow to stand for 5 minutes to blanch. Turn into a sieve or colander and drain *thoroughly*. Trim off any discolored areas. Transfer to a large plastic container with tightly fitting lid.

Combine oil, vinegar, paprika, crushed oregano and thyme, and cumin. Pour over mushrooms. Cover and toss *gently* to coat mushrooms well. Refrigerate for at least 12 hours, turning occasionally to insure uniform marination.

Turn into a sieve, set over a mixing bowl, and drain *very thoroughly* before serving—*all but 2 tablespoonfuls of the marinade should be recovered.**

Turn into a serving bowl and garnish with watercress sprigs and lemon wedges before serving.

Yields 5 servings
of about 6 mushrooms each
adequate for 3-5 people

Notes: *The recovered marinade may be reused. Refrigerate in a jar with a tightly fitting lid for no more than 2 weeks.

This recipe is easily halved or doubled, when required.

1/5 SERVING (i. e., about 6 mushrooms) –
PROTEIN = 1.9 g.; FAT = 3.2 g.; CARBOHYDRATE = 4.7 g.;
CALORIES = 51; CALORIES FROM FAT = 56%

GREEK BAKED *FETA* CHEESE WITH HONEY
Feta meh Mèli

TPT - 3 days and 28 minutes;
3 days = *feta* desalination period

Years and years ago, the very knowledgeable and patient cheese purveyor at our local Food of All Nations taught me to enjoy feta cheese without guilt. He would pick out a huge chunk of Greek feta and tell me to soak it in water for three days, changing the water twice daily. He said, "It isn't the salt; it's the cheese." As a consequence of his wisdom, we can enjoy this simple, yet exotic, Greek appetizer spread on a hot summer's evening out in the garden without worrying about the sodium.

We like to serve this Greek appetizer or "mezethes" on unsalted crackers or melba toast accompanied by fried artichoke hearts (angináres) and a Greek retsina wine.

One large 8-ounce chunk Greek *feta* cheese, packed in water

2 tablespoons local wildflower honey
1 large sprig fresh thyme—well-rinsed
1 small sprig fresh oregano *or* marjoram, if preferred—well-rinsed

1 tablespoon *extra virgin* olive oil

Freshly ground black pepper, to taste

GREEK BAKED *FETA* CHEESE WITH HONEY (cont'd)

Drain the briny water in which the *feta* is packed. Put the chunk of *feta* into a bowl and cover with cold water. Refrigerate. *Change the water twice-a-day.* Repeat this process for three days. Drain well.

Preheat the oven to 375 degrees F.

In a Turkish coffeepot or small sauce warmer set over *LOW* heat, combine honey and the sprigs of thyme and oregano. Allow to warm while the cheese is being baked.

Place well-drained chunk of *feta* cheese in an attractive oven-to-table baking dish coated with non-stick lecithin spray coating. Brush with olive oil. Bake in preheated 375 degree F. oven for about 7-8 minutes, until soft and *heated through, but not melted*. Remove from oven.

Switch the oven to BROIL and allow to preheat to about 400 degrees F.

Remove the thyme and oregano sprigs from the warm honey. Brush the honey over the warm cheese. Place the sprigs of thyme and oregano on top. Broil for about 3-5 minutes or until the honey turns a dark, caramel color, *being very careful not to allow it to burn*. Remove from the oven. Cool for a minute or two.

Grind black pepper over.

Serve at once with an assortment of unsalted crackers, melba toast, or toasted bread upon which the cheese and honey can be spread.

Yields 12-18 servings

1/12 SERVING – PROTEIN = 5.4 g.; FAT = 8.9 g.; CARBOHYDRATE = 4.1 g.;
CALORIES = 121; CALORIES FROM FAT = 66%

GREEK BAKED *RICOTTA* AND *FETA* PUDDING APPETIZER WITH FRESH FENNEL

Myzithropita Kalavryton

TPT - 24 hours and 54 minutes;
24 hours = *ricotta* draining period

The traditional Kalavrytan cheese pie or tart upon which this recipe is based, as indicated in the name, is made with "mysithra," a fresh whey cheese which is a secondary product in the feta production process. The availability of this specialty cheese in the United States is hit or miss unless you live in a city with a substantial Greek population. A good ricotta plus some feta cheese can be substituted so when the fennel fronds appear in the herb garden in the early spring, we plan this dish as a first course for a formal meal or as a light supper in the garden on a warm evening. It is so easy to prepare and a pleasure you will remember for a long time.

For two servings:
  1 cup *part-skimmed milk ricotta* cheese

  1 teaspoon butter

  2 tablespoons crumbled *feta* cheese
  1/4 cup *fat-free* pasteurized eggs (the equivalent of 1 egg)
  3 tablespoons snipped fennel leaves
  1/2 teaspoon AROMATIC GREEK SEASONING MIX *(Baharika kai Aromatika)* [see recipe which follows]

  1 cup *mesclún* mixture—well-washed and dried
  1 teaspoon *extra virgin* olive oil

Place *ricotta* into a fine sieve and set over a small bowl in the refrigerator to drain thoroughly—about 24 hours.

Preheat oven to 350 degrees F. Prepare a water bath. Butter two 6-ounce ramekins with 1/2 teaspoon butter.

In a mixing bowl, combine drained *ricotta* cheese, *feta* cheese, pasteurized eggs, snipped fennel leaves, and Greek seasoning mixture. Stir to combine thoroughly. Divide between the buttered ramekins. Place in water bath, being sure that water comes to about halfway up the ramekins. Bake in preheated oven for 30 minutes, or until puffed and golden. Remove from oven. Allow to sit in water bath for about 10 minutes. Run a knife around each ramekin and unmold onto salad plates.

Garnish with a handful of greens. Drizzle a little bit of olive oil over the greens and the baked cheese pudding.

Serve at once.

Yields 2 individual servings

Note: This recipe can be doubled or tripled, when required.

Europe–**Greece**

GREEK BAKED *RICOTTA* AND *FETA* PUDDING APPETIZER WITH FRESH FENNEL (cont'd)

1/2 SERVING – PROTEIN = 17.5 g.; FAT = 12.6 g.; CARBOHYDRATE = 10.4 g.;
CALORIES = 246; CALORIES FROM FAT = 46%

AROMATIC GREEK SEASONING MIX
Baharika kai Aromatika
TPT - 3 minutes

The word aroma does come from the Greek . . . We add a pinch of this wonderfully complex seasoning mix to an oil and lemon dressing to dress vegetable or green salads; and a pinch to melted butter to dress cauliflower or wilted greens. Added to diced or crushed tomatoes, it is a quick fix when you need a simple tomato sauce or a sauce for a Greek pizza.

2 teaspoons crushed, dried Greek oregano
2 teaspoons crushed, dried parsley
1 small bay leaf—broken
1 teaspoon crushed, dried mint
1 teaspoon crushed, dried basil
2 teaspoons garlic powder
2 teaspoons onion powder
1/2 teaspoon freshly ground black pepper
1/2 teaspoon ground cinnamon
1/2 teaspoon ground nutmeg
1/2 teaspoon salt
1/2 teaspoon celery seeds

In a SPICE and COFFEE GRINDER, or in a mortar, combine dried oregano, dried parsley, dried mint, dried basil, garlic powder, onion powder, black pepper, ground cinnamon, ground nutmeg, salt, and celery seeds. Grind herbs to a uniform mixture.

Turn into a small jelly or spice jar.* Cover tightly and shake to mix thoroughly. Store in a cool, dark place.

Yields about 8 teaspoonfuls

Notes: *Choose a small jar because the smaller the jar, the less air will come in contact with the herbs, and the longer the mix will keep its flavor.

This recipe can be halved and that is often a good idea since the flavor dissipates considerably due to the release of the volatile oils with crushing. It is advisable to replace the seasoning combination after about 3 months.

FOOD VALUES for such herb mixtures are almost negligible.

SALAD options

GREEK VILLAGE TOSSED SALAD
Horiatiki Salata
TPT - 17 minutes

There are precious few Long Island or New Jersey diners that do not serve a decent Greek country salad. Some actually serve a terrific Greek salad since there is more to the splendor than a handful of feta cheese, a couple of olives, and vinaigrette with oregano. Living on Long Island for so many years we become complacent, knowing that there was always a salad within range that could make us very contented people. Since this is not so across the width and breadth of our country, our version of this wonderful salad travels with us.

Hint: The ingredients can be varied with seasonal availability or personal taste but the following recipe outlines the basic formula for perfect contentment.

Europe–Greece

GREEK VILLAGE TOSSED SALAD (cont'd)

4 ounces *frozen* artichoke hearts—*defrosted*
1 cup *boiling* water

GREEK OREGANO *VINAIGRETTE*:
    2 tablespoons *extra virgin* olive oil
    1 tablespoon OREGANO FLOWER
      VINEGAR *[see index]* or other white
      vinegar, of choice
    1/4 teaspoon dried oregano—*crushed*
    2 slivers garlic
    Pinch freshly ground black pepper, or
      to taste

6 large, dark green romaine lettuce leaves—well-washed, dried, and sliced crosswise
2 vine-ripened tomatoes—cut into wedges and then halved *or* sliced crosswise, if preferred
1 small-medium, *organic* cucumber—well-washed, scored with the tines of a fork, quartered lengthwise, and sliced crosswise into wedges
1 green pepper—cored, seeded, and sliced into rings
1 small yellow onion *or* a sweet onion, if preferred—sliced into rings
4 radishes—trimmed, well-scrubbed, and sliced

3 ounces (about 3/4 cup) *feta* cheese—cut into slices, chunks, *or* crumbled, as preferred
10 ripe, black olives, preferably *Kalamata*
12 small capers
Chopped fresh parsley, for garnish
Sprinkling of dried oregano, for garnish

In a saucepan set over *MEDIUM* heat, cook thoroughly *defrosted* artichoke hearts for about 5 minutes. Remove from heat, drain thoroughly and pat dry, and allow to cool while salad is being assembled.

In a cruet, combine oil, vinegar, 1/4 teaspoonful *crushed* dried oregano, garlic slivers, and black pepper. Shake vigorously. Set aside until required.

In a large, shallow serving dish or salad bowl, or on a large platter, combine sliced romaine, sliced tomatoes, cucumber, green pepper, onion, and radishes, and artichoke hearts. Toss.

Sprinkle *feta* cheese over the vegetables. Scatter olives and capers among the other ingredients. Sprinkle parsley and remaining dried oregano over the whole assembly.

Again, vigorously shake the dressing. Serve the salad onto dinner plates or into soup plates. Pass dressing to accommodate individual tastes.*

                    Yields 4 main course servings
                       or 6 side salad servings

Notes: *If you prefer to dress the salad, dress it at the very last minute. It is preferable, in our opinion, to serve the dressing on the side.

This recipe can be halved or doubled, when required.

1/4 SERVING – PROTEIN = 5.8 g.; FAT = 13.8 g.; CARBOHYDRATE = 10.6 g.;
CALORIES = 187; CALORIES FROM FAT = 66%

GREEK BEET AND GARLIC SALAD
Patsarosalata

TPT - 1 hour and 36 minutes;
      30 minutes = flavor development period

I do look forward to the time of year when beets come to market from local farms. The roots remain attached, the beets are never shriveled, and the leaves are fresh and unwilted. How many times in my life have I been asked by a greengrocer if I want the beet greens removed from a bunch of beets? Of course not . . . and this is a simple salad to demonstrate how those beautiful, nutritionally-packed leaves will be consumed by everyone with enthusiasm.

2 tablespoons *extra virgin* olive oil
2 tablespoons GARLIC–BASIL VINEGAR *[see index]*, MIXED FLOWER VINEGAR WITH OREGANO *[see index]*, or other vinegar of choice
Pinch dry mustard
Freshly ground black pepper, to taste

1 bunch (about 2 pounds) beets with greens and root intact
3 quarts *boiling* water

2 garlic cloves—*very finely* chopped
Salt, to taste

VOLUME I - 162

Europe–**Greece**

GREEK BEET AND GARLIC SALAD (cont'd)

In a cruet, combine oil, vinegar, dry mustard, and black pepper. Shake vigorously and set aside.

Leaving 2 inches of leaf stem attached, cut off leaves and wash very well. *Discard any that are spotted or show evidence of insect activity.* Trim off tough stems. Set aside until required.

In a deep saucepan, cook the beets in the 3 quartfuls *boiling* water until tender—about 45 minutes. Drain. Rinse in *cold* water until it can be handled. Cut off root end and stem end. Slip off skin and cut into slices. Place in a serving bowl.

Add *very finely* chopped garlic and salt to taste. Toss. Add prepared *vinaigrette*. Toss. Set aside briefly.

Using a sharp knife, shred the reserved beet greens. Blanch greens for 1 minute in the 2 quartfuls *boiling* water. Drain. Add to dressed beets. Toss. Refrigerate for at least 30 minutes, or until required.

Serve chilled.

Yields 6 servings
adequate for 4 people

Note: This recipe can be halved or doubled, when required.

1/6 SERVING – PROTEIN = 0.6 g.; FAT = 3.8 g.; CARBOHYDRATE = 3.9 g.;
CALORIES – 51, CALORIES FROM FAT = 67%

GREEK APPLE SALAD WITH ONION AND *FETA*
Milo Salata

TPT - 35 minutes;
30 minutes = refrigeration period

Apples are a wonderful salad ingredient. They stand boldly on their own, as anyone who has eaten a Waldorf salad knows, but here they are challenged by the powerful tastes of onions and feta cheese, and the sparkle of cilantro. The apples both support these other flavors and compete with them. This is a very, very good salad.

2 medium apples—*unpeeled,* **cored, and** *chopped*
  —*Granny Smith apples are our choice*
1/2 large onion—*sliced into rings*
2 tablespoons PLAIN YOGURT *[see index]* **or**
  commercially-available plain yogurt
1 tablespoon freshly squeezed lemon juice
Freshly ground black pepper, to taste

3 tablespoons crumbled *feta* **cheese**
2 tablespoons chopped fresh coriander (*cilantro***)**

In a large mixing bowl, combine chopped apples, onion rings, yogurt, lemon juice, and black pepper. Stir *gently*, but *thoroughly* to combine well.

Turn into a serving bowl. Sprinkle crumbled cheese and chopped coriander (*cilantro*) over.

Refrigerate until ready to serve—for at least 30 minutes but for *no more than 1 hour*.

Serve well-chilled.

Yields 4-6 servings
adequate for 4 people

Note: This recipe is easily doubled or tripled, when required.

1/6 SERVING – PROTEIN = 0.6 g.; FAT = 0.8 g.; CARBOHYDRATE = 6.2 g.;
CALORIES = 35; CALORIES FROM FAT = 21%

GREEK MELON, TOMATO, AND OLIVE SALAD
Pepani Salata

TPT - 1 hour and 7 minutes;
1 hour = refrigeration period

The appearance of Sirius, the star group the ancient astrologers called the "Dog Star," in the summer sky over the Mediterranean signals the start of the "dog days," the sultry late July and August days. Appetites flag somewhat and exciting salads, such as this, are called into action to excite those appetites. Here, chilled fresh melon, a warm "from-the-vine" tomato, and sassy olives are dressed with a sweet lemon vinaigrette and garnished with fresh mint leaves from the herb garden.

Europe–**Greece**

GREEK MELON, TOMATO, AND OLIVE SALAD (cont'd)

1/2 medium cantaloupe melon—seeded, peeled, and coarsely chopped
1 large ripe tomato—peeled, seeded, and chopped
1/4 cup oil and salt-cured olives*

1 tablespoon freshly squeezed lemon juice
2 teaspoons *extra virgin* olive oil
1/4 teaspoon honey

Several fresh mint leaves—chopped

In a large mixing bowl, combine chopped melon and tomato with olives. Stir to mix well. Set aside.

In a small dish, combine lemon juice, olive oil, and honey. Stir well to integrate ingredients thoroughly. Pour this dressing over melon mixture. Stir to combine well.

Sprinkle chopped mint leaves over. Stir to distribute evenly.

Cover with plastic wrap and refrigerate for at least 1 hour to allow flavors to marry. Stir occasionally. Turn into serving dish of choice.

Serve well-chilled.

Yields 4-6 servings
adequate for 4 people

Notes: *Oil and salt-cured olives are available in both Greek and Italian delicatessens and at the delicatessen counters of some grocery stores. *Kalamata* olives may be preferred and can be substituted.

This recipe is easily halved or doubled, when required.

1/6 SERVING – PROTEIN = 1.0 g.; FAT = 10.2 g.; CARBOHYDRATE = 6.7 g.;
CALORIES = 115; CALORIES FROM FAT = 70%

~ ~ ~

GREEK EGG AND LEMON SOUP
Avgolemono Súpa
TPT - 28 minutes

Through the years I have heard people say "pasta is pasta; it's the sauce that matters." I have a great deal of difficulty in ignoring a comment like that because I am passionate in my opinion that the shape of pasta matters. Small pasta shapes are always on hand in an Italian kitchen. Most Americans may be aware of "pastina" for babies or "ditali" and" maruzzine" (tiny shells). "Orzo" is less used by Americans but is an important larder item in the kitchens of Italy and Greece.

We prefer orzo in this soup, to the more traditional rice, even when we serve it chilled in the summer.

5 cups VEGETARIAN WHITE STOCK *[see index]* **or VEGETABLE STOCK FROM SOUP** *[see index]*
1/4 cup high protein *orzo* macaroni*
1/8 teaspoon *very finely* and freshly grated organic lemon zest

2 tablespoons freshly squeezed lemon juice
6 tablespoons *fat-free* pasteurized eggs**
   (the equivalent of 1 1/2 eggs)

Salt, to taste
Freshly ground *white* pepper, to taste

4 thin lemon slices, for garnish
1 tablespoon chopped fresh parsley, for garnish

In a kettle set over *MEDIUM-HIGH* heat, bring stock to the boil. Add *orzo* and grated lemon zest. Boil for about 12 minutes. Remove from heat.

In a mixing bowl, using a wire whisk, beat pasteurized eggs into lemon juice until light in color. While beating, add 2 tablespoonfuls hot soup stock. Continue adding hot stock—*tablespoonful by tablespoonful*—until about *one-half* of stock has been added. While stirring the remaining warm stock with a wooden spoon, add egg–lemon–stock mixture. Set over *LOW* heat and blend thoroughly while heating through. *Do not allow soup to come to the boil again as the egg may curdle.*

Taste and season with salt and *white* pepper, as necessary. Pour into a heated soup tureen.

GREEK EGG AND LEMON SOUP (cont'd)

Serve at once into heated soup cups. Float a thin slice of lemon, sprinkled with chopped parsley, on each serving.

Yields four 1-cup servings

Notes: *Rice is traditionally used in GREEK EGG AND LEMON SOUP *(Avogolemono Súpa)* but the rice-shaped macaroni gives a substantial texture to this version. Try with rice too; you might prefer it.

**Because raw eggs present the danger of *Salmonella* poisoning, commercially-available pasteurized eggs are recommended for use in preparing this dish.

When required, this recipe may be doubled or tripled with ease.

1/4 SERVING – PROTEIN = 3.2 g.; FAT = 0.2 g.; CARBOHYDRATE = 6.8 g.;
CALORIES = 43; CALORIES FROM FAT = 4%

GREEK CHILLED CHICK PEA SOUP WITH ROASTED RED PEPPERS AND GARLIC
Súpa Revithia me Kokkines Pipperies ke Skórdha

TPT - 3 hours and 15 minutes;
2 hours = minimum flavor development period

Made from the most humble of ingredients, this soup is an exciting variation of the Greek classic puréed chick pea soup found throughout Greece. It is a winner whether served hot or cold.

4 sweet red bell peppers—perfect, unblemished, and well-washed
2 garlic cloves—*unpeeled*
Extra virgin olive oil

1 can (15.5 ounces) chick peas *(garbanzos)*—well-drained

5 cups VEGETABLE STOCK FROM SOUP *[see index]* **or** other vegetarian stock of choice

Freshly ground black pepper, to taste

6 tablespoons heavy whipping cream, for garnish

Preheat oven to 350 degrees F.

Place red peppers and garlic cloves on a cookie sheet. Brush peppers and garlic cloves lightly with olive oil. Roast in preheated oven for about 40 minutes, *turning frequently*.

Remove from oven and place roasted red peppers in a heavy brown paper bag in dry sink. Roll the top of the bag down and allow to steam for about 15 minutes.

Meanwhile, squeeze the softened garlic from the cloves into the work bowl of the food processor fitted with steel knife or into the container of the electric blender.

Remove stems, seeds, and membranes of roasted red peppers, peel, and coarsely chop. Add to garlic in work bowl of food processor.

Add drained chick peas and 1 cupful of stock. Process into a smooth purée. Add more of the remaining stock until soup base is very smooth.

Set a sieve over a mixing bowl or soup tureen. Strain the purée through the sieve, discarding any fibrous material and the seed coats which will not pass through the sieve. Add any remaining stock to sieved mixture. Season with black pepper.

Refrigerate, covered, for at least 2 hours, or overnight, to allow for flavor development.

Serve from a chilled soup tureen into chilled soup plates, garnishing each serving with a tablespoonful of cream poured into the center of the serving in a tiny pool.

Yields about 6 cupfuls

Note: This soup base freezes well which is a convenience for advance planning and for leftovers. At the end of the "chilled soup season," when red peppers are plenteous and inexpensive, we process up a double batch of this soup to secret in the freezer for reappearance on cold winter's evenings as a hot soup, served with lovely thick slices of bread.

Europe–**Greece**

GREEK CHILLED CHICK PEA SOUP WITH ROASTED RED PEPPERS AND GARLIC (cont'd)

1/6 SERVING (i. e., per cupful) –
PROTEIN = 4.8 g.; FAT = 8.0 g.; CARBOHYDRATE = 17.2 g.;
CALORIES = 128; CALORIES FROM FAT = 56%

GREEK VEGETABLE *KEBABS*
Souvlakis me Salatica

TPT -   2 hours and 30 minutes;
2 hours = marination period

When we first chose to commit ourselves to a vegetarian lifestyle, we struggled with summer entertaining since outdoor grilling and the backyard picnic were the norm among our friends. Soy protein burgers, hot dogs, and sausages came along much later to solve this dilemma for vegetarians but, back then, we created grain and bean burgers, served salads, and generally forgot about the barbecue. One of the first recipes we adapted was this recipe for vegetable kebabs by simply eliminating the meat component of our old "shish kebab" recipe. It was a start . . . .

8 small white boiling onions—peeled with an
   X cut into the root end of each

1 small eggplant—cut into 8 large chunks
1 green bell pepper—cut into 8 squares
12 large mushrooms (about 1/4 pound)
   —stemmed, rinsed, and cleaned well with a brush
8 large cherry tomatoes
1 small zucchini—sliced into 8 slices

GREEK MARINADE:
   2 tablespoons *extra virgin* olive oil
   1/4 cup dry red wine
   2 tablespoons freshly squeezed lemon juice
   1 small onion—sliced
   1 large garlic clove—*finely* chopped
   1/2 teaspoon dried oregano—crushed
   1/8 teaspoon dried basil—crushed— *or*
      1 1/2 teaspoons *finely* chopped fresh basil
   1/2 teaspoon paprika
   1/8 teaspoon freshly ground black pepper
   1 small bay leaf—broken

1 lemon, cut into wedges, for garnish

Parboil white onions in *boiling* water until just tender. Drain thoroughly.

In a large, heavy plastic bag, combine parboiled onions with eggplant chunks, green pepper squares, mushroom caps, cherry tomatoes, and zucchini slices. Set aside.

In a 2-cup measuring cup, combine oil, wine, lemon juice, onion slices, *finely* chopped garlic, crushed oregano and basil, paprika, black pepper, and bay leaf pieces. Pour over vegetables and securely close bag using a twist tie. Toss gently to cover vegetables with marinade. Refrigerate for at least 2 hours to allow vegetables to absorb the marinade. Turn vegetables often during the marination period.

Preheat broiler to 400 degrees F.*

Remove vegetables from marinade. Alternate them on four large skewers or "swords," beginning and ending with mushroom caps. Arrange on broiler pan.

Strain marinade and reserve for basting.

Broil about 4 inches below heat source. Brush *generously* with marinade often while broiling. Turn when *lightly browned. Be careful not to overcook or burn.*

Serve at once, on a bed of rice or pilaf, of choice. Garnish with lemon slices.

Yields 4 servings

Notes: *These are most successfully broiled over an open charcoal fire if cooked about 4 inches above *glowing coals.* Brush with marinade often and *keep any "flare-ups" under control.*

This recipe is easily increased or decreased proportionately, as required.

Apple wedges are an interesting addition, as are pineapple chunks.

1/4 SERVING – PROTEIN = 3.7 g.; FAT = 6.0 g.; CARBOHYDRATE = 16.8 g.;
CALORIES = 127; CALORIES FROM FAT = 43%

Europe–Greece

EGGPLANT BYZANTINE
Melitzanes Vizantiou

TPT - 55 minutes;
30 minutes = eggplant draining period

Because the eggplant is broiled instead of fried, this is much lighter than most eggplant dishes, which allows the smooth, flavorful Greek sauce to compliment the eggplant gently and perfectly.

1 medium eggplant—washed, trimmed, and sliced into 1/2-inch crosswise slices
Salt

1 tablespoon butter—*melted*

1 small onion—chopped
1/2 cup tomato purée *or* tomato sauce, preferably homemade
1/2 cup PLAIN YOGURT *[see index] or* commercially-available plain yogurt
1/2 cup water
1/2 teaspoon dried oregano leaves—crushed
Freshly ground black pepper, to taste
1/4 cup grated *pecorino Romano*, *Kefalotyri*, or *Parmesan cheese*, as preferred

Prepare a broiler pan by covering it with aluminum foil. Also prepare a 1 1/2-quart shallow baking dish, a large *au gratin* dish, a deep-dish pie plate, or a ceramic *quiche* dish by coating with non-stick lecithin spray coating or by oiling.

Salt eggplant slices generously and place them in a sieve or colander set in the sink. Place a plate on top and a weight—a large can or a tea kettle filled with water—on top of the plate. Allow to stand for about 30 minutes.

Preheat broiler to about 400 degrees F. and set oven rack about 6 inches below heat source.

Rinse eggplant slices well in cold water and pat dry. Arrange slices on prepared broiler pan and brush with melted butter. Broil for about 5 minutes, or until *golden*, but *not browned*. Turn slices, brush with remaining melted butter, and return to broiler for an additional 5 minutes, or until *golden* but, again, *not browned*. Remove broiler pan to top of stove. *Turn oven setting to BAKE* and set temperature at 350 degrees F.

Prepare sauce by combining chopped onion, tomato purée or sauce, yogurt, water, and crushed oregano in container of electric blender or in work bowl of food processor fitted with steel knife. Process for about 30 seconds. Taste and season with black pepper.

Arrange broiled eggplant slices in a single layer in prepared baking dish. Spoon a layer of sauce over. Arrange a second layer of eggplant and pour remaining sauce over. Sprinkle grated cheese evenly over.

Bake in preheated 350 degree F. oven for about 30 minutes, or until hot, bubbly, and *lightly browned* on top.

Serve at once.

Yields 6 servings
adequate for 4 people

Note: This recipe is easily doubled, when required.

1/6 SERVING – PROTEIN = 3.0 g.; FAT = 3.2 g.; CARBOHYDRATE = 5.7 g.;
CALORIES = 63; CALORIES FROM FAT = 46%

GREEK MACARONI AND "MEAT" CASSEROLE
Pastitso

TPT - 1 hour and 12 minutes

For some unexplainable reason, I missed this classic Greek dish when we gave up meat. It was not that I ever really liked ground beef or lamb but there was something in this dish that said "comfort." Many, many years later, actually twenty-nine years to be exact, a soy product gave me the opportunity to revisit this comfort. Since we never really missed meat, we do not use the faux beef very much, but in this dish, its texture is a compliment to the macaroni.

Europe–Greece

GREEK MACARONI AND "MEAT" CASSEROLE (cont'd)

3 quarts water
1 tablespoon lemon juice
1 3-inch strip lemon zest
1 cup high-protein, whole wheat, *or* Jerusalem artichoke elbow macaroni*

6 ounces vegetarian "ground beef"
1 small onion—*finely* chopped
3 tablespoons tomato purée
1 teaspoon crushed, dried Greek oregano
Pinch ground cinnamon
Freshly ground black pepper, to taste

1 tablespoon butter
1 tablespoon whole wheat flour
1 cup skimmed milk

2 tablespoons grated Greek *Kefalotyri* or *pecorino Romano* cheese

Ground cinnamon

Preheat oven to 325 degrees F. Prepare a 1 1/2-quart soufflé dish or other oven-to-table casserole by coating with non-stick lecithin spray coating.

In a large kettle set over *HIGH* heat, bring water to the boil. Add lemon juice and zest. Add macaroni. Boil for about 10-12 minutes. Pour into a strainer and allow to drain thoroughly. Discard lemon zest.

Prepare filling by combining, "soy meat," *finely* chopped onion, tomato purée, crushed oregano, ground cinnamon, and black pepper, in a mixing bowl. Set aside until required.

In a saucepan set over *LOW* heat, melt butter. Remove from heat and, using a wire whisk, make a *roux* by beating in flour. Return to heat and, stirring constantly, cook for 2 minutes, *being careful not to burn or overbrown the roux.* Remove from heat and gradually beat in milk. Return saucepan to heat and cook, stirring constantly, until thickened. *Remove from heat.*

Spread *one-half* of cooked and drained macaroni in prepared casserole dish. Spoon "soy meat" mixture evenly over the macaroni. Sprinkle 1 tablespoonful of grated cheese over. Spoon *one-half* of prepared white sauce over. Top with remaining macaroni. Spoon remaining white sauce over. Sprinkle with remaining tablespoonful of grated cheese. Sprinkle with cinnamon, to taste.

Bake in preheated 325 degree F. oven for approximately 30 minutes.

Serve at once.

Yields 8 servings
adequate for 4-5 people

Notes: *We find high-protein *ziti* macaroni sale-priced often, while elbows seldom are. A few minutes with a serrated knife produces a macaroni shape which is just perfect for this type of dish.

This recipe can be halved and prepared in a small casserole, if desired. Baking time will, necessarily, be reduced.

1/8 SERVING – PROTEIN = 7.1 g.; FAT = 2.1 g.; CARBOHYDRATE = 16.0 g.;
CALORIES = 114; CALORIES FROM FAT = 17%

GREEK TOMATO OMELET
Omelettar me Damates
TPT - about 16 minutes

The first time I encountered this dish, I was appalled with the enormous amount of olive oil used and although I ran into it a number of times through the years, I just turned a blind eye to the delicious and unusual possibility. Every once and while the idea surfaced in my mind until I finally evolved and tasted this version of the classic Greek omelet. It is incredibly delicious with just the touch of olive oil and butter as used in eastern Sicily where Greek influences can still be found.

Europe–Greece

GREEK TOMATO OMELET (cont'd)

1 teaspoon butter
1 teaspoon *extra virgin* olive oil
1 cup canned, *diced* tomatoes—*well-drained*
1 tablespoon dried basil—crushed
1 teaspoon dried oregano—crushed
Freshly ground black pepper, to taste

4 large eggs—well-beaten*
1 tablespoon grated (about 1/2 ounce) *pecorino Romano or* Parmesan cheese, as preferred

Preheat broiler to about 350 degrees F.

In a 9-inch skillet,** set over *MEDIUM* heat, heat butter and olive oil. Add chopped tomatoes, crushed basil and oregano, and black pepper. Sauté *gently* for several minutes.

Stir in beaten eggs, spreading evenly over pan surface. Cook, *undisturbed*, until set. Wrap pan handle with aluminum foil, if necessary, to protect it from burning. Sprinkle the omelet with grated cheese and place under preheated broiler until *lightly browned*. Be careful not to scorch eggs.

Slide out of skillet onto a heated round serving platter.

Serve at once, cut into wedges. Accompany with whole wheat French or Italian bread and olives.

Yields 4-5 servings
adequate for 3-4 people

Notes: *Four eggs make a thin omelet, quite adequate for three people. This is easily increased proportionately as needed using the same 9-inch or a 10-inch skillet although it will require a longer cooking period and produce a thicker omelet.

**We use a non-stick-coated skillet which we further coat with a non-stick lecithin spray coating to facilitate the release of the omelet for serving.

1/5 SERVING – PROTEIN = 5.9 g.; FAT = 6.4 g.; CARBOHYDRATE = 1.9 g.;
CALORIES = 78; CALORIES FROM FAT = 74%

GREEK SHREDDED WHEAT DESSERT
Pseftiko Kataifi

TPT - 3 hours and 4 minutes;
2 hours = cooling period

We always enjoyed the Greek pastries, among them "pseftiko kataifi," sold at the annual festivals held at Greek Orthodox churches on Long Island. A thread-like dough, known as kataifi, is used for several Greek and Syrian desserts but outside of Greek neighborhoods, it is difficult to find. When we moved to Pennsylvania, we knew that, unless we traveled to a Greek bakery over two hours away in Scranton, we were either going to have to forget about these treats or improvise. So we improvised just as do many of Greek descent. Shredded wheat is an acceptable substitute and, instead of the large shredded wheat pillows, we use the mini wheat squares to make both the assembly and serving easier.

1/4 cup *whole* milk
1 tablespoon corn starch

40 unsweetened mini shredded wheat squares*
Boiling water
1 tablespoon butter—*melted*

FILLING:
    1/2 cup *finely* chopped *preservative-free* walnuts
    1/2 teaspoon ground cinnamon

40 unsweetened mini shredded wheat squares*
Boiling water

1 tablespoon butter—*melted*

SYRUP:
    1 cup sugar
    1/2 cup water

    1/2 teaspoon pure vanilla extract
    1/2 teaspoon pure almond extract
    1/2 teaspoon freshly squeezed lemon juice

GREEK SHREDDED WHEAT DESSERT (cont'd)

Preheat oven to 350 degrees F. Prepare a 9 x 5 x 3-inch non-stick-coated loaf pan by coating with non-stick lecithin spray coating.

In a small bowl, combine milk and cornstarch. Whisk until cornstarch is in suspension. Set aside until required.

Pour *boiling* water into a small dish. Place two or three shredded wheat squares on a slotted spoon or spatula and dip them in and out of the *boiling* water *quickly*. Hold up in the air to drain and then transfer them to the prepared loaf pan, tucking them up against each other in a single layer. Continue until you have single layer covering the bottom of the loaf pan.

Drizzle 1 tablespoonful of *melted* butter over the layer of shredded wheat squares. Drizzle 2 tablespoonfuls of prepared milk–corn starch suspension over.

Prepare the FILLING by combining *finely* chopped walnuts and ground cinnamon. Stir to combine thoroughly. Sprinkle as evenly as possible over the layer of shredded wheat in the loaf pan.

Then, dip the remaining squares of shredded wheat in *boiling* water just as you had done for the first layer. Form a second layer by putting each square on top of a filling-covered square in the first layer.

Drizzle 1 tablespoonful of *melted* butter over the second layer of shredded wheat squares. Drizzle the remaining 2 tablespoonfuls of prepared milk–corn starch suspension over.

Bake in preheated 350 degree F. oven for 20 minutes. Remove to a wire rack.

Prepare the SYRUP. In a deep saucepan set over *MEDIUM* heat, combine sugar and water. Allow to come to the boil. Boil the sugar syrup until it reaches 200 degrees F. on a candy thermometer. Using a brush, brush down any sugar crystals on the side of pan. *Remove from heat.*

Stir vanilla and almond extracts and lemon juice into the sugar syrup. Pour immediately over the hot pastry. Allow to cool on the wire rack at room temperature for at least 2 hours before cutting.

Serve onto a dessert plate using a long spatula or two spatulas.

Yields 8 servings
adequate for 6-8 people

Notes: Original shredded wheat can be used but we use this opportunity to inject a bit more fiber into our diet buy using the wheat and bran variety.

This recipe can be doubled using a 9-inch square baking pan.

1/8 SERVING – PROTEIN = 2.6 g.; FAT = 3.5 g.; CARBOHYDRATE = 49.2 g.;
CALORIES = 225; CALORIES FROM FAT = 14%

Europe–Greece

GREEK FARINA CUSTARD
Poutika

TPT - 3 hours and 50 minutes;
3 hours = chilling period

There is incredible elegance in the simplicity of this classic dessert. It is beautifully complimented by a bowl of whole, unblanched, and unsalted almonds and an assortment of fresh fruit.

2 cups skimmed milk

1/4 cup enriched quick-cooking farina *or* **Cream of Wheat cereal**—*not instant*
1 tablespoon sugar

1/2 teaspoon pure vanilla extract
1 tablespoon butter
2 tablespoons *finely* **ground, preservative-free almonds** *or* **almond meal**
1 large egg—well-beaten

1/4 cup honey
1 teaspoon freshly squeezed lemon juice
2 tablespoons water

Ground cinnamon

Prepare a 7 x 3 x 2-inch loaf pan, a 1-quart soufflé dish, or other oven-proof mold by coating with non-stick lecithin spray coating.

In a saucepan set over *MEDIUM* heat, heat milk to the boiling point. Stir in farina and sugar. Cook, stirring frequently, for about 12 minutes, or until thickened. Remove from heat.

Beat in vanilla extract, butter, and *finely* ground almonds.

Preheat oven to 350 degrees F.

Add a tablespoonful of hot farina mixture to well-beaten egg and beat well. Beat egg mixture into hot farina.

Pour into prepared baking dish, spreading evenly. Bake in preheated 350 degree F. oven for 20 minutes. Set aside on a wire rack to cool slightly.

Prepare syrup by combining honey, lemon juice, and water in a saucepan. Bring to the boil over *MEDIUM* heat and sustain the boil for a full 5 minutes.

Pour syrup over baked custard and sprinkle generously with ground cinnamon. Using a thin bamboo skewer, poke holes about one-half way down into custard all across the surface.

Refrigerate for at least 3 hours to allow for syrup absorption.

Unmold onto serving dish. *Serve very cold,* spooning any remaining syrup over each serving.

Yields 5 servings
adequate for 4 people

Note: When doubled, a ring mold is perfect.

1/5 SERVING – PROTEIN = 6.4 g.; FAT = 6.9 g.; CARBOHYDRATE = 24.5 g.;
CALORIES = 185; CALORIES FROM FAT = 34%

Hungary

The Carpathian Basin was ruled by Romans, the Huns, and the Ostrogoths, a branch of the Goths who established the first and short-lived Kingdom of Italy in 497 AD under the Romanized, Theodoric the Great. The First Bulgarian Empire and Great Moravia were the rulers when semi-nomadic peoples from an area between the Volga River and Ural Mountains migrated into the Basin. They were unified in 895 AD by Árpád, becoming known as the Hungarians or Magyars. By the tenth century Hungary was a stable, settled Christian principality. The feudal state created by King (Saint) Stephen I and ruled by successive strong rulers was victim to the Mongol Invasion of 1241-1242 and it is believed that about two million people were killed by the Mongols. The return of the Mongols in 1286 was successfully repulsed due to the extensive and effective stone-castle fortification system built by King Belá. Hungary enjoyed a prosperous period that ended in the early sixteenth century when the Ottoman Empire, with whom they had been fighting on and off for more that 150 years, gained a foothold due to weak and ineffective rulers. With the Turkish conquest of Buda in 1526, Hungary was divided into three parts. The northwestern part was ruled by the Hapsburgs who declared themselves Kings of Hungary; the eastern part became the independent Principality of Transylvania; and the remaining central area, which included the capital of Buda, became known as the Pashalik of Buda. The country remained divided until Ottoman rule ended in 1718.

Recovery of the Hungarian identity was hampered by the Hapsburgs resettlement policies. The Austrian–Hapsburg government prohibited Hungarians from returning to the area of the Great Plain and settled Serbs and other Slavs in the depopulated southern areas. Germans were encouraged to settle in the lands vacated by the Ottoman Turks and Romanians immigrated in large numbers into Transylvania. The attempt to drive out the Hapsburg control was countered by Hapsburg Emperor Franz Joseph I, with the help of Czar Nicholas I of Russia, and the Austro–Hungarian Empire was created and persisted until the end of World War I.

In 1918 Hungary's union with Austria was dissolved. After what is often called the Aster Revolution, the First Republic of Hungary was declared and Mihály Károlyi was named its first president. Károlyi embraced the political philosophy of entente and called for full disarmament, leaving the country without a national defense system and vulnerable to invasion. When the opportunity presented itself, Romania took over Transylvania to which many ethnic Romanians had migrated during the Hapsburg period. Czechoslovakia saw opportunity too and took control of the northern areas while the southern parts of the country were invaded by a joint force of Serbian and French military. Each occupation included areas in which their nationals had settled but each took the opportunity to extend their control. Further, in 1919 the Communists took power in Hungary but brief as this Hungarian Soviet Republic was, it did establish a mindset that would accept the Soviet Communist occupation after World War II. In 1920 the Treaty of Trianon established new borders for Hungary with a loss of seventy-one percent of its territory and sixty-six percent of its population. Hungary resisted return of the monarchy and functioned as a parliamentary democracy, albeit autocratic, until the coming of war again in Europe. Hungary entered the war on the side of the Axis Powers and after World War II became a satellite state of the Soviet Union. Intellectuals and Hungarian nationalists were executed or imprisoned in labor camps by the Soviets leading to the 1956 Hungarian Revolution. Although Hungary remained well within the Soviet sphere of influence, a slight lifting of pressure by Moscow occurred with the reduction of military production, an increase in consumer priorities, and the introduction of free market elements. With changes in the Soviet Union, Hungary established the Third Hungarian Republic in 1989 and is today a parliamentary republic once more.

Europe – Hungary

Lecsó in *Phyllo* Nest
Lecsó Filó

or

Lecsó Omelet
Lecsó Tojassal

Hungarian Vegetable *Mélange*
Lecsó

~

Bean Soup and Pinched Dumplings
Bableves Ssipet Kevel

~~~~~~~~~~~~~~~~~~~~~

Meatless *Goulash*   and   Tomato and Cucumber Salad
Goulash   *Paradicson – Uborka Salata*

or

Celeriac Salad
Zellersalata

~~~~~~~~~~

Savoy Cabbage and Potatoes   Creamy Mushrooms with Paprika
Kelkáposzta – Fözelék   *Gombapaprikas*

and

Yellow Summer Squash with *Crème*
Tejfeles Tokkaposzta

Pepper Salad
Paprikasalata

~~~~~~~~~~~~~~~~~~~~

Chocolate Almond *Torte*   Toasted Hazelnut *Torte*
                                        Mogyoros Torta

Vanilla Buttercream Frosting

Applesauce with Sour Cream Sauce   Our Favorite Applesauce

Chestnut Purée with Whipped Cream
Gestenyepüré

~

Homemade Paprika

Hungarians generally do not serve a side vegetable if they include a salad in a menu. On the other hand, several vegetable dishes, such as those in the menu above, can be served as an entirely adequate entrée combination.

Europe–**Hungary**

LECSÓ IN *PHYLLO* NEST
Lecsó Filo

TPT - 54 minutes

Varying the way I prepare lecsó makes every one of those containers I freeze each fall welcome to cook and family. I serve it as a stew or over noodles and as an omelet filling, much like a frittata. Wanting the meal to be a bit more celebratory one day, I decided to create a phyllo tart. Phyllo or filo, introduced to Hungary from the Middle East by the Turks in the sixteenth century, is the model for the strudel pastry made with such skill by Hungarians. The thicker sheets of frozen commercial phyllo contain the lecsó more efficiently than would the paper-thin strudel sheets my grandmother and great-grandmother hung over the damp towel-covered kitchen chairs as they worked.

**3 cups HUNGARIAN VEGETABLE *MÉLANGE*
(Lecsó)** *[see recipe which follows]*—**well-drained**

6 sheets *frozen phyllo* **pastry**—*defrosted*
1 tablespoon soft butter spread
2 tablespoons dry breadcrumbs

1 tablespoon grated *pecorino Romano* **or
Parmesan cheese, as preferred**

Preheat oven to 350 degrees F. Prepare a 10-inch pie plate by coating with non-stick lecithin spray coating.

Set a fine sieve over a mixing bowl. Pour *defrosted lecsó* into the sieve and allow the *lecsó* to drain thoroughly while preparing the *phyllo* pastry nest.

Unroll *phyllo* pastry onto a clean, dry surface, cut each sheet in half, and cover with a dampened cotton towel.

Take one of the *half-sheets* of *phyllo* and place it on a dry work surface. Using a pastry brush, lightly brush the sheet with the soft butter spread. Place the buttered pastry sheet onto the pie plate, allowing it to hang over the edge of the plate. Take a pinch of the breadcrumbs and sprinkle them over the pastry surface. Take another *half-sheet* of *phyllo*, butter it, and place it on top of the first sheet at a 45-degree angle. Sprinkle with crumbs. Continue with four more *half-sheets* of *phyllo*, positioning each at a 45-degree angle from the previous sheet. Carefully, using both hands, tuck the flaps from these first six *half-sheets* of *phyllo* into the pie plate *under* the nest base. Continue adding buttered *half-sheets* of *phyllo* in the same manner with a sprinkling of breadcrumbs *but do not tuck these under, instead roll them gently toward the center*. Press the center down to form a nest. Bake in preheated oven until lightly browned—about 15-17 minutes.

While the pastry is baking, turn drained *lecsó* into a saucepan set over *LOW* heat. Allow to heat through, *stirring frequently to prevent the vegetables from sticking to the pan*. When heated through, set on a warming tray to keep warm. Also set a round serving platter on the warming tray.

When the pastry is baked and puffed, remove from oven and carefully transfer the crisp *phyllo* pastry nest to the heated serving platter. Use two spatulas to loosen the nest from the pie plate.

Pour the warm *lecsó* into the center of the nest.

Serve at once. Cut with a very sharp knife into pie-shaped wedges and transfer to each diner's plate. Sprinkle with grated cheese.

Yields 6 first-course servings
or 4 entrée portions

Note: This can be halved if required. Cut the *phyllo* sheets in half and arrange them in a 7-inch pie plate to make a perfect meal for two.

1/6 SERVING – PROTEIN = 2.6 g.; FAT = 3.9 g.; CARBOHYDRATE = 14.5 g.;
CALORIES = 104; CALORIES FROM FAT = 34%

Europe–**Hungary**

HUNGARIAN *LECSÓ* OMELET
Lecsó Tojassal
TPT - about 21 minutes

Lecsó in the freezer is meal insurance and this omelet is one of our favorite ways to get a really terrific dinner on the table quickly.

1 teaspoon CLARIFIED BUTTER *[see index]*
**1 cup HUNGARIAN VEGETABLE *MELANGÉ*
(Lecsó)** *[see recipe which follows]*

4 large eggs—well-beaten

**2 tablespoons grated (about 1/2 ounce) Parmesan
or aged Asiago cheese**, as preferred

2 tablespoons YOGURT *CRÈME* *[see index]* **or
fat-free dairy sour cream**, if preferred

Preheat broiler to about 350 degrees F.

In a 9-inch non-stick-coated skillet set over *MEDIUM-LOW* heat, heat the clarified butter until you are able to coat the pan's surface completely.

Add *lecsó* and, stirring constantly, heat through.

Stir in beaten eggs, spreading evenly over pan surface. Cook, *undisturbed*, until set. Wrap pan handle with aluminum foil, if necessary, to protect it from burning. Sprinkle the omelet with grated cheese and place under preheated broiler until *lightly browned. Be careful not to scorch eggs.*

Slide out onto a heated round serving platter. Spoon yogurt *crème* or sour cream into center of omelet.

Serve at once, cut into wedges.

Yields 4-5 servings
adequate for 3-4 people

Note: Four eggs make an omelet quite adequate for three people but perhaps a bit small for four, especially if any are hearty eaters. This is easily increased proportionately as needed using the same 9-inch or a 10-inch skillet. It will, however, require a longer cooking period and result in a thicker omelet. A luncheon dish for two can be prepared by halving the recipe and using a 7-inch skillet.

1/5 SERVING – PROTEIN = 7.0 g.; FAT = 7.0 g.; CARBOHYDRATE = 3.7 g.;
CALORIES = 106; CALORIES FROM FAT = 59%

HUNGARIAN VEGETABLE *MÉLANGE*
Lecsó
TPT - 55 minutes

This version of lecsó evolved as the result of the sharing of a family recipe by Judith Fulop of Seaford, Long Island, to whom I am eternally grateful. We make a big batch of lecsó in the fall when the produce is at its most luscious and freeze it for winter menus. It makes a quick, nutritious meal with poppy seed noodles or dumplings and a fascinatingly different appetizer for a formal dinner.

2 teaspoons CLARIFIED BUTTER *[see index]*
2 teaspoons vegetable oil
2 cups chopped onion

4 frying peppers—seeded and coarsely chopped
3 medium tomatoes—peeled, seeded, and coarsely chopped
1 red bell pepper—seeded and coarsely chopped
1 clove garlic—*finely* chopped
1 1/2 teaspoons HOMEMADE PAPRIKA *[see recipe which follows]* **or commercially-available Hungarian sweet paprika**
Pinch ground caraway seeds*
**Several dashes ground red pepper (cayenne),
or to taste**

In a large, heavy saucepan set over *LOW* heat, combine clarified butter, oil, and chopped onion. Sauté until *very soft* and *lightly golden,* being careful not to allow onion to brown.

Stir in chopped frying peppers, tomatoes, and red pepper, *finely* chopped garlic, paprika, ground caraway seeds, and ground red pepper (cayenne). Mix well. Simmer, uncovered, over *LOW* heat for about 30 minutes, or until a thick sauce results. Stir frequently.

Yields about 4 cupfuls

HUNGARIAN VEGETABLE *MÉLANGE* (cont'd)

Notes: *The caraway seeds are easily ground in a SPICE and COFFEE GRINDER or in a mortar using a pestle, if preferred.

This dish is often served in Hungary as an appetizer. As such, this would serve six people.

As a sauce for noodles, rice, or with dumplings, you can expect to serve four or five people.

1/6 SERVING – PROTEIN = 1.6 g.; FAT = 3.1 g.; CARBOHYDRATE = 8.9 g.; CALORIES = 68; CALORIES FROM FAT = 41%

HUNGARIAN BEAN SOUP AND PINCHED DUMPLINGS
Babléves Szipet Kevel

TPT - 13 hours and 48 minutes;
8 hours = bean soaking period

Soups, stews, casseroles, and salads that combine the complementary proteins of legumes and grains are found all over the planet. Before man figured out that certain edibles contained complete, complemented, proteins and that most plants did not, breads sopped up bean soups, Italians created minestrones in infinite variety, and the beans and rice cultures were eating very nicely, thank you. Here, much loved dumplings, whose grain protein is deficient in isoleucine and lysine, are boosted by isoleucine- and lysine-rich beans.

2 cups dry navy *or* Great Northern beans
1 quart water

2 quarts water

2 medium carrots—peeled or scraped and diced
1 medium parsnip—peeled and diced
2 tablespoons chopped fresh parsley
14 cups water

1 tablespoon butter
1 large onion—diced

2 tablespoons whole wheat flour

1 teaspoon HOMEMADE PAPRIKA *[see recipe which follows]* or **commercially-available Hungarian sweet paprika**
1/2 teaspoon freshly ground black pepper

1 cup unbleached white flour
1/4 teaspoon salt
1 large egg
2 tablespoons water

2 tablespoons chopped fresh dillweed, for garnish

Rinse dry white beans in several changes of water. Remove and discard any of poor quality. Place in a bowl with the 1 quartful water and soak overnight in the refrigerator.

Next morning, drain beans and place in a large kettle with the 2 quartfuls water. Bring to the boil, reduce heat to *LOW*, partially cover, and allow to simmer for 2 hours, stirring occasionally. Turn partially cooked beans into a sieve and drain.

PREPARE SOUP by placing drained beans, diced carrots and parsnip, chopped parsley, and 14 cupfuls water into a large kettle. Bring to the boil over *MEDIUM-HIGH* heat. Reduce heat to *LOW* and simmer for 2 hours, stirring frequently.

In a skillet set over *MEDIUM* heat, melt butter. Add diced onion and sauté until onion is soft and translucent, *being careful not to allow onions to brown*.

Stir in whole wheat flour, blend well to form a *roux*. Pour in 1 cupful of bean broth. Stir to blend well. Pour into soup.

Add paprika and black pepper. Continue cooking, stirring frequently, for about 1 hour, or until beans are tender and soup is thickened.*

Meanwhile, PREPARE PINCHED DUMPLINGS by sifting the 1 cupful flour and salt into a mixing bowl. Make a well in the center. Add the egg and the water to the well and, using a fork, stir to form a dough. Turn out onto a *lightly floured* surface. Knead until smooth. Roll out to 1/8-inch thickness and allow rolled dough to rest for 30 minutes.

Pinch off small pieces of dough with fingers and drop into boiling soup. Dumplings will rise to the surface and float when done.

HUNGARIAN BEAN SOUP AND PINCHED DUMPLINGS (cont'd)

Ladle into a heated soup tureen and serve into heated soup plates. Garnish each serving with chopped dillweed.

Yields 10 servings
adequate for 8-10 people

Notes: *If convenient, the soup may be frozen at this point for future menus.

This recipe may be halved or doubled, when required.

An interesting variation, HUNGARIAN BEAN SOUP AND PINCHED DUMPLINGS WITH VEGETARIAN FRANKS, may be prepared by dropping sliced low-fat vegetarian soy "hot dogs" into hot soup *just before serving*.

1/8 SERVING – PROTEIN = 10.7 g.; FAT = 2.5 g.; CARBOHYDRATE = 34.7 g.;
CALORIES = 205; CALORIES FROM FAT = 11%

HUNGARIAN MEATLESS *GOULASH*
Goulash
TPT - 1 hour

It was more than thirty-five years after we had chosen a vegetarian lifestyle that I even considered making Hungarian goulash. Goulash, as I remembered it from my living-on-campus college years, looked like it sounded. It was this mass of ketchup-coated shin beef and onions ladled over noodles with gritty paprika in every mouthful. Then, there were no considerations for vegetarians so we ate what was served or nothing. Occasionally, because one of our housemates waitressed, you could purloin an extra dessert as the tray sat carelessly, but intentionally, next to you for a few extra seconds. This opportunity could only happen if you were not sitting at the housemother's table for a lesson in table manners. Boy, did we scramble! An extra slice of pie or cake or rice pudding, if you were really lucky, could hold you until breakfast when you could satisfy your appestat with several servings of oatmeal.

To eliminate that smoky, often bitter, off flavor that you can get from smoked paprika, I use only sweet paprika; to eliminate the gritty paprika sensation, I do not add it directly to the stew but instead create a paste with roasted, red peppers and tomato paste using the food processor.* I also use the more complex vegetable stock that I make from soup. It adds considerable flavor.

2 cups *boiling* water
1 teaspoon SEASONING MIXTURE FOR DEHYDRATED SOY MEAT ANALOGUE
 [see index]
2 ounces So Soya+ dehydrated soy meat analogue slices/nuggets *or* other dehydrated meat analogue product

HUNGARIAN PAPRIKA CREAM:
 3 tablespoons HOMEMADE PAPRIKA
  [see recipe which follows] *or* commercially-available Hungarian sweet paprika
 1/3 cup ROASTED RED PEPPERS
  (Peperoni Arrosto) [see index]—well-drained if packed in oil**
 1 1/2 tablespoons tomato purée
 1 1/2 tablespoons tomato paste
 1 teaspoon distilled white vinegar

1 tablespoon butter
1 tablespoon canola oil
2 large *sweet* onions—such as Vidalia, Walla Walla, *or* Mayan or Texas Sweet—chopped

2 large carrots—scraped or pared and cut into 1/2-inch chunks
1 large bay leaf—broken in half
2 tablespoons water

1 cup VEGETABLE STOCK FROM SOUP [see index] *or* other vegetarian stock of choice

2 tablespoons *fat-free* dairy sour cream

Freshly ground black pepper, to taste

In a pie plate, combine *boiling* water and seasoning mixture. Stir to mix thoroughly. Add dehydrated meat analogue and allow the product to rehydrate for about 20 minutes. Drain thoroughly and set aside until required.

In the work bowl of food processor, combine paprika, roasted red peppers, tomato purée, tomato paste, and vinegar. Process until a smooth purée results. Transfer to a small bowl and set aside until required.

Europe–Hungary

HUNGARIAN MEATLESS *GOULASH* (cont'd)

In a kettle set over *MEDIUM* heat, heat butter and oil. Add chopped onion and sauté until onion is soft and translucent, *being careful not to allow the onion to brown.*

Add prepared PAPRIKA CREAM. Stir to combine well. Cook, stirring frequently, until onions begin to stick to the bottom of the kettle.

Add carrot chunks, reconstituted soy slices/nuggets, bay leaf pieces, and water. Stir to coat vegetables with the tomato–paprika mixture. *Reduce heat to LOW-MEDIUM.*

Add vegetable stock, cover, and allow to simmer for about 20 minutes, stirring occasionally. Remove and discard bay leaf pieces.

Taste and season with black pepper.****

When ready to serve, stir in sour cream. Serve over wide noodles, if desired.

Yields 6 serving
adequate for 4 people

Notes: *There is a hard-to-find product called HUNGARIAN PAPRIKA CREAM in which the paprika is combined with puréed bell pepper. This condiment, if available, will accomplish pretty much what my pepper–paprika purée accomplishes except that I introduce my tomato flavoring into the goulash in my paprika cream. My Hungarian Paprika Cream can be made in quantity and frozen for addition to casseroles and as a sauce, when needed. If you choose to use the commercial paprika cream, you will have to add tomato paste or purée to your stew.

**Commercially-available, jarred roasted red peppers can be substituted.

***Frozen soy bites, a soy analogue product of amazing texture, was available when I first evolved this recipe but was discontinued by several manufacturers and became increasingly difficult to obtain. A dehydrated version, available from a Canadian mail order firm and packaged under the name Soy Soya+, can be used but must first be rehydrated with vegetable stock or water.

****If you are making this early in the day or the day before, do not add the sour cream. Instead, refrigerate the stew and reheat it just before serving. The sour cream should be stirred in just before serving.

This recipe can be halved or doubled, when required.

1/6 SERVING (using dehydrated soy analogue) –
PROTEIN = 5.1 g.; FAT = 4.2 g.; CARBOHYDRATE = 13.1 g.;
CALORIES = 108; CALORIES FROM FAT = 35%

TOMATO AND CUCUMBER SALAD WITH PEPPERS
Paradiscom – Uborka Salata

TPT - 1 hour and 8 minutes;
1 hour = flavor development period

Fresh, vine-ripened tomatoes and a warm cucumber straight from the garden make the taste of this summer salad a refreshing accompaniment to the more heavily seasoned dishes common to the Hungarian cuisine. It is the kind of salad that no one ever thinks of as ethnic but it is a very popular salad in Hungary.

3 medium tomatoes—sliced
1 medium cucumber—peeled, scored, and sliced
2 red, yellow, and orange *baby* peppers—cored, seeded, and sliced into rings
1/2 medium onion—*thinly* sliced

[see next page]

VOLUME I - 178

TOMATO AND CUCUMBER SALAD WITH PEPPERS (cont'd)

1 garlic clove—*very finely* chopped
1 tablespoon *finely* snipped dillweed
2 tablespoons *extra virgin* olive oil
1 tablespoon red wine vinegar
1/2 teaspoon sugar
Salt, to taste
Freshly ground black pepper, to taste

In a large, shallow serving dish, arrange tomato slices. Layer the cucumber slices over the tomatoes. Layer the pepper rings over the cucumbers. Scatter the onion slices over.

In a small bowl, combine *very finely* chopped garlic clove, *finely* snipped dillweed, olive oil, vinegar, sugar, salt, and black pepper. Using a small wire whisk or a fork, stir vigorously to blend. Drizzle over the salad. Refrigerate for 1 hour to allow for flavor development.

Serve chilled. Using a broad, slotted serving spoon, spoon a selection of vegetables onto a salad plate.

Yields 6 servings
adequate for 4 people

1/6 SERVING – PROTEIN = 1.1 g.; FAT = 3.9 g.; CARBOHYDRATE = 5.4 g.;
CALORIES = 60; CALORIES FROM FAT = 59%

HUNGARIAN CELERIAC SALAD
Zellersaláta

TPT - 1 hour and 37 minutes;
1 hour = refrigeration period

The intense celery taste of the celeriac, also known as knob celery or celery root, gives a fresh taste to this winter salad that is served as a salad or as a side vegetable in Hungary. It is a most unusual vegetable dish.

2 cups water
1 tablespoon freshly squeezed lemon juice

1 medium-sized celeriac—peeled

1/4 cup white wine vinegar
1 teaspoon sugar
Salt, to taste
Freshly ground white pepper, to taste

1/2 medium onion—sliced into *very thin* slices
1 tablespoon *very finely* chopped parsley

1 1/2 teaspoons *light* olive oil

In a saucepan set over *LOW-MEDIUM* heat, combine water and lemon juice.

While the acidulated water is coming to the boil, plane the celeriac into *thin* slices using a cheese plane or a mandolin. Drop them into the acidulated water and boil until they are *crisp-tender*—about 12 minutes. Ladle them from the cooking water to a bowl and allow to cool. *Save the cooking water.*

Add the vinegar, sugar, salt, and white pepper to 1/2 cupful of the cooking water. Set over *MEDIUM-HIGH* heat and again allow to come to the boil and reduced by about one-half.

On a platter or dinner plate, sprinkle the *very thin* onion slices and *very finely* chopped parsley onto the platter. Pour the hot dressing over the onion and parsley.

Carefully transfer the celeriac slices to the platter. Sprinkle the olive oil over. Refrigerate for at least 1 hour.

Serve with a slotted spoon. Refrigerated leftovers which will keep well for a week or so.

Yields 6 servings
adequate for 4 people

Note: This recipe can be halved or doubled, when required.

1/6 SERVING – PROTEIN = 0.3 g.; FAT = 1.0 g.; CARBOHYDRATE = 3.0 g.;
CALORIES = 20; CALORIES FROM FAT = 45%

Europe–**Hungary**

HUNGARIAN SAVOY CABBAGE AND POTATOES
Kelkáposzta – Főzelék
TPT - 40 minutes

Savoy cabbage is a beautiful vegetable and it, too, winters well. I remember my grandparents' root cellar and there were always a couple of these cabbages among the cabbages for special holiday dishes. This creamy, comforting stewed vegetable dish contains no cream or cheese. It is one of those dishes I like to use to illustrate that vegetables do contribute protein to a meal . . . a little here . . . a little there . . .

4 1/2-inch head savoy cabbage

3 quarts *boiling* water
1/2 teaspoon caraway seeds
2 medium potatoes—peeled and diced

1 1/2 tablespoons butter
1 1/2 tablespoons unbleached white flour
3 tablespoons grated onion
1 garlic clove—crushed and *very finely* chopped
1/4 teaspoon HOMEMADE PAPRIKA [see recipe which follows] or commercially-available Hungarian sweet paprika
1/4 cup water
Salt, to taste
Freshly ground black pepper, to taste

Thin orange, red, or yellow bell pepper rings, to garnish

Separate cabbage leaves. Remove core and tough ribs. Rinse thoroughly. Cut cabbage into strips.

In a large saucepan set over *MEDIUM* heat, combine *boiling* water, caraway seeds, diced potatoes, and cabbage strips. Cook until potatoes and cabbage are tender. Drain.

In a skillet set over *LOW-MEDIUM* heat, melt butter. Remove from heat and make a *roux* by beating in flour. Return to heat and, stirring constantly, cook for 2 minutes, *being careful not to burn or overbrown the roux*. Remove from heat and add grated onion, *very finely* chopped garlic, paprika, and water. Return saucepan to heat and cook, stirring constantly, for just a minute or two.

Add cooked and drained cabbage and potatoes. Cook, stirring frequently, until almost "pulp-like."

Season with salt and black pepper. Turn into a heated serving bowl. Garnish with pepper rings.

Serve at once.

Yields 6 servings
adequate for 4 people

Note: This recipe can be halved or doubled, when required.

1/6 SERVING – PROTEIN = 1.8 g.; FAT = 2.1 g.; CARBOHYDRATE = 12.4 g.;
CALORIES = 72; CALORIES FROM FAT = 26%

CREAMY HUNGARIAN MUSHROOMS WITH PAPRIKA
Gombapaprikás
TPT - 1 hour and 20 minutes;
    1 hour = mushroom soaking period

Dried mushrooms give a complexity to the flavor of this classic dish, usually made with freshly gathered mushrooms. Most Hungarian sources direct that the mushrooms be fried in lard and, of course, that full-fat sour cream be used. We prefer this modern, lighter version over rice, pasta, or boiled pierogi or just as a side dish.

3 cups dried mushrooms*
1 quart *boiling* water

2 tablespoons butter
1 medium onion—*finely* chopped

1 teaspoon HOMEMADE PAPRIKA [see recipe which follows] or commercially-available Hungarian sweet paprika
Pinch or two *hot* Hungarian paprika, or to taste
2 tablespoons mushroom stock, drained from rehydrated mushrooms
2/3 cup *fat-free* dairy sour cream

Europe – **Hungary**

CREAMY HUNGARIAN MUSHROOMS WITH PAPRIKA (cont'd)

Put dried mushrooms into a mixing bowl. Pour *boiling* water over. Place a saucer on top to weigh down the mushrooms and keep them in contact with the water. Allow to rehydrate for about 1 hour. Drain, *but reserve mushroom stock.***

In a skillet set over *MEDIUM* heat, melt butter. Add *finely* chopped onions and sauté until soft and translucent, *being careful not to allow onions to brown.*

Reduce heat to LOW-MEDIUM. Add rehydrated mushrooms. Sprinkle paprika over sautéed onions. Add the 2 tablespoonfuls of mushroom stock. Stir to mix well. Cook, stirring frequently, until the liquid has been absorbed or has evaporated and the mixture is hot.

Add sour cream and cook, stirring constantly, until mixture is hot and bubbling. Thin with mushroom stock, if necessary.

Turn into a heated serving bowl.

Serve at once.

Yields 6 servings
adequate for 4 people

Notes: *We use our own dried *crimini* mushrooms for this recipe and add to it any dried wild mushrooms that we might have on hand, such as *porcini*, *shiitake*, and *morels*.

**Freeze leftover mushroom soaking water and use in soups and stews.

This recipe can be halved, when required.

1/6 SERVING – PROTEIN = 4.0 g.; FAT = 1.9 g.; CARBOHYDRATE = 12.7 g.;
CALORIES = 83; CALORIES FROM FAT = 21%

HUNGARIAN YELLOW SUMMER SQUASH WITH *CRÈME*
Tejfeles Tokkaposzta

TPT - 14 minutes

Hungarians are very fond of noodles and my first instinct with any Hungarian menu is to plan to serve noodles in some form. However, the shredded squash looks very noodle-like when presented so I have to remember to leave the noodles out of this menu.

2 large yellow summer squashes—peeled, seeded,*
  and shredded into long pieces** *or* cut into long
  julienne pieces
2 teaspoons freshly squeezed lemon juice

2 teaspoons butter
3 tablespoons *finely* chopped onion

1 tablespoon chopped fresh dillweed
3 tablespoons YOGURT *CRÈME* [see index]

Prepare a steamer. When ready, steam squash until *crisp-tender*—about 2 minutes. Toss with lemon juice. Set aside.

In a saucepan set over *MEDIUM-LOW* heat, combine butter and *finely* chopped onion. Sauté onion until soft and translucent, *being careful not to allow onions to brown.*

Add steamed yellow squash and, stirring constantly, cook until heated through.

Stir in chopped dillweed and YOGURT *CRÈME*. Cook, stirring constantly, until heated through. Turn into a heated serving bowl.

Serve at once.

Yields 6 servings
adequate for 4 people

Notes: *Save seed and pulp for stock pot.

**Without the special Hungarian shredder used for this preparation, the easiest way we have found is to first, quarter and seed the squashes. Then, using a vegetable peeler, pare long shreds from the sides of each quarter. That which can not be shredded can be finely sliced into long julienne pieces.

This recipe may be halved or doubled, when required.

1/6 SERVING – PROTEIN = 2.4 g.; FAT = 1.5 g.; CARBOHYDRATE = 6.7 g.;
CALORIES = 45; CALORIES FROM FAT = 30%

Europe–**Hungary**

HUNGARIAN PEPPER SALAD
Paprikasaláta

TPT - 2 hours and 12 minutes;
  1 hour = salting period;
  1 hour = flavor development period

In Hungary you find peppers of all kinds and colors used in profusion when they are in season in ways that we in the West could not even imagine. This salad is perfectly beautiful and the salting period allows for the pepper rings to wilt to an amazing texture.

1 *medium green* bell pepper—cored, seeded, and cut into rings
1 *medium red* bell pepper—cored, seeded, and cut into rings
1 *baby yellow* bell pepper—cored, seeded, and cut into rings
1 *baby orange* bell pepper—cored, seeded, and cut into rings

Salt

1 tablespoon safflower *or* sunflower oil
1 tablespoon white wine vinegar
1/4 teaspoon freshly squeezed lemon juice
1/2 teaspoon sugar
Freshly ground black pepper, to taste
HOMEMADE PAPRIKA *[see recipe which follows]* **or** commercially-available Hungarian sweet paprika

In a shallow serving bowl, combine pepper rings. Salt generously. Place a plate on top of the bowl and allow the peppers to stand at room temperature for 1 hour. Rinse thoroughly with cold water and drain well. Return the pepper rings to the serving bowl. Arrange the pepper rings attractively.

In a small bowl, combine oil, vinegar, lemon juice, and sugar. Using a small whisk, beat until emulsified. Pour over the pepper rings. Grind black pepper over. Lightly sprinkle paprika over. Refrigerate for 1 hour before serving.

Serve chilled. Refrigerate any leftovers.

Yields 6 servings
adequate for 4 people

Note: This recipe can be halved or doubled, when required.

1/6 SERVING – PROTEIN = 0.7 g.; FAT = 2.4 g.; CARBOHYDRATE = 3.6 g.;
CALORIES = 37; CALORIES FROM FAT = 58%

HUNGARIAN TOASTED HAZELNUT *TORTE*
Magyaros Torta

TPT - 1 hour and 26 minutes

Hungarian desserts are celebratory dishes; they can be rich and quite extreme. Back in the years when I was growing up such tortes as these were offered in tiny slivers as refreshment when my mother invited two tables of bridge or when she hosted my grandmother and her friends who loved to play pinochle. It was all very lovely, I remember, with beautiful hand-embroidered card table tablecloths, with corner pockets for your cards, and tiny, tea-time linen napkins.

1/4 cup butter—*softened to room temperature*
1/4 cup sugar
1 cup *fat-free* pasteurized eggs (the equivalent of 4 eggs)

4 ounces semi-sweet chocolate bits

1/2 cup whole wheat breadcrumbs
1/2 cup ground, *preservative-free* hazelnuts or filberts—*lightly toasted*

8 large egg whites

1 cup BASIC VANILLA BUTTERCREAM FROSTING *[see recipe which follows]**

1 tablespoon ground, *preservative-free* hazelnuts or filberts—*lightly toasted*

Preheat oven to 325 degree F. Line three 8-inch cake pans with waxed paper.

In the container of the food processor fitted with steel knife or using the electric mixer, cream butter until light and fluffy. Add sugar and pasteurized eggs. Process until thick and lemon-colored.

Melt chocolate over hot water. Remove from heat.

HUNGARIAN TOASTED HAZELNUT *TORTE* (cont'd)

In a mixing bowl, combine breadcrumbs and 1/2 cupful *toasted* ground hazelnuts. Add melted chocolate. Stir to combine thoroughly. Add egg mixture. Stir again to combine thoroughly.

Using an electric mixer fitted with *grease-free* beaters or by hand using a *grease-free* wire whisk, beat egg whites in a *grease-free* bowl until stiff peaks form. Using a wire whisk, *whisk-fold gently,* but *thoroughly,* into chocolate–nut–yolk mixture. When thoroughly combined, divide evenly among three prepared cake pans.

Bake in preheated 325 degree F. oven for 24 minutes, or until no depression remains when lightly touched with your finger. Remove from oven and allow to *cool completely in baking pans* on wire racks.

Remove one layer to cake dish covered with paper lace dollies. Spread with *one-third* of the VANILLA BUTTERCREAM FROSTING. Place next layer on top; frost with *one-half* of remaining frosting. Place last layer on top; frost *attractively* with remaining frosting. Dust with remaining *toasted* ground hazelnuts.

Slice into wedges as for a cake to serve.**

Yields 20 servings
adequate for 10-14 people

Notes: *We prefer a vanilla buttercream frosting on this *torte* but a coffee buttercream frosting is also very complimentary.

**If you refrigerate leftovers, be sure to bring the *torte* to room temperature before serving.

1/20 SERVING – PROTEIN = 12.0 g.; FAT = 10.1 g.; CARBOHYDRATE = 12.4 g.;
CALORIES = 246; CALORIES FROM FAT = 37%

BASIC VANILLA BUTTERCREAM FROSTING
TPT - 20 minutes

There is no limit to the flavoring or coloring variations that you can produce with this basic cake frosting recipe.

1/2 cup (1 stick) butter—*softened to room temperature*
1 cup confectioners' sugar
1 1/2 teaspoons pure vanilla extract

3-4 tablespoons skimmed milk
About 2 cups confectioners' sugar

Using an electric mixer, or food processor fitted with steel knife, or by hand, cream butter until light and fluffy. Gradually beat the 1 cupful confectioners' sugar into the creamed butter. Continue beating until smooth. Add vanilla extract. Mix well.

Beat in the remaining 2 cupfuls confectioners' sugar gradually alternating with milk, adding more of each until a smooth, spreadable consistency is achieved.

Use to frost cakes or cookies.*

Yields enough to frost two 9-inch
cake layers or about 24-30 cupcakes

Notes: *The consistency of this may readily be altered to produce a buttercream filling for pastries, *tortes*, and cakes or a substitute for fondant in making *petits fours*.

Prepared frosting freezes well.

This recipe may be doubled, when required. It should, however, be noted that if this is being prepared by hand, a double batch is unwieldy.

1/16 SERVING (i. e., that which would be used on a two-layer slice of cake exclusive of the cake) –
PROTEIN = 0.1 g.; FAT = 5.7 g.; CARBOHYDRATE = 2.9 g.;
CALORIES = 152; CALORIES FROM FAT = 34%

1/24 SERVING (i. e., that which would be used on a cupcake exclusive of the cupcake) –
PROTEIN = 0.1 g.; FAT = 3.8 g.; CARBOHYDRATE = 2.0 g.;
CALORIES = 101; CALORIES FROM FAT = 34%

Europe–**Hungary**

CHOCOLATE ALMOND *TORTE*
TPT - 48 minutes

The word torte used to frighten me as a teenager. I remember my mother preparing elaborate tortes and it seemed to me, with little experience in cooking at that stage of my life, that this dessert must be difficult and fussy. This recipe certainly is not difficult or fussy but it is rich and delicious, a perfect dessert for the holidays.

6 tablespoons butter—*softened to room temperature*
1 cup sugar

3/4 cup *fat-free* **pasteurized eggs (the equivalent of 3 eggs)**
2 teaspoons freeze-dried coffee granules

4 squares *unsweetened* **chocolate**—*melted*
1/2 cup *preservative-free* **almond meal** *or* **ground almonds**
1/4 cup dry breadcrumbs
1 tablespoon *Cointreau* **liqueur** *or* **Grand Marnier, if preferred**
1 teaspoon pure vanilla extract
1 tablespoon orange juice

Sweetened whipped cream, for garnish

Preheat oven to 375 degrees F. Prepare an 8-inch non-stick-coated cake pan by coating with non-stick lecithin spray coating for baking.

In the mixing bowl of the electric mixer fitted with paddle, cream softened butter until light and fluffy. Add sugar and continue creaming until again light and fluffy.

Dissolve coffee granules in pasteurized eggs.

Gradually, tablespoonful by tablespoonful, add eggs while continuing to beat. *Gradually* add melted chocolate. Add almond meal, breadcrumbs, *Cointreau* liqueur, and vanilla extract. Beat until smooth. Turn into prepared baking pan. Bake in preheated 375 degree F. oven for 23-25 minutes, or until a cake tester inserted in the center comes out clean. Remove from oven and transfer to wire rack, *but leave torte in pan*. Allow to cool for 5 minutes. Invert *torte* onto wire rack.

Drizzle orange juice over the top. Allow to cool completely Slide onto serving dish. Refrigerate if not to be served the same day.

Cut into wedges to serve. Garnish with whipped cream, if desired. Cover and refrigerate leftovers.

Yields 12 servings
adequate for 8-10 people

1/12 SERVING – PROTEIN = 5.6 g.; FAT = 18.8 g.; CARBOHYDRATE = 29.2 g.;
CALORIES = 290; CALORIES FROM FAT = 58%

APPLESAUCE WITH SOUR CREAM SAUCE
TPT - 3 minutes, if you have already canned the applesauce;
1 hour and 53 minutes, if you have to make the applesauce

Time demands can easily get in the way with today's busy life styles discouraging the thoughts of strudels and tortes as dessert options but this quickly prepared dessert recipe is an absolutely perfect ending to a Hungarian menu. Hungarians serve an applesauce with sour cream to accompany savory dishes so this seems quite appropriate.

SOUR CREAM SAUCE:
    5 tablespoons *fat-free* **dairy sour cream**
    1 1/2 tablespoons heavy whipping cream
    1 tablespoon sugar
    Several drops pure vanilla extract

4 cupfuls OUR FAVORITE APPLESAUCE *[see recipe which follows]*—*well-chilled*

In a small bowl, combine sour cream, cream, sugar, and vanilla extract. Stir to combine thoroughly. Turn into a small serving bowl. Refrigerate until ready to serve.

Apportion chilled applesauce into six serving dishes. Spoon about a tablespoonful of the sour cream sauce into the center to garnish.

Serve chilled.

Yields 6 servings

Note: This recipe can be halved or doubled.

1/6 SERVING – PROTEIN = 2.0 g.; FAT = 2.0 g.; CARBOHYDRATE = 21.9 g.;
CALORIES = 103; CALORIES FROM FAT = 18%

Europe–**Hungary**

OUR FAVORITE APPLESAUCE
TPT - about 1 hour and 50 minutes;
1 hour = chilling period

My great-grandmother, my grandmother, and my mother all canned their own applesauce from New York State apples and they all had their favorite recipes and their personal favorite apple variety. This is my favorite applesauce recipe. I love the seasoning, I love the texture, and, most importantly, I very much like knowing what is going into those jars.

8 large tart apples—*Cortland apples are our choice*
3/4 cup water, or less if preferred

2 tablespoons sugar
1/4 teaspoon freshly grated nutmeg*
1/4 teaspoon ground cinnamon*
1/2 teaspoon freshly grated lemon zest

Wash apples, scrubbing well with a vegetable brush. Core apples but *do not pare*. Slice thinly into a large saucepan with a tightly fitting lid. Add water.

Set over *MEDIUM-HIGH* heat and bring to the boil. Reduce heat to *LOW* and simmer, tightly covered, for about 20 minutes, or until apples are soft. Stir occasionally.

If apples are not soft enough to put through a FOOD MILL at this point, mash with a potato masher or chop about 1 cupful at a time in a food processor, fitted with steel knife, or in the electric blender, *being careful not to liquefy*. Put chopped apples through FOOD MILL into a clean saucepan and discard residue.

Add sugar, nutmeg, cinnamon, and lemon zest to applesauce. Cook over *LOW-MEDIUM* heat, stirring constantly, until sugar is completely dissolved.

Chill for at least 1 hour before serving or freezing.

Yields about 4 cupfuls

Notes: *If applesauce is to be frozen, increase amount of spices used by about twenty-five percent. Frozen storage lessens their strengths.

If apples are quite sweet, add a little lemon juice and reduce amount of sugar used. On the other hand, if apples are very tart, add a bit more sugar.

When required, this recipe is easily halved or doubled. When preparing larger quantities, stir often during cooking period so that apple slices will all be softened to the same degree.

This applesauce may be canned using the boiling-water-bath method. Process for 10 minutes.

1/8 SERVING (i. e., per 1/2 cupful) –
PROTEIN = 0.2 g.; FAT = 0.6 g.; CARBOHYDRATE = 21.6 g.;
CALORIES = 83; CALORIES FROM FAT = 7%

CHESTNUT PURÉE WITH WHIPPED CREAM
Gesztenyepüré
TPT - 10 minutes

I remember well the battered baking pan, the one Mom also used to make vanilla fudge, coming from the oven full of roasted chestnuts. I remember the whole family sitting on the hearth each with their own oven mitt. Shells flew as we broke open the hot shells to find the rich, roasted flesh. I also remember the smell of chestnuts roasting on the streets of New York as shoppers hurried by in the cold and venders rubbed their mittened hands over the hot coals. When the chestnut harvest comes to market, I will cook those chestnuts and make my own chestnut purée but jarred and exported chestnuts from France can take some of the work out of this really very simple dessert. I always accompany it with a bowl of fresh cherries, if they are in season, or sweet cherries that I have canned the summer before.

5 ounces jarred, peeled, chestnuts—about 3/4 cup

3 tablespoons confectioners' sugar
2 tablespoons light cream *or* half and half
1/2 teaspoon pure vanilla extract*

1 cup heavy whipping cream
2 teaspoons confectioners' sugar

Using the food processor fitted with steel knife, process chestnuts to a uniform purée.

CHESTNUT PURÉE WITH WHIPPED CREAM (cont'd)

Add confectioners' sugar, cream, and vanilla extract. Process until smooth. Using a ricer, rice the chestnut purée into the middle of a shallow serving bowl or onto a round platter. Chill until required.

Using the electric mixer fitted with *chilled* beaters or by hand using a *chilled* wire whisk, beat heavy cream in a *chilled* bowl until soft peaks form. While continuing to beat, add confectioners' sugar. Beat until stiff peaks form. Using a pastry bag, pipe the whipped cream around the mound of riced chestnut purée. Refrigerate for *no more than 15 minutes* before serving.

Serve chilled onto chilled dessert plates.

Yields 6 servings
adequate for 4-6 people

Notes: *For very adult parties, replace the vanilla extract with about 2 teaspoonfuls of rum.

This recipe can be halved, when required.

1/6 SERVING – PROTEIN = 2.3 g.; FAT = 14.3 g.; CARBOHYDRATE = 27.4 g.;
CALORIES = 247; CALORIES FROM FAT = 52%

HOMEMADE PAPRIKA
TPT - 72 hours and 20 minutes;
about 72 hours = dehydration process

The find of well-priced red bell peppers, especially when they come to market from local farms, results in bags of diced peppers in the freezer for addition to this and that, bags of red pepper squares in the freezer for stir-fries, and a small jar or two of homemade paprika. This paprika has a more pronounced red pepper flavored than do commercial paprikas, even those from Hungary; you can almost taste the late summer sun. The preparation does require a dehydrator but an easily obtainable and inexpensive dehydrator works just as well as do those expensive ones with digital "bells and whistles." What does not work for this project is the oven. The sugars in the peppers tend to brown or burn and give the paprika a slightly burned taste if the oven is used, even when set on the very lowest setting.

As you will note, paprika is used frequently in the recipes included in this chapter. What would Hungarian food be without paprika? Where would Hungarian cuisine be today without the visitation of the Ottoman Turks? Yes, the Turks introduced paprika to the people of the Carpathian Basin.

Red bell peppers—one or as many as you wish—very well-washed, seeded, and cored, trimmed of all residual membranous tissue, and chopped into large pieces

Place pepper pieces on the trays of the dehydrator, spreading them well. Stack trays in the dehydrator and turn on. Be sure vent is open to allow for the escape of the moisture during evaporation. Turn trays and rearrange trays as to their proximity to the heat source several times during the drying process. Allow to dry until the pepper pieces are almost crisp.

Prepare one or more 4-ounce jelly jars by sterilizing and drying jars, lids, and rings. Set aside.

Set a fine sieve over a small bowl or measuring cup.

Using a SPICE and COFFEE GRINDER, grind the dried pepper pieces in small batches. Pour from the grinder into the sieve. Shake to allow finely ground paprika to fall through. Return any chunks to the grinder and grind them again with the next batch.

Transfer the sieved paprika to the prepared jelly jars, seal, label, and store.

Iceland

Iceland, the westernmost country of Europe, was a sovereign state under the Danish monarchy until 1944 at which time the present republic was formed. It is a land of extremes with dense ice sheets, hot springs, and over one hundred volcanoes, many still active, at a point where the Earth's crust is thin. Because of the gulf stream, the climate is relatively mild for its latitude just south of the Arctic Circle but agriculture is limited to the costal region where most of the population resides.

I have included a menu from Iceland because it was a stop on the migration route that brought explorers and settlers to North America after the last ice age. In the ninth century, Irish monks settled in Iceland. Their work put in place a school system upon which the present education system is still based. They moved on with the arrival of the Norsemen and their Celtic wives and slaves in about 850 AD. The Norse settled and then explored beyond, eventually reaching the Canadian maritime provinces, the edge of my world.

Iceland belonged to Norway as a result of the signing of the Old Covenant and was taken over with Norway by Denmark in 1380 under the unification known as the Kalmar Union, remaining a part of Denmark after the Treaty of Kiel and through 1943 under the Act of Union. Nevertheless, its limited resources have not allowed for the extensive cuisine development seen in other Scandinavian countries. Yes, there is a form of *smorbrød*, called "*smurt brauõ*," rice pudding for Christmas, a traditional cold table, and of course herring but Iceland's hearty cooking requires creativity with a few ingredients, especially in the winter when hot-house or canned vegetables and canned or imported fruits are the norm. Even onions are imported. It is a meat/fish–root vegetable–cheese cuisine and a challenge to a vegetarian and, perhaps, almost an impossibility for a vegan. In an often inhospitable climate, the high level of fat consumed in Iceland is much less of a concern as would be the same diet further south so you will note some modifications of traditional ingredients.

Crudités
with
Creamy Cocktail Sauce
Kokkteilsósa

~

Christmas Slaw
Galasalat

~ ~ ~ ~ ~ ~ ~ ~ ~ ~

Potato Pudding with Cheese
Kartoflubuoingur meo Ostur

Beets with Chopped Egg
Rauorofer meo Sopnou Eggi

~ ~ ~ ~ ~ ~ ~ ~ ~ ~

Rhubarb Mousse   **Almond Cake**
Rabarbara meo Rjoma   *Mondlukaka*

Europe–Iceland

ICELANDIC CREAMY COCKTAIL SAUCE
Kokkteilsósa

TPT – 4 minutes

A condiment made simply from mayonnaise and ketchup, much like American Russian dressing, is ubiquitous in Iceland as the sauce of preference for French fries, grilled sausages, and fried foods. The addition of sour cream, favored by some, gives this sauce a smooth texture and makes it a good dip for chips and crudités or a dressing for salads and sandwiches. Instead of using ketchup, we prefer chili sauce for a more complex taste.

1/4 cup *fat-free* dairy sour cream
1/4 cup *calorie-reduced or light* mayonnaise

2 tablespoons *chili* sauce
1 teaspoon MUSTARD SAUCE *[see index]*
1-2 teaspoons SWEET AND TART CRANBERRY VINEGAR *[see index] or* vinegar of choice

In a mixing bowl, combine sour cream and mayonnaise. Using a wire whisk, beat until smooth.

Add *chili* sauce, mustard sauce, and vinegar. Beat until of uniform consistency. Add more or less vinegar to obtain the consistency you require. Turn into a serving bowl. Refrigerate until required.

Refrigerate leftovers.

Yields about 10 tablespoonfuls

Note: This recipe is easily doubled, when required.

1/10 SERVING (i. e., per tablespoonful) –
PROTEIN = 0.9 g.; FAT = 0.6 g.; CARBOHYDRATE = 3.7 g.;
CALORIES = 23; CALORIES FROM FAT = 24%

ICELANDIC CHRISTMAS SLAW
Jolasalat

TPT - 1 hour and 21 minutes;
1 hour = cabbage draining period

In 1996, we tried this salad as a replacement for the Finnish slaw with black currant jelly we usually served on our traditional Christmas "cold table," a tradition we had embraced with enthusiasm after a 1985 Christmas in Denmark. We were all in agreement that, whether you are a fan of rhubarb or not, this is an interesting and worthy salad for the holidays.

1/2 small red cabbage*
1/2 teaspoon salt

2 tablespoons red currant jelly
3 tablespoons rhubarb preserves *or* jam *or*
   ENGLISH STEWED RHUBARB *[see index]***
2 teaspoons freshly squeezed lemon juice

Finely shred cabbage. Wash well. Place in a sieve set over the sink. Salt shredded cabbage and toss well. Place a plate on top and a weight—a large can or a tea kettle filled with water—on top of the plate. Allow to stand for 1 hour.

Rinse cabbage well. Drain again. Spread drained cabbage on paper toweling and pat to dry well. Place in salad bowl.

In a small bowl, combine red currant jelly, rhubarb preserves or ENGLISH STEWED RHUBARB, and lemon juice. Stir to mix well. Add to cabbage. Toss.

Refrigerate until ready to serve.

Yields 6 servings
adequate for 4 people

Notes: *Commercially available, jarred red cabbage responds well to this sauce. Be sure to drain brine thoroughly before adding currant–rhubarb sauce mixture.

**Rhubarb preserves are often available in food specialty stores or at country farmers' markets.

This recipe can be halved or doubled, as required.

1/6 SERVING – PROTEIN = 2.0 g.; FAT = 0.2 g.; CARBOHYDRATE = 13.1 g.;
CALORIES = 56; CALORIES FROM FAT = 3%

Europe–Iceland

ICELANDIC POTATO PUDDING WITH CHEESE
Kartoflubuðingur með Ostur
TPT - 1 hour

I so often choose to make this dish on a cold winter night. Is it the comfort it provides or have I too been influenced by the name that fooled would-be settlers and invaders alike into thinking this beautiful and peaceful land was inhospitable?

8 medium, all-purpose potatoes—peeled and coarsely chopped
Boiling water

3 tablespoons skimmed milk, or more as required

1/4 cup grated *pecorino Romano* cheese *or* other hard, ewe's milk grating cheese*
3 tablespoons butter—*melted*

Prepare a 2-quart oven–to–table baking dish by coating with non-stick lecithin spray coating.

Cook chopped potatoes in *boiling* water to cover until soft. Drain well.

Preheat oven to 375 degrees F.

Using a ricer, rice the drained potatoes into the bowl of the electric mixer. Using the electric mixer, whip potatoes. Add milk to potatoes *one tablespoonful at a time* until potatoes are *creamy and light*. Add more milk *only if necessary*.

Turn warm, mashed potatoes into prepared baking dish, spreading evenly to the sides.

Sprinkle grated cheese evenly over the top. Drizzle *melted* butter over.

Bake in preheated 375 degree F. oven until heated through and *lightly browned*—about 20 minutes.

Keep warm on warming tray until ready to serve.

Yields 6 servings
adequate for 4 people

Notes: *Icelandic cheeses are rarely available in the United States. Pecorino Romano is an adequate substitute.

This recipe may be halved or doubled, when required. Be sure that the baking dish chosen is appropriate to the new volume.

1/6 SERVING – PROTEIN = 5.1 g.; FAT = 7.4 g.; CARBOHYDRATE = 31.3 g.; CALORIES = 211; CALORIES FROM FAT = 32%

BEETS WITH CHOPPED EGG IN THE STYLE OF ICELAND
Rauðrófer með Söpuðu Eggi
TPT – 11 minutes

Yes, this is a wonderfully simple way to serve beets, a method also used to prepare smoked herring in Iceland, which we find is welcome winter or summer. It is similar to a beet dish my mother used to make when we were young and I know she had never been to Iceland.

1 can (16 ounces) sliced beets *or* about 2 cups sliced, cooked, fresh beets*

2 hard-cooked eggs

1/4 cup *finely* chopped onion
Freshly ground black pepper, to taste

In a saucepan set over *MEDIUM* heat, heat beets. Drain well. Turn into heated serving bowl set on warming tray.

Discard the yolk of one hard-cooked egg. *Finely* chop whites and remaining yolk. Scatter chopped egg over warm beets. Scatter *finely* chopped onion over. Grind black pepper over.

Serve at once.

Yields 4 servings
adequate for 3-4 people

Notes: *The taste of fresh beets is infinitely better in this dish but sometimes convenience may have to take precedence.

**BEETS WITH CHOPPED EGG
IN THE STYLE OF ICELAND** (cont'd)

This recipe can be halved or doubled, when required. When doubling, use just one more hard-cooked egg, not two.

1/6 SERVING – PROTEIN = 2.3 g.; FAT = 1.0 g.; CARBOHYDRATE = 6.5 g.;
CALORIES = 43; CALORIES FROM FAT = 21%

ICELANDIC RHUBARB MOUSSE
Rabarbara með Rjóma

TPT – 1 hour and 53 minutes;
30 minutes = first gelling period;
1 hour = second gelling period

I had always marveled at the ingenuity of Irish homemakers, an instinct handed down to those of us who crossed the Atlantic. Icelandic women also, by necessity, create meals from a very small number of ingredients. Recent DNA testing, a passion of Icelanders, revealed the irony that most of the women were of Celtic descent, unlike the male population whose dominant heritage was Norse. There is a tempting conclusion here but I shall avoid the temptation. Coincidently, rhubarb is also a resource in both countries. Actually this rhubarb dessert is a very old recipe from my files. I never was able to search back and find its origins until one day I stumbled on it in an old Scandinavian cookbook that included a chapter on Iceland. I suspect it made its way to me through Canada, where many of "our family recipes" are "their family recipes." This is a rich, sweet, stick-to-the-ribs, cold, northern, spring dessert.

2 cups diced, young rhubarb—trimmed and well-washed*

1/3 cup firmly packed *light* brown sugar

1/4 cup *cold* water

1 tablespoon (1 envelope) unflavored gelatin**
1 tablespoon freshly squeezed lemon juice

1/2 cup heavy whipping cream

Place diced rhubarb in a heavy saucepan set over *LOW-MEDIUM* heat. Cover tightly and cook for about 10 minutes, or until juice is rendered.

Remove cover, stir in brown sugar, and continue to cook, uncovered, over *MEDIUM* heat until rhubarb is tender. Place in the refrigerator to cool.

Pour the 1/4 cupful *cold* water into a saucepan. Sprinkle gelatin over and allow to soften for 5 minutes. Set saucepan over *LOW* heat and heat until gelatin is completely dissolved. Remove from heat. Stir in lemon juice.

Refrigerate gelatin mixture until it *just begins to thicken*—about 20 minutes. Stir gelatin into slightly cooled rhubarb.

Using an electric mixer fitted with *chilled* beaters or by hand, using a *chilled* wire whisk, beat heavy cream in a *chilled* bowl until stiff. Pour the rhubarb–gelatin mixture down the side of the mixer bowl. Using a rubber spatula, fold stiffly whipped cream *gently*, but *thoroughly*, into rhubarb–gelatin mixture.

Turn into a serving dish or individual dessert dishes, as preferred. Refrigerate for about 1 hour, or until firm.

Serve chilled. Refrigerate leftovers.***

Yields 6 servings
adequate for 4 people

Notes: *Remember, *the leaves of the rhubarb plant are poisonous*. Discard them immediately when preparing rhubarb.

**Agar-agar or kosher gelatin may be substituted for plain gelatin, if preferred. Since preparation procedures differ for these products, be sure to follow package directions.

**I often serve leftovers of this dessert with sweetened, sliced fresh strawberries.

This recipe may be halved or doubled, when required.

1/6 SERVING – PROTEIN = 2.0 g.; FAT = 6.6 g.; CARBOHYDRATE = 4.6 g.;
CALORIES = 145; CALORIES FROM FAT = 41%

Europe–Iceland

ICELANDIC ALMOND CAKE
Möndlukaka

TPT - 2 hours;
1 hour = cooling period

An Icelandic cook would garnish this cake lavishly with sweetened whipped cream. Of course it is divine, but we choose to garnish the cake with confectioners' sugar instead.

1 cup sifted cake flour
1/2 teaspoon baking powder

4 large egg whites

1 cup (2 sticks) butter—*softened to room temperature*
2/3 cup sugar
1 cup *fat-free* **pasteurized eggs (the equivalent of 4 eggs)**
1 teaspoon pure vanilla extract
1/2 teaspoon pure almond extract
1/3 cup *preservative-free* **almond meal** *or finely* **ground almonds**

1/2 cup strawberry jam

Confectioners' sugar, for garnish

Preheat oven to 350 degrees F. Prepare two 9-inch round cake pans by coating with lecithin spray coating. Lightly flour each pan.

Into a large mixing bowl, sift cake flour and baking powder. Set aside.

Using an electric mixer fitted with *grease-free* beaters or by hand, using a *grease-free* wire whisk, beat egg whites in a *grease-free* bowl until *stiff*, but *not dry*. Set aside.

Using the electric mixer, cream butter until light and fluffy. Add sugar and continue creaming until again light and fluffy. While continuing to beat, gradually add pasteurized eggs, beating until smooth. Add vanilla and almond extracts and almond meal. Beat until smooth. While continuing to beat, add sifted cake flour and baking powder. Continue beating until flour is thoroughly integrated.

Whisk-fold beaten egg whites *gently*, but *thoroughly*, into batter. Divide between prepared cake pans.

Bake in preheated 350 degree F. oven for about 18-20 minutes, or until golden brown and a cake tester inserted in the center comes out clean.

Cool for 5 minutes in baking pans before removing to wire racks. Cool for at least 1 hour.*

When ready to serve. Cover cake plate with a paper lace doily. Place first layer flat-side-up on cake plate. Spread layer with strawberry jam. Place second layer flat-side-down on top of jam-spread layer. Place a lace paper doily on top of cake layers. Sieve confectioners' sugar over. *Carefully lift lace paper doily off* leaving decorative sugar lace pattern on top of cake.

Yields 12 servings
adequate for 8 people

Notes: *The cake layers may be prepared well in advance of serving, wrapped well, and refrigerated or frozen until required.

This batter is perfect for making small cakes or tartlets. Bake for about 10 minutes. Cool slightly before removing from tart pans. Serve either spread with strawberry jam or with a dollop of strawberry jam beside the tartlet. Sieve confectioners' sugar over.

1/2 SERVING (i. e., per layer *without* jam) –
PROTEIN = 30.4 g.; FAT = 112.4 g.; CARBOHYDRATE = 128.7 g.;
CALORIES = 1631; CALORIES FROM FAT = 62%

1/12 SERVING (i. e., a two layer slice with strawberry jam) –
PROTEIN = 5.1 g.; FAT = 18.7 g.; CARBOHYDRATE = 29.5 g.;
CALORIES = 303; CALORIES FROM FAT = 56%

1/44 SERVING (i. e., per tartlet with 1 tablespoon jam) –
PROTEIN = 1.4 g.; FAT = 5.1 g.; CARBOHYDRATE = 17.9 g.;
CALORIES = 121; CALORIES FROM FAT = 38%

Ireland

There I stood in Dublin in 1983, in the midst of a period of considerable unrest and violence, staring into a display case at the Book of Kels with a reverence that gave me chills. For me, it was one of those things that you say to yourself, "This is one place I must go in my lifetime." It is said that the knotwork that one sees in art and fabric in Celtic lands possibly came to Ireland sometime in the seventh century in manuscript form. These illuminations were most probably worked by Coptic monastics from Egypt or, maybe Syria. The tradition was then carried to Scotland (then, Pictland) and Dalriada, Wales, Northumbria, and to the land of the Norse, where Norwegian stave churches bear the knotwork in interlaced animal designs.

The potato arrived in Ireland in the second half of the sixteenth century upon which the Irish became over-dependent. It could be cultivated in small gardens where the soil was poor-to-dead and potatoes, unlike other crops, could provide enough nourishment for large families. In 1739 the Irish experienced the First Great Famine but it is the Great Irish Famine of 1845-1849, caused by the potato blight, with which most of us are acquainted—the famine that drove nearly three million people to emigrate; the famine that killed about one million of the approximately three million people, who remained on the island. This tragedy clearly showed that dependence on a few foods and dependence upon a limited number of cultivars of those foods are indeed recipes for disaster. The Irish were dependent, almost entirely, upon the blight-susceptible Lumper potato. Since then the lack of biodiversity has not been corrected but rather acerbated by the use of fertilizers and pesticides as mega farms systems become the norm.

Ireland is a land to which those who have emigrated around the globe return by keeping alive a legendary Ireland that may not be, that may not have ever been. They also brought with them a meat-and-potatoes culture to which Americans are still heir. My paternal grandmother who was born in Auburn, New York, and who never visited Ireland, loved the "old sod" and dearly loved her "murphys" often serving several potato dishes in one meal. When she came to live with us, no meal was satisfactory if there were no "murphys."

The use of honey can be traced to ancient times as can the use of native berries and hazelnuts, both of which have been unearthed at the Viking settlement at Wood Quay, near Dublin. From the Middle Ages until the introduction of the potato in the 1500s meat from herd animals, chickens, and pigs, milk, butter, buttermilk, cheese, oats, and barley sustained the poor. Mushrooms, wild garlic, watercress supplemented cabbage, kale, and parsley which could be grown in cottage gardens.

I have found the cuisine of Ireland the most fascinating of all cuisines, almost without exception. What an Irish cook can do with the few ingredients available, never ceases to fascinate me. As new combinations present themselves, I am proud of the creativity that has been handed down to me.

Europe–Ireland

Shirred Eggs with Cheddar and Onion Sauce in Ramekins
Raimicíní Uibheacha le hAnlann Caise Agus Oinniuin Friochta

Creamed Sorrel Sauce
Anlann Uachtar

Puffed Potato – Cheddar Omelet
Uibhegan Práta
with
Parsley Sauce
Anlann Peirsile

Brown Buttermilk Scones   **Savory Leek Wheaten Scones** (in season)
Bannaga Blathai

~

Golden Watercress and Potato Soup   **Red Lentil and Red Onion Cream Soup**
Anraith Pratai Agus Biolar

Vegetarian Irish Stew
Stobhach Gaelach

Sautéed Baby Artichoke Hearts with Cream and Mustard Sauce

Roasted Mushrooms and Shallots with Rosemary and Cheese

Buttered Cabbage
Cabaiste

~ ~ ~ ~ ~ ~ ~ ~ ~ ~ ~

Bread and Butter Pudding with Apricot Topping
Marog Arain Agus Ime

Blackberry Cobbler (in season)
Marog Smeara Dubh

IRISH SHIRRED EGGS WITH CHEDDAR AND ONION SAUCE IN RAMEKINS
Raimicíní Uibheacha le hAnlann Caise Agust Oinniuin Friochta
TPT- 1 hour and 13 minutes

The Irish prepare this egg dish by utilizing the same lengthy sweating technique used by the French to prepare "soubise." It is, to our mind, a much more delicious and harmonious ingredient than are caramelized onions.

VOLUME I - 193

Europe–Ireland

IRISH SHIRRED EGGS WITH CHEDDAR AND ONION SAUCE IN RAMEKINS (cont'd)

1 tablespoon butter
1/2 cup VEGETARIAN WHITE *or* BROWN STOCK *[see index]* ***or*** **VEGETABLE STOCK FROM SOUP** *[see index]*, **as preferred**
4 medium onions—*thinly* sliced*

1/4 cup light cream *or* half and half
Freshly ground *white* pepper, to taste

1/2 cup *shredded* (about 2 ounces) *sharp* Cheddar cheese

4 large eggs*

Preheat oven to 300 degrees F. Prepare a 1 1/2-quart oven casserole by spraying with non-stick lecithin spray coating. Set aside.

In a skillet set over *MEDIUM* heat, combine butter, stock, and *thinly* sliced onions. Sauté, stirring constantly, until onions are soft and translucent, *being careful not to allow onions to brown.*

Transfer sautéed onions with the liquid remaining in the skillet to prepared oven casserole. Cover tightly with aluminum foil. Bake in preheated 300 degree F. oven for about 45 minutes, or until moisture is absorbed and onions are *very* tender, *but not browned.* Remove from oven.

Add cream and *white* pepper to prepared onions.

Increase oven temperature to 325 degrees F. Prepare four individual 10-ounce soufflé dishes, *au gratin* dishes, or other small "oven-to-table" dishes by coating each with non-stick lecithin spray coating.

Spread 1/4 cupful of *hot* ONION SAUCE over the bottom of each baking dish. Sprinkle *shredded* Cheddar cheese over ONION SAUCE, evenly dividing it among dishes.

Bake in preheated 325 degree F. oven for about 3 minutes, just until dishes are heated and cheese begins to melt. Remove from oven.

Using the back of a spoon, make a wide depression in the center of the slightly melted cheese. Break an egg into a small dish. Slide it carefully into the depression in the cheese and onion mixture. Repeat with each egg.

Spoon remaining onion sauce over eggs, dividing it evenly among dishes.

Return to oven for about 10 minutes, or until egg whites are set.

Serve at once, setting individual soufflé dishes on large dinner plates. Leave room for accompanying vegetable.

Yields 4 individual servings

Notes: *Although common yellow onions or Spanish onions are most often used to prepare this dish, Italian red onions introduce an interesting taste variation.

**Two eggs may be used per serving to accommodate larger appetites without altering sauce amounts.

Remember that the eggs will continue to cook after being removed from the oven. If it is necessary to hold them for a few minutes to allow for first course dawdling, do undercook them slightly. *The yolks should be runny and the whites firm, but not hard.*

For variety, IRISH CREAMED SORREL SAUCE *[see recipe which follows]* may be substituted for the onion sauce when sorrel is in season.

This recipe is easily halved or doubled, when required.

1/4 SERVING – PROTEIN = 12.4 g.; FAT = 14.5 g.; CARBOHYDRATE = 10.9 g.;
CALORIES = 217; CALORIES FROM FAT = 60%

IRISH CREAMED SORREL SAUCE
Anlann Uachtar

TPT - 1 hour and 16 minutes

Irish cooking is not boring, as some would label it, because it is based on few ingredients. It is, instead, a creative cuisine because it is based on those few ingredients. This is a perfectly wonderful spring dish; it tastes of the new season. Peeled whole carrots and onions may be added, if appropriate to your menu plans.

IRISH CREAMED SORREL SAUCE (cont'd)

1/4 cup sweet *(unsalted)* butter
2 cups French sorrel (dock) leaves—well-washed and cut into julienne slices*
1/2 cup light cream *or* half and half, as preferred

Salt, to taste
Freshly ground *white* pepper, to taste

In a saucepan set over *LOW-MEDIUM* heat, melt sweet *(unsalted)* butter. Add julienned sorrel. Stir until it disintegrates. Add cream and seasoning. Simmer, stirring frequently, for about 10 minutes. *Do not allow to boil once the cream has been added.* Turn into a sauceboat.

Serve at once.

Yields 6 servings
adequate for 4 people

Notes: *Note that French sorrel, with its large leaves, is much less sour or acidic in taste than sour dock or garden sorrel. It is an easily grown, hardy perennial but if you do not have a kitchen–garden source, use spinach to prepare the sauce. Add a dash from freshly squeezed lemon juice to approximate the sorrel taste.

This recipe may be halved or doubled, as required.

1/10 SERVING (per tablespoonful) –
PROTEIN – 0.8 g.; FAT = 5.7 g.; CARBOHYDRATE = 1.6 g.;
CALORIES = 60; CALORIES FROM FAT = 86%

IRISH PUFFED POTATO – CHEDDAR OMELET
Uibhegan Prata
TPT - 18 minutes

I am a fan of "planned leftovers," not only for the next-day's lunch but as a planned ingredient for other recipes. Just like leftover rice becomes tomorrow's rice pudding, a portion of leftover mashed potatoes can become tomorrow's supper as in this recipe. This omelet makes a nice family supper dish any time of year but we enjoy it also as an appetizer, as in this menu, or for brunch.

Because there is always a danger of encountering Salmonella when eggs are cooked in this manner, please do use organic eggs; be careful to choose organic eggs not just natural cage-free eggs.

1 cup cooked, *riced, or mashed* potatoes
1/2 cup shredded *extra sharp* Irish Cheddar cheese
3 large egg yolks
1 tablespoon chopped chives
Freshly ground black pepper, to taste

3 large egg whites

1 tablespoon butter

1/4 cup shredded *extra sharp* Irish Cheddar cheese

In a mixing bowl, combine mashed potatoes, 1/2 cupful shredded cheese, egg yolks, chopped chives, and black pepper. Mix well.

Using an electric mixer fitted with *grease-free* beaters or by hand, using a *grease-free* wire whisk, beat egg whites in a *grease-free* bowl until *stiff,* but *not dry.* *Fold* beaten egg whites *gently,* but *thoroughly,* into potato mixture.

Preheat broiler to 400 degrees F.

In a 9-inch non-stick-coated skillet or omelet pan set over *MEDIUM* heat, melt butter. Turn omelet mixture into skillet, spreading it evenly to the edge of the skillet. Sprinkle 1/4 cupful shredded cheese over. Cook until omelet begins to pull away from the edges of the pan and is golden. Wrap the skillet handle with aluminum foil. Slide under the preheated broiler until *lightly* browned on top. Slide out onto a heated plate or round platter.

Serve at once. Tear into wedges with two forks to serve.*

Yields 6 servings
adequate for 4 people

Notes: *Serve with a sauce, if desired—the parsley sauce which follows or a mushroom sauce.

This recipe can be doubled and baked in a 10-inch skillet, when required, or halved and baked in a 7-inch skillet.

Europe–Ireland

IRISH PUFFED POTATO – CHEDDAR OMELET (cont'd)

1/6 SERVING – PROTEIN = 5.8 g.; FAT = 9.3 g.; CARBOHYDRATE = 5.5 g.;
CALORIES = 136; CALORIES FROM FAT = 61%

IRISH PARSLEY SAUCE
Anlann Peirsile
TPT – 13 minutes

Due to the generous rainfall that Ireland experiences, parsley plants grow to a lushness we do not see here in our valley where the late spring and midsummer drought conditions take their toll on our herb yield. As is always the case with Irish cooks, the parsley supply is put to good use. This dead simple sauce is great over Irish potato cakes, vegetables, and battered or breaded foods.

2 tablespoons butter
1 1/2 tablespoons unbleached white flour

1 cup *two-percent* milk*

1/4 cup *finely* chopped parsley
Two or three drops of freshly squeezed lemon juice
Pinch of salt
Freshly ground black pepper, to taste

In a saucepan set over *LOW* heat, melt butter. Remove from heat and, using a wire whisk, make a *roux* by beating in flour. Return to heat and, stirring constantly, cook for 2 minutes, *being careful not to burn or overbrown the roux.* Remove from heat and gradually beat in milk. Return saucepan to heat and cook, stirring constantly, until thickened.

Remove from heat and place on warming tray set at *MEDIUM*.

Add *finely* chopped parsley and lemon juice. Season with black pepper. Stir until thoroughly integrated.

Keep warm until ready to serve.

Yields about 20 tablespoonfuls

Notes: *If you want a richer sauce, the sauce may be prepared with whole milk or cream.

This recipe can be doubled, when required.

1/10 SERVING (i. e., 2 tablespoonfuls) –
PROTEIN = 1.0 g.; FAT = 2.8 g.; CARBOHYDRATE = 2.1 g.;
CALORIES = 37; CALORIES FROM FAT = 68%

IRISH BROWN BUTTERMILK SCONES
Bonnoga Blathai
TPT – 29 minutes

This scone recipe is, to me, a basic, honest scone of substance, the kind we ate for breakfast while traveling in the British Isles. Today, especially here in the United States, scone recipes are more often sweet cakes and this is decidedly not a sweet cake.

1 1/3 cups unbleached white flour
2/3 cup whole wheat flour
1 1/2 teaspoons baking soda
1 teaspoon cream of tartar
2 teaspoons sugar

3 tablespoons *cold* butter—diced

2/3 cup *unsalted*, cultured buttermilk*

Beaten *fat-free* pasteurized eggs *or* milk, to glaze, if desired

Preheat oven to 400 degrees F. Prepare a cookie sheet by coating with non-stick lecithin spray coating.

In the work bowl of the food processor, fitted with steel knife, combine white and whole wheat flours, baking soda, cream of tartar, and sugar.** *Pulse on and off* several times to combine well. Add diced *cold* butter and *pulse on and off* several times until of the consistency of coarse corn meal. *Be careful not to overwork the batter or allow the butter to melt.* Turn mixture into a large mixing bowl.

Add buttermilk, and, using a fork, stir the liquid into the flour mixture until a soft dough is formed.

IRISH BROWN BUTTERMILK SCONES (cont'd)

Turn out onto a lightly floured surface. Turn dough to coat with flour. Using a rolling pin, roll dough out into a rectangle about 4 inches by 10 inches and to a thickness of about 3/4 inch. Cut into wedges and place on prepared cookie sheet.*** If desired, brush with beaten egg or milk before baking.

Bake in preheated 400 degree F. oven for about 12 minutes, or until *golden brown*.

Serve warm with butter and any jelly or jam, of your choosing. Crab apple jelly is especially favored in Ireland.

Yields 10 scones
adequate for 4-5 people

Notes: *Powdered buttermilk is readily available from mail order firms and in natural food stores. Since a quart of fresh buttermilk often spoils because we use only a bit for a recipe, we find the powdered product to be useful addition to our larder.

**If a food processor is not available, the dough may be prepared by hand. Using a pastry blender, work *cold* butter into dry ingredients until the mixture is of the consistency of coarse corn meal. Using a spoon, combine thoroughly. Add milk and stir until a soft dough is formed. Then proceed as above.

***If preferred, these may be cut into round scones using a 2 1/2- or 3-inch biscuit cutter.

This recipe is easily doubled or halved, when required.

1/10 SERVING (i.e., per scone) –
PROTEIN = 3.0 g.; FAT = 5.0 g.; CARBOHYDRATE = 22.1 g.;
CALORIES = 124; CALORIES FROM FAT = 36%

IRISH SAVORY LEEK WHEATEN SCONES
Bonnoga Blathai
TPT – 29 minutes

When the tender, young leeks and chives are up, these scones will be on the supper menu in an Irish home. The freshness from the kitchen garden will be welcome as will the butter churned from the spring milk. When you eat what your land provides, the food dried and the food preserved gives way to spring and that is grandly received.

1 1/3 cups unbleached white flour
2/3 cup whole wheat flour
1 1/2 teaspoons baking soda
1 teaspoon cream of tartar
2 teaspoons sugar

1/4 cup *well-washed* and *very finely* chopped leek
　white portion only
2 tablespoons *finely* snipped fresh chives
2 tablespoons *finely* chopped, fresh Italian flat-
　leafed parsley
Freshly ground black pepper, to taste
Pinch red pepper (cayenne)

3 tablespoons *cold* butter   diced

2/3 cup *unsalted*, cultured buttermilk*

Beaten *fat-free* pasteurized eggs *or* milk, to glaze,
　if desired

Preheat oven to 400 degrees F. Prepare a cookie sheet by coating with non-stick lecithin spray coating.

In the work bowl of the food processor, fitted with steel knife, combine white and whole wheat flours, baking soda, cream of tartar, and sugar.** *Pulse on and off* several times to combine well. Add diced *cold* butter and *pulse on and off* several times until of the consistency of coarse corn meal. *Do not overwork the batter or allow the butter to melt.* Turn mixture into a large mixing bowl.

Add buttermilk, and, using a fork, stir the liquid into the flour mixture until a soft dough is formed.

Turn out onto a lightly floured surface. Turn dough to coat with flour. Using a rolling pin, roll dough out into a rectangle about 4 inches by 10 inches and to a thickness of about 1/2 inch. Using a 2-inch biscuit cutter, cut out about 15 scones and place on prepared cookie sheet. If desired, brush with beaten egg or milk before baking.

Bake in preheated 400 degree F. oven for about 12 minutes, or until *golden brown*.

IRISH SAVORY LEEK WHEATEN SCONES (cont'd)

Serve warm with butter.

Yields 10 scones
adequate for 4-5 people

Notes: *Powdered buttermilk is readily available from mail order firms and in natural food stores. Since a quart of fresh buttermilk often spoils because we use only a bit for a recipe, we find the powdered product to be useful addition to our larder.

**If a food processor is not available, the dough may be prepared by hand. Using a pastry blender, work *cold* butter into dry ingredients until the mixture is of the consistency of coarse corn meal. Using a spoon, combine thoroughly. Add milk and stir until a soft dough is formed. Then proceed as above.

This recipe is easily doubled or halved, when required.

1/10 SERVING (i. e., per scone) –
PROTEIN = 3.1 g.; FAT = 3.8 g.; CARBOHYDRATE = 22.4 g.;
CALORIES = 125; CALORIES FROM FAT = 27%

GOLDEN IRISH WATERCRESS AND POTATO SOUP
Anraith Pratai Agus Biolar

TPT – 1 hour and 5 minutes

Once again, with a few basic ingredients, the Irish have created a soup that is hearty, filling, nutritious, and, above all, satisfyingly delicious. Watercress, gathered among the rocks along the streambeds, certainly makes potato soup sing. Thank you my cousins all . . . .

1 tablespoon butter
1 large yellow onion—chopped
1/2 celery rib—trimmed and chopped
1 small carrot—pared or scraped and chopped

1 1/2 cups diced potato—about 3 medium potatoes
2 1/2 cups VEGETARIAN BROWN *or* WHITE STOCK [*see index*]
1/2 teaspoon salt

1/4 teaspoon freshly ground *white* pepper
2 cups *whole* milk

1 large bunch watercress—stems removed and leaves chopped

In a kettle, with cover, set over *MEDIUM* heat, melt butter. Add chopped onion, celery, and carrot. Sauté until onion is soft and translucent, *allowing none of the vegetables to brown.* Add diced potatoes, stock, and salt. Set over *MEDIUM-HIGH* heat and bring to the boil. Reduce heat to *MEDIUM-LOW,* partially cover, and simmer for about 30 minutes, or until vegetables are *very tender.* Stir occasionally.

Purée two or three ladlefuls at a time in the electric blender, or in the food processor fitted with steel knife, or mash finely and press through a fine sieve or FOOD MILL.* Turn into a clean saucepan.

Stir in *white* pepper and milk. Set over *MEDIUM-LOW* heat and heat until it is warm to the touch. Add *finely* chopped watercress and cook, stirring frequently, for about 10 minutes. Adjust seasoning, if necessary.

Turn into a heated soup tureen and serve into heated soup bowls.

Yields 6 first-course servings

Notes: *The puréed base for this soup may be prepared ahead to this point and refrigerated for a day or two or frozen for future use. Defrost in the refrigerator and proceed as directed above.

This recipe may be halved or doubled, when required. Be careful not to over-salt when doubling.

1/6 SERVING – PROTEIN = 4.2 g.; FAT = 4.5 g.; CARBOHYDRATE = 17.9 g.;
CALORIES = 128; CALORIES FROM FAT = 32%

Europe–Ireland

IRISH RED LENTIL AND RED ONION CREAM SOUP
TPT - 58 minutes

According to my mother, I, as a toddler, adored some jarred baby food called lamb and liver stew with lentils. Perhaps this favorite Irish soup, which would most often be made with lamb stock in Ireland, is homage to a long-suppressed amnesiac memory, not reinforced since lamb was never served in our house. This vegetarian version is rich, complex, smooth, and a gorgeous, inviting color, thanks to the red lentils, unlike that stew of my childhood.

1 cup dry red (orange) lentils

2 tablespoons oil
3 celery ribs *with leaves*—trimmed, well-washed, and chopped
1 leek—*white portion only*—trimmed, *very* well-washed, and chopped
1 carrot—scraped or pared and grated
1 parsnip—peeled and grated
1 medium Italian red onion—grated

5 cups VEGETARIAN BROWN STOCK *[see index]* **or VEGETABLE STOCK FROM SOUP** *[see index]*

1/4 teaspoon freshly ground black pepper, or to taste
Salt, to taste
3/4 cup light cream *or* **half and half**

Fresh parsley *or* **watercress sprigs, for garnish**

Pick over lentils and discard any of poor quality. Rinse thoroughly. Drain and set aside briefly.

In a large *non-aluminum** kettle set over *MEDIUM* heat, heat oil. Add chopped celery and leek and grated carrot, parsnip, and red onion. Sauté until vegetables soften.

Add lentils and stock. Bring to the boil. *Reduce heat and simmer, covered, for about 20-25 minutes, or until vegetables and lentils are tender.*

Using a food processor or electric blender, process soup in small batches until smooth. Pour puréed soup through a sieve into a clean saucepan set over *LOW-MEDIUM* heat.** Discard refuse or add to vegetables for soup stock.

Season with salt and pepper, to taste, and add cream. Allow to heat through. *Do not allow soup to boil once cream has been added.*

Turn into heated soup tureen and serve into heated soup bowls, garnishing with parsley or watercress, as preferred.

Yields about 7 cupfuls

Notes: *Since aluminum discolors lentils rather unpleasantly, avoid using aluminum cookware or serving bowls in this case.

The soup base can be conveniently frozen at this point.

1/7 SERVING (i. e., per cupful) –
PROTEIN = 9.6 g.; FAT = 6.0 g.; CARBOHYDRATE = 26.0 g.;
CALORIES = 106; CALORIES FROM FAT = 51%

VEGETARIAN IRISH STEW
Stobhach Gaelach
TPT - 1 hour

Back in the 1980s, when we visited Ireland, I had great hopes of finding authentic vegetarian interpretations of the classic Irish dishes with which I was familiar. We had very little luck finding restaurants that catered to, or even acknowledged, vegetarian preferences, even near Trinity College in Dublin. While in Ireland we had to resort to our "when-all-else-fails-while-traveling" dinner of canned vegetarian beans and canned rice pudding on two occasions.

My dad was not a fan of Irish stew since it had usually been made with mutton in his family and he, as a consequence, had a real aversion to lamb, claiming he could smell and taste the wool. Mom, therefore, usually made a beef stew on St. Patrick's Day. I think this vegetarian stew is actually better flavored than any version of "Irish stew" that I remember.

Europe–Ireland

VEGETARIAN IRISH STEW (cont'd)

1 tablespoon butter
1 package (8.5 ounces) *frozen* soy nuggets *or* chopped strips
2 slices smoky *tempeh* bacon *or* soy bacon—cut into 1/2 inch pieces
1 tablespoon unbleached white flour
3/4 cup water

1/2 cup canned, *crushed* tomatoes—a thick purée
1 cup stout beer*
1/4 cup *finely* chopped celery with leaves
2 large, *fresh* sage leaves
1 sprig *fresh* rosemary
1 sprig *fresh* thyme
1 tablespoon gingersnap crumbs
Freshly ground black pepper, to taste

24 baby carrots—trimmed and well-scrubbed
1 large potato—peeled and coarsely chopped
18 *frozen* white boiling onions

1/2 cup freshly shelled *or frozen* green peas

Chopped fresh parsley

In a kettle set over *MEDIUM* heat, melt butter. Add *frozen* soy nuggets and bacon pieces. Sauté until the nuggets separate and begin to soften. Add flour and stir to integrate, cooking and stirring for about 1 minute. While continuing to stir, *gradually, tablespoonful by tablespoonful*, add water.

Add tomatoes, beer, *finely* chopped celery leaves, sage leaves, rosemary sprig, thyme sprig, ground gingersnaps, and black pepper. Cook, stirring frequently, until it comes to the boil. *Reduce heat to LOW.*

Add carrots, chopped potato, and *frozen* onions. Cover and allow to cook over *LOW* heat for 40 minutes. Stir occasionally.

Add *frozen* green peas. Continue cooking for about 5 minutes more until peas are just heated through.

Turn into heated serving bowl. Remove and discard sage leaves, rosemary sprig, and thyme sprig.

Garnish with chopped parsley. *Serve at once.*

Yields 6 serving
adequate for 4 people

Notes: *A good Irish stout usually contains honey and is, therefore, not vegan. If that is a problem for you, substitute any beer of choice. If you wish, you can add half a teaspoonful of *agave* nectar.

The celery leaves and the meat substitutes provide plenty of sodium so do not be tempted to salt this stew further.

This recipe can be halved or doubled, when required.

1/6 SERVING – PROTEIN = 14.9 g.; FAT = 5.1 g.; CARBOHYDRATE = 25.5 g.; CALORIES = 193; CALORIES FROM FAT = 23%

SAUTÉED BABY ARTICHOKE HEARTS WITH IRISH CREAM AND MUSTARD SAUCE
TPT - 18 minutes

Although globe artichokes have been grown in Ireland and found in Irish cuisine since the Norman Conquest (1066 AD), I had never tasted them until I was an adult on my own. When I served them to my grandmother, she thought they were a waste of money "for what you get out of them." Since artichokes are thistles and need a long, damp growing season and mild winters, they have been successfully grown in the British Isles, especially in the Western coastal regions which are touched by the warm gulf stream currents. Due to the short growing season, if you encounter artichokes on menus or in produce markets in the British Isles, you will usually find the small, tender baby artichokes instead of the large flower heads that are most often sold here in the United States.

2 teaspoons butter
1 pound *frozen* baby artichoke hearts—*defrosted**

IRISH CREAM AND MUSTARD SAUCE:
    2 large shallots—*finely* chopped
    2 tablespoons MUSTARD SAUCE [see index]**
    2/3 cup light cream *or* half and half, as preferred

Watercress sprigs, for garnish

In a large, non-stick-coated skillet set over *LOW-MEDIUM* heat, melt butter. Add *defrosted* baby artichoke hearts. Cook, stirring frequently, for about 10 minutes, or until tender.

While the artichoke hearts are cooking, in a measuring cup or small bowl, combine *finely* chopped shallots, mustard, and cream. Stir to combine well.

SAUTÉED BABY ARTICHOKE HEARTS WITH IRISH CREAM AND MUSTARD SAUCE (cont'd)

When the artichokes are tender, pour the prepared IRISH CREAM AND MUSTARD SAUCE over. Stir to be sure that each artichoke heart is coated with the sauce ingredients. Continue to cook, stirring frequently, until the cream sauce is hot and begins to thicken slightly. *Do not allow the sauce to boil.*

Transfer artichoke hearts and sauce into a heated serving bowl and serve at once, garnished with watercress sprigs.

Yields 6 servings adequate for 4 people

Notes: *If you find fresh baby globe artichokes in a greengrocer or at a farmers' market, trim, clean, halve, and prepare them as directed above for preparation of the more frequently available frozen variety.

**Dijon* mustard, of choice, may be substituted, if preferred. However, country-style *Dijon* mustard is a bit too assertive for this dish.

This recipe may be halved, when required.

1/6 SERVING – PROTEIN = 2.9 g.; FAT = 4.4 g.; CARBOHYDRATE = 7.8 g.;
CALORIES = 80; CALORIES FROM FAT = 50%

IRISH ROASTED MUSHROOMS AND SHALLOTS WITH ROSEMARY AND CHEESE
TPT - 37 minutes

I used to make this in a skillet, instead of oven-roasting the vegetables. The aroma is so incredible, I could hardly get it to the table. A spoonful here and there on a piece of bread, just to test whether it was done yet, of course, soon emptied the skillet. It makes a simple but wonderfully flavorful side dish that everyone loves or, for more formal meals, a portion on a buttermilk biscuit half makes a very nice first course. No matter how much you make, there will never be leftovers, I can promise you that.

8 medium shallots—peeled and halved
1 quart *boiling* water

1/4 cup butter—*melted*
1 large garlic clove—smashed
1 teaspoon fresh *or* dried rosemary needles
Freshly ground black pepper, to taste
1 pound assorted mushrooms—stems trimmed, rinsed and cleaned well with a brush, and *thickly* sliced*

1/2 cup (2 ounces) *slivered* goat's cheese, *very ripe* Brie, *or* "green" *Caerphilly*, if available

Preheat oven to 400 degrees F. Line a jelly roll pan sheet with aluminum foil, curling up the sides to form a "basket."

Parboil shallot halves in *boiling* water for about 5 minutes. Drain.

In a mixing bowl, combine *melted* butter, smashed garlic clove, rosemary needles, black pepper, mushroom slices, and parboiled shallot halves. Toss to coat mushrooms and shallots well. Turn out onto foil-lined cookie sheet and spread vegetables across the baking surface.

Roast in preheated 400 degree F. oven for 20 minutes, stirring once and twice to insure even roasting. *Remove baking sheet from oven.* Turn roasted mushrooms and shallots into a warmed serving bowl.

Remove and discard garlic clove. Scatter cheese slivers over roasted vegetables. Keep warm on a warming tray until cheese melts.

Serve at once.

Yields 6 servings adequate for 3 people

Notes: *We use a mixture of white field *(Agaricus)*, shiitake, oyster, *porcini* (*Cèpes Secjes, Boletes,* or *Steinpilze*), morels, *and/or* crimini or baby bella. Reconstituted, dried mushrooms can be added to the assortment, if desired.

This recipe can be doubled, when required.

1/6 SERVING – PROTEIN = 3.9 g.; FAT = 10.4 g.; CARBOHYDRATE = 4.5 g.;
CALORIES = 125; CALORIES FROM FAT = 75%

Europe–Ireland

IRISH BUTTERED CABBAGE
Cabaiste

TPT - 7 minutes

Americans tend to think of cabbage as a pairing for corned beef at St. Patrick's Day but cabbage was and is a mainstay in Irish cooking. If you have ever bought a big freshly harvested cabbage head, used a bit, and stored it in your refrigerator, you will understand the importance of cabbage in so many cuisines. Well into the spring that head of cabbage is available for soups and salads and dishes such as this.

3 tablespoons water
1 tablespoon butter
1/2 teaspoon salt

1 pound savoy cabbage, well-washed and *thinly* sliced, but *not shredded*

Freshly ground black pepper, to taste

In a large skillet set over *LOW-MEDIUM* heat, combine water, butter, and salt. Bring to the boil.

Add sliced cabbage and cook, stirring constantly, for about 3-5 minutes, or until cabbage is wilted. Season with black pepper.

Turn into a heated serving bowl.

Yields 6 servings
adequate for 4 people

Note: This recipe may be halved or doubled, when required.

1/6 SERVING – PROTEIN = 1.0 g.; FAT = 2.0 g.; CARBOHYDRATE = 4.1 g.;
CALORIES = 35; CALORIES FROM FAT = 51%

IRISH BREAD AND BUTTER PUDDING WITH APRICOT TOPPING
Marag Arain Agus Ime

TPT - 2 hours and 5 minutes;
30 minutes = soaking period;
30 minutes = cooling period

Although this is generally served warm in Ireland, it may be served chilled or at room temperature. The chilled version is especially welcome as a brunch or summer breakfast presentation which can, conveniently, be made the evening before. Oh, it is a beautiful pudding with which to greet the "maidin" or end the "la."

3 thick slices oat *or* whole wheat bread—crusts removed*
1 tablespoon butter

1/4 cup *preservative-free dark* raisins

3/4 cup *fat-free* pasteurized eggs (the equivalent of 3 eggs)
1/3 cup sugar
1 2/3 cups (13-ounce can) *skimmed* evaporated milk
1 cup *boiling* water
1 teaspoon pure vanilla extract

1 cup (8-ounce jar) all-fruit apricot preserves

Prepare a 1- or 1 1/2-quart shallow baking dish, such as a ceramic quiche dish or deep-dish pie plate by coating with non-stick lecithin spray coating.

Lightly toast bread slices. Butter each and cut into cubes. (There should be about 2 heaping cupfuls.) Arrange bread cubes in the bottom of prepared baking dish. Scatter raisins among bread cubes. Set aside.

In a large mixing bowl, combine pasteurized eggs, sugar, and evaporated milk. Blend thoroughly. Stir in *boiling* water and vanilla extract. Pour custard mixture over bread cubes and raisins.

Allow to stand at room temperature for at least 30 minutes. Skim any remaining bubbles from surface.

Preheat oven to 325 degrees F.

IRISH BREAD AND BUTTER PUDDING WITH APRICOT TOPPING (cont'd)

Place bread pudding in baking pan in which a 1-inch water bath has been prepared. Bake in preheated oven for 35 minutes. *Do not allow water bath to simmer or boil—by adding cold water or ice cubes, if necessary.*

Remove bread pudding from oven after the initial 35-minute baking period. Spoon apricot jam over. Return pudding to oven for about 5 minutes to allow preserves to begin to melt. Again, remove pudding from oven and spread apricot preserves, *carefully*, over the pudding surface. Return to the oven and continue baking for about 10 minutes more, or until a knife inserted in the center comes out clean.

Allow pudding to cool at room temperature for at least 30 minutes before serving. If you want to serve this pudding chilled, refrigerate for at least 1 hour before serving. However, it is traditionally served slightly warm or at room temperature.

Yields 6 servings
adequate for 4 people

Notes: *Reserve crusts to make breadcrumbs.

Leftovers keep well, if covered and refrigerated.

1/6 SERVING – PROTEIN = 9.6 g.; FAT = 2.2 g.; CARBOHYDRATE = 60.1 g.;
CALORIES = 253; CALORIES FROM FAT = 8%

IRISH BLACKBERRY COBBLER
Marag Smeara Dubh

TPT - 1 hour and 50 minutes;
1 hour = cooling period

Blackberry seeds found in the food preparation areas of Iron Age archaeological sites in Ireland indicate that blackberries were used in cooking at least as far back as that period. The great big, freshly-picked blackberries that appear in our farmers' market in August are so plump and so sweet that I can barely get home without diving into a quart. Those that I freeze often find their way into this wonderful cobbler that nourished my ancestors.

1 quart fresh blackberries—well-washed—
  or frozen, if necessary
2 tablespoons honey

1/2 cup whole wheat flour
1/4 cup unbleached white flour
1/4 cup oat flour
1/2 cup sugar
1 1/2 teaspoons baking powder
2 tablespoons *toasted* wheat germ
1/4 cup *fat-free* pasteurized eggs (the equivalent of 1 egg)

Light cream *or* half and half

Preheat oven to 350 degrees F. Prepare a 9-inch pie plate or quiche dish by coating with non-stick lecithin spray coating.

Scatter washed blackberries evenly across the prepared pie plate. Drizzle honey over.

Into a large mixing bowl, sift whole wheat, white, and oat flours with sugar and baking powder. Stir in wheat germ. Add pasteurized eggs and mix well with a pastry blender or a fork until of the consistency of coarse corn meal. Sprinkle this mixture evenly over blackberries.

Bake in preheated 350 degree F. oven for 40 minutes, or until *lightly browned.*

Allow to cool to room temperature about 1 hour—or refrigerate, as preferred. Serve warm or chilled with cream.

Yields 6 servings
adequate for 4-6 people

Notes: Coffee and vanilla ice cream flavors compliment this dessert well.

This recipe may be halved or doubled, when required.

1/6 SERVING (without cream) –
PROTEIN = 5.3 g.; FAT = 1.5 g.; CARBOHYDRATE = 52.7 g.;
CALORIES = 233; CALORIES FROM FAT = 6%

Italy

There is no earthly way in which I could or would suggest a single menu and label it typical of Italy. Each village within each province has its specialties which may or may not have even traveled to nearby villages or provinces. Of course, many of those very local recipes have become part of our combined heritage in United States since they traveled with emigrating women. I have chosen four menus from four very different areas of Italy and beg for understanding of my admittedly "arbitrary" choices.

The different foods one finds in Northern Italy and the South have been introduced to the world outside of Italy and are well-known by most but the distinctive cuisines of the Piedmont and Calabria will surprise.

Vercelli, in Novara, was the site of Celtic settlement, a *laetus*, where "foreigners," who collected at the borders of the empire, were allowed to settle within the territorial bounds of the Roman Empire, acquiring Roman protection but committing, in return, to fight for Rome. The word *laetus* actually has a Germanic language derivation meaning serf but the "*barbari*" were not only Germans. Iberians, from present-day Spain and Portugal; nomadic horsemen from Persia; Arabs; Georgians; and Armenians all brought their households and their traditions.

Laeti settlements have also been identified in Calabria, a poor, mountainous area so inhospitable that the Romans cared little for its meager resources and committed little to his security. Even the Nazis and Mussolini side-stepped this province. Calabrian cuisine has consequently enjoyed an incubation that has avoided the integration of foods from other parts of Italy allowing Calabrian food traditions to persist to this day.

Calabria

The first chocolate manufactured in Europe was manufactured in Turino, Italy.

**Pan-Grilled *Portobello* Mushrooms with
Lentils, Escarole, Tomato, and Olives**
Lenticche, Scarola, e Pomódoro en Funghi

~~~~~~~~~~~~~~~~~~~~~

Traditional Salt Cod Stew for Christmas Eve
Without the Salt Cod
Zuppa di Baccala Sénza Baccala

Bread
Páne

~~~~~~~~~~~~~~~~~~~~~

**Stuffed Figs Cloaked in Chocolate
with Raspberry Sauce**
Fichi al Cioccolata

Lemon Sherbet   with   **Fig Sauce**
Salsa di Fichi

Anise Toast   **Roasted Chestnuts**
Aninci   *Castagne Arrosto*

PAN – GRILLED PORTOBELLO MUSHROOMS
WITH LENTILS, ESCAROLE, TOMATO, AND OLIVES
Lenticche, Scarola, e Pomodóro en Fungi
TPT - 56 minutes

If I find big, meaty portobello mushrooms in the produce section of my grocery, at an attractive price, I do not seem to be able to resist them. Besides contributing that "unami" taste, they anchor a portion of the plate in a more comfortable pattern for meat eaters who visit and they can be filled with the most amazing combinations. I thought about the traditional New Year's Eve dish from Calabria and decided to adapt it as a stuffing for the mushrooms to be served as a first course for the holidays and as a light, everyday supper main course nestled on a bed of linguini. The addition of thyme, sage, and marjoram from my summer garden emphasize for me that the winter will soon be over.

1/2 cup dry, brown (*or* green) lentils
1 1/2 cups VEGETARIAN BROWN STOCK
   [see index]
1 bay leaf—broken*

1 quart *boiling* water
6 cups coarsely chopped escarole—using only
   well-washed inner leaves, trimmed of bitter
   white portions
[see next page]

PAN-GRILLED PORTOBELLO MUSHROOMS WITH LENTILS, ESCAROLE, TOMATO, AND OLIVES (cont'd)

3/4 cup canned, *diced* tomatoes—well-drained— or 2 plum tomatoes—peeled, seeded, and diced
1/8 teaspoon freshly ground black pepper
1/4 teaspoon dried thyme—crushed
1/4 teaspoon crushed, dried sage
1/4 teaspoon crushed, dried marjoram

3/4 cup diced (about 3 ounces) *low-moisture, part-skimmed milk mozzarella* cheese***
6 tablespoons sliced, pitted *Kalamata* olives

6 large *portobello* mushrooms (1/2 pound)–trimmed, stems removed, rinsed, and cleaned well with a brush

Blanch chopped escarole in the 1 quartful *boiling* water for just 1 minute. Drain well and set aside until required.

Sort lentils and discard those of poor quality. Rinse thoroughly.

In a non-aluminum saucepan** set over *MEDIUM* heat, combine lentils, stock, and broken bay leaf.* Bring to the boil. Reduce heat to *LOW*, cover tightly, and simmer for about 30 minutes, or until lentils are tender. Drain, reserving liquid for soup stock and discarding bay leaf pieces. Turn into a mixing bowl.

Add par-boiled and drained escarole, diced tomatoes, black pepper, and crushed, dried thyme, and sage, and marjoram. Stir to mix well.

Add diced *mozzarella* and sliced olives. Stir to combine well.

Preheat grill pan. Coat with non-stick lecithin spray coating. Preheat a non-stick-coated skillet over *LOW* heat.

Place well-cleaned *portobello* mushroom caps, *gill-side-down*, on preheated grill pan. Allow caps to grill for about 5 minutes. Turn over. Spoon *one-sixth* of the vegetable mixture into each mushroom cap. Grill for about 5 minutes more or until the caps are "marked." Using two large spoons, transfer the caps to the preheated skillet and keep warm until the cheese is melted and you are ready to serve. Transfer each to a heated serving plate.

Serve at once.

Yields 6 individual servings

Notes: *The bay leaf pieces are most easily recovered if secured inside a tea ball during the simmering.

**Since aluminum discolors lentils rather unpleasantly, avoid use of aluminum cookware or serving bowls in this case.

***The cheese may be omitted if you are looking for a vegan entrée or if the rest of your menu contains sufficient protein making the extra cheese superfluous.

This recipe can be halved or doubled or tripled, when required.

1/6 SERVING – PROTEIN = 10.2 g.; FAT = 3.5 g.; CARBOHYDRATE = 15.9 g.;
CALORIES = 135; CALORIES FROM FAT = 23%

TRADITIONAL SALT COD STEW FOR CHRISTMAS EVE IN THE STYLE OF CALABRIA *WITHOUT THE SALT COD*
Zuppa di Baccala sense Baccala

TPT - 1 hour and 31 minutes

Zuppa di Baccala was a tradition in Ray's family since his father was born in Calabria. A cousin continued to make it for Christmas Eve for years after the immigrant generations were gone but the saltiness of soup/stew and the multi-day soaking of dried cod were never to my liking. When we visited Portugal and I saw the cod drying on racks, covered with flies and the constant target of circling gulls, I said, "NO" but did make it a few times to please others. Eventually I evolved a vegetarian version but I suppose it would then be CHRISTMAS EVE BACCALA senza BACCALA. It is the gathered family that is important not the baccala, at least to some!

Even if we have to dig down under the snow, the sprigs of thyme come from our herb garden for this dish. Actually the fact that Christmas Eve comes after the Winter Solstice and the hours of daylight are growing longer each day, however imperceptibly, the sprigs of thyme seem to give promise of the spring and the gardening season ahead.

TRADITIONAL SALT COD STEW FOR CHRISTMAS EVE IN THE STYLE OF CALABRIA *WITHOUT THE SALT COD* (cont'd)

2 tablespoons *extra virgin* olive oil
3 medium onions—*thinly* sliced
3 large garlic cloves—*finely* chopped

2 cups canned, *diced* tomatoes
3 cups water
1 large celery rib—diced
1 bay leaf—broken in half*
1/2 teaspoon crushed, dried thyme
1/2 teaspoon crushed, dried sage

3 sprigs fresh, Italian flat-leafed parsley
2 sprigs fresh thyme

4 medium all-purpose potatoes—peeled and cut into sixths *or* eighths
1/2 teaspoon salt, or to taste

20 OLIVES IN GREEK MARINADE *(Elyes meh Ladoxkitho)* [see index], pitted, ripe black olives, *Kalamata* olives, *or* oil-cured Italian black olives *(OPTIONAL)*

In a kettle set over *MEDIUM* heat, heat oil. Sauté onions and garlic until onions are soft and translucent, *allowing neither the onion nor the garlic to brown.*

Drain liquid from tomatoes and add liquid to sautéed onions and garlic. Chop tomatoes and add with water, chopped celery, broken bay leaf, and crushed thyme and sage to onions and garlic mixture. Stir to combine.

Tie the parsley and thyme sprigs together with a string. Add to kettle. Cook vegetable base for about 20-25 minutes, stirring frequently.

Add potato chunks and salt. Cook for about 50 minutes more, or until potatoes are tender.** Stir frequently. Add more water during this time period if stew becomes too thick.

Add black olives, if desired. Allow to just heat through. Turn into a heated soup tureen.

Ladle into heated soup plates. Serve with bread.

Yields 10 servings
adequate for 6-8 people

Notes: *The bay leaf pieces are most easily recovered if secured inside a tea ball during the simmering process.

**Slivers of seitin or an unbreaded soy meat analogue can be added at this point to give the mouth feel of the cod, if desired.

This recipe may be halved or doubled, when required. Do not double the oil or herb *bouquet garni* when increasing.

1/10 SERVING (without meat alternative addition) –
PROTEIN = 2.2 g.; FAT = 3.1 g.; CARBOHYDRATE = 13.9 g.;
CALORIES = 91; CALORIES FROM FAT = 31%

CALABRESE STUFFED FIGS CLOAKED IN CHOCOLATE WITH RASPBERRY SAUCE
Fichi al Cioccolata
TPT - 35 minutes

We always say that we really should have just fruit and cookies for dessert at Christmas instead of cakes and pastries and then this wonderful, very special Italian holiday fruit dessert pops into my mind and I agree. "We'll just have fruit and cookies." The nice thing about this dessert is that you can actually prepare it and plate it before you get involved in all your dinner preparations or, if you prefer, you can make them a day or two ahead of time and refrigerate in a closed container until required.

1/2 package (5 ounces) *frozen* raspberries in syrup
—defrosted

1/4 cup candied orange peel—*finely* chopped*
1/4 cup *finely* chopped, *toasted, preservative-free* almonds
Pinch ground cloves

12 soft, dried, *preservative-free* whole figs**

1/4 cup *coating* chocolate***—melted over simmering water in a double boiler

Using the food processor, purée the defrosted raspberries. Set a tea strainer or other fine sieve over a small bowl, press the raspberry purée through to remove the seeds. Refrigerate until required.

CALABRESE STUFFED FIGS CLOAKED IN CHOCOLATE WITH RASPBERRY SAUCE (cont'd)

In a small bowl, combine *finely* chopped candied orange peel, toasted almonds, and ground cloves. Stir to mix well.

Slit each fig on one side and, using a butter knife, press a portion of the orange peel–almond mixture into each fig.

Holding figs by the stems, dip each into the coating chocolate several times until well-coated. *Hold in the air until chocolate sets up* and then transfer to a waxed paper-covered surface to dry.

To serve, place a chocolate-coated, stuffed fig on each dessert plate. Spoon a portion of the raspberry purée along side. *Serve at room temperature.*

Yields 12 servings
adequate for 6-10 people

Notes: *Unsulfured, candied orange peel is available by mail order from the same mail order firms that supply candied lemon peel and citron, all of which are requisite for our Italian Christmas baking.

**Whole dried Calimyrna figs are available from bulk food mail order firms if not available in your natural food stores. Fresh figs can also be prepared in this manner.

***"Coating" chocolate is the chocolate used to make candy. It is available usually in little disks where candy-making items are sold. Since it sets up better than does the chocolate used to make chocolate chips and it dries to a beautiful sheen, it is perfect for this dessert.

This recipe can be halved or doubled, when required.

1/12 SERVING – PROTEIN = 1.3 g.; FAT = 2.9 g.; CARBOHYDRATE = 19.5 g.;
CALORIES = 100; CALORIES FROM FAT = 26%

FIG SAUCE IN THE STYLE OF CALABRIA
Salsa di Fichi

TPT - 58 minutes;
20 minutes = cooling period

During the first winter after my family moved down from upstate New York to Long Island, I noticed trees wrapped in tar paper. I found out that this was the way that fig trees were protected from winter, a winter I considered mild in comparison to those I lived through in Rochester. Until I tasted fresh figs, I could not understand why anybody would go to all that trouble. This recipe calls for dried figs since the few fresh figs we are able to buy each year are just eaten out of hand here with an enthusiasm not unlike the canopy-dwelling primates of the tropical rain forests.

**1 cup water
1 cup (about 4 1/2 ounces) stemmed and chopped, *preservative-free* dried *Calimyrna* figs
1/2 cup sugar
1 cinnamon quill
1/2 vanilla bean**

1 tablespoon rum

In a saucepan set over *LOW-MEDIUM* heat, combine water, chopped figs, sugar, and cinnamon quill.** Split vanilla bean in half and scrape seeds into sauce ingredients. (Save vanilla bean to flavor other desserts or sugar.) Cook sauce ingredients, stirring constantly, until sugar dissolves. *Increase heat to MEDIUM.* Cook, stirring frequently, until figs are *very tender* and sauce has thickened into a syrup—about 30 minutes. Remove cinnamon quill.

Add rum. Stir to combine well. Allow to cool for about 20 minutes.***

Serve at room temperature over sherbets, ice cream, cakes, or puddings.

Yields 2 cupfuls

Notes: *Dried figs are often treated with sulfiting agents, to which many people are sensitive. Unsulfited figs and other dried fruits are available in natural food stores and from mail order firms. Be aware that imported dried fruits frequently are unlabeled, but do contain preservatives.

Europe-Italy/*Calabria*

FIG SAUCE IN THE STYLE OF CALABRIA (cont'd)

**If you are going to serve this sauce over lemon sherbet or a lemon pound cake, add about 2 tablespoons freshly grated lemon zest, if desired. If your dessert would benefit from an orange flavoring, add orange zest.

***This sauce may be made early in the day or a day ahead of time and refrigerated. Bring to room temperature before serving.

This recipe may be halved or doubled, when required.

1/16 SERVING (about 2 tablespoonfuls) –
PROTEIN = 0.4 g.; FAT = 0.1 g.; CARBOHYDRATE = 15.6 g.;
CALORIES = 59; CALORIES FROM FAT = 2%

ANISE TOAST
Anicini

TPT - 50 minutes

Commercial anise toasts are so different from these real Italian biscotti, sometimes called biscotti d'anice. The double-baking technique, the creation of toasts if you will, was evolved in the third century by the Romans as a preservation technique and, if you can find a place to hide them from breakfast dunkers and after-school snackers, you will find that they keep well for weeks. After all, they survived for months on voyages with the Roman navy. Christmas morning without anicini would be unheard of and since they can be made weeks ahead of the holidays, there is no reason to disappoint.

3/4 cup unbleached white flour
3 1/3 tablespoons whole wheat flour
2 teaspoons soy flour
1/4 teaspoon baking powder

2 large eggs*
1/3 cup sugar

1 teaspoon anise seed

Preheat oven to 375 degrees F. Prepare a 9 x 5 x 3-inch loaf pan by coating with non-stick lecithin spray coating and then *lightly* flouring. Also, prepare a cookie sheet by oiling generously.**

Into a mixing bowl, sift white, whole wheat, and soy flours with baking powder. Set aside.

In a large mixing bowl, using a wire whisk, beat eggs and sugar together thoroughly. Set aside.

Using a mortar and pestle, crush anise seeds until quite fine. Add to egg mixture.

Using a wooden spoon, gradually stir in sifted dry ingredients until a stiff, smooth batter is achieved. Spread batter in prepared loaf pan and bake in preheated 375 degree F. oven for about 20 minutes, or until a bamboo skewer or toothpick inserted into the center comes out clean. *(This will not rise significantly so do not be alarmed when the pan is only about 1/4 full at the end of the baking period.)*

Reduce oven setting to 200 degrees F. and leave oven door open until temperature is, indeed, 200 degrees.

Meanwhile, remove entire loaf from pan and immediately slice into sixteen 1/2-inch thick slices. Place slices side-by-side on the prepared cookie sheet and return to oven—now at 200 degrees F. Bake until bottoms of slices are *lightly browned*—about 20 minutes. Using tongs, turn each slice and continue to bake for an additional 10 minutes, or until the remaining side is *lightly browned*.

Remove to wire rack and cool completely. Store in tightly sealed plastic bag.

Yields 16 slices

Notes: *Do not substitute pasteurized eggs in this recipe.

**A perforated *biscotti* pan, often sold to make baked French fries, allows for constant air and heat circulation. When this simple pan, available from several mail order firms, is used instead of a cookie sheet, the *biscotti* slices are evenly and lightly browned.

These are also a pleasant accompaniment to a continental breakfast menu or afternoon "milk-dunk" snack.

Although these toasts keep well at room temperature for a considerable period of time, if tightly sealed, they may be conveniently frozen.

1/16 SERVING (i. e., per slice) –
PROTEIN = 1.7 g.; FAT = 0.9 g.; CARBOHYDRATE = 10.0 g.;
CALORIES = 41; CALORIES FROM FAT = 20%

Piemonte

Bread – Cheese Soup
Zuppa Mitunn

~~~~~~~~~~~~~~~~~~~~

Asparagus with *Fontina*
Asparagi con Fontina

Rice with Eggs
Uova e Riso

Breadsticks
Grissini

~~~~~~~~~~~~~~~~~~~~

Asti Spumonti

~

Thin Slices of Melon
Melone

Cherries in Red Wine Sauce
Ciliege al Barolo

BREAD – CHEESE SOUP FROM THE PIEDMONT
Zuppa Mitunn
TPT - 34 minutes

I will never forget the experience of flying over the Italian Piedmont as our flight followed the coastline towards a landing in Rome—the Alps looming to our left, the Ligurian Gulf filling the windows to our right, and Genoa below. Soup is important in the land that sits facing the Mediterranean Sea in the northwest corner of Italy with its back to Switzerland and the European Alps and a woman gains significant respect for the flavor and richness of her soup broth. One of my most favorite minestrones is from Novara. Bagna clauda is a well-known regional specialty but here is another specialty that reminds one of the "classic" French onion soup with intense garlic overtones that in turn remind me of the garlic soups I tasted in Portugal and Spain. The Piedmont was once part of the Kingdom of Savoy which encompassed northwestern Italy and southeastern France. The province borders present-day France to its West, with Spain and Portugal beyond, and perhaps this more ancient soup is that which influenced French onion soup. I favor this Italian soup over the French or Portuguese and Spanish versions because this soup so clearly suggests the possibility of simultaneous evolution of an idea or, perhaps the influence of contact. Using my most flavorful vegetarian broth, I have evolved this peasant soup one step further.

1 tablespoon butter
1 medium yellow onion—*very thinly* sliced into rings

6 cups VEGETABLE BROWN STOCK *[see index]* or other vegetarian stock of choice

12 *thin* slices French style *baguette*—lightly toasted*
1 1/2 tablespoons GARLIC OIL *[see index]*

6 ounces *thinly* sliced *or* planed Swiss *Gruyère* cheese

2 tablespoons chopped *porcini* mushrooms —either fresh *or* rehydrated dried mushroom kibble
1 tablespoon grated Parmesan cheese *or* pecorino Romano, if preferred
Freshly ground black pepper, to taste

BREAD – CHEESE SOUP FROM THE PIEDMONT (cont'd)

In a saucepan set over *MEDIUM* heat, melt butter. Add onion rings and sauté until onions are soft and translucent, *being careful not to allow the onions to brown.*

Add stock and allow to come to the boil.

Meanwhile, generously brush both sides of each *toasted* bread slice with garlic oil. Set aside until required.

Preheat oven to 375 degrees F.

Using a slotted spoon, transfer the onions to an oven-to-table casserole, soufflé dish, or even a Dutch oven large enough to hold six slices in one layer. Place six slices of bread on top of the onions. Layer *one-half* of the *Gruyère* cheese on top of the bread. Place the remaining six slices of bread on top of the cheese.

Pour the hot broth over the bread.

Layer the remaining cheese slices on top of the broth-soaked bread. Sprinkle with chopped *porcini* mushrooms and grated cheese. Grind pepper over. Bake in preheated 375 degree F. oven for about 15 minutes, or until most of the broth has been absorbed by the bread. Remove from oven.

Serve at once into heated soup plates

Yields 6 servings

Notes: *A multigrain bread is ideal for this soup since it adds dimension.

This recipe can be halved, when required. Use a baking dish that will hold just three slices of bread in a single layer.

1/6 SERVING – PROTEIN = 11.4 g.; FAT = 14.3 g.; CARBOHYDRATE = 17.8 g.;
CALORIES = 242; CALORIES FROM FAT = 53%

ASPARAGUS WITH *FONTINA* IN THE STYLE OF THE PIEDMONT
Asparagi con Fontina
TPT - 18 minutes

We used to visit a store where we learned about cheese from a remarkable man who never failed to introduce our young daughter to a new cheese each time we visited. It reminded me of the stores of my childhood where slivers of cheese or sausage were always handed over the counter to the children who accompanied parents or grandparents to the butcher or cheese shop. That kindly gentleman, who really knew his cheeses, taught us the difference between French and Italian fontina cheeses. It is harder and harder to find the creamy, nutty cheese from the Piedmont but do search it out; it and no other cheese makes this regional specialty perfect. The use of butter, in preference to olive oil, and the wide incorporation of Italian fontina cheese instead of mozzarella are two distinctly different characteristics of the cooking of the northwestern area of Italy.

30 large asparagus spears—well-washed and ends trimmed, with spears cut to about equal lengths

3 tablespoons butter
1 teaspoon freshly squeezed lemon juice

Freshly ground *white* pepper, to taste

3 ounces Italian *fontina* cheese—*thinly* sliced

Set up steamer.

Steam asparagus spears until bright green and *crisp-tender*—about 4 minutes.

In a large skillet set over *LOW–MEDIUM* heat, melt butter. Stir lemon juice into the butter. Place steamed asparagus into the skillet in a single layer with all the flower tips facing the same direction.

Grind *white* pepper over and cook, shaking occasionally to distribute the butter and turn the asparagus spears, for about 4 minutes more. *Reduce heat to LOW.*

Lay the slices of cheese across the asparagus spears just below the tips. Cover the pan and cook only until the cheese is melted—about 2 minutes more.

Serve at once, directly from the skillet.

Yields 6 servings
of 5 spears each

Note: This recipe may be halved or doubled, when required.

1/6 SERVING – PROTEIN = 4.7 g.; FAT = 10.2 g.; CARBOHYDRATE = 4.2 g.;
CALORIES = 119; CALORIES FROM FAT = 77%

Europe–Italy/*Piemonte*

NORTHERN ITALIAN RICE WITH EGGS
Uova e Riso

TPT - 39 minutes

The descriptive phrase "the plains of Vercelli" carries the imagination away until one fact checks and realizes that on the "plains" between Novara and Vercelli one actually finds acres and acres of paddy fields which provide approximately sixty percent of the total rice consumed in Italy. Short-grained Arborio rice, the rice used to make risotto, is a major product of this area. We often prepare this rice dish, a favorite of our daughter from the time she was a toddler, without the eggs, especially if the rest of our menu provides sufficient protein. It is also a good way to use a quantity of leftover rice to accompany a vegetable entrée. Simply steam the cold, leftover rice, fold in a bit of melted butter and Parmesan cheese, and in minutes, you have dinner.

3 cups bottled water *or* refrigerated water*
1 1/2 cups short-grained Italian *Arborio* rice**

2 tablespoons butter—*melted*
3 tablespoons grated Parmesan cheese***

6 large eggs—*brought to room temperature*

Freshly ground black pepper, to taste
3 tablespoons chopped fresh parsley, for garnish

In a saucepan set over *HIGH* heat, bring water to the boil. Stir in rice, reduce heat to *LOW*, cover tightly, and allow to cook *undisturbed* for 20 minutes.

While rice is cooking, set up egg poacher.

Remove rice from heat. Remove cover from saucepan to allow steam to escape, replace cover, and allow rice to stand for just a few minutes. Stir in *melted* butter and grated cheese. Keep warm.

Poach eggs so that *yolks are still runny*.

Mound 1/2 cupful of rice mixture on each of four plates. Using a soup spoon or the base of a *demitasse* cup, make a depression in the rice large enough to hold the poached egg. Slip the egg into the depression.

Grind a bit of black pepper over each egg. Sprinkle with chopped parsley.

Serve at once. Pass extra grated cheese to accommodate individual tastes.

Yields 6 servings
adequate for 4-6 people

Notes: *Unless you are "on a well," as we are, your tap water is probably chlorinated. Since the chlorine in tap water destroys the B-vitamin thiamin in grains, it is advisable to use either bottled water or water that has been refrigerated for at least 24 hours to cook grains.

**Short-grained *Arborio* rice, grown in the northern Italian agricultural provinces of *Piemonte*, *Tuscana*, and *Lombardia*, is available in Italian groceries, food specialty stores, natural food stores, and from specialty mail order firms. Incidentally, rice grains taken from this area of Italy by Thomas Jefferson in 1787, in violation of the stringent Italian law of the period, became the seeds of the ultimately successful rice-growing industry of the American South.

***Although a stronger grating cheese, such as *pecorino Romano*, would be uncharacteristic of the North of Italy, the sharp taste is infinitely pleasing to us.

This recipe can be increased or decreased proportionately, as required.

1/6 SERVING (with eggs) –
PROTEIN = 11.0 g.; FAT = 10.6 g.; CARBOHYDRATE = 35.3 g.;
CALORIES = 280; CALORIES FROM FAT = 34%

1/6 SERVING (without eggs) –
PROTEIN = 4.6 g.; FAT = 4.9 g.; CARBOHYDRATE = 35.3 g.;
CALORIES = 202; CALORIES FROM FAT = 22%

Europe–Italy/*Piemonte*

CHERRIES IN RED WINE SAUCE IN THE STYLE OF THE PIEDMONT
Ciliege al Barolo

TPT - 1 hour and 36 minutes;
1 hour = cooling period

As a child I helped my great-grandfather and my grandmother pick currants from the bushes that grew in the backyard. I was taught to choose just the ripe berries and to carefully remove them to the basket. Grandma then made red currant jelly and I can not remember a time when currant jelly was not on the pantry shelves. It was used in so very many recipes by my grandmother that during the years of World War II, when extra sugar rations were given to those who canned, we helped her harvest currants from any yard where the owners were not going to use them, trooping down the street behind Grandma with our little sand pails. One of the first plants I planted, when we bought our house, was a red currant bush. I waited for my harvest attentively and one evening I decided that the next morning was to be the day. The next morning I found that the birds had visited my ripened currants earlier that morning and I was left with nothing. I allowed the birds that bush for the whole time we lived there and, instead, bought my red currant jelly.

If you do not enjoy Barola wines, any really robust red wine will do. I use a Shiraz wine from the Barossa Valley of Australia to make this dessert. If you do not can cherries, pit fresh cherries and double the sugar.

3 cups canned, pitted sweet cherries—juice-packed *or* canned in light syrup—drained
6 tablespoons sugar
1 1/2 cups *Barolo* wine *or* a full bodied red wine of choice
1 cinnamon quill
3 long strips of orange zest—cut into thin 1-inch strips

2 tablespoons red currant jelly

Whipped cream, for garnish

In a saucepan set over *MEDIUM* heat, combine drained cherries, sugar, wine, cinnamon quill, and orange zest. Cook, stirring frequently, until the mixture comes to the boil. *Reduce heat to LOW.* Continue cooking, stirring frequently for about 20 minutes. *Remove from heat.* Using a slotted spoon, transfer cherries and orange zest to a sieve set over the sink. Remove and discard cinnamon quill. *Return saucepan to heat. Increase heat to MEDIUM.*

Add currant jelly. Cook until jelly melts and is fully integrated.

Turn drained cherries and orange zest into serving bowl. Pour wine–jelly syrup over. Refrigerate for at least 1 hour before serving.

Serve into small dessert dishes, sherbet glasses, or, preferably, wine glasses. Garnish each serving with a dollop of freshly whipped cream.

Yields 6 servings

Notes: *Barolo* wines are produced from the Nebbiolo grape variety and grown only in the Piedmont, southwest of Alba. The aroma prior to airing, or the nose, of this variety is that of a pine tree, similar to *retsina* from Greece; the taste has overtones of roses and resin, described by some as tar. These wines must be well-aged, making them generally expensive. They are interesting wines but do not have universal appeal.

This recipe can be halved or doubled, when required.

1/6 SERVING (with 2 tablespoonfuls whipped cream) –
PROTEIN = 1.1 g.; FAT = 2.6 g.; CARBOHYDRATE = 39.0 g.;
CALORIES = 159; CALORIES FROM FAT = 15%

Sicilia

I find that there is way more than my share of the planet's protein in this menu but you can pick and choose, as do I, as this traditional holiday meal progresses and progresses and progresses...

Antipasto:

Cheeses

Roasted Mushrooms with *Pignoli*

Roasted Peppers with Oil and *Pignoli*

~

Blood Orange Salad with Shaved Fennel and *Pecorino*, and Pomegranate Garnish

Salade de Tarocco, Finocchio, Pecorino, e Melagrana

~~~~~~~~~~~~~~~~~~~~

Lasagne

Lasagne al Forno

or

Skillet *Lasagne* with Soymeat

Lasagne en Casseruola

Steamed Baby Zucchini   Steamed Baby Carrots

Zucchine   *Carota*

~~~~~~~~~~~~~~~~~~~~

Italian Stuffed Artichokes

Carciofi Imbottit

~

Ricotta Pudding with Citron and Chocolate

Budini di Crema di Ricotta alla Siciliana

Homemade *Ricotta* Cheese

Hot Cocoa Mix

or

Pastry

Pasticceria

Fruit

Fruttas

Assorted Nuts

Nōce

Europe–Italy/*Sicilia*

SICILIAN BLOOD ORANGE SALAD
WITH SHAVED FENNEL, *PECORINO*, AND POMEGRANATE
Salade de Tarocco, Finocchio, Pecorino, e Melagrana

TPT - 1 hour and 5 minutes;
1 hour = marination period

A friend recoiled when I served freshly squeezed blood orange juice for brunch and I could not persuade her to even try something that we actually had to chart a shopping trip to find. Every holiday we search and search for blood oranges and if we are very lucky, we carry home a true Sicilian treasure. Choose any of the three most common types of blood oranges, Tarocco, native to Italy; the Sanguinello, native to Spain but grown in Sicily; or the Moro, a newer cultivar developed from an ancient variety grown near Siracusa in Sicily which has an intensely dark flesh and wonderful sweetness. The delicious fruit is believed to be a very ancient hybrid between the pomelo and the tangerine. Too often in recent years the treasure has evaded our search. Then, this classic Italian salad recipe must be made with navel oranges which I soak in pomegranate juice for about an hour before plating.

6 blood oranges *or* small navel oranges, if you can not find the blood oranges—peeled and sliced into about 5 slices each
2 tablespoons *extra virgin* olive oil
3 tablespoons pure pomegranate juice

1 fennel bulb trimmed and shaved as thinly as possible*
1/2 cup fresh pomegranate seeds
Freshly ground black pepper, to taste
1 ounce *pecorino Romano* cheese—shaved**

Notes: *A mandolin is helpful in achieving the thin shavings of fennel required.

**A cheese plane or vegetable peeler is helpful in creating the long, thin shavings of cheese required.

This recipe can be halved, when required. If more convenient, especially for a buffet presentation, it can be served from the large shallow bowl in which the oranges have been marinated.

In a large shallow bowl or platter, arrange orange slices in an overlapping spiral. Sprinkle olive oil and pomegranate juice over. Cover with plastic wrap and allow to stand at room temperature for about 1 hour to allow for flavor development during which time the fennel can be prepared and the pomegranate seeds extracted.

Lift the oranges from the marinade with a spatula, and divide them among six salad plates. Arrange attractively.

Divide the shaved fennel among the servings. Sprinkle pomegranate seeds on top. Grind black pepper over each serving. Divide cheese shavings among the servings, scattering them over the top.

Yields 6 individual servings

1/6 SERVING – PROTEIN = 3.5 g.; FAT = 5.4 g.; CARBOHYDRATE = 19.3 g.;
CALORIES = 132; CALORIES FROM FAT = 37%

Europe–Italy/*Sicilia*

LASAGNE
Lasagne al Forno

TPT - 2 hours and 23 minutes;
1 hour = first resting period;
10 minutes = second resting period

Pasta is not necessarily just pasta to Italians. The shapes of pastas are important and not always interchangeable in recipes. You dash to the store because you may have fusilli in the house but you need conchiglie for your salad and you would never substitute linguini or spaghetti for capelli d'angelo. The farfalle which combine perfectly with tiny, freshly made balls of mozzarella and a seasoned dressing to make an exquisite and perfect salad could never be replaced with the tiny, thimble pasta ditali or ziti.

While in Italy, we experienced eggplant parmigiana and lasagna very unlike that we were used to in the New York metropolitan area of the United States. The Sicilian and Neapolitan immigrants who settled near New York had introduced multi-layered casseroles that were "the way it should be." The flavors in Italy were right but the folded-over pasta technique was "not the way it should be." When we, in North America, say the word "lasagna," the image of a casserole such as this recipe comes to mind but "lasagne al forno" means no more than "noodles to the oven" and what you put between the between the layers of noodles is entirely your own business.

The rather irregular method of cooking and cooling used to make our lasagne usually produces an easily-plated result. The large amount of ricotta cheese in this recipe and the less substantial sauce benefit greatly from this unorthodox method.

High protein *lasagne* noodles—determine number needed for 2 layers in your particular pan (recommended 13 x 9 x 2-inch pan requires 10 noodles as packaged—about 8 ounces)
1 tablespoon vegetable oil

2 pounds (32 ounces) *part-skimmed milk ricotta* cheese
3/4 cup *fat-free* pasteurized eggs (the equivalent of 3 eggs)
1/2 cup grated Parmesan *or pecorino Romano* cheese, as preferred
3 tablespoons *finely* chopped, fresh flat-leafed Italian parsley
1/2 teaspoon freshly ground black pepper, or to taste

1 pound (16 ounces) *low-moisture, part-skimmed milk mozzarella* cheese—thinly sliced

3 cups TOMATO MUSHROOM SAUCE *[see index]*

Grated Parmesan *or pecorino Romano* cheese, as preferred

Prepare *lasagne* noodles according to package directions. Add oil to cooking water just before the *al dente* state is reached. When *al dente*, drain and rinse with *cold* water. Allow to drain thoroughly.

In a mixing bowl, combine *ricotta* cheese, pasteurized eggs, grated cheese, *finely* chopped fresh parsley, and black pepper. Mix well.

Preheat oven to 375 degrees F.

Arrange *one-half* of cooked noodles in a 13 x 9 x 2-inch baking pan or dish—piecing, if necessary, in order to fill all spaces. Spread *one-half* of *ricotta* mixture evenly over noodles. Arrange *one-half* of sliced *mozzarella* over *ricotta*. Spread 1 1/2 cupfuls of the tomato mushroom sauce evenly over *mozzarella* layer. Repeat layers using up all ingredients.

Bake in preheated 375 degree F. oven for 30 minutes. Remove from oven and place in the refrigerator for 1 hour. Return to preheated 375 degree F. oven for an additional 20 minutes, or until bubbling hot. *Allow to stand for about 10 minutes on warming tray.*

Cut into squares and serve into warmed soup plates or *au gratin* dishes. Pass additional grated cheese separately.

Yields 12 servings
adequate for 8 people as
a main course offering

Note: Two 8 x 8-inch pans may be used if a smaller quantity is required for a single meal. The remaining prepared *lasagne* may be frozen most successfully. Actually, the frozen preparation, when reheated, serves more easily than that which has been freshly prepared.

1/12 SERVING – PROTEIN = 26.0 g.; FAT = 13.7 g.; CARBOHYDRATE = 34.3 g.;
CALORIES = 333; CALORIES FROM FAT = 37%

Europe–Italy/*Sicilia*

SKILLET *LASAGNE* WITH SOYMEAT
Lasagne en Casseruola

TPT - 1 hour and 9 minutes

"Lasagne al forno" is one of the most incredibly delicious Italian dishes you can make. It was my mother-in-law's first choice for the pasta course before the meat course at a holiday meal, after which I was always too full to continue. It was work, yes, but it was worth it. Huge pans, exclusively for making lasagne, sat in a cupboard or pantry room in every kitchen in the family. I too had to have that exclusive pan; it was requisite to running your household. These pans are perfect for large family gatherings but now that there are only two of us, lasagne was not on the menu until I worked out a skillet lasagne that eliminates the dry leftovers. This is different from my "al forno" recipe in that it has no ricotta and the lasagne (lasagna) noodles are not boiled first but allowed to cook in the tomato juice. Also, the protein level has been raised not with high fat cheese but with soy.

1 cup *boiling* **water**
1/2 teaspoon SEASONING MIXTURE FOR DEHYDRATED SOYMEAT ANALOGUE [see index]
1 ounce So Soya+ dehydrated ground soymeat *or* **other dehydrated meat analogue product**

1 1/2 teaspoons *extra virgin* **olive oil**
1/2 small onion—*finely* **chopped**

1 cup canned, *diced* **tomatoes packed in tomato purée**
Sprinkling of dried red pepper flakes, to taste
1 1/2 teaspoons dried basil—crushed
3 (about 2 ounces) short, curly-edged *lasagne* **noodles—broken into 2-inch pieces***
2/3 cup FRESH *MARINARA* **SAUCE (***Salsa Marinara***)** [see index]
1 tablespoon grated Parmesan *or* **pecorino Romano cheese, as preferred**

2 ounces fresh *mozzarella* **cheese—cut into 4 slices**
1 teaspoon grated Parmesan *or* **pecorino Romano cheese, as preferred**

In a pie plate, combine *boiling* water and seasoning mixture. Stir to mix thoroughly. Add dehydrated groundmeat analogue and allow the product to rehydrate for about 20 minutes. Drain thoroughly.

Coat a 1 1/2-quart, non-stick-coated wok or deep skillet further with non-stick lecithin spray coating.** Set over *LOW-MEDIUM* heat. Heat oil. Add *finely* chopped onion and *rehydrated* soymeat. Cook, stirring frequently, until onion is soft and translucent, *being careful not to allow onions to brown.*

Add diced tomatoes with juice, red pepper flakes, and crushed dried basil. Stir to mix well. Arrange *lasagne* noodle pieces over the tomatoes. *Do not stir.* Spoon the marinara sauce over the noodles, distributing evenly across the skillet. Sprinkle the 1 tablespoonful grated cheese evenly over the surface. Cover. Reduce the heat to *LOW* and allow to cook for about 25 minutes, or until the noodles are tender. Stir only if you sense that the bottom is beginning to stick.

Place *mozzarella* slices on top of cooked skillet *lasagna*. Sprinkle with remaining 1 teaspoonful grated cheese. Cover and allow to cook for 10 minutes more.

Using two large spoons, spoon servings into heated soup plates.

Yields 4 servings
adequate for 2-3 people

Notes: *SKILLET *LASAGNE* WITH *RAVIOLI* (*Lasagne en Casseruola con Ravioli*) is a variation which we enjoy immensely. Prepare by replacing the *lasagna* noodles with cheese *ravioli*.

**We have found that a flat-bottomed wok is the best "skillet" for this *lasagna*. Our small 1 1/2-quart, two-person wok is perfect; we use our larger wok when we double this recipe.

1/4 SERVING – PROTEIN = 6.6 g.; FAT = 6.2 g.; CARBOHYDRATE = 17.4 g.; CALORIES = 156; CALORIES FROM FAT = 36%

Europe–Italy/*Sicilia*

ITALIAN STUFFED ARTICHOKES
Carciofi Imbottiti

TPT - 1 hour and 47 minutes

Never having tasted artichokes until I married, I had a joyous journey into the appreciation of this extraordinary thistle. No holiday season would be complete for our family today if these artichokes did not appear at least once. At holiday meals in many Italian–American families, especially those of Sicilian extraction, this dish is traditionally served as a course after dinner and before dessert but we sometimes serve a huge, stuffed artichoke as a main course for a light holiday supper, accompanying it with a soup, salads, and a selection of desserts.

4 large *or* 6 small Globe artichokes*
1/2 lemon
1 quart water
1 tablespoon freshly squeezed lemon juice

6 tablespoons *finely* chopped onion
3 garlic cloves—*very finely* chopped
1 1/2 tablespoons *finely* chopped, fresh Italian flat-leafed parsley
1 1/2 teaspoons dried oregano—crushed
1 1/2 cups whole wheat breadcrumbs
3 tablespoons grated Parmesan *or pecorino Romano* cheese, as preferred
Freshly ground black pepper, to taste

1 cup water

2 tablespoons *extra virgin* olive oil
1/4 cup dry red wine**

Prepare artichokes one at a time. Cut stem flush with base to form a flat "seat." Remove outer tough and discolored petals. Using a sharp knife, cut about 1/2 inch from the tops of the petals. Using a kitchen scissors, snip sharp tips from all petals. Rub all cut surfaces with lemon. *Gently* spread the petals outward in order to get into the center. Remove the choke, the hairy or spiny surface covering the heart, by scraping *firmly*, but *not deeply*, with a teaspoon. Put prepared artichokes into the 1 quart of water to which 1 tablespoonful of lemon juice has been added.

Using the food processor fitted with plastic knife, electric blender, or by hand, prepare the stuffing by combining chopped onion, garlic, and parsley, crushed oregano, breadcrumbs, grated cheese, and black pepper.

Drain artichokes by placing them upside down on a drain board or on a wire rack.

Place a drained artichoke in a small, but deep, bowl. Spread petals *gently*. Sprinkle *one-quarter* of prepared stuffing (or *one-sixth* if six small artichokes are being prepared) down between the petals. Continue stuffing artichokes until all breadcrumb mixture has been used.

Pour water into a saucepan with cover, preferably ceramic, which is adequate for the number of artichokes being prepared. Fit stuffed artichokes into saucepan. Pour olive oil and wine over artichokes. Cover tightly and steam over *LOW-MEDIUM* heat for about 45 minutes, or until the base of an artichoke is easily pierced with the tines of a fork.*** Keep covered on a warming tray until ready to serve.****

Yields 4-6* servings
adequate for 4-6* people

Notes: *If this is to be served as a salad or appetizer course, six adequate servings may be prepared from this recipe. As a main course, however, preceded by a soup and accompanied by a salad, plan on preparing four large blossoms to serve four moderate appetites.

**Red wine may be omitted or, if preferred, VEGETARIAN BROWN STOCK *[see index]* may be substituted.

***If preferred, the artichokes may be baked, covered, in a 325 degree F. oven for about the same time period. Another method of preparation, very non-traditional but very successful, is to steam stuffed artichokes in a bamboo steamer set over a wok. The steaming time must be increased to about 1 hour and 15 minutes and the water level in the wok must be carefully monitored, but the result is an incredibly moist and tender artichoke. Don't tell the family, but this very non-traditional wok-steaming technique is actually our favorite preparation method!

****In lieu of expensive artichoke plates may we suggest a substitute? Set a saucer on a dinner plate. The artichoke sits well in the cup depression and petals to be discarded may be placed on the dinner plate under the saucer rim.

If convenient, the stuffing may be prepared in advance and frozen for a month or two. This can be a great time saver.

ITALIAN STUFFED ARTICHOKES (cont'd)

1/4 SERVING (i. e., 4 large blossoms) –
PROTEIN = 8.0 g.; FAT = 7.5 g.; CARBOHYDRATE = 23.5 g.;
CALORIES = 185; CALORIES FROM FAT = 37%

1/6 SERVING (i. e., 6 smaller blossoms) –
PROTEIN = 5.4 g.; FAT = 5.0 g.; CARBOHYDRATE = 15.6 g.;
CALORIES = 157; CALORIES FROM FAT = 37%

SICILIAN *RICOTTA* PUDDING WITH CITRON AND CHOCOLATE
Budini di Crema di Ricotta alla Siciliana

TPT - 48 hours and 18 minutes;
48 hours = *ricotta* draining period

Ricotta puddings are a specialty of Sicily and there is no limit to their variety. When made with ewes' milk ricotta, this pudding becomes a more authentic and very delicious memory of Sicily and of family celebrations in Sicilian–American homes. Cows' milk ricotta cheese is generally all that is available in our grocery stores. However, a small amount of ricotta salata cheese or mascarpone, if obtainable from an Italian grocery, can be added to cows' milk ricotta when processing to create a pudding with a more authentic taste. Another alternative is to make your own ricotta and I have included a recipe for homemade ricotta that I use. The texture of this pudding should be very stiff as is the filling of a cannoli. Indeed, you will recognize it as the cream filling for a Sicilian cannoli.

2 pounds *part-skimmed milk ricotta* cheese

1 1/2 cups confectioners' sugar
1 tablespoon orange flower water*
1 teaspoon pure vanilla extract

3 tablespoons *finely* chopped, *preservative-free* citron
  or candied orange and/or lemon peel**
1 1/2 ounces *bittersweet* chocolate—*finely* chopped

1/8 teaspoon freeze-dried coffee granules, for garnish
1/8 teaspoon HOT COCOA MIX *[see recipe which follows]*, **for garnish**
Finely ground pistachio nuts, for garnish

Place *ricotta* into a fine sieve or in a cheesecloth bag and set the sieve or hang the bag over a small bowl in the refrigerator to drain for 48 hours.

Using the food processor fitted with steel knife or an electric mixer, beat *very well drained ricotta* cheese until *very smooth*, scraping down the sides as necessary. Add confectioners' sugar, orange flower water, and vanilla extract. Process until, again, *very smooth*.

Turn cheese mixture into a small mixing bowl. Add *finely* chopped citron or peel and *bittersweet* chocolate.

Divide among individual champagne flutes or *demitasse* cups. Turn remainder into a single serving bowl to facilitate second helpings. Refrigerate until ready to serve.

Using a mortar and pestle, grind freeze-dried coffee until finely pulverized. In a small bowl, combine the pulverized instant coffee with the cocoa mix. Set aside.

Garnish each serving with a sprinkling of the coffee–cocoa mixture and a sprinkling of *finely* chopped pistachio nuts *just before serving*.

Yields 10 servings
adequate for 6 people

Notes: *Orange flower water is available in food specialty stores and from food specialty mail order firms. A teaspoonful of frozen orange juice concentrate can be added instead of the orange flower water. Although it is certainly not a substitute, it does give a subtle and interesting flavor.

**Citron is most often treated with sulfiting agents to keep the color light and "appealing." Sulfite-free citron and citrus peels are available through mail order firms.

This recipe may be halved, when required. When doubling, divide the draining *ricotta* into two batches to insure a well-drained result.

1/10 SERVING (exclusive of garnish) –
PROTEIN = 9.9 g.; FAT = 6.6 g.; CARBOHYDRATE = 30.2 g.;
CALORIES = 226; CALORIES FROM FAT = 26%

Europe–Italy/*Sicilia*

ITALIAN HOMEMADE *RICOTTA* CHEESE
Ricotta

TPT - 2 hours and 43 minutes;
20 minutes = draining period;
2 hours = chilling period

The first homemade cheese that I attempted was successful so there was no stopping my attempts to explore this realm of self-sufficiency. From Indian "paneer" I moved to cottage cheese in the form of a Belgian soft white cheese and then I found an uncomplicated recipe for Italian cottage cheese. Since we often serve commercial ricotta cheese as a dessert with a sweet herb syrup, I wondered how it would taste if the ricotta was so fresh that you knew every curd by name.

2 quarts *whole* **milk**
2 cups *cultured* **buttermilk**

Line a sieve with a double layer of culinary cheesecloth. Set the sieve over a mixing bowl. Set aside until required.

In a saucepan set over *MEDIUM-HIGH* heat and fitted with a candy thermometer, combine milk and buttermilk. Cook, stirring constantly, until milk begins to steam. *Stop stirring at this point.* Allow mixture to continue cooking until curds separate from whey at about 175 degrees F. Immediately remove from heat. Using a Chinese skimmer or a slotted spoon, ladle the curd into the cheesecloth-lined sieve. Reserve whey for bread baking or use to feed outdoor plants and/or compost pile. DO NOT POUR WHEY DOWN YOUR DRAINS IF YOU HAVE A SEPTIC SYSYEM.

Allow to drain for about 5 minutes. Gather the corners of the cheesecloth and twist gently, *without squeezing the curd*, to form a ball. Secure with a rubber band. Return the balled curd to the sieve and allow to drain for about 20 minutes more, or until the dripping of whey has stopped. Unwrap the cheesecloth and turn the cheese into an airtight container. Refrigerate for at least 2 hours before using.

If tightly covered and refrigerated, the fresh cheese will keep for 3-4 days. Use in any recipe that calls for *ricotta*, cottage, or farmers' cheeses.

Yields about 1 1/2 cupfuls cheese
and 8 cupfuls whey

Note: This recipe can be doubled successfully but I do prefer to make the smaller amount since it does not keep well

1/6 SERVING (about 1/4 cupful) –
PROTEIN = 9.3 g.; FAT = 9.6 g.; CARBOHYDRATE = 1.5 g.;
CALORIES = 133; CALORIES FROM FAT = 6.4%

HOT COCOA MIX
TPT - 2 minutes

In 1894 Hershey Food Corporation of Hershey, Pennsylvania, introduced hot cocoa mix—a mixture of unsweetened cocoa powder and sugar to be stirred into hot milk. Over 100 years later, the Hershey product is still a must on staple shelves in the winter all over the world, not just in Pennsylvania. The addition of dry milk powder in this version eliminates the need for fresh milk when hiking or camping, or when you are "snowed in."

1/2 cup *unsweetened* **cocoa powder**
1/2 cup plus 2 tablespoons sugar
1 1/4 cups non-fat dry milk powder
1 teaspoon corn starch

Vanilla bean

In a mixing bowl, combine cocoa powder, sugar, dry milk powder, and corn starch. Stir to combine thoroughly. Pour into a clean, dry glass jar; a canning jar is perfect.

Tuck the vanilla bean* down into the mixture. Seal tightly and store until required.

Two tablespoonfuls of mixture makes a most satisfactory cup of hot cocoa when mixed with hot milk or water. A mixture of half milk and half water might be preferred.

Yields 34 tablespoonfuls
adequate for 17 servings

Notes: *A vanilla bean can be used over and over. Just tuck it into the next batch.

This mix can be halved, doubled or tripled, for convenience

1/17 SERVING (i. e., 2 tablespoonfuls) –
PROTEIN = 2.6 g.; FAT = 0.6 g.; CARBOHYDRATE = 12.4 g.;
CALORIES = 65; CALORIES FROM FAT = 8%

Europe–Italy/*Toscano*

Toscano

This is a celebration of verdure; an adventure in greens.

Toasted Bread Appetizers with Escarole, Garlic, and Capers
Antipasto di Crostini con Escarole, Aglio, e Capperi

~

Soup in the Milanese Style
Minestrone alla Milanese

***Pesto* Sauce**
Pesto alla Genovese

~~~~~~~~~~~~~~~~~~~~

***Ravioli* with Spinach and Sage Butter**
Ravioli con Spinaci e Salvia

or

***Fettuccine* with Browned Butter Sauce and Fried Sage Leaves**
Fettuccine con Burro Sciolto e Salvia Frita

Pan–Grilled Radicchio
Grigliata di Radicchio

Sautéed Baby Artichokes with Lemon and Garlic
Carciofi Friti con Limone e Aglio

~~~~~~~~~~~~~~~~~~~~

Mixed Green Salad with Mushrooms and Capers
with Oil and Vinegar Dressing
Insalata Mista con Funghi e Capperi

Parmesan Toasts
Crostini Parmigiano

~

Cooked Cream Dessert
Panna Cotta

Little Rice Puddings
Budini di Riso

Europe–Italy/*Toscano*

TUSCAN TOASTED BREAD APPETIZERS WITH ESCAROLE, GARLIC, AND CAPERS
Antipasto di Crostini con Escarole, Aglio, e Capperi

TPT - 3 minutes

Escarole is not as widely used in this country as it could be. This vitamin A-rich green is wonderful in salads dressed with assertive dressings, soups, and as a sautéed vegetable with garlic and pine nuts (pignoli). The slight bitterness present in escarole, and its close relatives endive and chicory, is mitigated by blanching and sautéing.

1 pound escarole leaves—well-rinsed
1/4 cup water

1 small loaf *unseeded* Italian *or* French bread
  —sliced diagonally into 1/2-inch slices

2 teaspoons *extra virgin* olive oil
3 garlic cloves—*very finely* chopped

3 tablespoons preserved capers—well-drained
  and chopped
10 pitted, ripe, black olives—sliced
Freshly ground black pepper, to taste

Preheat oven to 200 degrees F.

Cut well-rinsed escarole leaves into 1/2-inch strips.

In a large pot set over *MEDIUM* heat, combine escarole strips and water. Cover and cook until tender—about 12 minutes. Drain escarole in a colander set over a mixing bowl to *reserve drained cooking liquid*. Press out as much liquid as possible.

Place bread slices directly on oven racks and allow bread to dry and *lightly toast*.

Meanwhile, in a non-stick-coated skillet set over *MEDIUM* heat, heat oil. Add *very finely* chopped garlic and sauté for a minute or two.

Reduce heat to *LOW*. Add chopped capers, sliced olives, cooked escarole, and about 1/2 cupful of escarole cooking water. Cook, stirring frequently, for 5 minutes. Season with black pepper to taste. Keep warm on a warming tray until required.

When ready to serve, apportion *hot* escarole mixture among *crostini* and spread mixture over bread surface. Arrange on a large round platter.

Serve warm.

Yields about 16 *crostini*

Notes: The escarole topping can be prepared as much as two days ahead of time, covered, and refrigerated. Reheat while *crostini* are being prepared. This is a great convenience for entertaining.

This recipe may be halved or doubled, when required.

1/16 SERVING (per *crostini*) –
PROTEIN = 2.8 g.; FAT = 1.6 g.; CARBOHYDRATE = 16.4 g.;
CALORIES = 91; CALORIES FROM FAT = 16%

SOUP IN THE MILANESE STYLE
Minestrone alla Milanese

TPT - 52 minutes)

If, as the Milanese, you love rice in your minestrone, all well and good. However, a medium potato could be substituted for the rice. Oh, but the Genovese and the Calabrians do include their pasta so substitute four ounces of broken high protein tagliatelle, vermicelli, or other pasta of choice, for variety. Both pasta and potato are included in some versions, if you are "of a mind." Additionally, try substituting cooked dry limas, kidney, or white beans, chick peas, or lentils. A minestrone is truly as individual as you are and its moods are as unlimited. We enjoy experimenting with vegetable combinations and seasoning but always aware that everyone has their own "correct" version and they may try to dissuade our independence.

Europe–Italy/*Toscano*

SOUP IN THE MILANESE STYLE (cont'd)

2 tablespoons *extra virgin* olive oil
1/4 cup coarsely chopped onion
1 small garlic clove—*very finely* chopped

1/2 cup diced carrot
1 medium celery stalk with leaves—diced
2 medium Italian plum tomatoes—peeled, seeded, and diced
1/2 cup *finely* shredded cabbage—as for slaw

1 quart *boiling* water
1/2 cup quick-cooking dry, green split peas—washed and sorted
2 tablespoons dry, long grain brown rice
2 tablespoons *finely* chopped fresh, Italian flat-leafed parsley
1/2 teaspoon dried basil—crushed
1/4 teaspoon freshly ground black pepper, or to taste

1 small *unpeeled* zucchini *or* 1 small *peeled* yellow summer squash—diced
3/4 cup *frozen* cut green beans

Grated Parmesan, pecorino Romano, or Asiago cheese, as preferred

In a large skillet with cover, heat oil over *MEDIUM* heat. Add chopped onion and *very finely* chopped garlic. Sauté, stirring constantly, until onion is soft and translucent, *allowing neither the onion nor the garlic to brown.*

Reduce heat to *LOW.* Add diced carrot, celery, and tomatoes with *finely* shredded cabbage. Cover skillet tightly and allow to simmer for about 5 minutes.

In a large kettle, combine these vegetables with *boiling* water. Add split peas, brown rice, *finely* chopped parsley, crushed basil, and black pepper. Cover and simmer gently for about 40 minutes, stirring occasionally, until peas and rice are tender but *not mushy.**

Add diced squash and undefrosted cut green beans. Continue cooking for an additional 10 minutes. Taste and adjust seasoning, if necessary.

Turn into heated soup tureen and serve into heated soup plates. Pass grated cheese separately to accommodate individual tastes.

Yields 6 servings
adequate for 6 as a first course offering;
adequate for 3-4 as a main course offering

Notes: *Prepare to this point and refrigerate soup overnight or freeze, if desired. This allows the flavors to marry. When ready to serve, bring to the simmer and continue from asterisk.

This recipe is easily doubled, when required.

PESTO SAUCE *[see recipe which follows]* compliments this soup beautifully. Pass the *pesto* sauce separately and allow diners to stir a spoonful into their serving.

1/6 SERVING – PROTEIN = 6.5 g.; FAT = 4.6 g.; CARBOHYDRATE = 20.3 g.;
CALORIES = 142; CALORIES FROM FAT = 29%

PESTO SAUCE
Pesto alla Genovese
TPT - 27 minutes

There are many interpretations of pesto sauce; some even include such bizarre ingredients as walnuts. In the region around Genoa you will find, what we consider to be, "real pesto sauce" and, provincial specialties aside, this pesto sauce has become very popular in Tuscany. This useful, flavorful paste does freeze well so we find it convenient to double or triple this recipe when fresh basil is available and to freeze the resultant sauce in small portions from which we can scoop a tablespoonful or so when needed.

1/3 cup loosely packed *fresh* basil leaves—well-washed and *thoroughly dried**
1/4 cup chopped *fresh* Italian flat-leafed parsley
2 large garlic cloves—peeled and coarsely chopped
1/2 cup freshly grated Parmesan *or pecorino Romano* cheese, as preferred
1/4 cup *additive-free* pine nuts (*pignoli*)

1/3 cup *extra virgin* olive oil

In the work bowl of the food processor, fitted with steel knife, or in the container of the electric blender, combine fresh basil leaves, chopped fresh parsley leaves, chopped garlic cloves, grated cheese, and pine nuts *(pignoli)*. Process or blend to chop *finely.* Carefully, stir ingredients down with a spatula.

Europe–Italy/Toscano

PESTO SAUCE (cont'd)

Add oil and blend until a smooth, thick paste is formed. Scrape paste into a large mixing bowl.

Use as condiment in soups, stews, sauces. Refrigerate or freeze leftovers.

Yields about 1 1/4 cupfuls

Notes: *Use fresh basil only!

**Since this sauce is used in small amounts to enhance the flavor of dishes, we have not reduced the fat content. Be aware that this is a high-fat condiment and, since the flavor is powerful, a little goes a long way.

This recipe may be increased or decreased proportionately as required.

1/20 SERVING (i. e., per tablespoonful) –
PROTEIN = 1.2 g.; FAT = 4.2 g.; CARBOHYDRATE = 0.4 g.;
CALORIES = 44; CALORIES FROM FAT = 86%**

RAVIOLI WITH SPINACH AND SAGE BUTTER IN THE STYLE OF TUSCANY
Ravioli con Spinaci e Salvia

TPT - 21 minutes

In mid-April, after the winter weather as subsided and you can smell spring, I can see the grayish patch of our "mountain garden" sage, Salvia officinalis 'Berggarten,' from the dining room window. Instead of thinking, "Oh, that needs to be cut back," I think "There are new leaves under that shroud," and this dish goes on the menu.

I found this to be an especially useful standby when friends came out into our valley from Long Island to explore and the hours of the day slipped away as we traveled about, or went to market, or just visited. The dinner hour was upon us long before the sun slipped behind the mountains. I usually washed up a big batch of spinach and prepared some raw vegetables before we began our day's exploration and refrigerated these in plastic bags. The spinach was quickly prepared and the simple butter sauce, made with sage gathered from our herb garden, the prepared crudités, and the convenience of store-bought ravioli got dinner on the table quickly. Homemade ice cream, made and secreted in the freezer the week before, an assortment of fruits, and a good bread were all that was needed.

3/4 pound fresh spinach—*very* well-washed and tough stems removed

2 tablespoons butter
6 large, fresh sage leaves—*very* well-washed and sliced crosswise into thin slices

4 quarts *boiling* **water**
1 1/2 pounds large, round cheese *ravioli*—homemade **or** commercially-available frozen variety*

Place the *well-washed* spinach, *with just the water that clings to the leaves*, in a saucepan with cover. Set aside.

In a small saucepan or Turkish coffeepot set over *LOW-MEDIUM* heat, combine butter and sliced sage leaves. Allow butter to melt and become infused with the aroma of the sage.

When you are just about ready to serve, add *ravioli* to *boiling* water. Cook for about 6-8 minutes, or according to package directions.

Simultaneously, place spinach over *MEDIUM* heat. Cook spinach just until it wilts. Remove from heat and drain thoroughly.

Arrange *well-drained* spinach on a heated serving platter.

Drain cooked *ravioli* thoroughly. Arrange on top of spinach. Pour melted sage butter over *ravioli*.

Serve at once.

Yields 6 servings
adequate for 4 people

Notes: *In Tuscany, the *ravioli* would be filled with an indescribably delicious *ricotta* made from ewe's milk. Here, we must settle for *ricotta* made from cow's milk.

This recipe may be halved or doubled, when required.

1/6 SERVING – PROTEIN = 11.1 g.; FAT = 9.8 g.; CARBOHYDRATE = 31.8 g.;
CALORIES = 259; CALORIES FROM FAT = 34%

Europe–Italy/*Toscano*

FETTUCCINE WITH BROWNED BUTTER SAUCE AND FRIED SAGE LEAVES
Fettuccine con Burro Sciolto e Salvia Frita
TPT - 19 minutes

The flavors of this dish are quite typical of the simplicity of Northern Italian cooking except that I brown the "burro sciolto," which intensifies the butter flavor, and I do not bread the sage leaves. One is tempted to just drag the dining room table and chairs to the back yard—"Italian family-style"—and enjoy a big plate of this pasta with an assortment of olives, fruit, and a good wine.

2 quarts *boiling* **water**
1 tablespoon freshly squeezed lemon juice
One 3-inch strip lemon zest
1/2 pound high-protein *fettuccine*

3 tablespoons butter
20 *fresh* **sage leaves—well-washed, well-dried, and trimmed of their stems***

Freshly ground black pepper, to taste
2 tablespoons grated *pecorino Romano* **cheese**

In a large kettle set over *HIGH* heat, add lemon juice and lemon zest to the *boiling* water. Add *fettuccine* and cook, stirring occasionally, over *HIGH* heat according to package directions. Drain thoroughly, discarding lemon zest.

While the *fettuccine* is cooking, in a small saucepan set over *MEDIUM* heat, melt butter. When the butter is bubbling, add the sage leaves. Cook, stirring frequently, until the butter darkens and the sage leaves curl. *Be careful not to allow the butter to burn.* Remove from heat. Carefully remove sage leaves to a saucer.

Turn hot, drained *fettuccine* onto heated platter. Pour browned butter over and toss to dress *fettuccine*. Scatter fried sage leaves over. Grind black pepper over and sprinkle with grated cheese.

Serve at once. Pass extra grated cheese separately.

Yields 6 servings
adequate for 4 people

Notes: **Salvia officinalis 'Berggarten'* is the sage which I prefer for this. It flowers infrequently and, therefore, the essential oils are not dissipated. It is equal, in my mind, to any imported Dalmatian sage. Although the variety *'Purprascens'* has comparable flavor, the slightly small, purple leaves are less attractive when fried.

This recipe is easily halved or doubled, when required.

1/6 SERVING – PROTEIN = 5.5 g.; FAT = 6.8 g.; CARBOHYDRATE = 27.7 g.;
CALORIES = 200; CALORIES FROM FAT = 31%

SAUTÉED BABY ARTICHOKES WITH LEMON AND GARLIC
Carciofi Friti con Limone e Aglio
TPT - 39 minutes

I finally wrote up this family dish when one of our supermarkets began to carry baby artichokes on a regular basis. Granted, the California-grown darlings have their tender stems chopped off, presumably for packaging purposes, unlike those that we found on our trip to Italy. Frozen artichoke hearts can be adapted to this recipe when necessary but they do not compare to the tiny, fresh baby artichokes at their peak in April and May.

2 pounds baby artichokes
1/2 lemon
1 quart water
1 tablespoon freshly squeezed lemon juice

2 tablespoons *extra virgin* **olive oil**
1 large garlic clove—*thinly* **sliced**
Freshly ground black pepper, to taste
1 tablespoon freshly squeezed lemon juice

2 teaspoons freshly grated *pecorino Romano* **cheese**

Prepare a steamer.

Prepare artichokes one at a time. Remove outer tough and discolored petals. Using a sharp knife, cut about 1/2 inch from the tops of the petals. Using a kitchen scissors, snip sharp tips from all petals. Rub all cut surfaces with lemon. Put prepared artichokes into the 1 quartful of water to which 1 tablespoonful of lemon juice has been added.

Europe–Italy/*Toscano*

SAUTÉED BABY ARTICHOKES WITH LEMON AND GARLIC (cont'd)

Drain artichokes. Place leaf–edge down in the steamer. Steam for about 15 minutes. Remove from steamer and cut each artichoke in half through the middle of the heart.

In a wok or skillet set over *MEDIUM-HIGH* heat, heat oil. Add garlic and sauté gently for about 30 seconds.

Add artichoke halves and *stir-fry* for about 5 minutes, or until *lightly browned. Be careful not to allow garlic to burn.*

Remove from heat. Add remaining tablespoonful of lemon juice and stir to *deglaze* the wok. Season with black pepper.

Turn onto a heated serving platter. Sprinkle grated cheese over.

Serve at once.

Yields 6 servings
adequate for 4 people

Note: This recipe can be halved, when required.

1/6 SERVING – PROTEIN = 4.2 g.; FAT = 4.6 g.; CARBOHYDRATE = 11.4 g.;
CALORIES = 93; CALORIES FROM FAT = 45%

PARMESAN TOASTS
Crostini Parmigiano

TPT - 16 minutes

We love to serve these toasts with a salad full of this and that or a bowl of minestrone for a light supper or lunch. They are also a good choice as an appetizer with a glass of wine. Under no condition try this unless you have a good, aged hunk of Parmigiano-Reggiano or pecorino Romano, if you prefer a ewe's milk cheese.

16 slices French bread—about 1/4-inch thick
2 teaspoons *extra virgin* olive oil
1/3 cup grated *Parmigiano-Reggiano* cheese
Freshly ground black pepper, to taste

Preheat oven to 375 degrees. Coat a *biscotti*/French fry baking pan with lecithin non-stick coating.*

Brush each side of the *baguette* slices with olive oil. Place them on the *biscotti* baking pan. Sprinkle grated cheese, about 1 teaspoonful, on each slice and grind black pepper over. Bake in preheated oven for about 10 minutes, or until the bread toasts and the cheese is beginning to melt. Transfer to a heated platter.

Serve warm.

Yields 16 *crostini*

Notes: *If you do not have a *biscotti* baking pan, use a cookie sheet.

This recipe can be halved or doubled.*

1/16 SERVING (1 *crostini*) –
PROTEIN = 3.4 g.; FAT = 1.5 g.; CARBOHYDRATE = 15.7 g.;
CALORIES = 90; CALORIES FROM FAT = 15%

NORTHERN ITALIAN COOKED CREAM DESSERT
Panna Cotta

TPT - 5 hours;
30 minutes = infusion period;
4 hours = setting period

Made with heavy cream, as it is throughout Northern Italy, "panna cotta" is a taste never to be forgotten but rarely to be sampled. Made here with a combination of light cream and whole milk, the memory can be revisited often. Although a cherry sauce, "salsa di ciliegie," often made from brandied cherries, is customary, most berries and berry sauces are infinitely complimentary.

Europe–Italy/*Toscano*

NORTHERN ITALIAN COOKED CREAM DESSERT (cont'd)

1 3/4 cups *whole* milk
1 cup light cream *or* half and half
1-inch piece vanilla bean—split lengthwise
1/2 cup confectioners' sugar

1/4 cup *whole* milk
1 tablespoon unflavored gelatin*

Fresh berries, a simple, lightly-thickened fresh berry cherry sauce, *or* a peach sauce, *or* AUSTRALIAN SIMPLE BLACKBERRY SAUCE *[see index]*

In a saucepan set over *LOW-MEDIUM* heat, combine 1 3/4 cupfuls milk with light cream. Scrape the seeds from the split vanilla bean into the milk–cream mixture. Add bean and confectioners' sugar. Allow to come to the simmer. Remove from heat, cover, and allow to infuse for 30 minutes.

Pour the remaining 1/4 cupful milk into a small bowl. Sprinkle gelatin over and allow to soften—about 5 minutes.

Pour hot cream mixture through a fine sieve into another saucepan. Discard vanilla bean pieces.

Using a rubber spatula, scrape *softened* gelatin into strained milk-cream mixture.

Return cream to *LOW-MEDIUM* heat and allow to heat until gelatin is completely dissolved.

Divide cooked cream mixture among four individual 8-ounce custard cups or individual soufflé dishes. Refrigerate for at least 4 hours.

Dip dessert dishes into *warm* water to loosen molded cream. Invert each into the center of a dessert plate and unmold.** Refrigerate until ready to serve.

Serve with sauce, of choice, spooned around the custards.

Yields 4 individual servings

Notes: *Agar-agar or kosher gelatin may be substituted for plain gelatin, if preferred. Since preparation procedures differ for these products, be sure to follow package directions.

**This dessert may also be served in sherbet glasses or wide-bowl champagne glasses as an interesting change-of-pace, if desired.

When required, this recipe may be halved or doubled.

1/4 SERVING – PROTEIN = 7.4 g.; FAT = 9.5 g.; CARBOHYDRATE = 24.4 g.;
CALORIES = 202; CALORIES FROM FAT = 42%

NORTHERN ITALIAN LITTLE RICE PUDDINGS
Budini di Riso

TPT - 1 hour and 57 minutes;
20 minutes = cooling period

Friends have said that I have not met a rice pudding I do not like. The creativity of cooks all over the world who combine rice, milk, and sugar in unimaginably different ways, fascinates me and I taste them everywhere I travel, in every deli, and at every diner. I will have to say that there are some that I do like better than others but these little charmers from Italy made a coffee bar in Rome my favorite haunt. I was so disappointed when I found out that they did not make them every day. Budini di riso are also prepared, in Italy and by Italian bakeries in the United States, as tarts in rich pie crust shells. Both versions can be found at coffee bars in the North of Italy and, occasionally, in Rome.

2 cups skimmed milk
One 3-inch strip orange zest
1/4 cup sugar

1/3 cup Italian medium-grained *Arborio* rice
—do not use precooked/converted variety

1/4 cup *preservative-free dark* raisins*

1/4 cup *fat-free* pasteurized eggs (the equivalent of 1 egg)
2 teaspoons pure vanilla extract
1 teaspoon freshly grated orange zest

NORTHERN ITALIAN LITTLE RICE PUDDINGS (cont'd)

Prepare four 6-ounce custard cups by coating with non-stick lecithin spray coating.

In a saucepan set over *LOW* heat, heat milk with sugar and orange zest until just below the boiling point.

Stir in rice, cover tightly, and cook, *undisturbed*, for 30 minutes. Stir, replace cover, and cook, *undisturbed*, for another 30 minutes. *Milk will be almost completely absorbed, but rice should not be solidified or dry.* Remove and discard orange zest.

Stir in raisins and transfer to a bowl to cool. Stir occasionally.

Preheat oven to 325 degrees F.

In a small bowl, beat pasteurized eggs well with a wire whisk. Add vanilla extract and grated orange zest. Mix well. Stir in the slightly cooled, cooked rice, *a few tablespoonfuls at a time* until all is incorporated. Apportion among prepared custard cups.

Set in baking pan in which a 1-inch water bath has been prepared. Bake in preheated 325 degree F. oven for about 25 minutes, or until filling is set. *Do not allow water bath to simmer or boil—by adding cold water or ice cubes*, if necessary.

Cool on a wire rack for about 20 minutes. Remove each to a dessert plate by running a knife *carefully* around the edge of the cups and then inverting onto the plate.

Serve while still warm.

Notes: *Traditionally, bleached, golden raisins are used for these puddings. We prefer to use dark, *preservative-free,* chemically-benign raisins available from natural food stores and mail-order firms.

This recipe may be doubled, when required.

These little puddings make an excellent brunch presentation accompanied by fresh fruit.

Yields 4 individual servings

1/4 SERVING – PROTEIN = 6.2 g.; FAT = 0.3 g.; CARBOHYDRATE = 42.2 g.;
CALORIES = 198; CALORIES FROM FAT = 1%

Latvia

Latvia, or Livonia as it was known, fell under German rule at the beginning of the thirteenth century. From 1558 to 1583 Livonia was contended for in what was known as the Livonia War with the result that the territory was divided between Poland and Lithuania. The northern part of present-day Latvia and Estonia came under the rule of the Grand Duchy of Lithuania. The eleven-year struggle for control of the eastern Baltic, known as the Polish–Swedish War, brought northern Livonia under Swedish rule in 1611. Other areas, which continued under Polish rule, actually experienced a progressive period in the seventeenth century. Although Russia had lost out in its attempt to gain control of the eastern Baltic during this period, the Russian Empire's desire for the Baltic ports did not end. In 1721, with the end of the Great Northern War, all of present day Latvia eventually became part of the Russian Empire. The vicious tactics of Peter the Great and the periods of plague and famine during the same period led to a loss of about forty percent of the Latvian population. Independence was proclaimed in 1918, corresponding to the Russian Revolution, and lasted only until 1939 when the Soviets took advantage of the fact that Latvia was a signatory to the Molotov–Ribbentrop Pact by offering to build bases in Latvia ostensibly as "protection" for the Latvians against the possibility of German violation of the non-aggression pact. In 1940 the Soviets marched their troops into Latvia and occupied the country with the cooperation of Latvian officials. With the onset of World War II, Latvians were conscripted by both the Soviets and by the Nazis. After Germany's defeat, Latvia was collectivized. Fearing rising nationalism, the Soviets deported thousands of Latvians, Lithuanians, and Estonians to Siberian gulags in 1949 in what was called Operation Priboi. Latvia remained a part of the U.S.S.R. until changes began to occur in Soviet Russia under the *glasnost* and *peristroika* policies initiated by, then, General Secretary Mikhail Gorbachev. With the changes occurring within the Soviet republic structure, Latvia saw an opportunity to regain its independence from the Soviet Union as did the other two nations that have come to be known together as the Baltic States. The people of the three countries called for a joint demonstration in 1989 protesting Soviet occupation. Called the "Singing Revolution," an estimated two millions Latvians, Lithuanians, and Estonians joined hands, stretching hand-to-hand across the three nations.

We often forget that the people of these three nations, albeit similar and certainly culturally related, are really very different in many ways. The Latvian language is similar to Lithuanian, both being classified as Indo-European languages, but very dissimilar when compared to Estonian, which is a Finno-Ugric language. The cuisines of the three nations, although influenced by the same occupying forces with which they had to contend and with the same food shortages which they had to endure, emerged with significant differences. Strict citizenship laws, elimination of Russian as the official language, and a concerted effort to bring Latvia's national identity to the fore by encouraging the re-emergence of folklore, cultural practices, religion, and cuisine have, indeed, reintroduced the Latvian identity to the Latvians and to the world.

Europe – Latvia

Stuffed Eggs
Olas

Solstice Cheese
Jani

~

Potato – Meatball Soup
Frikadelu Zupa

Chilled Pearl Barley Soup with Sour Cream
Skaba Putra

~

Mixed Greens
with Green Peas and Shredded Onion

~~~~~~~~~~~~~~~~~~~~~~~

Egg Noodles

Red Kidney Beans and Red Peppers
Pupinas Pipari Sakans

Sour Cream and Onion Sauce
Skabs Krejums Sipols Merce

Slow Cooker Sauerkraut with Apples
Skabi Kaposti Slads

~~~~~~~~~~~~~~~~~~~~~~~

Cranberry Pudding
Kisel iz Klyukay Po-Latyshski

Caraway Refrigerator Cookies
Cepumi

LATVIAN STUFFED EGGS
Olas

TPT - 25 minutes

These stuffed eggs are meant to be served warm and make an appropriate first course for a Latvian meal. I serve them on a bed of tiny mesclún greens and with a dollop of mayonnaise made with olive oil.

1/2 cup small *mesclún* greens—well-washed
  and well-dried
1 tablespoon *calorie-reduced or light* mayonnaise

6 hard-cooked eggs—chilled and shelled

2 tablespoons soft butter spread
2 tablespoons *finely* chopped fresh parsley
2 tablespoons *finely* chopped fresh dillweed
1 tablespoon light cream *or* half and half

1 1/2 tablespoons soft butter spread
1 1/2 tablespoons grated *pecorino Romano*
  cheese

Preheat oven to 250 degrees F. Prepare an oven-proof plate by coating it with non-stick lecithin spray coating. Set aside until required.

Prepare six salad plates by putting a portion of the *mesclún* greens on each. Place 1/2 teaspoonful mayonnaise at the side on each plate. Set aside until ready to serve.

Cut hard-cooked eggs in half lengthwise. Remove egg yolks to a mixing bowl; set egg whites aside.

LATVIAN STUFFED EGGS (cont'd)

Using a fork, mash egg yolks well. Add the 2 tablespoonfuls butter spread, *finely* chopped parsley and dillweed, and cream. Mash until smoothly blended. Add more cream, only if necessary. Divide the filling evenly among the egg white halves.

Using the soft butter spread, anchor each stuffed egg half to the prepared baking plates. Sprinkle a portion of the grated cheese over each egg half. Bake in preheated 250 degree F. oven for about 12-14 minutes. Transfer two baked egg halves to each of the prepared salad plates. Tuck the greens up against the eggs.

Serve at once.

Yields 6 first course servings

Note: This recipe may be halved or doubled, when required.

1/6 SERVING – PROTEIN = 6.8 g.; FAT = 12.9 g.; CARBOHYDRATE = 0.4 g.; CALORIES = 144; CALORIES FROM FAT = 81%

LATVIAN SOLSTICE CHEESE
Jani

TPT - 36 hours and 45 minutes;
36 hours = cheese-pressing period

When I was a little girl, summer cheese and summer butter were to be anticipated and savored. There was a difference then. The taste was grassy and the color of the butter was the bright yellow color we now see year round, thanks perhaps to the mechanism for dispensing food coloring into the bags of margarine during World War II. Butter was a pale affair during the winter months back then when cows were fed with silage and the margarine trick proved that we could have a butter look-alike any time we wanted it. Once the snow had melted and the grass shoots came up, sweet and vernal, the milk given by those cows and the cheese and butter made from that milk were different. Margarine had been around since the mid-1800s; manufacture of the butter substitute began in the United States in 1875 but there was great opposition to margarine by states where dairy farming was important. Vermont, West Virginia, and New Hampshire actually passed laws requiring margarine to be dyed pink, the color of milk from cows ill with mastitis. These laws were struck down by the United States Supreme Court in 1902. Margarine was important during the years of the two world wars but after World War II dairy lobbyists all over the world campaigned against the growth of margarine acceptance. Margarine producers were penalized by targeted taxing and rules in the United States. Today milk, cheese, and butter have a generally consistent and unvarying color and taste. Need I say . . . good old days?

Latvians still celebrate the Summer Solstice with this cheese. You will note that I use low-fat products to make this cheese since the amount of fat in Solstice cheese is considerable. You will also note that I add a bit of lemon juice to encourage the formation of the curd since our dairy products seem to lack the lactic acid needed for quick separation of the curd and the whey.

5 cups *two-percent* milk

8 ounces farmer's cheese *or* dry, skimmed milk cottage cheese
1/2 teaspoon freshly squeezed lemon juice

1/2 cup (1 stick) *melted* butter
1/2 cup *melted* soft butter spread
3 tablespoons *fat-free* pasteurized eggs
5 1/4 teaspoons *fat-free* dairy sour cream
Pinch salt
1 teaspoon caraway seeds

Europe – Latvia

LATVIAN SOLSTICE CHEESE (cont'd)

Set a sieve over a large bowl. Line the sieve with a double layer of culinary cheesecloth. Set aside until required.

In a large saucepan set over *LOW-MEDIUM* heat, bring milk to the boil.

Add cheese and lemon juice. Continue heating until the solids separate from the whey. Pour the cheese and whey into the cheesecloth-lined sieve and allow to drain well.* Gather the corners of the cheesecloth and compress the cheese into a ball, squeezing out excess liquid as you do so. Turn cheese into a clean saucepan.

Add *melted* butters, pasteurized eggs, sour cream, salt, and caraway seeds. Mix well. Place over *LOW* heat and cook, stirring constantly with a wire whisk, until the cheese is quite smooth and glossy. Remove from heat.

Rinse the cheesecloth well and again place it in the sieve. Turn the cheese into the cheesecloth and gather the corners of the cheesecloth to again form a ball. Secure the corners tightly by tying with string. Place the cheese ball on a bread board covered with a folded cotton tea towel. Place another bread board on top of the ball as a weight. Refrigerate for about 36 hours, or until cool and dry. Change the tea towel three or four times during this period. Transfer to a plate.**

Serve cold with bread, butter, and honey.

Yields about 30 servings

Notes: *The resulting whey that separates from the curd will be considerable—about 1 quartful. DO NOT DISCARD IT, specifically avoid discarding any down the drain since it can adversely effect septic tanks and pipe seals. It is a nutritious by-product of cheese and yogurt making that is loaded with protein, minerals, and enzymes. I use it instead of water in my bread recipes and add it to the cooking water for rice, pasta, and potatoes. When I soak oatmeal overnight, I soak it in whey. Add it to soups, stews, and smoothies, and if you still have some left over, refrigerate or freeze it. It is inadvisable to pour whey down the drain but do pour any excess on your compost pile or feed your acid-loving crops. Chickens and pigs are said to love it.

**This is a fresh cheese product with no preservatives so it will not keep too long. Salting or spreading with salted, melted butter will preserve the cheese for about a week.

This recipe can be doubled, when required.

1/30 SERVING – PROTEIN = 2.5 g.; FAT = 5.8 g.; CARBOHYDRATE = 2.5 g.;
CALORIES = 70; CALORIES FROM FAT = 45%

Note that these food values reflect the subtraction
of the values for 4 cupfuls whey.

LATVIAN POTATO – MEATBALL SOUP
Frikadelu Zupa
TPT - 23 minutes

Latvians are very fond of a soup made from a rich, beef broth in which tiny meatballs, potatoes, and carrots are cooked. A vegetarian version can be enjoyed using a well-flavored vegetable stock and soy meatballs. It is, of course, not the same but it is good and the texture is awesome.

6 cups VEGETABLE STOCK FROM SOUP *[see index]* **or other vegetarian stock of choice**
2 medium potatoes—*coarsely shredded*
2 medium carrots—*diced*

1 package (9 ounces) *frozen* **vegetarian "meatballs"**
2 tablespoons snipped chives

Salt, to taste
Freshly ground black pepper, to taste

Chopped fresh parsley, for garnish
Fat-free **dairy sour cream, for garnish**

In a kettle set over *MEDIUM* heat, bring soup stock to the boil. *Reduce heat to LOW-MEDIUM.* Add *coarsely shredded* potatoes, and *diced* carrots. Simmer for about 20 minutes.

Add "meatballs" and simmer until "meatballs" are heated through.

Turn into a heated tureen. Sprinkle with chopped parsley. Serve into heated soup bowls. Pass sour cream to accommodate individual taste.

Yields 6 servings
adequate for 4 people

Europe–**Latvia**

LATVIAN POTATO – MEATBALL SOUP (cont'd)

Notes: *The vegetable stock is, of course, nutritional but calculating its food values is difficult without chemical analysis techniques. For these reasons, we have chosen to treat these stocks merely as flavoring—omitting them from nutritional calculations but recognizing them as a food, quite rich in vitamins and minerals.

This recipe can be halved or doubled, when required.

1/6 SERVING (with 1 tablespoonful sour cream per serving) – PROTEIN = 10.9 g.; FAT = 2.7 g.; CARBOHYDRATE = 18.0 g.; CALORIES = 130; CALORIES FROM FAT = 19%*

LATVIAN CHILLED PEARL BARLEY SOUP WITH SOUR CREAM
Skaba Putra

TPT - 2 hours and 2 minutes;
1 hour = chilling period

This thick soup is a perfect choice for a warm spring or autumn evening since the nutritional punch is in before someone has the chance to say that it is just too warm to eat. I took this to a potluck picnic on a warm June afternoon with a freshly-made loaf of multi-grain bread and a compote of strawberries, blueberries, and blackberries. Of course, I really was pleased when I heard someone say, "You've got to try that barley dish."

2 tablespoons safflower **or** sunflower oil
1 pound *crimini* mushrooms—stems removed, rinsed and cleaned well with a brush, and *finely* chopped

1 large onion—*finely* chopped

1 1/2 tablespoons tomato paste
2 tablespoons freshly squeezed lemon juice
1 quart VEGETARIAN BROWN STOCK *[see index]* **or** VEGETABLE STOCK FROM SOUP *[see index]*

1 cup dry pearl barley
Freshly ground black pepper, to taste

1 cup *two-percent* milk*
1 cup *fat-free* dairy sour cream
3 tablespoons chopped fresh dillweed

2 hard-cooked eggs—chopped—for garnish

In a large kettle set over *MEDIUM* heat, heat oil. Add *finely* chopped mushrooms and cook for about 15 minutes, or until all of moisture extruded from mushrooms has evaporated. Stir frequently.

Add *finely* chopped onion and sauté until onions are soft and translucent, *being careful not to allow the onions to overbrown.*

Add tomato paste, lemon juice, and vegetable stock. Allow to come to the boil.

Reduce heat to LOW-MEDIUM. Add barley and black pepper. Simmer until barley is tender—about 30 minutes. *Remove from heat and allow to cool to room temperature.*

When the soup base has reached room temperature, stir in milk, sour cream, and chopped dillweed. Turn into a chilled tureen and refrigerate for at least 1 hour to allow flavors to meld.

Serve *well-chilled* soup into chilled soup bowls. Allow diners to garnish their portion with chopped egg.

Yields 8 servings
adequate for 6 people

Notes: *Buttermilk is generally used in this soup but I have found that buttermilk is very much an acquired taste for some, especially those of southern European and Asian descent.

This recipe is easily halved, when required.

Refrigerate leftovers. This soup *can not* be frozen successfully once sour cream has been added.

1/8 SERVING – PROTEIN = 10.9 g.; FAT = 5.8 g.; CARBOHYDRATE = 40.9 g.; CALORIES = 255; CALORIES FROM FAT = 20%

Europe–Latvia

LATVIAN RED KIDNEY BEANS AND RED PEPPERS
Pupinas Pipari Sakans
TPT - 17 minutes

This is a wonderfully simple way to introduce leguminous amino acids into a menu and it is a great way to use your harvest of red peppers when all those peppers seem to ripen at once. During those busy days when I am roasting red peppers and freezing raw peppers to fill the freezer for winter meals, I plan this dish for dinner. If you use canned beans, it takes just minutes.

2 teaspoons corn starch
2 tablespoons water

1 tablespoon *extra virgin* **olive oil**
1/4 cup chopped Italian red onion
1 red bell pepper—cored, seeded, and sliced into thin strips
1 small garlic clove—*very finely* **chopped**

1 cup *well-drained* **canned red kidney beans** *or* *cooked*, **dry beans, if preferred**
2/3 cup VEGETABLE STOCK FROM SOUP
  [see index] *or* **other vegetarian stock of choice**

Freshly ground black pepper to taste

In a small dish, combine corn starch and water. Stir until corn starch is in suspension. Set aside until required.

In a saucepan set over *LOW-MEDIUM* heat, heat oil. Add chopped onion, pepper strips, and *very finely* chopped garlic. Cook, stirring frequently, until onion is soft and pepper strips are tender.

Add beans and vegetable stock. Allow to come to the boil.

Stir corn starch suspension vigorously and add to the bean–pepper mixture. Cook, stirring with a wooden spoon, until the sauce is thickened and glossy.

Season with black pepper. Turn into a heated serving bowl.

Serve at once.

Yields 6 servings
adequate for 4 people

Note: This recipe can be doubled, when required.

1/6 SERVING – PROTEIN = 7.8 g.; FAT = 2.4 g.; CARBOHYDRATE = 23.6 g.;
CALORIES = 144; CALORIES FROM FAT = 15%

SOUR CREAM AND ONION SAUCE IN THE STYLE OF LATVIA
Skabs Krejums Sipols Merce
TPT - 10 minutes

Latvians serve this sauce with burgers called "kurzemes." Although I add dried mushrooms to this sauce when I serve it with veggie burgers, I have found the sour cream sauce to be ever so complementary to ever so many dishes. Trust me, noodles are not just noodles with this sauce.

2 tablespoons butter
1/2 cup *finely* **chopped onions**
1/4 teaspoon *very finely* **crushed dried thyme**

1 cup *fat-free* **dairy sour cream**
2 tablespoons water

In a non-stick-coated skillet set over *LOW-MEDIUM* heat, melt butter. Add *finely* chopped onions and *very finely* crushed thyme. Sauté until onions are soft and translucent, *being careful not to allow the onions to brown.*

Add sour cream and, using a wooden spoon, stir onions into sour cream. Add water and stir to create a smooth sauce. Add more water, if necessary to achieve the desired consistency. Allow to heat through, *stirring constantly.*

Turn into a heated serving dish.

Serve at once.

Yields about 1 1/2 cupfuls

Note: This recipe can be halved, when required.

1/12 SERVING (i. e., 2 tablespoonfuls) –
PROTEIN = 2.7 g.; FAT = 1.9 g.; CARBOHYDRATE = 8.7 g.;
CALORIES = 63; CALORIES FROM FAT = 27%

Europe–Latvia

SLOW COOKER LATVIAN SAUERKRAUT WITH APPLES
Skabi Kaposti Slads

TPT - 2 hours and 19 minutes;
[slow cooker: 2 hours at LOW]

Latvians are fond of the sweet and sour taste of this dish and I will have to say that we like it too. Most sauerkraut dishes allow only the salt and sour receptors on the tongue to become involved in the eating process but this dish also involves those receptors that respond to sweet. It is quite a different experience, if you have never experienced "sweet and sour sauerkraut."

1 can (14.4 ounces) *sulfite-free* sauerkraut*

1 tablespoon butter

2 apples—peeled, cored, and diced
1/4 cup *finely* chopped onion
2 tablespoons *light* brown sugar
1/2 teaspoon caraway seeds
1 bay leaf
Freshly ground black pepper, to taste
2 cups *boiling* water

Preheat slow cooker at LOW.

Drain sauerkraut and rinse in several changes of cold water. Drain well and, using your hands, squeeze out as much water as you can.

In a non-stick-coated skillet set over *MEDIUM* heat, melt butter. Add *well-drained* sauerkraut and cook, stirring constantly, until the sauerkraut just begins to brown. Transfer to the heated bowl of the slow cooker.

Add diced apples, *finely* chopped onion, brown sugar, caraway seeds, bay leaf, and black pepper. Add *boiling* water. Stir. Cover and allow to cook at LOW for 2 hours, or until all the water has evaporated. Stir frequently. Remove and discard bay leaf.

Turn into heated serving bowl.

Serve at once.

Yields 8 servings
adequate for 6 people

Notes: *To maintain whiteness, many food processors add sulfiting agents to sauerkraut. If you are sensitive to sulfites, check labels carefully.

This recipe can be doubled, when required.

1/6 SERVING – PROTEIN = 0.6 g.; FAT = 1.6 g.; CARBOHYDRATE = 9.5 g.;
CALORIES = 51; CALORIES FROM FAT = 28%

LATVIAN CRANBERRY PUDDING
Kisel iz Klyukvy Po-Latyshski

TPT - 1 hour and 35 minutes;
1 hour = refrigeration period

Kisels (kissels) are wonderful seasonal fresh fruit purées that are found throughout Russia and in the cuisines of the nations that comprised the former Soviet Union. This one from Latvia, which classically would be made with a native berry similar in taste to our cranberry, is tart, yet sweet. It can be made with the cranberries available in the United States.

8 ounces fresh *or* frozen cranberries
1/4 cup water

6 tablespoons sugar
1/4 cup water
1 cinnamon quill

2 teaspoons corn starch
1 tablespoon *cold* water

1 tablespoon sugar

1/4 cup heavy whipping cream—*softly whipped*—for garnish

LATVIAN CRANBERRY PUDDING (cont'd)

Rinse cranberries. Pick over and discard any of poor quality.

In a saucepan set over *LOW* heat, combine cranberries and 1/4 cupful water. Cover and allow to cook until skins pop.

Using a FOOD MILL, purée cranberries into a mixing bowl. Discard refuse. Press the resultant purée through a sieve into a clean saucepan.

Set saucepan over *LOW* heat, add the 6 tablespoonfuls sugar, remaining 1/4 cupful water, and cinnamon quill. Cook, stirring often, for about 8 minutes, or until sugar is completely dissolved and mixture is hot. Remove cinnamon quill, rinse, and store for future use.

In a small dish, combine corn starch with 1 tablespoonful *cold* water. Stir until corn starch is completely in suspension. Scrape corn starch suspension into hot cranberry mixture and cook, stirring constantly, until thickened. Remove from heat and allow to cool slightly.

Pour into 4 individual serving dishes or into a single serving dish, if preferred, and refrigerate for at least 1 hour. A firm surface will form as the pudding cools. When this surface forms, sprinkle remaining tablespoonful of sugar over.

Serve well-chilled, decorated with a garnish of *softly whipped* cream.

Yields 4 individual servings

Note: This recipe is easily doubled, when required.

1/4 SERVING – PROTEIN = 0.5 g.; FAT = 5.3 g.; CARBOHYDRATE = 32.5 g.; CALORIES = 174; CALORIES FROM FAT = 27%

LATVIAN CARAWAY REFRIGERATOR COOKIES
Cepumi

TPT - 5 hours and 7 minutes;
1 hour = first dough chilling period;
3 hours = second dough chilling period

Latvia is a small country with a small population and a sad history of occupation. It is so often lumped with Estonia and Lithuania as "The Baltic States" and was for so long part of the Soviet Union that we tend to forget that it does have a historical cuisine, carried by its expatriates all over the world. This lovely orange-flavored cookie is one of my favorite refrigerator cookies. Putting caraway seeds into a sweet took a bit of convincing but then I considered the anise seeds in our favorite biscotti and the fennel seeds in our Christmas panettone. Caraway seeds are a very pleasant surprise to your taste buds; a delight with a cup of tea.

1 1/4 cups unbleached white flour
1/2 cup whole wheat flour
1/4 teaspoon baking soda

1/2 cup butter—*softened to room temperature*
3/4 cup sugar
1 teaspoon pure vanilla extract
1/4 cup *fat-free* **pasteurized eggs (the equivalent of 1 egg)**
2 tablespoons freshly squeezed orange juice
2 teaspoons freshly grated orange zest
2 teaspoons caraway seeds

LATVIAN CARAWAY REFRIGERATOR COOKIES (cont'd)

Sift whole wheat and white flours with baking soda. Set aside.

Using an electric mixer or food processor fitted with steel knife, cream butter until light and fluffy. Add sugar and again cream until light.

Add vanilla extract, pasteurized eggs, orange juice, grated orange zest, and caraway seeds. Beat until well-combined. Gradually beat in sifted dry ingredients until again well-combined. Refrigerate for at least 1 hour to make dough easy to handle.

Divide dough into three balls. Working quickly, roll dough into 1 1/2-inch cylinders. Wrap each tightly in plastic wrap. Tightly twist ends. Refrigerate or freeze for at least 3 hours.

Preheat oven to 325 degrees F. Prepare cookie sheets by lining with parchment paper.*

Slice chilled or frozen cylinders of dough into 1/4-inch slices. Space 2 inches apart on prepared cookie sheets.**

Bake in preheated 325 degree F. oven for about 12-13 minutes, or until *lightly browned* around edges. Remove from oven and allow to cool for a minute or two on top of the stove before removing to a wire rack to cool thoroughly.

Store in an airtight container or plastic bag.

Yields approximately 32 cookies

1/32 SERVING (i. e., per cookie) –
PROTEIN = 1.0 g.; FAT = 3.2 g.; CARBOHYDRATE = 10.3 g.;
CALORIES = 71; CALORIES FROM FAT = 41%

Notes: *Culinary parchment paper for baking is available in food specialty and housewares stores, and from mail order firms, where it is now even available as an unbleached, environmentally friendly product. Rarely in the United States, unlike in Europe, do you find it on the shelves of small grocery stores. Lining baking sheets and pans with parchment paper, instead of greasing, buttering, or oiling, not only protects your baking sheets from scorching, it encourages the even browning of cookies, scones, cakes, etc.

**To keep cookies from spreading too much as they bake, be sure to keep the dough chilled and let the cookie sheets cool down to room temperature between batches.

Europe – Liechtenstein

Liechtenstein

Yes, German dishes are eaten in Lichtenstein; yes, Austrian dishes are eaten in Lichtenstein; yes, French dishes are eaten in Lichtenstein; and yes, Lichtenstein does have a cuisine unique onto itself but due in part to its historical alliances and in part to its present role as a crossroads of international banking, the influences upon its very cosmopolitan, continental cuisine extend way beyond its boundaries.

The dynastic family of Castle Liechtenstein in Lower Austria acquired lands from the territory that had once formed a part of the ancient Roman province of Raetia, seeking to gain political power through a seat in the Imperial diet of the Holy Roman Empire beginning in 1699. In 1719 Charles VI, Holy Roman Emperor, granted the status of *Fürstentum* or principality to the united Lordship of Schellenberg and the County of Vaduz. Of little interest, except for its political value, it was over one hundred and twenty years before a reigning Prince of Liechtenstein set foot in the principality. In 1815 Liechtenstein joined the German Confederation under the Emperor of Austria. It was not until 1818, when Liechtenstein was a granted a limited constitution, that a member of the house of Liechtenstein visited the principality. It took until 1842 for a sovereign prince to visit the land over which he was sovereign.

The Principality of Liechtenstein is situated in the Upper Rhine River valley, bordered by Switzerland to the west and by Austria to the east. Only 160 square kilometers (61.776 square miles) in size, it is the sixth smallest independent nation in the world by land area; its prince is the sixth richest leader in the world.

Lentil *Consommé*
Linsenbrühe

~

Vegetable Salad with White Beans and Corn
Gemüsesalat
with

Lovage – Chive Vinegar   or   Spicy Nasturtium Flower Vinegar
Kräuteressig

~~~~~~~~~~~~~~~~~~~~

**Mixed Wild Mushrooms and Asparagus
with Oregano and Fennel Oil**
Champignon und Spargel mit Olivernöl Kraut

**Liechtenstein's Tiny Dumplings with Cheese
and Caramelized Onions**
Käsknöpfle

Steamed Whole Carrots   or   Steamed and Buttered Kohlrabi

~~~~~~~~~~~~~~~~~~~~

Thin pancakes   with   **Sweet Fresh Pear Dessert**
Pfannkuchen   *Gebraten Birne*
or

Macerated Berry Compote Topped with Vanilla Ice Cream
and a Sprinkling of Cinnamon

Europe–Liechtenstein

LENTIL *CONSOMMÉ*
Linsenbrühe

TPT - 1 hour and 3 minutes

The flavors of Germany are strong in the cuisine of Liechtenstein. This vegetable consommé is a perfect first course for a meal and the fact that it can quickly be made from canned lentil soup is a bonus as are the leguminous amino acids it provides.

2 cans (14.5 ounces each) ready-to-eat vegetarian lentil soup
3 soup cans water

6 thin, whole green beans—trimmed—for garnish

In a saucepan set over *MEDIUM* heat, combine vegetable soup and water. Allow to come to the boil. Reduce heat to *LOW* and simmer for 30 minutes. Set a fine sieve over a mixing bowl and pour the lentil mixture into the sieve and allow to drain thoroughly.* Rinse a cotton tea towel in water and wring out well. Line a clean sieve with the tea towel and set it over another clean saucepan. Pour the sieved lentil mixture through the tea towel.

Place the strained *consommé* over *LOW-MEDIUM* heat and allow to heat through.

Drop green beans into the broth and blanch for 3 minutes. Remove and place a green bean in each of six heated soup plates. Apportion hot *consommé* over each.

Serve at once.

Yields 6 servings
adequate for 6 people

Notes: *Reserve the lentil mixture. Freeze to add to a stew or reconstitute with a little water and make a thick soup.

This recipe can be halved, when required.

Accurate food values for this broth will vary with the commercial soup chosen.

VEGETABLE SALAD WITH BEANS AND CORN
Gemüsesalat

TPT - 1 hour and 9 minutes;
1 hour = flavor development period

This beautiful salad combination will certainly be recognized by any vegetarian cook as a quick, protein-complemented way to feed a family on a hot summer evening or as a perfect salad meal to pack up and tote to a park or stream bed for a fall picnic. Spread a tablecloth and just pretend you have hiked into the mountains in the Principality of Liechtenstein.

1 can (15.5 ounces) Roman beans—well-drained
1 cup corn kernels—fresh cut from the cob *or* frozen
1/2 medium cucumber—peeled, seeded, and chopped into pieces about the size of the corn kernels
1/2 cup Italian red onion—chopped into pieces about the size of the corn kernels
1 large ripe tomato—peeled, seeded, and chopped
1 medium beet—cooked, peeled, and diced
Freshly ground black pepper, to taste
Pinch ground cinnamon

2 tablespoons *extra virgin* olive oil
1/2 teaspoon freshly squeezed lemon juice
2 tablespoons **LOVAGE–CHIVE VINEGAR** *[see recipe which follows]*, **SPICY NASTURTIUM FLOWER VINEGAR** *[see recipe which follows]*, *or* other herb vinegar, of choice

In a mixing bowl, combine well-drained beans, corn, chopped cucumber, onion, and tomato, diced beet, black pepper, and ground cinnamon. *Gently* toss to combine.

In a small dish, combine olive oil, lemon juice, and herb vinegar. Using a small wire whisk, beat until it forms an emulsion. Pour over vegetable ingredients. Gently toss to coat the vegetables with the *vinaigrette*. Turn into a serving dish. Refrigerate for at least 1 hour to allow for flavor development.

Serve chilled. Refrigerate leftovers.

Yields 8 servings
adequate for 6 people

1/8 SERVING – PROTEIN = 9.8 g.; FAT = 3.2 g.; CARBOHYDRATE = 12.9 g.;
CALORIES = 107; CALORIES FROM FAT = 27%

Europe – Liechtenstein

LOVAGE – CHIVE VINEGAR
TPT - 1 week and 6 minutes;
1 week = flavor development period

If you grow lovage, you already know the incredible flavor of what my grandmother called "celery plant." Removing the flowers to make the vinegar does double duty since the plant then does not "think" it has done its job for the season; it just keeps growing. Lovage and chives are an exciting combination and it's just a single trip to the herb garden.

1 1/2 cups rice wine vinegar
2 lovage flower heads—*well-washed*
4 lovage stems with leaves, about 6 inches long—*well-washed* and coarsely chopped
1/4 cup coarsely chopped chive blades—*well-washed*
8 whole black peppercorns

Sterilize a one-quart canning jar, lid, and ring.

Pack *well-washed* lovage flowers, chopped lovage stems and chopped chive blades into the sterilized canning jar.

Pour vinegar into sterilized condiment bottle. Add peppercorns. Using a chopstick, stir leaves for about 30 seconds to start the infusion. Seal the jar and place in a cool, dark place for 1 week.

Sterilize a clear, condiment bottle, or several if you are planning to give the vinegar as gifts.

Place a fine sieve over a one-quart measuring cup or mixing bowl. Strain. Discard flowers, leaves, and peppercorns.

Pour vinegar into sterilized condiment bottle or bottles. Cap and label.

Store at cool room temperature for up to six months.

Yields 1 1/2 cupfuls

Note: This recipe may be doubled or tripled or quadrupled with ease; helpful if you should want to give bottles as gifts.

1/20 SERVING (i. e., per tablespoonful) –
PROTEIN = 0.0 g.; FAT = 0.0 g.; CARBOHYDRATE = 0.7 g.;
CALORIES = 1; CALORIES FROM FAT = 0%

SPICY NASTURTIUM FLOWER VINEGAR
TPT - 1 week and 14 minutes;
1 week = flavor development period

With a very good extra virgin olive oil and a bit of Dijon mustard, this assertive, beautifully tinted vinegar makes a terrific vinaigrette for green and vegetable salads or as a marinade.

2 cups *home-grown, spray-free* nasturtium (*Tropaeolum majus*) flowers—pulled from flower stems, *very* well-washed, and well-dried, with *pistils, stamen, and sepals removed*
3 garlic cloves—peeled and halved
4 whole cloves
8 whole peppercorns
3 1/2 cups rice wine vinegar *or* white distilled vinegar, if preferred

Sterilize a 1-quart bottle or jar.

Pack well-washed and well-dried nasturtium flowers, halved garlic cloves, whole cloves, and whole peppercorns into sterilized 1-quart bottle or jar. Pour rice wine vinegar over blossoms, being sure to cover completely. Cap.

Allow to stand at room temperature in a dark cupboard for 1 week to allow for both flavor and color development.

Sterilize a clear, condiment bottle.

Strain vinegar from flowers and spices into sterilized condiment bottle.

Store vinegar at cool room temperature away from light for up to three months.

Yields 3 1/2 cupfuls

Note: This recipe may be doubled or tripled or quadrupled with ease; helpful if you should want to give bottles as gifts.

1/56 SERVING (i. e., per tablespoonful) –
PROTEIN = 0.0 g.; FAT = 0.0 g.; CARBOHYDRATE = 0.0 g.;
CALORIES = 0; CALORIES FROM FAT = 0%

Europe–Liechtenstein

MIXED WILD MUSHROOMS AND ASPARAGUS WITH OREGANO AND FENNEL OIL IN THE STYLE OF LIECHTENSTEIN

Champignon und Spargel mit Olivenöl Kraut

TPT - 6 hours and 18 minutes;
6 hours = oil preparation

This dish can be the centerpiece of a very nice dinner. Early in the morning I clip some oregano and a few fennel fronds from the herb gardens off the patio to prepare the herb-flavored oil. Mushrooms, foraged the day before from a nearby grocery that always carries a selection of wonderful mushrooms from chanterelles to gorgeous trumpets, will be sautéed in butter and dressed with the oil at dinnertime. I have used dried mushrooms to prepare this dish on occasion; it is quite a different flavor experience.

OREGANO AND FENNEL OIL:
    About 4 inches from the top of 2 fresh oregano stems *or* marjoram, if preferred—well-rinsed, *well-dried,* and snipped into 1-inch pieces
    2 fennel fronds—well-rinsed and *well-dried*
    1/4 cup *extra virgin* olive oil

2 pounds mixed mushrooms including *crimini*, or baby bella, *chanterelles*, and *porcini**—stems removed, rinsed and cleaned well with a brush, well-rinsed, and sliced

3 tablespoons butter

Boiling water
12 thin asparagus spears—all the same length—trimmed and well-rinsed

1 teaspoon freshly squeezed lemon juice
Freshly ground black pepper, to taste

In a quart canning jar, combine well-rinsed and *well-dried* oregano pieces and fennel fronds with olive oil. Cover tightly and shake to bring the oil into contact with the herbs. Set aside at room temperature for 6 hours to allow for flavor development. Shake occasionally to again bring the oil into contact with the herbs. Set a funnel into a cruet. Set a fine sieve into the funnel. Pour the oil through the sieve. Discard the herbs.

In a skillet set over *MEDIUM* heat, melt butter. Add sliced mushrooms and cook, stirring frequently, until mushrooms begin to color and most of moisture extruded has evaporated—about 7-10 minutes.

While the mushrooms are sautéing, set up a large skillet over *MEDIUM* heat. Fill to a depth of about 1 inch with *boiling* water. Add asparagus spears and allow to simmer for about 5 minutes—*no more,*

Add lemon juice to mushrooms and season with black pepper. Transfer to a heated serving platter leaving about *one-third* of the platter for the asparagus.

Pour about a tablespoonful of prepared oregano and fennel oil over. Arrange asparagus spears on the platter.

Serve at once. Pass the herb oil to accommodate individual tastes.*

                         Yields 6 servings
                      adequate for 4-6 people

Notes: *Leftover oil can be used to make a rather different *vinaigrette* for salads or used to brush *bruschetta*.

This recipe can be halved, when required.

1/6 SERVING – PROTEIN = 3.7 g.; FAT = 13.6 g.; CARBOHYDRATE = 7.2 g.;
CALORIES = 163; CALORIES FROM FAT = 75%

Europe–Liechtenstein

LIECHTENSTEIN'S TINY DUMPLINGS WITH CHEESE AND CARAMELIZED ONIONS
Käsknöpfle

TPT - 53 minutes;
30 minutes = dough resting period

Similar to the "spaetzle" that every young German and Austrian woman learns to perfect, these tiny egg noodles are found only in Liechtenstein. The recipe that I first encountered told you to take out your käsköpfle maker which stumped me right from the start. Käsköpfle should be much smaller than the spaetzle that my grandmother taught me to make and the "thumb technique" that I learned does not work well for these tiny dumplings. A request send out into cyberspace was graciously responded to with the suggestion that I press the noodle dough through the holes in a colander by sliding it back and forth, imitating the motion of the käsköpfle maker. I am sincerely indebted to this anonymous benefactor. A spaetzle maker or a ricer work quite well too and both are much easier to manage and to clean that is the colander method.

1 1/2 cups unbleached white flour
1/2 teaspoon salt

1/2 cup *fat-free* pasteurized eggs (the equivalent of 2 eggs)
2 teaspoons water

2 tablespoons butter
1 large onion—chopped
1 teaspoon sugar

3 quarts water

2/3 cup grated cheese—a mixture of *Gruyère* or *Emmentaler*, with Parmesan or *Romano*

In a mixing bowl, combine flour and salt. Stir to mix well.

In a small bowl, mix pasteurized eggs and water. Add to the flour–salt mixture and stir until bubbles appear in the thick batter. Cover the batter with a linen tea towel and set aside at room temperature for about 30 minutes.

Meanwhile in a skillet set over *LOW-MEDIUM* heat, melt butter. Add chopped onion and sauté until onion is soft and translucent, *being careful not to allow onion to brown*. Sprinkle sugar over and sauté for several more minutes. Remove from heat.

Preheat a warming tray or heat the oven to 170 degrees F.

In a kettle set over *MEDIUM* heat, bring the 3 quartfuls water to the boil. If you do not have a *käsköpfle* maker or a *spaetzle* maker or a ricer, gather up a hunk of the noodle dough and, using a sliding motion, press the dough through the holes of the colander into the boiling water. As soon as the little dumplings float to the surface remove them with a skimmer and transfer them to a sieve to drain. Continue until all the dough as been used. Turn the drained *käsköpfle* onto a heated platter. Place the platter on a preheated warming tray or in an oven set at 170 degrees F.

Sprinkle mixed cheeses over. Top with caramelized onions. Allow to sit on warming tray until the cheese melts.

Serve hot.

Yields 6 servings
adequate for 4 people

Note: This recipe can be halved, when required.

1/6 SERVING –   PROTEIN = 11.1 g.; FAT = 10.0 g.; CARBOHYDRATE = 25.9 g.;
CALORIES = 236; CALORIES FROM FAT = 38%

Europe–Liechtenstein

SWEET VANILLA PEAR DESSERT
Gebraten Birne

TPT - 32 minutes;
15 minutes = cooling period

Pancakes filled with various and sundry sweet fruit fillings can be found all over Europe. I was inspired by a menu from a Liechtenstein restaurant that simply said "pear-filled dessert pancakes." It was too much of a challenge to pass up.

4 *slightly ripened, firm* pears—*our choice are Bosc*
1 tablespoon freshly squeezed lemon juice

1 vanilla bean
3 tablespoons butter

3 tablespoons *superfine* sugar

Sweetened whipped cream

Peel and slice pears. Place in a shallow dish.

Add lemon juice and toss gently to coat pear slices.

Split open vanilla bean and scrape seeds into a non-stick-coated skillet. Add butter to skillet and set over *LOW-MEDIUM* heat. Heat until bubbling.

Drain pear slices through a sieve to remove excess lemon juice. Add to skillet and sauce until lightly browned. Remove from heat. Remove vanilla bean.

Sprinkle sugar over pear slices and *very, very gently* stir, being careful not to break pear slices. Sugar should dissolve without caramelizing this way. Allow to come to room temperature.

Divide among six dessert dishes or sherbet glasses.

Serve at room temperature garnished with whipped cream.

Yields 6 individual servings

Notes: If you wish to use this filling to stuff pancakes, apportion in the center of six large, *thin, hot crêpes* set on six dessert plates. Fold each *crêpe* over and *serve at once*.

This recipe can be halved or doubled, when required.

1/6 SERVING (exclusive of whipped cream) –
PROTEIN = 0.3 g.; FAT = 5.7 g.; CARBOHYDRATE = 15.2 g.;
CALORIES = 113; CALORIES FROM FAT = 45%

Lithuania

Humans have lived in this area of Europe since the end of the last glacial period some twelve thousand years ago. The name Lithuania is first recorded in a German manuscript entitled the "Annals of Quedlenberg" on March 9, 1009 AD. Why did I not know more about this ancient country? As a child born just as World War II began, Lithuania has always been, to me, part of another country; I did not know an independent Lithuania until 1990. How could a land that has been the object of aggression and subjugation, a land that has struggled to preserve one of the oldest languages in Europe, finally emerge again with national identity?

Initially populated by small Baltic tribes, united in the 1230s by Mindaugas, Lithuania grew in size and power to include Belarus, Ukraine, and even parts of Poland and Russia which were part of the Grand Duchy of Lithuania in the fourteenth century. At that time, Lithuania was the largest country in Europe. In 1569 Lithuania and Poland formed the Polish–Lithuanian Commonwealth; the union was to last for two hundred years. After the disintegration of the state, during the period between 1772 and 1795, Russia annexed most of Lithuania. Lithuania reasserted itself as a sovereign nation in 1918 and after twenty-two years of independence it was again occupied, first by the Soviet Union and, subsequently, by Nazi Germany, whose defeat in World War II gave way to a reoccupation by the Soviets. In March of 1990 Lithuania declared independence as the Soviet Union collapsed. One of the most exciting consequences of that independence has been the concerted effort to resurrect the national cuisine.

Although dishes vary from area to area, this can not be attributed to climatic differences because Lithuania, encompassing a territory of slightly more than 25,000 square miles, about the size of West Virginia, has a similar climate throughout the country and a remarkably consistent growing season. You may be surprised to know that *pierogi, blini, paskha, and borscht* are traditional dishes in Lithuania but the influences of Poland and Russia can not be denied. The reliance on pork and potato dishes clearly shows the influence of Germany upon the cuisine. Mushrooms and berries, gathered from the woods, are prized as is the case throughout this area of Europe. Meats and starches dominate meals with noodles, rye bread, rice, and, of course, the much-loved potato often included in a single menu.

One of the most delightful discoveries about the foods that are enjoyed in Lithuania was the fact that one of their favorite desserts is something we have also always enjoyed – fresh, young, unfermented white cheese, such as a cottage cheese or farmer's cheese with honey. We top our own homemade ricotta cheese with wildflower honey available from a local apiary. It is a dessert that makes you very aware of and very content with your food supply.

Europe – Lithuania

Fried Cheese Appetizer
Suris

Deviled Eggs   Black Rye Bread with Oil and Garlic
Įdaryti Kiaušiniai   *Kepta Duona*

~

**Cream of Summer Squash Soup
with Noodles**

~

**Beet and Apple Salad with Sour Cream
on Boston Lettuce**
Mišraine su Rukelis Obuolys

~~~~~~~~~~~~~~~~~~~~~~

Potato Pudding
Kugelis

Savory Cranberry Sauce with Mustard

Steamed Savoy Cabbage with Butter and Chopped Chestnuts
Kaputus su Kaštonas

Warm Pears with Buttered Crumbs

~~~~~~~~~~~~~~~~~~~~~~

Dessert Pancakes with Blueberry Sauce
Pannkoogid

Custard Rice Pudding with **Blueberry Sauce**
Ryžispatiekas

Fresh, Soft White Cheese – such as Cottage Cheese or *Ricotta*
[see index for recipe]

with Honey

FRIED CHEESE APPETIZER
Suris

TPT - 1 hour and 26 minutes;
1 hour = refrigeration period

Beautiful cheeses are produced in Lithuania and are sometimes available in upscale cheese shops in large cities here in the United States. Since the Lithuanians produce semi-soft cheeses similar to mozzarella, Edam, Gouda, Emmentaler, and Tilsit, I find the varieties of those cheeses, available in the imported cheese section of my grocery store, to be adequate substitutes in this recipe. It is fun to prepare several different cheeses in this manner for an appetizer presentation with sour cream and long chive blades.

1 1/2 cups breadcrumbs, or more as needed	12 1/4-inch-thick slices of cheese, about 2 1/2 x 1 inches each—*well-chilled*
3 tablespoons *fat-free* pasteurized eggs (the equivalent of 1 egg)	3 tablespoons butter
3 tablespoons skimmed milk	Sour cream
1/4 cup unbleached white flour	Chives, for garnish

VOLUME I - 245

FRIED CHEESE APPETIZER (cont'd)

Put breadcrumbs in a soup plate and set aside briefly.

In a second soup plate, combine pasteurized eggs, milk, and flour. Using a whisk or a fork, mix well.

Dip a cheese slice into the egg–milk mixture. Then, coat the cheese slice with breadcrumbs. Place on a *cold* plate. Repeat until all the cheese slices have been breaded. Refrigerate for at least 1 hour.

Place a serving plate on a warming tray.

In a large skillet set over *LOW-MEDIUM* heat, melt butter. Add breaded cheese slices, several at a time, and fry until browned, turning once. Transfer to heated serving plate on warming tray.

Garnish with long chive blades and serve with sour cream.

Yields 12 servings
adequate for 6 people

Note: This recipe can be halved or doubled, when required.

1/12 SERVING (exclusive of sour cream and chives) –
PROTEIN = 5.6 g.; FAT = 7.8 g.; CARBOHYDRATE = 5.7 g.;
CALORIES = 111; CALORIES FROM FAT = 63%

LITHUANIAN CREAM OF SUMMER SQUASH SOUP WITH NOODLES
TPT - 48 minutes

In the late summer, I cook and freeze yellow summer squash so that the vegetable option is available to us through the winter. In the spring, if there are any containers still remaining in the freezer, I just make this very beautiful soup. I know that not everybody freezes summer squash so the recipe given here addresses that probability. "Kukulaiciai," an egg noodle that is pinched into the simmering soup, is traditionally used by Lithuanians. If you wish to make your own noodles, it is really enjoyable and quite rewarding. If you prefer to buy dry egg noodles, choose small ones or break larger forms into small pieces.

**4 small yellow summer squash—about 3 pounds
—peeled and chopped**

**1 medium potato—preferably an Idaho—boiled or
steamed, peeled, and chopped**

1/4 cup chopped onion

**1 quart *two-percent* milk
Freshly ground black pepper, to taste**

1 1/2 cups small, twisted, dry egg noodles

1/4 cup light cream *or* half and half

Place chopped squash in a large kettle set over *LOW-MEDIUM* heat. Cook, stirring frequently, until liquid in extruded. *Increase heat to MEDIUM.* Cover and allow to cook, stirring occasionally, until tender. Drain an excess liquid from squash.

In the container of the electric blender or in the work bowl of food processor fitted with steel knife, combine drained squash, chopped potato, and onion with 1 cupful of milk. Process until *very smooth.* Turn into a clean kettle.

Add remaining milk and black pepper to the puréed squash. Using a wire whisk, stir well. Set over *LOW-MEDIUM* heat. Allow to cook until milk is hot, but *not boiling.* Stir frequently.

Add egg noodles and allow to cook until noodles are tender—about 20 minutes. Stir frequently to prevent soup from sticking to the bottom of the pan.

Add cream and allow to heat through. Turn into a heated soup tureen.

Serve into heated soup plates.

Yields 6 servings
adequate for 4-6 people

Note: This recipe can be halved or doubled, when required.

1/6 SERVING – PROTEIN = 11.5 g.; FAT = 5.7 g.; CARBOHYDRATE = 33.8 g.;
CALORIES = 231; CALORIES FROM FAT = 22%

Europe–Lithuania

BEET AND APPLE SALAD WITH SOUR CREAM ON BOSTON LETTUCE
Mitraine su Rukelis Obuolys

TPT - 9 minutes

I once saw a Lithuanian recipe for chopped beets and apples. It was served warm with sour cream as a vegetable side dish. As the years went by it became this salad, a salad much loved by us.

1 medium apple—peeled, cored, and cut into matchstick pieces*
1 teaspoon freshly squeezed lemon juice

2 cups cooked, sliced beets *or* canned, sliced beets—preferably without salt and well-drained—cut into matchstick pieces

SOUR CREAM – DILL DRESSING:
    2 tablespoons *fat-free* dairy sour cream
    1 tablespoon *calorie-reduced or light* mayonnaise
    2 teaspoons chopped fresh dillweed
    Freshly ground black pepper, to taste

6 Boston lettuce leaves *or* those of another soft lettuce—well-washed and dried
2 hard-cooked eggs—shelled and cut into wedges

In a mixing bowl, combine apple pieces and lemon juice. Toss to coat the apple with lemon juice to minimize browning from oxidation.

Add beets pieces. Toss to mix well.

In a small bowl, combine sour cream, mayonnaise, chopped dillweed, and black pepper. Mix well. Add to beet–apple mixture. Fold gently until the beet and apple are completely integrated. Refrigerate until required.

When ready to serve, arrange lettuce leaves on a platter or in a shallow serving bowl. Pile the salad mixture into the center of the lettuce-lined serving dish. Arrange hard-cooked egg wedges around the edge.

Serve at once.

Yields 6 servings
adequate for 4 people

Notes: *When Cortland apples are available, they are our choice for this salad since they have a crisp texture and do not brown upon exposure to air.

This recipe can be halved or doubled, when required.

1/6 SERVING – PROTEIN = 3.5 g.; FAT = 2.9 g.; CARBOHYDRATE = 10.6 g.;
CALORIES = 80; CALORIES FROM FAT = 33%

LITHUANIAN POTATO PUDDING
Kugelis

TPT - 47 minutes

This is my favorite version of "kugelis." The combination of cooked and raw potatoes is quite unique. Lithuanians often serve it with a cranberry sauce so I have included one of my favorite whole berry cranberry sauces in this menu which I think particularly compliments the potato casserole.

1 large potato—boiled, peeled, and coarsely chopped

4 medium potatoes—peeled and *shredded*

1 egg—*well-beaten*
6 tablespoons skimmed milk
1/4 cup *finely* chopped onion
1 1/2 teaspoons farina *or* Cream of Wheat cereal
1/2 teaspoon baking powder
2 tablespoons butter—*softened to room temperature*
Salt, to taste
Freshly ground black pepper, to taste

Fat-free dairy sour cream
SAVORY CRANBERRY SAUCE WITH MUSTARD *[see recipe which follows]*

LITHUANIAN POTATO PUDDING (cont'd)

Preheat oven to 350 degrees F. Prepare a 1 1/2 quart soufflé dish or other oven-to-table baking dish by coating with non-stick lecithin spray coating.

Combine chopped, boiled potato and shredded raw potato with *well-beaten* egg, milk, onion, farina, baking powder, and butter. Stir well to combine. Season with salt and pepper and again beat well. Turn into a prepared soufflé dish. Bake in preheated 350 degree F. oven for about 40 minutes, or until the top is lightly browned.

Serve at once with sour cream and with cranberry sauce.

Yields 6 servings
adequate for 4 people

Note: This recipe can be halved or doubled, when required.

1/6 SERVING (exclusive of sour cream and cranberry sauce) –
PROTEIN = 3.6 g.; FAT = 4.9 g.; CARBOHYDRATE = 21.8 g.;
CALORIES = 149; CALORIES FROM FAT = 30%

SAVORY CRANBERRY SAUCE WITH MUSTARD
TPT - 21 minutes

This is an unusual cranberry sauce which is an extraordinarily delicious compliment to roasted vegetables, baked sweetpotatoes, as well as soy and lentil entrées.

1/2 cup sugar
3/4 cup freshly squeezed orange juice

1/2 pound (2 cups) fresh *or* frozen cranberries
1 teaspoon crushed, dried thyme

2 tablespoons country-style *Dijon* mustard
2 tablespoons heavy whipping cream

Sprig of fresh thyme, for garnish

In a saucepan set over *LOW-MEDIUM* heat, combine sugar and orange juice. Cook, stirring frequently, until sugar is dissolved and the mixture has come to a gentle boil.

Meanwhile, wash cranberries thoroughly and discard any of poor quality. Drain well.

Add cranberries and crushed thyme. Cook, uncovered, until cranberries pop—about 10 minutes. Stir occasionally.

Reduce heat to *LOW*. Add *Dijon* mustard and cream. Stir well to integrate thoroughly. Cook, stirring constantly, until heated through. *Do not allow sauce to boil once cream has been added.*

Turn into a heated serving bowl or sauceboat. Garnish with sprig of thyme. *Serve at room temperature.*

Yields about 2 cupfuls

Notes: This recipe may be halved or doubled, when required.

Leftovers should be stored, covered, in the refrigerator. Bring to room temperature before serving or warm slightly on a warming tray. If necessary, thin leftover sauce with orange juice or cream, as preferred.

1/16 SERVING (i. e., 2 tablespoonfuls) –
PROTEIN = 0.3 g.; FAT = 0.9 g.; CARBOHYDRATE = 9.8 g.;
CALORIES = 46; CALORIES FROM FAT = 18%

Europe–Lithuania

STEAMED SAVOY CABBAGE
WITH BUTTER AND CHOPPED CHESTNUTS
Kopūtas su Kaštonas
TPT - 34 minutes

We find savoy cabbage to be a milder accompaniment to other foods than is its other green/white cabbage cousins. Its quite delicate texture does not just shout "cabbage" and the wrinkled leaves drape softly around each other making an attractive presentation.

1 head savoy cabbage (about 8 inches in diameter)
—outer leaves removed and discarded, halved, and rinsed well

1/4 cup butter
Freshly ground black pepper, to taste

1/4 cup chopped chestnuts—freshly roasted and shelled *or* jarred

Prepare a steamer.

Cut the cabbage halves into three wedges each, *leaving a portion of core attached to each wedge*. Place in steamer and allow to steam until crisp-tender—about 20 minutes.

In a large skillet set over *MEDIUM* heat, melt butter. Carefully, using two spatulas, transfer the cabbage to the skillet. Cook, turning occasionally to allow each surface to lightly brown. Grind black pepper over.

When butter begins to brown, add chopped chestnuts. Cook, stirring the chestnuts for several minutes. Transfer the steamed and braised wedges of cabbage to a heated platter or plate directly onto dinner plates. Spoon the chestnuts and browned butter over.

Serve at once.

Yields 6 servings

Note: This recipe can be halved, when required.

1/6 SERVING – PROTEIN = 1.9 g.; FAT = 7.7 g.; CARBOHYDRATE = 6.8 g.;
CALORIES = 127; CALORIES FROM FAT = 55%

WARM PEARS WITH BUTTERED CRUMBS
IN THE LITHUANIAN STYLE
TPT - 34 minutes

Here the pear is elevated from the salad plate or the dessert plate to the dinner plate and usually steals the show. Although fruits appear in many different guises around the world nobody expects to find a warm pear covered with buttered crumbs. There are always exclamations of surprise. Pears, fixed this way, are a luscious compliment to a meal. If I have ripened pears perfectly, I make this with fresh pears; otherwise, I use canned pear halves or slices.

6 Bartlett *or* Bosc pears—peeled, halved, cored, and seeded

2 tablespoons freshly squeezed lemon juice

1/4 cup butter
1/2 cup dry, white breadcrumbs

Preheat the oven to 170 degrees F. Prepare a large oven-proof soup plate or large plate by coating with non-stick lecithin spray coating.

Roll the pear halves in lemon juice to prevent browning. Slice each half and arrange the slices on the plate by nesting the slices against each other to form a "sun pattern." Place in the oven for about 20 minutes.

Meanwhile, in a small non-stick-coated skillet set over *LOW* heat, melt butter. Add breadcrumbs and cook, stirring frequently, until butter is absorbed and crumbs are lightly browned. Keep warm on warming tray.

When ready to serve, spoon the warm, sautéed crumbs over the warm pear slices.

Serve at once.

Yields 6 individual servings

Note: This recipe can be halved or doubled, when required.

1/6 SERVING – PROTEIN = 0.9 g.; FAT = 7.7 g.; CARBOHYDRATE = 14.4 g.;
CALORIES = 130; CALORIES FROM FAT = 53%

Europe–Lithuania

LITHUANIAN DESSERT PANCAKES WITH BLUEBERRY SAUCE
Pannkaagid

TPT - 1 hour and 23 minutes;
1 hour = batter resting period

Traditionally, these are served for dessert but they are wonderful in a brunch menu.

2 large egg yolks—*well-beaten*
1/2 cup unbleached white flour
1/2 cup whole wheat flour
2 tablespoons sugar
2 tablespoons PLAIN YOGURT *[see index] or*
   commercially-available plain yogurt
1 1/4 cups skimmed milk

2 large egg whites

1 teaspoon butter—*melted*

LITHUANIAN BLUEBERRY SAUCE:
   2 cups blueberries—*fresh or frozen,*
      as preferred
   1/4 cup sugar
   1 tablespoon water

   1 2-inch piece cinnamon quill
   8 whole cloves
   8 allspice berries

Using the electric mixer, combine well-beaten egg yolks, white and whole wheat flours, sugar, yogurt, and skimmed milk. Beat until a smooth batter results. Set aside at room temperature for 1 hour to allow batter to rest.

When ready to proceed, using the electric mixer fitted with *grease–free* beaters or by hand, using a *grease–free* wire whisk, beat egg whites in a *grease–free* bowl until *stiff*, but *not dry*.

Using a wire whisk, *whisk-fold* stiffly beaten egg whites into batter mixture.

Prepare a 6- or 7-inch non-stick-coated *crêpe* skillet by *lightly* brushing with *melted* butter. Heat over *MEDIUM* heat until butter is hot and bubbling. Add about 1/4 cupful of batter and *tilt quickly* so that batter covers pan surface evenly. When *evenly browned* on one side, turn*, and *lightly brown* remaining side. Transfer to heated serving platter in oven to keep warm while preparing remaining pancakes. Prepare all pancakes in the same manner, brushing pan *lightly* with butter, if more is necessary.

At the same time, in a saucepan set over *MEDIUM* heat, combine blueberries, sugar, and water.

In a spice bag or *bouquet garni* bag, combine cinnamon quill, whole cloves, and allspice berries. Bury in blueberries. Cook over *MEDIUM* heat, stirring frequently, until sugar is completely dissolved and mixture comes to a boil. Remove from heat and set aside until pancakes are prepared. Remove spice bag before turning into a sauceboat or serving bowl.

Serve pancakes hot with warm LITHUANIAN BLUEBERRY SAUCE.

Yields 14 pancakes
with 1 1/4 cupfuls sauce
adequate for 4 people

Notes: *Turning often can be a problem, especially with the first few executed. Flipping onto a lightly oiled plate and then back into the skillet can salvage some possible disasters. However, we do prefer to heat a second larger skillet into which we flip the *crêpes*. When the second side is browned, another *crêpe* will be half done and ready to flip. This method cuts your preparation time almost in half.

This recipe may be halved or doubled, when required.

1/7 SERVING (i. e., per two-pancake serving with sauce) –
PROTEIN = 7.7 g.; FAT = 2.8 g.; CARBOHYDRATE = 36.4 g.;
CALORIES = 198; CALORIES FROM FAT = 13%

Europe–Lithuania

LITHUANIAN CUSTARD RICE PUDDING
Ryžispatiekas

TPT - 3 hours and 38 minutes;
2 hours = chilling period

When I packed to move to Michigan to start my first research job after graduating from college, a small wooden recipe box, thoughtfully refinished for me by my dad and containing Grandma's and Mom's custard rice pudding recipe and a very few others, went into the ancient steamer trunk with my books, clothes, research notebooks, and one basic cookbook. I have tweaked that recipe a bit over fifty some years and collected dozens of rice puddings from all over the world. Then I discovered this rice pudding recipe which takes the basic sweet milk rice, that was often a supper for children in my family during the war years, and just keeps going to a richly beautiful baked rice pudding. Let's face it, you can never have too many rice pudding recipes.

1 cup *boiling* water
1/4 cup *preservative-free dark* raisins, if desired

1 1/4 cups skimmed milk
2 three-inch strips *organic* orange zest
1 three-inch strip *organic* lemon zest
1/4 cup sugar
1/2 cup long grain white rice—*do not use precooked/converted variety*

2 egg yolks
1/4 cup sugar
1/2 cup *fat-free* dairy sour cream
1 teaspoon pure vanilla extract

2 large egg whites

In a small bowl, combine *boiling* water and raisins. Allow the raisins to rehydrate while the pudding is being prepared.

In a saucepan set over *LOW* heat, heat milk with strips of orange and lemon zest and 1/4 cupful sugar until just below the boiling point. Stir frequently until sugar has dissolved. Reduce heat to *WARM*. Stir in rice, cover tightly, and cook, undisturbed, for 30 minutes. Stir, replace cover, and cook, undisturbed, for another 15 minutes. If all milk is absorbed at this point, remove MILK RICE from heat and proceed. If all milk is not absorbed, return to heat and continue cooking until it is. Remove and discard strips of orange and lemon zest.

Preheat oven to 350 degrees F. Prepare an 1 1/2-quart soufflé dish or other baking dish by coating with non-stick lecithin spray coating.

Drain raisins.

In a mixing bowl, beat egg yolks well with a wire whisk. Add remaining 1/4 cupful sugar, sour cream, and vanilla extract. Stir in raisins. Add to MILK RICE in saucepan. Gently fold the mixture together.

Using an electric mixer fitted with *grease-free* beaters or by hand, using a *grease-free* wire whisk, beat egg whites in a *grease-free* bowl until *stiff*, but *not dry*. Fold beaten egg whites *gently*, but *thoroughly*, into rice mixture. Turn into prepared baking dish.

Set in baking pan in which a 1-inch water bath has been prepared. Bake in preheated 350 degree F. oven for about 30 minutes, or until top of pudding is a golden brown. *Do not allow water bath to simmer or boil—by adding cold water or ice cubes*, if necessary.

Chill for at least 2 hours before serving.

Serve chilled with LITHUANIAN BLUEBERRY SAUCE *[see recipe which precedes]*.

Yields 6 servings
adequate for 3-5 people

1/6 SERVING – PROTEIN = 5.3 g.; FAT = 2.0 g., CARBOHYDRATE = 36.9 g.;
CALORIES = 199; CALORIES FROM FAT = 9%

Luxembourg

Siegfried, Count of Ardennes acquired Lucilinburhuc from the abbey of St. Maximin in Trier which became a fortress and is today known as Luxembourg Castle. A town developed around this fort. Strategically positioned, Luxembourg became highly influential to the extent that three Holy Roman Emperors in the fourteenth and fifteenth centuries were of the House of Luxembourg. In 1437 the territory was sold to Philip the Good of Burgundy due to the lack of a male heir to maintain the succession. As fortunes changed, the territory now occupied by the Grand Duchy of Luxembourg, was occupied by the Bourbons, the Hapsburgs, the Hohenzollerns, and then by the French under Napoléon. In 1815, with the defeat of Napoléon, Luxembourg was claimed by Prussia and The Netherlands. The Congress of Vienna created a Grand Duchy but with close alliances and obligations to both The Netherlands and to the German Confederation who maintained a Prussian-manned fortress within the territory. Luxembourg lost about one-half of its territory, principally the territory of its French speaking population, to Belgium during the Belgian Revolution of 1830-1839 but the Grand Duchy stood, maintaining its close ties with The Netherlands. The King of The Netherlands, as Grand Duke of Luxembourg, remained the head of state of Luxembourg until 1890 when the death of William III resulted in the ascension of his daughter Wilhelmina. Luxembourg, restricted by the Nassau Family Pact, had to choose a male heir and therefore ended its sovereign relationship with The Netherlands.

Luxembourg was invaded by Germany during both world wars. In 1940, the small duchy was annexed into the Third Reich, forcing the establishment of a government-in-exile in London. Luxembourgers participated in the Normandy Invasion and Luxembourg was liberated in September 1944.

The motto of Luxembourg, in Luxembourgish, says it all, "*Mir welle bleiwe wat mir sinn*' – 'We want to remain what we are." Luxembourg is a constitutional monarchy ruled by a grand duke, the only remaining sovereign grand duchy. Luxembourg is also a founding member of the Benelux Customs Union, together with Belgium and the Netherlands. To insure the movement of workers, capital, services, and goods in the region, the members of the Benelux Customs Union joined with West Germany, France, and Italy in 1951 to form the European Coal and Steel Community which became known as the Benelux Economic Union or Benelux Union, the earliest version of the what is known today as the European Union. One of the six founding members of the European Union, Luxembourg is a small nation slightly smaller than our state of Rhode Island, but it is a highly developed country with a GDP ranking of 68th by the IMF and by the World Bank.

This is very much a meat and potato culture and you will see that the main course selections presented here feature the vegetables dearest to Luxembourgers, potatoes, leeks, cabbage, and carrots. In Luxembourg, even in restaurants, food is prepared as it has been for centuries. The food choices and the food preparation strongly reflect the influence of France, Germany, and Austria but Luxembourgers do not, generally, choose to incorporate the more contemporary, light dishes of these influential cuisines. Food in Luxembourg is unaffected and very hearty; it reflects its geographical position in Europe as a historically-impacted crossroad culture. However, immigrants who have swelled the population during the last fifty years have contributed variety to the culture and to the cuisine. A census in 1997 showed that Portuguese, who immigrated to Luxembourg during the Portuguese revolutionary period in the 1970s, now constitute about thirteen percent of the population; Italians, five percent. In the same census it was revealed that the percentage of the population that was native born, which was ninety-three percent in 1947, had been reduced to sixty-seven percent.

Europe–Luxembourg

Watercress Omelet
Omelett mit Brunnenkresse

~

Creamed Leek and Potato Soup
Potage Parmentier

~

Tossed Mixed Greens
with Sautéed Croutons and Crumbled Blue-Veined Cheese
with

Garlic *Vinaigrette*

~~~~~~~~~~~~~~~~~~~~~~

Cabbage and Potato Pot Pie
Küchen mit Kohl und Kartoffel

or

Potato and Sauerkraut *Croquettes*
Krokette mix Kartoffel und Kohl

or

Potatoes with Leeks and Carrots in Cream Sauce
Kartoffeles mit Porree und Karottes

with

Savory Apples with Sour Cream
Pommes aux Crème Aigre

and

Steamed Whole Green Beans

~~~~~~~~~~~~~~~~~~~~~~

Chestnut Custard Ice Cream
Glace aux Crème de Marron

Fruit Tart
Quetschentaart

LUXEMBOURG WATERCRESS OMELET
Omelett mit Brunnenkresse

TPT - 21 minutes

When an omelet has as much flavor as does this Luxembourg specialty, it is never a matter of saying, "Oh, I guess we'll just have an omelet for dinner." These simple ingredients combine to create a main course or a first course that is full of flavor.

2 cups *boiling* water
2 cups watercress leaves—trimmed of hard stems and petioles, well-washed, and well-dried

2 shallots—*finely* chopped
Freshly ground black pepper, to taste
3 eggs—well beaten
1 tablespoon water *or* white wine, if preferred

1/2 cup shredded *Gruyère or* Cheddar cheese, as preferred

Place a platter on a warming tray or in a warm oven.

In a 9-inch skillet, combine *boiling* water and watercress leaves. When watercress has wilted, drain well.

LUXEMBOURG WATERCRESS OMELET (cont'd)

Spray skillet with non-stick lecithin spray olive oil coating and set over *MEDIUM* heat.

In a small bowl, combine drained watercress, *finely* chopped shallots, black pepper, well-beaten eggs, and water or wine. Using a fork, mix well. Turn into the heated skillet, spreading it evening across pan. Cook, *undisturbed*, for 1-2 minutes, or until set. As the eggs begin to congeal, push them back with a spatula and allow the still-liquid egg mixture to flow onto the pan. Cook until the edges of the omelet can be pulled away from the pan.

Sprinkle the shredded cheese over the half of the omelet furthest from you. Fold the half of the omelet closest to you over the cheese. Using a spatula, lift the folded omelet to loosen it. Slide and flip it onto the warm platter.

This omelet is adequate for 2 to 3 people and can be served at once. If a second omelet needs to be prepared, leave the first omelet on the warming tray or in a warm oven until the second is prepared.

Yields 4 servings
adequate for 2-3 people

1/6 SERVING – PROTEIN = 9.1 g.; FAT = 8.7 g.; CARBOHYDRATE = 1.3 g.;
CALORIES = 121; CALORIES FROM FAT = 65%

CREAMED LEEK AND POTATO SOUP
Potage Parmentier
TPT - 1 hour

Vichyssoise, the rich, chilled soup few of us can resist, is an American invention based on European leek and potato soups. This is actually the hot version of my Vichyssoise recipe. This version is much less rich than most you will have encountered. The richness has been somewhat compromised in an effort to increase the protein content and reduce the calories. Heavy cream may be added to enrich if desired. Luxembourgers are very fond of leek and potato soup. You will find it on restaurant menus noted in Luxembourgish, German, or, as here, in French.

1 cup *thinly* sliced leeks—*white and very light green portions only**

1 1/2 cups diced potato—about 2 medium potatoes
1/2 cup *finely* chopped yellow onion
3 cups water
1 teaspoon salt

1/4 teaspoon freshly ground *white* pepper
Dash freshly grated nutmeg
1 cup *whole* milk

1 tablespoon butter—*brought to room temperature*

2 tablespoons *finely* snipped chives

Wash *thinly* sliced leeks in several changes of cold water and, using your fingers, remove all sand and grit. Drain thoroughly.

In a large saucepan with cover, combine diced potatoes, sliced leeks, chopped onion, water, and salt. Set over *MEDIUM-HIGH* heat and bring to the boil. Reduce heat to *LOW-MEDIUM*, partially cover, and simmer for about 45 minutes, or until vegetables are *very tender*.

Purée two or three ladlefuls at a time in the electric blender, or in the food processor fitted with steel knife, or mash finely and press through a fine sieve or FOOD MILL.** Pour into a clean saucepan set over *LOW-MEDIUM* heat.

Stir in *white* pepper, nutmeg, and milk. Allow to heat through. Turn into a heated soup tureen.

Float the butter on top. Garnish with snipped chives.

Serve into heated cream soup cups or bowls.

Yields 6 first-course servings

Notes: *Save green portions for use in preparing soup stocks.

**The base for this soup may be prepared ahead to this point and refrigerated for a day or two or frozen for future use. Defrost in the refrigerator, season, add milk, and heat.

1 1/2 cupfuls of yellow onion may be used in seasons when leeks are unavailable or over-priced.

CREAMED LEEK AND POTATO SOUP (cont'd)

1/6 SERVING – PROTEIN = 4.7 g.; FAT = 3.3 g.; CARBOHYDRATE = 14.9 g.;
CALORIES = 99; CALORIES FROM FAT = 30%

GARLIC *VINAIGRETTE* IN THE STYLE OF LUXEMBOURG
Vinaigrette

TPT - 1 hour and 2 minutes;
1 hour = flavor development period

You may well think that this is simply a classic French dressing, borrowed from a neighbor, but there are a few twists that make it excitingly different.

1/2 cup *extra virgin* olive oil
2 tablespoons white wine vinegar
1 tablespoon freshly squeezed lemon juice
2 teaspoons *Dijon* mustard with wine
1 tablespoon crushed, dried mixed herbs—parsley,
    chives, chervil, thyme, and/or tarragon
Salt, to taste
1/8 teaspoon freshly ground black pepper, or to taste
2 average-sized garlic cloves—halved

In a jar with a tightly fitting lid or in a cruet with a tightly fitting top or cork, combine all ingredients. Shake vigorously and set aside for about 1 hour to allow for development of flavor.

Always shake vigorously before serving. To avoid rancidity, try to prepare dressing within an hour or two of serving.

Yields about 12 tablespoonfuls

Note: This recipe is easily doubled or tripled, when required.

1/12 SERVING (i. e., per tablespoonful) –
PROTEIN = trace; FAT = 7.4 g.; CARBOHYDRATE = 0.3 g.;
CALORIES = 68; CALORIES FROM FAT = 98%

LUXEMBOURG CABBAGE AND POTATO PIE
Küchen mit Kohl und Kartoffel

TPT - 1 hour and 30 minutes

If you grew up enjoying pot pies, as I did, this Luxembourg specialty is quite a different take on the pie crust-encapsulated pot pies you can now find in the freezer section of grocery stores. Cabbage and potatoes are pared extensively in Luxembourg as they are in Germany and this combination is a useful tool for the vegetarian visiting Luxembourg; just beware the propensity for adding bacon to such dishes. I make this with my own baking mixture but Bisquick works just as well and it is a quick solution to the time it would take to prepare a homemade baking mixture or a pie crust. This recipe can be halved and baked in an eight-inch pie plate. The smaller pie will feed two or three people on a snowy winter evening quite satisfactorily.

Europe–Luxembourg

LUXEMBOURG CABBAGE AND POTATO PIE (cont'd)

1 tablespoons butter
1/2 medium onion—chopped
1 garlic clove—*very finely* chopped

3 cups shredded cabbage
1/2 teaspoon dried, crushed red peppers flakes
1/4 teaspoon salt
Freshly ground black pepper—to taste

1 1/2 cups *reduced-fat* Bisquick baking mix
3/4 cup skimmed milk
1/4 cup *fat-free* pasteurized eggs (the equivalent of 1 egg)

2 medium potatoes—peeled and *thinly* sliced into cold water*

1/2 cup light cream *or* half and half
2 tablespoons *fat-free* pasteurized eggs

Preheat oven to 325 degrees F. Prepare a 9-inch deep-dish pie plate by coating with non-stick lecithin spray coating.

In a skillet set over *LOW-MEDIUM* heat, melt butter. Add chopped onion and *very finely* chopped garlic. Sauté until onion is soft and translucent, *being careful to allow neither the onion nor the garlic to brown.*

Add shredded cabbage, crushed red pepper flakes, salt, and black pepper. Continue sautéing until cabbage is wilted. Remove from heat.

Drain potatoes.

In a mixing bowl, combine baking mix, milk, and 1/4 cupful of pasteurized eggs. Stir with a fork until well-mixed. Pour *one-half* of crust mixture into the pie plate. Spread to the edges and up the side of the pie plate. Layer *one-half* of the thinly-sliced potatoes on top of the bottom crust. Spoon *one-half* of the cabbage–onion mixture over the potatoes. Arrange remaining potatoes on top of the cabbage–onion layer. Spoon the remaining cabbage–onion mixture evenly over the potatoes.

In a measuring cup, combine cream and the remaining 2 tablespoons of pasteurized eggs. Beat the eggs into the cream with a fork or small whisk. Pour over the pie ingredients.

Pour the remaining crust mixture on top. Spread to the edges of the pie plate. Using an apple corer, put a whole in the middle of the crust to allow for the steam to escape.

Bake in preheated 325 degree F. oven for about 1 hour, or until browned.

Cut in wedges to serve.

Yields 8 servings
adequate for 6 people

Notes: *A mandolin or a vegetable peeler can be used most effectively to create the very thin slices of potato necessary for this pie.

Refrigerate any leftovers and warm them up for lunch the next day.

1/8 SERVING – PROTEIN = 5.0 g.; FAT = 7.6 g.; CARBOHYDRATE = 25.9 g.;
CALORIES = 162; CALORIES FROM FAT = 42%

LUXEMBOURG POTATO AND SAUERKRAUT *CROQUETTES*
Krokette mix Kartoffel und Kohl

TPT - 2 hours and 23 minutes;
1 hour = refrigeration period

Without the western hemisphere's contribution of the potato to world cuisine we would not have whole books on the subject of the root vegetable that literally conquered the world . . . deliciously. Without potatoes, tomatoes, corn, and peppers from this side of the Atlantic, this volume would never have been possible. The skillet and the deep-fryer have given us French fries, home-fries, potato pancakes, croquettes, patties, potato omelets, and more. Here the potato is combined with sauerkraut for a very Central European take on the humble vegetable.

2 cups *sulfite-free* fresh *or* canned sauerkraut

4 quarts *boiling* water
4 large potatoes—peeled and chopped

1/2 cup *fat-free* pasteurized eggs (the equivalent of 2 eggs)*

1 tablespoon *Dijon* mustard with wine

Freshly ground black pepper, to taste

1/4 cup butter

VOLUME I - 256

LUXEMBOURG POTATO AND SAUERKRAUT *CROQUETTES* (cont'd)

Put sauerkraut into a bowl. Fill with cold water and allow the sauerkraut to soak while preparing the potatoes.

In a large saucepan set over *MEDIUM* heat, cook chopped potatoes in *boiling* water for about 30 minutes, or until soft. Drain thoroughly. Using a ricer, rice potatoes into a large mixing bowl.

Drain sauerkraut and add to riced potatoes.

In a small bowl, whisk pasteurized eggs with mustard. Add to potato–sauerkraut mixture. Mix well.

Season with black pepper. Mix well. Using your hands or two large serving spoons, form about twenty-four patties. Place them on a large platter. Refrigerate for at least 1 hour to allow patties to firm before frying.

Place a serving plate or platter on a warming tray or in a warm oven.

In a skillet set over *MEDIUM* heat, melt butter. Fry *croquettes* a few at a time until browned on both sides. Transfer to several layers of paper toweling to drain. Transfer *croquettes* to heated platter until all *croquettes* have been prepared. Add more butter, if necessary.

Serve at once.

Yields 24 *croquettes*
adequate for 6 people

Notes: *Because raw eggs present the danger of *Salmonella* poisoning, commercially-available pasteurized eggs are recommended for use in preparing this dish.

This recipe can be halved when required.

Leftover *croquettes* can be frozen for a future appearance. Just reheat them in a frying pan with a little more butter.

1/24 SERVING – PROTEIN = 1.1 g.; FAT = 1.9 g.; CARBOHYDRATE = 6.2 g.;
CALORIES = 45; CALORIES FROM FAT = 38%

LUXEMBOURG POTATOES WITH LEEKS AND CARROTS IN CREAM SAUCE

Kartoffeles mit Porree und Karotter

TPT - 3 minutes

Recipes like this are those wonderful tools one saves for winter evenings when you can not get into town for supplies and you have to rely on your larder. Luxembourgers use potatoes and leeks in many dishes; they pair quite naturally to my way of thinking.

4 medium potatoes—peeled and cut into 4 thick slices each
3 quarts *boiling* water

2 large leeks—*white and light green portions only*—sliced and *very well-rinsed*
2 medium carrots—scraped or pared and cut into 1/4-inch slices
1 quart *boiling* water

1 1/4 cups light cream *or* half and half
1 tablespoon *Dijon* mustard with wine
1 tablespoon white wine vinegar
Freshly ground black pepper, to taste

Preheat oven to 200 degrees F. Prepare a *quiche* dish or other oven-to-table dish by coating with non-stick lecithin spray coating.

At the same time, in a large saucepan set over *MEDIUM* heat, cook potato slices in the 3 quartfuls *boiling* water for 20 minutes. Drain. Arrange in prepared baking dish and place in preheated 200 degree F. oven.

In a saucepan set over *MEDIUM* heat, cook sliced leeks and carrots in the 1 quartful *boiling* water. Cook until carrots are tender—about 12 minutes. Drain well.

Add cream, mustard, and vinegar to the saucepan. Using a wire whisk, stir to mix well. Place over *LOW-MEDIUM* heat.

Add cooked leeks and carrots. Season with black pepper. Allow to heat through. Spoon vegetables and cream sauce over potatoes in 200 degree F. oven. Allow to heat through—about 5-7 minutes.

Serve at once.

Yields 6 servings
adequate for 4 people

Note: This recipe can be conveniently halved, when required.

1/6 SERVING – PROTEIN = 3.0 g.; FAT = 4.8 g.; CARBOHYDRATE = 18.2 g.;
CALORIES = 129; CALORIES FROM FAT = 33%

Europe–Luxembourg

LUXEMBOURG SAVORY APPLES WITH SOUR CREAM
Pommes aux Crème Aigre

TPT - 22 minutes

I can apples in the early fall using Honeycrisp apples whenever possible. They can be added to a compote or a quick dessert can take just minutes when you apportion the apples in onion soup crocks, sprinkle them with cinnamon and nutmeg, add a little butter, and slip them into a warm oven while you are finishing dinner. Here those apples, canned in light syrup, become the base for a classic savory accompaniment to a meal popular in Luxembourg.

2 pints canned apples—drained
2/3 cup *fat-free* **dairy sour cream** *or* **crème fraîche**
1 1/2 tablespoons grated *pecorino Romano* **or Parmesan cheese**

2 tablespoons pine nuts (*pignoli***)**

Preheat oven to 300 degrees F.

Arrange drained apple slices in an oven-to-table serving dish. Using a butter spreader, spread sour cream over the slices. Sprinkle grated cheese over. Place in the preheated 300 degree F. oven and allow to heat through—about 15 minutes.

Sprinkle pine nuts (*pignoli*) over.

Serve at once.

Yields 6 servings
adequate for 4 people

Note: This recipe can be halved, when required.

1/6 SERVING – PROTEIN = 4.9 g.; FAT = 1.7 g.; CARBOHYDRATE = 20.4 g.;
CALORIES = 112; CALORIES FROM FAT = 14%

CHESTNUT CUSTARD ICE CREAM
Glace aux Crème de Marron

TPT - 8 hours and 15 minutes;
8 hours = freezing period

I have prepared my own chestnut paste but we do prefer the consistency and convenience of the imported, commercially-available product. There is always some left over when I make cakes, tarts, or soups and I have to plan to use it up quickly, since it survives in the freezer for only a short time. This custard ice cream was evolved to use up that leftover chestnut paste . . . something as beautiful and rich as this, made from leftovers? Chestnuts and chocolate have always been paired in this part of the world. This dessert is my tribute to the exquisite palates of the French, the Belgians, and the Luxembourgers.

1 cup heavy whipping cream

2/3 cup *fat-free* **sweetened condensed milk**
1/2 cup *fat-free* **pasteurized eggs (the equivalent of 2 eggs)***
1/2 cup unsweetened chestnut purée*
1 teaspoon pure vanilla extract
Pinch ground cinnamon

Triangular pieces of chocolate, for garnish

Prepare a 7 x 3 x 2-inch non-stick-coated loaf pan by placing it in the freezer until required.

Using an electric mixer fitted with *chilled* beaters or by hand, using a *chilled* wire whisk, beat heavy cream in a *chilled* bowl until stiff. Set aside.

CHESTNUT CUSTARD ICE CREAM (cont'd)

In a large bowl, combine sweetened condensed milk, pasteurized eggs, vanilla extract, unsweetened chestnut purée, and ground cinnamon. Stir to blend thoroughly. *Whisk-fold* stiffly whipped cream *gently*, but *thoroughly*, into milk–egg mixture.

Pour mixture into chilled loaf pan. Spread evenly. Cover tightly with aluminum foil. Freeze overnight or until firm—about 8 hours.

Either scoop ice cream from pan to serve or remove entire block of ice cream from pan and slice. Imbed a triangle of chocolate into each serving.

Leftovers should be returned to the freezer, tightly covered.

Notes: *Because raw eggs present the danger of *Salmonella* poisoning, commercially-available pasteurized eggs are recommended for use in preparing this dish.

Unsweetened chestnut paste is available in food specialty stores and in well-stocked grocery stores. We prefer to use the unsweetened paste to *crème de marron*, which is a sweetened paste, also now widely available.

**This recipe is easily doubled, when required. Use a 9 x 5 x 3-inch non-stick-coated loaf pan.

Yields about eight 3/4-cup servings

1/8 SERVING (i. e., per 3/4 cupful without chocolate garnish) –
PROTEIN = 4.1 g.; FAT = 9.8 g.; CARBOHYDRATE = 21.1 g.;
CALORIES = 191; CALORIES FROM FAT = 46%

FRUIT TART IN THE STYLE OF LUXEMBOURG
Quetschentaart

TPT - 2 hours and 10 minutes;
1 hour = cooling period

This fruit tart from Luxembourg reminds me of the küchens my grandmother made each week during the late summer when the peaches and prune plums were available. She would make seven küchens with blue prune plums and peaches. Family members swung by Grandma and Grandpa's on the way home from work to pick up bread and a küchen on baking day. Luxembourgers generally use plums but the increasing difficulty in finding those wonderful late-season blue, prune plums often sends me searching for firm peaches, or even, if all else fails, firm, canned cling peach slices.

I have cut my grandmother's pastry recipe down so that a single nine-inch cake pan or pie plate can be used.

3/4 cup unbleached white flour
3/4 teaspoon baking powder
1/2 teaspoon ground cinnamon
1/8 teaspoon salt

3 tablespoons butter

2 tablespoons sugar

1 large egg

1 teaspoon pure vanilla extract
1/2 teaspoon pure almond extract

1/4 cup *fat-free* dairy sour cream

6 large German prune plums or 8 Italian prune plums—pitted and cut into wedges *or* the equivalent in peach slices, if preferred

2 tablespoons sugar
1/4 teaspoon ground cinnamon

Preheat oven to 350 degrees F. Prepare a 9-inch cake pan by lining it with culinary parchment paper and coating it with non-stick lecithin spray coating.*

In a mixing bowl, combine flour, baking powder, 1/2 teaspoonful ground cinnamon, and salt. Stir to mix. Set aside until required.

FRUIT TART IN THE STYLE OF LUXEMBOURG (cont'd)

Using the electric mixer fitted with paddle, cream butter until light and fluffy.

Add the 2 tablespoonfuls sugar and continue creaming until again light and fluffy. Scrape down sides of mixer bowl.

Add egg and mix well.

Add vanilla and almond extracts. Mix well. Scrape down sides of mixer bowl.

While mixer is running, add dry ingredients alternately with sour cream. Mix until a uniform batter forms. Turn batter into prepared baking dish and spread the batter to the side of the pan.

Arrange plum or peach slices in a spiral, pressing them into the batter.

Mix remaining 2 tablespoonfuls sugar and 1/4 teaspoon ground cinnamon. Sprinkle evenly over tart.

Bake in preheated 350 degree F. oven for 40 minutes, or until a cake tester comes out clean. Remove to a wire rack to cool for at least 1 hour.

Serve cut into wedges as for a pie.

Yields 8 servings
adequate for 6 people

Note: *A 9-inch pie plate can be substituted.

1/6 SERVING – PROTEIN = 3.0 g.; FAT = 5.1 g.; CARBOHYDRATE = 20.0 g.;
CALORIES = 137; CALORIES FROM FAT = 34 %

Macedonia

Philip II of Macedonia, father of Alexander the Great, set out to expand his kingdom in 336 BC. In this campaign he conquered the lands which had, in antiquity, been populated by Thracian tribes. The area of the Macedonian kingdom was expanded by his son Alexander as he built his empire. This ancient conquest was included in the Roman province of Macedonia and much of it is part of the present-day Republic of Macedonia.

Byzantine Emperor Basil II consolidated control over the Balkans, including Macedonia, in 1018 AD, re-establishing a presence that had previously lasted from about 580 AD to the seventh century when domination by the Bulgarian Empire supplanted the Byzantine control. The Bulgarian Empire once again reasserted dominance over some areas beginning in the tenth century as the Byzantine Empire's influence began to wane. Frequent changes in influence followed as the Bulgarians and Serbians fought for control of the region through the thirteenth and fourteenth centuries. Beginning in the fifteenth century the area we know as Macedonia was conquered by the Ottoman Empire and remained part of the Ottoman Empire for five centuries until the First Balkan War of 1912 when the area was annexed to Serbia.

Much of Macedonia was incorporated into the post-World War I state called the Kingdom of Serbs, Croats, and Slovenes which was renamed Yugoslavia in 1929. Most of historical Macedonia, however, remained part of Greece, outside of the Socialist Republic of Macedonia. Greek Macedonia was designated by the Greeks as Northern Greece although it was officially known as Macedonia. In 1991 the Republic of Macedonia officially left Yugoslavia and became an independent state but not without the outspoken opposition of Greece who claimed historical right to the name Macedonia.

About the size of our state of West Virginia, with a population of slightly more than two million, the Republic of Macedonia is still struggling to navigate its parliamentary democracy in the modern world. In 2009, the year following the global recession, its economy was ranked as the fourth out of 178 nations in terms of its success in reforming its economy from a socialist model to that of a democracy. Trade accounts for ninety percent of its GDP despite a continuation of political corruption and little effort to reform the problem-ridden legal system. In addition, unemployment is still very high as is the poverty rate.

Macedonian cuisine is similar to that of other Balkan cuisines reflecting to some extent the influences left by the comings and goings of the Italians, Germans, Turks, and Hungarians as they jockeyed for control of the area over the centuries. Sitting down to dinner in Macedonia might transport you the Middle East and then the next night you might feel that you were in Greece or Italy. Dishes are well-seasoned and often redolent with garlic; coffee, an important Macedonian beverage, is strong.

Europe – Macedonia

Feta Cheese Slices with Olive Oil and Kalamata Olives

Roasted Red Peppers

Breaded and Fried Eggplant Slices   Boiled Baby Potatoes   Beet Slices

with

Garlic – Walnut Dipping Sauce
Skordalia

~

Cream of Vegetable Soup with Large Pot Pie Noodles

Macedonian Lentil Soup
Lescha Soupa

~

Peach, Cantaloupe and Blueberry Salad
with Almond Syrup and Moscato Wine Sauce
Frúta Fréska Kombósta

Macedonian Vegetable Salad
Shopska Salata

Oregano Flower Vinegar

~~~~~~~~~~~~~~~~~~~~~

Rice and Onions with Egg and Lemon Sauce
Rizi meh Saltsa Avgolemono

Pan-Grilled Baby Red Peppers, Plum Tomato Halves,
Baby Eggplant Halves, and Asparagus Spears

~ ~ ~

Potato and Cheese Casserole
Mussaka

Green Peas Simmered in Tomato Sauce
Arakas Laderos

Sautéed Carrots with Pomegranate Glaze
Mörkov Kalinka

~~~~~~~~~~~~~~~~~~~~~

Kadota Fig Halves with Fresh Pear Slices

Orange Cake
Portogal Torta

Orange Buttercream Frosting

Vegan Almond Rice Pudding
Sutlijash

Europe–Macedonia

MACEDONIAN GARLIC – WALNUT DIPPING SAUCE
Skordalia
TPT - 12 minutes

Today the only dipping sauces that people seem to serve are salsas. Granted, they are a far cry from and a vast improvement on the mayonnaise- or sour cream-base dips that sat on every coffee table with chips in the 1950s and '60s but skordalia is a dipping sauce that is not often served in the United States and it is well worth knowing.

2 garlic cloves—coarsely chopped
1/4 teaspoon salt, or to taste

1/4 cup chopped *preservative-free* walnuts

1 1/2 cups crumbled dry bread, without crusts,
 soaked in water and squeezed dry

1/2 cup *extra virgin* olive oil
1 1/2 tablespoons red wine vinegar

Using the food processor fitted with steel knife, process garlic cloves and salt until they form a paste. Scrape down the sides of the work bowl as needed.

Add chopped walnuts and again process until the nuts are uniformly ground into a meal.

Add the bread that has been soaked and squeezed dry, and again process until thoroughly mixed into the garlic–walnut mixture.

Then, while the machine is running, dribble the olive oil and vinegar into the mixture in a thin stream. Continue mixing until you have a smooth, creamy sauce. Thin with water if desired. Turn into a serving bowl.

Serve at once to prevent the oil from separating.

Yields 1 3/4 cupfuls

Note: This recipe can be doubled, when required.

1/28 SERVING (i. e., per tablespoonful) –
PROTEIN = 0.4 g.; FAT = 4.1 g.; CARBOHYDRATE = 1.6 g.;
CALORIES = 45; CALORIES FROM FAT = 82%

MACEDONIAN LENTIL SOUP
Lescha Soupa
TPT - 3 hours;
2 hours = lentil soaking period

Somebody once asked me why I collected so many rice pudding and lentil soup recipes. "After all," she said, "when you find a recipe that you and your family like, there is no need to keep searching." Point taken, but there is no end to the interpretations of just those two dishes. The pepper taste transmitted by the red pepper and the fresh sparkle of mint in this lentil soup recipe from Macedonia is different from all others. To thicken this soup I add mashed butternut squash which not only adds to the beautiful color of the soup but also adds a dose of vitamins A and C, phytochemicals, potassium, manganese, and magnesium.

3/4 cup dry brown (*or* green) lentils
Boiling water

1 tablespoon *extra virgin* olive oil
1 large leek—*white and light green portions only*—
 very well-rinsed and *finely* chopped
2 large garlic cloves—*very finely* chopped

1/2 cup canned, *diced* tomatoes
1/2 teaspoon crushed, dried mint
1 teaspoon HOMEMADE PAPRIKA *[see Index]*
 or Hungarian sweet paprika
1/2 teaspoon salt, or to taste
Freshly ground black pepper, to taste

5 cups *boiling* water
1 large red bell pepper—cored, seeded, and
 quartered
1/2 cup *cooked*, mashed butternut squash
1 tablespoon red wine vinegar

Pick over lentils and discard any of poor quality. Rinse thoroughly. Drain. Pour into a mixing bowl and add *boiling* water to cover. Set aside at room temperature for 2 hours. Drain.

In a *non-aluminum** kettle set over *MEDIUM* heat, heat oil. Add *finely* chopped leek and *very finely* chopped garlic. Sauté until soft and transparent, *being careful to allow neither the leeks nor the garlic to brown*.

VOLUME I - 263

MACEDONIAN LENTIL SOUP (cont'd)

Add diced tomatoes, crushed, dried mint, paprika, salt, and black pepper. Cook, stirring constantly, for several minutes.

Add drained lentils, *boiling* water, the pieces of the red bell pepper, mashed butternut squash, and vinegar. Reduce heat to *LOW*, cover tightly, and simmer for about 40 minutes, or until lentils are tender. Remove the red pepper pieces and add them to your soup stock bag. Turn into a heated soup tureen.

Serve into heated soup plates.

Yields about 6 cupfuls

Note: This recipe can be doubled, when required.

1/6 SERVING (i. e., 1 cupful) –
PROTEIN = 7.7 g.; FAT = 2.1 g.; CARBOHYDRATE = 20.2 g.;
CALORIES = 130; CALORIES FROM FAT = 15%

PEACH, CANTALOUPE, AND BLUEBERRY SALAD WITH ALMOND SYRUP AND *MOSCATO* WINE SAUCE
Frúta Fréska Kambósta

TPT - 2 hours and 8 minutes;
2 hours = flavor development period

In my experience, Americans rarely think to add fruits to savory dishes yet I have eaten main courses throughout the world that achieve the nuances of flavor only because fruit has been added. Americans, however, do not balk at a fruit salad so that is a first step. Fruit salads are wonderful accompaniments to savory dishes and, as my mother-in-law used to say, it all gets mixed up anyway once you eat it.

1 tablespoon ALMOND SYRUP *(Sciroppo di Latte di Mandorle)* [see index] **or commercially-available almond syrup**
3/4 cup chilled *Moscato* **wine**

2 ripe peaches—peeled, pitted, and chopped
2 cups cantaloupe—chopped *or* **balled**
1/2 cup blueberries—well-rinsed*

In a serving bowl, combine almond syrup and wine. Stir to distribute the almond syrup.

Add chopped peaches and cantaloupe, and blueberries. Spoon the wine sauce over the fruit. Refrigerate for at least 2 hours. Turn fruit occasionally.

Using a slotted spoon, serve onto salad plates.

Notes: *Other berries can be substituted.

This recipe can be halved or doubled, when required.

Yields 6 servings
adequate for 4 people

1/6 SERVING – PROTEIN = 0.6 g.; FAT = 0.2 g.; CARBOHYDRATE = 10.5 g.;
CALORIES = 50; CALORIES FROM FAT = 4%

Europe–**Macedonia**

MACEDONIAN VEGETABLE SALAD
Shopska Salata
TPT - 9 minutes

This salad is served all over the Balkans and is similar to the classic village salad so popular in Greece and in every Greek diner in the United States. A vegetarian can always find a satisfying meal in Macedonia too where this ubiquitous salad is often referred to as the Bulgarian salad. It is said to have been created by Bulgarian chefs in the 1950s who named their creation for the Shopi people who reside in the region where the borders of Bulgaria, Serbia, and Macedonia meet. This appears to be the only one of the several versions of the socialist era salad, created for the tourist restaurants, that has survived.

Bulgarian sirene cheese is occasionally available in the cheese shops in major metropolitan areas and is similar to the cheese one would have available in Macedonia. It is saltier than Greek feta and often made from goats' milk. Feta cheese made from ewes' milk is readily available here in the United States.

1 1/2 tablespoons *extra virgin* olive oil
1 tablespoon OREGANO FLOWER VINEGAR
 [see recipe which follows] or other white
 vinegar of choice
2 garlic slivers
Pinch crushed, dried, oregano
Pinch freshly ground black pepper, or to taste

3 vine-ripened tomatoes—seeded and chopped
1 small-medium cucumber—scored with the
 tines of a fork, quartered lengthwise, and
 sliced crosswise into wedges
1/4 cup green bell pepper—cored, seeded, and
 chopped
1/4 cup red bell pepper—cored, seeded, and
 chopped
1 small yellow onion *or* a sweet onion, if
 preferred—chopped
1 cup chopped fresh parsley—well-washed and
 dried

3 ounces (about 3/4 cup) *feta* cheese—shredded

In a cruet, combine oil, vinegar, garlic slivers, crushed oregano, and black pepper. Shake vigorously. Set aside until required.

In a large, shallow serving dish or salad bowl, combine chopped tomatoes, cucumber, green pepper, red pepper, onion, and parsley. Toss.

Sprinkle shredded *feta* cheese over the vegetables.

Again, vigorously shake the dressing. Drizzle just a bit over the salad. Serve the salad onto dinner plates or into soup plates. Pass dressing to accommodate individual tastes.*

Yields 8 servings
adequate for 6 people

Note: This recipe can be halved or doubled, when required.

1/8 SERVING – PROTEIN = 3.1 g.; FAT = 15.0 g.; CARBOHYDRATE = 3.6 g.;
CALORIES = 157; CALORIES FROM FAT = 86%

OREGANO FLOWER VINEGAR
TPT - 1 week and 14 minutes;
1 week = flavor development period

Most Northern Europeans, especially those in Great Britain, prefer marjoram to oregano. Although both herbs are members of the genus Origanum, it is claimed by some that oregano, so favored in Southern Europe, is strong and wild in taste and overtakes other flavors and so they struggle to grow a tender perennial which in the North must be treated as an annual. This delightfully colored vinegar delivers just a touch of oregano, a bit more than a very mild marjoram but not as much as fresh oregano leaves or even dried leaves, and certainly could solve any dilemma, although I personally have never been able to understand the problem. Can't they just use a bit less oregano, if they want a light touch?

1 cup purple oregano flowers—pulled from
 flower stems, well-washed, and well-dried*
4-inch sprig of oregano leaves
1 1/2 cups rice wine vinegar—about 12 ounces

OREGANO FLOWER VINEGAR (cont'd)

Sterilize a 1-pint bottle or jar.

Pack well-washed and well-dried oregano flowers and sprig of oregano leaves into sterilized 1-pint bottle or jar. Pour rice wine vinegar over herb blossoms and leaves, being sure to cover completely. Using a chopstick, stir leaves for about 30 seconds to start the infusion. Seal tightly.

Allow to stand at room temperature in a dark cupboard for 1 week to allow for both flavor and color development.

Sterilize a clear, condiment bottle.

Place a fine sieve over a one-quart measuring cup or mixing bowl. Strain the vinegar, discarding the flowers and leaves recovered.

Pour vinegar into sterilized condiment bottle or bottles. Cap and label.

Store at cool room temperature away from light for up to three months.**

Yields 1 1/2 cupfuls

Notes: *Any of the many oregano and marjoram varieties may be used in this recipe.

**If this vinegar is stored in direct sunlight, the attractive pink/lavender color will fade.

This recipe may be doubled or tripled or quadrupled with ease; helpful if you should want to give bottles as gifts.

1/24 SERVING (i. e., per tablespoonful) –
PROTEIN = 0.0 g.; FAT = 0.0 g.; CARBOHYDRATE = 0.7 g.;
CALORIES = 2; CALORIES FROM FAT = 0%

MACEDONIAN RICE AND ONIONS WITH EGG AND LEMON SAUCE
Rizi meh Saltsa Avgolemono
TPT - 27 minutes

In Macedonia, rice is used to stuff grape leaves, to make rice pudding, and to augment soups and stews. In this recipe it is combined with the egg and lemon sauce so popular in both Macedonia and Greece to provide a hearty, protein-rich vegetarian entrée.

1 cup dry converted rice
1 medium onion—*finely* chopped
2 cups *boiling* water

2 tablespoons butter
1/4 cup snipped fresh dillweed
Freshly ground black pepper, to taste

1 1/4 cups EGG AND LEMON SAUCE *(Saltsa Avgolemono)* [see recipe which follows]

In a saucepan set over *LOW-MEDIUM* heat, combine rice, *finely* chopped onion, and *boiling* water. When the water returns to the boiling point, reduced the temperature to *MEDIUM*, cover, and allow to cook, *undisturbed*, for 20 minutes. Remove lid.

Add butter, snipped dillweed, and pepper. Stir to combine well.

Add prepared egg and lemon sauce. Return to *LOW-MEDIUM* heat and cook, stirring constantly, until heated through. Turn into a heated serving bowl.

Serve at once.

Yields 6 servings
adequate for 4 people

Notes: This recipe can be halved or doubled, when required.

The rice combination is a good filling for *dolmas* such as steamed zucchini, acorn squash halves, or hollowed-out jack-be-little pumpkins.

1/6 SERVING – PROTEIN = 3.8 g.; FAT = 5.8 g.; CARBOHYDRATE = 33.7 g.;
CALORIES = 212; CALORIES FROM FAT = 25%

Europe–**Macedonia**

EGG AND LEMON SAUCE
Saltsa Avgolemono
TPT -24 minutes

This sauce is a perfect example of the strong Greek influence found in Macedonian cuisine. It is a popular sauce in both nations and is served with both meat and vegetable dishes.

3 tablespoons freshly squeezed lemon juice
1/2 teaspoon unbleached white flour

2 egg yolks

2 egg whites

1 cup VEGETARIAN WHITE STOCK *[see index]* or other vegetable stock of choice—*heated to just below the boiling point*

1/4 teaspoon salt, or to taste
Freshly ground black pepper, to taste

In a mixing bowl, combine lemon juice and flour. Using a wire whisk, combine thoroughly.

Add egg yolks. Again whisk until well combined. Set aside briefly.

In the top half of a double boiler set over *warm, not boiling*, water, whisk egg whites until foamy. Place double boiler on LOW-MEDIUM heat.

While whisking constantly, slowly pour the egg yolk mixture into the beaten egg whites. Cook, whisking constantly, until mixture begins to thicken. *This can take several minutes.*

Continue whisking while slowly adding heated vegetable stock. Cook, stirring frequently, until sauce thickens sufficiently. Remove from heat to counter top.

Season with salt and pepper. Leave off-burner, but over hot water, until ready to serve.

Yields about 1 1/4 cupfuls

Note: This recipe can be halved, when required.

1/10 SERVING (i. e., about 2 tablespoonfuls) – -
PROTEIN = 1.3 g.; FAT = 1.1 g.; CARBOHYDRATE = 0.4 g.;
CALORIES = 17; CALORIES FROM FAT = 58%

MACEDONIAN POTATO AND CHEESE CASSEROLE
Mussaka
TPT - 1 hour and 3 minutes

Macedonians make mussaka which is a significantly different dish from moussaka as interpreted by Greeks and experienced by most Americans. This mussaka does not contain eggplant, although they do also make an eggplant mussaka, constructed with alternating layers of thinly sliced potatoes and meat. There is an alternative to this traditional potato and meat casserole that is made with shredded potato instead of sliced potato and cheese instead of meat. If I had decided to write a book solely on comfort food, this recipe would have been in that collection. This potato dish takes the humble potato in a direction that no other culture thought to go.

5 tablespoons unbleached white flour
1 teaspoon baking powder
Freshly ground black pepper, to taste

3 medium potatoes—peeled and grated into cold water
2 large garlic cloves—*very finely* chopped

1/4 cup *extra virgin* olive oil
1/4 cup *fat-free* pasteurized eggs (the equivalent of 1 egg)
1/4 cup skimmed milk
1 1/2 teaspoons *finely* crushed, dried oregano
1/2 teaspoon *finely* crushed, dried thyme

3/4 cup *feta* cheese

2 teaspoons grated *pecorino Romano* cheese

Preheat oven to 350 degrees F. Prepare a 1 1/2-quart soufflé dish or other oven-to-table dish by coating with non-stick lecithin spray olive oil coating.

In a large mixing bowl, combine flour, baking powder, and black pepper.

Drain grated potatoes, squeezing out as much water as possible. Turn into the mixing bowl with the flour mixture. Add *very finely* chopped garlic. Stir to combine.

MACEDONIAN POTATO AND CHEESE CASSEROLE (cont'd)

In a measuring cup or small bowl, combine oil, pasteurized eggs, milk, and finely crushed dried oregano and thyme. Using a small wire whisk, combine thoroughly. Add to potato mixture and stir with a wooden spoon.

Spoon a layer of the potato mixture into the bottom of the baking dish. Spoon a layer of *feta* cheese over. Repeat layers until all ingredients have been used up. End with a layer of the potato mixture.

Sprinkle the grated *Romano* cheese over the top. Bake in preheated 350 degree F. oven for about 40 minutes, or until the top is golden brown.

Serve at once.

Yields 6 servings
adequate for 4 people

1/6 SERVING – PROTEIN = 7.5 g.; FAT = 14.0 g.; CARBOHYDRATE = 16.7 g.;
CALORIES = 228; CALORIES FROM FAT = 55%

GREEN PEAS SIMMERED IN TOMATO SAUCE
Arakas Laderos

TPT - 20 minutes

Peas are often cooked in a spiced tomato sauce in Macedonia. In this very different vegetable dish, the peas are firm with a cool, clean taste while the sauce is soft and spicy to the tongue. Some recipes call for potatoes and carrots but this is our favorite version because the contrast between the peas and the tomato sauce is not blurred by other tastes. It sure beats a bunch of green peas rolling aimlessly around on the plate.

1 cup canned, *diced* tomatoes

1/4 cup chopped fresh parsley
Salt, to taste
Crushed red pepper flakes, to taste*

1 cup *frozen* green peas

In a non-stick coated skillet set over *LOW-MEDIUM* heat, heat tomatoes, stirring frequently until most of the extra liquid has evaporated and the mixture is thick.

Add chopped parsley, salt, and crushed red pepper flakes. Cook, stirring frequently, for several minutes.

Add *frozen* green peas. Cook, stirring frequently, until the peas have defrosted and the dish has heated through. Turn into a heated serving dish. *Be careful not to overcook the peas.*

Yields 6 servings
adequate for 4 people

Notes: *Add a few red pepper flakes or really "hot" it up.

This recipe can be halved or doubled, when required.

1/6 SERVING – PROTEIN = 1.4 g.; FAT = 0.1 g.; CARBOHYDRATE = 3.9 g.;
CALORIES = 21; CALORIES FROM FAT = 4%

MACEDONIAN SAUTÉED CARROTS WITH POMEGRANATE GLAZE
Morkov Kalinka

TPT - 29 minutes

Some people consider carrots to be a favorite vegetable—sweet when cooked, refreshing when eaten raw. However, getting carrots into someone who claims carrots are dull and uninteresting is often a difficult sell. "They are good for your eyes;" "Rabbits love them;" and all those platitudes of our childhood just do not work if someone remembers the mashed carrots fed to toddlers or has ever eaten canned carrots. I happen to love carrots but I share my life with someone who cares little for carrots. "Have some more carrots." "No thank you, I had some." Was I surprised when he took a second helping of this dish. The pomegranate juice certainly improves the reception that carrots receive in our house.

4 large carrots—scraped or pared

3 tablespoons butter
1/4 cup pure pomegranate juice*

Freshly ground black pepper, to taste

Cut the carrots into thirds crosswise. Halve each of those cuts and then cut the halves in half again or into thirds if they are large.

Europe–**Macedonia**

**MACEDONIAN SAUTÉED CARROTS
WITH POMEGRANATE GLAZE** (cont'd)

In a large skillet set over *LOW* heat, melt butter. Add carrots strips and pomegranate juice. Allow to cook, partially covered, until carrots are tender—about 20 minutes. Stir occasionally. Turn into a heated serving bowl, scraping any residual butter and pomegranate juice over the carrots.

Season with black pepper.

Serve at once.

Yields 6 servings
adequate for 4 people

Notes: *When fresh pomegranates are available, add a tablespoonful of seeds too.

This recipe can be halved or doubled, when required.

1/6 SERVING – PROTEIN = 0.5 g.; FAT = 5.8 g.; CARBOHYDRATE = 5.2 g.;
CALORIES = 87; CALORIES FROM FAT = 60%

MACEDONIAN ORANGE CAKE
Pörtogal Tärta

TPT - 50 minutes

Although this really delicious cake evolved from a recipe found in a collection of recipes used for the fast days of Orthodox Lent, it is a recipe than any vegan cook would appreciate adding to his or her repertoire. It makes a wonderful snack cake. A recipe for orange buttercream frosting follows, which can be added after the fast is over.

1/2 cup sugar
1/2 cup sunflower *or* safflower oil
1/2 cup freshly squeezed orange juice
Zest of 1 *organic* orange—about 3 tablespoons

1/2 teaspoon baking powder
1/2 teaspoon baking soda
1 cup plus 2 tablespoons unbleached white flour

1/2 cup *preservative-free* raisins
1/2 cup chopped *preservative-free* walnuts *or* pecans

Preheat oven to 350 degrees F. Prepare an 8 x 8-inch square non-stick-coated baking dish by coating with lecithin baking spray.

In the electric mixer fitted with paddle, combine sugar, oil, orange juice, and orange zest. Mix at MEDIUM speed for 10 minutes.

Add baking powder, baking soda, and flour. Beat until thoroughly mixed.

Add raisins and chopped nuts. Mix until distributed. Turn into prepared baking pan, spreading the batter evenly to the sides of the pan. Bake in preheated 350 degree F. oven for 30 minutes, or until a cake tester comes out clean. Transfer to a wire rack and allow the cake to cool in the baking pan before transferring to a serving plate.

Yields 12 servings
adequate for 6-8 people

1/12 SERVING   PROTEIN = 2.3 g.; FAT = 13.7 g.; CARBOHYDRATE = 25.8 g.;
CALORIES = 234; CALORIES FROM FAT = 53%

ORANGE BUTTERCREAM FROSTING

TPT - 20 minutes

No other flavoring or coloring is necessary since the result is a light orange frosting with a terrific fresh orange flavor.

1/2 cup (1 stick) butter—*softened to room temperature*
1 cup confectioners' sugar
1 teaspoon pure vanilla extract

3-4 tablespoons frozen orange juice concentrate
—*defrosted*
About 2 cups confectioners' sugar

Using an electric mixer, or food processor fitted with steel knife, or by hand, cream butter until light and fluffy. Gradually beat the 1 cupful confectioners' sugar into the creamed butter. Continue beating until smooth. Add vanilla extract. Mix well.

Beat in the remaining 2 cupfuls confectioners' sugar gradually alternating with the *defrosted* orange juice concentrate, adding more of each until a smooth, spreadable consistency is achieved.

Europe–**Macedonia**

ORANGE BUTTERCREAM FROSTING (cont'd)

Use to frost cakes or cookies or freeze until needed.*

Yields enough to frost two 9-inch cake layers or about 24-30 cupcakes

Note: *The consistency of this may readily be altered to produce a buttercream filling for pastries, tortes, and cakes or a substitute for fondant in making *petits fours.*

1/16 SERVING (i. e., that which would be used on a two-layer slice of cake exclusive of the cake) –
PROTEIN = 0.1 g.; FAT = 5.7 g.; CARBOHYDRATE = 30.0 g.;
CALORIES = 168; CALORIES FROM FAT = 31%

1/24 SERVING (i. e., that which would be used on a cupcake exclusive of the cupcake) –
PROTEIN = 0.1 g.; FAT = 3.8 g.; CARBOHYDRATE = 20.0 g.;
CALORIES = 112; CALORIES FROM FAT = 31%

VEGAN ALMOND RICE PUDDING
Sutlijash

TPT - 3 hours and 15 minutes;
2 hours = chilling period
[slow cooker: 1 hour at HIGH, 1 hour at LOW]

Another rice pudding . . . ? Oh yes, and this is one that I evolved to serve to those who do not eat dairy products. It is the certainly the best of both worlds since it is still a homey, "creamy," cottage-style rice pudding but with the sophistication of almond flavoring lavished with a white chocolate garnish for special occasions. Since Macedonians are very fond of rice pudding with almonds, I offer this.

2 3/4 cups *unflavored* almond milk*
1 tablespoon butter
Two 2-inch strips orange *or* lemon zest
1 cinnamon quill

1/2 cup dry Japanese short grain rice**
3 tablespoons sugar, or to taste

1 teaspoon pure vanilla extract
1 tablespoon SICILIAN ALMOND SYRUP
  (*Scirioppo di Latte di Mandorle*) [see index]***

1 ounce white chocolate—peeled into large curls,
  for garnish, if desired****
Toasted, slivered *preservative-free* almonds

Notes: *Almond milk is available in well-stocked grocery stores and in natural food stores on the grocery shelf next to the unrefrigerated soy milk.

**Japanese short grain rice results in a sticky rice, with a glutinous rice texture. *Do not rinse it first.*

***If you do not have Sicilian almond syrup on hand and do not have the time to make it, an almond bar syrup can be substituted. Almond extracts are too harsh, in our opinion, for this pudding.

****A vegetable peeler or a cheese plane can be used to make the decorative curls. Test out your system ahead of time because some white chocolates curl better than others and vegetable peelers differ significantly. If you are unable to manage the large curls of chocolate, long shreds are just as well received.

In a saucepan set over *LOW* heat combine almond milk, butter, orange or lemon zest, and the cinnamon quill. Bring milk to just below the boiling point.

Stir in rice and sugar. Cook, *undisturbed,* over *LOW* heat for about 1 hour and 15 minutes. Remove zest pieces and cinnamon quill.

Stir in vanilla extract and almond syrup. Remove from heat.

Turn into serving dish of choice, or individual dessert dishes, if preferred. Chill thoroughly—about 2 hours.

This recipe may be halved or doubled, when required.

If prepared using a slow cooker, the results are super creamy.

Yields 6 servings
adequate for 4-6 people

1/6 SERVING – PROTEIN = 1.8 g.; FAT = 4.8 g.; CARBOHYDRATE = 32.3 g.;
CALORIES = 180; CALORIES FROM FAT = 3%

Malta

Michelangelo Merisi Caravaggio spent fifteen months in exile in Malta during which time he painted seven of his magnificent paintings. I had seen his *Salome Receives the Head of John the Baptist* at the National Gallery in London, and I had compared it to his renditions of other beheadings, *Judith Beheading Holofernes* and *David with the Head of Goliath* in Rome. His dark, brutal rendition of *The Beheading of Saint John the Baptist*, commissioned by the Knights of Malta, hangs in St. John's Co-Cathedral in Valletta. How I wanted to see it *in situ*; how I wanted to visit this tiny country.

The earliest evidence of human occupation of Malta dates from about 5200 BC. Caves, which are believed to have served as shelter for Neolithic settlers, reveal that they farmed and fished. Fifteen megalithic structures remain which predate Stonehenge and the pyramids of Egypt by about 1,000 years. The theory that these wandering people came from Sicily is not far-fetched since it has been confirmed that the once-submerged ridge on which Malta is located, between the Eurasian and African tectonic plates, was lifted above the water due to tectonic activity creating a land bridge between North Africa and Sicily. Fossils of sea organisms at the highest elevations and bones of animals now exclusive to Africa as well as bones of animals native to Europe offer evidence of Malta's unique geographic history.

The Phoenicians saw the strategic advantage of controlling the archipelago of which Malta is just one of several islands. They seized the island and for 320 years they controlled the traffic on the Mediterranean. The Punic Wars, 264-146 BC, brought the fall of Carthage and Malta became part of the Roman Empire. With the division of the Roman Empire, Malta found itself under the Byzantine Empire from 395-870 AD. The western expansion of the Arabs led to the invasion of Malta in 870 AD, an invasion which literally destroyed the island and led to two centuries of Islamic rule. In 1048-1049 AD Malta was recolonized by Arabs from Sicily. The Norman Kingdom of Sicily took control in 1090 and effected a re-Europeanization. All Arabs were expelled in 1224 leaving a significant void in the male population. It was said that the entire male population of Celano in Abruzzo was deported to Malta to provide a non-Arabic gene pool. It was not legend, as some had once thought, since DNA testing confirms that most of the males of Malta have genes that can be traced to Celano.

As we move into the modern period of Maltese history, the twists and turns continue to be fascinating. We have all heard of the Knights of Malta but the story of this military religious order, created to care for pilgrims and crusaders, begins in the Holy Land in 1099 when the Order of St. John, also known as the Knights Hospitaller, was established by Blessed Gerard. In 1309 they relocated to Rhodes where they remained until 1522 when the increasing threat of Turkey made Malta an important defensive location against the Ottoman Turks and the expanding influence of Islam. The island was granted to the Order of St. John by the Holy Roman Emperor Charles V, the grandson of Ferdinand II and Isabella of Castille. From their base in Malta the knights fought those who spread Islam until the death of the Sultan Suleiman and the end of military advancement into Europe by the Ottomans.

In 1798 the French under Napoléon Bonaparte took Malta, freed Turkish prisoners, and expelled the Knights of Malta, who by this time had declined in power. The French remained for almost two years during which time they organized municipalities and a public finance system, abolished feudal rights and privileges, abolished slavery, and created a system of public education. The Congress of Vienna in 1815 transferred Malta to the control of the British. Self-government was restored in 1947 and Malta became a republic within the British Commonwealth in 1974.

With a complex history like this it is no small wonder that the cuisine of Malta is also complex.

Europe–Malta

Crostini with Olive Oil, Tomato, and Capers
Hobz Biz-Zejt u Tadem

Butter-Fried Cheese *Ravioli* with Black Pepper   or   Angel Hair Spaghetti with Eggs
Ravjul   *Tarja bil Bajd*

~

Vegetable Soup with Fine Noodles   Pumpkin Soup
Minestra   *Soppa tal-Qargha Hamra*

~

Salad with Butter Beans   Summer Vegetable *Mélange*
Fagola Bajda   *Kapunata*

~~~~~~~~~~~~~~~~~~~~~

Artichoke and Fava Bean Skillet with Eggs
Stuffat tal-Qaqocc

Sautéed or Pan-Grilled Baby Zucchini

~~~~~~~~~~~

Spicy Beans   and   Baked Rice with Eggs and Tomatoes
Bigilla   *Ross Il-Forn*

~~~~~~~~~~

Cheese and Pastry Pies
Pastizzi t'l-Irkotta

Sautéed Artichoke Hearts with Lemon   or   Shelled Fresh Peas
Qlub tal-Qaqocc bil-Lumi

~~~~~~~~~~~~~~~~~~~~

Vanilla Ice Cream
with Prickly Pear Cactus Syrup

Fresh, Ripe Peaches   or   Seville Oranges   or   Figs (in season)

Pastries with *Ricotta* and Honey
Quassatat

MALTESE *CROSTINI* WITH OLIVE OIL, TOMATO, AND CAPERS
Hobz Biz-Zejt u Tadem
TPT - 10 minutes

"Bread with oil" is often seen as a first course in Maltese restaurants and homes. Slices of French bread are liberally rubbed with a good, rich olive oil. Instead of sprinkling the top with garlic and dried oregano as some Italians do or piling each slice with seasoned, chopped tomato, the Maltese spoon a ribbon of tomato purée across the bread and then sprinkle finely chopped olives or capers over.

MALTESE *CROSTINI* WITH OLIVE OIL, TOMATO, AND CAPERS (cont'd)

Per serving:

    1 tablespoon *extra virgin* olive oil
    2 thin slices French bread

    1/2 teaspoon *finely* chopped preserved capers

    Freshly ground black pepper, to taste
    1 tablespoon tomato purée

Pour olive oil onto a plate. Place French bread slices on the oiled surface. Move them back and forth to insure that the whole slice is soaked with the oil.

Meanwhile, place *finely* chopped capers in a small dish. Cover with cold water. Turn into a fine sieve and drain. Set aside until required.

Place bread slices, oil-side-up, on a salad plate. Grind black pepper over each. Spoon a ribbon of tomato purée across each slice. Sprinkle *one-half* of the chopped, drained capers over each slice.

Serve at once.

                        Yields 1 serving

Note: This recipe can be multiplied to accommodate the number of diners.

      1 SERVING – PROTEIN = 5.0 g.; FAT = 11.7 g.; CARBOHYDRATE = 32.3 g.;
      CALORIES = 254; CALORIES FROM FAT = 41%

ANGEL HAIR SPAGHETTI WITH EGGS
Tarja bil Bajd
TPT - 14 minutes

The addition of beaten, raw eggs to cooked vegetables and pasta was a cooking technique that I had never encountered until I became acquainted with the cooking of Malta and it was not a cooking technique I explored until the pasteurized egg product, now so widely available, was introduced. Little bits of softly scrambled eggs give this a texture that is very unique. Maltese add the cheese to the spaghetti before serving; I prefer to allow diners to use as much or as little grated cheese as they choose.

4 quarts *boiling* water
8 ounces angel hair spaghetti *(capelli d'angelo* or, sometimes, *capellini)*

2 tablespoons butter

1/2 cup *fat-free* pasteurized eggs*
Freshly ground black pepper, to taste

Grated *pecorino Romano* cheese

In a large kettle set over *HIGH* heat, boil spaghetti in *boiling* water for about 3 minutes. Drain thoroughly.

Reduce heat to *LOW*.

Return spaghetti to kettle. Add butter. Toss until butter is melted. Return kettle to *LOW* heat.

While stirring constantly with a wooden spoon, add pasteurized eggs and black pepper. Cook until eggs congeal. Turn onto heated platter.

Serve at once with grated cheese.

                        Yields 6 servings
                      adequate for 4 people

Notes: *To avoid the possibility of introducing *Salmonella* bacteria, be sure to use pasteurized eggs to make this dish.

This recipe can be halved or doubled, when required.

You may want to serve this as a lunch or light supper entrée.

      1/6 SERVING (exclusive of grated cheese) –
      PROTEIN = 6.7 g.; FAT = 4.4 g.; CARBOHYDRATE = 31.0 g.;
      CALORIES = 182; CALORIES FROM FAT = 22%

Europe–Malta

VEGETABLE SOUP WITH FINE NOODLES IN THE STYLE OF MALTA
Minestra

TPT - 1 hour and 3 minutes

This minestrone from Malta, and truly it is a minestrone, illustrates how this soup, perhaps the best known vegetable soup in the world, is tweaked by those who have adopted it.

1 tablespoon safflower *or* sunflower oil
1/2 cup *finely* chopped onion

1 cup tiny cauliflower florets
3/4 cup diced (about 1/2-inch) butternut squash *or* pumpkin, if preferred
3/4 cup diced (about 1/4-inch) carrot
1/4 cup diced (about 1/4-inch) celery
1 garlic clove—*very finely* chopped
2 tablespoons tomato paste
6 cups VEGETABLE STOCK FROM SOUP
 [*see index*] *or* other vegetarian stock of choice
1/4 teaspoon salt, or to taste
1/4 teaspoon freshly ground black pepper, or to taste
1 tablespoon *preserved* basil*

1/2 cup *fine* egg noodles

12 pitted *Kalamata* olives

Freshly grated Parmesan cheese

In a large kettle set over *MEDIUM* heat, heat oil. Add chopped onion and sauté until onion is soft and translucent, *being careful not to allow onion to brown.*

Add cauliflower florets, diced butternut squash or pumpkin, carrot, and celery, *very finely* chopped garlic, and tomato paste. Stir to mix well. Add stock. Season with salt, black pepper, and preserved basil. Simmer gently for about 40 minutes until quite thick.

Add *fine* egg noodles. Continue cooking for an additional 6 minutes.

Add olives. Turn into heated soup tureen and serve into heated soup plates. Pass grated cheese.

Yields about 8 cupfuls

Note: *Preserved basil is generally available in produce departments.

This recipe is can be halved or doubled, when required.

1/8 SERVING (i. e., per cupful exclusive of cheese) –
PROTEIN = 1.2 g.; FAT = 2.6 g.; CARBOHYDRATE = 10.4 g.;
CALORIES = 74; CALORIES FROM FAT = 31%

PUMPKIN SOUP
Soppa tal-Qargha Hamra

TPT - 52 minutes

This simple soup is popular in the autumn and in the winter in Malta but I have made it even simpler by using canned pumpkin/squash purée which is available year round. The Maltese reserve tomato soup for summer meals making the hint of tomato in this soup welcome in the winter.

1 1/2 teaspoons butter
1 1/2 teaspoons *extra virgin* olive oil
1 medium onion—*very finely* chopped
2 garlic cloves—*very finely* chopped

1 can (15 ounces) pumpkin—*unsweetened and unseasoned*
1 quart VEGETABLE STOCK FROM SOUP [*see index*] *or* other vegetarian stock of choice
3/4 cup canned, *crushed* tomatoes *or* tomato purée

Salt, to taste
1/4 teaspoon freshly ground black pepper, or to taste

3 tablespoons chopped fresh parsley, for garnish

In a small kettle set over *MEDIUM* heat, melt butter. Add *very finely* chopped onion and sauté until onion is soft and translucent, *being careful not to allow onion to brown.*

Add pumpkin purée, vegetable stock, and tomatoes. Stir. Allow to come to the boil. Reduce heat to *LOW-MEDIUM* and allow to simmer for about 20 minutes.

Season with salt and pepper to taste. Turn into a heated soup tureen.

Garnish with chopped fresh parsley.

Serve into heated soup plates.

Yield 6 cupfuls

PUMPKIN SOUP (cont'd)

Notes: This soup freezes well.

When required, this recipe can be doubled.

1/6 SERVING (i. e., per cupful) –
PROTEIN = 1.6 g.; FAT = 2.2 g.; CARBOHYDRATE = 10.6 g.;
CALORIES = 63; CALORIES FROM FAT = 31%

SALAD WITH BUTTER BEANS
Fagola Bajda
TPT - 4 minutes

This side dish can be made with butter beans or fava beans. I make it with well-drained canned butter beans but, if you prefer, dry beans can be soaked and cooked instead. Both Italian and Middle Eastern influences can be seen in this recipe but I would put my money on some North African and Egyptian input as well. Serve it as an appetizer or as a salad. We like to take it on a picnic with a crusty, country loaf of bread, an assortment of crudités, and a fruit tart.

1 1/2 tablespoons *extra virgin* olive oil
1 large garlic clove—*smashed* and *very finely* chopped
6 drops *jalapeño chili* sauce, or to taste
Freshly ground mixed peppercorns—black, red, and white—to taste

1 can (16 ounces) large butter beans—well-drained
1/2 cup chopped, fresh parsley—well-washed and well-dried

In a mixing bowl, combine oil, *very finely* chopped garlic, *jalapeño* sauce, and ground mixed peppercorns. Stir to mix.

Add well-drained butter beans and chopped parsley. Toss to coat well with sauce.

Serve chilled or at room temperature. Refrigerate leftovers.

Yields 6 servings
adequate for 4 people

Notes: Canned beans do not need to be salted but if you use cooked, dried beans, you will need to season with salt.

This recipe can be doubled, when required.

1/6 SERVING – PROTEIN = 2.7 g.; FAT = 2.8 g.; CARBOHYDRATE = 10.3 g.;
CALORIES = 73; CALORIES FROM FAT = 35%

MALTESE SUMMER VEGETABLE *MÉLANGE*
Kapunata
TPT - 23 minutes

Caponata is to Sicilians as kim chi is to Koreans. The ingredients indigenous to a specific town are the only ingredients with which either can be made; this is not negotiable. It is very personal and when you do not make your own, brand loyalty is ferocious and panic sets in when that company changes something or, God forbid, goes out of business. My mother-in-law did not make her own caponata so a specific brand of caponata was the brand and, as luck would have it, the manufacturer stopped making it. We tried every brand we could find in search of a satisfying replacement. I am sure this version from Malta will not satisfy all who try it and I will thoroughly understand if you have to tweak it somewhat to please your family.

The following recipe is one that can be prepared throughout the year. In the summer we avail ourselves, as do the Maltese, of diced fresh tomatoes and finely chopped fresh marjoram and basil.

MALTESE SUMMER VEGETABLE *MÉLANGE* (cont'd)

2 tablespoons *extra virgin* olive oil
1 medium onion—sliced

1 small-medium eggplant—peeled and diced
2 Italian frying peppers (Cubanella)—cored, seeded, and chopped
3/4 cup canned, *diced* tomatoes
2 garlic cloves—crushed and *finely* chopped
1 tablespoon tomato paste
1 teaspoon crushed, dried marjoram
1 teaspoon crushed, dried basil
Salt, to taste
Freshly ground black pepper, to taste

6 pitted *Kalamata* olives
1 tablespoon preserved capers

In a large skillet set over *LOW-MEDIUM* heat, heat oil. Add onions and sauté until onion are soft and translucent, *being careful not to allow them to brown.*

Add diced eggplant, chopped frying peppers, diced tomatoes, *finely* chopped garlic, tomato paste, crushed marjoram and basil, salt, and pepper. Stir to combine. Cover and cook, stirring frequently, until the vegetables are soft.

Add olives and capers. Turn into a heated serving bowl.

Serve at once or, if preferred, refrigerate and serve cold.

Yields 6 servings
adequate for 4 people

Note: This recipe can be doubled, when required.

1/6 SERVING – PROTEIN = 1.8 g.; FAT = 5.0 g.; CARBOHYDRATE = 8.2 g.;
CALORIES = 80; CALORIES FROM FAT = 56%

MALTESE ARTICHOKE AND FAVA BEAN SKILLET WITH EGGS

Stuffat tal-Qaqoċċ

TPT - 10 hours and 14 minutes;
8 hours = bean soaking period;
1 hour and 30 minutes = bean cooking period

Every Italian and Greek cookbook I have has artichoke recipes, some containing as many as fifteen or twenty. Appreciation of the artichoke spread throughout the Mediterranean where each nationality integrated it into their cuisine. One of the first recipes I mastered from my husband's tradition was that for Sicilian stuffed artichokes, a dish that is worth all the work if you love artichokes. This stew, which is a specialty of Malta, not only makes wonderful use of the artichoke it includes broad beans, also known as fava beans, which are eaten in countries all around the Mediterranean. Although I prefer to soak and cook dry fava beans for this dish, I do avail myself of frozen artichoke hearts to save preparation time. This is a wonderful vegetarian main course dish which can become a wonderful vegan main course dish by just omitting the eggs and the goat cheese. Bread, noodles or pasta, or a non-dairy rice pudding dessert can easily provide amino acid complementation.

3 cups water
1/2 cup dry fava beans

2 quarts *boiling* water

1 tablespoon *extra virgin* olive oil
1 medium onion—*finely* chopped
2 garlic cloves—*very finely* chopped

2 cups *frozen*, quartered artichoke hearts
1 cup canned, *diced* tomatoes
1/2 cup freshly shelled *or* frozen green peas
1/2 cup chopped fresh parsley
1/2 cup water

1/4 teaspoon salt, or to taste
Freshly ground black pepper, to taste

3 ounces goat cheese—divided into six pieces*
6 eggs*

Europe–**Malta**

MALTESE ARTICHOKE AND FAVA BEAN SKILLET WITH EGGS (cont'd)

In a small bowl, combine water and dried fava beans. Refrigerate overnight. Drain and remove any seed coats.

In a saucepan set over *LOW-MEDIUM* heat, cook beans in the 2 quartfuls *boiling* water for about 1 1/2 hours, or until beans are tender. Drain.

In a large, non-stick-coated skillet, that can be taken directly to the dinner table, set over *MEDIUM* heat, heat oil. Add *finely* chopped onion and *very finely* chopped garlic. Sauté until onion is soft and translucent, *being careful not to allow the onion to brown.*

Add cooked fava beans, *frozen* artichoke heart pieces, tomatoes, green peas, chopped parsley, and 1/2 cupful water. Cook, stirring frequently until vegetables are soft.

Season with salt and pepper. *Reduce heat to LOW.*

Using a serving spoon, make six depressions into the vegetable mixture. Place a piece of goat cheese in each. Slide an egg into each depression. Cover. Allow to cook until the whites of the eggs congeal.

Serve at once, directly from the skillet.

Yields 6 servings
adequate for 4 people

Notes: *The amount of goat cheese and the number of eggs can be adjusted to the number of diners.

This recipe can be halved but doubling will require two batches in two separate skillets.

1/6 SERVING – PROTEIN = 16.1 g.; FAT = 11.7 g.; CARBOHYDRATE = 19.5 g.;
CALORIES = 237; CALORIES FROM FAT = 44%

MALTESE SPICY BEANS
Bigilla

TPT - 51 minutes

The origin of many dishes considered by the Maltese as "their dishes," can be attributed to contact with Italy including such obvious adaptations as "kannoli," "bragoli," "kapunata," "ravjul," and "minestra." "Bigilla" seems to have evolved due to other influences. This can be made by soaking and slow-cooking dried beans; broad beans or fava beans are favored. However, I have found another efficient way of enjoying the taste of this Maltese specialty. While in Great Britain I found that Heinz markets vegetarian beans, manufactured for them in Australia, which are not heavily seasoned, sauced, and salted as are the vegetarian baked beans we find in our markets. Even the product marketed by Heinz in our country is not the same as that we found in Great Britain. If you have the availability of the British product, which can be identified by its blue label, you may want to make this Maltese dish. If not, soak and cook beans of choice and then proceed with the unique Maltese seasoning mixture and cook it slowly in a low oven.

2 cans (blue–labeled) Heinz (13.7 ounces each) vegetarian baked beans
3/4 cup *boiling* water
2 tablespoons *extra virgin* olive oil
1/4 cup chopped fresh parsley
2 large garlic cloves—crushed and *very finely* chopped
4-6 drops *jalapeño chili* sauce, or to taste
1 tablespoon *finely* chopped, fresh marjoram
1 tablespoon *finely* chopped, fresh mint
Salt, to taste

Prepare a bean pot by coating with non-stick lecithin spray coating.

In a bean pot, combine the beans, *boiling* water, oil, parsley, *very finely* chopped garlic, *jalapeño chili* sauce, *finely* chopped marjoram and mint, and salt. Stir to mix. Cover. Place in cold oven. Heat oven to 300 degrees F. Allow to slowly cook for about 45 minutes until hot and fragrant.

Serve hot.

Yields 6 servings
adequate for 4 people

Note: This recipe can be halved, when required.

1/6 SERVING – PROTEIN = 3.2 g.; FAT = 3.7 g.; CARBOHYDRATE = 9.1 g.;
CALORIES = 87; CALORIES FROM FAT = 38%

Europe–Malta

MALTESE BAKED RICE WITH EGGS AND TOMATOES
Ross Il-Forn

TPT - 51 minutes

The Maltese developed a method of slow-cooking in earthenware pots which were placed on a stone hearth called a "kenur." Lacking sufficient forestation from which to obtain wood for burning, early peoples adapted to necessity. Communal village ovens were used for baking. This is one dish that is still baked that way in those villages where the tradition of "baker's ovens" has been maintained. Whether or not they live in a small village with a communal oven or whether they live in a city, homemakers in Malta still favor slow-cooking. Ross il Forn, literally translated as "rice in the oven," usually includes an assortment of meats—ground pork, sausages, bacon, chicken livers, and/or ground beef—but there is no reason that it cannot be prepared as an lacto-ovo entrée. This is a satisfying family casserole but when this rice dish is added to a buffet spread, it usually returns to the kitchen empty. Another candidate for comfort food perhaps ...

1 tablespoon *high-heat* safflower *or* sunflower oil
1 cup *finely* chopped onion

2 cups canned, *diced* tomatoes
1 cup VEGETABLE STOCK FROM SOUP *[see index]* or other vegetarian stock of choice
2 cups *cooked*, converted white rice
1 tablespoon tomato paste

3/4 cup *fat-free* pasteurized eggs (the equivalent of 3 eggs)
1/4 cup grated Parmesan cheese
2 tablespoons *finely* chopped fresh parsley
2 teaspoons crumbled, dried basil
Freshly ground black pepper, to taste

Preheat oven to 350 degrees F. Prepare a 2-quart soufflé dish or other oven-to-table baking dish by coating with non-stick lecithin spray coating.

In a deep, non-stick-coated skillet set over *LOW-MEDIUM* heat, heat oil. Add *finely* chopped onion and sauté until onion is soft and translucent, *being careful not to allow onion to brown.*

Add diced tomatoes, vegetable stock, cooked rice, and tomato paste. Stir to integrate thoroughly. Remove from heat.

In a mixing bowl, combine pasteurized eggs, grated cheese, *finely* chopped parsley, crumbled basil, and black pepper. Stir well.

Add tomato–rice mixture. Stir well. Turn into prepared baking dish. Bake in preheated 350 degree F. oven for about 35 minutes, or until set and lightly browned on top.

Serve at once.

Yields 8 servings
adequate for 6 people

Note: This recipe can be halved, when required.

1/8 SERVING – PROTEIN = 5.5 g.; FAT = 3.0 g.; CARBOHYDRATE = 16.2 g.;
CALORIES = 113; CALORIES FROM FAT = 24%

MALTESE CHEESE AND PASTRY PIES
Pastizzi t'l-Irkotta

TPT - 1 hour and 33 minutes;
10 minutes = cooling period

This is a rather unique Maltese specialty. The cheese filling is often made with what are called "gbejna" or "cheeselets." They are small round cheeses made from goat cheese and they too seem to be exclusive to Malta. This version, made with a combination of ricotta cheese and goat cheese, is a very satisfying lunch or dinner entrée.

3/4 cup *part-skimmed milk ricotta* cheese
3 ounces goat cheese
1 egg—slightly beaten
2 tablespoons *finely* chopped fresh parsley

2 sheets *frozen* puff pastry—*brought to room temperature*

2 tablespoons *fat-free* pasteurized eggs *or well-beaten* egg, if preferred
1 tablespoon water

Honey

MALTESE CHEESE AND PASTRY PIES (cont'd)

Remove pastry from refrigerator or freezer and allow to come to room temperature.

Preheat oven to 400 degrees F. Prepare two baking sheets by lining them with culinary parchment paper.

In a bowl combine *ricotta* cheese, goat cheese, egg, and *finely* chopped parsley. Using a fork, blend well.

Spread defrosted pastry out on a cool surface. Cut twelve 6-inch circles from each sheet.

Place *one-sixth* of the cheese mixture in the center of six of the circles. Place one of the remaining pastry circles on top of each of cheese-covered circles. Seal the edges of each pastry pie. Transfer to culinary-lined baking sheet.

Mix the 2 tablespoons well-beaten egg with water. Brush each pie with the egg wash.

Bake at 400 degrees F. for about 15 minutes, *checking to be sure that the pastry does not over-brown.* Switch top tray to bottom and bottom tray to top and reverse trays about 7 minutes into the baking process. When done, remove from oven and allow to cool for about 10 minutes on the baking sheet.

Transfer one baked pastry to each of six dessert plates. Drizzle a bit of honey around the plate.

Yields 6 individual servings

Notes: This recipe can be halved or doubled, when required.

If preferred, twelve small pies can be made for lunch or as a snack.

1/6 SERVING – PROTEIN = 13.1 g.; FAT = 8.1 g.; CARBOHYDRATE = 30.3 g.;
CALORIES = 432; CALORIES FROM FAT = 17%

MALTESE PASTRIES WITH *RICOTTA* AND HONEY
Quassatat

TPT - 1 hour and 12 minutes;
40 minutes = pastry room temperature adjustment;
10 minutes = cooling period

Many recipes from Malta hint strongly at the influence of Italy, especially Sicily, has had on this island nation. The ricotta-filled pastries, so popular in Malta, clearly support this assertion. "Kannoli" are sold in every pastry shop. This ricotta recipe, which can be made with pie dough, phyllo pastry, or puff pastry, is a simple recipe that can be easily be made at home.

1 sheet *frozen* puff pastry—*brought to room temperature*

6 tablespoons *part-skimmed milk ricotta* cheese
1 tablespoon honey

1 tablespoon pine nuts (*pignoli*)
Honey

Remove pastry from refrigerator or freezer and allow to come to room temperature.

Preheat oven to 400 degrees F. Prepare a baking sheet by lining it with culinary parchment paper.

Spread defrosted pastry out on a cool surface. Cut six 6-inch circles from the sheet.

Place a tablespoonful of *ricotta* cheese on one side of each pastry round. Make an indentation in each *ricotta* mound and spoon 1 teaspoonful of honey into each hollow. Fold the pastry over to form a half moon. Roll and crimp edges. Transfer to parchment-lined baking sheet.

Bake at 400 degrees F. for about 15 minutes, *checking to be sure that the pastry does not over-brown.* Remove from oven and allow to cool for about 10 minutes on the baking sheet.

Transfer one baked pastry to each of six dessert plates. Sprinkle 1/2 teaspoonful of pine nuts (*pignoli*) over each pastry. Drizzle a bit of honey around the plate.

Serve immediately to preserve the crispness of the baked pastry.

Yields 6 individual servings

Note: This recipe can be halved, when required.

1/6 SERVING – PROTEIN = 4.9 g.; FAT = 12.3 g.; CARBOHYDRATE = 17.7 g.;
CALORIES = 205; CALORIES FROM FAT = 54%

Moldova

The territory occupied by Moldova today, somewhat larger than our state of Maryland, is far less than that occupied by their ancestors during the Neolithic period when this was the political center of the Cucuteni-Trypillian culture that occupied lands to the East beyond the Dniester River into present day Ukraine and to the West beyond the Carpathian Mountains into present-day Romania. The Cucuteni-Trypillian influence in the area lasted from c. 5500 to c. 2750 BC. Its strategic position between Asia and Europe made it an area of frequent interest and conquest. As the centuries passed this area of Europe found itself to be the target of conquest by the Goths, Huns, Avars, Bulgarians, Magyars, Pechenegs, Cumans, Mongols, Tartars, Turks, and Russians. The Pechenegs were a nomadic people of the Asian steppes who were driven from their homeland in the first century AD. The Cumans, light-haired nomadic warriors from the area near the Yellow River in China, who are believed to be related to the Pechenegs and who eventually settled in the area and interbred with the other peoples of the region including the Moldovans, greatly affected the political structure of the medieval states of the region.

The Principality of Moldavia was established in 1359 AD. The western part of the ancient principality of Moldavia is now part of Romania while the eastern part of this historical region is known as the Republic of Moldova. In 1538 the principality became a vassal of the Ottoman Empire and remained so until 1812 when they ceded to Russia a considerable portion of their territory which had been invaded and annexed by Russia, hoping, in so doing, to satisfy Russia and forestall further aggression. Russia's position in the principality made it an easy move into the region. In 1917, with the onset of the Bolshevik Revolution, the Moldavian Democratic Republic was declared, a status and title within the Soviet Union that was changed as the Soviet Union consolidated its influence. In 1924 the Moldavian Autonomous Soviet Socialist Republic was formed. In 1940 the Soviets established firmer controls, declaring Moldavia a Soviet Socialist Republic, and sought to Russify the population by resettling Russians, Ukrainians, and Belarusians into the new republic. More than eleven percent of the Moldovan population still identify themselves as Ukrainian; over nine percent, as Russian. In 1990 Moldova declared its independence from the Soviet Union and held its first democratic elections just prior to the Soviet Union's fall.

In 2013 Russia applied strong economic pressure to force Moldova to join an economic union headed by Russia. Instead, a decision was made to join the European Union economies along with its neighbor Romania with whom it shares ethnicity and language. This move clearly signals Moldovan determination to proceed with development of their market economy and the democratic experiment begun in 1990. However, there has been movement toward recollectivisation of land and an increase in governmental control of private business.

Moldova's population looks to the future, not back to the deficiencies of their Soviet past, with a well-managed agricultural system and a wine industry that has received world recognition. Nevertheless, the economy is under pressure, ranking last among European nations in per capita income, resulting in the fact that an estimated twenty-five percent of the 3.5 million population has emigrated to work abroad.

With long borders between Romania and The Ukraine it should not be surprising that the Moldovan cuisine reflects Romanian and Russian influences but one also finds dishes that can be traced back to the Turks and to Hungary.

Europe – Moldova

Cheese-Stuffed Tomato Appetizers
Rosii Umplute Cu Feta

Celeriac Appetizer Salad
Salata de Telina

~

Chili Bean Soup

Puréed Vegetable Soup with Sour Cream
Supa de Zarsavat cu Smantana

~

Beetroot Salad with Garlic – Mayonnaise Dressing
Salata de Sfecia

~~~~~~~~~~~~~~~~~~~~~~

Fried Polenta Slices with *Mujdei* Sauce
Mamaliga cu Mujdei

with

Fried Pepper, Onion, and Tomato Salad with *Mujdei*
Salata de Pipere Prâjit au Mujdei

and

Garlic Sauce in the Style of Moldova and Romania
Mujdei

~ ~ ~

Moldovan Cheese *Soufflé* with Grated Cheese
Sufleu

Steamed Whole Green Beans
with Grated Cheese and Breadcrumbs

~ ~ ~

Cream of Wheat Croquettes
Crochete de Gris

Buttered Carrots

Fried Cabbage with Tomatoes
Varga Calita

~~~~~~~~~~~~~~~~~~~~~

Buttermilk Cake
Prajitura cu Zer

with

Marmalade and Whipped Cream

Sweet Noodles with Walnuts
Macaroane cu Nuci

Ranger Cookies

Europe–**Moldova**

MOLDOVAN CHEESE-STUFFED TOMATO APPETIZERS
Rosii Umplute Cu Feta

TPT - 10 minutes

When Campari tomatoes, also called cocktail tomatoes, were first introduced from Canada, we found a winter tomato that tasted more like the tomatoes we grow in the summer, the tomatoes that one remembers from one's childhood if one is of a certain age . . . Campari tomatoes are larger than cherry tomatoes which makes them a substantial appetizer item. If you wish, you can slice them after they are filled and present them as a first course salad on a leaf of soft lettuce.

12 Campari tomatoes—well-rinsed

3/4 cup *softened* **cream cheese spread**
1/2 cup crumbled *feta* **cheese**
3 tablespoon soft butter spread
3 tablespoons GARLIC OIL *[see index]*

1/4 cup *finely* **snipped dillweed**

Slice the ends with the stem scars off of each tomato and hollow out each tomato. Set aside until required.

In a mixing bowl, combine cream cheese spread, *feta* cheese, butter spread, and garlic oil. Using the back of a wooden spoon or a wooden garlic masher, mash the mixture together until smooth. Apportion *one-twelfth* of the cheese filling into each of the hollowed-out tomatoes. Place in a shallow serving bowl.

Sprinkle *finely* snipped dillweed over each stuffed tomato. Refrigerate until ready to serve.

Serve chilled.

Yields 12 servings
adequate for 6 people

Note: This recipe can be halved or doubled, when required.

1/12 SERVING – PROTEIN = 2.2 g.; FAT = 8.4 g.; CARBOHYDRATE = 2.2 g.; CALORIES = 93; CALORIES FROM FAT = 81%

MOLDOVAN CELERIAC APPETIZER SALAD
Salata de Telina

TPT - 15 minutes

As I stood in line at the grocery store with the celeriac that I had found, one of only three I might add, a man, who was also in line, commented that you do not see too many people buying celeriac anymore. He proceeded to ask me how I was going to prepare it. Fearing that the description of this rather complex Macedonian dish might put him off a bit, I said that part of it was going to be shredded for a salad and that the remainder was going to be sautéed in butter. He smiled, satisfied that I at least knew something about the potential of this rather ugly, but oh so delicious, vegetable.

1 large leek—*white and light green portions only*—**cut into 1/4-inch slices**

1 tablespoon *extra virgin* **olive oil**
1 medium potato—peeled and cut into matchstick slices
1/4 of a large celeriac (celery root or knob celery) peeled and cut into matchstick slices
1/2 teaspoon rosemary powder*
2 tablespoons pure pomegranate juice**
Salt, to taste
Freshly ground black pepper, to taste

Place leeks slices in a salad spinner. Rinse and spin and drain until all the sand has been removed. Spin dry.

In a large skillet set over *LOW-MEDIUM* heat, heat oil. Add leek slices, potato and celeriac matchstick slices, rosemary powder, pomegranate juice, salt, and pepper. Sauté until soft and translucent, *being careful not to allow vegetables to brown*. Reduce heat to *LOW*, cover, and continue cooking, stirring frequently, until all vegetables are *crisp-tender*. Turn into a serving bowl.

Serve at once onto heated salad plates.***

Yields 6 servings
adequate for 4 people

MOLDOVAN CELERIAC APPETIZER SALAD (cont'd)

Notes: *Rosemary powder can easily be made by grinding dried rosemary using a SPICE and COFFEE GRINDER. I like to use rosemary powder because the flavor distribution is more uniform.

**When fresh pomegranates are available, use 2 tablespoons of the pomegranate seeds with juice drained from the cut pomegranate.

***Try to consume this salad at one meal; leftovers discolor unpleasantly.

This recipe can be halved or doubled, when required.

1/6 SERVING – PROTEIN = 0.6 g.; FAT = 1.9 g.; CARBOHYDRATE = 6.6 g.; CALORIES = 41; CALORIES FROM FAT = 42%

CHILI BEAN SOUP
TPT - about 7 hours and 10 minutes;
2 hours = soaking period

When I was a little girl, my dad taught me to add chili sauce to navy bean soup. The soup became transformed to me; suddenly it was not just lunch anymore! On a trip to Washington as a teenager, we, of course, lunched on the United States Senate Bean Soup in the visitor's cafeteria after witnessing the convening of the Senate by the vice-president and I remember watching visitors pound ketchup into the famous soup. It made me giggle and wish I had had the nerve to recommend the more powerful condiment. The following recipe evolved from the flavor combination preserved in my memory, although the chili sauce which I remember was homemade and home-canned by my maternal grandmother. Moldovan cooks often add milk or cream to their puréed bean soup but this vegan version is still my favorite.

1 cup dry Navy beans, pea beans, *or* Great Northern beans
2 cups water

10 cups water
3 medium potatoes—peeled and diced

3 tablespoons butter
1 large onion—chopped

2 tablespoons tomato paste
3/4 cup commercial *chili* sauce
1 bay leaf—broken*
1/4 teaspoon freshly ground black pepper, or to taste

Rinse dry beans in several changes of water. Remove and discard any of poor quality. Place in a saucepan with the 2 cupfuls water. Bring to the boil over *MEDIUM-HIGH* heat, reduce heat, and simmer for 5 minutes. Cover tightly and allow to stand for 2 hours at room temperature. Drain thoroughly.

Transfer drained beans to a large kettle. Add the 10 cupfuls water and diced potatoes. Bring to the boil over *MEDIUM-HIGH* heat. Reduce heat to *LOW*, cover tightly, and allow to simmer for 2 hours.

In a skillet set over *MEDIUM* heat, combine butter and chopped onion. Sauté until onion is soft and translucent, *being careful not to allow onions to brown.*

When beans and potatoes have completed the preliminary cooking period, add sautéed onion with butter, tomato paste, *chili* sauce, broken bay leaf, and black pepper. Allow to simmer for an additional 2 hours, or until beans are very tender.

Remove and discard bay leaf pieces.

Using an electric blender or a food processor fitted with steel knife, purée soup in small batches until smooth. Press through a sieve into a clean kettle. Thin with water, if necessary.

Bring to the boil over *MEDIUM-HIGH* heat. Taste and adjust seasoning and consistency, if necessary.

Turn into heated soup tureen and serve into heated soup bowls.

Yields about 12 cupfuls

Notes: *The bay leaf pieces are most easily recovered if secured inside a tea ball during the simmering process.

***CHILI* BEAN SOUP** (cont'd)

Although this recipe can be halved, this soup freezes well. Retrieving a container of this terrific broth from the freezer can be the beginning of a meal since it is excellent base for hearty vegetable soups.

Small *pasta* of choice can be added. A mixture of shapes can be fun for children—*ditali*, *maruzzine* (tiny or baby shells), elbows, bows, half twists, *radiatore*, etc. Add 1 cupful *cooked pasta* to the 12-cup recipe.

> 1/12 SERVING of *CHILI* BEAN SOUP BASE –
> PROTEIN = 4.3 g.; FAT = 3.1 g.; CARBOHYDRATE = 18.8 g.;
> CALORIES = 117; CALORIES FROM FAT = 24%

> 1/12 SERVING of *CHILI* BEAN SOUP WITH *PASTA* –
> PROTEIN = 4.9 g.; FAT = 3.2 g.; CARBOHYDRATE = 22.2 g.;
> CALORIES = 134; CALORIES FROM FAT = 21%

MOLDOVAN PURÉED VEGETABLE SOUP WITH SOUR CREAM
Supa de Zarzavat cu Smantana

TPT - 1 hour and 21 minutes

How often have you heard, "Oh, I'm not really very hungry. A cup of soup will do." and your instinct is to nourish? Puréed soups are deceptively hearty and nutritious. The convenience of frozen mixed vegetables and canned tomatoes brings a whole different feeling to the loving labor of soup making. This soup is a nutritious family favorite which I have often served as a first course for a more formal dinner. Moldovans include parsley root in their vegetable soup, which you may or may not be able to find. The addition of a couple of handfuls of parsley leaves and stems not only fulfills Moldovan tradition but it gives the soup a fresh and very enjoyable flavor.

6 cups VEGETABLE STOCK FROM SOUP *[see index]* **or other vegetarian stock of choice**
4 cups *frozen* mixed vegetables—carrots, peas, green and lima beans, and corn
1 cup well-rinsed and coarsely chopped parsley leaves and stems
2 medium potatoes—peeled and diced
1 cup canned, *diced* tomatoes

2 tablespoons chopped, fresh dillweed

Salt, to taste
Freshly ground black pepper, to taste

1/2 cup *fat-free* dairy sour cream

In a large kettle set over *MEDIUM-HIGH* heat, combine stock, frozen vegetable mixture, parsley leaves and stems, diced potatoes, and diced tomatoes. Allow to come to the boil. Reduce heat to *LOW-MEDIUM* and allow to simmer for 1 hour.

Add chopped dillweed.

Using an electric blender or a food processor fitted with steel knife, purée soup in small batches until smooth. Press through a sieve into a clean kettle. Return to heat and allow to heat through.

Taste and season with salt and black pepper.* Turn into a heated soup tureen.

Serve into heated soup plates. Garnish with about 1 tablespoonful of sour cream. Pass sour cream to accommodate individual tastes.

Yields about 8 cupfuls

Notes: *At this point, the soup can be cooled and frozen in portions suitable to future menus.

This recipe can be halved, when required.

> 1/8 SERVING (i. e., 1 cupful) –
> PROTEIN = 5.3 g.; FAT = 0.5 g.; CARBOHYDRATE = 21.9 g.;
> CALORIES = 137; CALORIES FROM FAT = 3%

MOLDOVAN BEETROOT SALAD WITH GARLIC – MAYONNAISE DRESSING
Salata de Sfecia

TPT - 2 hours;
1 hour = flavor development period

Beets in the root cellar represent a security in the winter. Soups and salads of infinite variation can bring the humble beetroot to the table. Now that we do not dismiss the beet as simply a vegetable but instead as a superior source of brain nutrition, some repertoires will need updating. This simple Moldovan salad is a deceptive nutritional powerhouse . . . beets, garlic, and walnuts, too.

3 medium beetroots with root intact and 2-inches of leaf stem attached

GARLIC – MAYONNAISE DRESSING:
    2 garlic cloves—*very finely* chopped
    1/4 cup *calorie-reduced or light mayonnaise with olive oil*
    1 tablespoon freshly squeezed lemon juice

1/2 cup chopped, *toasted preservative-free* walnuts

In a large kettle, cook beets in boiling water until tender—about 20-30 minutes. Drain. Rinse in *cold* water until they can be handled. Cut off root end and stem end. Slip off skins. Rinse well and allow to cool to room temperature. When cool, grate beets. Set aside briefly.

In a mixing bowl, combine *very finely* chopped garlic, mayonnaise, and lemon juice. Mix thoroughly.

Add grated beets and chopped, *toasted* walnuts. Fold beets and walnuts into garlic–mayonnaise dressing. Turn into a serving bowl. Refrigerate for at least 1 hour to allow for flavor development.

Serve chilled.

Yields 6 servings
adequate for 4 people

Notes   This recipe can be halved, when required.

If preferred, beets can be baked instead of boiled *[see index for technique.]* The taste is quite different.

1/6 SERVING – PROTEIN = 2.4 g.; FAT = 12.0 g.; CARBOHYDRATE = 5.0 g.;
CALORIES = 138; CALORIES FROM FAT = 78%

MOLDOVAN FRIED PEPPER, ONION, AND TOMATO SALAD WITH *MUJDEI*
Salata de Pipere Prăjit au Mujdei

TPT - 43 minutes;
30 minutes = refrigeration period

The aroma of frying peppers and onions will usually elicit "I guess we are having Italian fried peppers and eggs tonight," but Italian kitchens are not the only places where this aroma attracts attention. Here that wonderful combination combines with chopped tomatoes and is chilled to provide a versatile dish for summer or winter that is popular in Moldova. Italian frying peppers (Cubanella) are my choice for this dish simply because they, as their name implies, have been bred for frying. However, strips of red, yellow or orange peppers make colorful additions.

1 1/2 tablespoons *extra-virgin* olive oil
4 large Italian frying peppers (Cubanella)
    —cored, seeded, and cut into strips
1 medium onion—*thinly* sliced

1/4 cup canned, *diced* tomatoes
Salt, to taste

1 tablespoon *finely* snipped fresh dillweed

1/4 cup GARLIC SAUCE IN THE STYLE OF
    MOLDOVA AND ROMANIA *(Mujdei)* *[see recipe which follows]*

MOLDOVAN FRIED PEPPER, ONION, AND TOMATO SALAD WITH *MUJDEI* (cont'd)

In a large skillet set over *LOW-MEDIUM* heat, heat oil. Add strips of pepper and *thinly* sliced onion. Cook stirring frequently until both the peppers and onions are soft.

Add tomatoes. Season with salt. Turn into shallow serving bowl. Refrigerate for 30 minutes.

Sprinkle with *finely* snipped dillweed.

Serve chilled or at room temperature with *mujdei*.

Yields 6 servings
adequate for 4 people

Note: This recipe can be halved, when required.

1/6 SERVING – PROTEIN = 1.6 g.; FAT = 3.5 g.; CARBOHYDRATE = 6.6 g.; CALORIES = 70; CALORIES FROM FAT = 45%

GARLIC SAUCE IN THE STYLE OF MOLDOVA AND ROMANIA
Mujdei

TPT - 11 minutes

Garlic and other members of the onion family are natural cardio-protective foods due to their production of sulfur-containing molecules which, when picked up by our red blood cells and converted to hydrogen sulfide gas, expand blood vessels. These vegetables are often touted as nature's "roto-rooter" system. In addition to its role as a facilitator of plaque removal, garlic improves iron metabolism and is an excellent source of selenium. Mujdei is strong and assertive but absolutely essential to the cooking of Moldova and Romania. If you are a garlic lover, you will swoon over this adornment; if you are not a garlic lover, you will endure the breaths of your dining companions or you can join in and soften the effect with sour cream.

4 garlic cloves

1/2 teaspoon salt

1 tablespoon sunflower oil
Freshly ground black pepper, to taste

1/4 cup *reduced-fat* dairy sour cream

Using a garlic press, press garlic cloves into a small bowl.

Add salt and using the pestle from your mortar and pestle set, grind salt into garlic purée until a paste is formed.

Add sunflower oil and black pepper. Beat well until well-integrated and fluffy. Turn into a small serving dish. Refrigerate until ready to serve.

Spoon sour cream into a matching serving dish.

Serve the *mujdei* and the sour cream, allowing diners to take some of each to temper the garlic to their liking.

Yields 12 servings
adequate for 6 people

Notes: This recipe can be halved, when required.

Some people add the sour cream to the *mujdei* and serve it already mixed. I prefer to allow for preferences.

1/12 SERVING (depending, of course, on how much sour cream is added) –
PROTEIN = 0.8 g.; FAT = 3.1 g.; CARBOHYDRATE = 1.3 g.;
CALORIES = 37; CALORIES FROM FAT = 75%

Europe–**Moldova**

MOLDOVAN *SOUFFLÉ* WITH GRATED CHEESE
Sufleu

TPT - 1 hour and 7 minutes

Grated ewe's milk cheese gives this soufflé a taste very different from the French soufflés to which most of us are accustomed. The dish may be different in this respect but it still is creamy, light, and fragile. It too does not wait for belated diners; diners had better be at the table waiting for it to appear, gloriously risen and browned from the oven.

2 tablespoons dry breadcrumbs

4 egg whites

1/3 cup butter
3 tablespoons unbleached white flour

2 cups skimmed milk

3/4 cup grated ewe's milk cheese, such as
   pecorino Romano*
4 egg yolks—well-beaten

Preheat oven to 400 degrees F. Prepare a 2-quart soufflé dish by spraying with non-stick lecithin spray coating. Coat with breadcrumbs, discarding any extra.

Using an electric mixer fitted with *grease-free* beaters or by hand, using a *grease-free* wire whisk, beat egg whites in a *grease-free* bowl until *stiff*, but *not dry*. Set aside until required.

In a saucepan set over *LOW-MEDIUM* heat, melt butter. Add flour and cook, stirring constantly, until a roux is formed, *being careful not to allow the mixture to brown*. Remove from heat. Gradually, *tablespoonful by tablespoonful at first*, beat the milk into the *roux* until smooth.

Return to the heat. *Increase heat to MEDIUM.* Cook, stirring constantly, until it begins to thicken.

While stirring constantly, add cheese and well-beaten egg yolks. Continue to cook until again smooth and thickened. Remove from heat.

Whisk-fold beaten egg whites *gently*, but *thoroughly*, into cheese sauce. Turn into prepared soufflé dish. Place soufflé in preheated 400 degree F. oven and *immediately turn heat down to 375 degrees F. Do not open the oven door for 20 minutes.* Bake for 25 to 30 minutes, or until soufflé has risen and the top is nicely browned.

Yields 6 servings
adequate for 4 people

Note: *A grated piece of aged provolone is a good addition to this cheese mixture.

1/6 SERVING –   PROTEIN = 10.6 g.; FAT = 16.8 g.; CARBOHYDRATE = 8.3 g.
CALORIES = 228; CALORIES FROM FAT = 66%

MOLDOVAN CREAM OF WHEAT *CROQUETTES*
Crochete de Gris

TPT - 2 hours and 49 minutes;
2 hours = refrigeration period

During the Soviet Era, The Ukraine was widely referred to as "the bread basket of the Soviet Union." The Ukraine, Romania, and Moldova all share ideal climate conditions for grain production, a bounty of which the former Soviet Union took full advantage to the extent that the populations of these republics did not have enough of their own harvest to survive. Recovery of their own resources has meant revival of interesting recipes such as this. When I make these delicate croquettes, I prepare them in the morning and refrigerate them until dinnertime. If allowed to set, they are less likely to crumble in the skillet.

MOLDOVAN CREAM OF WHEAT *CROQUETTES* (cont'd)

2 cups skimmed milk
1 cup Cream of Wheat cereal *or* farina

2 teaspoons *cold* butter
1/4 cup *fat-free* pasteurized eggs (the equivalent of 1 egg)
1/4 teaspoon salt

Unbleached white flour for preparing breadboard surface

2 tablespoons butter
2 tablespoons *extra virgin* olive oil

In a saucepan set over *MEDIUM* heat, bring milk to just below the boiling point.

While stirring, sprinkle in Cream of Wheat or farina. Cook, stirring frequently, until it thickens. Remove from heat.

Add *cold* butter. Stir until melted. Add pasteurized eggs. Stir until thoroughly mixed into wheat mixture. Add salt. Again, stir well.

Lightly coat a bread board with flour. Make sausage-shaped croquettes using about 1 tablespoonful of the thick, cooked farina mixture. Place on a platter and refrigerate for at least 2 hours.

In a non-stick-coated skillet set over *MEDIUM* heat, combine the 2 tablespoonfuls of butter and the oil. Fry *croquettes* in batches, until golden brown. Transfer to a heated platter.

Serve at once.

Yields 26 *croquettes*
adequate for 6 people

Note: This recipe can be halved or doubled, when required.

1/26 SERVING (per *croquette*, exclusive of flour) –
PROTEIN = 2.5 g.; FAT = 2.2 g.; CARBOHYDRATE = 12.7 g.;
CALORIES = 82; CALORIES FROM FAT = 24%

MOLDOVAN FRIED CABBAGE WITH TOMATOES
Varza Calita
TPT - 14 minutes

The cabbage finds a strong reception on every continent. As we traveled the world for this project we were surprised at how many times we found ourselves retrieving a cabbage from the vegetable drawer to round out a menu. We have access to the sweetest organic cabbages now which are in no way like the stale old, root-cellar cabbages of my youth. Cabbages, harvested in October, will keep straight through until the spring in the refrigerator so their usefulness is recognized even by cooks who know nothing about the root cellars or the winter food shortages of the 1930s and '40s.

2 tablespoons safflower *or* sunflower oil
6 cups *finely* shredded green or white cabbage
1/2 cup *thinly* sliced onion
1/2 teaspoon salt

1 large bay leaf—halved
5 whole black peppercorns
1 large garlic clove—*very finely* chopped
1 teaspoon crushed, dried oregano
2-3 tablespoons water

1 cup canned, *diced* tomatoes

In a large skillet set over *MEDIUM* heat, heat oil. Add shredded cabbage, onion slices, and salt. Cook, stirring frequently, until onion softens. Reduce heat to *LOW*.

Add bay leaf pieces, whole peppercorns, *very finely* chopped garlic. Cover and allow to cook, stirring frequently until the cabbage is soft. Add water, *tablespoonful by tablespoonful*, as needed to prevent browning.

When cabbage is done, add *diced* tomatoes. Stir to integrate. Cover again and allow to cook until all of liquid has evaporated. Turn into a heated serving dish. Remove bay leaf pieces and whole peppercorns.

Serve hot.

Yields 6 servings
adequate for 4 people

Note: This recipe can be halved, when required.

1/6 SERVING – PROTEIN = 1.9 g.; FAT = 4.7 g.; CARBOHYDRATE = 8.5 g.;
CALORIES = 78; CALORIES FROM FAT = 54%

Europe – Moldova

MOLDOVAN BUTTERMILK CAKE
Prajitura cu Zer

TPT - 1 hour and 45 minutes;
30 minutes = cooling period

The Moldovan buttermilk cake is quite similar to a historic cake which is known in the United States as the Lord Baltimore Cake, also called "Gold Cake" or "Egg Yolk Cake." However, the Moldovan cake calls for whole eggs, not egg yolks, and buttermilk, not skimmed milk. I make this cake in a loaf pan instead of using round cake pans because it cuts well and slices can be topped with sauces and fruits for dessert much as one would serve pound cake.

1 1/2 cups sifted cake flour
1 1/2 cups whole wheat flour
2 1/2 teaspoons baking powder

3/4 cup (1 1/2 sticks) butter—*softened to room temperature*
3/4 cup sugar
1 cup *fat-free* pasteurized eggs (the equivalent of 4 eggs)
1 1/2 teaspoons pure vanilla extract

1 1/4 cups unsalted buttermilk

Jam, sweetened whipped cream, confectioners' sugar, *or* fruit sauce of choice

Preheat oven to 375 degrees F. Prepare two 9 x 5 x 3-inch loaf pans by coating with non-stick lecithin spray coating. Dust with cake flour.

Into a large mixing bowl, sift cake and whole wheat flours with baking powder. Set aside.

Using the electric mixer or food processor fitted with steel knife, cream butter until light and fluffy. Add sugar and continue to cream until again light and fluffy. Beat in pasteurized eggs and vanilla extract. Continue beating, at *HIGH* speed if mixer is used, *for 2 full minutes*.

Reduce mixer speed. Add sifted flours alternately with milk, beating until batter is very smooth.

Divide between prepared pans. Rap each sharply on counter top to release any large bubbles.

Bake in preheated 375 degree F. oven for 25-30 minutes, or until surface springs back when lightly touched.

Cool *completely* on wire racks before removing cakes from pans.

Serve in slices garnished with jam or whipped cream; sift confectioners' sugar over; or serve with a fruit sauces.

Yields two 9 x 5 x 3-inch loaves
of 8 slices each

Notes: *I generally use buttermilk powder which can be reconstituted for baking by adding it to water. It is a useful pantry item that eliminates a trip to the store for a quart of buttermilk and the inevitable leftover.

This recipe is easily halved but the second loaf, in this case, can be frozen for a future menu.

1/2 SERVING (i. e., per loaf exclusive of garnish) –
PROTEIN = 37.3 g.; FAT = 70.5 g.; CARBOHYDRATE = 229.1 g.;
CALORIES = 1661; CALORIES FROM FAT = 38%

1/12 SERVING (i. e., per slice exclusive of garnish) –
PROTEIN = 4.7 g.; FAT = 8.8 g.; CARBOHYDRATE = 28.6 g.;
CALORIES = 208; CALORIES FROM FAT = 38%

Europe–**Moldova**

MOLDOVAN SWEET NOODLES WITH WALNUTS
Macaroane cu Nuci

TPT - 1 hour and 21 minutes;
1 hour = chilling period

Jewish delicatessens often offer sweet noodle puddings because Central and Eastern Europeans carried their recipes and their love for these pudding to their new homes. The Polish market near my grandmother's home in Rochester, New York, prepared a sweet noodle pudding once a week and at the holidays for their customers. Noodles and pasta offer an inviting blank canvas to creative cooks. We have even found that Bangladeshi often end a meal with a sweet pasta pudding, included elsewhere in this volume. Although certainly in the European tradition, this simple Moldovan version is not baked as are most European kugels and is generously sprinkled with ground walnuts, an obvious influence borrowed from the cuisines of the Middle East to which they were exposed over the centuries.

3 quarts *boiling* water
2 cups dry, short, twisted, broad egg noodles*
1 tablespoon freshly squeezed lemon juice

3 tablespoons ground *preservative-free* walnuts
   or pecans, if preferred
3 tablespoons light cream *or* half and half*
3 tablespoons sugar
1/2 teaspoon pure vanilla extract

Ground cinnamon

In a kettle set over *MEDIUM* heat, combine *boiling* water, egg noodles, and lemon juice. Cook according to package directions. Turn into a strainer and drain well.

In a mixing bowl, combine ground walnuts, cream, sugar, and vanilla extract. Using a wooden spoon, combine thoroughly.

Add well-drained egg noodles. Toss to coat egg noodles with the walnut mixture. Turn into a serving bowl. Refrigerate for at least 1 hour. Toss two or three times during the chilling period to keep the noodles in contact with the flavored sauce.

Serve chilled.

Yields 6 servings
adequate for 4 people

Notes: *If a vegan dessert is required, choose noodles that do not contain egg and replace the cream with almond milk.

This recipe can be halved, when required.

1/6 SERVING – PROTEIN = 6.3 g.; FAT = 7.3 g.; CARBOHYDRATE = 10.8 g.;
CALORIES = 218; CALORIES FROM FAT = 30%

RANGER COOKIES

TPT - 1 hour and 5 minutes

These are wonderfully substantial, old-fashioned cookies, full of good things, with a hardy "glad these are good-for-me" taste. The cookie that has appeared on our Christmas cookie platter for more than fifty years and for decades before that on the cookie platter presented by my mother, is a favorite cookie in Moldova. The versions shared with me by Moldovan cooks substituted crispy rice cereal for the multi-grain cereal flakes I prefer.

1 cup unbleached white flour
1 cup whole wheat flour
1 1/2 teaspoons baking powder

1 cup (2 sticks) butter
1/2 cup white sugar
1/2 cup firmly packed *light* brown sugar

1/2 cup pasteurized eggs (the equivalent
   of 2 eggs)
1 teaspoon pure vanilla extract

1 cup high-fiber cereal flake mixture
   —*preferably without preservatives and*
   sugar
1 cup quick-cooking rolled oats (*not instant*)
1 cup dried, shredded *unsweetened* and
   preservative-free coconut
1/2 cup chopped *preservative-free* walnuts

RANGER COOKIES (cont'd)

Preheat oven to 325 degrees F. Prepare cookie sheets by lining them with culinary parchment paper.*

Sift white and whole wheat flours with baking powder. Set aside.

Using the electric mixer or food processor fitted with steel knife, cream butter until light and fluffy. Add sugars and continue to cream until again light and fluffy.

Add pasteurized eggs and vanilla extract. Beat until smooth.

Gradually beat in sifted dry ingredients until a smooth dough results.

Turn into a large mixing bowl or kettle and, using a wooden spoon or rubber spatula, fold in cereal flakes, rolled oats, shredded coconut, and chopped nuts until well-mixed.**

Drop by teaspoonfuls onto prepared cookie sheets, spacing at least 2 inches between each.

Bake in preheated 325 degree F. oven for about 14-17 minutes. Cool completely on wire racks. Store in airtight containers or in plastic bags.***

Yields about 65 medium-sized cookies

1/65 SERVING (i. e., per cookie) –
PROTEIN = 1.2 g.*; FAT = 4.3 g.*; CARBOHYDRATE = 9.1 g.*;
CALORIES = 79*; CALORIES FROM FAT = 49%*

*Since the food values for cereals vary, these figures are approximate.

Notes: *Culinary parchment paper for baking is available in food specialty and housewares stores, and from mail order firms, where it is now even available as an unbleached, environmentally friendly product. Rarely in the United States, unlike in Europe, do you find it on the shelves of small grocery stores. Lining baking sheets and pans with parchment paper, instead of greasing, buttering, or oiling, not only protects your baking sheets from scorching, it encourages the even browning of cookies, scones, cakes, etc.

**Unbaked dough may be frozen most successfully.

***Baked cookies, also, may be frozen.

This tends to be an unwieldy batter if doubled. It is better to make two separate batches.

Montenegro

Montenegro was among the small modern-day republics referred to by both the Greeks and the Romans as Illyria. By the fifth century AD, Slavic tribes settled in this area of Europe that we call the Balkans. Subsequently, the area became part of a Serbian kingdom known as Duklja. Until 1042 AD Duklja was under the rule of the Byzantine Empire. Montenegro maintained its independence until the twelfth century when it was absorbed into the Serbian Empire as the province of Zeta. In 1499 the area was conquered by the Ottoman Turks who controlled the Balkans until the seventeenth century when in 1697 a theocratic Serbian–Orthodox government was established in Montenegro under the House of Petrovic–Njegos with overarching rule emanating from the Venetian Republic. This government structure survived until the end of World War I at which time Montenegro was bundled into the Kingdoms of Serbs, Croats, and Slovenes. In 1929 the politically-created state, created by the Treaty of Versailles, was officially named Yugoslavia.

Yugoslavia was invaded by Fascist Italy in 1941 and subsequently by Nazi Germany. In 1944 Yugoslavia was liberated by partisans led by Josip Broz Tito, who would later head the government as "President for Life." The monarchy was not re-established, instead a socialist federal republic was formed combining the Socialist Republics of Bosnia and Herzegovina, Croatia, Macedonia, Montenegro, Slovenia, and Serbia including the Socialist Autonomous Provinces of Kosovo and Vojvodina. Although Marshall Tito died in 1980, this union struggled on until Yugoslavia began to dissolve when Croatia and Slovenia declared independence in June 1991. Macedonia followed in September of the same year; Bosnia–Herzegovina declared their combined statehood in March 1992; Montenegro and Serbia became independent in May 2006 forming the combined state of Serbia and Montenegro; and, finally, Kosovo, although officially recognized by only a few nations, declared independence in February 2008. Montenegro declared its withdrawal from the combined statehood with Serbia in June 2006. In 2011 the House of Petrovic–Njegos was reinstalled with a ceremonial function and the royal standard of King Nikola I was adopted, with some modifications, as the official flag of Montenegro.

Today this ancient land, slightly smaller than Connecticut but with only about one-fifth of the population, is a young nation trying to make its way forward in the twenty-first century. The economy is essentially service-oriented at this point but the emphasis on education and on attracting foreign investment have and will profit Montenegro.

Montenegrin cuisine is an easy cuisine to visit; so many of the dishes are familiar, as you will note in the menu that follows. Montenegrins have adopted, perhaps better described as preserved, culinary treasures from their historical contacts. They have woven these into a unique unity that recognizes good food. You move easily from dishes that can be identified with those of the Middle East, Greece, Italy, Hungary, Romania, and Austria to those of other Balkan countries. Be forewarned, however, there is a great emphasis on meat and fish so it is not always easy to find a vegetarian meal in Montenegro.

Europe – Montenegro

Marinated Dried Cheese and Olive Appetizer

~

Chowder of Vegetables and Fine Noodles
Čorba

Cream of Mushroom Soup

~

Tomato and Cucumber Salad with Grated Cheese in the Style of the Balkans
Rajca Salata od Krastava

Shredded Lettuce and Scallions *Vinaigrette*
with Grated Cheese

~~~~~~~~~~~~~~~~~~~~~

Collard Greens and Kale with Potatoes and Carrots
Raštan

Whole Wheat Spaghetti, Buckwheat, or Soba Noodles
with *Feta* Cheese, Olive Oil, and Black Pepper

~~~~~~~~~~

Slow Cooker *Polenta*
Cecvara

Steamed Whole Green Beans	or	Oven-Roasted Mixed Vegetables
		Sataraš

~~~~~~~~~~

Scalloped Cabbage with Cream
Peceni Kupus

and

Sautéed Vegetarian Meatballs	or	Vegetarian Burgers
Ćufte		*Pljeskavica*

Mashed Potatoes	or	Baked Potato Halves with Yogurt or Cheese
Pire od Krumpira		*Krtoli*

~~~~~~~~~~~~~~~~~~~~~

Rice Pudding	with	Pomegranate Syrup
Oris na Vareniku		*Sok od Sipka*

Turkish-Style *Phyllo* Pastry
Baklava

Jelly Doughnuts
Krofne

~

Turkish Coffee	or	American Coffee	or	Mineral Water
Turska Kava		*Americki Aparat*		*Kisjela Voda*

Europe–**Montenegro**

MONTENEGRIN MARINATED DRIED CHEESE AND OLIVE APPETIZER

TPT - 48 hours and 16 minutes;
48 hours = *feta* marination period

Montenegrins marinate feta cheese just as do the Greeks but unlike the Greek product, you have to go to Montenegro to sample their version or make it yourself.

10 ounces *feta* cheese—cut into cubes
4-inch sprig of fresh rosemary—well washed
1 teaspoon crushed, dried marjoram
1 teaspoon crushed, dried basil
1/2 teaspoon ground mixed peppercorns—red, black, and white—or to taste
1 cup *extra virgin* olive oil

Pinch rosemary powder *[see index]*
1/2 jar (about 5 ounce ounces) pitted *Kalamata* ripe olives—well drained and sliced
Freshly ground black pepper, to taste

Whole grain crackers *or* dry toasts

Sterilize a quart canning jar. Also sterilize a lid and a sealing ring.

Put the *feta* cheese cubes into the jar. Add rosemary sprig, crushed marjoram and basil, and ground mixed peppercorns. Pour olive oil into jar, adding more if necessary to cover the cheese cubes. Seal tightly. *Gently* roll the jar to distribute the seasoning elements and the olive oil. Refrigerate for at least 48 hours. Roll the jar periodically to insure even flavoring.*

When ready to proceed with this appetizer, drain the cheese through a sieve. Remove and discard rosemary sprig and peppercorns. *Reserve the olive oil to use in salad dressings or to drizzle over appetizers or cheese or to start another batch of marinated cheese.*

In a small serving bowl, combine the well-drained marinated *feta* cheese cubes, rosemary powder, olive slices, and additional black pepper. Toss gently. Refrigerate until required.

Place the small serving bowl on a large plate, surround it with crackers or toasts, and serve. Allow diners to scoop the appetizer mixture with a slotted spoon onto a cracker.

Yields 12 servings
adequate for 6 people

Notes: *Refrigerated, this will keep for several weeks.

I prefer to use dried herbs for this appetizer but you can use fresh herbs in season.

This recipe can be halved or doubled, when required.

1/12 SERVING (exclusive of crackers or toasts) –
PROTEIN = 4.8 g.; FAT = 9.0 g.; CARBOHYDRATE = 1.8 g.;
CALORIES = 107; CALORIES FROM FAT = 75%

MONTENEGRIN CHOWDER OF VEGETABLES AND FINE NOODLES

Corba

TPT - 47 minutes

Montenegrin soups are generally chuck-full of meats and vegetables such as the unusual chowder filled with nettles. Shepherd's cream of mushroom soup is more of a soup, as we know it, than a chowder but it is thick with mushrooms and very satisfying. Soup in Montenegro is a delicious way to nourish the soul and the body. The soup that follows is thinned a bit to Western taste and, of course, meat has been omitted, but I assure you it will satisfy.

1 tablespoon butter
2 teaspoons *extra virgin* olive oil
1 medium carrot—scraped or pared and diced
1 medium potato—peeled and diced
1/2 cup diced yellow summer squash *or* zucchini, if preferred
1/4 cup *finely* chopped red pepper
1/4 cup *finely* chopped onion
1 large garlic clove—*very finely* chopped

1/2 cup canned *or* cooked red kidney beans
1/2 teaspoon crushed dried basil
5 cups VEGETABLE STOCK FROM SOUP *[see index]* or vegetarian stock of choice
1 1/2 cups liquid drained from canned tomatoes —*not* purée and *not* tomato juice
Salt, to taste
Freshly ground black pepper, to taste
2 cups (about 8 ounces) *fine* egg noodles

MONTENEGRIN CHOWDER OF VEGETABLES AND FINE NOODLES (cont'd)

In a small kettle set over *LOW-MEDIUM* heat, heat butter and oil. Add diced carrot, potato, and yellow summer squash, *finely* chopped red pepper and onion, and *very finely* chopped garlic. Sauté until onion begins to soften, *being careful not to allow any of the vegetables to brown.*

Add kidney beans, crushed basil, vegetable stock, and tomato liquid. Season with salt and pepper. Stir. Simmer for about 30 minutes.

Raise heat to MEDIUM and allow the soup base to come to the boil. Add noodles and cook as directed on the package. Turn into a heated tureen.

Serve into heated soup bowls. Refrigerate leftovers. Reheat gently and thin with more stock, if necessary.

Yields 7 cupfuls

Note: This recipe can be doubled, when required.

1/7 SERVING (i. e., per cupful) –
PROTEIN = 7.2 g.; FAT = 4.4 g.; CARBOHYDRATE = 31.0 g.;
CALORIES = 192; CALORIES FROM FAT = 21%

TOMATO AND CUCUMBER SALAD WITH GRATED CHEESE IN THE STYLE OF THE BALKANS
Raja Salata od Krastana
TPT - 4 minutes

Garden-fresh tomatoes and cucumbers often just become unceremonious additions to a tossed salad and that sweet, sun-ripened elegance is compromised. These wonderful summer moments should be celebrated, in our opinion. Montenegrins keep it simple and all that elegant flavor just melts in your mouth. This is actually my first thought when I go to our farmers' market very early on a summer's morning. The Mennonite farmers arrive with tomatoes, cucumbers, corn, and arm-filling heads of lettuces picked at first light that day and this wonderful produce is snapped up by the savvy in a couple of hours.

3 large ripe tomatoes—well-washed, cored, and *thinly* sliced
2 medium cucumbers—scored with a fork, if unwaxed *or* peeled and scored, if waxed, and *thinly* sliced
3 tablespoons grated *pecorino Romano* cheese

On a chilled platter or plate, arrange tomato slices in a spiral pattern. Arrange cucumber slices over the top of the tomatoes, repeating the spiral pattern. Sprinkle grated cheese generously over. Refrigerate until ready to serve.

Yields 6 servings
adequate for 4 people

Note: This recipe can be halved or doubled or prepared as individual salads, when required.

1/6 SERVING – PROTEIN = 2.4 g.; FAT = 1.3 g.; CARBOHYDRATE = 3.8 g.;
CALORIES = 36; CALORIES FROM FAT = 33%

COLLARD GREENS AND KALE WITH POTATOES AND CARROTS
Raštan
TPT - 22 minutes

Kale and collard greens, known as "raštan" in Montenegro, are so popular in the Balkans that this dish is simply named "raštan." The recipe for this really quite tasty, folic acid-rich dish changes from kitchen to kitchen. This is our version of it which, more often than not, is chosen as the vegetable to accompany a pot of baked beans.

COLLARD GREENS AND KALE WITH POTATOES AND CARROTS (cont'd)

3 cups *boiling* water
1/2 cup diced carrot
1/2 cup diced potato

1 tablespoon *extra virgin* olive oil
1 tablespoon butter

1/4 cup *finely* chopped onion
2 garlic cloves—*very finely* chopped

3 cups chopped collard greens—*well-rinsed*
3 cups chopped kale—tough petioles removed and *well-rinsed*

Freshly ground mixed peppercorns—red, black, and white—to taste

In a saucepan set over *MEDIUM* heat, combine *boiling* water and diced carrot and potato. Cook until *crisp-tender*—about 5 minutes. Drain. Set aside until required.

In a large skillet set over *MEDIUM* heat, combine oil and butter. Add *finely* chopped onion and *very finely* chopped garlic. Sauté until onion is soft and translucent, *being careful to allow neither the onion nor the garlic to brown.*

Add chopped collard greens and kale. Sauté until greens have wilted.

Add cooked carrot and potato pieces. Season generously with ground mixed peppercorns. Cook, stirring frequently, for about 5 minutes. Turn out onto a heated platter.

Serve hot.

Yields 6 servings
adequate for 4 people

Note: This recipe can be halved or doubled, when required.

1/6 SERVING – PROTEIN = 2.8 g.; FAT = 4.5 g.; CARBOHYDRATE = 11.4 g.;
CALORIES = 91; CALORIES FROM FAT = 44%

SLOW COOKER *POLENTA* IN THE STYLE OF MONTENEGRO
Cecvara

TPT - 6 hours (depending on setting) and 20 minutes;
2 hours = chilling period:
[slow cooker: about 4 hours on LOW*]

Cecvara is a most unusual version of polenta in that cheese and sour cream are added to the water as the corn meal is cooked to produce a creamy polenta like no other. It is popular in Serbia and in Montenegro especially at Christmas. The slow cooker method is a remarkable tool on a busy day and uses a whole lot less energy making polenta the traditional way. I find it convenient to make it when I have time and chill it in a loaf pan overnight or for even a day or two to accommodate our schedule.

1 tablespoon butter

1/8 teaspoon sweet paprika
Several dashes ground red pepper (cayenne)

3 cups *boiling* water
3/4 cup diced *low-moisture, part-skimmed milk mozzarella* cheese
1/2 cup *fat-free* dairy sour cream
1 cup fine yellow corn meal—*masa harina / amarilla fina*
1 tablespoon butter—*melted*
1/2 teaspoon salt

1 tablespoon butter

Using 1 tablespoonful of butter, coat the bowl of the slow cooker.

Sprinkle the paprika and ground red pepper (cayenne) into the bowl.

Preheat slow cooker to *HIGH*.

Add *boiling* water, diced *mozzarella*, sour cream, corn meal, the 1 tablespoon *melted* butter, and salt. Stir well. Cover and cook on *LOW* for 4 hours, stirring occasionally.

Spoon into a 7 x 3 x 2-inch non-stick-coated loaf pan which has been coated with non-stick lecithin spray coating. Refrigerate for at least 2 hours. Turn out onto bread board. Slice as many 1/4-inch slices as you will need. Replace loaf pan, covered with plastic wrap, into the refrigerator.

SLOW COOKER *POLENTA* IN THE STYLE OF MONTENEGRO (cont'd)

In a skillet set over *MEDIUM* heat, melt remaining tablespoonful of butter. Fry *polenta* slices until browned. Using a spatula, transfer to a heated serving platter.

Serve at once.

Yields 12 servings
adequate for 6 people

Notes: *The four-hour cooking period produces a texture which we prefer. Depending on your slow cooker, this time may be too long or too short and the cooking period will need to be adjusted.

This recipe can be doubled, when required.

1/12 SERVING (exclusive of the butter required for frying) –
PROTEIN = 4.8 g.; FAT = 4.1 g.; CARBOHYDRATE = 17.3 g;
CALORIES = 121; CALORIES FROM FAT = 30%

MONTENEGRIN SCALLOPED CABBAGE WITH CREAM
Peceni Kupus

TPT - 1 hour and 11 minutes

My family often prepared scalloped vegetables. It was a way to "gussy up" a simple vegetable while using up bread before the next baking day. Apples, eggplant, corn, onions, and tomatoes often appeared on our table topped with buttered breadcrumbs. Cabbage can also be prepared in this way, although my mother much preferred to make salads of the sturdy, crisp cabbages that wintered over so well in our northern climate. Recipes for vegetables of the cabbage family abound in the Balkans. Cabbage goes into stews and soups; it is braised, boiled, and baked. Montenegrins and Serbians use either evaporated milk or cream to prepare this baked side dish. The cabbage becomes soft and creamy and the breadcrumbs add a crunchy contrast.

1/4 cup butter
1 cup dry breadcrumbs

6 cups *finely* shredded white *or* green cabbage
  —well-rinsed and well-dried
1 cup light cream *or* half and half
1/2 cup *two-percent* milk
Salt, to taste
Freshly ground black pepper, to taste

Preheat oven to 325 degrees F. Prepare a 2-quart soufflé or other oven-to-table baking dish by coating with non stick lecithin spray coating.

In a skillet set over *LOW* heat, melt butter. Add breadcrumbs. Stir constantly until breadcrumbs have absorbed the butter. Remove from heat and set aside until required.

Put *finely* shredded cabbage into the prepared baking dish. Pour milk and cream over. Season with salt and pepper. Evenly scatter breadcrumbs over the top. Cover. Bake in preheated 325 degree F. oven for 30 minutes. Remove cover and continue to bake for about 20-25 minutes more, or until breadcrumbs are lightly browned.

Serve at once.

Yields 6 servings
adequate for 4 people

Note: This recipe can be halved or doubled, when required.

1/6 SERVING – PROTEIN = 5.5 g.; FAT = 12.2 g.; CARBOHYDRATE = 23.5 g.;
CALORIES = 222; CALORIES FROM FAT = 49%

The Netherlands

As a child, The Netherlands was a far-away land of wooden shoes, ice skates, windmills, tulips, wonderful cheeses, and the home of the fable of the boy who stuck his finger in the dike to save his country from being flooded over by the sea but this, one of three countries often referred to as the Low Countries, has a long and complicated national history. The Netherlands occupies that triangle formed by the delta of the Rhine, the Meuse, the Scheldt, and the Ems rivers in an area which extends from French Gravelines and Dunkirk north to the area of Dutch Delfzijl and German Eastern Frisia and then southeast to Luxembourg and French Thionville. Belgic tribes were replaced by Germanic tribes in the fourth and fifth century AD and by the eighth century much of this area was part of Francia. After the death of Charlemagne, Francia was divided among his three grandsons with the Low Countries becoming part of Middle Francia and ruled by Lothair I. The Netherlands did become a population and trading center in the twelfth century but through the years, after the death of Lothair I and through the period of the Middle Ages, the land now occupied by The Netherlands was invaded and occupied by many seeking to expand their influence, reach the sea through the Low Countries, and access trading routes. By 1519 the region was ruled by Charles V, Holy Roman Emperor and King of Spain, part of what was known as the Seventeen Provinces of the Netherlands. In 1568 the struggle to remove the yoke of Spanish domination began. Known as The Eighty Years' War it resulted in the formation of the Dutch Republic in 1581, which lasted until 1795. During this period, in 1614, Dutch influence reached our shores with the founding of New Amsterdam.

Regarded by some as the first capitalist nation in the world, The Netherlands boasted the first full-time stock exchange. Insurance and retirement funds were established and traded. With this capitalism came the famous tulip mania of 1636-1637, and asset-inflation bubbles and the patterns of economic booms and busts with which we are so familiar.

In 1795, after William V of Orange fled to England, the French Republic designated The Netherlands as the Batavian Republic and from 1806 to 1810 it was governed by Louis Bonaparte in an effort by Napoléon Bonaparte to control the population living in what was then known as the Kingdom of Holland. It was absorbed into the French Empire in 1810, after the abdication of King Louis Bonaparte, and the succession of his five-year-old son Napoléon Louis Bonaparte.

In 1815 the country was declared the United Kingdom of the Netherlands by the Congress of Vienna. Belgium, which was part of the original kingdom, rebelled and declared independence in 1830 and in 1890 Luxembourg also became independent. Today The Netherlands is a parliamentary democracy under a constitutional monarch. To safeguard the population, twenty-one percent of whom actually live below sea level, from encroachment by the Zees and the ocean beyond, a hugely important system of polder and dikes has been built. Systematic reclamation of land from the sea has resulted in a present-day Netherlands in which twenty percent of its land area is under water and fifty percent of the country actually lies less than one meter above sea level.

Europe–The Netherlands

An amazing number of words, too many to list here, that we take for granted as English have their origins in what has become known as Holland Dutch, rather than Pennsylvania Dutch which, of course, is, more accurately, German *Deutch* —

With all the nations that came and went through this delta one would think that there would have been influences upon the cuisine but little is seen except in the areas close to France. Donut franchises and pancake houses, not withstanding, residual food influences from Dutch Colonial America are less obvious in our twenty-first century America but as I have traveled through these cuisines I have seen a Dutch colonial influence in Southeast Asia and the Caribbean. More dramatically, there is a change in what the Dutch now eat; their cuisine is evolving and they are absorbing the tastes and variety from their former colonies and the other areas of the world in which they still trade. The Dutch menu that follows is, as far as I can determine, unencumbered by extraneous influences.

Eggs in White Sauce or Kampen Sturgeon

~

Black Bean Soup

Grauwe Eruten of Carucijersoep

Gerkins (a Dutch word)

Cheese Soup

Soep me Melk en Edam

~~~~~~~~~~~~~~~~~~~~~

Sweet and Sour Cabbage

Steamed Parsnips with Honey – Mustard Glaze

Boiled Potatoes

~~~~~~~~~~~~~~~~~~~~~

Waffles

Pancake, Quick Bread, and Waffle Mix   **Baking Powder Substitute**

Apple Syrup

Appel Stroop

Canned Blue Plums

with

Creamy Cinnamon Sauce

Kaneelsaus

Europe–The Netherlands

EGGS IN WHITE SAUCE or KAMPEN STURGEON
TPT - 22 minutes

I can not attest to whether this story is truth or fable but is so wonderful that I did have to develop a version of this recipe just so I could repeat the tale. Supposedly the Bishop of Munich was to honor Kampen, a city on the river Ijssel in the Dutch province of Overijssel, with a visit. Bells were tied around the neck of a sturgeon, which was to be the main course for the dinner celebrating the visit, and the fish was released into the canals to keep it fresh. It was assumed that the bells would help them keep track of the fish until it was time to prepare it. This dish is said to be the meal that was prepared to replace the sturgeon which obviously made its way silently to freedom.

6 hard-cooked eggs—shelled and halved

3 tablespoons butter
3 tablespoons unbleached white flour
2 cups skimmed milk

3 tablespoons *finely* **chopped celery** *or* **lovage leaves**
2 tablespoons *Dijon* **mustard with wine**
Freshly ground black pepper, to taste

Celery seeds, for garnish

Set the platter you will be using to serve this dish on a warming tray.

In a saucepan set over *LOW* heat, melt butter. Remove from heat and, using a wire whisk, make a *roux* by beating in flour. Return to heat and, stirring constantly, cook for 2 minutes, *being careful not to burn or overbrown the roux*. Remove from heat and gradually beat in milk. Return saucepan to heat and cook, stirring constantly, until thickened. Add more milk, *tablespoonful by tablespoonful*, if consistency is too thick.

Add *finely* chopped celery or lovage leaves, mustard, and black pepper, to taste. Continue whisking until integrated. Turn onto heated platter. Spread the sauce over the platter surface.

Nestle the egg halves, cut-side-down, into the sauce. Grind a bit of pepper over each egg half.

Sprinkle a few celery seeds on each egg half.

Serve at once.

Yields 6 servings
adequate for 4-6 people

Note: This recipe can be halved, when required.

1/6 SERVING – PROTEIN = 9.1 g.; FAT = 9.6 g.; CARBOHYDRATE = 6.7 g.;
CALORIES = 151; CALORIES FROM FAT = 57%

DUTCH BLACK BEAN SOUP
Grauwe Erwten of Carucijnersoep
TPT - 7 hours and 4 minutes;
2 hours = soaking period

Although this economical soup, often referred to as "brune bonensoep" or "plain brown soup" in The Netherlands, is an very old tried and true Dutch family standby, it does not seem to have made the transition into our New World cuisine although a popular restaurant chain now features a soup similar to this among its vegetarian soup selections. Old Colonial cookbooks from Long Island, the Hudson Valley, and New Netherlands seem to have neglected the legumes that undoubtedly sustained the poor. This soup is, however, substantial, flavorful, and with a freshly-baked loaf of bread and a salad, it becomes a nutritious meal.

1 cup dry black beans*
2 cups water

7 cups water
1 bay leaf—broken**
2 whole cloves**
4 whole, black peppercorns**

2 tablespoons butter
1 medium onion—chopped
1 small leek—*white and light green portions only*—**trimmed, split lengthwise,** *very well-washed,* **and sliced**
1/4 cup whole wheat flour
[see next page]

Europe–The Netherlands

DUTCH BLACK BEAN SOUP (cont'd)

1/2 cup sliced celery *with leaves*
1/2 cup sliced carrot
2 tablespoons tomato paste

Salt, to taste
Freshly ground black pepper, to taste
Dash of freshly grated nutmeg

Rinse dry beans in several changes of water. Remove and discard any of poor quality. Place in a saucepan with the 2 cupfuls water. Bring to the boil over *MEDIUM-HIGH* heat, reduce heat to *LOW-MEDIUM*, and simmer for 5 minutes. Cover tightly and allow to stand for 2 hours at room temperature. Drain thoroughly.

Transfer drained beans to a large kettle with the 7 cupfuls water, bay leaf pieces, whole cloves, and peppercorns.** Set over *MEDIUM-HIGH* heat and bring to the boil. Reduce heat to *LOW*, cover tightly, and allow to simmer for 3 hours. Remove and discard bay leaf pieces, whole cloves, and peppercorns.

Using an electric blender or a food processor fitted with steel knife, purée soup in small batches until smooth. Press through a sieve into a clean kettle. Discard residue.

In a skillet set over *MEDIUM* heat, combine butter, chopped onion, and sliced leek. Sauté until onion is soft and translucent, *being careful not to allow onions to brown*. Reduce heat to *LOW*. Add whole wheat flour and cook, stirring constantly, for a minute or two. Add 1/2 cupful of puréed bean base to onion *roux* and stir until smooth, adding more liquid if necessary. Add the onion *roux* to the puréed bean base.

Add sliced celery and carrot with tomato paste. Set over *MEDIUM* heat and bring soup just to the boil. Reduce heat to *LOW* and allow to simmer for an additional 1 1/2 hours until vegetables are very tender and flavor is well-developed. Stir frequently.

Taste and season with salt, pepper, and nutmeg.

Turn into heated soup tureen and serve into heated soup bowls with strips of toasted bread.

Yields 7 servings
adequate for 4-5 people

Notes: *This soup may be prepared using navy beans or pea beans.

**The bay leaf pieces, whole cloves, and peppercorns are most easily recovered if secured inside a tea ball or in a cheesecloth *bouquet garni* bag during the simmering process.

Leftovers freeze beautifully.

1/7 SERVING – PROTEIN = 7.4 g.; FAT = 3.8 g.; CARBOHYDRATE = 24.6 g.;
CALORIES = 158; CALORIES FROM FAT = 22%

DUTCH CHEESE SOUP
Soep met Melk en Edam
TPT - 52 minutes

Whether true or apocryphal, a story, published in" The [Vermont] Harbinger" on December 11, 1847, described a naval battle in which Commodore Coe of the Montevidian Navy defeated Admiral Brown of the Buenos Ayrean Navy by using Holland cheese for cannon balls. I do like Gouda cheese and it too could be used to make this soup, but I prefer the "crimson cannon balls" of Holland. Edam cheese from Holland, aged at least two years, is a beautifully flavored cheese to which domestic versions can not compare.

DUTCH CHEESE SOUP (cont'd)

2 quarts *boiling* water
1 large French white turnip—peeled and diced
2 medium Yukon gold potatoes—peeled and diced

2 1/2 cups *one-percent* milk

1 tablespoon butter
1 large onion—sliced

2 tablespoons unbleached white flour

6 ounces *Edam* cheese—diced

Freshly ground white pepper, to taste

Up to 1/2 cup *one-percent* milk

In a saucepan set over *MEDIUM* heat, cook diced turnip and diced potato in *boiling* water for 12 minutes. Drain thoroughly.

In a large saucepan set over *LOW-MEDIUM* heat, heat milk to *just below the boiling point*.

While milk is heating, in a saucepan set over *MEDIUM* heat, melt butter. Add onion slices and sauté until soft and translucent, *being careful not to allow onions to brown. Reduce heat to LOW*.

Add flour and cook, *stirring constantly*, to make a *roux*. Gradually, *tablespoonful by tablespoonful*, stir 1 cupful of the *hot* milk into the *roux*. Stir until mixture thickens. Add to the remaining *hot* milk in the saucepan. Using a wire whisk, stir until mixture thickens. Remove from heat.

Add cooked turnip and potato. Using a food processor fitted with a steel knife or an electric blender, purée the milk and vegetable mixture. Turn into a clean saucepan and continue cooking over *LOW-MEDIUM* heat.

Gradually add the diced cheese, stirring after every addition.

Season with *white* pepper.

Add as much of remaining 1/2 cupful milk to thin as necessary.

Turn soup into heated soup tureen and serve into heated soup plates.

Yields 8 servings
adequate for 6 people

Notes: This recipe may be halved or doubled, when required.

Add more milk, as needed, when reheating leftovers.

1/8 SERVING – PROTEIN = 10.9 g.; FAT = 7.1 g.; CARBOHYDRATE = 11.1 g.;
CALORIES = 169; CALORIES FROM FAT = 38%

DUTCH SWEET AND SOUR RED CABBAGE
Rode Kool
TPT - 1 hour

My husband's family did not make, buy, or eat sweet and sour red cabbage but it was always a vegetable choice in my family. When I grew up and set about collecting the family recipes, everyone was then using the jarred sweet and sour cabbage found in every grocery store right next to the pickled beets they also had always canned. When was the last time you made either from scratch? This recipe from The Netherlands is certainly not hard to make and you will find that is far less salty than are the grocery store brands.

1 small head red cabbage—about 8 cups

1/2 cup *boiling* water
1/2 teaspoon salt
1/4 teaspoon ground cloves
1/8 teaspoon freshly ground black pepper, or
  to taste

1/4 cup apple cider vinegar
2 tablespoons sugar

1 1/2 tablespoons butter

Europe–**The Netherlands**

DUTCH SWEET AND SOUR RED CABBAGE (cont'd)

Trim any discolored leaves from the red cabbage head and chop the cabbage leaves. Do not include the hard core. Turn the chopped cabbage into a salad spinner and rinse well. Turn into a large kettle set over *LOW-MEDIUM* heat.

Add *boiling* water, salt, ground cloves, and black pepper and cook for about 35 minutes. Stir frequently. Add more water, if necessary.

Add vinegar and sugar. Continue cooking, stirring frequently, for about 10 minutes more.

Add butter. Cook, stirring constantly, until butter has melted. Turn into a heated serving dish.

Serve at once. Refrigerate leftovers.

Yields 8 servings
adequate for 4-6 people

Note: This recipe can be halved, when required.

1/8 SERVING – PROTEIN = 2.0 g.; FAT = 2.3 g.; CARBOHYDRATE = 10.8 g.;
CALORIES = 65; CALORIES FROM FAT = 32%

STEAMED PARSNIPS WITH HONEY – MUSTARD GLAZE IN THE DUTCH STYLE
Pastinaak

TPT - 21 minutes

Parsnips are a root vegetable, a member of the Apiacae and related to parsley, fennel, carrots, celery, lovage, and chervil. This sweet root is so often neglected today but was a staple in The Netherlands before the introduction of the potato. The Dutch, in turn, introduced parsnips to the British, it is believed. My paternal grandfather always referred to parsnips as a reliable kitchen garden crop that has fed the poor for generations and "Remember," he said, "it is sweeter after a frost." I remember reading, as a child, that General John Sullivan had destroyed the parsnip stores of the Iroquois near Geneva, New York, in 1779, not far from where my family settled in the mid-1800s and not all that far from where I grew up. And, I had retrieved parsnips for my maternal grandmother from their straw beds in the root cellar so I decided to revisit this vegetable, recently, as a choice for our Christmas table. I ran all over trying to find them with no success. Either everybody in the valley was making this really good parsnip recipe for their holiday table or parsnips are falling further and further out of favor. I hope it is the former.

1 tablespoon safflower *or* sunflower oil
2 tablespoons *Dijon* mustard with wine
2 tablespoons honey

2 pounds small parsnips—peeled

Salt, to taste
Freshly ground black pepper, to taste

Set up a steamer.

In a non-stick-coated skillet set over *LOW* heat, combine oil, mustard, and honey. Allow to heat, stirring occasionally while parsnips are prepared.

Cut peeled parsnips into 3-4-inch sections. Steam until *crisp-tender*—about 8 minutes. Drain. Turn into the skillet. *Increase the heat to MEDIUM.* Cook, stirring frequently, until parsnips are coated with the glazing mixture—about 3-5 minutes.

Season with salt and pepper. Turn into a heated serving dish.

Serve at once.

Yields 8 servings
adequate for 4-6 people

Note: This recipe can be halved, when required.

1/8 SERVING – PROTEIN = 1.7 g.; FAT = 2.2 g.; CARBOHYDRATE = 22.6 g.;
CALORIES = 110; CALORIES FROM FAT = 18%

Europe–The Netherlands

WAFFLES
TPT - about 30 minutes;
10 minutes = batter resting period

There is nothing wimpy about these waffles. They stand up to any topping — savory or sweet.

1 1/2 cups PANCAKE, QUICK BREAD, AND WAFFLE MIX *[see recipe which follows]*
1 cup skimmed milk, whole milk, buttermilk, or PLAIN YOGURT *[see index]*, **as preferred**
1/2 cup light vegetable oil—*sunflower oil is our choice*

2 large egg whites

In a large mixing bowl, combine mix, milk, and oil. Beat until smooth. Allow to stand for 10 minutes before proceeding.

Meanwhile, preheat oiled waffle iron to *MEDIUM*.

Using an electric mixer fitted with *grease-free* beaters or by hand, using a *grease-free* wire whisk, beat egg whites in a *grease-free* bowl until *stiff,* but *not dry. Whisk-fold* beaten egg whites *gently,* but *thoroughly,* into batter.*

Depending upon the size of your waffle iron, ladle sufficient batter onto hot waffle iron. Keep open for about 30 seconds, close, and allow to cook until browned and no steam is seen emanating from the waffle iron. Using two forks, remove and transfer to a heated serving platter. Keep warm until the remainder are prepared. To maintain crispness, *do not cover.*

Serve with DUTCH APPLE SYRUP *[see recipe which follows]*, butter, honey, warm pure maple syrup, CINNAMON SYRUP *[see index]*, FAMILY'S CHOICE PANCAKE AND WAFFLE SYRUP *[see index]*, fruit syrups, applesauce or other fruit sauces, or crushed fresh fruit, as desired, for breakfast, lunch, or dinner. Top with creamed eggs or vegetables for lunch or dinner.

Yields fourteen 3 1/2-inch square waffles adequate for 4-6 people

Notes: *1/2 cupful crushed berries or chopped fresh fruit may be folded in at this point. Or, if preferred, 1/4 cupful nuts, seeds, or nut butter may be added.

Freeze leftovers and toast them, or wrap them in aluminum foil before oven warming, for a quick breakfast or lunch offering.

1/14 SERVING (i. e., per 3 1/2-inch square waffle) –
PROTEIN = 4.2 g.; FAT = 7.3 g.; CARBOHYDRATE = 9.2 g.;
CALORIES = 114; CALORIES FROM FAT = 58%

PANCAKE, QUICK BREAD, AND WAFFLE MIX
TPT - 5 minutes

This mix is based on that published by the irrepressible Adele Davis, who preached that health and healthful eating choices were a lifetime commitment and from whom I learned so very much. In the 1970s I was quite content with the "healthful heaviness," as I called it, but later in my life I replaced part of the whole wheat and soy flours in this mix with unbleached white flour. Forgive me Adele.

2 cups whole wheat flour
1 1/2 cups unbleached white flour
1/2 cup soy flour
1/2 cup non-fat powdered milk—*not instant*
2 tablespoons plus 2 teaspoons baking powder— preferably aluminum-free— *or* BAKING POWDER SUBSTITUTE *[see recipe which follows]*
1 teaspoon salt

1 1/4 cups *toasted* wheat germ

In a large mixing bowl, combine unsifted whole wheat and soy flours, powdered milk, baking powder, and salt. Sift this mixture into another large bowl.

Stir in wheat germ thoroughly.

Store mixture in tightly sealed containers in the refrigerator until required. Bring to room temperature before using.

PANCAKE, QUICK BREAD, AND WAFFLE MIX (cont'd)

To substitute in favorite recipes, use one cup of mix for each cup of flour specified. You may have to make adjustments for this rule if consistency of resultant batter is too thick or too thin. Omit salt, baking powder, and baking soda called for in the recipe.

Yields about 6 cupfuls

Notes: *Do not use instant dry milk powder.* Its volume will destroy the ingredient balance. Non-instant dry milk powder is readily available in natural food stores.

This recipe may be doubled, when required.

Although it might seem convenient to freeze this mixture, the loss of vitamin E through freezing would be considerable.

1/6 SERVING (i. e., per cupful) –
PROTEIN = 26.9 g.; FAT = 6.4 g.; CARBOHYDRATE = 81.5 g.;
CALORIES = 386; CALORIES FROM FAT = 15%

BAKING POWDER SUBSTITUTE
TPT - 1 minute

Although I had never been in that desperate situation of starting to bake and finding that I had run out of baking powder, I have always kept this idea in my file box just in case. Since baking powder can lose its leavening power and most commercial baking powders contain either sodium aluminum phosphate or the sulfate, having a fresh, aluminum-free alternative might come in handy during a blizzard, or such, when you can not get to the natural food store. Baking soda, bicarbonate of soda, acts only when an acid is present to chemically form carbon dioxide and, hence, the bubbles that leaven breads or cookies or cakes. Baking powder, on the other hand, is a mixture of baking soda and other ingredients, one of which, when added to your batter, either provides the acid with which the baking soda can react or, at least lowers the pH. Cream of tartar, a salt of tartaric acid, reduces the pH of the mixture and enhances leavening. So just in case you want to be totally self-sufficient or are house-bound in a blizzard and out of baking powder, here it is.

2 tablespoons cream of tartar
1 tablespoon baking soda
1 tablespoon corn starch

In a small bowl, combine all ingredients. Stir together *thoroughly*. Pass through a fine sieve several times.

Store in a cool place, tightly sealed, in a spice jar.

Use the same amount of this substitute as the amount of baking powder specified in recipe.

Yields 4 tablespoonfuls

Note: This is easily doubled and will keep up to 4 weeks, but it is most effective if made fresh.

Europe–**The Netherlands**

DUTCH APPLE SYRUP
Appel Stroop

TPT - 26 hours and 12 minutes;
24 hours = cooling period after canning

When the apples in the root cellar or, in later years, in the downstairs refrigerator began to shrivel a bit and lose their crisp texture, my family chopped them up and mixed them with other fruit, stewed them with sugar and spices, or fried them with cinnamon candies. Here is another way to enjoy the goodness of apples when the apples are not "bite-into-crisp." A bowl of fruit, a scoop of ricotta cheese, or a dish of ice cream with this simple, naturally sweetened syrup is a treat.

8 medium apples—very well scrubbed, but
  ***not peeled*, quartered, and cored**
1/4 cup water

If you plan to can the syrup, sterilize one 1/2-pint canning jar. Also sterilize a lid and a ring for the jar.

Put apples and water into a large kettle set over *LOW-MEDIUM* heat. Cover and cook the apples until very soft. Stir frequently. Once soft, mash the apples with a potato masher. Remove from heat and allow to cool for about 20 minutes.

Set a sieve over a large, clean saucepan. Spoon the apples into the sieve. Allow the juice to strain through into the saucepan—about 1 hour. (If you remove the apple skins, the apple residue can be used as a dessert.) Remove the sieve. Place the saucepan over *MEDIUM-HIGH* heat and cook until the juice becomes syrupy and drops from the spoon in a thread—about 15 minutes. *Remove from heat immediately.*

If you are planning to can the syrup, ladle into the hot, sterilized 1/2-pint canning jar. Carefully wipe the lip of the jar. Seal with the hot, sterilized lid and ring. Process in hot-water-bath canner for 10 minutes, *timing from the moment the water reaches a full rolling boil.* Remove to surface covered with thick towels or newspapers. Allow to cool for 24 hours *undisturbed*. Check to be sure the jar is sealed before labeling and storing in a dark, cool, dry place. Loosen or remove the ring before storing.

Yields about 3/4 cupful

Note: This recipe can be doubled, when required.

1/6 SERVING (i. e., 2 tablespoonfuls) –
PROTEIN = 0.2 g.; FAT = 0.3 g.; CARBOHYDRATE = 14.1 g.;
CALORIES = 54; CALORIES FROM FAT = 37%

Europe–The Netherlands

DUTCH CREAMY CINNAMON SAUCE
Kaneelsauce

TPT - 32 minutes

This sauce is delicious over all kinds of desserts including home-canned fruit such as plums or cherries. It is often served over rice or oat groats in Holland. Converted white rice should be used to authentically prepare "Rijst mit Kaneelsauce." The parboiled rice does most closely approximate that found in The Netherlands where a dry, separate grain rice preparation is preferred. The Dutch cook the rice for this dish in water; we, however, prefer to prepare the rice with equal measures of water and milk.

1 3/4 cups skimmed milk
1 three-inch cinnamon quill

1/4 cup unbleached white flour
1/4 cup sugar
1/4 cup skimmed milk

1/2 teaspoon pure vanilla extract

In a saucepan set over *MEDIUM* heat, combine 1 3/4 cupfuls milk and the cinnamon quill. Bring to the boil. Reduce heat to *LOW* and allow hot milk to become infused with the cinnamon flavor—about 20 minutes. Remove cinnamon quill.*

Meanwhile, in another saucepan, using a wire whisk, combine flour, sugar, and 1/4 cupful milk. Set over *LOW* heat and allow the mixture to cook and thicken. Stir frequently.

Using a wire whisk, beat hot milk into prepared thickened flour–sugar–milk base. Set over *LOW-MEDIUM* heat and cook, stirring constantly, until thickened—about 5 minutes.** Keep warm on a warming tray until ready to serve.

Although traditionally served warm, it can be served as a cold sauce. Refrigerate leftovers.

Yields about 2 cupfuls

Notes: *The cinnamon quill may be well-washed and thoroughly dried to be stored in a plastic bag for future use.

**If necessary, strain through a fine sieve to remove any lumps.

When required, this recipe may be halved or doubled.

1/8 SERVING (i. e., 1/4 cupful) –
PROTEIN = 1.3 g.; FAT = 0.5 g.; CARBOHYDRATE = 11.0 g.;
CALORIES = 49; CALORIES FROM FAT = 9%

— sloop, yacht, scow, skipper, ahoy, avast, stoker, bow, deck, dock, brackish, blow, freight, iceberg, keelhauling, mart, and excise, all words we still use today. Spook, stoop, stove, wagon, wiggle, slurp, smuggler, snack, snicker, skate, sketch, trigger, bluff, boodle, booze, boss, brawl, bumpkin, caboose, dope, holster, landscape, sled, slurp, golf, and still life all owe their origins to the Dutch language. And, of course, so do Knickerbocker, Brooklyn, Coney Island, Hoboken, waffle, cookie, buckwheat, gherkin and pickle, gin, knapsack, which translates literally to a "bag of snacks", and Santa Claus. Oh, the list goes on and on . . .

Norway

On St. Patrick's Day, Irish-Americans often quip that "all the world is Irish" but it might be more accurate to credit some of that universal heritage to Norway. During the age of Norse explorations, the Viking Age during the eighth through the eleventh centuries, Norwegians left the land united by Harald Fairhair (Harald Hårfagre) after the Battle of Hafsfjord in 872 AD to live in Iceland, Greenland, the Faroe Islands, and the British Isles, founding the cities of Limerick, Dublin, and Waterford.

Since World War II Norway's growth has been phenomenal due to industrialization and an incredible shipping industry. In 1969 and the early 1970s the discovery of large deposits of oil in the North Sea and in the Norwegian Sea catapulted Norway to a ranking today as the world's wealthiest nation with the third highest per capita capital reserve. Norway, now the seventh largest oil exporter, depends heavily on its oil reserves since twenty-five percent of its GDP comes from the petroleum industry. Ranked by the United Nations as the best country to live in, Norway has model universal healthcare and social security systems, with a subsidized higher education system. A leader in women's, minority, and LGBT rights, Norway is a founding member of the United Nations and NATO. Although, as yet, not a member of European Union, the Kingdom of Norway is one of the founding member of the Council of Europe and is closely allied with the EU and its member nations. It remains a hereditary, constitutional monarchy, descended from the German ruling House of Schleswig-Holstein, with a democratically-elected, unicameral parliamentary system.

Due to it high latitude and our earth's seasonal orbital changes, Norwegians experience long winters with no sunrise from November to late January and the phenomenon of the "Midnight Sun" is evidenced by the fact that the sun is never positioned below the horizon in certain northern areas of the country from May until July allowing for twenty hours of daylight per day. These considerations and a rugged topography, carved by glacial advances and retreats, are agricultural challenges to a country that must feed a population of almost five million. Few meals do not include root crops. Because Norwegians have long prepared for winter, the four to six months when the land is covered with snow and even the fishing industry is mending its nets, the "wintering" of potatoes, carrots, parsnips, rutabagas, beets, onion, hard squashes, nuts, and apples, together with the salting of fish and meats, have been and are important techniques to insure a food supply even though canning and freezing now save many the trip to the root cellar. The second largest exporter of seafood, after China, it is not surprising that fish and seafood are significant in the Norwegian diet but a hearty, filling meatless meal of "*god*" food can always be had in Norway.

Europe–Norway

Marinated and Seasoned *Edam* Cheese
Marinért Edamerost Appetitittaekker

Maple Multigrain Bread *[see index]* or other Dark Bread, of choice

~

Warm Leek, Celeriac, and Carrot Salad
Varm Grønsak Salat

~~~~~~~~~~~~~~~~~~~~

Baked Acorn Squash with Tomato Stuffing
Fylld Squash

Breaded Beetroot Cutlets
Rødbetsbiff

Wild Mushroom Sauce

Oven-Roasted Whole New Red Bliss Potatoes

and/or

Steamed Cauliflower

and/or

Steamed Snow Whole Green Beans

and/or

Steamed Whole Belgian Baby Carrots

with

Jarlsberg **Cheese Sauce for Vegetables**	or	**Brown Onion Sauce**
Ost Saus		*Løksaus*

Fried Apples
Stekte Epler

~~~~~~~~~~~~~~~~~~~~

Yogurt Cream Whip Pudding with Rhubarb
Yoghurt och Fløtekrem med Rabarber
(in the spring)

or

Red Wheat Pudding
Rødgrøt
(in the winter)

Gold Cake Tartlets

Europe–**Norway**

NORWEGIAN MARINATED AND SEASONED *EDAM* CHEESE
Marinert Edamrost Appetittaekker

TPT - 49 hours and 21 minutes;
48 hours = flavor development period

For many years we have enjoyed marinated feta cheese that is exported from Greece. It seems that the Norwegians have a similar appetizer. Edam cheese, the crimson Dutch "cannonballs" referred to by British as "red balls" and as "cat's heads" by the German, is marinated and spiced by Norwegian cooks to create an appetizer that, to our mind, takes a seriously mild mannered cheese to an interesting level. It is a very pleasant addition to a cheese board ("ostebretter") or to a salad such as a potato salad ("potetsalat"). Since it keeps well for about a month, I prepare a batch way ahead of the holidays and always have something to offer with small canapé-sized slices of black bread and a glass of wine if friends drop by.

1 red bell pepper—perfect, unblemished, and well-washed*

1 1/4 cups *extra virgin* olive oil
3/4 cup distilled white vinegar**
1 1/2 teaspoons crushed, dried oregano
1 1/2 teaspoons crushed, dried thyme
1 1/2 teaspoons whole black peppercorns *or* whole mixed peppercorns—black, red, and white—if preferred
2 whole garlic cloves

3/4 pound imported *Edam* cheese—cut into 1/4 cubes

Preheat oven to 350 degrees F. Sterilize two 1-pint canning jars and lids.

Place the red pepper on a cookie sheet. Roast in preheated oven for about 40 minutes, *turning frequently*.

Remove from oven and place in a heavy brown paper bag in dry sink. Roll the top of the bag down and allow to steam for about 15 minutes.

Remove stems, seeds, and membranes, peel, and slice into strips. Place in a saucepan.

Add oil, vinegar, crushed, dried, oregano and thyme, peppercorns, and whole garlic cloves. Set over *MEDIUM* heat. Allow to come to the boil. *Remove from heat immediately.*

Prick cheese cubes with a fork. Divide between the two sterilized jars.

Using a slotted spoon, remove the pepper pieces from the saucepan and divide between the two sterilized jars. Pour the marinade over, dividing it evenly between the jars. Wipe the rims of the jars to remove any oil. Seal and refrigerate for 48 hours. Remove and discard garlic cloves or use them in preparation of another dish. Keep marinated cheese refrigerated until required. Drain portion of marinade to be served.

Serve at room temperature.

Yields about 3 cupfuls

Notes: *ROASTED RED PEPPERS *(Peperoni Arrosto)*, that have been frozen in oil and well-drained, can substituted in this recipe.

**Any herbed vinegar you may have on hand can be used instead of white vinegar.

This recipe can be doubled or halved, when required.

1/16 SERVING (about 3 tablespoonfuls of roasted red pepper and cheese; marinade drained) –
PROTEIN = 5.9 g.; FAT = 5.7 g.; CARBOHYDRATE = 1.3 g.;
CALORIES = 80; CALORIES FROM FAT = 64%

NORWEGIAN WARM LEEK, CELERIAC, AND CARROT SALAD
Varm Gronsak Salat

TPT - 28 minutes

On a post-Christmas afternoon, with snow again falling, I surveyed the refrigerator and found one more leek and half of a celeriac root leftover from Christmas week meals. Carrots, of course, were at hand. Served with a hearty lentil soup, bread, and fruit that had been canned during the summer, it was a perfect repast as the snow blanketed the valley and the thermometer fell into the teens.

NORWEGIAN WARM LEEK, CELERIAC, AND CARROT SALAD (cont'd)

1 large leek— *white and light green portions only*
  —trimmed and well-washed

1 tablespoon butter

About 1/4 of a large celeriac (celery root)—peeled
  and diced to yield about 1 cup
2 medium carrots—pared or scraped and diced

1/2 teaspoon sugar
Salt, to taste
Freshly ground black pepper, to taste

1 tablespoon DANISH SPICED VINEGAR
  (Kryddereddike), [see index], CANADIAN
  CELERY VINEGAR [see index], *or* distilled
  white vinegar, as preferred
1 tablespoon chopped fresh parsley

Trim and slice leeks into thin rings. Put into a salad spinner or large bowl and spin or slosh about until all sand is dislodged. Using a slotted spoon, transfer leek slices to a colander or fine sieve and allow to drain thoroughly.

In a skillet set over *LOW* heat, melt butter.

Add drained leeks slices and diced celeriac and carrots. Cook, stirring frequently, until vegetables are tender.

Sprinkle sugar over. Season with salt and black pepper. Stir to integrate seasoning.

Add vinegar and chopped parsley. Stir into the vegetable mixture. Continue cooking for a minute or two. Turn into a heated serving bowl.

*Serve at once. Refrigerate leftovers.**

Yields 6 servings
adequate for 4 people

Notes: *Bring leftovers to room temperature before serving.

This recipe can be halved, when required.

1/6 SERVING – PROTEIN = 0.8 g.; FAT = 2.0 g.; CARBOHYDRATE = 4.9 g.;
CALORIES = 40; CALORIES FROM FAT = 45%

NORWEGIAN BAKED ACORN SQUASH WITH TOMATO STUFFING
Fylld Sqyash
TPT - 1 hour and 10 minutes

Norwegians refer to acorn squash as summer squash while we refer to these hard-shelled squashes as winter squashes because they go into our winter larder and are available throughout the cold months. The squashes we call summer squashes are referred to in Norway, and most European countries, as marrows. This savory rendition of the baked acorn squash is quite a pleasant change from the butter and brown sugar that has always adorned these squashes in our family.

3 medium-large acorn squashes—well-washed

1/2 cup butter—*melted*
1 cup canned, *diced* tomatoes
1 garlic clove—*very finely* chopped
1/8 teaspoon ground allspice, or to taste

3 tablespoons grated Parmesan cheese

Preheat oven to 350 degrees F.

Cut squash in half lengthwise and remove seeds. Place cut-side-down on a jelly roll pan or in a shallow baking pan with about 1/2-inch of water. Bake in preheated 350 degree F. oven for about 30 minutes, or until almost tender.

Turn squash cut-side-up. Return to oven for an additional 30 minutes.

Meanwhile, in a saucepan set over *MEDIUM* heat, combine butter, diced tomatoes, *very finely* chopped garlic, and ground allspice. Cook, stirring frequently, for about 10 minutes.

When squash has completed oven-cooking period, spoon a portion of the tomato–garlic mixture into each squash half. Sprinkle about 1 1/2 teaspoonfuls grated cheese over the tomato. Carefully transfer one filled squash half to each dinner plate to serve.

Yields 6 individual servings

Europe–**Norway**

**NORWEGIAN BAKED ACORN SQUASH
WITH TOMATO STUFFING** (cont'd)

Note: This recipe is easily halved or doubled, when required.

1/6 SERVING – PROTEIN = 4.9 g.; FAT = 16.4 g.; CARBOHYDRATE = 38.0 g.;
CALORIES = 245; CALORIES FROM FAT = 60%

BREADED BEETROOT CUTLETS
Rödbetsbiff

TPT - 1 hour and 53 minutes;
15 minutes = beet cooling period;
30 minutes = breading setting period

This most unusual recipe was evolved from a recipe credited to Norway by my source. It is so unusual that to exclude it because I can not absolutely confirm its origins, would seem to deny the reader a real adventure and those who "don't like beets too much" a chance to like beets. Most large beets, especially wintered beets, seem to just end up boiled, quartered or sliced, and buttered. Oven-roasting the beets, instead of boiling them, adds flavor but to then slice, bread, and fry them beats a veggie burger by a mile. Wish my family had thought of this when retrieved those big old beets from the root cellar half way through the winter.

I serve these with a wild mushroom sauce and fried onions ("Stekt lok").

4 large beets—well-scrubbed*

9 tablespoons *fat-free* pasteurized eggs

3/4 cup dry, whole wheat breadcrumbs
Salt, to taste
Freshly ground black pepper, to taste

1/4 cup butter

1/2 cup **WILD MUSHROOM SAUCE** *[see recipe which follows]* **or sautéed mushrooms**

Prepare a jelly roll pan—a baking sheet with low sides—or a roasting pan by coating with a thin film of *high heat* safflower oil. Preheat oven to 350 degrees F.

Cut the leaves from the beets, *leaving 2 inches of each petiole. Do not cut off the root tip.* Place beets on prepared baking pan. Bake in preheated oven for about 50 minutes, turning about every 10 minutes until beets are tender and skins have loosened. Allow to cool for about 15 minutes. Slip skins off and trim ends. Cut into 1/4 inch slices.

Set up two soup plates. Pour the pasteurized eggs into one. In the second soup plate combine breadcrumbs, salt, and black pepper. Stir to combine. Dip each beet slice into the pasteurized eggs and then into the seasoned breadcrumbs, coating it well. Transfer to a platter. When all the beet slices have been breaded, transfer the platter to the refrigerator and chill for at least 30 minutes.

In a skillet set over *MEDIUM* heat, melt butter. Fry the breaded beet slices until browned, turning once. Transfer to a heated platter.

Serve at once with **WILD MUSHROOM SAUCE.**

Yields about 16 cutlets servings
adequate for 4-5 people

Notes: *Pick large beets that will yield about four slices each.

This recipe can be halved or doubled, when required.

1/16 SERVING (per beet cutlet)-
PROTEIN = 1.4 g.; FAT = 3.3 g.; CARBOHYDRATE = 3.7 g.;
CALORIES = 50; CALORIES FROM FAT = 59%

Europe–**Norway**

WILD MUSHROOM SAUCE

TPT - 50 minutes;
30 minutes = mushroom soaking period

Western taste is defined by the classic and valid "sweet, sour (or acid), salt, and bitter." Definable areas of the taste buds on the tongue are sensitive to these sensations, as all school children are aware. However, there is another nuance of taste that is considered in all Asian cuisines. If you think about it, the flavor of mushrooms does not fall into any of the classic western categories and you are hard-pressed to define it, but you can taste it. That earthy, fleshy or meaty flavor which is said to derive from our detection of the carbosylate anion of L-glutamate, known in Japanese as umami, is a wonderful tool for the vegetarian cook. This taste finds its way into our diet in many foods—fermented and aged foods such as soy sauce, miso, and cheeses; fish, shellfish, cured meats (due to the addition of MSG), green tea, and vegetables such as ripe tomatoes, Chinese cabbage, spinach, celery, sea kombu, and, of course, mushrooms.

1/2 cup *dried, sliced* white *(Agaricus)* mushrooms —well-rinsed*
1/2 ounce *dried, sliced porcini* mushrooms—well-rinsed**
6 small *dried, whole, shiitake or Chinese black* mushrooms—well-rinsed***
2 cups *boiling* water

1 1/2 tablespoons butter
2 1/2 tablespoons unbleached white flour
1 cup MUSHROOM BROTH, *the liquid in which the dried mushrooms were soaked*****
1 teaspoon *miso*****
Tiny pinch of ground sage

2 tablespoons light cream *or* half and half, more or less as required
Freshly ground black pepper, to taste

In a mixing bowl, combine dried, sliced white and *porcini* mushrooms and dried, whole *shiitake* or black mushrooms, which have been *well-rinsed and brushed to remove any foreign material*. Add *boiling* water. Allow mushrooms to soak for 30 minutes, or until softened. Press mushrooms down into the soaking liquid occasionally to insure even reconstitution.

Using a slotted spoon, remove mushrooms from MUSHROOM BROTH to a small bowl. Cut stems from black mushrooms. Set both MUSHROOM BROTH and mushrooms aside until required.

In a saucepan set over *LOW* heat, melt butter. Add flour and cook, stirring constantly with a wire whisk, for a few minutes to allow flour taste to cook off. *Do not allow flour to brown*. Add 1/4 cupful of reserved MUSHROOM BROTH to *roux* and, using the wire whisk, integrate the broth. *Gradually, tablespoonful by tablespoonful, add broth and stir until smooth.***** Add *miso* and ground sage. Stir well to integrate. Increase heat to *MEDIUM* and cook, stirring frequently, until thickened.

Reduce heat to *LOW* again. Using a slotted spoon, transfer reserved mushrooms to sauce. Add cream and cook, stirring frequently, until heated through. *Do not allow sauce to boil once cream has been added.* Season, to taste, with black pepper.

Keep warm on a warming tray or over hot water until ready to serve.

Yields about 1 1/2 cupfuls

Notes: *Drying sliced, white cultivated mushrooms using one of the inexpensive dehydrators available, is a very simple process. By drying mushrooms yourself you can be assured that they are *well-cleaned, well-trimmed, and flawless*.

**Porcini* mushrooms (also known as *Cèpes Secjes, Boletes*, and *Steinpilze*) lend a superbly rich and complex flavor to any dish. Although expensive and scarce in the past, these wonderful mushrooms are now widely available in the dried form.

***Dried, Chinese black mushrooms *(Lentinus edodes)* are available in Asian groceries. They are distinctive and well worth adding to this recipe. As you search for these mushrooms you will find names such as black winter mushrooms, fragrant mushrooms, *shiitake* mushrooms, black forest mushrooms, brown oak mushrooms, or simply Chinese dried mushrooms, depending from which area of Asia or Southeast Asia they have come. The best quality are usually dried for export. The fresh and dried *shiitake* mushrooms, now grown in the United States and widely available, are inferior in taste. Try to obtain dried black mushrooms which are thick and show deep, white fissures on the caps. Their taste is superior. If you are fortunate enough to find superior dried, Chinese black mushrooms in quantity, ignore the price, buy them, and store in a cool, dry place. They keep well and, if well-sealed, can even be stored in the freezer.

WILD MUSHROOM SAUCE (cont'd)

****Save any extra MUSHROOM BROTH to use to prepare vegetable stocks or to flavor soups, stews, and sauces. When frozen in cubes in the ice cube tray, this broth can become a very useful addition to many dishes that just need "a little something extra."

*****Mugi miso is a paste of soybeans, barley, seaweed, and salt, aged to develop flavor. It is available in Asian groceries and in natural food stores. Kome miso is milder in taste, made from brown rice instead of barley. Hacho miso is stronger in taste since it is made from soybeans without the mellowing effect of grains.

This recipe may be halved or doubled, when required.

Reheat, if necessary, in a double boiler, adding more MUSHROOM BROTH or cream when needed.

1/6 SERVING (i. e., 1/4 cupful) –
PROTEIN = 0.6 g.; FAT = 3.4 g.; CARBOHYDRATE = 2.8 g.;
CALORIES = 44; CALORIES FROM FAT = 70%

JARLSBERG CHEESE SAUCE FOR VEGETABLES
Ost Saus

TPT - 20 minutes

Norwegian Jarlsberg cheese has become an American favorite. When we were first married, we had to travel to an international cheese store to buy it; it was not even mentioned in Bob Brown's 1955 "The Complete Book of Cheese." Almost every grocery store now offers wedges of this nutty, buttery, slightly sweet cheese with the distinctive yellow rind. It is not, as some say, the other Swiss cheese. Aged quite differently than is Emmentaler, residual moisture weeps into its irregular holes when it is cut. The flavor is far more distinctive than domestic Swiss-style cheeses, especially if allowed to come to room temperature. I have made this basic sauce for years and years and years.

1 tablespoon butter

1 tablespoon whole wheat flour*

1 cup *two-percent* milk**

1 cup shredded (about 4 ounces) Norwegian *Jarlsberg* cheese
Freshly ground *white* pepper, to taste

In a saucepan set over *LOW* heat, melt butter. Remove from heat and, using a wire whisk, make a *roux* by beating in flour. Return to heat and, stirring constantly, cook for 2 minutes, *being careful not to burn or overbrown the roux*. Remove from heat and gradually beat in cream or milk. Return saucepan to heat and cook, stirring constantly, until thickened. *Do not allow sauce to boil.*

Add shredded cheese and cook, stirring constantly, until cheese has melted and sauce is smooth. Season with white pepper.

Keep warm on a warming tray or over hot water. *Do not allow sauce to boil.*

Yields about 1 1/4 cupfuls
adequate to sauce about 1 pound of vegetables

Notes: *If preferred, unbleached white flour can be substituted.

**For a richer sauce, whole milk or light cream can be substituted.

This recipe may be doubled, when required.

Leftovers can be heated in a double boiler over simmering water. Beat well with a wire whisk as sauce heats.

1/5 SERVING (about 1/4 cupful) –
PROTEIN = 8.4 g.; FAT = 9.5 g.; CARBOHYDRATE = 4.3 g.;
CALORIES = 135; CALORIES FROM FAT = 63%

Europe–Norway

NORWEGIAN BROWN ONION SAUCE
Løksaus

TPT - 18 minutes

To achieve the deep brown color desired in this classic sauce/gravy Norwegian cooks use beef bouillon instead of vegetable stock, of course, and add Bovril or Kitchen Bouquet. The addition of wild mushroom stock and soy sauce do achieve a satisfactory "brown" sauce. Traditionally served with potatoes and meatballs in Norway, we serve it with soy meatballs and roasted potatoes. Lingonberry preserves, on the side, provide a nice, sweet-tart contrast.

2 tablespoons WILD MUSHROOM STOCK
  [see index]
1/2 teaspoon corn starch

2 tablespoons butter
1/2 cup *very finely* chopped onion

2 tablespoons unbleached white flour
About 1 1/4 cups BROWN VEGETABLE STOCK
  [see index] *or* VEGETABLE STOCK FROM
  SOUP [see index]

1 tablespoon *tamari* soy sauce
1 tablespoon apple cider vinegar
Pinch of sugar
Freshly ground black pepper, to taste

Additional vegetable stock, as needed

In a small bowl or cup, combine mushroom stock and corn starch. Stir until corn starch is in suspension. Set aside until required.

In a saucepan set over *LOW* heat, melt butter. Add *very finely* chopped onion and sauté until onion is soft and translucent, *being careful not to allow onions to brown*.

Remove from heat and, using a wire whisk, make a *roux* by beating in flour. Return to heat and, stirring constantly, cook for 2 minutes, *being careful not to burn or overbrown the roux*. Remove from heat and gradually beat in vegetable broth. Return saucepan to heat and cook, stirring constantly, until thickened.

Add mushroom stock–corn starch suspension and stir to combine thoroughly.

Add soy sauce, vinegar, sugar, and black pepper. Thin with additional vegetable stock, if necessary to obtain desired consistency.

Keep warm on warming tray until ready to serve.

Yields 36 tablespoonfuls

Note: This recipe can be doubled or tripled, as required.

1/18 SERVING (i. e., 2 tablespoonfuls) –
PROTEIN = 0.1 g.; FAT = 1.3 g.; CARBOHYDRATE = 1.2 g.;
CALORIES = 17; CALORIES FROM FAT = 69%

NORWEGIAN SWEET FRIED APPLES
Stekte Epler

TPT - 15 minutes

I enjoyed fried apples, flavored with red cinnamon candies, as a breakfast item in the restaurant of a resort in the Blue Ridge Mountains on a trip down the Skyline Drive in the late 1960s which I filed as a "brunch" idea. Years later, on the trip to Denmark, this version was on the side table with the hot vegetables at the Christmas Day cold table buffet where a few holidaying foreigners, like the three of us, celebrated with Swedish families who had come across on the ferry and multi-generational Danish families. As I served a portion of the apples onto my plate next to the Danish browned potatoes, sweet and sour red cabbage, and deviled eggs, I was informed by a Swedish lady that the apples were good, but that they were neither Danish nor Swedish; they were Norwegian. Thank you, whoever you were; they are indeed good and now they are in the right chapter.

Norwegians may shutter a bit but we often serve these as a dessert sauce over ice cream and we still often serve it with brunch.

Europe–**Norway**

NORWEGIAN FRIED APPLES (cont'd)

1/4 cup butter
1/2 cup brown sugar
1/2 teaspoon ground cinnamon
1/4 teaspoon ground cardamom

8 large apples—peeled, quartered, cored, and sliced

In a large non-stick-coated skillet set over *LOW* heat, melt butter. Add brown sugar, and ground cinnamon and cardamom. Stir until brown sugar has dissolved.

Add apple slices and cook until apples have softened. Stir frequently, basting the apples with syrup. Turn into a heated serving dish.*

Serve warm.

Yields 6 servings
adequate for 4 people

Notes: *The apples can be fried early in the day and reheated over *LOW* heat at serving time.

A few cinnamon candies, although certainly not traditional, do add a pink color that makes this dish very festive.

This recipe can be halved, when required.

1/6 SERVING – PROTEIN = 0.3 g.; FAT = 7.9 g.; CARBOHYDRATE = 37.1 g.;
CALORIES = 211; CALORIES FROM FAT = 34%

NORWEGIAN YOGURT CREAM WHIP PUDDING WITH RHUBARB

Yoghurt och Flötedrem med Rabarber

TPT - 4 hours and 8 minutes;
4 hours = yogurt draining period

I have a number of these yogurt-whipped cream creations in my files, since dairy desserts like this are popular in many countries and the ease of preparation and versatility invites creativity. Turks love dairy desserts such as this as a middle-of-the-afternoon snack; Mexicans adore it with chopped fruit; and I have even enjoyed an Irish version make with almond flavoring and toasted oatmeal. Since I had tasted Norwegian versions of rhubarb with yogurt and rhubarb with whipped cream, this combination just seemed like a natural.

Our English stewed rhubarb is made much the same way and can be used in this recipe. Use either freshly stewed rhubarb, in the spring, or frozen stewed rhubarb, in the winter, and be sure to drain the stewed rhubarb well.

1 1/2 cups VANILLA YOGURT *[see index]*
or commercially-available vanilla yogurt

1/2 vanilla bean

3/4 cup heavy whipping cream
3 tablespoons confectioners' sugar

1 1/2 cups sweetened, STEWED RHUBARB *[see index]*—*very well-drained*
1/2 teaspoon ground cardamom, or to taste

Prepare VANILLA YOGURT *CRÈME* by setting two automatic drip coffeemaker filters into a sieve over a medium-sized bowl or a yogurt filter over a 2-cup measuring cup. Pour the VANILLA YOGURT into the filters and set in the refrigerator. Allow to drain for about 4 hours.

Split the vanilla bean in half and scrape the seeds into the drained yogurt. Using a wire whisk, beat the seeds into the YOGURT *CRÈME*, until the *crème* is smooth and creamy. Set aside briefly.

Using the electric mixer fitted with *chilled* beaters or by hand using a *chilled* wire whisk, beat heavy cream in a *clean, chilled* bowl until stiff peaks form. While still beating, *gradually* add confectioners' sugar.

Add VANILLA YOGURT *CRÈME* and *whisk-fold* the whipped cream into the yogurt.

Stir the ground cardamom into the *very well-drained* stewed rhubarb. *Gently*, but *thoroughly*, fold the rhubarb into the yogurt–cream mixture.

Divide among six dessert dishes. *Refrigerate for no longer than 30 minutes to prevent separation.*

Serve chilled.

Yields 6 individual servings

Note: This recipe may be halved, when required.

Europe–**Norway**

NORWEGIAN YOGURT CREAM WHIP PUDDING
WITH RHUBARB (cont'd)

1/6 SERVING – PROTEIN = 3.4 g.; FAT = 10.4 g.; CARBOHYDRATE = 23.3 g.;
CALORIES = 200; CALORIES FROM FAT = 47%

NORWEGIAN RED WHEAT PUDDING
Rødgrøt

TPT - 2 hours and 36 minutes;
2 hours = refrigeration period

A few days after Christmas, when the leftovers and most of the cookies have finally been consumed, this favorite winter dessert makes an appearance, made possible by the sweet juices drained from our canned fruits that had been included in the Christmas morning compote. Farina or semolina, always on the winter larder shelf for breakfasts, is cooked with cherry or plum canning liquid, combined with the bit of juice extruded from the strawberries and raspberries when they were defrosted. It makes a beautiful and thoroughly delicious pudding.

**1 1/2 cups combined sweet, red fruit liquid
drained from canned or frozen fruits***
3/4 cup water
2 tablespoons sugar

1/3 cup dry, farina *or* Cream of Wheat cereal**

In a saucepan set over *LOW-MEDIUM* heat, heat fruit juice, water, and sugar. Allow to come to the boil.

Gradually, while stirring constantly, add farina. Cook, stirring frequently, until thickened—about 15 minutes. Turn into a serving bowl or divide among six dessert dishes. Refrigerate for at least 2 hours.

Serve chilled with a vanilla sauce, whipped cream, sour cream sauce, or vanilla ice cream, if desired.

Yields 6 servings
adequate for 4-6 people

Notes: *The sweet, fruit-flavored liquid in which fruits are canned and frozen can be drained from the fruit and frozen for use in gelled dishes or in desserts such as this.

**Cream of Rice, Cream of Rye, or Wheatena dry cereals can be substituted, if preferred.

1/6 SERVING – PROTEIN = 2.9 g.; FAT = 0.3 g.; CARBOHYDRATE = 55.3 g.;
CALORIES = 230; CALORIES FROM FAT = 1%

GOLD CAKE

TPT - 1 hour and 45 minutes;
30 minutes = cooling period

The Lord Baltimore Cake, also called "Gold Cake" or "Egg Yolk Cake," is said to have evolved as a way to use the yolks leftover when whites were used to prepare a Lady Baltimore Cake. In our whole wheat version of this old-fashioned golden cake, we have replaced the five egg yolks with fat-free pasteurized eggs to reduce the percentage of calories from saturated fats. Norwegians also use up their egg yolks in a very sweet "gold cake," similar to this albeit with more butter and sugar and without milk. I prefer the texture of this one made with milk. The three layers of a traditional American Lord Baltimore cake would be filled with a very sweet mixture of boiled frosting, macaroons, pecans, almonds, candied cherries, and sherry. Norwegian cooks have not borrowed this American colonial excess but I often frost this cake with an orange buttercream frosting.

Prepared with white flour and egg yolks, the cakes will be golden; prepared with whole wheat flour and fat-free pasteurized eggs, the dessert with be healthier.

Europe–**Norway**

GOLD CAKE (cont'd)

1 1/2 cups sifted cake flour
1 1/2 cups whole wheat flour
2 1/2 teaspoons baking powder

3/4 cup (1 1/2 sticks) butter—*softened to room temperature*
3/4 cup sugar
1 cup *fat-free* **pasteurized eggs (the equivalent of 4 eggs)**
1 1/2 teaspoons pure vanilla extract

1 1/4 cups skimmed milk

Preheat oven to 375 degrees F. Prepare two 9-inch round cake pans by coating with non-stick lecithin spray coating. Dust with cake flour.

Into a large mixing bowl, sift cake and whole wheat flours with baking powder. Set aside.

Using the electric mixer or food processor fitted with steel knife, cream butter until light and fluffy. Add sugar and continue to cream until again light and fluffy. Beat in pasteurized eggs and vanilla extract. Continue beating, at *HIGH* speed if mixer is used, *for 2 full minutes.*

Reduce mixer speed. Add sifted flours alternately with milk, beating until batter is very smooth.

Divide between prepared cake pans. Rap each sharply on counter top to release any large bubbles.

Bake in preheated 375 degree F. oven for 20-22 minutes, or until surface springs back when lightly touched.

Cool *completely* on wire racks before removing cake layers from pans.

Frost, if desired; sift confectioners' sugar over; or serve with a sweet sauce.*

Yields two 9-inch layers

Notes: *ORANGE BUTTERCREAM FROSTING *[see index]* compliments this cake beautifully. Or, use the cake as a base for a fruit sauce, a compote of choice, or FRESH ORANGE CUSTARD SAUCE *[see index]*.

This recipe is easily halved when a single layer is required but, since this cake freeze well, baking the full recipe is ultimately practical.

The batter for this cake is perfect for making small cakes or tartlets. Bake for about 9-10 minutes. Cool slightly before removing from tart pans.

1/2 SERVING (i. e., per layer) –
PROTEIN = 34.7 g.; FAT = 70.6 g.; CARBOHYDRATE = 227.0 g.;
CALORIES = 1691; CALORIES FROM FAT = 38%

1/12 SERVING (i. e., a two-layer slice without frosting) –
PROTEIN = 5.8 g.; FAT = 11.8 g.; CARBOHYDRATE = 37.8 g.;
CALORIES = 282; CALORIES FROM FAT = 38%

1/44 SERVING (i. e., per tartlet) –
PROTEIN = 1.6 g.; FAT = 3.2 g.; CARBOHYDRATE = 10.3 g.;
CALORIES = 77; CALORIES FROM FAT = 38%

Poland

The celebrated settlement discovered in 1934 at Biskupi, and since restored, dates to about 700 BC. The find of this fortified Lusation (Lausitz) village of perhaps 1,200 residents, with as many as one hundred houses laid out with eleven streets within a ring road, reveals a settled, communal lifestyle among the early settlers of this area of Europe. Whether they were Slavic people, or Germanic people as the mid-twentieth century Germans claimed, is still argued and until human remains are found at this site, there is no way that this argument will, perhaps, ever be resolved.

Poland's nationhood is generally dated from the adoption of Christianity in 966 AD, becoming a kingdom in 1025 and a partner in the Polish–Lithuanian Commonwealth in 1569. Partitioned in 1795 with the collapse of the Commonwealth, it was not until 1918 that Poland re-emerged as an independent state, referred to as the Second Polish Republic. After World War II, when it was invaded and ravaged by Nazi Germany, Poland fell under Soviet influence becoming a Socialist republic within the Eastern Bloc. In 1989 Poles threw off the oppressive yolk and emerged in what is known today as the Third Polish Republic. Her expatriates and descendents to the third and fourth generations still revel in a homeland that produced such giants as the astronomer Copernicus, the composer and pianist Frederic Chopin, actress Pola Negri, writer Joseph Conrad, Kasimierz Pulaski, to whom all Americans can be grateful, and the great researcher Marie Sklodowska Curie, who named the element she discovered for her native land, polonium.

Very early in my life I learned to appreciate the Polish sour rye bread and the freshly made sour cream at Peak's Market on Joseph Avenue in Rochester, New York, to which a pack of cousins was dispatched by Grandma with the awesome responsibility of transporting a clean, empty sour cream crock to the store and transporting home the *śmietana*-filled crock and two loaves of freshly-baked sour rye bread plus crisp Polish dill pickles fished from the pickle barrel for each of us. Our reward was always a slathering of the remarkable sour cream on a slice of the rye bread and our pickles. Polish-Americans are much like Italian-Americans in that they keep alive their heritage through food. They may never have visited the land from which their ancestors emigrated but they do visit that land in food that is always a part of family tradition especially at the holidays. Riverhead, Long Island, was my next exposure to the colorful Polish traditions and the Polish Festival was a not-to-be-missed event. Street signs poignantly remind you of how far you are from Warsaw and Krakow. Here in Pennsylvania *pierogi* are as common a dinner choice as are potatoes or *pasta* and we eat them just as do Poles in Warsaw and Krakow with onions fried in copious amounts of butter.

The knowledge necessary for successful and safe mushroom hunting to satisfy the Poles passion for mushrooms is passed down from generation to generation and the joy of mushroom hunting need not be forgotten in the winter since a portion of that which is collected is always dried for use in soups, stews and sauces. A simple, inexpensive dehydrator is indispensable for this item which is a staple in our larder. No, I do not trust my identification skills, although guides to mushroom gathering tout the varieties here in Pennsylvania. Instead, I gather from the increasingly varied offerings in grocery stores and dry a portion of those, especially when they are part of the store's weekly specials. That sour cream my Grandma used was gloriously rich and I would prefer to use that sour cream any day. Because of the high fat content of such sour creams, I recommend using a low-fat or a fat-free sour cream. Taste test those available to you; they vary considerably.

Europe–**Poland**

Poached Farina and Cheese Drop Dumplings
Knedle
with
Polish Sauce
Sauce Polonaise
Sos Polsku
or
Deviled Mushrooms
Pieczarkami z Sos Musziardowy

~

Pearl Barley and Vegetable Soup with Sour Cream
Krupnik ze Smietana

Beet and Mushroom Soup for Christmas Eve
Barszcz Wigilijny

~

Radish Salad with Sour Cream
Surowka z Rzodkiewki

~~~~~~~~~~~~~~~~~~~~~~

Cabbage and Noodle Skillet Supper
Kapusta Kluski z Smietana

Lima Beans

Shredded Carrot with Lemon and Sugar
Karotka Strzepió

Pickled Blue Plums
Marynowane Sliwki

~~~~~~~~~~~~~~~~~~~~~~

Pears in Spiced Vanilla Honey with Chocolate and Cherries
Gruszki w Czekoladzi z Czeresniami

POLISH FARINA AND CHEESE DROP DUMPLINGS
Knedle
TPT - 31 minutes

I can see my mother dropping dumpling batter, made from a biscuit dough with baking powder, into a kettle of chicken and vegetables; it was one of her favorite meals. "Knedle" are dumplings, usually filled with fruit or made from cheese and potatoes. These dumplings, which I offer as an appetizer possibility, are unusual in that they are formed from a mixture of farina and cottage cheese. The combination is so unique, you will always be asked, "What's in these dumplings?" because neither ingredient is immediately detectable. The egg whites give them unexpected lightness. Although these are perfect when served with a "Sos Polsku" ("Sauce Polonaise"), a recipe for which I have included, they are also delicious with a mushroom sauce, if preferred.

Europe–**Poland**

POLISH FARINA AND CHEESE DROP DUMPLINGS (cont'd)

1/4 pound (about 1 1/2 cups) farina *or* Cream of Wheat cereal
1/4 cup skimmed milk

1/2 pound *two-percent creamed* cottage cheese
1/3 cup *fat-free* pasteurized eggs *or* 2 egg yolks

2 egg whites

3 quarts *boiling* water

In a mixing bowl, combine farina or Cream of Wheat with milk. Using a wire whisk, stir to combine.

Press the cottage cheese through a fine sieve into a second mixing bowl. Add pasteurized eggs or egg yolks. Stir to combine. Add farina.

Using an electric mixer fitted with *grease-free* beaters or by hand, using a *grease-free* wire whisk, beat egg whites in a *grease-free* bowl until *stiff*, but *not dry*. Add to cottage cheese–egg–farina mixture. *Fold* beaten egg whites and farina *gently*, but *thoroughly*, into batter.

Pour the *boiling* water into a large saucepan and set over *LOW-MEDIUM* heat. Using two spoons, gather about 2 tablespoonfuls of the dumpling batter and drop into the *boiling* water. Cook a *few at a time* in the *boiling* water and allow to poach until the dumplings float—about 4 minutes. Using a skimmer or a slotted spoon, remove the dumplings from the poaching liquid and transfer to a heated shallow serving bowl set on a warming tray set at MEDIUM or in a warm oven. Continue cooking the dumplings in small batches.

When all dumplings have been poached, *serve hot* with Sos Polsku (Sauce Polonaise).

Yields about 24 dumplings
adequate for 6 people

Note: This recipe can be halved, when required.

1/24 SERVING (i. .e., per dumpling without sauce) –
PROTEIN = 2.6 g.; FAT = 0.3 g.; CARBOHYDRATE = 9.7 g.;
CALORIES = 53; CALORIES FROM FAT = 5%

POLISH SAUCE
(SAUCE POLONAISE)
Sos Polsku
TPT - 10 minutes

"Sauce Polonaise," sauce in the Polish style, is a well-deserved part of the classic French sauce repertoire. It compliments steamed carrots, Brussels sprouts and leeks, sautéed cabbage, and especially steamed asparagus and cauliflower. It is, at once, a sauce and a garnish.

6 tablespoons butter

3 tablespoons *fine, dry* breadcrumbs

3 drops freshly squeeze lemon juice
Pinch ground red pepper (cayenne), or to taste

In a skillet set over *MEDIUM* heat, melt butter. Cook, stirring constantly, until butter just begins to color.

Add breadcrumbs and cook, stirring constantly, until crumbs begin to brown. Remove from heat.

Add lemon juice and ground red pepper (cayenne).

Serve at once.

Yields about 6 tablespoonfuls

Note: This recipe can be doubled, when required.

1/6 SERVING (i. e., per tablespoonful) –
PROTEIN = 0.2 g.; FAT = 11.3 g.; CARBOHYDRATE = 0.8 g.;
CALORIES = 106; CALORIES FROM FAT = 95%

Europe–**Poland**

POLISH DEVILED MUSHROOMS
Pieczarkami z Sos Musztardowy
TPT - 17 minutes

This unusual variation of the creamed mushrooms of years gone by reminds us of a mushroom appetizer we enjoyed in a restaurant tucked into a birch forest just outside of Moscow. We serve it as a vegetable side or as an appetizer in tiny ramekins with toasts on the side for formal occasions or heaped on toasted Italian bread for less formal dinners. Good bakeries often offer an Italian bread loaf made with whole wheat flour and to which whole grains have been added. The heartier bread is a good choice if you are going to serve the mushroom mixture as an appetizer.

10 ounces whole *crimini* mushrooms

1 teaspoon freshly squeezed lemon juice
Pinch salt
Freshly ground black pepper, to taste

1/3 cup *fat-free* dairy sour cream
3 tablespoons *two-percent* milk
1 1/2 teaspoons MUSTARD SAUCE [see index]
1/4 teaspoon crushed, dried thyme leaves
Pinch ground red pepper cayenne
1 tablespoon unbleached white flour

1 tablespoon *finely* snipped fresh chives

1 tablespoon *finely* chopped fresh parsley *or* dillweed, for garnish

Prepare mushrooms by trimming, rinsing well, and cutting into quarters.

In a non-stick-coated skillet, liberally coated with non-stick lecithin olive oil spray, combine mushrooms, lemon juice, salt, and black pepper. Toss to distribute the lemon juice and seasonings. Place over *MEDIUM* heat and cook, stirring frequently, until mushrooms exude water and begin to brown. Using a slotted spatula, remove mushrooms to a small bowl. Set aside briefly. *Reduce heat to LOW*.

In another small bowl, combine sour cream, milk, mustard, ground red pepper (cayenne), and flour. Stir to mix thoroughly. Add to liquid in skillet. Cook, stirring constantly, until mixture thickens. Add mushrooms and *finely* snipped chives. Cook, stirring constantly, until heated through. Turn into heated serving bowl.

Garnish with *finely* chopped fresh parsley

Serve at once.

Yields 6 servings
adequate for 4 people

Note: This recipe is easily doubled, when required.

1/6 SERVING – PROTEIN = 3.6 g.; FAT = 0.4 g.; CARBOHYDRATE = 9.6 g.;
CALORIES = 56; CALORIES FROM FAT = 6%

POLISH PEARL BARLEY AND VEGETABLE SOUP WITH SOUR CREAM
Krupnik se Smietana
TPT - 45 minutes

I will leave it to you whether to stir the sour cream into the hot soup before serving, or use it as a garnish, or even to serve no sour cream at all, if that is your pleasure. Polish cooks have strong opinions on the subject of both sour cream and mushrooms. Although this recipe can be halved, we find it as good, if not better, when heated up the next day so we always make the large quantity and save dinner preparation time for a day or two.

POLISH PEARL BARLEY AND VEGETABLE SOUP WITH SOUR CREAM (cont'd)

6 cups *boiling* water
3 medium potatoes—halved and, then, sliced
2 medium carrots—scraped or peeled and sliced crosswise into coins
1 large celery stalk—sliced
1 leek—*very well-washed*, trimmed, and sliced crosswise
1 medium onion—sliced
1/2 cup *dried* wild mushrooms—broken into pieces

2 cups VEGETARIAN BROWN STOCK *[see index]* or VEGETABLE STOCK FROM SOUP *[see index]*
2 tablespoons butter
1/2 cup dry pearl barley

1 tablespoon chopped fresh dillweed
1 tablespoon chopped fresh parsley
Freshly ground black pepper, to taste
Salt, to taste

Fat-free dairy sour cream, for garnish

In a kettle set over *MEDIUM* heat, combine *boiling* water, sliced potatoes, carrots, celery, leek, and onion, and *dried* mushroom pieces. Simmer for about 20 minutes.

Meanwhile, bring vegetable stock and butter to the boil. Add barley and cook until barley is tender—about 10 minutes.

When vegetable soup has cooked for the initial 20 minutes, add cooked barley. Cook for an additional 20 minutes.

Add chopped dill and parsley. Season with salt, to taste. Turn into a heated tureen.

Serve into heated soup bowls with a garnish of sour cream.

Yields 8 servings
adequate for 6 people

1/8 SERVING (with 2 tablespoonfuls sour cream) –
PROTEIN = 6.5 g.; FAT = 3.1 g.; CARBOHYDRATE = 33.9 g.;
CALORIES = 187; CALORIES FROM FAT = 15%

POLISH BEET AND MUSHROOM SOUP FOR CHRISTMAS EVE
Barszcz Wigilijny
TPT - 2 hours and 44 minutes

During the fall harvest we make a triple batch of this lovely soup, to serve during the warm autumn as a chilled broth with chilled sour cream. A portion is always frozen for the busy holidays ahead. Because holiday preparations can often become overwhelming it is so nice to have this soup base in the freezer ready to go. Although it should be served with the traditional mushroom dumplings (Uszka z Grzybami), we have often substituted tortellini stuffed with ricotta cheese and porcini mushrooms.

2 cups VEGETARIAN BROWN STOCK *[see index]* or VEGETABLE STOCK FROM SOUP *[see index]*
3 cups water
3/4 cup *dried, sliced* white *(Agaricus)* mushrooms—*well-rinsed and brushed to remove any foreign matter**
1/2 ounce *dried, sliced* porcini mushrooms—*well-rinsed and brushed to remove any foreign matter*

8 medium beets—peeled and coarsely grated
2 quarts water
1/2 teaspoon salt, or more to taste

1/2 teaspoon sugar
Freshly ground black pepper, to taste
1 tablespoon freshly squeezed lemon juice—*strained*

In a large kettle, with cover, set over *MEDIUM-HIGH* heat, bring vegetable stock and 3 cupfuls water to the boil. Reduce heat to *LOW*. Add dried mushrooms, cover, and allow to simmer until mushrooms are tender—about 40 minutes. Using a slotted spoon, remove reconstituted mushrooms from MUSHROOM STOCK to a small bowl to be used in another dish or to prepare POLISH "LITTLE EAR" MUSHROOM DUMPLINGS *(Uszka z Grzybami)*, which are traditionally served with this dish.

Return the MUSHROOM STOCK to *MEDIUM-HIGH* heat, and cook until reduced to about 1 cupful—about 1 hour. Strain through a fine sieve. Set aside until required.

POLISH BEET AND MUSHROOM SOUP FOR CHRISTMAS EVE (cont'd)

While MUSHROOM STOCK is reducing, prepare BEET STOCK. In a large kettle, set over *MEDIUM-HIGH* heat, combine coarsely grated beets, 2 quartfuls water, and salt. Bring to the boil. Reduce heat to *LOW-MEDIUM* and simmer, uncovered, for about 30 minutes. Remove from heat.

Using an electric blender or the food processor fitted with steel knife, purée the beets in small batches. Strain through a fine sieve into a clean kettle, discarding beet residue. or reserving the residue in your soup container in the freezer.

Return kettle containing BEET STOCK to *MEDIUM* heat. Add the prepared 1 cupful of MUSHROOM STOCK, sugar, black pepper, and *strained* lemon juice. Bring to the boil.

Turn into a heated soup tureen and serve into heated soup bowls.

Notes: *Drying sliced, white cultivated mushrooms using one of the inexpensive dehydrators available, is a very simple process. By drying mushrooms yourself you can be assured that they are *well-cleaned, well-trimmed, and flawless.*

Leftover soup may be frozen.

This recipe may be doubled, when required.

Yields 6 servings
adequate for 4 people

1/6 SERVING – PROTEIN = 0.7 g.; FAT = 0.07 g.; CARBOHYDRATE = 5.1 g.;
CALORIES = 24; CALORIES FROM FAT = 3%

POLISH RADISH SALAD WITH SOUR CREAM
Surówka z Rzodkiewki
TPT - 6 minutes

Every spring I plant radishes partially because I have a reason to get out into the garden on the very first nice day and partially because they grow so quickly, satisfying my need to entice Persephone from the underworld. Then, we have to eat the harvest before they are ravaged by the burrowing and tunneling agents of Hades. No matter how hot the radishes are, this salad sufficiently mellows them.

1 pound (about 40) blemish-free red radishes
   —well-washed, trimmed, and sliced
1/8 teaspoon salt
1/2 teaspoon sugar

1/4 cup *fat-free* dairy sour cream

6 large lettuce leaves
1 tablespoon *fresh* dillweed leaves

In a mixing bowl, combine sliced radishes, salt, and sugar. Toss to distribute salt and sugar evenly.

Add sour cream. Using a rubber spatula, fold the sour cream into the radishes.

Line a serving dish or bowl with lettuce leaves or place a lettuce leaf on each of six salad plates. The prepared salad may be served from the common lettuce-lined serving bowl or apportioned as individual servings. In either case, garnish with fresh dillweed.

Chill in refrigerator until ready to serve.

Yields 6 servings
adequate for 4 people

Note: This recipe may be halved or doubled, when required.

1/6 SERVING – PROTEIN = 1.9 g.; FAT = 0.07 g.; CARBOHYDRATE = 6.9 g.;
CALORIES = 35; CALORIES FROM FAT = 2%

Europe–Poland

POLISH CABBAGE AND NOODLE SKILLET SUPPER
Kapusta Kluski z Smietana
TPT - 24 minutes

The introduction of pasta as the Roman Empire expanded its influence in Europe, the Middle East, and North Africa led to many versions of pasta and soon eggs were added to the wheat flour and water to become the noodles used in this dish which is popular in Germany and in many countries in Eastern Europe. Pasta has traveled the world just has the tomato or corn, as has the sweetpotato and have black-eyed peas. Many nations have evolved pasta recipes that could not in any way, shape, or form be thought of as Italian or Chinese. When the argument as to where spaghetti was first invented arises, as it does with annoying regularity, I think about our visit to the Soviet Union and how, claiming inventions can become a national obsession when the wonder of international cross-fertilization is the far more fascinating fact.

2 tablespoons butter
1/2 cup *thinly* sliced onion

4 cups chopped white cabbage—well-rinsed
1/2 teaspoon caraway seeds
1/4 teaspoon sugar
Freshly ground black pepper, to taste
Salt, to taste

4 quarts *boiling* water
4 ounces short, broad egg noodles*

1/4 cup *fat-free* dairy sour cream

In a large skillet set over *LOW-MEDIUM* heat, melt butter. Add onion slices and sauté until the onions are soft and translucent, *being careful not to allow the onions to brown.*

Add chopped cabbage, caraway seeds, sugar, black pepper, and salt. Continue to cook, stirring frequently.

Meanwhile, in a large kettle set over *MEDIUM-HIGH* heat, combine *boiling* water and egg noodles. Cook according to package directions. Drain thoroughly.

Add drained noodles to cabbage–onion mixture. Stir to combine well.

Add sour cream and cook for about 5 minutes, stirring frequently. Turn into a heated serving bowl.

Keep warm on warming tray until ready to serve.

Yields 6 serving servings
adequate for 4 people

Notes: *I prefer the short, twisted, commercially-available broad egg noodles for this recipe.

When required, this recipe can be halved or doubled.

1/6 SERVING – PROTEIN = 5.5 g.; FAT = 4.9 g.; CARBOHYDRATE = 22.1 g.;
CALORIES = 151; CALORIES FROM FAT = 29%

POLISH SHREDDED CARROTS
WITH SUGAR AND LEMON
Karotka Strzepió
TPT - 7 minutes

We make a concerted effort to substitute organic products whenever possible especially when buying greens, soft fruits, and root vegetables. Our market carries organic carrots that are so incredibly sweet I thought I must be imagining the major taste difference I experienced when I first tasted them. One day I mentioned this to a friend who exploded with the same enthusiasm for the product. This recipe is a favorite of ours because the carrot shreds are barely cooked and the taste is a very balanced taste bud experience and yet it is a warm vegetable.

1 tablespoon butter
7 medium carrots—scraped or pared and
  coarsely shredded

1/2 teaspoon sugar
1 teaspoon freshly squeezed lemon juice
Freshly ground black pepper, to taste

POLISH SHREDDED CARROTS WITH SUGAR AND LEMON (cont'd)

In a skillet set over *LOW* heat, melt butter. Add shredded carrots. Allow to heat through while stirring frequently to coat the carrot shreds with butter—about 4-5 minutes.

Sprinkle sugar, lemon and black pepper over. Toss to mix well. Turn into a heated serving bowl.

Serve at once.

Yields 6 servings
adequate for 4 people

Note: This recipe can be halved or doubled, when required.

1/6 SERVING – PROTEIN = 0.4 g.; FAT = 2.0 g.; CARBOHYDRATE = 4.2 g.;
CALORIES = 35; CALORIES FROM FAT = 51%

POLISH PICKLED BLUE PLUMS
Marynowane Śliwki

TPT - 29 hours;
1 hour = first soaking period;
1 hour = second soaking period;
2 hours = third soaking period;
24 hours = cooling period

Throughout Central Europe, in countries that were once part of the Austro-Hungarian Empire, plums are used to make prized and potent brandies. At the beginning of Act III in Johann Strauss' "Die Fledermaus," set in Vienna, Frosch the jailer declares, ". . . Ah, hier ist es. Der Slibowitz—ein Pflaumenschnaps. Lasset uns einen Obsttag einlegen." He gets the fruit to start his day from plum brandy, which he consumes to excess. So it is no surprise that Poles find a myriad of uses for plums from September soup to alcoholic beverages. Our pickled plums will leave you pleased, not plastered. These are the perfect garnish when you are looking for a sweet–sour taste accent.

3 pounds small, firm Italian blue plums—about 2 plums—*very well-washed**

1 quart distilled white vinegar
1 quart water

1 quart distilled white vinegar
1 quart water
5 cups sugar
9 whole cloves
2 large cinnamon quills—broken into 6 pieces

Pat well-washed plums dry and place in a mixing bowl.

In a saucepan set over *MEDIUM-HIGH* heat, combine 1 quartful of vinegar and 1 quartful of water. Bring to the boil. Pour *hot* liquid over plums. *Be sure plums are covered.* If not, add a bit more *boiling* water. Allow plums to soak in vinegar for 1 hour.

Pour only the liquid back into the saucepan. Again, bring the vinegar solution to the boil over *MEDIUM-HIGH* heat. Pour, again, over the plums and, again allow plums to soak in liquid for 1 hour.

Pour the plums and the liquid in which they had been soaking into a sieve set over the sink. Discard liquid and return plums to mixing bowl.

In a saucepan set over *MEDIUM-HIGH* heat, combine the remaining quartful of vinegar and quartful of water, sugar, cloves, and cinnamon quill pieces. Bring to the boil and cook, stirring frequently, until the sugar is dissolved. Pour the *hot*, seasoned vinegar–sugar solution over the plums. Set the bowl aside and allow to cool to room temperature—about 2 hours.

Meanwhile, sterilize six 1-pint canning jars. Also sterilize lids and rings for jars.

Using a slotted spoon, divide plums among the six hot, sterilized jars—about 12 plums per pint.

Strain liquid through a fine sieve into a clean saucepan set over *MEDIUM-HIGH* heat. *Reserve both whole cloves and cinnamon quill pieces.* Bring liquid to the boil.

Fill jars with hot, strained liquid to about 1/2 inch from top. Add 1 whole clove and a small piece of cinnamon quill to each quart. Carefully wipe rims of jars. Seal with hot, sterilized lids and rings. Process in hot-water-bath canner for 30 minutes, *timing from the moment the water reaches a full rolling boil.* Remove to surface covered with thick towels or newspapers. Allow to cool for 24 hours *undisturbed.* Check to be sure jars are sealed before labeling and storing in a dark, cool, dry place.** Loosen or remove rings before storing.

POLISH PICKLED BLUE PLUMS (cont'd)

Allow flavors to meld for at least 1 month before serving.

Yields six 1-pint jarfuls

Notes: *Italian blue plums are preferable for this recipe since they are smaller than those usually referred to as German prune plums. They are available for only a short period in the early fall.

**Any jars that do not seal can be stored in the refrigerator for several months or resealed using a *new lid*.

1/72 SERVING (i. e., per plum with syrup) –
PROTEIN = 0.07 g.; FAT = 0.0 g.; CARBOHYDRATE = 18.0 g.;
CALORIES = 69; CALORIES FROM FAT = 0%***

***These food values can only be approximated since the plums are most often served without the syrup and the carbohydrate uptake is difficult to determine.

POLISH PEARS IN SPICED VANILLA HONEY WITH CHOCOLATE AND CHERRIES
Gruszki w Czekoladzi z Czeresniami
TPT - 6 minutes

Although I prefer to poach fresh Bosc pears, I do not always have perfectly ripened pears on hand. This recipe makes those small, convenient canned pears into quite a special dessert. Sour cherries, which my grandmother canned by the bushel for pies and küchens, require less spraying because they suffer from few pests and diseases. The reverse side of that very positive coin, as far as orchard men are concerned, is that they are very, very attractive to birds so between the avian feastings and the small yield due to their self-pollinating habit these perfectly acidic cherries are falling out of favor. Before World War II over fifty varieties were grown in the British Isles alone. Fewer and fewer farmers on either side of the Atlantic maintain sour cherry trees and in my own farmers' market only one farming family brings sour cherries to market. If you have dried Morello cherries, their use would be more authentic in this recipe but the sweet cherries from the American Northwest, which I dry each summer, do very well.

6 tablespoons honey, of choice
2 teaspoons *boiling* water
1 teaspoon pure vanilla extract
1/8 teaspoon ground cinnamon
Pinch ground cloves

2 cans small pear halves (12 pear halves), packed in light syrup—*very thoroughly* chilled and *well-drained*
30 dried cherries—preferably Morello cherries*

3 tablespoons BASIC CHOCOLATE SYRUP
   [see index] **or** dark chocolate syrup

In a small dish, combine honey, *boiling* water, vanilla extract, ground cinnamon, and ground cloves. Stir to mix thoroughly.

Pour about 3 1/2 teaspoonfuls of the spiced vanilla honey mixture into the center of each of six large, *chilled* dessert plates. Place two chilled pear halves cut-side-down on each plate, sliding them around so that the cut sides come into maximum contract with the honey. Nestle five dried cherries into the honey next to the pears.

When ready to serve, garnish each serving rim-to-rim with about 1 1/2 teaspoonfuls of chocolate syrup using "Pollock-like" drip strokes.

Serve at once.

Yields 6 individual servings

Notes: *The Morello cherry is a sour cherry grown in Eastern Europe occasionally available dried from mail order firms.

This recipe can be halved, when required.

1/6 SERVING – PROTEIN = 1.3 g.; FAT = 0.9 g.; CARBOHYDRATE = 40.0 g.;
CALORIES = 163; CALORIES FROM FAT = 4%

Portugal

In 868 AD, during the *Reconquista* when Moors, *Moriscos*, and Sephardic Jews, exclusive of *Conversos* (or *Marranos*) and Protestants, were expelled from the Iberian Peninsula, the County of Portugal was established as a fief of the Kingdom of León, its name deriving from the Roman "*Portus Cale*" or "warm port." In 1139, after the Battle of Ourique, the county became the independent Kingdom of Portugal with successive monarchies until 1910. With the institution of the tribunal of the Inquisition in 1232, Portugal too became embroiled in the attempt to eliminate the residual non-Roman Catholic elements from the Iberian Peninsula whose presence had been tolerated in Portugal during the Middle Ages. Beginning in the late 1400s Portugal sought and received permission from the Papacy to drive out those not of the Catholic faith, especially the Jews, who had fled the Spanish Inquisition into Portugal. Those who openly professed religions other than Roman Catholicism in its colonies were not immune from the long arm of the Portuguese Inquisition. As historical case records show, those accused of breaching the tenants of orthodox Roman Catholicism were persecuted in the Portuguese colonies of Goa, in which Hindus were persecuted, Brazil, and Cape Verde until 1821.

With the Age of Discovery, Portugal opened up the world and became a great trading empire initiating the exchange of cultures and ideas with the "New World" that has been dubbed the "Columbian Exchange." Tomatoes, peppers, potatoes, corn, kidney beans, turkeys, and avocados sailed West in the ships of the returning explorers and took hold in Portugal becoming unassailably identified with the cuisine. The purpose of exploration was not just riches and spices but also for conquest and colonization. Brazil, from which had flowed a bounty of new foods, remained a colony until 1822. Unlike Spain, whose colonization in South America, Mesoamerica, and to some extent into western North America was extensive, Portugal turned it attentions to Africa and its trade routes, colonizing the coastal area of Kenya, Cape Verde, São Tomé and Principe, Guinea-Bissau, Angola, and Mozambique. Goa, Macau, and East Timor were colonized to support the trade with Asian markets. In this modern age of globalization, Portugal finally handed Macau over to China in 1999 and granted East Timor's independence in 2002.

One year after Portugal adopted its constitution and in the aftermath of the Portuguese Colonial War (1961-1974) and the left-wing military coup of 1974 known as the Carnation Revolution, we made our first trip to Europe, choosing to go to Portugal. We found our language skills greatly challenged despite the fact that the Portuguese language owes much to Latin and to Roman influences residual from the period during which it was the Roman province of Lusitania. Back in 1977 we found it impossible to maintain a vegetarian eating pattern but we explored the country from Évora and Braga to Faro in the South and along the Mediterranean in a "Mini-Minor" past huge sheets of cork being harvested from the cork oaks in the Alentejo, up the mountain roads with no guide rails and the remains, hundreds of feet below, of those unfortunates who could not navigate those roads, to the wonderful university city of Coimbra to see the library, to the resort areas of the Algarve, to the cliffs at Sagres overlooking the ocean, from which the explorers sailed, to see the site where Prince Henry the Navigator, son of King João I, established his school of navigation, stopping as we did to explore museums, castles, and gardens. It was a thrilling experience we shall never forget.

Europe–Portugal

Any meal in Portugal hints at its exploration of the world, its far-flung colonial empire, its continued ownership of The Azores from which fresh tropical produce arrives to fill the greengrocer's shelves, and its brief union with Spain between 1580 and 1640 in what was known as the Iberian Union. More than any other influence, however, is its geography which allows fresh fish at the table every day in a profusion that boggles the mind. It is not surprising at all, in view of my own visit to Portugal, to read the statistic that claimed that the Portuguese eat more fish than any other country in Europe.

Mayonnaise – Cheese Dip with **Easy, Light "Mayonnaise"**
Maionese de Leite
Assorted Olives
Chunks of Crusty Bread

or

Autumn Compote
Salada de Frutas

~

Garlic Soup
Açorda á Alentejana

~

Tomato, Onion, and Pea Salad
Salada de Tomate, Cebolas, e Ervilhas

~~~~~~~~~~~~~~~~~~~~~

Cauliflower Pudding
Couveflor Cozado em Crème

Potatoes with Bay Butter
Batatas com Louro

Braised Onions with Cheese
Cebolas con Quiejo

~~~~~~~~~~~~~~~~~~~~~

Country Corn Bread
Broa

~

Orange Custards with Honey and Cinnamon
Flan a Suco de Larange com Miel e Canela

Orange Torte
Torta de Laranga

Europe–**Portugal**

MAYONNAISE – CHEESE DIP
TPT - 4 minutes

Using the light eggless "mayonnaise," popular in the Alentejo region of Portugal always makes me think that I am being prudent with my saturated fats. As a base for a simple dip into which one can dip olives and bread, it is superb.

1 recipe, 18 tablespoons, PORTUGUESE EASY, LIGHT "MAYONNAISE" *(Maionese de Leite)*
[see recipe which follows]
1/4 cup grated *pecorino Romano* or Parmesan cheese
Freshly ground black pepper, to taste

In a small bowl, combine the "mayonnaise," grated cheese, and black pepper. *Gently* combine.

Refrigerate until ready to serve.

Serve with assorted olives and crusty bread. Refrigerate any leftovers.

Yields 12 servings
adequate for 6 people

1/6 SERVING – PROTEIN = 0.8 g.; FAT = 14.9 g.; CARBOHYDRATE = 0.5 g.;
CALORIES = 139; CALORIES FROM FAT = 96%

PORTUGUESE EASY, LIGHT "MAYONNAISE"
Maionese de Leite
TPT - 14 minutes

While traveling and eating in Portugal, I was overwhelmed to see the extravagant use of egg yolks. So it was rather a surprise to find that the origin of the eggless "mayonnaise," which has now become somewhat of a darling among the health conscious, was of Portuguese origin, from the rural area south of the Tagus River known as the Alentejo. The idea of cutting the calories and saturated fat in homemade mayonnaise made with egg yolks was an idea that appealed to me when I found a recipe that promised results that were similar to classic mayonnaise. It is, of course, not truly mayonnaise since mayonnaise must contain eggs and never contains milk and this emulsion is made with milk and contains no eggs. The first time I made it I had to admit that it was good, certainly head and shoulders above any of the commercial mayonnaise-like salad dressings because it contained no additives in the form of stabilizers and emulsifiers but it was in need of a bit of help. I added mustard to increase the stability of the emulsion and a combination of oils to improve the flavor. Although I do like the taste of many of the commercially-available calorie-reduced olive oil mayonnaises, the additives for shelf-life extension and the plastic bottles in which they are packaged are big, big turn-offs for us so this mayonnaise substitute has a respected place in our kitchen.

10 tablespoons safflower *or* sunflower oil
2 tablespoons *extra virgin* olive oil
1 tablespoon GARLIC OIL *[see index]*

1/3 cup *two-percent* milk*
1/2 teaspoon *Dijon* mustard with wine
1/2 teaspoon freshly squeezed lemon juice
1/4 teaspoon salt
1/8 teaspoon sugar

In a measuring cup, combine sunflower, olive, and garlic oils. Set aside until required.

In the work bowl of a mini-chop food processor, combine milk, mustard, lemon juice, salt, and sugar. Cover. Remove cover of feeding tube. Process while gradually adding the oils through the feeding tube in a steady stream. Process until an emulsion forms.

Transfer to a sterilized canning jar. Cover and refrigerate up to a week.

Yields 18 tablespoonfuls

PORTUGUESE EASY, LIGHT "MAYONNAISE" (cont'd)

Notes: *Whole milk or a combination of whole milk and half and half can be used instead of two-percent milk. I have had no problem making the emulsion with two-percent milk and I like the idea of yet another lower fat ingredient. In addition, this recipe can be used to make a credible vegan salad dressing if you substitute soy milk for cow's milk.

This recipe CAN NOT be doubled successfully.

If preferred, you can make this mayonnaise using an immersion blender. A better product results if you use the mini food processor or an immersion blender. The emulsion often does not form if a large food processor or an electric blender is used.

1/18 SERVING (i. e., per tablespoonful) –
PROTEIN = 0.1 g.; FAT = 9.6 g.; CARBOHYDRATE = 0.3 g.;
CALORIES = 88; CALORIES FROM FAT = 98%

PORTUGUESE AUTUMN COMPOTE
Salada de Frutas

TPT - 2 hours and 6 minutes;
2 hours = maceration period

We visited Portugal in the summer and did not have a chance to taste this fruit dessert while there, concentrating, as we were, on consuming with enthusiasm the fresh summer fruits offered. This mixture is refreshing yet darker and more complex, conveying the feeling that summer has ended. When little ones are at hand, the Port wine can be omitted.

2 firm, but ripe, pears—peeled and sliced lengthwise
1 large, firm banana—sliced
2 ripe blue, prune plums—halved and sliced
1/2 cup *preservative-free*, green seedless grapes*
3 tablespoons *preservative-free* dark raisins*

1/4 cup Port wine**
1/4 cup freshly squeezed orange juice
2 tablespoons freshly *squeezed* lemon juice

1/3 cup halved, *preservative-free* hazelnuts or filberts—*lightly toasted*

In a large shallow bowl, combine pear, banana, and plum slices with grapes and raisins.

In a measuring cup, combine Port wine, orange juice, and lemon juice. Pour over fruit mixture and toss *very gently*.

Refrigerate for at least 2 hours to allow flavors to marry. *Gently* turn fruit occasionally to insure even marination.

Turn into serving bowl. Just before serving, garnish with *toasted* hazelnut halves.

Yields 5 servings
adequate for 3-4 people

Notes: *A sulfite-free source of grapes and raisins is worth investigating.

**Remember, the Port wine may be omitted, if preferred.

This recipe is easily doubled, when required.

1/6 SERVING – PROTEIN = 5.4 g.; FAT = 8.5 g.; CARBOHYDRATE = 27.7 g.;
CALORIES = 192; CALORIES FROM FAT = 40%

PORTUGUESE GARLIC SOUP
Açorda à Alentejana

TPT - 53 minutes

An acorda is a "dry" soup, thickened with wonderfully yeasty, country-style bread. Italian bread is a poor, albeit convenient, substitute for the flavorful loaves available in the Alentajo region of Portugal. Winter or summer this soup is on the menu in Portugal. Although we have sampled it from Brago to Sagres and from Lisbon to Estremoz, we still like this version best.

Europe–Portugal

PORTUGUESE GARLIC SOUP (cont'd)

8 slices Italian bread—seeded *or* plain, as preferred

1 1/2 tablespoons *extra virgin* olive oil
12 average-sized garlic cloves—peeled and coarsely chopped

1/2 teaspoon coarse salt (or kosher salt)
4 whole coriander seeds—crushed
1/4 bay leaf—*finely* crushed
Pinch dried thyme—crushed
1/8 teaspoon paprika
Dash freshly grated nutmeg

1 quart VEGETARIAN BROWN STOCK *[see index]* or other vegetarian stock of choice

Freshly ground black pepper, to taste

4 large *organic* eggs—*brought to room temperature*

Chopped, fresh coriander (*cilantro*) leaves—for garnish—if available

In an oven set at *WARM*, dry Italian bread slices. Check often to be sure that they only dry and *do not brown*. Remove, set aside, and allow to cool.

In a 2-quart saucepan set over *MEDIUM* heat, heat olive oil. When hot, add chopped garlic cloves. Sauté for about 5 minutes allowing garlic to cook to a *golden color*, but *being careful not to allow garlic to brown*.

In a mortar, combine coarse salt, crushed coriander seeds, crushed bay leaf, crushed thyme, paprika, and nutmeg. Using a mortar and pestle, grind to a powder. Add to sautéed garlic and continue to cook, stirring constantly, for an additional 5 minutes.

Add stock and allow to come to the simmer. Simmer, uncovered, for about 20 minutes. Remove from heat and allow to cool slightly. Using either an electric blender or a food processor fitted with steel knife, purée mixture and force this purée through a fine sieve to recover as much garlic as possible and to remove as much fiber as possible. Return to the pan, add black pepper to taste, and bring just to the boil.

Meanwhile, place four soup crocks or bowls on a warming tray set at HIGH or in oven set at LOW. When hot, break eggs one at a time into a custard cup and slip each egg into one of the soup crocks. Wait approximately 1 minute and then apportion hot soup gently over eggs. Allow eggs to coddle—about 3 to 5 minutes.* Sprinkle each serving with chopped coriander (*cilantro*) leaves.

Serve at once, with two dried bread croutons per serving.

Yields 4 cupfuls
adequate for 4 people as a
main course offering**

Notes: *If preferred, prepare four softly poached or coddled eggs and slip these into soup-filled crocks at serving time.

**If this soup is to be offered as a first course, it will serve six quite easily. Serve, then, only one slice of dried bread per serving. You might also prefer to eliminate the coddled eggs.

Although this soup may be frozen, if desired, the garlic flavor is altered and, thus, a rather impotent broth results.

This recipe is easily doubled, when required.

1/4 SERVING – PROTEIN = 11.8 g.; FAT = 10.5 g.; CARBOHYDRATE = 37.0 g.;
CALORIES = 279; CALORIES FROM FAT = 34%

PORTUGUESE TOMATO, ONION, AND PEA SALAD
Salada de Tomate, Cebolas, e Ervilhas

TPT - 1 hour and 12 minutes;
1 hour = marination period

We were served this salad, usually without the peas, almost everyday during a July visit to Portugal in the late 1970s. Even today, when it is served, one or the other of us usually mentions Portugal...

3 medium tomatoes—well-washed and cored

1 medium onion—*thinly* sliced
2 tablespoons CLASSIC FRENCH DRESSING
  [see index]

6 lettuce leaves

1/4 cup freshly shelled *or defrosted, frozen* peas—for garnish

PORTUGUESE TOMATO, ONION, AND PEA SALAD (cont'd)

Cut tomatoes into quarters. Then, using a very sharp knife, slice each quarter into slices *(. . . much the way you slice an onion).*

In a large plastic container with a tightly fitting lid, combine sliced tomatoes and onions with CLASSIC FRENCH DRESSING. Cover tightly. Toss gently to coat.

Refrigerate for at least 1 hour, turning occasionally to insure even marination.

Turn into a sieve and drain off excess salad dressing— *at least 1 tablespoonful should be recovered.*

Turn into a lettuce-lined serving bowl and garnish with peas.

Serve at once.

Yields 6 servings
adequate for 4 people

Note: This recipe is easily halved or doubled, when required.

1/6 SERVING – PROTEIN = 1.1 g.; FAT = 1.6 g.; CARBOHYDRATE = 4.3 g.;
CALORIES = 35; CALORIES FROM FAT = 41%

PORTUGUESE CAULIFLOWER PUDDING
Couveflor Cozado em Crème
TPT = 1 hour and 8 minutes

When I first tasted this cauliflower dish, I was struck with how similar it was to a Brazilian recipe in my collection, a dish that dates back to the Jewish communities of the sixteenth and seventeenth century. I began to wonder if Portuguese Jews had also brought kosher dishes, such as this, to the homes of their Roman Catholic friends in an effort to maintain their kosher eating practices but still enjoy the meal to which they had been invited. I was not introduced to this dish in Portugal because our trip was a summer visit so I can not confirm the connection but I can speculate . . .

When the gorgeous orange cauliflowers are available, I always choose one over its white relative for this dish. The egg custard and the orange cauliflower florets make a striking presentation.

1 1/2 tablespoons unbleached white flour
1/8 teaspoon freshly ground black pepper, or
 to taste

3 quarts *boiling* water
2 cups *small* cauliflower florets

1/2 cup *fat-free* pasteurized eggs (the equivalent
 of 2 eggs)

2 tablespoons butter
3 tablespoons onion—*very finely* chopped

1 1/4 cups *two-percent* milk

2 tablespoons grated *pecorino Romano* or
 Parmesan cheese

Preheat oven to 325 degrees F. Prepare a 1-quart soufflé dish or other oven-to-table baking dish by coating with non-stick lecithin spray coating.

In a small dish, combine flour and black pepper. Set aside briefly.

In a saucepan set over *MEDIUM* heat, parboil cauliflower florets in *boiling* water for about 5 minutes. Drain and rinse thoroughly with cold water until cool. Drain thoroughly.

In a mixing bowl, combine the well-drained, cool cauliflower florets with pasteurized eggs. Stir to combine and set aside until required.

In a saucepan set over *MEDIUM* heat, melt butter. Add *very finely* chopped onion. Sauté until onion is soft and translucent, *being careful not to allow onion to brown.* Reduce heat to *LOW*.

While still stirring constantly, add flour mixture and stir for several minutes to form a *roux*.

Gradually add milk, stirring as you do with a wooden spoon. Increase heat to *MEDIUM* again and cook, stirring constantly, until the mixture comes to the boil and thickens slightly.

PORTUGUESE CAULIFLOWER PUDDING (cont'd)

Add grated cheese and cauliflower–egg mixture. Stir to integrate. Turn into prepared baking dish. Set in a baking pan in which a 1-inch water bath has been prepared. Bake in preheated 325 degree F. oven for about 30-35 minutes, or until a knife inserted into the center comes out clean. Check water level occasionally and add *cold* water, if needed. *Do not allow water bath to simmer or boil—add cold water or ice cubes,* if necessary. Remove baking dish from water and allow to stand for about 5 minutes before serving to allow for custard to firm.

Serve hot.

Yields 6 servings
adequate for 4 people

Note: This recipe can be doubled, when required.

1/6 SERVING – PROTEIN = 7.6 g.; FAT = 5.6 g.; CARBOHYDRATE = 7.1 g.;
CALORIES = 102; CALORIES FROM FAT = 49%

PORTUGUESE POTATOES WITH BAY BUTTER
Batatas com Louro
TPT - 39 minutes

If you have ever been to Portugal, you know that the aromatic leaf of the bay laurel, Laurus nobilis, is beloved. The aroma fills the air within restaurants and taverns. I must admit that I brought back few recipes from Portugal that do not contain bay leaves. This one is a favorite.

2 pounds small, new potatoes—well-scrubbed, but *unpeeled*
1 medium, *peeled* onion into which 2 whole cloves have been inserted
3 quarts *boiling* water

4 dried bay leaves*

1 tablespoon sweet (*unsalted*) butter
1 tablespoon *extra virgin* olive oil

Salt, to taste
Freshly ground black pepper, to taste

In a large kettle, with cover, set over *MEDIUM-HIGH* heat, cook *unpeeled* potatoes and onion with cloves in *boiling* water until tender, but *not crumbly*—about 20 minutes.

Using a mortar and pestle, grind bay leaves until they are crumbled quite finely.

While potatoes are cooking, in a non-stick-coated skillet set over *LOW* heat, heat butter and oil. Add *finely* crumbled bay leaves and allow the bay leaf pieces to steep until potatoes are done. Stir occasionally.

When potatoes are done, drain thoroughly. Discard onion *(or reserve for stock pot)*. Peel potatoes.

Using a fine sieve, strain the butter mixture, removing all but the smallest bay leaf pieces. Return strained butter to skillet set over *LOW-MEDIUM* heat. Add peeled potatoes and cook, stirring frequently, for about 5 minutes, or until *glazed and lightly browned*. Season with salt and pepper, to taste.

Turn into heated serving bowl and keep warm on warming tray or in a warm oven until ready to serve.

Yields 6 servings
adequate for 4 people

Notes: *Although *Laurus nobilis* is winter hardy only to Zone 8, it can be grown outside in northern herb gardens in the summer, potted, and brought indoors. Use well-washed fresh leaves in stews and soups or harvest leaves, wash thoroughly, dry, and store airtight to use in dishes such as this where the leaves must be ground or crumbled.

This recipe may be halved or doubled, when required.

1/6 SERVING – PROTEIN = 1.3 g.; FAT = 3.8 g.; CARBOHYDRATE = 10.5 g.;
CALORIES = 75; CALORIES FROM FAT = 46%

Europe–Portugal

PORTUGUESE BRAISED ONIONS WITH CHEESE
Cebolas con Quiejo

TPT - 1 hour and 25 minutes
[slow cooker: 2 hours at HIGH and 2 hours at LOW
plus final 5-minute oven period]

As with many Portuguese dishes, this is indeed a very simple recipe. The onions are infused with flavor during the slow-cooking process, complimenting other foods well. If you wish to enjoy this dish throughout the year, not just in the fall and winter when the wonderful, tiny, white boiling onions are available, as we do, prepare double batches, freezing half, to reappear when these lovely onions will seem very special indeed.

1 pound small white boiling onions, all approximately the same size—peeled—or *frozen* white boiling onions
1 tablespoon butter
1 large garlic clove—*finely* chopped
2 bay leaves—broken
6 whole peppercorns

Small pinch Spanish saffron—crushed
3/4 cup shredded (about 3 ounces) Hungarian Trappist, Dutch *Gouda,* or Dutch *Edam* cheese, as preferred
1 tablespoon grated *pecorino Romano,* Parmesan, *Asiago,* or *Kefalotyri* cheese, as preferred
2 small tomatoes—peeled, seeded, and chopped

Preheat oven to 275 degrees F.

Cut a small, shallow **X** into the root end of each peeled onion to insure that the onions will not fall apart during cooking. Put them in a heavy oven-to-table casserole, with tightly fitting cover, together with butter, *finely* chopped garlic, bay leaf pieces, and peppercorns. Place in preheated 275 degree F. oven, tightly covered, for about 1 1/4 hours, or until onions are succulently tender. Turn onions occasionally during cooking period to prevent excess browning. Remove casserole from oven. Remove and discard bay leaf pieces and peppercorns.*

Increase oven temperature to 325 degrees F.

Sprinkle crushed saffron over, then shredded cheese, then grated *Romano* cheese or other grated cheese of choice, and then chopped tomato. Return casserole to 325 degree F. oven, uncovered, and allow to cook *only until cheese is melted*—about 5 minutes.

Notes: *You might find it a time-saving convenience to prepare a double batch of these braised onions. If prepared only to this point and frozen, they may be defrosted and reheated most successfully. After reheating, proceed according to the recipe.

When doubling, a large oven casserole should be used; one that allows onions to remain in a single layer.

This is an ideal recipe for slow cooker cookery, if you choose to use frozen pearl onions. Cook at *HIGH* for 2 hours, reduce heat to *LOW*, and continue cooking for 2 more hours. Either freeze at this point or finish dish by combining the cooked onions with cheeses and tomato in a soufflé dish and bake in conventional oven, preheated to 325 degrees F. for about 5 minutes.

Yields 6 servings
adequate for 4 people

1/6 SERVING – PROTEIN = 5.6 g.; FAT = 5.2 g.; CARBOHYDRATE = 8.1 g.;
CALORIES = 98; CALORIES FROM FAT = 48%

Europe–Portugal

PORTUGUESE COUNTRY CORN BREAD
Broa

TPT - 3 hours and 10 minutes;
1 hour and 50 minutes = automated machine preparation period*

The influence of a population of about 40,000 gypsies upon Portuguese cuisine is minimal but their caravans and their handicrafts are colorful punctuations at markets and along the roads primarily in the South and in Lisbon where we could have had our palms read almost any day right there in Parque Eduardo VII. We had been traveling north from Lisbon to an area near the Spanish border. It had been a long time since we had eaten the continental breakfast served in the posada in which we had stayed and lunch time had passed; we were hungry. Loaves of this wonderful rustic bread and hunks of strong, unaged cheese were offered for sale on tables pulled from the gypsy caravans. It was like a waterhole in the desert to us.

I allow my Zojirushi bread machine or my mixer, fitted with a dough hook, to do the work of mixing and kneading this dough but I do not allow the bread machine to complete the process. Then, I simply bake it in the oven on tiles. This bread, because of its very dense texture, can be thinly sliced and oven-dried to create a remarkable melba-style toast.

3/4 cup water (105°-115° F.)**
1/2 cup *two-percent* milk (105°-115° F.)**
1 tablespoon canola oil

1 cup corn flour *or* stone-ground yellow corn meal***
2 1/2 cups bread flour
1/2 cup whole wheat flour
2 tablespoons sugar
3/4 teaspoon salt

1 tablespoon (1 envelope) *preservative-free active dried yeast*****

All ingredients except warm liquids should be at room temperature.

Put water, milk, and oil into the BREAD MACHINE pan.

Add corn flour, bread flour, whole wheat flour, sugar, and salt, spreading the ingredients over the liquid as you add them. *Do not stir.*

Using a spoon, create a depression in the dry ingredients, being very careful not to press down into the liquid layer below. Pour yeast into the depression.

Select the MANUAL SETTING cycle on the BREAD MACHINE. When the cycle has been completed, turn the dough out onto a floured surface and knead until smooth and all trace of stickiness is gone. Form into a ball and place on an oiled bread peel covered with a cotton tea towel. Allow the bread to rise in a warm, draft-free kitchen until doubled in volume—about 45 minutes.

Place a baking tile in the middle of the oven.*****
Preheat oven to 400 degrees F.

Transfer the loaf of bread from the bread peel to the preheated tiles and bake at 400 degrees F. for about 45 minutes, or until the loaf "thumps hollow" when rapped with your knuckles. Spritz the tiles with water every 10 minutes to create steam. Transfer loaf to a wire rack and allow to cool completely before slicing and serving.

Yields one 9-inch loaf
— about 16 slices

Notes: *Preparation time depends, of course, on the brand of bread machine which you are using.

**If you are using a bread machine which preheats before mixing and kneading, there is no reason to be concerned with the exact temperature of your liquids, as long as they have been brought to room temperature.

***Do seek out corn flour. Corn flour creates a much more authentic texture than does the granular corn meal available in the cereal section of grocery stores and widely used for corn meal mush and Southern-style cornbread. *Harina de Maíz*, labeled "*amarilla fina*" is available in most grocery stores and gives a good texture to this bread if you can not find a finely ground, stone-ground corn meal.

****Some packaged dried yeast available in grocery stores contain a preservative. Natural food stores carry an additive-free dried yeast. In addition, *do not use so-called fast action yeasts*. The results will not please you.

PORTUGUESE COUNTRY CORN BREAD (cont'd)

*****This loaf has a firm crust. A very hard crust can be achieved by placing a pan of water on the rack under the tile while baking.

Preparation time will vary depending upon whether you use a bread machine for the initial mixing and kneading process.

1/16 SERVING – PROTEIN = 3.9 g.; FAT = 1.5 g.; CARBOHYDRATE = 24.7 g.; CALORIES = 128; CALORIES FROM FAT = 1%

PORTUGUESE ORANGE CUSTARDS WITH HONEY AND CINNAMON
Flan a Suco de Larange com Miel e Canela

TPT - 10 hours;
30 minutes = first cooling period;
8 hours = refrigeration period

When I stumbled on this recipe, I could not help laughing, reminded as I was of our vain attempts to get orange juice when we visited Braganca, Portugal, in the 1970s in search of the Castilian connections in Portuguese history. We were always offered the sweet soda so popular there. In this dish, freshly squeezed orange juice provides a fresh natural flavoring for a rich, sweet, traditional custard. I enrich fat-free pasteurized eggs with a couple of egg yolks to make these custards, instead of using the eight to twelve egg yolks usually called for in such a recipe. In addition, the usual two cups of heavy cream, have been replaced with a combination of milk and light cream. And, I have reduced the sugar since Portuguese desserts are considerably sweeter than we are used to. A simple brown sugar–cinnamon sauce is our favorite adornment.

1 cup *two-percent* milk
1 cup light cream *or* half and half
1 cup freshly squeezed orange juice*
2/3 cup sugar

1 cup *fat-free* pasteurized eggs (the equivalent of 4 eggs)—*brought to room temperature*
2 egg yolks

3 tablespoons honey, of choice
1 tablespoon cinnamon–sugar**

Preheat oven to 325 degrees F. Prepare a water bath large enough to hold six custard cups. Prepare six custard cups, ramekins, or molds by coating with non-stick lecithin spray coating.

Pour milk, cream, orange juice, and sugar into a saucepan set over *MEDIUM* heat. Allow to come to a boil. *Remove immediately from heat.*

Pour pasteurized eggs and egg yolks into a second saucepan. Using a wire whisk, combine thoroughly. *Slowly, while stirring constantly*, add the hot liquid to the eggs. Place over *LOW* heat and cook, *stirring constantly with a wire whisk*, until thickened. Set a fine sieve over a mixing bowl. Pour the custard mixture through the sieve to remove bits of scrambled eggs and chalazae that may be in the custard mixture. Divide the custard mixture among the prepared six small custard cups or molds. Using a spoon, remove bubbles from the surface. Place the cups in the prepared water bath. Be sure water comes halfway up the cups.

Bake in preheated 325 degree F. oven for about 1 hour. Test with a wooden skewer or a knife to be sure center has set. Remove from oven and allow to cool completely on a wire rack—about 30 minutes. Transfer to the refrigerator for at least eight hours.

Run a sharp knife around the edge of each custard. Loosen the molded custards by dipping the molds into warm water. Unmold onto *chilled* dessert plates. Refrigerate until ready to serve.

Drizzle about 1 1/2 teaspoonfuls of honey over each unmolded custard. Sprinkle with cinnamon–sugar.

Serve chilled.

Yields 6 individual servings

Notes: *Orange juice can be replaced with tangerine juice or clementine juice, if preferred.

**Make your own cinnamon–sugar or use a commercial mixture that pleases you.

This recipe can be halved or doubled, when required.

1/8 SERVING – PROTEIN = 7.7 g.; FAT = 6.5 g.; CARBOHYDRATE = 32.5 g.; CALORIES = 219; CALORIES FROM FAT = 27%

Europe–**Portugal**

PORTUGUESE ORANGE *TORTE*
Tarta de Laranja

TPT - 4 hours and 38 minutes;
        4 hours = filling development period

Rice puddings, caramelized flans, rich almond and egg pastries, and fresh fruit were frequent desserts as we traveled the length and breadth of Portugal but one evening this gorgeous torte was served in the courtyard restaurant of a monastery. It was a dinner never to be forgotten as bats flew up against the glass enclosure and I was introduced to one of most divine desserts ever.

It may take you a couple of times to get the knack of this dessert since once it is removed from the oven it must be rolled very, very quickly.

1 tablespoon butter—*softened to room temperature*
2 tablespoons unbleached white flour

3/4 cup sugar

1/3 cup sugar
4 large eggs

Juice of 1 orange—about 1/4 cupful*
1 tablespoon *finely* **grated** *organic* **orange zest**
1/4 teaspoon pure vanilla extract
1/8 teaspoon ground cinnamon

Preheat oven to 400 degrees F. Prepare a 15 x 10 x 1-inch jelly-roll pan by lining it with waxed paper.** Butter the waxed paper and the sides of the pan generously and evenly. Sprinkle the flour over the buttered waxed paper. Move the pan from side to side to coat both the waxed paper and the sides of the pan with an even coating of flour. Set aside until required.

Place a cotton tea towel, larger than the jelly roll pan that you are using to bake the *torte*, on the counter top with the shorter side facing you. Sprinkle 1/3 cupful of sugar on the towel to cover evenly an area slightly larger than that of baking pan.

In the bowl of the electric mixer fitted with wire whip, combine the remaining 3/4 cup sugar and the eggs, Beat at HIGH speed for about 5 minutes. The consistency will be similar to that of mayonnaise.

Once the egg–sugar mixture has reached a volume about 2 1/2 – 3 times its original volume, *reduce mixer speed to LOW* and gradually add orange juice, *finely* grated orange zest, vanilla extract, and cinnamon. Pour batter into prepared jelly-roll pan and spread it evenly to the sides of the pan. Bake in preheated 400 degree F. for 8 minutes. *Reduce oven temperature to 350 degrees F.* Continue baking for about 5 minutes more, or until browned. *Do not try to even out the canyons that form; they are normal.*

Immediately upon removal from the oven, loosen the edges with a knife or spatula and *quickly invert* the pan onto the sugar-covered area of the tea towel. Remove the waxed paper. Using a sharp knife, trim off any crisp edges. Roll the *torte* by lifting the edge of the towel nearest to you and allowing the *torte* to roll over itself, just as you would for a jelly roll. *Leave the torte wrapped in the towel at room temperature for 4 hours to allow the jelly-like filling to develop.*

Carefully unwrap and place on a bread board.

To serve, slice the *torte* on the bias into thin slices, about 3/8-inch thick. Allow 2 slices per serving. Refrigerate leftovers.

                            Yields 12 slices
                            adequate 6 people

Notes: *A lemon *torte* can be made in the same manner. Use lemon juice and lemon zest. Omit cinnamon.

         **Do not use parchment paper; use only waxed paper.

1/12 SERVING – PROTEIN = 2.5 g.; FAT = 3.0 g.; CARBOHYDRATE = 23.7 g.;
CALORIES = 129; CALORIES FROM FAT = 20%

Romania

The Romania we see today is a complex amalgam of influences and customs. From 100 to 271 AD this area of the European continent was the Roman province of Dacia, rich in gold, silver, and other ores much desired by the Romans. As in most provinces of the Roman Empire, Latin was introduced and an intense effort of Romanization was pursued. Lost to barbarian invasions beginning in the third century and for centuries thereafter, it became part of the First Bulgarian Empire from the eighth to the tenth centuries through which Eastern Orthodox Christianity was introduced. In 1003 AD the area known as Transylvania became an autonomous province of the Kingdom of Hungary until 1571 when it became independent. Known as the Principality of Transylvania, it remained autonomous until 1711, even while technically under the rule of the Ottoman Empire. The large principalities of Wallachia and Modavia emerged in 1310 and 1352 respectively as the advance of the Ottoman Empire threatened their security. By 1541 all three principalities had been absorbed into the Ottoman Empire. The overlapping of foods and customs in this part of Europe attests to the years that the Kingdom of Romania, formed in 1859 by the merger of the principalities of Modavia and Wallachia under the Hohenzollern monarchy, remained under Turkish influence. Independence from the Ottoman Turks was declared in 1877. After World War I, the prospering kingdom added Transylvania, Bukovina, and Bessarabia. At the end of World War II Romania's territories were occupied by the Soviet Union and Romania became a socialist republic. Since 1989, with the overthrow of the neo-Stalinist, abusive rule of Nicolae Ceausescu which had brought the population to the brink of starvation, Romania has made a difficult but steady effort to overcome the country's financial difficulties and its reputation for corruption.

Romanian cuisine reveals its history in so very many ways and truly illustrates its geographic position as the meeting point of the Balkans, Eastern Europe, and Central Europe. One can see Turkish, Greek, Hungarian, and German recipes which have been integrated into the cuisine with touches that make them quite thoroughly Romanian. So similar are some foods that substitution is not a problem for the western cook. *Telemea*, the tangy white cheese, can be substituted with *bryndza* or a good Greek *feta*. When you need a grating cheese for a Romanian recipe, an ewes' milk or cows' milk *Romano* cheese can be substituted for *cașcaval*. The concept and the seasoning of *ghiveci*, a popular and complex vegetable stew, sets it apart from similar vegetable stews, such as Bulgarian *gjuvec* and Hungarian *lecsó*. German *schnitzel* have become *șnițel* in Romanian, doughnuts are called *gogoși*, but Romanians have not modified the names for the revered Turkish sweets *baklava* and *halva*, enjoying each as they have for centuries as part of the magnificent assortment of pastries, *prăjituri*, displayed in pastry shops and served at the end of formal meals.

Europe–**Romania**

Roasted Eggplant *Caviar*
Caviar de Vinete

Feta Cheese Spread
Antreuri de Telemea

Sour Cream Omelet
Omlete cu Smatana Agra

~

Vegetable Soup with Caraway
Supa de Chimen

~

Asparagus Salad with Capers
Salta de Sparanghel

Shredded Beetroot Salad
Salata de Sfecia Rosie

~~~~~~~~~~~~~~~~~~~~~

Corn Meal Pudding with Cheese
Mamaliga ala Telemea

Sautéed Cabbage with Fennel Leaves
Varza cu Frutas de Chimen Dulce

Marinated Dried Mushroom Salad with Herbs
Gombasalata

~~~~~~~~~~~~~~~~~~~~~

Raspberry Swirl Dessert
Satou de Smeura

Cream of Wheat with Cherries
Cris cu Lapte cu Compote de Cirese

ROMANIAN ROASTED EGGPLANT *CAVIAR*
Caviar de Vinete
TPT - 35 minutes

From India to the Near East, and then to Europe through the influences of the Ottoman Empire, the humble vegetable, which we know as eggplant, has found its way into many cuisines and into some very delicious dishes. This "caviar" is sometimes called "poor man's caviar." We beg to differ; this beats "fish eggs" by a mile!

1 medium eggplant—well-washed, but *unpeeled*

1 tablespoon *extra virgin* olive oil
1 tablespoon freshly squeezed lemon juice
1 teaspoon HOMEMADE PAPRIKA *[see index]*
  or commercially-available *sweet* Hungarian paprika
1/2 teaspoon salt, or to taste
1/4 teaspoon freshly ground black pepper, or to taste

2 tablespoons preserved capers—well-drained and coarsely chopped

1 medium onion—*finely* chopped

Preheat broiler to 400 degrees F. and set the oven rack about 8 inches from heat source.

Pierce the eggplant several times with a sharp knife, place it on a broiler pan so that the eggplant is about 4 inches below the heat source. Broil the eggplant for a total of about 20 minutes, *turning the eggplant with tongs frequently during the broiling period* so that the skins chars evenly. Remove eggplant from oven and wrap in a dampened cotton tea towel for 5 minutes to steam.

Europe–**Romania**

ROMANIAN ROASTED EGGPLANT CAVIAR (cont'd)

Remove the towel. Trim and peel eggplant. Coarsely chop. Using a FOOD MILL fitted with steel knife, purée the eggplant chunks.*

Turn puréed eggplant into a bowl. Stir in olive oil, lemon juice, *sweet* paprika, salt, and black pepper.

Serve at room temperature or chill until ready to serve.

Turn into one side of a divided serving dish. Sprinkle chopped capers over eggplant mixture. Place *finely* chopped onions in the other section. Encourage diners to add onions to their serving of "eggplant caviar" as their taste dictates.

Serve with *crudités*, of choice, and crackers or small breads.

Yields 8 servings
adequate for 4 people

Notes: *We prefer a FOOD MILL to a food processor to prepare this appetizer since the roasted eggplant has the tendency to liquefy when processed.

This recipe may be doubled, when required.

1/8 SERVING – PROTEIN = 0.5 g.; FAT = 1.4 g.; CARBOHYDRATE = 2.8 g.;
CALORIES = 25; CALORIES FROM FAT = 50%

FETA CHEESE SPREAD IN THE ROMANIAN STYLE
Antreuri de Telemea

TPT - 6 hours and 17 minutes;
4 hours = *feta* cheese desalination period;
1 hour = *feta* cheese draining period;
1 hour = flavor development period

Telemea is the name for the feta-type ewe's milk cheese cas, which has been stored in a salted brine. Neither cheese is exported from Romania in any quantity so you will have to substitute. Feta cheese is an acceptable substitute for Romanian telemea cheese I am told, although regretfully I have never tasted the original.

1 cup (about 4 ounces) *feta* **cheese**

1/4 cup sweet *(unsalted)* **butter**—*softened to room temperature*

3 tablespoons snipped fresh chives*
1 tablespoon snipped fresh fennel leaves*
1 tablespoon *finely* **chopped fresh parsley***
1/2 teaspoon caraway seeds
1/8 teaspoon Hungarian *hot* **paprika**

Place *feta* cheese in a bowl. Add *cold* water to cover and refrigerate. Replace the water with *cold* fresh water approximately every 1 hour. Remove from bowl and wrap in a cotton tea towel. Allow moisture to drain from cheese for about 1 hour.

Crumble drained cheese into a mixing bowl. Add *softened* butter and, using a wooden paddle or spoon, work the cheese and butter together to form a smooth spread.

Add snipped chives and fennel leaves, *finely* chopped parsley, caraway seeds, and paprika. Stir to distribute evenly.

Mold into a cone shape in the middle of a serving dish. Chill in the refrigerator for at least 1 hour to allow flavors to develop.

Serve with black olives, whole radishes, scallions, tomatoes, fennel sticks, and crackers or breadsticks.

12 tablespoonfuls
adequate for 4 people
as an appetizer

Notes: *Use only fresh herbs to prepare this dish.

This recipe is easily doubled, when required.

1/12 SERVING (i. e., per tablespoonful) –
PROTEIN = 1.4 g.; FAT = 5.8 g.; CARBOHYDRATE = 0.7 g.;
CALORIES = 61; CALORIES FROM FAT = 86%

Europe–**Romania**

ROMANIAN SOUR CREAM OMELET
Omlete cu Smantana Agra
TPT - 27 minutes

Until I tasted this omelet, I was quite satisfied with a classic French omelet as long as it was filled with extra sharp Cheddar cheese. This does not take much longer to prepare but the taste is quite different and, may I add, quite satisfying. We often serve these omelets with fruit as a brunch, for which we add one tablespoon sugar to the egg mixture and eliminate the black pepper and chives, or with a mushroom ragoût for lunch or a light supper. This recipe makes two omelets but can be multiplied as required.

3 large *organic* eggs
3 tablespoons *fat-free* dairy sour cream
Freshly ground black pepper, to taste

2 tablespoons unbleached white flour

1 tablespoon butter

Snipped fresh chives—for garnish—if desired
Fat-free dairy sour cream—for garnish—if desired

In a mixing bowl, combine eggs, sour cream, and black pepper. Using a wire whisk, lightly mix together.

Teaspoonful by teaspoonful, whisk flour into egg mixture.

Brush a thin coating of butter on 9-inch non-stick coated skillet. Set over *LOW-MEDIUM* heat.

In a 7-inch non-stick-coated skillet or omelet pan set over *MEDIUM* heat, melt butter. Ladle *one-half* of omelet mixture into skillet, spreading it evenly to the edge of the skillet. Cook until omelet begins to pull away from the edges of the pan and is golden. Flip the omelet into the 9-inch pan and allow it to brown on the other side. Slide out onto a heated plate or round platter and set on a warming tray.

While the first omelet is browning in the 9-inch skillet, prepare a second omelet using the remaining omelet mixture.

Serve at once sprinkled with chives, if desired.

Yields 2 individual servings

1/2 SERVING (i. e., per individual omelet, exclusive of garnish) –
PROTEIN = 13.7 g.; FAT = 14.3 g.; CARBOHYDRATE = 17.0 g.;
CALORIES = 254; CALORIES FROM FAT = 51%

ROMANIAN VEGETABLE SOUP WITH CARAWAY
Sopa de Chimen
TPT - 55 minutes

This root vegetable soup does not need a meat stock to enthrall a soup lover. Every simple element contributes big, satisfying flavor. In addition to replacing the stock with a good, rich, dark vegetable stock, I have had to, unfortunately, omit an ingredient that is traditional because it is rarely, if ever, available in produce departments in the United States. There are many cultivars of parsley root, Petroselinum crispum tuberosum (aka Petroselinum hortense), grown for its root and not for its leaves, but its popularity appears to have remained in Europe, principally in Central European cuisines. Therefore, I have substituted a parsnip for the parsley root or rock root that would traditionally be used to make this soup.

2 tablespoons butter
1 medium leek—*white and green portions only*
  —trimmed, halved lengthwise, sliced, and well-washed
1 large parsnip—peeled and cut into large dice
1/2 medium celeriac (celery root or knob celery)
  —peeled and cut into large dice
1 cup loosely-packed, chopped parsley stems
  —well-washed

2 quarts BROWN VEGETABLE STOCK *[see index] or* other vegetarian stock of choice
1 cup *boiling* water
1 tablespoon caraway seeds
1/4 teaspoon salt
Freshly ground black pepper, to taste

ROMANIAN VEGETABLE SOUP WITH CARAWAY (cont'd)

In a kettle set over *LOW-MEDIUM* heat, melt butter. Add sliced leeks, diced parsnip, diced celeriac, and chopped parsley stems. Sauté gently for about 5 minutes, *being careful not to allow the vegetables to brown.*

Add stock, *boiling* water, caraway seeds, salt, and pepper. Cook, stirring frequently, for about 45 minutes, or until vegetables are tender. Turn into a heated soup tureen.

Serve into heated soup bowls.

Yields 6 servings
adequate for 4 people

Note: This recipe can be halved or doubled, when required.

1/6 SERVING – PROTEIN = 1.0 g.; FAT = 4.0 g.; CARBOHYDRATE = 7.6 g.;
CALORIES = 68; CALORIES FROM FAT = 53%

ROMANIAN ASPARAGUS SALAD WITH CAPERS
Salata de Sparanghel

TPT - 30 minutes

Capers, the flower buds of Capparis spinosa, are immensely popular in the cooking of the Mediterranean, adding a sour and salty accent to many dishes. The tiniest ones, "nonparells" from France, are aromatic and have a delicate flavor while the larger varieties are stronger in flavor and less aromatic. Since these are hand-picked, the price can be steep, especially for the very prized "nonparells." We think they are worth the price and our daughter claims that she can not cook without them. This simple Romanian asparagus salad really demonstrates the flavor punctuation that capers can provide.

24 spears of fresh asparagus—trimmed and well-washed to remove any sand

Yolks *only* from 2 hard-cooked eggs
2 tablespoons *extra virgin* olive oil
1 tablespoon white wine vinegar
1 teaspoon *fat-free* sour cream

1 tablespoon *nonparell* capers, packed in brine —well-rinsed and dried
Freshly ground black pepper, to taste

Set up a steamer and a large bowl of *ice water*.

Steam asparagus spears over boiling water for about 8 minutes or until bright green and just tender. Plunge the asparagus into *ice water*. Allow to remain in the *ice water* for about 10 minutes. Drain thoroughly.*

Sieve hard-cooked egg yolks into a mixing bowl. Using a wire whisk, beat in olive oil, vinegar, and sour cream. Beat well.

Add capers and black pepper. Stir to integrate.

Pile asparagus in the center of a long platter. Spoon dressing over the asparagus spears. Refrigerate until ready to serve.

Serve chilled.

Yields 6 servings
adequate for 4 people

Notes: *Conveniently, the asparagus and the dressing can be prepared early in the day. Refrigerate the asparagus and you will have a significant head start on dinner.

This recipe can be halved or doubled, when required.

1/6 SERVING – PROTEIN = 1.8 g.; FAT = 5.7 g.; CARBOHYDRATE = 3.4 g.;
CALORIES = 65; CALORIES FROM FAT = 79%

Europe–**Romania**

ROMANIAN SHREDDED BEETROOT SALAD
Salata de Sfecia Rosie

TPT - 2 hours and 44 minutes;
2 hours = marination period

Throughout history, every attempt to unify Europe has met with nationalistic and regional obstacles that can be negotiated but whether or not people like beets seems to be non-negotiable. When you come from a heritage where this workhorse of a winter staple is valued and, yes, loved, you find it hard to understand why everybody doesn't like the sweet, versatile beet. I remember well the beets among the other winter vegetables in my grandparents' root cellars and the canned and pickled beets on my mother's canning shelves and the beautiful ones I grew in the sandy soil of Long Island. I remember also the promise of good food which they represented.

3 quarts *boiling* water
1 1/2 pounds fresh beets—4 medium beets—well-scrubbed, with roots intact and 2 inches of leaf stem

1 tablespoon *extra virgin* olive oil
1 tablespoon freshly squeezed lemon juice

3 tablespoons chopped fresh dillweed
1 1/2 tablespoons *finely* chopped fresh basil
Salt, to taste
Freshly ground black pepper, to taste

Several soft lettuce leaves, such as Boston or Bibb*

In a large kettle, cook beets in *boiling* water until tender—about 30 minutes. Drain. Rinse in *cold* water until they can be handled. Cut off root end and stem end. Slip off skins and cut into quarters.

Using a food processor fitted with shredding blade or by hand using the medium blade surface of a hand shredder, shred cooked beets. Discard any large pieces which can not be shredded. Turn into a plastic container with tightly fitting lid.

In a cruet, combine olive oil and lemon juice. Shake the *vinaigrette* well. Pour over the shredded beets. Seal container tightly and turn over and over to coat beet shreds with *vinaigrette*.

Refrigerate for at least 2 hours, turning the container occasionally to insure even marination.

When ready to serve, add chopped dillweed and basil. Season with salt and black pepper, to taste.

To serve, arrange lettuce leaves in a serving bowl. Pile marinated beets into the center.**

Yields 6 servings
adequate for 4 people

Notes: *Red-leafed Boston lettuce, if available, is particularly attractive as a base for this salad.

**If preferred, this may be served as a relish, rather than as a separate salad.

This recipe may be halved or doubled, when required.

1/6 SERVING – PROTEIN = 0.5 g.; FAT = 1.9 g.; CARBOHYDRATE = 3.2 g.;
CALORIES = 31; CALORIES FROM FAT = 55%

ROMANIAN CORN MEAL PUDDING WITH CHEESE
Mamaliga ala Telemea

TPT - 51 minutes

Since mamaliga is eaten at almost every meal in Romania, a variety of accompaniments can please those who might complain, "Oh, not mamaliga again." Consequently, sautéed onions and garlic, sauerkraut, all kinds of vegetable sauces, and meats are served with and over the corn meal pudding/bread. We especially like to serve it with a wild mushroom or herbed tomato sauce or with cheese, as in this recipe.

1 1/2 cups *cold* water
1 cup yellow corn meal

1 1/2 cups *boiling* water
1 tablespoon butter

1/4 cup crumbled Greek *feta* cheese*
1 tablespoon grated *pecorino Romano* cheese

1 tablespoon *cold* butter—diced
1/4 cup *fine, whole wheat* breadcrumbs

VOLUME I - 344

ROMANIAN CORN MEAL PUDDING WITH CHEESE (cont'd)

Preheat oven to 350 degrees F. Prepare a 1-quart soufflé dish or other oven-to-table baking dish by coating with non-stick lecithin spray coating.

In the top half of the double boiler, combine *cold* water and corn meal. Mix well. Place insert over simmering, *not boiling*, water. While stirring with a wooden spoon, add *boiling* water. Add butter and continue to stir until butter is melted and integrated. Cook, stirring frequently, until thickened and smooth.

Cover and allow to cook, stirring frequently, for about 10-15 minutes.

Mix crumbled *feta* cheese and grated Romano cheese together.

Spoon *one-third* of softly cooked *mamaliga* into prepared baking dish. Scatter *one-half* of combined cheeses over. Spoon *one-half* of remaining corn meal over and scatter remaining cheese mixture over. Top with a layer of remaining corn meal.

Dot top with diced butter and sprinkle breadcrumbs over the top.

Bake in preheated 350 degree F. oven for 15 minutes, or until lightly browned on top.

Yields 6 servings
adequate for 4 people

Notes: *Feta* cheese is an adequate substitute for Romanian *telemea* cheese, which is rarely found outside of Romania. *Telemea* is the name for the *feta*-type ewe's milk cheese *cas*, which has been stored in a salted brine.

Most recipes for *mamaliga* direct that the corn meal be added to boiling water. The method described above results in a lump-free porridge.

When required, this recipe may be halved or doubled.

1/6 SERVING – PROTEIN = 3.4 g.; FAT = 6.0 g.; CARBOHYDRATE = 17.3 g.;
CALORIES = 136; CALORIES FROM FAT = 40%

SAUTÉED CABBAGE WITH FENNEL LEAVES IN THE ROMANIAN STYLE
Varza cu Frunzas de Chimen Dulce
TPT - 13 minutes

All summer long the feathery leaves of the common, perennial fennel plants (Foeniculum vulgare) in our gardens sway in the breeze, suggesting that it is cooler than it really is. These flavorful fronds are often ignored by gardeners who seek a seed harvest or in the case of Florence fennel, "finocchio," the bulbs. The mouse moth and the anise swallowtail butterfly share our passion for the anise taste and add the fronds to their diet as do we. In the winter the feathery tops of the finocchio we buy from our produce departments must suffice. It is disappointing to see people breaking off the stems and leaves and discarding them in the store; the stems add enormous flavor to soup stock and the leaves can be added to salads and dishes like this simple cabbage skillet.

2 tablespoons butter
5 cups *thinly* sliced (as for slaw) white cabbage
—well-washed and well-dried
1/2 medium onion—*thinly* sliced

1/4 cup *loosely-packed* fennel leaves—trimmed
of hard stems

3/4 cup canned, *diced* tomatoes
Pinch salt
Freshly ground black pepper, to taste

1 tablespoon distilled white vinegar
3 tablespoons *fat-free* dairy sour cream

In a large skillet set over *MEDIUM* heat, melt butter. Add *thinly* sliced cabbage and onion. Cook, stirring frequently, until cabbage is wilted, *being careful to allow neither vegetable to brown.*

Add fennel leaves. Cook, stirring constantly, for a minute or two more.

Add tomatoes, salt, and pepper. Cook, stirring, until heated through.

Europe–**Romania**

SAUTÉED CABBAGE WITH FENNEL LEAVES IN THE ROMANIAN STYLE (cont'd)

Add vinegar and sour cream. Stir into vegetable mixture. Allow to heat through. Turn into heated serving bowl. Keep warm on warming tray until ready to serve.

Yields 6 servings
adequate for 4 people

Note: This recipe can be halved or doubled, when required.

1/6 SERVING – PROTEIN = 2.5 g.; FAT = 4.0 g.; CARBOHYDRATE = 8.7 g.; CALORIES = 81; CALORIES FROM FAT = 44%

ROMANIAN MARINATED DRIED MUSHROOM SALAD WITH HERBS
Gambasalata

TPT - 12 hours and 52 minutes;
40 minutes = mushroom soaking period;
12 hours = marination period

This is a feast of what the Japanese would call "umami" in the style of Romania where mushrooms are treasured ingredients for soups, salads, or vegetable side dishes.

3 cups *boiling* water
1 1/2 cups *dried, sliced* white *(Agaricus)* mushrooms
 —*well-rinsed and brushed to remove any foreign matter**
1/2 ounce *dried, sliced porcini* mushrooms *or* a mixture of *dried*, wild mushrooms—*well-rinsed and brushed to remove any foreign matter*
10 small *dried, whole,* Chinese black mushrooms
 —*well-rinsed and brushed to remove any foreign matter*

1/2 cup *extra virgin* olive oil
1/4 cup GARLIC–BASIL VINEGAR *[see index] or* red wine vinegar**
1 teaspoon HOMEMADE PAPRIKA *[see index] or* commercially-available Hungarian sweet paprika
1/2 teaspoon dried thyme—crushed
1/4 teaspoon dried tarragon—crushed
1/8 teaspoon ground cumin
1/8 teaspoon ground sweet marjoram

Lettuce leaves
1 lemon—cut into thin wedges—for garnish

Soak *well-cleaned*, dried mushrooms in *boiling* water for 40 minutes until softened. Drain well. Cut stems from black mushrooms.

Combine oil, vinegar, paprika, crushed thyme and tarragon, and ground cumin and sweet marjoram. Pour over mushrooms. Cover and toss to coat mushrooms well. Refrigerate for at least 12 hours, turning occasionally to insure uniform marination.

Turn into a sieve, set over a mixing bowl, and drain *very thoroughly* before serving—*all but 2 tablespoonfuls of the marinade should be recovered.*

Turn into a serving bowl lined with lettuce leaves. Garnish with lemon wedges before serving.

Yields 6 servings
adequate for 4 people

Notes: *Drying sliced, white cultivated mushrooms using one of the inexpensive dehydrators available, is a very simple process. By drying mushrooms yourself you can be assured that they are *well-cleaned, well-trimmed, and flawless.*

**ROMANIAN MARINATED DRIED MUSHROOM SALAD
WITH HERBS** (cont'd)

**Homemade, flavored vinegars are enjoyed by Romanians and are used expertly by many Romanian cooks to prepare marinades for both vegetable and meat dishes.

This recipe is easily halved or doubled, when required.

1/6 SERVING – PROTEIN = 1.1 g.; FAT = 2.0 g.; CARBOHYDRATE = 4.7 g.;
CALORIES = 41; CALORIES FROM FAT = 44%

ROMANIAN RASPBERRY SWIRL DESSERT
Satau de Smeura

TPT - 2 hours and 18 minutes;
2 hours = fruit maceration period

This is an extreme variation on the traditional Romanian pudding which is made from egg yolks and includes a great deal of sweet white wine.

2 cups frozen raspberries—*defrosted*—or fresh raspberries, in season
2 tablespoons sugar

1/2 teaspoon pure lemon extract

1 cup *fat-free* pasteurized eggs (the equivalent of 4 eggs)
3 tablespoons sugar

1 1/2 teaspoons freshly grated, *organic* lemon zest
—the grated zest of 1 large lemon

In a small bowl, combine defrosted raspberries and the 2 tablespoons sugar. Toss to mix well. Cover dish and set aside at room temperature for 2 hours.

Set a fine sieve over a bowl. Press raspberries through the sieve, removing as many seeds as possible. Sieve the raspberry purée again to remove any errant seeds. Stir in lemon extract. Set aside.

Using the electric mixer, beat pasteurized eggs and the remaining 3 tablespoons sugar at *MEDIUM-HIGH* speed until thick and tripled in volume.

Add lemon zest and continue to beat until the lemon zest is evenly dispersed. Refrigerate until ready to serve.

Just before serving, add raspberry purée and, using a rubber spatula, fold the purée *lightly* into the egg mixture, to *create a red swirl.** Turn into a large serving dish or into six individual sherbet glasses or other glass dessert dishes.

Serve at once.

Yields 6 servings
adequate for 4-6 people

Notes: *Although the egg base of this dessert can be prepared as much as an hour ahead of serving, the raspberry purée can not be added more than a few minutes before serving or the dessert turns a rather unappealing blue. For that reason, leftovers are equally unappealing.

This recipe may be halved or doubled, when required.

1/6 SERVING – PROTEIN = 4.3 g.; FAT = 0.07 g.; CARBOHYDRATE = 23.9 g.;
CALORIES = 113; CALORIES FROM FAT – <1%

Europe–**Romania**

ROMANIAN CREAM OF WHEAT WITH CHERRIES
Cris cu Lapte cu Compote de Cirese

TPT - 2 hours and 51 minutes;
30 minutes = cooling period
2 hours = cherry flavoring period

Young and old, the whole family enjoys this dessert. I prefer the richness of the farina when cooked in milk although some prefer to cook it in water and I often allow the cherries to sit in the vanilla-scented liquid overnight to intensify the vanilla flavor. A friend prepares a similar recipe in which fresh cherries are boiled and mashed and then combined with the cream of wheat.

2 pints sweet cherries canned in light syrup
  —drained, but canning liquid reserved
1 vanilla bean

1 cup light cream *or* **half and half**
1/2 cup *two-percent* **milk**
1/4 cup sugar

1/3 cup enriched quick, *but not instant,* **farina**
  or Cream of Wheat cereal, if preferred

1/2 teaspoon pure vanilla extract

In a large, shallow bowl, combine cherries and 1/2 cupful of canning liquid. Split the vanilla bean open and scrape the seeds from the vanilla pod into the bowl. Stir to disperse the seeds throughout the liquid. Add the pod for extra flavor. Cover and refrigerate for at least 2 hours.

In a saucepan set over *LOW* heat, heat cream and sugar *just to the boiling point.*

Add farina and cook, stirring constantly, until thickened. Stir pudding well. Add vanilla extract. Thin with more cream at this point, if necessary. Divide pudding among six sherbet glasses or other small dessert dishes. Refrigerate for at least 30 minutes before serving.

When ready to serve, remove the vanilla pod from the cherries and, using a slotted spoon, transfer the cherries to a serving dish. Spoon the cherries over the chilled farina or pass the cherries to accommodate individual tastes.

Yields 6 individual servings

Note: This recipe may be halved or doubled, when required.

1/6 SERVING – PROTEIN = 5.2 g.; FAT = 5.0 g.; CARBOHYDRATE = 41.2 g.;
CALORIES = 223; CALORIES FROM FAT = 20%

Europe–Russia

Russia

Russia is an incredibly vast country, the largest country in the world with one-quarter of the earth's fresh water reserves. To visit Russia and even to live in Russia is really not to know Russia. Archeological excavations in Kostenki on the Don River show that humans have visited here, or perhaps even lived here, for at least 35,000 years.

Russia is today a complex matrix overlaying a long and complex history in which both Byzantine and Slavic threads are intertwined. Kievan Rus', the first East Slavic state dates to the ninth century AD and by 988 AD Orthodox Christianity had been adopted from the Byzantine Empire. The Mongols invasion (1237-1240) resulted in the destruction of Kiev and the death of an estimated fifty percent of the population of Kievan Rus'. In the fourteenth century, at the beginning of the Little Ice Age, the Grand Duchy of Moscow, initially a part of Vladimir–Suzdal, asserted itself and reunified the principalities into which Kievan Rus' had divided after the invasion of the Mongols and their subsequent control. This union and the Novgorod Republic became Russia. Under Ivan III (Ivan, the Great) the Golden Horde was driven out of northern and central Rus', which then came under Moscow's rule. Ivan IV (Ivan, the Terrible) was the first ruler to use the title *Tsar* (Czar), derived from the Latin "Caesar," when he was crowned in 1547. The Rurikid Dynasty ended in 1598 since Ivan's sons had died and ended the line of succession. The Romanov Dynasty succeeded, coming to the throne in 1613, and by the eighteenth century Russia, then an empire, extended from Poland east to Alaska. *Tsar* Nicholas II, the last of the Romanoff rulers, was forced to abdicate during the February Revolution of 1917, after which a short-lived provisional government was established. The world's first socialist state, the Union of Soviet Socialist Republics, was established by the Bolsheviks under Vladimir Lenin later that year after the October Revolution.

In August 1991 a military coup against the Soviet leader Mikhail Gorbachev, who had instituted policies of openness (*glasnost*) and restructuring (*perestroika*), was unsuccessful but led instead to the collapse of the Soviet system. Boris Yeltsin was elected president in June 1991; by December of the same year the U.S.S.R. has dissolved into fifteen states.

We visited Russia in 1983, during the Soviet era, and found that *Pravda* had been running "health" articles which condemned vegetarianism and promoted the eating of red meat. My reading material, which included several vegetarian journals, was closely scrutinized and questioned by officials at the airport. Our Russian guide was beside herself with concern for our daughter, then sixteen. Restaurants and hotels were beside themselves trying to feed the five of us who chose to try to maintain our vegetarianism while on this trip. By the end of our visit, there were fourteen of us at the "meatless table" and our Russian guide had joined us. She said that it did not look like our health was suffering and she thought maybe she could control her weight with less meat. My fondest memories of meals in Russia include the lunch we ate in Vladimir where the flustered chef in the small family restaurant prepared the freshest fried eggs I have eaten and sautéed wild mushrooms for us since he had not been forewarned that members of the group would not eat tongue. And, I shall never forget the breakfasts that greeted us each morning at the hotels in Moscow and St. Petersburg (then, Leningrad) in which we stayed. Piles of the lightest *blini* or cheese and potato cutlets with melted butter, rich sour cream, and jams, served in huge silver punch bowls, meats and cheeses, and strong tea fortified us for the cold as we ventured into the almost day-long darkness of those December days.

Europe–Russia

Moscow Salad
Salat Moscovskii

~

Cabbage Soup
Kapustnye Shchi

Sorrel – Potato Soup
Zelyoniye Shchi

~~~~~~~~~~~~~~~~~~~~~~~

Potato Cheese Cutlets
Syrniki iz Tvoroga iz Kartofeyelya

Yogurt – Sour Cream Sauce

Shredded Fresh Beets
Sviokly

~~~~~~~~~~

Individual Sour Cream Omelets
Omlyet so Smyetanoy

Cucumbers Sautéed in Dill Butter
Ogurtsy so Buter s Ukropom

Stewed Mushrooms
Griby Tushonye

~~~~~~~~~~~~~~~~~~~~~~~

Yogurt *Crème* Mousse   and   **Walnut Sponge Cake**
Ryazhenka Muss   *Osnovnoi Orekhovyi Biskvit*

Apple Pudding with Breadcrumbs
Yamblochnyi o Krem

Orthodox Easter Dessert
Pashka

Orange Spiced Tea
Chai s Sok

Europe–**Russia**

MOSCOW SALAD
Salat Moscovskii

TPT - about 3 hours and 28 minutes;
30 minutes = potato chilling period;
2 hours = marination period

We were on our way by rail to St. Petersburg and, finding ourselves with an hour or two between train connections in Moscow, we ate a late supper in a hotel restaurant. It was in that restaurant that we first tasted this wonderful composed creation, beautifully prepared so that every element was the same size; nothing was larger than a pea. Upon returning home, I tried to remember the nuances of the remarkable appetizer which we had enjoyed and this recipe is the result of the experimentation and the never-to-be-forgotten memory of that pleasurable meal.

2 medium potatoes

1 large carrot—peeled or scraped and diced

1/4 medium cucumber—peeled, seeded, and diced
1/4 cup diced celery
3 large mushrooms—trimmed, rinsed, cleaned well with a brush, and diced
1 small kosher pickle—diced
1/3 cup freshly shelled *or defrosted, frozen* peas
2 medium scallions—trimmed, well rinsed, and sliced
3 preserved capers—*finely* chopped

1/4 cup CLASSIC FRENCH DRESSING *[see index]*

2 tablespoons *calorie-reduced or light* mayonnaise

Scrub potatoes thoroughly and place in boiling water to cover. Boil until cooked through, but still *firm*—about 25 minutes. *(They will yield to a fork, but not crumble.)* Drain thoroughly and chill for at least 30 minutes. Peel and dice.

Cook diced carrot in *boiling* water to cover until cooked through, but *still firm*—about 10 minutes. Drain thoroughly.

In a large bowl with cover, combine diced potatoes, carrot, cucumber, celery, mushrooms, and pickle with peas, sliced scallions, and *finely* chopped capers. Toss gently to combine.

Add French dressing and toss gently to coat thoroughly. Cover bowl and marinate in the refrigerator for at least 2 hours, occasionally tossing to redistribute settled marinade.

Just before serving, turn salad into a fine sieve and allow to drain *very thoroughly*. (About 2 tablespoonfuls of marinade should drain off.)

Turn drained vegetables into a large mixing bowl. Add mayonnaise. Toss *gently*, but *thoroughly*. Turn into a serving dish. Chill until required.

Serve into individual lettuce leaf cups, if desired.

Yields about 8 servings
adequate for 4-6 people

Note: This recipe is easily doubled, when required.

1/8 SERVING – PROTEIN = 1.3 g.; FAT = 6.5 g.; CARBOHYDRATE = 11.4 g.;
CALORIES = 109; CALORIES FROM FAT = 38%

Europe–**Russia**

RUSSIAN CABBAGE SOUP
Kapustnye Shchi
TPT - 1 hour and 33 minutes

We grew to love this soup, and the derivative sauce, and hoped each night that the Russian chef's response to our vegetarianism would be this body-warming, soul-warming specialty accompanied by thick slices of wonderful black bread, instead of a lecture on the Party's stand on nutrition. The Russians we met, in general, could not understand, if you could afford meat, why you did not eat meat —"since it is necessary for health and your sixteen-year-old daughter will have no energy and surely become stupid and die." The Soviet Russians were literally throwing meat at us at every meal to prove that there were no shortages in the U.S.S.R. When meat was rejected, sturgeon and dreadful deep-fried whole fish with their tales tucked unappealingly in their mouths appeared on our plates meal after meal. "Tell all your friends to come."

1 1/2 tablespoons vegetable oil
4 cups chopped cabbage
1 1/2 cups chopped onion
2 small garlic cloves—*very finely* chopped

1 cup VEGETARIAN BROWN STOCK *[see index]* or other vegetarian stock of choice
2 tablespoons freshly squeezed lemon juice
2 tablespoons whole wheat flour
1 teaspoon sugar
2 teaspoons caraway seeds
1/2 teaspoon freshly ground black pepper, or to taste

1 1/2 cups canned, *diced* tomatoes—drained and liquid retained
1 1/2 cups canned, *whole* tomatoes

In a large, heavy kettle set over *LOW* heat, heat oil. When hot, add chopped cabbage and onion with *very finely* chopped garlic. Sauté for about 15 minutes, or until vegetables are *soft*, but *not browned*.

In a mixing bowl, combine stock, lemon juice, flour, sugar, caraway seeds, and black pepper. Mix well. Add to sautéed vegetables in kettle. Add chopped, stewed tomatoes with liquid and whole tomatoes with liquid. Bring to the boil over *MEDIUM* heat. Reduce heat to *LOW* again and simmer for 1 hour. Stir occasionally.

Turn into warmed soup tureen to serve into warmed soup plates. Serve a whole tomato with each serving. Accompany with dark rye or pumpernickel bread.

Yields 8 servings
adequate for 4-6 people

Notes: This soup freezes well. Defrost in the refrigerator before heating or, if still frozen, heat in a double boiler over boiling water.

When required, this recipe may easily be doubled.

Russians often serve this as a sauce over mashed potatoes. Drain the liquid from the soup to form the thick RUSSIAN TOMATO AND CABBAGE SAUCE *(Sous z Kapustnye)*.

1/8 SERVING – PROTEIN = 2.5 g.; FAT = 2.5 g.; CARBOHYDRATE = 14.1 g.;
CALORIES = 82; CALORIES FROM FAT = 31%

RUSSIAN SORREL – POTATO SOUP
Zelyoniye Shchi
TPT - 1 hour and 6 minutes

Sorrel announces spring as surely as do crocuses and forsythia. In Russia the feeling is the same and you can tell because "same old, same old" potato soup is not "same old" anymore. It is spring! Although Russian cooks usually mix sorrel with spinach to make this soup, we prefer the gentle bite of the French sorrel.

RUSSIAN SORREL – POTATO SOUP (cont'd)

2 tablespoons butter
1 large shallot clove—*finely* chopped
4 large scallions—*white portions with one inch of green portions*—trimmed, well-rinsed, and *thinly* sliced

5 cups chopped *or* sliced French sorrel (dock) leaves*—ribs discarded
1/4 teaspoon dried thyme—crushed**
1/2 teaspoon dried dillweed—crushed— *or*
1 1/2 teaspoonfuls fresh dillweed—*finely* chopped

7 small potatoes—peeled and *thinly* sliced

2 cups VEGETARIAN BROWN STOCK *[see index]* or other vegetarian stock of choice
2 cups water
1/2 teaspoon salt

Freshly ground black pepper, to taste

Fat-free sour cream, for garnish***

In a kettle set over *MEDIUM-LOW* heat, melt butter. Add *finely* minced shallot and *thinly* sliced scallions. Sauté until soft and translucent, *allowing neither the shallot nor the scallions to brown.*

Add sorrel with crushed thyme and dillweed. Cook, stirring frequently, until sorrel wilts and turns dark.

Add *thin* potato slices. Stir to coat potatoes with sautéed ingredients and cook, stirring frequently, for about 10 minutes.

Add stock, water, and salt. Increase heat to *MEDIUM-HIGH* and allow soup to come to a boil. Reduce heat to *LOW* and cook, stirring frequently, for about 35-40 minutes, or until potatoes are tender.

Season with black pepper to taste.

Turn into a heated soup tureen and serve into heated soup plates. Garnish each serving with a dollop of sour cream.

Yields 6 servings
adequate for 4 people

Notes: *French sorrel, with its large leaves, is much less sour in taste than sour dock or garden sorrel.

**Any of the many varieties of the herb thyme may be used to prepare this dish. Our special favorite is lemon thyme *(Thymus vulgaris 'citriodorus')*. It compliments the sharp, lemony taste of the sorrel. Both the sorrel and lemon thyme are hardy perennials which will grow easily in your garden. About 3/4 teaspoonful fresh thyme may be substituted, when available.

***Sliced hard-cooked eggs and fresh chives are also traditional Russian garnishes for this soup and its variations.

This recipe may be halved or doubled, when required.

Leftovers may be reheated *gently* over *LOW* heat but this soup does not freeze well.

1/6 SERVING (with 1 tablespoonful *fat-free* sour cream) –
PROTEIN = 5.2 g., FAT = 4.1 g.; CARBOHYDRATE = 25.5 g.;
CALORIES = 142; CALORIES FROM FAT = 26%

RUSSIAN POTATO CHEESE CUTLETS
Syrniki iz Tvoroga iz Kartofeyelya

TPT - 49 hours and 24 minutes;
48 hours = *ricotta* draining period

Either blini or these divine cheese cutlets, formed into smaller cakes, were always on the menu at the lavish buffet breakfasts served in our Russian hotels. Since they freeze so beautifully, if layered with plastic wrap and securely sealed, we make a large quantity of the smaller cutlets when we take up the project. This is a wonderful convenience for breakfast or brunch menus and they heat up so quickly that one forgets the bit of effort it takes to make them.

RUSSIAN POTATO CHEESE CUTLETS (cont'd)

2 cups *part-skimmed milk ricotta* **cheese***

4 medium all-purpose potatoes
1 quart *boiling* **water**

3 large eggs—well-beaten
1/2 cup whole wheat flour

2 tablespoons butter

Unbleached white flour, as needed

YOGURT – SOUR CREAM SAUCE *[see recipe which follows]*
Cinnamon sugar *or* jam of choice

Place *ricotta* into a fine sieve and set over a small bowl in the refrigerator to drain for 48 hours. *(You should recover about 1 1/2 cupfuls of drained ricotta.)*

Rub the drained cheese through a sieve into a clean bowl to remove all lumps. Set aside.

Peel and dice potatoes. Cook, covered, in *boiling* water until tender—about 20 minutes. Drain thoroughly.

Using a RICER, rice potatoes into a clean bowl. Add sieved *ricotta* cheese and well-beaten eggs. Mix well. Beat in whole wheat flour to form a thick batter.

In a skillet set over *MEDIUM* heat, melt butter.

Turn potato–cheese mixture out onto surface floured with white flour. Form about 1/3-1/2 cupful of batter into a cutlet. Flop the batter over and over in the flour until it has enough substance to transfer into the hot skillet. Press down gently to form an oval cake. Cook several at a time, turning until evenly browned. Transfer to warmed platter on warming tray or in a warm oven to keep warm until all are prepared.

Serve with YOGURT – SOUR CREAM SAUCE and cinnamon sugar or with jam, if preferred.

Yields about 16 cutlets
adequate for 4-5 people

Notes: *Tvorog, Russian-style cottage cheese, is not available in the United States unless you make it yourself. Cottage and pot cheeses tend to be a bit too sour for our tastes. Drained *ricotta* approximates the texture and taste admirably.

If frozen, defrost in the refrigerator. Melt butter in a skillet, add cutlets, and heat through.

1/16 SERVING (i. e., per cutlet) –
PROTEIN = 6.9 g.; FAT = 4.3 g.; CARBOHYDRATE = 15.1 g.;
CALORIES = 118; CALORIES FROM FAT = 33%

YOGURT – SOUR CREAM SAUCE
TPT - 2 minutes

During our trip to Russia, I realized that my memory of that wonderful sour cream that my grandmother insisted upon was not just a glorification of the past. We had really gotten much too used to commercial sour cream. This mixture of sour cream and yogurt is closer to the taste that we experienced over our blini each morning in Russia and more like the sour cream from the Polish butcher on Joseph Avenue in Rochester, New York.

1/4 cup *fat-free* **dairy sour cream**
1/2 cup PLAIN YOGURT *[see index]* **or commercially-available plain yogurt**

In a small bowl, combine sour cream and yogurt. Using a wire whisk, whisk gently to form a smooth sauce.

Serve with RUSSIAN POTATO CHEESE CUTLETS (Syrniki iz Tvoroga iz Kartofyelya) *[see recipe which precedes]*, cheese *blintzes (Blinchatrye Piroski s Tvorogom)*, *blini*, over vegetables, or even as a salad dressing.

Yields 3/4 cupful

Note: This recipe is easily doubled or tripled, when required.

1/6 SERVING (i. e., 2 tablespoonfuls) –
PROTEIN = 2.3 g.; FAT = 0.3 g.; CARBOHYDRATE = 5.1 g.;
CALORIES = 22; CALORIES FROM FAT = 12%

Europe–**Russia**

RUSSIAN SHREDDED FRESH BEETS
Sviokly

TPT - 14 minutes

We were served this twice while visiting Russia in 1983. It is such a simple, fresh way to enjoy beets that I have served it often since then.

5 medium raw beets—trimmed and peeled
1 tablespoon butter

Using a food processor fitted with medium shredding disk or by hand, using a hand shredder, shred beets.

Put shredded beets into the top half of a double boiler set over simmering water. Add butter and cover tightly. Simmer over *MEDIUM* heat until beets are *crisp-tender* and deep red—about 10-12 minutes. Stir occasionally. Turn into heated serving dish

Serve at once.

Yields 6 servings
adequate for 4 people

Note: This recipe is easily halved or doubled, when required.

1/6 SERVING – PROTEIN = 0.7 g.; FAT = 1.9 g.; CARBOHYDRATE = 4.1 g.;
CALORIES = 52; CALORIES FROM FAT = 33%

INDIVIDUAL RUSSIAN SOUR CREAM OMELETS
Omlyet so Smyetanoy

TPT - 8 minutes

Although this recipe for omelets can be used to make a single, classic omelet, we enjoy these small extremely light, crêpe-like omelets for breakfast, lunch, or for a light supper. They are just perfect when children or grandchildren are sharing a meal. For more formal dinners, these omelets make perfect appetizers.

Per serving:
  1 large egg
  1 tablespoon *fat-free* dairy sour cream
  2 teaspoons water
  Freshly ground black pepper, to taste

  1/2 teaspoon butter

For each omelet, combine egg, sour cream, and water in a mixing bowl. Using a wire whisk, combine well. Season with black pepper. Again, beat well.

Place a non-stick-coated 7-inch skillet over *MEDIUM* heat. Brush heated pan with butter. Heat pan until a drop of water bounces up from the hot surface when dropped onto it.

Drop egg mixture onto *hot* skillet surface. *Lightly brown* on one side. Using a spatula, lift the edge and fold in half. Transfer folded omelets to a heated platter set on a warming tray or in a warm oven. Continue preparing omelets until all are completed.

*Serve warm.**

Yields 1 single–serving omelet

Note: *If preferred, these omelets may be served cold with jam or jelly.

1 SERVING (i. e., per individual omelet) –
PROTEIN = 8.4 g.; FAT = 7.6 g.; CARBOHYDRATE = 6.0 g.;
CALORIES = 127; CALORIES FROM FAT = 54%

Europe–**Russia**

RUSSIAN CUCUMBERS SAUTÉED IN DILL BUTTER
Ogurtsy so Buter s Ukropom
TPT - 14 minutes

Americans tend to do little more than cut up a cucumber and put it into a lettuce salad or serve them with crudités. Some admittedly do salt and wilt them for sweet and sour salads and occasionally someone will make a cucumber sauce for fish . . . but we do seem to ignore the potential of this vegetable. This Russian way of serving cucumbers suggests the French influence of the Czarist period. It is a luscious, yet light, vegetable dish.

2 tablespoons butter
2 tablespoons chopped, fresh dillweed

3 large cucumbers—peeled, seeded, and evenly chopped*

In a skillet, with cover, set over *LOW-MEDIUM* heat, melt butter. Add chopped dillweed. Cook, stirring constantly for about 30 seconds.

Add chopped cucumbers, cover tightly, and cook for about 5-7 minutes, or until cucumbers are *crisp–tender*. Stir occasionally. Turn into heated serving bowl.

Serve at once.

Notes: *Seeds and pulp can be added to vegetables being accumulated in the freezer for soup stock

This recipe may be halved or doubled, when required.

Yields 6 servings
adequate for 4 people

1/6 SERVING – PROTEIN = 0.6 g.; FAT = 3.9 g.; CARBOHYDRATE = 3.3 g.;
CALORIES = 49; CALORIES FROM FAT = 72%

RUSSIAN STEWED MUSHROOMS
Griby Tushonye
TPT - 28 minutes

We tasted this mushroom dish for the first time in a Russian restaurant nestled in a birch forest outside of Moscow in an area where beautiful traditional dachas still offered well-healed Russians escape from the city. Bottle after bottle of vodka was offered to ward off the bitter cold of that day but I remember the mushrooms.

1 1/2 teaspoons butter
1 medium onion—*thinly* sliced
1 small garlic clove—crushed and *finely* chopped

12 ounces fresh mushrooms—trimmed, rinsed, cleaned well with a brush, and sliced into 1/4-inch slices
1 1/2 tablespoons whole wheat flour

1 tablespoon butter

1/2 cup YOGURT *CRÈME* [see index]*

Chopped fresh dillweed *or* parsley, for garnish

In a non-stick-coated skillet set over *LOW-MEDIUM* heat, combine the 1 1/2 teaspoonfuls butter, onion slices, and *finely* chopped garlic. Sauté gently until onion slices are soft and translucent, *allowing neither the onions nor the garlic to brown.* Remove from heat and set aside.

Combine slightly damp mushroom slices and flour in a plastic bag. Shake gently to coat mushroom slices.

In a large skillet set over *LOW* heat, melt the 1 tablespoonful butter. Add mushrooms slices and sauté gently until liquid begins to be released. Add sautéed onion and garlic. Continue cooking, stirring frequently, until evenly browned—about 10 minutes.

Stir in YOGURT *CRÈME* and cook until just heated through.

RUSSIAN STEWED MUSHROOMS (cont'd)

Turn into heated serving dish or divide among four small heated individual soufflé dishes, custard cups, or small casseroles. Keep warm on a warming tray until ready to serve.

Garnish with chopped dillweed or parsley before serving.

Notes: *Fat-free sour cream may be substituted, if preferred.

This recipe is easily halved or doubled, when required.

Yields 4 servings
adequate for 4 people as an
appetizer or as a side dish

1/4 SERVING – PROTEIN = 7.5 g.; FAT = 4.6 g.; CARBOHYDRATE = 15.1 g.;
CALORIES = 135; CALORIES FROM FAT = 31%

YOGURT *CRÈME MOUSSE* IN THE RUSSIAN STYLE
Ryazhenka Muss

TPT - 2 hours and 28 minutes;
10 minutes = cooling period;
2 hours = chilling and setting period

Ryazhenka is a thick, sweet, and slightly brown yogurt made from evaporated milk, or baked milk, as the Russians say. Our "yogurt crème" is close to this product in taste, if taste memory serves us well. It does lack the dark "Russian baked milk taste," instead having a fresher, cleaner taste.

3 tablespoons *cold* water
2 teaspoons unflavored gelatin*

2 tablespoons orange blossom *or* wildflower honey, as preferred

1 cup light cream *or* half and half

1 cup thick YOGURT *CRÈME* [see index]
1 tablespoon frozen orange juice concentrate
—*defrosted*
1/2 teaspoon pure vanilla extract

Fresh strawberries, raspberries, *or* tiny mandarin orange sections, for garnish, if desired

Pour *cold* water into a saucepan, sprinkle gelatin over, and allow to soften for 5 minutes.

Add honey and heat over *LOW* heat until both gelatin and honey are dissolved.

Stir in cream. Allow to heat through until *tepid to the touch*. Set aside to cool slightly—about 10 minutes.

Stir *defrosted* orange juice concentrate and vanilla extract into yogurt *crème*. Blend thoroughly. Using a wire whisk, thoroughly whisk yogurt *crème* mixture into cream mixture. Pour into a serving bowl or into individual sherbet glasses. Refrigerate until firm—about 2 hours.

Garnish with fruit, of choice, before serving.

Yields 5 servings
adequate for 3-4 people

Notes: *Agar-agar or kosher gelatin may be substituted for plain gelatin, if preferred. Since preparation procedures differ for these products, be sure to follow package directions.

This recipe may be doubled, if required. However, the setting period must also be increased to 3 or 4 hours.

Additionally, this may be molded. To insure success, we would, however, suggest increasing the gelatin used to 1 tablespoonful.

1/5 SERVING – PROTEIN = 9.5 g.; FAT = 4.7 g.; CARBOHYDRATE = 18.4 g.;
CALORIES = 154; CALORIES FROM FAT = 27%

Europe–**Russia**

RUSSIAN WALNUT SPONGE CAKE
Osnovnoi Oreklovyi Biskvit

TPT - 2 hours and 20 minutes;
1 hour and 30 minutes = cooling period

When I baked this as a surprise for two dear friends, I was the one who was surprised and pleased because each remembered such a cake being baked on special occasions by their grandmothers and mothers who had been born in Eastern Europe and who had carried this tradition here.

1/3 cup chopped *preservative-free* walnuts

4 large egg yolks—*brought to room temperature*
1/4 teaspoon black walnut extract

1/3 cup cake flour
3/4 teaspoon baking powder

4 large egg whites—*brought to room temperature*
5 tablespoons sugar

Preheat oven to 250 degrees F.

Cut out a piece of waxed paper to fit into the bottom of an 8-inch springform pan. Coat waxed paper with lecithin spray coating or butter. Fit into the bottom of the pan. Set aside.

Spread walnuts on a baking sheet or in a pie plate and place in preheated 250 degree F. oven. Stir frequently until *evenly toasted*. Remove from oven and chop *finely* either by using a nut chopper or by hand. Set aside.

Increase oven temperature to 350 degrees F.

In a large mixing bowl, using a wire whisk, beat egg yolks until light and lemon-colored. Add black walnut extract. Combine well. Set aside.

Sift cake flour with baking powder. Set aside.

Using an electric mixer fitted with *grease-free* beaters or by hand, using a *grease-free* wire whisk, beat egg whites in a *grease-free* bowl until soft peaks form. While continuing to beat, gradually add the 5 tablespoonfuls of sugar. Continue beating until stiff peaks form and meringue is dense.

Whisk-fold a large dollop of beaten egg whites into egg yolks. When well-combined, using a rubber spatula, fold flour, walnuts, and remaining meringue *gently*, but *thoroughly*, into egg yolks. Alternately fold in these items to achieve thorough and even distribution without sacrificing the volume of the beaten egg whites.

Turn batter into prepared pan, spreading evenly to assure an even depth.

Bake in preheated 350 degree F. oven for about 22 minutes, or until cake is *lightly browned* and a cake tester inserted in the center comes out clean.

Remove from oven. Run a knife around the edge to loosen side, release spring on cake pan, and remove ring. Allow cake to cool on wire rack for about 1 hour before inverting and removing waxed paper and pan base. Replace cake, right-side-up, on wire rack and allow to cool completely.

Serve plain or fill with all-fruit jam or buttercream frosting and decorate, if preferred.* Cut into wedges.

Yields 8 servings
adequate for 6 people

Note: *If you plan to fill or decorate this cake, allow at least 4 hours of cooling before slicing horizontally for filling or attempting to spread a butter cream frosting or jam.

1/8 SERVING (unfrosted) –
PROTEIN = 4.5 g.; FAT = 3.3 g.; CARBOHYDRATE = 13.2 g.;
CALORIES = 136; CALORIES FROM FAT = 22%

Europe–Russia

RUSSIAN APPLE PUDDING WITH BREADCRUMBS
Yamblochnyi s Krem

TPT - 1 hour and 45 minutes;
1 hour = chilling period

There are two events that stand out in my memory in connection with this dessert. One of our daughter Katy's friends joined us for a picnic at "Caumsett," the former home of Marshall Field III on Long Island, now a New York State Park. I remember circling the car pouring cream into bowls sitting on top of the car, as the four of us polished off the eight servings of this dessert on that warm summer day. I am also reminded of a luncheon eaten in that restaurant in the woods near a dacha community outside of Moscow on that very cold winter day. There, we also tasted a simple fruit compote with huge berries. They tasted much like our blueberries and I was told that they were called snowberries. I guess that's why I love to garnish this dessert with a few blueberries, especially when I serve it for breakfast.

2 medium, cooking apples—peeled, cored, and shredded
2 teaspoons freshly squeezed lemon juice
1/2 cup *fat-free* pasteurized eggs (the equivalent of 2 eggs)
2/3 cup *whole* milk
1/4 cup sugar
1/2 cup whole wheat breadcrumbs
1 1/2 tablespoons butter—*melted*
1/2 teaspoon pure vanilla extract

Light cream *or* half and half

Preheat oven to 350 degrees F. Prepare a 9-inch pie plate by coating with non-stick lecithin spray coating.

In a large mixing bowl, combine shredded apples and lemon juice. Toss to coat apple. Add pasteurized eggs, milk, sugar, breadcrumbs, *melted* butter, and vanilla extract. Stir to mix well. Turn into prepared pie plate; spread evenly to edges.

Bake in preheated 350 degree F. oven for 35-40 minutes, or until *lightly browned*.

Chill for at least 1 hour before serving or serve at room temperature, if preferred. Serve in wedges, as for a pie, with cream.

Yields 8 servings
adequate for 4-5 people

Note: This makes a fine breakfast offering although we prefer to reduce the sugar to 2 tablespoonfuls in that case. Serve with blueberries, if desired.

1/8 SERVING (without cream) –
PROTEIN = 2.4 g.; FAT = 2.9 g.; CARBOHYDRATE = 13.8 g.;
CALORIES = 90; CALORIES FROM FAT = 29%

RUSSIAN ORTHODOX EASTER DESSERT
Paskha

TPT - about 99 hours and 48 minutes;
48 hours = *ricotta* draining period;
3 hours = fruit maceration period;
48 hours = refrigeration period

In Russia on Orthodox Easter, paskha is accompanied by kulich, the wonderfully fragrant sweet Russian Easter bread. Both are carried to the church on Saturday evening before Easter by the women of the family to be blessed and although the blessing is important, the admiration of women of other families is sought as well. An interesting fact is that only the children, not bound by the fasting rules of the church, judge the taste of the paskha as it is being prepared indebting the cook to the taste buds of her children. As a result, most Russians are greeted on Easter by paskhas much sweeter than ours.

VOLUME I - 359

RUSSIAN ORTHODOX EASTER DESSERT (cont'd)

2 pounds *part-skimmed milk ricotta* cheese*

1/2 cup mixed, chopped, *preservative-free* dried fruits, of choice
1 1/2 teaspoons pure vanilla extract

1/4 pound sweet (*unsalted*) butter—*softened to room temperature*
1/4 cup firmly packed *light* brown sugar

2/3 cup heavy whipping cream

1/2 cup *fat-free* pasteurized eggs** (the equivalent of 2 eggs)**

1/2 cup chopped *preservative-free* almonds

Whole, unblanched, *preservative-free* almonds, for garnish
Preservative-free dried fruit pieces, for garnish

Scrub a *new* 6-inch clay flowerpot well. Place in a 300 degree F. oven for an hour or two to dry. Allow to cool overnight. *(Use this same method to clean the flowerpot afterwards. Then store in a plastic bag until used again.)* If preferred, a 3 1/2-cup *coeur d' crème* mold can be used quite successfully.

Hang cheese in a culinary cheesecloth bag over a bowl in the refrigerator for 48 hours to drain.

In a small, shallow bowl, combine 1/2 cupful dried fruits and vanilla extract. Set aside for 3 hours.

Using an electric mixer, cream butter until light and fluffy. Add brown sugar and continue to cream until again fluffy. Add drained cheese and beat until a smooth mixture results. Set aside.

In a heavy, non-stick-coated saucepan set over *LOW* heat or in a double boiler over simmering water, heat heavy whipping cream until bubbles form around the edges.

Using a wire whisk, *gradually—tablespoonful by tablespoonful*—beat the scalded cream into the pasteurized eggs. Return to saucepan and cook over *LOW* heat, *stirring constantly,* until a smooth, thick custard is formed. Beat custard into cheese-butter mixture. When smooth, fold in vanilla-saturated fruits and chopped almonds.

Line prepared flowerpot or *coeur d' crème* mold with clean, washed culinary cheesecloth. Spoon *paskha* into lined mold and pack down well. Cover over with cheesecloth. Place a saucer on top (or a heart-shaped cover in the case of the *coeur d' crème* mold) and a 2- or 3-pound weight on top of the saucer. Refrigerate for 2 or 3 days.

Remove weight and saucer. Loosen sides of mold by pulling cheesecloth toward the center slightly and inserting a knife around the edges, if necessary. Turn cheesecloth ends back and invert on serving plate. *Carefully* peel cheesecloth off molded *paskha*. Press whole almonds and dried fruit pieces into *paskha* to decorate.***

After unmolding, this *paskha* will keep well for about a week, if refrigerated.

Yields 14 servings
adequate for 7-14 people

Notes: **Tvorog*, Russian-style cottage cheese, is not available in the United States unless you make it yourself. Cottage and pot cheeses tend to be a bit too sour for our tastes. Drained *ricotta* not only approximates the texture admirably, it also is a sweeter cheese necessitating less sugar.

**Because raw eggs present the danger of *Salmonella* poisoning, commercially-available pasteurized eggs are recommended for use in preparing this dish.

***Traditionally, the *paskha* is decorated with the letters XB representing "Christ risen."

1/14 SERVING – PROTEIN = 9.0 g.; FAT = 16.0 g.; CARBOHYDRATE = 24.7 g.;
CALORIES = 259; CALORIES FROM FAT = 56%

Europe–**Russia**

RUSSIAN ORANGE SPICED TEA
Chai s Sok

TPT - 15 minutes

A thoroughly peculiar beverage appeared on the scene some years ago that needs to be addressed by those of us who had enjoyed Russian spiced orange tea in Russia. I was astonished to see the widespread use of orange drink powders like Kool-Aid and Tang to try to recreate a classic taste that is easily made with the simple ingredients of the original—tea, orange juice, honey, and spice. I created this for my friend Ellen who loves the hint of orange in her tea cup and who was not with us on the overnight train to St. Petersburg to wake up to glasses of orange spiced tea after a night of talking and singing spurred on by bowls of freshwater shrimp and iced vodka and a supreme feeling of "mir."

1 quart strongly brewed black tea*
1 cinnamon quill
6 whole cloves

3 ounces frozen orange juice concentrate
   —thawed
1 tablespoons freshly squeezed lemon juice
3 tablespoons honey

In a saucepan set over *LOW-MEDIUM* heat, combine tea, cinnamon quill, and cloves. Allow to come to the boil. Remove cinnamon quill and cloves.

Add thawed orange juice concentrate, lemon juice, and honey. Stir to combine. Continue to heat until *hot,* but *not boiling.*

Place a spoon in each of six Russian tea glasses or Irish coffee glasses. Ladle hot tea into each glass. *Serve at once* with biscuits.

Yields 6 servings

Notes: *You might prefer, as I do, to make a full pot of strong brewed tea in the morning and refrigerate the extra for an afternoon glass of iced tea or a glass of this orange spiced tea.

This recipe can be doubled, when required.

1/6 SERVING – PROTEIN = 0.6 g.; FAT = 0.2 g.; CARBOHYDRATE = 15.6 g.;
CALORIES = 63; CALORIES FROM FAT = 3%

Serbia

The changes in the Balkans in my lifetime have been mind-boggling and I was challenged, as I started this project, to expunge from my memory every national border that I had learned in school. Today Serbia is slightly smaller than the state of Indiana encompassing 34,116 square miles, if you deduct the land mass of the southern province of Kosovo which is inhabited primarily by Muslims of Albanian heritage and which declared its independence from Serbia in 2008 after bitter conflict and significant bloodshed.

In 2006 Serbia finally stood as an independent state again after the dismantling of Yugoslavia, the nation into which it had been cobbled since 1929. Serbia, Croatia, Slovenia, Macedonia, Bosnia and Herzegovina, and Montenegro were included in this amalgamation formed as the Kingdom of the Serbs, Croats, and Slovenes in 1918 after World War I and ruled by King Peter I, a Serbian. The establishment of a Serbian ruling class did not sit well with the other nationalities and their authority was constantly challenged, especially by Croatian nationalists. Yugoslavia joined the Little Entente as the Germans began their march through Europe but by 1939 Yugoslavia's stand against the Axis powers had grown increasingly less firm. In March 1941 a military *coup d'etat* deposed the pro-Axis government but this was very short-lived as Yugoslavia was invaded in April 1941 by the combined forces of Germany, Hungary, Bulgaria, and Italy with the result that Serbia and Croatia fell under the Nazis and the remaining states were divided among the other Axis nations. The occupying forces were opposed by partisan forces. Their defiance may have led to the lifting of the Nazi yoke but it also led to a protracted civil war. In 1943 Marshal Josip Broz Tito came to power and with the help of the Soviets drove the Germans from Yugoslavian soil. Under his iron hand, a communist state was established and Yugoslavia began to have a national identity, albeit only an umbrella identity for the restless nationalists who wanted no more of the Kingdom of the Serbs, Croats, and Slovenes. Tumultuous years followed Marshal Tito's death in 1980. Slobodan Milošević rose to power in 1989 and in 1990 Serbia took a step toward democracy by establishing a multiparty democratic system, a move violently opposed by the ruling Socialist Party who went so far as to refuse to accept municipal election results. Milošević's clash with the communist leadership led to the secession from Yugoslavia of Slovenia, Croatia, Bosnia and Herzegovina, and Macedonia and his policy toward the Islamic minority in Kosovo led to his eventual overthrow, arrest, and trial by the World Court.

Twenty-one percent of the length of the Danube River passes through Serbia so it not surprising that many peoples found it suitable for agriculture. As early as 8,500 years ago Neolithic peoples, known as Starčevo and Vinča cultures, settled in the Balkans and it has been confirmed that they had settlements near present-day Belgrade. Thracians, Dacians, and Illyrians also farmed this region. In the fourth century BC the Greeks under Alexander the Great expanded into what is today southern Serbia. In the third century BC, as Greek power waned, Celtic tribes moved into Serbia in the third century BC. They established fortifications and cities, most notably Singidunum which today is the Serbian capital of Belgrade. The Celts were displaced by the rise of Roman imperialism. The Romans conquered parts of Serbia in the second century BC and established Sirmium, which served as one of the capitals of the Roman Empire during the Tetrarchy. Seventeen Roman Emperors were Serbian-born, notable among them was the Emperor Constantine. Through the centuries that followed Serbia became part of the Byzantine Empire, the Ottoman Empire, and the Austro-Hungarian Empire and through the decades of occupation Serbians survived as Serbians, adopting and adapting.

Europe–Serbia

Serbian cuisine, as do the cuisines of all the areas which were once part of the former country of Yugoslavia, reflects a myriad of other cuisines with Greek, Hungarian, Bulgarian, Turkish, and Austrian influences obvious in virtually every menu. "National dishes" have common origins with similar dishes found in Turkey and Greece. Vegetarians are hard-pressed to sample variety in Serbia since the main course of any meal is meat and soups are almost always made with meat stock. However, a dizzying variety of cheeses and other dairy products are popular, made from ewes', goats', cows', and even donkeys' milk. Serbians love eggs which are usually reserved for breakfast but, as we found when visiting Russia, most chefs will willing fry up eggs for you. A lacto-ovo vegetarian will find accommodation but vegans may be seriously challenged. Since one-third of the raspberries grown in the world are grown in Serbia, you could always opt for a bowl of fresh raspberries and cream.

Scrambled Eggs
Kajgana

Roasted Eggplant *Caviar*
Ajvar

Assorted Pickled Vegetables
Tursija

~

Onion Soup with Cheese
Corba od Luka

~

Beet Salad with *Feta* **Cheese**
Salata o Cvekla

~~~~~~~~~~~~~~~~~~~~~

Vegetable Stew with Brown Rice and Soymeat
Djuvec

Golden Buttermilk Cornbread
Proja

~~~~~~~~~~

Cabbage Casserole with Breadcrumbs
Ponac o Kupus

with

Buttered Noodles with Poppy Seeds   or   Steamed Baby Potatoes
Rezanci s Makom

~~~~~~~~~~~~~~~~~~~~~

Stuffed Pears with Sour Cream Sauce
Kruska Pavlaka

Pumpkin Pie in a *Phyllo* **Roll**
Bundevara

Fruit Sorbet, of choice, with Fresh Raspberries
Serbe

~

Tea   Plum Brandy   Pear Brandy
Sumadija   *Sljivovica*   *Vijamovka*

Europe–Serbia

SCRAMBLED EGGS
Kajgana

TPT - about 14 minutes

This recipe for scrambled eggs is not a filler although it might well seem to be since everybody "knows" how to scramble eggs. I too just thought that everybody scrambled eggs like I did. It is a choice for breakfast or dinner that most people think requires little thought. Urging the protein threads to unwind and urging the whole mass to lift into fluffy moist mounds takes some doing and it took me some thought a few years ago. In an episode of "Nero Wolfe" the detective created by Rex Stout instructs two young assistants in the art of scrambling eggs. His approach was a forty-five minute-constant stirring over very low heat. He was, with all due respect to one of my father's favorite mystery writers, partially correct but that constant stirring over low heat must occur at the end of the process. Shocking the protein strands over higher heat at the beginning of the process invites the unwinding process but maintaining that high heat to the end will only tighten the strands and not allow the moisture to lift the scramble, desirable for an omelet but not desirable for scrambled eggs. Over the years my eggs became less voluminous; they were beginning to look like the slabs of dry "scrambled" eggs that you usually get in a diner. What had I done? Well, for one thing I had replaced the cream or milk with water to cut down on the fat. I had eliminated the egg yolks, leftover from egg white recipes, to cut down on the chance of Salmonella contamination without taking into consideration the necessary water to fat ratio that helps to slow the coagulation process. I had eliminated the salt, assuming that the naturally occurring salt in the cells of the egg was sufficient to soften the proteins enough to prevent them from seizing tightly when cooked, and I no longer prepared the pan with butter, having switched to an oil cooking spray. M-m-m-m, I was onto something. I went back to the recipe I had learned from my grandmother and mother and there I was again with voluminous clouds of cooked eggs. Serbians love scrambled eggs and I offer my favorite recipe here as a first course.

8 large *organic* eggs
2 *organic* egg yolks
2 tablespoon light cream *or* **half and half**
1/4 teaspoon salt
Freshly ground black pepper, to taste

2 teaspoons butter

In a mixing bowl, combine eggs, egg yolks, cream, salt, and pepper. Using a fork, combine but do not overbeat.

In a non-stick-coated 9-inch skillet set over *MEDIUM-HIGH* heat, heat butter. Add egg mixture and, using a wooden spatula, *stir the eggs until they begin to coagulate*. Remove from heat. *Reduce heat to LOW*. Put the eggs back on the burner and *cook over LOW-MEDIUM heat, moving the eggs almost constantly with the wooden spatula*. When the eggs are soft and fluffy, *and still moist*, turn onto a heated platter.

Serve at once.

Yields 6 servings
adequate for 4 people

Note: This recipe can be halved, when required.

1/6 SERVING – PROTEIN = 9.6 g.; FAT = 11.3 g.; CARBOHYDRATE = 0.2 g.;
CALORIES = 142; CALORIES FROM FAT = 72%

SERBIAN ROASTED EGGPLANT AND PEPPER *CAVIAR*
Ajvar

TPT - 25 hours and 55 minutes;
24 hours = flavor development period

You will find vegetable "caviars" throughout Central Europe. This Serbian version is beautiful due to the use of yellow, orange, and red peppers which are not included in the Romanian version that I shared in the previous chapter. I have made it with the more traditional green peppers but do love the effect that the colored peppers contribute. If someone in your family loves eggplant, they will enjoy this. It actually gets better and better as the flavors meld.

Europe–Serbia

SERBIAN ROASTED EGGPLANT AND PEPPER *CAVIAR* (cont'd)

1 medium eggplant—well-washed, but *unpeeled*

2 garlic cloves—*very finely* chopped
1 tablespoon *extra virgin* olive oil
1 1/2 teaspoons freshly squeezed lemon juice
1/4 – 1/2 teaspoon red *jalapeño chili* sauce, more or less to taste
1/4 teaspoon freshly ground black pepper, or to taste
Pinch salt, or to taste

1 yellow *or* orange bell pepper—unblemished, and well-washed
1 red bell pepper—perfect, unblemished, and well-washed

1 medium onion—*finely* chopped
2 hard-cooked eggs—*finely* chopped

Preheat broiler to 400 degrees F. and set the oven rack about 8 inches from heat source.

Pierce the eggplant several times with a sharp knife, place it on a broiler pan so that the eggplant is about 4 inches below the heat source. Broil the eggplant for a total of about 20 minutes, *turning the eggplant with tongs frequently during the broiling period* so that the skin chars evenly. Remove eggplant from oven and wrap in a dampened cotton tea towel for 5 minutes to steam.

Set oven at BAKE and reduce temperature to 350 degrees F.

Remove the towel. Trim and peel eggplant. Coarsely chop. Using a FOOD MILL fitted with coarse blade, purée the eggplant chunks.*

Turn puréed eggplant into a bowl. Stir in *very finely* chopped garlic, olive oil, lemon juice, *jalapeño* sauce, black pepper, and salt.

Place yellow or orange and red peppers on a cookie sheet. Roast in preheated oven for about 40 minutes, *turning frequently*.

Remove from oven and place in a heavy brown paper bag in dry sink. Roll the top of the bag down and allow to steam for about 15 minutes.

Remove stems, seeds, and membranes, peel, and chop peppers. Add to eggplant mixture. Stir to mix thoroughly. Cover and refrigerate for about 24 hours to allow for flavor development.

Turn into one section of a divided three-sectioned serving dish. Place *finely* chopped onions and *finely* chopped hard-cooked egg in the other sections. Encourage diners to add onions and egg to their serving of "eggplant caviar" as their taste dictates. Also provide a salt seller since some do want their vegetable "caviar" to taste more like salty fish eggs.

Serve with *crudités,* of choice, and crackers or small breads

Yields 20 servings
adequate for 10 people

Notes: *We prefer a FOOD MILL to a food processor to prepare this appetizer since the roasted eggplant has the tendency to liquefy when processed.

This recipe may be doubled, when required.

1/20 SERVING (exclusive of the onions) –
PROTEIN = 1.0 g.; FAT = 1.2 g.; CARBOHYDRATE = 2.0 g.;
CALORIES = 22; CALORIES FROM FAT = 49%

ONION SOUP WITH CHEESE
Corba od Luka
TPT - 50 minutes

Before we chose to become vegetarians I had the best, albeit traditionally prepared, French onion soup recipe. We missed the wonderful flavors of that soup; we missed the memories of those bistros in which we had warmed body and soul when we were young. As a result, I evolved another version to comfort the soul—this time, the vegetarian soul. Serbians enjoy thick soups usually with meat, beans, noodles, and always with meat stocks. The traditional onion soup in Serbia differs from this and I am sure, as is the case in so many countries, cooks will say, "Well, it is not like my onion soup," but this version is thick and full of the richness of caramelized onions, and satisfying.

ONION SOUP WITH CHEESE (cont'd)

2 tablespoons butter

6 medium onions—peeled, sliced, and separated into rings *(use white, Spanish, or Bermuda onions, if available)*

2 teaspoons *light* brown sugar

2 tablespoons whole wheat flour

5 cups VEGETARIAN BROWN STOCK *[see index]* or other vegetarian stock of choice

2 bay leaves—broken in half

Freshly ground black pepper, to taste

About 1/2 cup shredded or coarsely grated (about 2 ounces) Serbian *Kačkavalj* or *Caciocavallo* ewe's milk cheese or Italian aged *provolone*

In a non-stick-coated skillet set over *MEDIUM-LOW* heat, melt butter. Add onion rings. Sauté until onion rings are a soft, translucent, and golden in color, *being careful not to allow onions to brown. Add a bit of water to keep onions from overbrowning, if necessary.*

Add brown sugar and continue cooking and stirring until sugar caramelizes.

Add whole wheat flour and blend well with onion–butter mixture. Add 1 cupful of stock, stirring well to blend thoroughly.

Turn entire mixture into a 2-quart saucepan with cover. Set over *MEDIUM* heat. Add remaining 4 cupfuls stock and bay leaf pieces. Bring to the boil while stirring constantly. Reduce heat to *LOW*, cover, and simmer gently for about 20 minutes. Remove and discard bay leaf pieces. Taste and season with black pepper. Turn into a heated soup tureen.

Serve at once into heated soup bowls or crocks. Pass shredded cheese and large chunks of country or French bread, of choice.

Yields six 1-cup servings
adequate for 4 people
as a main course offering

Notes: This recipe is easily doubled, when required.

Leftover soup freezes well.

1/6 SERVING (i. e., per cupful) –
PROTEIN = 6.9 g.; FAT = 9.8 g.; CARBOHYDRATE = 13.3 g.;
CALORIES = 162; CALORIES FROM FAT = 54%

SERBIAN BEET SALAD WITH *FETA* CHEESE
Salata o Cvekla
TPT - 51 minutes

Serbians serve salads with the main course, as is generally the custom in the United States for family dinners. This very simple salad is a perfect salad to accompany many dishes because it does not present a complication in flavors that interferes with flavors in other dishes. Beets are often overlooked but their phytonutrient contribution is enormous. Betalains, antioxidants which support detoxification, and the carotenoids lutein and zeaxanthin, which have been shown to important phytonutrients in maintaining eye health especially concerns of age-related eye problems that involve the macula and the retina. Bright red, orange, and yellow vegetables should be on our radar or one might muse that when we shop for produce, we should "be seeing red."

4 quarts *boiling* water

3-4 large, fresh beets (about 2 pounds)—well-scrubbed, with roots intact and 2 inches of leaf stem attached*

2 tablespoons *very finely* chopped red onion

2 tablespoons crumbled Serbian *Sirenje* or Greek *feta* cheese

Freshly ground black pepper, to taste

In a deep saucepan or small kettle, cook the beets in *boiling* water until tender—about 45 minutes. Drain. Rinse in *cold* water until it can be handled. Cut off root end and stem end. Slip off skin and cut into large round slices. Place beets on plate. Refrigerate until ready to serve.

Sprinkle *very finely* chopped onion and crumbled Serbian *Sirenje* or Greek *feta* cheese over. Grind black pepper over.

SERBIAN BEET SALAD AND *FETA* CHEESE (cont'd)

Serve chilled.

Yields 6 servings
adequate for 4 people

Notes: *Canned beets can be substituted, if necessary, but the taste of fresh beets is superior.

This recipe can be halved or doubled, when required.

1/6 SERVING – PROTEIN = 1.4 g.; FAT = 1.1 g.; CARBOHYDRATE = 5.3 g.; CALORIES = 35; CALORIES FROM FAT = 28%

SERBIAN VEGETABLE STEW WITH BROWN RICE AND SOYMEAT
Djuvec

TPT - 1 hour and 36 minutes;
20 minutes = dehydrated soymeat rehydration period

Described as a mellow, succulent dish with the complex flavors of meat and vegetables, it is usually made with beef and pork, or lamb and is popular throughout the countries that once composed the post-war country known as Yugoslavia. Unlike most recipes for djuvec that I have found, I start the unique layering technique by caramelizing the onions and I use a red bell pepper for increased flavor complexity. I also do not add as much olive oil as do most Serbian cooks. Although we make this casserole without the soymeat most of the time and freeze it as such in the fall for winter menus, the soymeat gives a more authentic mouthfeel and the protein level is then elevated to the point that little else except a chunk of good country wheat or corn bread need accompany it.

1 cup *boiling* water
1/2 teaspoon SEASONING MIXTURE FOR DEHYDRATED SOY MEAT ANALOGUE [see index]
1 ounce So Soya+ dehydrated soy meat analogue slices/nuggets *or* other dehydrated meat analogue product*

1 small eggplant—trimmed and cubed**
1/2 large red bell pepper—diced
1 large stalk celery—diced
1/3 cup chopped fresh parsley
1 tablespoon *extra virgin* olive oil
1/2 teaspoon salt
1/4 teaspoon ground mixed peppercorns—black, red, and white—or to taste

1 tablespoon *extra virgin* olive oil
2 large onions—sliced into large, thick rings

1 tablespoon water
1 1/2 teaspoons sugar

1 cup canned, *crushed* tomatoes—*divided into two portions*

2 1/2 tablespoons dry long grain brown rice

1 1/2 cups canned, *whole* tomatoes

Preheat oven to 325 degrees F.

In a pie plate, combine *boiling* water and seasoning mixture. Stir to mix thoroughly. Add dehydrated meat analogue and allow the product to rehydrate for about 20 minutes. Drain thoroughly and set aside until required.

In a mixing bowl, combine chopped eggplant, diced pepper and celery, chopped parsley, 1 tablespoonful olive oil, salt, and ground pepper. Mix well. Set aside briefly.

In a large Dutch oven set over *MEDIUM* heat, heat oil. Add onion rings and cook, stirring constantly, until they begin to soften.

Add water and sugar and stir constantly until onions are soft and translucent.

SERBIAN VEGETABLE STEW WITH BROWN RICE AND SOYMEAT (cont'd)

Add in the following order, *layering it over the onions without stirring*:

> *one-half* of canned, crushed tomatoes;
> *one half* of the mixed vegetables;
> *all* of uncooked rice;
> *all* of rehydrated soymeat;
> remaining mixed vegetables;
> remaining crushed tomatoes;
> *all* of canned, whole tomatoes

Cover and bake in preheated 325 degree F. oven for 45 minutes. Remove cover and continue to bake for about 15 minutes more.

Serve directly from the Dutch oven into heated soup plates.

Yields 6 servings
adequate for 4 people

Notes: *This can also be made with unbreaded, frozen soy meat analogue products.

**A lavender Asian or Japanese eggplant is the perfect size for this recipe and its mild flavor is appropriate.

Leftovers should not be removed from the Dutch oven. Refrigerate and reheat in a 300 degree F. oven.

1/6 SERVING – PROTEIN = 6.0 g.; FAT = 4.0 g.; CARBOHYDRATE = 22.6 g.;
CALORIES = 149; CALORIES FROM FAT = 24%

GOLDEN BUTTERMILK CORNBREAD
Proja

TPT - 25 minutes

Draining yogurt for desserts, results in a considerable amount of nutritious whey which I use in baking to replace water where possible. Dehydrated whey is also available from mail order firms. The dehydrated product is a useful protein supplement for vegetarians and can be reconstituted to use in the following recipe. This cornbread has become a staple for legume complementation in our menu planning. Low in fat, but high in flavor, it is wonderful with bean salads, stews, or soups. Serbians generally make their cornbread with water so if you prefer authenticity, replace all the buttermilk or yogurt whey and evaporated milk with water.

1 cup yellow corn meal*
1/2 cup whole wheat flour
2 teaspoons soy flour
1 tablespoon *light* brown sugar
1 tablespoon baking powder

1/2 cup *fat-free* pasteurized eggs (the equivalent of 2 eggs)
3/4 cup *unsalted,* cultured buttermilk *or* yogurt whey, if available
3 tablespoons evaporated *skimmed* milk
3 tablespoons butter—*melted*

Preheat oven to 400 degrees F. Prepare an 8- or 9-inch square pan—non-stick-coated, if possible—by coating generously with non-stick lecithin spray coating.

Sift yellow corn meal, flours, brown sugar, and baking powder into a large mixing bowl. Add pasteurized eggs and buttermilk. Beat well using a wooden spoon. Then, beat in evaporated milk and *melted* butter.

Pour into prepared pan. Bake in preheated 400 degree F. oven for about 15 minutes, or until a cake tester inserted in the center comes out clean.

Cut into squares. *Serve hot*, wrapped in the whitest linen napkin you have. Pass butter.

Yields nine 3-inch squares
adequate for 4-5 people

Notes: *White corn meal can not be used interchangeably in this recipe.

Leftovers may be frozen quite successfully. Either reheat wrapped in foil or toast for a breakfast or served sliced as a base for a creamed main course.

This recipe may be halved. Bake in a 9 x 5 x 3-inch loaf pan. Or, if preferred, divide full recipe between two loaf pans. Freeze the second baked loaf for a future menu.

1/9 SERVING – PROTEIN = 4.9 g.; FAT = 4.6 g.; CARBOHYDRATE = 20.1 g.;
CALORIES = 141; CALORIES FROM FAT = 29%

Europe–Serbia

SERBIAN CABBAGE CASSEROLE WITH BREADCRUMBS
Janac o Kupus

TPT - 1 hour and 8 minutes

Since cabbage is a cold-weather crop and since it can be over-wintered well, it has found an important position in the cuisines of central and northern Europe. On a cool summer evening I often choose to "use up" the remains of a wintered cabbage by preparing this very simple recipe which I generally serve with steamed baby potatoes.

8 cups *finely* green/white shredded cabbage—well-washed and well-dried
Freshly ground black pepper, to taste
1 1/3 cups light cream *or* half and half
1 cup dry breadcrumbs
1/2 cup *cold* butter—diced

Preheat oven to 350 degrees F. Prepare a 3-quart soufflé dish or other oven-to-table baking dish by coating with non-stick lecithin spray coating.

Put *finely* shredded cabbage in prepared baking dish. Season with black pepper. Pour cream over. Sprinkle breadcrumbs over. Dot with butter. Cover tightly with aluminum foil. Bake in preheated 350 degree F. oven for 30 minutes. Remove aluminum foil. Continue baking in 350 degree F. oven for 30 minutes more, or until breadcrumbs are lightly browned and crisp.

Serve at once.

Yields 6 servings
adequate for 4 people

Note: This recipe can be halved, if required.

1/6 SERVING – PROTEIN = 5.7 g.; FAT = 20.6 g.; CARBOHYDRATE = 24.8 g.;
CALORIES = 302; CALORIES FROM FAT = 61%

SERBIAN STUFFED PEARS WITH SOUR CREAM SAUCE
Крушка Павлака

TPT - 11 minutes

Pears are grown in Serbia to satisfy the Serbian love for pears, pear nectar, and for viljamovka, a truly luxurious pear brandy. However, despite the enormous national consumption, Serbian orchardmen harvest over fifty thousand tons of pears annually allowing for a lucrative export of both fresh pears and canned pears. This dessert is a bit unusual but a family favorite when I have poached perfectly ripened pears. The extensive use of sour cream is characteristic of cuisines throughout central Europe and Serbians, too, use the cultured milk product in a variety of dishes so it is no surprise, really, that sour cream and their beloved pears are often paired. Here I make this interestingly different dessert with pears canned in light syrup so that it can be enjoyed even if you do not have the time to perfectly ripen those pears.

1/3 cup *finely* chopped, *toasted, preservative-free* walnuts
2 tablespoons sugar
1 tablespoon *fat-free* dairy sour cream*
1/4 teaspoon pure vanilla extract

12 small canned pear halves

SERBIAN SOUR CREAM SAUCE:
    1/3 cup *fat-free* dairy sour cream
    2 tablespoons light cream *or* half and half
    1 tablespoon sugar
    1/4 teaspoon pure vanilla extract

12 *toasted, preservative-free* walnut halves

In a small bowl, combine the *finely* chopped, *toasted* walnuts with 2 tablespoonfuls sugar, 1 tablespoonful sour cream, and 1/4 teaspoonful vanilla extract. Stir to blend well.

Apportion the nut stuffing among the pear halves, mounding it into the depression created when the pears were cored. Refrigerate stuffed pear halves until required.

In a small bowl, prepare the sauce by combining the remaining 1/3 cupful sour cream, cream, the remaining tablespoonful sugar, and the remaining 1/4 teaspoonful vanilla extract. Stir well to blend thoroughly.

**SERBIAN STUFFED PEARS
WITH SOUR CREAM SAUCE** (cont'd)

Serve pears chilled. Allow two pear halves per serving. Pour a dollop of the sour cream sauce over each pear before serving and garnish each plate with two *toasted* walnut halves.

Yields 6 individual servings

Notes: *Full fat or reduced fat sour cream can be substituted, if your menu can tolerate the increased fat.

This recipe can be halved or doubled, when required.

1/6 SERVING – PROTEIN = 4.0 g.; FAT = 7.1 g.; CARBOHYDRATE = 27.2 g.;
CALORIES = 188; CALORIES FROM FAT = 34%

SERBIAN PUMPKIN PIE IN *PHYLLO* ROLL
Bundevara

TPT - 1 hour and 35 minutes;
30 minutes = cooling period

The word pie, or "pita" in Serbian which is very unlike a Greek "pita," is a more complicated concept in Serbia than it is here in the United States and, for that matter, in most countries. There are pies made with pastry called "strudla" which are nut rolls, not at all our concept of a strudel. Then there are "pita," made with phyllo pastry, called "kore" in Serbian. These can be sweet or savory. Bundevara is an example of a sweet pie called a "savijaša" in Serbian which is usually make with "kore." If made as a pastry roll, it would be a "štrudla." This is a pumpkin pie like no other you have seen and certainly bears no resemblance to our Thanksgiving pumpkin pies. I have seen many versions of this dessert over the years but this is my favorite.

Safflower *or* **sunflower oil**
Warm water
9 sheets (9 x 14 inches) *phyllo* **pastry**—*defrosted*

1/2 large acorn squash *or* **the equivalent in fresh pumpkin**—**coarsely grated***

6 tablespoons sugar

Ground cinnamon

Preheat oven to 350 degrees F. Prepare 9 x 13-inch baking pan by light oiling.

Place oil in a small dish. Place warm water in a small dish. Spread one *phyllo* sheet out on bread board covered with a cotton tea towel. Using a basting brush dipped in oil, sprinkle the *phyllo* sheet. Then sprinkle with water. Repeat with two more sheets of *phyllo*. Spread *one-sixth* of the grated pumpkin out on the *phyllo* sheets. Sprinkle one tablespoonful of the sugar over the pumpkin. Sprinkle *lightly* with ground cinnamon. Using the tea towel, roll the pastry tightly and place in the prepared baking pan.

Repeat with three more *phyllo* sheets, grated pumpkin, sugar, and cinnamon until you have made six "*savijăsa*" and all of the ingredients have been used. Leave a space between the pastry rolls. Bake in preheated 350 degree F. oven for about 40 minutes until browned. Remove from oven and place a thoroughly dampened cotton tea towel over the baked pastry. Allow to stand for 30 minutes. Using two spatulas, transfer the pastry rolls to a bread board. Cut in half and transfer to a serving platter.

Serve at room temperature.

Yields 12 "*savijăsa*" rolls
adequate for 6 people

Notes: *Although pumpkin is used in Serbia for this dessert, acorn or golden nugget squash are less watery and work well as a filling.

This recipe can be halved or doubled, when required.

1/12 SERVING – PROTEIN = 1.3 g.; FAT = 0.6 g.; CARBOHYDRATE = 16.3 g.;
CALORIES = 76; CALORIES FROM FAT = 7%

Slovakia

The nation of Slovakia encompasses 18,931 square miles, making it about the size of Vermont and New Hampshire combined but much of that land mass is occupied by the Carpathian Mountains. With a population of about five and a half million people, it is twice as populated as are the two U. S. states. Eighty-five percent of those claiming citizenship also claim to be ethnically Slovak but it has long puzzled me how this can be a valid statistic considering all those who occupied and ruled this region of Europe and with all the immigration and emigration that Slovakia has experienced.

Humans may have occupied this land as early as 270,000 BC, a date set through radiocarbon-dating of stone tools found. Other archaeological excavations have unearthed stone tools and a Neanderthal skull that attest to continued occupation during the Middle Paleolithic Period. The manufacture and trade of arms, shields, dishes, jewelry and other decorative items during the Bronze Age have been attributed to a culture known as the Lusatian who learned to mine and work the abundant copper ore available in the central regions and in the northwest area of the present country. The Lusatians appear to have been quite a successful culture, a conclusion supported by the remains of large permanent buildings and complex fortifications from the period. The advance of the Scytho–Thracian people and the Celtic tribes dispersed or absorbed these settlements and by about 500 BC the area was settled principally by Celts. By the second century AD the Romans had expanded their empire into the area of present-day Slovakia creating the province of Pannonia which subsequently became a base for the Huns for seventy-five years at the end of the first century BC and into the beginning of first century AD. This area became home base for the Huns to which they returned after their raids into Western Europe. Attila died in 45 AD and from that point onward the Huns withdrew and disappear from Slovak history to be succeeded by the Avars, a proto-Mongol tribe who occupied the Pannonian Plain. The Avars, as did the Huns, raided their neighbors in the Middle Danube area and lived by the profits of the booty they collected. The Avars established an empire which dominated the Carpathian Basin until 804 AD.

Slavic tribes had begun to settle in the area in the fifth century and were unified into Great Moravia in about 830 AD by Moimir I. Hungary annexed the territory after the fall of the Great Moravian Empire at the beginning of the tenth century and controlled the area into the present era. In 1918, at the end of World War I, Slovakia, Bohemia, Moravia, and Silesia, in rejection of Austro-Hungarian control, joined to form Czechoslovakia which was recognized as a sovereign European nation in 1919 but this challenging sovereignty lasted for only twenty years. In March 1939 Germany occupied Czechoslovakia and continued its occupation until the end of World War II. In 1948, after the defeat of the Axis Powers, the Communist Party took power in Czechoslovakia under a centralized Czech government. It was not until 1969, however, that Slovakia gained full recognition within the U.S.S.R. and became known as the Slovak Socialist Republic. Slovakians struggled under the Soviet yoke as they had under the Germans. In 1989 democratic political reform began with the fall of the Soviet Union and in 1991 the Republic of Slovakia declared itself a nation separate from the Czech Republic. The two republics again are moving forward on their own agendas, with their own national identities. Slovakia is now a market-driven, stable economy that is attractive to foreign investment because of its well-educated work force, low taxes, and low wages.

Europe–Slovakia

Appetizer Cheese Spread
Bryndzová Natierka
with
Thin Toasts
or
Goat Cheese, Tomatoes and Olives with *Vinaigrette*

~

Sour Green Bean and Potato Soup
Polievka zo Zelenej

Mushroom and Potato Soup
Fazule Hubová Polievka

~

Celery and Apple Salad
Salat od Zeler i Jabiko

Whole Campari or Cherry Tomatoes
Filled with Freshly-Made Mayonnaise

Cucumber Salad
Uhorkový Salat

~~~~~~~~~~~~~~~~~~~~~

Noodle and Cheese Custard Pudding
Nudle s Tvarohem Pundik
or
Eggplant and Tomato Casserole
Zapekaný Baklažán
or
Breaded and Fried *Semolina* with Cranberry Garnish
Semolina Smažit i pri Brusnicas

with

Pumpkin with Cream	Beet and Horseradish Relish
Tekvicový Prívarok	*Chren*

~~~~~~~~~~~~~~~~~~~~~

Strawberry Tart
Jahoola Ovocný

Peach or Apricot Halves garnished with Plum Jam
and sprinkled with
Gingersnap Crumbs or Ground Hazelnuts

Europe–Slovakia

SLOVAK APPETIZER CHEESE SPREAD
Bryndzová Natierka

TPT - 36 minutes;
20 minutes = refrigeration period

Unlike the Croatian cheese spread, included elsewhere in this book, which is made from a cream cheese, the Slovak version is made from the ubiquitous, Slovak Bryndza cheese. In addition, the Slovaks season it with paprika and onions. It is a feta-like cheese so I substitute a Greek reduced-fat feta. This spread is delicious and it is often one of my choices when we decide to have one of our cheese and crackers suppers.

1/4 cup *reduced-fat feta* cheese—brought to room temperature
1/4 cup *soft, whipped* butter spread
1 teaspoon light cream *or* half and half

1/2 teaspoon MUSTARD SAUCE *[see index] or* Dijon mustard with wine
1/8 teaspoon HOMEMADE PAPRIKA *[see index] or* commercially-available Hungarian sweet paprika
Freshly ground black pepper, to taste

2 medium scallions—*white and light green portions only*—trimmed, well-washed, and *finely* chopped

In a mixing bowl, crumble *feta* cheese. Add butter and, using a wooden paddle or a wooden garlic "mushroom," work the *feta* and butter together until smooth and completely integrated. Gradually, *drop by drop*, work cream into the mixture until the consistency is to your liking.

Add paprika and black pepper. Work them into the cheese–butter mixture until the mixture is a light pink.

Add scallion slices and stir to integrate. Using a rubber spatula, scrape it from the bowl into a small serving bowl or crock.* Refrigerate until required.

Remove from the refrigerator at least 20 minutes before serving.

Yields 9 tablespoonfuls

Notes: *If I am going to serve it right away, I put it into a serving dish and, using a metal spreader knife, swirl it up into a small volcano. I then refrigerate it so that, when presented, it holds its attractive sculpture.

This recipe can be halved or doubled, when required.

1/6 SERVING – PROTEIN = 1.0 g.; FAT = 4.5 g.; CARBOHYDRATE = 0.6 g.;
CALORIES = 46; CALORIES FROM FAT = 88%

SLOVAK SOUR GREEN BEAN AND POTATO SOUP
Polievka zo Zelenej Fazule

TPT - 38 minutes

Sauerkraut and sausage soup is not the only soup eaten in Slovakia, although some writers would make you think so. Fresh green beans and dried beans are also used to make simple, filling soups. Slovakian cooks usually thicken this soup using flour. I prefer to allow the starch from the potatoes and the sour cream to do the thickening. Consequently, my soup is not as thick as are most Slovak presentations. In addition I generally use a vegetable stock instead of water to add another layer of flavor.

1/2 pound green beans—trimmed, well-washed, and cut into pieces about one half inch long
1 medium potato—peeled and cubed
1 quart VEGETABLE STOCK FROM SOUP *[see index] or* other vegetable stock of choice
1/2 teaspoon salt

1/4 cup *fat-free* dairy sour cream
1 tablespoon light cream *or* half and half
1 1/2 teaspoons sugar
1/2 teaspoon HOMEMADE PAPRIKA *[see index] or* commercially-available Hungarian sweet paprika

1/2 teaspoon GARLIC–BASIL VINEGAR *[see index] or* other vinegar of choice
3 tablespoons well-washed and chopped fresh dillweed

In a kettle set over *LOW-MEDIUM* heat, combine chopped beans, cubed potatoes, *boiling* water or stock, and salt. Allow to come back to the boil, cover and allow to cool for about 20 minutes, or until the beans and potatoes are tender.

SLOVAK SOUR GREEN BEAN AND POTATO SOUP (cont'd)

In a small bowl, combine sour cream, cream, sugar, and paprika. Using a small wire whisk, combine well. While stirring, gradually add several ladlefuls of the soup broth to the cream mixture until smooth. Whisk until smooth. While stirring the soup in the kettle, slowly add the cream mixture. Keep stirring until heated through.*

Remove from heat. Add vinegar and chopped dillweed. Stir to integrate. Taste and add more salt, if necessary. Turn into a heated soup tureen.

Serve into heat soup plates.

Yields 6 servings
adequate for 4 people

Notes: *If the soup is not thickened to your liking at this point, stir in a ball of *buerre manie* [see index].

This recipe can be halved or doubled when required.

1/6 SERVING – PROTEIN = 2.4 g.; FAT = 0.3 g.; CARBOHYDRATE = 11.2 g.;
CALORIES = 61; CALORIES FROM FAT = 4%

SLOVAK MUSHROOM AND POTATO SOUP
Hubová Polievka

TPT - 40 minutes

How often, as I have assembled this work, have I found myself pursuing another interesting mushroom soup. You will find, in addition to this Slovak soup, mushroom soups from Poland, the Czech Republic, Germany, and Austria, each with it own distinct identity. Family excursions to gather mushrooms are common to each country and the cuisines of these countries as well as their political histories are forever intertwined. If you seek out a restaurant or even a home cook to whom you have confided your vegetarianism, this soup will be suggested but do not be too quick to accept the recommendation since smoked bacon and bacon grease are used to make it and no Slovak will understand why this would not be vegetarian. Bacon is considered a flavoring agent, its drippings are simply a flavorable fat for frying. Its porcine origins do not seem to be a consideration.

5 cups *boiling* water
2 large potatoes—peeled and cut into cubes

2 tablespoons butter
8 ounces fresh *crimini* mushrooms—well-washed and chopped
2 ounces fresh shaggy mane *or* pom pom mushrooms—well-washed and chopped
2 tablespoons *finely* chopped dried *porcini* mushrooms *or* porcini kibble

1 tablespoon unbleached white flour

2 tablespoons *fat-free* dairy sour cream
Salt, to taste
Freshly ground black pepper, to taste

In a large kettle set over *MEDIUM* heat, combine *boiling* water and potato cubes. Allow to simmer for about 20 minutes.

Meanwhile, in a skillet set over *MEDIUM* heat, melt butter. Add chopped fresh *crimini* and shaggy main mushroom, and *finely* chopped dried *porcini* mushrooms. Cook, stirring frequently, until extruded mushroom water has evaporated and mushroom pieces are browned. Remove from heat.

Add flour to mushrooms and stir to combine thoroughly. Add to cooking potatoes. Cook, stirring frequently, until potatoes are tender and soup is thickened.

Add sour cream, salt, and pepper. Stir well and allow to heat through. Turn into a heated soup tureen.

Serve into heated soup plates.

Yields 8 cupfuls

1/8 SERVING (i. e., per cupful) –
PROTEIN = 2.3 g.; FAT = 3.0 g.; CARBOHYDRATE = 11.5 g.;
CALORIES = 89; CALORIES FROM FAT = 30%

Europe–Slovakia

SLOVAK CELERY AND APPLE SALAD
Salat ad Zeler i Jabiko
TPT - 7 minutes

I have always saved the celery heart and the inner ribs for a sit-in-front-of-the-fire treat for my favorite people or for a celery salad. The sweet, bleached center of the celery is really a treat. This salad from Slovakia is similar to the celery slaw I have made since I first started to cook, since I was first trusted with a chef's knife. I remember well my grandmother's words. I had been asked to make a salad and could find no lettuce in the icebox. It was winter and the kitchen garden was not an option either. All my grandmother said was, "Well, what else in the icebox?" That question has been a life-long guide.

4 ribs celery—trimmed, well-washed, and *thinly* sliced
1 small apple—peeled, cored, and shredded

2 tablespoons *calorie reduced or light* mayonnaise
1 tablespoon white wine
1/4 teaspoon sugar
Freshly ground white pepper

6 radishes—cut into small wedges—for garnish

In a mixing bowl, combine *thinly* sliced celery and shredded apple. Toss.

In a small bowl, combine mayonnaise, wine, sugar, and white pepper. Using a small wire whisk, beat until smooth. Add to celery–apple mixture. Toss to coat. Turn into a serving bowl.

Garnish with radish wedges. Refrigerate until required.

Yields 6 servings
adequate for 4 people

Note: This recipe can be doubled, when required.

1/6 SERVING – PROTEIN = 0.5 g.; FAT = 1.7 g.; CARBOHYDRATE = 4.8 g.;
CALORIES = 35; CALORIES FROM FAT = 44%

SLOVAK CUCUMBER SALAD
Uharkovy Salat
TPT - 6 hours and 9 minutes;
  4 hours = cucumber salting period;
  2 hours = flavor development period

When Slovaks or Slovak–Americans are asked to share their cucumber salad, they respond generously and with enthusiasm for their particular twist on this specialty. How often did I hear, "This is my favorite." Of the five responses I received from the area of Trnava, each recipe was slightly different from the others. I share this recipe with trepidation since I am sure someone will be say that my version is not quite authentic.

4 medium cucumbers—peeled and *very thinly* sliced
1/2 teaspoon salt

1 small garlic clove—*crushed and very finely* chopped
3 tablespoons white wine vinegar
3 tablespoons water
1 tablespoon sugar
Freshly ground white pepper, to taste

3 tablespoons *thinly* slivered onion
2 tablespoons chopped fresh parsley

Fat-free dairy sour cream, to garnish
Hungarian sweet paprika, to garnish

Place thin cucumber slices in a mixing bowl. While turning the slices gently, sprinkle salt over. Refrigerate for 4 hours. Rinse cucumber slices several times. Place in a clean mixing bowl filled with cool water and allow to soak until ready to proceed. Drain thoroughly.

In a serving bowl, combine *very finely* chopped *crushed* garlic, vinegar, water, sugar, and white pepper.

Add onion slivers, chopped parsley, and well-drained cucumber slices. Stir to coat the vegetables with the seasoning mixture. Refrigerate for 2 hours to allow for flavor development.

SLOVAK CUCUMBER SALAD (cont'd)

Serve with a slotted spoon. Garnish with sour cream and or paprika, if desired.

Yields 6 servings
adequate for 4 people

1/6 SERVING – PROTEIN = 0.6 g.; FAT = 0.1 g.; CARBOHYDRATE = 5.8 g.;
CALORIES = 24; CALORIES FROM FAT = 4%

SLOVAK NOODLE AND CHEESE CUSTARD PUDDING
Nudle s Tvarohem Pundik

TPT - 2 hours and 14 minutes;
1 hour = refrigeration period

Noodle puddings are very typical of the cuisines of central Europe and have been brought to the United States by many immigrant groups. Although I do not remember my German-born great-grandmother and grandmother making such a pudding, my grandmother often used the noodles leftover from the night before to prepare a "grandchild lunch," that I do remember well. The noodles were reheated and topped with a sweetened cottage cheese and plumped raisins.

3 quarts water
1 tablespoon lemon juice
1 3-inch strip lemon zest
3 cups (about 1/3 pound) broad egg noodles

1/2 cup *fat-free* pasteurized eggs (the equivalent of 2 eggs)
1 1/2 cups *two-percent* milk
1/2 cup *part-skimmed milk ricotta* cheese*
1 teaspoon pure vanilla extract
1/4 cup sugar
1/4 cup *preservative-free dark* raisins

Preheat oven to 350 degrees F. Prepare a 2-quart baking dish by coating with non-stick lecithin spray coating.

In a large kettle set over *HIGH* heat, bring water to the boil. Add lemon juice and zest. Add egg noodles. Boil for about 8 minutes. Pour into a strainer and allow to drain thoroughly. Discard lemon zest.

In a mixing bowl, combine pasteurized eggs, milk, *ricotta* cheese, vanilla extract, and sugar. Mix well to combine thoroughly. Using a rubber spatula, fold in raisins and cooked noodles. Turn *gently* to coat noodles well. Turn into prepared baking dish.

Set in baking pan in which a l-inch water bath has been prepared. Bake in preheated 350 degree F. oven for about 50 minutes, or until pudding sets and separates from the sides of baking dish. If the noodles begin to brown, lay a piece of aluminum foil over the baking dish to prevent further browning.

Refrigerate for at least 1 hour before serving with jam or cinnamon, if desired.

Yields 6 servings
adequate for 4 people

Notes: *The farmers' cheeses found in central Europe, are not available in the United States unless you make it yourself. Cottage and pot cheeses tend to be a bit too sour for our tastes. Drained *ricotta* not only approximates the texture admirably, it also is a sweeter cheese necessitating less sugar.

This recipe may be doubled, when required.

1/6 SERVING – PROTEIN = 9.3 g.; FAT = 3.2 g.; CARBOHYDRATE = 42.9 g.;
CALORIES = 202; CALORIES FROM FAT = 14%

Europe–Slovakia

SLOVAK EGGPLANT AND TOMATO CASSEROLE
Zapekaný Baklažán

TPT - 2 hours and 5 minutes;
1 hour = eggplant salting period

When you gather the ingredients for this recipe you will recognize these ingredients as common to Mediterranean dishes, but when you put it together in the Slovak way, you will be amazed at the different taste sensation. Bryndza cheese is a cheese made from goat or ewe's milk throughout the Balkans, in Romania, and in Hungary. It is a salty, crumbly cheese, much like Greek feta so if you can not find a cheese shop that stocks it, you can substitute feta. It is an essential taste in Slovak cooking and makes this dish a very tasty vegetarian choice. It is one of very few that is enjoyed in Slovakia without the addition of meat. The first time I tasted this casserole I detected a strong, yet wonderful creamy, cheese taste between the layers. I later found out it was a cheese akin to brie so when I make this, I add very well-aged brie.

1/2 cup dry breadcrumbs

1 small eggplant
Salt

4 small tomatoes—sliced

8 ounces *crimini* mushrooms—stems removed, rinsed, cleaned well with a brush, and sliced

2 garlic cloves—*finely* chopped
4 ounces aged *Brie*—diced

1 cup crumbled *feta* cheese

Prepare a 3-quart soufflé dish, *au gratin* dish, or other oven-to-table casserole by coating with non-stick lecithin spray coating. Sprinkle the breadcrumbs evenly over the bottom of the baking dish. Set aside until required.

Salt eggplant slices generously and place them in a sieve or colander set in the sink. Place a plate on top and a weight—a large can or a tea kettle filled with water—on top of the plate. Allow to stand for 1 hour.

Preheat oven to 350 degrees F.

Rinse eggplant slices well in cold water and pat dry. Place *one-half* of the eggplant slices in a layer in the prepared baking dish.

Layer *one-half* of the tomato slices over.

Layer *one-half* of the mushroom slices over.

Scatter *finely* chopped garlic over.

Scatter the diced *Brie* over.

Layer remaining eggplant slices, tomato slices, and mushroom slices. Bake in preheated 350 degree F. oven for 35 minutes. Remove from oven.

Scatter remaining *feta* cheese over. Return to oven and allow to bake for about 10 minutes more.

Serve directly from oven casserole.

Yields 6 servings
adequate for 4 people

Notes: When required, this recipe can be doubled.

The casserole can be baked and frozen, if convenient. Bring to room temperature, cover, and reheat in a 250 degree F. oven until heated through.

1/6 SERVING – PROTEIN = 12.1 g.; FAT = 16.5 g.; CARBOHYDRATE = 20.8 g.;
CALORIES = 235; CALORIES FROM FAT = 63%

Europe–Slovakia

BREADED AND FRIED *SEMOLINA* WITH CRANBERRY GARNISH
Semolina Smažit i pri Brusnicas

TPT - 9 hours and 57 minutes;
8 hours = first refrigeration period;
1 hour = second refrigeration period

When I first set up housekeeping as a young genetics researcher, Mom was not there to present a breakfast and getting out the door in the morning to get to work was just as much a rush as had it had been when I was in college and graduate school. Living in the Midwest, I had become acquainted with corn meal mush and tried making a large batch on the weekend so that I could slice and fry a slice or two in the morning for breakfast. I really was not thrilled so the whole breakfast plan had to be revised and that is when I took to soaking oatmeal in milk overnight and heating it the morning. When I found this Slovakian use of semolina, I remembered my experiments back in the early 1960s and thought, "Here I go again." But these soft, delicate, sweet, fried semolina "cutlets" create a very nice side dish or not-so-sweet dessert.

1 3/4 cups *two percent* **milk**
Pinch salt

1 cup dry *semolina*, **farina,** *or* **Cream of Wheat cereal**
Pinch ground nutmeg
1/4 cup *fat-free* **pasteurized eggs (the equivalent of 1 egg)**

1/2 cup *fat-free* **pasteurized eggs (the equivalent of 2 eggs)**
About 1 cup dry breadcrumbs

1 cup fresh *or* **frozen cranberries—sorted and well-washed**
1 tablespoon sugar

3 tablespoons butter

10 canned apricot halves, for garnish

Prepare a 5 x 3 x 2-inch loaf pan by coating with lecithin non-stick spray coating. In a saucepan set over *MEDIUM* heat, heat milk until it reaches the boil. Add salt. Reduce heat to *LOW-MEDIUM*.

While stirring with a wire whisk, add *semolina*, nutmeg, and the 1/4 cupful pasteurized eggs. Cook, stirring constantly, until mixture is very well thickened. Turn into prepared loaf pan and refrigerate for at least 8 hours, or overnight. *It should be solid enough to slice at this point.* Turn out onto a board and slice into 1/2-inch slices to yield 10 slices.

Assemble two soup plates. In one, pour the 1/2 cupful pasteurized eggs. In the other, put dry breadcrumbs.

Supported by a spatula, dip the slices of *semolina* first in the eggs and then in the breadcrumbs until thoroughly covered with the breading. Transfer to a platter. Repeat with each slice of *semolina*. Refrigerate for at least 1 hour to allow the breading to set.

Put well-washed cranberries and sugar into a saucepan set over *LOW-MEDIUM* heat. Cover and allow to cook, stirring frequently, until all the cranberries have popped. Place on a warming tray and keep warm until ready to serve.

In a large skillet set over *MEDIUM* heat, melt butter. Fry breaded *semolina* until brown on both sides. Transfer to a heated serving platter.

Garnish the platter with well-drained canned apricot halves.

Turn cranberries into a serving bowl.

Serve at once with an apricot half and cranberries on the side.

Yields 10 servings
adequate for 4-5 people

1/6 SERVING – PROTEIN = 6.4 g.; FAT = 4.2 g.; CARBOHYDRATE = 31.7 g.;
CALORIES = 191; CALORIES FROM FAT = 32%

Europe–Slovakia

SLOVAK PUMPKIN WITH CREAM
Tekvicový Prívarok

TPT - 16 minutes

I have seen many versions of this simple Slovak recipe, made with potatoes, lentil, and beans, and, admittedly, I have tried most of them. This is my favorite which I make not only with pumpkin but also with acorn, delicata, butternut, and kabocha squashes. It is a wonderful way to add the nutritional wonder of the yellow gourds to your family table and the sweet and sour taste is an adventurous change from the "three sisters" preparations which I grew up with in Iroquois country although I must admit beans and corn also accompany this dish well . . .

1 tablespoon *extra virgin* olive oil
1 tablespoon butter
3/4 cup *finely* chopped onion

1 1/2 cups unsweetened mashed cooked pumpkin*
1 teaspoon HOMEMADE PAPRIKA *[see index]*
 or commercially-available Hungarian sweet paprika
Salt, to taste

3/4 cup light cream *or* half and half
3 tablespoons unbleached white flour
2 tablespoons chopped fresh dillweed

1 1/2 teaspoons distilled white vinegar, or to taste
3/4 teaspoon sugar

In a large non-stick-coated skillet set over *MEDIUM* heat, heat oil and butter. Add *finely* chopped onion and sauté until onion is soft and translucent, *being careful not to allow onion to brown. Reduce heat to LOW-MEDIUM.*

Add mashed pumpkin, paprika, and salt and cook, stirring often, until pumpkin is soft.

In a small bowl combine cream, flour, and chopped dillweed. Using a small wire whisk, combine thoroughly. Add to pumpkin. Stir to combine. Cook, stirring frequently, until the mixture begins to boil.

Add vinegar and sugar. Stir well to combine. Turn into a heated serving bowl.

Serve at once.

Yields 6 servings
adequate for 4-5 people

Notes: *Canned pumpkin purée is a real convenience for this recipe if you do not want to take the time to cook and mash pumpkin or squash.

This recipe can be halved, when required.

1/6 SERVING – PROTEIN = 1.7 g.; FAT = 6.6 g.; CARBOHYDRATE = 8.2 g.;
CALORIES = 102; CALORIES FROM FAT = 58%

SLOVAK BEET AND HORSERADISH RELISH
Chren

TPT 1 week and 10 minutes;
 1 week = flavor development period

When we first moved to central Pennsylvania, I was unable to find the creamy, sulfite-free, preserved horseradish that was so popular in the New York metropolitan area. Those of German and central European extraction grated fresh horseradish and preserved it themselves as my own great-grandparents had done. I asked the manager of the grocery store if he planned to carry the brand I was used to purchasing but I did not hold much hope for his response. On a trip back to Long Island, I gathered up jars of the horseradish sauce and brought it back to Pennsylvania only to find out that my store manager had complied. We have lots of horseradish sauce on hand now.

This is so good with a hunk of cheese, hard-cooked eggs, or soy sausages.

1 pound *well-drained* canned beets *or cooked* fresh beets
2 ounces *sulfite-free* creamy horseradish sauce

Sterilize a canning jar, lid, and ring. Set aside until required.

SLOVAK BEET AND HORSERADISH RELISH (cont'd)

In the work bowl of the food processor fitted with steel knife, combine beets, and horseradish sauce. Process until of uniform consistency. Turn into sterilized jar. Seal. Refrigerate for 1 week to allow for flavor development.

Keep refrigerated.

Yields 1 1/2 cupfuls

Note: This recipe can be halved or doubled, when required.

1/24 SERVING (i. e., per tablespoonful) –
PROTEIN = 0.2 g.; FAT = 0.02 g.; CARBOHYDRATE = 2.0 g.;
CALORIES = 7; CALORIES FROM FAT = 3%

SLOVAK STRAWBERRY TART
Jahoola Ovocnj

TPT - 1 hour and 20 minutes

Slovakians, who seem to be very fond of sweet, gooey desserts, usually add a marshmallow cream layer to this dessert but the gelatin element of this product is not an appropriate choice for most vegetarians. I like this dessert because all the ingredients can be prepared in advance and then assembled as you clear the table and pour the coffee.

4 cups hulled, well-washed, and sliced fresh strawberries*
2 tablespoons sugar

5 ounces Maria biscuits *or* British digestives**
1/4 cup butter—*melted*

1 tablespoon corn starch

1 cup heavy whipping cream

1 Maria biscuit—crushed to crumbs for garnish

Prepare a 7-inch, two-piece tart pan by coating with non-stick lecithin spray for baking.

In a saucepan or mixing bowl, if preferred, sprinkle sugar over sliced strawberries. Toss to coat all the berry slices with sugar. Set aside until the strawberries extrude juice—about 30 minutes.

Meanwhile, using the food processor fitted with steel knife, grind cookies to an even crumb. While the machine is running, pour *melted* butter through the feed tube. Process until mixture sticks together. Turn into prepared tart pan and press evenly across the surface to form a crust. Refrigerate or freeze until ready to assemble.

Measure about 3 tablespoons of the extruded strawberry juice into a small dish. Add corn starch and stir until the corn starch is in suspension.

Set the saucepan with the strawberries over *LOW-MEDIUM* heat. Heat until strawberries soften. Add corn starch suspension and cook, stirring constantly, until the mixture thickens. Refrigerate until completely cooled.

Using the electric mixer fitted with *chilled* beaters or by hand using a *chilled* wire whisk, beat heavy cream in a *clean, chilled* bowl until stiff peaks form. Set aside or refrigerate until ready to assemble.

Just before you are ready to serve, spoon *one-half* of the whipped cream into the biscuit crust. Spread evenly to the edges. Spoon cooled strawberry mixture over. Spread it evenly over the surface. Spoon remaining whipped cream over, spreading it to the edges. Sprinkle biscuit crumb garnish over. Remove tart ring and slide the tart onto a serving plate.

Serve at once. Cut into wedges and, using a pie server, carefully transfer to dessert plates.

Yields 6 servings
adequate for 4 people

Notes: *Other berries can be substituted, if preferred.

**Maria biscuits are available in the United States under the Goya label.

This can be doubled using a 9-inch tart pan or halved using a 6-inch tart pan. I have even made individual tarts which present very dramatically.

1/6 SERVING – PROTEIN = 5.4 g.; FAT = 27.0 g.; CARBOHYDRATE = 33.0 g.;
CALORIES = 351; CALORIES FROM FAT = 69%

Slovenia

In 1991 Yugoslavia, a nation created after World War I comprising six regions, Serbia, Croatia, Bosnia and Herzegovina, Macedonia, Montenegro, and Slovenia, dissolved and in the aftermath Slovenia emerged as an independent nation. It borders Italy to the west, the Adriatic Sea to the southwest, Croatia to the south and east, Hungary to the northeast, and Austria to the north. Slovenia has been part of the Roman Empire; the Republic of Venice; the principality of Cartantania; the Holy Roman Empire; the Austro-Hungarian Empire; the Kingdom of Serbs, Croats, and Slovenes, which became the Kingdom of Yugoslavia in 1929; and the Socialist Federal Republic of Yugoslavia from 1945 until independence was possible because of the dissolution of Yugoslavia. It is small wonder that the cuisine of this nation is the cuisine of many nations.

Recipes even for the same foodstuffs vary from area to area with some saying that there are as many as forty distinct cuisines. Pork, beef, poultry, potatoes, beans, mushrooms, and *regrat*, dandelion, are eaten throughout the country but recipes for even these common denominators vary dramatically with often challenging complex preparations to differentiate traditions and create variety.

Since I grew up knowing only the post-World War II, cobbled-together entity of Yugoslavia, the appearance of the independent nation of Slovenia challenged me to separate the recipes in my files so as to discover the foods of Slovenia, Serbia, Croatia, Bosnia–Herzegovina, Macedonia, and Montenegro from that which had been collectively filed as Yugoslavian. It allowed cuisines to see the light of day, cuisines that had been masked by their political identity. There has been much cross-fertilization, not only between the nations that comprise the region but from the cuisines of Italy, Austria, and Hungary from whom much was borrowed and adapted. It was years before I began to recognize the space between eating habits and preparation preferences and could see that almost everything borrowed or begged eventually had a Slovenian fingerprint.

Meat eaten in the form of sausages is so important in this cuisine that I have included distinctive dishes adapted for the vegetarian using soymeat products now generally available. Since Slovenian dishes can be rather rich and heavy, especially those considered to be winter dishes, I have chosen to include several popular salads. The salad portion of this menu could actually be enjoyed as a buffet-style presentation all by itself. You will note that I have not included a recipe for chocolate cake. I simply did not have the courage to choose; every Slovenian has their own recipe and is passionate about their choice. Just choose your favorite chocolate cake recipe or favorite bakery cake and you will be thinking like a Slovenian.

Europe–Slovenia

Vermicelli with Buttered Breadcrumbs
Vermicelli alla Carrettiera

~

Slow Cooker Tomato – Squash Stew
Paradižnikova Juhu

~~~~~~~~~~~~~~~~~~~~

Soy Sausages in Sweet Wine Sauce
Klobasa s Slaščica Polivka

or

Sweet Soy Meatballs and Caramelized Onions
Cevapcici

Mixed Sautéed Wild Mushrooms
with Yogurt

Savory Potato – Apricot Dumplings
Marelični Cmoki

~~~~~~~~~~~~~~~~~~~~

Green Bean and Garlic Salad with *Romano* Cheese
Zelen Fižol Česen Solato

Potato Salad with Dandelion Leaves
Krompirjeva Regatova Solato

Kidney Bean Salad with Eggs
Nizek Fižol Orientalski Pozdrav s Eggs

Cabbage Slaw
Zelje Solato

~

Baked Apple Dessert   or   **Chocolate Cake**
Jabolko Narezek

SLOVENIAN *VERMICELLI* WITH BUTTERED BREADCRUMBS
Vermicelli alla Carrettiera
TPT - 33 minutes

Americans, who learned their pasta eating practices from Italians who emigrated from southern Italy, so often smother pasta in sauce and grated cheese. The rest of Italy and the rest of Europe, for that matter, approaches a bowl of cooked spaghetti quite differently. One of my favorite ways to eat spaghetti is an ancient Roman recipe where a little oil, black pepper, and grated cheese are mixed with the cooked spaghetti. This Slovenian take on spaghetti is a wonderfully simple first course which can be made with either thin spaghetti, vermicelli, or with compact nests of angel hair pasta, capelli d'angelo or capellini. It is not fussy; it is family. Be sure to use the most flavorful olive oil you can buy.

Europe–**Slovenia**

SLOVENIAN *VERMICELLI* WITH BUTTERED BREADCRUMBS (cont'd)

2 tablespoons *extra virgin* olive oil
2 tablespoons butter
1/2 cup *finely* chopped onion

1 large garlic clove—*very finely* chopped

3/4 cup dry breadcrumbs
1/2 teaspoon *finely* crushed dried oregano
2 teaspoons *finely* chopped fresh parsley

4 quarts *boiling* water
1 tablespoon freshly squeezed lemon juice
1 3-inch piece lemon zest
1/2 pound high protein or whole wheat vermicelli*

1 1/2 teaspoons *extra virgin* olive oil
Freshly ground black pepper, to taste**

In a skillet set over *MEDIUM* heat, combine the 2 tablespoonfuls olive oil and butter. Add *finely* chopped onion and sauté until onion is soft and translucent, *being careful not to allow onion to brown.*

Add *very finely* chopped garlic and sauté for a minute more. Reduce heat to *LOW*.

Add breadcrumbs, *finely* crushed dried oregano, and *finely* chopped fresh parsley. Cook, stirring frequently, until breadcrumbs have absorbed the butter and oil and are light brown. Place on a warming tray set at HIGH until required.

In a large kettle set over *HIGH* heat, add lemon juice and lemon zest to *boiling* water. Break spaghetti in half. Add spaghetti and cook, stirring occasionally, over *HIGH* heat according to package directions. Drain *very briefly*, discarding lemon zest.

Turn *pasta* into a heated serving bowl. Add the 1 1/2 teaspoonfuls of olive oil. Toss. Season well with black pepper. Toss to distribute the pepper evenly. Pour the breadcrumbs over the *pasta*.

Serve at once.

Yields 6 appetizer servings
adequate for 4 people

Notes: *Instead of thin spaghetti, *vermicelli*, angel hair *pasta* (*capelli d'angelo* or *capellini*) can be substituted. The compact nests, available in most well-stocked grocery stores or from mail order firms, make a more formal presentation possible.

**Do not substitute packaged ground black pepper. This dish deserves the taste of freshly cracked pepper.

This recipe may be halved or doubled, when required.

1/6 SERVING – PROTEIN = 6.7 g.; FAT = 10.0 g.; CARBOHYDRATE = 68.0 g.;
CALORIES = 279; CALORIES FROM FAT = 32%

SLOW COOKER SLOVENIAN TOMATO – SQUASH STEW
Paradižnikova Juha

TPT - 2 hours and 25 minutes;
[slow cooker: 1 hour at HIGH;
1 hour and 15 minutes at LOW]

Much like the minestras of Italy, soups vary in Slovenian from province to province, from village to village, and from family to family. The most important consideration is to use the produce at hand. An unusual relish, common to all the nations that once formed the country of Yugoslavia, ajvar is the subtle signature that distinguishes this thick soup/stew. Ajvar is one of those "prepare for the winter" foods, or "zimnica," that all Slovenian cooks tackle just as soon as the peppers and eggplant can be harvested. If you do not make ajvar yourself, it is available in specialty food stores and from mail order firms. Whether you sit in the garden with a chilled bowl of this soup on a warm summer evening or whether you serve it hot in the dining room on a cold winter evening, you can not help but appreciate the texture, the flavors, the comfort.

Europe–Slovenia

SLOW COOKER SLOVENIAN TOMATO – SQUASH STEW (cont'd)

1 cup canned, diced tomatoes with juice
1 cup canned, crushed tomatoes with juice
6 tablespoons SERBIAN ROASTED EGGPLANT CAVIAR (Ajvar) *[see index]**
1/2 medium onion–diced—to yield about 1 1/2 cupfuls
1 garlic clove—*very finely* chopped
1 small zucchini—well washed and diced
1 small yellow summer squash—peeled and diced
1/2 cup diced carrot
2 tablespoons chopped fresh basil leaves
1/1/2 teaspoons red wine vinegar
1/4 teaspoon sugar
2 or 3 drops *jalapeño* **sauce** *or* **Tabasco Sauce, or to taste***
Pinch salt, or to taste
Freshly ground black pepper, to taste
1/2 cup *boiling* **water**

In the bowl of the slow cooker set at HIGH, combine diced and crushed tomatoes, *ajvar*, diced onion, *very finely* chopped garlic, diced zucchini, diced yellow summer squash, diced carrot, chopped basil leaves, vinegar, sugar, salt, black pepper, and *boiling* water. Stir to mix thoroughly and allow to cook for 1 hour. Reduce the slow cooker setting to LOW, and allow to cook for about 1 hour and 15 minutes more. Stir occasionally. Add more *boiling* water if needed.

Turn into heated soup tureen or serving bowl and serve into heated soup plates.

Yields 6 servings
adequate for 6 people

Notes: *If the *ajvar* that you use is hot, omit the extra hot sauce addition to the stew.

Although this can be made in a heavy kettle or Dutch oven set over *LOW* heat, we prefer the slow cooker method since you do not have to worry about burning or sticking.

This recipe can be doubled, when required.

Conveniently, this stew freezes well.

1/6 SERVING – PROTEIN = 2.8 g.; FAT = 1.4 g.; CARBOHYDRATE = 10.1 g.;
CALORIES = 62; CALORIES FROM FAT = 20%

SOY SAUSAGES IN SWEET WINE SAUCE IN THE STYLE OF SLOVENIA
Klobasa a Slaščica Polivka

TPT - 35 minutes

This recipe was created as homage to an extraordinary Carniolian sausage dish. The debate over the most authentic recipe for "kranjske klobase" has spread to Internet forums; Slovenians are that passionate about this national treasure. It takes a bit of courage to step into this arena but whether you eat meat or eschew meat, as do we, the sauce that gives their sausages incredible flavor can be enjoyably replicated.

1 1/2 tablespoons butter
1 large garlic clove—smashed
1 sprig fresh rosemary—well-washed
1 sprig fresh thyme—well-washed

2 tablespoons apricot jam
2 tablespoons red currant jelly
1 tablespoons lemon juice
1/2 teaspoon MUSTARD SAUCE *[see index]*

3 tablespoons red wine

1 package (8 ounces/10 per package) soy sausages—brought to room temperature

In a saucepan set over *LOW* heat, melt butter. Add garlic clove, rosemary, and thyme. Cook, stirring frequently, for about 10 minutes to allow the flavor of the garlic and the herbs to permeate the butter. *Be careful not to allow garlic to brown.*

Add apricot jam, currant jelly, lemon juice and mustard. Continue cooking and stirring until jam and jelly melt. *Increase heat to MEDIUM.*

Add red wine and continue cooking for about 12 minutes, stirring frequently. Set a fine sieve over a clean saucepan. Pour the mixture through removing garlic, rosemary, thyme, and jam pieces.

Europe–Slovenia

**SOY SAUSAGES IN SWEET WINE SAUCE
IN THE STYLE OF SLOVENIA** (cont'd)

Add soy sausages to the sweet wine sauce. Set over *LOW-MEDIUM* heat and allow sausages to heat through. Stir frequently to prevent the sauce from sticking to the bottom of the pan. When heated through, turn sausages with sauce into a shallow, heated serving bowl. Keep warm on a warming tray until ready to serve.

Yields 10 sausages
adequate for 5 people

Note: This recipe can be doubled, when required.

1/10 SERVING (i. e., per sausage with sauce) –
PROTEIN = 4.5 g.; FAT = 3.2 g.; CARBOHYDRATE = 6.7 g.;
CALORIES = 77; CALORIES FROM FAT = 37%

SWEET SOY MEATBALLS AND CARAMELIZED ONIONS IN THE STYLE OF SLOVENIA

Čevapčiči *

TPT - 28 minutes

Living in the New York metropolitan area for many years, I have lunched or snacked on the wares of street vendors, especially those who sell roasted chestnuts and hot pretzels with mustard. Food vendors are found in almost every city in the world offering their own unique specialties—bowls of soup, bits of this and that on a stick, hunks of this and that in a bread wrap, some of which boggles the mind. Slovenians are fond of well-seasoned meatballs made from a mixture of ground meats and served on skewers. A variety of spicy and sweet sauces are provided by the vendors. I adapted this Slovenian street snack as a main course using vegetarian soy meatballs. The caramelized onions not only form a bed for the serving, they add flavor and eliminate the need for an additional sauce.

Non-stick lecithin *high heat* spray coating

1/3 cup all-fruit apricot preserves
3 tablespoons *chili* sauce
1 1/2 tablespoons *Dijon* mustard with wine
2 tablespoons water

1 package (9 ounces) vegetarian "meatballs"

**4 cups *thinly* sliced Italian red onion—about
    1 pound—separated into rings**
Non-stick lecithin *high-heat* spray coating

1 teaspoon sugar
**Freshly ground mixed peppercorns—red, black,
    and white—to taste**

Preheat a grill pan or skillet over *MEDIUM* heat. Coat lightly with the *high heat* cooking spray.

In a saucepan set over *MEDIUM-LOW* heat, combine apricot preserves, *chili* sauce, *Dijon* mustard, and water. Cook, stirring frequently with a wire whisk, until the jam, has melted and the sauce is smooth.

Add meatballs and cook, stirring frequently with a wooden spoon, for about 10 minutes, or until meatballs are heated through.

While meatballs are heating, put onion rings on the preheated grill pan. Spray the onion rings with the *high heat* cooking spray. Toss and spray again.

Cook, stirring and turning frequently with a wooden fork, until onions have softened.

Sprinkle sugar over. Toss. Grind pepper over. Toss. Continue cooking and stirring until most of the juice as evaporated and onions are soft. Transfer to the heated platter on which the entrée is to be served. Transfer the heated meatballs to the same platter.

Yields 4 servings
adequate for 3-4 people

Notes: *Čevapčiči* are, unlike the round meatballs to which we are accustomed, more like hand rolled sausages in shape. Variations of these are popular in many countries in the region. The name is derived from the Arabic *kebab*.

This recipe can be doubled, when required.

Europe–Slovenia

**SWEET SOY MEATBALLS AND CARAMELIZED ONIONS
IN THE STYLE OF SLOVENIA** (cont'd)

1/4 SERVING – PROTEIN = 13.8 g.; FAT = 3.5 g.; CARBOHYDRATE = 32.4 g.;
CALORIES = 17; CALORIES FROM FAT = 17%

SLOVENIAN SAVORY POTATO – APRICOT DUMPLINGS
Marelični Cmoki

TPT - 47 minutes

My grandmother used to drop little balls of mashed potatoes into soup. We simply called them potato balls because light, billowy, flour dumplings were the specialty of the cooks of German descent in my family. Those potato balls of my childhood visits to my grandparents were never filled with fruit as they are in Slovenia so the first time I made these dumplings was the first time I experienced that divine sensation as the flavor of the sweet, slightly cooked apricot flesh and the potato pastry set off the taste buds.

I use canned apricot halves because fresh apricots are rarely sweet enough or firm enough to use but I use fresh plum halves for plum dumplings, češplijevi cmoki, because the canned plums are too soft to use.

1 tablespoon butter
1/2 cup fine, dry breadcrumbs

2 cups *mashed* **potatoes**
1 1/3 cups unbleached white flour
1 tablespoon butter—*softened to room temperature*
1/4 cup *fat-free* **pasteurized eggs (the equivalent of 1 egg)**
Pinch salt

**3 canned apricot halves in juice or light syrup
—pitted, well-drained, and sliced into 12 slices ***

4 quarts *boiling* **water**

In a small skillet set over *LOW-MEDIUM* heat, melt 1 tablespoonful butter. Add breadcrumbs and cook, stirring frequently, until the butter has been absorbed by the breadcrumbs and the breadcrumbs are browned. Remove from heat and set aside until required.

In a mixing bowl, combine mashed potatoes, flour, *softened* tablespoonful of butter, pasteurized eggs, and salt. Mix well until it begins to form a dough. Knead until the dough is smooth. Add more flour as needed. Turn out onto a floured surface and roll to about 1/2-inch thickness. Cut into twelve squares.

Place an apricot slice in the center of one of the twelve squares. Draw the pastry square up and around the apricot half and form a ball. Repeat to form 12 dumplings.

In a large kettle set over *LOW-MEDIUM* heat, bring the *boiling* water to a gentle simmer. Poach four of the dumplings at a time until they float—about 8-10 minutes. Remove with a slotted spoon or skimmer and transfer to a heated serving platter placed on a warming tray.

When all dumplings have been cooked and transferred to the serving platter, sprinkle the buttered crumbs over.

Serve at once.

Yields 12 dumplings
adequate for 6 people

Notes: *Fresh plum slices can be used, if preferred.

This recipe can be halved or doubled, when required.

1/12 SERVING – PROTEIN = 3.0 g.; FAT = 2.1 g.; CARBOHYDRATE = 17.7 g.;
CALORIES = 99; CALORIES FROM FAT = 1%

Europe–Slovenia

SLOVENIAN GREEN BEAN AND GARLIC SALAD WITH *ROMANO* CHEESE

Zelen Fižol Česen Solato

TPT - 1 hour and 6 minutes;
      1 hour = flavor development period

The cuisine of a land that once was a part of the Republic of Venice, that once was part of the Austro-Hungarian Empire, and which borders on the Asiatic Sea could hardly ignore its ancestry. The garlic, grating cheese, and seasoning in this simple bean salad clearly show these historic influences. This is a really great garlicky accompaniment to a grainburger.

1 pound *frozen* tiny whole green beans
  —trimmed and cut into 1-inch pieces
2 medium garlic cloves—*very finely* chopped

1 tablespoon olive oil
1 tablespoon walnut oil
2 tablespoons GARLIC–BASIL VINEGAR *[see index]* or other vinegar, of choice
1/2 teaspoon AROMATIC GREEK SEASONING MIX *(Baharika kai Aromatika) [see index]*

1/2 ounce *pecorino* Romano cheese—shaved into long strips—for garnish*

In a shallow serving bowl, combine green bean pieces and garlic.

In a jar, with tightly-fitting lid, combine olive and walnut oils, vinegar, and Greek seasoning. Tightly close and shake vigorously and pour over salad ingredients. Toss. Cover with plate and allow to marinate at room temperature for 1 hour.

Garnish with shaved Parmesan cheese slices.

Serve at once with a slotted spoon.

Yields 6 servings
adequate for 4 people

Note: This recipe is easily halved, when required.

1/6 SERVING – PROTEIN = 2.1 g.; FAT = 4.8 g.; CARBOHYDRATE = 5.2 g.;
CALORIES = 70; CALORIES FROM FAT = 61%

SLOVENIAN POTATO SALAD WITH DANDELION LEAVES

Krompirjeva Regatana Solato

TPT - 4 hours and 20 minutes;
      2 hours = potato chilling period;
      2 hours = flavor development period

North Americans are always amazed when they encounter a potato salad dressed only with a vinaigrette, salt, and pepper. We are so accustomed to mayonnaise-drowned salad mixtures. Even European delis serve overly mayonnaised potato salads. When I make my family German potato salad, I sprinkle the vinegar mixture on the hot potato cubes to allow the flavor to permeate the potatoes. Slovenians, as do many other Europeans, chill the cooked potatoes and then dress them with a vinaigrette. The end result is that the potato flavor dominates. In the spring, when tender dandelion leaves can be foraged, this becomes the vehicle for the much loved green.

5 medium all-purpose potatoes *(not Idaho)*
  —preferably Red Bliss, if available—
  unpeeled but well-scrubbed
3 quarts *boiling* water

1 medium onion—chopped
1 garlic clove—*very finely* chopped
1/4 cup Italian flat-leafed parsley—well-washed and chopped

2 tablespoons SAGE VINEGAR *[see index]* or other herbed or plain apple cider vinegar, of choice
2 tablespoons *extra virgin* olive oil
1/4 teaspoon ground black pepper, or to taste
Salt, to taste

1 cup coarsely chopped *spray-free* dandelion leaves—well-washed and dried*

VOLUME I - 387

SLOVENIAN POTATO SALAD WITH DANDELION LEAVES (cont'd)

Cook potatoes in *boiling* water until *firm-tender*—about 18-20 minutes. Peel and place in a large mixing bowl. Refrigerate for at least 2 hours, or until thoroughly chilled and easily sliced. Slice potatoes into the mixing bowl.

Add chopped onion, *very finely* chopped garlic, and chopped parsley.

In a cruet or small jar, combine vinegar, oil, black pepper, and salt. Shake vigorously to combine. Sprinkle oil–vinegar mixture over vegetables. Toss *very gently*. Refrigerate for 2-3 hours. Turn potatoes occasionally to insure uniform distribution of the dressing.

Pour marinated salad into a sieve to allow excess marinade to drain through. Turn salad into a serving bowl.

Add chopped dandelion leaves. Refrigerate until required.

Serve cold.

Yields 6 servings
adequate for 4 people

Notes: *If you live in a city where foraging dandelions is not an option, some greengrocers do stock dandelions.

This recipe may be doubled or tripled, when required.

1/6 SERVING – PROTEIN = 2.4 g.; FAT = 3.9 g.; CARBOHYDRATE = 20.3 g.;
CALORIES = 124; CALORIES FROM FAT = 28 %

SLOVENIAN KIDNEY BEAN SALAD WITH EGGS
Nizek Fižol Orientalski Pozdrav s Eggs

TPT - 9 hours and 9 minutes;
8 hours = flavor development period

In Slovenia, bacon and potatoes usually show up in this salad and if it is spring and there is an ample supply of dandelion greens, well, you can expect them to be added to the salad too. I have, however, simplified the ingredients to accommodate this salad menu. This is a pretty salad and if the beans are allowed to marinate overnight, the taste is transcendent.

Instead of the salty soy bacon, I have found that a soy breakfast link reinforces the spirit of the original and provides a bit more protein and less sodium to this main course salad.

1 can (16 ounces) dark red kidney beans—well-drained*
1 *precooked, frozen* soy breakfast link
  —*defrosted* and chopped

2 large fresh sage leaves—*very finely* chopped
3 tablespoons *finely* chopped onion

3 tablespoons SAGE VINEGAR *[see index] or*
  apple cider vinegar
1 tablespoon *extra virgin* olive oil
1/2 teaspoon caraway seeds
Freshly ground black pepper, to taste

3 hard-cooked eggs—peeled and cut in round slices**

3 cups *mesclún*—*well-washed* and *well-dried*

In a large plastic container, combine well-drained kidney beans, chopped soy sausage link, *very finely* chopped sage leaves, and *finely* chopped onion. Gently stir to combine well.

In a cruet, combine vinegar, olive oil, caraway seeds, and black pepper. Shake vigorously and pour over bean mixture. Cover and refrigerate for at least 8 hours, turning frequently to insure uniform marination. Turn into shallow serving bowl or onto a platter, if preferred.

Arrange egg slices attractively on top of the marinated kidney bean mixture.

Serve chilled over a bed of greens.

Yields 4 main course servings

**SLOVENIAN KIDNEY BEAN SALAD
WITH EGGS** (cont'd)

Notes: *If you have the time and the inclination, cook dried kidney beans.

**An inexpensive egg slicer is indispensable for this dish.

This recipe can be halved or doubled, when required.

1/4 SERVING – PROTEIN = 12.7 g.; FAT = 7.9 g.; CARBOHYDRATE = 20.4 g.;
CALORIES = 203; CALORIES FROM FAT = 35%

SLOVENIAN CABBAGE SLAW
Zelje Solato

TPT - 1 hour and 8 minutes;
1 hour = flavor development period

This cabbage slaw from Slovenia is quite different from the coleslaw, which always contained mayonnaise, that I learned to make from the German cooks in my family, and it is different from the coleslaw with oil and vinegar that my Italian in-laws made. The caraway seasoning clearly places this salad in the countries influenced by German cuisine but the Greek seasoning called for in this recipe suggests an influence that few would suspect but an influence that is obvious in many dishes to be found in Slovenian cuisine.

5 cups *finely* shredded green cabbage
1/4 cup slivered onion

1 tablespoons *extra virgin* olive oil
2 teaspoons GARLIC–BASIL VINEGAR *[see index]* **or vinegar of choice**
1 teaspoon caraway seeds
1/2 teaspoon AROMATIC GREEK SEASONING MIX *(Baharika kai Aromatika)* *[see index]*
1/4 teaspoon sugar

Salt, to taste
Freshly ground black pepper, to taste

1 teaspoon grated Parmesan *or pecorino Romano* cheese

In a mixing bowl, combine shredded cabbage and slivered onion. Toss.

In a cruet, combine olive oil, vinegar, caraway seeds, Greek seasoning mixture, and sugar. Shake vigorously. Add to shredded vegetables. Toss to combine thoroughly.

Season with salt and pepper. Toss to combine thoroughly. Turn into a serving bowl. Refrigerate for 1 hour to allow the salad to wilt. Toss occasionally to insure even marination.

Sprinkle grated cheese over to garnish.

Serve chilled.

Yields 6 servings
adequate for 4 people

Note: This recipe can be halved or doubled, when required.

1/6 SERVING – PROTEIN = 1.5 g.; FAT = 4.2 g.; CARBOHYDRATE = 6.3 g.;
CALORIES = 55; CALORIES FROM FAT = 69%

Europe–Slovenia

SLOVENIAN BAKED APPLE DESSERT
Jabolko Narezek

TPT - 9 hours;
8 hours = raisin soaking period

My family called these stewed apples but Slovenians would interpret that as a sort of marmalade, which would be too mushy for my taste. Certainly this is not a dessert exclusive to Slovenia because wherever apples are grown, cooks make this or something very similar.

1/4 cup *preservative-free dark* raisins
2 tablespoons rum *or* brandy*
1 tablespoon water

4 large cooking apples—peeled, seeded, and sliced

2 tablespoons *melted* butter

1/2 cup sugar
1/2 teaspoon cinnamon

3 tablespoons *finely* chopped, *toasted* walnuts

3 tablespoons *fat-free* dairy sour cream

In a small dish, combine raisins, rum, and water. Stir to mix well. Place a saucer over the dish and allow to sit at room temperature for 8 hours, or overnight. Drain well.

Preheat oven to 300 degrees F. Prepare six oven-to-table individual baking dishes, such as onion soup crocks, by coating with non-stick lecithin spray coating.

Combine apple slices and raisins. Divide mixture among the serving dishes.

Sprinkle *melted* butter over the apples and raisins in each serving dish.

Combine sugar and cinnamon. Sprinkle some over each serving. Toss each serving to distribute the butter, sugar, and cinnamon. Bake in preheated 300 degree F. oven until the apples are soft, about 45 minutes. Remove from heat.

Sprinkle 1 1/2 teaspoonful of the *finely* chopped, *toasted* walnuts over each serving. Set aside to cool.

Garnish each serving with 1 1/2 teaspoonfuls sour cream. *Serve at room temperature.*

Yields 6 individual servings

Notes: *If you do not have rum or brandy in your liquor cabinet, buy one of the small one-serving bottles at your local liquor store. They are convenient to have on hand for a dish like this.

This recipe can be halved, when required.

1/6 SERVING – PROTEIN = 2.0 g.; FAT = 7.3 g.; CARBOHYDRATE = 44.3 g.;
CALORIES = 240; CALORIES FROM FAT = 27%

Spain

My most vivid memory of Spain is a mental postcard I will carry with me for always. A hassle of considerable proportions developed as we tried to cross over into Spain from Portugal in July 1977. I remember only the rifle-toting military and my frustrated repeating of the phrase "*no esta verde, esta azul*" when asked for a green travel document by a border official who wore a Portuguese uniform hat as we entered and switched to a Spanish uniform hat as he moved to the other side of the room to complete the Spanish entry form. When we finally crossed the border, we were met with rolling hills, enormous, round hay bails drying in the hot Andalusian sunshine, and acres of sunflowers in bloom.

Wheat and its cultivation were introduced by the Iberians to Aquitaine and the Celtic areas. Spanish wheat became known as the best wheat in the Roman Empire with that endorsement and its consequence economic advantage, the cash crop spread to Greece and Egypt. Olives came to Spain with the Phoenicians; garlic came with the Romans; tomatoes, potatoes, and peppers were brought back to Spain from the Americas during the Period of Exploration. Lentils, fava beans, and garbanzo beans have been known from antiquity. Bread soups/sops, *panzella*, popular in Italy from the period of the Roman Empire could well have traveled to Spain with the Roman legions giving us the soup/salad we revere as Spanish gazpacho. But most obvious even to the casual visitor is the Moorish influence which is, in our experience, everywhere, but nowhere more intensely than in Andalusia and to the east to Valencia where over five hundred years of Moorish rule brought many kinds of fruits including blood oranges, nuts, short-grained rice, exotic spices such as saffron, cinnamon and nutmeg, and agricultural practices to Spain. The art, the literature, the dialect variations, the customs of religious observance even today, and, of course, the cuisine, reflect the history of this land that is Europe one moment and North Africa the next.

Andalusia now produces *arroz largo* or *arroz varidad Americana*, the long-grained rice popular in the United States. It is used for salads and *pilaf* dishes instead of the short-grained rice, introduced by the Moors, which is used for *paella*. When people love to eat, as the Spanish do, they continue to explore the world.

Europe–Spain

Fried *Calamarata* with Garlic Mayonnaise
Calamares a la Romano

~

Vegetable Soup in the Style of Andalusia
Gazpacho Andaluz

~~~~~~~~~~~~~~~~~~~~~

Scrambled Eggs with Greens and Mushrooms
Huevos Revueltos con Verduras y Setas

or

Rustic Noodle, Mushroom, and Sausage Skillet
Fideuá a la Cazuela

Asparagus in Bitter Orange Sauce
Espárrago con Salsa de Naranja Sevilla

Sautéed Chick Peas with Sage
Garbanzos con Salvia

~~~~~~~~~~~~~~~~~~~~~

Walnut Rice Cream
Crema de Arroz Morisco

FRIED *CALAMARATA* WITH GARLIC MAYONNAISE
Calamares a la Romano

TPT - 1 hour and 37 minutes;
1 hour = refrigeration period

Squid is a popular protein source in other parts of the world especially in Asia and in the countries that border the Mediterranean—cooked whole, grilled, stuffed, and served with sauces appropriate to the cuisine; stir-fried; and in salads. An attempt in the 1970s to promote squid in the United States as a protein source was so unsuccessful that I imagine few of my readers will have ever tasted squid. One popular way of preparing squid was to cut the squid into rings, coat them in batter, deep-fry them, and serve them with a spicy tomato-based sauce. It appeared on the menus of hip restaurants for years and aficionados would seek out this pleasure The Spanish name for this dish suggests that the dish was, however, introduced to Spain by the Romans but I did not find it on menus in Italy; the last time I saw fried squid on a menu was in Spain where it was part of a tapas menu in Seville. Battered and fried squid, in this style, is still a popular dish in Italy, Greece, Spain, Cyprus, Albania, Turkey, and South Africa, where it is often an option in fish and chip shops.

Calamarata pasta is a useful pasta shaped to imitate squid and just chewy enough to suggest the texture of squid. The protein in this dish is not at all shabby either.

GARLIC MAYONNAISE:
    3/4 cup *calorie-reduced or light* mayonnaise
    1/4 cup *fat-free* dairy sour cream
    2 tablespoons GARLIC OIL *[see index]*

3 quarts *boiling* water
3/4 pound *calamarata pasta*

1/2 cup *fat-free* pasteurized eggs (the equivalent of 2 eggs)

1 cup dry breadcrumbs

High-heat safflower *or* sunflower oil for deep-frying

Salt, to taste

Europe–**Spain**

FRIED *CALAMARATA* WITH GARLIC MAYONNAISE (cont'd)

In a small bowl, combine mayonnaise, sour cream, and garlic oil. Using a small wire whisk, combine thoroughly. Cover and refrigerate until required.

In a large kettle, set over *MEDIUM-HIGH* heat, cook *pasta* in *boiling* water according to package directions. Plunge into cold water to stop further cooking. Drain well.

Using a scissors, cut each *pasta* ring in half to form two narrow rings. Place in a mixing bowl. Add pasteurized eggs. Toss to coat *calamarata* well.

Scoop egg-coated *pasta* into another mixing bowl. Add breadcrumbs. Toss to coat *pasta* well. Refrigerate for at least 1 hour.

Heat oil for deep-frying to 375 degrees F.

Deep-fry breaded *calamarata*, a handful at a time, until lightly browned. Transfer to several layers of paper toweling to absorb excess oil.

Serve at once with prepared garlic mayonnaise.

Yields 8 servings
adequate for 4 people

Notes: This recipe can be halved or doubled, when required.

FRESH *MARINARA* SAUCE *(Salsa Marinara) [see index]* is also a good dip for the fried *calamarata*.

1/6 SERVING – PROTEIN = 9.6 g.; FAT = 14.0 g.; CARBOHYDRATE = 47.7 g.;
CALORIES = 364; CALORIES FROM FAT = 35%

SPANISH VEGETABLE BREAD SOUP IN THE STYLE OF ANDALUSIA

Gazpacho Andaluz

TPT - 3 hours and 17 minutes;
3 hours = chilling period

Believe it or not, Mary Randolph, in her 1824 cookbook "The Virginia House-wife," actually gives a recipe for Spanish "gaspacha" on page 107. I guess we were not quite as provincial as some might have thought. Her version is far simpler and the flavors and garnishes are far less complex as is mine. Such a "gazpacho" as mine should really be categorized as a salad and in Andalusia it is. This version is as good as any we ate there.

3 medium tomatoes—peeled, quartered, and seeded
1/2 medium green pepper—seeded and chopped
1 medium cucumber—peeled, seeded, and chopped
1 small onion—chopped

1 garlic clove

1/2 slice whole wheat bread

1 tablespoon *extra virgin* olive oil

2 teaspoons wine vinegar
1 1/2 teaspoons freshly squeezed lemon juice
1/2 cup tomato vegetable juice—preferably homemade and unsalted
Freshly ground black pepper, to taste
Dash ground red pepper (cayenne)

GARNISHES:
Finely chopped onion (red, Bermuda, Spanish, yellow, or green, as preferred)
Finely chopped fresh parsley
Finely chopped cucumber
Finely chopped green and/or red bell pepper
Peeled, seeded, and *finely* chopped tomatoes
Chopped, hard-cooked eggs
Tiny, dry whole wheat croutons

Europe–**Spain**

**SPANISH VEGETABLE SOUP
IN THE STYLE OF ANDALUSIA** (cont'd)

In the work bowl of the food processor fitted with steel knife or in the container of the electric blender, combine quartered tomatoes with chopped green pepper, cucumber, and onion. Process or blend for a few seconds until *finely chopped,* but *not puréed*. Press garlic through a garlic press into the tomato mixture. Again, process or blend for a few seconds.

Soak bread in water. Squeeze out as much excess moisture as possible. Add to vegetables and, again, process or blend for a few seconds.

Turn into a large bowl. Gradually beat in olive oil, *drop by drop*. Stir in wine vinegar, fresh lemon juice, and tomato vegetable juice. Season with black and red (cayenne) peppers. Turn into a soup tureen.

Chill for several hours in the refrigerator.

Serve with a selection of garnishes in individual dishes arranged around the soup tureen. If too thick, float an ice cube in each serving. As it cools and melts, it will thin to desired consistency.

Yields 8 servings
adequate for 4-8 people

Note: This recipe is easily doubled or tripled, when required.

1/8 SERVING (exclusive of garnishes) –
PROTEIN = 1.2 g.; FAT = 1.6 g.; CARBOHYDRATE = 5.9 g.;
CALORIES = 44; CALORIES FROM FAT = 34%

SPANISH SCRAMBLED EGGS
WITH GREENS AND MUSHROOMS
Huevos Revueltos con Verduras y Setas

TPT - 44 minutes;
30 minutes = mushroom soaking period

The first time I served this version of scrambled eggs, I was met with a very positive statement, "As far as I'm concerned you could serve scrambled eggs this way from now on." You rarely get a more positive endorsement of an experiment than that. It is very different and very exciting.

1 tablespoon *dried* wild mushrooms
1/2 cup *boiling* water

1 teaspoon butter
1 teaspoon *extra virgin* olive oil
2 cups tiny spring leaves such as turnip, kale, and spinach—*well-washed* and *well-drained* and chopped*
1 small garlic clove—*very finely* chopped

6 large eggs
1 tablespoon light cream *or* half and half
Freshly ground black pepper, to taste

Grated Parmesan, *pecorino Romano,* **or** *Manchego*
  cheese from La Mancha, if available

Soak dried mushrooms in *boiling* water for 30 minutes. Drain thoroughly.

In a 9-inch skillet, set over *MEDIUM* heat, heat butter and olive oil. Add chopped greens, *well-drained* mushrooms, and *very finely* chopped garlic. Sauté *gently* for a minute or two.

In a small bowl combine eggs and cream. Using a wire whisk, combine thoroughly. Season beaten eggs with black pepper. Add beaten eggs to vegetables in skillet. Scramble *gently* until eggs are cooked, but *still soft*. Turn onto a heated platter.

Serve at once, with a light sprinkling of grated cheese. Accompany with thick slices of a coarse, crusty peasant-style bread.

Yields 4 servings
adequate for 3-4 people

Notes: *A salad spinner is useful to wash and dry leaves.

This recipe can be halved or doubled, when required.

1/4 SERVING – PROTEIN = 10.9 g.; FAT = 11.1 g.; CARBOHYDRATE = 1.4 g.;
CALORIES = 149; CALORIES FROM FAT = 68%

Europe–**Spain**

RUSTIC SPANISH NOODLE, MUSHROOM, AND SAUSAGE SKILLET
Fideuá a la Cazuela

TPT - 45 minutes

The Catalan specialty "fideuá" was often on the menu when we traveled in Spain but, of course, I never tried it since it is usually made with fish stock, pork and / or other meats, sausage, and shellfish. Today, a vegetarian chorizo product can be used in this unusual country dish which celebrates the wonderful flavors of wild mushrooms in a garlicky tomato sauce and the texture of a fine noodle called "fideuá" similar to angel hair pasta and for which angel hair pasta can be substituted. A variety of vegetables can be chosen such as artichoke hearts and sliced carrots, as in this version, asparagus tips, or green beans and I have seen it served with parboiled cubed potatoes. The uniquely Spanish way of cooking this fine pasta is really worth trying.

1 tablespoon *extra virgin* Spanish olive oil
3 ounces angel hair *pasta, (capelli d'angelo* or, sometimes, *capellini*)—broken into 2-inch pieces

1 teaspoon GARLIC OIL *[see index]*
1/2 medium Italian red onion—chopped
1 1/2 cups sliced mixed wild mushrooms, of choice
6 ounces soy *chorizo (chouriço)*—sliced into 1/4-inch-thick slices
1/2 small red bell pepper—cut into squares
2 garlic cloves—*very finely* chopped
2 tablespoons chopped fresh parsley
1/4 teaspoon *smoked* paprika
2 drops liquid smoke

1/2 cup canned, *diced* tomatoes
1/2 cup canned, *crushed* tomatoes *or* tomato purée
1/2 cup WILD MUSHROOM STOCK *[see index] or* other vegetable stock of choice

1/2 cup *frozen* artichoke hearts *or* other vegetable of choice
1/2 cup *parboiled*, thick carrot slices

GARLIC MAYONNAISE *[see index – BLENDER MAYONNAISE variations]*
Grated ewe's milk cheese – Spanish *Manchego* cheese *or* Italian *pecorino Romano*

In a wok, a *paella* pan, or in large non-stick-coated skillet set over *LOW-MEDIUM* heat, heat 1 tablespoonful oil. Add angel hair *pasta* and sauté until lightly browned and opaque. Using a spatula, transfer the *pasta* to paper toweling to drain until required.

Add garlic oil to the wok. Add chopped onion, sliced mushrooms, sliced *chorizo* sausage, red pepper squares, *very finely* chopped garlic, chopped parsley, smoked paprika, and liquid smoke. *Stir-fry* mixture for about 10 minutes, or until most of liquid has evaporated.

Add well-drained, fried angel hair *pasta*, diced tomatoes, tomato purée, and stock. Cover and simmer for about 5 minutes. Stir frequently.

Preheat oven to 350 degrees F.

To the mixture in the wok, add artichoke hearts and parboiled carrot slices, or other vegetables selected. Cover and simmer for about 5 minutes more, or until the *pasta* is softened. Stir frequently. Transfer *fideuá* from the wok to a skillet or oven-to-table baking pan Place in preheated 350 degree F. oven for about 10 minutes, or until the *pasta* on top becomes crisp. Watch carefully because the pasta can burn very easily.

Serve directly from skillet or *paella* pan or transfer to a clay casserole.* Accompany with GARLIC MAYONNAISE and grated cheese.

Yields 6 servings
adequate for 4 people

Notes: *If you have a *paella* pan, by all means use it instead of the skillet. Spaniards serve *fideuá* in a clay casserole. I use the bottom portion of my Moroccan *tagine* cooker; it keeps the casserole warmer at table than does a metal pan. It is an appropriate casserole dish in which to serve *fideuá* because the name, and possibly the recipe, has roots in the period of Muslim domination of Spain.

This recipe can be halved, when required.

1/6 SERVING (exclusive of mayonnaise and /or cheese garnishes] –
PROTEIN = 7.2 g.; FAT = 5.6 g.; CARBOHYDRATE = 19.9 g.;
CALORIES = 153; CALORIES FROM FAT = 33%

Europe–Spain

SPANISH ASPARAGUS IN BITTER ORANGE SAUCE
Esparrago con Salsa de Naranja Sevilla
TPT - 21 minutes

While visiting the Iberian Peninsula, we met a couple from California who wanted a glass of orange juice so badly that the man went into the kitchen to "show" the waiter how to squeeze oranges. We too had tired of the orange soda that passes for orange juice in Portugal and Spain and Italy but I was concerned that we would just end up with a glass of juice from Seville oranges, have to add sugar, and then be right back to the "naranjada" again. Fortunately we were refreshed on that hot July day because the oranges he found in the kitchen were sweet not "Citrus aurantium," the orange know as bitter or sour orange. Seville oranges are much less sweet than are our navel oranges. They are perfect for marmalade, as the Scots have found. Finding a Seville orange in a grocery store in the middle of Pennsylvania in March is an unusual event but if I do, this is the recipe I prepare. Tender asparagus is just coming into the markets and this recipe is a very pleasant change from a Hollandaise sauce or just lemon butter. It does not overwhelm the asparagus.

1 cup freshly squeezed Seville orange juice*
2 tablespoons *light* **brown sugar**
2 tablespoons butter
Pinch of salt

24 asparagus spears—well-rinsed and trimmed

Set up a steamer over *MEDIUM* heat.

In a saucepan set over *MEDIUM* heat, combine the orange juice, brown sugar, butter, and salt. Bring to the boil. Allow to thicken, stirring frequently, while preparing asparagus.

Meanwhile, steam asparagus in steamer until just *crisp-tender*. Transfer to a heated platter. Pour the orange sauce over.

Serve at once.

Yields 6 servings
adequate for 4 people

Notes: *If Seville oranges are unavailable, use 3/4 cupful freshly squeezed orange juice and 1/4 cup freshly squeezed lemon juice.

This recipe can be halved or doubled, when required.

1/6 SERVING – PROTEIN = 1.0 g.; FAT = 3.9 g.; CARBOHYDRATE = 9.6 g.;
CALORIES = 77; CALORIES FROM FAT = 45%

SPANISH SAUTÉED CHICK PEAS WITH SAGE
Garbanzos con Salvia
TPT - 1 hour and 13 minutes;
1 hour = flavor infusion period

Chick peas, prepared in this manner, are a delightful accompaniment to bruschetta as an appetizer. We especially like to serve them with a wild mushroom bruschetta and with brie and chive toasts. These are really a nice addition to an "I'm-not-too-hungry-cheese-and-crackers-dinner." They are also excellent in a salad, as part of an antipasto platter, as part of a tapas offering with sherry or wine before a Spanish meal, or mixed into a pasta or rice dish.

2 tablespoons *extra virgin* **olive oil** *or* **walnut oil, if preferred**
1 large garlic clove—peeled and halved
4 large sage leaves—well-washed

1 can (19 ounces) chick peas (*garbanzos***)—well-drained, rinsed, well-dried, and seed coats removed**

Freshly ground black pepper, to taste
Salt, if desired

In a skillet large enough to hold the chick peas in a single layer and set over *LOW-MEDIUM* heat, heat oil with garlic and sage leaves until the combined aroma begins to be apparent. *Remove from heat.*

Check to be sure that seed coats have been removed from each chick pea. Add well-dried chick peas to skillet. Set aside for 1 hour to allow the flavors to infuse the chick peas.

Sauté gently for several minutes for *MEDIUM* heat. *Shake the pan frequently as you sauté.* Discard garlic and sage leaves.

Europe–**Spain**

SPANISH SAUTÉED CHICK PEAS WITH SAGE (cont'd)

Using a slotted spoon, transfer chick peas to a heated bowl. Grind black pepper over and salt, if desired.

Serve warm.

Yields 6-8 servings
adequate for 4 people

Note: This recipe can be doubled, when required.

1/6 SERVING – PROTEIN = 2.0 g.; FAT = 3.4 g.; CARBOHYDRATE = 4.7 g.
CALORIES = 59; CALORIES FROM FAT = 52%

SPANISH WALNUT RICE CREAM
Crema de Arroz Marisco

TPT - 2 hours and 50 minutes;
2 hours = chilling period

This is one of the most unusual rice puddings we have ever collected. Each flavor, rather distinct on its own, becomes part of a fabric so subtle that only the garnishes give a hint of the ingredients. It is unusual and it is one of our favorite desserts for a North African menu. If you can find blood oranges to garnish, so much the better!

2 cups *one-percent* **milk**

1/4 cup powdered brown rice*

1/3 cup firmly packed *light* **brown sugar**

1/2 teaspoon freshly grated lemon zest
1/2 teaspoon freshly grated orange zest
Pinch freshly grated nutmeg

1/2 teaspoon pure vanilla extract
1/8 teaspoon pure black walnut flavoring

1/2 cup heavy whipping cream—*stiffly-whipped***—for garnish****
4 thin orange slice twists or "butterflies," for garnish
3 teaspoons *toasted,* **chopped,** *preservative-free* **English walnuts** *or* **black walnuts, if available—for garnish****

In the top half of a double boiler set directly over *MEDIUM* heat, bring milk carefully to the boil.

Set double boiler inset containing milk over boiling water. Stir in powdered rice, cover, and allow to cook for about 10 minutes until it thickens slightly.

Add brown sugar, stirring to disperse evenly. Cover again and allow to cook for 15 minutes.

Add grated lemon and orange zests, and nutmeg. Cook, *uncovered,* for an additional 3 minutes, stirring frequently.

Remove double boiler inset from heat and allow to cool for about 10 minutes. Stir in vanilla and black walnut extracts. Divide mixture evenly among four sherbet glasses or other dessert dishes. Chill in the refrigerator for 2 hours.

Just before serving, garnish each serving with a dollop of stiffly whipped cream. Nestle a twisted orange slice into the cream and sprinkle with *toasted,* chopped walnuts.

Yields 4 individual servings

Notes: *Prepare powdered rice by blending 5 tablespoonfuls of brown rice at *HIGH* speed in a *dry* electric blender or in a food processor, fitted with steel knife, until *finely powdered.*

**Instead of whipped heavy cream, heavy pouring cream may be passed with garnished servings, if the thinner consistency is preferred.

***Prepare toasted walnuts by placing chopped walnuts in a 250 degree F. oven for about 15 minutes, or until *lightly browned.*

This recipe is easily doubled but cooking times may have to be increased slightly to allow for volume.

1/4 SERVING – PROTEIN = 6.1 g.; FAT = 13.0 g.; CARBOHYDRATE = 37.7 g.;
CALORIES = 290; CALORIES FROM FAT = 40%

Sweden

As with other countries in the far North, there is evidence in Sweden of settlement by bands of Late Paleolithic peoples at the edge of the retreating glacial ice sheet, c. 12,000 BC, with continued occupation through the Bronze and Iron Ages. Without interruption by Roman occupation, a primitive Swedish culture grew in a more gradual, linear manner, although seriously underdocumented. The Viking Age extended from the eighth to the eleventh centuries during which the Swedish Vikings, know as "Rus," raided as far south as Turkey. Documentation of this period relies on runestones found all over Sweden. Information revealed by these runestones does date the last major expedition of Ingvar the Far-Travelled. In 1041 his contingent traveled down the Volga River to the land of the Saracens (Serkland), probably with the intension of reopening old trade routes.

The union formed between Sweden and Norway in 1319 was reorganized in 1397 as they joined with Denmark to create the Kalmar Union. Sweden became an independent kingdom in 1523 under King Christian I after the repulsion of the Danish attempt to conquer Sweden in 1520. Militaristic expansion by Sweden under King Gustavus Adolphus during the seventeenth century created a Swedish Empire. Later, during the Thirty-Years' War, the Swedish king invaded and claimed close to fifty percent of the states that had formerly comprised the Holy Roman Empire, planning, it is said, to proclaim himself the new Holy Roman Emperor. Most of their territorial claims were lost during the eighteenth and nineteenth century. Among these claims was modern-day Finland which was lost to Russia in 1809. In 1814 Sweden militarily forced Norway into a union which survived until 1905. Since then a foreign policy of non-alignment as been observed under a constitutional monarchy.

Household self-sufficiency, when little if anything was purchased, has led to a people, a nation, of great strength. Centuries of producing your own food and planning for the seasons of the year creates a practical approach to not only basic survival but also to your view of the world and your place in that world. Swedes are practical people with an insight into world affairs that is unique on a national scale. Those that I met on our trip to Scandinavia in 1985 were even practical about their choices at the Christmas cold table.

Although most vegetables, especially root vegetables, are popular today in Sweden, the earliest vegetables of importance in Sweden appear to be onions and cabbage. Turnips, rutabagas ("Swedes"), celeriac, beets, parsnips, carrots, leeks, peas, broad beans, and, of course, the potato followed. The potato which, although known in the seventeenth century, did not take on the importance it has today until the nineteenth century when it was found that it could replace precious grain, essential for bread flour and for alcohol production. Fifteen percent of Sweden lies north of the Arctic Circle, which significantly limits grain cultivation since grains, other than barley, do not grow well in such northern climates. The need for grain and the importance of bread in the Swedish diet can not minimized. Flatbreads were generally made from barley which grows well in colder climates but which does not rise well, hence the characteristic flatbread with the hole in the center which facilitates the drying process. In the not-so-distant past a supply of flatbreads was made twice a year, at Christmas and at Midsummer. The management of the bread supply was an important responsibility of a housewife. Eggs, from domesticated birds and from wild birds, were considered a spring or summer food since the low-light level of the darker months limited egg production. Even milk was not consumed fresh in cases other than for children or the sick. The oceans which surround Sweden and the extensive forests provided and provide seafood and game which can be salted for winter use. The high salt and high fat intake characteristic of the Swedish cuisine is fortunately changing today.

Europe–Sweden

Yellow Pea Soup
Ärter Soppa

Potato Soup with Cheese
Potatissoppa med Ost

Uncooked Mustard
Hemlagad Senap

~

Ruby Pear Salad with Lingonberries
Sellad Päron Samt Lingosylt

~~~~~~~~~~~~~~~~~~~~~~

Vegetable Omelet with Oven-Roasted Root Vegetables with Cheese
Grønsakeromelette Rotsaksgratäng

Sautéed Peas in the Pod
Ärtskida

or

Sautéed Kale with Cream
Längkål

~~~~~~~~~~~~~~~~~~~~~~

Lingonberry Cream Dessert
Sur Gradde med Lingon

YELLOW PEA SOUP IN THE SWEDISH STYLE
Ärter Soppa

TPT - 2 hours and 25 minutes

This is a "no nonsense," "stick-to-the-ribs" winter soup that satisfies hunger well, comforts fully, pleases the eye, and nourishes splendidly. Americans, if they use split peas at all, usually choose green peas, so back in the 1970s this was a new experience for us. It is a soup to which we turn each winter with anticipation and pleasure

1 pound dry yellow split peas
2 quarts water

2/3 cup sliced scallions
1 small onion—chopped
3 medium carrots—diced
2 celery ribs with leaves—diced
1 teaspoon dried parsley—crushed
1/4 teaspoon dried thyme—crushed
1/4 teaspoon freshly ground black pepper, or to taste
1 small bay leaf—broken*
2 tablespoons butter
1/4 cup light cream *or* half and half

Unbuttered whole wheat croutons

Rinse dry split peas thoroughly, sort, and discard any of poor quality. Put peas in a large heavy saucepan, with cover. Add water and set over *MEDIUM-HIGH* heat. While stirring, bring to the boil. Reduce heat to *LOW*, cover, and simmer for about 30 minutes, or until peas are *very soft*—stirring frequently.

Using an electric blender or a food processor fitted with steel knife, purée peas and liquid. Pour puréed mixture through a sieve into a clean, large, heavy saucepan.**

Europe–Sweden

YELLOW PEA SOUP IN THE SWEDISH STYLE (cont'd)

Add sliced scallions, chopped onion, diced carrots and celery, crushed parsley and thyme, black pepper, bay leaf, and butter. Set over *LOW* heat and simmer gently, uncovered, for about 1 1/2 hours, or until of desired thickness with vegetables still *al dente*. Stir often to prevent sticking.***

Stir in cream. Allow soup to heat through but *do not allow it to boil*. Remove and discard bay leaf.

Pour into heated soup tureen and serve into heated soup plates or bowls. Pass croutons separately.

Yields 8 main course servings
adequate for 4-6 people

Notes: *The bay leaf pieces are most easily recovered if secured inside a tea ball during the simmering process.

**If desired, this soup base may be frozen successfully at this point.

***If preferred, the completed soup may be frozen at this point. But, in this case, *defrost completely in refrigerator before heating through* to preserve the texture of the vegetables.

1/8 SERVING – PROTEIN = 14.5 g.; FAT = 4.1 g.; CARBOHYDRATE = 39.3 g.;
CALORIES = 247; CALORIES FROM FAT = 15%

SWEDISH POTATO SOUP WITH CHEESE
Potatissoppa med Ost

TPT - 15 minutes

This potato soup, Swedish in origin, is very, very different from any potato soup that I have made over the years. It is quickly prepared from grated raw potatoes rather from peeled, cooked, and puréed potatoes. Grated cheese gives it an extraordinary taste. A mug of this soup early on a cold, clear January morning, after watching the Quadrantid meteorite shower, is one of those winter memories that is never forgotten.

1 1/2 cups *grated* raw potatoes—about 2 medium—
  grated, not shredded
1/2 cup grated Parmesan *or pecorino Romano*
  cheese, as preferred
2 1/4 teaspoons unbleached white flour
1/8 teaspoon freshly ground white pepper, or
  to taste
1/2 cup *whole* milk

2 cups *boiling* water
1 1/2 tablespoons butter

1 cup light cream *or* half and half

In a kettle, combine *grated* potatoes, grated cheese, flour, white pepper, and whole milk. Stir to form a paste.

Set kettle over *MEDIUM* heat. Gradually, while stirring constantly, add *boiling* water. Add butter. Cook, stirring frequently, until hot and thickened.

Add cream, thinning to the desired consistency. Cook, until heated through.

Turn into a heated tureen. Ladle into heated soup plates or mugs.

Yields about 5 cupfuls

Note: This recipe can be doubled, when required.

1/5 SERVING (i. e., per cupful) –
PROTEIN = 9.2 g.; FAT = 14.3 g.; CARBOHYDRATE = 17.9 g.;
CALORIES = 237; CALORIES FROM FAT = 54%

Europe–Sweden

SWEDISH UNCOOKED MUSTARD
Hemlagad Senap

TPT - 8 hours and 20 minutes;
15 minutes = water absorption period;
8 hours = mellowing period

My cooked mustard sauce and the Danish mustard sauce (sennepsaus), made from course-grained Dijon mustard, [see index for both] have been my consistent choices over the years, so much so that I had rarely looked left or right for another mustard recipe. Neither of my standbys were appropriately assertive enough to accompany a Swedish smorgasbord so I began to explore the Swedish method of making mustard and was pleased to add this recipe to my repertoire.

1/4 cup English-style dry mustard
2 tablespoons unbleached white flour
6 tablespoons *boiling* water

3 tablespoons sugar
Pinch salt
2 tablespoons white wine vinegar

2 tablespoons heavy whipping cream, or to taste*

In a mixing bowl, combine dry mustard, flour, and *boiling* water. Stir to combine thoroughly. Set aside for about 15 minutes.

Add sugar, salt, and vinegar. Mix thoroughly.

Set a fine sieve over a bowl. Pour mustard base into sieve and gently stir press through the sieve. Turn into a jar or mustard cup. Refrigerate overnight to allow mustard to mellow.

Just before serving, add heavy cream. Stir to integrate thoroughly. Cover and refrigerate any leftovers.

Yields about 15 tablespoonfuls

Notes: *Fat-free dairy sour cream can be used instead of cream, if preferred

This recipe can be doubled, when required.

1/45 SERVING (i. e., per teaspoonful) –
PROTEIN = 0.2 g.; FAT = 0.4 g.; CARBOHYDRATE = 1.3 g.;
CALORIES = 9; CALORIES FROM FAT = 40%

SWEDISH RUBY PEAR SALAD WITH LINGONBERRIES
Sellad Päron Samt Lingosylt

TPT - 38 minutes;
30 minutes = chilling period

The tartness of these fruits is the perfect foil for the soft, sweetness of the pears and the bright berries plated against the whiteness of the pears is so very pretty. This could also be used as a dessert or just as a plate garniture.

12 canned, juice-packed pear halves—well-drained
6 tablespoons lingonberry preserves

6 tablespoons OUR GRANOLA [see index]

Slice pear halves lengthwise, keeping slices together. Place two pear halves on each of six dessert plates. Spread each into an attractive fan. Spoon 1 tablespoonful of lingonberry preserves over pear slices.

Refrigerate for at least 30 minutes.

Sprinkle 1 tablespoonful granola over each serving.

Serve at once.

Yields 6 individual servings

Note: This recipe may be increased or decreased proportionately as required.

1/6 SERVING – PROTEIN = 3.0 g.; FAT = 2.6 g.; CARBOHYDRATE = 32.1 g.;
CALORIES = 160; CALORIES FROM FAT = 14%

Europe–Sweden

SWEDISH VEGETABLE OMELET
Gransakeromelette Rotsaksgratäng

TPT - 50 minutes

The first time I ever had this rolled Swedish omelet it was stuffed with fresh crabmeat in an extravagant cream sauce and was very rich. The recipe languished in my files for years because we had chosen to eliminate fish and seafood from our protein choices because of the contamination of the planet's fishing grounds and because seafood is routinely "kept white" by the use of sulfiting compounds which we wanted to avoid. One winter day this came to me in a flash. It is perfectly, and authentically, accompanied by a dilled cream sauce, if desired, and pickled beets.

FILLING:
    SWEDISH OVEN-ROASTED ROOT VEGETABLES WITH CHEESE
    (***Rotsaksgratäng***) *[see recipe which follows]*

OMELET:
    Unbleached white flour

    3 tablespoons butter
    3 tablespoons unbleached white flour
    4 tablespoons whole wheat flour
    1 cup skimmed milk
    3 large eggs
    Pinch freshly grated nutmeg

Thin lemon slices, for garnish
Fresh dill sprigs, for garnish

Prepare root vegetable filling as directed in recipe which follows. Stir in cream. Set aside on a warming tray set at *MEDIUM* until required.

Preheat oven to 375 degrees F. Prepare a non-stick-coated 9 x 11-inch cake pan or small jelly roll pan by coating with non-stick lecithin spray coating. Line prepared pan with waxed paper. Coat top of waxed paper liner with non-stick lecithin spray coating. Dust lightly with unbleached white flour. Set aside.

In a saucepan set over *LOW* heat, melt 3 tablespoonfuls butter. Remove from heat. Using a wire whisk, make a *roux* by beating in the 3 tablespoonfuls of white flour and the 4 tablespoonfuls of whole wheat flour. Return to heat and, stirring constantly, cook for 2 minutes, *being careful not to burn or overbrown the roux.*

Remove from heat and gradually beat in the 1 cupful milk. Return saucepan to heat and cook, stirring frequently, until thickened and smooth. Remove from heat.

In a mixing bowl, using a wire whisk, beat eggs. Add nutmeg to beaten eggs. Gradually, *tablespoonful by tablespoonful*, whisk hot white sauce into eggs. When thoroughly combined, pour batter into prepared pan.

Bake in preheated 350 degree F. oven until *puffed and golden*, about 25 minutes. Prick large bubbles if they form.

Line counter top work area with waxed paper. Lift edges of baked omelet with spatulas. *Carefully*, invert cooked omelet onto paper. Peel paper from bottom of omelet. Spread omelet with prepared vegetable filling leaving a border of about 3/4 inch without filling, *reserving about 1/4 cupful for garnish*. Starting at the short end lift paper and roll omelet up as for a jelly roll. Transfer to heated serving platter.

Garnish with lemon slices and dill sprigs.

                                  Yields 8 servings
                              adequate for 4-6 people

Note: This is easily doubled. Use an 11 x 17-inch jelly roll pan.

1/8 SERVING – PROTEIN = 5.6 g; FAT = 9.3 g; CARBOHYDRATE = 14.2 g;
CALORIES = 161; CALORIES FROM FAT = 52%

SWEDISH OVEN-ROASTED ROOT VEGETABLES WITH CHEESE
Rotsaksgratäng

TPT - 35 minutes

Root vegetables inevitably become somewhat boring as the winter months grind slowly on to spring, tempting you to buy the asparagus from Peru and the fresh baby vegetables flown in from Guatemala. Roasting the vegetables, as in this recipe from Sweden, can still tempt the taste buds when the family sees you heading for the root cellar or wherever root vegetables are stored in your house. Although being sent out to the root cellar to retrieve potatoes and carrots or leeks from the straw or whatever was a chore in the snow when I was a child, it was all stored in the same place and one trip was all you needed. Root vegetables are often baked in the oven with cream and cheese in Sweden. Here they are oven-roasted and sprinkled with grated cheese. Doubled, this can be served simply as a very satisfying au gratin vegetable dish.

SWEDISH OVEN-ROASTED ROOT VEGETABLES WITH CHEESE (cont'd)

1 teaspoon butter

3 *quarts* boiling water
1 medium French turnip—peeled and cut into 1/4-inch dice
2 medium carrots—scraped or pared and cut into 1/4-inch dice
1/4 cup diced celeriac (root celery)

2 small potatoes—peeled and diced into 1/4-inch dice

1 tablespoon *high-heat* safflower oil
1 small leek, *white portion only*—well-washed and sliced

Freshly ground black pepper, to taste
2 tablespoons grated Parmesan cheese, *pecorino Romano, or* other salty grating cheese, of choice

Preheat oven to 400 degrees F. Prepare an *au gratin* dish or other oven-to-table dish by lightly coating with butter. Set aside until required.

In a saucepan set over *MEDIUM* heat, combine *boiling* water, diced turnip, carrots, and celeriac. Parboil for about 6 minutes.

Add diced potatoes and cook for another 6 minutes. Drain well. Turn *parboiled* vegetables into a Dutch oven or roasting pan.

Add oil and leek slices. Roast in preheated 400 degree F. oven, stirring frequently, until vegetables are browned. *Be careful not to allow vegetables to burn.* Remove roasting pan from oven. *Reduce oven temperature to 350 degrees F.*

Transfer vegetables to prepared *au gratin* dish. Grind black pepper over. Sprinkle grated cheese over. Bake in 350 degree F. oven until cheese just begins to color. Remove from oven.

Serve at once or use as filling for a SWEDISH VEGETABLE OMELET *[see recipe which precedes]*.

Yields 6 servings
adequate for 4 people

Note: This recipe can be halved or doubled, when required.

1/6 SERVING – PROTEIN = 2.2 g.; FAT = 3.7 g.; CARBOHYDRATE = 10.0 g.;
CALORIES = 82; CALORIES FROM FAT = 40%

SWEDISH SAUTÉED PEAS IN THE POD
Ärtskida
TPT - 6 minutes

Of course, I still plant my peas on St. Patrick's Day just as my grandmother did but I no longer tempt the animals that come and go in our unfenced Pennsylvania gardens. Instead, I plant them in large patio pots close to the house using tomato cages to control the vines. The rabbits can not reach the peas; the deer rarely come that close to the house. To be able to just step out the door in the late spring and pick sweet, unsprayed edible pod peas, eat a couple on the way to the kitchen, and toss the rest into a skillet is a joy which my grandmother never knew. When she cooked peas in their pods, she had to pick very young peas and parboil them in order to soften the fibrous pod tissue. The hint of orange that I add gives a simple vegetable side dish a bright "little something."

3 tablespoons butter

36 small, edible pod sugar snap peas—well-washed and ends trimmed
1 tablespoon freshly squeezed orange juice

In a large skillet set over *MEDIUM* heat, melt butter.

Add well-washed and trimmed pea pods and orange juice. Cook stirring constantly for about 3 minutes. Turn into a heated serving bowl.

Serve at once.

Yields 6 servings
adequate for 4 people

Note: Of course, this recipe can be halved, doubled, or decreased and increased proportionately.

1/6 SERVING (i. e., 6 whole sugar snap pea pods) –
PROTEIN = 0.7 g.; FAT = 3.8 g.; CARBOHYDRATE = 1.7 g.;
CALORIES = 36; CALORIES FROM FAT = 95%

Europe–Sweden

SWEDISH SAUTÉED KALE WITH CREAM
Långkål

TPT - 39 minutes

After the first frost, we always took a trip to the east end of Long Island to seek out kale, cauliflower, squashes, and the undersized "salad potatoes" culled from the fields after the main harvest. Today we still look for the sweet post-frost kale at market or at a local farm stand. Kale fell out of favor for a considerable period of our married life, being relegated to decoration on salad bars. It is gratifying to see the resurgence in popularity for just the right reasons. It is a good food, rich in beta carotene, vitamin K, and all the cancer-fighting sulforaphane for which the members of the cabbage family are to be valued. Aniti-inflammatory and antioxidant properties are impressive.

2 cups VEGETARIAN BROWN STOCK *[see index]* **or other vegetarian stock of choice**

1 large bunch fresh kale—well-washed, trimmed or tough stems, and chopped to yield about 6 cupfuls*

1 tablespoon butter

1/4 cup light cream *or* **half and half**

Freshly ground *white* **pepper, to taste**
Pinch sugar

In a saucepan set over *MEDIUM* heat, combine stock and chopped kale. Allow to come to boil. *Reduce heat to LOW-MEDIUM.* Simmer for about 15 minutes. Drain thoroughly.

In a skillet set over *LOW* heat, melt butter. Add drained kale and sauté.

Add cream and simmer for about 15 minutes.

Add white pepper and sugar. Turn into a heated serving bowl.

Serve at once.

Yields 6 servings
adequate for 4 people

Notes: *Kale is occasionally available frozen. Parboiled for 2 minutes, kale can be frozen at home for winter use.

This recipe can be halved or doubled, when required.

1/6 SERVING – PROTEIN = 4.5 g.; FAT = 3.6 g.; CARBOHYDRATE = 6.4 g.;
CALORIES = 66; CALORIES FROM FAT = 49%

SWEDISH LINGONBERRY CREAM DESSERT
Sur Gradde med Lingon

TPT - 10 minutes

We became drawn, irresistibly, to "cold tables" and lingonberry desserts for Christmas menus after our 1985 Christmas in Denmark. This may look like just a simple "whip," but it is, in truth, a quick return to Scandinavia for us.

3 tablespoons heavy whipping cream

1 cup *fat-free* **dairy sour cream**

6 tablespoons *fat-free* **sweetened condensed milk**
1/4 cup lingonberry preserves
1/4 teaspoon ground cardamom

Using the electric mixer fitted with *chilled* beaters or by hand using a *chilled* wire whisk, beat heavy cream in a *clean, chilled* bowl until stiff peaks form. Transfer whipped cream from mixer bowl to a mixing bowl. Set aside.

Put sour cream into the mixer bowl. Using the electric mixer whip sour cream until light and fluffy.

Add sweetened condensed milk, lingonberry preserves, and ground cardamom. *Whisk-fold* the mixture *gently,* but *thoroughly,* into the whipped sour cream.

Add whipped heavy cream. Again, *whisk-fold* the mixture *gently,* but *thoroughly.*

Apportion among six sherbet glasses or other dessert dishes, of choice.

Serve at once.

Yields 6 individual servings

Note: This recipe can be halved or doubled, when required.

1/6 SERVING – PROTEIN = 6.3 g.; FAT = 2.5 g.; CARBOHYDRATE = 29.1 g.;
CALORIES = 164; CALORIES FROM FAT = 14%

Switzerland

Switzerland, the small land-locked nation in the European Alps, presents a coming together of three of western civilization's greatest cuisines. Albeit small, a little less than three times the size of the state of Connecticut, Switzerland's cantons offer distinct regional specialties which correspond, as do the languages spoken, to the ancestry of the residents. Here, preserved as in no other single nation, are the distinct heritages of Italy, Germany, and France. Ethnic and linguistic identities remain while an overall sense of belonging endures based on the shared values of federalism, direct democracy, and a fierce pride in the history and the beauty of the land in which they live. Both Zurich and Geneva offer a high quality of life and have been ranked high among the world's most livable cities. Switzerland and her people boast the highest wealth per adult of any country in the world with a ranking of nineteen by nominal GDP.

The two central cantons of Uri and Schwyz, and Unterwalden, a forest canton which has since been divided and whose lands have been renamed, formed the precursor to the present nation by uniting in a loosely structured protective confederation in 1291 to insure peace on the mountain trade routes. However, human and pre-human occupation has been documented as early as 150,000 years ago. A farming settlement known as *Goldäcker* at Gächlingen at the northern border of the modern nation has been dated to c. 6000 BC. The western part of Switzerland became part of the realm of the Burgundian monarchy in the fourth century AD. By the fifth century Suevi, also known as the Alemanni, a confederation of Germanic tribes who had settled on the upper Rhine River, began to create settlements in Switzerland but were driven out by the Franks at the Battle of Tobiac. The date of the battle is disputed but evidence puts the defeat of the Alemanni as approximately 491-506 A.D. The entire region became part of the Frankish Empire at that time and remained so until the eighth century AD. By 1200 AD, the Swiss plateau was ruled by the houses of Savoy, Zahringer, Habsburg, and Kyburg but the central area was granted the right to form the protective confederation previously mentioned. By 1460 the Confederacy, now composed of eight cantons, controlled most of the territory south and west of the Rhine to the Alps and Jura mountains. Victories over the Hapsburgs, over the Burgundian King Charles the Bold, and over the Swabian League of Emperor Maximilian I in 1499 effectively positioned Switzerland as a *de facto* autonomous state within the Holy Roman Empire.

Switzerland was conquered by Napoleon's revolutionary forces in 1798 and became known as Helvetic Republic. It was then overrun by the Russians and the Austrians but the Swiss refused to fight with the French against France's enemies. The Congress of Vienna in 1815 restored Switzerland's independent status and recognized its neutrality; Switzerland has not been in a state of belligerence since that date. Its neutrality has been respected by its European neighbors, leaving Switzerland completely surrounded by Axis nations during World War II and today by EU nations since Austria's entry into the EU in 1995. The Swiss political mentality is clearly reflected in the fact that Switzerland is not a member of the European Economic Area and still uses the Swiss franc as its official currency.

The Swiss Federal Constitution of 1858, based to some degree on the United States constitution, had eliminated the unrest that began to arise due to regional differences, granting cantons autonomy and the ability to preserve the heritage of their ancestry, one of the things that makes this nation so very unique.

Europe–Switzerland

Deviled Cheese Toasts
Diablotins

Stuffed Appetizer Mushrooms
Champignons mit Gruyere

Open-faced Sandwiches with Mushrooms
Käeschnitten mit Champignons

~

Potato and Celeriac Chowder
Weisse Kartoffel und Salleriesuppe

~

Apple and Cheese Salad
Chilled Baby Beets
with
Remoulade Sauce with Cornichons and Capers
Sauce Remoulade

~~~~~~~~~~~~~~~~~~~~~~

Cauliflower, Spinach, and Fennel Gratin   or   **Leek and Potato Gratin**
Chou-Fleur, Epinades, et Fennouil au Gratin   *Lauch und Pomes de Terre au Gratin*

Fried Potato Cakes
Kaserosti

~~~~~~~~~~

Bernase Onion Tart
Berner Zwiebelwabe

Sautéed Baby Spinach   **Boiled Dumplings**
Knöpfli

~~~~~~~~~~

either *Fondue Alice* or *Fondue Herren*
with Bread Chunks and Assorted *Crudités*
or
Pan-Fried Cheese Sandwiches
Einfache Gebackene Käseschnitten

Riced Potatoes and Pears   **Fried Parsley**
Kartoffelstock mit Birnen   *Pressemolo Fritto*

~~~~~~~~~~~~~~~~~~~~~~

Italian Blue Prune Plum Cobbler   **Uncooked Applesauce**
Pflaumenpudding   *Robes Apfelmus*

Carrot Cake   **Chocolate Mousse** *Kahlua*
Aaegauer Rübli Torte   *Mousse au Chocolat*

Europe–Switzerland

SWISS DEVILED CHEESE TOASTS
Diablotins

TPT - 12 minutes

Only the best imported Swiss Gruyère will do for this lovely rustic appetizer. Oh, a good Swiss Appenzeller is acceptable too. Since all the ingredients for this appetizer can be prepped ahead of time with just a few minutes of last minute assembly, this is an excellent choice for a hot hors d'oeuvre selection or an in-from-the-cold snack after a winter walk.

10 slices Italian bread—about 1/4-inch thick—each cut in half and *lightly toasted*

4 ounces Swiss *Gruyère* cheese—grated *or finely* shredded
1/2 cup *fat-free* pasteurized eggs (the equivalent of 2 eggs)*
1 teaspoon *Dijon* mustard with wine
Several dashes of paprika
Several dashes ground red pepper (cayenne), or to taste

Preheat oven to 400 degrees F.

In a mixing bowl, combine grated or shredded cheese, pasteurized eggs, mustard, paprika, and ground red pepper (cayenne).

Divide the cheese–egg mixture among the *lightly toasted* bread halves. Spread it evenly across the bread surface. Place on a baking sheet. Bake in preheated 400 degree F. oven for about 4-5 minutes, or until cheese is bubbling. *Be careful not to let the edges of the toast brown too much.*

Serve at once.

Yields 20 servings
adequate for 6-8 people

Notes: *Because raw eggs present the danger of *Salmonella* poisoning, commercially-available pasteurized eggs are recommended for use in preparing this dish.

This recipe can be halved or doubled, when required.

1/16 SERVING (i. e., per toast half) –
PROTEIN = 4.0 g.; FAT = 2.8 g.; CARBOHYDRATE = 12.1 g.;
CALORIES = 82; CALORIES FROM FAT = 31%

SWISS STUFFED APPETIZER MUSHROOMS
Champignons mit Gruyère

TPT - 30 minutes

Hot, stuffed mushrooms were a must for the cocktail party or cocktail hour when we first married. Everybody had their closely guarded recipe which they constantly refined after tasting a friend's version which contained a "secret ingredient," an ingredient rarely divulged. It was the silliest game. This Swiss version is superb.

18 large *crimini* mushrooms—trimmed, rinsed, and cleaned well with a brush*

1 tablespoon *extra virgin* olive oil
1/4 cup *finely* chopped onion
1 large shallot bulb—*finely* chopped

1 tablespoon *finely* chopped fresh French tarragon leaves*
1/4 cup whole wheat breadcrumbs
2 teaspoons country-style *Dijon* mustard
1 tablespoon preserved capers—*well-rinsed* and *well-drained*

2 ounces Swiss *Gruyère* or Swiss *Appenzeller* cheese, if preferred, cut into small cubes**

Several large sprigs French tarragon, for garnish

Preheat oven to 350 degrees F. Prepare a cookie sheet or broiler pan by lining with aluminum foil.

Remove stems from mushrooms. Chop quite finely.

In a non-stick-coated skillet set over *MEDIUM* heat, heat oil. Add *finely* chopped onion and shallot. Sauté until soft and translucent, *allowing neither the onion nor the shallot to brown. Reduce heat to LOW.*

Add *finely* chopped mushroom stems and continue to cook until most of moisture extruded from the mushroom stems has evaporated.

SWISS STUFFED APPETIZER MUSHROOMS (cont'd)

Remove from heat. Add *finely* chopped fresh tarragon leaves and breadcrumbs. Stir to combine. Add *Dijon* mustard. Stir to integrate well. Add capers. Stir to distribute evenly.***

When ready to fill mushrooms, stir cheese cubes into the breadcrumb mixture. *Do not add too far ahead or cheese will begin to melt from the heat of the sautéed ingredients.*

Divide the filling among the mushrooms, heaping it into the mushroom cavities. Arrange mushrooms on foil-lined baking sheet or, if preferred, use a large baking dish of glass or ceramic.

Bake in preheated 350 degree F. oven until mushrooms begin to soften and stuffing begins to brown on top—about 18-20 minutes.

Transfer to a warmed platter. Keep warm on a warming tray until ready to serve. Garnish the serving platter with sprigs of tarragon just before serving as "sit-down, knife-and-fork" appetizers, "stand-up" cocktail party appetizer, or as a side dish vegetable offering with your main course.

Yields 4-6 servings
adequate for 4-6 people

Notes: *French tarragon *(Artemisia dracunculus 'sativa')* has a distinctive anise flavor. Generally hardy in Zones 4-8, it is best grown from cuttings or nursery stock since the seeds produced are rarely viable. So-called Russian tarragon (also, *Artemisia dracunculus)*, sold often in garden centers as tarragon and much less flavorful, can not be successfully substituted.

**Swiss *Appenzeller* cheese is a uniquely-flavored, semi-soft cheese, stronger in taste than either *Emmentaler* or *Gruyère*. It will hold its own with the *Dijon* mustard in this recipe. There are two types available. The common *Appenzeller* is made from skimmed milk and is cured in brine while the whole milk version is steeped in wine, or sometimes in cider. *Appenzeller* has been produced in Switzerland since the first century AD.

***If convenient, the stuffing may be prepared as much as two days in advance.

This recipe may be halved or doubled, when required.

1/18 SERVING (i. e., per mushroom) –
PROTEIN = 1.2 g.; FAT = 1.7 g.; CARBOHYDRATE = 2.5 g.;
CALORIES = 26; CALORIES FROM FAT = 58%

OPEN-FACED SANDWICHES WITH MUSHROOMS
Käeschnitten mit Champignons
TPT - 43 minutes

Mushroom hunters trail up and down the mountains and through the forested valleys in search of the treasures that can make or break the perfection of a dish. We settle for mushrooms that appear in our grocery stores, although living in Pennsylvania gives one a singular edge in terms of cultivated mushroom variety and quality. This mushroom-loaded toast appetizer makes a perfect light supper entrée. The Swiss often top each serving with a poached egg. Just remember, the more diverse the mushrooms, the more delicious the experience.

3 tablespoons butter
6 slices firm whole wheat or whole grain bread*

4 1/2 ounces Swiss *Gruyère* cheese—*thinly* sliced

1/4 cup butter
1 pound mixed wild mushrooms of choice
   —cleaned well with a brush, trimmed, and sliced

1/3 cup *finely* chopped onion
1/2 teaspoon freshly squeezed lemon juice
Freshly ground black pepper, or to taste
Salt, to taste

In a large skillet set over *MEDIUM-HIGH* heat, melt the 3 tablespoonfuls butter. Brown bread slices on both slides in the hot melted butter and arrange in a baking pan that will hold all comfortably or on a cookie sheet.

Preheat oven to 350 degrees F.

OPEN-FACED SANDWICHES WITH MUSHROOMS (cont'd)

Divide the *thinly* sliced cheese among the toasts, keeping it within 1/4 inch of the edge of each slice.

In a large skillet set over *MEDIUM* heat, melt the remaining 1/4 cupful butter. Add mushrooms and cook, stirring frequently, until the mushrooms are browned.

Add *finely* chopped onion and cook, stirring constantly, until onions soften.

Add lemon juice and season with black pepper and salt. Spoon mushrooms on top of toasts, apportioning the mushrooms evenly among the toasts. Bake in preheated 350 degree F. oven for about 10 minutes, or until the cheese is melted. Remove from oven.

Using a wide spatula, lift the toasts, one at a time, from the baking pan onto heated salad or dessert plates.

Serve at once.

Yields 6 servings
adequate for 4 people

Note: *The bread slices can be trimmed of the crusts, if preferred.

1/6 SERVING – PROTEIN = 10.6 g.; FAT = 20.3 g.; CARBOHYDRATE = 17.0 g.;
CALORIES = 289; CALORIES FROM FAT = 63%

SWISS POTATO AND CELERIAC CHOWDER
Weisse Kartoffel und Salleriesuppe
TPT - 54 minutes

This is an unusually refreshing potato soup. Ugly old knob celery, when peeled, is a beautiful vegetable, just full of flavor. The lovage garnish adds another layer of celery flavor.

Bouquet garni:
  1 bay leaf—broken
  1 tablespoon fresh thyme—chopped

1 tablespoon butter
1 medium yellow onion—*thinly* sliced

1 1/2 tablespoons unbleached white flour
1 cup water

1 knob celery (celeriac)—chopped into 1/4-inch
  cubes, to yield about 1 1/2 cups

2 medium all-purpose or russet potatoes—peeled,
  quartered lengthwise, and sliced into 1/4-inch
  slices—to yield about 3 cups
1/2 teaspoon salt, or to taste
1 1/2 cups water

1 cup *whole* milk
Freshly ground *white* pepper, to taste

Fresh parsley florets, for garnish
Fresh lovage leaves, for garnish, if in season*

In a tea ball or in a cheesecloth *bouquet garni* bag, prepare a *bouquet garni* of bay leaf pieces and chopped fresh thyme. Set aside until required.

In a large kettle with cover, set over *LOW-MEDIUM* heat, melt butter. Add onion slices and sauté until soft and translucent, *being careful not to allow onions to brown.*

Prepare a *roux* by stirring flour into sautéed onions and cook, stirring constantly, for a minute or two to allow the flour taste to "cook off."

Using a wire whisk, *gradually* stir the 1 cupful water into the *roux*. Add *bouquet garni* and diced celery root. Cover and allow to simmer over *LOW-MEDIUM* heat for about 15 minutes, stirring frequently.

Add potato slices, salt, and remaining 1 1/2 cupfuls water. Increase heat to *MEDIUM*, and allow to come to the boil. Reduce heat to *LOW-MEDIUM*, cover, and simmer for about 15 minutes, or until potatoes are *tender*, but *still firm*.

Reduce heat to *LOW*. Add milk and *white* pepper. Heat, stirring frequently, until heated through. *Do not allow soup to boil once milk has been added.*

Turn into a heated soup tureen and serve into heated soup plates, garnished with fresh parsley florets.

Yields about 6 cupfuls

SWISS POTATO AND CELERIAC CHOWDER (cont'd)

Notes: *If you do not have fresh lovage leaves on hand, but do have celery leaves, celery leaves can be quite satisfactorily substituted.

This recipe may be halved or doubled, when required.

This soup does not freeze well since a firm potato texture is desired.

1/6 SERVING (i. e., per cupful) –
PROTEIN = 3.4 g.; FAT = 3.4 g.; CARBOHYDRATE = 15.9 g.;
CALORIES = 104; CALORIES FROM FAT = 29%

SWISS APPLE AND CHEESE SALAD
TPT - 6 minutes

This salad is very similar to the American salad known as a Waldorf Salad, which was created by Oscar Tschirky, known as "Oscar of the Waldorf," the maitre d'hotel of the Waldorf–Astoria Hotel from the hotel's opening in March 1893 until his death in 1950. Walnuts were not an ingredient in the original salad but have long ago become part of the American favorite. The Swiss add the walnuts too, albeit as a garnish, but they do add Swiss cheese to the apple mixture and we have found that both Gruyère and Emmentaler add their special taste to the salad and, hence, to the meal. Onion is also added to this version. It is different; it is good but tastes even better with homemade mayonnaise.

3 medium red-skinned apples—*very well-scrubbed**
—*Cortland or Braeburn apples are our choices*
3 inner, white celery ribs—well-trimmed and diced
to yield about 1 cupful
3 tablespoons chopped onion—yellow, sweet, or
Italian red, as dictated by your menu
1 cup shredded Swiss *Emmentaler or* Swiss
***Gruyère* cheese, as preferred**

Freshly ground black pepper, to taste

1/4 cup *calorie-reduced or light* mayonnaise
1 teaspoon *Dijon* style mustard with wine
1 teaspoon freshly squeezed lemon juice*

1/4 cup coarsely chopped, *preservative-free* walnuts

Core and coarsely chop apples without peeling.

In a large mixing bowl, combine chopped apple, celery, onion, and shredded cheese. Toss well.

Season with black pepper and toss again.

In a small bowl, combine mayonnaise, mustard, and lemon juice thoroughly. Add mayonnaise mixture to apple mixture and toss to coat well.

Turn into a serving dish and refrigerate until required.

Garnish with chopped walnuts over and *serve at once*.

Yields 6 servings
adequate for 4 people

Notes: *If Cortland apples, which do not require acidulation for salad making, are not available, use other red-skinned apples but toss chopped apple with about 2 teaspoonfuls freshly squeezed lemon juice.

This recipe is easily doubled, when required.

1/6 SERVING – PROTEIN = 6.6 g.; FAT = 13.3 g.; CARBOHYDRATE = 10.9 g.;
CALORIES = 188; CALORIES FROM FAT = 64%

Europe–Switzerland

SWISS *REMOULADE* SAUCE WITH CORNICHONS AND CAPERS
Sauce Remoulade

TPT - 40 minutes:
30 minutes = caper soaking period

Both cornichons and preserved capers are too salty for our taste. By using my homemade, less-salty mayonnaise combined with a bit of yogurt and by soaking the capers, we find this to be an enjoyable, less-salty version of the classic Swiss sauce to use as an appetizer or as an accompaniment to a cold supper of assorted cheeses, breads, and crudités. This is very complimentary to beets so such a supper might well include a bowl full of tiny, tiny whole beets too.

4 teaspoons tiny, preserved capers—*well-drained*
1 cup *cold* water

6 tablespoons BLENDER MAYONNAISE *[see index]* or *calorie-reduced* or *light* mayonnaise, if preferred
2 tablespoons PLAIN YOGURT *[see index]* or commercially-available plain yogurt
2 tablespoons *finely* chopped fresh parsley
4 teaspoons *finely* chopped, *well-drained* cornichons
1 teaspoon freshly squeezed lemon juice

Place *well-drained* capers in a small bowl. Add *cold* water. Soak capers in the water for at least 30 minutes, *changing the water once or twice*. Drain well. Chop the capers quite *finely*.

In a small bowl, blend mayonnaise and yogurt. Stir in *finely* chopped capers, parsley, and cornichons. Add lemon juice. Combine thoroughly.

Refrigerate until ready to serve.

Yields about 12 tablespoonfuls

Note: When required, this recipe is easily doubled or tripled.

1/12 SERVING (i. e., per tablespoonful) –
PROTEIN = 0.3 g.; FAT = 4.6 g.; CARBOHYDRATE = 0.3 g.;
CALORIES = 44; CALORIES FROM FAT = 94%

SWISS CAULIFLOWER, SPINACH, AND FENNEL *GRATIN*
Chou-Fleur, Epinades, et Fennouil au Gratin

TPT - 1 hour

As you move from province to province in Switzerland, subtle changes remind you that this is a country where German, French, and Italian are spoken and where the influences of three countries are strong. It is a country where the butter and cream culture confronts and then lives with the olive oil culture of southern Europe quite comfortably. It is a country where wonderful cheeses can be sprinkled over the dishes of each tradition, uniting them. This gratin is a welcome dish on our table when the fresh cauliflower, "chou-fleur" or "blumenkohl," and fennel, "feinouil" or" finocchio," have come to market and the seasons are changing.

3 quarts *boiling* water
1 tablespoon lemon juice
1 pound cauliflower florets—trimmed and halved, if too large

3 tablespoons *coarse*, whole wheat breadcrumbs
1 teaspoon FRENCH COUNTRY HERB SEASONING MIXTURE *(Herbes de Provence)* *[see index]*

1 tablespoon butter
1 small fennel bulb—trimmed, well-washed, and cut into 1/4-inch strips to yield about 2 cups

2 garlic cloves—*finely* chopped

1 10-ounce package baby spinach—trimmed, *very well-washed* and patted dry
Freshly ground black pepper, to taste

1/4 cup skimmed milk
2 tablespoons corn starch

1/2 cup skimmed milk
1/2 cup light cream *or* half and half

1/4 cup (1 ounce) shredded Swiss *Gruyère* cheese

SWISS CAULIFLOWER, SPINACH, AND FENNEL *GRATIN* (cont'd)

Preheat oven to 350 degrees F. Prepare a shallow oven-to-table baking dish such as a *quiche* dish or *au gratin* dish by coating with non-stick lecithin spray coating.

In a kettle set over *MEDIUM* heat, combine *boiling* water and lemon juice. Parboil cauliflower florets for 3-4 minutes. Drain and immerse in cold water to stop cooking. Drain again.

In a small bowl, combine breadcrumbs and the *herbes de Provence* mixture. Stir and set aside until required.

In a skillet set over *MEDIUM* heat, melt butter. Add fennel strips and sauté for about 4 minutes.

Add *finely* chopped garlic and continue to sauté for another 2 minutes.

Add spinach leaves and sauté for another minute or two, or until wilted. Season with black pepper.

Add 1/2 cupful each of milk and cream. Cook, *stirring frequently*, for about 5 minutes. *Remove skillet from heat.*

In a small bowl, combine the 1/4 cupful skimmed milk and corn starch. Stir until corn starch is thoroughly in suspension. Add to ingredients in skillet. Stir to disperse the corn starch suspension.

Place parboiled cauliflower in prepared baking dish. Pour skillet ingredients over.

Sprinkle *one-half* of prepared breadcrumb mixture evenly over the top of the vegetables in sauce. Sprinkle shredded cheese over the breadcrumbs. Sprinkle the remaining breadcrumbs over the cheese.

Bake in preheated 350 degree F. oven for about 35 minutes, or until *lightly* browned and bubbling.

Serve at once.*

Yields 6 servings
adequate for 4 people

Notes: *Although leftovers can be reheated, the texture of the vegetables is compromised.

This recipe can be halved or doubled, when required.

1/6 SERVING – PROTEIN = 7.0 g.; FAT = 5.7 g.; CARBOHYDRATE = 12.9 g.;
CALORIES = 123; CALORIES FROM FAT = 42%

LEEK AND POTATO GRATIN
Lauch und Pomes de Terre au Gratin
TPT - 1 hour and 5 minutes

Vegetarian Thanksgiving menus can be filled with wonderful vegetable dishes that do celebrate the harvest. As a child I remember being thankful for the plenty that graced our table but I also remember being full way too soon to enjoy everything. Now I can indulge in all those side dishes because they are the centerpieces of our feast today.

3 large leeks—*very well-washed*

1 tablespoon butter
1 teaspoon *extra virgin* **olive oil**

3 medium potatoes—peeled and sliced with a vegetable peeler as you would for potato chips
1 teaspoon *extra virgin* **olive oil**

1/2 ounce *pecorino Romano* **cheese—sliced with a vegetable peeler into long shreds**
Freshly ground black pepper, to taste

Preheat oven to 375 degrees F. Prepare a 9-inch shallow, *au gratin* dish by coating with non-stick lecithin spray coating.

Trim the tops and root ends from the leeks. Cut the white portion of the leeks into 1/2-inch slices. Wash well in several changes of water to remove all sand.

In a skillet set over *LOW* heat, combine 1 tablespoonful butter and 1 teaspoonful olive oil. Add sliced and well-washed leeks. Allow to cook until leeks are wilted. Turn into prepared *au gratin* dish.

Toss the potato slices with the remaining 1 teaspoonful olive oil. Arrange potato slices attractively in consecutive circles or in a spiral pattern on top of the leeks.

Sprinkle shredded cheese over. Grind black pepper over.*

Bake in preheated 375 degree F. oven 35-40 minutes, or until potatoes are brown and the dish is heated through.

Serve at once.

Yields 6 servings
adequate for 4 people

LEEK AND POTATO GRATIN (cont'd)

Notes: *The dish can be assembled to this point ahead of time. Bring to room temperature before putting into hot oven.

When required, this recipe can be halved or doubled.

1/6 SERVING – PROTEIN = 3.5 g.; FAT = 3.7 g.; CARBOHYDRATE = 11.4 g.; CALORIES = 88; CALORIES FROM FAT = 38%

SWISS FRIED POTATO CAKES
Kaserosti

TPT - 2 hours and 12 minutes;
1 hour = potato chilling period

I suppose if the Swiss were surveyed on their favorite potato dish, consistent with the three component ethnic groups, French, Italian, and German, there would be strong differences of opinion. However, this potato dish would win hands-down in German-speaking Switzerland. We like it especially because the potatoes can be prepared early in the day or even the night before, saving time when we have overnight guests. The potato cakes are a delicious choice for breakfast, brunch, or lunch especially when accompanied by cinnamon–fried apples.

2 quarts *boiling* **water**
4 medium all-purpose potatoes—about 1 pound
  —well-scrubbed and *unpeeled*

1 tablespoon butter
1 medium onion—*finely* **chopped**
1/2 teaspoon freshly ground black pepper, or
  more to taste

1/3 cup shredded (about 1 1/2 ounces) Swiss
  ***Emmentaler* or Swiss *Gruyère* cheese**

Drop *unpeeled* potatoes into *boiling* water and cook for 30 minutes. Refrigerate for at least 1 hour.

In an 8-inch non-stick-coated skillet* with cover set over *MEDIUM* heat, melt 1 1/2 teaspoonfuls butter. Add half of the chopped onions and sauté until onions are soft and translucent, *being careful not to allow onions to brown.*

Meanwhile, peel chilled potatoes and coarsely grate.

Preheat oven to 200 degrees F.

Add *one-half* of the grated potatoes to the sautéed onion and season with *one-half* of the black pepper. Sauté until potatoes are coated with butter. Using a wooden spatula, press potatoes flat to form a cake. Cover and cook until the bottom of the potato cake is *brown and crisp*—about 10 minutes. Shake gently now and then to prevent scorching. *Carefully* fold over in omelet fashion and slide onto an oven-proof platter. Transfer to preheated 200 degree F. oven until second cake is finished.

Prepare a second cake in exactly the same manner using the remaining 1 1/2 teaspoonfuls butter, onions, grated potatoes, and black pepper.

Fold over second potato cake in omelet fashion and slide onto the oven-proof platter with the first potato cake. Sprinkle shredded cheese over both. Return to 200 degree F. oven just long enough for cheese to melt.

Serve at once.

Yields 6 servings
adequate for 4 people

Notes: *We do feel that a non-stick-coated skillet is absolutely essential to form a perfect cake.

This recipe may be halved or doubled, when required.

1/6 SERVING – PROTEIN = 3.7 g.; FAT = 4.2 g.; CARBOHYDRATE = 15.7 g.; CALORIES = 115; CALORIES FROM FAT = 33%

Europe–Switzerland

BERNASE ONION TART
Berner Zwiebelwabe

TPT - 1 hour and 36 minutes;
10 minutes = post-baking setting period

Each year in Bern, Switzerland, the onion harvest is celebrated with an onion festival. Granted, it is not the only onion festival in the world, but this onion tart is one-of-a-kind. We prefer to make it in a whole wheat pie crust and we use yogurt crème while you might prefer to use sour cream.

WHOLE WHEAT PIE CRUST for 10-inch pie
[see index]

1 tablespoon butter
5 medium onions—*thinly* sliced
2 tablespoons whole wheat flour
2 tablespoons unbleached white flour
1/8 teaspoon freshly grated nutmeg
1 teaspoon dry mustard
1 cup skimmed milk

1/4 cup *fat-free* pasteurized eggs (the equivalent of 1 egg)
1 large egg white
1 cup YOGURT *CRÈME* [see index]*

1 cup shredded (about 4 ounces) Swiss *Gruyère* cheese

Preheat oven to 350 degrees F. Prepare ceramic quiche dish by coating with non-stick lecithin spray coating or by oiling.

Roll pie crust out to a diameter of about 12 inches. Fit into prepared quiche dish. Flute edges and set aside until required.

In a large non-stick-coated skillet set over *LOW-MEDIUM* heat, melt butter. Add onion slices and sauté until *very* soft and translucent, *being careful not to allow onions to brown.*

Stir in whole wheat and white flours, nutmeg, and dry mustard. Cook, stirring constantly, for several minutes. Gradually stir in milk and, stirring constantly, cook until sauce thickens. Remove from heat and set aside.

In a large mixing bowl using a wire whisk, beat pasteurized eggs and egg white together until thick and lemon-colored. Add yogurt *crème* and beat until thoroughly combined. Stir in shredded cheese. Stir sautéed onion mixture into egg–cheese mixture. Combine thoroughly. Pour into prepared pie crust.

Bake in preheated 350 degree F. oven for 50-55 minutes, or until golden and filling is firm when dish is gently shaken.

Allow to cool for 5-10 minutes before serving in wedges.

Yields 8 servings
adequate for 4-6 people

Note: *Fat-free dairy sour cream may be substituted for yogurt *crème*, if desired.

1/8 SERVING – PROTEIN = 14.6 g.; FAT = 12.1 g.; CARBOHYDRATE = 28.3 g.;
CALORIES = 276; CALORIES FROM FAT = 39%

BOILED DUMPLINGS
Knöpfli

TPT - 56 minutes;
30 minutes = dough resting period

Spaetzli were a special treat when my grandmother made them as a substitute for bread or potatoes or to expand a soup or stew when necessary. I still make those precious little dumplings, each spaetzle like a tiny winged noodle being. I do not serve them with gravy, as she did, but instead with my own British Gravy "Without the Sunday Roast" [see index] or with butter and cheese. Spaetzli or Knöpfli or Hörnli are Switzerland's take on those German dumplings.

1 1/2 cups unbleached white flour
Pinch salt

1 large egg—*well beaten*
1/2 cup *cold* water

3 quarts *boiling* water

Freshly ground black pepper, to taste
3 tablespoons *melted* butter
3 tablespoons grated Parmesan *or* pecorino *Romano* cheese

BOILED DUMPLINGS (cont'd)

In a mixing bowl, combine flour and salt.

In a measuring cup or small dish, combine *well-beaten* egg and *cold* water. Using a fork, combine thoroughly. Gradually, while stirring constantly, stir egg into flour. Beat until smooth.* Set aside for 30 minutes.

Using a *spaetzle* maker press a portion of the dough through the holes into the *boiling* water.** Cook for about 3 minutes until tender. The dumplings will float to the top. Scoop out using slotted spoon or skimmer and transfer to a sieve to drain. Repeat until all the dumplings have been made. Turn into a heated serving dish.

Add black pepper to taste and the *melted* butter. Toss to coat the dumplings with the butter. Sprinkle grated cheese over.

Serve at once.

Yields 6 servings
adequate for 4 people

Notes: *Add a bit more water, if necessary; add a bit more flour, if necessary.

**To make the small dumpling called *knöpfli* ("little buttons") or *hörnli* ("little horns"), you can press the dough through the holes of a colander if you do not have a *spätzle* (*spaetzle*) maker. *Spätzle* ("little sparrows") are usually made by cutting the dough into small pieces with a sharp knife.

This recipe can be doubled, when required.

1/6 SERVING – PROTEIN = 5.6 g.; FAT = 9.6 g.; CARBOHYDRATE = 21.4 g.;
CALORIES = 190; CALORIES FROM FAT = 45%

FONDUE ALICE
TPT - 16 minutes

In the 1960s American hostesses turned to one of the most delightful meals on the planet—the fondue. Fondues are pleasurably intimate and encourage conversation so for entertaining or for family evenings, they are a natural. They have declined in popularity a bit in recent years but the fondue will not be forgotten for long; it is just too good. The residual crust left in the bottom of the pot at the end of the meal is considered a special treat and we agree. Remember to serve the same wine used in the fondue for drinking if wine is to be served.

6 ounces Swiss *Emmentaler* cheese—shredded and at room temperature
6 ounces Swiss *Gruyère* cheese—shredded and at room temperature
2 1/3 tablespoons whole wheat flour

1 garlic clove—cut in half

1 1/4 cups dry white wine
2 teaspoons fresh lemon juice
Freshly ground black pepper, to taste

In a large mixing bowl, combine shredded cheeses and flour. Set aside.

Rub the inside of a FONDUE POT thoroughly with cut garlic; then discard garlic or reserve for other purposes. Set FONDUE POT control to *LOW*. Pour in wine and heat slowly just to the boiling point—when bubbles begin to rise.

Add lemon juice. Using a wooden spoon, stir in cheese *gradually—spoonful by spoonful*—allowing cheese to melt before each addition. Stir constantly. Regulate heat to prevent boiling.

When all the cheese has been added and the mixture is creamy, smooth, and barely simmering, add a light grinding of black pepper. Stir to blend well.

Lower FONDUE POT heat setting to *WARM*. Serve at once, with bite-sized "dunkables" of choice.

Adequate to serve 4 people
as a main course offering
or for 8 as an appetizer

Notes: This recipe is easily doubled, when required, if fondue pot is sufficiently large.

A dusting of freshly grated nutmeg gives variety when desired.

A handful of minced fresh chives added will give you *FONDUE A' LA CIBOULETTE*.

FONDUE KUMMEL results when 1 teaspoonful of caraway seeds, which have been soaked in hot water for 15 minutes, is added.

FONDUE ALICE (cont'd)

1/4 SERVING (exclusive of dunkables) –
PROTEIN = 25.3 g.; FAT = 26.9 g.; CARBOHYDRATE = 7.7 g.;
CALORIES = 373; CALORIES FROM FAT = 65%

FONDUE HERREN
TPT - 16 minutes

This is a bit more assertive than is the classic "Fondue Alice" but it is definitely not just for gentlemen. The mistress (herrin) loves this version too.

6 ounces Swiss *Emmentaler*—shredded and at room temperature
6 ounces Swiss *Gruyère* cheese—shredded and at room temperature
2 1/3 tablespoons whole wheat flour
1 garlic clove—cut in half
1 1/4 cups dry white wine
2 teaspoons fresh lemon juice
1/2 teaspoon MUSTARD SAUCE *[see index]*, **or more to taste**
Dash ground red pepper (cayenne)
Freshly ground black pepper, to taste

In a large mixing bowl, combine shredded cheeses and flour. Set aside.

Rub the inside of the FONDUE POT thoroughly with cut garlic; then discard garlic or reserve for other purposes. Set FONDUE POT control on *LOW*. Pour in wine and heat slowly just to the boiling point—when bubbles begin to rise.

Add lemon juice. Using a wooden spoon, stir in cheese *gradually—spoonful by spoonful*—allowing cheese to melt before each addition. Stir constantly. Regulate heat to prevent boiling.

When all cheese has been added and the mixture is creamy, smooth, and barely simmering, stir in mustard sauce, ground red pepper (cayenne), and black pepper. Stir to blend well.

Lower FONDUE POT heat setting to *WARM*.

Serve at once, with bite-sized "dunkables" of choice.

Adequate to serve 4 people as
a main course offering
or for 8 people as an appetizer

Notes: This recipe is easily doubled when required, if fondue pot is sufficiently large.

Remember to serve the same wine used in the fondue for drinking, if wine is to be served.

The residual crust left in the bottom of the pot at the end of the meal is considered a special treat.

1/4 SERVING (exclusive of dunkables) –
PROTEIN = 25.3 g.; FAT = 27.0 g.; CARBOHYDRATE = 8.1 g.;
CALORIES = 376; CALORIES FROM FAT = 65%

Suggested "dunkables" for main course cheese fondues:

Chunks of French or Italian bread, each with a side of crust
Raw zucchini or yellow squash chunks
Parboiled artichoke heart wedges
Raw green or red pepper squares
Parboiled cauliflower florets
Parboiled broccoli florets
French fried onion rings
Parboiled celery chunks
Parboiled green beans
Raw cherry tomatoes
Raw cucumber slices
Raw mushroom caps
Vegetable fritters
Potato puffs

Europe–Switzerland

SWISS PAN–FRIED CHEESE SANDWICHES
Einfache Gebackene Käseschnitten
TPT - 25 minutes

My mother had the most beautiful silver waffle iron you can imagine; so beautiful, in fact, that it could be taken to the dining room table for Sunday night suppers, an important family ritual in the 1940s and '50s. One side of the removable plates could be used to make waffles and other side was used to grill sandwiches. I loved this Sunday night specialty but I also loved the pan-fried sandwiches that my German-born grandmother made in her big cast iron skillet. This appears to be one of those Swiss dishes contributed by those of Germany ancestry.

12 teaspoons (1/4 cup) butter

12 thin slices bread, of choice*

12 teaspoons (1/4 cup) MUSTARD SAUCE
 [see index]

12 slices (about 6 ounces) Swiss *Emmentaler, Gruyère,* or *Appenzeller* cheese

Prepare a large non-stick-coated skillet or griddle by coating with non-stick lecithin spray coating.

In a SAUCE WARMER set over *LOW* heat, melt butter.

Lay the slices of bread out on a bread board. Spread each bread slice with one-half teaspoonful of mustard sauce. Place one slice of cheese on each of six of the bread slices. *Be sure to tuck the cheese well in from the edge of each slice.* Place the remaining bread slices, *mustard–side–down*, on top of the cheese.

Using a pastry brush, brush 1/2 teaspoonful of butter evenly across the surface of each sandwich.

Place prepared skillet or griddle by preheating it over *MEDIUM* heat for several minutes.

Invert as many sandwiches as will fit, *butter-side-down*, onto the heated skillet or griddle. Pan-fry, pressing the sandwiches down against the hot surface, until *lightly browned*.

Brush the unbuttered top bread slices with *melted* butter and, using a spatula, turn each sandwich and pan-fry on the remaining side until the cheese is melting and the bread surface is *lightly browned*. Transfer to a heated platter set on a warming tray or in a warm oven.

Continue cooking until all are prepared.

Cut sandwiches in half and return to the heated platter.

Serve at once.

Yields 6 sandwiches
adequate for 4 people

Notes: *Use a firm, white or light whole wheat homemade bread, if possible.

This recipe is easily increased or decreased proportionally, as required.

1/6 SERVING   PROTEIN = 13.5 g.; FAT = 19.1 g.; CARBOHYDRATE = 32.1 g.
CALORIES = 352; CALORIES FROM FAT = 48%

SWISS RICED POTATOES AND PEARS
Kartoffelstock mit Birnen
TPT - 52 minutes

Still a popular way to prepare potatoes in rural areas, especially in cantons dominated by those of German ancestry, this mashed potato and pear dish is surely related to "kartoffel apfelpuree," the mashed potato and apple dish which is so frequently served with roast pork in Germany.

4 quarts *boiling* water
3 large potatoes—peeled and diced

3 pear halves—canned in light syrup—well-drained*

2 tablespoons butter—*softened to room temperature*
1/8 teaspoon ground cinnamon
Pinch ground cloves
Salt, to taste
Freshly ground black pepper, to taste

Europe–Switzerland

SWISS RICED POTATOES AND PEARS (cont'd)

In a small kettle set over *MEDIUM* heat, combine *boiling* water and diced potatoes. Cook, until potatoes are tender—about 20-25 minutes. *Drain thoroughly.*

Using a ricer, rice potatoes into a mixing bowl.

Rice pear halves into the same bowl. Stir to combine. Turn the potato and pear mixture into a clean saucepan set over *LOW-MEDIUM* heat.

Add *softened* butter and ground cinnamon and cloves. Again mix well. Season to taste with salt and black pepper. Allow to heat through, stirring to prevent the mixture from sticking to the bottom of the pan. Turn into a heated serving dish.

Serve at once.

Notes: *Some people add sugar to this dish but because I use the sweeter canned pears, I do not add sugar. If you choose to use peeled and cored, ripe, fresh pears, you may find that you need to add some sugar.

This recipe can be halved or doubled, when required.

Yields 6 servings
adequate for 4 people

1/6 SERVING – PROTEIN = 1.6 g.; FAT = 3.9 g.; CARBOHYDRATE = 21.7 g.;
CALORIES = 130; CALORIES FROM FAT = 19%

SWISS FRIED PARSLEY
Pressemolo Fritto

TPT - 13 minutes

Deep–fried parsley is one of the most unexpectedly delicious garnishes ever. There are few menus that would not profit from the addition of this wonderful taste. It is a bit tricky so do make sure that the parsley is very well-dried and that the oil is at the proper temperature.

Vegetable oil for deep-frying

3 cups fresh curly-leafed parsley florets—stemmed, well-washed, and *very well-drained**

Preheat oil for deep-frying to 375 degrees F. in deep-fryer or in a wok. *(Oil must be just at the smoking point. If it is not hot enough, the parsley will be limp; if it is too hot, the parsley will be brown.)*

Using a frying basket, deep-fry parsley, *one cupful at a time,* for about 1 or 2 minutes, or *until no sizzling sound is heard.*

Drain briefly on paper toweling.

Serve at once, spooned onto the same platter as your main course offering, garnish-style.

In Belgium, where this is also extensively used as a garnish, it is called *persil frit* and is prepared in the same manner.

Yields 1 1/2 cupfuls
adequate for 4 people

Notes: *Parsley must be *absolutely dry.*

1/4 SERVING – PROTEIN = 0.5 g.; FAT = 1.3 g.; CARBOHYDRATE = 1.1 g.;
CALORIES = 18; CALORIES FROM FAT = 65%

Europe–Switzerland

ITALIAN BLUE PRUNE PLUM COBBLER
Pflaumenpudding

TPT - 51 minutes

This dessert is one of our all time "best favorites." We have found that requests for seconds are the rule with this dish, not the exception, so it is advisable to plan for seconds when having guests. You will find that coffee, vanilla, and butter pecan ice cream flavors compliment this dessert well.

1 pound or about 16 large, blue prune plums
 —well-washed, halved, and pitted
2 tablespoons honey
1/2 teaspoon ground cinnamon

1/2 cup whole wheat flour
1/4 cup unbleached white flour
1/4 cup soy flour
1/2 cup sugar
1 1/2 teaspoons baking powder
2 tablespoons *toasted* wheat germ
1/4 cup *fat-free* pasteurized eggs (the equivalent of 1 egg)

Light cream *or* **half and half**

Preheat oven to 350 degrees F. Prepare an 8- or 9-inch square baking pan or a 9-inch deep-dish pie plate by coating with non-stick lecithin spray coating.*

Arrange plum halves cut-side-up in prepared pan. Drizzle honey over and sprinkle with cinnamon.

Into a large mixing bowl, sift whole wheat, white, and soy flours with sugar and baking powder. Stir in wheat germ. Add pasteurized eggs and mix well with a pastry blender or a fork until of the consistency of coarse corn meal. Sprinkle this mixture evenly over plums.

Bake in preheated 350 degree F. oven for 40 minutes, or until *lightly browned.*

Serve warm or chilled, as preferred, with cream or ice cream.

Yields 6 servings
adequate for 4-6 people

Note: *This recipe may be baked in two 9 x 5 x 3-inch loaf pans to provide 3-4 servings each. The second cobbler may then be frozen for a future appearance since this dessert does freeze well.

1/6 SERVING (without cream) –
PROTEIN = 5.9 g.; FAT = 1.4 g.; CARBOHYDRATE = 59.3 g.;
CALORIES = 265; CALORIES FROM FAT = 5%

UNCOOKED APPLESAUCE IN THE SWISS STYLE
Rahes Apelmus

TPT - 14 minutes

When the Cortland apples are in the markets in the fall, I try to make several batches of this uncooked applesauce. Cortland apples, which do not experience oxidation when cut, allow me to use less lemon juice and, thus, the apple taste is even more intense. Once the Cortland apples are no longer available I must turn to apples like Gala or Fiji and add more lemon juice. The Swiss are very fond of uncooked fruit purées *and they are, I must admit, a good way to end a rich meal.*

6 tablespoons freshly squeezed lemon juice

4 large firm, *organic* apples—very well-scrubbed,
 quartered, cored, and seeded

1/4 cup sugar, or to taste
1/4 cup heavy whipping cream*

UNCOOKED APPLESAUCE IN THE SWISS STYLE (cont'd)

Pour lemon juice into a mixing bowl.

Shred apples, skin and all, into the lemon juice. Stir frequently to prevent the apple from browning.

Add sugar and heavy cream. Stir well.

Turn into a chilled serving bowl.

Serve at once.

Yields 6 servings
adequate for 4 people

Notes: *If preferred, the heavy cream can be whipped and used as a topping instead.

This recipe can be doubled, when required.

1/6 SERVING – PROTEIN = 0.3 g.; FAT = 3.7 g.; CARBOHYDRATE = 20.4 g.;
CALORIES = 111; CALORIES FROM FAT = 30%

CARROT CAKE
Aargauer Rubli Torte

TPT - 1 hour and 50 minutes;
1 hour = cooling period

Although carrots have been baked into cakes and tortes for centuries, the resurgence of popularity in the 1960s set us off testing and tasting. This is the best carrot cake we have ever tried—moist and sweet, but a nutritional improvement over most versions.

3 cups *finely* grated, *not shredded,* carrots—about
  1 pound trimmed and peeled medium carrots

1 1/2 cups unbleached white flour
1/2 cup whole wheat flour
1 1/2 teaspoons ground cinnamon
1/2 teaspoon ground mace *or* nutmeg
1 teaspoon baking soda
1 teaspoon baking powder
1/2 teaspoon salt

1 cup *fat-free* pasteurized eggs (the equivalent
  of 4 eggs)
1 1/3 cups white sugar
1/3 cup firmly packed *light* brown sugar
1 cup light vegetable oil—*our choice is sunflower oil*
1 teaspoon pure vanilla extract
1 teaspoon freshly grated orange zest

Preheat oven to 325 degrees F. Prepare a 13 x 9 x 2-inch baking pan by coating with non-stick lecithin spray coating.

Sift white and whole wheat flours, ground cinnamon and mace, baking soda, baking powder, and salt into a mixing bowl. Set aside until required.

Using an electric mixer, beat pasteurized eggs *briefly* until well-mixed. Add grated carrots, white and brown sugars, oil, vanilla extract, and grated orange zest. Beat until thoroughly blended. Add sifted flour and spice mixture. Beat at LOW speed until moistened—*do not overbeat.**

Turn into prepared baking pan, spreading evenly to the sides.

Bake in preheated 325 degree F, oven for about 35-40 minutes, or until a cake tester inserted in the center comes out clean. Cake should spring back when pressed with your finger. Transfer to a wire rack and allow to cool completely—at least 1 hour.

When thoroughly cooled, frost with a cream cheese frosting of choice or serve with a cream sauce or, if preferred, just sprinkle with confectioners' sugar.

Yields 21 servings

Notes: *If desired, 1/2 to 1 cupful of chopped, *preservative-free* nuts—walnuts, black walnuts, or hazelnuts—may be added at this point as may *preservative-free* dark raisins or currants.

Although this recipe may be halved and baked in a 9 x 9-inch baking pan, this cake actually profits from a day or two of aging, so the larger cake is often a good idea. When halving this recipe, baking time will be reduced, but not halved, so do watch carefully and test frequently.

1/12 SERVING – PROTEIN = 2.8 g.; FAT = 11.0 g.; CARBOHYDRATE = 30.1 g.;
CALORIES = 226; CALORIES FROM FAT = 44%

Europe–Switzerland

CHOCOLATE *MOUSSE KAHLUA*
Mousse au Chocolat

TPT - 24 hours and 25 minutes;
24 hours = setting period

This was always, bar none, our favorite chocolate mousse recipe. I even tried to carry a bowl full of mousse, packed in ice and blankets, to our daughter's college campus for a birthday celebration. However, it is very fragile and did not travel well . . . On another occasion I made the mousse and refrigerated it just as a power failure hit. Six hours passed as the temperature inside the refrigerator slowly rose. The resulting mousse had not set well. The Swiss version of this French classic is usually made with Crème de Cacao, Grand Marnier, brandy, or kirschwasser.

1 cup *whole* milk

6 ounces semi-sweet chocolate bits
1 ounce unsweetened baking chocolate—chopped into small bits

1/2 cup *fat-free* pasteurized eggs* (the equivalent of 2 eggs)
2 tablespoons *Kahlua* liqueur**

2 tablespoons *Salmonella*–negative pasteurized egg white powder**
6 tablespoons *warm* water

1 cup heavy whipping cream
1 teaspoon confectioners' sugar
1/2 teaspoon pure vanilla extract

In a heavy saucepan set over *LOW-MEDIUM* heat, heat milk *just to the boiling point.* Remove from heat.

In the container of the electric blender, combine both semi-sweet chocolate and unsweetened chocolate bits. Add heated milk and blend at LOW speed until extremely smooth. Remove top and, while blender is still running, add pasteurized eggs in thin, steady stream. Add *Kahlua.* Cover again and blend until *very smooth.* Turn into a large mixing bowl and set aside to cool slightly.

In the *grease-free* mixer bowl of the electric mixer, combine egg white powder and *warm* water. Stir gently for several minutes until completely dissolved. Using the electric mixer fitted with *grease-free* beaters or by hand using a *grease-free* wire whisk, beat egg whites until stiff peaks form.

Gently, but *thoroughly, whisk-fold* whipped egg whites into chocolate mixture. Turn into a single 2-quart soufflé dish or into individual dishes, as preferred.

Refrigerate for 24 hours, or overnight, before serving.

Just before serving, using either an electric mixer fitted with *chilled* beaters or by hand using a *chilled* wire whisk, beat heavy cream in a *chilled* mixing bowl until soft peaks form. Gradually beat in confectioners' sugar and vanilla extract. Continue to beat until stiff peaks form.

Adorn each serving of *mousse* with a generous dollop of whipped cream.***

Yields 8 servings
adequate for 4-8 people

Notes: *Because raw eggs present the danger of *Salmonella* poisoning, commercially-available, *Salmonella*-negative pasteurized eggs and *Salmonella*-negative dried egg whites are recommended for use in preparing this dish.

**If preferred, the *Kahlua* liqueur may be omitted or another liqueur of choice can be used.

***Although whipped cream is a fitting crown for this glorious dessert, it is entirely optional as far as we are concerned.

Rather than doubling this recipe, it is far more advisable to repeat the recipe and allow each batch to set separately. On the other hand, one-half of this recipe is easily prepared and the resultant quantity discourages over-indulging.

Return leftovers to the refrigerator quickly.

1/8 SERVING (with whipped cream garnish) –
PROTEIN = 5.4 g.; FAT = 20.2 g.; CARBOHYDRATE = 29.3 g.;
CALORIES = 262; CALORIES FROM FAT = 69%

1/8 SERVING (without whipped cream garnish) –
PROTEIN = 4.8 g.; FAT = 10.4 g.; CARBOHYDRATE = 27.9 g.;
CALORIES = 167; CALORIES FROM FAT = 56%

Ukraine

Trade routes were established through which the Trypillians, who inhabited the region from 4500 to 2000 BC, were able to market the cultivated crops that grew easily in the rich soil—notably barley, millet, rye, and wheat. It is estimated that fifty-seven percent of the Ukraine is suitable for agriculture. The steppes are considered among the most fertile plains on earth. Its designation for centuries as the "breadbasket of Europe" is understandable and traces back to its very early history. The Ukraine was a strategically important republic to the Soviets since it was the most productive agricultural area of the former Soviet Union, providing twenty-five percent of all Soviet Union grain production, twenty percent of dairy and meat production, and more than half of its sugar beet production. Despite the profound influence upon the Ukraine during the two-hundred-year rule by Czarist Russia and, subsequently, by the Soviet Union, other influences can be noted especially when one analyzes the cuisine. Important foods like sausages and sauerkraut came to the Ukraine from Poland. Cabbage stuffed with rice can be traced to Turkey, as can other stuffed vegetables, and the breading of meats and fish, strudels, both sweet and savory, and desserts such as cheesecake and tarts can be traced to the period of the Austro–Hungarian Empire.

Although the Greek, Roman, and Byzantine Empires all established colonies in what is today's Ukraine, its national identity flows from the founding of Kievan Rus' by the Rus' people of Scandinavian origin, who settled around Ladoga and Novgorod. The Rus' gradually moved southward and archaeological evidence indicates than they reached the area of Kiev about 800 AD.

In 1654 Ukraine asked the Czar of Moscovy for protection from Poland. The agreement was taken by Moscow as an invitation to take over Kiev. The Ukrainian state became part of the Russian Empire and remained so until 1918, when it declared its independence, an independence short-lived when it was again taken by the Russians and became a Soviet republic. The Ukraine was one of the founding states of the Soviet Union and remained a part of the Soviet Union until the demise of the Soviet state in 1991. In 2014, during a period of political unrest, Russia annexed the far eastern part of Ukraine, Crimea, to regain the warm water port it had lost in 1991. Agitation by Russia suggests that Ukraine's agriculture significance may also be an object of Russian interest again.

Agricultural festivals evolved into religious festivals with the coming of Christianity and today's festivals still have elements of those early celebrations of the land. If you visit the Ukraine at Christmas time you will find the traditional Christmas Eve feast not only a delicious meatless experience but also an inspiration. Twelve meatless dishes are usually included at a large family gathering. Although traditional dishes differ from family to family, just as such food traditions do in most families, among the most common dishes for this feast are a meatless borsch, mushroom-filled *vushka*, little dumplings somewhat like Italian *tortellini*, rice-stuffed cabbage rolls, dumplings, a fish dish, a dried fruit compote, an ancient or modern version of flummery, yeast-raised doughnuts, and preserves.

Ukrainians from Galicia and Bukovyna seeking religious freedom settled in Canada in the late 1890s. These vegetarian pacifists brought their cuisine with them, preserving it as has almost no other immigrant group. Most of the foods they had grown in Europe could be grown in the area of western Canada where they settled but at this higher latitude the growing season was truncated. As a result, the high grain/carbohydrate diet of their homeland was modified and Ukrainian–Canadians increased their dairy consumption. In addition, the lower humidity of the western plains of Canada limited the availability of mushrooms and honey. They introduced *varenyky*, potato-filled dumplings, not only to their Canadian neighbors but also to the United States. The name was changed to *pierogies* and under their new English name this simple food became a staple on both sides of the border, available sometimes freshly-made and always frozen in almost every grocery store in Canada and in the United States.

Europe – Ukraine

Deep-Fried Straw Potatoes
Kartoplia Solimkoi

Uncooked Horseradish and Sour Cream Sauce
Smetana z Khronom

~

Cucumber Salad with Dill and Garlic Mayonnaise
Salata z Orgurtsov

Cabbage Slaw with Onion and Apple
Salat iz Kapusty z Iabloki

~

Doukhobor Beet Soup from British Columbia
Boracht

~~~~~~~~~~~~~~~~~~~~

Mushroom Casserole with Sour Cream
Gribnoy iz Smetanoy z Bringi

~~~~~~~~~~

Fried Egg Noodles with Mushrooms
Lokshyna z Gribney

~~~~~~~~~~

Potato-Filled *Pierogies*
Varenyky
with

Caramelized Onions

Pickled Beets

~~~~~~~~~~~~~~~~~~~~

Crustless Pineapple Cheese Pie
Syrnyk Ananas

Sweet Wheat Fritters
Slastony z Manykh Krupio

Preserves

Europe–Ukraine

UKRAINIAN DEEP-FRIED STRAW POTATOES
Kartoplia Solimkoi

TPT - 40 minutes

I remember my grandmother standing at the big old black iron stove frying up a batch of straw potatoes as a snack one Saturday night. Nuts that had dried in the attic and a hunk of cheese kept the card players fueled and the grandkids whizzing about "stealing" the straw potatoes out from under the noses of the game participants. Canned potato sticks, a salty convenience snack that preceded the onslaught of chips, were introduced and the making of straw potatoes seems to have become a lost art. Ukrainians love them and we especially like them with just dot of the Ukrainian horseradish and sour cream sauce, the recipe for which follows.

Oil for deep-frying heated to 365 degrees F.

5 medium potatoes—peeled
3 quarts *ice* water

Salt

In a deep heavy saucepan set over *MEDIUM-HIGH* heat, heat oil to 365 degrees F.

Slice the peeled potatoes into thin "sticks," about one-sixteenth inch wide.* As you cut the potato sticks, transfer them to the *ice* water while you are preparing the rest. Drain thoroughly. Transfer to a cotton tea towel and pat dry with another towel.

Deep-fry in small batches until golden and crisp, *being careful not to allow potato straws to over-brown.* Remove with a skimmer and transfer to paper-toweling to allow for excess oil to drain. Turn into a serving bowl. Add salt, to taste.

Serve warm with or without the horseradish and sour cream sauce.

Yields 6 servings
adequate for 4 people

Notes: *Grandma always cut up the potatoes in the afternoon and placed them in ice water in the ice box until she was ready to fry them.

This recipe can be halved or doubled, when required.

1/6 SERVING – PROTEIN = 1.7 g.; FAT = 3.8 g.; CARBOHYDRATE = 17.4 g.;
CALORIES = 112; CALORIES FROM FAT = 31%

UKRAINIAN UNCOOKED HORSERADISH AND SOUR CREAM SAUCE
Smetana z Khronom

TPT -   1 hour and 2 minutes;
        1 hour = flavor development period

Horseradish sauce, as an accompaniment to meats, especially cold smoked meats, is common to many cuisines in Eastern Europe. There is never a time of year that a hunk of horseradish root is not displayed in the produce sections of our grocery stores in central Pennsylvania. Mennonites and others of German and Russian descent, who live in this region of the United States, do still grate their own horseradish. I greatly prefer the convenience of the prepared horseradish sauce which is jarred and usually available in the dairy case. However, be aware that if you keep it around too long, it will lose its potency. Ukrainians use both cooked and uncooked horseradish sauces and they do, of course, grate their own horseradish.

1 1/2 tablespoons prepared horseradish sauce*
1/2 teaspoon distilled white vinegar
1/2 cup *full-fat* dairy sour cream
2 teaspoons sugar

In a small, non-metallic bowl, combine horseradish sauce, vinegar, sour cream, and sugar. Using a small wire whisk, mix until the horseradish has been thoroughly integrated. Turn into a small serving dish. Cover and refrigerate for at least 1 hour.**

Yields 9 tablespoonfuls

**UKRAINIAN UNCOOKED HORSERADISH
AND SOUR CREAM SAUCE** (cont'd)

Notes: *The commercially-available horseradish sauce which I buy already has vinegar, salt, and some sugar added to the grated horseradish.

**If the sauce is too thick, thin with a bit of light cream.

This recipe can be halved or doubled, when required.

1/9 SERVING (per tablespoonful) –
PROTEIN = 0.2 g.; FAT = 0.4 g.; CARBOHYDRATE = 2.2 g.;
CALORIES = 12; CALORIES FROM FAT = 30%

CUCUMBER SALAD WITH DILL AND GARLIC MAYONNAISE
Salata of Ogurtsov
TPT - 8 minutes

In the Ukraine vegetables are more apt to be served as part of cooked dishes than as raw salads. However, summer menus will frequently include a salad as a first course or as a replacement for the soup course. When you cross off the meat and fish first-course salads favored by Ukrainians, you are left with few dishes that fit our definition of a salad. This unusual cucumber salad is a lively salad that we are glad we took the time to find. This should not be confused with "mizeria," which is a popular cucumber salad that is dressed with sour cream and does not contain garlic.

1 large cucumber—peeled, quartered, seeded, and diced
1/4 cup *finely* chopped onion
Freshly ground black pepper, to taste
2 tablespoons chopped dillweed

2 garlic cloves removed from preserved garlic used to make GARLIC OIL *[see index] or* GARLIC WITH THYME AND BAY IN OIL *[see index]—very finely* chopped*
2 tablespoons *calorie-reduced or light* mayonnaise

In a mixing bowl, combine diced cucumber, *finely* chopped onion, black pepper, and chopped dillweed. Toss to mix well.

In a small dish, combine *very finely* chopped *preserved* garlic and mayonnaise. Mix well. Add to cucumber mixture. Toss to combine. Turn into a serving dish. Refrigerate until ready to serve.

Serve chilled as a salad or as a relish accompaniment to other dishes.

Notes: *Do not substitute raw garlic in this dish. The preserved garlic, which has been cooked, gives a sweet taste to this dish that raw garlic can not achieve.

This recipe can be halved or doubled, when required.

Yields 6 servings
adequate for 4 people

1/6 SERVING – PROTEIN = 0.3 g.; FAT = 1.7 g.; CARBOHYDRATE = 2.3 g.;
CALORIES = 25; CALORIES FROM FAT = 61%

Europe–Ukraine

UKRAINIAN CABBAGE AND CARROT SLAW WITH ONION AND APPLE
Salat iz Kapusty y Yabloki

TPT - 1 hour and 8 minutes;
     1 hour = flavor development period

Ukrainians and Russians eat cabbage in more ways than I had ever imagined, even though I had grown up in a family of German descent in northern New York State. We did not make cabbage pudding; we did not layer pancakes with cabbage; we did not stew cabbage with beans; we did not bake cabbage with sour cream; we did not make cabbage strudels; we did not stuff cabbages; we did not make cabbage patties, and the list seems to go on and on. However, cabbage was used to make sauerkraut, soups, and cabbage salads which were major menu items in the middle of winter. This cabbage slaw from Kiev is quite different from the coleslaw that I learned to make from the German cooks in my family; it is different from the coleslaw that my Italian in-laws made; and it will not be recognized by those who frequent delis and diners in the United States. The addition of grated cheese and sugar to the dressing and an apple to the slaw are remarkable.

5 cups shredded cabbage
1 medium carrot—scraped or pared and coarsely shredded
1 medium apple—well scrubbed and slivered—*our choice is a Fuji or a Honeycrisp apple*
1/4 cup slivered onion
1 tablespoon freshly squeezed lemon juice
Freshly ground black pepper, to taste

1 tablespoon grated *pecorino Romano* **cheese**
2 tablespoons *calorie-reduced or light* **mayonnaise**
1/4 teaspoon sugar
2 tablespoons chopped fresh parsley
1 tablespoon chopped fresh basil*

In a mixing bowl, combine shredded cabbage, and carrot, slivered apple, and onion, lemon juice, and black pepper. Toss to coat well.

In a small bowl, combine grated cheese, mayonnaise, sugar, and chopped parsley and basil. Mix well. Add to shredded vegetables. Toss to combine thoroughly. Turn into a serving bowl. Refrigerate for 1 hour to allow the salad to wilt.

Serve chilled.

Yields 6 servings
adequate for 4 people

Notes: *Basil can be omitted, or a sprinkling of dried basil can be added, in the winter when your gardens are no longer supplying fresh basil.

This recipe can be halved or doubled, when required.

1/6 SERVING – PROTEIN = 1.6 g.; FAT = 3.1 g.; CARBOHYDRATE = 8.9 g.;
CALORIES = 56; CALORIES FROM FAT = 50%

DOUKHOBOR BEET SOUP FROM BRITISH COLUMBIA
Borscht

TPT - 1 hour and 30 minutes

The Doukhobor (Dukhobor) communities of western Canada were founded in the 1890s by refugees from Russian oppression seeking religious freedom. This controversial Christian sect, which embraces both vegetarianism and pacifism, arose in the Ukraine in the 1700s. Their name translates to "spirit wrestlers" but they are more properly known as the "Union of Spiritual Communities of Christ." In Czarist Russia, they met with much opposition to their beliefs, especially to their collective rejection of the Orthodox church, Czarist authority, and conscription. Between 1898-1899, approximately 7,500 members of this sect were helped by Leo Tolstoy, also a vegetarian, and English Quakers to emigrate to Canada where they established communal farms and flourished, but not without controversy. They brought with them their Russian culinary heritage and reinvented it with the bounty they grew in the western Canadian prairies of, first, Saskatchewan and, later, British Columbia. It is believed that about 30,000 Doukhobors still live in Canada with an equal number spread out and assimilated into the cultures of Russia and the provinces of the former Soviet Union including the Ukraine (from which they came), Siberia (to which they were banished), and Georgia (to which they fled). A small community was also established in Paraguay.

This soup is a meal in itself. Accompany with a hearty bread such as our Russian black bread (Chernyi Khlib).

DOUKHOBOR BEET SOUP FROM BRITISH COLUMBIA (cont'd)

**2 large, unpeeled beets with root intact and
2-inches of leaf stem attached—well-washed
2 quarts** *boiling* **water**

**2 medium potatoes—peeled and diced
1 quart** *boiling* **water**

**1 tablespoon butter
1/2 cup diced carrot
1/4 cup diced green pepper
1/2 cup shredded green cabbage**

**2 teaspoons chopped fresh dillweed
1/2 teaspoon salt, or to taste
1/2 cup** *whole* **milk**

1 medium tomato—peeled, seeded, and diced *or*
canned, diced tomato, if necessary

1/2 cup light cream *or* **half and half**

6 tablespoons *fat-free* **dairy sour cream, for garnish**

Cook beets in the 2 quartfuls *boiling* water until tender—about 25 minutes. Trim off the tops and bottoms, slip off the skins, and dice the beets. Set aside until required.

Cook the diced potato in the 1 quartful *boiling* water for 10 minutes. Drain potatoes through a strainer set over a mixing bowl in order to *reserve the potato cooking water.*

In a kettle set over *MEDIUM-LOW* heat, melt the butter. Sauté diced carrot and green pepper, and shredded cabbage for about 5 minutes, or until vegetables are softened, *being careful to allow none of the vegetables to brown.*

Add *one-half* of the diced, cooked potato and all of the potato cooking liquid to the sautéed vegetables.

Mash the remaining cooked potato in a bowl. Add chopped dillweed and salt. Continue mashing. *Gradually* add the milk, working it into the potato–dillweed mixture. Add this mixture to the ingredients in the kettle with the reserved, diced beets and the diced tomato.

Reduce heat to LOW and cook for about 30 minutes. Simmer gently, but *do not allow soup to boil.*

Add cream and allow to heat through. *Do not allow soup to boil.*

Turn into a heated soup tureen and serve into heated soup bowls. Garnish each serving with 1 tablespoonful of sour cream.

Yields 6 servings
adequate for 4 people

Note: Leftovers may be *gently* reheated in a double boiler. *Do not boil.*

1/6 SERVING – PROTEIN = 4.5 g.; FAT = 2.9 g.; CARBOHYDRATE = 18.5 g.;
CALORIES = 120; CALORIES FROM FAT = 22%

Europe–Ukraine

UKRAINIAN MUSHROOM CASSEROLE WITH SOUR CREAM
Gribney iz Smetanoy z Brinzi
TPT - 48 minutes

Wild mushrooms, "hryby," are dearly loved by Ukrainians, where families set out into the woods in September on a dry day after a rainy spell. The cry "Idu na hryby!" or "move on the mushrooms" can probably be heard as the hunters move on to their favorite "hunting" sites to search out and gather the freshest fungi. Just the thought of gently carrying the treasures home in baskets and then cleaning, quickly frying, and serving with freshly cultured sour cream, sets the taste buds tingling.

1 pound whole mushrooms—trimmed, rinsed, cleaned well with a brush
1 1/2 tablespoons whole wheat flour

1 1/2 tablespoons sweet *(unsalted)* butter
1 large leek—*white and light green portions only*— trimmed, well-rinsed, and *thinly* sliced

1/2 cup *fat-free* dairy sour cream
1/4 cup *whole* milk

1/4 cup (1 ounce) *feta* cheese—preferably Bulgarian, if available—crumbled*

Preheat oven to 325 degrees F. Prepare a 1 1/2-quart baking dish or soufflé dish by coating with non-stick lecithin spray coating.

Combine slightly damp mushroom slices and flour in a plastic bag. Shake *gently* to coat mushroom slices.

In a large skillet set over *MEDIUM-LOW* heat, melt butter. Add leek slices and sauté for just a minute or two. Add flour-dredged mushrooms and sauté gently until liquid begins to be released.

In a mixing bowl, combine sour cream and *whole* milk. Using a wire whisk, combine until smooth. Add to mushrooms in skillet, *gently* stirring to combine well.

Turn into prepared baking dish. Scatter the crumbled *feta* cheese over.

Bake in preheated 325 degree F. oven for about 30 minutes. Mushroom mixture will be bubbling and top will be *very lightly browned.*

Yields 6 servings
adequate for 4 people

Notes: *In the Ukraine an ewe's milk cheese similar to Rumanian *brynza* would be used. If *brynza* is available, by all means use it. *Feta* is, however, an adequate substitution.

This recipe may be halved or doubled, when required.

1/6 SERVING – PROTEIN = 5.9 g.; FAT = 4.1 g.; CARBOHYDRATE = 13.4 g.;
CALORIES = 92; CALORIES FROM FAT = 40%

FRIED EGG NOODLES WITH MUSHROOMS IN THE STYLE OF THE UKRAINE
Lokshyna z Gribney
TPT - 1 hour and 35 minutes;
1 hour = dried mushroom reconstitution period

Ukrainians cook noodles in more ways that you will ever have time to try. This fried noodle skillet supper is remarkably similar to a fried penne dish popular in northern Italy. Dry-toasting the egg noodles gives them a flavor nuance that is unusual and compatible with the dried mushroom.

Europe–Ukraine

FRIED EGG NOODLES WITH MUSHROOMS IN THE STYLE OF THE UKRAINE (cont'd)

1 ounce dried mushroom pieces—well-brushed and well-rinsed*
Warm water, to cover

3/4 pound broad egg noodles

1 teaspoon *extra virgin* olive oil
1 teaspoons butter
1 small onion—*finely* chopped

1 2/3 cups VEGETARIAN WHITE STOCK *[see index]*
1/2 cup *reserved* mushroom–soaking liquid
Freshly ground black pepper, to taste
Several dashes ground red pepper (cayenne), or to taste

2 tablespoons light cream *or* half and half

1/2 cup crumbled, dry farmers' cheese
2 tablespoons chopped, fresh parsley

Place dried mushroom pieces into a small bowl or measuring cup. Cover with *warm* water and allow to reconstitute for about 1 hour. Drain, *reserving liquid*. Chop roughly into small pieces.

Put dry *egg noodles* into a *large, non-stick-coated* skillet, with cover, set over *MEDIUM* heat. *Toast* for about 5-7 minutes, stirring constantly. *Do not allow the egg noodles to brown.*

Add oil, butter, *finely* chopped onion, and reconstituted mushrooms. Sauté only until onion begins to soften.

Add stock and mushroom liquid. Season with black pepper and ground red pepper (cayenne) to taste.

Allow to come to the boil. Reduce heat to *LOW-MEDIUM*, cover tightly, and allow to cook for about 15 minutes. Stir occasionally to be sure that the egg noodles do not stick to the bottom of the skillet. Remove cover and cook, stirring constantly, until liquid is almost totally evaporated.

Add sautéed onions, mushroom pieces, the olive oil and butter remaining in the skillet in which they were sautéed, and the cream. Stir to combine well and cook only until heated through. Season with black pepper and red pepper (cayenne).

Turn out onto heated serving platter. Sprinkle crumbled farmers' cheese over. Garnish with chopped parsley.

Serve at once.

Yields 6 servings
adequate for 4 people

Notes: *Try to include dried *porcini* mushrooms in the mixture. Even a few give dishes like this so much flavor.

This recipe may be halved, when required.

1/6 SERVING – PROTEIN = 10.8 g.; FAT = 9.4 g.; CARBOHYDRATE = 38.1 g.; CALORIES = 268; CALORIES FROM FAT = 32%

Europe–Ukraine

UKRAINIAN CRUSTLESS PINEAPPLE CHEESE PIE
Syrnyk Ananas

TPT - 2 hours and 17 minutes;
1 hour = cooling period

Most cheese cakes with which we are familiar have some sort of crust, usually a sweet crumb crust. In the Ukraine that crust is more often a baked sour cream pastry crust. "Syrnyk pyrih" is the name by which a traditional Easter cheese cake is known, "pyrih" being a term rather generically applied to a turnover or a food in which a soft filling has been enclosed in an edible case. This is certainly not a New York cheesecake by any stretch of the imagination. It is an unusual dessert with a light texture that is not really a pudding, not really a cake, and not really a pie.

3/4 pound *part-skimmed milk ricotta* cheese*

1/2 cup *fat-free* pasteurized eggs (the equivalent of 2 eggs)
1/2 cup sugar
Grated zest of 1/2 lemon—about 1/4 teaspoon
1 tablespoon freshly squeezed juice

1 tablespoon unbleached white flour
1/2 cup *crushed*, juice-packed pineapple—drained

2 large egg whites *or* 4 teaspoons *Salmonella*-negative pasteurized egg white powder beaten with 4 tablespoonfuls warm water

1/4 cup *finely* chopped, *preservative-free* walnuts

Sweetened, softly whipped cream—as garnish—if desired

Preheat oven to 300 degrees F. Prepare a 9-inch glass pie plate by coating with non-stick lecithin spray coating.

Set a sieve over a mixing bowl. Press the *ricotta* cheese through the sieve. Set aside until required.

Using the electric mixer, combine pasteurized eggs, sugar, grated lemon zest, and lemon juice. Beat until well-combined.

Add sieved cheese and beat well.

Add flour and crushed pineapple. Again, mix well.

Using an electric mixer fitted with *grease-free* beaters or by hand, using a *grease-free* wire whisk, beat egg whites in a *grease-free* bowl until *stiff*, but *not dry*. Whisk-fold beaten egg whites *gently*, but *thoroughly*, into cheese mixture. Turn into prepared pie plate, spreading evenly to the edges of the pie plate.

Sprinkle *finely* chopped walnuts evenly over the surface.

Bake in preheated 300 degree oven for 1 hour. Remove from oven and place on a wire rack. Allow to *cool completely in a warm room*—about 1 hour. *(This method eliminates the cracked top surface resultant from "in-oven" cooling.)*

Do not remove from baking dish. Instead, *serve directly from pie plate in which it was baked.* Serve at room temperature or chilled, as preferred. Cut in wedges as you would for a pie and serve with whipped cream, if desired. Refrigerate any leftovers.

Yields 6 servings
adequate for 4 people

Note: *The more traditional dry cottage cheese or farmer's cheese can be substituted, if preferred. *Ricotta* cheese given this cheese cake a better texture, in our opinion.

1/6 SERVING (exclusive of whipped cream garnish) –
PROTEIN = 11.0 g.; FAT = 7.4 g.; CARBOHYDRATE = 28.6 g.;
CALORIES = 228; CALORIES FROM FAT = 29%

Europe–Ukraine

UKRAINIAN SWEET WHEAT FRITTERS
Slastony z Manykh Krupiv

TPT - 53 minutes
20 minutes = porridge cooling period

Ukrainians prepare fritters from all kinds of grains and legumes. Fritters are easily and quickly prepared and are as much of a "meal-on-the-run" for Ukrainians as are burgers and fries in America or fish and chips in Great Britain, Australia, and New Zealand. These nutritious vegetarian snacks are available at stalls in bazaars and markets and from vendors on street corners. Dessert fritters are a bit more work but these, made from quick-cooking wheat cereal, are divinely light and just beg for a fruit sauce. We adore them for breakfast on special occasions, like Tuesdays!

1 cup skimmed milk
1/2 cup quick-cooking Cream of Wheat cereal
  ***or* farina**

1/2 teaspoon baking powder
2 tablespoons sugar
1/2 cup skimmed milk
1/3 cup *fat-free* pasteurized eggs (the equivalent of about 2 egg yolks)
1/2 teaspoon pure vanilla extract

2 large egg whites

1/4 cup butter

Sour cream or fruit sauce *or* sweetened, whipped, cream

In a saucepan set over *LOW-MEDIUM* heat, heat the 1 cupful milk to boiling. *Reduce heat to LOW.* While stirring, add cream of wheat and cook, stirring frequently, until porridge has thickened. Remove from heat and allow to cool for 20 minutes.

Turn *cooled* porridge into a mixing bowl. Add baking powder, sugar, and remaining 1/2 cupful skimmed milk. Using a wire whisk, combine well. Add pasteurized eggs and vanilla extract. Blend well.

Using an electric mixer fitted with *grease-free* beaters or by hand, using a *grease-free* wire whisk, beat egg whites in a *grease-free* bowl until *stiff*, but *not dry*. Whisk-fold beaten egg whites *gently*, but *thoroughly*, into porridge mixture.

In a non-stick-coated skillet set over *MEDIUM* heat, melt butter. Drop fritter batter by tablespoonfuls into hot butter. Using a spatula, turn so that both sides are golden brown. Transfer cooked fritters to a serving plate set on a warming tray or in a warm oven until all are prepared.

Serve warm, with prepared sauce or whipped cream.

Yields about 30 small fritters
adequate for 6 people

Note: This recipe can be halved or doubled, when required.

1/8 SERVING (exclusive of whipped cream or fruit sauce) –
PROTEIN = 1.3 g.; FAT = 1.6 g.; CARBOHYDRATE = 3.6 g.;
CALORIES = 34; CALORIES FROM FAT = 42%

England

A large flint cache, recently discovered in Norfolk, has extended the 700,000-year marker that has been the accepted date when hominoids visited this land mass. Habitation by modern humans in the British Isles is documented to 35,000 years ago but the owners of the flints traveled this way some 840,000 years ago could move easily from what is today continental Europe to the islands we know as Great Britain. The Devensian glaciation, comparable to the Wisconsin glacier in this hemisphere, forced these people South and it was not until about 11,000 years ago, with the retreat of the last Ice Age, that humans, moving along the Southern edge of the glaciation, again returned to and settled in these islands. Just as the early proto-humans had done, these post-ice age migratory hunters and gathers traveled easily from Europe about 8,500 years ago via the land bridge. As ocean levels rose, due to the glacial melt and outwash, the land bridge was eliminated, isolating the people who had settled there by creating the islands we know today as the British Isles. The people who came after would be seafaring people.

Many have contributed to what is now Britain. The Celts arrived from Central Europe during the Iron Age. They were finally successfully conquered by the Romans in 43 AD and during the 367 years of Roman occupation the disparate and illiterate tribes benefited through the introduction of education, hygiene, religion, agricultural practices, public water supply techniques, and the introduction of a legal system as well as exposure to architecture and literature. The retrenchment of the Romans to the continent with the decline of the Roman Empire left the Islands open to invasion and influence by the Saxons, the Jutes, the Norse, and, of course, the Norman French led by William the Conqueror, who introduced feudalism. As Britain was influenced so has it influenced, spreading its influence around the world and leaving its influences behind as its imperial era ended.

One of the first vegetarian cookbooks I bought was a 1960s British book. I assumed that because the author discussed restaurants and restaurant dishes, we would not find meals to be the difficult part of our travels in Great Britain. Amazingly, that was not the case and several evenings we resorted to "the can of vegetarian baked beans and the can of rice pudding dinner" we kept in reserve. When we rented a flat just off the High Street in London in 1983, our daily trips to the market had to be early in the morning because produce was depleted by noon and shelves were incredibly empty by the time we returned after a day of adventuring.

Restaurants of many nationalities can be found in London but the search for truly English food was more elusive. I returned home to examine the foods that my family ate and there, strangely, I found what I had been looking for in the "receipt' books and boxes" of my own relatives, on this side of the Atlantic. Pan-fried Cheddar sandwiches, sturdy jellies, jam tarts, gingerbread, mincemeat, summer pudding, curds, cream of celery soup, and macaroni and cheese were all right there in our kitchens, brought to America by the women of my family. Included among the following recipes you will find several desserts because seasonality is key to British cooking. You do not find that tremendous diversity of options in British markets that we are now so used to in this country.

Europe – United Kingdom – England

Baked Mushroom Pâté

Baked Oat – Cheddar Savory Appetizers with Herbs

~

Cream of Celery Soup with Stilton

~

Tossed Salad with Blueberries, and Hazelnuts

with

Celery Seed Dressing

Deviled Eggs

~ ~ ~ ~ ~ ~ ~ ~ ~ ~ ~ ~ ~ ~ ~ ~ ~ ~ ~ ~

A Remarkably Fine Macaroni and Cheese

or

Simmered Potato Slices in Casserole with Stilton Cheese

Deviled Pearl Onions

Vicarage Beets with Fresh Herbs

~ ~ ~ ~ ~ ~ ~ ~ ~ ~

Pan-Fried Cheddar Sandwiches

Crudités

~ ~ ~ ~ ~ ~ ~ ~ ~ ~ ~ ~ ~ ~ ~ ~ ~ ~ ~ ~

Easy Vanilla Ice Cream with Pear Mincemeat   Pear Mincemeat with Pecans

Christmas Pudding with Pear Mincemeat

Gingerbread

with

Lemon Curd Sauce   or   English Toffee Sauce

Yorkshire Summer Pudding

My Strawberry – Blueberry Summer Pudding, in season

English Stewed Rhubarb

~

Whole Wheat Hot Cross Buns

BRITISH BAKED MUSHROOM *PÂTÉ*

TPT - 4 hours and 10 minutes;
       1 hour = mushroom rehydration period;
       2 hours = refrigeration period

It is a fact that way too much food is eaten in our house during the holidays. I designate one evening as a "cheese and cracker" supper but instead of a boring cheese board and assorted grocery store crackers, I make this pâté and accompany it with the most beautiful wedge of English Stilton I can find and two Cheddars, one mild and one sharp. A holiday dessert or cookies and a good wine are all you need to add.

2 cups mixed dried mushrooms—white field (*Agaricus*), shiitake, oyster, *porcini,* and/or *crimini* or baby bella—*well-rinsed and brushed to remove any foreign matter*
3 cups *boiling* water

1/3 cup fresh breadcrumbs—*divided into two portions**
1 teaspoon crushed, dried mixed herbs of choice
[see next page]

BRITISH BAKED MUSHROOM *PÂTÉ* (cont'd)

1 1/2 tablespoons butter
1 medium onion—chopped
2 garlic cloves—*finely* chopped

2 tablespoons *ready-to-serve* cream of mushroom soup

1 cup fresh breadcrumbs*
1 large egg
Freshly ground black pepper, to taste

In a mixing bowl, combine well-cleaned dried mushrooms and *boiling* water. Cover with plate and weight the mushrooms down. Set the mushrooms aside for about 1 hour to rehydrate. Drain thoroughly.

Preheat oven to 325 degrees F. Line a 2 1/2-cup *pâté* terrine with strips of buttered culinary parchment, fitting the strips tightly into the terrine, *butter-side-in.* Allow the edges to hang over the sides of the dish to allow for easy removal of the *pâté.***

In a small bowl combine the 1/3 cupful breadcrumbs and dried herbs. Mix well. Sprinkle *two-thirds* of this mixture onto the butter sides and bottom of the prepared terrine. Pat it in place to cover the surface evenly.

In a skillet set over *MEDIUM* heat, melt butter. Add chopped onion and *finely* chopped garlic. Sauté until onion is soft and translucent, *being careful to allow neither the onion nor the garlic to brown.*

Add rehydrated and drained mushrooms. Sauté for several minutes more. Turn into the work bowl of the food processor fitted with steel knife. Process until mixture is uniformly and quite finely chopped. Add mushroom soup and again process.

Add the 1 cupful breadcrumbs, egg, and black pepper. Process, scraping down the sides of the work bowl, as necessary.

Spoon the mixture, *carefully*, into the lined terrine and spread to the edges. Press the top of the *pâté* firmly using a meat mallet or wooden garlic crusher to eliminate air pockets.

Sprinkle the remaining *one-third* of the herbed crumb mixture on top.

Bake, *uncovered*, in preheated 325 degree F. oven for 40 minutes. Remove from oven. Refrigerate for at least 2 hours.

Using the paper strips, lift the *pâté* from the terrine onto a rectangular serving dish. *Carefully* peel the culinary paper off. Refrigerate until required.

Provide a sharp knife and a cheese or pie server to facilitate the transfer of slices to a salad plate. Serve with slices of sharp Cheddar and English Stilton cheeses.

Yields 8 servings

Notes: *I prefer to use white breadcrumbs for this *pâté*. A day-old baked round Italian or French loaf is the perfect texture for this dish.

**Either a porcelain terrine or a metal one will do quite nicely. Metal ones with sides that drop away for easy removal have an advantage too.

1/6 SERVING – PROTEIN = 5.4 g.; FAT = 8.3 g.; CARBOHYDRATE = 33.1 g.;
CALORIES = 178; CALORIES FROM FAT = 42%

BRITISH BAKED OAT – CHEDDAR SAVORY APPETIZERS WITH HERBS
TPT - 53 minutes

These simple appetizers combine very basic British country ingredients. They are a nice accompaniment to a soup or salad supper too.

2 cups quick rolled oats *(not instant)*
1 1/2 cups shredded (about 6 ounces) *sharp* Cheddar cheese
1/4 cup *fat-free* pasteurized eggs (the equivalent of 1 egg)

1 tablespoon *finely* chopped *fresh* rosemary needles
1/2 teaspoon crushed, dried thyme
Pinch ground red pepper (cayenne), or to taste
1/4 cup butter—*melted*

BRITISH BAKED OAT – CHEDDAR SAVORY APPETIZERS WITH HERBS (cont'd)

Preheat oven to 350 degrees F. Prepare an 8-inch square non-stick-coated baking pan by coating with non-stick lecithin spray coating.

In a mixing bowl, combine rolled oats, shredded Cheddar cheese, and pasteurized eggs. Stir to combine well.

Add *finely* chopped rosemary, crushed thyme, and ground red pepper (cayenne) to *melted* butter. Stir to mix well. Add to oat–Cheddar–egg mixture in mixing bowl. Mix very *thoroughly*.

Press mixture into the prepared baking pan, pressing the mixture evenly to the edges and into the corners. Bake in preheated 350 degree F. oven for 30-35 minutes, or until lightly browned.

Transfer pan to a wire rack. *While still hot*, using a sharp knife, cut the baked cheese bread into twenty-four squares.

Serve while still warm.

Yields 24 servings

1/24 SERVING – PROTEIN = 3.3 g; FAT = 4.8 g; CARBOHYDRATE = 6.6 g; CALORIES = 83; CALORIES FROM FAT = 52%

ENGLISH CREAM OF CELERY SOUP WITH STILTON
TPT - 45 minutes

Oh, how the British love celery—raw celery with salt in the summer and celery soup in the winter. This is a beautifully textured soup to which the English add the queen of all blue-veined cheeses. Before you dismiss it as a peasant soup, try it as a first course for a holiday meal.

4 1/2 cups diced celery
1 medium onion—peeled and chopped
1/2 cup chopped fresh parsley
2 cups *boiling* water
1/2 teaspoon freshly ground *white* pepper
Pinch ground mace

1 cup *whole* milk*
1 tablespoon butter
1 cup Stilton cheese—crumbled or chopped

1/4 cup chopped celery leaves, for garnish

In a kettle set over *MEDIUM* heat, combine diced celery, chopped onion, chopped parsley, *boiling* water, *white* pepper, and ground mace. Cover and cook for about 30 minutes, or until *very tender*. Stir occasionally.

Using a food processor or electric blender, purée celery–onion mixture. Strain the purée through a fine sieve into a clean saucepan. Set over *MEDIUM* heat again.**

Add milk, butter, and crumbled Stilton cheese. Cook, stirring frequently, for about 10 minutes, or until cheese is melted and soup is smooth. Taste and adjust seasoning, if necessary

Turn into a heated soup tureen. Garnish with celery leaves. Serve into heated soup bowls.

Yields about 7 cupfuls
adequate 4-6 people

Notes: *On very special occasions we have been known to use light cream or half and half instead of milk.

**Conveniently, this soup can be prepared to this point and the base frozen. It is helpful, we find, for holiday menu planning.

This recipe is easily halved or doubled, when required.

1/6 SERVING (i. e., per cupful) –
PROTEIN = 6.5 g.; FAT = 9.0 g.; CARBOHYDRATE = 6.0 g.;
CALORIES = 129; CALORIES FROM FAT = 63%

Europe–United Kingdom–England

BRITISH TOSSED SALAD WITH BLUEBERRIES AND HAZELNUTS
TPT - 5 minutes

Although blueberries are not as common in Great Britain as they are here in the United States, varieties of fruits and vegetables are becoming increasingly available as a result of European Union trade with much greater variety available, even in the North, than when we were there in the 1980s. The native British berries are considerably less sweet, as I remember, than are our native blueberries. On a hot, summer evening, this salad, as a main course, offers delightfully different sensations with each mouthful. It goes a long way to revive the spirit.

We add about two ounces of cubed, ripe Brie to this salad when it becomes the center of a summer menu.

3 cups torn *soft* lettuce leaves, such as Bibb or Boston—well-washed and well-dried
3 cups torn red-leafed lettuce—well-washed and well-dried
1 cup *fresh, baby* spinach leaves—well-washed and well-dried
1 tablespoon *tiny, fresh* mint leaves—well-washed

Pinch freshly grated nutmeg

1 cup *fresh* blueberries—stemmed, well-washed and well-drained*
2 ounces *chilled Brie*—cubed
3 tablespoons chopped, *toasted, preservative-free* hazelnuts

CELERY SEED DRESSING *[see recipe which follows]* **or CLASSIC FRENCH DRESSING (Vinaigrette)** *[see index]*

In a salad bowl, combine bite-sized soft lettuce and red-leafed lettuce pieces, *baby* spinach leaves, and *tiny* mint leaves. Toss to mix well.

Grate a bit of nutmeg over the combined lettuce leaves. Again, toss.

Scatter blueberries, cubes of *Brie* cheese, and *toasted* hazelnuts over the top.

Serve into salad bowls or onto salad plates. Pass salad dressing to accommodate individual tastes.**

Yields 6-8 servings
adequate for 4 people

Notes: *Use only *fresh* blueberries, *not frozen*, to prepare this salad.

**We, personally, prefer this salad without dressing.

This recipe may be halved or doubled, when required.

1/8 SERVING (without dressing) –
PROTEIN = 2.2 g.; FAT = 5.0 g.; CARBOHYDRATE = 4.0 g.;
CALORIES = 61; CALORIES FROM FAT = 74%

CELERY SEED DRESSING
TPT - 4 minutes

. . . a good choice for a complex greens mixture!

2 tablespoons chopped onion

1/2 cup vegetable oil, of choice
1/4 cup tarragon wine vinegar
1 tablespoon honey
1 1/2 teaspoons celery seed
1 teaspoon paprika
1/4 teaspoon dry mustard

Using the food processor fitted with steel knife or the electric blender, chop onion. Add remaining ingredients and process until smooth.

Pour into a cruet. Serve over mixed greens, or over vegetable and fruit salads.*

Yields about 14 tablespoonfuls

Notes: *If the dressing separates upon standing, reprocess in the food processor or blender before serving.

This recipe may be doubled, when required.

1/14 SERVING (i. e., per tablespoonful) –
PROTEIN = trace; FAT = 6.3 g.; CARBOHYDRATE = 0.2 g.;
CALORIES = 58; CALORIES FROM FAT = 98%

Europe–United Kingdom–England

DEVILED EGGS
TPT - 9 minutes

While rummaging in a used book store on Craig Street in Pittsburgh, I found a small, well-used 1963 British cookbook which I gathered up as a treasure. The previous owner had inked out the word "deviled" wherever it appeared in the book. It has never ceased to amuse me since I just can not image anyone thinking that the designation of "deviled" in the name of dishes containing mustard is morally dangerous or politically incorrect. Nor do I think that eating deviled eggs can elicit the spirits of the underworld. Whatever she called them, I hope she ate them. Deviled eggs, and particularly these deviled eggs, are the only way I really, really enjoy eggs.

6 hard-cooked eggs—chilled and shelled

2 tablespoons *calorie-reduced* or *light* mayonnaise
1 tablespoon MUSTARD SAUCE *[see index]*

Cut hard-cooked eggs in half lengthwise. Remove egg yolks to a mixing bowl; set egg whites aside.

Using a fork, mash egg yolks well. Add mayonnaise and mustard sauce. Combine thoroughly. Add additional mayonnaise or mustard sauce to achieve a smooth consistency.

Using a pastry bag fitted with a star tube, fill egg white halves with deviled yolk mixture or spoon filling into egg white halves, if preferred.

Place filled egg halves on an egg plate or other serving dish. Refrigerate until ready to serve.

Yields 12 egg halves
adequate for 6 people

Notes: This recipe may be halved or doubled, when required.

Stuffed eggs may be garnished with parsley sprigs, dill sprigs, a sprinkling of paprika, a colorful strip of well-drained fresh tomato or roasted red pepper, scallion slices, selected *mesclún* or even a sliver of smoked salmon for those who eat fish; whatever is appropriate to your menu.

1/12 SERVING – PROTEIN = 3.4 g.; FAT = 3.8 g.; CARBOHYDRATE = 1.2 g.;
CALORIES = 52; CALORIES FROM FAT = 66%

A REMARKABLY FINE MACARONI AND CHEESE
TPT - 1 hour and 10 minutes

Strangely enough institutionally-prepared and packaged macaroni and cheese have not completely destroyed the American affinity for this, often badly rendered, dish. The French abhor it, and they have a point in this case if they have judged this dish by some that we have suffered; but the French do abhor a lot of things . . . Just about everybody has their own version of this casserole, which actually originated in Great Britain after pasta was introduced to the British Isles by the Romans in the first century A.D. They added their justly famous Cheddar cheese to cooked pasta and the result is certainly history.

3 quarts water
1 tablespoon lemon juice
1 3-inch strip lemon zest
1 cup high-protein, whole wheat, *or* Jerusalem
    artichoke elbow macaroni
1 tablespoon vegetable oil

2 ounces Danish *Havarti* cheese *(also known as
    Danish Butter cheese)*—cubed
2 ounces *sharp* Cheddar cheese—cubed
1/2 teaspoon freshly ground black pepper, or
    to taste
1 cup skimmed milk

1 tablespoon butter
1/2 cup whole wheat breadcrumbs
1 tablespoon millers' wheat bran
1/2 teaspoon crushed, dried parsley

Preheat oven to 325 degrees F. Prepare a 1 1/2-quart soufflé dish or other oven-to-table casserole by coating with non-stick lecithin spray coating.

In a large kettle set over *HIGH* heat, bring water to the boil. Add lemon juice and zest. Add macaroni. Boil for about 10-12 minutes. Just before the end of the cooking period, add oil. Pour into a strainer and allow to drain thoroughly. Discard lemon zest.

VOLUME I - 437

A REMARKABLY FINE MACARONI AND CHEESE (cont'd)

Turn well-drained macaroni into a large mixing bowl. Add cubed cheeses and black pepper. Toss to combine well. Turn into prepared casserole. Pour milk over. Set aside.

In a small skillet set over *LOW* heat, melt butter. Stir in breadcrumbs, bran, and crushed parsley. Stir until all butter has been absorbed. Sprinkle evenly over the top of prepared casserole.*

Bake in preheated 325 degree F. oven for approximately 45 minutes, or until all of milk has been absorbed.

Serve at once.

Yields 6 servings
adequate for 4 people

Note: *This dish may be prepared in advance to this point and refrigerated until about 1 hour before required serving time.

1/6 SERVING – PROTEIN = 9.0 g.; FAT = 8.1 g.; CARBOHYDRATE = 13.5 g.; CALORIES = 163; CALORIES FROM FAT = 45%

SIMMERED POTATO SLICES IN CASSEROLE WITH STILTON CHEESE IN THE BRITISH STYLE
TPT - 43 minutes

I found a gorgeous chunk of Blue Stilton in my local market and on that fortuitous January day this dish was born. Stilton is not a blue for the faint of heart. It is to my mind one of the most perfect adventures man has ever taken to explore the world of "Penicillium." Only six English dairies in Leicestershire, Nottinghamshire, and Derbyshire, notably not in Stilton, are licensed to produce the "Queen of Cheeses." Blue Stilton is made from pasteurized cows' milk into which the mold spores of "Penicillium roqueforti" are introduced. It is eaten as a young cheese and is not pressed. It is offered for sale at nine weeks; at sixteen weeks, by the time we buy it as consumers, the sharp bite will have mellowed. A white Stilton is also produced in the same regions.

The wild mushroom stock, in which the potatoes are simmered in this dish, stands up well to the strong cheese.

5 medium, waxy, all-purpose potatoes—well-scrubbed and peeled

3 cups WILD MUSHROOM STOCK *[see index]*
plus additional stock, as required
Freshly ground black pepper, to taste

2 ounces Stilton cheese—crumbled

3 tablespoons light cream *or* **half and half**

Preheat oven to 350 degrees F. Prepare a 2-quart soufflé dish or other oven-to-table baking dish by coating with lecithin non-stick spray coating.

Thinly slice peeled potatoes and scatter evenly in a large skillet.

Add mushroom stock and black pepper. Allow to come to the boil over *MEDIUM* heat. *Reduce heat to LOW-MEDIUM.* Stir to keep potatoes submerged and cook until potatoes are *crisp-tender, but still firm.* Add more stock, if necessary. *Remove from heat.* Place *one-third* of the partially-cooked potatoes in the prepared baking dish. Sprinkle *one-half* of the crumbled Stilton cheese over. Layer another *one-third* of the potatoes; the rest of the Stilton cheese; and, then, the remaining potatoes.

Pour stock remaining in skillet over the potatoes. Pour cream evenly over the potatoes. Grind more black pepper over. Bake in preheated 350 degrees F. oven for about 15 minutes, or until most of liquid has evaporated and potatoes on top begin to harden.

Serve at once.

Yields 6 servings
adequate for 4 people

Note: This recipe can be halved, when required.

Europe–United Kingdom–England

**SIMMERED POTATO SLICES IN CASSEROLE
WITH STILTON CHEESE IN THE BRITISH STYLE** (cont'd)

1/6 SERVING – PROTEIN = 4.5 g.; FAT = 4.4 g.; CARBOHYDRATE = 17.9 g.;
CALORIES = 131; CALORIES FROM FAT = 30%

BRITISH DEVILED PEARL ONIONS
TPT - 22 minutes

Our mustard sauce could legitimately be described as an English-style mustard sauce, which makes it entirely appropriate for this dish. If you do not want to go to all the trouble of preparing pearl onions, small white onions are conveniently available as a frozen product.

10 ounces small white boiling onions—*peeled*

2 quarts *boiling* **water**

3 tablespoons butter
3 tablespoons light cream *or* **half and half**
2 tablespoons MUSTARD SAUCE *[see index]*

Cut an **X** in the root end of each peeled onion to prevent the onions from falling apart.

Place kettle of *boiling* water over *MEDIUM* heat. Drop *peeled* onions into the *boiling* water. Cook for about 15 minutes, or until tender. Drain.

In a non-stick-coated skillet set over *LOW* heat, melt butter. Add cream and mustard sauce.

Stir to mix well. Add drained, cooked onions and cook only until heated through. Turn into a heated serving bowl.

Serve at once.

Yields 6 servings
adequate for 4 people

Note: This recipe can be halved or doubled, when required.

1/6 SERVING – PROTEIN = 2.3 g.; FAT = 7.0 g.; CARBOHYDRATE = 10.0 g.;
CALORIES = 107; CALORIES FROM FAT = 59%

BRITISH VICARAGE BEETS WITH FRESH HERBS
TPT - 53 minutes

Although we now revere beets as a brain food, early British and Colonial American cookbook authors frequently directed that red foods were inappropriate for fine dining. Beets especially were considered "food of the peasants" and as such were eaten only by those whose incomes were limited and at family meals, away from criticizing eyes. I have always felt that the tiniest beets are a real treat. They are so very sweet and tender...

1 tablespoon butter

1 jar (16 ounces) tiny whole beets

1 tablespoon *finely* **chopped fresh parsley**
1 tablespoon snipped fresh chives

Place a serving bowl on a warming tray set as *MEDIUM*. Add butter and allow to melt.

In a saucepan set over *MEDIUM* heat, heat beets in their canning liquid until hot. Drain thoroughly. Pour drained beets into serving bowl with melted butter. Spoon butter over beets.

Garnish with *finely* chopped parsley and snipped chives.

Serve at once.

Yields 6 servings
adequate for 4 people

Notes: *Freshly cooked beets can be substituted, if available. The taste of fresh beets is infinitely superior.

This recipe can be doubled, when required.

1/6 SERVING – PROTEIN = 0.7 g.; FAT = 2.0 g.; CARBOHYDRATE = 5.5 g.;
CALORIES = 41; CALORIES FROM FAT = 44%

Europe–United Kingdom–England

BRITISH PAN–FRIED CHEDDAR SANDWICHES
TPT - 25 minutes

These are the "grilled cheese sandwiches" I grew up with and it is this that most British and Canadian children first experience. They are so very, very good that you never forget the comfort of those lunches and Sunday-night suppers where these simple sandwiches were the stars and your fingers "got all sticky."

12 teaspoons (1/4 cup) butter

12 slices bread, of choice, such as MAPLE OATMEAL BREAD *[see index]* **or COLONIAL-STYLE BREAD** *[see index]*

12 teaspoons (1/4 cup) MUSTARD SAUCE *[see index]*

12 slices (about 6 ounces) *extra sharp* **Cheddar cheese***

Prepare a large non-stick-coated skillet or griddle by coating with non-stick lecithin spray coating.

In a SAUCE WARMER set over *LOW* heat, melt butter.

Lay the slices of bread out on a bread board. Spread each bread slice with one-half teaspoonful of mustard sauce. Place one slice of Cheddar cheese on each of six of the bread slices. *Be sure to tuck the cheese well in from the edge of each slice.* Place the remaining bread slices, *mustard-side-down*, on top of the Cheddar cheese.

Using a pastry brush, brush 1/2 teaspoonful of butter evenly across the surface of each sandwich.

Place prepared skillet or griddle by preheating it over *MEDIUM* heat for several minutes.**

Invert as many sandwiches as will fit, *butter-side-down*, onto the heated skillet or griddle. Pan–fry, pressing the sandwiches down against the hot surface, until *lightly browned.*

Brush the unbuttered top bread slices with *melted* butter and, using a spatula, turn each sandwich and pan-fry on the remaining side until the cheese is melting and the bread surface is *lightly browned.* Transfer to a heated platter set on a warming tray.

Continue cooking until all are prepared.

Cut sandwiches in half and return to the heated platter.

Serve at once.

Yields 6 sandwiches
adequate for 4 people

Notes: *Other cheeses may be substituted for or used in combination with the Cheddar. Swiss and *provolone* are especially good choices since they melt well and are well-complimented by mustard.

**If preferred, a non-stick-coated electric waffle/sandwich iron can be used. Lightly coat the sandwich grill plates with non-stick lecithin spray coating before grilling sandwiches. We find we use less butter when we use the electric iron.

This recipe is easily increased or decreased proportionally, as required.

1/6 SERVING – PROTEIN = 12.4 g.; FAT = 19.3 g.; CARBOHYDRATE = 32.2 g.;
CALORIES = 368; CALORIES FROM FAT = 47%

EASY VANILLA ICE CREAM WITH PEAR MINCEMEAT
TPT - 8 hours and 12 minutes;
8 hours = freezing period

Although some say that they could never, nor would they ever, trade their mince pie or mince tarts for ice cream, we always celebrate the holidays with several different kinds of homemade ice cream, including this one created from the memory of my dad's favorite flavor of "the twenty-eight flavors," rum raisin. This mincemeat ice cream keeps the pie lovers from having a complete "meltdown." In fact, melting vanilla ice cream is really a dreamy sauce for the mincemeat.

2/3 cup *fat-free* **sweetened condensed milk**
1/2 cup *fat-free* **pasteurized eggs*** **(the equivalent of 2 eggs)**
2 teaspoons pure vanilla extract

1 cup PEAR MINCEMEAT WITH PECANS *[see recipe which follows]*—*well-drained*

1 cup heavy whipping cream

PEAR MINCEMEAT WITH PECANS, for garnish, if desired

EASY VANILLA ICE CREAM WITH PEAR MINCEMEAT (cont'd)

Prepare a 9 x 5 x 3-inch non-stick-coated loaf pan by placing it in the freezer until required.

In a large bowl, combine sweetened condensed milk, pasteurized eggs, and vanilla extract. Stir to blend thoroughly.

Add well-drained mincemeat. Fold *gently* until well-combined.

Using an electric mixer fitted with *chilled* beaters or by hand, using a *chilled* wire whisk, beat heavy cream in a *chilled* bowl until stiff. *Whisk-fold* stiffly whipped cream *gently*, but *thoroughly*, into egg–milk–mincemeat mixture. Pour mixture into chilled loaf pan. Spread evenly. Cover tightly with aluminum foil. Freeze overnight or until firm—about 8 hours.

Either scoop ice cream from pan to serve or remove entire block of ice cream from pan and slice. Garnish with a bit of the pear mincemeat, if desired.

Leftovers should be returned to the freezer, tightly covered.

Yields about ten 1/2-cup servings

Notes: *Because raw eggs present the danger of *Salmonella* poisoning, commercially-available pasteurized eggs are recommended for use in preparing this dish.

This recipe is easily doubled, when required. Use a 9 x 5 x 3-inch non-stick-coated loaf pan.

1/10 SERVING (i. e., per 1/2 cupful) –
PROTEIN = 3.6 g.; FAT = 9.3 g.; CARBOHYDRATE = 27.4 g.;
CALORIES = 207; CALORIES FROM FAT = 40%

PEAR MINCEMEAT WITH PECANS
TPT - about 1 hour and 10 minutes,
exclusive of canning procedure

Oh, how my dad loved mince pie at the holidays. I helped my mom and her mother make "green tomato mincemeat" when I was quite young. I even walked to the butcher to get the suet to make the mincemeat. It was an economical event: the suet or back fat was a throw-away item of butchering back then, so it was free; the green tomatoes were harvested at the end of the season, and despite all kinds of "systems," never ripened sufficiently indoors after the frost; apples came up from our root and fruit cellars. This fruity, meatless version of mincemeat would not have been considered to be economical back then but it is good and there is enough industry required in this homemade mincemeat preparation to qualify it as an autumn "getting-ready-for-the-holidays-food."

1 large navel orange—well-washed

2 cups sugar
1/2 cup cranberry–apple juice
1/2 cup freshly-squeezed orange juice
1/4 cup freshly-squeezed lemon juice
1/2 teaspoon ground cinnamon
1/2 teaspoon freshly grated nutmeg
1/4 teaspoon ground cloves
Pinch kosher salt or pickling salt
1 1/2 teaspoons Calvados (apple brandy) *or*
   several drops brandy flavoring, if desired

2 Gala *or* Golden Delicious apples—peeled,
   cored, and chopped
4 large *firm*, ripe pears—peeled, cored, and
   chopped
3 cups *preservative-free dark* raisins
1 cup chopped, *toasted, preservative-free* pecans

If you wish to can the mincemeat for future use, sterilize four 1-pint jars before starting to prepare the mincemeat. Also sterilize lids and rings for jars.

Using a vegetable peeler, peel rind from orange. Chop rind and adhering pith *finely* and put into a kettle. Halve peeled orange. Juice orange halves. Add juice and pulp to rind in kettle.

Add sugar, cranberry–apple juice, orange juice, lemon juice, ground cinnamon, nutmeg, and cloves, kosher salt, and brandy or brandy flavoring, if desired.

On a large chopping board, combine chopped apples and pears, raisins, and *toasted* pecans. Using a sharp chef's knife, chop the ingredients to create a uniformly, *finely* chopped mixture.* Add to ingredients in kettle. Set over *LOW-MEDIUM* heat. Cook, stirring frequently, until almost all of liquid is absorbed—about 40 minutes, or until thickened. Remove from heat.

If to be used within a day or two, transfer to a mixing bowl and refrigerate.

PEAR MINCEMEAT WITH PECANS (cont'd)

If you wish to can the mincemeat, ladle hot mincemeat into the sterilized 1-pint canning jars. Carefully wipe lips of jars. Seal with hot, sterilized lids and rings.

Process in hot-water-bath canner for 25 minutes, *timing from the moment the water reaches a full rolling boil.* Remove to surface covered with thick towels or newspapers. Allow to cool for 24 hours *undisturbed*. Check to be sure jars are sealed before labeling and storing in a dark, cool, dry place. Loosen or remove rings before storing.

Notes: *If preferred, a food / meat grinder, fitted with the coarse blade can be used. Although I would use the grinder for conventional mincemeat, I prefer the coarser texture of the knife-chopped fruit ingredients in this recipe even though it takes a bit longer to prepare.

A cupful of *preservative-free, dried* currants can be added, if available.

Yields 8 cupfuls

1/16 SERVING (about 1/2 cupful) –
PROTEIN = 1.3 g.; FAT = 7.3 g.; CARBOHYDRATE = 64.8 g.;
CALORIES = 319; CALORIES FROM FAT = 21%

CHRISTMAS PUDDING WITH PEAR MINCEMEAT

TPT - 1 hour and 25 minutes;
1 hour = refrigeration period

Oh, the Christmas pudding, ceremoniously borne into the dining room . . . In no way is this the traditional British Christmas plum pudding with its pound of suet or figgy pudding to which suet is also added. Our pear mincemeat, used as a garnish, for this rich corn starch pudding conveys the spirit of the pudding served at Christmas lunch in Great Britain and keeps all the vegetarians on track.

3/4 cup sugar
2 1/2 tablespoons corn starch
2 cups *two-percent* **milk**

1/4 cup *fat-free* **pasteurized eggs (the equivalent of 1 egg)***

1 tablespoon butter
1 teaspoon pure vanilla extract

1/2 cup PEAR MINCEMEAT WITH PECANS *[see recipe which precedes]*
2 tablespoons *biscotti* **crumbs** *or* **plain digestive cookie crumbs**

In a saucepan, combine sugar and corn starch. Stir to mix well. Gradually add milk, while stirring with a wire whisk. Set over *LOW-MEDIUM* heat and cook, stirring constantly, until mixture begins to thicken and all sugar is dissolved.

Put pasteurized eggs into a small bowl. While stirring vigorously with a wire whisk, gradually mix about 1 cupful of the thickened milk mixture into the eggs. Then, while stirring the milk mixture in the pan, beat the egg–pudding mixture into the hot mixture.

Continue stirring while adding butter and vanilla extract. Stir until butter is dissolved and mixture is thickened and smooth.** Turn into a serving bowl. Cover with plastic wrap and refrigerate for at least 1 hour.***

When ready to serve, spread pear mincemeat over the surface of the pudding. Sprinkle *biscotti* or cookie crumbs over the mincemeat.

Serve at room temperature or chilled, as preferred.

Yields 6 servings
adequate for 4 people

Notes: *On very special occasions I replace the fat-free pasteurized eggs with six *organic* egg yolks.

**Occasionally, even though you are very conscientious about stirring, corn starch puddings can become lumpy. Press through a sieve into a clean saucepan and continue cooking over hot water until uniformly thickened.

***This pudding can be made, and refrigerated for up to three days, if necessary.

When required, this recipe can be doubled.

1/6 SERVING – PROTEIN = 4.1 g.; FAT = 4.9 g.; CARBOHYDRATE = 49.0 g.;
CALORIES = 253; CALORIES FROM FAT = 17%

Europe–United Kingdom–England

GINGERBREAD
TPT - 1 hour and 4 minutes;
20 minutes = cooling period

Warm gingerbread is part of growing up in America. Many children only experience real gingerbread if they are lucky enough to visit a historic colonial house where it is served. Don't disappoint your children; bake gingerbread!!

1/2 cup dark *unsulfured* molasses
3/4 cup *boiling* water
1/4 cup butter—*softened to room temperature*
1/2 teaspoon baking soda

1 cup unbleached white flour
1/2 cup whole wheat flour
1/3 cup sugar
1 1/2 teaspoons baking powder
1 1/2 teaspoons freeze-dried coffee granules
1 teaspoon ground ginger
1 teaspoon ground cinnamon
1/8 teaspoon ground cloves

1 large egg—well-beaten

Preheat oven to 350 degrees F. Prepare a 9-inch square baking pan by coating with non-stick lecithin spray coating. Dust lightly with flour.

In a large mixing bowl, combine molasses, *boiling* water, *softened* butter, and baking soda. Stir well. Set aside.

Into a large mixing bowl, sift white and whole wheat flours, sugar, baking powder, coffee granules, and ground ginger, cinnamon, and cloves.

Using an electric mixer or by hand using a wooden spoon, beat sifted dry ingredients gradually into molasses mixture. Add well-beaten egg. Beat well. Turn batter into prepared baking pan.

Bake in preheated 350 degree F. oven for 30 minutes, or until a cake tester inserted into the center comes out clean. Cool on a wire rack for at least 20 minutes.

Garnish with candied orange peel or ginger preserves and serve while slightly warm or at room temperature with:

LEMON CURD SAUCE
   [see recipe which follows],
ENGLISH TOFFEE SAUCE
   [see recipe which follows],
PINEAPPLE–LEMON SAUCE
   [see index],
CUSTARD SAUCE
   [see index],
FRESH ORANGE CUSTARD SAUCE
   [see index],
or LEMON SAUCE
   [see index].

Yields 9 servings
adequate for 6 people

1/9 SERVING (without sauce) –
PROTEIN = 3.0 g.; FAT = 5.9 g.; CARBOHYDRATE = 34.6 g.;
CALORIES = 201; CALORIES FROM FAT = 26%

LEMON CURD
TPT - 1 hour and 30 minutes;
1 hour = chilling period

Commercially-available jarred lemon curd is a travesty, an appallingly bogus substitute for the fresh lemon taste of the real thing. Fat-free pasteurized eggs do not change the taste memory from our trip to Great Britain, they just allow us to visit that memory more often. Served as a dessert or as a dessert sauce, there is nothing to equal the sensual texture of lemon, orange, or pineapple curd.

1 lemon—well-rinsed

1/2 cup *fat-free* pasteurized eggs* (the equivalent of 2 eggs)

2 tablespoons butter
3 tablespoons sugar

Grate lemon zest from lemon into the top half of a double boiler.

Juice lemon and strain through a sieve into the top half of the double boiler. Discard residue.

Pour pasteurized eggs into the top half of the double boiler set over *hot*, but *not boiling*, water. Stir in butter and sugar. Cook, stirring constantly with a wire whisk, until thickened. Remove from heat.

Divide among three *demitasse* cups. When cool, cover with plastic wrap. Refrigerate until *thoroughly chilled*—about 1 hour.

Serve with *demitasse* spoons. Accompany with SHORTBREAD petticoats, ROLLED SUGAR COOKIES *[see index]*, or other cookies, if so desired.

LEMON CURD (cont'd)

Yields 3 servings
adequate for 3 people

Notes: *Because raw eggs present the danger of *Salmonella* poisoning, commercially-available pasteurized eggs are recommended for use in preparing this dish.

This recipe may be doubled, when required.

If desired, this may be served as a LEMON CURD SAUCE with such desserts as GINGERBREAD *[see recipe which precedes]*. Additionally, you might like to try this between cake layers as a LEMON CURD CAKE FILLING or in baked tart shells for LEMON CURD TARTS.

1/3 SERVING – PROTEIN = 4.2 g.; FAT = 7.6 g.; CARBOHYDRATE = 18.8 g.;
CALORIES = 158; CALORIES FROM FAT = 43%

ENGLISH TOFFEE SAUCE

TPT - about 50 minutes;
30 minutes = cooling period

Count Carrocioli, who served as Neapolitan ambassador to London in the 18th century, appears to have had more than his fill of the, admittedly, ever-present British custard sauce and is quoted as saying "There are in England sixty different religions, and only one sauce." The dessert sauce selection in the British Isles has changed considerably since Carrocioli's visit. We like to serve this sauce with sliced bananas, ice cream, gingerbread, and over all kinds of cakes, especially as a crowning for my very favorite Lady Baltimore Cake.

3/4 cup *two-percent* milk
1/4 cup *light* brown sugar
1/3 cup butter

1/4 cup *cold* light cream *or* half and half
2 teaspoons corn starch

1/2 teaspoon pure vanilla extract
1/8 teaspoon pure almond extract

In a heavy saucepan set over *LOW* heat, or in a double boiler set over hot water, combine milk, sugar, and butter. Cook, stirring frequently, until the mixture just comes to the boil.

Combine 1/4 cupful *cold* cream with corn starch. Stir until corn starch is completely in suspension. Stir into hot mixture and, stirring constantly, cook until sauce is smooth and thickened. Remove from heat.

Stir in vanilla and almond extracts. Set aside and allow to cool at room temperature—about 30 minutes.

Yields 1 1/4 cupfuls

Note: Refrigerated leftovers can be *gently* reheated to restore desired consistency.

1/5 SERVING (i. e., per 1/4 cupful) –
PROTEIN = 1.1 g.; FAT = 12.6 g.; CARBOHYDRATE = 13.9 g.;
CALORIES = 171; CALORIES FROM FAT = 66%

YORKSHIRE SUMMER PUDDING

TPT - 24 hours and 53 minutes;
30 minutes = cooling period;
24 hours = setting period

Old-fashioned...traditional...comforting...yummy... This traditional British dessert made its way to the United States and became a standard summer dessert in years-gone-by. As I grew up, this dessert appeared with the same regularity in the spring and summer as did strawberry shortcake and was received with the same enthusiasm. We favor our maple oatmeal bread or a sweet egg bread for this dessert.

8 thin slices bread—about 1/4 inch thick—*crusts* removed*
1 tablespoon light cream, half and half, *or* whole milk, as preferred

3 cups red raspberries—fresh *or* frozen without sugar
1 cup fresh black and red currants; hulled and sliced strawberries; pitted and halved cherries; *or* blueberries—or a mixture, of choice—*well-washed* and *dried*
1 cup sugar
[see next page]

Europe–United Kingdom–England

YORKSHIRE SUMMER PUDDING (cont'd)

3 tablespoons red *or* black currant jelly**

1/4 cup *fresh* raspberries—*well-washed* and *dried*—for garnish

Sweetened whipped heavy cream—for garnish— if desired

Prepare a 1-quart mold, bowl, or "pudding basin" by coating with non-stick lecithin spray coating.

Brush bread slices lightly with cream or milk. *Do not soak bread slices.*

Fit pieces of bread into prepared mold, reserving enough to cover top of mold completely. Set aside until required.

In a saucepan set over *MEDIUM* heat, combine all berries and sugar. Cook until sugar melts and juices run. Remove from heat.

Transfer about 3 tablespoonfuls of the extruded berry juice to a small bowl. Refrigerate and reserve until required.

Add currant jelly to fruit mixture and stir until it is melted. Allow to cool, at room temperature, for 30 minutes.

Spoon fruit and remaining juice into the bread-lined mold. Cover the fruit-filled mold with the remaining bread slices. Fit a plate into the mold on top of the bread slices and place a two-pound weight on top. Refrigerate for 24 hours.

When ready to serve, unmold onto a large platter or into a large shallow bowl. *Pour the reserved juice over any areas of the bread that have not been colored by the filling.*

Serve cold with whipped cream in soup plates.

Yields 6 servings
adequate for 4 people

Notes: *There should be enough bread to line the mold and to top the mold.

**Both red and black currant jellies of excellent quality are shipped to the United States by British firms. These are usually available in food specialty stores or, often, in gift shops.

If doubled, this can be an awkward dessert. It is far better to make two molds and bring out "the second for seconds."

1/6 SERVING (exclusive of whipped cream) –
PROTEIN = 2.5 g; FAT = 0.7 g ; CARBOHYDRATE = 73.4 g;
CALORIES = 302; CALORIES FROM FAT = 2%

MY STRAWBERRY – BLUEBERRY SUMMER PUDDING
TPT - 1 hour and 8 minutes;
1 hour = maceration period

Instead of the wonderful traditional molded Yorkshire pudding that requires raspberries and currants for authenticity, I often make a modified summer pudding from strawberries and blueberries, thus beating the astronomical summer by several weeks and giving me a quickly prepared family pudding. This is also a dessert that can be adjusted for just two or three or four or five.

6 thin slices bread*—*crusts removed* and quartered into triangles
6 tablespoons light cream *or* half and half
6 tablespoons cherry juice *or* the light syrup in which cherries have been canned

2 cups well-rinsed, stemmed, and sliced fresh strawberries
1 cup well-washed and stemmed blueberries
3 tablespoons sugar
1/4 cup red *or* black currant jelly—*melted***

Sweetened whipped heavy cream—for garnish— if desired

Arrange four triangles of bread in the bottom of each of six soup plates.

Pour a tablespoonful of cream and a tablespoonful of cherry juice over the bread in each serving. Cover the plates and set aside until required.

In a mixing bowl combine sliced strawberries, blueberries, sugar, and *melted* jelly. Toss to mix well.

Cover and set aside at room temperature for 1 hour to allow fruit to macerate.

Apportion fruit on top of the bread in each of the six soup plates.

MY STRAWBERRY – BLUEBERRY SUMMER PUDDING (cont'd)

Serve, garnished with whipped cream.

Yields 6 servings
adequate for 4 people

Notes: *You may prefer white bread or a sweet egg bread but we prefer a maple multigrain bread or a barley loaf that we bake in our bread machine.

**Both red and black currant jellies of excellent quality are shipped to the United States by British firms. These are usually available in food specialty stores or, often, in gift shops.

1/6 SERVING (exclusive of whipped cream garnish) –
PROTEIN = 2.7 g; FAT = 1.9 g; CARBOHYDRATE = 44.0 g;
CALORIES = 198; CALORIES FROM FAT = 9%

ENGLISH STEWED RHUBARB

TPT - 1 hour and 15 minutes;
1 hour = chilling period

Rhubarb, of course, is a vegetable but one that is used in the American diet as a fruit. Therefore, we have collected it with fruit recipes for menu convenience. Tomatoes, on the other hand, although botanically classified as fruits, are used principally as vegetables in cooking. Anyway, for those who love rhubarb as I do, this is spring! Canadians add orange juice to this basic recipe.

**2 pounds young rhubarb—cut into 3/4-inch pieces
  to yield about 4 cupfuls
1/2 cup sugar
1/2 cup water
Thin lemon slice**

In a large kettle, with cover, combine all ingredients. Bring to the boil over *MEDIUM* heat. Reduce heat to *LOW* and simmer, *tightly covered,* for about 7 minutes, or until *tender,* but *not mushy.* Stir occasionally. Remove from heat. Remove and discard lemon slice.

Refrigerate until completely cooled, at least 1 hour.

Turn into serving dish or into individual sherbet glasses. Serve plain or with light cream or half and half, if desired. This is also a very pleasant spread for toast.

Yields about 3 cupfuls
adequate for 4 people

Notes: Rhubarb freezes so easily that we secret a store throughout the spring and early summer. Simply remove and discard leaves, which incidentally are poisonous, and any tough strands or "strings." Wash and dry stems thoroughly. Chop into 3/4-inch pieces. Bag in freezer bags, label, and freeze.

Stewed rhubarb may also be frozen but its consistency after freezing is more that of a sauce. However, it is a delightful sauce when served as such.

This recipe is easily increased or decreased proportionately, when required.

1/4 SERVING – PROTEIN = 0.8 g.; FAT = 0.1 g.; CARBOHYDRATE = 32.5 g.;
CALORIES = 140; CALORIES FROM FAT = trace only

WHOLE WHEAT HOT CROSS BUNS

TPT - about 2 hours and 43 minutes;
1 hour = first rising period;
30 minutes = second rising period;
20 minutes = cooling period

Hot cross buns originated in the pre-Christian period, long before anyone ever thought up the ecclesiastical season of Lent. These simple buns were baked by the ancient Britons, Romans, and Greeks. Although they are typically square today, they were round, a shape which represented the source of life, the sun. The cross dividing the bun surface into four even sections then represented either the four seasons, according to some historians, or possibly the four phases of the moon, as alleged by others. Even after they became a Lenten fast-breaking treat, they were credited with magical powers and thought to ward off disasters so they were available in bakeries year round. It was not until the fourteenth century that they became closely associated with Christian religious rituals and that was through the efforts of the monks in an abbey in England who used leftover dough from the baking of the sacramental bread to bake such buns for the poor who came to the abbey door.

Europe–United Kingdom–England

WHOLE WHEAT HOT CROSS BUNS (cont'd)

2/3 cup skimmed milk

1/4 cup *warm* water (105-110 degrees F.)
Pinch sugar
2 tablespoons (2 envelopes) *preservative-free* active dry yeast*
3 tablespoons sugar
1/2 cup butter—*softened to room temperature*
3/4 cup *fat-free* pasteurized eggs (the equivalent of 3 eggs)
1 cup whole wheat flour
2/3 cup *preservative-free* dried currants
1/4 cup *preservative-free* candied mixed fruit peel *or* citron
1/2 teaspoon ground cinnamon

1 cup whole wheat flour
2 cups unbleached white flour

Additional flour, as required for kneading

1 egg white well-beaten

About 1 tablespoon skimmed milk
1/2 cup confectioners' sugar
4 drops pure vanilla extract

Prepare a large bowl by *lightly*, but *thoroughly*, oiling. Prepare a cookie sheet by coating with non-stick lecithin spray coating.

In a small saucepan set over *MEDIUM* heat, scald milk. Remove from heat and allow to cool until lukewarm to the touch.

In a small bowl, combine warm water and the pinch of sugar. Sprinkle dry yeast over and allow to proof.

Into a large mixing bowl, pour the lukewarm milk. Using a wooden spoon, stir in the 3 tablespoonfuls sugar, *softened* butter, pasteurized eggs, and 1 cupful whole wheat flour. Stir to combine well. Stir in proofed yeast, currants, citron, and cinnamon.

When well-combined, gradually beat in remaining 1 cupful whole wheat and white flours. Turn out onto lightly floured surface and knead lightly until dough can be gathered into a ball. Dough should be softer than bread dough so *do not knead out all stickiness.*

Place in oiled bowl. Turn to coat all sides with oil. Cover bowl with plastic wrap and a cotton tea towel and allow to rise in a draft-free, warm (75-80 degree F.) place until doubled in bulk—about 1 hour.

Turn dough out onto floured surface. Knead gently, adding additional flour if dough is too sticky to handle.**

Roll dough out to 3/4-inch thickness. Cut out buns using a floured 3-inch biscuit cutter. Square off into buns and place side-by-side, but *not tightly against each other,* in several rows on prepared cookie sheet.

Brush buns with beaten egg white and allow to rise for about 30 minutes in warm, draft-free place until puffy.

Little-by-little, mix milk with confectioners' sugar and vanilla extract to form a thin frosting. Set aside until required.

Preheat oven to 350 degrees F.

Bake risen buns for about 15 minutes, or until *golden brown.* Remove to a wire rack set over a large piece of waxed paper and allow to cool for at least 20 minutes.

Using a pastry bag with a plain tip or a carefully controlled spoon, drizzle frosting over buns to form a cross on each, dividing the bun's surface into four equal quadrants.

Yields 16 large buns

Notes: *Some packaged dried yeast available in grocery stores contain a preservative. Natural food stores carry an additive-free dried yeast.

**Dough may be frozen most successfully at this point, divided into quantities sufficient for your needs. Allow to defrost in the refrigerator for about 5-8 hours or overnight. Roll out dough and proceed as above. This convenient method makes it easy to have hot, fresh buns for breakfast without much work at all.

These buns are really at their best when freshly baked. However, leftover and frozen or day-old buns may be warmed to near first-day freshness if crosses are eliminated. A Chinese bamboo steamer is ideal for this purpose.

1/16 SERVING (i. e., per bun)
PROTEIN = 5.8 g., FAT = 6.3 g., CARBOHYDRATE = 39.5 g.;
CALORIES = 238; CALORIES FROM FAT = 24%

Europe–United Kingdom–Scotland

Scotland

I am, proudly, of Scottish descent, from the Clan Taylor (*Clann an Taillear Dibh Chamronach*) a sept of Clan Cameron. I have visited Scotland; I have walked at the top of the world in the remarkable Highlands; I have, of course, *seen* Nessie; but I have not eaten haggis and that is how it will stay, no matter that some have evolved a "vegetarian haggis."

Although confirmation of very early occupation of the land we know as Scotland was erased by the frequent advances and retreats of the glacial mass during and after the Pleistocene period, it is known that about 12,800 years ago hunter-gathers arrived. Village settlement dates back over 6,000 years and evidence of habitation can be dated back 9,500 years. The clan structure descends from the tribes of Caledonia, the Picts, who formed a union in the sixth century known as the Kingdom of the Picts, literally the "land of the painted people," in opposition to the Roman advance into the land that we know as Scotland. Little is really known about the Picts but much has been romantically fabricated in film and fiction. The Vikings came and went and in their wake the Picts declined to obscurity. By the tenth century this kingdom was infused with Gaelic culture.

True, the traditional foods of Scotland reflect a frugality, not of spirit but of resources—the seasons of the hunt and the seasons of the harvest. The ways of the hunter-gather are still alive and well in Scotland. Breakfasts are hearty; lunches and suppers are generally light, with suppers often little more than tea and a cold plate. We found that a substantial Scottish breakfast could carry us to the middle of the afternoon without even a desire for a snack or a noon meal.

Red Pottage

Oat Scones **Ginger Scones**

English Cream

~ ~ ~ ~ ~ ~ ~ ~ ~ ~ ~ ~ ~ ~ ~ ~ ~ ~ ~ ~

Barley with Wild Mushrooms and Sage

Sautéed Soy Sausages

Sautéed Leeks and Baby Carrots with Celery Sauce and "Curvies"

or

Freshly Shelled Green Peas, *in season*

~ ~ ~ ~ ~ ~ ~ ~ ~ ~ ~ ~ ~ ~ ~ ~ ~ ~ ~ ~

Compote of Chopped Pears and Stewed Prunes

with

Rum Cream from Caledonia

or

Citrus and Honey Sauce

Oatmeal Lace Cookies

Europe–United Kingdom–Scotland

SCOTTISH RED POTTAGE
TPT - 1 hour

Lunch in a small cafeteria in Inverness included a soup called "red pottage." It was a cool, rainy August morning and the warmth was welcome. They assured us that the soup was not made with chicken or meat stock and was I ever glad that I had opted for it because it was delicious. My mother, who was traveling with us, commented that it just looked like tomato soup. It certainly was not "just tomato soup;" it was wonderfully complex. I puzzled and could not figure out what was in the soup and was delighted when they graciously shared the list of vegetables with me. This soup is the result of the notes I jotted down and it never ceases to transport me back to that summer on the loch.

A similar soup is made in Scotland, not with kidney beans but, with red lentils. Either is a great choice a soup-and-salad meal.

2 tablespoons butter
1/2 cup chopped onion
1 large stalk celery—chopped

1 can (15 ounces) red kidney beans—*well-drained*— or cooked, dried red kidney beans, if preferred
1 can (28 ounces) diced tomatoes in tomato purée*
1 medium *raw* beet—peeled and diced
6 cups water
1/2 teaspoon paprika
1 large bay leaf—broken in half

Salt, to taste
Freshly ground black pepper, to taste

Set a sieve over a clean saucepan. Set aside until required.

In a kettle set over *MEDIUM* heat, heat butter. Add chopped onion and celery. Sauté until vegetables are soft, *being careful not to allow either vegetable to brown*.

Add well-drained kidney beans, tomatoes with purée in which they were canned, diced beet, water, paprika, and bay leaf pieces. Stir to combine well. Allow to come to the boil. Reduced heat to *LOW-MEDIUM* and simmer for about 30 minutes.

Using an electric blender or food processor fitted with steel knife, purée soup mixture a cup or two at a time. Pour the purée into the sieve set over the clean saucepan. Place over *MEDIUM* heat to reheat. Discard residue in sieve or save for soup stock.

Season to taste with salt and black pepper.

When soup has reheated, turn into a heated soup tureen.

Serve into heated soup plates.

Yields about 13 cupfuls

Notes: *Although I am tempted to make this with fresh summer tomatoes, the tomatoes canned in purée give the soup significant body.

The puréed soup freezes well.

1/13 SERVING (i. e., per cupful) –
PROTEIN = 2.8 g.; FAT = 1.9 g.; CARBOHYDRATE = 10.6 g.;
CALORIES = 68; CALORIES FROM FAT = 25%

SCOTTISH OAT SCONES
TPT - 29 minutes

. . . classic and comforting!! There is almost nothing on Earth as delicious as fresh-baked oat scones.

3/4 cup unbleached white flour
1/4 cup whole wheat flour
1 cup *old-fashioned* rolled oats
1/2 teaspoon baking soda
1 teaspoon cream of tartar
2 teaspoons sugar

1/4 cup *cold* butter—diced

1/2 cup skimmed milk

VOLUME I - 449

Europe – United Kingdom – Scotland

SCOTTISH OAT SCONES (cont'd)

Preheat oven to 400 degrees F. Prepare a cookie sheet by coating with non-stick lecithin spray coating.

In the work bowl of the food processor, fitted with steel knife, combine white and whole wheat flours, rolled oats, baking soda, cream of tartar, and sugar.* *Pulse on and off* several times to combine well. Add diced *cold* butter and *pulse on and off* several times until of the consistency of coarse corn meal. Turn mixture into a large mixing bowl.

Add milk, and, using a fork, stir the liquid into the flour mixture until a soft dough is formed.

Turn out onto a lightly floured surface. Turn dough to coat with flour. Using a rolling pin, roll dough out into a rectangle about 4 x 10-inches by and to a thickness of about 3/4 inch. Cut into wedges and place on prepared cookie sheet. Bake in preheated 400 degree F. oven for about 12-15 minutes, or until *golden brown*.

Serve warm with butter or ENGLISH CREAM *[see recipe which follows]*, if preferred.

Yields 8 scones
adequate for 4 people

Notes: *If a food processor is not available, the dough may be prepared by hand. Using a pastry blender, work *cold* butter into dry ingredients until mixture is of the consistency of coarse corn meal. Using a spoon, combine thoroughly. Add milk and stir until a soft dough is formed. Then proceed as above.

**Do not overwork the dough or allow the butter to melt.* The texture of the resulting baked product will be disappointing.

This recipe is easily doubled or halved, when required.

1/8 SERVING (i. e., per scone) –
PROTEIN = 4.1 g.; FAT = 6.9 g.; CARBOHYDRATE = 22.2 g.;
CALORIES = 167; CALORIES FROM FAT = 37%

SCOTTISH GINGER BUTTERMILK SCONES
TPT - 45 minutes

These are more refined, less traditional Scottish scones. They are, however, every bit as wonderful as oat scones and add something very special to a brunch menu.

1 large egg
3/4 cup *unsalted* cultured buttermilk

1 1/4 cups unbleached white flour
3/4 cup whole wheat flour
3 tablespoons sugar
2 1/2 teaspoons baking powder
2 teaspoons ground ginger
1/2 teaspoon baking soda

1/2 cup (1 stick) *cold* butter

2 tablespoons freshly grated orange zest

2 tablespoons sugar

Preheat oven to 400 degrees F. Prepare cookie sheets by coating with non-stick lecithin spray coating.

In a small bowl or measuring cup, using a fork, beat egg until thick and lemony. Add *unsalted* buttermilk. Stir to combine well. Set aside.

In the work bowl of the food processor, fitted with steel knife, combine white and whole wheat flours, sugar, baking powder, ground ginger, and baking soda.* *Pulse on and off* several times to combine well. Add diced *cold* butter and *pulse on and off* several times until of the consistency of coarse corn meal. Turn mixture into a large mixing bowl.**

Add blended egg and buttermilk with grated orange zest and, using a fork, stir the liquid into the flour mixture until a soft dough is formed.***

Divide dough in half. Turn each onto a well-floured surface. Knead lightly. Press into a circle about 3/4 inch thick. Using a floured sharp knife, cut each round into six wedges. Press 1/2 teaspoonful of sugar gently into the top of each wedge.

Place the twelve wedges onto prepared cookie sheets.

SCOTTISH GINGER BUTTERMILK SCONES (cont'd)

Bake in preheated 400 degree F. oven for about 14 minutes, or until *lightly browned*. If more than one cookie sheet is used, *bake one batch at a time.*

Serve warm with sweet *(unsalted)* butter, and jam, jelly, marmalade, honey, or ENGLISH CREAM *[see recipe which follows]*, as preferred.

Yields 12 scones
adequate for 6 people

Notes: *If a food processor is not available, the dough may be prepared by hand. Using a pastry blender, work *cold* butter into dry ingredients until mixture is of the consistency of coarse corn meal. Using a spoon, combine thoroughly. Add blended egg and buttermilk and stir until a soft dough is formed. Then proceed as above.

**If convenient, this recipe may be prepared to this point the night before, covered, and refrigerated.

***Do not overwork the dough or allow the butter to melt.* The texture of the resulting baked product will be ruined.

This recipe may be halved, when required.

Although these scones may be frozen, when reheated, they are not nearly as wonderful as when they are freshly prepared!

1/12 SERVING (i. e., per scone) –
PROTEIN = 3.4 g.; FAT = 8.3 g.; CARBOHYDRATE = 22.0 g.;
CALORIES = 174; CALORIES FROM FAT = 43%

ENGLISH CREAM
TPT - 5 minutes

The English, and those who have visited the British Isles, treasure the taste of Devonshire cream or clotted cream, the very thick sweet cream made from the top milk of milk which has not been homogenized. It is delicious as a topping for fruits and desserts, as a filling for pastries, and as a spread for breads and scones. It is rarely available fresh in the United States and the jarred version, in our opinion, is very disappointing, if you have tasted the real thing. The following recipe has the fresh sweet dairy taste one expects. Although not authentic clotted cream, it is a pleasant substitute and the lowered fat is an obvious bonus.

3 tablespoons heavy whipping cream
1 1/2 tablespoons confectioners' sugar

1/2 cup YOGURT *CRÈME* [see index]
1/4 teaspoon pure vanilla extract

Using an electric mixer fitted with *chilled* beaters, or by hand using a *chilled* wire whisk, beat heavy cream in a *chilled* mixing bowl until soft peaks form. Add confectioners' sugar and continue beating until stiff.

Using a rubber spatula or a flat mixer attachment, *carefully*, but *thoroughly*, fold YOGURT *CRÈME* and vanilla extract into stiffly beaten cream.

Turn into serving bowl and chill until required. Serve with scones, unfrosted tea cakes, muffins, sweet breads, or fruits.

Yields about 3/4 cupful

Notes: Fat-free dairy sour cream may be substituted for the YOGURT *CRÈME*, if desired.

This recipe may be doubled, when required.

1/12 SERVING – PROTEIN = 1.5 g.; FAT = 1.3 g.; CARBOHYDRATE = 3.4 g.;
CALORIES = 23; CALORIES FROM FAT = 51%

Europe–United Kingdom–Scotland

SCOTTISH BARLEY WITH WILD MUSHROOMS AND SAGE

TPT - 3 hours and 25 minutes;
2 hours = mushroom soaking period;
2 hours = barley soaking period

Most Scottish cookbooks and those who post family recipes on the internet seem to omit this recipe with considerable more emphasis on oats choosing to relegate barley to malt brewing and cattle feed. Even in the United States, barley, over half of which is used for animal feed, takes a backseat to other grains. Barley is one of the earliest cereal grains to be cultivated by man, documented back to the Stone Age in Europe. Its reliability season to season, its annual rebirth if you will, seems to have been used by both the cults of Osiris in Egypt and Demeter in Greece as support for and a celebratory example of resurrection. We enjoy this dish year after year, season after season. Since barley contains all eight amino acids, it, like soybeans, does not need to be complemented in vegetarian dishes such as this one although, on occasion, we expand leftovers not with potatoes as is common in Eastern Europe, but with chick peas.

A similar recipe is popular in the Maritime Provinces of Eastern Canada, no doubt, brought in the recipe collections of those who traveled from the British Isles and settled in Nova Scotia or carried by loyalists from Long Island and other areas of the Colonies who fled to Nova Scotia with the patriot victory in the American Revolution.

1 cup dry pearl barley*
2 cups water

3 cups assorted *dried* wild mushrooms—well-brushed and rinsed**
5 cups *boiling* water

1 tablespoon *extra virgin* olive oil
1 medium onion—*finely* chopped

3 tablespoons *finely* chopped fresh sage***

1/3 cup grated *pecorino Romano or* Parmesan cheese, as preferred
1 tablespoon butter—*melted*
Freshly ground black pepper, to taste

In a bowl, combine *dry* barley and the 2 cupfuls water. Allow to stand at room temperature for 2 hours. Drain.

Put *dried* mushrooms into a second bowl. Pour *boiling* water over. Set a bowl down into the mushrooms to hold them under the water. Allow to stand at room temperature for 2 hours. Drain, reserving the soaking liquid.

Turn mushroom soaking liquid (WILD MUSHROOM STOCK) into a saucepan set over *MEDIUM* heat. Allow to heat until required.

In a Dutch oven or large, heavy saucepan, set over *MEDIUM* heat, sauté chopped onion in the olive oil until onion is soft and translucent, *being careful to allow neither the onion nor garlic to brown.*

Add mushrooms and 1/2 cup of hot WILD MUSHROOM STOCK. Cook, stirring constantly until the mushrooms are soft and browned—about 7 minutes.

Add drained barley and *finely* chopped sage plus about 2 cupfuls of mushroom soaking liquid (WILD MUSHROOM STOCK). While stirring frequently, allow to heat almost to the boil. Reduce heat to *LOW*, cover, and simmer for about 30 minutes. Continue to simmer until the barley is tender and most of the liquid has been absorbed—about 20 minutes more. Remove from heat.

Add grated cheese, *melted* butter, and black pepper. Stir *gently* to integrate. Turn into a heated serving bowl.

Keep warm on warming tray until ready to serve.

Yields 8 servings
adequate for 4-6 people

Notes: *Quick-cooking barley *can not* be substituted in this recipe.

**Including a variety of mushrooms, such as *shiitake*, button, *crimini*, oyster, and/or portobello, adds interest to this dish.

***Although we can even dig down under a coat of snow and find sage leaves in our herb garden, crumbled, dried sage leaves, not powdered sage, can be substituted if the snow is too deep.

This recipe may be halved or doubled, when required.

1/8 SERVING – PROTEIN = 3.9 g.; FAT = 4.1 g.; CARBOHYDRATE = 24.0 g.;
CALORIES = 145; CALORIES FROM FAT = 25%

Europe–United Kingdom–Scotland

SAUTÉED LEEKS AND BABY CARROTS WITH CELERY SAUCE AND "CURVIES"

TPT - 1 hour and 4 minutes

To look at the cookbooks and articles written, you'd think there were no vegetables other than stovies and neps served in the whole of Scotland.

1 cup water
3 stalks celery—trimmed, fibers removed, and diced

2 quarts *boiling* water
24 baby carrots uniform in size

1 tablespoon butter
1 teaspoon *extra virgin* olive oil

3 large leeks—*very well-washed*

3/4 cup *whole* milk*

1 tablespoon butter
2 tablespoons *whole* wheat flour *or* unbleached white flour, if preferred
Freshly ground black pepper, to taste

1/2 teaspoon caraway seeds

In a saucepan with cover, bring water to the boil. Add chopped celery and cook, covered, until *tender*—about 15 minutes. Drain, reserving liquid from celery for sauce.

In a second saucepan set over *MEDIUM* heat, parboil the carrots for about 8 minutes in *boiling* water. Drain.

Trim the tops and root ends from the leeks. Cut the white portion of the leeks into 1/2-inch slices. Wash well in several changes of water to remove all sand.

In a skillet set over *LOW* heat, combine 1 tablespoonful butter and 1 teaspoonful olive oil. Add sliced and well-washed leeks and par-boiled carrots. Allow to cook until leeks are wilted.

While vegetables are cooking, combine celery water with whole milk to yield 1 cupful of liquid. Set aside briefly.

In a saucepan set over *LOW* heat, melt butter. Remove from heat and, using a wire whisk, make a *roux* by beating in flour. Return to heat and, stirring constantly, cook for 2 minutes, *being careful not to burn or overbrown the roux*. Remove from heat and gradually beat in the 1 cupful liquid composed of mixture of milk and celery cooking water. Return to saucepan to heat and cook, stirring constantly, until thickened.

Add cooked celery. Turn into a heated sauceboat. Keep warm on a warming tray until vegetables are ready to sauce.

Turn cooked leeks and carrots into a heated serving dish. Sprinkle caraway seeds ("*curvies*") over. Spoon several tablespoons of sauce over the vegetables.

Serve at once, accompanied by the sauceboat of celery sauce to accommodate individual tastes.

Yields 6 servings
adequate for 4-6 people

Notes: This recipe can be halved, when required.

By the way, this celery sauce is delicious over "*stovies*" too.

1/6 SERVING – PROTEIN = 3.9 g.; FAT = 5.6 g.; CARBOHYDRATE = 10.6 g.;
CALORIES = 93; CALORIES FROM FAT = 54%

Europe–United Kingdom–Scotland

SCOTTISH RUM CREAM FROM CALEDONIA
TPT - 5 minutes

Some say that the long limbs and red hair used to describe the Caledonians suggests a Teutonic or Germanic or Norse origin. With all the comings and goings in the land that became known as Alba or Scotland, it is not surprising. Caledonia is the Roman name for the area of Scotland north of the Firths of Clyde and Forth, home of the Pictish tribe, the "Caledonii"— into which sailed many invaders and from which sailed the great ships built in the shipyards of the firths. My most intense memory of that part of Scotland is watching a cricket match from the window of my B and B. It was summer and the "permanent dusk" at the summer solstice allowed the game to continue well after 11 PM with the light still sparkling on the firth beyond.

I would be remiss not to mention the phenomenon which is Dundee orange marmalade, sold by the firm of James Keiller & Son which was established in 1897. Made from Seville oranges, Mrs. James Keiller is said to have invented the marmalade that has no peer. I bought Dundee marmalades in Harrods for 42 pence a jar in 1983 and weighted down our luggage considerably only to arrive home to find that a local store was now selling my beloved marmalade. I have always countered the continued heavy luggage jibs by reminding everyone that the marmalade was $2.50 a jar in my store. This is a divine sauce that can be made with brandy, if preferred, but Scottish marmalade is the only marmalade to use. We serve it as an adornment for desserts as mundane as baked or stewed apples, stewed prunes, chopped compotes of citrus fruits, and pound cake and it the perfect topping for Scottish crumpets, which are truly ethereal crêpes, unlike the English tea crumpet. Trust me, these dessert suggestions are far from mundane with this sauce.

3 ounces *fat-free* cream cheese
2 tablespoons heavy cream
1 tablespoon light cream *or* half and half
1 tablespoon Scottish marmalade
1 tablespoon rum *or* brandy
1 teaspoon lemon juice
1 1/2 tablespoons sugar

Combine cream cheese, heavy and light cream, marmalade, rum, lemon juice, and sugar in the work bowl of the food processor filled with steel knife. Process until smooth, scraping down the sides of the bowl as required. Turn into a serving dish.

Cover leftovers and store in the refrigerator.

Yields about 11 tablespoonfuls

Note: This recipe can be doubled, when required.

1/7 SERVING (about 1 1/2 tablespoonfuls) –
PROTEIN = 2.0 g.; FAT = 2.9 g.; CARBOHYDRATE = 6.1 g.;
CALORIES = 59; CALORIES FROM FAT = 44%

SCOTTISH CITRUS AND HONEY SAUCE
TPT - 43 minutes

A Mesolithic rock drawing in Valencia, Spain, clearly shows that people 10,000 years ago collected honey from wild bees so should we be surprised to find a traditional sauce with honey in this oh so ancient land. We are fortunate to have an apiary near us, fortunate in that we enjoy his wildflower honey and fortunate in that his bees visit out gardens on their rounds each day and in so doing pollinate our plants in return for that which they gather. How long has man had such an arrangement with these industrious insects? How long will he have such an arrangement if we continue to use pesticides and herbicides?

Scots serve this sauce over puddings, pancakes, and fruits; my dad loved it with a jelly omelet and I enjoy it over ricotta cheese for dessert. When I am in the mood, I make it and it is there in the refrigerator when I need it.

SCOTTISH CITRUS AND HONEY SAUCE (cont'd)

1/2 cup wildflower honey *or* heather honey, if available
1/2 cup plus 1 tablespoon water

1 tablespoon freshly squeezed orange juice
1 tablespoon freshly squeezed lemon juice
1/2 teaspoon freshly grated *organic* orange zest
1/2 teaspoon freshly grated *organic* lemon zest
1 teaspoon butter

2 tablespoons *fat-free* pasteurized eggs

Sterilize a pint canning jar. Also sterilize a lid and a ring for the jar.

Bring water to the simmer in the bottom half of a double boiler set over *MEDIUM* heat.

In the top half of the double boiler, combine honey and water. Using a wire whisk, combine thoroughly.

Add orange and lemon juice, orange and lemon zest, and butter. Using the wire whisk, again combine thoroughly.

Add pasteurized eggs and whisk thoroughly. Set over simmering water and cook, stirring frequently, until thickened—about 20 minutes.

Ladle into the hot, sterilized canning jar. Carefully wipe lip of jar. Seal with hot, sterilized lid and ring. Refrigerate.

Yields about 1 cupful

Note: This recipe can be doubled, when required.

1/8 SERVING (about 2 tablespoonfuls) –
PROTEIN = 0.6 g.; FAT = 0.5 g.; CARBOHYDRATE = 17.0 g.;
CALORIES = 69; CALORIES FROM FAT = 7%

SCOTTISH OATMEAL LACE COOKIES
Haureflarn
TPT - 50 minutes

These are somewhat tedious cookies to make and they must be stored carefully with waxed paper between the layers, but, at the same time, they are fun to make and any broken cookies or crumbs make a fine topping for ice cream, puddings, custards, or even stewed fruit. If shaped when they are still hot and flexible, oatmeal lace baskets may be formed by pressing the cookies into a muffin tin. These make a lovely presentation when filled with ice cream or sherbet.

3/4 cup quick-cooking rolled oats *(not instant)*
3 tablespoons sugar
3 tablespoons unbleached white flour
2 tablespoons whole wheat flour
1/4 teaspoon baking powder

6 tablespoons butter—*melted*
2 tablespoons skimmed milk
2 tablespoons *light* corn syrup

Preheat oven to 325 degrees F.

In a mixing bowl, combine oats, sugar, white and whole wheat flours and baking powder. Stir to mix well.

Add *melted* butter, milk, and corn syrup. Combine thoroughly.

Drop by level tablespoonfuls on an *ungreased* baking sheet, leaving plenty of space between each cookie. (Four or five cookies per cookie sheet are sufficient.)

Bake in preheated 325 degree F. oven for 6 minutes, or until *lightly browned around edges*. Remove cookie sheet from oven and place on top of stove for about a minute or two before *carefully* removing cookies to wire rack to cool completely.

Carefully transfer cookies to a flat basket or plate, lined with a lace doily, to serve.

Yields 16 cookies

Note: This recipe may be halved or doubled, when required.

1/16 SERVING (i. e., per cookie) –
PROTEIN = 1.1 g.; FAT = 4.7 g.; CARBOHYDRATE = 9.8 g.;
CALORIES = 85; CALORIES FROM FAT = 50%

Wales

Because Wales was free of the glaciation of the last ice age between 12,000-10,000 BC, it has been continually inhabited by *homo sapiens* for at least 29,000 years. *Cymru*, Wales, is considered to be one of the Seven Celtic Nations. The word nation suggests a more formal confederation than the more probable tribal structure. Nevertheless, the Celtic tribes swept across Europe, dominating what we know as Europe from Ireland in the west to Spain and even Turkey in the east, sometimes called the "Celt Belt" or the "Celtic Crescent," until Germanic and Roman periods of invasion and dominance changed the face of Europe forever. Celtic influences are still strong in many of the nations once in the Celtic sphere and the relationship of the peoples that comprised this loose federation is still evident.

The Welsh national identity can be traced to the fifth century after the Romans withdrew from Britain. The Anglicized name Wales actually comes from the Germanic word *Wahl* (*Waelisc*) which designates foreigners who have been Romanized. Conquered by Edward I after his defeat at Llewelyn in 1282, Wales began centuries of English occupation. Wales was incorporated into England with the Laws in Wales Acts 1535-1542. It was not until 1955 that Wales declared Cardiff its capital city.

If you have ever visited Wales, you know that it is different from the rest of the British Isles; that it is a country where people do not just live, they survive with courage; and that it is country of fiercely independent, nationalistic, and proud people. The mountains of gray slag will for always be in my memory. They are not just the residue from mining operations, they are the residue of lives, hard lived.

We were warmly welcomed to *Cymru*, Cumbric for "land of comrades," by a Welsh family with whom we stayed near Cardiff. They in no way had accepted the fact that Wales was part of Great Britain other than the fact that they were bilingual which made it a whole lot easier for us. One son in the family was, at that time, studying at a Welsh college where all instruction was in Welsh. This family very proudly personified the Welsh drive for preservation of heritage and customs.

Although eighty percent of the land of Wales is designated agricultural, most of this consists of grazing land for herd animals. We observed large herds of sheep, correlating to the number of lamb dishes we found on menus, but we did also see many dairy cows, whose milk and cheese were, gratifyingly, found on the same menus. We bypassed *selsig morgannwg*, known as *glamorgan* sausage, the first time we encountered it. Once the vegetarian "sausage," made from cheese, eggs, and breadcrumbs, was explained to us and once we tasted it, we went out of our way to seek them out since no two cooks seem to have the same recipe.

Europe–United Kingdom–Wales

True and Ancient Welsh Rabbit (Rarebit), or Roasted Cheese
Caws Pobi

~

Potato and Watercress Soup with Herbs
Cawl Berw Dwr â Thatws

Lettuce Soup
Cawl Letysen

~~~~~~~~~~~~~~~~~~~~~~

***Glamorgan* Sausages**
Selsig Morgannwg

Sautéed Leeks in Creamy Orange Sauce
Cennin Mewn Saws Oren

Steamed Root Vegetables Julienne

~~~~~~~~~~~~~~~~~~~~~~

Yogurt *Crème* with Sweet Oatmeal Topping
Yoghurt Blawd Ceirch

Fresh Mixed Berries

TRUE AND ANCIENT WELSH RABBIT (RAREBIT) or ROASTED CHEESE
Caws Pobi

TPT - 8 minutes

In Wales, as throughout Great Britain, savories are often served after the main course, sometimes altogether replacing a sweet dessert. On the other hand, in the United States this might well be served as an appetizer.

8 slices crisp, *unbuttered, whole wheat* toast
—bread slices should be quite thin

1/2 pound *Caerphilly* cheese, if available—if not, a *mild* Cheddar cheese will do—sliced into 8 slices*

Set two slices of toast on each of four *warmed* plates. Place on a warming tray or in an oven set at *WARM*.

Set a non-stick-coated griddle or large skillet over *MEDIUM* heat. When hot, place cheese slices on the hot surface. Turn to toast both sides, allowing each slice to toast only until heated through. *Cheese should be heated to the point of just melting but the slice should not be oozing.*

Transfer a slice of roasted cheese onto a slice of toast.

Serve at once, with a knife and fork as an appetizer, light supper or luncheon main course.

Yields 4 servings**

Notes: *Low-fat Cheddar cheese varieties are widely available but they vary considerably in taste and texture. Most, that we have tried, are not suitable for this recipe because they do not melt well.

VOLUME I - 457

TRUE AND ANCIENT WELSH RABBIT (RAREBIT) (cont'd)

**If served as a savory or as an appetizer, this recipe would be quite adequate for eight people.

This recipe may be halved or doubled, when required.

1/8 SERVING – PROTEIN = 14.0 g.; FAT = 18.7 g.; CARBOHYDRATE = 26.0 g.; CALORIES = 348; CALORIES FROM FAT = 48%

WELSH POTATO AND WATERCRESS SOUP WITH HERBS
Cawl Berw Dwr â Thatws

TPT - 1 hour and 12 minutes

One of the joys of the British Isles is the watercress that suddenly appears in the spring at the foot of small waterfalls and along the shores of streams. It, at once, delights and shocks the taste buds after the long winter. Ladies can be seen, scissors in hand, searching along a stream embankment just as spring brings out the scissor-armed dandelion aficionados in Italy and on Long Island too. Watercress, as used in this recipe, can make a "from-the-residuals-in-the-root-cellar" soup base really sing. Instead of the traditional bouquet garni that is used to flavor this soup, I add fresh herbs from my garden or a mixture of dried herbs in the winter.

1 tablespoon butter
1/2 cup chopped onion

2 large potatoes—peeled and diced to yield about 3 cupfuls
2 cups watercress leaves—well-washed
1 tablespoon fresh lemon thyme *or* **1 teaspoon dried, crushed thyme**
1 tablespoon *fresh or frozen* **parsley*** *or* **2 teaspoons dried, crushed parsley**
1 tablespoon dried winter savory needles
2 small fresh *or* **dried sage leaves**
A sprig of celery leaves
A sprig of winter savory
5 1/2 cups VEGETARIAN BROWN STOCK *[see index]* **or VEGETABLE STOCK FROM SOUP** *[see index]*
1/2 teaspoon salt, or to taste

Pinch freshly grated nutmeg
Freshly ground black pepper, to taste

2 tablespoon light cream *or* **half and half, for garnish**

In a kettle set over *LOW-MEDIUM* heat, melt butter. Add chopped onion. Sauté until the onion is soft and translucent, *being careful not to allow onion to brown.*

Add chopped potatoes, well-washed watercress, thyme, parsley, sage, celery leaves, winter savory, vegetable stock, and salt. Increase the heat to *MEDIUM-HIGH* and allow to come to the boil. *Reduce the heat to LOW-MEDIUM again immediately.* Cover and allow to simmer for about 45 minutes, or until all the vegetables are soft. Stir occasionally. Remove from heat and allow the soup to cool slightly.

Purée the soup in batches using the electric blender. Purée thoroughly until *very smooth.* Set a fine sieve over a clean kettle or large saucepan and press the purée through the sieve.** Discard residue or freeze and add to vegetables for soup stock. Set sieved, puréed mixture over *LOW-MEDIUM* heat and allow to heat through. Season with nutmeg and pepper to taste. Transfer to a heated soup tureen.

Serve into heated soup bowls or mugs. Using a spoon, garnish each serving with a spoonful of cream swirled on top of the serving.

Yields 6 cupfuls

**WELSH POTATO AND WATERCRESS SOUP
WITH HERBS** (cont'd)

Notes: *When our parsley plants are huge and green and full of summer goodness, we harvest, wash and dry and freeze the florets in plastic containers for the winter. Granted, you can not garnish with the frozen florets but the flavor of the parsley that has been frozen is infinitely superior to that of dried parsley.

**A FOOD MILL, if you have one, is very useful at this stage.

This recipe can be doubled and since the puréed soup freezes well, we generally double this recipe. It can also be halved, when required.

1/6 SERVING (i. e., per cupful) –
PROTEIN = 1.5 g.; FAT = 2.4 g.; CARBOHYDRATE = 12.6 g.;
CALORIES = 79; CALORIES FROM FAT = 27%

WELSH LETTUCE SOUP
Cawl Letysen
TPT - 46 minutes

The first time I had this soup, I must admit that I did not expect the lettuce to be flavorful enough but I was surprised at the subtle pleasure of the taste. I do not recommend this soup as a winter soup when the prices are astronomical but in the summer, when the garden gives and gives and gives, a mug of this soup is a pleasant choice for a cool evening. I prefer to use romaine lettuce but any lettuce will do if you find a blessing of excess in your kitchen garden. As my grandmother always said, "It's amazing, dear, what you can do with a single potato."

2 tablespoons safflower *or* sunflower oil
1 tablespoon butter
2 medium onions—chopped
1 large potato—peeled and chopped

2 heads of lettuce—well-washed and chopped
4 cups VEGETARIAN WHITE STOCK *[see index]**
1/2 cup light cream *or* half and half

Salt, to taste
Freshly ground white pepper, to taste

2 tablespoon light cream *or* half and half, for garnish
Snipped fresh chives, for garnish

In a kettle set over *LOW-MEDIUM* heat, heat oil and butter. Add chopped onion and chopped potato. Sauté until potato is golden and the onion is soft and translucent, *being careful not to allow either vegetable to brown.*

Add well-washed lettuce and vegetable stock. Increase the heat to *MEDIUM-HIGH* and allow to come to the boil. *Reduce the heat to LOW-MEDIUM again immediately.* Cover and allow to simmer for about 20 minutes, or until all the vegetables are soft. Stir occasionally. Remove from heat and allow the soup to cool slightly.

Purée the soup in batches using the electric blender or the food processor fitted with steel knife. Purée thoroughly until *very smooth*. Turn into a clean kettle or large saucepan set over *LOW-MEDIUM* heat and allow to heat through. Stir in cream. Season with salt and pepper to taste. Transfer to a heated soup tureen.

Serve into heated soup bowls or mugs. Garnish each serving with snipped chives.

Yields 8 cupfuls

Notes: *Be sure to use a very light-colored vegetable stock. Stocks made with tomatoes can ruin the lovely green color of this soup.

This recipe can be doubled or halved, when required.

1/8 SERVING (i. e., per cupful) –
PROTEIN = 1.6 g.; FAT = 6.2 g.; CARBOHYDRATE = 6.3 g.;
CALORIES = 86; CALORIES FROM FAT = 65 %

Europe–United Kingdom–Wales

WELSH *GLAMORGAN* SAUSAGES
Selsig Morgannwg

TPT - 2 hours and 39 minutes;
2 hours = refrigeration period

I tasted Caerphilly cheese for the first time in a deli-type store in a small village in Wales where I was foraging for a bread and cheese lunch to take back to Mom and Katy, who were minding our drying laundry. Although readily available in cheese stores on the East Coast, it is only occasionally available in our grocery stores out here in Pennsylvania. When I find it, I do put this dish on the menu. Every vegetarian planning to visit Wales should be familiar with glamorgan sausages. It is meatless heaven in a country where few restaurants have thought to include a vegetarian dish other than a salad or pasta, neither of which lets you experience a real Welsh dish. All you need is a skillet to prepare these very delicious protein-filled cheese, leek, and breadcrumb rolls. We serve them with buttered carrots or peas or red onion jam/marmalade cooked slowly on a grill pan.

Since the mixture can be frozen, quite successfully, I often double the recipe if I have windfall of breadcrumbs. I form the "sausages." wrap them in plastic wrap, and freeze them in a freezer bag. It is a great convenience to pull two or three out for a quick, delicious, and very nutritious lunch.

2 1/2 cups white breadcrumbs
4 ounces *Caerphilly* cheese—shredded*
1 large leek—*white portion* only—trimmed, very well-rinsed, and *finely* chopped
1 tablespoon *very finely* chopped parsley
1 tablespoon *very finely* chopped fresh thyme
Freshly ground black pepper, to taste

1 tablespoon coarse grain (country-style) *Dijon* or Welsh mustard
5 tablespoons *fat-free*-pasteurized eggs**
Up to 1/4 cup skimmed milk, *only if necessary*

1/4 cup butter

1/2 cup fresh white breadcrumbs

In the work bowl of the food processor, combine the 2 1/2 cupfuls breadcrumbs, shredded cheese, *finely* chopped leek, *very finely* chopped parsley, fresh coriander (*cilantro*), and thyme, and black pepper. Process to combine well.

In a small bowl, combine mustard and pasteurized eggs. Mix well. Add to breadcrumb–cheese mixture. Process until mixture begins to stick together. Divide the mixture into 12 portions. Using your hands, squeeze and roll each portion into a sausage shape. Place on a cold plate and refrigerate for 1 hour. Add a little milk as you are shaping the *glamorgan, only if necessary,* to achieve a workable texture.

Remove plate from refrigerator and reshape each sausage, compressing the ingredients as firmly as you can. Replace the plate in the refrigerator for another hour.

In a non-stick-coated skillet set over *LOW-MEDIUM* heat, melt butter.

Remove the plate from the refrigerator. Pour the remaining 1/2 cupful breadcrumbs onto the plate. Roll the sausages in the breadcrumbs and transfer to the skillet, using two spoons or two wooden spatulas. Cook, turning frequently, until lightly browned. Transfer to a heated serving platter and keep warm on a warming tray or in a warm oven until ready to serve.

Yields 12 servings
adequate for 4-6 people

Notes: *A mild Cheddar or a *Fontina* cheese can be substituted for *Caerphilly* cheese, if not available.

**Fresh eggs may be substituted for pasteurized eggs, which we choose not only to keep the fat level down but also to eliminate the danger of *Salmonella* poisoning since the method of cooking the *glamorgan* is not hot enough or thorough enough to completely eliminate the danger of lingering *Salmonella* bacteria.

This recipe can be halved or doubled, when required.

1/12 SERVING (i. e., per sausage) –
PROTEIN = 4.6 g.; FAT = 7.0 g.; CARBOHYDRATE = 8.9 g.;
CALORIES = 116; CALORIES FROM FAT = 54%

Europe–United Kingdom–Wales

WELSH SAUTÉED LEEKS IN CREAMY ORANGE SAUCE
Cennin Mewn Saws Oren

TPT - 23 minutes

"Cennin," or alternately "ceninen," is both the Welsh name commonly used for the leek and for the daffodil, each Welsh symbols. It is recorded that the leek was worn in the buttonholes and hats of the Welsh for national identity as early as 1536. On St. David's Day today, the leek is most often replaced by a daffodil in the buttonhole. This very lovely dish is a wonderful way to celebrate "Dydd Gŵyl Dewi Sant," St. Tavy's Day, on March 1st.

5 large leeks—*white and light green portions*—trimmed and well-rinsed

2 tablespoons butter

2 tablespoons unbleached white flour

3 tablespoons freshly squeezed orange juice
1 tablespoon freshly squeezed lemon juice

Pinch salt
Freshly ground black pepper, to taste

1 cup *two percent* milk

1 teaspoon freshly grated *organic* orange zest

Trim the tops and root ends from the leeks. Cut the white portion of the leeks into thin slices. Wash well in several changes of water to remove any sand.

In a skillet set over *LOW-MEDIUM* heat, melt butter. Add leek slices, cover, and allow to cook, stirring frequently, until leeks are wilted.

Pull leek slices to one side of pan. Add flour and stir it into the butter in the bottom of the pan to form a *roux*.

While stirring constantly, add orange juice and lemon juice. When juices are fully integrated into the flour and are beginning to thicken, pull leek slices back into mixture.

Season with salt and black pepper.

Add milk. Stir until evenly distributed and cook over *LOW-MEDIUM* heat, stirring frequently until heated through and thickened.

Add orange zest. Turn into heated serving bowl.

Serve at once.

Yields 6 servings
adequate for 4 people

Note: This recipe can be halved, when required.

1/6 SERVING – PROTEIN = 2.1 g.; FAT = 4.6 g.; CARBOHYDRATE = 6.9 g.;
CALORIES = 77; CALORIES FROM FAT = 54%

YOGURT *CRÈME* WITH SWEET OATMEAL TOPPING IN THE STYLE OF WALES
Yoghurt Blawd Ceirch

TPT -   17 minutes;
         8 hours and 17 minutes,
         if you have to make the yogurt *crème*

Ever since we visited Wales in 1983 I have chosen to top my yogurt with the sweet oatmeal crunch I had tasted at a food counter/snack bar at the boat dock in Swansea. It was available as a snack or quick breakfast item in a paper cup for those arriving and departing on the ferries. We had come across on a night passage and were waiting for daybreak to continue our trip. The yogurt that I found that morning was so welcome. One day, with a batch of yogurt crème ready for dinner dessert, I decided to adapt the crunchy, sweet oatmeal breakfast topping to make a yogurt dessert. Maybe this is not strictly Welsh but I created it to remember that trip and the Wales we met that summer.

We serve this with a bowl of fresh berries or sliced peaches on the side in the summer. Since this topping is delicious on buttered toast, a small bowl of it sits beside the jams at breakfast when we have overnight guests.

**YOGURT *CRÈME* WITH SWEET OATMEAL TOPPING
IN THE STYLE OF WALES** (cont'd)

2 cups YOGURT *CRÈME* [see index]
1 tablespoon white sugar
2 tablespoons light cream *or* **half and half**

1/4 cup quick rolled oats (*not instant*)
2 tablespoons *light* brown sugar

In a mixing bowl, combine yogurt *crème* with white sugar and cream. Stir to combine thoroughly. If necessary, add more cream to get the desired consistency. Divide among six sherbet glasses, wine glasses, or other small dessert dishes. Refrigerate until ready to serve.

Preheat oven to 300 degree F.

Spread rolled oats out in a glass pie plate. Sprinkle brown sugar over the oatmeal as evenly as possible. Bake in preheated oven until sugar melts—about 10 minutes. Remove it immediately and allow to cool. *Be careful not to allow the sugar to burn.*

When ready to serve, sprinkle a portion of the crunchy, sweet oatmeal over each portion.

Yields 6 individual servings

Note: This recipe can be halved or doubled, when required.

1/6 SERVING – PROTEIN = 12.2 g.; FAT = 1.0 g.; CARBOHYDRATE = 27.6 g.;
CALORIES = 170; CALORIES FROM FAT = 5%

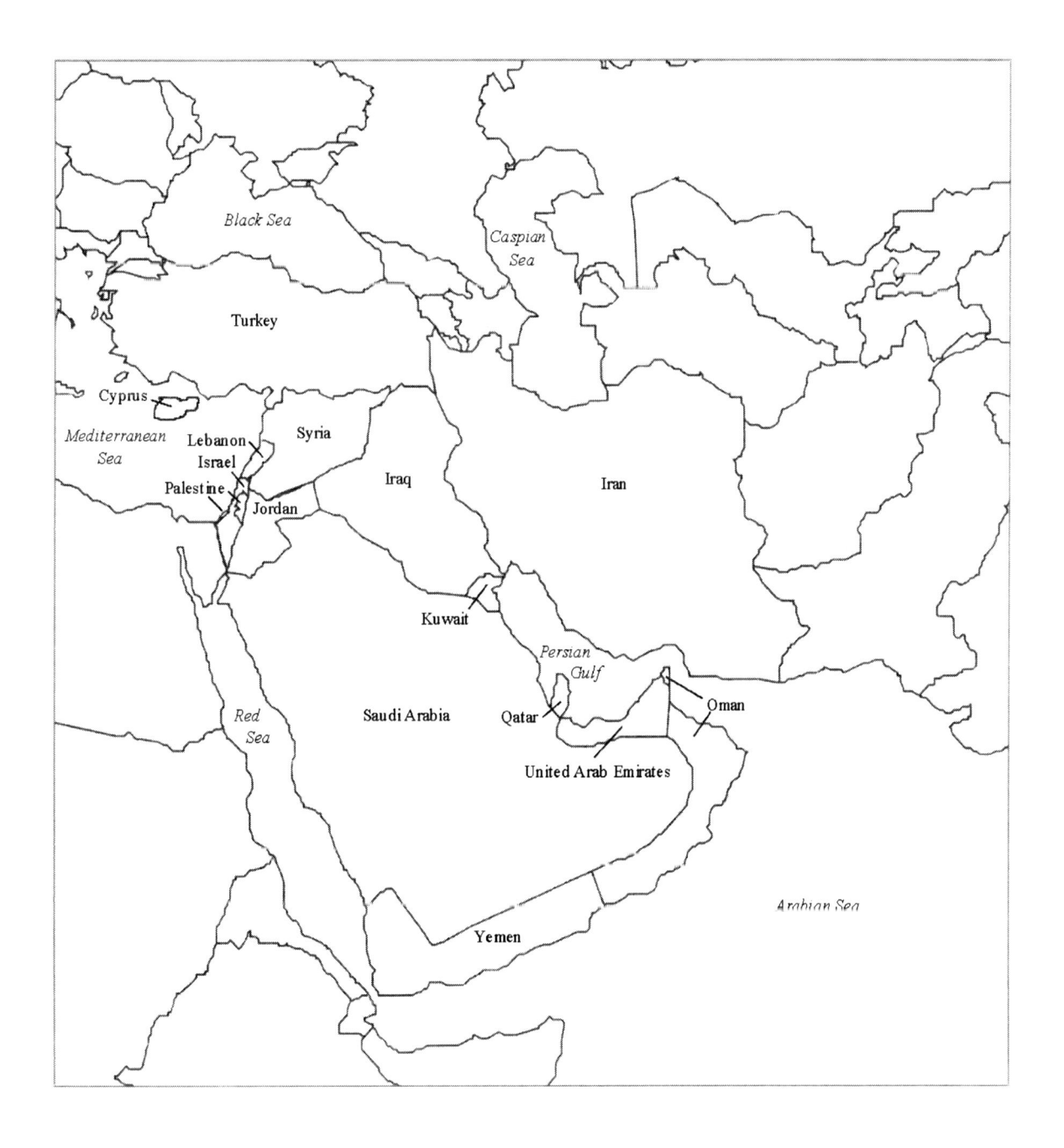

Middle East

Middle East

Cyprus	. .	465
Iran	. .	475
Iraq	. .	485
Israel	. .	492
Jordan	.	501
Kuwait	.	511
Lebanon	. .	521
Oman	.	535
Palestine	. .	543
Saudi Arabia	. .	551
Syria	.	561
Turkey	.	565
Yemen	.	576

Cyprus

The story of Cyprus is really a story of two Cypruses. The area under control of the Republic of Cyprus encompasses about fifty-nine percent of the island nation which is approximately twice the size of the State of Rhode Island. About thirty-six percent of the island declared itself the Turkish Republic of Northern Cyprus in 1983 and is not recognized by the international community, with the exception of Turkey. The explanation for this situation is complicated and reconciliation of the two mind-sets seems to be even more complicated. Since the Turkish invasion in 1974, the northern portion of Cyprus has been settled by Turkish followers of Sunni Islam and is occupied by Turkish forces.

It has been a long road under many flags for this 3,500-square-mile island on which Stone Age water wells and Neolithic settlements have been uncovered dating human settlement to at least 8400 BC. Ceramic chards support the theory that settlements were built by Neolithic peoples from the Levant.

Mycenean Greeks came to Cyprus in the second millennium BC. In 708 BC it came under the rule of the Assyrians and remained so for a century. After a brief period of Egyptian rule, the expansion of the great Persian Empire reached Cyprus in 545 BC. In 333 BC Alexander the Great seized the island. Following Alexander's death in 623 BC and the division of his kingdom, Cyprus was incorporated into Ptolemaic Egypt and then in 58 BC Cyprus became part of the Roman Empire and its successor in the region, the Byzantine Empire. Byzantium ruled the strategically-positioned island for eight hundred years until the period of the crusades. In 1570 the Ottoman Turks invaded, eliminating the feudal system and ousting the Italian aristocracy that had settled there after Venice had annexed the island in 1489. Administration by Great Britain after the Russo–Turkish War in 1878 carried through until after the periods of the two world wars. Independence was declared in 1960 but Greece and Turkey continued to vie for control. A *coup d'etat* in 1974 by Greek military officers who supported Greek acquisition of the island was responded to by Turkish forces. Although Turkey was a signatory to the Zürich and London Agreement which created the new nation, Turkish forces invaded in 1974 displacing an estimated 150,000 Greek Cypriots.

You can only imagine the influences left behind by these occupations and how they have led to a fascinating cuisine, a cuisine where threads lead all over the Mediterranean and the Middle East. Until I researched Cyprus, I, like so many other people, thought Cypriot cuisine was Greek food. It is remarkably similar to food eaten in the islands of the Dodecanese, often to the use of the same name. When tasted side by side, however, those remarkable threads of influence that have allowed for the evolution of this cuisine become evident.

Maintaining a water supply that depends on rainfall and storage of that water has challenged Cypriots since early peoples first came to the island. The Kyrenia Mountains in the North do not provide the elevation to encourage rainfall but the Troodos mountain range in the South, with peaks some 900 feet higher than those of the Kyrenia, do provide the lift that results in precipitation as clouds move North across the Mediterranean from November to April. This enables the collection of rainwater and snowmelt in the South to supply the agricultural area through an extensive dam and reservoir system. Changes in rainfall patterns have challenged the agriculture of the island in the last decade impacting the production of fresh vegetables and the wide assortment of fruits that can be grown in this warm subtropical climate.

Middle East – Cyprus

Tomato Omelet
Kalymniotiko Avgozoumo

Fresh Black-Eyed Peas with Caramelized Onions
Ta Papfouthia

Cauliflower Pickles   Olives   Rice-Stuffed Grape Leaves
Koupepia

~

Meatball Soup with Rice and Lentils
Giouvarlakia

~

Cabbage Salad with Shredded Carrot
Lahanosalata

**Tomato Salad with Shredded *Halloumi*
with Lemon Zest, and Celery and Parsley Leaves**
Tomatasalata me Halloumi

~~~~~~~~~~~~~~~~~~~~~

Lentils and *Orzo* with Caramelized Onions
Fakes me Kritharaki kai Syvasi

Steamed and Mashed Pumpkin

Steamed Baby Artichokes

***Trahana* with Yogurt and *Gorgonzola* Cheese**
Trahana

~ ~ ~

***Tagliatelle* with Chick Peas**
Matsi me Revithia

Halloumi* Cheese and Tomato *Kebabs
Halloumi Souvlakia

Breaded and Deep-Fried Okra with Tomato Sauce
Bamies me Tomata

Olive Oil Bread with *Hummus* and Mint
Eliopsomo

~~~~~~~~~~~~~~~~~~~~~

Mixed Melon Balls with Fresh Mint

Nectarine, Peach, or Apricot Slices Sautéed in Butter and Sugar

Greek Yogurt with **Savory Forest Honey with Rosemary,
Winter Savory, and Juniper Berries**

Middle East–**Cyprus**

CYPRIOT TOMATO OMELET
Kalymniotiko Avgozoumo

TPT - 12 minutes

While traveling back in the 1980s we stopped for breakfast along the Southern Tier of New York State and found that the health department would no longer allow restaurants to serve poached eggs. Salmonella contamination had become that widespread a concern. Until organic eggs became widely available, raw, poached, shirred, and undercooked eggs, such as in this recipe, were off our menus. This simple, delicious dish, popular in Cyprus and throughout the Greek Islands, can be made more safely with organic eggs. However, in Cyprus the dish is served before the eggs have really cooked; the eggs are still quite runny. It is difficult to serve and egg safety is still a concern so we have evolved a firmer, omelet version that plates well as a first course or for a light lunch.

1 tablespoon *extra virgin* olive oil
1 1/2 cups canned, *crushed* tomatoes
1/2 cup *finely* chopped Italian red onion
1/2 teaspoon *finely* crushed dried thyme
1 large bay leaf—broken in half
Salt, to taste
Freshly ground mixed peppercorns—black, red, and white—to taste

6 *organic* eggs
2 tablespoons water

In a 9-inch non-stick-coated skillet set over *MEDIUM* heat, heat oil. Add *crushed* tomatoes, *finely* chopped red onion, *finely* crushed thyme, bay leaf pieces, salt, and ground mixed peppercorns. Allow to simmer until most of the liquid has evaporated, stirring frequently. Remove and discard bay leaf pieces.

In a small bowl, combine eggs and water. Using a fork or a small wire whisk, beat the eggs until no large areas of white are visible. Add to the tomato mixture. Stir vigorously to combine. Cook, stirring frequently, until eggs are softly set. Slide the omelet onto a heated, round platter. *Do not fold.*

Serve at once in wedges.

Yields 6 servings
adequate for 4 people

Note: This recipe can be halved or doubled, when required. Be sure to use a small skillet if you halve the recipe and a larger skillet if you double.

1/6 SERVING – PROTEIN = 7.0 g.; FAT = 7.7 g.; CARBOHYDRATE = 3.3 g.;
CALORIES = 110; CALORIES FROM FAT = 63%

MEATBALL SOUP WITH RICE AND LENTILS
Giouvarlakia

TPT - 34 minutes

According to those who have experienced this cuisine first-hand, Cypriot cooks make amazing meatballs to which they add rice. Although the fast days of the Orthodox Church require fasting for about one-third of the year, making Cyprus a very welcoming country to vegetarians, we, who have chosen a vegetarian/vegan lifestyle must, however, bypass those meatballs and the chicken stock used to make soups. The following soup was evolved to appreciate Cypriot soups as vegetarians.

5 cups VEGETARIAN STOCK FROM SOUP *[see index]* or other vegetarian stock of choice
1/2 cup canned vegetarian lentil soup
1/2 cup dry converted rice
3 tablespoons *very finely* chopped celery leaves
1 garlic clove—*very finely* chopped
Pinch crushed, dried oregano
1 large bay leaf, broken in half

12 small *frozen* vegetarian meatballs

In a kettle set over *MEDIUM-HIGH* heat, combine stock, lentil soup, rice, *very finely* chopped celery leaves, *very finely* chopped garlic, crushed oregano, and bay leaf pieces. Allow to come to just below the boil. Stir. *Reduce heat to LOW-MEDIUM.* Cover and allow to simmer for about 20 minutes, or until the rice is tender.*

Add meatballs and continue cooking until meatballs are heated through. Remove and discard bay leaf pieces. Turn into a heated tureen.

MEATBALL SOUP WITH RICE AND LENTILS (cont'd)

Serve at once into heated soup plates.

Yields 6 servings

Notes: *The soup can be prepared to this point and frozen.

This recipe can be halved or doubled, when required.

1/6 SERVING (about 1 cupful with 2 meatballs) –
PROTEIN = 8.2 g.; FAT = 2.4 g.; CARBOHYDRATE = 205 g.;
CALORIES = 132; CALORIES FROM FAT = 16%

CYPRIOT CABBAGE SALAD WITH SHREDDED CARROT
Lahanosalata

TPT - 1 hour and 10 minutes;
1 hour = flavor development period

I suggested to a retired friend of mine that a good old fashioned, "scrape-your-knuckles" grater was the best tool to use to prepare this slaw. He said that he did not think they had one so he used the food processor. You want the vegetables to be fairly uniform but not all mushed up like the coleslaw in the grocery store so unless you have a food processor with shredding disks, find a "knuckle scraper." My mother-in-law's four-sided aluminum grater, on which she grated cheese before every meal, is perfect for this and dozens of other shredding and grating jobs.

3 cups *very finely* shredded green *or* white cabbage
1 cup *very finely* shredded carrot
1/4 cup shredded sweet onion—Vidalia, Walla Walla, *or* Mayan *or* Texas Sweet
3 tablespoons *finely* chopped fresh parsley leaves
2 tablespoons *finely* chopped fresh coriander (*cilantro*) leaves

2 tablespoons *extra virgin* olive oil
1 tablespoon freshly squeezed lemon juice

1/4 teaspoon sugar
1/8 teaspoon salt, or to taste
1/8 teaspoon freshly ground black pepper, or to taste

In a salad bowl, combine *very finely* shredded cabbage and carrots, shredded sweet onion, and *finely* chopped parsley and fresh coriander (*cilantro*). Toss.

In a cruet, combine olive oil and lemon juices. Shake vigorously. Pour over vegetables. Toss.

Sprinkle sugar, salt, and black pepper over. Again, toss. Cover with plastic wrap and refrigerate for 1 hour to allow for flavor development.

Serve chilled.

Yields 6 servings
adequate for 4 people

Note: This recipe can be halved or doubled, when required.

1/6 SERVING – PROTEIN = 1.0 g.; FAT = 3.9 g.; CARBOHYDRATE = 5.5 g.;
CALORIES = 65; CALORIES FROM FAT = 54%

Middle East–**Cyprus**

CYPRIOT TOMATO SALAD AND SHREDDED *HALLOUMI* WITH LEMON ZEST, CELERY AND PARSLEY LEAVES

Tomatasalata me Halloumi

TPT - 10 minutes

This simple Cypriot salad demonstrates how a few ingredients can present complex nuances of flavors that simply amaze and confound. You taste something and then the lemon aroma and taste mask it slightly and, yes, your taste buds are confounded. I usually make this about an hour before serving and set it, covered by another plate or platter, on the table. The flavors marry beautifully in that time period.

4-5 small, firm, ripe tomatoes—*thinly* sliced
1 ounce *Halloumi* cheese—slivered
1/2 teaspoon shredded, *fresh organic* lemon zest
1 1/2 teaspoons *finely* chopped fresh celery leaves
1 1/2 teaspoons *finely* chopped fresh parsley leaves
Freshly ground black pepper, to taste

1 tablespoon *extra virgin* olive oil
1 teaspoon red wine vinegar

Arrange tomato slices on a large round plate or platter. Scatter slivered cheese, shredded lemon zest, and *finely* chopped celery and parsley leaves over the tomatoes. Generously grind black pepper over.

In a cruet, combine oil and vinegar. Shake vigorously. Drizzle over tomatoes.*

Serve at room temperature.

Yields 6 servings
adequate for 4 people

Note: This recipe can be halved, when required.

1/6 SERVING – PROTEIN = 1.7 g.; FAT = 3.4 g.; CARBOHYDRATE = 2.7 g.;
CALORIES = 47; CALORIES FROM FAT = 65%

CYPRIOT LENTILS AND *ORZO* WITH CARAMELIZED ONIONS

Fakes me Kritharaki kai Syvasi

TPT - 1 hour and 43 minutes;
1 hour = lentil soaking period

The odds are that caramelized onions will turn up in your meal in Cyprus; they are that popular. Recipes for caramelized onions appear in several other places in this volume so there is really no need to dwell on that aspect of this recipe. The fact that this dish presents the vegetarian with both grain and legume proteins, thus complementing the amino acids, is worth emphasizing. There is often reference to the beans and rice cultures of Latin American to our south but people in the United States do not seem to be as familiar with the myriad of ways in which grain and legume proteins are incorporated into cuisines all over the world. Lentils and orzo are probably right there in your larder even if you do not live on an island in the Mediterranean.

1/2 cup dry brown (*or* green) lentils
3 cups *boiling* water

2 1/2 cups *boiling* water
1/2 cup red wine

1/2 medium *sweet* onion—Vidalia, Walla Walla,
or Mayan or Texas Sweet—*finely* chopped
2 tablespoons canned, *crushed* tomatoes
2 teaspoons crushed, dried oregano

2 bay leaves—broken in half
1/2 teaspoon salt

1/3 cup dry *orzo pasta*

Freshly ground black pepper, to taste
1 tablespoon *extra virgin* olive oil

2 cups *hot* CARAMELIZED ONIONS *[see index]**

Middle East–**Cyprus**

**CYPRIOT LENTILS AND *ORZO*
WITH CARAMELIZED ONIONS** (cont'd)

Pick over lentils and discard any of poor quality. Rinse thoroughly. Drain. Pour into a mixing bowl and add 3 cupfuls *boiling* water. Set aside at room temperature for 1 hour. Drain.

In a large *non-aluminum*** saucepan set over *MEDIUM-LOW* heat, combine drained lentils, 2 1/2 cups of *boiling* water, red wine, *finely* chopped onion, *crushed* tomatoes, crushed oregano, bay leaf pieces, and salt. Simmer until lentils are *almost* tender—about 20 minutes.

Add *orzo*. Simmer until the *orzo* is tender and most of the liquid has been absorbed.

Season with black pepper and more salt, if necessary. Add olive oil and allow to briefly heat through. Turn into heated serving bowl. Retrieve and discard bay leaf pieces.

Top with *hot* caramelized onions.

Serve at once.

Yields 6 servings
adequate for 4-6 people

Notes: *My large grill pan can accommodate five big sweet onions. Frozen, these are a real convenience.

**Since aluminum discolors lentils rather unpleasantly, avoid using aluminum cookware or serving bowls in this case.

This recipe can be doubled, when required.

1/6 SERVING – PROTEIN = 6.7 g.; FAT = 2.2 g.; CARBOHYDRATE = 17.8 g.;
CALORIES = 129; CALORIES FROM FAT = 15%

CYPRIOT *TRAHANA* WITH YOGURT AND *GORGONZOLA* CHEESE
Trahana

TPT - 43 minutes;
  30 minutes = *trahana* soaking period

Trahana is an ancient product of Cyprus, a product historically prepared after the growing season that allowed the Cypriots to survive. It is one of the region's oldest processed foods, versions of which are eaten in Crete, Thrace, Greece, and Macedonia. There is sour trahana, made from wheat flour and either buttermilk or yogurt, and sweet trahana, made from cracked wheat simmered in fresh milk. The wheat product is dried in the sun and then crumbled. Trahana is used to make a remarkable soup and to stuff vegetables, it is eaten for breakfast and, with an addition of this and that, it can become a side dish to your main meal.

1/2 cup sweet *trahana**
1 cup *two-percent* milk

1/4 cup PLAIN YOGURT *[see index]* **or
  commercially-available plain yogurt**
1/4 cup crumbled *Gorgonzola* cheese
Additional *two-percent* milk, as needed

1 small tomato—seeded and chopped—for garnish

In a saucepan, combine *trahana* and milk. Allow to soak for 30 minutes.

Add yogurt and *Gorgonzola* cheese. Stir to combine. Add more milk if necessary. Set over *LOW-MEDIUM* heat and cook until heated through. Turn into a heated serving bowl.

Garnish with chopped tomato.

Serve at once.

Yields 6 servings
adequate for 4 people

Notes: *Both sweet and sour *trahana* are available from mail order firms.

This recipe can be halved or doubled, when required.

1/6 SERVING – PROTEIN = 8.0 g.; FAT = 3.1 g.; CARBOHYDRATE = 16.9 g.;
CALORIES = 89; CALORIES FROM FAT = 31%

Middle East–**Cyprus**

TAGLIATELLE WITH CHICK PEAS
Matsi me Revithia

TPT - 58 minutes

Some dishes said to be local specialties of the Island of Rhodes are found in Cyprus with the same claim. You would be hard-pressed to identify the nationality of the cook should you be presented with a dish such as this one. A rich cuisine has developed at the crossroads of three continents and the influences of each of the three continents is in evidence. Cooking in the Dodecanese, the group of fourteen islands in the southeastern Aegean, is often mistaken for the cooking of Cyprus, and vice versa. This is such a dish, popular in both Cyprus and Rhodes and very similar to a simple family spaghetti and broccoli dish which always pleased.

1 cup canned chick peas—*undrained**
1/2 cup *finely* chopped Italian red onion
1/2 cinnamon quill
3 whole allspice berries
1 large bay leaf—broken in half

3 quarts *boiling* water
1 tablespoon freshly squeezed lemon juice
1 3-inch piece lemon zest
8 ounces dry imported *tagliatelle* or *fettucine*

1 cup canned, *petite diced* tomatoes
2 tablespoons *extra virgin* olive oil
1 tablespoon red wine
Freshly ground black pepper, to taste

In a saucepan set over *LOW–MEDIUM* heat, combine *undrained* canned chick peas, *finely* chopped onion, cinnamon quill, whole allspice berries, and bay leaf. Cover and allow to cook for about 25-30 minutes. Remove and discard any seed coats that have floated free, the cinnamon quill, allspice berries, and bay leaf pieces. Turn into a sieve and allow to drain while you are preparing the *pasta*.

In a large kettle set over *HIGH* heat, add lemon juice and lemon zest to *boiling* water. Break *tagliatelle* in half and add to *boiling* water. Cook, stirring occasionally, over *HIGH* heat according to package directions, but *only until al dente*. Drain thoroughly, discarding lemon zest. Turn into a large skillet set over *LOW-MEDIUM* heat.

Add drained chick peas, *diced* tomatoes, olive oil, red wine, and lots of black pepper. Toss. Cook until heated through. Turn into a heated serving bowl.

Serve at once.

Yields 6 servings
adequate for 4 people

Notes: *If preferred, dry chick peas can be soaked and cooked. Add the spices to the dry chick peas as you simmer them so that they become infused with the flavors.

This recipe is easily halved or doubled, when required.

1/6 SERVING – PROTEIN = 7.2 g.; FAT = 4.6 g.; CARBOHYDRATE = 37.1 g.;
CALORIES = 220; CALORIES FROM FAT = 19%

HALLOUMI CHEESE AND TOMATO KEBABS
Halloumi Souvlakia

TPT - 14 minutes

Halloumi cheese is an unusual cheese that is, in our opinion, one of Cyprus' greatest treasures. This wonderful cheese originated in Cyprus and its origins can be traced back to the era when Cyprus was part of the Byzantine Empire. It is traditionally made from a mixture of ewe's and goat's milk and you do not have to travel to Cyprus to enjoy Halloumi. It can be found in well-stocked groceries and specialty shops in the United States but it can also be ordered online from purveyors of Greek foods. Because it can be successfully frozen for up to a year, it is advisable to stock up when you locate a supply. Due to its high melting point, it can be fried or grilled and thus become the centerpiece of a meal.

1 teaspoon *finely* crushed, dried mint*
2 tablespoons *extra virgin* olive oil

1 package (8 ounces) *Halloumi* cheese—cut into
  24 cubes
3 *firm* Roma tomatoes—cut into 30 small wedges

Middle East – Cyprus

HALLLOUMI CHEESE AND TOMATO *KEBABS* (cont'd)

Heat grill pan over *MEDIUM* heat.

On a platter, long enough to accommodate the bamboo skewers chosen, combine *finely* crushed mint and olive oil. Set aside.

Thread four cubes of *Halloumi* cheese and five wedges of tomato alternately on six *very thin* bamboo skewers. Place on platter with mint and oil. Roll kebabs in oil.

Place *kebabs* on *hot* grill pan. Roll over and over until cheese is browned and tomato wedges are blistered.

Serve at once as an appetizer or as a side dish with your main meal.

Notes: *If preferred, crushed oregano can be used instead of mint.

This recipe can be halved or doubled, when required.

Yields 6 servings
adequate for 4 people

1/6 SERVING – PROTEIN = 8.3 g.; FAT = 12.6 g.; CARBOHYDRATE = 1.3 g.;
CALORIES = 144; CALORIES FROM FAT = 79%

BREADED AND DEEP-FRIED OKRA WITH TOMATO SAUCE
Bamies me Tomata

TPT - 36 minutes;
39 minutes = okra soaking period

Okra is a vegetable one often sees on menus in the Middle East and in Africa. Greeks serve it with fish and it is baked in a tomato sauce in Cyprus. Deep-fried okra is really quite delicious and when served with a tomato sauce, it makes a different and complimentary side dish or appetizer, if preferred. When pre-treated with vinegar, the mucilaginous nature of okra is moderated.

Oil for deep-frying

6 tablespoons distilled white vinegar
1 teaspoon crushed red pepper flakes

15 firm okra—well-washed and trimmed

1/2 cup unbleached white flour
1/4 cup *very finely* ground corn meal, such as masa harina
1/4 teaspoon salt

1 cup canned, *crushed* tomatoes
1 tablespoon GARLIC OIL *[see index]*

Pour oil into a deep frying pan or kettle to a depth of about 1/2 inch. Set over *MEDIUM* heat and allow to preheat to 365 degrees F.

In a pie plate, combine vinegar and crushed red pepper flakes,

Slice okra in half lengthwise. Add to vinegar mixture and allow to marinate for at least 10 minutes.

Put flour, corn meal, and salt into a mixing bowl. Form a paste by adding a tablespoonful of the vinegar mixture at a time.

Using a spatula, lift out the okra pieces and add to flour mixture. Using a spoon, gently stir to coat the okra with the flour mixture. Deep-fry in the hot oil in batches until crisp and browned. Transfer to paper toweling to drain off excess oil. Turn into a skillet set over *LOW* heat.

Add crushed tomatoes and garlic oil. Spoon it around the okra. Heat, stirring occasionally, until heated through.

Yields 30 pieces
adequate for 6 people

Note: This recipe can be halved, when required.

1/30 SERVING – PROTEIN = 0.5 g.; FAT = 0.8 g.; CARBOHYDRATE = 3.0 g.;
CALORIES = 21; CALORIES FROM FAT = 34%

Middle East–**Cyprus**

(BREAD MACHINE) OLIVE OIL BREAD WITH *HUMMUS* AND MINT IN THE STYLE OF CYPRUS

Eliopsomo

TPT - 2 hours and 11 minutes;
15 minutes = garlic oil preparation period;
1 hour and 50 minutes = automated machine preparation period*

This is a high protein specialty bread with the earthy flavors of olive oil, garlic, and sesame as well as that of hummus making it an excellent accompaniment to any Mediterranean or Middle Eastern menu. Although similar breads are found throughout the cuisines of the Mediterranean, mint clearly identifies this as Cypriot.

1/4 cup *extra virgin* olive oil—*heated to about 105 degrees F.*
1 large garlic clove—smashed

1/4 cup *fat-free* pasteurized eggs (the equivalent of 1 egg)
3/4 cup skimmed milk—*heated to about 95 degrees F.*

2 cups bread flour
1 cup whole wheat flour
1 1/2 teaspoons sugar
1/2 teaspoon salt
1/3 cup sesame seeds—*toasted*
1 cup commercially-available *hummus* (chick pea dip)**
1 tablespoon *finely* crushed dried mint leaves

1 tablespoon (1 envelope) *preservative-free* active dried yeast***

Bring all ingredients except warm milk to room temperature.

Place smashed garlic clove in *hot* olive oil. Allow to infuse for 15 minutes. Remove garlic from garlic oil and discard.

Put prepared garlic oil, pasteurized eggs, and warm milk into the BREAD MACHINE pan.

Add bread flour, whole wheat flour, sugar, salt, toasted sesame seeds, *hummus*, and *finely* crushed mint leaves, spreading the ingredients over the liquid as you add them. *Do not stir.*

Using a spoon, create a depression in the dry ingredients, being very careful not to press down into the liquid layer below. Pour yeast into the depression.

Select MANUAL SETTING and push START.

Prepare a cookie sheet by coating with non-stick lecithin spray coating.

Remove dough from baking pan when MANUAL cycle is completed. On a bread board coated with flour, knead until dough is smooth. Form into a round loaf and place on prepared cookie sheet.**** Allow the loaf to rise in a warm, draft-free kitchen until doubled in volume—about 45 minutes. Bake in preheated 350 degree F. oven for about 40-45 minutes, or until you get a hollow sound when you knock on top of the loaf. Remove from cookie sheet and cool completely on a wire rack before slicing and serving.

Yields 1 large loaf
— the equivalent of about 32 slices

Notes: *Preparation time depends, of course, on the brand of bread machine which you are using; my bread machine is from Zojirushi.

**Although you can make your own *hummus* (*hummous*) *[see index]*, the *hummus*, available in the deli department, saves time and makes an excellent bread.

***Some packaged dried yeast available in grocery stores contain a preservative. Natural food stores carry an additive-free dried yeast. In addition, *do not use so-called fast action yeasts*. The results will not please you.

****If preferred, you can form two round loaves and freeze one for a future menu.

1/32 SERVING (i. e., per slice) –
PROTEIN = 2.6 g.; FAT = 3.1 g.; CARBOHYDRATE = 10.3 g.;
CALORIES = 76; CALORIES FROM FAT = 37%

Middle East–**Cyprus**

SAVORY FOREST HONEY
WITH ROSEMARY, WINTER SAVORY, AND JUNIPER BERRIES

TPT - 32 minutes;
10 minutes = flavor infusion period

A friend from Croatia, whose tastes run to the more exotic and who enjoys Ray's homemade Calabrese limoncello, inspired this honey. I knew we were going to have a lovely wheel of Brie at our Thanksgiving gathering and I had a bumper crop of rosemary and winter savory ... so ... We took a jar as a gift to enhance the winter stews and meat dishes, especially pork and wild game, that both Amani and Nick enjoyed. It is also lends a flavorful taste to root vegetables and, of course, we enjoy it with a good ripe piece of Brie. A similar herb-flavored honey is popular on Cyprus. A thyme flavored version is especially popular as a dessert sauce.

1/2 cup fresh rosemary needles
1/2 cup fresh winter savory needles

8 dried juniper berries*
1 cup (a 16-ounce jar) wildflower honey

Sterilize a honey jar and its lid.

Cover a bread board with waxed paper. Place rosemary and winter savory needles on the waxed paper. Using a rolling pin, release the flavorful oils in the needles by rolling back and forth. Turn into a small saucepan.

Add juniper berries and honey.

Set the saucepan over *LOW-MEDIUM* heat and, *while carefully watching*, allow the honey to come to the boil. Reduce heat to *LOW*. Allow to simmer for 5 minutes. Remove from heat. Allow to stand for 10 minutes.

While still warm, strain through a fine strainer into the sterilized jar. Place a piece of waxed paper on top and allow to come to room temperature before putting lid on jar. *Store*, as you would any honey, *at room temperature.*

Notes: *For some reason, we have encountered several people in whom juniper berries elicit an allergic reaction. Those people usually also avoid gin. For this reason we always prepare a label and list the ingredients.

Several jars of this honey can be prepared at once, bottled, and stored for gift giving. A cap made from a very rich Mediterranean fabric tied with raffia or a gold cord is perfect for gift giving.

Yields 1 cupful

1/16 SERVING (i. e. per tablespoonful) –
PROTEIN = 0.1 g.; FAT = 0.0 g.; CARBOHYDRATE = 16.5 g.;
CALORIES = 61; CALORIES FROM FAT = 0%

Iran

Archeological evidence of urban settlement dating to the fourth millennium BC suggests that pre-historic peoples settled in this area of Eurasia hundreds of years before civilizations became established in nearby Mesopotamia. Present-day Iran is the site of one of the world's oldest continuous major civilization centers. The Elamite kingdom, the first Iranian dynasty, was formed in 2800 BC. It is shortly after unification by the Medes in 625 BC, during the period known as the Sassanid Empire, that the earliest use of the name Iran is recorded. International use of the name Iran dates only from 1935. However, the language spoken by the majority of the population and the country itself are still referenced by the pre-1935 name Persia. Iran gradually became more and more Islamized but, unlike other countries in the region, Arab influence was minor.

The Islamic Republic of Iran, as the country is known today, is a theocratic state in which eighty-nine percent of the population practices *Shia* Islam and approximately two-thirds of the seventy-four million inhabitants are under the age of thirty. Educational emphasis, begun during the Pahlavi Dynasty, has resulted in a literacy rate of eighty-three percent. As a result of the Iranian Revolution (also known as the Islamic Revolution), the more secular, westward-looking Pahlavi Dynasty collapsed and the Shah of Iran fled into exile. The theocratic constitution under which Iran is governed was adopted in December 1979, twelve months after the Shah was forced from the Peacock throne.

Today Iran is about the size of the United Kingdom, France, Spain, and Germany combined making it the eighteenth largest country in the world but the great Persian Empire, from which it descends, extended from the Indus and Oxus rivers in the east to the Mediterranean Sea in the west and from Anatolia (Turkey) south to Egypt, spread Persian culture and learning far beyond the borders of modern-day Iran. During their voyages and conquests, Persia introduced food, literature, philosophy, medicine, art, and scientific achievements, to the world during the period known as the Islamic Golden Age, a period which reached a height of astounding learning and cultural achievements during the tenth and eleventh centuries AD.

Hospitality in the Islamic tradition is very food oriented. Courtesy demands that food be shared with the poor and that no visitor leave your home hungry. Persian food preferences today show evidence of centuries of "give and take" with the lands to which their ancestors traveled and the foods introduced by those who happened by via "the silk road." Rice, which is eaten at every meal, most probably came to Iran from India. The eggplant, referred to as the "potato of Iran," is native to Nepal, India, Bangladesh, Pakistan, and Sri Lanka. Iranians stuff vegetables and call them "*dolmehs*"; Turks also stuffed vegetables and call them "*dolmas*." A salty cheese called "*panir*," suspiciously close to the Indian word for cheese "*paneer*," is much like Greek *feta* cheese. And, it should be noted that the Persian word for bread is *nan,* the same name given to *tandoori* flatbreads in the Indian subcontinent.

Middle East–**Iran**

Cheese and Mixed Fresh Herbs on Bread

Fried Eggs on Flatbread with Garlic – Yogurt Sauce
Nimru ba Mast

~

Hot Yogurt Soup with Rice and Chick Peas
Ashe Mast

~

Baby Beet Salad with Yogurt and Mint
Borani Chogondar
Sliced Goat Cheese

Cucumber Salad with Pomegranate *Vinaigrette*
Salad-e-khiar-o-Onar

~~~~~~~~~~~~~~~~~~~~~

Skillet Meal with Black-Eyed Peas, Leeks and Spinach
Khoresh-e Lubia

~~~~~~~~~~

Sautéed Soymeat and Peaches
Khoresh-e Hula

Persian Spice Mixture for *Khoresh*
Advieh-ye Khoresh

Dried Citrus Zest
Khelale Narangi

Cauliflower and Garlic Pickle
Torshi-e Gol-e Kalam

~~~~~~~~~~~~~~~~~~~~

Sweet Rice Flour Pudding with Rose Water
Shir Berenji

Assortment of Nuts, Seeds, and Dried Fruits
including Dates, Apricots, Pistachios
or
Fresh Fruit, of choice, in season

IRANIAN FRIED EGGS ON FLATBREAD WITH GARLIC – YOGURT SAUCE
Nimru ba Mast
TPT - 25 minutes

Lavash is a Middle Eastern shepherd's bread generally associated with Armenia but popular throughout the region. It is occasionally available with other flatbreads and wraps in the deli departments of well-stocked grocery stores. Although traditionally served over lavash, nan or any flatbread can be substituted in this recipe if you are unable to find lavash. It is a most unusual but thoroughly delicious way to serve eggs; not your run-of-the-mill poached egg presentation.

IRANIAN FRIED EGGS ON FLATBREAD WITH GARLIC – YOGURT SAUCE (cont'd)

GARLIC – YOGURT SAUCE:
- 2 cups PLAIN YOGURT *[see index]* or commercially-available plain yogurt
- 2 teaspoons GARLIC OIL *[see index]*
- 2 large garlic cloves preserved in oil —*very finely* chopped *[see index]*

1 large loaf of *lavash* or 2 loaves of *nan*

1 tablespoon butter
1 tablespoon *extra virgin* olive oil
6 *organic* eggs

Freshly ground black pepper, to taste

In a saucepan set over *LOW* heat, combine yogurt, garlic oil, and *very finely* chopped garlic. Stir to combine. Allow to heat through *but do not allow to boil*. Turn into a heated sauceboat or bowl.

Place bread in *WARM* oven to heat.

In a *large* skillet set over *MEDIUM* heat, combine butter and olive oil. When hot, slip the shelled eggs—one at a time—into the heated fat. When the whites have congealed, remove from heat. Using a spatula, cut through the whites to separate the fried eggs.

Place *warm* bread on a heated platter. Using the spatula, transfer the eggs—one at a time—onto the bread, spreading them out so that cutting the bread will not be a problem.

Grind black pepper over.

Serve at once by cutting through the bread and transferring one egg to each diner's plate. Accompany with garlic–yogurt sauce.

Yields 6 servings of one egg each

Note: This recipe can be halved.

1/6 SERVING (i. e., one egg per serving) –
PROTEIN = 12.8 g.; FAT = 14.2 g.; CARBOHYDRATE = 23.3 g.;
CALORIES = 278; CALORIES FROM FAT = 46%

PERSIAN HOT YOGURT SOUP WITH RICE AND CHICK PEAS
Ashe Mast
TPT - 54 minutes

Soups utterly laden with ingredients are the norm in Iran and soups containing meats, beans, grains, eggs, and yogurt are not unusual. When I asked about vegetarian soups, the answer was, "Why?" When I suggested that I did not wish to consume more than my fair share of the earth's protein at just the soup course, the response was again, "Why?" My search continued unassisted until I found a soup similar to this in an old cookbook of mine. It is typical of the thick soups, "ashe," that are favored in Iran and would contain meatballs when served, but it is somewhat more appropriate, in my mind, as a soup course for a multi-course meal. I don't know about you, but I generally expect a chilled soup when someone serves a yogurt soup. Iranians do serve chilled yogurt soups but their love of rich, thick soups has also resulted in hot yogurt soups.

2 tablespoons CLARIFIED BUTTER *[see index]*
1 cup *finely* chopped onion

2 cups PLAIN YOGURT *[see index]* or commercially-available plain yogurt
2 1/2 cups water
3 tablespoons *fat-free* pasteurized eggs

1/2 cup *cooked* converted rice
1/4 teaspoon salt
1/4 teaspoon freshly ground black pepper

1/4 cup chopped parsley
2 scallions—well-washed, trimmed, and *thinly* sliced
1 tablespoon chopped dillweed
1/2 cup well-drained, canned chick peas (*garbanzos*)—seed coats removed

1 large garlic clove—*very finely* chopped
2 tablespoons dried mint leaves—ground to a powder

In a small kettle set over *MEDIUM* heat, heat clarified butter. Add *finely* chopped onion and sauté onion until soft and translucent, *being careful not to allow the onions to brown*. Reduce heat to *LOW*.

PERSIAN HOT YOGURT SOUP WITH RICE AND CHICK PEAS (cont'd)

Add yogurt, water, and pasteurized eggs. Using a wire whisk, combine thoroughly.

Add cooked rice, salt, and pepper. Cook, stirring frequently with a wooden spoon, for about 20 minutes.

Add chopped parsley, sliced scallions, chopped dillweed, and chick peas. Continue cooking, for about 15 minutes more. *Stir frequently to prevent curdling.* Turn into a heated soup tureen. Place the *very finely* chopped garlic and mint-leaf powder in a small bowl.

Spoon a bit of the garlic–mint powder mixture into the center of each heated soup plate. Ladle soup over.*

Yields 6 3/4 cupfuls

Notes: This recipe can be halved, when required.

Leftovers can not be frozen and do not reheat well.

1/9 SERVING (i. e., about 3/4 cupful)-
PROTEIN = 4.3 g.; FAT = 3.5 g.; CARBOHYDRATE = 10.2 g.;
CALORIES = 92; CALORIES FROM FAT = 39%

IRANIAN BABY BEET SALAD WITH YOGURT AND MINT
Borani Chogondar
TPT - 3 minutes

Adding a bit of salt to the beets before you add the yogurt allows the beets, in a chameleon-like manner, to develop a taste quite akin to corn. I was taught this by my very wise grandmother, who salted and buttered beets to fool the palate of a family member who had always said that he did not like beets. I was never able to fool "he who also is not all that fond of beets" or his mother for that matter, nor were they swayed by the fact that beets are real "brain food." However, inexplicably, this recipe was always well-received. A similar salad is popular in Turkey where the mint is omitted and garlic is added and still further north in central Europe and Germany the mint is replaced with fresh dillweed.

1 jar (16 ounces) baby beets—drained and quartered
Pinch or two of salt, or to taste

2/3 cup PLAIN YOGURT *[see index]* **or commercially-available plain yogurt**
3 tablespoons *finely* chopped fresh mint*
Freshly ground black pepper, to taste

In a mixing bowl, combine drained baby beets and salt. Toss.

Add yogurt, *finely* chopped mint, and black pepper. *Gently*, but thoroughly, fold ingredients together. Turn into a serving bowl and refrigerate until required.

Serve chilled.

Notes: *Fresh mint leaves are obviously the best choice here but if, in the winter, you want to present this salad, you can use about 2 teaspoons dried mint.

This recipe can be halved, when required.

Yields 6 servings
adequate for 4 people

1/6 SERVING – PROTEIN = 1.8 g.; FAT = 0.5 g.; CARBOHYDRATE = 9.1 g.;
CALORIES = 49; CALORIES FROM FAT = 9%

Middle East—**Iran**

IRANIAN CUCUMBER SALAD WITH POMEGRANATE *VINAIGRETTE*
Salad-e-khiar-o-Onar

TPT - 1 hour and 9 minutes;
1 hour = flavor development period

Cucumbers are treated as the fruit they, in fact, are in Iran. They are even eaten for dessert and it is, I have found, a refreshing ending to a meal. The complex flavoring that takes the rather innocuous taste of cucumber to very lofty heights in this refreshing salad presents an exciting challenge to the taste buds. Our version is less salty than would usually be the case in an Iranian home because instead of salting yellow onions to mellow them, as they do, I prefer to use a sweet Vidalia onion. At Thanksgiving, when pomegranates appear in our Pennsylvania groceries, we garnish this salad with pomegranate seeds in the traditional style.

POMEGRANATE *VINAIGRETTE*:
- 2 tablespoons *extra virgin* olive oil
- 2 tablespoons GARLIC OIL [see index]
- 1/4 teaspoon sesame oil
- 3 tablespoons pure pomegranate juice
- 2 tablespoons freshly squeezed lime juice
- 2 teaspoons honey
- 1/8 teaspoon Tabasco Sauce, or to taste

2 medium cucumbers—peeled, halved, seeded, and chopped into bite-sized chunks
1/2 cup coarsely chopped sweet Vidalia onion
1/4 cup sliced ripe black olives

1 teaspoon crushed dried mint
1/4 teaspoon angelica powder*

1/4 cup chopped, *toasted preservative-free* walnuts
2 tablespoons crumbled plain *feta* cheese
Freshly ground black pepper, to taste

In a cruet, combine olive, garlic, and sesame oils, pomegranate and lime juices, honey, and Tabasco Sauce. Shake vigorously. Set *vinaigrette* aside briefly.

In a mixing bowl, combine cucumber chunks, chopped onion, and olive slices.

Pour three tablespoonfuls of prepared *vinaigrette* into a small bowl. Add crushed dried mint and angelica powder. Pour over vegetables. Toss. Cover and refrigerate for about 1 hour to allow for flavor development. Turn into a shallow serving bowl.

Sprinkle *toasted* walnuts and crumbled *feta* cheese over. Grind black pepper over.

Serve at once. Accompany with remaining *vinaigrette*.

Yields 8 servings
adequate for 4-6 people

Notes: *Angelica powder is available in Middle Eastern groceries and from mail order firms.

This recipe can be halved, when required.

1/8 SERVING – PROTEIN = 1.8 g.; FAT = 10.6 g.; CARBOHYDRATE = 8.0 g.;
CALORIES = 125; CALORIES FROM FAT = 76%

IRANIAN SKILLET MEAL WITH BLACK-EYED PEAS, LEEKS, AND SPINACH
Khoresh-e Lubia

TPT - 15 minutes

Skillet meals, referred to as "khoresh" are very popular in Iran but most contain meat. I was delighted to find an authentic meatless "khoresh," graciously shared by an online cook, from which I created a bean-based "khoresh" of my own. Although I prefer to use black-eyed peas because they are an ancient food which probably originated in India before making its way to the Western Hemisphere via the Middle East and Africa, if you prefer, pinto beans (Lubia chiti) or kidney beans (Lubia quermez) can be substituted.

IRANIAN SKILLET MEAL WITH BLACK-EYED PEAS, LEEKS, AND SPINACH (cont'd)

1 tablespoons butter
1 tablespoon GARLIC OIL [see index]
2 large leeks—*white portion only*—halved, rinsed thoroughly to remove all sand, and chopped

5 ounces fresh baby spinach—petioles removed and well-washed

1 can (15 ounces) black-eyed peas—drained and rinsed*
1 teaspoon PERSIAN SPICE MIXTURE FOR KHORESH (Advieh-ye Khoresh) [see recipe which follows]
2 *dehydrated* lime slices**
3 tablespoons pure pomegranate juice

In a large non-stick-coated skillet set over *MEDIUM* heat, combine butter and garlic oil. When hot, add leeks and sauté until onion is soft and transparent, *being careful not to allow onion to brown.*

Add spinach, cover, and cook until spinach wilts.

Add drained black-eyed peas, Persian spice mixture, dried lime slices, and pomegranate juice. Stir to integrate. Cook, stirring gently, *only until heated through.* Turn into a heated serving bowl.

Serve at once over rice or *chelow*, if preferred.

Yields 6 servings
adequate for 4 people

Notes: *Canned black-eyed peas are often available as "Southern-style" in which bacon and bacon fat are used in the preparation. Your vegetarian lifestyle not withstanding, you do not want the "Southern style" for this dish.

**Dried, fresh, organic lime slices are infinitely sweeter and more flavorful than in the Persian dried lime powder that is available in Middle Eastern markets.

This recipe can be doubled, when required, but do use a sufficiently large skillet.

1/6 SERVING – PROTEIN = 6.3 g.; FAT = 3.9 g.; CARBOHYDRATE = 13.3 g.;
CALORIES = 103; CALORIES FROM FAT = 34%

IRANIAN SAUTÉED SOYMEAT AND PEACHES
Khoresh-e Hula
TPT - 15 minutes

I probably have collected about a dozen Persian "khoresh" recipes for chicken with peaches looking for seasoning that I could use successfully with a meat substitute. Without the slow rendering of the chicken fat, the spices could become too assertive. This is a dish we love.

1 tablespoon dried tangerine zest—DRIED CITRUS ZEST (Khelale Narangei) [see recipe which follows]
1/4 cup *boiling* water

1 1/2 tablespoons butter
1 tablespoon GARLIC OIL [see index]
1/4 cup *finely* chopped onion

8 ounces soy meat analogue strips

12 *preservative-free* walnut halves
1 teaspoon PERSIAN SPICE MIXTURE FOR KHORESH (Advieh-ye Khoresh) [see recipe which follows]
2 *dehydrated* lime slices
3 tablespoons pure pomegranate juice

2 cups peach slices, canned in light syrup—*well-drained*

In a small dish, combine dried tangerine zest and *boiling* water. Allow to soak until required.

In a large non-stick-coated skillet set over *MEDIUM* heat, combine butter and garlic oil. When hot, add *finely* chopped onion and sauté until onion is soft and transparent, *being careful not to allow onion to brown.*

Add soymeat and sauté gently until soymeat begins to brown.

Drain tangerine zest. Add zest to soymeat with walnut halves, spice mixture, dried lime slices, and pomegranate juice. Stir to integrate.

IRANIAN SAUTÉED SOYMEAT AND PEACHES (cont'd)

When pomegranate juice begins to bubble, add peach slices. Cook, stirring gently, *only until heated through*. Turn into a heated serving bowl.

Serve at once over rice or *chelow*, if preferred.

Yields 6 servings
adequate for 4 people

Note: This recipe can be doubled, when required, but do use a large skillet.

1/6 SERVING – PROTEIN = 16.2 g.; FAT = 8.7 g.; CARBOHYDRATE = 18.8 g.;
CALORIES = 207; CALORIES FROM FAT = 38%

PERSIAN SPICE MIXTURE FOR *KHORESH*
Advieh-ye Khoresh

TPT - 3 minutes

While living in Ann Arbor, Michigan, in 1960, I learned from an Indian friend how very useful spice mixtures could be and how they could be used to pinpoint the origin of the cook. The aroma of the cooking of many, many locales could be detected when I visiting Sue and Chandi in an apartment building that housed exchange families. I had a chance to revisit that memory when we lived for six months in an apartment next to a family from the subcontinent. Every morning as I worked at my computer, I could hear her grinding her spices and by the time her husband came home for lunch the aroma wafting from their apartment was so inviting I wanted to go next door and ask if I could join them. I, shamefully trained to take spice bottles from the spice cupboard, do not prepare a spice mixture like this Persian spice combination each time I plan to cook with it. Instead, I do mix up a batch and store it so that I do not have to add spice preparation to my time schedule each time I will need it.

2 tablespoons ground cinnamon
1 1/2 teaspoons ground cardamom
1 teaspoon ground angelica*
1 teaspoon ground nutmeg
1 teaspoon ground cumin
1 teaspoon ground coriander
1/2 teaspoon freshly ground black pepper
1/4 teaspoon sugar

1/4 cup *dried, home-grown, spray-free* rose petals*

In a small jelly jar or spice jar, combine ground cinnamon, cardamom, angelica, nutmeg, cumin, and coriander, black pepper, and sugar. Stir to mix well.

In a SPICE and COFFEE GRINDER, or in a mortar, grind dried rose petals into small pieces of uniform size. Add to ground spices in spice jar.

Cover tightly and shake to mix thoroughly. Store in a cool, dark place.

Notes: *Ground angelica can be found in natural food stores and in Middle Eastern groceries.

**Many roses grown today have little to no scent. Be sure to dry flower petals that are scented. Also do not dry petals from florist roses; they have been sprayed.

Dried lime powder (*limu-omani*) is often added to this seasoning mixture. I, instead, slice and dehydrate organic limes, when they are available, and add a dried lime slice or two to the *khoresh* as it is simmering. The flavor of the dried lime slice adds, in my opinion, a fresher nuance to the dish than does the dried powder, which is often bitter because the seeds are generally not removed before grinding.

This recipe can be doubled, if desired.

Yields 5 1/2 tablespoonfuls

FOOD VALUES for such herb mixtures are almost negligible.

Middle East–**Iran**

DRIED CITRUS ZEST
Khelale Narangi

TPT - approximately 1 hour and 30 minutes

The peel or zest of citrus fruits is intensely flavorful. I have made it one of my winter tasks to seek out organic tangerines to squeeze and peel. Iranian cooks perform the same task for addition to all sorts of soups and khoreshs and also seem, as I am, to be particularly partial to tangerine zest. Organic oranges, lemons, and limes get the same treatment from me so that I have these useful flavoring agents on hand. I have always been amazed at how many times I reach for those little jars to add just the right touch to a dish.

Although I use a dehydrator to prepare the zest, a warm oven works well too.

4 *organic* tangerines, oranges, lemons, or limes —*very well-washed*

Using a vegetable peeler, peel the zest from the fruit. Using a very sharp knife, remove the bitter, white pith from the inside of the peel. Slice the peel into thin strips about 1-inch in length. Spread out on an oven-proof plate.

Using a food dehydrator or an oven that has been preheated to 200 degrees F. and then turned off, dry the prepared zest for about 1 hour. Continue drying in the dehydrator or oven, if necessary, until thoroughly dried.

Store in a clean, dry 1/2-cup jelly jar for use as needed.

1 tablespoonful (about 6 grams) –
PROTEIN = 0.1 g.; FAT = 0.025 g.; CARBOHYDRATE = 1.0 g.;
CALORIES = 0.25; CALORIES FROM FAT = 10%

IRANIAN CAULIFLOWER AND GARLIC PICKLE
Torshi-e Gol-e Kalam

TPT - 25 hours and 20 minutes;
24 hours = flavor development period

The annual garlic festival held in Meadville, Pennsylvania, introduced me to garlic varieties that I had never known and now can never be without, many of which were introduced into the United States in 1989 when the USDA was finally allowed into the former Soviet Union to collect the many varieties of garlic not available to growers and cooks in the West. Garlic can be the mild grocery-store variety or it can be stronger and, then, even stronger. Although the mild garlic will work in this recipe, seek out a German Red or a Porcelain variety or even a braided soft-necked Silverskin garlic.

The hot summers in Iran encourage the preservation of cool weather crops such as cauliflower and, as in Greece, cauliflower is paired with garlic. Although I have come to know that pickling is a technique used to a greater or lesser extent in most cuisines, I was somewhat surprised to find several versions of this cauliflower pickle in Iranian recipe sources. No, it is not chow-chow nor is it the mustard pickle so loved by my family, but it is a perfect salad foil to a khoresh. It can be made with white cauliflower but I think the yellow cauliflower, developed by Cornell University and now widely available, makes the most beautiful pickle.

2 garlic bulbs—separated into cloves, peeled, and grated
1/4 cup fresh mint leaves—*well-washed, well-dried*, and *finely* chopped
1 1/2 tablespoons salt

1 pound cauliflower—yellow *or* white, as preferred —separated or cut into small florets
4 quarts *boiling* water

About 6 cups rice wine vinegar, or more as needed*

Sterilize 2 quart canning jars. Also sterilize lids and rings for jars.

In a mixing bowl, combine grated garlic, *finely* chopped mint, and salt. Mash together well. Set aside until required.

In a large kettle, blanch cauliflower florets in *boiling* water for 1 minute. Drain thoroughly.

Spoon a layer of blanched cauliflower into each sterilized canning jar. Spoon some of the garlic mixture over the cauliflower. Repeat layers until all jars are full to about 1 inch from the top of the jar. Pour vinegar into each jar, covering the vegetables. Seal and refrigerate for 24 hours to allow for flavor development.

Yields 2 quartfuls

IRANIAN CAULIFLOWER AND GARLIC PICKLE (cont'd)

Notes: *Distilled white vinegar may be substituted, if preferred.

Carefully wipe lips of jars. Seal with hot, sterilized lids and rings. Process in hot-water-bath canner for 15 minutes, *timing from the moment the water reaches a full rolling boil.* Remove to surface covered with thick towels or newspapers. Allow to cool for 24 hours *undisturbed.* Check to be sure jars are sealed before labeling and storing in a dark, cool, dry place. Loosen or remove rings before storing. Any jars that do not seal can be stored in the refrigerator for several months or resealed using a *new lid*.

1/20 SERVING – PROTEIN = 0.9 g.; FAT = 0.5 g.; CARBOHYDRATE = 2.3 g.; CALORIES = 13; CALORIES FROM FAT = 35%

IRANIAN SWEET RICE FLOUR PUDDING WITH ROSE WATER
Shir Berenji

TPT - 2 hours and 23 minutes;
2 hours = refrigeration period

All through the Middle East, Eurasia, and South Asia sweet puddings are found, some with rice flour, as in this case, others with just corn starch, and some with farina. I have loved puddings with this soft consistency all my life since they are reminiscent of the first comfort foods I remember. Leftover cereal grains were frequently made into desserts for the evening meal and no child growing up in America is a stranger to the comfort of corn starch puddings. "Shir berenji," said to have originally been the food of angels and often called "ice in heaven," is the dish that legend says was served to Mohammed when he entered heaven. It is always served during the meal that breaks the fast after sunset during Ramadan. Here, a celebratory Iranian version combines both concepts and is a perfect foil in texture to a bowl of dried fruits, nuts, and seeds as an ending to a Persian menu.

6 tablespoons brown *or* white rice flour
2 cups *two-percent* milk

1/2 cup corn starch
2 cups *cold* water

1 cup sugar
2 tablespoons rose water*

2 tablespoons crushed pistachio nuts
Ground cardamom

In a saucepan set over *MEDIUM* heat, combine rice flour and milk. Using a wire whisk, stir to combine thoroughly.

In a mixing bowl, combine corn starch and cold water. Using a wire whisk, stir until corn starch is in suspension. While stirring constantly, add corn starch suspension to rice–milk mixture in saucepan. Cook, stirring frequently, until mixture comes to the boil. *Reduce heat to LOW-MEDIUM.*

Middle East–Iran

IRANIAN SWEET RICE PUDDING (cont'd)

Add sugar and rose water. Cook, stirring constantly, until mixture becomes *very thick*. Remove from heat. Set a sieve over a mixing bowl. Press the pudding mixture through the sieve to remove any lumps which may have formed. Pour the sieved pudding into 2 1/2-cup square dish.* Shake until surface is level and mixture has spread to the edges of the dish. Swirl the surface attractively. Refrigerate for at least 2 hours.

Sprinkle with crushed pistachio nuts and ground cardamom.

Cut into squares to serve.

Yields 9 servings
adequate for 6 people

Notes: *A large, square black dish is especially complimentary.

This recipe can be halved or doubled, when required.

1/9 SERVING – PROTEIN = 2.6 g.; FAT = 1.5 g.; CARBOHYDRATE = 39.7 g.;
CALORIES = 179; CALORIES FROM FAT = 8%

Since the Iranian climate ranges from arid to subtropical, deserts in the eastern portion and rain forests in the North separated by high mountains, the fruits available are remarkably diverse. Choose from:

apples	apricots	cherries	cucumbers	grapes	lemons	limes	oranges	peaches
persimmons	pomegranates	quinces	rhubarb	tangerines	watermelon			

Iraq

Mesopotamia, "the land between the rivers," is the name by which Iraq has been known since antiquity. The name derives from its geographic position on the plains formed by the Tigris and Euphrates rivers, located between the great empires of the Babylonians and the Assyrians. Continuously occupied by a succession of successful societies, a highly advanced civilization was thriving there as early as 4000 BC. Here, recorded history was born with the creation of the wedge-shaped writing known as cuneiform writing. This advance was preceded by pictogram writing that has been dated to 3500 BC through excavations at Tell Asmar in Iraq. Through the millennia the land we now know as Iraq, at the crossroads of the trade routes from East to West, was the center of the Sumerian, Akkadian, Assyrian, Babylonian, Hellenistic, Parthian, Sassanid, and Abbasid empires and under the rule of the Achaemenid, Roman, Rashidun, Umayyad, Mongol, Safavid, Afsharid, Ottoman, and British Empires. It came under the British Mandate of Mesopotamia and its borders were created in 1920 by the League of Nations under the Treaty of Sevres which divided the Ottoman Empire after World War I. The Kingdom of Iraq was established in 1921. It gained its independence from Britain in 1932. The monarchy was overthrown in 1958 and the Republic of Iraq came into being under control of the Arab Socialist Ba'ath Party. Iraq began its journey to democracy on June 28, 2004, with the invasion by United States and British military forces and the subsequent collapse of the brutal dictatorship of Saddam Hussein and removal of the Ba'ath Party from power.

Although there are dishes that are prepared in a manner unique to Iraq, the cuisine borrows from other cuisines in the region. It is a cuisine that has existed for 10,000 years, borrowing as it goes, from the Sumarians, the Akkadians, the Babylonians, the Assyrians, the Persians, and from Turkey, Iran, and Lebanon. A high cuisine evolved in the medieval period which extended until the destruction of Baghdad by the invading Mongols in 1258 AD. Wealth brought through the Mediterranean trade led to a revival of the historic cuisine in the 1700s but that historic body of recipes became more tangled since it was then generally interpreted by Jewish chefs, who had traveled in Europe, especially Italy, and who became the most sought-after chefs for restaurants and for the homes of the prosperous. Untangling a true Iraqi recipe from the files of ex-patriots can further complicate the project as the influences of adopted countries also infuse tradition.

Iraqis generally end a meal with dates and enjoy dates with coffee any time of day. Some one hundred and twenty varieties of dates are grown in the hot, humid south but other fruits are also grown due to the diverse climate of the country. They are renowned for the variety and quality of their melons, grown in the hot, dry central region of the country. Nuts, peaches, plums, pears, and apples are grown in the north where cold winters allow for these crops.

Middle East–**Iraq**

Lentil Salad
Zalatat Adas
with
Fried or Toasted *Pita* Bread

Baked Eggplant Slices with Yogurt
Misaqua'at Betinjan bil Laban

~

Spinach Soup with Leeks and Dillweed
Shorbat Sbenagh Kurrath

~~~~~~~~~~~~~~~~~~~~

Macaroni in Spicy Sauce with Mushrooms
Ma'karoni

Grilled Corn–on–the–Cob with the Taste of Iraq
Balal

~~~~~~~~~~~~~~~~~~~~~~

Yogurt with Chopped Dates and Cream

Melon Slices

IRAQI LENTIL SALAD
Zalatat Adas

TPT - 3 hours and 34 minutes;
3 hours = marination period

One finds many wonderful lentil salad recipes throughout this region of the world. The seasoning in this Iraqi version is similar to that used in the Lebanese bulgur wheat salad "tabbouleh," albeit redolent of garlic as are so many Iraqi dishes. It is a wonderful way to complement grain proteins elsewhere in your menu. The legume protein can be complemented with a loaf or two of warm pita bread and served as a very enjoyable light summer main course.

1/2 cupful quick-cooking, dry, brown (*or* green) lentils
1 garlic clove—*whole and unpeeled*

1 scallion—trimmed, well-rinsed, and *thinly* sliced
1 small tomato—peeled, seeded, and chopped
1/4 cup parsley—well-washed and *finely* chopped
2 tablespoons *finely* chopped fresh mint
2 tablespoons shredded carrot
1/4 teaspoon ground cumin
Pinch ground red pepper (cayenne), or to taste
Pinch salt
Freshly ground black pepper, to taste

1 tablespoon *extra virgin* olive oil
1 tablespoon freshly squeezed lemon juice

Pick over lentils and discard any of poor quality. Rinse thoroughly. Put lentils and *unpeeled* garlic clove into a large *non-aluminum* kettle set over *MEDIUM* heat.* Add water to a level of about 1 inch above lentils. Bring to the boil. *Reduce heat to LOW* and simmer, covered, for 15 to 20 minutes, or until *tender*, but *not mushy*. Drain *thoroughly* until each lentil is dry and separate. Turn into a mixing bowl.

Remove garlic clove. Grip the root end tightly and squeeze the soft garlic pulp into a saucer. Mash the garlic pulp and add it to the lentils.

Add *thinly* sliced scallion, chopped tomato, *finely* chopped parsley and mint, shredded carrot, ground cumin and red pepper (cayenne), salt, and black pepper. Toss *gently*.

IRAQI LENTIL SALAD (cont'd)

Add olive oil and lemon juice. Toss *gently*.

Cover tightly and refrigerate for several hours or overnight to allow for flavor development. Turn occasionally to insure uniform marination.

Correct seasoning, if necessary. Turn into serving bowl.

Yields 6 servings as a side salad
Yields 3 servings as a main course salad
adequate for 3-4 people

1/6 SERVING – PROTEIN = 5.0 g.; FAT = 2.3 g.; CARBOHYDRATE = 12.7 g.;
CALORIES = 89; CALORIES FROM FAT = 23%

Notes: *Since aluminum discolors lentils rather unpleasantly, avoid the use of aluminum cookware or mixing bowls in this case.

This recipe may be doubled, when required.

IRAQI BAKED EGGPLANT SLICES WITH YOGURT
Misaqua'at Betinjan bil Laban

TPT - 1 hour and 45 minutes;
1 hour = eggplant salting period

Eggplants were an important part of the Iraqi cuisine in the medieval period during what has been described as the period of high cuisine which preceded the Mongol invasions and the destruction of Baghdad. Unlike the Armenians, Iraqis and Afghanis, who enjoy the very same dish, do not bread the eggplant slices before frying. The slices are then served with a garlicky yogurt dressing. Baked instead of fried, this traditional eggplant dish is considerably healthier. Although we generally serve this as a summer salad, it is a good choice for meze or as an appetizer as well.

1 medium eggplant, about 1 pound—washed, trimmed, and sliced into 1/4-inch crosswise slices
Coarse or kosher salt

1 large garlic clove—smashed and, then, *very finely* chopped
1/2 teaspoon salt

1 1/2 cups PLAIN YOGURT *[see index]* or commercially-available plain yogurt
Pinch ground cumin
Pinch ground coriander

3 tablespoons safflower *or* **sunflower oil**

1 small tomato—well washed, seeded, and chopped—for garnish
Ground red pepper (cayenne), to taste

Salt eggplant slices generously and place them in a sieve or colander set in the sink. Place a plate on top and a weight—a large can or a tea kettle filled with water—on top of the plate. Allow to stand for 1 hour. Rinse eggplant slices well in cold water and pat dry.

While eggplant is draining, place garlic clove and salt on a cutting board and chop until salt is integrated and garlic is almost a paste.

Put yogurt into a small bowl. Add garlic paste, ground cumin, and ground coriander. Mix until thoroughly combined. Set aside until required.

Place a rimmed cookie sheet in oven to heat. Preheat oven to 375 degrees F.

Remove preheated baking sheets from oven. Pour about 3 tablespoonfuls of oil on each pan; brush to edges. Arrange eggplant slices on each of prepared baking sheets. Bake in preheated 375 degree F. oven for 10 minutes. Remove baking sheets from oven. Turn each eggplant slice. Return to oven for about 10 minutes more, or until each slice is crisp and well-browned. Drain eggplant slices *thoroughly* on several thicknesses of paper toweling.

Arrange eggplants slices, overlapping, on a platter. Spoon the yogurt mixture over. Sprinkle the chopped tomato over and sprinkle with ground red pepper (cayenne).

Yields 8 servings
adequate for 6-8 people

Note: If you find baby eggplants in your greengrocer, you can cut them lengthwise and prepare them as above. This allows the recipe to be halved or even quartered to serve two people.

Middle East—Iraq

IRAQI BAKED EGGPLANT SLICES WITH YOGURT (cont'd)

1/8 SERVING – PROTEIN = 2.7 g.; FAT = 6.0 g.; CARBOHYDRATE = 4.9 g.;
CALORIES = 86; CALORIES FROM FAT = 63%

IRAQI SPINACH SOUP WITH LEEKS AND DILLWEED
Shorbat Sbenagh Kurrath
TPT - 35 minutes

I have found that most Iraqi soups are too heavy to be used as the soup course of a western menu. Some, granted, can be converted into vegetarian meals but to find a light soup that can function in a multi-course meal plan is a challenge. This soup includes leeks (kurrath) that have been used in recipes in the region for centuries. The wild leeks that are used in Iraqi cooking are different from ours in that the white bulb portion is not well-developed; the leeks are, instead, chosen for green leaves. Iraqis use the stem and greens in many dishes. Here, it gives both color and flavor to this milk-based soup.

1 1/2 tablespoons *extra virgin* olive oil
2 medium leeks—*both white and green portions*—trimmed, *very well-rinsed*, and chopped

2 tablespoons unbleached white flour
3 cups *two-percent* milk

10 ounces baby spinach—trimmed of tough stems, *very well-rinsed*, and *finely* chopped
1/4 cup chopped fresh dillweed
1/2 teaspoon ground coriander
1/4 teaspoon freshly ground black pepper, or to taste
1/8 teaspoon salt, or to taste

Lemon wedges, for garnish

In a large kettle set over *MEDIUM* heat, heat oil. Add chopped leeks and sauté until leeks are wilted, *being careful not to allow the leeks to brown.*

Add flour and, using a wooden spoon, make a *roux* by beating flour into the oil and leeks in the kettle. Cook for 2 minutes, stirring constantly. *Be careful not to burn or overbrown the roux.* Remove from heat and gradually beat in milk. Return saucepan to heat.

Add *finely* chopped spinach, chopped dillweed, ground coriander, black pepper, and salt. Cook, stirring frequently, for about 15-20 minutes, or until thickened. Turn into a heated tureen.

Serve into heated soup bowl. Garnish each serving with a lemon wedge.

Yields about 5 cupfuls

Note: This recipe can be doubled, if required. It does not freeze well but since it reheats well, it can be a menu planner for the next day.

1/5 SERVING (i. e., per cupful) –
PROTEIN = 6.0 g.; FAT = 6.4 g.; CARBOHYDRATE = 12.4 g.;
CALORIES = 133; CALORIES FROM FAT = 43%

Middle East–Iraq

IRAQI MACARONI IN SPICY SAUCE WITH MUSHROOMS
Ma'karoni

TPT - 2 hours and 42 minutes;
2 hours = mushrooms rehydration period

Perhaps you will look at this recipe and question why such a modern ingredient as macaroni is used in an Iraqi dish. You may conclude that it was introduced to Iraq by the British or the Americans but this is far from the case. The connection between the Arab world and Sicily may have led to the introduction of macaroni to Europe. Even the origin of the word macaroni may be from the Arabic. It is only in the last fifty years that the word "maqarna" has been replaced by ma'karoni in Iraq. The Arab world was most probably introduced to this flour and water product via the silk road trade with the Far East since written evidence in China dates noodles between 25 and 220 AD, during the Chinese East Han Dynasty. Medieval cookbooks are full of recipes for noodles but increasingly rice became the choice in the Middle East. Rice is still considered the Iraqi staple but the convenience of dry pasta products has returned noodle and ma'karoni dishes to Iraqi menus. This has been evolved as a vegetarian dish by eliminating the traditional lamb. Its flavor is wonderful.

2 cups mixture of *dried* mushrooms—*porcini, crimini,* lobster, *chanterelles,* morels, *shiitake,* oyster, black trumpet mushrooms, and/or any others of choice—*well-rinsed and brushed to remove any foreign matter*

1 quart *boiling* water

2 tablespoons *extra virgin* olive oil
1 small onion—*finely* chopped

1 cup canned, *diced* tomatoes
1/2 cup canning liquid from tomatoes
1/2 cup chopped red bell pepper
1/2 teaspoon crushed red pepper, or to taste
1 teaspoon honey *or agave* nectar
2 teaspoons tamarind concentrate*
2 teaspoons chopped fresh sage *or* 1 teaspoon crushed, dried sage
1/4 teaspoon ground turmeric
1/4 teaspoon ground coriander
1/4 teaspoon ground cumin
1/4 teaspoon ground ginger
1/4 teaspoon mustard powder
1 bay leaf—broken
Freshly ground black pepper, to taste

6 ounces macaroni—*castellane, campanella,* or *ziti*
3 quarts *boiling* water

In a mixing bowl, combine dried mushrooms mixture, which have been *well-rinsed and brushed to remove any foreign material.* Add the 1quartful *boiling* water. Allow mushrooms to soak for at least 2 hours, or until softened. Press mushrooms down into the soaking liquid occasionally to insure even reconstitution.

Using a slotted spoon, remove mushrooms from mushroom broth to a small bowl. Set aside until required. Reserve WILD MUSHROOM STOCK for future recipes.

In a large skillet set over *MEDIUM* heat, heat oil. Add *finely* chopped onion and *sauté* until onion is soft and translucent, *being careful to allow neither the onion nor the garlic to brown. Reduce heat to LOW-MEDIUM.*

Add drained, rehydrated mushrooms, diced tomatoes, tomato liquid, chopped red pepper, crushed red pepper, honey or *agave* nectar, tamarind concentrate, sage, ground turmeric, coriander, cumin, and ginger, mustard powder, broken bay leaf, and black pepper. Stir to combine well. Reduce heat to *LOW,* cover, and simmer for 15 minutes.

Meanwhile, in a saucepan set over *MEDIUM* heat, cook macaroni is 3 quartfuls *boiling* water for 12 minutes. Drain. Add to tomato–mushroom sauce mixture in skillet. Stir to coat the macaroni with the sauce. Cover and allow to cook for another 10 minutes. Remove and discard bay leaf pieces. Turn out onto a heated serving platter.

Serve at once.

Yields 6 servings
adequate for 4 people

Notes: *Tamarind concentrate is available in Middle Eastern, Indian, and Thai groceries and in most grocery stores in the international food section. This sour fruit paste, which keeps almost indefinitely in the refrigerator, gives a unique flavor to this dish and to many other dishes.

This recipe can be halved, when required.

1/6 SERVING – PROTEIN = 4.7 g.; FAT = 4.4 g.; CARBOHYDRATE = 26.0 g.;
CALORIES = 164; CALORIES FROM FAT = 24%

Middle East–**Iraq**

GRILLED CORN – ON – THE – COB
WITH THE TASTE OF IRAQ
Balal

TPT - about 45 minutes

Piles of corn, grilled directly over hot coals, greet hungry Iraqi as they peruse the wares of the street venders. Maybe a soup or stew with bread for lunch and why not add a couple of ears of sweet, salty corn to the impromptu menu? Since the charcoal fires of the street vendors of Baghdad are not a fixture in my home, I prepare the corn by wrapping each ear in aluminum foil when the meal and cooking have moved inside but I also find that the aluminum foil wrap allows for succulent corn without the burned kernels that result when the outdoor grill is used. This a delicious way to serve corn, especially if the corn might have been picked the day before and the sugar has begun to turn to starch.

Salt
5 teaspoons firmly packed *light* brown sugar

6 freshly husked, large ears of corn

Prepare a moderately hot charcoal fire of glowing coals.*

Place each ear of corn in the middle of a square of heavy-duty aluminum foil. Generously salt each ear. Sprinkle 1 teaspoonful of brown sugar over each ear. Roll each ear over and over to distribute the salt and brown sugar. Wrap ears and seal ends. Using a second square of heavy-duty aluminum foil, double wrap each ear.

When coals are *white hot,* place wrapped corn ears on grill about 4 inches above coals. Grill for about 25-30 minutes, turning occasionally. When done, these can be set on the back of the grill for a *few* minutes until other grilled items are done.

Serve in aluminum wraps to keep them hot and moist.

Yields 6 servings
adequate for 3-6 people**

Notes: *These can also be prepared in the oven, if preferred. Bake at 375 degrees F. for about 30 minutes.

**It is wise to know each guest's *corn quota*. For most moderate appetites, one ear is usually sufficient. Half ears may also be prepared to accommodate smaller appetites, especially those of children.

This recipe may be halved, doubled, or tripled with ease, when required.

1/6 SERVING (i. e., per ear) –
PROTEIN = 4.8 g.; FAT = 1.5 g.; CARBOHYDRATE = 34.3 g.;
CALORIES = 147; CALORIES FROM FAT = 9%

YOGURT WITH CHOPPED DATES AND CREAM

TPT - 1 hour and 16 minutes;
1 hour = yogurt draining period

The slim, hard pits of the fruit of the date palm have given us one clue to the eating habits of early man. It is now known that dates were part of the diet of those who lived in the Middle East as early as 50,000 BC. Yogurt, drained of the whey, is frequently used as an ingredient in Middle Eastern cooking. The drained product we revere as "yogurt crème" for its rich smoothness is often called yogurt cheese or" labneh" in Lebanon or just Greek-style yogurt. It is useful for salads and for desserts and is stirred into all sorts of soups and stews and skillet dishes. Yogurt is popular in Iraq and, although this recipe is not Iraqi but of my own creation, it is a cooling end to a hot and spicy meal and most respectfully submitted.

2 1/2 cups VANILLA YOGURT *[see index]*
  or commercially-available vanilla yogurt

2 tablespoons sugar
1/2 teaspoon pure vanilla extract
1/2 teaspoon pure almond extract

1/2 cup heavy whipping cream
1 teaspoon confectioners' sugar

3/4 cup chopped *preservative-free* dates—about 15 medium

YOGURT WITH CHOPPED DATES AND CREAM (cont'd)

Prepare VANILLA YOGURT *CRÈME* by setting two automatic drip coffeemaker filters into a sieve over a medium-sized bowl or a yogurt filter over a 2-cup measuring cup. Pour the VANILLA YOGURT into the filters and set in the refrigerator. Allow to drain for about 1 hour. Turn into mixing bowl.

Add sugar, vanilla extract, and almond extract. Using a wire whisk, beat the yogurt until smooth and creamy. Set aside briefly.

Using the electric mixer fitted with *chilled* beaters or by hand using a *chilled* wire whisk, beat heavy cream in a *clean, chilled* bowl until soft peaks form. While continuing to beat, add confectioners' sugar. Beat until stiff peaks form.

Divide the yogurt mixture among six custard cups or ramekins. Scatter a portion of the chopped dates over the yogurt in each cup. Spoon a portion of the whipped cream over each serving. Refrigerate until required.

Serve chilled.

Yields 6 individual servings

Notes: *A cupful of fresh raspberries or blackberries, well-washed and well-dried can be substituted for the dates.

This recipe can be halved, when required.

1/6 SERVING – PROTEIN = 5.0 g.; FAT = 2.2 g.; CARBOHYDRATE = 31.7 g.;
CALORIES = 222; CALORIES FROM FAT = 9%

Israel

"Storybook dolls," as they were known when I was a little girl, were Christmas gifts to be treasured. They were small dolls with pretty ceramic faces, beautifully costumed in tiny silk dresses. My "bride" doll is the angel on our Christmas tree. In 1948 I received a most unusual doll dressed in a blue and white silk dress, a commemorative "storybook doll" that celebrated the founding of the State of Israel. I knew little about this new nation then but in 1954 a classmate left with her family to live on a *kibbutz* in Israel. Before she left school, Lee told us about her family's plan and the country to which she was going. Years later I was to realize that Israel presented an opportunity to observe the emergence of a new cuisine and that my classmate was part of this enormous experiment.

Carving a state in the Levant, out of the inhospitable desert with unfriendly neighbors, was no small task but the feeding of those who came was equally daunting, also because of the desert. Irrigation was critically important. From irrigated land came the orchards and the fields, food for people and food for animals. The cuisines that the diverse immigrant population had left behind could not be reproduced in Israel; a cuisine, which their new land could produce, was going to evolve. Today, we tend to concentrate on all that the Israelis have brought from the soil, especially the cultivation of fruits and vegetables through the *kibbutz* system that have been so successful, but it was not an easy process. Suddenly, due to the Law of Return, the population grew daily and those people had to be fed. Someone once told me that because of the scarcity of animal protein in the early years, cottage cheese, *kaese*, was a crucial source of protein and a major tool in the creative cook's hand.

This soup and salad menu may help you to begin to understand the modern cuisine that evolved, that is still evolving, thanks to the heritage of Africans, Europeans, and North Americans who have come to live in the Middle East.

Herbed Yogurt "Cheese" and **Vegan "Chopped Liver"**
Gehackte Leber"
with *Pita* bread and Olives

Roasted Beetroot and Garlic Dip with *Hummus*
or
Hard-cooked Eggs with *Matbucha* Sauce

Warm *Pita* Bread

~

Puréed Butternut Squash Soup with Soymeat

~~~~~~~~~~~~~~~~~~~~

Israeli *Couscous* and Chick Pea Salad with Cucumber, Cherries, and Dates

~~~~~~~~~~

Prickly Pear Salad
Sabra Salad

~~~~~~~~~~

Roasted Red Peppers with Yogurt and Pecans

~~~~~~~~~~

Avocado and Egg Salad

~~~~~~~~~~

Zucchini Salad *Vinaigrette*

~~~~~~~~~~~~~~~~~~~~

Orange Wheat Pudding   **Grapefruit Dessert with Yogurt**

Middle East–**Israel**

ISRAELI HERBED YOGURT APPETIZER
TPT - 10 minutes

We have enjoyed the taste, the nutrition, and the culinary adaptability of drained yogurt for some forty years, since we first began to make out own yogurt. The product we call "yogurt crème" is called "yogurt cheese" by those in the Middle East who also appreciate the nutrition and versatility of the dense, smooth result of draining yogurt. It can be sweetened and incorporated into desserts, used as a nutritious garnish in place of whipped cream or as a substitute for sour cream in savory dishes such as this herbed dip, popular in Israel. Summer savory ("Satureja hortensis") is an annual I grow and dry each year as did my grandmother, an herb that has been used to flavor food for over 2,000 years. Little used except in herb mixtures and for seasoning green beans and lentils, in the German style, it has a subtle, but recognizable, peppery taste that begs to be used more.

1/4 teaspoon celery seeds
1 teaspoon dried chives
1/4 teaspoon dried summer savory

1 teaspoon sesame seeds
1/4 teaspoon salt, or to taste
1/8 teaspoon ground cumin
1/8 teaspoon ground red pepper (cayenne)

2 cups YOGURT *CRÈME* [see index]*

1 tablespoon *extra virgin* olive oil

Pita bread triangles, assorted olives, tomato
  wedges, and assorted *crudités*, of choice

Using a mortar and pestle, grind celery seeds, dried chives, and dried summer savory to a powder. Turn into a small bowl.

Add sesame seeds, salt, ground cumin, and ground red pepper (cayenne). Stir to mix well.

Pack yogurt *crème* into a small mixing bowl or cereal bowl. Invert bowl onto a serving platter and unmold yogurt. Drizzle oil over the yogurt. Sprinkle the seed–herb mixture over. Refrigerate until ready to serve.

When ready to serve, surround the herbed yogurt *crème* with *pita*, olives, and selected vegetables

Provide salad plates, salad forks, and butter knives for convenience.

Yields 2 cupfuls
adequate 6-8 people

Notes: *I begin the draining process of freshly made yogurt for the yogurt *crème* the evening before I plan to serve this so that the texture is very dense and the yogurt flavor is very fresh.

This recipe can he halved.

1/8 SERVING (exclusive of pita, olives, and vegetables chosen) –
PROTEIN = 8.7 g.; FAT = 1.8 g.; CARBOHYDRATE = 13.1 g.;
CALORIES = 104; CALORIES FROM FAT = 16%

VEGAN "CHOPPED LIVER"
Gehackte "Leber"
TPT - 45 minutes

In the New York metropolitan area, "chopped liver," a finally chopped mixture of chicken livers and hard-cooked eggs" is found in large trays in every German–Jewish delicatessen, attesting to its widespread popularity. It was an appetizer or snack that was not left behind by Europeans and North Americans who emigrated to Israel. This vegan version is equally as good as a spread for crackers or toasts and as a dip for crudités. If you have access to crimini or baby bella mushrooms, they are preferable due to the increased flavor and the dark color, which adds authenticity.

1 cup chopped *preservative-free* walnuts*

3 tablespoons safflower *or* sunflower oil
8 ounces *crimini* or baby bella mushrooms
  —stems removed, rinsed, and cleaned well
  with a brush and chopped

1 medium onion—chopped

Salt, to taste
Freshly ground black pepper, to taste

VOLUME I - 493

VEGAN "CHOPPED LIVER" (cont'd)

Using the food processor fitted with steel knife, chop the walnuts into a uniformly chopped meal. Turn into a bowl. Set aside until required.

In a non-stick-coated-skillet set over *MEDIUM* heat, heat oil. Add chopped mushrooms and onion. Sauté until mushrooms have released water and most of that water has been evaporated—about 8 minutes. Turn into the work bowl of the food processor fitted with steel knife.

Add chopped walnut meal. Process until very smooth, scraping down the sides of the work bowl as necessary.

Season with salt and pepper, to taste. Stir to integrate seasoning uniformly. Turn into a serving dish, smooth the top surface using a butter spreader, cover, and refrigerate until required.

Serve chilled.

Yields about 1 cupful

Notes: *Toasting the walnuts adds another layer of flavor.

This recipe can be halved or doubled, when required.

1/16 SERVING (i. e., about 1 tablespoonful) –
PROTEIN = 2.1 g.; FAT = 9.0 g.; CARBOHYDRATE = 3.1 g.;
CALORIES = 101; CALORIES FROM FAT = 80%

ISRAELI ROASTED BEETROOT AND GARLIC DIP WITH *HUMMUS*
TPT - 1 hour and 34 minutes

Almost every ethnic group in Israel can be said to be fond of beets. It may surprise some people that beetroots are even eating in the cuisines of the Middle East and in North Africa but the number of recipes I have found over the years confirms that this wonderful brain-food root is eaten around the Mediterranean with gusto. The nuances of its preparation from cuisine to cuisine truly deserve a dedicated volume. This appetizer displays the amalgamation of influences that have given Israel a cuisine of its own.

3 large fresh beets—well-scrubbed

3 large garlic cloves—*finely* **chopped**

1/4 cup TURKISH CHICK PEA DIP *(Hummus)*
[see index] or **commercially-available** *hummus*
of preference
2 tablespoons *extra virgin* **olive oil**
1 tablespoon red wine vinegar
1 teaspoon ground coriander
1/2 teaspoon ground cumin

Prepare a jelly roll pan—a baking sheet with low sides —or a roasting pan by coating with a thin film of *high heat* safflower oil. Preheat oven to 375 degrees F.

Cut the leaves from the beets, *leaving 2 inches of each petiole. Do not cut off the root tip.* Place beets on prepared baking pan. Bake in preheated oven for about 50 minutes, turning about every 10 minutes until beets are tender and skins have loosened. Allow to cool for about 15 minutes. Remove skins and chop. Put into work bowl of food processor fitted with steel knife. Process until *finely* chopped.

Add *finely* chopped garlic cloves and process until finely puréed.

Add *hummus*, oil, vinegar, and ground coriander and cumin. Process until uniform in color and consistency. Turn into a serving bowl.

Serve at room temperature with *pita* bread, crackers, chips, or *crudités*. Refrigerate leftovers.

Yields 24 servings
adequate for 6 people

Note: This recipe is easily halved, when required.

1/24 SERVING – PROTEIN = 0.3 g.; FAT = 2.3 g.; CARBOHYDRATE = 1.3 g.;
CALORIES = 27; CALORIES FROM FAT = 77%

Middle East–**Israel**

ISRAELI TOMATO AND PEPPER APPETIZER SALAD
Matbucha

TPT - 4 hours and 6 minutes;
2 hours = refrigeration period

Matbucha is a sauce-like salad, very popular in Israel, which probably came to Israel with Sephardic immigration from North Africa. It is a fabulous "salad" into which hard-cooked eggs or pita or challah bread can be dipped as an appetizer; it is a terrific sauce to mix into hummous or serve over entrees. We also serve it on the side with soy analogue fish filets. If you have roasted red peppers in the freezer and a can of diced tomatoes, you can quickly be on your way to a very interesting taste experience.

1 ROASTED RED PEPPER *[see index]*—*finely* chopped
2 cups canned, *petite diced* tomatoes—well-drained
3 garlic cloves—*finely* chopped
1 teaspoon Hungarian hot paprika
1/4 teaspoon ground coriander
Pinch ground red pepper (cayenne)
Pinch coarse, kosher salt, or to taste

1/4 cup *extra virgin* olive oil

Lemon wedges

In a saucepan set over *MEDIUM* heat, combine *finely* chopped roasted red pepper, tomatoes, *finely* chopped garlic, paprika, ground coriander, ground red pepper (cayenne), and salt. Stir to combine.

Pour oil over. Allow to come to the simmer. Reduce heat to *LOW*. Cover and allow to cook for about 1 1/2 to 2 hours, or until most of the liquid has evaporated. Stir occasionally to prevent sticking. Turn into a serving dish and refrigerate for at least 2 hours to allow for flavor development.

Serve chilled, garnished with lemon wedges.

Yields 8 servings

Note: This recipe can be halved or doubled, when required.

1/8 SERVING – PROTEIN = 0.9 g.; FAT = 5.7 g.; CARBOHYDRATE = 3.6 g.; CALORIES = 67; CALORIES FROM FAT = 77%

ISRAELI PURÉED BUTTERNUT SQUASH SOUP WITH SOYMEAT

TPT - 1 hour and 22 minutes

The very phrase "soup and a salad" congers up a pleasant, light lunch or supper and this Israeli soup is a good, nutritious choice. More often than not there is a container of mashed butternut squash or puréed pumpkin in the freezer in May when I inventory the freezer in preparation for the summer and autumn produce to come so part of the work for this soup is already done and on a cool spring or summer evening, what could be a more enjoyable entrée.

1 tablespoon *extra virgin* olive oil
1/2 cup chopped onion
2 garlic cloves—*finely* chopped

1 tablespoon *extra virgin* olive oil
1/2 cup chopped onion
2 garlic cloves—*finely* chopped

1 1/2 cups canned, *diced* tomatoes
1/8-1/4 teaspoon jalapeño red *chili* sauce *or* Tabasco Sauce, or more to taste
1/2 teaspoon ground coriander
1/4 teaspoon paprika
1/4 teaspoon ground cumin

1 quart water
1 pound butternut squash *or* pumpkin, if preferred—peeled, seeded, and chopped to yield about 5 cupfuls

1/2 teaspoon grated orange zest
Salt, to taste
Freshly ground black pepper, to taste

2 ounces chopped *or* slivered *frozen* soy meat analogue

Set a sieve over a clean saucepan. Set aside until required.

In a kettle set over *MEDIUM* heat, heat oil. Add chopped onion and garlic. Sauté until vegetables are soft, *being careful to allow neither the onion nor the garlic to brown.*

Add tomatoes with purée in which they were canned, *jalapeño* red *chili* sauce, ground coriander, paprika, and cumin. Stir to combine well. Allow to come to the boil, stirring constantly.

VOLUME I - 495

ISRAELI PURÉED BUTTERNUT SQUASH SOUP WITH SOYMEAT (cont'd)

Add water and chopped or mashed squash. Allow to come to the boil. Reduce heat to *LOW-MEDIUM*. Allow to simmer for about 45 minutes.

Using an electric blender or food processor fitted with steel knife, purée soup mixture a cup or two at a time. Pour the purée into the sieve set over the clean saucepan.** Place over *MEDIUM* heat to reheat. Discard residue in sieve or save for soup stock.

Season to taste with grated orange zest, salt, and black pepper.

Add slivered soymeat. When soup has reheated, turn into a heated soup tureen.

Serve into heated soup plates.

Yields about 9 cupfuls

Notes: *Jalapeño* sauce is available in Hispanic groceries, food specialty stores, and in most grocery stores throughout the Southwest.

**The puréed soup freezes well at this point.

This recipe can be halved or doubled, when required.

1/9 SERVING (i. e., per cupful) –
PROTEIN = 2.9 g.; FAT = 1.7 g.; CARBOHYDRATE = 5.2 g.;
CALORIES = 55; CALORIES FROM FAT = 27%

ISRAELI *COUSCOUS* AND CHICK PEA SALAD WITH CUCUMBER, CHERRIES, AND DATES
TPT - 41 minutes

Israeli couscous, mughrabiye, or pearl couscous is really a commercial version of the North African pasta product brought to Israel in the 1950s. It was introduced as an alternative for rice and was preferred by immigrants from North Africa and eastern Arab countries. Although often a challenge to find, mughrabiye is well worth seeking out. It is made from the same toasted semolina as is regular couscous, but the balls of pasta are larger and more useful in recipes because they actually add substance to the dish when stirred into the other ingredients while regular couscous has to be used as base over which the ingredients are served.*

The combination from the Eastern Mediterranean sounded strange at first but I persisted and I am very glad that I did. This is a substantial, well-flavored, diversely textured, one-dish vegan meal that would be typical of an Israeli settlement community supper and that can withstand the trip to a picnic ground, a day's travel, or an early prep schedule. It is certainly not "your same old" pasta salad.

3 quarts *boiling* water
1 tablespoon freshly squeezed lemon juice
1 3-inch strip lemon zest
1 cup Israeli *couscous (mughrabiye)*

2 cups well-washed and dried young spinach
—heavy ribs and stems removed

1 cup fresh *or* canned sweet cherries—pitted and halved
1/2 cucumber—peeled, seeded, and chopped into 1/4-inch dice to yield about 1 1/2 cupfuls
1 cup canned chick peas (*garbanzos*)—well-drained, well-rinsed, and well-dried
1/4 cup *finely* chopped red onion
1/3 cup chopped, pitted *preservative-free* dates
Freshly ground black pepper, to taste

1 1/2 tablespoons PLAIN YOGURT *[see index] or* commercially-available plain yogurt
1 1/2 tablespoons *calorie-reduced or light* mayonnaise
1 teaspoon *very finely* chopped garlic

2 tablespoons slivered, *toasted preservative-free* almonds

In a kettle set over *MEDIUM-HIGH* heat, combine *boiling* water, lemon juice, lemon zest, and the *couscous*. Boil for 10 minutes. Drain. Plunge *couscous* into a bowl of ice water to stop further cooking and to chill. Allow to stand for about 10 minutes. Drain thoroughly. Turn into a large mixing bowl.

Roll the well-washed and dried spinach leaves into tight rolls and, using a sharp knife, cut the leaves into slivers. Add to *couscous*.

Add cherry halves, diced cucumber, well-drained chick peas, *finely* chopped red onion, and chopped dates. Toss gently.

Season with black pepper.

ISRAELI *COUSCOUS* AND CHICK PEA SALAD WITH CUCUMBER, CHERRIES, AND DATES (cont'd)

In a small dish, combine yogurt, mayonnaise and *very finely* chopped garlic. Stir to combine. Add to salad mixture and gently toss to coat ingredients. Turn into a serving bowl.

Sprinkle *toasted* almonds over the top.

Refrigerate until required.

Yields 6 servings
adequate for 4 people

Notes: *Palestinian *maftoul* is quite different. It is made from *bulgur* and flour, not from *semolina*.

Refrigerate leftovers are just as good the next day.

This recipe can be halved or doubled, when required.

1/6 SERVING – PROTEIN = 5.9 g.; FAT = 5.4 g.; CARBOHYDRATE = 30.3 g.;
CALORIES = 168; CALORIES FROM FAT = 29%

ISRAELI PRICKLY PEAR SALAD
Sabra Salad
TPT - 5 minutes

A distinctive cuisine, perhaps the most significantly new cuisine on the planet, has been developing in Israel since 1948. Because of their determination to make the desert give back the land to agriculture, they have successfully established orchards of all kinds with the help of irrigation. The clever use of greenhouse and hydroponic culture of vegetables has augmented field crops, further enabling them to feed their people. This salad clearly reflects their success and, one might add, their latitude and longitude.

2 tablespoons freshly squeezed orange juice
2 tablespoons freshly squeezed lemon juice
1 tablespoon *walnut* oil
1/2 teaspoon ground cardamom

2 prickly pears (cactus pears, *sabras*, Indian figs, *ficos d'India*, Barbary figs, *or tunas*)—peeled, halved and sliced*
1 large Gala apple—*very well-washed*, quartered, cored, seeded, and *thinly* sliced
6 large dates—chopped**
1 medium red bell pepper—cored, seeded and cut into strips
2 tablespoons slivered Italian red onion

In a large mixing bowl, combine, orange and lemon juices, *walnut* oil, and ground cardamom. Using a wire whisk, combine thoroughly.

Add prickly pear and *unpeeled* apple slices, chopped dates, and red pepper strips. Toss to coat ingredients with dressing. Turn into a serving bowl. Refrigerate until ready to serve.

Serve chilled. Leftovers will keep, refrigerated, for a day or two.

Yields 6 servings
adequate for 4 people

Notes: *Prickly pear fruits, from the United States Southwest and imported, are widely available from October through January, in greengrocers and increasingly in the specialty produce sections of grocery stores. Choose small, firm pears and ripen at room temperature. Be sure to remove the roots of the spines when peeling prickly pears. The seeds are edible although bothersome to dental work if you are not careful!

**The easiest way to "chop" dates is to cut them with scissors.

This recipe can be doubled, when required.

1/6 SERVING – PROTEIN = 0.8 g.; FAT = 2.7 g.; CARBOHYDRATE = 19.8 g.;
CALORIES = 97; CALORIES FROM FAT = 25%

Middle East–**Israel**

ISRAELI ROASTED RED PEPPERS WITH YOGURT AND PECANS
TPT - 1 hour and 12 minutes

Although a classic Sephardic breakfast dish, served throughout Israel, we find this to be a most satisfying summer salad or luncheon dish.

3 large red bell peppers

2 cups PLAIN YOGURT *[see index]* **or commercially-available plain yogurt**
Salt, to taste
Freshly ground black pepper, to taste

1/4 cup coarsely chopped, *toasted preservative-free* **pecans**
1/4 cup chopped fresh mint leaves

Preheat oven to 350 degrees F.

Place red peppers on a cookie sheet. Roast in preheated oven for about 40 minutes, *turning frequently.*

Remove from oven and place in a heavy brown paper bag in dry sink. Roll the top of the bag down and allow to steam for about 15 minutes.

Remove stems, seeds, and membranes, peel, and divide roasted peppers into large sections. Set aside.

Put yogurt into a mixing bowl. Season with salt and black pepper to taste.

Put about 1/3 cupful seasoned yogurt in the center of each of six salad plates. Apportion roasted red pepper pieces among the salad plates, arranging them over the yogurt.

Serve at once, garnished with *toasted* pecans and chopped mint leaves.

Yields 6 individual servings

Note: This recipe can be halved or doubled, when required.

1/6 SERVING – PROTEIN = 5.2 g.; FAT = 6.2 g.; CARBOHYDRATE = 9.0 g.;
CALORIES = 97; CALORIES FROM FAT = 58 %

ISRAELI AVOCADO AND EGG SALAD
TPT - 10 minutes

The delicious, nutritionally-packed avocado is a more recent fruit crop in Israel and not yet an export crop. Avocados are very popular in Israel which suggests that at the present rate of consumption it is unlikely that we will find Israeli avocados in our local grocery here in the middle of Pennsylvania. They are eaten out-of-hand, as garnishes for both salads and meat dishes, and in composed tossed and vegetable salads. In this simple salad they are combined with hard-cooked eggs. By removing two of the egg yolks, the fat content of this salad can be considerably decreased.

4 hard-cooked eggs—peeled

2 small, ripe avocados
2 tablespoons freshly squeezed lemon juice

1 small onion—*finely* **chopped**

Freshly ground black pepper, to taste

Paprika

Remove the yolks of three of the hard-cooked eggs. (Refrigerate yolks to use for another purpose.) Chop the whites of these three eggs and the white and yolk of the fourth egg. Set aside briefly.

Peel and dice avocados into a mixing bowl. Add lemon juice. *Gently* toss to coat the avocado pieces with lemon juice to prevent browning.

Add *finely* chopped onion and chopped hard-cooked eggs. *Toss gently*. Turn into a serving bowl.

Sprinkle with paprika.

Serve at once.

Yields 6 servings
adequate for 4 servings

Note: This recipe can be halved or doubled, when required.

1/6 SERVING – PROTEIN = 4.6 g.; FAT = 11.9 g.; CARBOHYDRATE = 4.7 g.;
CALORIES = 139; CALORIES FROM FAT = 77%

ZUCCHINI SALAD *VINAIGRETTE* IN THE STYLE OF ISRAEL

TPT - 1 hour and 9 minutes;
1 hour = marination period

Squashes similar to the present-day marrows (zucchini) and yellow summer squash existed in the Middle East in ancient times. Summer squashes are grown today in Israel. I thought it might be appropriate to create this for an Israeli-inspired salad buffet which I planned for a "two-sleep visit" by our grandson when he was nine years old. His interest in the world and in different foods amazed and thrilled me.

2 small zucchini—*very thinly* sliced on the diagonal to create elliptical slices*

2 tablespoon *extra virgin* olive oil
1 teaspoon acacia *or* wildflower honey
2 tablespoons MIXED FLOWER VINEGAR WITH OREGANO *[see index] or* other herb vinegar of choice
1/8 teaspoon freshly ground black pepper

1 tablespoon pine nuts (*pignoli*), for garnish

In a shallow serving dish, arrange zucchini slices in a spiraling pattern.

In a cruet or jar, combine oil, honey, vinegar, and black pepper. Shake vigorously. Pour over zucchini slices. Cover dish tightly with plastic wrap and refrigerate for at least 1 hour.

Garnish with pine nuts (*pignoli*).

Serve chilled using a slotted pie server.

Yields 6 servings
adequate for 4-6 people

Notes: *If desired, yellow summer squash slices can be alternated with the zucchini. The combination makes a beautiful presentation.

**The food value calculation assumes that about two-thirds of the marinade is residual.

This recipe can be halved, when required.

1/6 SERVING – PROTEIN = 0.8 g.; FAT = 1.9 g.; CARBOHYDRATE = 3.0 g.;
CALORIES = 25; CALORIES FROM FAT = 68%**

ISRAELI ORANGE WHEAT PUDDING

TPT - 1 hour and 44 minutes;
15 minutes = cooling period;
1 hour = refrigeration period

Wheat is used all over the Middle East and North Africa, and not just for breads. Semolina and farina desserts, couscous, and bulgur salads from Palestine, Greece, Turkey, Lebanon, Morocco, Syria, and Egypt have found their way into our recipe files. The present occupants of the Levant in the State of Israel have, however, introduced another variable because the cultivation of fruit trees has been so very successful. Many of their desserts and salads may reflect the cuisines that surround them in the eastern Mediterranean but these traditional dishes, more often than not, have the added nutrition and flavor of fruits. Sweet, juicy oranges are plentiful and useful, as shown by this recipe. This dessert is a really good choice if you plan to serve a bean or lentil soup or even a chili.

1/2 cup sugar
2 cups water

2/3 cup skimmed milk
1/3 cup frozen orange juice concentrate—*thawed*
3/4 cup farina, preferably whole wheat , *or* Cream of Wheat cereal

2 teaspoons pure vanilla extract
1/2 cup *cold* light cream *or* half and half*

Cinnamon sugar

Sweetened whipped cream, to garnish, if desired
Jarred mandarin orange sections, to garnish, if desired

In a saucepan set over *MEDIUM* heat, combine sugar and water. Bring to a boil.

Meanwhile, in a small bowl, combine milk, *thawed* orange juice concentrate, and farina. Mix well.

ISRAELI ORANGE WHEAT PUDDING (cont'd)

While stirring the *boiling* sugar water, add farina mixture. Continue stirring until mixture thickens. Remove from heat and allow to cool for about 15 minutes. Turn into bowl of electric mixer.

Add vanilla extract and cream. Using the electric mixer set at LOW speed, beat the vanilla extract and milk into the farina mixture. Increase the mixer speed to HIGH and beat for 5 minutes until light and fluffy. Turn into serving bowl and refrigerate for at least 1 hour.

Sprinkle with cinnamon sugar.

Spoon into sherbet glasses or individual dessert dishes. Serve with a garnish of whipped cream and a mandarin orange section or two, if desired. Refrigerate any leftovers.

Yields 8 servings
adequate for 6 people

Notes: *If preferred, the cream may be replaced with milk to increase the protein and reduce the saturated fat content of the pudding.

This recipe can be halved or doubled, when required.

1/8 SERVING (exclusive of garnishes) –
PROTEIN = 3.3 g.; FAT = 1.1 g.; CARBOHYDRATE = 34.4 g.;
CALORIES = 160; CALORIES FROM FAT = 6%

ISRAELI GRAPEFRUIT DESSERT WITH YOGURT
TPT - 11 minutes

It surprises me that yogurt companies have not struck upon the idea of yogurt with grapefruit. It is a wonderful combination. Here, in this very simple dessert, the tart and the sweet play very perfectly at the end of a meal.

2 pink grapefruits—*chilled*—or 2 *chilled* cans red grapefruit sections—well-drained

3/4 cup PLAIN YOGURT *[see index]* **or commercially-available plain yogurt**
2 tablespoon honey of choice
Ground cinnamon, to taste

Peel grapefruits and separate into segments. Divide among six soup plates. Arrange in fans. Alternately, divide *well-drained*, canned sections among the six soup plates.

Spoon 2 tablespoonfuls of yogurt into the center of each grapefruit fan. Drizzle honey back and forth over each serving. Sprinkle with ground cinnamon.
Serve chilled.

Yields 6 servings

Note: This recipe can easily be adjusted for two or four servings.

1/6 SERVING – PROTEIN = 2.2 g.; FAT = 0.6 g.; CARBOHYDRATE = 16.6 g.;
CALORIES = 75; CALORIES FROM FAT = 7%

Jordan

Situated in the Levant region of the Fertile Crescent and in the center of the area occupied by many early civilizations, Jordan shares an ancient history with many neighboring nations influenced by the ebb and flow of power in this still very volatile part of the world. The area was controlled by the Babylonians and the Canaanites. It was home to many ancient kingdoms in the second and first millennia BC—Nabatean Petra, which is said to have originated Arabic script, and Edom, Ammon, and Moab kingdoms whose wars with and defeats of the Israelites are recorded on ancient clay tablets and in the Bible's Old Testament. It fell under the rule of Pharonic Egypt during Egypt's wars with the Babylonians and the Hittites. The Greeks, the Persians, and the Romans all came and went as did the soldiers of the later Byzantine Empire. In the seventh century Jordan became part of the Arabic Islamic Empire allowing for a period of relative stability during which the tribal people of this region assumed the present Arabic Islamic cultural identity. By the eleventh century, however, Jordan became a battlefield as the Christian Crusaders invaded the Middle East. In 1516 the area became part of the Ottoman Empire and remained so until the period of World War I when in 1918 the so-called Army of the Great Arab Revolt took control and secured the area for local tribes, a period colorfully chronicled by T. E. Lawrence. Despite agreements in 1916 and 1917 with Great Britain that were thought to be a basis for the formation of an expansive and inclusive Arab state, in 1921 an area only slightly larger that South Carolina was allotted under the British League of Nations mandate and became known as The Emirate of Transjordan. It was not until 1946 that it became the sovereign state known as the Hashemite Kingdom of Jordan.

Despite its latitude and longitude and a logical expectation of desert conditions, Jordan presents a fascinatingly unexpected Mediterranean climate—semidry in the summer with average temperatures in the high 80s F. and relatively cool in the winter with temperatures often in the mid 30s F. in some areas. Most of the precipitation can be expected during the winter when the humidity is relatively high. Surprisingly, snow is not at all unusual in the capital of Amman which is at 4,199 feet above sea level. Most of the country receives less than twenty-four inches of rain a year but the Jordan Valley receives about thirty-five inches of rain per year so it is small wonder that agriculture is centered in the fertile land of this huge rift valley. Because of limited groundwater, most irrigation projects have been designed to increase the productivity of this region rather than redirecting water to the smaller agricultural lands in the North where olive trees are cultivated and where orchards of fruit and almond trees can be found. Even though some fruits and vegetables are exported to neighboring countries, Jordan's comfortable economic position depends on its large deposits of phosphates and uranium. Shale oil and natural gas industries have expanded in recent years. Tourism, both conventional and medical, is increasingly important to Jordan. A well-developed tourism industry is expanding and increasing the accessibility to a large number of sites that chronicle the art and architecture of the many peoples who have occupied this land.

Jordanian cuisine stands back and surveys the Middle East with an eye to flavor and the very Jordanian concept of dining together. Perhaps the best way to enjoy the cornucopia of the collected culture and their interwoven histories is to gather friends and partake of a comprehensive *mezze*.

Middle East – **Jordan**

MEZZE

Falafel with Fava Beans and Chick Peas
Falafel

Pan-Grilled *Halloumi* Cheese
J'ibna Bedhah

Turkish Chick Pea Dip *[see index]*
Hummus

Assorted Olives
Zatun

Roasted Chick Peas with Nuts
Leblebi

Yogurt with Za'atar *[see index]*
Labaneh Za'atar

Pita bread
Kubz

SALADS

Bulgur Wheat Salad
Tabbouleh

Pickled Vegetables

Artichoke Hearts in Oil
Ardishawki Bzeit

~

Jordanian Stewed Tomatoes
Galayet Badora

~~~~~~~~~~~~~~~~~~~~~~

Roasted Eggplant Pie in *Phyllo* Crust
Batinijaan bi Fillo

or

Meatballs in *Tahini* Sauce with Potatoes
Kafta bi Tahini

Baked Fennel in the Style of the Middle East
Bizbas

~~~~~~~~~~~~~~~~~~~~~~

Raspberry Curd

Sweet Cheese Pastry
Kunafa

Coffee with Cardamom Pods

Middle East–**Jordan**

JORDANIAN *FALAFEL* WITH FAVA BEANS AND CHICK PEAS

TPT - 2 hours;
1 hour = refrigeration period

Stuffing a pita half with falafel, cucumber, tomatoes and a yogurt–garlic sauce is almost as common a sandwich choice in the New York metropolitan area as it is in the countries of the Levant, where every country claims falafel as its own. There are street vendors who appear at midday with warm pitas and all the fixings and this wonderful vegetarian staple is also available in Israeli and Middle Eastern delicatessens in any East Coast city. New Yorkers who eat street food will gladly direct you to the best of the many. I have made falafel from a number of recipes using only chickpeas but never had I encountered a combination of beans such as this recipe. I do think this is the best of all those that fill a folder in my files. Note that Jordanians make small falafel and serve them with a dipping sauce. They do not make the large falafel patties usually found in New York City and on the streets of Israeli cities.

1 can (15.5 ounces) chick peas (*garbanzos*)—well-drained
1/2 cup cooked *or* canned and drained fava beans

1 large onion—*finely* chopped
3 large garlic cloves—*finely* chopped
1/4 cup fresh parsley—*finely* chopped
1/2 teaspoon ground coriander
1 1/2 teaspoons ground cumin
1/4 teaspoon ground allspice
2 1/2 tablespoons unbleached white flour
Freshly ground black pepper

Oil for deep-frying

Remove the seed coats on the chick peas and on the fava beans. Place in the work bowl of the food processor, fitted with steel knife.

Add *finely* chopped onion, garlic, and parsley, ground coriander, cumin, and allspice, flour, and black pepper. Process to form a thick paste.

Using two teaspoons, roll the bean paste into small balls and set them on waxed paper or a cold plate. Refrigerate for 1 hour to allow *falafel* to solidify.

Pour oil in a deep skillet or small kettle to a depth of about 2 inches. Heat oil to 350 degrees F.

Fry *falafel*, a few at a time, in hot oil until golden brown about 3-5 minutes. Transfer to paper toweling to drain.

Place the dip of choice in the center of a heated plate. Arrange hot *falafel* around the dip dish.

Serve at once. Provide small forks such as cocktail forks or even fondue forks for dipping.

Yields about 30 *falafel*

Notes: Because I use canned chick peas, I do not add salt. If you cook dried beans from scratch, you may find that you need to add salt.

This recipe can be halved or doubled, when required.

1/30 SERVING – PROTEIN = 1.1 g.; FAT = 1.0 g.; CARBOHYDRATE = 4.7 g.;
CALORIES = 24; CALORIES FROM FAT = 38%

JORDANIAN ROASTED CHICK PEAS WITH NUTS

Leblebi

TPT - 26 minutes

Chick peas as a roasted snack may well have its origins in the ancient Anatolia region, that is, modern-day Turkey. Enjoyment of this snack appears to have traveled throughout the Ottoman Empire. Today roasted chick peas are eaten in most of the countries that border the Mediterranean. Although Jordanians do not add a crouton element to this snack, it is very similar to a snack that is enjoyed in Italy. We think it is a really, really great way to add the nutrition of legumes to the diet. Our grandson, who seemed to enjoy countering our vegetarianism with pronouncements of his carnivorism, just thought they were snack food worthy of consuming during his self-proclaimed "Tyrannosaurus Rex period" . . .

JORDANIAN ROASTED CHICK PEAS WITH NUTS (cont'd)

1 can (19 ounces) chick peas (*garbanzos*)—well-drained

1 1/2 tablespoons *extra virgin* olive oil
2 large garlic cloves—peeled and halved

1 cup *salted* mixed, *preservative-free* nuts with peanuts*

Freshly ground black pepper, to taste
Pinch or two dried basil—*finely* crushed
Pinch or two dried parsley—*finely* crushed
1 tablespoon *extra virgin* olive oil
2 tablespoons grated *pecorino Romano* or Parmesan cheese, as preferred

Preheat oven to 400 degrees F.

Spread *well-drained* chick peas out on a layer of paper toweling. Place another layer of paper toweling over the chick peas. Pat and roll to dry. Discard and loosened seed coats.

While the chick peas are drying, prepare a jelly roll pan or cookie sheet with sides by oiling *evenly* with the 1 1/2 tablespoonfuls oil. Rub garlic halves—*cut side down*—all over the pan, leaving the garlic halves on the pan to flavor and roast.

Scatter towel-dried chick peas over the prepared baking sheet.

Bake in preheated 400 degree F. oven for about 15 minutes, or until chick peas are *lightly* toasted. *Shake the pan frequently during the baking period to insure even browning.* Remove from oven. Discard garlic.

Add nuts. Stir to coat the nuts with any residual garlicky oil. Transfer roasted chick peas and nuts to a heated bowl.

Add black pepper and crushed, dried, basil and parsley. Toss to mix well. Sprinkle remaining tablespoonful of olive oil and grated cheese over. Again toss well.

Serve while still warm as part of *mezze* spread or allow to cool and add to a salad.

Yields 20 servings

Notes: *Jordanians prefer a salty mixture. If desired, unsalted nuts can be used in this recipe.

This recipe may be doubled, when required.

1/20 SERVING – PROTEIN = 3.6 g.; FAT = 6.3 g.; CARBOHYDRATE = 5.1 g.;
CALORIES = 87; CALORIES FROM FAT = 65%

BULGUR WHEAT SALAD
Tabbouleh

TPT - 1 hour and 16 minutes;
1 hour = wheat soaking period

We happen to find "tabbouleh" to be one of the most wonderful taste sensations in the world. It is simple and, yet, simply wonderful. This salad, too, found its way onto the buffet for our daughter's wedding reception luncheon because Fischer's in Huntington, Long Island, catered the luncheon and they made a truly not-to-be-missed version. For less formal occasions, pita "pockets" filled with this salad mixture make unusual and, we think, wonderful sandwiches. It is popular all over the Middle East and this version may well have come to the Jordanian mezze from Lebanon. The chapter devoted to Lebanon includes a version of "tabbouleh" made with millet.

3/4 cup dry bulgur (*bulghur*) wheat*
1 1/2 cups *cold* water

4 scallions—trimmed, well-rinsed, and sliced
1 cup chopped Italian flat-leafed parsley
1/4 cup fresh mint leaves—chopped
2 tablespoons *extra virgin* olive oil
2 tablespoons freshly squeezed lemon juice
Freshly ground black pepper, to taste

6 large Romaine lettuce leaves

2 medium, ripe tomatoes—peeled, seeded, and chopped—for garnish

Rinse bulgur wheat well and remove any extraneous material. Place in a mixing bowl. Cover with *cold* water and allow to soak for 1 hour.

Turn soaked wheat into a strainer and drain thoroughly. Squeeze out any excess moisture.

In a mixing bowl, combine wheat, sliced scallions, and chopped parsley and mint. Toss *gently* with a fork to mix well. Add olive oil and lemon juice. Toss again with fork to mix well. Season with black pepper.**

Line a serving bowl with lettuce leaves. Pile prepared wheat salad into center. Garnish with chopped tomato.

Middle East – **Jordan**

BULGUR WHEAT SALAD (cont'd)

Serve at once.

Yields 6 servings
adequate for 4 people

Notes: *Bulgur (*bulghur*) wheat, cracked wheat, or crushed wheat is available in natural food stores and in Middle Eastern groceries. It is a par-boiled product and, therefore, needs no further cooking.

**This recipe may be prepared to this point several hours ahead of time and refrigerated.

When required, this recipe may be doubled.

Fresh coriander (*cilantro*) leaves make a nice addition to this salad, as does *finely* chopped garlic, if desired.

1/6 SERVING – PROTEIN = 2.7 g.; FAT = 4.1 g.; CARBOHYDRATE = 15.9 g.;
CALORIES = 110; CALORIES FROM FAT = 34%

ARTICHOKE HEARTS IN OIL
Ardishawki Bzeit

TPT - 1 hour and 20 minutes;
30 minutes = cooling period

Cooking vegetables in oil was a technique common to many areas of the so-called Fertile Crescent, an arc from the Nile River to the Tigris and Euphrates rivers. Today's cooks in the nations that now form that ancient cradle of civilization development, Jordan, Lebanon, Syria, Iraq, Israel, and the disputed West Bank area of Palestine, still cook vegetables in oil. I find the easiest way to serve this dish as part of a mezze is to use frozen artichoke hearts; the preparation is greatly reduced and the quartered artichoke hearts are easily served and eaten. It is also a perfect side dish for a main course entrée.

24 *frozen, quartered* artichoke hearts
2 tablespoons freshly squeezed lemon juice
3 tablespoons *extra virgin* olive oil
2 tablespoons water
1/2 teaspoon sugar*
Salt, to taste
Freshly ground black pepper, to taste

In a non-stick-coated skillet set over *LOW-MEDIUM* heat, combine artichoke hearts, lemon juice, oil, water, sugar, salt, and black pepper. Allow to come to the boil. Stir. *Reduce heat to LOW.* Simmer for 45 minutes, stirring occasionally.

Using a slotted spoon, remove artichoke hearts to a heated serving bowl. Allow to stand for about 30 minutes.

Serve at room temperature.

Yields 6 servings
adequate for 4 people

Notes: *The bit of sugar added to this recipe brings out the sweetness that every artichoke lover knows and loves so do not leave it out.

**In reality there are far less calories from fat than this calculation would suggest. It is impossible to determine how much actually returns to the skillet when the artichoke hearts are spooned into a serving dish.

This recipe can be halved or doubled, when required.

1/6 SERVING – PROTEIN = 0.8 g.; FAT = 5.7 g.; CARBOHYDRATE = 2.9 g.;
CALORIES = 64; CALORIES FROM FAT = 80%**

JORDANIAN STEWED TOMATOES
Galayet Bandora
TPT - 12 minutes

There are few memories that can impact my heart and my taste buds simultaneously as can the memory of sitting at my grandmother's table with a bowl of stewed tomatoes and my family around me. Grandma would send one of us to the fruit cellar to get jars of the tomatoes she had canned the autumn before. In my mind's eye I can still lift the layers of newspapers that insulated the jars from the cold as I selected from the jars with lead screw-on tops that were used back then. The stewed tomatoes were brought to the boil with sugar and butter and ladled into bowls. Crackers were crushed into the tomatoes and we "set to it" with gusto. Jordanians enjoy stewed tomatoes too but their version is redolent with garlic, onion, and spices. Instead of crackers, chunks of flat bread are added to the hot soup.

Mom and I canned tomatoes but the generations that have followed no longer have the pleasure of seeing those beautiful jars on the shelves of a fruit cellar.

1 tablespoon CLARIFIED BUTTER or *GHEE*
[see index]
1 tablespoon *extra virgin* olive oil
1 large onion—*finely* chopped
2 large garlic cloves—*very finely* chopped

Pinch ground cumin, or to taste
Pinch Spanish *smoked* paprika
2 or 3 drops *jalapeño chili* sauce

10 ripe tomatoes—peeled, seeded, and chopped

2 tablespoons pine nuts (*pignoli*), for garnish

Warm, fresh *pita* or Jordanian *shrak* bread, if available

In a saucepan set over MEDIUM heat, heat clarified butter and olive oil. Add *finely* chopped onion and very *finely* chopped garlic. Sauté until soft and translucent, *being careful to allow neither the onion nor the garlic to brown.*

Add cumin, *smoked* paprika, and *jalapeño chili* sauce. Stir for a minute or two.

Add chopped tomatoes and cook, stirring frequently, until the tomatoes are cooked and soft. Turn into heated serving bowl.

Serve into heated soup bowls. Garnish each serving with a few pine nuts (*pignoli*). Accompany with warm bread.

Yields 6 servings
adequate for 4 people

Notes: This recipe can be doubled, when required, and canned in sterilized jars using the hot water-bath method for canning tomatoes.

Stewed tomatoes, prepared this way, make a very pleasant side dish for a meal.

1/6 SERVING – PROTEIN = 3.0 g.; FAT = 5.9 g.; CARBOHYDRATE = 9.8 g.; CALORIES = 101; CALORIES FROM FAT = 53%

ROASTED EGGPLANT PIE IN *PHYLLO* CRUST
Batinjaan bi' Fillo
TPT - 2 hours and 32 minutes

Although I am not the biggest fan of eggplant, I find this pie to be one the most exquisitely seasoned dishes on the planet; that's why I prefer to just call it "batinjaan," which would be recognized everywhere simply as eggplant. And, the textural juxtapositions are utterly amazing. What can I say; this is a stunning, fragrant, and thoroughly delicious dish. It is found with many names across the Eastern Mediterranean and whether it originated in Turkey or in Greece or somewhere else, it doesn't matter.

ROASTED EGGPLANT PIE IN *PHYLLO* CRUST (cont'd)

2 medium, firm eggplants—about 1 pound

2 tablespoons *extra virgin* olive oil
1 medium onion—*finely* chopped
1 orange bell pepper—cored, seeded, and *finely* chopped
2 tablespoons *finely* chopped fresh mint
1 teaspoon anise seeds
2 teaspoons ground cumin
1 teaspoon Spanish *smoked* paprika
1/2 teaspoon red pepper flakes

1 1/2 cups canned, *diced* tomatoes—*well-drained*
2 tablespoons tomato paste

2 large garlic cloves—*very finely* chopped

12 sheets (9- x 14-inch) *phyllo* pastry—*defrosted*
2 tablespoons dry breadcrumbs

2 tablespoons *trans-fat-free soft* butter spread *or* whipped butter—*brought to room temperature*

1 large Italian plum tomato—sliced

Preheat oven to 350 degrees F. Prepare a 10-inch pie plate by coating with non-stick lecithin spray coating.

Pierce the eggplants and place them on a baking sheet. Bake in preheated 350 degree F. oven for about 50 minutes, or until soft. Turn occasionally during the baking period. When the eggplants are soft, transfer to a bread board and scoop the flesh from the skin into the work bowl of the food processor. Process to form a smooth purée. Set aside briefly.

In a large non-stick-coated skillet set over *MEDIUM* heat, heat oil. Add *finely* chopped onion, pepper, and mint, anise seeds, ground cumin, smoked paprika, and red pepper flakes. Sauté until onion is soft and translucent, *being careful to allow neither the vegetables or the spices to brown. Reduce heat to LOW-MEDIUM*

Add well-drained tomatoes and tomato paste. Cook, stirring frequently, until thickened—about 8 minutes.

Add eggplant purée and *very finely* chopped garlic. Cook, stirring frequently, for about 10 minutes. Be careful not to allow the mixture to stick to the bottom of the skillet. Set aside briefly.

Take one of the half-sheets of *phyllo* and place it on a dry work surface. Using a pastry brush, lightly brush the sheet with the soft butter spread. Place the buttered pastry sheet onto the pie plate, allowing it to hang over the edge of the plate. Take a pinch of the breadcrumbs and sprinkle them over the pastry surface. Take another half-sheet of *phyllo*, butter it, and place it on top of the first sheet at a 45-degree angle. Sprinkle with crumbs. Continue with four more half-sheets of *phyllo*, positioning each at a 45-degree angle from the previous sheet. Carefully, using both hands, tuck the flaps from these first six half-sheets of *phyllo* into the pie plate under the nest base. Continue adding buttered half-sheets of *phyllo* in the same manner with a sprinkling of breadcrumbs but do not tuck these under, instead roll them gently toward the center. Press the center down to form a nest.

Spoon eggplant filling into the *phyllo* crust. Arrange tomato slices attractively over. Bake in preheated oven until lightly browned—about 55 minutes.

When the pastry is baked and puffed, remove from oven and transfer to a round serving platter or set the pie plate on a platter.

Serve at once. Cut with a very sharp knife into pie-shaped wedges and transfer to each diner's plate. Refrigerate leftovers.

Yields 8 servings
adequate for 4-6 people

Note: This recipe can not be doubled.

1/8 SERVING – PROTEIN = 3.4 g.; FAT = 5.1 g.; CARBOHYDRATE = 19.4 g.;
CALORIES = 135; CALORIES FROM FAT = 37%

Middle East–**Jordan**

MEATBALLS IN *TAHINI* SAUCE WITH POTATOES
Kofta bi Tahini
TPT - 1 hour and 34 minutes

I remember the chore of making meatballs and meatloaves when I was a kid. First my mother sent me to the butcher to buy a specific cut of pork, lean ground beef, and lean veal. I asked him to grind the meat twice as instructed. Home with my purchase, we then started adding the onion, breadcrumbs, and seasonings. Then we rolled lumps of the meat mixture into balls, refrigerated them, and finally fried them before adding them to the dish that was being prepared. The rest of the ground meat was made into my mom's special meatloaf. When I think back, it was an all-day event. "Kofta," as prepared in Jordan, takes time too but soy meatballs really speed up the preparation of this delicious dish which is popular in neighboring countries too.

1 package (9 ounces) vegetarian "meatballs"
2 small-medium potatoes—peeled, halved, and thinly sliced into half-moon slices*
3/4 cup water

TAHINI **SAUCE:**
    1/2 cup sesame *tahini*
    1/2 cup water
    1/4 cup freshly squeezed lemon juice
    Salt, to taste

Preheat oven to 350 degrees F. Prepare a 1 1/2-quart soufflé dish by coating with non-stick lecithin spray coating.

Arrange meatballs in a single layer in the prepared baking dish. Arrange potato slices over the meatballs. Pour the 3/4 cupful water over the potatoes. Cover tightly with aluminum foil. Bake in preheated 350 degree F. oven for 40 minutes. Remove from oven.

While the casserole is baking, in a mixing bowl, combine sesame *tahini*, water, and lemon juice. Using a wire whisk or an immersion blender, blend until smooth. Add salt to taste.

Pour the *tahini* sauce over the potatoes and return to the oven, *uncovered*, for about 30 minutes more. The sauce should reduce and the top will be lightly browned.

Serve at once.

Yields 6 servings
adequate for 4 people

Notes: *A cheese plane produces thin slices which are perfect for this dish.

        This recipe can be doubled, when required, but be sure to choose an oven-to-table baking dish that can hold the meatballs in a single layer.

1/6 SERVING – PROTEIN = 11.3 g.; FAT = 9.3 g.; CARBOHYDRATE = 12.5 g.;
CALORIES = 166; CALORIES FROM FAT = 50%

BAKED FENNEL IN THE STYLE OF THE MIDDLE EAST
Bizbas
TPT - 55 minutes

The bulb of Florence fennel has a slightly sweet, anise flavor. Its fresh, clean taste makes it a favorite throughout the Mediterranean—raw or cooked. Here it is baked in a tomato sauce and garnished with its own fronds. Some eastern Mediterranean cooks use fennel as a dolma and fill the halves with a variety of stuffings but this simple recipe makes an unusual and very enjoyable side dish.

1 cup water
1 cup canned, *crushed* **tomatoes**
1 tablespoon chopped fresh oregano
Freshly ground black pepper, to taste

3 fennel bulbs—well-washed, trimmed, and halved

2-3 tablespoons chopped fresh fennel fronds —well-washed—for garnish

Preheat oven to 350 degrees F.

In a baking dish adequate to accommodate all six fennel bulb halves, combine water, crushed tomatoes, chopped fresh oregano, and black pepper.

Nestle the fennel bulb halves cut-side-down into the tomato mixture. Cover and bake in preheated 350 degree F. oven for 45-50 minutes, or until bulbs have softened. Transfer to a heated serving platter. Garnish with fennel fronds.

Middle East–**Jordan**

BAKED FENNEL IN THE STYLE OF THE MIDDLE EAST (cont'd)

Serve at once.

Yields 6 servings
adequate for 4-6 people

Note: This recipe can be halved, when required.

1/6 SERVING – PROTEIN = 2.1 g.; FAT = 2.3 g.; CARBOHYDRATE = 5.9 g.;
CALORIES = 29; CALORIES FROM FAT = 9%

RASPBERRY CURD

TPT -   1 hour and 30 minutes;
1 hour = chilling period

Sweet pastries are consumed in Jordan just as they are throughout the Middle East. Usually these are reserved for celebrations and are purchased at shops that specialize in one or the other pastry, just as we would choose a pastry shop for Italian pastries. You would probably be offered such a pastry if you were invited for dinner by a Jordanian family because your presence at their table would be viewed as a celebration. Kunafa is a Jordanian syrup-soaked sweet made with the shredded pastry kataifi popular in Greek desserts, together with nuts, and cheeses. Fruit curds, enjoyed in Jordan since the days of British influence, are satisfyingly nutritious, and quite easy to make for an everyday meal. Commercially-available jarred curds are an entirely inadequate substitute for the real thing. Fat-free pasteurized eggs do not change the taste memory from our trip to Great Britain, they just allow us to visit that memory more often. Served as a dessert or as a dessert sauce, the sensual texture is such a perfect way to end a meal.

12 ounces well-rinsed fresh raspberries *or* frozen, if necessary, *or* blackberries, if preferred

1/4 cup freshly squeezed lemon juice
5 tablespoons sugar

3/4 cup *fat-free* pasteurized eggs* (the equivalent of 3 eggs)
2 tablespoons butter

Using a food processor fitted with steel knife, purée raspberries. Turn into a saucepan set over *LOW-MEDIUM* heat.

Add lemon juice and sugar. Cook, stirring frequently, for about five minutes. Set a fine strainer, such as a tea strainer. Using the back of a spoon, press the purée through the strainer. Discard residue.

Add pasteurized eggs and butter to the fruit purée in the top half of the double boiler. Set over *hot*, but *not boiling*, water. Cook, stirring constantly with a wire whisk, until thickened. Remove from heat.

Divide among four *demitasse* cups or small custard cups. When cool, cover with plastic wrap. Refrigerate until *thoroughly chilled*—about 1 hour.

Serve with *demitasse* spoons.

Yields 4 individual servings

Notes: *Because raw eggs present the danger of *Salmonella* poisoning, commercially-available pasteurized eggs are recommended for use in preparing this dish.

This recipe may be doubled, when required.

1/4 SERVING – PROTEIN = 5.1 g.; FAT = 5.8 g.; CARBOHYDRATE = 27.7 g.;
CALORIES = 271; CALORIES FROM FAT = 19%

Middle East–**Jordan**

JORDANIAN SWEET CHEESE PASTRY
Kunafa

TPT - 2 hours and 58 minutes;
1 hour = raisin soaking period;
1 hour = cooling period

The cuisine of Jordan is the result of the incorporation of dishes from other areas of the Levant. Kunafa is a sweet served on celebratory occasions especially during the month-long Muslim celebration of Ramadan. Of Palestinian origin, it is a much loved, rich dessert, but it is not at all as difficult to make as are some of the phyllo-based sweets of the Middle East. My first contact said that I should just buy a package of kataifi. That is a lot easier said than done in most areas of the United States but frozen phyllo pastry is available in most well-stocked grocery stores and kataifi can easily be made by cutting the frozen phyllo sheets into fine shreds. My contact also recommended using Naboulsi or Akawi cheese. That too was a problem but I have since found that ricotta and fresh mozzarella, blended together, can be substituted quite satisfactorily.

1/4 cup *preservative-free dark* **raisins**
1 cup *boiling* **water**

SUGAR SYRUP:
   1/2 cup sugar
   1/2 cup water
   1 tablespoons freshly squeezed lemon juice
   Pinch saffron

   1/2 teaspoon orange blossom water

CHEESE FILLING:
   1 cup *part-skimmed milk ricotta* **cheese**
   1/2 cup fresh *mozzarella*—**shredded**

1/2 pound *frozen phyllo* **pastry**—*brought to room temperature*
3 tablespoons CLARIFIED BUTTER or GHEE
   [see index]

Soak raisins in *boiling* water for at least 1 hour.

Prepare a 9 x 5 x 3-inch non-stick-coated loaf pan or an 8-inch Pyrex pie plate by coating with non-stick lecithin spray coating.

In a saucepan set over *MEDIUM-HIGH* heat, combine sugar, water, lemon juice, and saffron. Stir. Allow to come the boil. Reduce heat to *LOW-MEDIUM* heat and allow to simmer until syrupy—about 12 minutes. Remove from heat.

Add orange blossom water. Stir to integrate. Set aside to cool.

Using the food processor fitted with steel knife, combine *ricotta* and shredded fresh *mozzarella* cheeses. Process until thoroughly combined. Set aside until required.

Slice *phyllo* pastry into thin strips. Put into a mixing bowl. Add clarified butter or *ghee* and toss to coat the *phyllo* strips with the *ghee*. Spread *one-half* of the *phyllo* strips in the bottom of the prepared pan or pie plate. Press down lightly.

Spoon the cheese mixture over the *phyllo* strips, spreading it evenly.

Spoon the rest of the *phyllo* strips over. Bake in preheated oven for about 30-35 minutes, or until lightly golden. Remove from oven and *immediately* pour the prepared, cold sugar syrup evenly over. Set aside and allow to cool to room temperature.

When cooled, invert onto a platter.

Drain raisins thoroughly and scatter over the unmolded *kunafa*.

Slice into squares to serve. Using a wide spatula, carefully lift a serving to a dessert plate.

               Yields 8 servings
               adequate for 6 people

Notes: This is customarily garnished with blanched almond slices, chopped cashews or walnuts, and either golden raisins or chopped dried dates that have been sautéed in more *ghee*.

When required, this dish can be doubled. When doubling, use an 8 x 8-inch non-stick-coated baking pan or a 10-inch Pyrex pie plate.

1/6 SERVING – PROTEIN = 7.5 g.; FAT = 8.6 g.; CARBOHYDRATE = 22.4 g.;
CALORIES = 263; CALORIES FROM FAT = 29%

Kuwait

In 123 BC a major Persian Gulf port in the trade route between Mesopotamia and India known as Characene occupied the northeastern edge of the Arabian Peninsula. The port and surrounding area remained under the control of the Parthian Empire until 224 AD when rule shifted to the Sassanid Empire who renamed the port Hajar. Part of a caliphate from the fourteenth to the seventeenth centuries, its population consisted of nomadic tribes and associated clans who were eventually absorbed into the expanding Ottoman Empire. In 1756 Sabah I bin Jaber emerged as the first Emir of Kuwait, ruling semi-autonomously under the Ottoman Turks. Al-Sabah, the ruling family of Kuwait, has descended from Sabah I bin Jaber. Subsequent to the establishment of the emirate, nomadic tribes that roamed the Arabian Peninsula began to move to the coastal area that is now Kuwait City.

In 1899 Sheikh Mubarah Al-Sabah signed a treaty with Great Britain through which Kuwait would receive, as a British protectorate, aid and naval protection should the Ottoman Empire decide to bring Kuwait firmly under their rule and should the Germans decide to expand their influence to the Persian Gulf. This protectorate status ended with Kuwaiti independence in 1961. Kuwait was annexed by Iraq in 1990 after years of dispute over oil resources. In 1991 Kuwait was liberated by United States and coalition troops during the Gulf War. Destruction of oil wells and the resultant contamination of the soil, caused by the Iraqi "scorched earth" retreat, left eastern and southeastern regions of Kuwait uninhabitable. The oil deposited by the spills created a semi-asphalt surface in large areas of the desert eliminating both habitation and agriculture. Coastal fishing and pearling, once a major industry, were also adversely impacted.

The ancient tropical jungles that covered this part of our planet and the animals that lived there are buried now beneath the desert and have become the oil that has made life possible in this now inhospitable climate. Coastal effect not withstanding, Kuwait experiences a hot, dry desert climate. The average July high temperature is 117 degrees F. with an overnight low temperature average of 84 degrees F. Ten percent of the world's oil reserves are beneath the Kuwaiti desert, an enormous resource for a state only about three-quarters the size of the Commonwealth of Massachusetts. Discovered in 1937, this wealth of oil allows Kuwait to produce 2.8 million barrels a day. The prosperity from this oil has brought a very comfortable lifestyle to the Kuwaiti population of about three million, 1.3 million of whom are actually non-nationals since Kuwaiti law does not allow for naturalization. There are no taxes and the unemployment rate is only 2.2 percent. Due to this economic windfall that oil provided, an effort began in the 1950s, while still a British protectorate, to modernize the kingdom's infrastructure and to improve the educational system in an effort to provide an educated and skilled work force in anticipation of independence. Today, the ruling Al-Sabah family is making an effort to change Kuwait's almost total dependence upon the oil industry as a hedge against the possibility of world petroleum consumption changes as had occurred in the early 1980s.

Because of their wealth, compared to that of other countries in the region, Kuwaiti eat well and also because of their wealth, Kuwaiti eat meat, fish, and/or cheese at every meal. Restaurants that serve vegetarian and vegan meals are few and far between and those usually specialize in diverse Indian cuisines. Since a significant amount of the food eaten in Kuwait is imported due to the lack of land suitable for agriculture, the Kuwaiti cuisine is a more global cuisine. An infusion of Indian, Persian, Mediterranean, especially Lebanese, and Najdi cuisines underlie menu choices. This amalgamation is said to have begun with the date trade. Dates from Iraq were moved overland by caravan and by sea under the sails of nomadic traders. In return they brought spices back to the Arabian Peninsula, introducing the tastes of the subcontinent and the Far East to their own tables. Kuwaiti have adopted many dishes from other cuisines and patronize restaurants from all corners of the world.

Middle East – **Kuwait**

Spinach and Yogurt Salad
Borani

~

Puréed Lentil Soup with Potatoes

Sweet Corn Soup

~~~~~~~~~~~~~~~~~~~~

Basmati Rice with Peas and Dillweed

Steamed Kaboucha Squash

Middle Eastern Bread and Vegetable Salad
Fattoush

Grilled Vegetable Salad
Mechouia

~~~~~~~~~~~~~~~~~~~~

Vegetables with *Vermicelli* and Rice
Maraq Bamiya

Kuwaiti Spice Mixture
Baharat

~~~~~~~~~~

Vegetable *Kebabs* with Lemon
Kebabs

Basmati Rice

~~~~~~~~~~~~~~~~~~~~

Mascarpone Mousse

Custard with Saffron and Rose Water
Khabees Al-Nasha

Dates

KUWAITI SPINACH AND YOGURT SALAD
Borani
TPT - 21 minutes

The taste of frozen spinach does not hold a candle to that of steamed, fresh spinach. Kuwaiti devotion to that fresh spinach taste can be seen in this unusual salad. It may be difficult and expensive to buy fresh spinach in Kuwait City but those who love this salad demand the freshest spinach and, as one author stated, "We just wait." This is a frequent summer salad for us because it refreshes and that little extra dairy protein is welcome.

Middle East–Kuwait

KUWAITI SPINACH AND YOGURT SALAD (cont'd)

10 ounces fresh baby spinach—trimmed and well-washed

1/8 teaspoon salt

1/2 cup **PLAIN YOGURT** *[see index]* or commercially-available plain yogurt
2 tablespoons freshly squeezed lemon juice
1 tablespoon *very finely* chopped onion

1 tablespoon *finely* slivered fresh mint

In a small kettle set over *LOW* heat, place washed spinach. Cover and steam in just the water adhering to the leaves. Drain very well. Using several thicknesses of paper toweling, press out any remaining water. Transfer spinach to a cutting board and chop finely. Turn into a small bowl.

Add salt. Stir well.

Add yogurt, lemon juice, and *very finely* chopped onion. Fold over and over until thoroughly mixed. Turn out on a small platter or into a shallow serving bowl.

Sprinkle mint over the salad. Refrigerate until ready to serve.

Serve chilled.

Yields 6 servings
adequate for 4 people

Note: This recipe can be halved or doubled, when required.

1/6 SERVING – PROTEIN = 3.0 g.; FAT = 0.2 g.; CARBOHYDRATE = 4.7 g.;
CALORIES = 30; CALORIES FROM FAT = 6%

KUWAITI PURÉED LENTIL SOUP WITH POTATOES
TPT - 1 hour and 23 minutes

There are probably hundreds of lentil soup variations. My files contain several dozen comforting lentil soups that we have enjoyed and each is, believe it or not, different. The addition of lemon slices, tomato paste, and cumin gives the classic lentil–onion–garlic–potato combination a taste that is decidedly unique. It is certainly not black lentil soup from Nepal nor is it the taste of German or French lentil soups.

1 cup dry brown (*or* green) lentils

1 tablespoon **CLARIFIED BUTTER** *or* **GHEE** *[see index]*
2 garlic cloves—crushed and *finely* chopped
2 teaspoons ground cumin

1 quart *boiling* water
1/2 medium onion—coarsely chopped

6 cups **VEGETARIAN BROWN STOCK** *[see index]* *or* water
3 tablespoons tomato paste
3 dried lemon slices
1/2 teaspoon salt, or to taste
1/4 teaspoon ground cardamom

2 medium potatoes—peeled and diced

Pick over lentils and discard any of poor quality. Rinse thoroughly. Set aside briefly.

In a large *non-aluminum** kettle set over *LOW-MEDIUM* heat, heat clarified butter. Add *finely* chopped garlic cloves and ground cumin. Sauté the garlic for several minutes.

Add the 1 quartful *boiling* water, chopped onion, and lentils. Cook, stirring occasionally, until most of the water has boiled away and the lentils are soft—about 40 minutes. Transfer lentil–onion–garlic mixture to the container of the electric blender. Blend thoroughly. Turn into a clean kettle set over *MEDIUM* heat.

Add the 6 cupfuls stock or water, tomato paste, dried lemon slices, salt, and ground cardamom. Allow to come to the boil.

Add diced potato and cook for about 15 minutes. Turn into a heated soup tureen.

Serve into heated soup bowls.

Yields about 8 cupfuls

Notes: *Since aluminum discolors lentils rather unpleasantly, avoid using aluminum cookware or serving bowls in this case.

This recipe can be halved, when required.

1/8 SERVING (i. e., per cupful) –
PROTEIN = 7.9 g.; FAT = 2.1 g.; CARBOHYDRATE = 24.1 g.;
CALORIES = 144; CALORIES FROM FAT = 13%

Middle East–**Kuwait**

SWEET CORN SOUP
TPT - 23 minutes

The introduction of canned vegetables and meats during the British colonial period led to many dishes that would never be expected in a desert climate. The fact that Kuwaiti have adopted soups seemed almost unbelievable but the relative cool months of December, January, and February together with wide-spread air conditioning, have made a vast variety of soups regular items on restaurant menus. Canned sweet corn is an example of a resource welcomed by both Kuwaiti and Omani, a resource that expands what could otherwise be a restricted cuisine.

4 teaspoons CLARIFIED BUTTER *or* **GHEE**
[see index]
2 teaspoons *extra virgin* **olive oil**
1 cup *finely* **chopped onion**
4 garlic cloves—*very finely* **chopped**

2 cans (14 3/4 ounces each) *low-sodium* **creamed corn**
1 cup liquid drained from canned tomatoes*
1 cup *two-percent* **milk**
6 scallions—trimmed, well-rinsed, and sliced
2 *dehydrated* **lime slices**
Freshly ground black pepper, to taste
Several dashes ground red pepper (cayenne)

In a kettle set over *MEDIUM* heat, heat clarified butter and olive oil. Add *finely* chopped onion and *very finely* chopped garlic. Sauté until onion is soft and translucent, *being careful to allow neither the onion nor the garlic to brown. Reduce heat to LOW-MEDIUM.*

Add creamed corn, tomato canning liquid, milk, sliced scallions, and black pepper. Cook, stirring frequently, until soup is hot—about 10 minutes. Turn into a heated soup tureen.

Serve into heated soup bowls.

Yields 8 cupfuls

Notes: *Be careful not to add any large pieces of tomato or the authentic texture of the final soup will be compromised.

This recipe can be halved, when required. Since the soup freezes well, we usually make the eight-cup recipe to provide a freezer-stashed meal-maker.

1/8 SERVING (i. e., per cupful) –
PROTEIN = 2.8 g.; FAT = 4.1 g.; CARBOHYDRATE = 17.3 g.;
CALORIES = 110; CALORIES FROM FAT = 34%

KUWAITI BASMATI RICE
WITH PEAS AND DILLWEED
TPT - 58 minutes

Whenever I find organic limes, half of them are peeled and juiced; the strips of zest are dried using the dehydrator; and the juice is frozen. The rest of the limes are sliced and dried in the dehydrator after which they can be stored for years if kept dry. The dried slices are a useful flavoring tool for dishes like this. Limes and lemons are culinary treasures to cooks in hot climates. I remember the astonishment the son of Filipino friends showed when he went to the store with me and saw piles of limes and lemons. Citrus fruits can dehydrate and mold quickly so Kuwaitis too dehydrate zest and slices. You will find many Kuwaiti dishes that call for dried lime slices such as this one which reminds me of the northern Italian dish "rizi e bizi," in which grain and legume proteins have been complementing each other for centuries, albeit notably without the addition of lime and dillweed.

2 tablespoons safflower *or* **sunflower oil**
3/4 cup *finely* **chopped onion**

1 cup dry basmati rice

2 cups water
2 *dehydrated* **lime slices**
About 1/2 cup chopped fresh dillweed
1/2 teaspoon ground cardamom
Generous pinch saffron

1/2 cup freshly shelled *or* **frozen peas**

In a large skillet set over *MEDIUM* heat, heat oil. Add *finely* chopped onion and sauté until onion is soft and translucent, *being careful not to allow onion to brown.*

Add rice and sauté for several minutes.

Add water, lime slices, chopped dillweed, cardamom, and saffron. Stir to combine thoroughly. Bring to the boil and then reduce heat to *LOW*. Cover and allow to simmer until rice is cooked—about 35 minutes. Remove and discard lime slices.

KUWAITI BASMATI RICE WITH PEAS AND DILLWEED (cont'd)

Add peas and cook for 5 minutes. Turn onto a heated platter.

Serve at once.

Yields 6 servings
adequate for 4 people

Note: This recipe can be halved or doubled, when required.

1/6 SERVING – PROTEIN = 3.0 g.; FAT = 4.6 g.; CARBOHYDRATE = 34.1 g.; CALORIES = 175; CALORIES FROM FAT = 24%

MIDDLE EASTERN BREAD AND VEGETABLE SALAD
Fattoush

TPT - 10 minutes

"The bread left in the bread basket is to be immediately thrown away." That is what I was told by the older waitress who trained me for a waitressing job the summer before my freshman year in college. It was not even given to the sea gulls that ran reconnaissance to see if the garbage dumpster was open. When we traveled in Portugal I was pleased to see that extra hard rolls left over from breakfast were recycled as toasts in the evening bread basket. Bread, when freshly baked, is soft and pliable but it becomes hard as a board if it is not stored in a plastic bag. We have all experienced that phenomenon, I am sure, and bags of breadcrumbs in our freezers attest to our alternative to feeding the birds. Bread salads in Italy and the Middle East have evolved in order not to waste "the staff of life." Fattoush, a bread salad as popular in Kuwait as it is in Lebanon, where it most probably originated, is one of those salads that addresses leftover bread. This version, which may have been adapted from an old magazine article, makes a satisfying main course salad on a hot summer evening.

DRESSING:
  1 tablespoon *extra virgin* olive oil
  1 tablespoon freshly squeezed lemon juice
  1 tablespoon LEBANESE POMEGRANATE
    MOLASSES *(Dibs Rimman)* [see index]
  1 small garlic clove—*very finely* chopped
  2 teaspoons GARLIC–BASIL VINEGAR [see index] *or* white wine vinegar if preferred
  2 teaspoons NORTH AFRICAN SUMAC
    SEASONING MIXTURE *(Zahtar or Zaatar)*
    [see index]
  Freshly ground black pepper, to taste

1 *pita* bread loaf—white *or* whole wheat, as preferred
2 tablespoons *extra virgin* olive oil
Salt, to taste

1 large, ripe tomato—chopped
1 small cucumber—peeled, quartered lengthwise, and *thinly* sliced crosswise into wedges
3 medium scallions—trimmed, well-rinsed, and *thinly* sliced
4 cups Romaine lettuce—shredded crosswise into 3/4 cup strips—well-washed, and well-dried
1 cup purslane leaves*
1 cup fresh parsley florets—well-washed and dried
1/4 cup slivered fresh mint leaves

In a cruet or small jar, combine 1 tablespoonful oil, lemon juice, pomegranate molasses, *very finely* chopped garlic, vinegar, sumac seasoning mixture, and black pepper. Cover cruet tightly and shake vigorously. Set aside until required.

Break *pita* loaf into bite-sized pieces and place in salad bowl.

MIDDLE EASTERN BREAD AND VEGETABLE SALAD (cont'd)

Pour 2 tablespoonfuls of oil into the salad bowl. Toss until *pita* bread is coated with oil. Sprinkle with salt. Toss again.

Add chopped tomato, sliced cucumber, *thinly* sliced scallions, lettuce strips, purslane leaves, parsley florets, and slivered mint leaves. Toss.

Add 2 tablespoonfuls of the prepared sumac dressing. Toss.

Serve at once. Pass the cruet of dressing to allow diners to add more if desired.

Notes: *Purslane is a frequent "weed" in most gardens but to assure the quality of your purslane, plant it in your herb bed. Remember it is an invasive plant so if you do not control its flowering and seed-setting, you will have much more purslane than you want.

This recipe can be doubled, when required.

Yields 6 servings
adequate for 4 people

1/6 SERVING – PROTEIN = 1.5 g.; FAT = 6.2 g.; CARBOHYDRATE = 12.8 g.;
CALORIES = 113; CALORIES FROM FAT = 49%

KUWAITI GRILLED VEGETABLE SALAD
Mechouia

TPT - 1 hour and 32 minutes

Chilled, grilled vegetables were served as a side in a posada in Portugal, according to my journal from a 1977 summer visit. While on an early September trip to Rome, I enjoyed several visits to a small restaurant for lunches of cold, grilled vegetables and fresh cheese. The vegetables were similar and in both incidents the vegetable selections were dressed with fresh-pressed olive oil and vinegar. Cold, grilled vegetables are often on the menu in summer and fall in southern Europe and this dish has made its way to the tables of Kuwait where it is a year-round option.

6 baby artichokes

12 *frozen* white boiling onions
3 large red bell peppers—halved and seeded
6 large garlic cloves

2 tablespoons *extra virgin* olive oil
1 teaspoon crushed, dried oregano
Pinch ground red pepper (cayenne), or to taste

1 tablespoon freshly squeezed lemon juice

2 tablespoons crumbled *feta* cheese

Wash and trim artichokes well. Remove any dry outside leaves. Snip the sharp tips off the leaves with a sharp knife or with a scissors. Slice the artichokes in half from the base through the leaves. Put into a mixing bowl.

Preheat grill pan over *MEDIUM-HIGH* heat.*

Add boiling onions, red pepper halves, and garlic cloves to the artichokes.

In a small dish, combine olive oil, oregano, and ground red pepper (cayenne). Stir to mix well. Add to vegetables. Toss to coat each vegetable with oil and to distribute the oregano. Place vegetables on hot grill pan. Grill, turning as the vegetables brown, until all the vegetables are tender. Transfer to a platter.

Sprinkle with lemon juice. Refrigerate for at least 1 hour.

Sprinkle *feta* cheese over just before serving.

Yields 6 servings
adequate for 4 people

Note: *Although I prefer to use a grill pan since it offers better control when it comes to burning, the vegetables can be grilled over hot coals. When cooking over a charcoal fire, it is advisable to choose an oil that is more tolerant of high heat than is olive oil. I use a high-heat safflower or sunflower oil if I cook outdoors.

This recipe can be halved, when required, and other vegetables can be substituted, if preferred.

1/6 SERVING – PROTEIN = 4.8 g.; FAT = 5.0 g.; CARBOHYDRATE = 17.8 g.;
CALORIES = 122; CALORIES FROM FAT = 37%

Middle East–**Kuwait**

KUWAITI VEGETABLES WITH *VERMICELLI* AND RICE
Maraq Bamiya
TPT - 1 hour and 10 minutes

I bypassed this dish many times before I could wrap my mind around the idea of mixing pasta and rice together and then adding potatoes to the vegetable mixture that topped it. In my family the carbohydrate was either spaghetti or rice or potatoes or bread. Bamiya is Arabic for okra and it is mixed with other vegetables including potatoes, simmered to an unctuous wonderfulness, and served over the vermicelli and rice mixture. There are many approaches to maraq but few are meatless, a puzzlement to me because this is delicious.

1 tablespoon *high heat* **safflower** *or* **sunflower oil**
2 ounces *vermicelli pasta*—broken into thirds

1/2 cup dry converted rice
1 cup *boiling* **water**

1 tablespoon *high heat* **safflower** *or* **sunflower oil**

1/2 pound okra—trimmed and sliced

1 medium potato—peeled and diced
2 large garlic cloves—crushed and *very finely* chopped
1 1/2 cups canned, *diced* **tomatoes**
1/2 teaspoon ground turmeric
1/2 teaspoon KUWAITI SPICE MIXTURE (*Baharat*) [see recipe which follows]
1 teaspoon freshly squeezed lemon juice

Salt, to taste

PLAIN YOGURT [see index] **or commercially-available plain yogurt**

In a large saucepan set over *MEDIUM* heat, heat 1 tablespoonful of oil. Add *vermicelli* pieces and sauté until the spaghetti is golden and begins to give off a toasted smell.

Add rice and water. Stir. Allow to come to the boil. Reduce heat to *LOW-MEDIUM*. Cover and allow to cook for 25 minutes. Remove from heat and set aside for about 10 minutes.

While the rice is cooking, in a small kettle set over *MEDIUM-HIGH* heat, heat the remaining 1 tablespoonful of oil. Add sliced okra and quickly sauté for a minute or two. Remove from heat. *Reduce heat to LOW-MEDIUM*.

Return kettle to heat. Add diced potatoes, *very finely chopped* garlic, diced tomatoes, ground turmeric, Kuwaiti spice mixture, and lemon juice. Cook, stirring frequently, for about 30 minutes. Thin with water if the stew is too thick for your taste.

Season with salt.

Turn the cooked rice and *vermicelli* out onto a platter. Spoon the *maraq* over the rice.

Serve at once with yogurt.

Yields 6 servings
adequate for 4 people

Note: This recipe can be halved, when required.

1/6 SERVING (exclusive of yogurt) –
PROTEIN = 4.2 g.; FAT = 5.0 g.; CARBOHYDRATE = 30.4 g.;
CALORIES = 267; CALORIES FROM FAT = 17%

KUWAITI SPICE MIXTURE
Baharat
TPT - 2 minutes

I sometimes wonder if sharing my spice mixtures is any more helpful to cooks than are those drab spice and herb mixtures you can pick up in the grocery store. Tasting and seasoning a dish is such a personal moment. If we could invite a roomful of people to season a dish, I am sure that no two people would combine the same spices in exactly the same way. Although I feel that I am venturing where angels fear to tread, I will recommend my favorite combination for seasoning Kuwaiti dishes. Most versions of this spice mixture contain far more ground red pepper and more or less of the warm spices, ginger, cloves, cinnamon and nutmeg but this is the mixture that we have come to enjoy. Start with this and then make it your own.

KUWAITI SPICE MIXTURE (cont'd)

2 tablespoons freshly ground black pepper
1 teaspoon ground red pepper (cayenne)
3/4 teaspoon ground cumin
1/2 teaspoon ground coriander
1/2 teaspoon ground ginger
1/4 teaspoon ground cinnamon
1/4 teaspoon ground cloves
1/4 teaspoon ground nutmeg

In a small jar, combine black pepper, ground red pepper (cayenne), and ground coriander, cumin, ginger, cinnamon, cloves, and nutmeg. Tightly seal jar. Shake to mix spices. Store in a cool, dry place.

Yields 10 teaspoonfuls

Note: This recipe is easily doubled to tripled, when required.

FOOD VALUES for such spice mixtures are almost negligible.

KUWAITI VEGETABLE *KEBABS* WITH LEMON
Kebabs

TPT - 2 hours and 30 minutes;
2 hours = marination period

Sure we love our Greek "souvlakia me salatica" but sometimes a change is an adventure worth the detour. Skewering lemon wedges onto the spears and grilling them with the vegetables was a new adventure. After all, lemon wedges are garnishes for kebabs in Greece. What an experience we had when we first bit into a grilled lemon wedge! No longer are lemon wedges just a garnish when we grill.

8 small, white boiling onions—peeled with an X cut into the root end of each

1 organic lemon—very well-scrubbed and rinsed

1 small eggplant—cut into 8 large chunks
1 green bell pepper—cut into 8 squares
1 small zucchini—sliced into 8 slices

1/4 cup *extra virgin* olive oil
3 tablespoons freshly squeezed lemon juice
1 tablespoon MIXED FLOWER VINEGAR WITH OREGANO *[see index]* or other herb vinegar of choice
1 small onion—sliced
1 large garlic clove—*finely* chopped
1/2 teaspoon dried oregano—crushed
1/8 teaspoon dried basil—crushed— *or*
   1 1/2 teaspoons *finely* chopped fresh basil

1/2 teaspoon KUWAITI SPICE MIXTURE
   (**Baharat**) *[see recipe which precedes]*

Parboil white onions in boiling water until just tender. Drain thoroughly.

Slice lemon in half lengthwise. Slice each half in half lengthwise. Slice each quarter in half crosswise.

In a large, heavy plastic bag, combine parboiled onions and lemon wedges with eggplant chunks, green pepper squares, and zucchini slices. Set aside.

In a 2-cup measuring cup, combine oil, lemon juice, vinegar, onion slices, *finely* chopped garlic, crushed oregano and basil, and spice mixture. Pour over vegetables and securely close bag using a twist tie. Toss gently to cover vegetables with marinade. Refrigerate for at least 2 hours to allow vegetables to absorb the marinade. Turn vegetables often during the marination period.

Preheat broiler to 400 degrees F.*

Remove vegetables and lemon wedges from marinade. Alternate them on four large skewers. Arrange on broiler pan.

Strain marinade and reserve any remaining marinade for basting.

KUWAITI VEGETABLE *KEBABS* WITH LEMON (cont'd)

Broil about 4 inches below heat source. Brush *generously* with marinade often while broiling. Turn when *lightly browned*. *Be careful not to overcook or burn.*

Serve at once, on a bed of rice.

Yields 4 servings

Notes: *These are most successfully broiled over an open charcoal fire if cooked about 4 inches above *glowing coals.* Brush with marinade often and *keep any "flare-ups" under control.*

This recipe is easily increased or decreased proportionately, as required.

1/4 SERVING – PROTEIN = 3.6 g.; FAT = 11.3 g.; CARBOHYDRATE = 18.3 g.; CALORIES = 178; CALORIES FROM FAT = 57%

MASCARPONE MOUSSE
TPT - 8 minutes

Although obviously adapted from the cuisines of Italy and France, this rich, calorie-laden mousse is popular in Kuwait and can be served elegantly as a mousse, with or without fruit such as berries, or, if preferred, over pound cake or Arabic honey cake. One of my favorite ways to serve it is to pile it on top of fresh, ripe peach halves.

1/4 cup heavy whipping cream

4 ounces *mascarpone* **cheese**
1/4 cup sugar
1/4 cup *fat-free* **pasteurized eggs (the equivalent of 1 egg)**
1/2 teaspoon pure vanilla extract
1/8 teaspoon ground cinnamon

Using the electric mixer fitted with *chilled* beaters or by hand using a *chilled* wire whisk, beat heavy cream in a *clean, chilled* bowl until stiff peaks form. Set aside. If you do not have a second mixing bowl for your electric mixer, transfer the cream to a small bowl and set aside until required.

In the bowl of the electric mixer fitted with a paddle, combine *mascarpone* cheese, sugar, pasteurized eggs, vanilla and ground cinnamon. Mix until thoroughly combined.

Add whipped cream and slowly fold the cream into the *mascarpone*–egg mixture.

Divide among wine glasses. Or, turn into a serving bowl if you are going to serve it over cake. Refrigerate until required.

Serve chilled.

Yields 6 individual servings

Note: This recipe can be halved or doubled, when required.

1/6 SERVING – PROTEIN = 2.5 g.; FAT = 11.3 g.; CARBOHYDRATE = 10.2 g.; CALORIES = 181; CALORIES FROM FAT = 56%

Middle East–**Kuwait**

KUWAITI CUSTARD WITH SAFFRON AND ROSE WATER
Khabees Al-Nasha

TPT - 18 minutes

Most cooks, set to the task of making a corn starch pudding, would probably not use water as the liquid base nor would they think of checking their pantry for saffron and rose water. Perhaps this dessert is not a custard as we generally know it, but Kuwaiti love these pudding-like desserts. There are many variations of this recipe enjoyed in the Arab Gulf states. These are often the dish offered to the returning family to break the day-long fasting during the month of Ramadan. In this version the costly seasoning elements of saffron and cardamom honor the guest and bring honor to the home.

1 tablespoon rose water
A pinch of saffron threads

1 cup water
1 cup corn starch
3/4 cup sugar

1/4 cup butter

3/4 teaspoon ground cardamom

2 tablespoons *toasted* **pine nuts (***pignoli***), for garnish**

2 tablespoons chopped pistachio nuts, for garnish

In a small dish, combine rose water and saffron. Set aside until required.

In a bowl, combine water and corn starch. Stir until thoroughly combined and all lumps have dissolved. Add sugar and stir again until well-combined. Set aside briefly.

In a saucepan set over *LOW-MEDIUM* heat, melt butter.

Add corn starch–sugar mixture. Stir until thickened and smooth. *Reduce the heat to LOW*.

Add rose water with saffron and cardamom. Stir constantly for several minutes. Turn out onto a heated serving plate or platter.

Sprinkle *toasted* pine nuts (*pignoli*) and chopped pistachio nuts over.

Serve warm.

Yields 6 servings
adequate for 4-6 people

Note: This recipe can be halved, when required.

1/6 SERVING – PROTEIN = 1.3 g.; FAT = 9.4 g.; CARBOHYDRATE = 38.9 g.;
CALORIES = 293; CALORIES FROM FAT = 29%

Lebanon

I remember the amazement and joy that I experienced when I was given a book in the 1960s showing the exquisite architecture of the Lebanese capitol of Beirut, a world banking hub at that time for which it was nicknamed "The Switzerland of the East." Photograph after photograph showed a cultured, wealthy society and a cuisine to die for; I looked forward to a day when I would visit this beautiful country. Then came the Lebanese Civil War in 1975 and suddenly this sophisticated country was changed. The war ended in 1990 and Lebanon began to rebuild just as it had had to rebuild after the sixth century earthquake and tsunami. Recovery was interrupted by the war between Israel and Hezbollah in 2006 and, again, the Lebanese are rebuilding.

One of the oldest continuously occupied cities on earth is located along the coast of Lebanon. Archeological evidence dates Byblos, the capital of ancient Phoenicia, to before 5000 BC. We call the people who occupied this land from 3000 BC to 539 BC Phoenicians but the name Phoenicia is actually a general Greek term used to designate the major Canaanite port towns. Early documents show that the Phoenicians called themselves *Kenaani* or *Kinaani* meaning Canaanites. The Phoenicians were maritime traders who sailed from these ports and opened up the Mediterranean to trade and commerce reaching their zenith between 1200 and 800 BC. Alexander the Great captured the important port of Tyre in 332 BC, after which the area we know as Lebanon was ruled by Hellenistic rulers and, subsequently, by the Ptolemies of Egypt. The Romans destroyed the Phoenician city of Carthage, on the Bay of Tunis in present-day Tunisia, in 146 BC causing the Phoenicians to retreat back to the eastern end of the Mediterranean. Then, eighty-one years later, in 65 BC, Pompey incorporated the mainland area of Lebanon into the Roman province of Syria. The Persian, Assyrian, and Ottoman empires left their marks too. In 1918 Lebanon became part of the French Mandate ending four hundred years of Turkish rule and in 1926 the Lebanese Republic was formed. Authorized by the Free French led by General Charles de Gaulle, Lebanon declared independence in 1941, taking the step toward self governance during World War II while France was under German occupation. When elections were held in 1943 and the Lebanese abolished the French Mandate, the new leaders were imprisoned by the French Vichy government. The crisis precipitated an international protest and the French backed down, releasing the Lebanese government officials and recognizing Lebanon's independence in November of that year. The 1948 the Arab–Israeli War added the burden of Palestinian refugees to the young nation's post-World War II recovery since Israel blocked their repatriation after the hostilities; 400,000 Palestinian refugees remain in Lebanon with more than half of them still in refugee camps. Additional refugee populations have been sheltered in Lebanon with an estimated 50,000 from war-torn Iraq and 4,500 from the Sudan.

Lebanon, comparable in land mass to that of Connecticut, is at an important geographical crossroads at the eastern end of the Mediterranean and at the western end of the Asian trade roots. This small country has been the recipient of influences that have given its culture a complexity that dwarfs our "melting pot culture." As a result of this constant exposure to and dependence upon those who came and went from east and west, Lebanon has adopted from these diverse encounters. An astounding sense of cuisine has created a national menu of exotic, yet somehow familiar, dishes.

Meat, especially lamb, and grains, bulghur wheat, milled wheat, millet, and rice, are ubiquitously present in Lebanese recipes. Having eliminated meat from our diet some forty years before I began this writing project, I found many Lebanese recipes in my files, recipes from a glorious period in Lebanese history, when Beirut was a cultured capital, often referred to as "The Paris of the Middle East." When I began to put together the following menu to share with you, I was perplexed by the number of Lebanese recipes I had come to treasure that were grain-based.

Middle East – Lebanon

Roasted Eggplant Appetizer
Baba Ghannuj

Za'atar **Toast**

North African Sumac Seasoning Mixture
Za'atar or *Zahtar*

Rice- and Lentil-Stuffed Grape Leaves With Currants
Warak Dawali

Thick Greek-style Yogurt
Laban

~

Spinach and Rice Soup
Shourabit Sababikh

~

Millet *Tabbouleh*
Tabbouleh

~~~~~~~~~~~~~~~~~~~~~

Vegetable *Ragoût* **with Soymeat, Roasted Green Peppers, and Artichoke Hearts**
Ardishowki mah "Laham"

Seasoned Butter and Oil for Lebanese Cooking

Mediterranean Dry Marinade for Vegetables

Pomegranate Molasses
Dibs Rimman

~~~~~~~~~~

Broad Beans with Eggs Scramble   or   **Eggs Shirred in Cooked Yogurt**
Fool mah Bayd   *Schmamit*

Grilled Vegetables, of choice,
with

Pine Nut Sauce with *Tahini*
Taratour bi Snoobar

Sautéed Potatoes with Sumac
Batata bi Summa

~~~~~~~~~~~~~~~~~~~~

Apples Cooked in Syrup with Cloves
Tiffeho

Semolina Snack Cake with *Tahini*
Nammura

Middle East–**Lebanon**

LEBANESE ROASTED EGGPLANT APPETIZER
Baba Ghannuj

TPT - 2 hours and 15 minutes;
30 minutes = cooling period;
1 hour = chilling period

Tahini, a traditional paste made from ground sesame seeds, is used to make many Middle Eastern appetizers. The eggplant lover in our family is very, very glad that the Lebanese combined tahini and roasted eggplant and came up with baba ghannuj.

2 small-medium eggplants—well-washed and unpeeled, but with stems removed

6 unpeeled garlic cloves

1 tablespoon *extra virgin* olive oil
2 tablespoons sesame *tahini* (sesame paste or sesame butter)*
1/2 cup chopped, fresh Italian flat-leafed parsley
Freshly ground black pepper, to taste

1 tablespoon freshly squeezed lemon juice

Lemon wedges, for garnish
Red onion rings, for garnish

Preheat oven to 400 degrees F.

Place whole eggplants on a baking sheet and bake in preheated 400 degree F. oven for about 30 minutes, or until flesh is soft.

Place garlic cloves on the baking sheet with the eggplants and continue baking a few more minutes until garlic cloves are soft. Remove both eggplant and garlic from oven. Allow to cool for about 30 minutes.

When cool, using a sharp knife, slice eggplants in half lengthwise. Scoop out eggplant pulp. Using a FOOD MILL or by hand, using a fork, mash eggplant and softened garlic.**/*** Turn into a large mixing bowl. Add oil, *tahini*, chopped parsley, and black pepper. Stir to combine well. Then, stir in lemon juice. Chill for at least 1 hour before serving.

Turn into a serving bowl or dip bowl or into individual saucers. Garnish with lemon wedges and red onion rings.

Serve with pieces of *pita* bread, crackers, tiny sesame breadsticks, or *crudités*, of choice.

Yields about 1 1/2 cupfuls
adequate for 4-6 people as an appetizer
or for 4 people as a side dish

Notes: *Tahini* is readily available in natural food stores and in stores specializing in Middle Eastern products. It can also be made at home using a food processor.

**We prefer a FOOD MILL to a food processor to prepare this appetizer since the roasted eggplant has the tendency to liquefy when processed.

***The eggplant–garlic purée may be made in advance and frozen, if convenient to menu planning.

This recipe may be halved or doubled, when required.

We enjoy a truly American adaptation of this dish. Spread on a toasted English muffin, sprinkled with freshly squeezed lemon juice, and topped with onion rings, it transforms an English muffin into an OPEN–FACED ONION SANDWICH WITH LEBANESE EGGPLANT SPREAD.

1/24 SERVING (i. e., per tablespoonful) –
PROTEIN = 0.4 g.; FAT = 5.5 g.; CARBOHYDRATE = 1.1 g.;
CALORIES = 14; CALORIES FROM FAT = 59%

LEBANESE *ZA'ATAR* TOAST
TPT - 2 minutes

Lebanese, Palestinians, Jordanians, and Syrians often start the day with warm bread or toast spread with the seasoning mixture known as za'atar and especially encourage their children to do so, believing that the mixture helps to keep the mind alert. This seasoning mixture which is popular throughout the Middle East and across North Africa contains herbs, salt, sesame seeds, and seeds of the indigenous sumac. The seasoning is made into a dip, eaten with olive oil and pita bread, used as a dry marinade for meats and vegetables, and, in Oman, steeped in boiling water to make a traditional herbal tea. The Lebanese roll cured balls of labneh, yogurt cheese, in za'atar.

Middle East–**Lebanon**

LEBANESE *ZA'ATAR* TOAST (cont'd)

Per serving:
> A 6-inch warmed *pita* bread *or* 2 slices of toasted bread
> 1/2 teaspoon NORTH AFRICAN SUMAC SEASONING MIXTURE (*Za'atar* or *Zahtar*) [see recipe which follows]
> 1 teaspoon *extra virgin* olive oil

Sprinkle toast or pieces of warmed *pita* bread with the seasoning mixture. Drizzle olive oil over the bread.

Eat.

Yields 1 serving

1 SERVING – PROTEIN = 3.7 g.; FAT = 10.9 g ; CARBOHYDRATE = 42.2 g.;
CALORIES = 240; CALORIES FROM FAT = 41%

NORTH AFRICAN SUMAC SEASONING MIXTURE
Zahtar or *Zaatar*

TPT - 28 minutes;
15 minutes = sesame seed cooling period

The mixture is found, under various names and in various proportions, from Turkey all through the Middle East and across North Africa. It lends a slightly acidic taste and is often found as a table condiment.

2 tablespoons sesame seeds

2 tablespoons ground sumac seeds*
1 tablespoon ground thyme
1/8 teaspoon ground red pepper (cayenne), or more to taste
Pinch salt *unless sumac seeds have been ground with salt*

In a non-stick-coated skillet set over *MEDIUM* heat, dry-roast sesame seeds for about 5 minutes, stirring frequently. *Be careful not to allow seeds to burn.* Cool for at least 15 minutes.

Using a mortar and pestle or a SPICE and COFFEE GRINDER, grind roasted and cooled sesame seeds, ground sumac seeds, ground thyme, and ground red pepper (cayenne) to uniform consistency. Turn into a glass jar to store.**

Use to season *tuajen* [plural of *tagine*] and vegetables, or season oil with the mixture to spread on bread.

Yields 3 tablespoonfuls

Notes: *Ground or dried, whole sumac seeds are available in Middle Eastern groceries and from mail order spice firms.

**This mixture stores well for 3 to 4 months before it begins to lose flavor. However, do check for rancidity if stored for an extended time period.

Za'atar, an oregano-like herb (*Origanum cyriacum*) used in Morocco, is often confused with *zahtar*. It is not a mixture and, therefore, can not be substituted.

1/18 SERVING (i. e., per 1/2 teaspoonful) –
PROTEIN = 0.2 g.; FAT = 0.06 g ; CARBOHYDRATE = 0.2 g.;
CALORIES = 7; CALORIES FROM FAT = 8%

Middle East–**Lebanon**

LEBANESE RICE- AND LENTIL-STUFFED GRAPE LEAVES WITH CURRANTS

Waraq Inab bi Zeyt

TPT - 6 hours and 38 minutes;
4 hours = cooling period

Stuffed grape leaves are usually served when one orders a "horiatiki salata," a village salad or simply a Greek salad, in a good Greek diner on Long Island or in New Jersey. Often homemade versions are available in Greek delis. However, stuffed grape leaves are not exclusive to Greece and this Lebanese specialty is a wonderful protein-complemented choice to accompany a luncheon salad or as part of a vegetarian meze.

Because this takes a bit of time, I sometimes make a double batch and freeze the lentil–rice stuffing mixture for a future menu.

26 jarred, imported grape leaves

FILLING:
  1/4 cup brown (*or* green) lentils
  2 cups *boiling* water

  2 tablespoons *extra virgin* olive oil
  1 1/2 tablespoons freshly squeezed lemon juice
  1/4 cup dry converted rice
  3 scallions—trimmed, well-rinsed, and *finely* chopped
  1/4 cup *finely* chopped fresh mint leaves
  1 1/2 tablespoons dried *preservative-free* currants
  1/4 teaspoon ground cumin
  1/8 teaspoon ground cinnamon
  1/8 teaspoon ground allspice
  Freshly ground black pepper, to taste

3/4 cup canned, *crushed* tomatoes
1/2 cup water

2 tablespoons pine nuts (*pignoli*), for garnish

Trim off the stems of the grape leaves and place the leaves in a large bowl or kettle under the sink faucet. Allow warm water to run for several minutes to rinse the leaves of the excessive brine. Transfer the leaves to a bowl filled with hot water. Soak for about 5 minutes; change the water and allow to soak for an additional 5 minutes. Remove the leaves one at a time from the hot water and carefully drape over a sieve or colander to drain. Set the colander on a tray and refrigerate until required.

Rinse lentils well and discard any of poor quality.

In a saucepan set over *MEDIUM* heat, combine lentils and *boiling* water. Cook for only 15 minutes; *they will complete their cooking when the grape leaf rolls are baked.* Drain. Turn into a mixing bowl.

Add oil, lemon juice, *raw converted* rice, *finely* chopped scallions and mint, dried currants, and ground cinnamon, allspice, cumin, and black pepper. Mix well.

Prepare a casserole or pie plate by coating with non-stick lecithin spray olive oil coating. Place six grape leaves and any small pieces flat over the bottom of the baking dish. Set aside.

Place a grape leaf on a large plate with the point of the leaf facing away from you. Place a spoonful of filling on the leaf about halfway down. Fold the bottom of the leaf up over the filling. Fold the sides in toward the center of the leaf. Tightly roll the leaf from the bottom toward the point of the leaf, being careful to keep the sides tightly folded in. Place the rolled grape leaf in the bottom of the grape-leaf lined baking dish. Repeat until all the filling and/or all the grape leaves have been used up.

Preheat oven to 325 degrees F. Prepare a cookie sheet by covering it with aluminum foil.

In a small bowl combine the crushed tomatoes and water. Stir to combine well. Pour over grape leaves. Cover baking dish with aluminum foil. Bake in preheated 325 degree F. oven for 1 1/2 hours. Check occasionally and add more water if necessary. Remove from oven. Allow to come to room temperature. Refrigerate for 4 hours before serving or freezing.

Sprinkle with pine nuts (*pignoli*).

Serve at room temperature.

Yields 20 stuffed grape leaves
adequate for 5-6 people as a first course

1/20 SERVING (per stuffed grape leaf roll with sauce) –
PROTEIN = 1.7 g.; FAT = 1.5 g.; CARBOHYDRATE = 5.7 g.;
CALORIES – 46, CALORIES FROM FAT = 29%

Middle East–**Lebanon**

SPINACH AND RICE SOUP
Shourabit Sabanikh

TPT - 50 minutes

Lebanese soups are generally thick, heavy affairs of beans or pulses and meat which are, in truth, a meal in and of themselves. This soup, evolved from a meat soup with spinach, can be served as a separate soup course and is perfect for a luncheon entrée. Be sure to choose a rich vegetable stock and to simmer it slowly as you add the onion and garlic flavors.

7 cups VEGETABLE STOCK FROM SOUP *[see index]* **or other vegetarian stock of choice**
1 medium onion—coarsely chopped
2 garlic cloves—chopped

1/4 cup dry converted rice

1/8 teaspoon ground cinnamon
1 pound spinach—well-washed, trimmed, and chopped*

Finely **chopped parsley, for garnish**

In a large saucepan set over *LOW-MEDIUM* heat, combine vegetable stock with chopped onion and garlic. Allow to slowly come to the boil. *Reduce heat* and simmer for about 20 minutes. Set a sieve over a kettle and pour the stock into the kettle. Discard the onion and garlic or add to the soup stock bag in your freezer.

Set the kettle over *MEDIUM* heat and allow the stock to come to the boil. *Reduce heat to LOW.* Add rice. Cover tightly and allow the rice to cook for 20 minutes.

Add cinnamon and *finely* chopped spinach. Stir. Allow the soup to cook until the spinach is wilted—about 10 minutes. Turn into a heated soup tureen.

Serve at once into heated soup plates. Garnish with chopped parsley.

Yields 6 servings
adequate for 4-6 people

Notes: *I roll the well-washed and trimmed spinach leaves into a tight roll and just slice. It is the perfect texture for this soup.

This recipe can be halved or doubled, when required.

Leftovers can be frozen.

1/6 SERVING – PROTEIN = 3.5 g.; FAT = 0.3 g.; CARBOHYDRATE = 9.6 g.;
CALORIES = 64; CALORIES FROM FAT = 4%

MILLET *TABBOULEH*
Tabbouleh

TPT - 34 minutes

Millet is an ancient grain, cultivated and, according to palaeoethnobotanists, used by man for as long as 10,000 years. One of the more exciting finds in northern China was a bowl still containing noodles made from foxtail millet dating to 6500 BC. The small seeds come from several grass species and are not too unlike wheat in nutritional value but, unlike wheat, millets do not contain gluten and are, therefore, useful for making flatbreads and as an alternative for those suffering from celiac disease. Millets survive well in areas prone to drought. Teff, the grain used to make injera in Ethiopia, is a millet. My first encounter with millet as a food was in the Soviet-period literature of Russia where today millet is no longer eaten for survival but is still eaten as a porridge with milk and sugar or added to meat and vegetable stews. Millets still have a place in the cuisines of China and Germany. The seeds can be cooked to mushy porridge consistency or, as is the case here, for a short period of time to create a couscous-like texture. It can replace couscous or bulgur wheat in recipes.

1 tablespoon safflower *or* sunflower oil
1/2 cup millet—well-rinsed and well-drained

3 cups *boiling* water
[see next page]

Middle East–**Lebanon**

MILLET *TABBOULEH* (cont'd)

3 scallions—trimmed, well-rinsed, and sliced
1 cup chopped Italian flat-leafed parsley
1/4 cup fresh mint leaves—chopped
2 tablespoons *extra virgin* olive oil
2 tablespoons freshly squeezed lemon juice
Freshly ground black pepper, to taste

6 large Romaine lettuce leaves

2 medium, ripe tomatoes—peeled, seeded, and chopped—for garnish

1 small cucumber—peeled, seeded, and chopped—for garnish

In a skillet set over *LOW-MEDIUM* heat, heat oil. Add millet and cook, stirring frequently until the seeds are dry and there is fragrant aroma.

Add *boiling* water. Reduced heat to *LOW*, cover, and allow to cook for 15 minutes. Drain and rinse well in cold water. Drain well and turn into a mixing bowl.

Add sliced scallions, and chopped parsley and mint. Toss *gently* with a fork to mix well. Add olive oil and lemon juice. Toss again using a fork to mix well. Season with black pepper.*

Line a serving bowl with lettuce leaves. Pile prepared millet salad into center. Garnish with chopped tomatoes and cucumber.

Serve at once.

Yields 8 servings
adequate for 6 people

Notes: *This recipe may be prepared to this point several hours ahead of time and refrigerated.

When required, this recipe may be doubled.

1/8 SERVING – PROTEIN = 2.4 g.; FAT = 4.9 g.; CARBOHYDRATE = 10.8 g.;
CALORIES = 95; CALORIES FROM FAT = 46%

VEGETABLE *RAGOÛT* WITH SOYMEAT, ROASTED GREEN PEPPERS, AND ARTICHOKE HEARTS IN THE STYLE OF THE EASTERN MEDITERRANEAN

Ardishowki mah "Laban"

TPT - 51 minutes

Any Lebanese cookbook can give you at least two or three versions of lamb stew and perhaps a dozen different lamb and vegetable stews. Patterned on a Middle Eastern lamb ragoût I encountered, this vegetable ragoût can feel sinfully unctuous and yet, oh, so sophisticated at the very same time. It delivers on both taste and texture, and as it is cooking, the house is filled with the wonderful aromas of the region. We serve it over Israeli couscous or with large chunks of boiled potato to add a contrasting texture and to provide a display "canvas" for the very appealing colors.

Green peppers are more popular in Lebanon than are red peppers but either roasted green or red peppers can be used in this stew.

2 tablespoons SEASONED OIL AND BUTTER
  FOR LEBANESE COOKING *[see recipe which follows]* or *extra virgin* olive oil
1 large onion—peeled and coarsely chopped
3 medium celery ribs—coarsely chopped
2 medium carrots—scraped or pared and coarsely chopped

1/4 cup canned, *crushed* tomatoes
1 cup water
1/2 cup *full-bodied* red wine
1/2 teaspoon MEDITERRANEAN DRY
  MARINADE FOR VEGETABLES *[see recipe which follows]*, **or to taste**
3 drops mesquite smoke seasoning liquid

1 tablespoon butter
3/4 cup coarsely chopped, *frozen* artichoke hearts

6 ounces *frozen* soy meat analogue strips or slices

1/2 cup large pieces of *roasted* green peppers*

In a saucepan set over *MEDIUM* heat, heat oil. Add chopped onion, celery, and carrots and sauté until onions begin to soften.

VEGETABLE *RAGOÛT* WITH SOYMEAT, ROASTED RED PEPPER, AND ARTICHOKE HEARTS IN THE STYLE OF THE EASTERN MEDITERRANEAN (cont'd)

Add crushed tomatoes, water, red wine, the Mediterranean dry seasoning mixture, and mesquite smoke seasoning liquid. Stir to combine. Reduce heat to *LOW-MEDIUM* and allow to cook, stirring frequently, until the vegetables are cooked and liquid has reduced by about one-half—about 20 minutes.

In a large skillet set over *MEDIUM* heat, melt butter. Add chopped artichoke hearts and cook, stirring frequently, for about 4 minutes.

Add soymeat and sauté *gently* until soymeat begins to brown.

Add roasted green pepper pieces. Cook, stirring constantly, for a minute or two.

Add cooked vegetables with liquid. Increase temperature to *MEDIUM*. Cook, stirring frequently, until desired consistency is achieved. Turn into a heated serving bowl.

Serve with *couscous* or with large pieces of boiled potato.

Yields 6 servings
adequate for 4 people

Notes: *Green peppers can be roasted and frozen in oil just like red peppers. *See index* for ROASTED RED PEPPERS.

This recipe can, of course, be halved, but because it freezes well, we make the full recipe to enjoy at a future menu.

1/6 SERVING – PROTEIN = 13.3 g.; FAT = 7.5 g.; CARBOHYDRATE = 12.6 g.;
CALORIES = 157; CALORIES FROM FAT = 43%

SEASONED OIL AND BUTTER FOR LEBANESE COOKING
TPT - 8 minutes

This is in no way an authentic Lebanese recipe. It is, instead, my way. Lebanese generally cook with a seasoned meat rendering, lard, or olive oil. Dehen is a lamb kidney fat rendering, popular in the rural areas of Lebanon, which is used for frying. The seasoning of the rendered fat fascinated me so I created an oil and butter mixture to try to capture the same unique flavor nuances so that it could be used with meatless ingredients.

1/2 cup CLARIFIED BUTTER or *GHEE* [see index]
1/2 cup *extra virgin* olive oil

1 teaspoon ground cinnamon
1 teaspoon ground allspice
1 teaspoon salt
3/4 tablespoon freshly ground black pepper

In a saucepan set over *LOW* heat, combine clarified butter and olive oil. Allow to heat until butter liquefies. Using a small wire whisk, stir to combine.

Add ground cinnamon and allspice, salt, and black pepper. Stir well. Allow to cook for about 5 minutes. Remove from heat. Transfer to a jar or crock. Allow to *cool completely.* Cover tightly and store in the refrigerator until ready to use.

Yields 1 cupful

Note: This recipe can be doubled, when required. Since it keeps well in the refrigerator, doubling is a good idea if you think you will be using the mixture during the next six months or so.

1/16 SERVING (i. e., per tablespoonful) –
PROTEIN = 0.0 g.; FAT = 12.6 g.; CARBOHYDRATE = 0.0 g.;
CALORIES = 114; CALORIES FROM FAT = 100%

Middle East–Lebanon

MEDITERRANEAN DRY MARINADE FOR VEGETABLES
TPT - 1 hour and 1 minute;
1 hour = vegetable pre-grill marinade period

Using a dry marinade can make vegetables sing but often, if very flavorful, as in this case, the seasoning can overpower other flavors in the meal. However, I have learned that a dry marinade such as this can be the salvation to leftover grilled vegetables. Returning them to the grill or the grill pan for just a few minutes, just long enough to heat through, can be the making of the next day's lunch or supper.

1 teaspoon dried thyme—crushed
1 teaspoon dried marjoram—crushed
1 teaspoon onion powder
1 teaspoon garlic powder
1/4 teaspoon dried rosemary—crushed
1/4 teaspoon dried sage—crushed

1 tablespoon grated *pecorino Romano* cheese
1/4 teaspoon freshly ground black pepper

In a mortar, combine dried thyme, marjoram, onion powder, garlic powder, rosemary, and sage. Using the pestle, grind herbs to a uniform consistency. Turn into a small bowl.

Add grated cheese and black pepper. Stir to combine.

One hour before cooking, rub dry marinade into vegetables that are to be grilled. Set aside until ready to grill. Grill over a charcoal fire or broil under *MEDIUM* heat, *being sure that vegetables are 4-6 inches from heat source.* Or, if preferred, grill over a burner using a grill pan.

Yields about 2 1/2 tablespoonfuls

Notes: This recipe can be halved so it is especially useful as a leftover tool.

A small quantity of this dry marinade is used to flavor the vegetables before grilling. Little remains after grilling so the calories available from this marinade are almost negligible.

LEBANESE POMEGRANATE MOLASSES
Dibs Rimman
TPT - about 1 hour and 5 minutes

Unable to find a source of Lebanese pomegranate molasses, except via an internet mail order source, I searched for the possible experimentation of others dealing with the same dilemma. Of course, I had pomegranate juice, sugar, and lemon juice in the house on the icy morning that I began my successful experimentation. It doesn't get any easier than this! This recipe combines the postings of several others out there in the cyber cooking community and to them I am grateful.

2 cups unsweetened pomegranate juice
1/4 cup sugar
1 1/2 teaspoons freshly squeezed lemon juice

Sterilize a 1/2-pint canning jar or jelly jar, lid, and ring.

In a large saucepan set over *MEDIUM* heat, combine pomegranate juice, sugar, and lemon juice. Cook, stirring occasionally, until sugar has dissolved. Reduce heat to *LOW* and cook, stirring occasionally, until the ingredients have formed about 1/2 cupful of thick syrup—about 1 hour.* *Do not allow syrup to boil or it will become too thick.* Using a rubber spatula, pour into sterilized jar and allow to cool to room temperature.

When cool, cover tightly with lid and ring. Refrigerate.**

Notes: *If you prefer pomegranate syrup to the molasses, cook down to only 3/4 cupful—about 50 minutes.

**If tightly sealed and kept refrigerated, either pomegranate molasses or pomegranate syrup will keep for 6-8 months.

This recipe can be doubled.

Yields 1/2 cupful

1/8 SERVING (per tablespoonful of molasses) –
PROTEIN = 0.1 g.; FAT = 0.0 g.; CARBOHYDRATE = 16.6 g.;
CALORIES = 65; CALORIES FROM FAT = 0%

Middle East–**Lebanon**

LEBANESE BROAD BEANS AND EGGS SCRAMBLE
Fool mah Bayd
TPT - 18 minutes

Broad beans have been cultivated in the Old World for centuries. Speculation is that this bean became part of the Mediterranean diet as early as 6000 BC. Unlike most legumes, broad beans can be successfully cultivated in soils with high salinity and they can withstand extremes of cold that other beans will not tolerate. Broad beans or fava beans, as they are also known, are a good choice for a rotation crop system in areas of poor soil or in areas where the soil has been worn out by the repeated planting of crops that feed heavily because the nitrogen-fixing bacteria in their root nodules refresh the soil and their extensive root systems help to control erosion. When we lived in the New York metropolitan area, broad beans or fava beans, if not fresh at least canned, were always available, but are not stocked by stores in the area to which we moved. We always bring some back when we go to visit family on Long Island or we purchase online from mail order companies or we just use butter beans, canned or frozen, or lima beans. If fresh beans are available, be sure to choose young ones; they are the most tender.

With the addition of salt and cream to the beaten eggs and the temperature adjustment described below, the protein threads in the eggs unwind slowly and the eggs lift to give a rich, fluffy finish.

5 large eggs
Pinch salt
2 tablespoons light cream *or* **half and half**

1 1/2 tablespoons SEASONED OIL AND BUTTER FOR LEBANESE COOKING *[see recipe which precedes]*
1 medium onion—chopped

1 jar (16 ounces, drained weight) *or* **1 can (19 ounces, drained weight) broad or** *fava verdi* **beans** *or* **butter beans—well-drained and well-rinsed—about 2 cups**
Pinch or two ground cumin

In a small bowl, combine eggs, salt, and cream. Using a small wire whisk or a fork, beat until no trace of white can be seen. Set aside briefly.

In a non-stick-coated skillet set over *MEDIUM* heat, heat seasoned oil/butter mixture. Add onion and sauté until onion is soft and translucent, *being careful not to allow the onion to brown.*

Add beans and ground cumin. Stir to combine. *Increase temperature to MEDIUM-HIGH.*

Add beaten eggs and move them gently with a spatula to prevent them from sticking to the bottom of the pan. *The minute they show signs of congealing, turn the temperature down to LOW.* Keep moving the eggs until they have congealed into light clouds of cooked eggs. Transfer to a heated serving platter.

Serve at once.

Yields 6 servings
adequate for 4 people

Note: This recipe can be halved, when required. Use three medium or two extra large eggs when halving.

1/6 SERVING – PROTEIN = 10.1 g.; FAT = 8.5 g.; CARBOHYDRATE = 13 g.;
CALORIES = 168; CALORIES FROM FAT = 46%

LEBANESE EGGS SHIRRED IN COOKED YOGURT
Schamit
TPT - 45 minutes

I have shirred eggs with honey in the Russian style and with mozzarella cheese and tomato sauce in the Italian style; in fact, I have tried dozens of shirred egg recipes from dozens of countries. This version from Lebanon was a surprise and an unqualified success. A well-seasoned mixed grain pilaf and grilled vegetables accompany it well for a family supper.

LEBANESE EGGS SHIRRED IN COOKED YOGURT (cont'd)

1 tablespoon corn starch
1 tablespoon yogurt whey

1 tablespoon butter
4 garlic cloves—crushed and *finely* chopped

1 3/4 cups *low-fat* or *fat-free, plain* yogurt—*do not use thick Greek-style yogurt*
Pinch salt

6 large eggs

2 teaspoons *crushed dried* mint leaves
Freshly ground black pepper, to taste

Preheat oven to 300 degrees F. Prepare a 10-inch pie plate by lightly buttering.

In a small dish, combine corn starch and yogurt whey. Stir to combine well. Set aside briefly.

In a skillet set over *LOW-MEDIUM* heat, melt butter. Add *finely* chopped garlic and sauté until garlic is soft and translucent, *being careful not to allow the garlic to brown*. Set aside briefly.

In a large saucepan, combine yogurt and salt. Using a wire whisk, beat until yogurt is of a smooth liquid consistency. Set over *LOW-MEDIUM* heat. Add corn starch mixture. Stir to mix. Cook, stirring almost constantly, until yogurt comes to the boil and thickens. Remove from heat. Add sautéed garlic. Stir to combine. Turn yogurt into prepared baking dish, spreading it evenly across the dish.

Using a large spoon, make an indentation in the yogurt surface. Break an egg into a small dish and slide the whole egg into a depression made in the yogurt. Repeat until all eggs are in place. Bake in preheated oven for about 15-17 minutes, or until the whites of the eggs have set. Remove from oven.

Sprinkle the crushed mint over the eggs. Grind black pepper over each egg.

Serve at once. Use two large spoons or a large spoon and a spatula to transfer one shirred egg with yogurt to each dinner plate.

Yields 6 servings
adequate for 4 people

Note: This recipe can be halved. Use a 7- or 8-inch pie plate.

1/6 SERVING – PROTEIN = 8.9 g.; FAT = 8.4 g.; CARBOHYDRATE = 4.8 g.;
CALORIES = 133; CALORIES FROM FAT = 57%

LEBANESE PINE NUT SAUCE WITH *TAHINI*
Taratour bi Snoobar
TPT - 6 minutes

Taratour is the Lebanese name for a sauce made from garlic and tahini, the intensely flavored paste of ground white sesame seeds. Here, the basic sauce is further enhanced by the addition of ground pine nuts. The creamy texture of the sauce makes it a good choice for dipping fried vegetables or crudités.

1 large garlic clove—peeled
1/4 teaspoon salt

1/2 cup pine nuts (*pignoli*)*

1/4 cup freshly squeezed lemon juice
2 tablespoons water
1 tablespoon sesame *tahini* (sesame paste or sesame butter)**

Finely chopped fresh parsley—for garnish—
    if desired

Place peeled garlic clove on a cutting board. Using the flat side of a large chef's knife, smash garlic clove. Sprinkle salt on crushed garlic clove and continue to crush it using the knife blade. *Finely* chop crushed garlic clove. Turn into the work bowl of the food processor fitted with steel knife or into the container of the electric blender.

Add pine nuts (*pignoli*) to garlic. Process to chop finely.

LEBANESE PINE NUT SAUCE WITH *TAHINI* (cont'd)

Add lemon juice, water, and sesame *tahini*. Process until sauce is thick and creamy.

Refrigerate until ready to serve. Garnish with parsley, if desired. Refrigerate any leftovers.

Yields 11 tablespoonfuls

Notes: *When selecting pine nuts in your store or online, be sure to avoid the small, dull, oval nuts. These have been reported to leave an unpleasant aftertaste for days in those sensitive to a malady known as PNS, Pine Nut Syndrome. These generally are an export product of China, although they may be labeled as a product of Korea or Russia. Choose instead pine nuts grown in the Mediterranean. The large, elongated, brown-tipped pine nuts from Italy are the most desirable, and, unfortunately, the most expensive.

**Tahini* is readily available in natural food stores and in stores specializing in Middle Eastern products. It can also be made at home using a food processor.

This recipe can be doubled, when required.

1/11 SERVING (i. e., per tablespoonful) –
PROTEIN = 1.9 g.; FAT = 3.0 g.; CARBOHYDRATE = 1.2 g.;
CALORIES = 37; CALORIES FROM FAT = 73%

LEBANESE SAUTÉED POTATOES WITH SUMAC
Batata bi Summa
TPT - 33 minutes

Potatoes fried and seasoned in this Lebanese manner are almost addictive. Yes, they are that good. Home-fried potatoes, as we know them in the United States, really can not compete with this taste of these potatoes. The flavor contributed by the sumac seasoning to the potato, onion, and garlic mixture is unique in all the world. I use the garlic confit because the garlic has been slowly braised and is, I think, a very sweet and complimentary addition.

3 tablespoons *extra virgin* olive oil
5 large potatoes—peeled and diced
1 teaspoon salt

1 large onion—halved and sliced
6 cloves of GARLIC WITH THYME AND BAY IN OIL *[see index]*—**well-drained**— *or* **3 large raw garlic cloves, if preferred**—*finely* **chopped**
2 tablespoons NORTH AFRICAN SUMAC SEASONING MIXTURE (*Zahtar* or *Zaatar*)
[see recipe which precedes]

In a large non-stick-coated skillet set over *MEDIUM* heat, heat oil. Add diced potatoes. Sprinkle with salt. Cook, stirring frequently, until potatoes are lightly browned and tender. *Reduce heat to LOW-MEDIUM.*

Add onion slices, *finely* chopped garlic, and sumac seasoning mixture. Cook, stirring constantly, until onions are soft and translucent, *being careful not to allow the vegetables to burn.* Turn onto a heated platter.

Serve at once.

Yields 6 servings
adequate for 4 people

Note: This recipe can be halved, when required.

1/6 SERVING – PROTEIN = 4.6 g.; FAT = 5.9 g.; CARBOHYDRATE = 33.4 g.;
CALORIES = 208; CALORIES FROM FAT = 26%

Middle East – **Lebanon**

LEBANESE APPLES COOKED IN SYRUP WITH CLOVES
Tiffeho
TPT - 28 minutes

Although apples are cooked with fish and lamb in Turkey, I would have not expected to find a dessert of apples in the collection of a Lebanese cook. Barring that surprise, I would have expected the syrup to be scented with rose water or maybe geranium leaves. The extra surprise of cloves in this dessert was enough to send me quickly to the kitchen. What a lovely ending to a Middle Eastern meal—sweet, but not the cloying sweetness of pastries. We save those pastry recipes for tea time.

3/4 cup *boiling* water
1 cup sugar

4 large cooking apples—*our preference would be for a small Rome apple or a Cortland*—well-washed and cored
18 whole cloves

1/2 cup heavy whipping cream

Choose a saucepan just the right size to hold the four apples upright. Combine *boiling* water and sugar in the saucepan and set over *MEDIUM* heat. Cook, stirring frequently, until the sugar is completely dissolved.

Insert four whole cloves in the stem end of each *cored* apple and two cloves to the poaching liquid. Place in saucepan, stem-side-up. Baste with syrup. *Reduce heat to LOW.* Cover pan. Allow to simmer for about 12-15 minutes, or until the apples are *just tender*. Remove from heat and allow to cool slightly.

Meanwhile, using the electric mixer fitted with *chilled* beaters or by hand using a *chilled* wire whisk, beat heavy cream in a *clean, chilled* bowl until stiff peaks form.

Transfer each apple to a dessert dish. Spoon residual syrup over each.

Serve warm or at room temperature, topping each apple with a portion of the whipped cream.

Yields 4 individual servings

Note: This recipe can be halved or increased proportionally to accommodate the number of diners. Be sure to choose a saucepan that will hold the apples upright.

1/4 SERVING – PROTEIN = 1.0 g.; FAT = 11.0 g.; CARBOHYDRATE = 58.2 g.;
CALORIES = 312; CALORIES FROM FAT = 32%

LEBANESE SEMOLINA SNACK CAKE WITH *TAHINI*
Nammura
TPT - 1 hour and 17 minutes

This cake is obviously very different from our Western perception of a cake. The technique for preparation is strikingly similar to that for an Armenian farina cake, which is also drenched with sweet syrup. Remember to use regular Cream of Wheat, if you must substitute. Do not use the instant product.

1 cup PLAIN YOGURT *[see index] or* commercially-available plain yogurt
3/4 teaspoon baking soda

1 tablespoon sesame *tahini* (sesame paste or sesame butter)*

1 1/2 cups (8 ounces) semolina #1, farina, *or regular* Cream of Wheat cereal**
5 tablespoons sugar

1 teaspoon pure vanilla extract
1/4 cup butter—*melted,* but *not hot*

12 pine nuts (*pignoli*)

SUGAR SYRUP:
    1/2 cup sugar
    1/4 cup water
    1 teaspoon freshly squeezed lemon juice—*strained*

    1/2 teaspoon rose water *or ma ward****

In a small bowl, combine the yogurt and baking soda. Allow to stand for 15 minutes.

Preheat oven to 350 degrees F. Prepare an 8-inch square pan by brushing the sesame *tahini* over the bottom and sides.

LEBANESE SEMOLINA SNACK CAKE WITH *TAHINI* (cont'd)

In a mixing bowl, combine the semolina or farina and sugar. Stir to mix well.

Stir vanilla extract into *melted* butter. Stir butter and vanilla extract into yogurt and pour this mixture over the semolina and sugar in the mixing bowl. Using a wooden spoon, stir to form a stiff dough. Spread this dough evenly in prepared baking pan. *Do not press down on dough as you spread it.* Using a sharp knife, cut dough in a criss-cross pattern to form twelve diamonds.

Bake in preheated 350 degree F. oven for about 40 minutes, or until surface is golden and the edges are just beginning to brown. Remove to a wire rack.

While cake is baking, prepare SUGAR SYRUP by placing the sugar and water in a heavy saucepan set over *MEDIUM* heat. Bring to the boil, stirring frequently. When the sugar is dissolved and syrup is boiling, add *strained* lemon juice, *reduce heat to LOW*, and simmer for about 10 minutes, or until syrup feels very sticky.

Stir rose water into syrup. Remove from heat and set aside to cool slightly as cake bakes.

Using the sharp knife, score diamonds all the way to the bottom of the pan. Place a pine nut (*pignoli*) in the center of each diamond. Pour the sugar syrup over the hot cake.

Return to the 350 degree F. oven for about 5 minutes, or until the syrup is absorbed. Allow cake to cool on a wire rack. Carefully remove cake diamonds from pan and transfer to a serving plate.

Serve warm or at room temperature, as preferred.

Yields 12 servings
adequate for 6 people

Notes: *Tahini*, sesame paste, is available in natural food stores and in Middle Eastern groceries. It can also be made at home using a food processor.

**The granular wheat flour, semolina, is available in Middle Eastern groceries, natural food stores, and food specialty stores. It is called *smid* in Lebanese. Semolina is milled from hard, durum wheat and, if available, buy semolina #1. It gives this cake a unique texture. Farina or regular (*not instant*) Cream of Wheat cereal may be substituted.

***Both French and Lebanese rose water products are available in food specialty stores.

Refrigeration causes the syrup to harden. Instead, store the cake at room temperature. It will keep well for two days.

1/12 SERVING – PROTEIN = 4.4 g.; FAT = 5.3 g.; CARBOHYDRATE = 35.8 g.;
CALORIES = 219; CALORIES FROM FAT = 22%

Oman

Muscat, the capital of Oman, is a modern, clearly Islamic city that, despite its modernity, looks like it has always been there, guarding the entry to the Persian Gulf forever. It is situated on the 1,000-mile-long coastal plain on the southeast coast of the Arabian Peninsula. In a way, the city, as we know it, is ancient albeit modern in form, having been a wealthy trading center for many centuries before the formation of the Sultanate of Oman. The nearby city of Ibri is the site of what is believed to the first settlement, dating to 8000 BC and an archeological site, dating to about 106,000 years ago, revealed stone tools specific to the African lithic of the so-called Arabian Nubian Complex.

The strategic positioning of the settlement and its copper resources were important leading to domination in turn by the empires of the Achaemenids, Parthians, and the Sassanids.

In the seventh century AD a very conservative form of Islam was adopted and today it is the only country in the Islamic world where Ibadism is the predominate form of Islamic practice. With Islam came rule by successive Islamic regimes—the Abbasids, the Qarmatians, the Byids, and the Suljuks. European influence did not come to Oman until 1498 AD when the Portuguese moved to protect shipping lanes by taking Muscat. The area was under control of the Portuguese for one hundred and forty-three years until they were driven out of Muscat by the Ottoman Turks between 1581 and 1588. Tribesmen from the Uman region of Yemen eventually controlled the area and may well have contributed the name by which we now know the county. At that point Oman became a sultanate. In 1774 the ruling sultan accepted the protection of Great Britain and Oman remained a British protectorate until 1951. The independent monarchy we know today was officially formed in 1970. Although it is an absolute monarchy, ruled by the Sultan of Oman, it has a parliament with limited powers.

Oil reserves, modest by comparison to other countries in the region, have enabled a high standard of living but, limited as those reserves are, dependency upon oil revenues does not bode well for future prosperity. Diversification of industrial development to areas other than that related to the oil industry has lagged and the drop in oil prices in 1998 demonstrated the need for other sources of income for a population of close to four million people. Guest workers send an estimated $30 billion out of the country annually to their home countries in Asia and Africa. An effort to promote tourism has been launched but unrest in the Middle East has discouraged visitors from Europe and the Western Hemisphere.

This is a hot, dry desert nation with an average rainfall amount of only about four inches. Attempts to maintain water supplies has led to over use of fossil water supplies and increased salinity, impacting agriculture which is possible on only about one percent of the land mass. Despite the development of an extensive greenhouse agricultural system, Oman is still a net importer of food and will probably be so well into the future. As a result, one experiences an international cuisine with seasoning overtones from South Asia.

Middle East–**Oman**

Coffee with Cardamom
Khawa

Dates

~ ~ ~

Roasted Eggplant Appetizer *[see index]*
Baba Ghanoush

Warm Pita Bread

~

Banana, Mango, and Pineapple in Golden Mango–Yogurt Sauce

Microgreens, Baby Spinach, and Watercress
with Slivered Onion and Grated Cheese

~

Melon Soup with Fresh Mint

Vegetable Soup with Oatmeal or Barley
Shurbah

~ ~ ~ ~ ~ ~ ~ ~ ~ ~ ~ ~ ~ ~ ~ ~ ~ ~ ~ ~

Orzo with Spinach and Tomatoes

Steamed, Shredded Carrot

Mashed Fava or Butter Beans with Olive Oil and Grated Cheese

~ ~ ~

Beans, Carrots, and Creamed Corn

Baby Potatoes in Spicy Tomato Sauce

Steamed Rice

~ ~ ~ ~ ~ ~ ~ ~ ~ ~ ~ ~ ~ ~ ~ ~ ~ ~ ~ ~

Coffee Cream

Farina Dessert with Rose Water　　　**Tapioca Pudding with Warm Spices**
Khabeesa　　　*Sako*

Coconut Cake *with* Fresh Pineapple Slices
Juz al-Hind

Middle East–**Oman**

BANANA, MANGO, AND PINEAPPLE IN GOLDEN MANGO – YOGURT SAUCE
TPT - 13 minutes

Tropical fruits can always be found in the markets and hotels in Oman and in any grocery in America today. A simple salad like this does make the most of the bounty.

3 mangoes—peeled pitted

1/2 cup **PLAIN YOGURT** *[see index]* or commercially-available plain yogurt

6 pineapple slices
4 large bananas—peeled and sliced

Slicing parallel to the pit, slice two large slices from each peeled mango. Set aside briefly until ready to assemble. Chop the remaining mango from the pits and put the *chopped* mango in the work bowl of the food processor, fitted with steel knife, or in the container of the electric blender.

Add yogurt. Blend until a smooth sauce results.

Place a mango slice and a pineapple slice on each of six salad plates. Apportion banana slices over the pineapple slices. Spoon prepared mango–yogurt sauce over each serving.

Refrigerate until ready to serve.

Serve chilled.

Yields 6 servings
adequate for 4 people

Notes: This recipe can be decreased or increased proportionately, as required.

This also makes a very nice, light dessert.

1/6 SERVING – PROTEIN = 3.1 g.; FAT = 1.3 g.; CARBOHYDRATE = 46.9 g.;
CALORIES = 239; CALORIES FROM FAT = 5%

OMANI MELON SOUP WITH FRESH MINT
TPT - 1 hour and 10 minutes;
1 hour = flavor development period

Fruits, both dried and fresh, add their sweet deliciousness to so many Middle Eastern dishes. What would a koresh be without the beautiful apricots or peaches grown in Iran? Omani cooks use fruits beautifully and a fresh soup like this is not just a soup course, it is instead an invitation to the next course. Melons are said to have originated in the Middle East and this Omani soup showcases, most simply, any of the descendants of those early species that you might prefer—cantaloupe, honeydew, casaba, Persian, or the casaba x Persian hybrid known as the Crenshaw melon. I tend to prefer the bright sweetness of a honeydew melon for this soup. Follow your soup course with a spicy stew and then bring your taste buds back to the starting point by ending the meal with fruit and you will have found the Middle Eastern way to add fruit to a menu. When I first discovered this recipe, the herb garden was many months from presenting me with the mint I needed and the melons in our markets were still coming from South America. I had to wait but I must say it was worth the wait.

1 pound, about 4 cups, chopped sweet melon
—peeled and seeded
1 tablespoon sugar, *as required**
Pinch salt
1/4 cup *very finely* chopped fresh mint leaves
Water, to thin, if necessary

In the work bowl of food processor fitted with steel knife, combine chopped melon, sugar if required, salt, and *very finely* chopped fresh mint leaves. Process until uniformly smooth. Add water, as necessary, to get the desired consistency. Turn into a pitcher or decanter. Refrigerate for at least 1 hour.

Divide among four chilled soup plates.

Serve at once.

Yields 4 servings
adequate for 4 people

Notes: *Sweet, summer melons should not require added sugar.

This recipe can be halved or doubled, when required.

1/6 SERVING – PROTEIN = 0.9 g.; FAT = 0.3 g.; CARBOHYDRATE = 11.5 g.;
CALORIES = 48; CALORIES FROM FAT = 6%

Middle East – **Oman**

OMANI VEGETABLE SOUP WITH OATMEAL OR BARLEY
Shurbah

TPT - 1 hour and 3 minutes

This soup, a particular favorite of Omani, is made with rolled oats by some cooks, others chose bulgur wheat or barley. I most frequently use this soup as a vehicle to get more barley into our diet; we get plenty of oats in our bread and breakfast cereal choices.

2 tablespoons CLARIFIED BUTTER *or* **GHEE**
[see index]
1 cup *finely* **chopped onion**

6 cups VEGETABLE STOCK FROM SOUP *[see index]*, **other vegetable stock of choice,** *or* **water**
1 cup canned, *petite diced* **tomatoes**
1/2 cup old-fashioned rolled oats *or* **dry pearl barley**
1/2 cup grated carrot
1/2 cup *finely* **chopped cabbage**
2 teaspoons NORTH AFRICAN SUMAC SEASONING MIXTURE *(Zahtar or Zaatar)* *[see index]**
1/2 teaspoon ground cardamom

Salt, to taste
Freshly ground black pepper, to taste

In a kettle set over *MEDIUM* heat, melt clarified butter. Add *finely* chopped onion and sauté until onions are soft and translucent, *being careful not to allow onions to brown.*

Add vegetable stock or water, diced tomatoes, oatmeal or barley, *grated* carrot, *finely* chopped cabbage, *zahtar* seasoning, and ground cardamom. Allow to come to the boil. Reduce heat to *LOW-MEDIUM* and simmer for about 40 minutes.

Season with salt and pepper. Turn into heated soup tureen.

Serve into heated soup bowl or plates.

Yields 7 cupfuls

Notes: **Zahtar* or *zaatar* is also available from mail order spice firms and is a stable in Middle Eastern groceries.

This recipe can be halved or doubled, when required.

1/7 SERVING (i. e., per cupful) –
PROTEIN = 1.8 g.; FAT = 4.7 g.; CARBOHYDRATE = 10.3 g.;
CALORIES = 92; CALORIES FROM FAT = 46%

OMANI *ORZO* WITH SPINACH AND TOMATOES

TPT - 45 minutes

Semolina is a product of durum wheat, a hard wheat which gives a beautiful and firm pasta product. If your pasta has an ivory color, then it was probably made from semolina, although some manufacturers go out of their way to "fool the public," as my dad would say. I prefer a semolina orzo to pasta made with soft wheat, more popular in the southern provinces of Italy, since semolina gives a firm result when cooked and holds up better to wet ingredients as in this dish from Oman. This is not a complicated dish but the resulting flavors intertwine and challenge each other. I always make the full recipe because this is one of our favorite next-day luncheon warm-ups.

1 cup dry *orzo* **semolina** *pasta*
1 quart *boiling* **water**

1 tablespoon *extra virgin* **olive oil**
1 5-ounce package baby spinach—trimmed and well-washed
Pinch salt
Freshly ground black pepper, to taste

1 tablespoon *extra virgin* **olive oil**
1/4 cup pine nuts *(pignoli)*

2 large garlic cloves—smashed and *very finely* **chopped**

1 cup canned, *diced* **tomatoes—well-drained**

2 tablespoons grated *pecorino Romano* **cheese**

In a saucepan set over *MEDIUM* heat, combine *pasta* and *boiling* water. Cook according to package directions. Drain and set aside until required.

OMANI *ORZO* WITH SPINACH AND TOMATOES (cont'd)

In a large skillet set over *LOW-MEDIUM* heat, heat 1 tablespoonful oil. With the water still adhering to the leaves, add spinach leaves with salt and black pepper. Sauté until spinach is wilted. Remove spinach to a small bowl and set aside briefly.

Add the second tablespoonful of oil to the skillet. Return to *LOW-MEDIUM* heat. Add pine nuts (*pignoli*) and sauté until pine nuts are golden brown.

Add *very finely* chopped garlic and sauté for 3 or 4 minutes.

Add tomatoes, spinach with liquid, and cooked *orzo*. Cook, stirring frequently, for about 7 minutes or until heated through. Turn out in a serving bowl or onto a heated serving platter.

Sprinkle with grated cheese or pass cheese to allow for individual tastes.

Yields 6 servings
adequate for 4 people

Note: This recipe can be doubled, when required.

1/6 SERVING – PROTEIN = 5.7 g.; FAT = 7.0 g.; CARBOHYDRATE = 17.2 g.;
CALORIES = 153; CALORIES FROM FAT = 41%

OMANI BEANS, CARROT, AND CREAMED CORN
TPT - 10 minutes

This might be called Omani mixed vegetables but it is certainly a different approach to mixed vegetables as served in U. S. restaurants and it is not as boring. Omani make use of canned products, by necessity, but add fresh and frozen vegetables that may be available. The creamed corn functions as a sauce in this mixture and makes a nice sauce over a veggie patty or over boiled potatoes.

2 tablespoons CLARIFIED BUTTER *or* GHEE
[see index]
2 scallions—well-washed, trimmed, and sliced
1 medium carrot—scraped or pared and cut into small dice
1/2 cup *frozen* green beans—chopped into 1/2-inch pieces
1/4 cup *frozen* lima beans *or* butter beans

1 cup canned, *low sodium* creamed corn
Pinch sugar
Salt, to taste
Freshly ground black pepper, to taste

In a skillet set over *LOW* heat, heat clarified butter. Add scallion slices, diced carrot, chopped green beans, and lima beans. Cover and allow to cook, stirring occasionally, until carrots and frozen beans are tender. Increase heat to *LOW-MEDIUM*.

Add creamed corn, sugar, salt, and black pepper. Cook, stirring frequently, until heated through. Turn into a serving bowl.

Serve hot.

Yields 6 servings
adequate for 4 people

Note: This recipe can be halved or doubled, when required.

1/6 SERVING – PROTEIN = 1.7 g.; FAT = 5.0 g.; CARBOHYDRATE = 10.8 g.;
CALORIES = 84; CALORIES FROM FAT = 54%

OMANI BABY POTATOES IN SPICY TOMATO SAUCE
TPT - 46 minutes

The influence of Indian cuisine upon the evolving cuisines of the Arabian Peninsula is obvious in the seasoning. This dish seems to have borrowed from the dishes introduced by South Asian traders in a number of ways. Although Omanis prepare chicken in this manner, chicken maraq, the base clearly references the spicy meatless potato dishes found throughout South Asia. The spice mixture is typical of both Oman and Kuwait and it is a good mixture to have on hand for those creative moments.

Middle East–**Oman**

OMANI BABY POTATOES IN SPICY TOMATO SAUCE (cont'd)

2 tablespoons CLARIFIED BUTTER *or* GHEE
   [see index]
1 medium onion—*finely* sliced
2 large garlic cloves—*very finely* chopped

2 cups canned, *diced* tomatoes
1 cup VEGETABLE STOCK FROM SOUP *[see index]* **or** other vegetarian stock of choice
1/2 teaspoon KUWAITI SPICE MIXTURE (***Baharat***) *[see index]*, **or** to taste
2 *dehydrated* lime slices*

24 baby potatoes—about 2 pounds—well-scrubbed and sliced in half

1/2 cup chopped fresh coriander (*cilantro*), for garnish

In a large skillet set over *MEDIUM* heat, melt clarified butter. Add onion slices and *very finely* chopped garlic. Sauté until onion is soft and translucent, *being careful to allow neither the onion nor the garlic to brown.*

Add *diced* tomatoes, vegetable stock, spice mixture, and *dehydrated* lime slices. Stir until well-combined. *Reduce heat to LOW-MEDIUM.*

Add potato halves. Cover and allow to simmer until potatoes are tender—about 30 minutes.** Stir occasionally. Turn into a heated serving bowl.

Garnish with chopped fresh coriander (*cilantro*).

Serve at once.

Yields 6 servings
adequate for 4 people

Notes: *If you have a dehydrator, slices of organic limes can be preserved for a dish like this.

**3/4 cupful canned chickpeas or red kidney beans can be added at this point if appropriate to your menu.

This recipe can be halved or doubled, when required.

1/6 SERVING – PROTEIN = 3.9 g.; FAT = 5.0 g.; CARBOHYDRATE = 26.4 g.;
CALORIES = 160; CALORIES FROM FAT = 28%

OMANI COFFEE CREAM
TPT - 35 minutes
15 minutes = brown sugar "melting" period

Oman does not boast large herds of milk cattle so the importation of dairy products has become an important business, a business well-patronized by the affluent population of this oil-rich state. Rich desserts are always found on the restaurant menus in Oman and an Omani hostess always includes a sinfully rich dessert at her dinner parties. This is a very simply prepared dessert which need not be served in large portions to satisfy.

1 tablespoon freeze-dried coffee granules
1 tablespoon *boiling* water

1 cup heavy whipping cream
1 tablespoon confectioners' sugar

2 tablespoons ground almonds *or* almond meal

6 teaspoons *light* brown sugar

In a small dish, combine coffee granules and *boiling* water. Stir to dissolve. Set aside until required.

Using the electric mixer fitted with *chilled* beaters or by hand using a *chilled* wire whisk, beat heavy cream in a *chilled* bowl until soft peaks form. While continuing to beat, add confectioners' sugar. Beat until stiff peaks form.

Gently fold coffee and ground almonds into whipped cream. Apportion in six sherbet glasses or wine glasses, if preferred. Sprinkle 1 teaspoonful of brown sugar over each serving. Set aside, at room temperature, for 15 minutes to allow the brown sugar to absorb some of the moisture from the coffee cream.

Serve within 30 minutes.

Yields 6 individual servings

Note: This recipe can be halved or doubled, when required.

1/6 SERVING – PROTEIN = 1.7 g.; FAT = 15.8 g.; CARBOHYDRATE = 8.3 g.;
CALORIES = 179; CALORIES FROM FAT = 79%

Middle East–**Oman**

OMANI FARINA DESSERT WITH ROSE WATER
Khabeesa

TPT - 1 hour and 26 minutes;
   1 hour = refrigeration period

The perfume of rose water flows through the Middle East from cuisine to cuisine. It is a production to make your own rose water but, of course, I had to try it at least once. When I think back to the Rube Goldberg-apparatus I constructed and to the amount of time it took for all the rose petals in our gardens to produce a tiny amount of distillate, I am quite content to buy a bottle of Lebanese or French rose water and to bless their patience. Until I found this recipe, it had never occurred to me to flavor a dessert with saffron, cardamom, and rose water but this simple dessert compliments so many Middle Eastern dishes, so beautifully, that it is now one of those treasures to which I turn frequently.

1/4 teaspoon saffron threads

2 cups *two-percent* **milk**

1/3 cup farina *or* **Cream of Wheat cereal**
1/2 cup *fat-free* **sweetened condensed milk**

1 tablespoon CLARIFIED BUTTER *or* **GHEE**
   [see index]
1 tablespoon rose water
1/2 teaspoon ground cardamom

In a marble mortar, grind saffron threads with the pestle until powderized. Set aside briefly.

In a saucepan set over *MEDIUM* heat, bring milk to just below the boiling point.

While stirring, sprinkle in farina or Cream of Wheat. Continue stirring while adding sweetened condensed milk. Cook, stirring frequently, until it thickens.

Add saffron powder, clarified butter, rose water, and ground cardamom. Stir until well-mixed. Turn into a serving bowl. Refrigerate for at least 1 hour.

Serve chilled.

Yields 6 servings
adequate for 4 people

Note: This recipe can be halved or doubled, when required.

1/6 SERVING – PROTEIN = 7.3 g.; FAT = 4.1 g.; CARBOHYDRATE = 37.3 g.;
CALORIES = 219; CALORIES FROM FAT = 17%

OMANI TAPIOCA PUDDING WITH WARM SPICES
Sako

TPT - 2 hours and 30 minutes;
   1 hour = saffron soaking period;
   1 hour = refrigeration period

I buy quick-cooking tapioca in bulk so instead of making this with pearl tapioca, I make it with the quick-cooking tapioca; it saves time because there is no need to soak as with pearl tapioca. However, the first time I made it, using the recipe of a generous Omani cook, I had a sticky mess with large clumps of tapioca. A potato masher, a sieve, the electric mixer . . . none completely rid me of the hard tapioca clumps. This recipe delivers the sweet, spicy taste of the Omani original but it had been adjusted to use quick-cooking tapioca.

1/2 teaspoon saffron
2 tablespoons water

3/4 cup sugar

2 1/2 cups water
1/4 cup *quick-cooking* **tapioca**
1/4 cup butter
1 tablespoon rose water
1 1/2 teaspoons ground cardamom
1/2 teaspoon ground cinnamon

1/4 teaspoon ground ginger
Ground pistachio nuts—for garnish—if desired

In a small dish, soak saffron threads in the 2 tablespoonfuls of water for 1 hour.

In a heavy saucepan set over *LOW-MEDIUM* heat sugar until it melts and caramelizes. Be careful not to allow it to burn. *The sugar will crystallize into chunks that will dissolve after you add the water. Reduce the heat to LOW.*

OMANI TAPIOCA PUDDING WITH WARM SPICES (cont'd)

Add the saffron and the water in which it was soaked, 2 1/2 cups water, tapioca, butter, rose water, and ground cardamom, cinnamon, and ginger. Allow to come to the boil over the *LOW* heat. The sugar chunks will dissolve and the pudding will thicken. Add more water, if necessary.

Divide among six small dessert dishes or sherbet glasses or, if preferred, turn into a serving bowl. Refrigerate for at least 1 hour to allow for firm setting.

Serve chilled, garnished with ground pistachio nuts, if desired.

Refrigerate leftovers.

Yields 6 servings
adequate for 4 people

1/16 SERVING (exclusive of nut garnish) –
PROTEIN = 0.1 g.; FAT = 0.0 g.; CARBOHYDRATE = 44.0 g.;
CALORIES = 211; CALORIES FROM FAT = 0%

OMANI COCONUT CAKE
Juz al-Hind

TPT - 1 hour and 48 minutes;
1 hour = cooling period

Fresh coconuts were not a fruit that we saw often in upstate New York in the 1940s and '50s. I remember a neighbor bringing a duffel full of coconuts home from a Florida trip. They were gifted to friends and neighbors as if they were something new and exciting. To many they were something very new because desiccated coconut and Mounds or Almond Joy candy bars were just about the only coconut we saw. Today you can pick up a coconut in almost every grocery store and occasionally young fruits that have not formed a shell sit there in the produce department like pretty tropical huts. This is a lovely tasting cake even though the texture is a bit foreign to Western taste buds.

Most Omanis use vanilla powder to flavor this cake because of religious alcohol restrictions. I use pure vanilla extract because it is more readily available. In addition, I use fresh cow's milk while Omani bakers usually have to resort to reconstituted dry milk.

SUGAR SYRUP:
    1 cup sugar
    1 1/2 cups water

1/2 cup unbleached white flour
1/2 cup farina, semolina, *or* Cream of Wheat cereal
1/3 cup sugar
1 1/2 tablespoons baking powder
1 cup shredded, desiccated *preservative-free* coconut

1 cup *two-percent* milk
1/2 cup *fat-free* pasteurized eggs (the equivalent of 2 eggs)
1 1/2 teaspoons pure vanilla extract

Preheat oven to 350 degrees F. Prepare a 9-inch-square non-stick-coated baking pan by lining it with culinary parchment and then spraying the parchment with non-stick lecithin baking spray.

In a large saucepan set over *MEDIUM* heat, combine the 1 cupful sugar and water. Allow to come to a full boil. Boil for 5 minutes until a thin syrup forms. Remove from heat and set aside until required.

In a mixing bowl, combine white flour, farina, 1/3 cupful sugar, baking powder, and coconut. Mix well. Set aside briefly.

In the electric mixer bowl, combine the milk, eggs, and vanilla extract. Beat at MEDIUM speed for several minutes.

Add dry ingredients. Mix until moistened. Turn into prepared baking pan. Bake in preheated 350 degree F. oven for 25 minutes, or until a cake tester inserted in the middle of the cake comes out clean. Remove from oven to a wire rack. Immediately pour sugar syrup over cake. Allow to cool completely—about 1 hour.

Either serve from baking pan or lift, using two wide spatulas, onto a cake plate to serve.

Yields 9 servings
adequate for 6 people

1/9 SERVING – PROTEIN = 4.8 g.; FAT = 4.8 g.; CARBOHYDRATE = 56.1 g.;
CALORIES = 285; CALORIES FROM FAT = 15%

Palestine

In 2012 the Palestinian Territories, as they have been known, were declared a state, a dream of these people for decades. Although the United Nations turned down their bid for representation and few nations have endorsed their declaration, the idea that the descendants of the nomadic peoples who occupied this ancient land would someday stand shoulder to shoulder with those of other nations in the Middle East is now not entirely a dream. The boundaries of Palestine have changed over the centuries as has the name of the region. First referenced as Palestine in the fifth century BC and defined as the entire area between Phoenicia and Egypt, it has been known as the Land of Canaan, Zion, Jund Filastin, Outremer, Syria Palaestina, and even Southern Syria. The 1920 Franco–British boundary agreement and the Transjordan Memorandum of 1922, clarified the boundaries to include not just the Palestinian Territories, for which nationhood is sought, but land now occupied by the nations of Jordan and Israel.

One of the earliest areas of civilization and historically a political, religious, and cultural collision point, the Territories still experience the turbulence that has been characteristic of the region presumably since the period of pre-history. The Levant was occupied by the Egyptians from 3000 to 1850 BC and then for another three hundred years between 1500 and 1200 BC. During the latter period an alliance was led against the Egyptians by the Canaanites. Beginning in the late eleventh century BC the armies of the Philistines and Israelites fought for control of this vast region. As the centuries progressed the area was invaded and held by Assyria, Babylon, Persia, Greece, the Roman Empire, Byzantium, the Crusaders, and the Ottoman Empire, whose control ended in 1917 during World War I. Stability has not been a characteristic of Palestine. In 1922 the British were given a mandate to govern the region. The Muslim population rose up against British rule in 1920 before the mandate was even in place and again in 1929 and 1936. In 1947 the British terminated the mandate and the United Nations voted to partition the territory into a Jewish state and an Arab state. The partition was accepted by the Jewish population but the Arab leadership rejected the plan. In 1948 the state of Israel was formed, precipitating the Arab–Israeli War, during which Israel incorporated a further twenty-six percent of the territory beyond the partition boundaries, Jordan captured the region known as the West Bank, and Egypt captured the Gaza Strip. In the Six-Day War in 1967 Israel captured the remaining mandate territory including the West Bank and Gaza.

The Palestinian National Charter defines their homeland in the terms of the original Mandate Palestine excluding the Transjordan but including lands still controlled by Israel. In 2004 Israel withdrew all settlers and most of its military presence from the Gaza in a unilateral disengagement plan but Israel still occupies the West Bank claiming control as a matter of national security. A first step was achieved in November 2012 when the United Nations general assembly voted to approve Palestine's petition for observer state status. Full statehood for Palestine will depend on continued diplomacy and negotiated agreements that are infinitely difficult in this very volatile region of the world.

The cuisines of the nations of the Middle East have borrowed many dishes from those who lived in Palestine and have made them their own. Compare the stewed tomato dish loved by Jordanians to the tomato soup included here. Compare the eggplant dishes found throughout the region to the simple eggplant dish popular in Palestine. The threads that weave these cuisines together are strong.

Middle East–Palestine

Red Pepper and Walnut Dip
Muhammara

Yogurt with Green *Chilies*
Mish

Pita Bread

~

Tomato Soup with Green Peas
Bazella

Slow Cooker Lentil Soup with Potatoes and Spinach
Shorabat Adas

~~~~~~~~~~~~~~~~~~~~~

Twice-Baked Potatoes
Batata Mahshi

Baked Eggplant with *Laban*
Batinjan Imfashakh

Coriander in Yogurt   or   **Parsley Salad with *Tahini***
Kuzbara bi Laban   *Bajidiibsiyyeh*

~~~~~~~~~~~

Steamed Rice with Butter

Sliced Zucchini or Cauliflower Florets
Fried in Olive Oil

Baked Tomatoes

~~~~~~~~~~~~~~~~~~~~~

Wheat and Coconut Dessert with Sweet Syrup
Harisa Qatr

PALESTINIAN RED PEPPER AND WALNUT DIP
Muhammara
TPT - 17 minutes

In the fall, when the local red bell peppers appear in the farmers' market and in our grocery stores, the work begins but it is not without reward in the months that follow. This Palestinian recipe, also popular in Syria and Lebanon, is easily made from the peppers that were roasted and frozen in oil. If you have pomegranate molasses or syrup in the house, add directly to the food processor mixture instead of concentrating it further as you sauté the garlic.

- 2 tablespoons *extra virgin* olive oil
- 2 large garlic cloves—*finely* chopped
- 3 tablespoons unsweetened pomegranate juice
- 2 large ROASTED RED PEPPERS—*well-drained, if packed in oil* [see index]
- 2 cups chopped, *toasted preservative-free* walnuts
- 1/2 teaspoon salt
- Freshly ground black pepper, to taste

PALESTINIAN RED PEPPER AND WALNUT DIP (cont'd)

In a small skillet set over *MEDIUM* heat, heat oil. Add *finely* chopped garlic and pomegranate juice. Sauté until garlic is soft and translucent and pomegranate juice is thickened. *Be careful not to allow garlic or pomegranate molasses to burn.* Turn into the work bowl of the food processor fitted with steel knife.

Add roasted red pepper pieces, *toasted* walnuts, salt, and pepper. Process until a smooth sauce results. Turn into a small bowl.

Serve at room temperature with pieces of *pita* bread or crudités. Refrigerate leftovers.

Yields 2 cupfuls

Note: This recipe can be halved or doubled, when required.

1/16 SERVING (about 2 tablespoonfuls) –
PROTEIN = 3.3 g.; FAT = 14.4 g.; CARBOHYDRATE = 4.3 g.;
CALORIES = 160; CALORIES FROM FAT = 81%

PALESTINIAN YOGURT WITH GREEN *CHILIES*
Mish
TPT - 4 minutes

This dish can be made to please anyone since the type of hot peppers you can add can be the mild green chilies we favor or something more assertive. This slightly sour mixture, "mish" actually means sour, is an unusual sensation to the western palate that can be served as a salad or as a condiment or as an appetizer. It makes an interesting addition to a snacks-and-drinks menu or a cheese-and-crackers supper.

1 cup Greek-style plain yogurt
2 tablespoons *finely* chopped mild green *chilies*
1/2 lemon—peeled, pith removed, seeded, and
 finely chopped
1 medium tomato—*finely* chopped
1 tablespoon *extra virgin* olive oil
Salt, to taste

In a small mixing bowl, combine yogurt and *finely* chopped green *chilies*, lemon flesh, and tomato. Stir to mix well. Add olive oil and season with salt. Stir to combine well. Turn into a serving dish. Refrigerate until ready to serve.

Serve with pieces of *pita* bread as a dip.

Yields 18 servings
adequate for 6 people

Note: This recipe can be halved, when required.

1/18 SERVING – PROTEIN = 0.7 g.; FAT = 0.9 g.; CARBOHYDRATE = 1.2 g.;
CALORIES = 16; CALORIES FROM FAT = 51%

PALESTINIAN TOMATO SOUP WITH GREEN PEAS
Bazella
TPT - 33 minutes

Bazella is usually made with lamb meat but when a Palestinian cook does not have meat to make a stew, she makes a vegetarian soup that is thoroughly satisfying. I accompany this soup with pita bread or rice cooked in the Palestine way with butter.

1 tablespoon butter
1 medium onion—*finely* chopped
3 cups canned, *whole* tomatoes in tomato purée
1 cup freshly shelled *or frozen* peas
1 cup tomato juice *or* tomato-vegetable juice
1/4 teaspoon sugar

1/4 teaspoon ground allspice
Salt, to taste
Fresh ground black pepper, to taste

PALESTINIAN TOMATO SOUP WITH GREEN PEAS (cont'd)

In a large saucepan set over *MEDIUM* heat, melt butter. Add *finely* chopped onion and sauté until onion is soft and translucent, *being careful not to allow onion to brown.*

Add tomatoes, green peas, water, sugar, allspice, salt, and pepper. Simmer until heated through—about 15 minutes. Turn into a soup tureen.

Serve into heated soup plates.

Yields 6 servings
adequate for 4 people

1/6 SERVING – PROTEIN = 2.1 g.; FAT = 2.1 g.; CARBOHYDRATE = 10.2 g.;
CALORIES = 66; CALORIES FROM FAT = 29%

SLOW COOKER PALESTINIAN LENTIL SOUP WITH POTATOES AND SPINACH
Shorabat Adas

TPT - 6 hours and 35 minutes
[slow cooker: 6 hours and 30 minutes]

I have adapted a classic recipe from the historic and troubled land of Palestine to the very gadget-oriented world of the Western kitchen since I find the slow cooker to be a tremendous help for cooking lentils and the like. I come and go, doing errands, writing, gardening, walking, and it attends the pot all day, cooking the lentils to perfection. If I have mushroom stock on hand, I often substitute a cupful of the stock for a cupful of water.

5 cups *boiling* water

1/2 cup dry brown (*or* green) lentils—well-rinsed and sorted to remove any debris

2 medium potatoes—peeled and diced
Pinch ground red pepper (cayenne), or to taste
Pinch ground cumin, or to taste
Pinch salt
1 tablespoon tomato paste

2 cups fresh spinach leaves—trimmed, well-washed, and chopped— *or* 1 cup *frozen* and chopped spinach

Prepare the bowl of the slow cooker by coating with lecithin non-stick spray. Set temperature at *LOW*.

Combine *boiling* stock, and lentils. Cover and allow to cook, stirring occasionally for 4 hours.

Add diced potatoes, ground red pepper (cayenne), ground cumin, salt, and tomato paste. Stir to integrate well. Continue to cook for 2 hours more.

Add spinach. Stir to integrate and allow to cook for an additional 30 minutes.

Turn into a heated soup tureen and serve into heated soup plates.

Yields about 6 cupfuls

Note: Leftovers can be frozen.

1/6 SERVING (i. e., per cupful) –
PROTEIN = 6.3 g.; FAT = 0.4 g.; CARBOHYDRATE = 19.7 g.;
CALORIES = 104; CALORIES FROM FAT = 3%

Middle East–**Palestine**

PALESTINIAN TWICE-BAKED POTATOES
Batata Mahshi

TPT - 2 hours and 8 minutes

Here again, potatoes and tomatoes, foods from the New World, are important today to people whose ancestors lived in this land long before the Spanish and Portuguese explorers introduced their finds to the Old World. Palestinians use ground lamb to stuff the potatoes but the substitution of ground soymeat turns a simple baked potato into a protein-rich, vegetarian main course that fills and nourishes.

6 baking potatoes—well-scrubbed

2 tablespoons butter *or* oil, if preferred
1 cup *frozen* vegetarian "ground beef"
6 canned, *whole* tomatoes—*finely* chopped
1 cup *finely* chopped onion
3/4 teaspoon ground cumin
Freshly ground mixed peppercorns—red, black, and white—to taste

Preheat oven to 350 degrees F.

Cut an **X** in the top of each potato and place in the preheated oven. Bake for about 1 1/4 hours. Remove from oven and allow to cool slightly.

In a large skillet set over *LOW-MEDIUM* heat, heat butter or oil. Add ground soymeat, *finely* chopped tomatoes and onion, ground cumin, and ground mixed peppercorns. Cook, stirring frequently, until onion softens.

Using a sharp knife, cut an oval in the top of each potato. Remove the ovals.* Using a teaspoon, scoop the cooked potato flesh from each potato leaving a shell. Chop the potato flesh and add it to the mixture in the skillet. Stir to mix well. Apportion the potato mixture among the baked potato shells, packing it tightly into each shell. Arrange stuffed potatoes in a 10-inch pie plate. Return to oven and bake for about 20 minutes.

Serve at once.

Yields 6 servings
adequate 4 for people

Notes: *The ovals can be buttered and salted and, then, baked to be served as an appetizer.

This recipe can be halved, when required.

1/6 SERVING – PROTEIN = 10.6 g.; FAT = 4.9 g.; CARBOHYDRATE = 68.3 g.;
CALORIES = 349; CALORIES FROM FAT = 13%

BAKED EGGPLANT WITH *LABAN*
Batinjan Imfashakh

TPT - 2 hours and 53 minutes;
    1 hour = eggplant draining period;
    1 hour = refrigeration period

Here is a dish that can make my husband smile; he is very fond of eggplant, from any cuisine. Many Palestinian cooks fry the eggplant but since eggplant soaks up oil like a sponge, I prefer to bake it.

Coarse or kosher salt

3 tablespoons *extra virgin* olive oil

2 small, firm eggplants—peeled and sliced

1 large garlic clove
1/2 teaspoon salt

1 cup PLAIN YOGURT [see index] *or*
commercially-available plain yogurt

Salt eggplant slices generously and place them in a sieve or colander set in the sink. Place a plate on top and a weight—a large can or a tea kettle filled with water—on top of the plate. Allow to stand for 1 hour.

Rinse eggplant slices well in cold water and pat dry.

Place rimmed cookie sheets in oven to heat. Preheat oven to 350 degrees F.

Remove preheated baking sheets from oven. Pour about 1 1/2 tablespoons of oil on each pan; brush to edges. Arrange eggplant slices on each of prepared baking sheets. Bake in preheated 350 degree F. oven for 10 minutes. Rotate baking sheets and switch racks. Continue baking for an additional 10 minutes. Remove baking sheets from oven. Turn each eggplant slice. Return to oven for about 10 minutes more. Drain eggplant slices *thoroughly* on several thicknesses of paper toweling.

BAKED EGGPLANT WITH *LABAN* (cont'd)

Transfer baked eggplant slices to bread board. Using a large knife, chop until the eggplant has been mashed. Transfer to a mixing bowl.

Using the blade of a large knife, crush garlic cloves on the bread board. Sprinkle salt on the garlic and continue chopping until *very finely* chopped. Turn garlic and salt into the mixing bowl containing the mashed eggplant. Stir to mix well.

Add yogurt. Stir to mix well. Turn into a serving dish. Refrigerate for at least 1 hour.

Serve chilled. Refrigerate leftovers.

Yields 6 servings
adequate for 4 people

1/6 SERVING – PROTEIN = 2.6 g.; FAT = 6.3 g.; CARBOHYDRATE = 6.0 g.;
CALORIES = 93; CALORIES FROM FAT = 61%

PALESTINIAN CORIANDER IN YOGURT
Kuzbara bi Laban
TPT - 7 minutes

Ground coriander is found in almost every cuisine in the Middle East and in North Africa so use of the leaves of the coriander plant is certainly not unexpected. Fresh coriander leaves, also known as cilantro, have a bright taste that is not overwhelmed by the yogurt and the garlic. This can be served as a salad or just as a side dish. In Palestine and other nations of the Levant it is always served with roast lamb. We find it to be a wonderful way to cleanse the palate when the main course is spicy or heavy.

2 garlic cloves
1/2 teaspoon salt

2 cups PLAIN YOGURT *[see index] or*
  commercially-available plain yogurt
2 cups well-washed and *finely* chopped fresh
  coriander leaves (*cilantro*)

Using the blade of large knife, crush garlic cloves on a bread board. Sprinkle salt on the garlic and continue chopping until *very finely* chopped. Turn garlic and salt into a small mixing bowl.

Add yogurt, and *finely* chopped fresh coriander (*cilantro*). Mix well. Turn into a serving dish. Refrigerate until required.

Serve cold. Refrigerate leftovers.

Yields 12 servings
adequate for 4-6 people

Note: This recipe can be halved, when required.

1/12 SERVING (about 1/4 cupful) –
PROTEIN = 2.2 g.; FAT = 0.7 g.; CARBOHYDRATE = 2.9 g.;
CALORIES = 28; CALORIES FROM FAT = 23%

PALESTINIAN PARSLEY SALAD WITH *TAHINI*
Bajidiibsiyyeh
TPT - 3 minutes

Americans never think of parsley salads, for that matter they do not think of celery as the main ingredient in a salad either. This salad may well change your mind about parsley, the "forever garnish." The first time I tasted this salad, I said, "Oh, do please pass the salad again."

2 tablespoons *tahini*
1 tablespoon freshly squeezed lemon juice
Salt, to taste
2-3 tablespoons water

4 cups *curly* parsley florets—well washed and dried

In a small bowl, combine *tahini*, lemon juice, and salt. Using a small wire whisk combine thoroughly. Add water, as needed to create a smooth dressing.

Put parsley in a mixing bowl. Add *tahini* dressing. Toss until parsley is covered with the dressing. Turn into a serving bowl.

Middle East–**Palestine**

PALESTINIAN PARSLEY SALAD WITH *TAHINI* (cont'd)

Serve at once.

Yields 6 servings
adequate 4 for people

1/6 SERVING – PROTEIN = 1.4 g.; FAT = 1.6 g.; CARBOHYDRATE = 2.9 g.;
CALORIES = 32; CALORIES FROM FAT = 45%

PALESTINIAN BAKED TOMATOES
TPT - 37 minutes

This dish, called "duqous" in some parts of the Middle East, is said to have originated in Palestine. Although it is most frequently prepared in a skillet on top of the stove, I find it convenient to bake it. These spicy tomatoes make a wonderful side dish and it is a good recipe to have on hand when you have hot-house tomatoes or "winter" tomatoes that leave something to be desired in the taste department.

3 large, firm tomatoes—*thinly* sliced

1/4 cup water
3 tablespoons *extra virgin* olive oil
1/4 cup *finely* chopped fresh coriander (*cilantro*)
1 teaspoon garlic powder
1/2 teaspoon salt
1/4 teaspoon HOMEMADE PAPRIKA *[see index] or* commercially-available Hungarian sweet paprika
1/4 teaspoon ground cumin
1/4 teaspoon ground coriander
1/4 teaspoon chili powder

Preheat oven to 350 degrees F. Prepare a baking dish or 10-inch pie plate by coating with non-stick lecithin spray coating.

Arrange tomato slices in prepared baking dish or pie plate, overlapping as necessary.

In a small bowl, combine water, olive oil, *finely* chopped fresh coriander (*cilantro*), garlic powder, salt, paprika, ground cumin and coriander, and chili powder. Mix well. Spread evenly over tomatoes. Bake in preheated 350 degree F. oven for about 25-30 minutes.

Serve at once.

Yields 6 servings
adequate for 4 people

Note: This recipe can be halved, when required.

1/6 SERVING – PROTEIN = 0.6 g.; FAT = 5.7 g.; CARBOHYDRATE = 2.2 g.;
CALORIES = 63; CALORIES FROM FAT = 81%

PALESTINIAN WHEAT AND COCONUT DESSERT
WITH SWEET SYRUP

Harisa Qatr

TPT - 5 hours and 50 minutes;
1 hour = pre–baking absorption period;
4 hours = cooling period

Syrup- and honey-soaked pastries are found all over the Middle East. This does not pretend to be "baklawa;" it is, instead a simply-prepared, delicious, celebratory treat beloved by a people torn by conflict for decades. It is a crumbly, treat that makes you forget your troubles . . . .

PALESTINIAN WHEAT AND COCONUT DESSERT WITH SWEET SYRUP (cont'd)

1 1/2 cups enriched quick-cooking farina *or* Cream of Wheat cereal—*not instant*
1/2 cup powdered unsweetened, *preservative-free* desiccated coconut
1/4 cup butter—*softened to room temperature*

1/3 cup sugar
1/2 cup skimmed milk
1 teaspoon rose water *or ma ward**

QATR:
    1/2 cup sugar
    1 cup water
    1 tablespoon freshly squeezed lemon juice
    1/4 teaspoon ground cinnamon

1/4 cup chopped, *toasted preservative-free* almonds

Prepare an 8-inch square non-stick-coated baking pan by coating with non-stick lecithin spray coating.

In a large bowl, combine farina, powdered coconut, and softened butter. Using a pastry cutter, combine dry ingredients with butter until you achieve a consistency of coarse corn meal. Spread mixture into the bottom of prepared pan.

Pour 1/3 cupful sugar into a second bowl. While stirring, add milk and stir until well-combined. Add rose water and mix thoroughly. Pour sugar–milk mixture *as evenly as possible* over the top. Allow to stand at room temperature for 1 hour.

Preheat oven to 350 degrees F.

Bake in preheated oven for about 35 minutes, or until top is *lightly browned*.

While *harisa* is baking, prepare the *qatr*, sugar syrup, by mixing the 1/2 cupful sugar, water, lemon juice, and cinnamon in a saucepan. Cook over *MEDIUM* heat until it comes to a *full boil*. *Remove from heat.*

Remove baked farina–coconut base from oven. Sprinkle *toasted* almond pieces over the surface. Pour sugar syrup over. Refrigerate for at least 4 hours to allow the dessert to firm so that it may be cut more easily.

Cut into sixteen pieces and remove with a narrow spatula or wide knife.

Serve at room temperature.

                              Yields 16 servings

Notes: *Both French and Lebanese rose water products are available in food specialty stores.

        This recipe can be doubled, when required.

1/16 SERVING – PROTEIN = 2.9 g.; FAT = 5.2 g.; CARBOHYDRATE = 28.5 g.;
CALORIES = 172; CALORIES FROM FAT = 27%

Saudi Arabia

The roots of the modern nation of Saudi Arabia, founded in 1932, go back some thirty years before that date when Abdul-Aziz bin Saud began conquering tribal lands to form an Islamic state, eventually controlling an area more than three times the size of our state of Texas. Ibn Saud, as he was known, was the leader of the House of Saud which rules the Kingdom of Saudi Arabia to this day.

Saudi Arabia is the keeper of the two sites most holy to Moslems, *Al-Masjid al-Haram* in Mecca, which contains Islam's most sacred place, the *kaaba*, and *Al-Masjid al-Nabawi* in Medina, which contains the tomb of the Prophet Muhammad. Muhammad was born in Mecca c. 571 AD and in the seventh century united the tribes of the Arabian Peninsula. Upon his death in 632 the territory established by Muhammad as an Islamic political state was vastly expanded by his followers who carried the teachings of the *Koran* to the West as far as the Iberian Peninsula and to the East all the way to Pakistan. The dynasty known as the House of Saud or *Al Saud*, was founded by Muhammad bin Saud during the sixteenth century when the Arabian Peninsula came under the rule of the Ottoman Empire. By 1891 *Al Saud* had been driven into exile by a rival Arabian family, the *Al Rashid*, and stayed out of the political scene until 1902 when the ancestors of today's ruling family began their military campaigns to establish their family as the ruling family. The British, immersed in World War I and their own battle against the Ottoman Turks, saw their opportunity to enlist the cooperation of the House of Saud to drive the Ottoman Empire from the Arabian Peninsula. In 1916 they backed the House of Saud and their Arab allies in their revolt against Ottoman rule with the objective of forming a united Arab state. The Arab Revolt which lasted from 1916 to 1918 was not successful but the Allied victory in World War I did end Ottoman control of Arabia and allowed for establishment of an Arab state. Consolidation of power by the House of Saud was achieved by 1925 and the Kingdom of Saudi Arabia was declared in 1932. It is an absolute monarchy in which the king is not only the seat of executive power but also controls legislative and judicial functions; the *Koran* is the constitution. With an estimated 7,000 princes who are appointed to posts by the king, all levels of government are closely controlled with little transparency.

The Kingdom of Saudi Arabia was a vastly different country in 1932 than it is today. This newly minted nation was a vast desert with limited agriculture and unexplored natural resources. Revenues from pilgrimages by the Islamic faithful represented the most significant percentage of the national income; it was, in truth, one of the poorest countries on Earth. In 1938 fortunes dramatically changed for the Saudis with the discovery of the world's second largest oil reserve. Saudi Arabia became a major player on the world geo-political stage and was able to vastly improve the economic conditions of its population. Oil now accounts for ninety-five percent of exports and some seventy percent of government revenues. Oil exploration and drilling not withstanding, forty percent of the population was still nomadic in 1950. By 1992 seventy-five percent of the population was living in urban settings. With fifty percent of the over twenty-eight million population under the age of twenty, the government has been seriously challenged to stimulate job creation and eliminate the chronic unemployed state of its young people.

A rather interesting cuisine has evolved, albeit heavily influenced by nomadic traditional foods, Turkish and Persian dishes, and influences from North Africa.

Middle East—**Saudi Arabia**

Roasted Eggplant and Red Peppers

Lentils and Potatoes with Lemon Juice
Adas bil Hamod

Spiced Eggs
Aijet Beytat

Wheat Flatbread
Kimaje

~

Chilled Cucumber and Mango Soup

Puréed Root Vegetable Soup

~~~~~~~~~~~~~~~~~~~~

Couscous with Raisins, Pine Nuts, and *Feta* Cheese
Couscous

Wheat Flatbread
Kimaje

~~~~~~~~~~

Braised Vegetables in Olive Oil

Chick Peas and Finely Chopped Onions with *Tahini* Sauce
Foul

~~~~~~~~~~

Yellow Summer Squash Custard Casserole

Spicy Sautéed Cauliflower Florets
Qarnabeet

~~~~~~~~~~~~~~~~~~~~

Rice Pudding with Dates   Carrot Pudding
Ruz bil Laban

Phyllo Pastries
Samboosak Hilwah

ROASTED RED PEPPER AND EGGPLANT APPETIZER IN THE STYLE OF SAUDI ARABIA
TPT - 1 hour and 20 minutes

Roasted red peppers and grilled or baked eggplant flesh combine so beautifully. I have made a dish combining these two vegetables for decades but with Italian seasoning. When you mash them together with onion, garlic, lemon juice, and seasoning, you have a spread that is complimentary to almost all meze dishes.

ROASTED RED PEPPER AND EGGPLANT APPETIZER IN THE STYLE OF SAUDI ARABIA (cont'd)

2 large red bell peppers—perfect, unblemished, and well-washed
2 small eggplants—well washed

2 teaspoons *extra virgin* olive oil
1 teaspoon freshly squeezed lemon juice

1/4 cup *very finely* chopped onion
1 small garlic clove—*very finely* chopped
1/4 teaspoon chili powder, or to taste
Salt, to taste
Freshly ground black pepper, to taste

Preheat oven to 350 degrees F.

Place red peppers and eggplants on a cookie sheet. Roast in preheated oven for about 40 minutes, *turning frequently*. Remove from oven.

Place red peppers in a heavy brown paper bag in dry sink. Roll the top of the bag down and allow to steam for about 15 minutes. Remove stems, seeds, and membranes, peel, and chop finely. Place in a shallow bowl.

Peel eggplant and chop flesh. Add to the chopped, roasted red peppers. Using a potato masher, mash the two vegetables together.

Add olive oil and lemon juice. Mash again.

Add *very finely* chopped onion and garlic, chili powder, salt, and pepper. Mash again. Turn into a serving dish set on a large plate or platter. Surround with *pita* bread pieces, small toasts, or crackers, if preferred.

Serve at room temperature. Refrigerate leftovers.

Yields 18 servings
adequate for 6 people

Note: *Instead of chopping the roasted peppers, large pieces can be conveniently frozen in oil for future menus. For this reason, I roast a large number of peppers whenever I roast peppers.

This technique, of course, can be used to roast green, yellow, and orange peppers too.

When required, this recipe can be halved.

1/6 SERVING – PROTEIN = 0.4 g.; FAT = 0.5 g.; CARBOHYDRATE = 2.3 g.; CALORIES = 15; CALORIES FROM FAT = 30%

SAUDI ARABIAN BLACK LENTILS AND POTATOES WITH LEMON JUICE

Adas bil Hamod

TPT - 60 minutes

You want to choose a very firm lentil for this dish such as French green lentils or black lentils. Black lentils are readily available and do give this appetizer salad a very beautiful look. We generally serve this as a salad but it is an excellent choice for a meze table.

1 cup black lentils—well-washed and sorted
3 cups *boiling* water

1 large potato—peeled and diced

1 tablespoon *extra virgin* olive oil
2 garlic cloves—*very finely* chopped
1/2 cup chopped fresh coriander (*cilantro*)

2 tablespoons freshly squeezed lemon juice
Salt, to taste
Freshly ground black pepper, to taste

In a saucepan set over *MEDIUM* heat, combine black lentils and *boiling* water. Allow to boil for 15 minutes.

Add diced potatoes and allow to boil for 15 minutes more. Drain and return to saucepan.

In a skillet set over *LOW-MEDIUM* heat, heat oil. Add *very finely* chopped garlic cloves and chopped coriander (*cilantro*). Sauté until garlic is soft. Add to lentil-potato mixture and return to *LOW-MEDIUM* heat. Cook, stirring frequently to prevent sticking, for about 10 minutes more.

Add lemon juice, salt, and black pepper. Turn into a serving dish.

Serve warm or cold with *pita* bread.

Yields 6 servings
adequate for 4 people

Note: This recipe can be doubled, when required.

SAUDI ARABIAN BLACK LENTILS AND POTATOES WITH LEMON JUICE (cont'd)

1/6 SERVING – PROTEIN = 6.3 g.; FAT = 2.8 g.; CARBOHYDRATE = 42.6 g.;
CALORIES = 220; CALORIES FROM FAT = 11%

SPICED EGGS IN THE STYLE OF SAUDI ARABIA
Aijet Beytat
TPT - 15 minutes

These spiced eggs are enjoyed as an appetizer, as a snack, or for breakfast in Saudi Arabia. We like to serve them with a vegetable dish or two as a summer supper. Chilled, they can be a nice item for a picnic.

3/4 teaspoon paprika
3/4 teaspoon freshly ground black pepper
1/4 teaspoon ground cinnamon
1/2 teaspoon salt
Pinch ground red pepper (cayenne)

6 *hard-cooked* eggs

1 1/2 teaspoons *extra virgin* olive oil
1 tablespoon butter

In a small dish, combine paprika, pepper, cinnamon, salt, and ground red pepper (cayenne). Mix well. Set aside.

Shell eggs. Using a bamboo skewer, prick each egg all over. Place in a saucepan.

Add olive oil and butter. Set over *MEDIUM* heat and allow eggs to brown slightly—about 5-6 minutes. Shake frequently. Turn into a heated serving bowl.

Sprinkle spice mixture over.

Serve at once.

Yields 6 servings

Note: This recipe can be halved, when required.

1/6 SERVING (i. e., per egg) –
PROTEIN = 6.4 g.; FAT = 8.5 g.; CARBOHYDRATE = 0.0 g.;
CALORIES = 103; CALORIES FROM FAT = 74%

SAUDI ARABIAN CHILLED CUCUMBER AND MANGO SOUP
TPT - 8 minutes

From a very warm part of the Middle East comes a refreshing cold soup that is perfect as a first course for a summer meal. The unexpected taste of the mango and cucumber combination stimulates the taste buds and anyone who said that they weren't hungry changes that declaration rather quickly.

1 large mango—peeled, pitted, and chopped
1 small cucumber—peeled, quartered, seeded, and chopped
1 large garlic clove—chopped
3 scallions—trimmed, well-rinsed, and chopped
1 cup Greek-style plain yogurt

1/2 cup water
1/8 teaspoon salt

In the work bowl of the food processor, fitted with steel knife, or in the container of the electric blender, combine chopped mango, cucumber, garlic, and scallions with yogurt. Process or blend until a smooth purée forms.

Add water and salt. Again, process.

*Serve chilled.**

Yields 6 small soup cup servings
adequate for 4-6 people

Notes: *I store any leftovers in the container of the electric blender and simply process them again to serve the next day.

This recipe can be doubled, when required. When doubling, purée in batches, turn into a chilled soup tureen, and stir well.

1/6 SERVING – PROTEIN = 2.4 g.; FAT = 0.8 g.; CARBOHYDRATE = 12.3 g.;
CALORIES = 63; CALORIES FROM FAT = 11%

Middle East–**Saudi Arabia**

PURÉED ROOT VEGETABLE SOUP IN THE STYLE OF SAUDI ARABIA
TPT - 53 minutes

This soup, popular in Saudi Arabia, is very similar to a soup that I have made for years, which I dubbed "underground soup" because it depends upon root vegetables. It freezes beautifully and is always available when needed. Chicken stock and chicken are added by Saudis but I see no reason to add meat. This thick soup stands up well as a vegetarian first course or as choice for lunch.

1 quart VEGETABLE STOCK FROM SOUP *[see index]* **or other vegetarian stock of choice**
3/4 teaspoon ground cumin
1/2 teaspoon ground coriander
Freshly ground black pepper, to taste
2 bay leaves—broken in half and secured in a tea ball

1 medium potato—peeled and diced or shredded
1 medium carrot—scraped or pared and diced or shredded
1 medium French turnip—peeled and diced or shredded
1 large onion—*finely* **chopped**
1 large garlic clove—*very finely* **chopped**
1/4 cup *finely* **chopped fresh coriander leaves (***cilantro***)** *or* **parsley, if preferred**

1 cup *whole* **milk, half and half,** *or* **light cream, as preferred**
Salt, to taste

In a large kettle set over *MEDIUM* heat, combine vegetable stock, ground cumin and coriander, black pepper, and tea ball containing bay leaves. Allow to come to boil. *Reduce heat to LOW-MEDIUM.*

Add dice or shredded potato, carrot, and turnip, *finely* chopped onion, *very finely* chopped garlic, and *finely* chopped fresh coriander (*cilantro*) or parsley. Allow to cook until vegetables are tender—about 30 minutes.* Remove from heat. Remove tea ball and discard bay leaves.

Using a food processor fitted with steel knife or electric blender, process vegetables and stock carefully in small batches until puréed. Add a little of the milk if purée becomes too thick for the machine to manage. Turn into a clean saucepan or kettle set over *LOW-MEDIUM* heat.

Using a wire whisk, stir milk or cream into puréed soup base. Salt to taste. Allow to heat through—about 5 minutes. Turn into heated soup tureen. Serve into heated soup plates.

Yields about 6 cupfuls

Notes: *This recipe may be prepared ahead to this point and refrigerated or frozen. Reheat and proceed as described above.

When required, this recipe can be doubled.

1/6 SERVING (i. e., per cupful) –
PROTEIN = 2.3 g.; FAT = 1.4 g.; CARBOHYDRATE = 9.3 g.;
CALORIES = 57; CALORIES FROM FAT = 22%

SAUDI ARABIAN *COUSCOUS* WITH RAISINS, PINE NUTS, AND *FETA* CHEESE

Couscous

TPT - 1 hour and 36 minutes;
1 hour = raisin soaking period

Couscous is enjoyed throughout North Africa, down into Central Africa, and in the Middle East. Saudis combine the couscous with the sweet of raisins, the crunch of pine nuts, and the taste of dry, salty cheese. A good Greek feta cheese, usually available in our grocery stores, adds just the right taste. Please note that omission of the cheese results in a splendid vegan entrée and crumbled feta can be served as a condiment for those who wish to add it to their serving of couscous.

SAUDI ARABIAN *COUSCOUS* WITH RAISINS, PINE NUTS, AND *FETA* CHEESE (cont'd)

3 tablespoons *preservative-free dark* raisins
1 cup *boiling* water

1 tablespoon butter
1/4 cup *finely* chopped onion
1/4 cup *finely* chopped carrot

3/4 cup VEGETARIAN WHITE STOCK *[see index]**
1/2 cup dry, quick-cooking, whole wheat *couscous***

2 tablespoons pine nuts (*pignoli*)
2 tablespoons *well-drained* and crumbled *feta* cheese
Freshly ground black pepper, to taste

Lemon wedges, for garnish

In a small bowl, soak raisins in *boiling* water until hydrated and plump—about 1 hour. Drain well.

In a saucepan set over *MEDIUM* heat, melt butter. Add *finely* chopped onion and carrot. Sauté until vegetables have softened.

Add vegetable stock and allow to come to the boil. Reduce heat to *LOW* and stir in *couscous*. Cover tightly and allow to cook for about 5 minutes. Remove from heat and allow *couscous* to steam for about 10 minutes. *All water should be absorbed.*

When *couscous* is steamed and *all water has been absorbed*, fluff cooked *couscous* with a wooden fork. Turn onto a warmed platter. Spread.

Sprinkle pine nuts (*pignoli*) and *feta* cheese over. Grind black pepper over to taste.

Serve at once with lemon wedges.

Yields 4 servings
adequate for 3 people

Notes: *VEGETARIAN WHITE STOCK does not discolor this dish. Other vegetable stocks, especially those which contain tomatoes, are not suitable.

**Couscous is packaged by several companies and is now generally available in grocery stores and food specialty stores as well as in Middle Eastern groceries and in natural food stores.

This recipe may be doubled, when required.

1/4 SERVING – PROTEIN = 5.4 g.; FAT = 6.5 g.; CARBOHYDRATE = 26.5 g.;
CALORIES = 184; CALORIES FROM FAT = 32%

SAUDI ARABIAN BRAISED VEGETABLES IN OLIVE OIL WITH RICE
TPT - 57 minutes

Dishes which combine leeks and carrots are certainly not unusual as you travel the world, but when braised in olive oil, the dish becomes spectacular. This is an amazingly versatile dish that can be served hot or cold. It is a perfect choice for a buffet.

1/2 cup *extra virgin* olive oil
2 medium leeks—trimmed, sliced into 1/2-inch slices, and *very well-rinsed*
2 medium carrots—scraped or pared, cut in half lengthwise, and cut into half-moon slices

1/4 cup dry converted rice
1 teaspoon sugar
1/4 teaspoon salt, or to taste
1 teaspoon freshly squeezed lemon juice
1 1/2 cups *boiling* water

In a large saucepan set over *LOW-MEDIUM* heat, heat oil. Add leek and carrot slices. Cover and cook, stirring frequently, for about 25 minutes.

Add rice, sugar, salt, lemon juice, and *boiling* water. Cover and allow to cook for 25-30 minutes, until water has been absorbed and rice is tender. Stir frequently. Turn into a heated serving bowl.

Serve warm with flatbread, or, if preferred, at room temperature, or even chilled.

Yields 6 servings
adequate for 4 people

Note: This recipe can be halved, when required.

1/6 SERVING – PROTEIN = 1.0 g.; FAT = 14.9 g.; CARBOHYDRATE = 7.5 g.;
CALORIES = 182; CALORIES FROM FAT = 74%

Middle East – **Saudi Arabia**

SAUDI ARABIAN YELLOW SUMMER SQUASH CUSTARD CASSEROLE
TPT - 1 hour and 41 minutes

Yellow summer squash was just that, a yellow squash available only in the summer. September meant the end of this vegetable option and if you had not frozen a portion or two of mashed summer squash and made your ratatouille, you just had to wait until the next summer's harvest. Now it is readily available year-round. The first time I saw this recipe on a Middle Eastern menu I felt sure that it just could not be an authentic Saudi Arabian recipe. Since then I have found several similar recipes so I guess there is every reason to include this tasty dish.

1 large yellow summer squash—about 1 pound— peeled, halved, pitted, and shredded
6 tablespoons dry breadcrumbs
1 garlic clove—*very finely* chopped
3 tablespoons *finely* chopped fresh parsley

1 cup *two-percent* milk
1/2 cup *fat-free* pasteurized eggs (the equivalent of 2 eggs)
2 tablespoons *melted* butter
1/4 teaspoon salt
Pinch of ground red pepper (cayenne)
Freshly ground black pepper, to taste

2 tablespoons grated *pecorino Romano* cheese

Preheat oven to 350 degrees F. Prepare a soufflé dish or other oven-to-table baking dish by coating with non-stick lecithin spray coating. Create a water bath by setting the baking dish into a larger baking dish or roaster pan in which about 1 inch of water has been poured.

In a mixing bowl combine shredded yellow squash, breadcrumbs, *very finely* chopped garlic, and *finely* chopped fresh parsley. Stir to mix well.

In a 2-cup measuring cup, combine milk, pasteurized eggs, *melted* butter, salt, ground red pepper (cayenne), and black pepper. Stir to mix well. Pour over squash mixture. Mix thoroughly. Turn into prepared soufflé dish. Place the soufflé dish and its water bath in the preheated 350 degree F. oven. Allow to bake for about 1 hour and 10 minutes.

Pull rack out of oven. Sprinkle grated cheese over. Push rack back into oven and allow to bake for 10-15 minutes more, or until a knife inserted in the center comes out clean. Check water level occasionally and add *cold* water, if needed. *Do not allow water bath to simmer or boil—add cold water or ice cubes*, if necessary.

Serve at once.

Yields 6 servings
adequate for 4 people

1/6 SERVING – PROTEIN = 5.7 g.; FAT = 5.3 g.; CARBOHYDRATE = 12.1 g.;
CALORIES = 117; CALORIES FROM FAT = 40%

SPICY SAUTÉED CAULIFLOWER FLORETS IN THE SAUDI STYLE
Qarnabeet
TPT - 15 minutes

Every fall, without fail, I have heard people going on and on about the piles of beautiful pumpkins and squashes. Nobody seems to get all warm and fuzzy about cauliflowers but freshly harvested, snowy white or golden heads of locally-grown cauliflower are equally beautiful and equally symbolic of the season. The over-sized, unmarketable cauliflower were always available at farm stands on eastern Long Island and we took advantage of the plenty. In October we would drive Out East and buy cauliflower, broccoli, cabbages, squashes, salad potatoes, beets, a few duck eggs, and, of course, a Halloween pumpkin. The cauliflowers were frozen, whole, if small, or as florets, if large. Trimmings were cooked and processed into a creamy soup base. The discovery of this recipe was a real find because we now have another way to enjoy this beautiful and very healthful vegetable.

2 tablespoons butter
4 cups fresh cauliflower florets—well-rinsed
1/4 cup *finely* chopped onion
1/4 teaspoon chili powder, or to taste
Salt, to taste

2 tablespoons *finely* chopped fresh coriander (*cilantro*), for garnish
Lemon wedges, for garnish

SPICY SAUTÉED CAULIFLOWER FLORETS IN THE SAUDI STYLE (cont'd)

In a large non-stick coated skillet or saucepan set over *LOW-MEDIUM* heat, melt butter. Add cauliflower florets, *finely* chopped onion, chili powder, and salt. Cook, stirring frequently until cauliflower is tender—about 10 minutes. *Be careful not to allow onion to brown.* Turn into a heated serving bowl.

Garnish with *finely* chopped fresh coriander (*cilantro*) and lemon wedges.

Serve at once.

Yields 6 servings
adequate for 4 people

Note: This recipe can be halved or doubled, when required.

1/6 SERVING – PROTEIN = 1.9 g.; FAT = 3.9 g.; CARBOHYDRATE = 4.2 g.;
CALORIES = 55; CALORIES FROM FAT = 64%

SAUDI ARABIAN RICE PUDDING WITH DATES
Ruz bil Laban

TPT - 3 hour and 20 minutes;
2 hours = refrigeration period

The Saudis, due to their unique geographical position atop oil reserves of enormous financial potential, have a comfortable life. Nevertheless, the desert and its agricultural limitations must still be calculated. Grazing animals convert into body weight only about six-percent of the grasses on which they feed. Grains are completely edible by humans while only about two-thirds of the butchered animals are eaten. Amazing as it may seem, ninety-six percent of the calories that would be available if one ate the primary grasses has literally been wasted in the serving of meat on the dinner plate. The grass we know as rice has provided South America, Africa, Asia, Central Asia, and the Middle East with an economical source of nutrition and a variety of rice puddings to cheer the soul. The flavor of star anise in a rice pudding was an amazing new experience for me; and I thought there was no rice pudding variation I had not tried. In addition, dates are added to this Saudi Arabian specialty along with the ubiquitous touch of rose water. This is a rice pudding like no other.

3 1/2 cups *two-percent* milk
1/2 cup dry short grain white rice*
2 whole star anise seedpods
6 tablespoons sugar

1 teaspoon rose water
6 large *preservative-free* dates—*finely* chopped**

In a large saucepan set over *MEDIUM* heat, combine milk, rice, star anise seedpods, and sugar. Allow to come to the boil. Reduce heat to *LOW-MEDIUM* and simmer for about 1 hour, stirring frequently to avoid sticking.

When the rice is soft and most of the milk has been absorbed, add rose water and *finely* chopped dates. Stir well. Continue cooking for about 7 minutes more. Remove from heat. Remove and discard star anise pods. Turn into a serving bowl. Refrigerate for at least 2 hours before serving.

Serve chilled or at room temperature.

Yields 6 servings
adequate for 4 people

Notes: *Some Saudis make this pudding with converted white rice. I prefer to use short grain rice; the texture is soft and rich.

**Dates are more easily "chopped" into little pieces using a scissors than with a knife.

This recipe can be halved or doubled, when required.

1/6 SERVING – PROTEIN = 6.3 g.; FAT = 2.8 g.; CARBOHYDRATE = 42.6 g.;
CALORIES = 220; CALORIES FROM FAT = 11%

Middle East–**Saudi Arabia**

SAUDI ARABIAN CARROT PUDDING
TPT - 1 hour and 3 minutes;
20 minutes = cooling period

My grandfather always wanted to know what was for dessert so that he could measure his intake of the rest of the meal. If it meant cutting back on vegetables to maintain room for a favorite dessert, he generally took small servings while my grandmother pressed the vegetables saying, "Have some more vegetables, George." A particular brand of organic carrots available in our grocery stores is so sweet that there is always a comment when I steam them for dinner and I think grandpa would have been hard-pressed to refuse my grandmother's request when carrots were served. When the dessert placed on the table is as beautiful and as sweetly satisfying as is this dessert, you probably will not even hear a comment about the fact that it is a vegetable. And, there is, in our experience, little difficulty encouraging a second serving. Grandpa could have justifiably said that he would wait for dessert for the extra serving of vegetables.

BUERRE MANIE:
- 1 tablespoon *softened* butter
- 1 tablespoon unbleached white flour

3 large carrots—pared or peeled

1/2 cup sugar
1 cup *two-percent* milk
1/4 teaspoon ground cardamom
1 teaspoon grated *organic* lemon zest—fresh or dried

1 tablespoon *finely* chopped pistachio nuts, for garnish
1 tablespoon *finely* chopped, *toasted preservative-free* almonds—for garnish

Put flour and butter into a mixing bowl. Using a wooden spoon or paddle, work the mixture until combined and smooth. Set aside until required.

Shred carrots and transfer them to a food processor fitted with steel knife. Process until carrots are uniformly grated. Turn into a saucepan.

Add sugar, milk, ground cardamom and grated lemon zest. Place over *MEDIUM* heat and allow to come to the simmer, stirring frequently. Cook for about 15 minutes.

While stirring, scrape *buerre manie* into the carrot mixture. Cook, stirring constantly, until pudding thickens. Turn into a serving bowl.

Sprinkle *finely* chopped pistachios and almonds over. Set aside until pudding comes to room temperature.

Serve into small dessert dishes. *Serve at room temperature* but refrigerate any leftovers.

Yields 6 servings
adequate for 4 people

Note: This recipe can be doubled, when required.

1/6 SERVING – PROTEIN = 2.2 g.; FAT = 3.7 g.; CARBOHYDRATE = 5.8 g.;
CALORIES = 136; CALORIES FROM FAT = 24%

SAUDI ARABIAN *PHYLLO* PASTRIES WITH ROSE WATER AND HONEY
Samboosak Hilwah

TPT - 54 minutes;
15 minutes = saffron soaking period

Standing in the food department of Harrods' in London, I was impressed with the Middle Eastern pastries available. Having just bought pastries in an Iranian bakery to serve for dessert, I passed them by. For years I thought it would be too difficult to make them but the general availability of phyllo pastry in the frozen food departments of grocery stores encouraged me and soon I was making pastries that I would have never believed possible. This recipe is quick and simple; it is a good place to start your adventure with phyllo pastry. Both Tunisians and Lebanese make a similar pastry but neither saffron nor cardamom are added by either country. Tunisians add grated orange zest while Lebanese substitute walnuts for almonds and add cinnamon and nutmeg.

SAUDI ARABIAN *PHYLLO* PASTRIES WITH ROSE WATER AND HONEY (cont'd)

1 pinch saffron—crumbled
2 tablespoons rose water

1/2 cup ground *preservative-free* almonds *or* almond meal
1/3 cup sugar
1 teaspoon ground cardamom

12 *phyllo* pastry leaves—*brought to room temperature*
2 tablespoons *melted* butter

3 tablespoons honey*

Preheat oven to 375 degrees F. Prepare a cookie sheet by lining it with culinary parchment paper.

In a small dish, combine crumbled saffron and rose water. Allow to soak for 15 minutes.

In a marble mortar, combine ground almonds, sugar, and cardamom. Using a pestle, grind them together until of uniform consistency.

Add rose water and saffron. Grind until you form a paste.

On a cutting board, cut the *phyllo* leaves into 3 1/2-4-inch strips. Cover the strips with a damp tea towel to keep them from drying out.

Lay one strip on the cutting board and using a brush, brush with *melted* butter. Lay a second strip on top of the first and brush it with *melted* butter. Spoon about 2 teaspoonfuls of the filling into the lower right hand corner of the strip about 1 inch from the bottom. Fold the edge of the strip up and then fold the filled corner over to the left to form a triangle. Continue to fold into triangles as you would to fold a flag, alternating from left to right and then right to left. Dip your fingers in a little water and seal. Place on the prepared cookie sheet. Continue until you have made 24 pastries.

Bake in preheated 375 degree F. oven for 15-18 minutes until browned. Using a spatula transfer to a serving dish.

Drizzle honey over pastries.*

Serve at once.

Yields 24 servings
adequate for 4 people

Notes: *If preferred, sugar can be sprinkled over the pastries before baking. The sugar will caramelize while the pastries bake.

This recipe can be halved or doubled, when required.

1/24 SERVING – PROTEIN = 0.8 g.; FAT = 1.7 g.; CARBOHYDRATE = 8.3 g.; CALORIES = 56; CALORIES FROM FAT = 27%

Syria

Whether or not you have heard of the seventh century Islamic Umayyad Empire or the later Mamluk Empire, you surely have heard of Damascus, the present-day capital of the present-day country of Syria. Damascus served as the capital of both those ancients empires and is considered to be one of the oldest continuously-occupied cities in the world. Modern Syria occupies only a small portion of the larger footprint of the ancient land of Syria which comprised the entire Levant. Since the period of the Roman Empire, Syria shares the ancient territory with Israel, Jordan, and the Palestinian Territories, formerly known as Judaea and named Palaestina in 135 AD, and Lebanon, formerly the area known as Phoenicia. Within its borders also was the civilization cradle of Mesopotamia and near the present city of Idlib is the now partially excavated capital of an empire referred to as the Eblan civilization, an early Semitic empire, established about 3000 BC, extending from the Red Sea north to Turkey and east to Mesopotamia. This Semitic empire prospered into the second millennium BC, falling then to the Hittites.

Syria is considered to be an Arabized population due to the cultural, linguistic, and religious adaptations made by the indigenous population with the arrival of Arabian Muslims. This not withstanding, they are genetically more closely related to those whose borders they share.

Lamb is omnipresent on Syrian menus, so much so that a vegetarian can be truly challenged but if one remembers the number of fast days in the Syrian calendar, one can pretty much bet on a grain or legume dish to satisfy hunger and principle. Typical family cooking, especially outside of the cities, reveals dishes shared by other nations in the area such as *tabbouleh* and *hummus* which are, I would wager to guess, as beloved in the West as they are in Middle East. Refinements in cuisine experienced under the period of the French mandate following World War I are more apparent in the cities but culinary clues to the long centuries under the Ottoman Empire are also obvious;" ba'lawa" is still, perhaps, the most favored dessert for special occasions.

Cheese Spread with Garlic
Kareeshee mi Thume

Syrian String Cheese
Gibbneck Masahllale

Syrian Bread or Pita Bread
Khubz

~

Tomato and Onion Salad
Salatat Banadoora

~~~~~~~~~~~~~~~~~~~~

Noodles with Lentils
Rishta

Beet and *Tahini* Salad with Eggs
Salatat Shamandar bi Taheena

~~~~~~~~~~~~~~~~~~~~

Dates, Figs, and Dried Apricots

Middle East–**Syria**

SYRIAN CHEESE SPREAD WITH GARLIC
Kareeshee mi Thume
TPT - 5 minutes

This spread is perfect for an appetizer in the Middle Eastern manner, at table, or as an offering for a party set on the coffee table or on the picnic table while the rest of the meal is being prepared. On a night when we are "not that hungry," we often make this spread and serve it with pita or flatbread, crudités, and a bowl of black olives. We always find we were more hungry than we thought.

1 cup *feta* cheese*

1 garlic clove—*finely* chopped
2 tablespoons fresh parsley—chopped
1 tablespoon fresh dillweed—chopped

1 cup *part-skimmed milk ricotta* cheese
6 tablespoons soft butter spread

10 *preservative-free* walnut halves—*toasted*

Warm *pita* bread pieces

Using the food processor fitted with steel knife, process *feta* cheese until uniformly crumbly.

Add *finely* chopped garlic, parsley, and dillweed. Process until a smooth mixture results.

Add *ricotta* cheese and butter and process until very smooth. Turn into a small serving bowl and chill until required.

Before serving, garnish with *toasted* walnut halves.

Serve chilled or at room temperature with warm *pita* bread pieces. Refrigerate leftovers.

Yields 10 servings
adequate for 6 people

Notes: *Packaged seasoned *feta* is sold in most grocery stores. It adds an additional dimension to this spread.

This recipe can be halved or doubled, when required.

1/10 SERVING (exclusive of bread) –
PROTEIN = 5.9 g.; FAT = 11.2 g.; CARBOHYDRATE = 2.4 g.;
CALORIES = 136; CALORIES FROM FAT = 74%

SYRIAN TOMATO AND ONION SALAD
Salatat Banadoora
TPT - 1 hour and 12 minutes;
1 hour = marination period

This salad, popular in both Syria and Lebanon, is strikingly similar to a tomato and onion salad served in Portugal, where it is so popular that we ate it almost daily during a summer trip to the Iberian Peninsula. In the Middle East, however, a refreshing lemon vinaigrette with thyme and mint is the classic dressing. "Fattoush," a salad meal akin to the Greek salad "horiatiki salata" is also popular in Syria and from that we have borrowed the capers, black olives, and garlic croutons that adorn our "salatat bandadoora."

3 medium tomatoes—well-washed and cored

1/2 medium Spanish onion

1/4 cup *finely* chopped scallions—*both white and green portions*
1 large garlic clove—*crushed*
Pinch salt
Freshly ground black pepper, to taste

2 tablespoons *extra virgin* olive oil
2 tablespoons freshly squeezed lemon juice
1/4 teaspoon *dried* thyme—crushed
1 teaspoon *dried* mint—crushed

2 tablespoons *extra virgin* olive oil
1 large garlic clove—*crushed*

2 slices bread—trimmed and cut into four triangles

2 tablespoons pitted *Kalamata* olives —quartered
1 tablespoon marinated capers—well-rinsed

SYRIAN TOMATO AND ONION SALAD (cont'd)

Cut tomatoes into quarters. Then, using a very sharp knife, slice each quarter into slices *(. . . much the way you slice an onion)*.

Cut onion half into slices just as the tomatoes were sliced.

In a large plastic container with a tightly fitting lid, combine sliced tomatoes and onions, *finely* chopped scallions, and a crushed garlic clove. Season with salt and pepper.

In a cruet or jar, combine 2 tablespoons oil, lemon juice, and crushed thyme and mint. Pour over vegetables in the plastic container. Cover tightly. Toss gently to coat.

Refrigerate for at least 1 hour, turning occasionally to insure even marination. Turn into a sieve and drain off excess salad dressing—*at least 1 tablespoonful should be recovered*. Remove and discard crushed garlic clove.

While the vegetables are marinating, heat the 2 tablespoonfuls oil and a second crushed garlic in a skillet set over *LOW-MEDIUM* heat. Stir frequently for about 5 minutes. Remove and discard garlic clove.

Fry bread triangles, turning once, until lightly browned. Remove from skillet and set aside on a wire rack until required.

Turn salad into a shallow serving bowl or platter. Scatter capers and black pepper pieces over. Garnish with fried bread triangles.

Serve at once.

Yields 6 servings
adequate for 4 people

Note.   This recipe is easily halved or doubled, when required.

1/6 SERVING – PROTEIN = 2.2 g.; FAT = 8.1 g.; CARBOHYDRATE = 10.6 g.;
CALORIES = 123; CALORIES FROM FAT = 59%

SYRIAN NOODLES WITH LENTILS
Rishta
TPT - 55 minutes

Complementing amino acids in a casserole or soup or skillet meal has always seemed to me to be an efficient route for vegetarians, especially for vegans, but I have found that it is also the route for busy families all over the world. We often hear reference to the rice-and-beans-cultures but, of course, the grain does not always have to be rice and the legume does not always have to be beans. We enjoy an Italian lentil sauce over pasta and we often add noodles to lentil soup so this Syrian recipe seemed at once familiar but worth exploring further. It is a rather thick soup, more like what we would call a stew, but it is served in soup plate to contain the broth.

1 cup dry brown (*or* green) lentils

6 cups water *or* VEGETARIAN BROWN STOCK
  [see index] or **other vegetarian stock of choice**

2 tablespoons butter
1 large onion—*finely* **chopped**
2 large garlic cloves—*finely* **chopped**
3 tablespoons *finely* **chopped fresh coriander (cilantro)**

4 ounces *fine* **egg noodles***
1/2 teaspoon dried basil—*crushed*
1/4 teaspoon ground coriander
Pinch ground red pepper (cayenne)
Salt, to taste
Freshly ground black pepper, to taste

1 tablespoon freshly squeezed lemon juice

Large, fresh basil leaves, to garnish, if desired

Sort lentils and discard any of poor quality.

In a non-aluminum kettle set over *MEDIUM* heat, combine washed lentils, and water or stock. Bring to the boil. Reduce heat to *LOW*, cover tightly, and simmer for about 25 minutes, or until lentils are tender, but *not mushy*.

While the lentils are cooking, in a skillet set over *LOW-MEDIUM* heat, melt butter. Add *finely* chopped onion, garlic, and fresh coriander (*cilantro*). Sauté until onion is soft and translucent, *being careful not to allow any of the vegetables to brown*. Add to lentils.

SYRIAN NOODLES WITH LENTILS (cont'd)

Increase temperature to MEDIUM. Add noodles, crushed, dried basil, ground coriander, and ground red pepper (cayenne). Season to taste with salt and black pepper. Add more water or stock, if necessary. Cook for about 10 minutes, or until noodles are tender.

Add lemon juice. Turn into a heated serving bowl or small tureen.

Serve into heated soup plates. Garnish each serving with a large, fresh basil leaf, if desired.

Yields 6 servings
adequate for 4 people

Notes: *For a vegan soup/stew, use fine, flour and water noodles that do not contain eggs.

This recipe can be halved, when required.

1/6 SERVING – PROTEIN = 12.6 g.; FAT = 4.4 g.; CARBOHYDRATE = 39.2 g.;
CALORIES = 249; CALORIES FROM FAT = 15%

SYRIAN BEET AND TAHINI SALAD WITH EGGS
Salatat Shamandar bi Taheena

TPT - 35 minutes;
30 minutes = refrigeration period

Growing up where beets were buttered and salted, it was an enormous leap when I discovered this recipe from Damascus. It is probable that the beetroot originated in the Mediterranean basin. However, evidence unearthed at a Neolithic site in The Netherlands suggests that the wild beet was being eaten, perhaps just for its leaves, earlier and further north than had previously been known. Excavations in Thebes, Egypt, at the Sakkara step-pyramid, which dates to the Third Pharonic Dynasty during the reign of Zoser (2700-2650 BC), show evidence that beetroots were included for the pharaoh's journey into the afterlife. Early Roman recipes do suggest that beetroot cultivars were grown in the first century BC even though it has long been thought that the leafy forms, like chard, were the only culinary use of this species at the time. Beets are now being recognized for the fact that they contain phytonutrients called betalains and they also contribute two important carotenoids, lutein and zeaxanthin. Their role in eye health, especially in age-related maladies involving both the macula and the retina, is being intensely studied. The nutritional value of beets can not be underestimated and to anticipate all this nutrition from a salad as interesting as is this, makes life just a little better. Although this can be a perfect side salad with a soup, it can also be a nutritious and interesting lunch or just as an appetizer with Syrian bread.

1/4 cup sesame *tahini* sauce*
1/3 cup thick, Greek-style yogurt
1/4 teaspoon freshly grated nutmeg
Freshly ground black pepper, to taste

3 medium beets—boiled or baked, peeled, and *finely* chopped*

3 hard-cooked eggs—peeled and quartered

In a mixing bowl, combine *tahini* sauce, yogurt, grated nutmeg, and black pepper. Mix to thoroughly combine.

Add chopped beets. Stir to combine. Spread mixture on a small platter. Refrigerate for about 30 minutes.

Arrange egg wedges on top.

Serve chilled or at room temperature.

Yields 6 servings
adequate for 4 people

Notes: *Tahini* sauce or paste is available in Middle Eastern groceries and in most well-stocked grocery stores.

**When you are in a hurry, well-drained canned beets can be substituted.

1/6 SERVING – PROTEIN = 6.7 g.; FAT = 6.2 g.; CARBOHYDRATE = 5.4 g.;
CALORIES = 103; CALORIES FROM FAT = 54%

Turkey

Evidence of some of the earliest human settlements in the world can be found on the Anatolian peninsula. Today modern Turkey occupies most of this land, a land continually inhabited since the Neolithic period. Anatolia not only straddles the millennia, it also straddles the continents with ninety-five percent of present-day Turkey in Asia and five percent in Europe.

In the eleventh century people from the Seljuk Empire migrated to the eastern regions of Anatolia. The defeat of the Seljuk Empire by the Mongols in 1243 allowed the tribal principality headed by Osman I to gain control of most of the Anatolian peninsula. Osman I, from whom the name Ottoman derives, headed one of the Ghazi emirates in western Anatolia and rose to lead. In the course of some two hundred years his successors would lead the powerful Ottoman Empire, which lasted from 1299-1923. Osman I ruled as sultan from 1281-1326 and expanded settlement to the edge of the then weakened Byzantine Empire, establishing a capital at Bursa. After his death Ottoman rule was extended over the Eastern Mediterranean and the Balkans. With the conquest of Constantinople, the capital of the Byzantine Empire, in 1453, recognition of Ottoman preeminence in southeastern Europe, North Africa, and the eastern Mediterranean was secured. Their hold on the Mediterranean and land routes to the East spurred sovereigns like Queen Isabella and King Ferdinand of Spain and those of Portugal to finance exploration in search of a westward route to Asia. Wars reversed the expansion of the empire and stagnation set in the late 1600s. As was also true of the Roman Empire, managing the far-flung territories became economically impossible and the rise of nationalistic movements heralded the end of the Ottoman Empire. The casualties suffered in World War I can not be minimized as a contributing factors. The Sultanate was abolished in 1922 and the democratic and secular Republic of Turkey was declared in 1923 but the six hundred years of influence throughout the Middle East, across North Africa, and into Europe extends far beyond the borders of Turkey. With six centuries of political and cultural influence, it is small wonder that the foods, customs, and religion of what we now know as the Republic of Turkey can be seen on three continents.

A dinner in Turkey is almost a tour of the Ottoman Empire and foods that they encountered in their travels have long ago become "Turkish." Ruled by the Hittites, Seljuks, Persians, Greeks, and Romans, the Turkish cuisine has also profited by these encounters. The Greeks introduced wine cultivation in Anatolia and where would Turkish cuisine be without the sweets, sugar, and rice introduced by the Persians. One food appears at every meal and that is yogurt. It is not the commercial yogurt of the little grocery store cartons. It is soft and sour and luscious. I have included my own yogurt recipe which is easy, extremely satisfying to make, and luscious too.

Our search in the Middle East for comfortable meatless meals has been frustrated at many turns since meat or meat stock is added to so many dishes that really need no further protein addition. Another obstacle to safe vegetarian or vegan eating is the fact that, as in Buddhist countries in Asia, many Middle Eastern cultures do not regard chicken or fish as meat. Learning the phrases "*Ben vejeteryan*," – "I am a vegetarian," and "*Hic et yemiyorum*," – "I never eat meat," can be very helpful to the vegetarian encountering food in the Middle East without a translator. But "*Et suyu bile yemiyorim*," – "I don't even eat meat stock," is also a good one to master.

Middle East – Turkey

The zeytinagli, the course often referred as the olive oil course, has been incorporated into the more western menu I have chosen to share.

mergeler:

Feta-Filled *Phyllo* Pastries
Ispanakli Börek

Chick Pea Dip   *Pita* bread
Hummus

Assorted olives

~

Puréed Red Lentil and Bulgur Soup
Bulgurlu Merciment Çorbasi

Puréed Cream of Chick Pea and Celeriac Soup
Norhut Çorbasi

~

Artichoke Salad with Leeks and Carrots
Zeytinyagli Enginar

~~~~~~~~~~~~~~~~~~~~

Fried Cheese with Eggs
Yumurta Peynirli

Vegetable-Stuffed Zucchini
Kabak Dolma

Marinated Roasted Sweet Italian Long Frying Peppers
Sirkeli Sarmisakli Buber Izgara

Plain Yogurt

~~~~~~~~~~~~~~~~~~~~

Squash Dessert in Sweet Syrup with Walnuts
Kabak Tatlisi

Coffee Soft Egg Custard
Khave Yumarta Krema

Custard Bread Sweet
Pasha

Dried figs   Dried apricots
Incir   *Kayisi*

Middle East–Turkey

FETA-FILLED *PHYLLO* PASTRIES
Ispanakli Börek

TPT - 51 minutes

"Börek" are Turkish snack and appetizer pastries that can be complex compositions or divinely simple, as in this recipe. Ready-made phyllo pastry, "yufka" in Turkish, which is available in the frozen food department of most grocery stores, bakes to a buttery, flakiness around a filling which is just a bit of this and that.

2 tablespoons butter

18 half-sheets of frozen *phyllo* pastry
 —defrosted
3 ounces plain *feta* chunk cheese
1 1/2 cups *finely* chopped fresh spinach
1/3 cup *thinly* slivered onion
1 1/2 teaspoons grated *Romano* cheese

Preheat oven to 400 degrees F. Prepare a baking sheet by lining with parchment paper.

In a small dish or Turkish coffee pot, melt butter.

Place a single half-sheet of *phyllo* pastry on a work surface. Using a brush, lightly coat it with *melted* butter. Place a second half-sheet on top and brush that with butter. Place a third half-sheet on top and brush with butter. Place a one-half ounce slice of *feta* cheese on the buttered *phyllo* sheets at an angle about 2 inches from one corner of the pastry. Sprinkle 1/4 cupful *finely* chopped spinach on top of the cheese. Scatter a portion of the onions on top of the spinach. Sprinkle 1/2 teaspoonful of grated cheese on top.

Fold the corner over the cheeses and vegetables. Bring the sides to the center and continue folding the bundle to the opposite corner, creating a package about 2 x 4 inches or, if preferred, fold into tight overwrapped triangles. Place folded side down on parchment-lined baking sheet. Brush the top with butter.

Repeat until all *börek* are formed. Bake in preheated 400 degree F. oven for about 15 minutes, or until evenly browned. Transfer to a heated serving platter.

Serve at once.

Yields 6 servings
adequate for 6 people
as first course;
adequate for 3 people
as a luncheon entrée

1/6 SERVING – PROTEIN = 7.4 g.; FAT = 10.4 g.; CARBOHYDRATE = 20.3 g.;
CALORIES = 208; CALORIES FROM FAT = 45%

TURKISH CHICK PEA DIP
Hummus

TPT - 40 minutes;
30 minutes = chilling period

Why would you buy commercial hummus when it can be made so easily and quickly? Spice it up to suit your family's taste with a pinch of this and a pinch of that to achieve a signature flavor. Finely chopped roasted red peppers or sun-dried tomatoes are nice additions too.

1 can (15 ounces) chick peas (*garbanzos*)–seed
 coats removed*

1/8 teaspoon freshly ground black pepper
2 garlic cloves—crushed
1/2 cup *extra virgin* olive oil
2 tablespoons sesame *tahini* oil or paste**
1/2 cup freshly squeezed lemon juice

2 tablespoons *finely* chopped fresh Italian flat-
 leafed parsley

1/2 teaspoon paprika
Curly parsley florets, for garnish

Drain skinned chick peas in a sieve and wash under cold running water until water runs clear. Drain thoroughly.

In the work bowl of the food processor, fitted with steel knife, or in the container of the electric blender, combine drained chick peas, black pepper, crushed garlic cloves, olive oil, sesame *tahini* oil or paste, and lemon juice. Process until a smooth paste forms. The blender should be turned off occasionally and ingredients scraped from sides with a rubber spatula.

TURKISH CHICK PEA DIP (cont'd)

Turn paste into a mixing bowl. Add *finely* chopped parsley and combine well.

Spread into individual serving dishes or saucers for table service or into a single serving bowl for community dipping. Garnish with paprika and parsley florets. Chill for at least 30 minutes before serving.

Serve as a dip with Arab, Syrian, or *pita* bread, sesame crackers, sesame breadsticks, or *crudités*.

Yields 2 cupfuls
or about 8 servings

1/8 SERVING (i. e., per 1 1/2 tablespoonfuls) –
PROTEIN = 1.6 g.; FAT = 12.2 g.; CARBOHYDRATE = 4.7 g.;
CALORIES = 135; CALORIES FROM FAT = 81%

Notes: *If desired, dry chick peas may be soaked and cooked to use in this recipe.

**Sesame *tahini* oil or paste is available in specialty food stores, natural food stores, and in Asian and Middle Eastern groceries.

This also makes an interesting sandwich filling or spread for canapés, celery fingers, and Romaine lettuce leaves.

When required, this recipe is easily doubled.

PURÉED TURKISH RED LENTIL AND BULGUR SOUP
Bulgurlu Merciment Çorbasi
TPT - 1 hour and 12 minutes

We have long enjoyed a Turkish main course salad which combines legumes and grains, a salad that quickly addresses the protein issue. In the winter we now enjoy the same protein combination in a soup which can be puréed to make a soothing, warm lunch. I love to take a mug of this out into the spring garden just as the mint plants come back to life. There is no fresher garnish.

1 tablespoon *extra virgin* olive oil
1 tablespoon butter
3/4 cup *finely* chopped onion

2 tablespoons whole wheat flour

2 tablespoons tomato paste

1/2 cup dry *fine* or *medium* bulgur (*bulghur*) wheat—well-rinsed and extraneous material removed*
1/2 cup dry split *red* lentils *or masur dal***
7 cups VEGETARIAN BROWN STOCK [see index] **or other vegetarian stock of choice**

2 tablespoons *dried* mint leaves—crushed
1 teaspoon *dried* thyme—crushed
1 teaspoon red pepper flakes

Fresh mint leaves, for garnish, if available

In a large kettle set over *LOW-MEDIUM* heat, heat oil and butter. Add *finely* chopped onion and sauté until onion is soft and translucent, *allowing neither the onion nor the garlic to brown.*

Add flour and cook, stirring constantly, until a paste has formed.

Add tomato paste. Cook, stirring constantly, for another minute or two.

Add lentils, well-rinsed bulgur, and stock. Allow to come to the boil. Cover and simmer for 30 minutes, or until the lentils are soft.

Add dried mint leaves and thyme and red pepper flakes. Allow to cook for another 10 minutes. Remove from heat.***

Purée the soup in batches using the electric blender. Purée thoroughly until *very smooth*. Turn into a clean kettle or large saucepan set over *LOW-MEDIUM* heat and allow to heat through. Turn into a heated soup tureen.

Serve into heated soup plates or mugs, if preferred. Garnish each serving with a fresh mint leaf, if available.

Yields 9 cupfuls

Notes: *Bulgur (*bulghur*) wheat, cracked wheat, or crushed wheat is available in natural food stores and in Middle Eastern groceries. It is a par-boiled product and, therefore, needs no further cooking. We prefer to use fine bulgur for this recipe.

Middle East–**Turkey**

PURÉED TURKISH RED LENTIL AND BULGUR SOUP (cont'd)

**Red lentils, sometime referred to as pink or orange lentils or even Egyptian lentils, are found in groceries that specialize in Middle Eastern foods. Indian or Pakistani groceries carry red lentils as *masur dal*. If you do not have them in your larder, try the recipe with French brown lentils. You may prefer the taste.

***Although we do prefer this as a puréed soup, it can just be ladled into soup plates at this point.

This recipe may be halved or doubled, when required, and since it freezes well, a double batch is a good plan.

1/9 SERVING (i. e., per cupful) –
PROTEIN = 4.5 g.; FAT = 2.8 g.; CARBOHYDRATE = 16.4 g.;
CALORIES = 99; CALORIES FROM FAT = 25%

TURKISH PURÉED CREAM OF CHICK PEA AND CELERIAC SOUP
Nokhut Çorbasi
TPT - 54 minutes

The inclusion of celery root and both parsley and cilantro gives this rich, puréed vegetable soup nuances that are challenging to identify and red bell pepper contributes both flavor and an irresistible color. Usually made with poultry or meat stock, it is equally delicious when made with a robust vegetable stock.

2 tablespoons butter
1 large yellow onion—chopped
1 medium carrot—pared or scraped and chopped
3/4 cup chopped celeriac (celery root)
1 large red bell pepper—cored, seeded, and chopped
3 tablespoons chopped parsley leaves
2 tablespoons chopped fresh coriander (*cilantro*) leaves

1 can (15 ounces) chick peas (*garbanzos*) —undrained
1 1/2 cups VEGETABLE STOCK FROM SOUP [see index] *or* VEGETARIAN BROWN STOCK [see index]

1 cup *whole* milk
3 tablespoons *finely* chopped fresh parsley leaves
2 tablespoons *finely* chopped fresh coriander (*cilantro*) leaves

In a large saucepan set over *LOW-MEDIUM* heat, melt butter. Add chopped onion, carrot, celeriac, red pepper, parsley, and fresh coriander (*cilantro*). Sauté until vegetables have softened, *being careful not to allow them to brown*.

Add *undrained* chick peas and vegetable stock. Cover and allow to cook for about 30 minutes.

Purée the soup in small batches using the electric blender or the food processor fitted with steel knife. Set a sieve over a clean saucepan and sieve the puréed soup mixture. Discard debris or freeze in a bag with other soup stock items. Place the saucepan over *LOW-MEDIUM* heat again.

Add milk and *finely* chopped parsley and fresh coriander (*cilantro*) leaves. Stir to combine well. Allow to heat through.* Turn into a heated soup tureen.

Ladle into heated soup bowls.

Yields about 6 cupfuls

Notes: *Thin, if necessary, with additional vegetable stock.

This recipe can be doubled, when required.

1/6 SERVING (i. e., per cupful) –
PROTEIN = 7.7 g.; FAT = 5.2 g.; CARBOHYDRATE = 18.3 g.;
CALORIES =140; CALORIES FROM FAT = 33%

Middle East–**Turkey**

TURKISH ARTICHOKE SALAD WITH LEEKS AND CARROTS
Zeytinyagli Enginar

TPT - 48 minutes;
30 minutes = flavor development period

If a rich first-pressing olive oil is used in the preparation of this salad, the taste will persist and that is just what you want in this Middle Eastern artichoke salad, popular in both Turkey and Greece. We substitute frozen artichoke hearts in this salad so that we can enjoy it year round. The traditional use of fresh baby artichokes would limit us to the harvest season and send us far and wide in search of a green grocer with baby artichokes; it is hard enough to find a good source of frozen artichoke hearts.

3 tablespoons *extra virgin* olive oil
9 ounces *frozen* artichoke hearts—*defrosted*
3 medium carrots—scraped or pared, sliced lengthwise and cut into 2-inch julienne pieces
1 large leek—white and light green portions only—trimmed, v*ery well-rinsed*, and cut crosswise into 1/8-inch slices
1 garlic clove—*finely* chopped

2 tablespoons water
2 tablespoons freshly squeezed lemon juice
1 teaspoon freshly grated lemon zest
Salt, to taste
Freshly ground black pepper, to taste

3 tablespoons *finely* chopped fresh dillweed

In a Dutch oven or kettle with cover, set over *MEDIUM* heat, heat oil. Add artichoke hearts, carrot pieces, leek slices, and *finely* chopped garlic. Sauté, until leeks are soft, about 5 minutes.

Add lemon juice, grated lemon zest, salt, and black pepper. *Reduce heat to LOW* and simmer, partially covered, for about 10 minutes, or until the vegetables are *crisp-tender*. Stir frequently.

Turn into a serving bowl and place in the refrigerator for about 30 minutes.

Sprinkle *finely* chopped dillweed over.

Serve at room temperature—neither hot nor chilled.

Yields 6 servings
adequate for 4 people

Note: This recipe may be halved or doubled, when required.

1/6 SERVING – PROTEIN = 1.5 g.; FAT = 5.9 g.; CARBOHYDRATE = 5.8 g.;
CALORIES = 77; CALORIES FROM FAT = 69%

TURKISH FRIED CHEESE WITH EGGS
Yumurta Peynirli

TPT - 15 minutes

Fried cheese, "frico" in Italian, is popular in Trieste but it is also popular in Turkey. The Turks have carried it a bit further and place a fried or poached egg on top of the cheese. Although this makes an unusual appetizer for a Turkish menu, is also a delightful lunch or light supper entrée for the two of us.

Per serving:

1 large *organic* egg*

2 teaspoons butter
2 slices (4 inches x 4 inches) Swiss *Gruyère* cheese—*about 1 ounce*
2 slices (4 inches x 4 inches) Cheddar cheese—*about 1 ounce**

Freshly ground black pepper, to taste

Using an egg poacher or in a deep skillet filled with *gently boiling* water, prepare a poached or coddled egg.

Meanwhile, in a 7-inch skillet set over *LOW-MEDIUM* heat, melt butter.

Place the slices of cheese, overlapping, in the center of the skillet. Cook the cheese until melted. Remove skillet from heat and allow the skillet to cool for a minute or two during which time the cheese will harden. Slide the cheese onto a heated dinner plate. Slide the poached egg onto the cheese.

Grind black pepper over.

Serve at once.

Repeat the process as needed.**

Yields 1 serving

TURKISH FRIED CHEESE WITH EGGS (cont'd)

Notes: *Since the egg will be slightly undercooked, it is preferable to use organic eggs to minimize the chance of *Salmonella* exposure.

**If you have several skillets, you can decrease the preparation time since several servings can be prepared simultaneously.

1 SERVING – PROTEIN = 21.7 g.; FAT = 31.3 g.; CARBOHYDRATE = 1.1 g.; CALORIES = 372; CALORIES FROM FAT = 76%

TURKISH VEGETABLE-STUFFED ZUCCHINI
Kabak Dolma
TPT - 35 minutes

This presents so beautifully; it's like saying, "Here are your vegetables."

3 medium zucchini squashes

2 tablespoons *extra virgin* olive oil
2 medium onions—slices into rings

4 large garlic cloves—*very finely* chopped

1 cup canned, *diced* tomatoes
2 teaspoons sugar
Salt, to taste

2 tablespoon fresh dillweed—chopped

Preheat oven to 350 degrees F.

Trim ends from zucchini. Wash thoroughly, but *do not peel*. Cut in half lengthwise and, using a small spoon, scoop out pulp to form "boats."*

In a skillet set over *MEDIUM* heat, heat oil. Add onion rings and cook, stirring frequently, until they have softened.

Add *very finely* chopped garlic. Cook, stirring constantly, for several minutes.

Add tomatoes and sugar. Salt, to taste.

Apportion vegetables mixture among zucchini "boats." Arrange filled "boats" in prepared baking pan. Add about 1/2 inch of boiling water. Bake in preheated 350 degree F. oven for 15 minutes. *Be careful not to overcook.* Transfer to a serving platter or serve directly onto heated dinner plates using two large serving spoons.

Serve at once.

Yields 6 servings
adequate for 4 people

Notes: *Reserve pulp for soup stock.

This recipe is easily halved or doubled, when required.

1/6 SERVING – PROTEIN = 2.1 g.; FAT = 3.9 g.; CARBOHYDRATE = 9.9 g.; CALORIES = 77; CALORIES FROM FAT = 46%

Middle East–**Turkey**

TURKISH MARINATED ROASTED SWEET ITALIAN LONG FRYING PEPPERS
Sirkeli Sarmisakli Buber Izgara

TPT - about 4 hours and 15 minutes;
3 hours = marination period

The smell of peppers and onions on a hot grill at an Italian street fair is an incredibly enticing smell to us. We know these as Italian frying peppers, as do most East Coast cooks, and frequently have to explain them to young, non-ethnic cooks who think they are hot peppers simply because they are long and narrow and not bell-shaped. Ray's mother taught me to prepare peppers and eggs in the Italian style and I do freeze these peppers, sliced for frying, in the fall to provide for a pepper and egg sandwich or two. I was surprised to see that Turkish cooks prepare these sweet peppers, as we roast and marinate red peppers. I guess we will have to stop referring to them as "Italian frying peppers" now that we know that they are actually roasted much further to the East in the Mediterranean.

6 large, long, sweet "Italian frying peppers" (also called cubanella)—perfect, unblemished, and well-washed

2 garlic cloves—*very finely* chopped
1/4 cup *extra virgin* olive oil
1 tablespoon distilled white vinegar
1/4 teaspoon dried thyme—crushed
1/4 teaspoon dried oregano—crushed
Salt, to taste
Freshly ground black pepper, to taste

Preheat oven to 350 degrees F.

Place peppers on a cookie sheet. Roast in preheated oven for about 25-30 minutes, *turning frequently*.

Remove from oven and place in a heavy brown paper bag in dry sink. Roll the top of the bag down and allow to steam for about 15 minutes.

Remove stems, seeds, and membranes, peel, and cut into large pieces.

In a deep pie plate combine *very finely* chopped garlic, olive oil, vinegar, crushed thyme and oregano, and salt and black pepper, to taste. Transfer the roasted pepper pieces to the marinade and gently bathe them in the marination mixture and place them in the bowl. Cover the pie plate with plastic wrap and allow to marinate for three hours, turning the pepper pieces, carefully, several times during that marination period.

Refrigerate, if not to be served immediately.

Pour peppers and marinating liquid into a sieve and allow to drain thoroughly.

Serve at room temperature as a side dish.

Yields 6 servings
adequate for 4 people

Note: This recipe can be halved or doubled, when required.

1/6 SERVING – PROTEIN = 1.5 g.; FAT = 2.2 g.; CARBOHYDRATE = 7.4 g.;
CALORIES = 49; CALORIES FROM FAT = 40%

PLAIN YOGURT

TPT - 10 hours and 10 minutes;
4 hours = first incubation period;
4 hours = second incubation period;
2 hours = chilling period

The use of the cultured milk product we know as yogurt has a long history. Praise of its nutritional and medicinal virtue finds disciples in many, many countries and has been consumed for these benefits for hundreds of years. Evidence suggests that kiselo mlyako, or literally soured milk, was part of the Balkan diet as far back as 3500 BC. One of my favorite anecdotes tells about the suffering and remarkable curing of Francis I, of France. Beset with chronic diarrhea, the king was said to have been cured by the yogurt fed to him by a doctor sent by Suleiman the Magnificent.

For years and years, from the time our daughter was born until we retired, we made our own yogurt using this recipe which was evolved from that of Adele Davis. The yogurt was good and economical, and, in addition, making it was a task that I always enjoyed doing. I may return to that pleasure one of these days.

PLAIN YOGURT (cont'd)

1 teaspoon yogurt culture* or 1/2 cup *additive-free*, commercially available plain yogurt**
4 cups *instant* non-fat dry milk powder
2 cups *warm* water—100-110 degrees F.

3 cups *warm* water—100-110 degrees F.
1 can (13 ounces) evaporated *skimmed* milk

Preheat oven to 250 degrees F.

Assemble 2 quart jars, 5 pint jars, 5 one-pound plastic yogurt or butter tubs, or 8 coffee mugs—as preferred—plastic wrap cut into squares to cover each container (or fold-over plastic sandwich bags, if preferred), a cookie sheet or baking pan, and a couple of large, thick towels.

In the container of the electric blender, combine the yogurt starter, non-fat dry milk powder, and 2 cupfuls of *warm* water. Blend until smooth.

In a *large* mixing bowl, combine the 3 cupfuls *warm* water and evaporated milk. Add blended mixture and stir well.

Using either a ladle or a pitcher, apportion the yogurt among the containers chosen. Cover each with a square of plastic wrap or a sandwich bag. Set on the cookie sheet or in the baking pan and cover with the towels, tucking them around the yogurt containers.

Turn the oven off!!

Place yogurt into oven and allow to culture for 4 hours.

Remove tray of culturing yogurt *carefully* from oven. Reheat oven to 250 degrees F. *Turn the oven off!!* Return tray to oven and allow culture to develop for another 4 hours, or until culture is developed to your liking. (This may take some experimentation.)

Place containers in refrigerator and chill for at least 2 hours before using.

This yogurt will keep well for about 5 days but in our experience it is better to make a new batch every 3-4 days.

Yields about 8 cupfuls

Notes: *Bulgarian yogurt cultures are available at natural food stores.

**If a fresh culture is used each time, the result will be a fresher, less acid product. Be sure to select a brand that indicates that it contains "live yogurt culture."

If the temperature of the culturing medium is too high, the organisms will be destroyed and your yogurt will not thicken. On the other hand, the organisms will remain inactive if the temperature is too low with an uncultured liquid resultant.

Chilled plain yogurt may be flavored with pure vanilla extract or other flavorings, sugar, crushed fruit, or frozen juice concentrate.

1/8 SERVING (i. e., per cupful) –
PROTEIN = 17.1 g.; FAT = 0.3 g.; CARBOHYDRATE = 25.7 g.;
CALORIES = 177; CALORIES FROM FAT = 2%

TURKISH SQUASH DESSERT IN SWEET SYRUP WITH WALNUTS
Kabak Tatlisi

TPT - 2 hours;
1 hour = chilling period

What a way to add another vegetable to your "daily five!" Less sweet and less calorific than classic versions of "kaback tatlisi," it is appealing to the Western palate in this form. Although pumpkin is usually used to make this dessert, I always use one of the acorn squashes that nestle on my bakery rack from October to mid-spring. The rich flesh is very well suited to this sweet treatment. If you have a pumpkin left over from Halloween, this is a good way to use the pumpkin for something other than a compost pile adornment. Hubbard squash, although beautiful to look at, is a bland, watery squash but it also works well in this recipe.

1 two-pound acorn squash—well-scrubbed, halved, and seeded*

1 cup sugar
1/2 cup heavy whipping cream

1/2 cup chopped, *toasted preservative-free* walnuts

Cut seeded squash halves into large pieces. Put in a large kettle and add water to a level of about half way up the squash pieces. Set over *MEDIUM* heat, cover, and cook for about 50 minutes, or until tender. *The liquid will then be reduced by about one-half.*

TURKISH SQUASH DESSERT IN SWEET SYRUP WITH WALNUTS (cont'd)

Add the sugar to the liquid around the squash pieces. Cover and continue cooking until the sugar is dissolved. *Reduce heat to LOW.* Remove cover and simmer gently until syrup thickens. Remove from heat and place on a serving dish. Pour syrup over the squash pieces. Refrigerate for at least 1 hour.

Meanwhile, using the electric mixer fitted with *chilled* beaters or by hand using a *chilled* wire whisk, beat heavy cream in a *clean, chilled* bowl until stiff peaks form. Turn into a serving bowl and set aside until required.

When ready to serve, sprinkle the *toasted* walnuts over the chilled squash. Serve with whipped cream. Provide spoons to enable the removal of the sweet flesh from the squash rind.

Yields 6 servings
adequate for 4 people

Notes: *Gold Nugget squash can be substituted for acorn squash, if preferred, and, as mentioned, both pumpkin and Hubbard squash can also be used to make this dessert.

This recipe can be halved or doubled, when required.

1/6 SERVING – PROTEIN = 3.4 g.; FAT = 15.2 g.; CARBOHYDRATE = 28.5 g.;
CALORIES = 258; CALORIES FROM FAT = 53%

TURKISH COFFEE SOFT EGG CUSTARD
Kahve Yumarta Krema

TPT - 4 hours and 22 minutes;
4 hours = cooling and setting period

I always wondered if leftover sweet, thick Turkish coffee was creatively incorporated into a dessert by thrifty Turkish women. Someone of Turkish descent told me that there was never any coffee leftover if there was a Turkish man in the house but years later I found a recipe for a rich top-of-the-stove egg custard using leftover Turkish coffee. Ours is considerably less rich. The orange juice concentrate gives the pudding a caramel color and adds the perfect nuance of flavor. Espresso is an adequate stand-in for the boiled Turkish coffee if you do not have leftover Turkish coffee, for whatever reason.

1 cup light cream *or* **half and half**
3/4 cup *two-percent* **milk**
1 tablespoon *frozen concentrated* **orange juice**
1 teaspoon unflavored gelatin*

1/3 cup *light* **brown sugar**
2 tablespoons *Crème de Cocoa or Kahlua*
2 tablespoons *instant espresso* **powder**
3/4 teaspoon ground cardamom

1/2 cup *fat-free* **pasteurized eggs (the equivalent of 2 eggs)****

Whipped cream lightly sweetened with *Crème de Cocoa or Kahlua*, **for garnish, if desired**
Ground cardamom, for garnish, if desired

Pour cream, milk, and orange juice concentrate into a saucepan. Sprinkle gelatin over cream and allow gelatin to soften for 5 minutes.

Set the saucepan over *LOW-MEDIUM* heat. Add brown sugar, *crème de cocoa* or *Kahlua*, espresso powder, and ground cardamom. Using a wire whisk combine thoroughly and allow to cook until gelatin, sugar, and coffee granules are completely dissolved. Remove from heat.

Pour pasteurized eggs into a small bowl. Using a wire whisk, *gradually, tablespoonful by tablespoonful*, beat 1/2 cupful of cream–coffee mixture into eggs. Integrate thoroughly. While stirring, add egg mixture to cream–coffee base in saucepan. Return to heat and, *stirring constantly*, cook until thickened.

Divide the pudding evenly among six sherbet glasses or other small dessert dishes or six *demitasse* cups, if preferred. Refrigerate for at least 4 hours, or until set.

Garnish with a dollop of coffee liqueur-flavored whipped cream and a sprinkling of ground cardamom, if desired.

Serve well-chilled.

Yields 6 individual servings

Middle East–**Turkey**

TURKISH COFFEE SOFT EGG CUSTARD (cont'd)

Notes: *Agar-agar or kosher gelatin may be substituted for plain gelatin, if preferred. Since preparation procedures differ for these products, be sure to follow package directions.

**Because raw eggs present the danger of *Salmonella* poisoning, commercially-available pasteurized eggs are recommended for use in preparing this dish.

This recipe can be halved or doubled, when required.

1/6 SERVING (exclusive of whipped cream garnish) –
PROTEIN = 4.7 g.; FAT = 4.4 g.; CARBOHYDRATE = 18.4 g.;
CALORIES = 140; CALORIES FROM FAT = 28%

TURKISH CUSTARD BREAD SWEET
Pasha

TPT - 1 hour and 50 minutes;
30 minutes = milk absorption period

Many, many very, very sweet treats come from Middle Eastern cuisines. A trip to a Middle Eastern bakery can make your teeth hurt just anticipating the intense sweetness of the displays filled with nuts and honey. This sweet, unlike any I have ever tasted, is less sweet, less caloric, and it is a surprisingly adequate source of protein. It is, therefore, a dessert that will not leave you feeling guilty. Leftovers are no problem in our family. We cut leftover pasha into squares and put it on a plate, wrapped with plastic wrap, to serve for a breakfast the next morning. Oh, is this a treat!

1 eight-ounce French wheat bread loaf—crusts removed and shredded
3 cups *two-percent* milk

3/4 cup *fat-free* pasteurized eggs (the equivalent of 3 eggs)
3 tablespoons confectioners' sugar
1/2 teaspoon ground cinnamon
3 tablespoons butter—*melted*

SYRUP:
    1/4 cup confectioners' sugar
    1 teaspoon freshly squeezed lemon juice
    1 cup water

Preheat oven 325 degrees F. Prepare a 15 x 10 1/2 x 1 inch-jelly roll pan by lining with parchment paper.

In a mixing bowl, combine shredded bread and milk. Set aside for about 30 minutes to allow bread to soak up milk.

Add pasteurized eggs, the 2 tablespoonfuls confectioners' sugar, ground cinnamon, and *melted* butter. Stir until well-mixed. Using a strainer, ladle the bread onto the prepared jelly roll pan, spreading it evenly across the pan surface. Ladle the liquid over the bread.* Bake in preheated 325 degree F. oven for about 50 minutes, or until browned on both the top and the bottom.

About 20 minutes before the baking period is completed, in a saucepan set over *MEDIUM* heat, combine the 1/4 cupful confectioners' sugar, lemon juice, and water. Allow to come to the boil. Reduce heat to *LOW-MEDIUM* and allow to simmer for 15 minutes, or until it thickens.

Remove baked dessert from oven. Pour syrup evenly over. Allow to cool completely.

Cut into squares to serve. Refrigerate leftovers.

Yields 24 servings
adequate for 8-12 people

Notes: *It is helpful to place the bread-filled tray into the oven and then ladle the liquid over. It prevents the possibility of sloshing the liquid as you transfer it from the counter top to the oven.

If you have a small baking pan, this can be halved.

1/24 SERVING – PROTEIN = 2.6 g.; FAT = 0.8 g.; CARBOHYDRATE = 9.5 g.;
CALORIES = 70; CALORIES FROM FAT = 36%

Yemen

Over two hundred islands in the Arabian Sea and in the Gulf of Aden claimed by Yemen, many of which are volcanic, contribute to a land mass of about 203,849 square miles making it approximately twice the size of Colorado, or a little smaller than Texas. It is the only nation in the Arabian Peninsula to have a Republican form of government but the unrest of 2011, dubbed "The Arab Spring," did not spare Yemen where the unemployment level is in excess of forty percent. Corruption; a lack of foreign investment, save the hydrocarbon industry; extreme poverty; and the insidious spread of Islamic extremism have frustrated the population and the government.

Dating perhaps from as early as 3000 BC, the Arabs of the southern peninsula were united under Qahtan and their union continued until the eighth century BC when they fell under the rule of the Kingdom of Saba (Sheba). Sabaean rule continued for about fourteen centuries. Subsequently conquered and ruled by the Himyarites, Romans, Abyssinians (Ethiopians), and the Sassanids of ancient Persia, a national identity emerged when Yemen was conquered in the seventh century AD by Muslim Arabs. In the sixteenth century Yemen came under the Turks as the Ottoman Empire spread across the Near East and North Africa. Yemen evolved an Islamic state in relative isolation from other states within the Ottoman sphere of influence and became an important coffee trader, utilizing the talents that had made them so successful and prosperous in the earlier spice trade. During the Ottoman period the walled city of Shibam was built. It is a very early example of vertical construction as part of an urban plan. "Skyscrapers" and city walls survive in what is now a World Heritage Site. In 1918, after the defeat of the Turks in World War I and their withdrawal from Yemen, the northern part of Yemen became independent and in 1962 declared itself a republic. South Yemen, consisting of several British protectorates, became The Peoples' Republic of South Yemen shortly after the British withdrew in 1967 and closely aligned itself with the Soviet Union. North and South Yemen united in 1990 after the fall of the Soviet Union.

The exodus of Yemenis over the centuries has led to large populations of Yemeni origin all over the world. Trade with the Far East led to the relocation of Yemenis to Indonesia, Malaysia, and Singapore with the result that an estimated four million Indonesians and about ten thousand Singaporeans were born in or are descended from emigrants from the Hadramawt coastal region of South Yemen on the Gulf of Aden The Hadramis also emigrated to the Indian subcontinent and into East Africa. In Mauitania Yemeni Arabs were the dominant demographic group by the end of the seventeenth century. The sizable Jewish population that called Yemen home was decreased to just a few hundred individuals in the mid-twentieth century as Arab Jews were welcomed into Israel under what was known as Operation Magic Carpet. Due to civil war, Islamic extremism, and lack of opportunity in Yemen, the Yemeni diaspora in the United Kingdom is now estimated at about eighty thousand, that in France is about two thousand, and close to twenty thousand Yemeni expatriates now reside in the United States. And yet, with all this emigration the population is growing at the rate of close to three-quarters of a million per year due to refugees and asylum seekers from Arab countries in turmoil and also due to the extraordinarily high birthrate. With over forty-five percent of the population under the age of fifteen, the needs of the refugees, and the lack of productivity, the government is hard pressed to provide services. Add to this these two important facts—a large percentage of those Yemenis who are employed depend on the oil industry for employment and the government depends to a very large extent on revenue from oil taxes. The government and these oil employees must now face the fact that the supply of this precious commodity is dwindling and it is estimated that the oil reserves will be depleted by 2017.

Middle East–**Yemen**

Fenugreek Seasoning Paste
Hulbah

Fenugreek and Vegetable Appetizer Dip
Hulbah
with Pita Bread

~

Yogurt and Bread Soup
Shafut

~

Tomato and Coriander Salad   **Eggplant – Tomato Salad**
Banadura Salata b'Kizbara

~~~~~~~~~~~~~~~~~~~~~~

Chick Peas with Tomatoes and Apricots
Tamaatin Mishmash Feeha Houmous
or

Soymeat and Melon Skillet
Melon Baal Canaf

Sautéed Greens

~

Yemeni Spice Mixture
Hawayil

~~~~~~~~~~~~~~~~~~~~~~

Date Balls with Coconut

Platter of Fruit – Mango, Guava, Banana, and/or Melon
drizzled with Yemeni Royal *Sidr* Honey

YEMENI FENUGREEK SEASONING PASTE
Hulbah

TPT - 24 hours and 15 minutes;
24 hours = seed soaking period

When we were first married, we frequented a cheese and food specialty store called Food of All Nations in which a man of Greek descent was one of the most knowledgeable culinary teachers I had ever met to that point. I remember standing next to a lady who was picking up an order of spices. One of the spices she needed for her Greek Easter meals was fenugreek which was presented to her in a tightly wrapped paper parcel. I had found a new passion as I then began to explore this exciting, but much under-appreciated, spice. At first I researched its medicinal uses and found that steeping fenugreek seeds in hot water created a herbal tea that was effective in clearing the mucous membranes which turned out to be very useful knowledge. The Dutch, French, Germans, Italians, Portuguese, Spanish, and Russians all use it and it is also popular in North Africa and in Southeast Asia and the Indian subcontinent where it is an important ingredient in curry mixtures. The astringent, but edible, leaves are used in the United States principally as animal fodder and the seeds are used to make imitation maple syrup. However, the Yemeni are probably its greatest champions, adding it as a condiment to almost every non-sweet food—soups, stews, vegetables, skillet meals, salad dressings, and appetizer dips. [See appetizer dip recipe which follows.]

YEMENI FENUGREEK SEASONING PASTE (cont'd)

1 tablespoons *finely* **ground fenugreek seeds**
1 cup water

Up to 2 tablespoons water

In a small bowl, combine fenugreek seeds and the 1 cupful of water. Cover the bowl with a saucer and allow to stand at room temperature for 24 hours. Drain the bitter liquid off. Rinse well and drain again. Turn the seeds into a marble mortar and grind with a pestle until a paste forms.* Add a little water at a time and keep grinding until a bubbly paste forms. Turn into a small dish, cover, and refrigerate.

It will keep well for a week.

Yields about 3 tablespoonfuls

Notes: *A mini food processor, if you have one, is the perfect tool for preparing this paste.

This recipe can be doubled, when required.

YEMENI FENUGREEK AND VEGETABLE APPETIZER DIP
Hulbah
TPT - 5 minutes

This appetizer dip, served with pita bread, is unique, healthy, and remarkably satisfying.

1 1/2 tablespoons YEMENI FENUGREEK SEASONING PASTE (*Hulbah*) [see recipe which precedes]
2 firm tomatoes—peeled, seeded, and diced
1 garlic clove—*very finely* chopped
1/2 cup *finely* **chopped fresh coriander (*cilantro*)**
4 teaspoons *finely* **chopped mild green *chilies*,** more or less to taste
1 tablespoon freshly squeezed lemon juice
Salt, to taste

Warm **pita bread, broken into pieces**

In the work bowl of the food processor fitted with steel knife or in the container of the electric blender, combine the prepared fenugreek seasoning mix, diced tomato, *very finely* chopped garlic, *finely* chopped fresh coriander (*cilantro*), *finely* chopped green *chilies*, lemon juice, and salt. Process or blend until frothy. Turn into a dipping bowl.

Place dipping bowl in the middle of a plate. Surround with pieces of warm *pita* bread or other flatbread of choice.

Serve at once.

Yields 3/4 cupful

Note: This recipe can be doubled, when required.

1/12 SERVING (i. e., per tablespoonful exclusive of bread) –
PROTEIN = 0.2 g.; FAT = 0.1 g.; CARBOHYDRATE = 1.0 g.;
CALORIES = 5; CALORIES FROM FAT = 18%

YEMENI YOGURT AND BREAD SOUP
Shafut
TPT - 7 minutes

Of all the yogurt soups from countries in the Middle East east through Central Asia that we have tasted, this quickly-prepared soup from Yemen stands out. Some prefer to make it with buttermilk but you have to be a fan of buttermilk; we prefer the sweetness of a milk/yogurt combination. Injera, pita, naan, or any flatbread you have on hand works well for this very tasty and very healthy soup.

YEMENI YOGURT AND BREAD SOUP (cont'd)

3 cups PLAIN YOGURT *[see index]* or
   commercially-available plain yogurt
1 1/2 cups *two-percent* milk
1 cup fresh coriander (*cilantro*) leaves—chopped
1 1/2 teaspoons red *jalapeño chili* sauce, or to taste
2 garlic cloves—chopped
Pinch ground ginger

4 cups *warmed* flatbread—broken into bite-sized pieces

In the container of the electric blender or in the work bowl of the food processor fitted with steel knife, combine yogurt, milk, chopped fresh coriander (*cilantro*) leaves, *jalapeño* sauce, chopped garlic, and ground ginger. Process until very smooth. Allow to remain at room temperature until required.*

When ready to serve, divide the warmed flatbread pieces among six soup plates. Pour *one-sixth* of the soup over the bread in each of the six soup plates.

Serve at once.

Yields 6 servings

Notes: *If you make this soup early in the day, refrigerate and then bring to room temperature before serving.

This recipe can be halved or doubled, when required.

1/6 SERVING − PROTEIN = 10.8 g.; FAT = 5.5 g.; CARBOHYDRATE = 29.0 g.;
CALORIES = 213; CALORIES FROM FAT = 23%

YEMENI TOMATO AND CORIANDER SALAD
Banadura Salata b'Kizbara
TPT - 5 minutes

Fresh coriander, or cilantro as it is known in Latin America and here in the United States, is one herb that I do not grow. It bolts so quickly in our climate that I have settled for that which is available in the produce section of my grocery store. Whenever I buy a bunch, I have to plan its use efficiently since it does not keep well in the refrigerator even when it is placed in a glass of water and wrapped with a "plastic-bag turban." Nothing could be simpler than is this salad.

4 ripe tomatoes—well-washed and sliced
1/2 cup well-washed and chopped fresh coriander (*cilantro*) leaves

1 tablespoon *extra virgin* olive oil
Pinch ground coriander
Pinch salt

Place tomatoes on a serving plate. Sprinkle chopped fresh coriander (*cilantro*) over.

In a small dish, mix olive oil, ground coriander, and salt. Drizzle it over the tomatoes.

Serve at once.

Yields 6 servings
adequate for 4 people

Note: This recipe can be halved or doubled, when required.

1/6 SERVING − PROTEIN = 0.8 g.; FAT = 2.3 g.; CARBOHYDRATE = 3.0 g.;
CALORIES = 34; CALORIES FROM FAT = 61%

YEMENI EGGPLANT – TOMATO SALAD
TPT - 5 hours;
30 minutes = eggplant draining period;
4 hours = flavor development period

You will recognize immediately that this is not a salad in the strictest Western sense and, in truth, this dish could and does function in Yemen as a vegetable side dish. I usually seek out an Asian eggplant for this recipe or two baby eggplants, choosing male fruit, because they have less seeds.

Middle East – Yemen

YEMENI EGGPLANT – TOMATO SALAD (cont'd)

1 pound eggplant—well-washed and trimmed, but *unpeeled*
1 teaspoon salt

1 tablespoon *extra virgin* olive oil
1 medium onion—*finely* chopped
1 large tomato—peeled, seeded, or chopped *or* about 3/4 cup canned, *diced* tomato
3/4 teaspoon ground cumin
3/4 teaspoon ground allspice
Pinch ground red pepper (cayenne), or to taste

3 large garlic cloves—*very finely* chopped
1/2 cup dried, *preservative-free* currants

2 tablespoons *extra virgin* olive oil

3 tablespoons slivered fresh mint leaves
3 tablespoon chopped fresh coriander (*cilantro*)
Freshly ground black pepper, to taste

Chop unpeeled eggplant into 1/2-3/4-inch cubes to yield about 3 cupfuls. Place in a fine sieve and sprinkle with salt. Allow to drain for about 30 minutes. Rinse well and allow to drain until required.

In a large skillet set over *LOW-MEDIUM* heat, heat 1 tablespoonful of oil. Add *finely* chopped onion, chopped tomato, and ground cumin, allspice, and ground red pepper (cayenne). Cook, stirring frequently, until onion is soft and translucent, *being careful not to allow the onion to brown*. Add *very finely* chopped garlic and dried currants. Continue cooking, stirring constantly, for about 3 minutes. Pour into a mixing bowl.

Add the remaining 2 tablespoons oil to the skillet. Return to heat. Add eggplant and cook, stirring frequently, until onion is tender—about 10 minutes. Add to tomato–onion mixture in bowl.

Add slivered mint, chopped fresh coriander (*cilantro*), and black pepper. Toss to mix. Refrigerate for at least 4 hours to allow for flavor development.

Serve *chilled*.

Yields 6 servings
adequate for 4 people

Note: This recipe can be halved or doubled, when required.

1/6 SERVING – PROTEIN = 1.6 g.; FAT = 9.7 g.; CARBOHYDRATE = 9.6 g.;
CALORIES = 132; CALORIES FROM FAT = 66%

YEMENI CHICK PEAS WITH TOMATOES AND APRICOTS
Tamaatin Mishmash Feeha Houmous
TPT - 30 minutes

In Israel, a nation that has only existed, as such, since 1948 and whose population has gathered from all over the world, the evolution of a national cuisine is very much an ongoing process, gathered too from all over the world. Most travelers will more than likely encounter this dish in Israel, where it is very popular. The truth is that it most probably originated in Yemen. It can be served hot or cold so when we serve it hot over couscous for dinner, we plan enough leftovers for a cold lunch, with bread or perhaps a bit of rice pudding, the next day.

My version of the Arabic name for this dish, whether or not it is entirely accurate, may help you to order it in a restaurant.

1 tablespoon *extra virgin* olive oil *or* GARLIC OIL *[see index]*, if preferred
1 cup chopped onion
3 garlic cloves—*finely* chopped

2 cups canned, *diced* tomatoes
1 can (15 ounces) chick peas (*garbanzos*)—well-rinsed and *well-drained or* the equivalent in cooked, dry chick peas
1 cup pitted and chopped juice-canned apricots*
2 teaspoons dried Greek *or* Italian oregano —crushed
1 teaspoon ground cumin
Freshly ground black pepper, to taste

In a large saucepan set over *MEDIUM* heat, heat oil. Add chopped onion and *finely* chopped garlic. Sauté until onion is translucent, *being careful not to allow onion or garlic to brown*.

Add *diced* tomatoes, *well-drained* chick peas, chopped apricots, crushed oregano, ground cumin, and black pepper. Allow mixture to come to the boil, stirring frequently. *Reduce heat to LOW*, cover, and cook, for about 15-20 minutes. Stir occasionally to prevent burning. Add a couple of tablespoonfuls of tomato purée in which the tomatoes were canned if necessary. Turn into a heated serving bowl.

Middle East–**Yemen**

YEMENI CHICK PEAS WITH TOMATOES AND APRICOTS (cont'd)

Serve *hot* over *couscous*, if desired. Refrigerate leftovers.

Yields 6 servings
adequate for 4 people

Notes: *Chopped, dried apricots can be used and may be more traditional. However, the sauce created when canned apricots are used is especially tasty.

This recipe can be doubled, when required.

1/6 SERVING – PROTEIN = 3.4 g; FAT = 2.8 g; CARBOHYDRATE = 14.3 g;
CALORIES = 65; CALORIES FROM FAT = 38%

SOYMEAT AND MELON SKILLET WITH THE TASTE OF YEMEN
TPT - 23 minutes

Chicken with melon, "Melon Baal Canaf," is an unusual combination to the western palate. It is, however, a very popular dish in Yemen in which chicken and rice are cooked and stuffed into scooped-out melon halves. Here, I have adapted the commercially-available soy meat analogue products now available to vegetarians to provide a stir-fried dish that can be enjoyed as a first course or as a light entrée over rice.

1/2 cantaloupe melon

1 tablespoon *extra virgin* **olive oil**
1/2 cup *finely* **chopped onion**

6 ounces *frozen* **soy meat analogue strips**—*defrosted*
1 tablespoon freshly squeezed lemon juice
1/2 teaspoon YEMENI SEASONING MIXTURE
   (*Hawayli***), or to taste** *[see recipe which follows]*
Chopped fresh parsley, to garnish

Seed and peel cantaloupe half. Chop into 3/4-inch pieces. Set aside until required.

In a skillet set over *LOW-MEDIUM* heat, heat oil. Add onion and sauté until onion is soft and translucent, *being careful not to allow the onion to brown.*

Add soymeat pieces and allow to heat through—about 5 minutes. Stir frequently.

Add melon pieces and allow to heat through, stirring frequently.

Add lemon juice and seasoning mixture. Stir to integrate. Turn into a heated serving bowl.

Garnish with chopped parsley.

Serve warm as a first course or as a main course over rice.

Yields 6 servings
adequate for 4 people

Note: This recipe can be halved, when required.

1/6 SERVING (exclusive of rice) –
PROTEIN = 12.1 g.; FAT = .3.7; CARBOHYDRATE = 9.5 g.;
CALORIES = 113; CALORIES FROM FAT = 29%

YEMENI SEASONING MIXTURE
Hawayli
TPT - 9 minutes

Turmeric has been widely known since ancient days as an antibacterial and an anti-inflammatory agent. The roles of this spice and folk medication in detoxifying the liver and its possible role in cancer prevention and treatment have long been investigated by researchers. Since it has recently been shown to enhance the effects and reduce the side effects of chemo drugs, research has redoubled to find the exact mechanism of its action.

The extravagant use of true saffron and unexpected taste of caraway and cardamom amazed me when I was first introduced to the seasonings used in Yemen. A pinch here, a pinch there . . . unusual and interesting . . . and perhaps, very good for us.

YEMENI SEASONING MIXTURE (cont'd)

3 teaspoons black peppercorns

1 1/2 teaspoons caraway seeds
1/2 teaspoon saffron threads

1/2 teaspoon ground cardamom
1 teaspoon ground turmeric

In a SPICE and COFFEE GRINDER, or in a mortar, combine peppercorns, caraway seeds, and saffron threads. Grind spices to a uniform mixture.

Turn into a small jelly or spice jar.* Add ground cardamom and ground turmeric. Cover tightly and shake to mix thoroughly. Store in a cool, dark place.

Yields about 4 teaspoonfuls

Notes: When required, this recipe can be doubled.

FOOD VALUES for such spice mixtures are almost negligible.

YEMENI DATE BALLS WITH COCONUT
TPT - 25 minutes

Date balls, as prepared in Yemen, are easy to make and do provide a really sweet end to a meal. Maria cookies, a product of Spain and readily available in the international aisle of most grocery stores, were introduced to Yemen through trade with Andalusia and British digestives were introduced by the British during the years right after World War I when South Yemen was a protectorate. These cookies and coconut are used to give the balls substance and sweetness since no sugar is added.

1 1/4 cups pitted *preservative-free* dates—*finely* chopped*
1/4 cup shredded coconut—fresh *or* desiccated
1 tablespoon white sesame seeds
1/2 teaspoon ground cardamom

6 Maria cookies

2 tablespoons butter

In a mixing bowl, combine *finely* chopped dates, shredded coconut, sesame seeds, and ground cardamom. Mix well.

Using your hands, grind the cookies as finely as possible over a mixing bowl. Pick out any large pieces and grind them again. Add to date mixture and mix until very well-combined. Take about a soup spoonful and roll into a ball. Set on waxed paper until all are formed.

In a skillet set over *LOW-MEDIUM* heat, melt butter. Fry the date balls, a few at a time. Roll them around with a spatula. Fry until heated through—about 5 minutes. *Do not allow to brown.* Transfer to a heated serving dish.

Serve warm.

Yields about 14 date balls

Notes: *Dates are most easily cut with scissors. After they have been cut into small pieces, they can be chopped more easily.

This recipe can be doubled or halved, when required.

1/14 SERVING (per confection) –
PROTEIN = 0.7 g.; FAT = 2.5 g.; CARBOHYDRATE = 12.0 g.;
CALORIES = 66; CALORIES FROM FAT = 34%

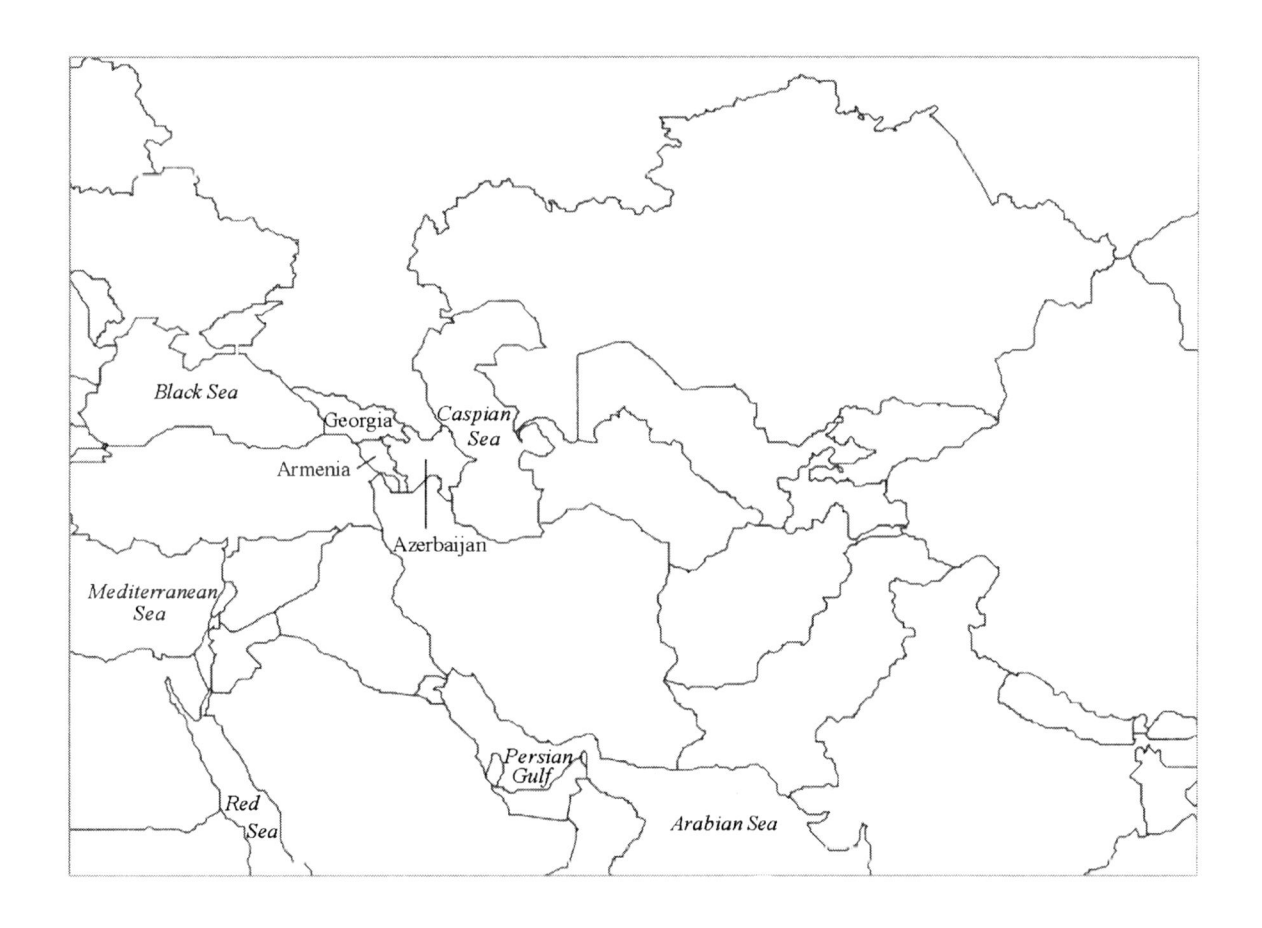

Caucasus

Black Sea
Georgia
Caspian Sea
Armenia
Azerbaijan
Mediterranean Sea
Red Sea
Persian Gulf
Arabian Sea

Caucasus

Armenia	.	.	585
Azerbaijan	.	.	600
Georgia	.	.	610

Armenia

Christianity spread into Armenia as early as 40 AD and Christianity was declared the state religion in 301 AD, making Armenia the first Christian nation some ten years before the Roman Empire under Galerius accepted Christianity. It is an ancient civilization which legend says was founded by Hayk (or Haik or Haig), a descendant of Noah. Archeology places this early civilization in the area near Lake Van, which is now part of Turkey at the base of Mount Ararat, the mountain upon which the Old Testament says that the ark of Noah came to rest. Ararat is still highly revered by Armenians, who consider the mountain and the surrounding area to be their ancient homeland since their ancestors settled in the kingdom of Urartu (Ararat), the former land of the Hittite Empire, sometime in the sixth century BC.

Armenia reached the height of its power under Tigrane the Great (95-55 BC). Today it is a fraction of the size of its ancient predecessor which extended from the Caspian Sea west to the Mediterranean. Although land-locked and situated in a cold, mountainous terrain, Armenia's position at the crossroads of "the silk road" between the Black and Caspian seas, gave exposure to and allowed for assimilation of the cultures of many, many peoples who came and went. Among those who came and went were countless invaders and Armenia endured conquest by Greeks, Romans, Persians, Byzantium, nomadic Mongols, and Arabs. The Ottoman Turks controlled major portions of Armenia from the sixteenth century AD through World War I, during which Armenian suffering was almost indescribable. Thousands of Armenians were massacred by the Turks and in 1915 the horrific genocide, still described by Turkey as a civil war, took place whereby an estimated 600,000 to perhaps 1.5 million Armenians were murdered or died of starvation when the Turks deported the Armenian population to the deserts of Syria and Mesopotamia. In 1918, after World War I and the defeat of the Turks, the Republic of Armenia declared its independence. This period of independence was brief. In May 1920 Armenia was annexed by the Soviet Union. In 1922 Armenia, Georgia, and Azerbijan became part of a Soviet republic, the Transcaucasion Soviet Socialist Republic, and in 1930 became a separate Soviet republic. Independence from the U.S.S.R was declared, as the Soviet Union collapsed in 1991.

Expatriate communities were established by those who fled the Turkish and Soviet occupation of their homeland but the Armenian identity remains strong. Although many Armenians live abroad, their loyalty through business, literature, and direct contribution is an important element of their lives. An example of this can be seen in the community of Armenian vintners who immigrated to California, established vineyards, and make wine in the tradition handed down to them by their ancestors, an ancient practice as confirmed by excavations in southern Armenia that have uncovered a wine-making facility that dates back about 6,000 years making it the oldest wine press ever found.

Caucasus–Armenia

Parsley and Scallion Omelets
Azadkeghov Tzuazegh or Ijjah

Baby Zucchini with *Feta* and Roasted Red Peppers
Titoumi Dolma

~

Stewed Tomatoes, Wheat Berries, and Meatballs with Yogurt
Kololik Gekharkuni

Red Lentil and Bulgur Soup with Apricots
Vosbabour

Tomato and Spinach Soup with Bulgur Wheat and Mint
Tzavarabour

~

Potato and Chick Pea Salad
Kednakhintzor Siser Aghtsan

Fresh *Edamame* Salad with Armenian String Cheese and Chive Oil
Piaz tel Paneer a Ghtzan

~~~~~~~~~~~~~~~~~~~~~~

Cabbage Rolls Stuffed with Lentils, *Bulghur*, and Dried Fruit
Dolma Mujaddarah

Artichokes and Onions in Tomato Sauce
Enguinar

Shepherds' Flatbread
Lavash

~~~~~~~~~~~

Breaded Eggplant and Cheese Sandwiches
Dabgvadz Simpoogov yev Banirov Sandvich

Beets with Chive Oil
Gegentegh Tzitayough

Minted Yogurt Sauce
Anonoukhov Madzoon

~~~~~~~~~~~~~~~~~~~~

Stewed Fruit Compote with Walnuts
Khoshab

Milk Pudding
Muhallebi

Melon and Walnut Compote
Kompot iz Dyni i Orekhov

Christmas Porridge with Dried Fruit and Wheat Berries
Anoush Abour

Caucasus–Armenia

ARMENIAN PARSLEY AND SCALLION OMELETS
Azadkeghov Tzuazegh or Ijjah

TPT - 25 minutes

Omelets and crêpes filled with chopped scallions are found in many cuisines—both East and West. Traditionally these omelets are served at Easter time in their region of origin, but we find that they make a wonderfully different brunch offering year round.

2 large eggs
1/2 cup *fat-free* pasteurized eggs (the equivalent of 2 eggs)
1 tablespoon water
1/4 cup chopped parsley
3 scallions—*including 2 inches of green portions*—trimmed, well-rinsed, and *thinly* sliced
1 garlic clove—*finely* chopped
Freshly ground black pepper, to taste

1 teaspoon *extra light* olive oil

In a mixing bowl, combine eggs, pasteurized eggs, and water. Using a wire whisk, combine well. Add chopped parsley, sliced scallions, and *finely* chopped garlic. Beat until well-integrated. Season with black pepper. Again, beat well.

Place a non-stick-coated griddle or skillet over *MEDIUM* heat. Brush heated pan with olive oil. Heat pan until a drop of water bounces up from the hot surface when dropped onto it.

Drop egg mixture *one tablespoonful at a time* onto *hot* griddle or skillet surface. *Be careful not to crowd omelets.* Using a spatula, carefully contain any egg mixture which runs. Brown on one side; turn and brown on the other side.* Transfer omelets to a heated platter set on a warming tray. Continue preparing omelets until all are completed.

*Serve warm.***

Yields 24 three-inch omelets
adequate for 4 people

Notes: *To speed preparation, set up a second skillet over *MEDIUM* heat. Brush lightly with olive oil. After one side of each omelet is browned, transfer the omelet to the second pan to brown the second side while starting new omelets on the first skillet surface.

**If preferred, these omelets may be served cold.

This recipe may be halved or doubled, when required.

1/24 SERVING (i. e., per omelet) –
PROTEIN = 1.1 g.; FAT = 0.6 g.; CARBOHYDRATE = 0.5 g.;
CALORIES = 11; CALORIES FROM FAT = 49%

BABY ZUCCHINI WITH *FETA* AND ROASTED RED PEPPERS
Titoumi Dolma

TPT - 21 minutes

Baby zucchini are often available in well-stocked produce departments. They are generally less watery and the perfect size for a sophisticated appetizer presentation. This recipe is adapted from an Armenian dolma recipe which called for larger zucchini. If you roast and freeze red peppers in oil, as we do, you will find this a quickly prepared first course with lots of flavor.

6 tablespoons chopped ROASTED RED PEPPERS *[see index]*
3 scallions—*white and light green portions only*—trimmed, well-rinsed, and *thinly* sliced
6 tablespoons crumbled dry *feta* cheese
1/2 teaspoon dried oregano—crushed
Freshly ground black pepper, to taste

6 baby zucchini—ends trimmed and halved lengthwise

Set up a steamer. Preheat broiler to 400 degrees F.

In a small bowl, combine chopped roasted red peppers, *thinly* sliced scallions, *feta* cheese, crushed, dried oregano, and black pepper. Mix well and set aside until required.

Hollow out each zucchini half into a small boat using the smallest end of a melon baller. Place in steamer, hollow-side-down. Steam for about 4 minutes. Remove to counter top. Place in a pie plate or *au gratin* dish.

BABY ZUCCHINI WITH *FETA* AND ROASTED RED PEPPERS (cont'd)

Apportion the red pepper–*feta* filling among the zucchini boats.* Broil under preheated 400 degree F. broiler for about 2 minutes, or until cheese is melted and beginning to color. Remove from broiler. Transfer two zucchini halves to each of six dessert plates.

Serve at once with a fruit knife and a salad fork.

Yields 6 individual servings

Notes: *If the roasted red peppers you are using were not packed in olive oil, you may want to drizzle a teaspoonful of olive oil over the prepared *dolmas*.

This recipe can be halved or doubled, when required.

1/6 SERVING – PROTEIN = 2.9 g.; FAT = 3.1 g.; CARBOHYDRATE = 3.3 g.; CALORIES = 51; CALORIES FROM FAT = 55%

STEWED TOMATOES, WHEAT BERRIES, AND MEATBALLS WITH YOGURT
Kololik Gekharkuni
TPT - 1 hour and 10 minutes

When I was young, a side dish of stewed tomatoes was often served not only at home but in restaurants. The waitress would tick off the vegetable offerings which were not the most interesting of vegetables—peas, carrots, corn, stewed tomatoes. The food options were often thin during the waning years of the Great Depression and the years during and after World War II. "Kololik gekharkuni" is the name given to a meatball and wheat stew similar to this vegetarian version which is made with either bulgur wheat or wheat berries. It is not that side of stewed tomatoes served in restaurants; it is an interesting side dish, first course, or soup and it can also be a nutritious and easily prepared main course offering for a family meal or lunch. Spices rarely overpower a dish in Armenia but the introduction of spices from the Far East by travelers is evident. In this dish I tried to approximate a taste memory and found that the Indian spice mixture "garam masala" gave just the exotic hint I remembered. When augmented with oregano and mint, it was perfect. "Mahdzoon," yogurt, is part of almost every meal in Armenia often being the principal ingredient in a soup or beverage. Here it is a topping or garnish that can be stirred into the stew to the satisfaction of each diner.

The protein level of this simple dish will astound you.

1/2 cup whole wheat berries (*dzedzaz*)—sorted carefully and well-rinsed*
3 cups *boiling* water

1 can (28 ounces) *whole* tomatoes
1/4 cup canned, *crushed* tomatoes
2 tablespoons fresh mint leaves—well washed and *finely* chopped
2 tablespoons fresh Greek oregano leaves—well-washed and *finely* chopped
1/2 teaspoon OUR INDIAN SPICE MIXTURE (*Garam Masala*) [see index] or commercially-available mixture

18 small, *frozen* "vegetarian meatballs"

1/2 cup PLAIN YOGURT [see index] or commercially-available plain yogurt

In a saucepan set over *LOW* heat, cook wheat berries in *boiling* water until tender—about 1 hour.

In a large saucepan set over *MEDIUM* heat, combine whole tomatoes with liquid, crushed tomatoes, *finely* chopped mint and oregano leaves, and *garam masala*. Stir to combine. Cook until mixture begins to boil. Reduce heat to LOW-MEDIUM.

STEWED TOMATOES, WHEAT BERRIES, AND MEATBALLS WITH YOGURT (cont'd)

Add cooked wheat berries and soy meatballs. Cook, stirring frequently, until meatballs are thoroughly heated through. Turn into a heated serving bowl.

Serve at once into small dishes. Pass yogurt.

Yields 6 servings
adequate for 4 people

Notes: *Many recommend that wheat berries be soaked overnight before cooking. This is not necessary. The chewy texture desired can be achieved by cooking over direct heat at *LOW* for about 1 hour.

This recipe can be halved, when required.

1/6 SERVING – PROTEIN = 20.1 g.; FAT = 6.0 g.; CARBOHYDRATE = 22.3 g.;
CALORIES = 202; CALORIES FROM FAT = 27%

ARMENIAN RED LENTIL AND BULGUR SOUP WITH APRICOTS
Vosbabour

TPT - 1 hour and 9 minutes

The oldest Christian state in the world, Armenia has been invaded and reinvaded, divided and subdivided, for centuries. The influences of those who occupied its mountainous landscape and its fertile river valleys have left their marks evidenced in the cuisine and in many, too many, other ways. Lentils and other pulses have been raised in the valleys of the Tigris and Euphrates Rivers for thousands of years. Apricots, and cherries too, began their travels to the cuisines of the world from this ancient nation.

1 cup (about 1/3 pound) dry split *red* lentils *or* masur dal *

9 cups VEGETARIAN BROWN STOCK *[see index]* or water

2 tablespoons *extra virgin* olive oil
1 large onion—*finely* chopped
1 large garlic clove—*finely* chopped

6 tablespoons dry *coarse* bulgur *(bulghur)* wheat
—well-rinsed and extraneous material removed**
1 cup canned, *diced* tomatoes
1/2 teaspoon ground cumin, or to taste
1/2 teaspoon dried thyme—crushed
1/2 teaspoon dried tarragon—crushed
Salt, to taste
Freshly ground black pepper, to taste

2 tablespoons freshly squeezed lemon juice
1/2 cup chopped, *preservative-free* dried apricots
—about 10 halves

Chopped fresh parsley, for garnish

Pick over lentils and discard any of poor quality. Rinse thoroughly. Put lentils into a large *non-aluminum**** kettle set over *MEDIUM* heat. Add stock or water and allow to come to the boil. *Reduce heat to LOW.*

Meanwhile, in a skillet set over *LOW-MEDIUM* heat, combine oil with *finely* chopped onion and garlic. Sauté until onion is soft and translucent, *allowing neither the onion nor the garlic to brown.*

Add sautéed onion and garlic to ingredients in kettle. Cover tightly and allow to simmer for about 25 minutes. Stir occasionally.

Add bulgur wheat, chopped tomato, ground cumin, crushed, dried thyme and tarragon, salt, and black pepper. Cook, uncovered, for an additional 20 minutes.

When you are just about ready to serve, remove two or three ladlefuls of soup to the container of the electric blender or food processor, fitted with steel knife. Purée and return to the soup in the kettle.**** Stir in chopped, dried apricots and lemon juice. Allow to heat through—about 5 minutes more.

Turn into heated soup tureen and serve into heated soup bowls. Garnish each serving with chopped parsley.

Yields about 2 quartfuls
or 8 servings

ARMENIAN RED LENTIL AND BULGUR SOUP WITH APRICOTS (cont'd)

Notes: *Red lentils, sometime referred to as pink lentils or even Egyptian lentils, are found in groceries that specialize in Middle Eastern foods. Indian or Pakistani groceries carry red lentils as *masur dal*.

**Bulgur (*bulghur*) wheat, cracked wheat, or crushed wheat is available in natural food stores and in Middle Eastern groceries. It is a par-boiled product and, therefore, needs no further cooking.

***Since aluminum discolors lentils rather unpleasantly, avoid using aluminum cookware or serving bowls in this case.

****This soup may be frozen at this point. Apricots added before freezing tend to disintegrate during the reheating process.

1/8 SERVING – PROTEIN = 8.4 g.; FAT = 3.3 g.; CARBOHYDRATE = 27.3 g.;
CALORIES = 166; CALORIES FROM FAT = 18%

ARMENIAN TOMATO AND SPINACH SOUP WITH BULGUR WHEAT AND MINT
Tzavarabour

TPT - 34 minutes

This is a satisfying and filling soup featuring bulgur wheat, as do many Armenian soups and stews. We like to accompany this soup with a fava or kidney bean salad sprinkled with walnuts.

1 quart VEGETARIAN BROWN STOCK *[see index]*, **VEGETABLE STOCK FROM SOUP** *[see index]*, **or water**

1 tablespoon butter
2 cups canned, *whole* tomatoes—*finely* chopped— or 4 medium ripe tomatoes—peeled, seeded, and *finely* chopped

1/2 cup dry, coarse bulgur *(bulghur)* wheat*

1/2 pound spinach—*very well-washed*, hard stems removed, and chopped
1 garlic clove—peeled
Freshly ground black pepper, to taste

1 tablespoon freshly squeezed lemon juice—*strained*
1 teaspoon dried mint leaves *or* lemon balm leaves, if preferred**

In a kettle set over *MEDIUM* heat, bring stock or water to the boil.

Meanwhile, in a saucepan set over *LOW-MEDIUM* heat, melt butter. Add *finely* chopped tomatoes and cook for about 5 minutes. Stir the tomatoes frequently, mashing with a wooden spoon as you stir.

Add bulgur wheat and cook for about 5 minutes, stirring frequently.

Add the tomato–wheat mixture and the chopped spinach to the *boiling* stock in the kettle. Press the peeled garlic clove through a garlic press directly into the soup mixture. Discard any residue. Season with black pepper. Stir to integrate garlic and black pepper.

Reduce heat to LOW. Cover kettle and simmer for about 20 minutes until bulgur is *tender*, but *not mushy*. Stir frequently.

Stir in *strained* lemon juice and crushed mint. Turn into a heated soup tureen.

Serve at once, into heated soup bowls.

Yields 6 servings
adequate for 4 people

Notes: *Bulgur (*bulghur*) wheat, cracked wheat, or crushed wheat is available in natural food stores and in Middle Eastern groceries. It is a par-boiled product and, therefore, needs little further cooking.

**The dried leaves of any member of the mint family, which you prefer, may be used in this recipe. However, peppermint is, we feel, a bit too strong. On the other hand, lemon balm (*Melissa officinalis*), which is an easily grown perennial herb, hardy in Zones 4-9, adds just the right combination of mint and lemon to compliment this soup.

Caucasus–Armenia

ARMENIAN TOMATO AND SPINACH SOUP WITH BULGUR WHEAT AND MINT (cont'd)

This recipe may be doubled, when required.

Leftover soup does not freeze well.

1/6 SERVING – PROTEIN = 3.3 g.; FAT = 2.3 g.; CARBOHYDRATE = 13.6 g.;
CALORIES = 83; CALORIES FROM FAT = 25%

ARMENIAN POTATO AND CHICK PEA SALAD
Kednakhintzor Siser Aghtsan

TPT - 4 hours and 20 minutes;
2 hours = marination period;
2 hours = flavor development period

By cubing and then cooking the potatoes, you can avoid the inevitable crumbling which occurs when hot potatoes are cut. As I do when I make my family German potato salad, I sprinkle the vinegar mixture on the hot potato cubes. The flavor then permeates the potatoes. A garnish of hard-cooked egg slices is beautiful, albeit not traditional.

5 medium all-purpose potatoes *(not Idaho)*
—preferably Red Bliss, if available—peeled and cut into 1/2-inch cubes
3 quarts *boiling water*

2 tablespoons vinegar, of choice—*our preference is for* ROSEMARY VINEGAR *[see index]* or GARLIC– BASIL VINEGAR *[see index]*
2 tablespoons *extra virgin* olive oil
1/2 teaspoon dry mustard
1/4 teaspoon ground black pepper, or to taste
Salt, to taste

1 can (15 ounces) chick peas *(garbanzos)*—*well-drained*
1/2 cup Italian flat-leafed parsley—well-washed and *finely* chopped
2 small scallions—*both green and white portions*—trimmed, well-rinsed, and *thinly* sliced

Cook potato cubes in *boiling* water until *firm-tender*—about 8 minutes. Place in a large mixing bowl.

In a cruet or small jar, combine vinegar, oil, dry mustard, black pepper, and salt. Shake vigorously to combine. Sprinkle oil–vinegar mixture over *hot* potato pieces. Toss *very gently*.

Refrigerate for 2 hours. Turn potatoes occasionally to insure uniform distribution of the dressing.

Add *well-drained* chick peas, *finely* chopped parsley, and *thinly* sliced scallions. Toss gently. Cover and refrigerate for an additional 2 hours.

Pour marinated salad into a sieve to allow excess marinade to drain through. Turn salad into a serving bowl. Refrigerate until required.

Serve cold.

Yields 6 servings
adequate for 4 people

Note: This recipe may be doubled or tripled, when required.

1/8 SERVING – PROTEIN = 4.5 g.; FAT = 4.7 g.; CARBOHYDRATE = 24.1 g.;
CALORIES = 160; CALORIES FROM FAT = 26%

FRESH *EDAMAME* SALAD WITH ARMENIAN STRING CHEESE AND CHIVE OIL
Piaz tel Paneer a Ghtzan

TPT - 34 minutes

While Ray was interviewing a family for a book we were writing, he was introduced to frozen edamame. We are very fond of green soybeans and their wide availability, shelled, precooked, and frozen, is a real help to vegetarians who do other things beside food prep all day. Thank you, Joy Taylor.

As far as I can tell, chive oil is an uniquely Armenian flavoring tool that can be used in so many ways that you will never stop experimenting. The inspiration for this wonderful salad was an Armenian salad made with fresh fava beans. This salad can be made with fava beans or baby limas, if preferred.

Caucasus–**Armenia**

FRESH *EDAMAME* SALAD WITH ARMENIAN STRING CHEESE AND CHIVE OIL (cont'd)

CHIVE OIL:
    1 cup *boiling* water
    1/3 cup chopped fresh chives

    1/4 cup *extra virgin* olive oil
    Pinch kosher salt

3 quarts *boiling* water
14 ounces *frozen edamame*
3 quarts *ice* water

2 teaspoons *finely* chopped fresh mint
1 teaspoon *extra virgin* olive oil
1/4 teaspoon freshly ground black pepper, or to taste

4 large Romaine *or* butter lettuce leaves—well-washed and dried
2/3 cup (about 3 ounces) Armenian string cheese —*pulled out* into long shreds

In a small bowl prepare CHIVE OIL by combining the 1 cupful *boiling* water and the chopped fresh chives. *Immediately*, pour through a sieve to drain. Transfer par-boiled chives to paper toweling and pat dry. Place chives in the work bowl of the food processor.

Add the 1/4 cup olive oil and salt. Process until smooth, scraping down the sides of the work bowl as needed. Set a funnel into a cruet. Set a small sieve into the funnel. Pour the chive mixture through. Allow to drain thoroughly. Discard chives.

In a saucepan set over *MEDIUM* heat, combine *boiling* water and *frozen edamame*. Cook for about 5 minutes, or until defrosted. Plunge *edamame* into *ice* water. Allow to cool for about 5 minutes. Drain thoroughly.

In a mixing bowl, combine drained *edamame*, *finely* chopped mint, the 1 teaspoonful olive oil, and black pepper.**

Arrange lettuce leaves on a plate or small platter. Pile the salad onto the lettuce leaves. Heap the strings of the string cheese over the beans.

Serve chilled with prepared CHIVE OIL.

                Yields 6 servings
               adequate for 4 people

Notes: *Freshly prepared or leftover chive oil can be refrigerated until required. Bring to room temperature before serving.

        **The salad can be prepared to this point early in the day and refrigerated until required.

        This recipe can be doubled, when necessary.

1/6 SERVING – PROTEIN = 11.5 g.; FAT = 12.4 g.; CARBOHYDRATE = 11.5 g.; CALORIES = 201; CALORIES FROM FAT = 56%

ARMENIAN CABBAGE ROLLS STUFFED WITH LENTILS, *BULGHUR*, AND DRIED FRUIT
Dolma Mujaddarah
TPT - 1 hour and 40 minutes

The large outside leaves of the cabbage were always stuffed with mashed potatoes in my family. This dolma, of Arabic origin, is an adventure in flavors and texture. When I do not have cabbage leaves, I even use this as a filling for an open ravioli.

1/4 cup coarse bulgur (*bulghur*)
2 cups *warm* water

1 tablespoon butter
1 tablespoon *extra virgin* olive oil
1 medium onion—*finely* chopped
1 garlic clove—*very finely* chopped

1/2 cup *well-drained* organic lentil soup*

3 tablespoons chopped, *preservative-free* dried apricots
2 tablespoons dried, *preservative-free* currants
1/4 cup *finely* chopped fresh coriander (*cilantro*)
2 tablespoons *finely* chopped fresh mint leaves
2 tablespoons *finely* chopped fresh summer savory
1/4 teaspoon freshly ground black pepper, or to taste

8 large, well-washed cabbage leaves

2 tablespoons grated Parmesan, *pecorino Romano*, or *Kefalotyri* cheese
2 tablespoons pine nuts (*pignoli*), for garnish

ARMENIAN CABBAGE ROLLS STUFFED WITH LENTILS, *BULGHUR*, AND DRIED FRUIT (cont'd)

Prepare a 9- or 10-inch pie plate or other oven-proof plate by coating with non-stick lecithin spray coating.

Soak *bulgur* in warm water for 30 minutes. Drain thoroughly.

In a skillet set over *LOW-MEDIUM* heat, combine oil and butter. Add *finely* chopped onion and *very finely* chopped garlic. Sauté until soft and translucent, *allowing neither the onion nor the garlic to brown.*

Add soaked and drained bulgur, *well-drained* lentil soup, chopped apricots, currants, *finely* chopped coriander (*cilantro*), mint leaves, and summer savory, and black pepper. Stir to combine. Remove from heat.

Bring a large kettle of water to the boil or, if preferred, set up a steamer. Boil or steam cabbage leaves for about 5-7 minutes, or until just soft and pliable. *Drain thoroughly.*

PREPARE CABBAGE ROLLS by placing *one-eighth* portion of the filling mixture along the thick edge of each cooked cabbage leaf. Turn sides toward the center and roll up by turning filled side toward center. Place prepared cabbage rolls, seam-side-down and side-by-side in prepared pie plate. Refrigerate until ready to proceed.**

Preheat oven to 300 degrees F.

Bake in preheated oven for about 25 minutes, or until heated through.

Sprinkle grated cheese over and garnish with pine nuts (*pignoli*).***

Serve cabbage rolls directly from baking dish. Accompany with *lavash*.****

Notes: *Although the lentil soup reduces the preparation time considerably and adds another level of flavor, lentils can be cooked from scratch for this recipe, if preferred. In a non-aluminum saucepan set over *MEDIUM* heat, combine 1/4 cupful lentils, 3 cupfuls vegetable stock, and a broken bay leaf.* Bring to the boil. Reduce heat to *LOW*, cover tightly, and simmer for about 30 minutes, or until lentils are tender. Drain, reserving liquid for soup stock and discarding bay leaf pieces.

**The stuffed cabbage rolls may be prepared early in the day and conveniently refrigerated until about 45 minutes before serving time.

***If you have any of the lentil soup leftover, it makes a very complimentary sauce.

****Lavash, a very flat shepherd's bread, is readily available and usually found in deli departments of large grocery stores. It is now widely appreciated as a sandwich wrap.

This recipe may be halved or doubled, if required.

Yields 8 rolls
adequate for 4 people

1/8 SERVING – PROTEIN = 3.8 g.; FAT = 4.7 g.; CARBOHYDRATE = 10.9 g.;
CALORIES = 96; CALORIES FROM FAT = 44%

ARMENIAN ARTICHOKES AND ONIONS IN TOMATO SAUCE
Enguinar

TPT - 2 hours and 42 minutes;
[slow cooker: 30 minutes at HIGH;
then, 2 hours at LOW]

Having several large bags of artichoke hearts in the freezer is a convenience on which I have become dependent. Whether it is just a sauté with grated cheese or something more substantial, such as this slow cooker version of a traditional Armenian vegetable dish, artichoke hearts are a very useful ingredient. The long, slow cooking of this dish fills the house with an aroma that is irresistible. Not only is this a nice vegetable side dish, it is often enjoyed as a first course in Armenia.

ARMENIAN ARTICHOKES AND ONIONS IN TOMATO SAUCE (cont'd)

1 tablespoon *extra virgin* olive oil

1 large onion—*very thinly* sliced

1/2 cup water
12 ounces *frozen* artichoke hearts
1 1/2 cups canned, *diced* tomatoes with purée
2 tablespoons *finely* snipped fresh dillweed *or*
  1 tablespoon dried dillweed—crushed
1 tablespoon freshly squeezed lemon juice

2 tablespoons *finely* chopped fresh parsley
Salt, to taste
Freshly ground black pepper, to taste

1/4 cup crumbled *feta* cheese

Pour the olive oil into the bowl of the slow cooker set at HIGH. Allow to heat for several minutes.

Add *very thinly* sliced onion. Toss to coat with oil. Allow the onion to sweat for 30 minutes, stirring frequently.

Add artichoke hearts, diced tomatoes, crushed dillweed, and lemon juice. Reduce the slow cooker temperature to *LOW*, cover, and allow to cook for about 2 hours. Stir occasionally. Add a tablespoonful or two of water if you get too much evaporation and the mixture begins to dry out.*

Add *finely* chopped fresh parsley. Season with salt and pepper. Turn into a serving bowl.

Scatter crumbled *feta* cheese over.

Serve at once.

Yields 8 servings
adequate for 6 people

Notes: *This recipe can be frozen at this point.

When required, this recipe can be halved or doubled.

1/8 SERVING – PROTEIN = 3.1 g.; FAT = 3.2 g.; CARBOHYDRATE = 7.8 g.; CALORIES = 66; CALORIES FROM FAT = 43%

ARMENIAN BREADED EGGPLANT AND CHEESE SANDWICHES
Dabgvadz Simpoogas yev Banirov Sandwich

TPT - 1 hour and 53 minutes;
30 minutes = eggplant draining period;
1 hour = refrigeration period

Anyone who fries breaded eggplant slices, usually has a few leftover—intentionally in our house. Eggplant sandwiches seem to be rather a universally planned leftover for next-day menus in those nations where eggplant cutlets are part of the cuisine. This is an Armenian version.

1 medium eggplant
Salt

1/2 cup *fat-free* pasteurized eggs (the equivalent of 2 eggs)

1 cup whole wheat breadcrumbs

1 tablespoon butter—*melted*
1 tablespoon *extra virgin* olive oil

16 slices *diagonally-cut* Italian bread *or* French bread
8 slices Danish *Havarti,* plain or seasoned, *or* Italian *Bel Paese* cheese

Slice eggplant crosswise into 1/2-inch slices to yield eight slices. Sprinkle each generously with salt. Place in a colander, cover with a small saucer, and place a weight of about 2-3 pounds on top. Allow to drain over a plate or in the sink for about 30 minutes. Rinse *very thoroughly* to remove salt and pat as dry as possible with paper toweling.

Put pasteurized eggs and breadcrumbs into *separate* soup plates or pie plates.

Coat eggplant slices with breadcrumbs; dip into eggs; and then coat well with breadcrumbs. Place on a large platter and refrigerate for about 1 hour before proceeding with the frying process.*

Preheat oven to 300 degrees F. Arrange eight of the bread slices on a cookie sheet.

ARMENIAN BREADED EGGPLANT AND CHEESE SANDWICHES (cont'd)

Coat a large non-stick-coated skillet with non-stick lecithin spray coating. Set over *MEDIUM* heat. When hot, add breaded eggplant slices. When breading begins to brown, add *melted* butter and oil. Cook for about a minute more; turn and brown the remaining side. Add more *melted* butter to prevent overbrowning, if necessary. Transfer fried eggplant slices to drain on paper toweling. Pat the slices with paper toweling to remove excess butter before proceeding.

Transfer a hot, breaded eggplant slice onto a slice of bread on the cookie sheet. Place a slice of cheese on top of the eggplant slice and place a slice of bread on top of cheese. Repeat until all sandwiches are assembled.

Place the cookie sheet in the preheated 300 degree F. oven and allow sandwiches to bake until cheese begins to melt. Transfer to a heated serving platter.

Serve at once.

Yields 8 servings
adequate for 4-6 people

Notes: *Breaded eggplant slices may be prepared ahead of time to this point and refrigerated until required. Place on a cookie sheet in a slow oven and allow to heat through before proceeding.

This recipe may be halved or doubled, when required.

1/8 SERVING – PROTEIN = 10.4 g.; FAT = 8.4 g.; CARBOHYDRATE = 36.4 g.;
CALORIES = 256; CALORIES FROM FAT = 30%

ARMENIAN BEETS WITH CHIVE OIL
Gegentegh Tzitayough
TPT - 8 minutes

Here is another example of how the diverse influences of invaders and neighbors, sometimes one in the same, are chronicled in the foods of this ancient nation. And here, also, is proof of Armenian respect for the tastes of individual ingredients, a truth I came to recognize in my study of the Armenian cuisine.

2 jars of baby beets *or* the equivalent in cooked, fresh baby beets

1/4 cup CHIVE OIL *[see recipe which precedes]*
Freshly ground black pepper, to taste

In a saucepan set over *MEDIUM* heat, heat beets until heated through. Drain thoroughly. Return beets to saucepan over *MEDIUM* heat.

Add CHIVE OIL and black pepper. Allow to heat through. Turn into a heated serving bowl.

Serve at once with a slotted spoon.

Yields 6 servings
adequate for 4 people

Note: This recipe can be halved, when necessary.

1/6 SERVING – PROTEIN = 1.4 g.; FAT = 7.6 g.; CARBOHYDRATE = 11.4 g.;
CALORIES = 117; CALORIES FROM FAT = 58%

ARMENIAN MINTED YOGURT SAUCE
Anonoukhov Madzoon
TPT - 2 minutes

We fill dessert dishes or sherbet glasses with an assortment of berries, lavender blossoms, and a few happy pansy faces and then we pass this sauce.

1 cup PLAIN YOGURT *[see index]* **or commercially-available plain yogurt**
1 1/2 tablespoons wildflower honey

1 tablespoon *very finely* chopped fresh mint

ARMENIAN MINTED YOGURT SAUCE (cont'd)

In a small bowl, combine yogurt and honey. Using a wire whisk, whisk gently to form a smooth sauce.

Add *very finely* chopped fresh mint. Stir to combine. Turn into a small serving bowl. Refrigerate until required.

Serve chilled.

Note: This recipe is easily doubled or tripled, when required.

Yields 1 cupful

1/8 SERVING (i. e., 2 tablespoonfuls) –
PROTEIN = 2.2 g.; FAT = 0.04 g.; CARBOHYDRATE = 6.4 g.;
CALORIES = 34; CALORIES FROM FAT = 1%

ARMENIAN STEWED FRUIT COMPOTE WITH WALNUTS
Khoshab

TPT - 10 hours and 30 minutes;
8 hours = fruit rehydration period;
2 hours = cooling period

On celebratory occasions, such as New Year's Day, Armenians often serve this winter compote and we have adopted their tradition, using fruits from our winter fruit larder. We tasted Armenian brandy for the first time when we visited the Soviet Union and upon our departure on New Year's Eve 1983, a bottle of that wonderful brandy was in our luggage secured in a roll of 1984 calendars. We add our dried cherries to the fruit mix and often include dried apple pieces and serve it either straight-up as a fruit dessert or over desserts such as puddings and ice cream.

1/2 cup *preservative-free* dried apricots
—quartered
1/4 cup pitted, *preservative-free* prunes
1/4 cup *preservative-free* dried cherries
1/2 cup *preservative-free* dark raisins

1/2 cup water
2 tablespoons confectioner's sugar
1 cinnamon quill
2 whole cloves
Pinch ground allspice
1 thin slice fresh lemon

1/4 cup chopped *preservative-free* walnuts
2 tablespoons Armenian brandy *or* French cognac

Rinse the dried fruits well under cold running water. Drain well. Turn into a large mixing bowl and add enough water to cover the fruit. Cover the bowl with plastic wrap and allow the fruits to rehydrate for about 8 hours or overnight. Turn into a saucepan.

Set the saucepan over *MEDIUM-HIGH* heat and allow to come to the boil. Reduce heat to *MEDIUM-LOW* and simmer the fruits for 10 minutes.

Add the extra 1/2 cupful of water, confectioner's sugar, cinnamon quill, whole cloves, ground allspice, and lemon slices. Stir to combine. Continue to cook for an additional 5-10 minutes. Turn into a mixing bowl. Refrigerate for at least 2 hours. Remove and discard cloves. Remove and wash the cinnamon quill well; dry and store to reuse.

Using a slotted spoon, transfer the fruits to a chilled serving bowl.

Serve well-chilled, topping each serving with chopped walnuts and a splash of brandy.

Yields 6 servings
adequate for 4-6 people

Note: This recipe can be halved or doubled, when required.

1/6 SERVING – PROTEIN = 3.2 g.; FAT = 9.1 g.; CARBOHYDRATE = 29.0 g.;
CALORIES = 201; CALORIES FROM FAT = 41%

ARMENIAN MILK PUDDING
Muhallebi

TPT - 5 hours and 27 minutes;
       1 hour = cooling period at room temperature;
       4 hours = chilling period

I would wager to bet that almost everyone in the United States has a box of corn starch sitting in their cupboard, for thickening sauces, for puddings, etc. Not so in Armenia or Turkey, where this rice pudding is also popular due to the presence of an Armenian minority. Some say "muhallebi" is Turkish and that it was introduced to Armenia by the Turks; some say its popularity in Turkey is due to the influence of Armenians. I would never get into the middle of that one. Instead of corn starch, rice flour is used to thicken the pudding. Armenians prefer cinnamon flavoring while rose water is often used to flavor milk pudding in Turkey. Bitter orange and orange blossoms are used to flavor a similar pudding in Cyprus.

1/2 cup dry brown rice flour *or* rice powder*
1 cup *cold skimmed* milk

2 cups *skimmed* milk*
1 cup heavy cream
1/2 cup sugar

1 teaspoon pure vanilla extract

2 teaspoons ground cinnamon, for garnish**
2 tablespoons *finely* chopped, *unsalted* pistachio nuts, for garnish

In a small bowl, combine rice flour and 1 cupful *cold* milk. Stir until rice flour is dissolved and in suspension. Set aside briefly.

In the top half of a double boiler set over *boiling* water, combine the remaining 2 cupfuls milk, heavy cream, and sugar. Cook, stirring occasionally until sugar is dissolved and milk is hot. *Reduce heat to LOW-MEDIUM.*

Add dissolved rice flour and continue cooking over simmering water until thickened—about 30 minutes. Stir frequently with a wire whisk.

When thickened, add vanilla extract. Stir to integrate. Remove from heat.

Turn into a serving bowl. Sprinkle ground cinnamon evenly over the pudding surface. Allow to cool to room temperature. Cover with plastic wrap and refrigerate for at least four hours.

Garnish with *finely* chopped pistachio nuts. *Serve cold.*

Notes: *Brown rice flour can be purchased in Asian groceries and in most natural food stores.

**Ground cardamom is a delightful garnish for this dessert also.

This recipe *can not* be doubled successfully but it can be halved, when necessary.

Occasionally, even though you are very conscientious about stirring, rice flour puddings can become lumpy. Press through a sieve into a clean saucepan and continue cooking over hot water until uniformly thickened.

Yields 6 servings
adequate for 4 people

1/6 SERVING – PROTEIN = 5.6 g.; FAT = 14.0 g.; CARBOHYDRATE = 33.7 g.;
CALORIES = 279; CALORIES FROM FAT = 45%

Caucasus–**Armenia**

ARMENIAN MELON AND WALNUT COMPOTE
Kompot iz Dyni i Orekhov

TPT - 19 minutes;
15 minutes = maceration period

Versions of this compote, found in the cuisines of Armenia, Georgia, and Uzbekistan, would assuredly be much sweeter than the version presented here. This, we feel, is more to the taste of the American palate.

1 medium cantaloupe, honeydew, *or* **casaba melon, as preferred—halved, seeded, and cubed to yield about 6 cupfuls**
1/4 cup honey—*a hearty wildflower honey is our choice*

1/2 cup coarsely chopped, *preservative-free* **walnuts**

Place cubed melon in a shallow serving bowl. Add honey and coat melon by tossing *gently*. Allow to stand for 15 minutes to allow melon juice to flow.

Stir in chopped walnuts.

Serve into small, individual salad bowls.

Yields 6 servings
adequate for 4 people

Note: This recipe may be halved or doubled, when required.

1/6 SERVING – PROTEIN = 2.8 g.; FAT = 8.7 g.; CARBOHYDRATE = 20.6 g.;
CALORIES = 165; CALORIES FROM FAT = 47%

ARMENIAN CHRISTMAS PORRIDGE
WITH DRIED FRUIT AND WHEAT BERRIES
Anoush Abour

TPT - 9 hours and 38 minutes;
8 hours = wheat berry soaking period

No matter how many Armenian desserts I chose to include in this manuscript, I would be remiss not to include a version of the ancient Armenian sweet porridge, "anoush abour." This porridge may date to before the 40 AD introduction of Christianity into Armenia. Oh yes, it is a very, very ancient dish, as good today as it was way back then. Armenians all over the world prepare this dish for their January 6th celebration of Christmas. Some say that the touch of rose water is the magic. All I know is that it is good and good for you and that makes me feel very good.

1/2 cup whole wheat berries (*dzedzaz***)—sorted carefully and well-rinsed***
3 cups *boiling* **water**

1/2 cup water
1 cup dried fruit—a mixture of apples and *preservative-free dark* **raisins, peaches, or apricots**
1/4 cup sugar
1/2 teaspoon pure vanilla extract

1/2 vanilla bean
1 teaspoon rose water*
1 tablespoon ground, *preservative-free* **almonds** *or* **walnuts, as preferred**
Pinch ground cinnamon

VOLUME I - 598

**ARMENIAN CHRISTMAS PORRIDGE
WITH DRIED FRUIT AND WHEAT BERRIES** (cont'd)

In a saucepan set over *LOW* heat, cook wheat berries in *boiling* water until tender—about 1 hour. Transfer the saucepan to the refrigerator and allow to soak overnight. *Cover once it has cooled down to refrigerator temperature.* Allow to remain refrigerated overnight.

Drain any remaining liquid from the wheat berries. Return to saucepan and set over *LOW* heat.

Add 1/2 cup water, dried fruit mixture, sugar, vanilla extract, and vanilla bean. Cook, stirring frequently, until liquid has been absorbed, and a thick porridge results. Turn into a serving bowl. Remove vanilla bean, wash, dry, and store for reuse.

Sprinkle pudding with rose water. Stir. Sprinkle ground nuts and ground cinnamon over.

Serve at room temperature or, refrigerate and serve slightly chilled.

Yields 6 servings
adequate for 4 people

Notes: *Both French and Lebanese rose water or *ma ward* products are available in food specialty stores.

This recipe can be halved or doubled, when necessary.

1/6 SERVING – PROTEIN = 2.5 g.; FAT = 1.7 g.; CARBOHYDRATE = 37.2 g.;
CALORIES = 187; CALORIES FROM FAT = 8%

Azerbaijan

Only about eighteen percent of Azerbaijan's land mass can be classified as arable. An estimated fifty-percent of the mud volcanoes on the planet are located here, geologic features that did not seem to have discouraged our wandering ancestors from moving to and through this land. Archaeological records show that this area of the Near East was inhabited in the late Stone Age; settled by the Scythians in the ninth century BC; and then by the Iranian Medes who built a large empire beginning in 900 BC. The Medes Empire became part of the Archaemenids Empire in c. 550 BC. The Archaemenids were followers of Zoriaster, a Persian religious leader whose religious model evolved from that of nature worship. The expansion of the Archaemenids Empire led to the spread of Zoriasterism. The religion was revived during the feudal era by the Sassanidae after the religion almost became extinct during the Greek period under Alexander the Great. It survives in the beliefs of the Ghebers in Iran and the Parsis in India.

Through the Treaties of Gulitan and Turkamanchai, 1813 and 1828 respectively, Russia acquired territory from Persia which remained under Soviet rule until the Bolshevik Revolution in 1918 when Azerbaijan declared its independence. However, the extensive oil and gas reserves in the Baku were not resources that the Soviets would allow to slip from their control and the period of independence lasted only twenty-three months. In 1922 the republic was annexed into the Transcaucasian Soviet Socialist Republic until 1936 when it was established as a separate Soviet republic. In 1991, with the collapse of the Soviet Union, Azerbaijan declared independence once again.

Azerbaijan is still disputing the Armenian claim to the southern region known as Nagorno–Karabakh bringing it into conflict with Iran due to Iran's support of Armenia and its opposition to Azerbaijan's pro-western trade agreements. Unlike the predominately Shia Muslim population of Azerbaijan, the majority of the population in Nagorno–Karabakh identify themselves as Armenian Christians and wish to be annexed into Armenia.

Azerbaijan has been most successful in privatization and economic development since the Soviet era although the political road has not been smooth as they have moved toward a western-looking democracy. In addition, their conflicts with Armenia have not been resolved despite United Nations resolutions ordering Armenia to withdraw from and to return Azerbaijani territory.

Armenian, Iranian, and Russian influences can be expected, and are found, in both cuisine and culture making for an exciting cuisine. Albeit meat-based, there are wonderful dishes that can be adapted and enjoyed by vegetarians. There are many meatless dishes but soy meat analogue products can replace meat for a closer approximation of many other dishes one would typically find in Azeri homes and restaurants. The following menu recommendations provide wonderful mix and match options. Any of the entrée suggestions can be paired with an appetizer or a salad or a soup for a very satisfying meal. Sticky, sweet, nut-filled pastries, typical of Middle Eastern cuisines, are favored by Azerbaijani for holidays and festive events. You will find *pakhlava*, *halva*, *shakarbaro*, and *girmapadam* in pastry shops and, trust me, you will want to try every one. Family dinners, however, usually end with fruit.

Caucasus – Azerbaijan

Eggplant and Onions with Yogurt
Kashkeh Badenjan

Baked or Fried and Chilled Eggplant Slices
and Chilled, Roasted Red and Green Bell Peppers

with

Mayonnaise

Nan or other *Tandoori* Bread

Cucumber and Olive Salad
Salat Xijar Zeytun

~

Yellow Split Pea Soup with Meatballs
Kufta Bozbash

Pumpkin Soup with Pomegranate Seeds
Balgabag Shorbasi

Walnut and Rice Soup	Rice Soup with Yogurt
Qoglu Siyig	*Kelekosh*

~

Tossed Vegetable Salad
Salati

~~~~~~~~~~~~~~~~~~~~

Herb Omelet
Kuku

with

Yogurt

Mashed Potato Kebabs
Lyulya Kebab

~~~~~~~~~~

Noodles with Soymeat and Yogurt – Garlic Sauce
Khangal

~~~~~~~~~~

Mixed Grain Pilaf with Fruits and Nuts
Shirin Plov

~~~~~~~~~~~~~~~~~~~~

Fresh or Canned Apricot Halves with Honey   Fresh Cherries
garnished with Fig Preserves

~

Black Tea

AZERBAIJANI EGGPLANT AND ONIONS WITH YOGURT
Kashkeh Badenjan
TPT - 43 minutes

This appetizer was undoubtedly introduced to Azerbaijan by the Persians since it is known by the same name in Azerbaijan as it is known in Iran. It is, however, popular all over Azerbaijan and not just in the southern regions where one might expect a strong Iranian influence. A thick, soured whey product known as kashk is called for but thick, Greek-style yogurt or sour cream can be substituted, if you can not find kashk. Any flatbread makes a good accompaniment but we generally serve it with warm nan and sometimes with toasts.

3 tablespoons *extra virgin* olive oil
1 tablespoon dried mint leaves

1 large onion—*thinly* sliced

1 tablespoon *extra virgin* olive oil
1 medium Asian eggplant—peeled and cubed
2 large garlic cloves—crushed and *finely* chopped

2 tablespoons canned, *crushed* tomatoes *or* tomato purée, if preferred
2 tablespoons thick, Greek-style yogurt *or* YOGURT CRÈME [see index]

1/4 teaspoon ground turmeric
Salt, to taste
Freshly ground black pepper, to taste

1 tablespoon thick, Greek-style yogurt *or* YOGURT CRÈME [see index]

In a skillet set over *LOW* heat, heat the 3 tablespoonfuls olive oil with dried mint leaves until the fragrance becomes pronounced. Remove from heat and strain the oil into a small dish. *Be sure to remove all bits of mint leaves.*

Add 1 tablespoonful of mint-infused onion to the skillet. Set over *MEDIUM* heat. Add *thinly* sliced onion. Sauté until onion is soft and translucent, *being careful not to allow onion to brown.* Remove from heat.

In a non-stick-coated skillet set over *MEDIUM* heat, combine the 1 tablespoon olive oil with the rest of the mint-infused oil. Add eggplant pieces and *finely* chopped garlic. Stir-fry until eggplant is soft—about 10 minutes.

Add tomatoes, 2 tablespoonfuls of yogurt, and about three-quarters of the fried onions. Stir to combine. Cover and allow to cook for about 5 minutes, stirring occasionally. Remove from heat and turn into a mixing bowl. Using a potato masher, mash eggplant into small bits.

Add ground turmeric, salt, and pepper. Mix thoroughly. Spoon out onto a small platter or into a large soup plate. Spread it across the surface.

Garnish with remaining tablespoonful of yogurt and remaining fried onions.

Serve at room temperature. Refrigerate leftovers.

Yields 18 servings
adequate for 6 people

Note: This recipe can be doubled, when required.

1/18 SERVING – PROTEIN = 0.7 g.; FAT = 2.5 g.; CARBOHYDRATE = 2.5 g.; CALORIES = 35; CALORIES FROM FAT = 64%

AZERBAIJANI CUCUMBER AND OLIVE SALAD
Salat Xijar Zeytun
TPT - 13 minutes

Olives have been grown just to the west of the capital Baku since the eighth century and are still an important food to Azerbaijanis. The green olives are harvested and preserved in October; the fully ripe black olives are harvested in November. This wonderfully simple salad often appears on our table because it is a salad that compliments so many dishes.

AZERBAIJANI CUCUMBER AND OLIVE SALAD (cont'd)

1 medium cucumber—peeled and scored*

3 tablespoons pitted, black olives—*thinly* sliced into rounds
3 tablespoons pitted, green olives—*thinly* sliced into rounds
Freshly ground mixed peppercorns—red, black, and white—to taste
1 tablespoon grated *pecorino Romano* cheese

Slice cucumber into thin slices. Arrange on a chilled plate or platter.

Scatter black and green olive slices over the cucumber slices. Grind mixed peppercorns over. Scatter grated cheese over. Refrigerate until ready to serve.

Serve chilled.

Yields 6 servings
adequate for 4 people

Notes: *If the cucumber is organic and unwaxed, there is no need to peel. Simply score and slice.

This recipe can be halved or doubled, when required.

1/6 SERVING – PROTEIN = 0.8 g.; FAT = 1.7 g.; CARBOHYDRATE = 1.7 g.; CALORIES = 43; CALORIES FROM FAT = 36%

There are so many satisfying Azerbaijani soups that it was really impossible to chose. Instead, if you will indulge my enthusiasm, I offer you the next four recipes and sincerely hope you enjoy them as much as we do.

AZERBAIJANI YELLOW SPLIT PEA SOUP WITH MEATBALLS
Kufta Bozbash

TPT - 9 hours and 16 minutes;
8 hours = split pea soaking period

Azerbaijani make a split pea and lamb soup which is simmered for hours. They are also fond of split pea soup with meatballs made from ground lamb meat. The name for the meatballs actually means "gray meatballs" so the commercially-available soy meatballs I buy look just like the lovingly-formed meatballs being made in an Azeri kitchen.

3/4 cup (about 6 ounces) quick-cooking, dry, yellow split peas
2 cups water

1 tablespoon *extra virgin* olive oil
1 small carrot—*thinly* sliced into rounds
1 celery rib—well-scrubbed, trimmed, and *thinly* sliced into half-moon slices
1/4 cup chopped onion

1 quart vegetarian stock, of choice
1 small potato—peeled and diced
2 teaspoons crushed, dried mint
Salt, to taste
Freshly ground black pepper, to taste

1 package (9-ounces) *frozen* vegetarian "meatballs"
1 tablespoon chopped fresh dillweed

Wash and sort split peas, discarding those of poor quality.

In a large saucepan or small kettle, combine dry, yellow split peas and water. Cover and refrigerate for 8 hours, or overnight.

Place saucepan or kettle over *LOW-MEDIUM* heat.

Meanwhile, in a skillet set over *MEDIUM* heat, heat oil. Add carrot and celery slices and chopped onion. Sauté until vegetables begin to soften, *being careful not to allow onion to brown*. Add to kettle with split peas.

Add vegetable stock, diced potato, crushed mint, salt, and pepper. Allow to come to the simmer. Cover, and simmer until peas are tender—about 45 minutes. Stir frequently.

**AZERBAIJANI YELLOW SPLIT PEA SOUP
WITH MEATBALLS** (cont'd)

Add frozen meatless meatballs and chopped dillweed. Continue cooking until meatballs are heated through. Check seasoning. Turn into a heated soup tureen.

Serve into heated soup plates.

Yields 6 servings

Note: This recipe can be halved, when required.

1/6 SERVING – PROTEIN = 15.4 g.; FAT = 4.8 g.; CARBOHYDRATE = 33.3 g.;
CALORIES = 229; CALORIES FROM FAT = 19%

AZERBAIJANI PUMPKIN SOUP WITH POMEGRANATE SEEDS
Balgabag Shorbasi
TPT - 52 minutes

Creamed pumpkin and squash soups are frequent items on autumn and winter menus here in the Northeast. It takes a very good soup to pry creamed soup devotees away from their favorite squash bisque or cream of pumpkin soup but this pumpkin soup from Azerbaijan is a very worthy alternative. Pomegranates and pumpkins appear in our markets at about the same time and their respective flavors greatly compliment each other. You will see that I use canned pumpkin/squash purée because the consistency of the purée is always uniform and not watery.

1 cup vegetarian stock, of choice
2 cups water

1 can (15 ounces) pumpkin—*unsweetened and unseasoned*
1/4 cup dry short grain white rice
1 tablespoon sugar
1/4 teaspoon salt

3 tablespoons butter
1 medium onion—*finely* chopped

3 tablespoons chopped fresh coriander (*cilantro*)
  or parsley, if preferred

Seeds from 1 pomegranate
Sugar, for garnish

In a small kettle set over *MEDIUM* heat, combine vegetable stock and water. Allow to come to the boil.

Add pumpkin purée, rice, sugar, and salt. Reduce heat to *LOW-MEDIUM*. Cover and allow to cook for 30 minutes or until rice is tender.

While rice is cooking, in a skillet set over *LOW-MEDIUM* heat, melt butter. Add onion and sauté until onion is soft and translucent, *being careful not to allow onion to brown*. Remove from heat and set aside until required.

Once rice is tender, add sautéed onion to soup. Turn into a heated soup tureen.

Garnish with chopped fresh coriander (*cilantro*) or parsley.

Serve into heated soup plates. Allow diners to add pomegranate seeds and sugar to their taste. Refrigerate leftovers and reheat over *LOW* heat.

Yields 6 cupfuls

Notes: *Add more water or stock, if necessary to maintain a soup-like liquidity. Azerbaijani prefer a very thick soup, much like a Russian pumpkin porridge. Adjust the consistency to your taste.

This soup freezes well.

When required, this recipe can be doubled.

1/6 SERVING (i. e., per cupful) –
PROTEIN = 2.0 g.; FAT = 6.0 g.; CARBOHYDRATE = 19.0 g.;
CALORIES = 146; CALORIES FROM FAT = 37%

Caucasus–Azerbaijan

AZERBAIJANI WALNUT AND RICE SOUP
Ooglu Siyiq
TPT - 30 minutes

This soup strongly reflects Azerbaijan's Caucasus geography and as with other countries in the region, such as Georgia, one sees the creative and prominent use of walnuts. Although traditionally this is a very thick soup, a porridge, we thin it down a bit and enjoy it as a soup course and garnish it with thick, Greek-style yogurt or sour cream.

5 cups *boiling* water
1 cup dry short grain white rice

1 medium onion—*finely* chopped
1 cup ground *preservative-free* walnuts *or* walnut meal

2 tablespoons CLARIFIED BUTTER *or* GHEE *[see index]*
1/2 teaspoon caraway seeds
1/4 teaspoon salt

6 tablespoons *fat-free* dairy sour cream *or* thick, Greek-style yogurt, if preferred

In a small kettle set over *LOW-MEDIUM* heat, combine *boiling* water and rice. Cover and allow to simmer for about 10 minutes.

Add *finely* chopped onion and ground walnuts. Cover and allow the soup to simmer for about 15 minutes. The nut oil will be floating on the surface when it is done.

Add clarified butter, caraway seeds, and salt. Add more water, if necessary. Heat through and stir to integrate the butter. Turn into a heated soup tureen.

Serve into heated soup plates. Garnish each serving with yogurt or sour cream.

Yields 6 cupfuls

Note: This recipe can be halved or doubled, when required.

1/6 SERVING (i. e., per cupful) –
PROTEIN = 7.1 g.; FAT = 22.0 g.; CARBOHYDRATE = 19.5 g.;
CALORIES = 304; CALORIES FROM FAT = 65%

AZERBAIJANI RICE SOUP WITH YOGURT
Kelekosh
TPT - 48 minutes

In the West, the soup course in a multi-course formal meal is supposed to encourage the appetite. Once again, this soup is lighter than most Azeri soups and works very well if the soup is only one of many courses. I have tasted many yogurt-based soups over the years but this one from Azerbaijan is quite special. The bite of the chopped garlic and the palate-tingling mint make it a very refreshing pleasure.

1 tablespoon safflower *or* sunflower oil
1 medium onion—*finely* chopped

3 cups PLAIN YOGURT *[see index] or*
commercially-available plain yogurt*
1 1/2 tablespoons unbleached white flour

3 cups water
1/2 cup *fat-free* pasteurized eggs (the equivalent of 2 eggs)
1/4 cup *cooked* short grain white rice
2 tablespoons crushed, dried mint leaves
1 large garlic clove—crushed and *very finely* chopped
1/2 teaspoon sugar

Salt, to taste
Freshly ground black pepper, to taste

In a small kettle set over *MEDIUM* heat, heat oil. Add onions and sauté until soft and translucent, *being careful not to allow onions to brown.*

Add yogurt, and flour. Stir until flour is thoroughly integrated.

Gradually stir in water and pasteurized eggs. Add rice, crushed mint, *very finely* chopped garlic, and sugar. Allow to come to the simmer. Reduce heat to *LOW-MEDIUM*. Cook, stirring frequently, until soup has thickened and rice is tender—about 20-25 minutes.

Season with salt and black pepper, to taste. Turn into a heated soup tureen.

AZERBAIJANI RICE SOUP WITH YOGURT (cont'd)

Serve into heated soup plates.

Yields 7 cupfuls

Notes: *Greek-style yogurt is too thick to give this soup the desired texture.

**Refrigerated leftovers will thicken overnight and may need to be thinned with water when reheated.

This recipe can be halved when required.

1/7 SERVING (i. e., per cupful) –
PROTEIN = 7.8 g.; FAT = 3.6 g.; CARBOHYDRATE = 16.2 g.;
CALORIES = 131; CALORIES FROM FAT = 25%

AZERBAIJANI TOSSED VEGETABLE SALAD
Salati
TPT - 9 minutes

Just before the tasteless hot house tomatoes come to market, the pomegranates begin to appear in our markets here in the Northeast so this salad becomes a menu possibility. The small sweet tomatoes, marketed as Campari tomatoes or cocktail tomatoes, are now available year round and these help to extend the season for the exciting combination of tomatoes and pomegranate.

4 cups torn romaine lettuce—well-washed and dried

3 large tomatoes—well-washed and diced
1 small cucumber—peeled, seeded, and diced
2 green bell peppers—well-washed, cored, seeded, and diced
2 large scallions—trimmed, well-rinsed and *finely* chopped

2 tablespoons *extra virgin* olive oil
1 tablespoon pomegranate juice
1 teaspoon freshly squeezed lemon juice, of choice
Salt, to taste
Freshly ground black pepper, to taste

1/4 cup pomegranate seeds

In a salad bowl or on a large platter, scatter romaine lettuce pieces as a base.

In a small bowl, combine diced tomatoes, cucumbers, and green pepper with *finely* chopped scallions. Toss.

In a small bowl, combine oil, pomegranate juice, lemon juice, salt, and black pepper. Using a small wire whisk, beat well. Add to vegetable mixture. Toss. Pour over romaine lettuce.

Sprinkle pomegranate seeds over.

Toss at the table. *Serve at once.*

Yields 6 servings
adequate for 4 people

Note: This recipe can be halved or doubled, when required.

1/6 SERVING –   PROTEIN = 1.2 g.; FAT = 4.0 g.; CARBOHYDRATE = 6.4 g.;
CALORIES = 66; CALORIES FROM FAT = 55%

AZERBAIJANI HERB OMELET
Kuku
TPT - 16 minutes

Kuku are generally prepared as individual omelets. Served at room temperature as an appetizer with yogurt, they are a delicious way to begin a meal. I use the concept to prepare a vegetarian entrée omelet.

AZERBAIJANI HERB OMELET (cont'd)

5 large eggs—beaten
Salt, to taste
Freshly ground black pepper, to taste

2 teaspoons safflower *or* sunflower oil
2 teaspoons CLARIFIED BUTTER or *GHEE* [see index]

1 1/2 cups shredded spinach—well-rinsed and dried
1/4 cup chopped fresh dillweed—well-washed and dried
1/4 cup chopped fresh coriander (*cilantro*)—well-washed and dried
2 scallions—trimmed, well-rinsed, and *thinly* sliced

1/4 cup crumbled *feta* cheese

Plain yogurt

Preheat broiler to about 350 degrees F. Place a large, round, oven-proof serving plate in a warm oven or on a warming tray.

In a small bowl, beat eggs with a fork. Season with salt and pepper. Set aside until required.

In a 9-inch non-stick-coated skillet set over *MEDIUM-LOW* heat, heat the oil and clarified butter until you are able to coat the pan's surface completely.

Add shredded spinach, chopped dillweed, chopped fresh coriander (*cilantro*), and scallion slices. Stir for a minute or two.

Stir in beaten eggs, spreading evenly over pan surface. Cook, *undisturbed*, until set. Wrap pan handle with aluminum foil, if necessary, to protect it from burning. Sprinkle the omelet with the crumbled cheese and place under preheated broiler until *lightly browned*. Be careful not to scorch eggs.

Slide out onto a heated round serving plate.

Cut into wedges. *Serve at once*, with yogurt.

Yields 6 servings
adequate for 4 people

Note: This recipe can be halved and prepared in a 7-8-inch skillet; it can be doubled using a 10-inch skillet.

1/6 SERVING (exclusive of yogurt) –
PROTEIN = 7.3 g.; FAT = 10.3 g.; CARBOHYDRATE = 1.6 g.;
CALORIES = 125; CALORIES FROM FAT = 73%

MASHED POTATO KEBABS
Lyulya Kebab
TPT - 1 hour and 40 minutes

Prior to World War II, my dad ran summer camping trips to Hudson Bay Outpost during which young men learned to leave behind the comforts of civilization and explore their own strengths. Although hunting and fishing were the main sources of food, some staples were packed-in. The taste of a baked potato roasted in the ashes of the fire became a very "big deal" for those campers. When I was young, we baked potatoes in the ashes in our backyard barbecue and it was a treat for us too. Have you ever chopped potatoes into large chunks, fed them onto bamboo skewers, and grilled the potatoes over a charcoal fire or on a grill pan? If you have, then you know that the potato takes rather well to grilling but I bet you never thought of turning mashed potatoes into kebabs as do the Azerbaijani.

4 quarts *boiling* water
4 large all-purpose potatoes—peeled and chopped
2 large garlic cloves—*very finely* chopped

1 tablespoon ground coriander
1 teaspoon salt
1/4 teaspoon ground turmeric
1/4 teaspoon freshly ground black pepper, or to taste

2 tablespoons *extra virgin* olive oil

Prepare a charcoal grill or a grill pan by preheating.

In a kettle set over *MEDIUM* heat, boil potatoes and *very finely* chopped garlic in *boiling* water until potatoes are soft. Drain thoroughly. Using a potato ricer, rice potatoes and garlic into a mixing bowl to avoid lumps that would occur with hand mashing.

Add ground coriander, salt, turmeric, and black pepper. Mix thoroughly. Form the mashed potatoes and garlic into twelve very tightly-packed sausage-shaped logs.* Place in a non-stick skillet set over *MEDIUM* heat.

MASHED POTATO KEBABS (cont'd)

Add olive oil. Brown potato logs until golden brown. Remove from heat.

When cool enough to handle, push a bamboo skewer through each potato kebab.

Grill on a grill pan or over the glowing coals of a charcoal grill until hot and flecked with burned bits. Place on a heated platter.

Serve at once.

Yields 12 servings
adequate for 6 people

Notes: *If the potatoes are not very tightly compacted, they will break apart on the grill.

This recipe can be halved, when required

1/12 SERVING – PROTEIN = 1.0 g.; FAT = 1.9 g.; CARBOHYDRATE = 10.6 g.;
CALORIES = 65; CALORIES FROM FAT = 26%

AZERBAIJANI NOODLES WITH SOYMEAT AND YOGURT – GARLIC SAUCE
Khangal
TPT - 29 minutes

Azerbaijani cooks make and boil squares of dough similar to a noodle product popular among German and Mennonite cooks in the United States. The noodles available as "pot pie" ["bott boi"] squares are used for stews and soups and to cover pot pies, in lieu of pastry. In Azerbaijan the pasta squares become a base for ground meat and a yogurt sauce. I find this recipe, prepared with ground soymeat crumbles, to be a rather different first course and a perfectly adequate luncheon or light supper offering.

AZERI YOGURT – GARLIC SAUCE:
    1 cup PLAIN YOGURT *[see index]* **or commercially-available plain yogurt**
    1 large garlic clove—crushed and *very finely* chopped

2 tablespoons butter
1/2 cup *finely* chopped onion

4 ounces *frozen* vegetarian "ground beef"
Freshly ground mixed peppercorns—black, red, and white—to taste
1/2 teaspoon crushed, dried mint leaves

6 ounces *dry* pot pie squares (*bott boi*)
4 quarts *boiling* water

In a small bowl, combine yogurt and *very finely* chopped garlic. Combine thoroughly. Turn into a sauce dish. Set aside until required.

In a skillet set over *LOW-MEDIUM* heat, melt butter. Add onion and sauté until onion is soft and translucent, *being careful not to allow onion to brown.*

Add soymeat, ground mixed peppercorns, and crumbled mint leaves. Cook, stirring frequently, until hot.

While soymeat–onion mixture is cooking, cook *pasta* squares in *boiling* water according to package directions. Drain thoroughly. Turn onto heated platter. Spoon soymeat mixture over.

Serve at once with prepared yogurt–garlic sauce.

Yields 6 servings
adequate for 4 people

Note: This recipe can be halved or doubled, when required.

1/6 SERVING – PROTEIN = 8.9 g.; FAT = 5.7 g.; CARBOHYDRATE = 25.5 g.;
CALORIES = 193; CALORIES FROM FAT = 27%

Caucasus—Azerbaijan

MIXED GRAIN *PILAF* WITH FRUITS AND NUTS IN THE STYLE OF AZERBAIJAN

Shirin Plov

TPT - 1 hour and 50 minutes;
1 hour = rehydration period

Plov, pilaf, is probably the dish to which Azerbaijani from all over the country would give the nod. However, there will be as many different recipes as there are nods. It is a dish that is always a part of festive meals and those served at family holiday gatherings. Since we prefer a mixture of grains, we choose a commercially-available grain mixture consisting of wild rice, Wehani rice, and long grain brown rice.

3 tablespoons *preservative-free dark* raisins
12 small *preservative-free* dates
12 small dried chestnuts
2 cups *boiling* water

1 cup VEGETABLE STOCK FROM SOUP *[see index]* **or other vegetarian stock of choice**

1/2 cup dry wild rice and rice *pilaf* mixture*

1 tablespoon butter
Freshly ground black pepper, to taste

1 tablespoon slivered *preservative-free* almonds

Notes: *Several mail-order bulk food suppliers market interesting *pilaf* mixtures that are neither seasoned nor salted which work well in this dish. Or, make your own pilaf mixture from grains in your larder.

This recipe can be halved or doubled, when required.

In a small bowl, combine raisins, dates, chestnuts, and *boiling* water. Allow to stand for 1 hour until the fruits and chestnuts are rehydrated. Drain well. Break chestnuts into small pieces. Set aside briefly.

In a saucepan set over *MEDIUM* heat, heat vegetable stock until it boils. *Reduce heat to LOW-MEDIUM.*

Add cooked wild rice and rice pilaf mixture. Stir. Cover and allow the rice to cook for about 30 minutes, or until the liquid has been absorbed.

Add butter and black pepper. Stir to mix. Add rehydrated raisins, dates, and chestnuts. Stir to mix. Allow to continue cooking, stirring frequently, until heated through. Turn onto a heated platter.

Sprinkle slivered almonds over.

Serve at once.

Yields 6 servings
adequate for 4 people

1/6 SERVING – PROTEIN = 2.1 g.; FAT = 3.2 g.; CARBOHYDRATE = 34.7 g.;
CALORIES = 165; CALORIES FROM FAT = 17%

Georgia

I was so disappointed when our plans to visit Tilbilsi corresponded to a period of enormous political unrest, a Soviet crackdown, and the automatic denial of visa applications by writers. The Caucasus has been an eternal fascination for me. With the collapse of the Soviet Republic structure and the subsequent changes which allowed for Georgian independence in 1991, I again find myself thinking about visiting Georgia, meeting these strong, independent people, who do not call themselves Georgians but *Kartvelebi*, and enjoying their unique cuisine.

The present Republic of Georgia, whose monarchy adopted Christianity in the fourth century, can trace it origins back to the ancient kingdoms of Iberia and Colchis, the location of the mythological Golden Fleece sought by Jason and the Argonauts in *Argonautica*. It is interesting to note that sheep's fleeces were used to sift gold dust from rivers in Colchis and this practice may well have been known by the third century BC head librarian at the Library of Alexandria Apollonius of Rhodes, the Hellenistic Egyptian author of the epic poem. This area of the Caucasus has been inhabited since the early Stone Age with archaeological evidence confirming political organization and advanced metallurgy dating back to at least the seventh century BC.

Here live a unique people with a unique position in Western Europe since they can not be classified as members of the main ethnic categories of Europe and Asia nor does their language, one of the oldest living languages on earth with its own distinct alphabet, show Indo-European, Turkic, or Semitic origins. A crossroads of the advances and retreats of the Persian, Byzantine, Greek, and Roman Empires, Georgia is a mixture of cultural influences.

In the twelfth and thirteenth centuries Georgia experienced a period often referred to as the Georgian Renaissance during the reign of David the Builder and Queen Tamar. This chivalric Golden Age has left us a body of philosophic writings, romantic poetry and literature, monasteries, and cathedrals. The Golden Age came to an end as the Black Death decimated the population in 1366. In 1386 the Mongols under Tamerlane saw opportunity and invaded Georgia eight times eventually subjugating the population. The Peace of Amasia in 1555 between the Ottoman Turks and Safarid Persians left Georgia in a divided and unsettled position with Turkish influence in the west and Persian (Iranian) influence in the east. Georgia became a part of the Russian Empire when East Georgia was annexed in 1801 under Czar Paul I in violation of the 1783 treaty. Briefly independent following the Russian Revolution in 1917 when it joined with Azerbaijan and Armenia to form an anti-Bolshevik union known as the Transcausian Federation, it was incorporated into the Soviet Union in 1922, following an internal communist revolution. The transformation of Georgia from an agrarian society to a predominately urban, industrial society under the Soviets aided its economic development as it again emerged as an independent state after the fall of the Soviet Union. Although today a representative democracy, its conflicts with Russia are not at an end. In August 2008 a dispute arose over the provinces known as Albkhazia and South Ossetia, which Russia claimed and in which Russia began to establish a military presence. Unresolved, the Georgian government has declared these two provinces to be "Russian-occupied territories." Maybe I am just not meant to visit *Sarkartvelo*, not meant to meet *Kartvelebi* in the beautiful land that they believe God was saving for himself.

Caucasus–Georgia

If there is a theme to this menu, it is to introduce the many wonderful ways walnuts enter the Georgian cuisine.

Chilled Baby Vegetables with Walnut and Garlic Sauce
Postneuli Nigozit Satsebela

~

Chilled Yogurt Soup with Rice
Matsonis Schechamandi

Hearty Tomato Winter Soup with Walnuts and *Vermicelli*
Bostneulis Kharcho

Georgian Herbed Seasoning Mixture
Khmeli - Suneli

~

Bean Salad with Walnuts
Salat iz Fasoli's Orekhami

~~~~~~~~~~~~~~~~~~~~~

Cauliflower and Onion Omelet
Chirbuli

Grits with Cheese
Elardzhi

Beets with Tart Cherry Sauce and Fresh Herbs
Charkhlis Chogi

or

Fresh Spinach and Beet Salad with Traditional Yogurt Dressing
Ispanakhi Charklis Matsunit

~~~~~~~~~~~~~~~~~~~~~

Peaches (fresh when in season)   Small Cakes with **Peach Jam**

Honey-Sweetened Walnuts
Gozinaki

Caucasus–Georgia

CHILLED BABY VEGETABLES
WITH GEORGIAN WALNUT AND GARLIC SAUCE
Postneuli Nigvzit Satsebela

TPT - 54 minutes;
30 minutes = flavor development period for sauce

When we were in Rome in late October, the restaurant that we frequented for a week always had steamed, chilled vegetables ready for lunch, which we enjoyed with a ball of fresh mozzarella, bread, and wine. The Georgians do the same thing except that they are more likely to serve the vegetables with this walnut and garlic sauce, yogurt, and bread. Baby artichokes, eggplants, patty-pan squashes, and zucchini are available from local farms and greenhouses in season and imported from South America in winter. We combine one or more of these tiny darlings with long green beans, Brussels sprouts, and mushrooms, cook and refrigerate them early in the day, and leisurely prepare the sauce after we come in from a long day of gardening. Sometime we have them with mozzarella and sometimes we have them with yogurt.

Walnut sauces are probably the most well-known of the sauces used in Georgia. They can be tweaked and varied to compliment meat, fish, and vegetables. These beautiful walnut sauces not only add complex flavoring to a dish, the amino acids they contain add to the day's amino acid total, contributing to the protein complementation process to provide the body with the eight essential protein amino acid building blocks. In addition, with higher levels of omega 3 fatty acids when compared to other nuts, walnuts play a very positive roll in lowering LDL cholesterol.

GEORGIAN WALNUT AND GARLIC SAUCE:
  1 tablespoon *warm* water
  1/2 teaspoon saffron threads

  1 cup VEGETARIAN WHITE STOCK
    [see index]

  3/4 cup *preservative-free* walnut pieces
  2 large garlic cloves
  1/4 teaspoon ground mixed peppercorns
    —red, white, and black—or to taste*
  3 tablespoons fresh parsley leaves
  Pinch coarse (kosher) salt, or more to taste

  1/2 teaspoon ground coriander
  1/4 teaspoon HOMEMADE PAPRIKA *[see index]* or commercially-available
    Hungarian sweet paprika
  1/4 ground fenugreek**

  1 tablespoon red wine vinegar

About 2 pounds baby vegetables—crisp-cooked, whole, and chilled*

Pour the *warm* water into a marble mortar. Add saffron threads. Using a pestle, grind saffron.

In a saucepan set over *LOW-MEDIUM* heat, combine ground saffron and stock. Bring to the gentle simmer.

Meanwhile, in the work bowl of the food processor fitted with steel knife, combine walnut pieces, garlic cloves, ground mixed peppercorns, fresh parsley, and salt. Process until thoroughly pulverized, scraping down the sides of the work bowl when required. Add a few tablespoonfuls of vegetable stock, if necessary to achieve a smooth paste.

Add processed walnut mixture to ingredients in saucepan and cook for about 5 minutes. *Do not allow to boil.*

Add ground coriander, paprika, and ground fenugreek. Cook for an additional 5 minutes. *Do not allow to boil.* Remove from heat. Stir in red wine vinegar. Refrigerate for at least 30 minutes to allow flavors to develop and *to allow sauce to cool to room temperature.*

When ready to serve, arrange crisp-cooked, whole, baby vegetables attractively on a platter. Turn chilled GEORGIAN WALNUT AND GARLIC SAUCE (*Nigvzit Satsebela*) into a sauceboat or small serving bowl. Pass separately to accommodate individual tastes.

Yields 6 servings
adequate for 4 people

Notes: *Minced hot red or green pepper may be substituted, if appreciated. A dash or two of *jalapeño* sauce might also be to your liking.

**Ground fenugreek is best known perhaps as an ingredient in Southern Indian spice mixtures used for curries. This spice, cultivated in Asia and the Middle East for centuries, is an indispensable ingredient in many Middle Eastern and North African dishes. Georgia, on the ancient spice route from Asia, has also incorporated this spice into their sauces and lamb dishes for centuries.

VOLUME I - 612

CHILLED BABY VEGETABLES WITH
GEORGIAN WALNUT AND GARLIC SAUCE (cont'd)

***Steamed new potatoes in their jackets, pared or scraped Belgian baby or finger carrots, asparagus, green or yellow wax beans, cauliflower or broccoli florets, tiny beets (peeled after steaming or use jarred baby beets), tiny Brussels sprouts, whole *crimini* mushrooms, whole, tiny yellow squash or zucchini, baby patty-pan squashes, and baby artichokes are all good choices for this dish.

This recipe may be halved or doubled, when required.

Although this recipe is usually served as a cold dish, freshly steamed vegetables can be just as easily served with a warmed sauce, making it a very interesting main course for a light supper menu.

This GEORGIAN WALNUT AND GARLIC SAUCE (*Nigvzit Satsebela*) is also an excellent choice for dressing roasted vegetables and as a dip for *crudités*.

1/6 SERVING – PROTEIN = 5.3 g.; FAT = 13.1 g.; CARBOHYDRATE = 13.4 g.;
CALORIES = 199; CALORIES FROM FAT = 59%

CHILLED GEORGIAN YOGURT SOUP WITH RICE
Matsunis Schechamandi

TPT - 1 hour and 20 minutes;
1 hour = chilling period

Georgians consume rich, thick yogurt on a daily basis. Despite the depictions in the popular commercials connecting the longevity of Georgians to their consumption of a popular brand of yogurt, their yogurt does not come from the dairy department of grocery stores in little plastic cups. Made in most homes every few days from either cow's milk or water buffalo milk, a crock of the fresh, slightly sour local yogurt can be found on Georgia's celebrated supra table or at any family dinner. This soup can be served warm or chilled and is, for us, a much-loved summer supper dish served with a shredded carrot or beet salad. It is the first recipe that pops into my mind when we have rice leftover from the night before.

2 cups **PLAIN YOGURT** *[see index]* or
commercially-available plain yogurt
1 cup *cold* water
Pinch salt

6 tablespoons *chilled, cooked*, long grain
brown rice

1 tablespoon butter
1 tablespoon **GARLIC OIL** *[see index]*
1 small-medium onion—*finely* chopped

3 tablespoons *finely* chopped fresh coriander
(cilantro)
2 tablespoons *finely* chopped fresh dillweed

In a mixing bowl, combine yogurt, cold water, and salt. Using a wire whisk, mix well.

Add *chilled* rice. Stir with a wooden spoon. Set aside briefly.

In a skillet set over *MEDIUM* heat, combine butter and garlic oil. Add *finely* chopped onion and sauté until onion is soft and translucent, being careful not to allow onion to brown. Remove from heat and allow to cool for about 10 minutes.* Add to yogurt–rice mixture.

Add *finely* chopped fresh coriander (*cilantro*) and dillweed to yogurt mixture. Refrigerate for at least 1 hour.

Serve chilled.

Yields 8 servings
adequate for 6 people

Notes: *If you prefer to serve this soup hot, add the sautéed onion to the yogurt mixture. Turn into a saucepan set over *LOW-MEDIUM* heat and allow the soup to heat through. *Do not allow it to boil.* Add the fresh herbs just before serving.

Some people prefer to add mint to this soup; I prefer to season it with dillweed.

This recipe can be halved or doubled, when required.

CHILLED GEORGIAN YOGURT SOUP WITH RICE (cont'd)

1/8 SERVING – PROTEIN = 3.4 g.; FAT = 3.8 g.; CARBOHYDRATE = 7.0 g.;
CALORIES = 76; CALORIES FROM FAT = 45%

HEARTY GEORGIAN TOMATO WINTER SOUP WITH WALNUTS AND *VERMICELLI*
Bostneulis Kharcho

TPT - 56 minutes

This soup is often referred to as a vegetarian version of "kharcho," a popular Georgian beef soup, an attribution to which I do not subscribe since the only three similarities are that it is a soup and it contains fresh herbs and garlic. The garlicky tomato base with fresh herbs, onions, and walnuts is quintessentially Georgian but then you stumble on vermicelli and the question arises, "Vermicelli?" The traditional addition of pasta to this soup, and to many Georgian dishes, is said to be a Turkish influenced addition brought to the Caucuses by the armies of the Ottoman Empire in the late 1500s.

2 large garlic cloves—*very finely* **chopped**
1 1/2 teaspoons GEORGIAN HERBED SEASONING MIX (Khmeli-Suneli) [see recipe which follows]

1 cup chopped, *preservative-free* walnuts

2 tablespoons butter
2 medium onions—*finely* **chopped**

1 can (28 ounces) diced tomatoes packed in tomato sauce—**drained**
5 cups water
1 ounce *vermicelli*—broken into pieces to yield about 3/4 cup
1 large bay leaf—broken in half and secured in a tea ball

3 tablespoons chopped parsley
3 tablespoons chopped fresh coriander (*cilantro*)

In a marble mortar, combine *very finely* chopped garlic and spice mix. Using a pestle, grind the herbs, spices, and garlic to a paste. Set aside until required.

Using a SPICE and COFFEE GRINDER, grind walnut meats to a fine consistency. *Be careful not to over-grind or walnut oil will be released and walnut butter will form.* Set aside until required.

MEDIUM heat, melt butter. Add *finely* chopped onion and sauté until onion is soft and translucent, *being careful not to allow onion to brown.*

Add the prepared spiced garlic paste, *finely* chopped walnuts, drained, *diced* tomatoes, water, *vermicelli* pieces, and the bay leaf. Allow to come to the simmer. *Reduce heat to LOW-MEDIUM*, cover, and simmer for about 20 minutes. Stir occasionally. Remove and discard bay leaf pieces.

Add chopped parsley and fresh coriander (*cilantro*). Stir to integrate. Cook uncovered for an additional 5-10 minutes. Turn into a heated soup tureen.

Serve into heated soup plates.

Yields about 10 cupfuls

Notes: *An Italian *mesa-luna* is a good tool to use to chop the walnuts. It does take a bit of effort and time but the consistency is more easily controlled.

This recipe can be halved, when required, but since I have successfully frozen it, I generally make the entire recipe.

1/6 SERVING – PROTEIN = 4.7 g.; FAT = 12.8 g.; CARBOHYDRATE = 13.2 g.;
CALORIES = 195; CALORIES FROM FAT = 59%

Caucasus–Georgia

GEORGIAN HERBED SEASONING MIXTURE
Khmeli - Suneli

TPT - 3 minutes

There is a taste to Georgian dishes, especially salads, that always seemed hard for me to capture. A bean salad with walnuts and garlic would taste good, but not great, until I started to explore the seasoning more closely. This mixture is great for soups and stews and simple vegetable dishes too. Mixed with a really good olive oil, it is wonderful when spread on a slice of a good country loaf of bread.

2 teaspoons crushed, dried basil
2 teaspoons ground coriander seed
2 teaspoons crushed, dried dillweed
2 teaspoons dried marjoram
2 teaspoons dried summer savory
1 teaspoon crushed, dried *Calendula* petals
1 teaspoon crushed, dried fenugreek
1 teaspoon crushed, dried mint
1 teaspoon crushed, dried parsley
1/2 teaspoon freshly ground black pepper
1 large bay leaf—crushed

In a SPICE and COFFEE GRINDER, or in a mortar, combine all ingredients. Grind herbs to a uniform mixture.

Turn into a small jelly or spice jar.* Cover tightly and shake to mix thoroughly. Store in a cool, dark place.

Notes: *Choose a small jar because the smaller the jar, the less air will come in contact with the herbs, and the longer the mix will keep its flavor.

This recipe can be halved and that is often a good idea since the flavor dissipates considerably due to the release of the volatile oils with crushing. It is advisable to replace the seasoning combination after about 3 months.

Yields about 12 teaspoonfuls

FOOD VALUES for such herb mixtures are almost negligible.

GEORGIAN BEAN SALAD WITH WALNUTS
Salat iz Fasoli s Orekhami

TPT - 12 hours and 15 minutes;
      30 minutes = flavor development period;
      8 hours = overnight bean soaking period*

Georgians make good use of filling and nutritious legumes; their larders are economically stocked for the winter. Amazingly each Georgian soup, stew, or salad, and there are many, is uniquely seasoned. When I decide that a bean salad is appropriate, the first cuisine I visit is the incredible cuisine of Georgia because I rarely need to adventure further.

1 cup dry cranberry *or* Roman beans
3 cups water

3 cups water

1 tablespoon safflower *or* sunflower oil

1/2 cup chopped, *preservative-free* walnuts
2 garlic cloves—*finely* chopped
1/2 teaspoon dried tarragon—crushed

2 tablespoons red wine vinegar

1 medium Italian red onion—*finely* chopped
Freshly ground black pepper, to taste

1/2 cup chopped, fresh dillweed**

Rinse dry beans in several changes of water. Remove and discard any of poor quality. Place in a bowl with the 3 cupfuls water and soak overnight in the refrigerator.*

In the morning, drain beans and place in a large saucepan with 3 cupfuls water. Bring to the boil over *MEDIUM-HIGH* heat. When the water boils, reduce heat to *LOW*, cover tightly, and allow to simmer for about 2 1/2 hours, or until beans are tender, but *not soft*. Drain thoroughly and place in a mixing bowl.

While still warm, add oil to beans. Toss well to coat beans with oil.

VOLUME I - 615

GEORGIAN BEAN SALAD WITH WALNUTS (cont'd)

In a mortar, combine chopped walnuts, *finely* chopped garlic, and crushed tarragon. Using a pestle, grind to form a paste. Add vinegar to walnut paste. Stir to combine well. Add paste to beans. Toss well.

Add *finely* chopped onion and black pepper. Toss to combine.

Refrigerate for at least 30 minutes, or even overnight, to allow flavors to marry.

Just before serving, add dillweed and toss gently to combine.

Yields 8 servings
adequate for 4-6 people

Notes: *If soaking overnight is inconvenient, there is an alternative method. Put beans and water into a saucepan. Bring to the boil over *MEDIUM-HIGH* heat, reduce heat, and simmer for 5 minutes. Cover tightly and allow to stand at room temperature for 2 hours before proceeding with cooking as if beans had been soaked overnight.

**If preferred, chopped fresh *coriander* (*cilantro*) leaves can be used instead of dillweed in this salad.

This recipe may be halved or doubled, when required.

1/8 SERVING – PROTEIN = 6.9 g.; FAT = 8.4 g.; CARBOHYDRATE = 17.2 g.;
CALORIES = 176; CALORIES FROM FAT = 43%

GEORGIAN CAULIFLOWER AND ONION OMELET
Chirbuli

TPT - 18 minutes

When we visited the former Soviet Union in the winter, we found the use of sprouting onions as a fresh substitute for scallions fascinating. Ever after I have harvested those green tips for omelets in the winter when chives are unavailable and scallions are not in my vegetable drawer. Add these to this omelet, if you have any "growing onions" in your onion bin.

4 large eggs
1/4 cup water
Freshly ground black pepper, to taste
2 tablespoons chopped fresh dillweed
2 tablespoons chopped fresh parsley

1 tablespoon butter
1/2 cup *finely* chopped onion
2 cups *tiny fresh* cauliflower florets

Fat-free **dairy sour cream, for garnish**

In a mixing bowl, using a wire whisk, beat eggs and water thoroughly. Add black pepper, to taste, chopped dillweed and chopped parsley. Again, mix well. Set aside briefly.

In a 9-inch non-stick-coated skillet, set over *LOW-MEDIUM* heat, heat butter. Add chopped onion and cauliflower florets. Sauté until onions are soft and translucent, *being careful not to allow onions to brown*.

Preheat oven to 350 degrees F.

Stir beaten eggs into vegetables in skillet, spreading evenly over pan surface. Cook, *undisturbed*, until set. Wrap pan handle with aluminum foil, if necessary to protect it from burning. Place in preheated oven until eggs are set—about 5 minutes. Slide out onto a heated round serving platter. Cut into five wedges.

Serve at once, with sour cream.

Yields 5 servings
adequate for 3 people

Notes: *Four eggs make a thin omelet, quite adequate for three people. This is easily increased proportionately as needed using the same 9-inch or a 10-inch skillet although it will require a longer cooking period and produce a thicker omelet.

**We use a non-stick-coated skillet which we further coat with a non-stick lecithin spray coating to facilitate the release of the omelet for serving.

1/5 SERVING (without sour cream) –
PROTEIN = 6.1 g.; FAT = 6.9 g.; CARBOHYDRATE = 3.1 g.;
CALORIES = 97; CALORIES FROM FAT = 64%

GEORGIAN GRITS WITH CHEESE
Elardzhi

TPT - about 13 minutes

"Gomi," which is simply cooked coarse-ground corn meal grits, is a mainstay of the Georgian cuisine and is, in effect, served as a bread. With cheese added to the cooked grits, this simple peasant dish becomes something very special. Children always love it.

3 cups bottled water *or* refrigerated water*
3/4 cup quick-cooking *white* hominy grits

3/4 cup (about 3 ounces) shredded *low-moisture, part-skimmed milk mozzarella* cheese
1 tablespoon butter—*softened to room temperature*

Bring the water to the boil in a saucepan. Add grits, *being careful not to allow water to stop boiling.* Continue to boil for 1 minute, *stirring constantly.* Reduce heat to *MEDIUM-LOW* and cook for an additional 4 minutes, or until thickened.

Blend the shredded cheese with the *softened* butter. Using a rubber spatula, fold this mixture thoroughly into the cooked grits. Stir until cheese melts.

Turn out onto a platter or onto a marble cheese board and allow to cool slightly. Using a spatula, slice to serve as a "bread."

Notes: *Since the chlorine in tap water destroys the B-vitamin thiamin in grains, it is advisable to cook grains in either bottled water or water that has been refrigerated uncovered for at least 24 hours.

This recipe is easily halved or doubled, when required.

Yields 6 servings
adequate for 3-4 people

1/6 SERVING – PROTEIN = 5.5 g.; FAT = 5.8 g.; CARBOHYDRATE = 15.1 g.;
CALORIES = 120; CALORIES FROM FAT = 44%

GEORGIAN BEETS WITH TART CHERRY SAUCE AND FRESH HERBS
Charkhlis Chogi

TPT - 53 minutes

Jars of both sweet and sour cherries stood side by side in my grandmother's fruit cellar. I would lift the newspaper insulation and read the labels to be sure that I brought the right jar upstairs. Sour cherries, picked by grandchildren from the tree in Grandma and Grandpa's backyard and canned each summer by Grandma, were designated only for pies and küchens, as far as I remember. Georgians use Cornelian cherries, which, to my knowledge, are not available in the United States. However, I can sour cherries each year, during the very brief period when they can be found at our local farmers' market. Since these are canned in a light syrup, the sweet and sour taste of the cherry sauce is enhanced which plays beautifully against the sweetness of the beets and the tang of the onions.

3 quarts *boiling* water
3-4 large, fresh beets (about 2 pounds)—well-scrubbed, with roots intact and 2 inches of leaf stem attached*

1 tablespoon butter
1 large onion—*finely* **chopped**

1 1/2 cups canned tart or sour cherries—drained, but liquid reserved**

1/4 cup *finely* chopped fresh parsley
1/4 cup *finely* chopped fresh dillweed

GEORGIAN BEETS WITH TART CHERRY SAUCE AND FRESH HERBS (cont'd)

In a deep saucepan, cook the beets in *boiling* water until tender—about 45 minutes. Drain. Rinse in *cold* water until it can be handled. Cut off root end and stem end. Slip off skin and cut into large round slices. Place beets in a shallow serving bowl. Keep warm on a warming tray or in a warm oven until ready to serve.

In a skillet set over *MEDIUM* heat, melt butter. Add *finely* chopped onion and sauté until onion is soft and translucent, *being careful not to allow onions to brown.*

Using a FOOD MILL or a sieve set over a saucepan, force cherries through. Discard residue. Set saucepan over *LOW-MEDIUM* heat. If the sauce needs to be thinned a bit, use the reserved canning syrup.

Assemble to serve by spooning sautéed onion over warm beets in a heated serving bowl. Then, spoon cherry sauce over the onions. Scatter *finely* chopped parsley and dillweed over.

Serve at once.

Yields 6 servings
adequate for 4 people

Notes: *Canned beets can be substituted, if necessary, but the taste of fresh beets is superior.

**Dried Morello cherries are available from the mail order firm in the northwestern United States. Their tart cherries are very much like the cherries available in Georgia. If I have them on hand, I soak the cherries and use them in this recipe.

This recipe can be halved or doubled, when required.

1/6 SERVING – PROTEIN = 1.4 g.; FAT = 2.1 g.; CARBOHYDRATE = 9.5 g.;
CALORIES = 60; CALORIES FROM FAT = 32%

GEORGIAN FRESH SPINACH AND BEET SALAD WITH TRADITIONAL YOGURT DRESSING
Ispanakhi Charklis Matsvnit
TPT - 12 minutes

Although the simple spinach and yogurt salad, ispanakhi matsvnit, a cold, cooked spinach dish, is more generally eaten in the Georgian home, salads such as this are becoming increasingly popular and are often found in restaurants catering to European and American travelers. In Georgia this salad would be dressed with the yogurt dressing before being served.

1/4 cup fresh coriander *(cilantro)* leaves—*finely* chopped
1 garlic clove—*finely* chopped
1/4 teaspoon salt
Pinch sugar

1 cup PLAIN YOGURT *[see index]* or commercially-available plain yogurt

3/4 pound fresh spinach—well-washed, hard stems removed, torn into bite-sized pieces, and well-dried*
1 jar (1 pound) whole baby beets—well-drained and quartered
1 small onion—sliced into rings
Freshly ground black pepper, to taste

2 hard-cooked eggs—cut into wedges—for garnish
8 large, pitted, ripe, black olives—slivered—for garnish
2 tablespoons *finely* chopped, *preservative-free* walnuts, for garnish, if desired

In a mortar, combine *finely* chopped coriander *(cilantro)* leaves and garlic, salt, and sugar. Using a pestle, pound and grind the mixture to a paste. Add this paste to the yogurt and stir to combine well. Set aside until required.

In a salad bowl, combine well-dried spinach pieces, beet pieces, and onion rings. Toss. Season with black pepper, to taste.

GEORGIAN FRESH SPINACH AND BEET SALAD WITH TRADITIONAL YOGURT DRESSING (cont'd)

Garnish with hard-cooked egg wedges, black olive slivers, and chopped walnuts, if desired, before serving. Pass yogurt dressing to accommodate individual tastes.

Yields 8 servings
adequate for 4-6 people

Notes: *Either pat the spinach leaves dry or use a salad spinner to remove excess moisture.

This recipe may be halved or doubled, when required.

1/8 SERVING (with walnut garnish) –
PROTEIN = 6.1 g.; FAT = 5.0 g.; CARBOHYDRATE = 8.7 g.;
CALORIES = 102; CALORIES FROM FAT = 44%

PEACH JAM

TPT - 25 hours and 3 minutes;
24 hours = cooling period

When we lived on Long Island, we drove Out East to the Davis Peach Farm every August and chose just the right, sweet, locally-grown freestone peaches for canning and for making this jam, a recipe I have used since the mid-1960s. It was and is a must for our winter larder. There really is nothing like the taste of summer peaches spread on a slice of toast as the snow falls.

4 cups *finely* chopped, fresh, ripe peaches—about 3 pounds
1/4 cup freshly squeezed lemon juice
1 teaspoon butter*
7 1/2 cups sugar

1 pouch (3 ounces) liquid pectin

Sterilize nine 1/2-pint canning jars. Also sterilize lids and rings for jars.

In a large, non-aluminum kettle, combine *finely* chopped peaches, lemon juice, and butter. Stir in sugar. Place over *MEDIUM-HIGH* heat and bring to a *full boil—a boil which can not be stirred down.*

While stirring with a metal spoon, add fruit pectin. Continue stirring constantly while allowing mixture to return to the boil. *Boil for 1 minute.* Immediately, remove from heat. Stir and skim off all foam.

Ladle into nine hot, sterilized 1/2-pint canning jars. Carefully wipe lips of jars. Seal with hot, sterilized lids and rings. Process in hot-water-bath canner for 10 minutes, *timing from the moment the water reaches a full rolling boil.* Remove to surface covered with thick towels or newspapers. Allow to cool for 24 hours *undisturbed.* Check to be sure jars are sealed before labeling and storing in a dark, cool, dry place.** Loosen or remove rings before storing.

Yields nine 1/2-pint jarfuls

Notes: *The addition of butter prevents a foam or scum from forming at the surface. The butter can be omitted but, if omitted, it is recommended that the surface be skimmed with a metal spoon before pouring into jars.

**Any jars that do not seal can be stored in the refrigerator for about one month or resealed using a *new lid.*

1/144 SERVING (i. e., per tablespoonful) –
PROTEIN = 0.3 g.; FAT = 0.03 g.; CARBOHYDRATE = 12.3 g.;
CALORIES = 45; CALORIES FROM FAT = <1%

HONEY-SWEETENED WALNUTS
Gozinaki

TPT - 2 hours and 15 minutes;
2 hours = drying period

Walnuts are much-loved in Georgia and those who have visited often comment on the sweet nuts that accompany fresh fruit desserts. The result of the simple honey caramelizing in this recipe can lead to an addiction of serious proportions.

1/4 cup wildflower honey

2 cups *preservative-free* **walnut halves**—*lightly toasted*

Prepare a large plate or platter by lightly rubbing with vegetable oil.

In a non-stick-coated skillet set over *LOW-MEDIUM* heat, heat honey until it just begins to bubble.

Add *toasted* walnut halves. Stir until walnuts are coated with the thickening honey—about 8 minutes. *Stir and turn often to prevent burning.* Remove from heat. Spread walnuts out on the oil-treated plate or platter, being sure that they do not touch. Allow to cool in a cool, dry kitchen for about 2 hours. *They should no longer be sticky.* Transfer to a serving dish or plate.

Yields 2 cupfuls

Note: This recipe can be halved, when required.

1/16 SERVING (about 2 tablespoonfuls) –
PROTEIN = 1.6 g.; FAT = 6.5 g.; CARBOHYDRATE = 5.7 g.;
CALORIES = 86; CALORIES FROM FAT = 68%

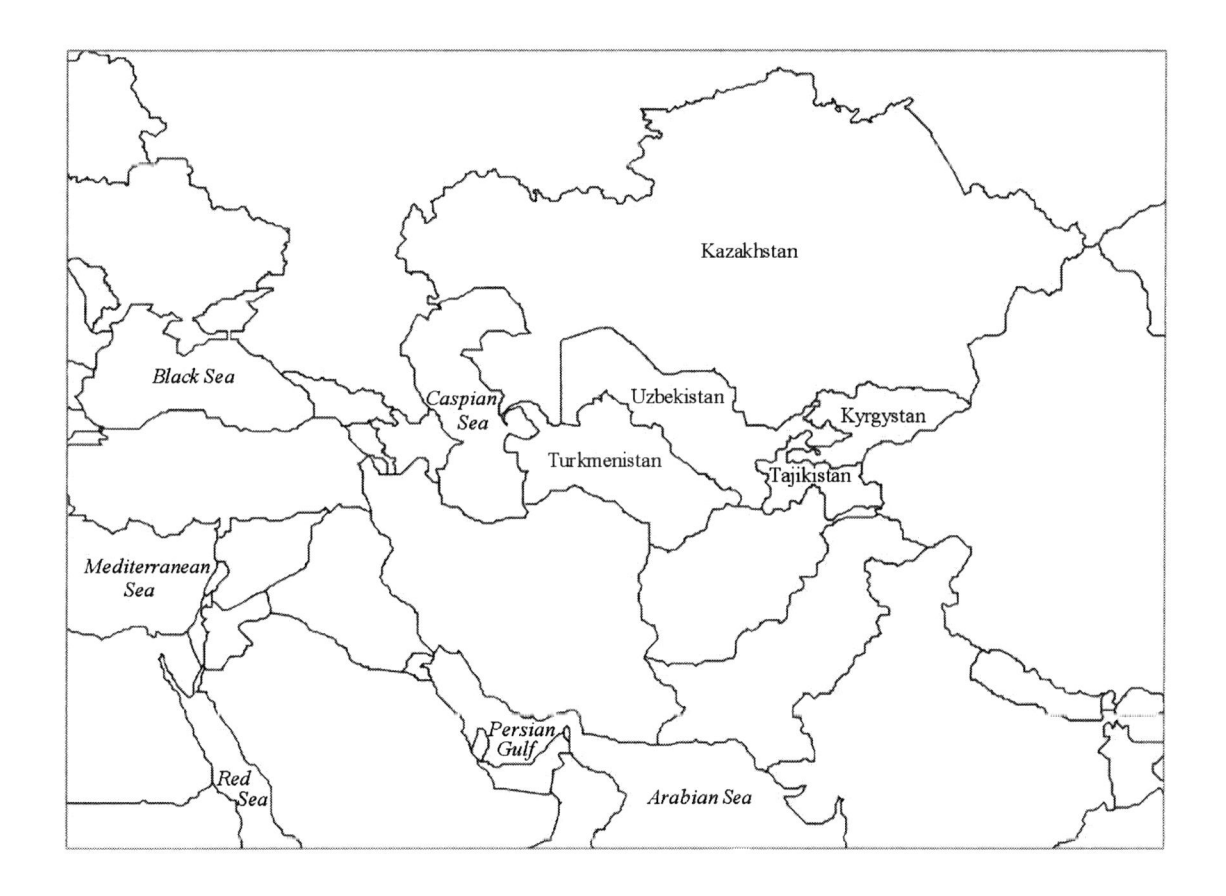

Central Asia

Central Asia

Kazakhstan

Kyrgyzstan

Tajikistan

Turkmenistan

Uzbekistan

Central Asia

Central Asia was defined by the geographer Alexander von Humboldt in 1843. Once called Turkistan, Central Asia has become a collective designation for a number of nations, new and old that share customs, food, and through which the Silk Road ran. Uzbekistan, Tajikistan, Turkmenistan, and Kyrgyzstan, the southern Soviet republics which became independent after the collapse of the Soviet Union, together with Kazakhstan and Xinjiang, China, are generally accepted to comprise Central Asia. The Turks migrated and settled in this region and during the period prior to the spread of Islam the sedentary population was mostly of Persian origin so it is not remarkable that some social historians try to expand the concept of Central Asia to include those nations and parts of nations that share language or religious roots such as the Caucasus, Turkey, Azerbaijan, and even parts of Siberia. Others include Mongolia, Iran, Afghanistan, northern India, all or part of Pakistan, and even Tibet. The most extreme definition, in my view, is that laid down by UNESCO that used climate as a basis for the defining of Central Asia.

The countries of Central Asia sit at the crossroads of historic trade routes that easily allowed for the movement of aggressive adversaries. The Huns, Mongols, and, later, the Russians pushed down from the North into Central Asia; the Chinese pushed from the East. The desire for influence in this region has continued for centuries. Alexander the Great, India under the British, and Persia, and now Iran, all have competed for influence. Today the United States and other western powers, seek to counteract the continued influence of Russia in the post Cold War period and that of Iran in an era when fossil fuel reserves often govern political diplomacy.

The influence of Persia on religion and culture and the contributions of the Mongols can not be denied but many came and went, visited and stayed, conquered and ruled along this route between west and east. The Uighurs and Dungans, who fled the northwest province of China, Xinjiang, in the late nineteenth century brought many culinary influences including the use of noodles in soups, common to these cuisines. Noodle dishes and hot peppers, brought by the Chinese who relocated, are especially evident in the cuisines of the Uzbeks, the Kazaks, and that of the Kyrgyz. The influence of Koreans, who were settled in Uzbekistan during the Stalin era, can be seen also in the noodle dishes, specifically those made from sweetpotatoes, and in the vegetable salads, now so much a part of the cuisine.

Influenced by the Greeks and the Chinese, the people of this region view foods in terms of the ancient concept of humors. Nutrition is medicinal; foods are either *sardi* (hot) or *garmi* (cold). Spices are also viewed with an eye to their influence on the health of the body. Although the use of spices is more pronounced in the eastern part of the region, spicing to a greater or lesser degree is part of an overall view of the medicinal importance of food.

Hospitality to family and friends over the first course is traditional here as it is throughout Eurasia. All manner of delights are presented from breads and cheese to sweets. This is usually followed by a soup and then a variety of dishes appear. The variety which is presented below is a collection of meatless dishes from which to choose, some of which are specific to certain nations and other which can be found in one form or another throughout the region. These are followed by sweet dishes and tea, always tea.

Central Asia

Yogurt *Katyk*   or   Clotted Cream
with Bread

Dried Fruits including Dried Melon – Turkmenistan

Mixed Nuts

Smoked *Mozzarella* Cheese – Turkmenistan
Peynir

Sweets including *Halwa*

~

Noodle Soup with Kidney Beans – Tajikistan and Uzbekistan / Dungan
Ugra

~

Red Onion Salad – Uzbekistan   **Pickled Eggplant with Dill** – Turkmenistan
Piez Salati

Carrot Slaw – Kazakhstan   **Potato Salad and Mayonnaise** – Turkmenistan
Kartofelnyi Salat

~~~~~~~~~~~~~~~~~~~~

Vegetable Stew – Uzbekistan
Dimlama

Brown Rice – Garlic *Pilaf* – Tajikistan and Uzbekistan
Sirkaniz Palov

Steamed Pumpkin with Fried Onions – Turkmenistan
~~~~~~~~~~

Carrot *Pilaf* – Kazakhstan   **Flatbread and Cheese** – Tajikistan
Palov or *Plov*   *Qurutob*

Yogurt *Katyk*

~~~~~~~~~~~~~~~~~~~~

Fried Walnut Fritters – Uzbekistan   **Pumpkin Porridge with *Couscous*** – Kazakhstan
Samsa   *Tykvennaia Kasha*

Rock Candy *Nabat* – Tajikistan

Yogurt Drink – Uzbekistan
Airan

or

Watermelon Punch – Uzbekistan, Tajikistan, Turkmenistan, Kazakhstan
Tarauz Kompoti

~

Green Tea   or   **Chilled Spiced Honey Tea** – Uzbekistan
with sugar, milk, butter, or fruit preserves   *Dolchinli Asal Choi*

Central Asia

NOODLE SOUP WITH KIDNEY BEANS
Ugra

TPT - 37 minutes

In Uzbekistan and in Tajikistan a cooking pot is set over heat and this and that, often whatever you have, are added; the process is quite simple but recipes are a bit serendipity. Several kinds of soup are popular and with the exclusion of meat and meat stock, these can be prepared vegetarian or vegan with amazingly satisfying results. "Shurpa" and "mastava" are stews made with meats to which vegetables are added. "Ugra" soups are more liquid and contain homemade noodles, meat, and vegetables. "Chuchvara," a favorite in these republics, is a soup that is crammed full of small dumplings that look very much like tortellini. These dumplings, which are small versions of the large, popular dumplings called "manty" are filled with meat and poached in water, bouillon, or "suzma," a soured milk product that is greatly enjoyed by the population.

1 tablespoon butter
2 large carrots—scraped or pared and chopped into 1/4-inch cubes
1 large potato—peeled and chopped into 1/4-inch cubes
1 medium onion—diced

3 tablespoons canned, *crushed* tomatoes

6 cups VEGETABLE STOCK FROM SOUP *[see index]* or other rich vegetarian stock of choice

1/2 cup canned red kidney beans—well-drained
Salt, to taste
Freshly ground black pepper, to taste

1 cup *fine* egg noodles—dry *or* freshly made

In a skillet set over *MEDIUM-HIGH* heat, melt butter. Add chopped carrots, potato, and onion. Sauté just until vegetables begin to brown. Remove skillet from heat.

Add crushed tomatoes and stir mixture together.

In a saucepan set over *MEDIUM* heat, allow vegetable stock to come to the boil. Add sautéed vegetable mixture and kidney beans. Season with salt and pepper to taste. Cook, stirring frequently, for about 10 minutes.

Add egg noodles and simmer until tender—about 4 minutes. Turn into a heated soup tureen.

Serve at once into heated soup plates.

Yields 6 servings
adequate for 4 people

Note: This recipe can be halved, or doubled. when required.

1/6 SERVING – PROTEIN = 3.0 g.; FAT = 2.3 g.; CARBOHYDRATE = 15.5 g.; CALORIES = 99; CALORIES FROM FAT = 21%

UZBEK RED ONION SALAD
Piez Salati

TPT - 1 hour and 15 minutes;
1 hour = salting period

Samarkand always seemed so exotic and so very romantic from the prospective of a child growing up in upstate New York. Then, I would never have thought that something as mundane as an onion salad would be a specialty of people who existed in my mind wrapped in gossamer as they floated about on magic carpets. There is, however, a degree of magic in this recipe that transforms the strong onion flavor into a mild, sweet accompaniment appropriate to many dishes. The onions are salted and allowed to wilt. Then they are dressed with a touch of sweetness and bright contrast of fresh coriander leaves and just a touch of pomegranate juice.

1 large Italian red onion—trimmed and *thinly* sliced into rings
Salt

2 tablespoons pure pomegranate juice
1 tablespoon red wine vinegar
1/2 teaspoon sugar

1/4 cup chopped fresh coriander (*cilantro*) leaves

Several dashes ground red pepper (cayenne), or to taste

UZBEK RED ONION SALAD (cont'd)

Put onion slices in a bowl. Sprinkle salt over and toss to coat the onion slices with salt. Allow to sit at room temperature for 1 hour. Pour into a sieve and drain thoroughly. Rinse the bowl well and fill with cold water. Add onions and swish around to rinse any residual salt from the onion rings. Pour back into the sieve and then rinse well under running water. Drain well. Turn into a serving dish.

In a small dish combine pomegranate juice, vinegar, and sugar. Add to onions. Toss well.

Add chopped fresh coriander (*cilantro*) leaves. Toss well.

Garnish with ground red pepper (cayenne).*

Serve at room temperature but refrigerate any leftovers.

Yields 6 servings
adequate for 4 people

Notes: *During the holidays, when I have a pomegranate or two on hand, I garnish this salad generously with pomegranate seeds. The sweet/sour result is quite exciting.

This recipe can be doubled, when required.

1/6 SERVING – PROTEIN = 0.7 g.; FAT = 0.02 g.; CARBOHYDRATE = 4.7 g.;
CALORIES = 12; CALORIES FROM FAT = 2%

PICKLED EGGPLANT WITH DILL
TPT - 25 hours and 43 minutes;
24 hours = cooling period

In Turkmenistan cooks pickle eggplant to extend the harvest. Since they do not add the oregano and basil leaves one would find in a jar of eggplant pickles prepared by an Italian cook but instead add dillweed, it is probable that this delight was another preparation introduced during the years of Soviet influence. One can find eggplant pickles, canned for export from Central Asia to your doorstep, from online mail order firms but it is an easy process and so satisfying to make from scratch.

4 firm, mini or baby eggplants—trimmed

1 tablespoon coarse salt (kosher salt)

1 cup distilled white vinegar
2 cups water
2 garlic cloves—sliced
1/2 teaspoon dried red pepper flakes

3 small inner stalks of celery with leaves—well-washed and trimmed, if necessary
3 tablespoons chopped fresh dillweed

1 1/2 cups safflower *or* sunflower oil*

Prepare three one-pint canning jars by sterilizing. Also sterilize lids and rings.

Peel eggplant and cut in half crosswise and then cut in half lengthwise. Cut each of those pieces into thin spears about 2 1/2 inches long. Place in a colander or in an over-the-sink strainer.

Sprinkle with salt. Toss to distribute the salt. Place a plate on top and a weight—such as a large can—on top of the plate. Allow to stand for 1 hour. Transfer to a bowl and rinse in several changes of cold water to remove excess salt. Squeeze the eggplant pieces gently to remove excess liquid.

In a saucepan set over *MEDIUM* heat, combine vinegar, water, garlic slices, and dried red pepper flakes. Allow to come to the boil. Remove from heat.

Add eggplant pieces.

Place a celery stalk and a tablespoonful of chopped fresh dillweed in each jar.

Divide the eggplant mixture, with liquid, among sterilized jars leaving about 1 inch below the jar rim. Pour olive oil to about 1/4 inch below the jar rim. Wipe rim of jars and seal with hot, sterilized lids and rings. Process in hot-water-bath canner for 10 minutes, *timing from the moment the water reaches a full rolling boil*. Remove to surface covered with thick towels or newspapers. Allow to cool for 24 hours *undisturbed*. Check to be sure jars are sealed before labeling and storing in a dark, cool, dry place.** Loosen or remove rings before storing.

Yields about 4 servings per pintful

Notes: *Cheaper cottonseed oil is generally used in Turkmenistan but you will appreciate the clean, neutral taste of safflower or sunflower oil.

PICKLED EGGPLANT WITH DILL (cont'd)

**Any jars that do not seal can be stored in the refrigerator for about two months or resealed using a *new lid*.

1/12 SERVING – PROTEIN = 0.7 g.; FAT = 2.4 g.; CARBOHYDRATE = 4.8 g.;
CALORIES = 42; CALORIES FROM FAT = 51%

KAZAKH CARROT SLAW
TPT - 5 minutes

My grandmother would often say, "Oh, we need a salad," and out would come the grater and carrots. Peeled and ready to go, you were admonished to watch your knuckles. Minutes later, after a little of Grandma's magic touch, we sat down to dinner with salad. This carrot slaw is considerably different from my grandmother's slaw which included raisins, orange zest, cinnamon, cloves, and mayonnaise. I had to go half way around the world to find this savory carrot slaw to love. In the markets of Kazakhstan you will find large trays of this salad redolent of the local garlic. As you see, we prefer to make it with the garlic oil which we prepare and store each year but we do prepare the oil from the wonderful garlic varieties from Central Asia which became available after the demise of the Soviet Union. These cultivars, so different from the grocery store garlic, are now grown by specialty farmers in the United States.

4 large carrots—*finely* shredded*
1/4 teaspoon freshly ground black pepper, or to taste
1/4 teaspoon chili powder, or to taste

1 tablespoon GARLIC OIL *[see index]*
2 teaspoons distilled white vinegar
Pinch salt
Pinch sugar

Notes: *In choosing large carrots take care not to select them so large that they have become "woody."

This recipe is easily halved or doubled, when required.

In a mixing bowl, combine *finely* shredded carrots, black pepper, and chili powder. Toss well.

In a small dish, combine garlic oil, vinegar, salt, and sugar. Using a small wire whisk, combine well. Add to shredded carrots. Again, combine well. Turn into a serving dish. Chill until ready to serve.

Yields 6 servings
adequate for 4 people

1/6 SERVING – PROTEIN = 0.3 g.; FAT = 1.9 g.; CARBOHYDRATE = 2.6 g.;
CALORIES = 44; CALORIES FROM FAT = 39%

POTATO SALAD WITH MAYONNAISE IN THE STYLE OF TURKMENISTAN
Kartofelnyi Salat
TPT - 1 hour and 17 minutes;
1 hour = flavor development period

Influenced by seventy years of exposure to Russian cuisine during the period that they were a republic in the former Soviet Union, the Turkmen modernized their food choices. An expansion of vegetable choices led to an increase in the eating of salads and salads dressed with mayonnaise can be found on practically every restaurant menu and in the stalls of every market. Unlike Russian and German potato salads, however, there is little emphasis on seasoning in Turkmenistan . . . a little salt, a little, not a lot of, pepper, and maybe some fresh dillweed. Turkmen consider the mayonnaise alone sufficient seasoning.

POTATO SALAD WITH MAYONNAISE IN THE STYLE OF TURKMENISTAN (cont'd)

2 large all purpose potatoes—peeled and cut into large dice
1 quart *boiling* water

1/4 teaspoon salt

2 tablespoons *calorie-reduced or light* mayonnaise
Freshly ground black pepper, to taste

3 tablespoons chopped fresh dillweed

In a saucepan set over *MEDIUM* heat, cook diced potatoes in *boiling* water until *crisp-tender*—about 12-14 minutes. Drain thoroughly. Turn into a mixing bowl.

While still hot, sprinkle with salt. Toss *gently*.

Add mayonnaise and black pepper. Toss *gently* to coat the potato pieces with mayonnaise. Turn into a serving bowl. Refrigerate for at least 1 hour to allow salad to cool and to allow for flavor development.

Garnish with chopped dillweed before serving.

Yields 6 servings
adequate for 4 people

Note: This recipe can be doubled, when required.

1/6 SERVING – PROTEIN = 1.1 g.; FAT = 1.7 g.; CARBOHYDRATE = 10.9 g.; CALORIES = 48; CALORIES FROM FAT = 32%

UZBEK VEGETABLE STEW
Dimlama

TPT - 1 hour and 42 minutes
[slow cooker: 4-6 hours at LOW]

Dimlama is usually made with fatty chunks of lamb or beef and large chunks of whatever vegetables are in season and are favored by the family. Everything is layered in a large kettle and allowed to simmer, covered, until every ingredient is mouth-wateringly tender. This is my version which can be prepared in the oven or in a slow cooker, if preferred.

1 cup VEGETABLE STOCK FROM SOUP *[see index]*
  or other vegetarian stock of choice
2 medium potatoes—peeled and cut into large dice
3 medium carrots—scraped or pared and chopped
1 large French turnip—peeled and chopped
3/4 cup canned, *whole* tomatoes
Freshly ground black pepper, to taste
1/8 teaspoon cumin seed
1/2 cup *frozen*, vegetarian "ground beef" *or* rehydrated dried ground soymeat
1 large red bell pepper—cored, seeded, and cut into long strips
1 cup small, white boiling onions—peeled
3/4 cup canned, *whole* tomatoes
Freshly ground black pepper, to taste
1/8 teaspoon cumin seeds
1 small apple—peeled, cored, and chopped*
1/2 cup *frozen*, vegetarian "ground beef" *or* rehydrated, dried "ground soymeat
1 medium potato—peeled and cut into large dice
4 *whole* garlic cloves—peeled
2 tablespoons cold butter—diced
8 large cabbage leaves—well-washed and left whole

UZBEK VEGETABLE STEW (cont'd)

Pour vegetable stock into a Dutch oven set over *LOW* heat. Then layer remaining ingredients as listed below:

> Scatter the diced pieces from two potatoes as a first layer.
>
> Layer chopped carrots over potatoes.
>
> Layer chopped turnip over.
>
> Layer 3/4 cupful tomatoes over.
>
> Season with black pepper and 1/8 teaspoon cumin seeds.
>
> Layer 1/2 cupful ground soymeat over.
>
> Layer red pepper strips over.
>
> Layer small boiling onions over.
>
> Add another layer of an additional 3/4 cupful tomatoes.
>
> Again, season with black pepper and an additional 1/8 teaspoonful of cumin seeds.
>
> Layer chopped apple.
>
> Add another layer of 1/2 cupful ground soymeat.
>
> Scatter the diced pieces from one potato.
>
> Scatter whole garlic cloves over.
>
> Scatter diced butter over.
>
> Place cabbage leaves on top, pressing them down as a dome over the vegetables, positioned so that there is no place for steam to escape

Preheat oven to 325 degrees F.

Place Dutch oven in preheated 325 degree F. and allow to gently simmer for about 1 hour and 20 minutes. Remove the cabbage leaves to a serving bowl or platter. Ladle the vegetables over the cabbage.

Serve at once into large soup plates.

Yields 8 servings
adequate for 6-8 people

Notes: *Uzbeks are more apt to add a chopped quince to this stew than an apple. Quinces are infrequently found in markets in some areas of the United States so I have chosen to recommend the addition of an apple.

This recipe can be doubled, when required.

If prepared in a slow cooker, expect it to take about 4-6 hours at LOW setting.

1/8 SERVING – PROTEIN = 4.9 g.; FAT = 3.7 g.; CARBOHYDRATE = 19.0 g.;
CALORIES = 124; CALORIES FROM FAT = 27%

BROWN RICE – GARLIC *PILAF*

Sirkaniy Palav

TPT - 2 hours and 42 minutes;
2 hours = raisin soaking period

The classic picture of the father-of-the-house carving the holiday turkey is not just a nostalgic nod to the artist Norman Rockwell. All through my younger years, the male head-of-the-house stood at the head of the table, carved, and served. It was a fascinating irony to find that men in Central Asia pride themselves on their cooking of palov (pilaf). The preparation of "palov" or "osh" differs from region to region but only as to ingredients, not as to preparation. The rice mixture is cooked over an open flame, which is no small challenge, and in front of guests with great pride and skill.

Barberry has been grown for centuries and used as a folk medicinal. The sharp taste can be mellowed with sugar as in Estonia, Lithuania, and the Ukraine where it is made into a popular candy, the name for which translates to "Barberis," the genus to which all the many barberry species belong. In Iran and in Patagonia (Argentina/Chile) it is made into a rather unique preserve. In Uzbekistan and in Tajikistan the barberries are chopped and added to many dishes including palov.

BROWN RICE – GARLIC PILAF (cont'd)

1/2 cup *preservative-free dark* raisins
1 cup *boiling* water

1 tablespoon butter
1/2 cup *finely* chopped onion
4 large garlic cloves—*very finely* chopped

1/2 cup dry long grain brown rice

4 *preservative-free* dried apricot halves—chopped
1 tablespoon well-washed fresh or dried barberries, if available—chopped
1/4 teaspoon freshly ground black pepper, or to taste
Pinch ground cumin

1 1/2 cups VEGETARIAN BROWN STOCK *[see index]* or other vegetarian stock of choice

In a measuring cup or small bowl, combine raisins and *boiling* water. Allow to stand for at least 2 hours. Drain well.

In a non-stick-coated wok, with cover, set over *MEDIUM* heat, combine the butter with *finely* chopped onion and garlic. Sauté until onion is soft and translucent, *allowing neither the onion nor the garlic to brown*.

Add brown rice. Sauté for an additional 2 or 3 minutes.

Add rehydrated raisins, chopped apricots, chopped barberries, black pepper, cumin, and stock. Allow to come to the boil, *stirring constantly*. Reduce heat to *LOW*, cover, and allow to cook for about 10 minutes, or until the rice has absorbed most of the stock and the grains begin to soften. Continue cooking, stirring frequently, until all of the stock has been absorbed and rice grains are separate. Turn onto a heated platter.

Serve at once.

Yields 5 servings
adequate for 3-4 people

Note: This recipe is easily decreased or increased proportionately, when required.

1/5 SERVING – PROTEIN = 1.9 g.; FAT = 2.7 g.; CARBOHYDRATE = 33.2 g.;
CALORIES = 163; CALORIES FROM FAT = 15%

KAZAKH CARROT *PILAF*
Palav or *Plav*

TPT - 1 hour and 42 minutes;
1 hour = raisin soaking period

This pilaf (palov/plov) is unique in that the shredded carrots are fried before they are added to the rice mixture. We use a combination of butter and oil; in Kazakhstan cooks would generally use lamb tail fat to fry the carrots.

10 pitted, *preservative-free* prunes—chopped
1 cup *boiling* water

1 tablespoon butter
1 tablespoon canola oil
1/2 cup *finely* chopped onion
3 large carrots—scraped or pared and *coarsely* shredded

1/2 cup dry converted rice
2 tablespoons slivered *preservative-free* almonds

1/4 teaspoon freshly ground black pepper, or to taste
Pinch ground cumin
1 1/2 cups water *or* VEGETARIAN BROWN STOCK *[see index]*

In a measuring cup or small bowl, combine chopped prunes and *boiling* water. Allow to stand for at least 1 hour. Drain well.

In a non-stick-coated wok, with cover, set over *MEDIUM* heat, heat butter and oil. Add *finely* chopped onion and shredded carrot. Sauté until onion is soft and translucent, *allowing neither the onion nor the carrots to brown*.

Add rice and slivered almonds. Sauté for an additional 2 or 3 minutes.

KAZAKH CARROT PILAF (cont'd)

Add rehydrated prunes, black pepper, cumin, and water or stock. Allow to come to the boil, *stirring constantly*. *Reduce heat to LOW*, cover, and allow to cook for about 10 minutes, or until the rice has absorbed most of the stock and the grains begin to soften. Continue cooking, stirring frequently, until all of stock has been absorbed and rice grains are separate. Turn out onto a heated platter.

Serve at once.

Yields 5 servings
adequate for 3-4 people

Note: This recipe is easily decreased or increased proportionately, when required.

1/5 SERVING – PROTEIN = 3.1 g.; FAT = 6.7 g.; CARBOHYDRATE = 33.6 g.;
CALORIES = 215; CALORIES FROM FAT = 28%

TAJIK FLATBREAD AND CHEESE
Qurutob

TPT - 21 minutes

Qurutob is a vegetarian dish that is extremely important in the diet of the Tajks. Dried balls of salt cheese, "qurut," are dissolved in water to create a pourable liquid cheese. It is poured over strips of "patyr," a thin flaky flatbread. Fried vegetables, usually onions, top this traditional dish. It is delicious but a bit difficult to reproduce here in the middle of Pennsylvania. I have worked out a substitute that does not require dried cheese and which uses an easily obtainable flatbread.

This is traditionally eaten from a communal bowl or platter but can be served onto dinner plates, if desired.

8 ounces *crumbled* plain *feta* cheese
1/2-3/4 cup *boiling* water

2 tablespoons safflower *or* sunflower oil
2 medium onions—peeled and sliced

2 loaves Indian *nan* bread

Freshly ground black pepper, to taste

Preheat oven to 170 degrees F.

In a saucepan set over *LOW-MEDIUM* heat, combine crumbled cheese and *boiling* water. Cook, stirring frequently until the cheese has melted and has mixed completely with the water. Stir with a wire whisk until smooth as possible. Set aside on warming tray briefly.

In a skillet set over *LOW-MEDIUM* heat, heat oil. Add onion slices and sauté until onions are soft and translucent, *being careful not to allow the onions to brown*.

At the same time, place bread in warm oven to heat.

When ready to serve, slice the bread into large strips and place on a platter. Whisk the melted cheese again to insure smoothness. Pour over the bread. Scatter fried onions over. Grind black pepper over.

Serve at once.

Yields 6 servings
adequate for 4 people

Note: This recipe can be doubled, when required.

1/6 SERVING – PROTEIN = 6.0 g.; FAT = 14.8 g.; CARBOHYDRATE = 23.3 g.;
CALORIES = 260; CALORIES FROM FAT = 51%

UZBEK FRIED WALNUT PASTRIES
Samsas
TPT - 35 minutes

Fried fritters, called samsas, are very popular in Central Asia. Much like pierogi or ravioli or wontons, they can be filled with meats, meat and vegetables, just vegetables, eggs, and a whole host of imaginative combinations including this walnut version from Uzbekistan. You can make your own thin pastry but I have found that commercially available wonton skins (wrappers) or egg roll wrappers save time.

1 cup *high-heat* safflower *or* sunflower oil for deep-frying

4 ounces *preservative-free* walnuts—ground in a nut grinder or food processor

1 1/2 tablespoons butter—*brought to room temperature*

1 1/2 tablespoons sugar

20 *wonton* wrappers *or* 20 two-inch by two-inch pieces of egg roll wrapper

2 teaspoons confectioners' sugar

In a small wok, heat oil for deep-frying to 375 degrees F.

In a mixing bowl, combine ground walnuts, softened butter, and sugar. Mix well to form a paste.

Place a portion of the walnut mixture in the center of a pastry (*wonton*) square. Draw the corners up to form a bundle. Wet your fingers to seal the edges and secure the bundle.

When all are prepared, deep-fry them, a few at a time, in the hot oil until golden brown. Transfer to paper toweling and allow excess oil to drain. Allow oil to reheat between batches. Transfer to a serving plate.

Sprinkle lightly with confectioners' sugar.

Yields about 20 fritters

Note: This recipe can be halved or doubled, when required.

1/20 SERVING (i. e., per fritter) –
PROTEIN = 1.0 g.; FAT = 4.1 g.; CARBOHYDRATE = 4.4 g.;
CALORIES = 56; CALORIES FROM FAT = 66%

KAZAKH PUMPKIN PORRIDGE WITH *COUSCOUS*
Tykvennaia Kasha
TPT - 13 minutes

The first time I tasted this porridge was at breakfast in a Leningrad (St. Petersburg) hotel in 1983. Many years later I was informed that it was a Kazakh dish. Suddenly I found myself catapulted into the dilemma as to origin, much like the endless debate as to whether peach melba originated in Australia or New Zealand. We enjoy this as a dessert and can have it throughout the year by using the canned pumpkin/squash product available in the United States instead of having to limit it to fall and early winter menus when fresh pumpkins are available. Served as a dessert, or for a breakfast or lunch, it is a convenient and nutritious offering.

2 cups *canned* pumpkin—*unseasoned* and *unsweetened*

1 1/2 cups skimmed milk

3 tablespoons sugar

1/4 cup dry, quick-cooking *couscous or* coarse ground semolina*

1 tablespoon butter

Sugar *or* honey

In a saucepan set over *MEDIUM* heat, combine pumpkin purée, milk, and sugar. Using a wire whisk, stir to create a smooth mixture. Cook, stirring frequently, until mixture boils.

Reduce heat to *LOW*. Stir in *couscous* or semolina and simmer for 5 minutes. Stir in butter.

Serve warm with sugar or honey or, if preferred, chill in the refrigerator for 1 hour before serving.

Yields 8 servings
adequate for 6 people

Notes: *Avoid using finely ground semolina or farina; the grind is usually too fine to give the texture that this dish should have. The grain should be visible in the finished porridge.

KAZAKH PUMPKIN PORRIDGE WITH *COUSCOUS* (cont'd)

Instead of semolina, cooked millet can be used. Also rice is often enjoyed in this porridge. Add rice at the beginning of the cooking process and allow the rice to cook for at least 15 minutes.

When required, this recipe may be halved or doubled.

1/6 SERVING – PROTEIN = 2.0 g.; FAT = 1.8 g.; CARBOHYDRATE = 16.4 g.;
CALORIES = 88; CALORIES FROM FAT = 18%

UZBEK YOGURT DRINK
Airan

TPT - 5 minutes

The Mongol hoards thundered west across Asia and into Europe bringing the taste of cultured milk to those they met and conquered. Milk from mares, ewes, and camels was carried in leather bags over their saddles and as they galloped along the milk curdled. Mythology suggests that people believed that the milk clabbered due to lightning but any wild bacteria will curdle milk and those skin bags were certainly not sterile containers. Soured milk products and yogurt were known in the hot humid countries of Central Asia and the Middle East as early as 2000 BC. Today we do not depend on wild bacteria, although exposure will quickly sour milk as any cook knows. The isolation of Lactobacillus bulgaricus by Dr. Elie Metchnikoff, the Russian bacteriologist and Nobel Prize winner, resulted in the ability to produce a consistent, sweet cultured product that is a staple in our kitchens today. Make your own yogurt ("katyk") or buy a low-fat vanilla yogurt to make this beverage which accompanies a Central Asian meal well.

16 ounces VANILLA YOGURT *[see index]* **or
  commercially-available vanilla yogurt***
1 cup plain seltzer water
Salt, to taste

In a large mixing bowl, using a wire whisk, whisk yogurt until very smooth. Turn into a pitcher or decanter.

When ready to serve, add seltzer water and salt. Stir *gently, but thoroughly.*

Serve into small glasses.

Yields 3 cupfuls

Notes: *We like a slightly sweet taste. If you prefer a tart beverage, use plain yogurt.

This recipe can be increased or decreased proportionately to accommodate more or fewer people.

1/6 SERVING (i. e., per cupful) –
PROTEIN = 3.3 g.; FAT = 1.1 g.; CARBOHYDRATE = 9.6 g.;
CALORIES = 46; CALORIES FROM FAT = 22%

Central Asia

CENTRAL ASIAN WATERMELON PUNCH
Tarang Kompoti

TPT - 2 hours and 23 minutes;
2 hours = chilling period

We were driving along a road south of Moscow back in the 1980s in a December snow storm. Our driver stopped to clean off the windshield with snowballs and as we looked around we noted several trucks broken down along the side of the road. It was not an unusual sight in the Soviet Union considering the level of automotive engineering efficiency during that period but what was unusual was that several of the truck drivers were offloading melons as they prepared to fix their trucks. Melons in December . . . from where? We later found that melons from the Central Asian Soviet republics were trucked up to Moscow and Leningrad (St. Petersburg) weekly. Turkmenistan is probably most famous for its melon farming, producing about four hundred varieties. The mystery of the cantaloupe-slice garnish on our dinner plates was solved.

We choose to use the small sugar baby watermelons for this refreshing summer drink which is a common summer accompaniment to a meal in all the Central Asian nations except Kyrgyzstan where the desert climate and the nomadic, herdsman habit of the population limit farming,

6 cups water*
1 cup sugar

2 1/2 cups seeded and cubed watermelon

In a large saucepan set over *MEDIUM* heat, combine water and sugar. Bring to the boil, stirring frequently, until the sugar dissolves. Reduce the heat to *LOW-MEDIUM* and allow to simmer for about 10 minutes.

Add watermelon pieces and allow to return to the boil. Simmer for about 5 minutes more. Remove from heat and refrigerate for about 2 hours, or until thoroughly cool. Turn into a pitcher.

To serve, pour liquid and watermelon pieces into wine glasses or watermelon flutes. *Serve chilled.*

Yields 8 cupfuls

Notes: *We have the great good fortune of delicious, clean, untreated water which we draw directly from a deep artesian well. If your tap water has been chlorinated, use bottled water for this drink since chlorination will distort the taste of the watermelon.

This recipe can be halved or doubled, when required.

1/8 SERVING (i. e., per cupful) –
PROTEIN = 0.3 g.; FAT = 0.2 g.; CARBOHYDRATE = 30.4 g.;
CALORIES = 126; CALORIES FROM FAT = 1%

CHILLED SPICED HONEY TEA
Dolchinli Asal Chai

TPT - 2 hours and 3 minutes;
2 hours = chilling period

If you enjoy drinking cold tea in the summer, as I do, this Uzbek variation will certainly appeal. A glass can be just the thing for dessert with cookies, pastries, or biscotti or as an afternoon pick-me-up. Add cream if you like cream in your tea or omit the cream . . . your choice.

1 quart hot brewed black tea
1 tablespoon honey, of choice
1 cinnamon quill

Cream, if desired

Pour tea into a heat-proof refrigerator jar or pitcher. Add honey. Stir to mix well. Add cinnamon quill. Refrigerator for at least 2 hours.

Serve well-chilled in Russian tea glasses or Irish coffee glass mugs. Pass cream for those who desire it.

Yields 4 cupfuls

Note: This recipe is easily halved or doubled, when required.

1/4 SERVING (i. e., per cupful without cream) –
PROTEIN = 0.025 g.; FAT = 0.0 g; CARBOHYDRATE = 4.1 g.;
CALORIES = 15; CALORIES FROM FAT = 0%

South Asia

South Asia

Afghanistan	. .	637
Bangladesh	. .	644
Bhutan	. .	655
India	. .	663
Nepal	. .	680
Pakistan	. .	689
Sri Lanka	. .	698

South Asia–**Afghanistan**

Afghanistan

The modern state of Afghanistan was founded in 1747 but excavations by a team of archaeologists from the University of Pennsylvania have verified occupation for at least 50,000 years. Afghanistan has known more than its share of invaders and occupiers over the centuries, in addition to its home-grown struggles for power. It was conquered by the Empires of the Median and the Persians, Alexander the Great, the Seleucids, the Indo-Greeks, the Indians, the Turks, and the Mongols. Then came the British, the Soviets, and the United States and its "coalition of the willing." . . . a hard life in a land of geographical extremes not made easier by its strategic position. Today, according to the Human Development Index, Afghanistan is the second least developed country in the world and UNICEF has declared it to be the most dangerous place on earth for a child to be born.

The city of Kabul, Afghanistan's present capital, was established during the period of Aryan occupation, 2000-1500 BC. The Zoroasterian religion, founded by the Persian religious leader Zoroaster, was introduced during this same period but replaced by Buddhism with the reign of King Kanishka of India in 50 AD. Islam was introduced in about 600 AD by the Arabs and even the invasion of the Mongols under Genghis Khan in 1219 did not interrupt its spread and eventual dominance. Viewing Buddhism as idolic, the Taliban systematically obliterated Afghanistan's historic Buddhist culture and its art. In their campaign to create a conservative Islamic state, the Taliban destroyed many ancient treasures of the pre-Islamic period declaring them to be violations of *Sharia* law. They destroyed historic monuments and art that reflected the more progressive, secular culture of the preceding centuries, that which had been conserved in museums and historical phenomena such as the exquisite sixth century Buddhas of the Banyan Valley, in the Hindu Kush, carved into the rock at the site of ancient Buddhist monasteries on the Silk Road route between East Asia and West Asia.

Here a cuisine endures that clearly shows Persian, Indian, and Mongolian influences. Some sharing is obvious such as a rice preparation I first found in Iran, Indian spices and spice mixtures, and noodles introduced by the Mongols. Many, many other adaptations become evident as one explores Afghan cuisine. Of note is the Afghan love of and the totally unique use of the tomato. It is very much a meat-based cuisine, in which seriously large amounts of protein are consumed at a single meal. Because of the rigors of the climate and life style, the large amounts of fat consumed are tolerated by Afghans. The following recipes have been adjusted to the western palate and lifestyle.

South Asia – Afghanistan

Fried Scallion Turnovers
Bulanee Gandana

~

Creamed Tomato Soup with Yogurt
Sherwa-e-Lawang

Flatbread or *Nan*

~~~~~~~~~~~~~~~~~~~~~~

**Linguine, Chick Peas, and Red Kidney Beans
with Seasoned Soymeat**
Aush

Spiced Yogurt Marinade

Fresh Coriander Sauce
Chatni Gasneez

Baked Eggplant with Yogurt
Burani Baunijan

~~~~~~~~~~~~~~~~~~~~~~

Almond and Coconut Corn Starch Pudding
Kajkool-e-Fugara

AFGHAN FRIED SCALLION TURNOVERS
Bulanee Gandana
TPT - 20 minutes

Over the centuries influences from Pakistan, Iran, China, and Russia have very much affected the cuisine of this ancient, fiercely proud, and historically poor country. With few electrical appliances in Afghani kitchens, most food is prepared over open fires. Although Afghani cooks usually use only the green portion of spring onions or sprouting winter onions, we use the whole scallion or salad onion to fill these turnovers, which make a very interesting first course or a luncheon main course that is light but very satisfying.

15 scallions *or* **2 large Vidalia salad onions**
—washed, trimmed, and *finely* chopped to yield about 1 1/2 cups
1 medium garlic clove—crushed and *very finely* chopped
1/2 teaspoon freshly ground black pepper
Salt, to taste

8 egg roll skins*

1/2 cup vegetable oil

1/2 cup chilled PLAIN YOGURT [*see index*] or commercially-available plain yogurt, for garnish
8 *iced* **radish roses, for garnish**

In a small bowl, combine *finely chopped* scallions or salad onions, *very finely chopped* garlic, black pepper, and salt. Blend well.

Spread out an egg roll skin on a flat surface. Using your finger, rub the perimeter with water. Spoon *one-eighth* of scallion mixture onto one side of the skin, shaping the filling into a triangle. Fold skin over to form a triangle. Press moistened edges to seal. Repeat until all eight turnovers have prepared.

In a large skillet set over *MEDIUM* heat, heat the 1/4 cupful oil. Add turnovers and fry until golden brown on each side, about 2 minutes on each side. Transfer to paper toweling to drain.

South Asia – **Afghanistan**

AFGHAN FRIED SCALLION TURNOVERS (cont'd)

Serve at once, with chilled yogurt and radish roses.

Yields 8 servings
adequate for 4 people

Notes: *Egg roll skins are available in specialty food markets, Chinese markets, and in most grocery stores. Extras, well-wrapped, can be frozen.

This recipe can be doubled, when required.

1/8 SERVING (with 1 tablespoon yogurt) –
PROTEIN = 3.4 g.; FAT = 3.2 g.; CARBOHYDRATE = 4.5 g.;
CALORIES = 89; CALORIES FROM FAT = 32%

AFGHAN CREAMED TOMATO SOUP WITH YOGURT
Shorwa-e-Lamang

TPT - 3 hours and 21 minutes;
3 hours = yogurt *crème* preparation period

In Afghanistan the word "chaka" is used for yogurt that has been tied up in a muslin or cheesecloth bag and drained in much the way I make my yogurt crème. I do use my yogurt crème for "chaka" preparation but I drain it for no more than three hours since the soup requires liquid, just not too much liquid. We accompany this with flatbread or nan and a salad.

Since this soup can be served cold or at room temperature, doubling can provide an easy lunch option the next day.

2 tablespoons CLARIFIED BUTTER or *GHEE*
 [see index] **or butter**

2 large garlic cloves—crushed and *very finely* chopped

2 cups canned, *diced* tomatoes

1 1/2 cups YOGURT *CRÈME* [see index]
1 1/2 tablespoons unbleached white flour
1 cup *two-percent* milk
1/2 teaspoon ground turmeric

In a saucepan set over *MEDIUM* heat, melt *ghee* or butter. Add *very finely* chopped garlic cloves and sauté until soft and translucent, *being careful not to allow the garlic to brown.*

Reduce heat to LOW. Add chopped tomatoes and cook, stirring frequently.

In the container of the electric blender, combine yogurt *crème,* flour, milk, and ground turmeric. Blend thoroughly.

Add tomato–garlic mixture to blender container. Blend until very smooth. Return to saucepan set over *LOW-MEDIUM* heat. Cook until hot and thickened. *Do not allow it to boil while it is heating.* Turn into a heated soup tureen.

Serve into heated soup bowls.

Yields 6 servings
adequate for 4 people

Note: This recipe can be doubled to be reheated. It can not, however, be frozen successfully.

1/6 SERVING – PROTEIN = 11.0 g.; FAT = 5.8 g.; CARBOHYDRATE = 19.7 g.;
CALORIES = 174; CALORIES FROM FAT = 30%

South Asia–**Afghanistan**

AFGHAN *LINGUINE*, CHICK PEAS, AND RED KIDNEY BEANS WITH SEASONED SOYMEAT

Aush

TPT - 18 minutes

Long wheat noodles hang to dry on kitchen racks or dowels balanced between two dining room chairs in an Afghan home much the way one would find fresh pasta in Italian homes. Traditional "aush" is prepared by cooking these long wheat noodles, dressing them with yogurt, and serving with meatballs but this version of "aush" is a vegetarian's dream. Homemade spaghetti or fresh linguine is preferable but commercially-available dried linguine can be used. Fettuccine are too wide; spaghetti and angel hair pasta would be too thin. It is usually topped with meat so I have replaced it with crumbled soy meat seasoned with a most wonderful Afghan yogurt sauce.

1 cup (about 2 ounces) *frozen* **vegetarian "ground beef"** *or* **dehydrated and reconstituted vegetarian "ground beef"**
1/4 cup tomato purée
3 tablespoons AFGHAN YOGURT MARINADE
[see recipe which follows]

1/2 cup canned chick peas (*garbanzos***)—undrained***
1/2 cup canned red kidney beans—undrained*

4 quarts *boiling* **water**
One 3-inch strip lemon zest
1 tablespoon freshly squeezed lemon juice
1/2 pound whole wheat, high protein, *or*
   Jerusalem artichoke *linguine*

1 1/4 cups PLAIN YOGURT *[see index]* **or commercially-available plain yogurt**

AFGHAN FRESH CORIANDER SAUCE (*Chatni Gashneez***)** *[see recipe which follows]*

In a mixing bowl, combine defrosted or reconstituted crumbled soymeat, tomato purée, and AFGHAN YOGURT MARINADE. Stir to combine thoroughly. Turn into a small non-stick-coated skillet and set over *LOW* heat. Allow to heat through. Stir frequently.

In a small saucepan set over *LOW* heat, combine undrained chick peas and red kidney beans. Allow to heat through. Stir frequently.

In a large kettle set over *HIGH* heat, add lemon zest and lemon juice to *boiling* water. Add *linguine* and cook, stirring occasionally, over *HIGH* heat according to package directions. Drain thoroughly, discarding lemon zest. Turn drained *linguine* into a mixing bowl.

Add heated beans and yogurt. Gently fold ingredients together.* Turn out onto a heated platter.

Pour heated soymeat sauce over.

Serve at once with AFGHAN FRESH CORIANDER SAUCE.

Yields 6 servings
adequate for 4 people

Notes: *If consistency is too thick, add a tablespoon or two of the canning liquid from the canned beans or a bit of the cooking water from the *linguine*.

This recipe can be halved or doubled, when required.

1/6 SERVING – PROTEIN = 12.3 g.; FAT = 2.2 g.; CARBOHYDRATE = 42.0 g.;
CALORIES = 252; CALORIES FROM FAT = 7%

AFGHAN SPICED YOGURT MARINADE

TPT - 4 minutes

Yogurt is often used in meat marinades since there is a noticeable effect upon tough connective tissue. Tenderizing action aside, these seasoned yogurt marinades can add flavor to non-meat dishes. Such is this sauce, frequently used to marinate meats in Afghanistan, which can be a useful tool for vegetables and soy products. I often add this sauce to the water used to reconstitute a convenient dehydrated soy meat analogue product that otherwise would be very bland. The sauce is flavorful and works well as both a table sauce and as a marinade.

South Asia—**Afghanistan**

AFGHAN SPICED YOGURT MARINADE (cont'd)

1 large onion—peeled and *finely* chopped
1 cup PLAIN YOGURT *[see index]* **or**
 commercially-available plain yogurt
2 teaspoons ground cumin
2 teaspoons ground coriander
1/2 teaspoon lemon juice
1 teaspoon GARLIC OIL *[see index]*
1/2 teaspoon ground ginger
1/4 teaspoon ground turmeric
1/8 teaspoon ground red pepper (cayenne),
 or to taste
Freshly ground black pepper, to taste

Put everything into the work bowl of food processor or into the container of the electric blender. Process until liquefied.

Store in a sterilized condiment bottle in the refrigerator until required.

Yields 21 tablespoonfuls

Notes: This recipe can be halved, when required.

The spicing can be easily modified to taste.

1/21 SERVING (per tablespoonful) –
PROTEIN = 0.7 g.; FAT = 0.4 g.; CARBOHYDRATE = 1.3 g.;
CALORIES = 13; CALORIES FROM FAT = 27%

AFGHAN FRESH CORIANDER SAUCE
Chatni Gashneez *

TPT - 8 hours and 8 minutes;
 8 hours = flavor development period

Fresh coriander (cilantro or Chinese parsley) is native to southern Europe, North Africa, and southwestern Asia so it is not surprising to find it used in Afghan cooking. Archaeological excavations have confirmed its use in the region since the early Neolithic Period. The taste of the leaves is a fresh, bright taste to those who love it and a rather soapy taste to the unfortunate. Coriander seeds, the seeds of this same plant have a spicy lemony taste which is usually not perceived as objectionable to those who dislike the leaves. The inspired combination of coriander leaves, garlic, jalapeño sauce, lemon juice, and walnuts creates a complex, assertive sauce, versions of which can be found as far away as India and the Republic of Georgia.

1 cup loosely packed fresh coriander (*cilantro*)
 —stemmed, well-rinsed, and dried
1/2 cup coarsely chopped *preservative-free* walnuts
3 medium garlic cloves *or* garlic cloves from
 GARLIC OIL preparation *[see index]*
 —coarsely chopped

1/4 cup freshly squeezed lemon juice
1/2 teaspoon *green jalapeño chili* sauce
1/4 teaspoon ground cumin
1/4 teaspoon freshly ground black pepper, or to
 taste
1/4 teaspoon salt

2-3 tablespoons water, or as needed

In the work bowl of the food processor, fitted with steel knife, or in the container of the electric blender, combine coriander leaves, walnuts, and chopped garlic cloves. Process until coarsely chopped, scrapping down the sides of the work bowl or blender container as needed.

Add lemon juice, *jalapeño* sauce, ground cumin, black pepper, and salt. Again process.

Gradually add water, processing after each addition, until of desired consistency. Turn into a sterilized condiment bottle. Cover tightly and allow to stand overnight in the refrigerator before serving.

Serve at room temperature.

Yields about 1 cupful

Notes: **Chatni*, which translates as chutney, is frequently used for sauces that are quite different from the chutneys of the Indian subcontinent with which we are more familiar.

This recipe can be halved or doubled, when required.

1/32 SERVING (i. e., about 1 1/2 teaspoonfuls) –
PROTEIN = 0.5 g.; FAT = 1.6 g.; CARBOHYDRATE = 0.7 g.;
CALORIES = 19; CALORIES FROM FAT = 75%

South Asia—**Afghanistan**

AFGHAN BAKED EGGPLANT WITH YOGURT
Burani Baunjan

TPT - 1 hour and 30 minutes;
1 hour = eggplant salting period

"Burani" is an Afghani culinary term referring to vegetable dishes served with yogurt-based sauces. No two people stepping into their kitchen today to make this dish will make it the same way. I am confident of this declaration. To say it is a traditional Afghan "burani" recipe requires large quotation marks around the word traditional. Aubergines, eggplants, are used often in Afghan cooking and a yogurt sauce is, more often than not, used with eggplant but that is where the uniformity in a dish such as this ends. Some add tomatoes, some do not; some add onions and peppers, some do not. Garlic is essential but it can be added raw to the yogurt or it can be sautéed and added to the sauce. Personally, I prefer to bake the eggplant slices rather than fry them. I also layer not only the yogurt sauce but a second sauce composed of sautéed garlic and tomatoes onto the platter as I serve.

1 cup PLAIN YOGURT *[see index]* **or commercially-available plain yogurt**
1 teaspoon crushed, dried mint

1 large eggplant—washed, trimmed, and sliced into 1/4-inch crosswise slices
Coarse or kosher salt

3 tablespoons *high heat* **safflower** *or* **sunflower oil**

1 tablespoon *extra virgin* **olive oil**
3 garlic cloves—*finely* **chopped**

3/4 cup *diced* **tomatoes canned in tomato purée**
1/8 teaspoon ground red pepper (cayenne), or to taste
Pinch ground cinnamon

Salt eggplant slices generously and place them in a sieve or colander set in the sink. Place a plate on top and a weight—a large can or a tea kettle filled with water—on top of the plate. Allow to stand for 1 hour. Rinse eggplant slices well in cold water and pat dry.

Place a rimmed cookie sheet in the oven to heat. Preheat oven to 350 degrees F.

Remove preheated baking sheet from oven. Pour about 3 tablespoons *high-heat* safflower oil on pan; brush to edges. Arrange eggplant slices on the prepared baking sheet. Bake in preheated 350 degree F. oven for 8-10 minutes. Turn each eggplant slice over. Return to oven for an additional 5-8 minutes, or until baked through and browned on each side. Keep warm on a warming tray.

While eggplant is baking, in a skillet set over *MEDIUM* heat, heat the 1 tablespoonful olive oil. Add *finely* chopped garlic and sauté until garlic is soft, being careful not to allow the garlic to brown.

Add diced tomatoes, ground red pepper (cayenne), and ground cinnamon. *Reduce heat to LOW and allow to heat through.*

At the same time, in a small saucepan set over *LOW* heat, heat yogurt and crushed, dried mint just until warmed. Stir to create a smooth sauce.

Spoon about *one-half* of the yogurt mixture onto a heated platter. Arrange the baked eggplant slices on top of the yogurt. Spoon the tomato-garlic sauce over the eggplant slices. Top with remaining yogurt.

Serve warm.

Yields 6 servings
adequate for 4 people

Note: This recipe can be halved using a small eggplant, when required. This is a perfect vegetable side dish for many menus.

1/6 SERVING – PROTEIN = 2.8 g.; FAT = 9.3 g.; CARBOHYDRATE = 5.7 g.;
CALORIES = 118; CALORIES FROM FAT = 70%

South Asia–**Afghanistan**

AFGHAN ALMOND AND COCONUT CORN STARCH PUDDING

Kajkool-e-Fuqara

TPT - 1 hour and 18 minutes;
1 hour = chilling period

"Kajkool-e-Fuqara," I am told, actually translates to "beggar's bowl" It is the Afghan name for a rich, smooth pudding probably of Persian origin but known elsewhere the Middle East as "Keshkul-e-fuquara." Similar to "firnee," which is made with cow's milk, this dessert is made with almond milk and coconut which are prepared from scratch by Afghani women. I have made both from scratch and I understand why this dessert is only made on special occasions. The wide availability of additive-free almond milk and canned coconut milk, in almost every grocery store and natural foods store in the United States, makes this an easy family dessert for us.

1/2 cup sugar
6 tablespoons corn starch
1 1/2 cups *cold* unflavored almond milk—*chilled*

1 1/2 cups *light, sulfite-free* coconut milk

1 teaspoon rose water, or to taste*
1/2 teaspoon ground cardamom

2 teaspoons *finely* ground, *preservative-free* almonds
  or almond meal, for garnish
2 teaspoons ground, shelled pistachio nuts, for
  garnish

In a saucepan, combine sugar, corn starch, and *cold* almond milk. Using a wire whisk, stir until corn starch is thoroughly dissolved. Place over *MEDIUM* heat. Cook, stirring frequently, until pudding begins to thicken. *Reduce heat to LOW-MEDIUM.*

Gradually, stir in coconut milk. Continue cooking, stirring almost constantly with a wire whisk, until pudding is uniformly thickened. Set aside to cool slightly.

Add rose water and ground cardamom, stirring to integrate thoroughly.

Divide among six sherbet glasses. Refrigerate for at least 1 hour.

Combine *finely* ground almonds and ground pistachio nuts. Stir well. Garnish each serving with a portion of the ground mixed nuts before serving.

Serve chilled.

Notes: *The strength of rose water varies considerably. It is available from French and Middle East distributors but the strength must be evaluated with each new bottle.

This recipe *can not* be doubled successfully but it can be halved, when necessary.

Occasionally, even though you are very conscientious about stirring, corn starch puddings can become lumpy. Press through a sieve into a clean saucepan and continue cooking over hot water until uniformly thickened.

Yields 6 individual servings

1/6 SERVING – PROTEIN = 1.8 g.; FAT = 5.1 g.; CARBOHYDRATE = 37.1 g.;
CALORIES = 196; CALORIES FROM FAT = 23%

Bangladesh

For many, the familiarity with Bangladesh extends only as far as the headlines reporting the all too frequent flooding experienced by the nation that occupies a low plain formed by the combined delta of the Ganges and Brahmaputra rivers. These rivers provide water for agriculture but when you live in a tropical monsoon climate, the same rivers can be devastating especially when the majority of the nation is less than forty inches above sea level. Recent monsoons have been particularly destructive as the oceans rise and weather patterns change due to atmospheric changes. It is estimated that ten percent of Bangladesh would be inundated should ocean levels rise three feet. In April 1991 one hundred and thirty-one thousand died; in May 1997, eight hundred thousand were made homeless; storms from July to September 1998 killed fourteen hundred people and the monsoon flooding stranded thirty million.

For one hundred years beginning in 1757 the British East India Company ruled India. With the company's dissolution the period known as the British *Raj* began. In 1905 Bengal was partitioned but it was not until 1947, after World War II, that the independent states of India and Pakistan were created and the present borders were defined. That which is today Bangladesh was known first as East Bengal and then, beginning in 1955, as East Pakistan. It was separated from Pakistan by a 994-square-mile area of India which encouraged political exclusion and economic neglect by Pakistan. Its unsatisfactory relationship with Pakistan ended with the adoption of a constitution in 1972 after the Indo–Pakistani War of 1971, alternately referred to as the Bangladesh Liberation War of 1971. Approximately 161 million people live is this area of just 56,977 square miles, an area about the size of Iowa.

From 750 AD to 1000 AD Buddhist kings of the Pala Empire ruled the entire subcontinent. They were replaced by Hindu rulers. Today only about ten percent of the population of Bangladesh practices Hinduism; eighty-nine percent are Muslims who settled there after the region was conquered by Muslim invaders in the twelfth century. The majority of Muslims are Sunni with minority populations of Twelver Shia and Sufi Muslims. Islam was declared the state religion in the 1980s, a move that some felt threatened the secular principles of the 1972 constitution. However, a potential constitutional crisis was averted and the constitution, ratified after the Bangladesh Liberation War against Pakistan, was preserved.

Since independence, the life expectancy of Bangladeshi has increased about twenty-three years with both men and women now expected to live into their fifty-sixth year. Education has been a major goal and the effort to raise the literacy rate from thirty-eight percent has resulted in a government-subsidized, three-tier school system. There are now thirty-four public and sixty-four private universities.

Ninety-seven percent of the population are ethnic Bengali who speak Bengali which explains the cuisine that is similar to that of the regional cooking of northern India. It is a cuisine familiar to those in the West, especially those in the United Kingdom where eighty percent of Indian restaurants are said to be owned by Bangladeshi emigrants. If you have ever traveled in the British Isles, you can surely attest to the number of Indian take-away restaurants and if you have sought out a shop to find a vegetarian dinner while traveling there, you have probably enjoyed Bangladeshi cooking.

South Asia – Bangladesh

Breaded and Fried Cauliflower Florets

Spicy Fried Okra *Bhindi Pakora*

Baked or Fried Eggplant Slices *Begun*

with

Spicy Yogurt Dipping Sauce

Fried *Puppodum* Chips
with Chutney Dipping Sauce

~~~~~~~~~~~~~~~~~~~~~~

Potatoes and Cabbage in Tomato Sauce
Banda Kopir Tartari

Mashed *Tofu* and Garlic

~~~~~~~~~~

Curried Tomato and Onion with Eggs

Stir-fry of Sweetpotatoes and Snowpeas

Nan

~~~~~~~~~~

Red Lentil Stew with Bengali Five-Seed Spice Mixture
Masoor Dal

Bengali Five-Seed Spice Mixture
Panch Phoran

Steamed Fragrant Mekong Rice

Oven-Roasted Carrots

~~~~~~~~~~~~~~~~~~~~~~

Sweet *Pasta* Dessert with Almonds and Raisins
Sherai Jorda

Uncooked Sweet Yogurt Dessert
Misti Doi

Yogurt *Crème*

BANGLADESHI BREADED
AND FRIED CAULIFLOWER FLORETS
TPT - 22 minutes

The cauliflower is said to have originated in the northeast Mediterranean basin. From there it traveled to Europe where it was embraced and hybridized. As with so many foods, this divinely beautiful and adaptable vegetable traveled the world finding its way into the cuisines of Asia where it has become a favorite vegetable in Bangladesh, throughout the Indian Subcontinent, and in the island nation of Indonesia.

South Asia – Bangladesh

**BANGLADESHI BREADED
AND FRIED CAULIFLOWER FLORETS** (cont'd)

Oil for deep-frying

**2 quarts *boiling* water
3 cups fresh cauliflower florets**

**1/4 cup corn starch
1 teaspoon chili powder**

**1 large garlic clove—*finely* chopped and mashed
to a paste
2 tablespoons *tamari* soy sauce**

Water to form a paste

Heat oil in a deep kettle set over *MEDIUM* heat to about 365 degree F.

In a kettle set over *HIGH* heat, parboil cauliflower florets in *boiling* water for 3 minutes. Drain well and pat dry.

In a mixing bowl combine corn starch and chili powder. Stir to mix well.

Add mashed garlic and soy sauce. Again, stir to mix well.

Add water, *a tablespoonful at a time*, until a thick paste is formed. Add parboiled cauliflower. Toss gently until the florets are coated with the corn starch paste.

Using tongs, transfer a portion of the cauliflower florets to the hot oil. Fry, turning as necessary until crispy and browned. Remove to paper toweling to allow excess oil to drain. Continue to deep-fry until all cauliflower has been prepared.

Transfer to a serving platter and serve at once or, if necessary, transfer to a pie plate and keep warm in the oven until the rest of the meal has been prepared.

Serve hot with a sauce, of choice, for dipping.

Yields 6 servings
adequate for 4-6 people

1/6 SERVING – PROTEIN = 1.5 g.; FAT = 3.9 g.; CARBOHYDRATE = 9.0 g.;
CALORIES = 74; CALORIES FROM FAT = 47%

BANGLADESHI SPICY FRIED OKRA
Bhindi Pakora

TPT - 38 minutes

Okra, or lady fingers as they are often called, or bhindi, as they are called in Bangladesh, are not as popular in the United States as they are in the Middle East, Asia, and Africa. The mucilaginous texture of cooked okra is somewhat of a turn-off but that very texture is an asset for thickening stews without the addition of flour or potatoes. If okra is first marinated in vinegar and then breaded and quickly fried, the result is quite delicious.

Oil for deep-frying

**6 tablespoons distilled white vinegar
1 teaspoon crushed red pepper flakes
2 teaspoons turmeric
2 teaspoons ground coriander
2 teaspoons OUR *TANDOORI* SPICE MIXTURE
(Chaat Masala) [see index] *or* commercially-available mixture**

15 firm okra—well-washed and trimmed

3/4 cup unbleached white flour

Place an oven-proof dish in a warm oven to heat.

Pour oil into a deep frying pan or kettle to a depth of about 1/2 inch. Set over *MEDIUM* heat and allow to preheat to 365 degrees F.

In a mixing bowl, combine vinegar, crushed red pepper flakes, turmeric, ground coriander, and *chaat masala*.

Slice okra in half lengthwise. Add to vinegar mixture and allow to marinate for at least 10 minutes.

Put flour in a mixing bowl. Form a paste by adding a tablespoonful of the vinegar mixture at a time.

Using a spatula, lift out the okra pieces and add to flour mixture. Using a spoon, gently stir to coat the okra with the flour mixture. Deep-fry in the hot oil in batches until crisp and browned. Transfer to paper toweling to drain off excess oil. Transfer to the dish in the warm oven and keep warm until ready to serve.

Yields 30 pieces
adequate for 6 people

Note: This recipe can be halved, when required.

South Asia – **Bangladesh**

BANGLADESHI SPICY FRIED OKRA (cont'd)

1/30 SERVING – PROTEIN = 0.5 g.; FAT = 0.8 g.; CARBOHYDRATE = 0.9 g.;
CALORIES = 20; CALORIES FROM FAT = 36%

BANGLADESHI SPICY YOGURT DIPPING SAUCE
TPT - 7 minutes

This sauce is the perfect sauce for a vegetable side dish of baked or fried eggplant slices or, as in this menu, as a dipping sauce for an assortment of vegetables.

1 cup PLAIN YOGURT *[see index]* **or**
   commercially-available plain yogurt
2 tablespoons *very finely* chopped mild green *chilies*
1 teaspoon *very finely* chopped onion—mashed to a paste
1 teaspoon *very finely* chopped gingerroot—mashed to a paste
1 teaspoon sugar
1/2 teaspoon ground cumin
1/2 teaspoon ground coriander
1/2 teaspoon turmeric
1/2 teaspoon salt
1/2 teaspoon ground cardamom
1/4 teaspoon chili powder

2-3 tablespoons water

In a mixing bowl, combine yogurt, *very finely* chopped green *chilies*, the onion paste, the gingerroot paste, sugar, ground cumin, ground coriander, turmeric, salt, ground cardamom, and chili powder. Stir well to distribute the spicing ingredients.

Add water, *a teaspoonful at a time*. Stir after each addition. Continue adding water until you have a dipping sauce of the consistency desired. Turn into a serving bowl. Refrigerate until required.

Serve chilled or at room temperature. Refrigerate leftovers.

Yields about 20 tablespoonfuls

Note: This recipe can be halved, when required.

1/20 SERVING (per tablespoonful) –
PROTEIN = 0.6 g.; FAT = 0.2 g.; CARBOHYDRATE = 1.0 g.;
CALORIES = 9; CALORIES FROM FAT = 20%

DEEP-FRIED *POPPODUM* CHIPS WITH CHUTNEY DIPPING SAUCE
TPT - about 20 minutes

A persisting influence of the diverse cuisines of India and the introduction of foods by the British, during the period of Empire, can be seen in many Bangladeshi dishes. Here we have combined the popular fried, lentil-flour poppodum breads and the chutney that has practically become a British institution. This is a wonderful "chip-and-dip" appetizer which provides a healthy amount of leguminous protein to the meal.

About 1 cup *high-heat* safflower oil for deep-frying—brought to 365 degrees F.

6 loaves (disks) commercially-available, dehydrated *poppodum* bread*

1/2 cup Major Grey *or* mango chutney, as preferred

Pour oil for deep-frying into a deep kettle to the depth of about 1/2 inch. Preheat oil to 365 degrees F.

Break *poppodum* disks into about six pieces each. Deep-fry in batches until puffed and golden brown. Using a skimmer, remove to paper toweling to allow excess oil to be drained. Transfer to a heated serving plate.

Serve at once with a bowl of chutney for dipping.

Yields approximately 36 chips
adequate for 4-6 people

Notes: **Poppodum* bread loaves (disks) are available, packaged seven to a package, in the international aisles of most well-stocked grocery stores. There are usually two kinds available. One is unspiced and the second variety is spicy; both are made from lentil flour.

This recipe can be halved or doubled, when required.

VOLUME I - 647

**DEEP-FRIED *POPPODUM* CHIPS
WITH CHUTNEY DIPPING SAUCE** (cont'd)

1/36 SERVING (per chip with about 1/2 teaspoon chutney) –
PROTEIN = 0.3 g.; FAT = 0.7 g.; CARBOHYDRATE = 19.9 g.;
CALORIES = 16; CALORIES FROM FAT = 39%

BANGLADESHI POTATOES AND CABBAGE IN TOMATO SAUCE

Banda Kapir Tartari

TPT - 41 minutes

When this fragrant skillet dinner is brought to the table, it is no surprise to my family because the perfectly wonderful aroma has already captured their attention. This is a winter dish in Bangladesh and, once tried, it became a staple in our winter menu plans too. I always accompany it with warm nan so that none of the delicious juices need be left behind.

**1 tablespoon *high heat* safflower *or* sunflower oil
1/2 teaspoon ground turmeric**

3 medium potatoes—peeled and diced

**1 tablespoon *high heat* safflower *or* sunflower oil
1/2 medium onion—*finely* chopped**

**1/4 teaspoon ground cumin
1/4 teaspoon ground ginger
1/4 teaspoon chili powder
1 bay leaf**

1 1/2 cups canned, *diced* tomatoes

1 cup shredded green cabbage

**1/3 cup freshly shelled *or* frozen peas
Salt, to taste**

In a heavy skillet set over *LOW-MEDIUM* heat, heat 1 tablespoonful oil and turmeric for just a minute or two.

Add diced potatoes and stir-fry them for about 7 minutes. Using a spatula, remove the potatoes to a dish and set aside briefly.

Add the second tablespoonful of oil and *finely* chopped onions to the skillet. Sauté until onions are soft and translucent, *being careful not to allow onions to brown.*

Add ground cumin, ground ginger, chili powder, and bay leaf. Sauté for several minutes to allow for the release of the flavorful oils in the spices.

Add tomatoes and cook, stirring frequently, for about 5 minutes.

Add cabbage. Stir to introduce the cabbage to the spicy mixture. Cover and allow to cook for about 5 minutes.

Just before serving, add the partially cooked potato pieces and the peas. Season with salt. Cover and allow to cook for about 5 minutes more. Remove and discard bay leaf. Turn into a heated serving bowl.

Serve hot. Refrigerate any leftovers and gently reheat for lunch the next day.

Yields 6 servings
adequate for 4 people

Note: This recipe can be doubled, when required.

1/6 SERVING – PROTEIN = 2.3 g.; FAT = 4.6 g.; CARBOHYDRATE = 11.9 g.;
CALORIES = 110; CALORIES FROM FAT = 38%

South Asia – **Bangladesh**

MASHED *TOFU* AND GARLIC IN THE STYLE OF BANGLADESH
TPT - 16 hours and 23 minutes;
8 hours = freezing period;
8 hours = beancurd draining period

A favorite dish of Bangladesh is a mashed mixture of fish, garlic, and spices. Here, using readily available tofu and a little culinary magic, the exotically spiced essence of this dish can be enjoyed by vegans.

1 package (10.5 ounces) *extra firm silken tofu*

2 tablespoons *tamari* soy sauce
1 teaspoon kelp powder *or* ground sea vegetable
1/2 teaspoon turmeric
1 teaspoon chili powder

1 1/2 tablespoons GARLIC OIL *[see index]*
4 garlic cloves—*very finely* chopped
1/2 cup *finely* chopped onion
2 tablespoons *finely* chopped mild green *chilies*

3 tablespoons chopped fresh coriander (*cilantro*) leaves

Freeze the package of *tofu* overnight. The next day remove the frozen *tofu* from the package and wrap it in several cotton tea towels. Place a bread board on top and allow the *tofu* to drain for an additional 8 hours. Change the towels when they become too wet. Turn the block of soy beancurd into a bowl and, using a fork, mash to the consistency of tuna fish.

Add soy sauce, seaweed powder, turmeric, and chili powder. Stir to mix well. Set aside until required.

In a skillet set over *MEDIUM* heat, heat garlic oil. Add *very finely* chopped garlic, *finely* chopped onion, and *finely* chopped green *chilies*. Sauté until onion and garlic are soft and translucent, *being careful not to allow the vegetables to brown.*

Add shredded *tofu* and spice mixture. Continue cooking for several minutes until heated through.

Add chopped fresh coriander leaves. Stir to mix well. Turn into a heated serving dish.*

Serve at once.

Yields 6 servings
adequate for 4 people

Notes: *Instead of serving as a hash, the mixture can be rolled into balls, about the size of a small meatball.

This recipe can be halved or doubled, when required.

1/6 SERVING – PROTEIN = 3.9 g.; FAT = 3.4 g.; CARBOHYDRATE = 3.5 g.;
CALORIES = 59; CALORIES FROM FAT = 52%

BANGLADESHI CURRIED TOMATO AND ONION WITH EGGS
TPT - 46 minutes

This curry certainly illustrates the influence of those who sailed west from Europe in search of the spices of Asia. The foods that they gathered in our hemisphere when they bumped into these two big continents were introduced to Asia as the spice trade continued. This dish uses the spices of the Indian Subcontinent to turn the tomato that was introduced from South America into a spectacular dish that is most often served over rice. If you do not grow the curry plant in your summer herb garden, the leaves are available dried from mail-order spice firms or you can add a pinch or two of curry powder.

We eat this dish as a main course with hard-cooked eggs but, without the eggs, it is a flavorful vegetable side dish.

VOLUME I - 649

South Asia–Bangladesh

BANGLADESHI CURRIED TOMATO AND ONION WITH EGGS (cont'd)

1 tablespoon safflower *or* sunflower oil
1/2 teaspoon mustard seeds

2 medium onions—*finely* chopped
5 large garlic cloves—crushed and *very finely* chopped
10 fresh curry leaves

1 teaspoon chili powder
1/2 teaspoon ground coriander
1/4 teaspoon turmeric
1/2 teaspoon salt

5 large tomatoes—peeled, seeded, and chopped

Up to 1/2 cup water, *ONLY if your tomatoes have not released sufficient liquid*
1 tablespoon *light* brown sugar
6 hard-cooked eggs—shelled with several knife slits cut on a diagonal

1/4 cup chopped *fresh* coriander (*cilantro*) leaves

In a large skillet set over *LOW-MEDIUM* heat, heat oil. Add mustard seeds and allow them to heat until they pop.

Add the *finely* chopped onions, *very finely* chopped garlic, and curry leaves. Cook, stirring frequently, until onions are soft and translucent, *being careful to allow neither the onions nor the garlic to brown.*

Add chili powder, ground coriander, turmeric, and salt. Combine well. Allow to cook, while stirring, for a minute or two.

Add chopped tomatoes. Cook uncovered, stirring frequently, for about 8 minutes. Cover and cook for an additional 5 minutes.

Add water, if necessary, and brown sugar. Stir well. Add hard-cooked eggs. Cover and allow to cook for about 15 minutes, or until of the desired consistency. Turn into a heated serving bowl.

Garnish with fresh coriander (*cilantro*) leaves.

Serve over rice or in soup plates as a stew with breads like *chapattis* or *nan*.

Yields 6 servings
adequate for 4 people

Note: This recipe can be halved, when required.

1/6 SERVING – PROTEIN = 8.1 g.; FAT = 8.2 g.; CARBOHYDRATE = 6.9 g.;
CALORIES = 145; CALORIES FROM FAT = 51%

BANGLADESHI STIR-FRY OF SWEETPOTATOES AND SNOWPEAS
TPT - 26 minutes

Snowpeas, known as mangetout in Bangledesh and in northern India, have always been a favorite of mine for a quick stir-fry when a vegetable is needed. With the addition of thinly sliced sweetpotatoes and toasted spices, a rather beautiful and very tasty vegetable dish results.

1 teaspoon whole cumin seeds
1 teaspoon whole coriander seeds

1 tablespoon safflower *or* sunflower oil
1 teaspoon ground turmeric
1/4 teaspoon *smoked* paprika
2 large bay leaves
1 teaspoon salt

2 small sweetpotatoes—peeled and *thinly* sliced

1/2 cup water, *ONLY if necessary*

1/2 pound (about 50) snowpeas—trimmed and cut in half on a diagonal, if large

In a large, heavy, dry skillet set over *LOW-MEDIUM* heat, toast cumin and coriander seeds but they begin to brown and you can begin to smell the spices. Remove from heat and transfer to a mortar. Using a pestle, crush thoroughly. Set aside briefly.

Add oil to the skillet and return to the heat. Add turmeric, smoked paprika, bay leaves, and salt. Allow to heat for about 1 minute, stirring constantly.

Add sweetpotato slices and cook, stirring frequently, until the sweetpotato slices begin to soften.

South Asia – **Bangladesh**

BANGLADESHI STIR-FRY OF SWEETPOTATOES AND SNOWPEAS (cont'd)

Add the ground, toasted cumin and coriander. Cover and allow to cook for about 10 minutes, or until the potatoes are soft. Add water, if necessary. *Be careful not to allow the water to boil away completely or to let the potatoes stick to the pan or brown.* Remove and discard bay leaves.

Turn the heat up to MEDIUM-HIGH. Add the snowpeas and stir-fry briefly—no more than 2 minutes. Turn onto a heated serving platter.

Serve at once.

Yields 6 servings
adequate 4 for people

1/6 SERVING –   PROTEIN = 2.2 g.; FAT = 2.4 g.; CARBOHYDRATE = 13.7 g.;
CALORIES = 80; CALORIES FROM FAT = 27%

BANGLADESHI RED LENTIL STEW WITH BENGALI FIVE-SEED SPICE MIXTURE
Masoor Dal

TPT - 1 hour and 3 minutes

Dals of all sorts can be found in the cuisines of the subcontinent and I am sure that an expert could just about pinpoint the village of origin with one taste. The spices differ from one kitchen to the next and I am no expert but I know that I could identify this dal anywhere; the seasoning is that distinctive.

3/4 cup red lentils *or masur dal*—well-rinsed and picked over to remove any stems or small stones
2 cups *boiling* water
1/2 teaspoon turmeric

1/2 teaspoon salt

2 teaspoons safflower *or* sunflower oil
2 teaspoons BENGALI FIVE-SEED SEASONING MIXTURE (*Panch Phoran*) [*see recipe which follows*]

1/2 cup *finely* chopped onion
1 large garlic clove—*very finely* chopped

1 teaspoon *finely* chopped and *crushed* fresh gingerroot
1/2 cup canned, *diced* tomatoes
1/4 cup *boiling* water
Pinch crushed, dried red pepper flakes

In a saucepan set over *MEDIUM* heat, combine well rinsed red lentils, 2 cupfuls *boiling* water, and turmeric. Allow to come to the boil. Reduce heat to *LOW-MEDIUM* and simmer for about 25 minutes.

Add salt. Remove from heat and set aside until required.

In a large, deep skillet set over *LOW-MEDIUM* heat, heat oil. Add *panch phoran* and cook, stirring constantly, until the seeds begin to burst open.

Immediately, add *finely* chopped onion and *very finely* chopped garlic. Sauté until onion is soft and translucent, *being careful to allow neither the onion nor the garlic to brown.*

Add *finely* chopped and *crushed* fresh gingerroot, diced tomatoes, the remaining 1/4 cup *boiling* water, and crushed, dried red pepper flakes. Cook, stirring frequently, for about 5 minutes.

Add cooked lentils. Cook for about 10 minutes more, stirring frequently. Turn into a heated serving bowl.

Serve at once, either with or without rice as preferred.

Yields 6 servings
adequate for 4 people

Note: This recipe can be doubled, when required.

1/6 SERVING –   PROTEIN = 7.4 g.; FAT = 1.9 g.; CARBOHYDRATE = 1.9 g.;
CALORIES = 120; CALORIES FROM FAT = 14%

South Asia – Bangladesh

BENGALI FIVE-SEED SPICE MIXTURE
Panch Phoran
TPT - 2 minutes

Often the taste of a familiar dish in an Indian restaurant will surprise your taste buds and that may well be the result of the addition of panch phoran. It is a five-seed mixture that is used as a coating on roasted meats or sprinkled by Bengali cooks on breads and vegetable dishes, especially on those made with lentils, eggplant, cauliflower, and potatoes. The mixture is available by mail order but it simply prepared and a worthy addition to your seasoning arsenal. There is a huge dispute among those loyal to this seasoning as to whether the mixture should include black mustard seeds or radhuni seeds, for which celery/lovage seeds can be substituted. I won't get into the argument but I have tried it both ways and found that I do prefer the refreshing taste of the lovage seeds which I harvest from my herb gardens each summer.

2 tablespoons celery *or* lovage seeds
2 tablespoons nigella seeds*
2 tablespoons cumin seeds
2 tablespoons fennel seeds
1 tablespoon fenugreek seeds*

In a small jar with a tightly fitting lid, combine all the seeds. Store in a cool, dark cabinet until required. Some Bengali recipes will call for sizzling the seeds in a skillet until they burst; others will simply direct that the mixture be sprinkled over the dish.

Note: *Nigella and fenugreek seeds are available from mail order firms.

Yields 10 tablespoonfuls

BANGLADESHI SWEET *PASTA* DESSERT WITH ALMONDS AND RAISINS
Sherai Jarda
TPT - 58 minutes;
30 minutes = raisin soaking period

It may seem strange to you to find a pasta dessert in Bangladesh but noodles are eaten all over Asia and if you have ever gone to the trouble to make your own noodles and spaghetti, you well know that packaged pasta products are a convenience that is not to be ignored. It may also seem strange to you to even find pasta used in a dessert. When one considers the noodle puddings or kugels of Eastern Europe, maybe it is not so strange.

1/4 cup *preservative-free dark* raisins
1 cup *boiling* water

1/2 cup *fat-free* pasteurized eggs (the equivalent of 2 eggs)
1 cup *two-percent* milk
1/2 cup sugar
Pinch salt

1/4 cup CLARIFIED BUTTER *or* GHEE [see index]
2 whole pods cardamom
1 cinnamon quill—broken in half
2 whole cloves
1 bay leaf—halved
2 tablespoon chopped *or* slivered, *preservative-free* almonds

2 cups *cooked and well-drained* angel hair *pasta* (*capelli d'angelo* or, sometimes, *capellini*)

In a small bowl, combine raisins and *boiling* water. Set aside for about 30 minutes. Drain well. Set aside until required.

In another small bowl, combine pasteurized eggs, milk, sugar, and salt. Stir to mix well. Set aside until required.

In a large skillet set over *LOW-MEDIUM* heat, combine clarified butter, cardamom pods, cinnamon quill pieces, whole cloves, bay leaf pieces, and almonds. Allow to heat gently, while stirring constantly, until the almonds just begin to brown.

BANGLADESHI SWEET *PASTA* DESSERT WITH ALMONDS AND RAISINS (cont'd)

Add *cooked pasta*. Cook, *stirring constantly*, until *pasta* is heated through. *Remove from heat.* Fish cardamom pods, cinnamon quill pieces, whole cloves, and bay leaf pieces out to the skillet. *Return to heat.*

Add plumped raisins and sweet egg–milk mixture. Mix very thoroughly. Cover and allow to cook for several minutes. Remove cover and cook, *stirring constantly*, until mixture congeals and separates from the skillet in a custardy mass. Turn into a heated serving dish.

Serve at once.

Yields 6 servings
adequate for 4 people

1/6 SERVING – PROTEIN = 6.2 g.; FAT = 11.9 g.; CARBOHYDRATE = 46.0 g.;
CALORIES – 316; CALORIES FROM FAT – 34%

UNCOOKED SWEET YOGURT DESSERT
Misti Doi

TPT - 4 minutes

Milk desserts are prevalent in Bengali cuisine and are enormously popular with Bangladeshi living in Bangladesh and those living abroad. You will always find milk-based desserts on the menus of Bangladeshi restaurants. Over the years I have come to value the low-fat dessert possibilities when the refrigerator presents yogurt, sour cream, and sweetened condensed milk and found that Bangladeshi cooks pride themselves on a similar yogurt dessert but, unlike my quick, uncooked dessert, the wonderful combination of dairy products is baked. My uncooked version combines cream, yogurt, and sweetened condensed milk into a finale for a meal that takes just minutes and is absolutely delicious. Although it is most frequently served as a family dessert in our house, the response to a large bowlful of doi on a holiday buffet table is remarkable.

2 cups YOGURT *CRÈME* [see recipe which follows]
1/2 cup *fat-free* sweetened condensed milk
1/2 cup sugar

2 tablespoons light cream *or* half and half—more or less as needed for desired consistency

In a mixing bowl, combine yogurt *crème*, sweetened condensed milk, and sugar. Using a wire whisk, combine thoroughly.

Gradually whisk in cream until you have a pudding consistency. Turn into six individual serving dishes, wine glasses, or sherbet glasses, or, if preferred turn into a single serving bowl. Refrigerate until required.

Yields 6 individual servings

Note: This recipe can be halved or doubled easily, when required.

1/6 SERVING – PROTEIN = 13.6 g.; FAT = 0.4 g.; CARBOHYDRATE = 43.3 g.;
CALORIES = 234; CALORIES FROM FAT = 2%

YOGURT *CRÈME*

TPT - about 8 hours and 5 minutes;
8 hours = yogurt draining period

Although this recipe is often called "yogurt cheese" by food writers, it is not a cheese in terms of taste or use. We prefer to call this "yogurt crème" because of its rich, thick, creamy consistency which is ideal for use in desserts; as a base for chilled soups; as a substitute for sour cream and crème fraîche; or as a condiment with Middle Eastern menus. We evolved it as a substitute for sour cream many years before we ever found reference to it and before fat-free sour cream appeared in the dairy case.

3 cups PLAIN YOGURT *[see index]* ***or***
commercially-available plain yogurt

Set two automatic drip coffeemaker filters into a sieve over a medium-sized bowl or a yogurt filter over a 2-cup measuring cup. Pour the PLAIN YOGURT into the filters and set in the refrigerator. Allow to drain for about 8 hours, or until of the consistency appropriate for your use.*

Turn prepared YOGURT *CRÈME* into a bowl and proceed as directed in the recipe which you wish to prepare. If not to be used immediately, cover bowl with plastic wrap and refrigerate for not more than 3 days.

Yields approximately 1 1/2 cupfuls

Note: *This is well-accomplished overnight but the time must be experimented with to give you the consistency which pleases you. It should be noted that the yield will, of course, vary as the final product is more or less concentrated.

1/24 SERVING (i. e., per tablespoonful) –
PROTEIN = 2.6 g.; FAT = 0.04 g.; CARBOHYDRATE = 3.2 g.;
CALORIES = 22; CALORIES FROM FAT = 2%

Bhutan

The Kingdom of Bhutan was formed in the seventeenth century AD by Shabdrung Ngawang Namgyal, a Tibetan military leader and lama who fled religious persecution in Tibet and united the warring fiefdoms that occupied the region. Although archaeological evidence that includes large stone structures, stone tools, and weapons suggest that Bhutan was occupied as early as 2000 BC, the intervening ancient civilizations are for the most part undocumented. Further, a devastating fire swept through the ancient capital Punakha in 1827 destroying the little of Bhutan's history that actually had been recorded.

Shabdrung Ngawang Namgyal was so important to the unity of the country that his death in 1651 was kept secret until 1705. When it was known that this revered leader had been dead for fifty-four years, a period of internal unrest was precipitated which was followed by decades of militarism. Bhutan successfully repulsed the Mughal Empire whose leaders had seen opportunity in the governmental disarray in the small kingdom. In 1772 an incursion by Bhutan into the Kingdom of Cooch Behar in the south was repulsed with the help of the British East India Company and Bhutan was forced back into its pre-1730 borders. Border incidents with the British forces continued for the next hundred years culminating in the Duar War, which saw the defeat of the Bhutanese and the end of hostilities between the British and the Bhutanese. A series of civil wars, which followed shortly thereafter, brought Ugyen Wangchuck to the throne. His descendants still rule Bhutan. In the late 1980s the young king Jigme Singye Wangchuck, whose father had established a legislature, set up a Royal Advisory Council, and formed a cabinet thus transforming the nation of more than 708,000 people from an absolute monarchy into a constitutional monarchy, began an expulsion of those of Nepali origin—about one-fifth of the population. Their citizenship was revoked and their homes were burned in an effort to preserve Tibetan Buddhist culture and identity. More than one hundred thousand Bhutanese, mainly Hindu Lhotshampas from the south, who were living in camps inside the Nepali border, have been given refugee status in other nations including the United States. The expulsion was accompanied by the establishment of rigid cultural dress codes which require wearing of the nation dress, the *gho* for men and the *kira* for women, in public areas and a return to emphasis on the Buddhist culture which so strongly influences everyday life. Buddhism was first introduced to Bhutan in the seventh century AD. Vajrayan Buddhism is the state religion and is practiced by about two-thirds of the population.

Although the official language of the Kingdom of Bhutan is Dzongkha, a Dzongkha dictionary was not published until 2006. English is the second official language which is advantageous to business, commerce, and tourism. Although tourism has become an important source of income for the kingdom, it is rigidly controlled. Only 21,000 tourists are granted visas annually with the exception of Indian citizens, whose visitations are not restricted. Tourists must contract with Bhutanese tour operators, book on the Bhutanese airline, stay in approved government accommodations, and pay 100% duty on any tobacco products brought in for personal use since tobacco and smoking are banned.

. The cuisine depends heavily upon meat and rice, especially a red rice variety that will grow successfully at such high altitudes. The short growing season of this small Himalayan kingdom does limit agriculture. Bhutan, located on the southern slopes of the eastern Himalayan mountains, experiences a climate that varies dramatically with elevation. In the south you will find subtropical plains gradually shifting to a temperate climate in the highlands. In the north a polar climate prevails with year-round snow so it is not a total surprise that a limited number of ingredients reappear and reappear in Bhutanese dishes but it is a surprise to find that every dish is blessed with hot *chilies*. The recipes which follow have been modified from the fiery hot, preferred by Bhutanese, to a milder "warm" to which the western palate is more receptive. Both tomatoes and potatoes have found their way from the New World to the Top of the World and have expanded the limited variety one finds where the growing season is short and crop choice is limited.

South Asia – **Bhutan**

Potato and Mushroom *Momos* in *Tukpa* Broth
Motak

~

Cucumber Salad with Cheese

Mango Slices with Mango – Lime Dressing
Am Chu Kuleh

~ ~ ~ ~ ~ ~ ~ ~ ~ ~ ~ ~ ~ ~ ~ ~ ~ ~ ~ ~

Buckwheat Noodles with Egg and Green Onion
Bumthang Putta

Steamed Asparagus
over Sautéed Onion
with Crumbled Farmers' Cheese

~ ~ ~ ~ ~ ~ ~ ~ ~ ~

either *Chilies* and Cheese   or   **Mushroom Stew**
Ema Datsi   *Tshoem*

over

Red and White Rice
Eue Chhum

~ ~ ~ ~ ~ ~ ~ ~ ~ ~

Rice with Vegetables
Zow Shungo

~ ~ ~ ~ ~ ~ ~ ~ ~ ~ ~ ~ ~ ~ ~ ~ ~ ~ ~ ~

Watermelon Chunks

Mango Slices

Sago with Coconut Milk

POTATO AND MUSHROOM *MOMOS* IN *TUKPA* BROTH
Motak

TPT - 1 hour and 38 minutes

Momos, Himalayan ravioli or pierogi so to speak, are popular additions to a simple broth in both Tibet and Bhutan. Although the dough for these is usually made in the home and is of the consistency of a ravioli, wonton wrappers result in a more delicate momo. Some versions contain spinach or cabbage, garlic, greens onions, and gingerroot but this potato and mushroom version has become a favorite dumpling of ours. Potatoes were introduced to the Himalayan kingdoms by the British about two hundred years ago and are widely incorporated into dishes whose origins might be hundreds and hundreds of years older. The present Dalai Lama is said to like this combination immensely and that endorsement did not lead us astray. Delicious . . .

South Asia – Bhutan

POTATO AND MUSHROOM *MOMOS* IN *TUKPA* BROTH (cont'd)

2 medium potatoes—peeled and chopped
3 quarts *boiling* water

1/4 cup *feta* cheese
2 tablespoons *finely* chopped fresh coriander (*cilantro*)
Pinch HOMEMADE PAPRIKA *[see index]* or commercially-available paprika

1 tablespoon sunflower *or* safflower oil
1 medium onion—*very finely* chopped

4 ounces assorted wild mushrooms—well-rinsed, trimmed, and *finely* chopped

Salt, to taste
Freshly ground mixed peppercorns—red, black, and white—to taste

24 *wonton* wrappers (skins) *or* round Japanese *gyoza* wrappers, if available

6 cups TIBETAN VEGETABLE BROTH (*Tukpa*) *[see index]*

In a saucepan set over *MEDIUM* heat, cook chopped potatoes in *boiling* water for about 20 minutes. Drain thoroughly. Turn into a mixing bowl and mash well.

Add *feta* cheese, *finely* chopped fresh coriander (*cilantro*), and paprika. Set aside briefly.

Set up a steamer.

In a non-stick-coated skillet set over *MEDIUM* heat, heat oil. Add *finely* chopped onions and sauté until onions are soft and translucent, *being careful not to allow the onions to brown.*

Add *finely* chopped mushrooms. Sauté until mushroom are brown and most of water extruded by mushrooms has evaporated. Add onion–mushroom mixture to potato–cheese mixture. Gently combine.

Season with salt and ground mixed peppercorns. Stir to combine.

Lay *wonton* wrappers out on a work surface. Divide the *momo* filling among the *wonton* wrappers. Gather each *momo* up in one hand and pleat and seal the tops with the other hand. Place in steamer set over *simmering* water and steam for 20 minutes. Put *momos* in a heated soup tureen.

Pour *tukpa* broth into a kettle set over *MEDIUM* heat. Allow to come to the boil. Pour boiling broth over the *momos* in the soup tureen.

Serve at once into heated soup bowls.

Yields 6 servings
of about 1 cup broth and four *momos* each

1/6 SERVING – PROTEIN = 4.9 g.; FAT = 4.3 g.; CARBOHYDRATE = 21.8 g.;
CALORIES = 159; CALORIES FROM FAT = 24%

BHUTANESE CUCUMBER SALAD WITH CHEESE
TPT - 2 hours and 5 minutes;
2 hours = flavor development period

Unlike " ema datshi" which is a fiery hot dish of chilies in a spicy cheese sauce and is considered the national dish of Bhutan by some, this salad incorporates mild green chilies and cucumber with farmers' cheese for an uncharacteristically mild Bhutanese summer specialty.

1 large cucumber—peeled, halved, seeded and chopped
1/2 cup *finely* chopped Italian red onion
1/3 cup *feta* cheese—crumbled
2 tablespoons canned mild green *chilies*—*finely* chopped

Salt, to taste
Freshly ground black pepper, to taste

In a mixing bowl, combine chopped cucumber, *finely* chopped onion, crumbled cheese, and *finely* chopped green *chilies*. Cover bowl and refrigerate for at least 2 hours. Remove from refrigerator. Toss gently.

Season with salt and pepper. Turn into serving bowl.

Serve chilled.

Yields 6 servings
adequate for 4 people

South Asia – **Bhutan**

BHUTANESE CUCUMBER SALAD WITH CHEESE (cont'd)

Note: This recipe can be doubled, when required.

1/6 SERVING – PROTEIN = 2.1 g.; FAT = 2.7 g.; CARBOHYDRATE = 2.6 g.;
CALORIES = 44; CALORIES FROM FAT = 55%

MANGO SLICES WITH MANGO – LIME DRESSING
Am Chu Kaleh
TPT - 19 minutes

Whenever I get the opportunity to buy a bag of organic limes, I do buy the whole bag. No, I do not worry about them molding or drying out in the refrigerator anymore because I immediately slice and dehydrate some and juice most of the rest. This way I have the juice in the freezer for future needs and the dehydrated slices can be tossed into stews, stir-fries, or drinks or they can be ground to a powder as in this recipe to accent all kinds of dishes.

1 small dehydrated, *organic* lime slice

1/4 cup freshly squeezed lime juice
1 teaspoon honey
Pinch ground red pepper (cayenne), or to taste

3 ripe mangoes

Using a SPICE and COFFEE GRINDER, grind the dehydrated lime slice to a powder. Pour it through a tea strainer into jar or cruet. Discard residue.

Add lime juice, honey, and ground red pepper (cayenne). Shake well.

Peel mangoes. Slice each peeled mango into large, flat slices by slicing straight down, parallel to the pit, to create two slices on each side of the pit. Lay two slices, overlapping, on each of six salad plates.

Slice the remaining bits of mango off the pit and chop into small pieces. Add to lime juice mixture. Shake vigorously. Pour a portion of the lime dressing over the mango slices on each salad plate.

Refrigerate until required or serve at once.

Yields 6 servings
adequate for 4 people

Note: This recipe can be halved or doubled, when required.

1/6 SERVING – PROTEIN = 0.6 g.; FAT = 0.4 g.; CARBOHYDRATE = 22.9 g.;
CALORIES = 89; CALORIES FROM FAT = 4%

BHUTANESE BUCKWHEAT NOODLES
WITH EGG AND GREEN ONION
Bumthang Putta
TPT - 40 minutes

Buckwheat is an important grain crop in Bhutan. In the steep drylands both sweet buckwheat (Fagopyrum esculentum) and bitter buckwheat (Fagopyrum tataricum) are grown. The latter is used mostly for the treatment of hoof and mouth disease in cattle. Both species are important agricultural products for the Bhutanese population, especially in areas of the country where red rice can not be grown. Sweet buckwheat is not grown simply for the grain, although this is vitally important. The tender young leaves are used in a soup and the straw remaining after grain winnowing is used to feed cattle and dried to provide bedding. At one time simply regarded as "poor man's food," buckwheat has taken on a bit of panache here in the West so you will have no trouble locating buckwheat noodles, sold as soba noodles, for this recipe or, if you prefer to make your own noodles, buckwheat flour is available in most well-stocked grocery stores and in natural food stores.

South Asia – **Bhutan**

**BHUTANESE BUCKWHEAT NOODLES
WITH EGG AND GREEN ONION** (cont'd)

1 teaspoon safflower *or* sunflower oil
2 large eggs—slightly beaten

2 teaspoons safflower *or* sunflower oil
1/4 cup *finely* chopped onion

1/4 cup canned, *crushed* tomatoes
2 teaspoons *tamari* soy sauce*

4 ounces *soba* noodles—broken into thirds*
4 quarts *boiling* water

1/2 cup *thinly* sliced scallion—*both white and green portions*
Freshly ground mixed peppercorns—red, white, and black—to taste

In a 7-inch non-stick-coated skillet set over *MEDIUM* heat, heat the 1 teaspoonful oil. Add *one-half* of the beaten egg. Allow to spread across the pan. Lift egg as it sets to allow liquid egg to reach the hot pan surface. Fold over as for an individual omelet and slide from the pan to a cutting board. Cook the remaining egg in the same manner to form a second omelet. Allow both omelets to cool slightly. Cut into strips. Set aside until required.

Add the 2 teaspoonfuls of oil to the skillet again set over *MEDIUM* heat. Add *finely* chopped onion and sauté until onion is soft and translucent, *being careful not to allow the onions to brown.*

Add crushed tomatoes and soy sauce. Remove from heat.

In a wok, set over *MEDIUM* heat, cook the *soba* noodles in *boiling* water for about 8 minutes. Drain well. Return the drained soba noodles to the empty wok. Reduce heat to *LOW-MEDIUM*. Add tomato-onion mixture and stir constantly as you coat the noodles with the sauce.

Add egg strips and scallion slices. Continue cooking while tossing the ingredients together until heated through. Turn into a heated serving bowl or onto a heated serving platter.

Serve at once.

Yields 6 servings
adequate for 4 people

Notes: *Soba* buckwheat noodles are available in well-stocked natural food stores and from mail order firms.

This recipe can be halved, when required.

1/6 SERVING – PROTEIN = 5.1 g.; FAT = 4.5 g.; CARBOHYDRATE = 18.2 g.;
CALORIES = 118; CALORIES FROM FAT = 34%

BHUTANESE *CHILIES* AND CHEESE
Ema Datshi
TPT - 31 minutes

Ask any Bhutanese what the national dish is and they will say, without hesitation, "ema datshi." That is as far as agreement goes on the subject because most Bhutanese will use the hottest peppers they can find. Western palates wither at the Bhutanese tolerance for fiery hot peppers but can usually be accommodated by local restaurateurs who will prepare dishes like this with milder green chilies. Ema datshi is always served in western restaurants that bill themselves as Himalayan and, yes, there are more in the United States, than you might imagine. Reviews of these restaurants, which presumably cater to immigrants from the nations of the Himalayan region, are, without exception, critical of the execution of this dish. Our version is made with green chilies and cow's milk cheeses instead of a cheese made from the milk of a dri, the female yak. By all means, replace the mild green chilies with hotter chilies as your tolerance grows.

1 cup *boiling* water
4 1/2 ounces whole mild green *chilies*—seeded and cut into wide strips—or to taste
1/2 sweet onion—Vidalia, Walla Walla, *or* Texas or Mayan Sweet—*thinly* sliced
2 teaspoons canola oil

3/4 cup canned, *diced* tomatoes
3 large garlic cloves—crushed and *finely* chopped

5 ounces *feta* cheese—chopped
3 ounces English Stilton cheese *or* Danish blue cheese—chopped

2 tablespoons chopped fresh coriander (*cilantro*)

VOLUME I - 659

BHUTANESE *CHILIES* AND CHEESE (cont'd)

In a saucepan set over *MEDIUM* heat, combine *boiling* water, green *chili* strips, *thinly* sliced onion, and oil. Allow to cook for about 10 minutes.

Add *diced* tomatoes and *finely* chopped garlic. Continue to boil for about 4 minutes more, stirring frequently.

Add chopped cheeses. Cook, stirring frequently, until cheese is melted. Remove from heat.

Add fresh coriander (*cilantro*). Stir. Cover and allow to stand 3 minutes before turning into a heated serving bowl.

Serve hot over rice, preferably Bhutanese red rice.

Yields 8 servings
adequate for 6 people

Note: This recipe can be doubled, when required.

1/8 SERVING – PROTEIN = 8.6 g.; FAT = 12.1 g.; CARBOHYDRATE = 5.1 g.;
CALORIES = 169; CALORIES FROM FAT = 64%

BHUTANESE MUSHROOM STEW
Tshoem

TPT - 30 minutes

Tshoem translates into English from Dzongkha as curry but in Bhutan the concept of curry refers not to the spicing of the dish, as it does in India, but instead simply denotes a hearty stew. Bhutanese are very fond of mushrooms and use the some four hundred varieties that they gather in many ways. I have made the following dish using just mushrooms but the name "tshoem" did not seem entirely appropriate. In this version a soy analogue product substitutes for the beef that is usually used in this dish and gives the stew the substance of the original.

1 large garlic clove—chopped
1 tablespoon chopped fresh gingerroot

3 tablespoons butter
4 ounces *frozen* soy meat analogue strips *or*
  nuggets, as preferred
1 medium onion—chopped
3/4 cup water

3 tablespoons chopped mild green *chilies*
3 cups fresh oyster mushrooms—trimmed,
  cleaned well with a brush, and well-rinsed
Freshly ground black pepper, to taste

On a chopping board, chop the garlic and gingerroot together until *finely* chopped. Set aside briefly.

In a large saucepan set over *LOW-MEDIUM* heat, melt butter. Add soy meat analogue product and chopped onion. Sauté for a few minutes until soymeat is defrosted and onion softens. Add water and allow to come to the simmer.

Add *finely* chopped garlic and gingerroot mixture, chopped green *chilies*, oyster mushrooms, and black pepper. Cook, stirring frequently, until mushrooms are tender—about 10-15 minutes. Turn into a heated serving bowl.

Serve hot, over rice.

Yields 6 servings
adequate for 4 people

Note: This recipe can be doubled, when required.

1/6 SERVING – PROTEIN = 5.9 g.; FAT = 6.9 g.; CARBOHYDRATE = 4.2 g.;
CALORIES = 99; CALORIES FROM FAT = 62%

South Asia–**Bhutan**

BHUTANESE RED AND WHITE RICE
Eue Chhum Ja Chhum
TPT - 42 minutes

Bhutanese red rice is a chewy, reddish-brown grain that has a nutty flavor. In this very traditional dish it is mixed with white rice. This most unique red rice is the only true rice that will grow at this high altitude. Instead of ordinary grocery store white rice, I prefer to use the fragrant Mekong Flower rice grown in the Mekong River delta in this dish. Both these unusual rice varieties are available from mail order firms.

1/2 cup dry Bhutan red rice
1 1/2 cups *boiling* water

1/2 cup dry Mekong Flower rice *or* long grain white rice, of choice
1 1/2 cups *boiling* water

In a saucepan set over *LOW* heat, combine red rice and *boiling* water. Cover and allow to steam for about 20-30 minutes, or until all of the water as been absorbed. Remove cover and allow steam to escape.

In a second saucepan set over *LOW* heat, combine white rice and *boiling* water. Cover and allow to steam for about 20 minutes, or until all the water has been absorbed. Remove cover allow steam to escape.

Add the white rice to the red rice. Stir with a wooden fork to mix and fluff the rice. Turn into a heated serving bowl and place on a warming tray set at MEDIUM-HIGH until other dishes are ready to serve.

Serve hot.

Yields 6 servings
adequate for 4 people

Note: This recipe can be doubled. The leftover rice can be reheated and used to prepare *zow shungo* [see recipe which follows] which is, quite simply, rice with leftover vegetables.

1/6 SERVING – PROTEIN = 2.1 g.; FAT = 0.06 g.; CARBOHYDRATE = 25.1 g.; CALORIES = 109; CALORIES FROM FAT = <1%

RICE WITH VEGETABLES IN THE BHUTANESE STYLE
Zow Shungo
TPT - 20 minutes

"Zow shungo" describes a dish that is simply reheated, leftover vegetables served over rice. This recipe was evolved to make this simple vegetarian dish when there were no leftover vegetables in the refrigerator. Instead of stir-frying or sautéing, the Bhutanese boil their vegetables with copious amounts of butter. The technique we use preserves the Bhutanese method and is also kinder to the nutritional content of the vegetables.

3 tablespoons butter
1/4 cup water

1 small potato – peeled and diced
1 cup well-washed and trimmed fresh mushrooms of choice—sliced
1 cup fresh well-rinsed and trimmed asparagus pieces
1/4 cup *finely* chopped onion

1/4 cup canned, *diced* tomatoes*
1/4 cup tightly packed green pea tendrils, if available
2 tablespoons diced mild green *chilies*
Crushed red pepper flakes, to taste

1/2 cup chopped fresh coriander (*cilantro*) leaves —well-rinsed

6 cups hot, steamed rice, preferably BHUTANESE RED AND WHITE RICE (*Eue Chhum Ja Chhum*) [see recipe which precedes]

In a large saucepan set over *MEDIUM* heat, combine butter and water. Allow to heat for several minutes.

Add diced potato, mushroom slices, asparagus pieces, and *finely* chopped onion. Cook, stirring frequently, for about 8-10 minutes. Add more water, as needed.

Add diced tomatoes, green pea tendrils, and diced green *chilies*. Season with crushed red pepper flakes. Cook, stirring frequently, for several more minutes. Add a bit more water, if necessary.

South Asia – **Bhutan**

**RICE WITH VEGETABLES IN
THE BHUTANESE STYLE** (cont'd)

Add chopped fresh coriander (*cilantro*). Turn into a heated serving dish.

Serve at once over hot, steamed rice.

> Yields 6 servings
> adequate for 4 people

Notes: *Petite diced tomatoes are preferable for this recipe.

This recipe can be halved or doubled, when required.

> 1/6 SERVING – PROTEIN = 5.2 g.; FAT = 17.0 g.; CARBOHYDRATE = 50.9 g.;
> CALORIES = 285; CALORIES FROM FAT = 53%

SAGO WITH COCONUT MILK
TPT - 2 hours and 20 minutes;
2 hours = chilling period

My grandmother's tapioca pudding, made with the large, "fish-eye" tapioca, was very popular with her grandchildren. After much watching and measuring, I learned to make that absolutely luscious dessert but I must say that I did think that it should be named "All-Day Tapioca Pudding." Before quick-cooking tapioca was available, tapioca pudding took an expenditure of hours and hours of cooking fuel and time. Quick-cooking tapioca/sago and canned coconut milk, exported from Thailand, are both available to the Bhutanese cook. Since the Bhutanese turn most of their milk into butter or cheese, this is a more unusual dish for this cuisine and would more probably be served in hotel restaurants than in the average home.

I add an egg and vanilla extract to my version of this pudding. These can be omitted, if preferred. In addition, water can be substituted for milk if a vegan dessert is desired. When available, sliced bananas are often added to this pudding in Bhutan.

**1 1/2 cups skimmed milk
1 can (13-14 ounces)** *light, sulfite-free* **coconut milk
1/4 cup quick-cooking tapioca
6 tablespoons sugar**

1/4 cup *fat-free* **pasteurized eggs (the equivalent of 1 egg)
1 teaspoon pure vanilla extract**

In a large saucepan set over *LOW-MEDIUM* heat, combine milk, coconut milk, tapioca, and sugar. Using a wire whisk, combine well. Allow mixture to come to a boil, stirring *very* frequently. *Remove from heat.*

In a mixing bowl, combine pasteurized eggs and vanilla extract. Whisk to combine.

While stirring the eggs with a wire whisk, add two or three tablespoonfuls of the tapioca mixture. Beat well. Then, add two or three tablespoonfuls more of the tapioca mixture. Again, beat it into the egg mixture. *Gradually*, while stirring the tapioca mixture in the saucepan with a wire whisk, add the egg mixture to the tapioca pudding. Whisk until thoroughly combined. Place over *LOW* heat and cook, stirring constantly, until the pudding thickens slightly.

Stir in vanilla extract. Turn into a serving bowl. Refrigerate for at least 2 hours, until cold and firmly set.

Serve chilled.

> Yields 8 servings
> adequate for 6 people

> 1/8 SERVING – PROTEIN = 2.3 g.; FAT = 1.1 g.; CARBOHYDRATE = 17.6 g.;
> CALORIES = 88; CALORIES FROM FAT = 11%

South Asia—India

India

Paleolithic era petroglyphs, found in caves in Madhya Pradesh, record the presence of prehistoric hunter-gathers who first came to the Indus Valley. They may have moved on or they may have been the ancestors of those who established the first known permanent settlements which date to about 6500 BC. These settlements appear to have developed into what has became known as the Indus Valley Civilization which dates to about 3400 BC. The foundations for Hinduism were laid during the succeeding Vedic Period which ended about 500 BC. Then began the period of the Mahajanapadas with independent kingdoms and republics spread across the country. These empires grew and ebbed culminating in a period beginning in the third century AD known the "Golden Age" of ancient India. Under the Gupta Dynasty and through the patronage of succeeding rulers art, science, mathematics, astronomy, literature, and technology together with logic, religion, and philosophy flourished laying the cultural foundation for the India we know today.

At the crossways of trading routes and as the source of spices coveted by the world, trading posts were set up by nations such as Portugal, The Netherlands, France, and Great Britain, each seeking influence in the area. These nations took advantage of conflicts and quickly expanded their trading posts into colonies. In 1857, with most of India under the control of the British East India Company, an insurrection known as the Sepoy Mutiny challenged the British control but the instability it precipitated was followed by British consolidation and India was brought under the direct rule of Great Britain. The non-violent campaign led by Mahatma Gandhi, which attracted millions of followers, contributed, in no small way, to eventual independence in 1947 and the concurrent formation of the Moslem nation of Pakistan. India, the second most populous nation in the world, with over one billion people as of the 2001 census, is a parliamentary republic within the British Commonwealth. Its democratic journey has not always been an easy journey since both China and Pakistan have challenged India seeking territorial gains.

Regional differences have actually developed into distinctive cuisines within the term "Indian cuisine." Kashmiri, Punjabi, and Rajasthan cuisines hint strongly at influences incorporated during the period between the tenth and twelfth centuries when much of northern India was ruled by invading peoples from Central Asia and, later, by the Mughal (Moghul) Empire. The Mughal emperors, descendants of the Timurids and of Turco–Mongol ancestry, first came to power in 1526 and ruled until 1857 when the last Mughal emperor was deposed by the British. Foods here are rich and there is a heavy use of meat in these regions with only a small nod to vegetarianism. Kashmiri cuisine is an ancient cuisine strongly influenced by the cultures who invaded Kashmir from the region of present-day Uzbekistan and clearly traceable to the cuisines of Central Asia and Persia. The food in the Punjab is usually cooked with lots of *ghee*, cream, and *masala* spicing. Ground grains like farina are found in many dishes. The *tandoor* is the favored cooking pot for meats and breads like *nan* (*naan*). *Rajput* is an arid area of India. Rajasthan foods are most frequently cooked in milk or *ghee* and, as a result, dishes are quite rich to the western taste. *Besan* flour (chick pea flour) is a staple of the people of Rajput and it is from this area that *boondi*, an addictive snack, found its way to our kitchen. Uttar Pradesh has given us *paneer*, *dal*, *roti*, and *pooris* but rice, not wheat, is the staple here. Assam cuisine is strongly spiced but due less to ground spices as in other regions of India, and more to local herbs. Bihar cuisine is predominately vegetarian with dishes containing dairy products favored, although fish is also widely consumed. The spicy potato mixture that forms the filling for *samosas* comes from Bihar. Bengali cuisine emphasizes fish, lentils, rice, and sweet desserts. Dishes common to Orissa are subtly spiced and never, never have to be requested as "mild please" by westerners unlike the cuisine of Andhra Pradesh in the South where spices and *chilies* are added with a heavy hand. In Karnataka you can legitimately start your meal with a dessert. The cuisine of Kerala includes many dishes with coconut and coconut milk. Fish, rice, and manioc are included in most meals and everything is well spiced, but not hot. I have favorite lentil and legume recipes from Tamil

Nadu, using a warm spice blend that includes rose water, and wheat and lentil recipes with coconut from Maharashtra, which is a coastal province on the Arabian Sea. Goa, also on the Arabian Sea, has a cuisine which includes many dishes that hint at its Portuguese past. The inhabitants of Nagaland, Sikkim, Arunachal Pradesh, and Tripura, all in the shadow of the Himalayas, have their own challenges to survival and, consequently, their own cuisines based on vegetables that can be grown and the animals they can raise in the climates of these northern provinces, far different from the provinces in the south of India.

India is unique in that, unlike other countries, those who have come and gone have not significantly changed what is Indian, maybe, in part, because the food of India was already diverse and was relished by those who first tasted it. The colonial occupiers took Indian food home to Europe with them instead of persisting in bringing Europe to their Indian homes. Case in point: you can find an Indian take-away with a good *vindaloo* in almost every neighborhood in London. The divisions in what was often referenced as the Indian Subcontinent have fortunately left intact one of the most beautiful and diverse cuisines in the world. Hinduism, Buddhism, Jainism, and Sikhism originated in Indian and Zoroastrianism, Judaism, Christianity, and Islam were introduced in the first century AD, each bringing their own reverence for foods. These religious beliefs have influenced the cuisine making it richer and more complex. To a vegetarian looking for sustenance, India is home and mother. No other nation in the world produces cooks with the unique sense of spicing. An Indian spice box sits on my book shelves reminding me always that one must open several drawers to achieve variety and health.

The many vegetable-rich dishes of the diverse cuisines of India offer so much variety to the vegetarian whether you choose a vegan or lacto-ovo lifestyle. When we visit a new area of the United States, we try to locate a nearby Indian restaurant. First we might explore their interpretations of old favorites; then we immerse ourselves in their specialty dishes. Lunches and lunch buffets available in family-owned Indian restaurants satisfy the soul as well as the hunger of a traveling vegetarian.

~

Included are many of the Indian dishes we love most from which you can select or create a buffet to thrill your guests.

South Asia – India

Baked *Samosa* Casserole
Aloo Samosa

Mango Powder
Amchur

Chick Pea Dumplings in Yogurt Sauce
Boondi Raita

~

Tomato Soup in the Style of Mumbai
Tamatarshorva

~

Cucumber and Tomato Salad with *Chaat Masala*
Kachoomar Chaat Masala

Mixed Fruit Salad with *Chaat Masala*
Phalon ki Chaat Masala

Orange, White Radish, and Onion Salad with Cumin
Santre au Mooli

Cucumber – Yogurt Salad
Kheere ka Raita

~~~~~~~~~~~~~~~~~~~~

Potatoes Braised in Aromatic Cream Sauce
Rogani Aloo

Northern Indian Roasted Eggplant
Bharta

~~~~~~~~~~

Curried Eggs and Rice

Cheese and Red Peppers in Spinach Sauce   or   **Cheese with Peas**
Saag Paneer   *Mattar Paneer*

Clarified Butter
Ghee

Indian Cheese
Paneer

~~~~~~~~~~~~~~~~~~~~~

Baked Cheese Sweet in the Style of Calcutta with Tropical Fruit Garnish
Channa ki Mithi

Cardamom Wheat Pudding in the Style of Northern India
Sooji Elaichi

Indian-Style Mango Ice Cream
Aam Kulfi

~

Our Indian Spice Mixture
Garam Masala

Our *Tandoori* Spice Mixture
Chaat Masala

South Asia–**India**

BAKED INDIAN *SAMOSA* CASSEROLE
Aloo Samosa

TPT - 1 hour and 18 minutes

Ordering samosas as an appetizer at our favorite Indian restaurant results in little appetite for the rest of their phenomenal meal, and we have to travel a distance to visit this restaurant . . . dilemma upon dilemma . . . because their samosas are so very good, albeit deep-fried. Much as I love the pastry crust, less might be more. Instead of packing the filling into large rounds of pastry I decided to pack the filling into a pie crust. It makes a satisfying lunch served with a fruit salad. Cut as a pie and served as an appetizer, there is room for other dishes, and it allows diners to maximize filling or crust as they choose. In addition, it is another way for me to eliminate some unbleached white flour from our diet.

1/2 recipe WHOLE WHEAT PIE CRUSTS, i. e., single crust *[see index]*

1 tablespoon black mustard seeds
1/2 teaspoon OUR INDIAN SPICE MIXTURE (Garam Masala) *[see index]* **or CURRY POWDER** *[see index]**
1 teaspoon INDIAN MANGO POWDER (Amchur) *[see recipe which follows]*
1 teaspoon ground ginger
1/2 teaspoon ground cumin

5 medium Yukon potatoes—peeled and quartered
3 quarts *boiling* **water**

1 tablespoon canola oil
1 medium onion—*finely* **chopped to yield 1 cupful**
1 medium carrot—scraped or pared and *finely* **chopped to yield about 1/2 cupful**

2 garlic cloves—*very finely* **chopped**

1 cup freshly shelled *or frozen* **peas**
1 tablespoon *finely* **chopped mild green** *chilies*
3/4 cup vegetarian stock of choice
1 tablespoon sugar

Preheat oven to 375 degrees F. Prepare a 10-inch pie plate by coating with non-stick lecithin spray coating. Set aside.

On a pastry board, roll out the pie crust into an 11-inch circle. Fold in quarters (bottom to top; then right to left), lay in upper left quadrant of prepared 9-inch pie plate, and unfold. Trim around edge leaving about 1/2 inch beyond rim. Turn excess under and crimp—pressing down slightly as you go to give a rather firm attachment and thus reducing shrinkage somewhat. Set aside until required.

In a small bowl, combine mustard seeds, *garam masala* or curry powder, mango powder, ground ginger and cumin, and red pepper flakes. Set aside until required.

In a large saucepan set over *MEDIUM* heat, cook quartered potatoes in *boiling* water until tender—about 15 minutes. Drain. Using a potato ricer, rice the potatoes into a mixing bowl.** Set aside briefly.

In a skillet set over *MEDIUM* heat, heat oil. Add *finely* chopped onion and carrot. Cook, stirring frequently, for several minutes, or until vegetables begin to soften.

Add *very finely* chopped garlic. Sauté for several minutes more. Push onion–carrot–garlic mixture to the side of the pan.

Add spicing mixture and, while stirring, toast the spices until the aroma release is apparent—only about 45 seconds to a minute.

Add peas, *finely* chopped green *chilies*, vegetable broth, and sugar. Stir to thoroughly combine. Add to riced potatoes and stir to combine. Turn into crust-lined pie plate, spreading the filling evenly to the sides of the baking dish.***

Bake in preheated 375 degree F. oven for about 30 minutes, or until crust is golden.

Serve hot, cut into wedges as for a pie.

Yields 10 appetizer servings

Note: *Both *garam masala* or curry powder can be homemade or commercial and either can be increased or decreased, depending on your taste.

**The texture of the potatoes is greatly improved if you rice them rather than mash.

***The *samosa* casserole can be made in advance to this point, covered securely, and frozen. Uncover, defrost to room temperature before baking.

This does make a terrific lunch dish too.

BAKED INDIAN *SAMOSA* CASSEROLE (cont'd)

1/10 SERVING – PROTEIN = 3.7 g.; FAT = 6.4 g.; CARBOHYDRATE = 23.3 g.;
CALORIES = 165; CALORIES FROM FAT = 35%

INDIAN MANGO POWDER
Amchur

TPT - 24 hours and 25 minutes;
24 hours = dehydration period

Tandoori food is invariably seasoned with a mixture than includes amchur which is a powder made from green mangoes. Unable to obtain it except by mail order at a price that seemed unreasonable, I decided to buy rock-hard green mangoes and make my own. Yes, I was now able to add this unique seasoning to my own tandoori spice mixture but the flavor of the amchur is so unique and so interesting that it has proved more useful on more occasions than I could have ever expected.

2 *very hard, green* mangoes

Sterilize a 1/2-pint jar. Also sterilize a lid and ring for jar.

Using a vegetable peeler, peel the mangoes. Using a sharp knife, slice the flesh into *thin* slices by sliding the knife down and along the large pit. Arrange the slices on the drying trays of a dehydrator. Dry the mango slices until hard, alternating the drying trays several times a day.

Grind the *dried* mango slices, a few at a time, using a SPICE and COFFEE GRINDER, until powderized. Transfer the powder to the clean, dry jelly jar and seal with a lid and ring. Store in a cool, dry place.

Yields about 3/4 cupful

1/36 SERVING (per teaspoonful) –
PROTEIN = 0.06 g.; FAT = 0.03 g.; CARBOHYDRATE = 2.0 g.;
CALORIES = 8; CALORIES FROM FAT = <1%

CHICK PEA DUMPLINGS IN YOGURT SAUCE
Boondi Raita

TPT - 1 hour and 5 minutes;
30 minutes = dumpling chilling period

The first time I tasted this dish at the India Pavilion in State College, Pennsylvania, I was ready to go back the next day and eat them until I could eat no more. They were that good. These divine dumplings, which originate in the North of India, often turn up on Indian buffet tables labeled lentil balls made with lentil flour instead of chick pea flour. They are a warm weather favorite of ours. We serve them either on the side in a small dish or over basmati rice as a light supper or lunch dish.

The sauce presented here is similar to the one we use with our Punjabi kidney bean salad with nuts. When the two dishes are served together the flavor continuity makes them remarkable companions.

South Asia–India

CHICK PEA DUMPLINGS IN YOGURT SAUCE (cont'd)

1 cup *boondi**
1 cup *warm* water

INDIAN YOGURT SAUCE:
    3/4 cup PLAIN YOGURT *[see index] or* commercially-available plain yogurt
    5 tablespoons unsalted, cultured buttermilk *or* 2 tablespoons dried buttermilk powder plus 5 tablespoons water
    1 tablespoon honey *or agave* nectar, if preferred
    1 tablespoon chopped mild green *chilies*
    1 tablespoon *finely* chopped fresh coriander (*cilantro*)
    1/2 teaspoon OUR *TANDOORI* SPICE MIXTURE (*Chaat Masala*) *[see index] or* commercially-available mixture
    1/4 teaspoon ground cumin
    1/4 teaspoon freshly ground black pepper

In a shallow mixing bowl, combine *boondi* and warm water. Allow to stand until the crisp chick pea pearls soften. Using a potato masher, mash the *boondi* until a mash is formed. *Add more water, if necessary.* Gather a portion of the softened pearls and squeeze the water out. Form into a ball. Place in a soup plate. Continue until all the pearls have been formed into dumplings. Refrigerate the dumplings for at least 30 minutes.

Prepare sauce in a small bowl, combine yogurt, buttermilk, honey or *agave* nectar, chopped green *chilies, finely* chopped fresh coriander (*cilantro*), ground cumin, and black pepper. Refrigerate until ready to serve.

Pour yogurt sauce over dumplings.

Serve chilled, with prepared yogurt sauce.

                Yields about 12 dumplings
        adequate for 6 people as a first course

Notes: *Boondi are crisp, seasoned balls or pearls made from chick pea flour, a specialty of the Punjab region. They are eaten as snacks or added to salads and yogurt for added protein and for textural interest. They can be made at home but are conveniently available in Indian groceries and through mail order.

This recipe can be halved or doubled when required.

1/6 SERVING – PROTEIN = 3.9 g.; FAT = 0.5 g.; CARBOHYDRATE = 2.7 g.;
CALORIES = 31; CALORIES FROM FAT = 15%

INDIAN TOMATO SOUP IN THE STYLE OF MUMBAI
Tamatarshorva
TPT - 55 minutes

The use of tomatoes in Indian cuisine is still infrequent, but it is increasing. Some Hindu sects, specifically the Brahmins and Jains, do not eat plant foods that are red, such as tomatoes, red peppers, beets, and watermelons, because the color is too much like meat. The flavoring of this soup, typical of the Indian subcontinent, is like that of no other tomato soup in the world.

4 cups peeled, seeded, and chopped fresh tomatoes *or* canned, *diced* tomatoes
1 medium red bell pepper—cored, seeded, membranes removed, and coarsely chopped

1 can (6 ounces) tomato paste
2 cups VEGETARIAN BROWN STOCK, VEGETARIAN WHITE STOCK, VEGETABLE STOCK FROM SOUP *[see index]*, *or* water

2 teaspoons ground cumin
2 teaspoons ground cinnamon
2 teaspoons ground coriander
1/4 teaspoon red pepper (cayenne), or to taste

1/4 cup freshly squeezed orange juice*
2 tablespoons *light, sulfite-free* coconut milk
2 tablespoons *finely* chopped fresh coriander (*cilantro*) leaves *or* parsley, if preferred

Freshly ground black pepper, to taste

Ground *preservative-free* almonds *or* almond meal, for garnish

South Asia – **India**

INDIAN TOMATO SOUP IN THE STYLE OF MUMBAI (cont'd)

Using the electric blender or food processor fitted with steel knife, process fresh or canned tomatoes and chopped red pepper until a smooth purée is formed. Pour through a sieve to remove seeds. (Reserve residue to make soup stock.)

In a large kettle set over *MEDIUM* heat, combine prepared tomato and pepper purée, tomato paste, stock, and ground cumin, cinnamon, coriander, and red pepper (cayenne). Using a wire whisk, combine the ingredients thoroughly. Allow the soup base to *slowly* come to the boil, reduce heat to *LOW-MEDIUM*, and simmer for about 30 minutes.

Add orange juice, coconut milk, *finely* chopped fresh coriander *(cilantro)*, and black pepper. Stir to integrate well. Continue to simmer for another 10 minutes, or until heated through. Turn into a heated soup tureen.

To serve, ladle into heated soup bowls. Garnish with a sprinkling of ground almonds.

Yields about 7 cupfuls
adequate for 4-5 people

Notes: *The western palate is more receptive to orange juice in a dish such as this, although lime juice would more probably be the citrus juice of choice in India. Lime juice may be substituted, if desired.

This recipe may be halved or doubled, when required.

The complex flavoring of this soup is adversely affected by freezing but leftovers can be reheated over *LOW* heat, when required.

1/7 SERVING (i. e., per cupful) –
PROTEIN = 2.5 g.; FAT = 1.1 g.; CARBOHYDRATE = 14.9 g.;
CALORIES = 74; CALORIES FROM FAT = 13%

INDIAN CUCUMBER AND TOMATO SALAD WITH *CHAAT MASALA*
Kachoomar Chaat Masala

TPT - 4 minutes

I had occasionally chosen the spicy Indian cucumber and tomato soup offered by a favorite Long Island restaurant but it was years later before the salad possibility occurred to me. The chaat masala elevates a simple cucumber and tomato relish to amazing heights. Served with a simple omelet and sliced papaya as foils, this is a great way to nourish on a hot summer's evening.

1 small cucumber—peeled, seeded, and
  chopped into 1/4-inch pieces
1 large tomato—cored, seeded, and chopped
1/2 cup chopped red onion
2 tablespoons chopped fresh coriander (*cilantro*)
1/4 teaspoon *very finely* chopped fresh gingerroot
1/8 teaspoon *toasted* cumin seeds

2 tablespoons freshly squeezed lime juice
1 teaspoon OUR *TANDOORI* SPICE MIXTURE
  (**Chaat Masala**) *[see index]*

Salt, if desired, to taste

In a mixing bowl, combine chopped cucumber, tomato, onion, and fresh coriander (*cilantro*), *finely* chopped gingerroot, and *toasted* cumin seeds. Toss *gently*. Refrigerate until ready to serve.

Just before serving, combine lime juice and *chaat masala*. Sprinkle over salad vegetables. Season with salt, if desired. Toss *gently*. Turn into serving bowl.

Serve at once.

Yields 6 serving
adequate for 4 people

Note: This recipe can be doubled or halved, when required.

1/6 SERVING – PROTEIN = 0.4 g.; FAT = 0.1 g.; CARBOHYDRATE = 3.0 g.;
CALORIES = 13; CALORIES FROM FAT = 7%

South Asia–**India**

INDIAN MIXED FRUIT SALAD WITH *CHAAT MASALA*
Phalon ki Chaat Masala

TPT - 35 minutes;
30 minutes = maceration period

Chaat [alternately chat] masala, the traditional tandoori spice mixture, does wonders for a simple fruit mixture. Cups full of spicy fruit mixtures like this are sold by street vendors in Delhi and are a great pick-me-up when your blood sugar and/or energy levels have experienced a dip. I love to serve this salad as a counterpoint to a mildly seasoned dal or potato dish. Other fruits can be added to this mixture; use what you like and what is available. At Christmas I often top this salad with a few pomegranate seeds.

2 tablespoons pure pomegranate juice
1 teaspoon freshly squeezed lemon juice
2 teaspoons OUR *TANDOORI* SPICE MIXTURE (*Chaat Masala*) [see index]
1 teaspoon sugar
1/4 teaspoon *finely* crushed dried mint *or* lemon verbena, if desired

1/2 small cucumber—peeled, seeded, and chopped into 1/4-inch pieces
1/2 Granny Smith apple—peeled, cored, and chopped into 1/4-inch pieces
1 pear—peeled, cored, and chopped into 1/4 inch pieces
1/2 cup canned mandarin orange sections—well-drained
1 kiwifruit—peeled and chopped into 1/4 inch pieces

In a mixing bowl, combine pomegranate juice, lemon juice, *chaat masala*, sugar, and *finely* crushed dried mint. Mix well.

Add chopped cucumber, apple, pears, mandarin orange sections, and chopped kiwifruit. Toss *gently*. Turn into a serving bowl. Refrigerate for 30 minutes to allow for flavor development.

Serve at room temperature.

Yields 6 servings
adequate for 4 people

Note: This recipe can be doubled or halved, when required.

1/6 SERVING – PROTEIN = 0.4 g.; FAT = 0.1 g.; CARBOHYDRATE = 10.4 g.;
CALORIES = 30; CALORIES FROM FAT = 3%

INDIAN ORANGE, WHITE RADISH, AND ONION SALAD WITH CUMIN
Santre au Mooli

TPT - 12 minutes

Humans are unable to made vitamin C, ascorbic acid, due to the lack of the enzyme L-gulonalactone oxidase and, therefore, must seek out the vitamin in their food choices as do apes, guinea pigs, fruit bats, some insect groups, and some birds. This can be solved with orange juice in the morning or fruit at lunch or supplements but it is far more enjoyable to add the necessary nutrient by preparing desserts and salads with citrus fruits. In India, the concept of "salad" is quite different than that with which we have grown up. Raita is used to designate yogurt and vegetable salads but dishes like this fruit salad are more often referred to as savories or snacks. I simply call it "oranges and white radishes" but it is really more than that. This recipe is also popular in North Africa, from which it most probably was introduced into India. I have found it seasoned with hot chilies, cayenne pepper, and harissa; I use bottled jalapeño sauce. It is a great afternoon pick-me-up with a hunk of warm naan or it can be served as a conventional side salad with dinner.

6 large lettuce leaves—well-washed and dried

4 navel oranges—peeled

1/2 medium Italian red onion—*very thinly* sliced
2 inches of daikon radish—well-washed, trimmed, and *thinly* planed
2 tablespoons freshly squeezed lime juice

1 tablespoon *extra virgin* olive oil
1/2 teaspoon ground cumin, or to taste
1/8 teaspoon red *jalapeño chili* sauce, or to taste*
Pinch salt

South Asia—**India**

INDIAN ORANGE, WHITE RADISH, AND ONION SALAD WITH CUMIN (cont'd)

Arrange lettuce on a serving platter or large plate.

Using a very sharp knife, remove the bitter pith from each peeled orange. Slice each orange into *thin* slices. Arrange on a serving platter on top of lettuce.

Scatter *thin* onion and radish slices over.

In a mixing bowl, combine lime juice, olive oil, cumin, *jalapeño chili* sauce, and salt. Whisk until emulsified. Pour over assembled salad ingredients.

In a mixing bowl, combine lime juice, olive oil, cumin, *jalapeño chili* sauce, and salt. Whisk until emulsified. Pour over assembled salad ingredients.

Serve at once.

Notes: **Jalapeño* sauce is available in Hispanic groceries, food specialty stores, and in most grocery stores throughout the Southwest.

This recipe can be halved or doubled, when required.

Yields 6 servings
adequate for 4 people

1/6 SERVING – PROTEIN = 1.2 g.; FAT = 2.9 g.; CARBOHYDRATE = 16.7 g.;
CALORIES = 85; CALORIES FROM FAT = 31%

INDIAN CUCUMBER – YOGURT SALAD
Kheere ka Raita

TPT - about 2 hours and 13 minutes;
2 hours = draining period

Raita translates loosely to " raw or cooked vegetables or fruits mixed into seasoned yogurt," which sounds simple enough. The flavor and function of this classic Indian dish belies such a simple translation. It so beautifully compliments or contrasts with so many highly flavored dishes that it is indeed appropriate to almost any Indian menu and is especially helpful as a protein source for vegetable–based meals that do not include complemented proteins.

1 medium cucumber
1 teaspoon salt

1 cup PLAIN YOGURT *[see index]* **or**
 commercially-available plain yogurt
1 tablespoon *finely* **chopped fresh, Italian flat-leafed parsley** *or* **fresh coriander** *(cilantro),* **if available**
1/4 teaspoon ground cumin
Pinch garlic powder
Pinch ground red pepper (cayenne)
1 tablespoon freshly squeezed lemon juice
1 medium tomato—peeled, seeded, and chopped

Peel and seed cucumber, reserving seeds for soup stock. Chop into bite-sized pieces. Place in a bowl and sprinkle with salt. Set aside in the refrigerator for 2 hours. Rinse cucumber pieces well and allow to drain thoroughly.

In a small bowl, combine yogurt with *finely* chopped fresh parsley or coriander *(cilantro)*, ground cumin, garlic powder, ground red pepper (cayenne), and lemon juice. Mix well. Stir in chopped tomato and *well-drained,* chopped cucumber.

Turn into serving bowl and chill until ready to serve.

Yields 5 servings
adequate for 4 people

Notes: A tablespoonful of chopped onion may be added with cucumber, if desired.

This recipe is easily doubled or tripled, when required.

1/5 SERVING – PROTEIN = 3.2 g.; FAT = 1.0 g.; CARBOHYDRATE = 6.0 g.;
CALORIES = 46; CALORIES FROM FAT = 20%

South Asia – India

MOGHUL – STYLED POTATOES BRAISED IN AROMATIC CREAM SAUCE
Rogani Aloo
TPT - 50 minutes

A mellow, gentle, soft, sweet dish from India that became a family favorite after the very first mouthful, this wonderful potato casserole is an excellent foil for spicier dishes.

3/4 cup PLAIN YOGURT *[see index]* or
   commercially-available plain yogurt
1 cup light cream *or* half and half
1 medium onion—coarsely chopped
2 teaspoons chopped fresh gingerroot
3 tablespoons slivered *preservative-free* almonds
1 tablespoon ground coriander
3/4 teaspoon ground cardamom
1/2 teaspoon freshly ground black pepper

4 medium all-purpose potatoes (about 1 pound)
   —peeled and quartered

Light cream *or* half and half to thin sauce, if necessary

Preheat oven to 300 degrees F.

In the container of the electric blender or in the work bowl of the food processor fitted with steel knife, combine yogurt, light cream, coarsely chopped onion, chopped gingerroot, slivered almonds with ground coriander, cardamom, and black pepper. Blend or process until *very smooth*.

Bake, covered, in preheated 300 degree F. oven for about 45 minutes. Baste potatoes occasionally with sauce and turn potatoes to prevent sticking. If necessary, thin sauce with light cream.

Keep warm on warming tray until ready to serve.*
Serve directly from oven casserole or turn into heated serving bowl, if preferred.

                         Yields 6 servings
                      adequate for 4 people

Notes: *If more convenient, prepare this dish early in the day. About 20 minutes before serving, reheat in 300 degree F. oven. This time period allows the flavors to marry beautifully.

This recipe may be easily doubled, when required.

1/6 SERVING – PROTEIN = 5.4 g.; FAT = 6.5 g.; CARBOHYDRATE = 22.2 g.;
CALORIES = 167; CALORIES FROM FAT = 35%

NORTHERN INDIAN ROASTED EGGPLANT
Bharta
TPT - 1 hour and 50 minutes

One of us loves eggplant in almost any form, but one of us takes small portions. Once I tasted this eggplant dish, however, small portions were a thing of the past and I ate the whole meal with relish. Actually I now judge an Indian restaurant by their bharta.

To prepare this dish traditionally, the eggplant is smoked for about two hours over a smoking wood fire or, at the very least, roasted over a gas flame. Many, and we are among those, have electric ranges. This dish, to really be appreciated, must be eaten in an Indian restaurant where the eggplant is prepared traditionally. However, once tasted, you will long for it and this version is one way to achieve at least the essence of the dish. If you have a smoker or can use a gas grill to prepare the eggplant, by all means use either to smoke the eggplant.

1 large eggplant—about 1 1/2 pounds

1 large onion—chopped
1 garlic clove—chopped
1 1/2 teaspoons *very finely* chopped gingerroot
3 tablespoons water

1 tablespoon GHEE *[see index]*

1/2 teaspoon ground cumin—*dry-pan roasted*
Pinch ground turmeric
Pinch paprika
Pinch sugar
1/8 teaspoon salt
[see next page]

NORTHERN INDIAN ROASTED EGGPLANT (cont'd)

1/2 of a small green *chili*—seeded and *very finely* chopped
1 cup canned, *diced* tomatoes

1/4 teaspoon OUR INDIAN SPICE MIXTURE
  (*Garam Masala*) *[see recipe which follows]* or commercially-available mixture
2 tablespoons PLAIN YOGURT *[see index]* or commercially-available plain yogurt
1 tablespoon chopped fresh coriander *(cilantro)* leaves

Preheat oven to 400 degrees F. With a small knife, make two slits about 1/2-inch deep into the eggplant. Place the eggplant on a non-stick coated baking sheet and bake for about 45-50 minutes, or until very tender.

Remove eggplant from oven and halve. Place in a sieve and set over the sink to allow bitter liquid to drain away. Remove pulp to a mixing bowl. Discard eggplant skin. Mash pulp. Set aside.

In the container of the electric blender, combine chopped onion and garlic, *very finely* chopped gingerroot, and water. Blend until a smooth paste forms. In a skillet set over *MEDIUM* heat, heat ghee. Add roasted cumin, ground turmeric, paprika, sugar, and salt. Sauté briefly. Add blended onion–garlic paste and cook, stirring frequently, for about 15 minutes.

Add *very finely* chopped green *chili* and chopped tomato. Cook, stirring frequently, for about 10 minutes.

Reduce heat to *LOW*. Add mashed eggplant and cook, stirring frequently, until almost all of the moisture in the pan has evaporated—about 15 minutes.*

Remove from heat. Add *garam masala*, yogurt, and chopped coriander (*cilantro*) leaves. Stir to combine well.

Serve at once with an Indian bread of choice. Hot *pooris, nan,* and *chapatis* accompany this well. Sesame *pita* bread is also a good choice if you do not have time to prepare Indian loaves.

Yields 6 servings
adequate for 4 people

Notes: *This recipe may be frozen at this point, if more convenient to your menu planning. Defrost completely in the refrigerator. Heat and then proceed from *.

When necessary, this recipe is easily doubled.

Leftovers do not reheat well. Most *garam masala* mixtures do not maintain their flavor when heated. A fresh pinch of *garam masala* might, however, make heated leftovers suitable for a quick lunch.

1/6 SERVING – PROTEIN = 1.7 g.; FAT = 2.5 g.; CARBOHYDRATE = 7.1 g.;
CALORIES = 55; CALORIES FROM FAT = 41%

CURRIED EGGS AND RICE
TPT - 35 minutes

This is a family favorite that evolved year by year since the late 1970s when we first started experimenting with its fascinating taste combinations and textures. The yogurt and mayonnaise bake to a phenomenal custard-like consistency that is stupendous.

1/2 cup *calorie-reduced or light* mayonnaise
1/2 cup PLAIN YOGURT *[see index]* or commercially-available plain yogurt
2 teaspoons dry white wine
3/4 teaspoon HOMEMADE CURRY POWDER
  [see index] or commercially-available mixture of choice
1/8 teaspoon freshly ground black pepper

2 cups *cooked* Indian *basmati* rice,* converted rice, *or* long grain brown rice, as preferred
1 can (15 ounces) small, peeled Chinese straw mushrooms—well-drained and thoroughly rinsed in cold water**
4 hard-cooked eggs—shelled and sliced

Preheat oven to 325 degrees F. Prepare a 1 1/2-quart soufflé dish or other oven-to-table baking dish by lightly oiling or by spraying with non-stick lecithin spray coating.

In a saucepan set over *LOW* heat, combine mayonnaise, yogurt, wine, curry powder, and black pepper. Stir with a wire whisk until well-blended. Cook for about 3 minutes until warmed through. Set aside until required.

Pour rice into prepared baking dish, spreading it evenly over bottom of dish. Arrange straw mushrooms over rice and then arrange egg slices over mushrooms. Spoon curried mayonnaise–yogurt mixture evenly over egg slices.

CURRIED EGGS AND RICE (cont'd)

Bake, uncovered, in preheated 325 degree F. oven for about 25 minutes until heated through and until curried mayonnaise–yogurt mixture is *set*, but *not browned*.

Serve at once.

Yields 5 servings
adequate for 3-4 people

Notes: *Indian *basmati* rice is available in Indian groceries, Asian groceries, and natural food stores.

**If preferred, fresh mushroom slices may be substituted.

This recipe may be halved to serve two or doubled, when required. When doubled, choose a baking dish such as a quiche dish which provides a large surface area.

1/5 SERVING – PROTEIN = 9.8 g.; FAT = 13.2 g.; CARBOHYDRATE = 24.4 g.;
CALORIES = 258; CALORIES FROM FAT = 46%

INDIAN CHEESE AND PEPPERS IN SPINACH SAUCE
Saag Paneer

TPT - 8 hours and 50 minutes;
8 hours and 22 minutes = cheese preparation

This is a relatively mild dish done this way. We enjoy it more than we do the highly spiced versions found in many cookbooks and served in many restaurants. The flavors of the homemade cheese, the different vegetables, and spices are delightful to the taste buds and too good to blunt with hot peppers, in our opinion.

5 cups fresh spinach

1/2 medium, sweet green pepper—cored, seeded, and coarsely chopped

1 1/2 teaspoons safflower *or* sunflower oil
2 teaspoons CLARIFIED BUTTER *or* GHEE [see recipe which follows]
1/2 recipe INDIAN CHEESE *(Paneer)* made from 2 cups milk [see recipe which follows]—**cut into 1 x 1/2-inch pieces**
2 tablespoons whole wheat flour

3/4 cup *finely* chopped onion
1 tablespoon *finely* chopped fresh gingerroot
1/4 teaspoon ground turmeric

1/4 cup water
1 medium, sweet red pepper—cored, seeded, and chopped

1 teaspoon OUR INDIAN SPICE MIXTURE (*Garam Masala*) [see recipe which follows] **or commercially-available mixture***

Wash spinach *very thoroughly,* remove tough stems, and place in a small saucepan. Cook over *LOW-MEDIUM* heat until leaves are wilted. No water other than that clinging to the washed leaves need be added.

Using the food processor fitted with steel knife or the electric blender, purée the cooked spinach with the green pepper until very smooth. Set aside.

In a large non-stick-coated skillet with cover, set over *LOW-MEDIUM* heat, combine oil and *ghee*. Dust cheese pieces with whole wheat flour. Sauté gently until *lightly browned* on both sides. Using a slotted spoon or spatula, remove cheese to a dish until required.

Add chopped onion to skillet and sauté until onion is soft and translucent, *being careful not to allow onion to brown.* Add grated gingerroot and sauté for an additional minute or two. Add ground turmeric. Stir to incorporate thoroughly. Stir in spinach purée and water. Combine well. Add chopped red pepper, cover tightly, and allow to cook for about 2 minutes. Fold cheese pieces gently into the mixture. Allow to heat through thoroughly—about 2 or 3 minutes.

Just before serving, stir in *garam masala*.

Yields 6 servings
adequate for 4 people

Notes: *Garam masala* is available in most Asian groceries.

This recipe is easily doubled or halved, when required.

Paneer [see recipe which follows] may be prepared a day in advance, if more convenient.

South Asia–India

INDIAN CHEESE AND PEPPERS IN SPINACH SAUCE (cont'd)

1/6 SERVING – PROTEIN = 5.1 g.; FAT = 5.4 g.; CARBOHYDRATE = 11.8 g.;
CALORIES = 112; CALORIES FROM FAT = 43%

INDIAN CHEESE WITH PEAS
Mattar Paneer
TPT - 25 minutes

"Mattar paneer" and "bharta" are two of my all time favorites and when I am in an Indian restaurant, I am hard pressed to choose. I usually try to convince someone else at the table to choose one and promise to share. I was thrilled when I learned to make paneer at home and although it is fun to go out to dinner or even cook up a store-bought version of this wonderful classic dish, making mattar paneer gives me a very special joy.

1 recipe INDIAN CHEESE *(Paneer)* [see recipe which follows]—cut into 1 x 1/2-inch pieces
2 tablespoons CLARIFIED BUTTER *or* GHEE [see recipe which follows]

1 cup *finely* chopped onion
2 tablespoons *finely* shredded fresh gingerroot
2 small garlic cloves—*finely* chopped
3 or 4 drops Tabasco Sauce
1 teaspoon OUR INDIAN SPICE MIXTURE (*Garam Masala*) [see recipe which follows] *or* commercially-available mixture*
1/4 teaspoon ground cardamom

1/2 cup water *or* 1/4 cup reserved whey from making cheese
2 large tomatoes—peeled, seeded, and chopped *or* 2 cups canned, *diced* tomatoes—well-drained
1 1/2 cups freshly shelled *or frozen* peas

In a 10-inch skillet set over *MEDIUM-LOW* heat, heat ghee or clarified butter. Add Indian cheese (*paneer*) squares and fry gently on each side for about 2 minutes. *Be sure to keep them well-separated* or they will stick together. Remove to a plate and set aside until required.

To ghee remaining in pan, add *finely* chopped onion and garlic, *finely* shredded gingerroot, Tabasco Sauce, garam masala, and ground cardamom. Cook over *LOW* heat, stirring constantly, until the onions are soft and translucent, *being careful not to allow onions to brown.* The aroma will be heavenly!

Stir in water or reserved whey, chopped tomato, and peas. Continue cooking over *LOW* heat, stirring frequently, for about 8 minutes.

Add cheese squares and allow to heat through.

Turn into heated serving bowl or onto a large heated serving platter.

Yields 6 servings
adequate for 4 people

Notes: *Garam masala* is available in Indian groceries and in many food specialty stores.

This recipe can be halved, when required.

1/6 SERVING – PROTEIN = 7.6 g.; FAT = 10.2 g.; CARBOHYDRATE = 16.4 g.;
CALORIES = 186; CALORIES FROM FAT = 49%

CLARIFIED BUTTER
TPT - 17 minutes

Clarified butter keeps for months when refrigerated. Additionally, it does not burn at high temperatures as does regular butter because clarified butter is pure fat. The clarifying process removes the water in the whole butter, which holds the temperature down, and the solids, which tend to smoke and burn.

1 pound butter

In a heavy saucepan set over *MEDIUM* heat, allow butter to melt completely. Remove from heat and *skim off all foam.* Strain the remaining hot liquid through a sieve lined with a cotton tea towel. *Be sure to discard all milky residue remaining in the bottom of the pan* because elements of this are what cause butter to become rancid.

Allow strained clarified butter to *cool completely.* Cover and refrigerate.

Yields about 1 1/2 cupfuls

Note: GHEE, the Indian version of clarified butter, is prepared in exactly the same manner except that it is carefully allowed to brown to give a dark, nutty flavor.

CLARIFIED BUTTER (cont'd)

1/24 SERVING (i. e., per tablespoonful) –
PROTEIN = 0.0 g.; FAT = 14.1 g.; CARBOHYDRATE = 0.0 g.;
CALORIES = 124; CALORIES FROM FAT = 100%

INDIAN CHEESE
Paneer

TPT - 8 hours and 22 minutes;
8 hours = cheese setting period

The owner of an Indian restaurant in Smithtown, Long Island, gave me the secret to perfect paneer and to him I will always be indebted since I do love Indian dishes that include this wonderful, albeit simply prepared, cheese.

1 quart whole milk
1/4 cup PLAIN YOGURT *[see index]* **or commercially-available plain yogurt**—*at room temperature*
1 tablespoon freshly squeezed lemon juice—**strained**

Fold a cotton tea towel so that it will fit into the bottom of a 7 x 3 x 2-inch loaf pan. Let the ends of the towel hang over the ends of the pan. Press the folded layers of the towel firmly into the bottom of pan.

Bring milk to the boil over *LOW-MEDIUM* heat. Boil for 1 full minute. Remove from heat and allow to cool down for 3-5 minutes. Bring to the boil again and boil for 1 full minute.

Remove from heat and immediately stir in yogurt and lemon juice. Continue to stir until curd is completely separated from whey.

Line a sieve with a double layer of culinary cheesecloth. Pour curds and whey into lined sieve and allow to drain and cool completely. When most of whey has drained through, gather corners of cheesecloth and squeeze out as much of whey as possible. Put into the loaf pan, on top of the towel, and press curds into a rectangle. Fold the cheesecloth over. Press the curds firmly again. Refrigerate for 8 hours.

Unwrap cheese, cut into small squares. Place on a plate, cover with plastic wrap, and refrigerate until required.

Yields about 3/4 cupful

Notes: *Alternately, if you have sufficient room in your refrigerator, compress curds into a rectangle about 3/4 inch thick and, still wrapped in cheesecloth, place on a bread board. Place another bread board on top and weight with cans, a brick, or a heavy pot—approximately 10 pounds. (A 12-inch square marble cheese board is a perfect weight.)

This recipe may be doubled or halved with ease.

1/6 SERVING (i. e. per 2 tablespoonful serving) –
PROTEIN = 5.3 g.; FAT = 5.3 g.; CARBOHYDRATE = 7.8 g.;
CALORIES = 100; CALORIES FROM FAT = 49%

INDIAN BAKED CHEESE SWEET IN THE STYLE OF CALCUTTA WITH TROPICAL FRUIT GARNISH
Channa ki Mithi

TPT - 5 hours and 32 minutes;
30 minutes = room temperature cooling period;
4 hours = chilling period

Channa (or chenne) is a dense, sweet-tasting Indian cottage cheese used in India to make this dessert. It is not available here so we use ricotta cheese which, although not a perfect substitute, is an adequate substitute.

South Asia–India

INDIAN BAKED CHEESE SWEET IN THE STYLE OF CALCUTTA WITH TROPICAL FRUIT GARNISH (cont'd)

10 cardamom pods

1 1/2 pounds *part-skimmed milk ricotta* cheese
1/4 cup unbleached white flour
1/2 cup sugar
1 teaspoon pure vanilla extract

Mango slices *or* fresh pineapple spears, for garnish

Preheat oven to 300 degrees F. Prepare a 9 x 5 x 3-inch non-stick-coated loaf pan by further coating with non-stick lecithin spray coating.

Over a clean, dry mixing bowl, carefully open cardamom pods and remove the tiny black seeds. Transfer the cardamom seeds to a mortar and, using a pestle, crush the seeds. Remove and discard any pieces of the pods which might have inadvertently been transferred to the mortar.

In a mixing bowl, combine *ricotta* cheese, flour, sugar, vanilla extract, and the crushed cardamom seeds. Mix well. Turn into prepared baking pan, spreading the mixture evenly to the sides.

Bake in preheated 300 degree F. oven for 55 minutes, or until the pudding is *lightly browned* on top and a knife inserted in the center comes out clean. Remove to a wire rack and allow the pudding to cool for 30 minutes at room temperature. Cover it with plastic wrap and refrigerate for at least 4 hours, or overnight, if more convenient.

Cut into squares, using a spatula. Garnish each serving with mango slices or a pineapple spear, as preferred.

Yields 8 servings
adequate for 4-6 people

Note: This recipe may be doubled, when required. Use an 8-inch square, non-stick-coated baking pan when doubling. Increase the baking time to about 1 1/4 hours in this case.

1/8 SERVING – PROTEIN = 9.7 g.; FAT = 5.0 g.; CARBOHYDRATE = 30.1 g.;
CALORIES = 206; CALORIES FROM FAT = 22%

CARDAMOM WHEAT PUDDING IN THE STYLE OF NORTHERN INDIA
Sooji Elaichi

TPT - 1 hour;
20 minutes = first cooling period;
30 minutes = second cooling period

Although this dessert may not be authentically Indian, it accompanies Indian vegetarian dishes well providing a substantial protein source. I tasted and enjoyed a similar dish many, many years ago, while in graduate school, in the home of a New Delhi family transplanted to a research community in Cold Spring Harbor, Long Island.

2 1/2 cups *one-percent* milk
1/4 cup enriched quick, *but not instant*, farina, *or* Cream of Wheat cereal
1/4 cup sugar

1 teaspoon ground cardamom
1 teaspoon pure vanilla extract
1 cardamom seed pod

2 teaspoons shredded carrot

In a saucepan set over *LOW-MEDIUM* heat, heat milk *just to the boiling point.* Add farina and sugar. Cook, stirring constantly, until thickened. Refrigerate for about 20 minutes to cool slightly.

Stir in ground cardamom, vanilla extract, and cardamom seed pod. Refrigerate for about 30 minutes, stirring occasionally to move the seed pod around.

Remove cardamom seed pod and discard. Stir pudding well and thin with milk at this point, if necessary. Divide pudding among four sherbet glasses or other dessert dishes. Refrigerate until ready to serve.

Garnish each serving with a sprinkling of shredded carrot.

Yields 4 individual servings

Notes: *Firni*, a dessert more typical of southern regions of India and often found on restaurant menus, may be prepared by substituting Cream of Rice cereal for the farina. The rice-based version is most often flavored with almonds and rose water.

**CARDAMOM WHEAT PUDDING
IN THE STYLE OF NORTHERN INDIA** (cont'd)

This recipe may be halved or doubled, when required.

1/4 SERVING – PROTEIN = 7.4 g.; FAT = 2.1 g.; CARBOHYDRATE = 32.2 g.;
CALORIES = 177; CALORIES FROM FAT = 11%

INDIAN-STYLE MANGO ICE CREAM
Aam Kulfi

TPT - 8 hours and 16 minutes;
8 hours = freezing period

This method of preparing Indian ice cream is quite unorthodox but the simplicity and convenience of preparation strongly outweigh tradition. A high-protein, low-fat dessert, this smooth, sweet ice cream finishes off the simplest meal with style.

**3/4 cup mango purée—freshly puréed from
1 large ripe mango** *or* **commercially-available canned variety** *(alfanzo)*
1 can (14 ounces) *fat-free* **sweetened condensed milk**

1 cup heavy whipping cream

Prepare six, small 5-ounce soufflé dishes by coating with non-stick lecithin spray coating.

In a mixing bowl, combine mango purée and sweetened condensed milk.

Using an electric mixer fitted with *chilled* beaters or by hand, using a *chilled* wire whisk, beat heavy cream in a *chilled* bowl until stiff. Pour milk–mango mixture down the side of the mixer bowl. *Whisk-fold* stiffly whipped cream *gently*, but *thoroughly*, into milk–mango mixture.

Divide among prepared soufflé dishes. Cover each tightly with aluminum foil and freeze for at least 8 hours, or overnight.

Serve in soufflé dishes or unmold, if preferred.

Yields 6 individual servings

Note: When required, this recipe is easily doubled.

1/6 SERVING – PROTEIN = 6.2 g.; FAT = 13.2 g.; CARBOHYDRATE = 50.7 g.;
CALORIES = 345; CALORIES FROM FAT = 34%

OUR INDIAN SPICE MIXTURE
Garam Masala

TPT - 17 minutes

Commercial preparations of this very aromatic spice mixture, which originated in northern India during the Moghul reign, are readily available in Indian and Pakistani groceries but the blend can easily be personalized. As you can see, this version contains more of the "warm spices" than do many. This is not a "curry powder," since it does not contain turmeric, but can bring life and complexity to any recipe in which it is substituted for the mundane curry taste.

10 green cardamom pods *(elaichi)*

10 *whole* **cloves** *(laung)*
1 two-inch piece of cinnamon quill—crushed
  (dalchini)
1 teaspoon freshly grated nutmeg *(jaiphul)*
1/4 teaspoon ground mace *(javitri)*

2 tablespoons *whole* **coriander seeds** *(dhania)*
1 tablespoon *whole* **black peppercorns**
1 1/2 tablespoons *whole* **cumin seeds** *(jeera)*

Peel cardamom pods, removing seeds to a SPICE and COFFEE GRINDER.*

South Asia–**India**

OUR INDIAN SPICE MIXTURE (cont'd)

Add *whole* cloves, *crushed* cinnamon quill, freshly grated nutmeg, and ground mace. Grind the mixture just to the point where the cloves and cinnamon are broken into small pieces. Set aside briefly.

In a non-stick-coated skillet set over *MEDIUM* heat, dry-roast *whole* coriander seeds, *whole* black peppercorns, and *whole* cumin seeds for about 5-6 minutes. Stir frequently and shake the pan so that the seeds *roast* and *do not burn*.**

Add roasted seeds to crushed spices. Grind until mixture is *uniformly fine* but *not powderized*

Turn *garam masala* into a jar, with tightly fitting lid. Store, tightly covered, in a cool dry place.***

Yields about 6 tablespoonfuls

Notes: *If you do not have a SPICE and COFFEE GRINDER, grind spices in a mortar, using a pestle.

**Instead of pan roasting, the coriander seeds, peppercorns, and cumin seeds can be oven-roasted in a 375 degree F. oven, if preferred.

***This seasoning can be stored several months without rancidity.

When required, this recipe can be halved or doubled. However, please note, the fresher the mixture is, the more wonderful the flavor!!

FOOD VALUES for such spice mixtures are almost negligible.

OUR *TANDOORI* SPICE MIXTURE

TPT - 4 minutes

Of course, as vegetarians, we do not choose to rub this spice mixture on the parts of all sorts of unfortunate creatures and then pop them into a tandoori oven but we have found it to be a useful mixture for salads, sauces, and vegetables, giving the mundane an authentically ethnic flavor. Adding a complexity of flavors to our own "warm spice" garam masala, has given us another low-sodium spice mixture to which we often turn.

1 1/2 teaspoons fennel seeds (*saunf – Foeniculum vulgare*)
1 teaspoon *dried* spearmint (*podina – Mentha spicata*)
1/4 teaspoon ground red pepper (*cayenne*)
1/4 teaspoon ground ginger (*sonth*)
1 tablespoon INDIAN MANGO POWER (*Amchur*) [see recipe which precedes]*

1 teaspoon OUR INDIAN SPICE MIXTURE (*Garam Masala*) [see recipe which precedes] or commercially-available mixture

Using a SPICE and COFFEE GRINDER,** grind fennel seeds, mint, ground red pepper (cayenne), ground ginger, and mango powder.

Add *garam masala* and grind until the mixture is of uniform consistency.

Turn *chaat masala* into a jar, with tightly fitting lid. Store, tightly covered, in a cool dry place.***

Yields about 2 tablespoonfuls

Notes: *Amchur powder is a tart seasoning made from dried mangoes. It presents a signature flavor in this mixture and should not be excluded. If you do not make your own, a recipe for which you will find elsewhere in this chapter, it is available in Indian and Asian grocery stores, in the international section of well-stocked grocery stores, and from mail order firms.

**If you do not have a SPICE and COFFEE GRINDER, grind spices in a mortar, using a pestle.

***This seasoning can be stored several months without rancidity.

When required, this recipe can be halved or doubled. However, please note, the fresher the mixture is, the more wonderful the flavor.

Classic *chaat masala* mixtures contain rock salt, or black salt as it is referred to in Indian cooking, and a tablespoonful of that would be ground into this mixture. We choose to omit the salt because of our preference for a low-sodium seasoning.

FOOD VALUES for such spice mixtures are almost negligible

Nepal

My first knowledge of Nepal came when I was in eighth grade through the climbing exploits of the courageous hero, Sir Edmund Hillary, the New Zealander who stood atop Mount Everest with his Sherpa guide Tenzing Norgay in May 1953. To many of us, Nepal still represents that ultimate ascent of man to the highest point on the planet, Mount Everest/*Sagarmatha* at 29,029 feet, and the ultimate descent of man into the deepest gorge on Earth, Kali Gandaki Gorge. Nine of the ten highest mountain peaks on Earth are to be found in Nepal and during the climbing season climbers from all over the world accept the challenge.

The dramatic changes in elevation in this small nation, which is actually only about the size of the state of Illinois, result in five climatic zones from tropical, below 3,937 feet, to arctic, above 14,436 feet. Agriculture in Nepal is greatly challenged by these climatic extremes together with the fact that Nepal experiences five seasons, summer, monsoon, autumn, winter, and spring. The length of each season understandably varies from region to region. In addition, Nepal is in a very active earthquake zone, lying as it does completely within the subduction zone of the tectonic plates that formed and continue to form the Himalayan Mountains and the Tibetan Plateau.

Nepal, now a federal republic with a constituent assembly, has been a monarchy for most of its history. The Kirata people were the first to settle. They are said to have ruled for 2,500 years but no one can accurately date their rule due to the lack of a recorded history or substantiating artifacts. In 1768 Prithvi Narayan Shah united the small kingdoms and obtained neutrality agreements with Nepal's Indian neighbors. The Shah dynasty ruled until the 1990s. It was a tumultuous period with incursions into Tibet and Northern India, a war with Britain called the Anglo-Nepalese War from 1815-1816 over the British East India Company's annexation of border states, palace intrigue and power struggles between the king and the government, and, finally, in 1996, a significant move by the Communist Party of Nepal to take over the assembly and create a Maoist state. In June 2001 Crown Prince Dipendra killed his father King Birendra, his mother Queen Aiswarya, and seven other members of the royal family over the fact that his parents would not approve his marriage to the woman he had chosen to be his wife. Dipendra subsequently died of self-inflicted wounds. His brother Gyanendra took the throne, dismissed the entire government, and using executive power, tried to eliminate the Maoist movement. Because the Maoists were firmly entrenched in local governments outside of Kathmandu, King Gyanendra was successful only in negotiating a three-month ceasefire. In 2006 King Gyanendra agreed to relinquish sovereign power reinstating the House of Representatives. The representative government declared Nepal a federal republic and abolished the monarchy. Jhala Nath Khanl of the Communist Party of Nepal, whose philosophy is best described as Marxist-Leninist, became prime minister in 2011. His government fell in May of 2012 and Barburam Bhattarai, a Maoist, became prime minister.

The cuisine of Nepal reveals exchanges with the other nations that have been carved out of the peaks and valleys of the Himalayan Mountains. Many dishes show a similarity to those served in Tibet and Bhutan but still stronger connections to the cuisines of India and China are very evident. Spicing mixtures show clearly the same incredible facility as one would find in India for making the most mundane ingredients exciting. Also as in India, fried vegetable fritters, *pakoda*, albeit more assertively spiced, are often an appetizer or a snack. The abundance of recipes which include cucumbers, potatoes, and chick peas, rice and noodles suggests strong threads to neighboring cuisines and a history of accommodation to the climate and to a food supply that is limited by the growing season, transportation, and the necessity to turn the food supply into products that can be available in some form during the long winter.

South Asia–Nepal

Black Lentil Soup
Kalo Mass ko Dal

~

Grapefruit sections with Sesame Seeds	or	Cucumber and Red Onion Salad
Bhogate Sadeko		*Sanden ko Kandro*

~ ~ ~ ~ ~ ~ ~ ~ ~ ~ ~ ~ ~ ~ ~ ~ ~ ~ ~ ~

Egg Curry with Green Peas	or	Curried Chick Peas
Phul ko Tarkari		*Thulo Chana ko Tarkari*

Nepali Curry Mixture
Tarkaru

Steamed Fragrant Mekong Rice

~ ~ ~ ~ ~ ~ ~ ~ ~ ~

Stir-Fried *Tofu*

Crushed Potatoes
Alu Dum

~ ~ ~ ~ ~ ~ ~ ~ ~ ~ ~ ~ ~ ~ ~ ~ ~ ~ ~

Potato Pickle with Green *Chilies*
Alu ko Achar

or

Cabbage Pickle	or	**Cucumber Pickle**
Banda ko Achar		*Kamkro ko Achar*

~

Sour Cream Dessert
Dahi Barfi

Semolina Pudding
Suji

BLACK LENTIL SOUP IN THE STYLE OF NEPAL
Kalo Mass ko Dal
TPT - 61 minutes

Black lentils are, first and foremost, one of the most beautiful pulses/peas/beans in my larder. Just looking at the canning jar in which I keep them satisfies the need for beauty in this world. When cooked and included in a soup, stew, or salad, that beauty translates into a presentation that is dramatic and enticing and that translates into happy diners. Probably most important is the taste and adaptability since black lentils, beluga black lentils or dal makhani (also available as kaali dal or maa di dal), are almost buttery in taste and contribute to dishes in a wide ethnic spectrum from Indian dals to French salads. This is a relatively mild first-course version of a dish to which Nepali cooks add hot red peppers.

South Asia – Nepal

BLACK LENTIL SOUP IN THE STYLE OF NEPAL (cont'd)

1 cup dry, Beluga black lentils*
2 quarts *boiling* water

1 tablespoon CLARIFIED BUTTER *or* GHEE
[see index]
2 tablespoons *grated* onion
2 tablespoons *very finely* chopped fresh gingerroot
1 small garlic clove—*very finely* chopped
1/2 teaspoon ground turmeric
Pinch ground red pepper cayenne, or to taste

1 quart VEGETARIAN WHITE STOCK *[see index]*, VEGETARIAN BROWN STOCK *[see index]*, TIBETAN VEGETABLE BROTH (*Tukpa*) *[see index]*, or other vegetarian stock of choice
Salt to taste

Pick over lentils and discard any of poor quality. Rinse thoroughly. Combine lentils and *boiling* water in a large *non-aluminum*** kettle set over *MEDIUM* heat. Add water and allow to come to the boil. *Reduce heat to LOW.* Cook for about 30 minutes, or until lentils are soft and most of water has been absorbed. Drain and plunge into ice water to stop further cooking. Drain thoroughly. Set aside until required.

In a skillet set over *MEDIUM* heat, heat clarified butter. Add grated onion, *very finely* chopped gingerroot and garlic, turmeric, and ground red pepper (cayenne). Sauté until onion is soft and translucent, *being careful not too allow any of the ingredients to brown.* Turn into a clean kettle set over *LOW-MEDIUM* heat.

Add vegetable stock and cooked, drained lentils. Season with salt to taste. Allow to come to the boil again. Turn into a heated soup tureen.

Serve into heated soup bowls.

Yields 6 cupfuls

Notes: *Beluga black lentils are available from mail order firms. They are a treasure.

**Since aluminum discolors lentils rather unpleasantly, avoid using aluminum cookware or serving bowls in this case.

This recipe can be halved or doubled, when required.

1/6 SERVING (i. e., per cupful) –
PROTEIN = 9.5 g.; FAT = 2.8 g.; CARBOHYDRATE = 22.2 g.;
CALORIES = 155; CALORIES FROM FAT = 16%

NEPALI-STYLED CUCUMBER AND RED ONION SALAD
Sanden ko Kandro
TPT - 1 hour and 20 minutes

This salad is not so different from salads enjoyed all over the world and, for that reason, it is a good first step when exploring Nepali cuisine. We find this salad to be a welcome palate refresher.

2 medium cucumbers—*not peeled, if organic, and peeled if not organic*—scored with tines of a fork
1/4 red onion—*thinly* sliced into rings
1 small garlic clove—crushed and *very finely* chopped
Salt, to taste
Freshly ground mixed peppercorns—black, red, and white—to taste
1 tablespoon safflower *or* sunflower oil
2 teaspoons freshly squeezed lemon juice
2 tablespoons *finely* chopped fresh coriander (*cilantro*)

Using a very sharp knife, slice cucumbers into thin slices. Arrange cucumber slices attractively on a plate or platter. Cover the cucumber slices with *thinly* sliced onion rings. Sprinkle *very finely* chopped garlic over. Sprinkle generously with salt and grind mixed peppercorns over. Drizzle oil and lemon juice over. Sprinkle *finely* chopped fresh coriander (*cilantro*) over.

Refrigerate until ready to serve—up to 1 hour.

Yields 6 servings
adequate for 4 people

Note: This recipe can be halved or doubled, when required.

1/6 SERVING – PROTEIN = 0.4 g.; FAT = 2.3 g.; CARBOHYDRATE = 2.8 g.;
CALORIES = 28; CALORIES FROM FAT = 74%

South Asia–Nepal

NEPALI EGG CURRY WITH GREEN PEAS
Phul ko Tarkari

TPT - 30 minutes

Do not let the list of spices discourage you. It is a wonderful, subtle combination that takes the ho-hum out of scrambled eggs. I have served this over fried potatoes instead of rice and saw in it the eggs and potato breakfasts that drive Americans to diners. But here, scrambled eggs never tasted so good.

1/2 teaspoon ground cumin
1/4 teaspoon ground coriander
1/4 ground turmeric
Pinch ground cardamom
Pinch ground cloves
Pinch ground cinnamon
Pinch ground mace
Pinch ground red pepper (cayenne), or to taste
Pinch freshly grated nutmeg
1/4 teaspoon salt

1 tablespoon safflower *or* sunflower oil
1 tablespoon butter
1 medium onion—*finely* chopped
2 garlic cloves—*very finely* chopped
1 tablespoon *very finely* chopped fresh gingerroot

6 large eggs—beaten

1/2 cup freshly shelled or *frozen* peas

In a small dish, combine ground cumin, coriander, turmeric, cardamom, cloves, cinnamon, mace, and red pepper (cayenne), freshly grated nutmeg, and salt. Stir to combine. Set aside briefly.

In a non-stick-coated skillet set over *MEDIUM* heat, combine oil and butter. Add *finely* chopped onion, and *very finely* chopped garlic and gingerroot. Sauté until onions are soft and translucent, *being careful not to allow vegetables to brown.*

Add spice mixture. Cook, stirring constantly, for about a minute. *Reduce heat to LOW*.

Add beaten eggs. Stir to mix well. Cook, stirring frequently, for 8-10 minutes, or until eggs have congealed.

Add peas and cook, stirring frequently, for about 5 minutes more.

Serve hot over steamed rice.

Yields 6 servings
adequate for 4 people

Note: This recipe can be halved, when required.

1/6 SERVING – PROTEIN = 7.3 g.; FAT = 9.8 g.; CARBOHYDRATE = 3.3 g.;
CALORIES = 131; CALORIES FROM FAT = 67%

NEPALI CURRIED CHICK PEAS
Thulo Chana ko Tarkari

TPT - 38 minutes

If I have time, I will cook dried chick peas to make this dish but my schedule, albeit now "retired," does not always allow me the luxury of being home to supervise the simmering process even if I choose to use the slow cooker. Organic chick peas are available canned and are so convenient for soups, stews, salads, and dishes like this that I rarely cook dried beans. The taste of this dish will amaze you and your taste buds. If you prefer a vegan dish, omit the yogurt.

2 tablespoons safflower *or* sunflower oil
1 medium onion—*thinly* sliced
1 teaspoon *very finely* chopped garlic
1 teaspoon *very finely* chopped fresh gingerroot

3 1/4 teaspoons NEPALI CURRY MIXTURE
   (**Takari**) *[see recipe which follows]*
[see next page]

VOLUME I - 683

NEPALI CURRIED CHICK PEAS (cont'd)

1 can (15.5 ounces) chick peas (*garbanzos*)—well-drained
1/4 cup canning purée from canned, *whole* tomatoes *or* tomato juice if preferred
2 tablespoons chopped mild green *chilies*

2 tablespoons PLAIN YOGURT [see index] *or* commercially-available plain yogurt

1 teaspoon freshly squeezed lemon juice

2 tablespoons *thinly* sliced uncooked onion, for garnish

In a saucepan set over *MEDIUM* heat, heat oil. Add *thinly* sliced onion and *very finely* chopped garlic and gingerroot. Sauté until onion is soft and translucent, *being careful not to allow any of the vegetables to brown.*

Add curry spice mixture. Cook, stirring constantly, to allow oils to be released.

Add well-drained chick peas, tomato purée or juice, and chopped green *chilies*. Cook, stirring frequently, until heated through.

Stir in yogurt and cook for another minute.

Add lemon juice. Stir to combine. Turn into heated serving dish.

Garnish with raw onion slivers.

Serve at once.

Yields 8 servings
adequate for 6 people

1/6 SERVING – PROTEIN = 3.2 g.; FAT = 5.7 g.; CARBOHYDRATE = 11.9 g.;
CALORIES = 86; CALORIES FROM FAT = 59%

NEPALI CURRY MIXTURE
Tarkari
TPT - 2 minutes

Nepali do wonders with vegetables. Herbs and spices turn the simple into a complex divinity that is good for the karma as well as the palate. The combination can be changed to suit your particular preference but this is the mixture we favor and I share it gladly.

4 teaspoons ground cumin
4 teaspoons ground coriander
4 teaspoons freshly ground black pepper
1/2 teaspoon ground turmeric
1/2 teaspoon ground cloves
1/2 teaspoon ground cardamom
1/2 teaspoon ground mace
1/2 teaspoon salt
1/2 teaspoon lovage seeds *or* celery seeds*

In a small jelly or spice jar, combine ground cumin, coriander, black pepper, turmeric, cloves, cardamom, and mace, salt, and lovage seeds.** Cover tightly and shake to mix thoroughly. Store in a cool, dark place.

Yields 15 teaspoonfuls

Notes: *Commercially-available celery seeds are usually lovage seeds that are produced by a single plant in great abundance. If you do not grow your own lovage, grocery store "celery" seeds can be substituted.

**Choose a small jar because the smaller the jar, the less air will come in contact with the herbs, and the longer the mix will keep its flavor.

This recipe can be halved and that is often a good idea since the flavor dissipates considerably due to the release of the volatile oils. It is advisable to replace the seasoning combination after about 3 months.

FOOD VALUES for such herb mixtures are almost negligible.

South Asia–**Nepal**

STIR-FRIED *TOFU*
TPT - 6 hours and 13 minutes;
6 hours = *tofu* draining period

Buddhists in the high mountains of the Himalayas believe that peppercorns, cloves, garlic, and onion stabilize the wind that inevitably comes with the rain. This dish incorporates the cuisine elements that stabilize the wind and tastes remarkably good.

1 package (12.3 ounces) *extra firm* silken soybean curd (*tofu*)

2 tablespoons *tamari* soy sauce
1 tablespoon Thai sweet *chili* sauce
1 teaspoon barley *miso* (*mugi*)
1/2 teaspoon *white* peppercorns—*roasted and ground*
Pinch corn starch
Pinch ground red pepper (cayenne)
Pinch ground cloves

1 tablespoon *high-heat* safflower *or* sunflower oil
1 clove garlic—*very finely* chopped

1 scallion—trimmed, well-rinsed, and *thinly* sliced
1/2 teaspoon sesame oil

Wrap the *tofu* in several cotton tea towels. Place on a bread board and place a second bread board on top. Allow the *tofu* to drain for 6 hours. Remove wraps and cut into small, bite-sized pieces. Set aside briefly.

In a small dish, combine soy sauce, sweet *chili* sauce, *miso*, roasted and ground *white* peppercorns, corn starch, ground red pepper (cayenne), and ground cloves. Stir to mix well. Set aside until required.

In a wok set over *MEDIUM-HIGH* heat, heat oil. Add garlic and stir-fry for 1 minute. Add chopped *tofu* and sauce mixture. Stir-fry for several minutes.

Add scallion slices and sesame oil. *Remove from heat immediately*. Turn into a heated serving dish.

Serve at once over rice.

Yields 6 servings
adequate for 4 people

Note: This recipe can be doubled, when required.

1/6 SERVING – PROTEIN = 5.2 g.; FAT = 3.7 g.; CARBOHYDRATE = 4.0 g.;
CALORIES = 70; CALORIES FROM FAT = 48%

CRUSHED POTATOES
Alu Dum
TPT - 45 minutes

Tracking the potato and the tomato around the world has been a fascinating adventure. Indians, Chinese, and those in the Himalayan nations at the top of the world also grow, cook, and bring their special ethnic magic to the foods of our hemisphere. This unusual dish, popular in rural China and in the Himalayan nations, makes wonderful use of the small new potatoes that we find at our farmers' market. Aloo dum is an Indian dish in which whole potatoes are served in a curry sauce. In Nepal whole potatoes are also served with sauces but alu dum, which literally means whole potato, can also be used to describe this dish in which the potatoes at least do start off whole.

1/4 cup *tamari* soy sauce
1 medium scallion—trimmed, well-rinsed, and *finely* chopped
2 teaspoons sugar
1 teaspoon salt
1 teaspoon ground turmeric
1 teaspoon granulated garlic *or* garlic powder

12 small red potatoes—unpeeled and well-scrubbed
4 quarts *boiling* water

1/2 cup *high-heat* safflower *or* sunflower oil

Freshly ground black pepper, to taste

Place several layers of paper toweling on a large plate. Place on a warming tray heated to MEDIUM. Also place a serving platter on the warming tray.

In a small dish, combine soy sauce, *finely* chopped scallion, sugar, salt, turmeric, and garlic powder. Stir to mix well. Set aside until required.

In a large saucepan or small kettle set over *MEDIUM* heat, cook potatoes in *boiling* water for about 20 minutes, or until tender *but not falling apart*. Drain well.

CRUSHED POTATOES (cont'd)

Set a potato on a cutting board. Using the bottom of a small plate, gently press the potato down. *The skin should hold the potato together and the crushed potato cake should not stick to the cutting board.* Repeat with each potato. Loosen the bottoms of the potato "cakes" by sliding a knife along the board or by sliding a thin, metal spatula under each crushed potato.

Spoon a bit of the spiced soy sauce mixture into each crushed potato.

In a large non-stick-coated skillet set over *MEDIUM-HIGH* heat, heat the oil. Working in batches, cook potato "cakes" for about 4-5 minutes.

Grind black pepper over. Remove from skillet and transfer onto the paper towel-lined serving platter set on a warming tray.

Add more oil to the skillet if needed. Repeat until all potato "cakes" have been cooked.

Transfer crushed potatoes to the heated serving platter.

Serve at once, garnished with chopped, fresh coriander (*cilantro*).

Yields 12 potato "cakes"
adequate for 6 people

Note: This recipe can be halved, when required. If you need to double, it is advisable to have two skillets working simultaneously.

1/12 SERVING – PROTEIN = 1.0 g.; FAT = 1.2 g.; CARBOHYDRATE = 11.8 g.;
CALORIES = 63; CALORIES FROM FAT = 17%

NEPALI POTATO PICKLE WITH GREEN *CHILIES*
Alu ko Achar

TPT - 1 hour and 15 minutes;
30 minutes = tamarind preparation period;
1 hour = flavor development period

When you serve this to the uninitiated and call it a pickle, you will get some very funny looks. This is more like our western view of a vegetable dish than are most of the Nepali pickles that I have tasted. Potato pickle is probably the most popular "achar" in Nepal where a pickle is generally served at every meal. This spicy potato dish is usually served over rice which also raises a few eyebrows in the West.

4 quarts *boiling* water
8-10 small, new potatoes—well-scrubbed, but unpeeled

1/4 cup *warm* water
2 tablespoons tamarind pulp

1/4 cup sesame seeds

1/4 cup chopped mild green *chilies*, or to taste
1 teaspoon salt
1/4 teaspoon ground turmeric
1/8 teaspoon ground red pepper (cayenne), or to taste

2 tablespoons snipped fresh chives*

In a kettle set over *MEDIUM* heat, combine *boiling* water and potatoes. Boil for 15 minutes. Drain. Refrigerate until required.

In a small dish, combine water and tamarind pulp. Using the back of a spoon, mash the tamarind pulp. Stir well. Allow to soak for at least 30 minutes. Strain through a tea strainer; retain liquid, discard pulp. Set aside until required.

In a non-stick-coated skillet set over *LOW-MEDIUM* heat, dry roast sesame seeds. Shake the skillet to prevent the seeds from burning. Remove from heat.

Using a mini-chop food processor, grind dry-roasted sesame seeds until they are reduced to a fine powder.

Add tamarind liquid, green *chilies*, salt, turmeric, and ground red pepper (cayenne). Process until the mixture has been reduced to a paste. Set aside until required.

Remove potatoes from the refrigerator. Slice potatoes and place on a serving plate. Pour sesame paste–tamarind mixture over the potatoes.

Serve warm or at room temperature, traditionally, over rice or as a vegetable side dish.

Yields 6 servings
adequate for 4 people

NEPALI POTATO PICKLE (cont'd)

Notes: *Instead of chives, an herb called *jimbu* is used in Nepal. It is available from mail order firms. *Jimbu* is a herb composed of two species of onion, *Allium hypsistum* and *Allium przewalskianum*. This herb mixture is used almost exclusively in Nepal.

This recipe can be halved, when required.

1/6 SERVING – PROTEIN = 2.7 g.; FAT = 3.5 g.; CARBOHYDRATE = 12.5 g.;
CALORIES = 92; CALORIES FROM FAT = 34%

NEPALI CABBAGE PICKLE
Banda ko Achar
or
NEPALI CUCUMBER PICKLE
Kankro ko Achar

TPT - 1 hour and 23 minutes;
1 hour = flavor development period

Either shredded cabbage or thin strips of cucumber can be made into a traditional Nepali accent, certainly not pickles in the Japanese or Western traditions, but referred to as pickles, achar, nonetheless in Nepal. Although alu ko achar, potato pickle, is probably the most popular of the Nepali pickled vegetables, pickled cabbage and cucumber are salad-like alternatives enjoyed in Nepal when potatoes are on the menu in another guise. The amount of ground red pepper (cayenne) can be adjusted to family tastes or menu requirements.

1/4 cup sesame seeds

2 tablespoons water
1 tablespoon freshly squeezed lime juice *or* lemon juice, if preferred

2 1/2 cups shredded cabbage as for slaw

or

2 cucumbers—cut into quarters, then halved, seeded, and cut into thin, lengthwise slices
1 teaspoon salt
Pinch ground red pepper (cayenne), or to taste

2 tablespoons safflower *or* sunflower oil
1/4 teaspoon ground turmeric

In a non-stick-coated skillet set over *LOW-MEDIUM* heat, dry roast sesame seeds. Shake the skillet to prevent the seeds from burning. Remove from heat.

Using a mini-chop food processor, grind dry-roasted sesame seeds until they are reduced to a fine powder.

Add water and lime juice and process until the mixture has been reduced to a paste.

In a mixing bowl, combine shredded cabbage (or, alternately, sliced cucumbers), salt, ground red pepper (cayenne), and the prepared sesame paste. Mix thoroughly.

In a small non-stick-coated skillet set over *MEDIUM*, heat oil. Add turmeric. Cook, stirring constantly, until the oil begins to smoke. Pour over cabbage (or cucumber) mixture. Toss to integrate. Refrigerate for at least 1 hour to allow for flavor development.

Turn into a serving bowl. *Serve chilled or at room temperature.*

Yields 10 servings
adequate for 8 people

1/10 SERVING (made with cabbage) –
PROTEIN = 1.1 g.; FAT = 4.8 g.; CARBOHYDRATE = 2.2 g.;
CALORIES = 55; CALORIES FROM FAT = 78%

1/10 SERVING (made with cucumbers) –
PROTEIN = 0.8 g.; FAT = 4.7 g.; CARBOHYDRATE = 1.2 g.;
CALORIES = 50; CALORIES FROM FAT = 84%

South Asia–Nepal

NEPALI SOUR CREAM DESSERT
Dahi Barfi

TPT - 1 hour and 35 minutes;
1 hour = refrigeration period

Sour cream, yogurt, and cheese are useful ways to preserve excess fresh milk in many cultures around the world. In Nepal the milk from cows and the milk from the female yak, the dri, are cultured and made into rich sour cream and yogurt. Paneer, the soft cheese we so often label as Indian, is also made in Nepal. These ingredients are very welcome to the traveling vegetarian.

2 cups *fat-free* dairy sour cream
5 tablespoons *fat-free* sweetened condensed milk
1/4 teaspoon baking powder

1 tablespoon slivered *preservative-free* almonds
1 tablespoon chopped *preservative-free* cashews

2 tablespoons *preservative-free dark* raisins—each cut in half

Preheat oven to 325 degrees F. Prepare a 9 x 5 x 3-inch loaf pan by coating with non-stick lecithin baking spray.

In a mixing bowl, combine sour cream, sweetened condensed milk, and baking powder. Stir to mix well.

Chop almonds and cashews into small, uniform pieces on a bread board. Add to sour cream mixture.

Add raisins. Stir to mix the nuts and raisins into the mixture. Turn into the prepared baking pan. Bake in preheated 325 degree F. oven for about 25 minutes, or until edges of the dessert pull away from the walls of the pan. Remove from oven and refrigerate for at least 1 hour.

Cut into serving-sized pieces and *serve chilled.*

Yields 8 servings
adequate for 6 people

Note: This recipe can be doubled. Use an 8-inch square pan or Pyrex baking dish if you double.

1/8 SERVING – PROTEIN = 5.5 g.; FAT = 1.3 g.; CARBOHYDRATE = 22.7 g.;
CALORIES = 125; CALORIES FROM FAT = 9%

SEMOLINA PUDDING
Suji

TPT - 1 hour and 26 minutes;
1 hour = refrigeration period

Semolina is frequently used in Nepali desserts. Dishes such as "laddu," a semolina ball filled with raisins, nuts, and coconut, or a simple pudding like this are always welcomed by the palate challenged through several courses of dishes with complex spicing.

1/4 cup *preservative-free dark* raisins
1 cup *boiling* water

2 1/2 cups water
6 tablespoons semolina, farina, *or* Cream of Wheat cereal

1 teaspoon ground cardamom
6 tablespoons *fat-free* sweetened condensed milk

In a small dish, combine raisins and the 1 cupful *boiling* water. Set aside to allow the raisins to plump.

In a saucepan set over *MEDIUM* heat, bring the 2 1/2 cupfuls water to the boil. Gradually, while stirring constantly, add semolina. Cook, stirring almost constantly, until thickened.

Add ground cardamom and sweetened condensed milk. Stir well to integrate.

Drain raisins and add to thickened semolina. Turn into a serving bowl. Refrigerate for at least 1 hour to cool and solidify.

Serve chilled into dessert dishes.

Yields 6 servings
adequate for 4 people

Note: This recipe can be halved or doubled, when required.

1/6 SERVING – PROTEIN = 3.0 g.; FAT = 0.1 g.; CARBOHYDRATE = 28.1 g.;
CALORIES = 128; CALORIES FROM FAT = <1%

Pakistan

About twice the size of the state of California, Pakistan is strategically located to the east of Afghanistan and Iran and to the west of India. Today the region is struggling, a struggle that is made difficult due to opposing goals within its own population and the pressures from other countries. Pakistan, situated on the trade roots across Asia, is no stranger to visitors welcome and unwelcome and to the external pressure from East and West.

The area we know today as Pakistan was part of British India from the mid-nineteenth century until the Indian subcontinent was partitioned along religious lines in 1947. One can therefore correctly expect that both Indian culture and British traditions have influenced this area of Asia. Islam was introduced to Pakistan in about 711 AD and with it came influences from the cultures of the Persians, Greeks, Arabs, Afghans, and Turks, all of whom invaded. From the sixteenth century until the coming of the British, the area was part of the Mogul Empire. Food preparation and spicing in some areas of Pakistan show the long exposure to the Mongols. Barbecuing and *tandoori* cooking are certainly linked to this period of their history. The heavy spicing of food in some regions can be traced to those who moved to Pakistan from India after Partition. As in India, the cuisine of Pakistan varies from region to region, with climate a major modifying factor.

Most of the population lives in the fertile Indus Valley which has attracted settlement since the Neolithic Period. The Indus River, said to be 1,000 miles long, and its tributaries flow through Pakistan from the Kashmir region south to the Arabian Sea. Its waters feed the fields that provide ample fresh fruits and vegetables for its 170 million inhabitants enabling irrigation of grasslands to feed cattle and other grazing animals. Because of the river and the sub-tropical climate, rice paddies flourish where basmati rice, the best basmati rice in the world according to some, can be grown.

If your gathering is large and celebratory, all of the dishes in the following menu would be served at the same time. Please note that each of the entrée dishes can be served alone as a family meal.

South Asia – Pakistan

Cabbage and Carrot Slaw with Peanuts
Phool Gobhi Salad
and / or
Mango Salad with Vegetables
Kachumer Salad

~~~~~~~~~~~~~~~~~~~~~

Spicy Potatoes and Baby Spinach
Aaloo Palek

Spicy, Slow-Cooked Chick Peas
Chola

Bananas in Aromatic Sauce
Kela Kofta

Steamed Basmati Rice

~~~~~~~~~~~

Corn Curry with Garlic and Onions
Makai ki Karhi

Cauliflower in Spicy Tomato Sauce
Guncha-O-Keema

Pakistani Evaporated Milk
Khoya

Loaves of Fresh *Naan, Roti,* or *Chappati*

Yogurt

~~~~~~~~~~~~~~~~~~~~~

Cardamom Rice Pudding
Firini

Mango Smoothie
Sharbat

PAKISTANI CABBAGE AND CARROT SLAW WITH PEANUTS
Phool Gobi Salad
TPT - 7 minutes

Here is a salad concept that is a world away from the usual coleslaw or carrot salad with raisins. Pakistanis generally include a salad in their evening meal and this salad is one to which we often turn. It transforms mundane winter salad ingredients into something quite different.

2 cups *thinly* shredded green/white cabbage
2 cups *thinly* shredded carrots
2 tablespoons chopped mild green *chilies*
1/2 cup *roasted, but unsalted*, peanuts—*crushed*
1/4 cup chopped fresh coriander leaves (*cilantro*)

1/2 teaspoon sugar
Several dashes chili powder, to taste
2 teaspoons peanut oil

1 teaspoon freshly squeezed lemon juice
Salt, to taste

PAKISTANI CABBAGE AND CARROT SLAW WITH PEANUTS (cont'd)

In salad bowl, combine shredded cabbage and carrots, chopped green *chilies*, crushed peanuts, and chopped coriander leaves (*cilantro*). Toss to mix well.

Sprinkle sugar and chili powder over. Add oil. Toss to mix well. Refrigerate until required.

When ready to serve, add lemon juice and salt. Toss well again.

Serve at once.

Yields 6 servings
adequate for 4 people

Note: This recipe can be halved or doubled, when required.

1/6 SERVING – PROTEIN = 4.9 g.; FAT = 5.4 g.; CARBOHYDRATE = 7.9 g.;
CALORIES = 135; CALORIES FROM FAT = 36%

PAKISTANI MANGO SALAD WITH VEGETABLES
Kachumer Salad

TPT - 10 minutes

Americans seem adverse to mixing fruits and vegetables and fruits with meat but in other parts of the world the fruits we call vegetables are recognized for what they really are. Fruit has a sweet designation to most Americans, a designation which puts it either at the end of meal, in a salad with other fruits, or in a fruit compote. If I could take you back to the heirloom tomatoes that I enjoyed in my childhood, perfectly ripened, warm from the vine, and so sweet, you could understand why tomatoes and red peppers were some people's favorite fruit – they contain the seeds of the next generation; they are fruits. But I digress . . . This salad takes full advantage of the taste of the ingredients and does not bury their flavor under the unnecessary flavors of a dressing.

The ingredients are frequently all diced and chopped to make a salad that is more a relish or a fresh salsa. I prefer to slice the mangoes into extravagantly large slices and top those slices with a relish made from the remainder of the traditional ingredients.

3 large mangoes—peeled

1 large, firm tomato—peeled, seeded, and *finely* chopped
1 red bell pepper—cored, seeded, membrane removed, and *finely* chopped
1/2 cup *finely* chopped Italian red onion
1/2 cup chopped fresh coriander (*cilantro*) leaves

Salt, to taste
Freshly ground black pepper, to taste

Standing each peeled mango on its end with the flat pit perpendicular to you, slice with a sharp knife to make two to three large slices from each side of the pit. Arrange slices on six individual salad plates or on a large serving plate.

Dice any mango remaining at the ends and sides of the pits. Put into a mixing bowl.

Add *finely* chopped tomato and red pepper, diced red onion, chopped coriander (*cilantro*) leaves. Toss to mix thoroughly. Spoon on top of mango slices.

Sprinkle salt, to taste, over the salad. Grind black pepper over. Refrigerate until ready to serve.

Serve chilled or at room temperature, as preferred.*

Yields 6 servings
adequate for 4 people

Note: *Be sure to provide knives for this salad.

1/6 SERVING – PROTEIN = 5.4 g.; FAT = 0.4 g.; CARBOHYDRATE = 22.4 g.;
CALORIES = 89; CALORIES FROM FAT = 4%

South Asia–Pakistan

PAKISTANI SPICY POTATOES AND BABY SPINACH
Aaloo Palak
TPT - 30 minutes

The combination of potatoes and spinach appears frequently on the Pakistani table but these vegetables are found less frequently in the same dish in India, although both potatoes and spinach appear in many Indian dishes. However, the seasoning, especially in the eastern area of Pakistan, is a complex mixture with which any Indian chef would also be familiar. Pakistani cuisine owes much to Afghani, Turkish, and Iranian cuisines but the spices in this dish would be enjoyed by Pakistani and Indian alike in the area of the Punjab.

2 quarts *boiling* water
3 medium potatoes—peeled and diced

1 tablespoon safflower *or* sunflower oil
1/2 teaspoon mustard seeds
1/4 teaspoon ground turmeric

2 tablespoons chopped mild green *chilies*

6 cups trimmed and well-washed fresh baby spinach
4 canned, *whole* tomatoes
1/4 cup water, or more if necessary
Salt, to taste
2 teaspoons OUR INDIAN SPICE MIXTURE *(Garam Masala)* [see index] *or* commercially-available mixture
1 teaspoon INDIAN MANGO POWDER *(Amchur)* [see index]

In a saucepan set over *MEDIUM* heat, combine *boiling* water and diced potatoes. Cook until potatoes are tender but still firm—about 8 minutes. Drain and set aside until required.

In a large non-stick-coated skillet set over *LOW-MEDIUM* heat, heat oil. Add mustard seeds and ground turmeric. Cook, stirring, constantly, until mustard seeds begin to sizzle and spit.

Add chopped green *chilies* and continue cooking for several minutes more.

Add cooked potato, chopped spinach and tomatoes, and water. Stir to mix well. Add salt, *garam masala*, and mango powder. Cook, stirring frequently, until heated through and spinach is wilted. Turn into a heated serving bowl.

Serve at once.

Yields 6 servings
adequate for 4 people

Note: This recipe can be halved or doubled, when required.

1/6 SERVING – PROTEIN = 3.3 g.; FAT = 2.6 g.; CARBOHYDRATE = 14.7 g.;
CALORIES = 95; CALORIES FROM FAT = 25%

PAKISTANI SPICY, SLOW-COOKED CHICK PEAS
Chola
TPT - 12 hours and 38 minutes;
8 hours = overnight soaking period
[slow cooker: 4 hours at HIGH]

I guess what I really like best about this dish from the Punjab is that the chick peas are cooked in tea. I cook the dried chick peas, after soaking overnight, in the slow cooker on a day when I know that I will be in and out. I often serve the chola over boiled potatoes.

1/2 cup dry chick peas (*garbanzos*)
2 cups water

5 cups *boiling* water
1 green tea bag
1 black tea bag

2 tablespoons safflower *or* sunflower oil
1/2 teaspoon cumin seeds
1 small onion—*finely* chopped
1 small piece fresh gingerroot—*very finely* chopped
1 large garlic clove—*very finely* chopped

2 teaspoons OUR *TANDOORI* SPICE MIXTURE *(Chaat Masala)* [see index] *or* commercially-available mixture
2 teaspoons INDIAN MANGO POWDER *(Amchur)* [see index]
1 teaspoon Korean red chili powder, or to taste
1/2 teaspoon ground coriander
1/2 teaspoon ground cumin
Pinch ground turmeric
Salt, to taste

3/4 cup water

South Asia–Pakistan

PAKISTANI SPICY, SLOW-COOKED CHICK PEAS (cont'd)

Rinse dry beans in several changes of water. Remove and discard any of poor quality. Place in a bowl with the 2 cupfuls of water and soak overnight in the refrigerator.

Preheat slow cooker to HIGH.

In the morning, drain chick peas and place in the bowl of the slow cooker. Add *boiling* water. Attach a clothespin to the tags on the tea bags. Drop the tea bags into the water with the chick peas and dangle the clothespin over the edge of the slow cooker bowl. Cover and cook in slow cooker for 4 hours at HIGH.* Drain. Discard tea bags.

In a large non-stick-coated skillet set over *LOW-MEDIUM* heat, heat oil. Add cumin seeds. When the seeds crackle and spit, add *finely* chopped onion, and *very finely* chopped gingerroot and garlic. Sauté, stirring constantly, until onions are soft and translucent. *Be careful not to allow the vegetables to brown.*

Add *tandoori* spice mixture (*chaat masala*), mango powder (*amchur*), chili powder, ground coriander, cumin, and turmeric, and salt. Sauté for several minutes allowing the spice mixture to release its essence.

Add the 1/2 cupful water and the cooked chick peas. Mix thoroughly. Allow to simmer, stirring frequently, for about 10 minutes. Turn into a heated serving bowl. Keep warm on a warming tray until ready to serve.

Yields 6 servings
adequate for 4 people

Note: This recipe can be doubled or halved, when required.

1/6 SERVING – PROTEIN = 2.0 g.; FAT = 4.9 g.; CARBOHYDRATE = 6.8 g.; CALORIES = 78; CALORIES FROM FAT = 57%

BANANAS IN AROMATIC SAUCE
Kela

TPT - 55 minutes

Cavendish bananas are more and more often the only bananas available in our markets. I find them to be utterly dull and tasteless and refuse to get used to something that has been completely spoiled by controlled breeding for marketing advantage. There are hundreds of varieties of bananas but their cultivation was squelched by the growers who sought to control the growth of, the genetics of, and the marketing of the banana. This too, as with the Lumper potato, is an example of the collapse of biodiversity due to the excesses of those who planted and farmed for commercial gain. It too led to bio-tragedy and deaths in what have been termed the Banana Wars, fought to control the commercial interests of the United States in the Caribbean and in Latin America. Today, with the rapid spread of a fungus disease, in the same category as the Dutch Elm Disease, known as Panama Disease Race 4, that lack of biodiversity is now threatening the supply of bananas to consumers who are said to eat more bananas than any other fruit. The average consumption in the United States adds up to 26.2 pounds per year. I, for one, rarely eat bananas because of the lack of taste now consistently found in the bananas in our stores and I do not choose to buy Cavendish bananas. Baby bananas with their hint of pineapple, although a descendant of Cavendish bananas, are infinitely more satisfying as are Red Dacca bananas, a triploid cultivar of the wild banana which is all too infrequently available in American groceries.

Pakistanis are fond of banana koftas or fritters which are then simmered in a beautiful spicy broth with onions and tomatoes. The broth offers a complexity of flavors that is beyond delicious. To avoid the added fat of deep-frying, I lightly sauté very firm banana chunks and then simmer them in the broth.

2 tablespoons safflower *or* sunflower oil
1/3 cup *finely* chopped onion
2 garlic cloves—*very finely* chopped to a paste
2 tablespoons very *finely* chopped mild green *chilies*
2 tablespoons *finely* chopped fresh coriander (*cilantro*) leaves
1 tablespoon *finely* chopped gingerroot
Freshly ground *white* pepper, to taste

1-inch piece of cinnamon quill
6 whole cardamom pods
4 whole cloves
1/2 cup canned, *crushed* tomatoes
Several dashes Korean red chili powder, or to taste*
Pinch salt
Pinch ground mace
[see next page]

South Asia – Pakistan

BANANAS IN AROMATIC SAUCE (cont'd)

1 cup water

1 tablespoon heavy whipping cream

1 tablespoon butter
2 large peeled, chopped firm red bananas or "cooking" Cavendish bananas, if necessary —cut into large chunks

Heat oil in a *kadhai*, a wok, or a skillet over *LOW-MEDIUM* heat.

Add the *finely* chopped onion, *very finely* chopped garlic, *very finely* chopped gingerroot and green *chilies*, *finely* chopped fresh coriander (*cilantro*) leaves, and white pepper, to taste. Sauté until onions are soft and translucent, *being careful not to allow the onions to brown.*

Add cinnamon quill, cardamom pods, and whole cloves. Stir until the cardamom pods begin to sizzle. Add crushed tomatoes, chili powder, salt, and mace. Cook, stirring constantly, for several minutes.

Add water. Allow to come to the simmer for about 10 minutes. Set a sieve over a Dutch oven and pour the sauce into the sieve. Press the sauce through the sieve. Discard the sieved remainders.

Add cream to the broth. Stir gently.

Preheat oven to 275 degrees F.

In a skillet set over *MEDIUM* heat, melt butter. Add banana chunks and sauté, stirring constantly, until they just begin to brown. Remove from skillet with a slotted spoon and transfer to the Dutch oven. Bake in preheated 275 degree F. oven, uncovered, for about 15 minutes. Transfer to a heated serving bowl.

Serve at once over steamed basmati rice.

Yields 6 servings
adequate for 4 people

Notes: *Korean red chili powder is available in Asian markets.

This recipe can be halved, when required.

1/6 SERVING – PROTEIN = 0.9 g.; FAT = 7.4 g.; CARBOHYDRATE = 10.7 g.;
CALORIES = 109; CALORIES FROM FAT = 61%

PAKISTANI CORN CURRY WITH GARLIC AND ONIONS
Makei ki Karhi

TPT - 21 minutes

Corn has found its way from the Americas all the way around the world and just as have the tomato and the potato it has become an important element in diverse cuisines. If you have never had corn in one of its Asian incarnations, you will be surprised and pleased with this Pakistani dish. Although in Pakistan corn is most often simply boiled, roasted, or steamed, it is also used creatively as a protein source in stews, especially in vegetarian preparations. The seasoning in this corn curry is complex and exciting.

2 medium onions—coarsely chopped
6 tablespoons chopped mild green *chilies*
2 tablespoon grated coconut—desiccated *or* fresh
6 garlic cloves—*finely* chopped
2 large slices of fresh gingerroot—*finely* chopped
1 cup fresh coriander (*cilantro*) leaves
1 teaspoon ground turmeric

3 tablespoons safflower *or* sunflower oil

2 cinnamon quills
2 whole cloves
2 whole cardamom pods

4 teaspoons freshly squeezed lemon juice

4 cups green (fresh) *or frozen* corn kernels
2/3 cup *two-percent* milk
Salt, to taste

In the work bowl of the food processor fitted with steel knife, combine chopped onion, chopped green *chilies*, grated coconut, *finely* chopped garlic and gingerroot, fresh coriander leaves, and ground turmeric. Process until the mixture forms a paste, scraping down the sides of the work bowl as needed.

In a large saucepan set over *MEDIUM* heat, heat oil. Add onion paste and fry for a minute or two.

Add cinnamon quills, whole cloves, and whole cardamom pods. Cook, stirring constantly, for several minutes. Remove cinnamon quills, whole cloves, and cardamom pods. Discard cloves and cardamom pods; rinse cinnamon quills and dry thoroughly to use in a future recipe.

Add lemon juice. Using a wooden spoon, mix well.

PAKISTANI CORN CURRY WITH GARLIC AND ONIONS (cont'd)

Add corn, milk, and salt. Stir to combine well. Cook, stirring frequently, for about 10 minutes. Turn into a heated serving bowl.

Serve at once.

Note: This recipe can be halved when the meal consists of several dishes as in this menu. It can be doubled when required.

Yields 8 servings
adequate for 6-8 people as a side dish

1/6 SERVING – PROTEIN = 6.6 g.; FAT = 7.7 g.; CARBOHYDRATE = 37.9 g.;
CALORIES = 222; CALORIES FROM FAT = 31%

PAKISTANI CAULIFLOWER IN SPICY TOMATO SAUCE
Guncha-O-Keema

TPT - 18 minutes

I like to make this dish with the yellow/orange cauliflowers now so common in our markets, albeit not in Pakistan I suspect. The carotene-rich cultivar represents a boost in vitamin A in our diet and when the golden cauliflower is simmered in this beautifully spiced and fragrant tomato sauce, it is a boost to the appetite and a feast for the eyes. It has become one of our autumn "can't-wait-for-the-cauliflower-to-come-to-market" dishes.

1 tablespoon peanut oil
2 garlic cloves—*very finely* chopped

6 cups cauliflower florets—trimmed and well-washed
1/2 teaspoon ground turmeric
3/4 teaspoon chili powder, or to taste
Salt, to taste

2 tablespoons butter
1/4 cup diced red bell pepper
1/4 cup canned, *diced* tomatoes

1/4 cup PAKISTANI EVAPORATED MILK
  (*Khoya*) [see recipe which follows] or powdered dry milk
1/4 cup canned, *crushed* tomatoes
2 tablespoons water

1 teaspoon OUR *TANDOORI* SPICE MIXTURE
  (*Chaat Masala*) [see index] *or* commercially-available mixture
1 teaspoon OUR INDIAN SPICE MIXTURE
  (*Garam Masala*) [see index] *or* commercially-available mixture
1 1/2 teaspoons freshly squeezed lemon juice

Fresh coriander leaves (*cilantro*), for garnish

In a non-stick-coated skillet, *kadhai*, or wok set over LOW-MEDIUM, heat oil. Add *very finely* chopped garlic and sauté for about 2 minutes.

Add cauliflower florets, ground turmeric, chili powder, and salt. Cook, stirring frequently, until cauliflower is *crisp-tender, being careful not to overcook*. Remove pan from heat and set aside briefly.

Add butter, diced red pepper, and *diced* tomatoes. Cook for a minute to two.

Add *khoya* or powdered dry milk. Cook, stirring constantly, until the milk becomes granular. Remove from heat.

Add *crushed* tomatoes and water. Stir frequently until heated through.

Add *chaat masala*, *garam masala*, and lemon juice. Stir to integrate. Turn into a heated serving bowl.

Garnish with coriander leaves (*cilantro*).

Serve at once.

Yields 6 servings
adequate for 4 people

Note: This recipe can be halved or doubled, when required.

1/6 SERVING – PROTEIN = 3.1 g.; FAT = 5.9 g.; CARBOHYDRATE = 7.1 g.;
CALORIES = 87; CALORIES FROM FAT = 61%

South Asia–Pakistan

PAKISTANI EVAPORATED MILK
Khoya

TPT - about 35 minutes

Khoya is in no way the liquid evaporated milk we buy in cans; it is almost a solid. This way of preserving milk may seem like a lengthy process for those of us whose refrigerators and pantries contain all kinds of milk products including powdered dry milk. Try it once and you will surely have an appreciation how much more difficult it can be to cook in Pakistan. Full-fat buffalo milk is preferred by many cooks but cow's milk will do.

2 cups *two-percent* milk

In a thick-bottomed saucepan set over *MEDIUM* heat, heat milk until it boils. Reduce heat to *LOW-MEDIUM* and keep the milk simmering. Using a wooden spatula, stir frequently, being careful to scrape the bottom of the pan each time, until milk has been reduced to about 6 tablespoonfuls. It will become so thick as to be almost solid—about 30 minutes. *Be careful not to allow the milk to stick to the bottom of the pan.*

Turn into a small dish or crock and refrigerate. It will keep for about 10-14 days.

Yields 5 tablespoonfuls

Notes: This recipe can be doubled, when required.

Certain Pakistani dishes call for *khoya* including several sweets like *pedha*, *gulab jamun*, *burfi*, *gujia*, and *halwa*, and the cauliflower dish included in this chapter. Making *khoya* does make your dinnertime visit to Pakistan more authentic but powdered dry milk can be substituted.

1/5 SERVING (i. e., per tablespoonful) –
PROTEIN = 3.2 g.; FAT = 1.9 g.; CARBOHYDRATE = 4.6 g.;
CALORIES = 51; CALORIES FROM FAT = 4%

PAKISTANI CARDAMOM RICE PUDDING
Firini

TPT - 1 hour;
20 minutes = first cooling period;
30 minutes = second cooling period

On very special occasions such as weddings and at the birth of a child, this simply prepared, creamy rice pudding is served to guests who share the parents' pride. Rice is a symbol of fertility in many eastern cultures and thus this simple food takes on a very different meaning at important moments in a family's history. Depending upon a family's financial position, you may find that saffron has been added to the pudding and presented as a gold orb on a fine plate or silver foil leaves may decorate the top.

2 1/2 cups *two-percent* milk
1/4 cup enriched Cream of Rice cereal
3 tablespoons sugar

1/2 teaspoon ground cardamom

2 tablespoons slivered pistachios
2 tablespoons slivered *preservative-free* almonds

In a saucepan set over *LOW-MEDIUM* heat, heat milk *just to the boiling point.* Add Cream of Rice and sugar. Cook, stirring constantly, until thickened.

Stir in ground cardamom. Refrigerate for about 20 minutes to cool slightly.

Stir pudding well and thin with milk at this point, if necessary. Divide pudding among four sherbet glasses or other dessert dishes or spread out onto a plate in the Pakistani fashion. Refrigerate until ready to serve.

Garnish each serving pistachio and almond slivers.

Yields 4 individual servings

Note: This recipe may be halved or doubled, when required. It may also be made with whole milk or light cream for special occasions. On those occasions you may want to decorate the top with silver foil leaves (*chandi varak*) which are sold in Indian and Pakistani groceries.

PAKISTANI CARDAMOM RICE PUDDING (cont'd)

1/4 SERVING – PROTEIN = 7.3 g.; FAT = 6.0 g.; CARBOHYDRATE = 28.0 g.;
CALORIES = 190; CALORIES FROM FAT = 28%

MANGO SMOOTHIE
TPT - 4 minutes

Rich, sweet, and refreshing . . . all that you could possible want in a dessert? Yes, this does make a wonderful dessert after a spicy meal.

2 mangoes—peeled and chopped
1 1/2 tablespoons sugar

1 cup light cream *or* **half and half**
2 1/2 tablespoons *fat-free* **pasteurized eggs**
1/2 teaspoon pure vanilla extract

In the container of the electric blender, combine chopped mango and sugar. Blend until smooth.

Add cream, pasteurized eggs, and vanilla extract. Blend until light and frothy. Pour into six champagne flutes.

Serve at once.

Yields 6 servings

1/6 SERVING – PROTEIN = 1.9 g.; FAT = 3. 9 g.; CARBOHYDRATE = 16.7 g.;
CALORIES =106; CALORIES FROM FAT = 33%

Sri Lanka

Cinnamon is native to Sri Lanka but the discovery of cinnamon in ancient Egypt and the dating of that cinnamon to c. 1500 BC revises our understanding of the "spice trade" considerably. Other evidence confirms that Sri Lanka had an active trade with the Roman Empire. Most fascinating to me was the fact that Cesarean, the seventeen-year-old son of Julius Caesar and Cleopatra, was destined, it is said, for exile in Sri Lanka, when he was whisked from Alexandria ahead of the advancing armies of Octavian and sent for safety to Berenice, the Egyptian port on the Red Sea where he was assassinated. The small Pacific nation of Sri Lanka, about the size of our state of West Virginia, was very much a world player in the ancient world.

Tracing the paths of early man from African cradles of human evolution across the planet has been a fascinating hobby for me, as I have sat on the sidelines of social history and archaeology. Hardly a word uttered by my ninth grade history teacher, Miss West, or the textbook we studied seem to have held up as fact during my lifetime as the world has plunged ahead discovering its past and sculpting its future. Sri Lanka, the small island nation in the Pacific to the southeast of India was home to our migrating ancestors as early as 37,000 BC. Further archaeological evidence dates the Island to about 125,000 BC as *Homo erectus* and other early pre-human groups spread out across the planet.

The *Mahūvamsa*, an ancient chronicle written in the Pāli language, records that Vijaya landed in Sri Lanka in 543 BC. He and his seven hundred followers sailed some eight hundred miles from West Bengal on eight ships. Vijaya was the first ruler of a long succession of native rulers who ruled until the early years of the nineteenth century. Although a monarchy for all these years, Sri Lanka was not isolated from the world. Trade across the globe continued as it seems to have from almost the earliest days of settlement. In 1638 AD a treaty with the Dutch East India Company resulted in the expulsion of the Portuguese from the coastal regions which they had controlled since 1619, changing once again Sri Lanka's relationship with its trading partners. In 1796 the British displaced the Dutch, fearing that the French control of The Netherlands during the Napoleonic Wars might lead to French occupation of the lucrative Dutch Pacific colonies. In 1815 the last Sri Lankan ruler was exiled to India. Sri Lanka, called Ceylon by the British, remained a British Crown Colony until after World War II. In 1948 it was granted dominion status.

Ceylon, the oldest democratic republic in South Asia, became a republic in 1972, declaring itself the Free Sovereign and Independent Republic of Sri Lanka. In 1977 the name of the nation was changed to the Democratic Socialist Republic of Sri Lanka. Consumed by a civil war for three decades, which only officially ended in 2009, Sri Lanka moved away from plantation agriculture into an aggressive industrialization which emphasizes food processing, textiles, telecommunications, and finance. A huge growth in GDP in 2010 clearly underlines their progress and a literacy rate of 92.5% illustrates a strong potential for growth and development.

Seventy percent of the population still follows the teaching of Siddhartha Gautama, the Buddha, born just twenty years before the arrival of Vijaya and his followers. The Buddha began his search for enlightenment at the age of twenty-nine, in c. 534 BC, and his teachings, then still oral, reached Sri Lanka in 250 BC with the arrival of the son of the Indian Emperor Ashoka. It is said that the first written records of the teachings of the Buddha were compiled on the island. Sri Lankans have been the cradle of preservation of the ancient religion and the principles of Buddhism can been seen in all aspects of daily life including the cuisine. Also reflected in food and culture, in some areas of the country, are the influences brought by traders from The Netherlands and Portugal as well as are food practices introduced by the Moorish traders from the Middle East whose descendants still populate the island.

South Asia – Sri Lanka

Sautéed Greens with Cashews

Tomato and Onion *Sambol*
Sambol

~ ~ ~ ~ ~ ~ ~ ~ ~ ~ ~ ~ ~ ~ ~ ~ ~ ~ ~ ~

Steamed Fragrant Mekong White Rice

with

Eggplant Curry with Tomatoes	**Green Bean Curry**
Brinjal Pahie	*Bonchi Curry*

Beet Slices Sautéed in *Ghee*

Diagonally-Cut Banana Slices

~ ~ ~ ~ ~ ~ ~ ~ ~ ~

Hearts of Palm Curry	**Onion Salad with Coconut Milk**
Pol Bada	*Luna Miris*

~ ~ ~ ~ ~ ~ ~ ~ ~ ~

Beetroot Curry
Rata ala Curry

Sautéed Snowpeas

~ ~ ~ ~ ~ ~ ~ ~ ~ ~

Steamed Bhutan Red Rice

with

Spicy Yams with Coconut Milk from Kandalama
Kahilia Temperadu

or

Soy *Smore*

~ ~ ~ ~ ~ ~ ~ ~ ~ ~ ~ ~ ~ ~ ~ ~ ~ ~ ~ ~

Sri Lankan Curry Powder

Lime Pickles
Luna Dehi

~

Milk Rice
Kiri Bath

Sweetpotato and Coconut Pudding

"Curds and Treacle"

Tapioca Pudding

Chilled Lychees   Papaya with Honey

South Asia–Sri Lanka

SRI LANKAN TOMATO AND ONION *SAMBOL*
Sambol

TPT - 1 hour and 6 minutes
1 hour = flavor development period

Sri Lankans do not eat the kind of salads with which we are most familiar. Vegetable relishes or sambols, of which the variety is vast, fulfill the function of salads with panache.

1/2 cup *finely* chopped onion
2 tablespoons *finely* chopped mild green *chilies*
1/2 cup freshly squeezed lime juice
1/2 teaspoon salt
1/4 teaspoon freshly ground black pepper
2 drops *jalapeño* pepper sauce
1 cardamom seed

3 firm, ripe tomatoes—sliced *thinly*

In a small bowl, combine *finely* chopped onion and green *chilies*, lime juice, salt, black pepper, *jalapeño* pepper sauce, and the cardamom seed. Stir to mix well. Allow the mixture to marinate for 1 hour.

Arrange tomato slices on a plate or on a small platter. Pour onion–chili mixture over.

Serve chilled or at room temperature, as preferred.

Yields 6 servings
adequate for 4 people

Note: This recipe can be halved or doubled when required.

1/6 SERVING – PROTEIN = 0.7 g.; FAT = 0.2 g.; CARBOHYDRATE = 5.1 g.;
CALORIES = 22; CALORIES FROM FAT = 8%

SRI LANKAN EGGPLANT CURRY WITH TOMATOES
Brinjal Pahie

TPT - 1 hour and 10 minutes;
45 minutes = eggplant preparation period

Although I am not overly fond of curried dishes, especially those where the taste of the spices is lost in the" fire," this curry has a lovely creamy texture and the warm spices are beautifully balanced. It is a dish that will be greatly enjoyed by those who love eggplant.

1 medium-large eggplant, about 2 pounds
  —unpeeled
Salt

Oil for deep-frying

1/2 teaspoon ground turmeric

2 teaspoons safflower *or* sunflower oil
1/4 cup chopped onion
2 garlic cloves—*finely* chopped
2 teaspoons *finely* chopped fresh gingerroot
1/2 bay leaf—broken
1 1-inch piece of cinnamon quill

1 cup canned, *diced* tomato *or* peeled, seeded, and coarsely chopped tomato
1 tablespoon OUR INDIAN SPICE MIXTURE
  (Garam Masala) *[see index] or* commercially-available mixture*
2 teaspoons dry mustard
1 teaspoon paprika
1/4 teaspoon ground cardamom
2 tablespoons thick COCONUT CREAM *[see index]*, *sulfite-free*, canned coconut cream, *or* water, if preferred

Lime slices, for garnish

10 tablespoons PLAIN YOGURT *[see index] or* commercially-available plain yogurt

Cut the *unpeeled* eggplant lengthwise into strips and then cut these strips into 1 1/2-inch pieces. Sprinkle generously with salt and place in a strainer set over the sink or a bowl. Set aside for about 45 minutes.

Rinse eggplant *very thoroughly* to remove as much salt as possible. Dry *thoroughly* with paper toweling

Place dried eggplant pieces in a mixing bowl. Sprinkle turmeric over. Toss *gently*, but *thoroughly* to coat evenly.

Preheat oil for deep-frying to 375 degrees F.

Deep-fry eggplant pieces until *lightly browned*. Drain *very thoroughly*, on paper toweling.

SRI LANKAN EGGPLANT CURRY (cont'd)

In a skillet set over *LOW-MEDIUM* heat, heat 2 teaspoonfuls oil. Add chopped onion, *finely* chopped garlic and gingerroot with bay leaf and cinnamon pieces. Sauté until onion is soft and translucent, *allowing none of the vegetables to brown.* Remove and discard bay leaf and cinnamon pieces.

Add chopped tomato, *garam masala*, dry mustard, paprika, cardamom, and water or coconut cream. Continue to cook for about 5 minutes, or until a thick sauce forms. Stir frequently.

Add deep-fried and *well-drained* eggplant pieces. *Cook only until heated through.*

Turn onto heated platter. Garnish with lime slices.

1/5 SERVING (without rice, but with 2 tablespoonfuls yogurt) –
PROTEIN = 2.7 g.; FAT = 6.2 g.; CARBOHYDRATE = 12.4 g.;
CALORIES = 117; CALORIES FROM FAT = 48%

Serve at once, with yogurt over steamed rice.

Yields 5 servings
adequate for 3-4 people

Notes: *Garam masala* is available in Indian groceries.

This recipe is a bit unwieldy to double but it can be done, when required.

SRI LANKAN GREEN BEAN CURRY
Bonchi Curry
TPT - 21 minutes

Although tiny, whole green beans can be prepared in this manner, French cut green beans, available frozen or easily prepared in your own kitchen, are admittedly easier to get from plate to mouth, especially if you have children at the table or are eating this delight with chopsticks. Served over rice, this beautifully spiced stir-fried vegetable dish, albeit very mild as Sri Lankan curries go, is a delight for the taste buds.

2 tablespoon *high-heat* safflower *or* sunflower oil
3/4 teaspoon whole mustard seeds
3/4 teaspoon fenugreek seeds
6 curry leaves*

2 cups *French cut* green beans

1/2 cup *thinly* sliced onions

3/4 teaspoon chili powder
1/2 teaspoon salt, or to taste
1/8 teaspoon OUR INDIAN SPICE MIXTURE (*Garam Masala*) *[see index]* or SRI LANKAN CURRY POWDER *[see recipe which follows]*, as preferred

1/2 cup *light, sulfite-free* coconut milk
2 tablespoons water
3 tablespoons *roasted, unsalted, preservative-free* cashew halves

In a wok set over *MEDIUM* heat, heat oil. Add mustard seeds, fenugreek seeds, and curry leaves. Stir-fry until mustard seeds pop.

Add beans. Stir-fry for 2-3 minutes.

Add *thinly* sliced onions. Stir-fry until onions begin to soften—5-7 minutes.

Add chili powder, salt, and *garam masala*. Stir to integrate. Remove wok from heat. *Reduce heat to LOW.*

Add coconut milk, water, and cashew halves. Stir to mix well. Return to *LOW* heat. Allow to reheat. Turn into a shallow heated serving bowl or onto a small platter.

Serve at once over steamed rice.

Yields 6 servings
adequate for 4 people

Notes: *Curry plants are available in our climate as a summer annual. Dried for winter use, they are a great convenience. Failing that, they are available from mail order spice firms.

SRI LANKAN GREEN BEAN CURRY (cont'd)

This recipe can be halved or doubled, when required.

1/6 SERVING – PROTEIN = 3.1 g.; FAT = 10.9 g.; CARBOHYDRATE = 7.7 g.;
CALORIES = 134; CALORIES FROM FAT = 73%

SRI LANKAN HEARTS OF PALM CURRY
Pol Bada

TPT - 45 minutes

You need not think of hearts of palm as simply an expensive garnish for a salad. Although I often broil them with a topping of grated cheese, that is a long way from using them as main course. The cooks who feed the "pol kadana minihas," the men who harvest the coconuts and maintain the palms grown for their fiber in Sri Lanka, await the sports or buds that are lopped off as part of the palm maintenance program by these skillful tree climbers. The hearts are removed from these buds and a remarkable delicious curry is served to the plantation workers.

1 tablespoon CLARIFIED BUTTER or GHEE
[see index]
1/2 cup *finely* **chopped red onion**

6 dried curry leaves*
2 tablespoons *finely* **chopped mild green** *chilies*
2 teaspoons SRI LANKAN CURRY POWDER
[see recipe which follows]**
1 teaspoon ground turmeric
1/4 teaspoon freshly ground black pepper

1 can (14 ounces) hearts of palm—drained and sliced into 3/4-inch slices
3/4 cup *light, sulfite-free* **coconut milk**

1/2 teaspoon salt
1/2 teaspoon ground mustard powder
2 teaspoons *light, sulfite free* **coconut milk**

In a non-stick-coated skillet set over *LOW-MEDIUM* heat, heat clarified butter or *ghee*. Add onion and sauté until onion is soft and translucent, *being careful not to allow the onion to brown*.

Add curry leaves, *finely* chopped green *chilies*, curry powder, turmeric, and black pepper. Cook, stirring constantly, for a minute or two.

Add slices of hearts of palm and 3/4 cupful coconut milk. Allow to come to the simmer over the *LOW* heat. Cover and cook for about 15 minutes. Stir frequently.

In a small saucepan set over *MEDIUM* heat, combine the salt, mustard powder, and the 2 teaspoonfuls coconut milk. Cook, stirring constantly, until well-combined and thick. Add to curry in skillet. Stir it into the sauce and continue cooking for another 10 minutes. Turn into a heated serving bowl or onto a small, deep, heated platter.

Serve at once over steamed rice.***

Yields 6 servings
adequate for 4 people

Notes: *If you do not grow the curry plant in your herb garden, dried curry leaves are available from several specialty spice online mail order firms.

**There are two types of Sri Lankan curry powder; one is made from roasted spices, the other is not. Use which ever one you prefer.

***I prefer the fragrant rice grown in the Mekong River Valley but any rice will do.

This recipe can be halved or doubled, when required.

1/6 SERVING – PROTEIN = 2.6 g.; FAT = 4.2 g.; CARBOHYDRATE = 4.2 g.;
CALORIES = 60; CALORIES FROM FAT = 63%

South Asia–Sri Lanka

SRI LANKAN ONION SALAD WITH COCONUT MILK
Luna Miris

TPT - 1 hour and 5 minutes;
1 hour = flavor development period

An onion salad, credited to Ceylon, has been in the drawer containing my vegetables salad recipes for years. I find that I still reach into the drawer for that old, yellowed card. The recipe is much the way it was back in the 1960s when I first found it although I have crossed out Ceylon and I now use sweet onions.

1 large sweet onion—Vidalia, Walla Walla, *or* Texas or Mayan Sweet—peeled and *thinly* sliced into rounds
1 tablespoon freshly squeezed lime juice
1 1/2 teaspoons sugar
1/4 teaspoon salt
Freshly ground mixed peppercorns—red, black, and white—to taste

1 teaspoon *very finely* chopped mild green *chilies*
2 tablespoons thick coconut milk

In a large plastic container with lid, combine onion slices, lime juice, sugar, salt, and ground mixed peppercorns. Shake gently to combine ingredients. Refrigerate for at least 1 hour to allow the onions to wilt slightly and develop flavor. Shake occasionally to distribute flavoring liquid. Turn into a shallow serving dish.

Add *very finely* chopped green *chilies* and coconut milk. Toss gently.

Serve with tongs or two forks.

Yields 6 servings
adequate for 4 people

Note: This recipe can be halved or doubled, when required.

1/6 SERVING – PROTEIN = 0.7 g.; FAT = 0.2 g.; CARBOHYDRATE = 2.6 g.;
CALORIES = 21; CALORIES FROM FAT = 8%

SRI LANKAN BEETROOT CURRY
Rata ala Curry

TPT - 35 minutes

The main ingredient in this curry was not a vegetable I expected to find in Sri Lanka but this specialty of the South Indian Brahmin community is a very popular dish. It is delicious made with just beets but I was introduced to a variation to which carrots are added and that is the recipe I share below.

1 tablespoon CLARIFIED BUTTER *or* GHEE
[see index]
1 medium onion—sliced

6 dried curry leaves*
1 tablespoon *finely* chopped mild green *chilies*, or more to taste

2-3 medium beetroots—peeled and diced
1 medium carrot—scraped or pared and diced
1 tablespoon distilled white vinegar
1 1/2 teaspoons SRI LANKAN CURRY POWDER
[see recipe which follows], or more to taste**
1/4 teaspoon ground turmeric
1/4 teaspoon freshly ground black pepper

3/4 cup *light, sulfite-free* coconut milk
1/2 teaspoon salt

In a non-stick-coated skillet set over *LOW-MEDIUM* heat, heat clarified butter or *ghee*. Add onion and sauté until onion is soft and translucent, *being careful not to allow the onion to brown.*

Add curry leaves and *finely* chopped green *chilies*. Cook, stirring constantly, for a minute or two.

Add diced beetroots and carrot, vinegar, curry powder, turmeric, and black pepper. Mix well.

Add coconut milk and salt. Allow to come to the simmer over *LOW* heat. Cover and cook for about 25 minutes. Stir frequently.

Serve at once over steamed rice.***

Yields 6 servings
adequate for 4 people

South Asia – Sri Lanka

SRI LANKAN BEETROOT CURRY (cont'd)

Notes: *If you do not grow the curry plant in your herb garden, dried curry leaves are available from several specialty spice online mail order firms.

**There are two types of Sri Lankan curry powder; one is made from roasted spices, the other is not. Use the raw or unroasted curry powder for this recipe.

***I prefer the fragrant rice grown in the Mekong River Valley but any rice will do.

This recipe can be halved or doubled, when required.

1/6 SERVING – PROTEIN = 0.8 g.; FAT = 3.5 g.; CARBOHYDRATE = 4.1 g.;
CALORIES = 48; CALORIES FROM FAT = 66

SPICY YAMS WITH COCONUT MILK FROM KANDALAMA
Kahilia Temperadu
TPT - 33 minutes

More like a relish to our Western eyes, this dish is typical of those carried to the rice fields by farm women or their children to provide lunch for the men so that the men do not have to walk back home for lunch and then back out to the fields to continue the afternoon's farm tasks. Farm/ranch wives in our American West did the very same thing.

1 tablespoon safflower *or* sunflower oil
2/3 cup *finely* chopped onions
2 garlic cloves—*finely* chopped
2 whole mild green *chilies—finely* chopped
5 curry leaves—*finely* chopped*

1/2 teaspoon mustard seeds

1 medium yam—peeled and cut into thin strips to yield about 2 1/2 cupfuls
1/2 cup canned, *diced* tomatoes
1 teaspoon fenugreek seeds
1 1/2 teaspoons chili powder
1 1/2 teaspoons SRI LANKAN CURRY POWDER
 [see recipe which follows], **or more to taste** **
1 teaspoon turmeric
1/2 teaspoon salt

1 1/2 cups *light, sulfite-free* coconut milk

In a deep skillet set over *LOW-MEDIUM* heat, heat oil. Add *finely* chopped onions, garlic, and green *chilies*, and curry leaves. Sauté until onions and garlic are soft and translucent, *being careful to allow none of the vegetables to brown*.

Add mustard seeds and continue stirring until mustard seeds burst.

Add *thinly* cut yam, diced tomato, fenugreek seeds, chili powder, curry powder, turmeric, and salt. Sauté for several minutes.

Add coconut milk. Allow to come to the boil. *Reduce heat to LOW.* Simmer, stirring occasionally for about 15 minutes, or until yams are tender. Turn into a heated serving bowl.

Serve over rice or as an accompaniment to other dishes.

Yields 6 servings
adequate for 4 people

Notes: *If you do not grow the curry plant in your herb garden, you can obtain dried leaves from mail order spice firms.

This recipe can be halved, when required.

1/6 SERVING – PROTEIN = 1.4 g.; FAT = 4.6 g.; CARBOHYDRATE = 8.6 g.;
CALORIES = 78; CALORIES FROM FAT = 53%

South Asia–Sri Lanka

SRI LANKAN SOY *SMORE*
TPT - 30 minutes

A simple dish of meat simmered in a spicy coconut milk sauce has survived from the period of Dutch colonization and is a favorite of Sri Lankans who do eat meat. It is very different from the culinary dishes left behind here in the United States by the Dutch. A vegetarian version of this truly delicious dish is easily made with a frozen soymeat product, which absorbs the flavors beautifully. I serve this with rice but over a base of stir-fried snowpeas.

2 tablespoons CLARIFIED BUTTER *or* GHEE
  [see index]
8 ounces *frozen* soy meat analogue strips

1 tablespoon distilled white vinegar
Freshly ground black pepper

10 curry leaves*
1 inch lemongrass—*thinly* sliced
2 large shallots—*thinly* sliced
2 tablespoons *finely* chopped mild green *chilies*,
  or to taste
1/2 teaspoon chili powder

1 cup *light, sulfite-free* coconut milk

In a large skillet set over *LOW-MEDIUM* heat, heat clarified butter or *ghee*. Add soymeat strips. Stir-fry for several minutes until soymeat begins to brown.

Add vinegar and black pepper. Cook, stirring until all bits of soymeat have been loosened from the bottom of the pan.

Add curry leaves, *thinly* sliced lemongrass and shallots, *finely* chopped green *chilies*, and chili powder. Stir for several minutes.

Add coconut milk. Stir it into the meat and spice mixture. *Reduce heat to LOW*. Cover and simmer for about 15 minutes, or until the coconut milk and spices form a thick sauce. Turn onto a heated serving platter.

Serve at once over stir-fried snowpeas, if desired. Accompany with rice or bread.

Yields 6 servings
adequate for 4 people

Notes: *Curry leaves can be grown and dried as an annual in most northern climates. They are also available from online herb/spice mail order firms.

This recipe can be halved or doubled, when required.

1/6 SERVING – PROTEIN = 10.9 g.; FAT = 8.5 g.; CARBOHYDRATE = 3.9 g.;
CALORIES = 131; CALORIES FROM FAT = 58%

SRI LANKAN CURRY POWDER
TPT - 3 minutes

Sri Lankans generally have two curry powders on hand, one is roasted and contains ground rice and a number of spices including cinnamon, cloves, and cardamom while the other is a simpler formula which allows the cook to add preferred seasonings to a dish without interference. For vegetable dishes I prefer this curry powder.

3 tablespoon coriander seeds
3 tablespoons cumin seeds
1 teaspoon ground turmeric
1 1/2 tablespoons fennel seeds
1 teaspoon ground turmeric
1/2 teaspoon ground ginger
1/2 teaspoon mustard seeds
1/2 teaspoon ground cardamom

Using a mortar and pestle or a SPICE and COFFEE GRINDER, grind spices to form a fine powder.

Store in a jar-tightly sealed; away from light and heat.

Yields about 4 1/2 tablespoonfuls

Note: This recipe may be doubled or tripled, when required, although it easier to grind in a mortar if a smaller amount is used.

FOOD VALUES for such spice mixtures are almost negligible.

LIME PICKLES
Luna Dehi

TPT - 6 months, four days, and 21 minutes;
3 days = salting period;
about 24 hours = dehydration period;
6 months = pickling period

Lime pickles offer a sweet and sour condiment that does compliment Sir Lankan curries. They are usually sun-dried for three days after the salting procedure but mold and other contaminates are real problems here in our rural farming area. I, therefore, use the dehydrator for the drying process and avoid the mold possibility. Be sure to seek out small limes for this recipe.

10 small, organic limes—well-washed, well-dried, and quartered
2 tablespoons coarse kosher salt

3 cups white distilled vinegar
1 1/2 cups sugar

Prick each lime half with a fork and placed in a saucepan. Add salt. Toss to coat lime halves with salt. Cover pan and set aside for 3 days.

Transfer the salted lime halves to the trays of a dehydrator. Dehydrate completely—about 24 hours, depending on the kind of dehydrator used.

Sterilize two quart canning jars. Sterilize lids and rings too.

Divide dehydrated lime halves between the sterilized jars. Pour 1 1/2 cupfuls vinegar in each jar. Pour 3/4 cupful sugar in each jar. Wipe edge of jars with a wet paper towel. Seal each jar. Store in a cool place, a refrigerator or canning cellar, for about six months before using. Refrigerate after opening.

Yields 40 pickles

1/40 SERVING (i. e., pickled lime quarter) –
PROTEIN = 0.1 g.; FAT = 0.03 g.; CARBOHYDRATE = 11.1 g.;
CALORIES = 40; CALORIES FROM FAT = 1%

SRI LANKAN MILK RICE
Kiri Bath

TPT - 32 minutes

I can remember sitting down at the dinner table to a huge bowl of milk rice made with rice and cow's milk and served with sugar and cinnamon. Mom often made this German version of milk rice when my dad was not going to be home for the meal. I found that the Sri Lankan version is very different from that which stills stirs memories of my childhood. Kiri bath is served, often quite ceremonially, for breakfast at celebratory events such as weddings. Sri Lankans are very fond of it and for good reason.

1 cup dry short grain rice
1 cup *boiling* water

1 cup light, sulfite-free coconut milk
1/4 teaspoon sugar
Pinch salt

In a non-stick-coated saucepan set over *LOW-MEDIUM* heat, combine rice and *boiling* water. Allow to simmer for about 10 minutes.

Add coconut milk, sugar, and salt. Stir to combine. Cover and allow to cook for about 15 minutes or until all the liquid as been absorbed. Remove from heat. Scoop rice into the middle of a heated plate. Using a knife, square-off the rice mound and press it down to form a square about 1 1/2 inches in height.

Serve warm or at room temperature. Cut into squares or diamonds to serve. Refrigerate leftovers.

Yields 8 servings
adequate for 6 people

Note: This recipe can be halved or doubled, when required.

1/6 SERVING – PROTEIN = 4.5 g.; FAT = 1.3 g.; CARBOHYDRATE = 47.3 g.;
CALORIES = 225; CALORIES FROM FAT = 5%

South Asia – **Sri Lanka**

SWEETPOTATO AND COCONUT PUDDING

TPT - 1 hour and 9 minutes;
1 hour = refrigeration period

Since there are only two of us now, there are always leftovers. Granted, most get consumed for lunch the next day but our freezers are generally full of little containers of this and that. This pudding can be an efficient, nourishing, and really very delicious way of using up mashed sweetpotatoes. It is made in Sri Lanka and The Philippines with rassawalli yams, a purple fleshed yam. Rassawalli yams are not available here but the idea is still a good one so I worked out an adaptation of "raja alla" that allows me to use up the cup or two of mashed sweetpotatoes that might have found its way to the back of a freezer shelf.

2 cups *buttered and well-mashed* sweetpotatoes

1/2 cup *light, sulfite-free* coconut milk
1/2 cup sugar
1/2 teaspoon ground cardamom

In a saucepan set over *LOW* heat, combine mashed sweetpotatoes, coconut milk, sugar, and cardamom. Using a wire whisk, beat until the coconut milk has been thoroughly integrated into the sweepotato. Continue cooking, stirring frequently with a wooden spoon, until the sugar has been dissolved. Turn into a serving dish or into six dessert dishes. Refrigerate for at least 1 hour.

Serve chilled.

Yields 6 servings
adequate for 4 people

Note: This recipe can be halved, when required.

1/6 SERVING – PROTEIN = 1.2 g.; FAT = 1.2 g.; CARBOHYDRATE = 28.2 g.;
CALORIES = 124; CALORIES FROM FAT = 9%

SRI LANKAN "CURDS AND TREACLE"

TPT - 2 minutes

You can stop for a refreshing cup of "curds and treacle" as you walk along the streets of Sri Lankan cities. It is an easy protein-rich dessert, made from the milk of water buffalo, that can be prepared in seconds. I am not a fan of treacle unless it is baked into a cookie or into "Indian Pudding" so I make this with corn syrup.

Per serving:
    1/2 cup Greek-style yogurt *or* YOGURT
        CRÈME *[see index]*
    2 tablespoons corn syrup*

Scoop yogurt into a chilled dessert dish. Pour corn syrup over.

Serve chilled.

Yields 1 serving

Note: Golden syrup can be substituted.

1/6 SERVING – PROTEIN = 17.4 g.; FAT = 0.3 g.; CARBOHYDRATE = 54.7 g.;
CALORIES = 288; CALORIES FROM FAT = <1%

index

Achiote oil (Ecuador), v. II, 572
AFGHANISTAN, v. I, 637-43
ALBANIA, v. I, 3-13
ALGERIA, v. II, 3-9
amaranth, adobe bread (Native America), v. II, 660
ANDORRA, v. I, 14-21
ANGOLA, v. II, 10-16
appetizer dips and spreads
    avocado and pineapple spread (Côte d'Ivorie), v. II, 62-63
    avocado and tomato dipping sauce (Venezuela), v. II, 630
    avocado dip with lime (Sierra Leone), v. II, 226-27
    avocado dip with tomato (Zambia), v. II, 292
    black olive *tapenade* with pine nuts, v. II, 190
    cheese and *chili* dip (Native America), v. II, 653
    cheese dip with mayonnaise (Portugal), v. I, 330
    cheese spread (Croatia), v. I, 84
    cheese spread (Romania), v. I, 341
    cheese spread (Slovakia), v. I, 373
    cheese spread with garlic (Syria), v. I, 562
    chick pea dip (Turkey), v. I, 567-68
    dipping sauce (Brunei), v. II, 306-307
    dip with corn and walnuts (Mexico), v. II, 579
    dip with roasted beets and *hummus* (Israel), v. I, 494
    feta cheese spread (Romania), v. I, 341
    fenugreek and vegetable appetizer dip (Yemen), v. I, 578
    garlic dipping oil with yogurt (Eritrea), v. II, 85
    garlicky lime mayonnaise (Peru), v. II, 611-12
    garlic-walnut dipping sauce (Macedonia), v. I, 263
    garlic-yogurt sauce with *tahini* (Tunisia), v. II, 272
    goat cheese and yogurt spread (Libya), v. II, 139-40
    herbed yogurt "cheese" (Israel), v. I, 493
    lemon dipping sauce (Egypt), v. II, 80-81
    mayonnaise-cheese dip (Portugal), v. I, 330
    mung bean sauce with tomatoes and garlic (Uganda), v. II, 285-86
    mustard-soy dip (China), v. II, 325
    olive and caper *tapanade* (Panama), v. II, 597-98
    pumpkin appetizer dip (Libya), v. II, 139
    red pepper and walnut dip (Palestine), v. I, 544-45
    roasted beets and *hummus* (Israel), v. I, 494
    roasted eggplant appetizer (Lebanon), v. I, 523
    roasted eggplant *caviar* (Romania), v. I, 340-41
    roasted eggplant and pepper *caviar* (Serbia), v. I, 364-65
    spicy yogurt dipping sauce (Bangladesh), v. I, 647
    sweetpotato and black bean appetizers (Caribbean) v. II, 491
    tamarind dipping sauce (Cambodia), v. II, 316
    tomato and pepper appetizer salad (Israel), v. I, 495
    tomato dipping sauce (The Gambia), v. II, 100
    vegan "chopped liver" (Israel), v. I, 493-94
    with fenugreek (Yemen), v. I, 578
    yogurt and peanut butter appetizer dip (Sudan), v. II, 252
    yogurt with green *chilies* (Palestine), v. I, 545
apples
    and beetroot salad (Uruguay), v. II, 624
    and beet salad with sour cream (Lithuania), v. I, 247
    and celeriac soup (Australia), v. II, 450
    and celery salad (Slovakia), v. I, 375
    and cheese salad (Switzerland), v. I, 410
    applesauce, v. I, 185
    applesauce with sour cream sauce (Hungary), v. I, 184
    baked dessert (Slovenia), v. I, 390
    cabbage and carrot slaw with (Ukraine), v. I, 426
    cheese-stuffed zucchini with lentils and fruit (Mexico), v. II, 583-84
    compote with *Brie* and raisins (South Africa), v. II, 243-44
    deviled beet, potato, apple, and egg salad (Estonia), v. I, 111-12
    dried, fruit salad (Uganda), v. II, 283-84
    fruit cream (Belgium), v. I, 55-56
    granola, v. II, 696
    meatballs and fruit in curry sauce (Mozambique), v. II, 183-84
    meat pies (Botswana), v. II, 21
    mixed fruit salad with *chaat masala* (India), v. I, 670
    peanut-apple crumble v. II, 469-70
    pear mincemeat with pecans (England), v. I, 441-42
    porridge with apples and oatmeal (Belarus), v. I, 41-42
    prickly pear salad with dates (Israel), v. I, 497
    pudding with breadcrumbs (Denmark), v. I, 108-109
    pudding with breadcrumbs (Russia), v. I, 359
    salad, with celery (Slovakia), v. I, 375
    salad, with onion and *feta* (Greece), v. I, 163
    savory, with sour cream (Luxembourg), v. I, 258
    slow cooker dried fruit curry (South Africa), v. II, 247-48
    soup, savory (Andorra), v. I, 17
    sweet fried (Norway), v. I, 315-16
    syrup (The Netherlands), v. I, 306
    syrup with cloves (Lebanon), v. I, 533
    uncooked applesauce (Switzerland), v. I, 419-20
    vegetable stew (Uzbekistan), v. I, 628-29
    with sauerkraut (Latvia), v. I, 235
apricots
    breaded and fried *semolina* with cranberry garnish (Slovakia), v. I, 378
    brown rice *pilaf* (Central Asia), v. I, 629-30
    chick peas with tomatoes (Yemen), v. I, 580-81
    dried, fruit salad (Uganda), v. II, 283-84
    dumplings, with mashed potatoes (Slovenia), v. I, 386
    lentil and bulgur cabbage rolls (Armenia), v. I, 592-93
    red lentil and bulgur soup (Armenia), v. I, 589-90
    salad, with mango and pineapple (Niger), v. II, 198
    sauce, for papaya and mango dessert (Tanzania), v. II, 265
    stewed fruit compote with walnuts (Armenia), v. I, 596
    tart (Austria), v. I, 31
    tea-infused dried fruits with whipped cream (Chad), v. II, 58

index

ARGENTINA, v. II, 507-13
ARMENIA, v. I, 585-99
artichokes, hearts
    and onions in tomato sauce (Armenia),
        v. I, 593-94
    cream soup (Brazil), v. II, 524
    grilled vegetable salad (Kuwait), v. I, 516
    in oil (Jordan), v. I, 505
    salad, with leeks and carrots (Turkey), v. I, 570
    salad, with preserved lemons and honey
        (Morocco), v. II, 173
    skillet stew with eggs and fava beans (Malta),
        v. I, 276-77
    summer vegetable stew (Tunisia), v. II, 276-77
    vegetable and cheese pies (Uruguay), v. II, 624-25
    vegetable *ragoût* (Lebanon), v. I, 527-28
    vegetable salad (Albania), v. I, 7
    village tossed salad (Greece), v. I, 161-62
    with angel hair *pasta*, mushrooms, and *chorizo* in
        skillet (Spain), v. I, 395
    with Irish cream and mustard sauce (Ireland),
        v. I, 200-201
artichokes, whole
    baby, sautéed with lemon and garlic (Italy),
        v. I, 225-26
    baby, with lemon dipping sauce (Egypt), v. II, 80-81
    stuffed (Italy), v. I, 218-19
asparagus
    and mushrooms with oregano and fennel oil
        (Liechtenstein), v. I, 241
    and *wonton* noodles with egg sauce (Japan),
        v. II, 364-65
    cream soup (Belgium), v. I, 48-49
    cream soup (German), v. I, 143-44
    in bitter orange sauce (Spain), v. I, 396
    rice with vegetables (Bhutan), v. I, 661-62
    salad, with capers (Romania), v. I, 343
    salad, with raspberry *vinaigrette* (Australia),
        v. II, 451
    sautéed with hazelnuts (Austria), v. I, 27
    with *fontina* (Italy), v. I, 211
AUSTRALIA (Oceania), v. II, 447-59
AUSTRIA, v. I, 22-31
avocados
    and egg salad (Colombia), v. II, 537
    and egg salad (Israel), v. I, 498
    and grapefruit salad (Somalia), v. II, 234-35
    and ice cream dessert (Indonesia), v. II, 358
    and mayonnaise salad (Ghana), v. II, 110
    and pineapple appetizer spread (Côte d'Ivoire),
        v. II, 62-63
    and pineapple salad (Central African Republics),
        v. II, 47
    and shallots in tomato soup (Australia), v. II, 449-50
    and tangerine dessert (Mozambique), v. II, 185-86
    and tomato dipping sauce (Venezuela), v. II, 630
    appetizer *guacamole* with egg and cheese (El
        Salvador), v. II, 559-60
    cream dessert (Venezuela), v. II, 635
    creamy, puréed, vegetable soup (Venezuela),
        v. II, 632-33
    dip with lime (Sierra Leone), v. II, 226-27
    dip with tomato (Zambia), v. II, 292
    fruit platter with lime *vinaigrette* (Caribbean),
        v. II, 496
    fruit salad (Central African Republics), v. II, 53
    fruit salad with citrus *vinaigrette* (Côte d'Ivoire),
        v. II, 66
    halves, with spicy dressing (Guinea), v. II, 118
    halves, stuffed with tomato salad (New Zealand),
        v. II, 463
    layered fruit salad (Cameroon), v. II, 34-35
    millet and corn salad with avocado (Central African
        Republics), v. II, 47-48
    nasturtium blossoms stuffed with avocado (Native
        America), v. II, 655
    potato and cheese soup (Ecuador), v. II, 552-53
    pudding (Western Sahara), v. II, 167-68
    salad, with cabbage and pickled red onion relish
        (Ecuador), v. II, 551
    salad, with mango, orange, and citrus dressing
        (Senegal), v. II, 219
    salad, with papaya and grapefruit (Kenya), v. II, 126
    salad, with peaches and tomato (Mozambique),
        v. II, 181
    soup, chilled (Côte d'Ivorie), v. II, 64
AZERBAIJAN, v. I, 600-609

Baking powder substitute, v. I, 305
bamboo shoots
    and greens (Uganda), v. II, 287
    rice noodle and meatball soup (Laos), v. II, 386
    stir-fried vegetables with coconut (Brunei),
        v. II, 311
    stir-fried with mushrooms (Tibet) v. II, 344
    with sesame seeds (Laos), v. II, 388-89
    wonton appetizers (China), v. II, 323-24
bananas, *see also* plantains
    and chocolate in pastry (Côte d'Ivoire), v. II, 68-69
    and deep-fried black-eyed peas (Niger),
        v. II, 199-200
    and flax cake (The Gambia), v. II, 107-108
    and lime whip (Pacific Islands), v. II, 484
    and mango salad (The Gambia), v. II, 102
    and rice curry with peanut butter (Angola), v. II, 14
    and semolina dessert (Guinea), v. II, 121-22
    and soymeat stew (Liberia), v. II, 134-35
    and sticky rice sweet (Cambodia), v. II, 321
    autumn compote (Portugal), v. I, 331
    baby, salad with peanuts (The Philippines),
        v. II, 420-21
    baked (Gabon), v. II, 52-53
    banana custard cornbread (Caribbean), v. II, 501
    banana nectar beverage dessert (Ghana), v. II, 115
    bean and celery soup (Burundi), v. II, 27-28
    biscuits (Pacific Islands – Fiji), v. II, 476-77
    cheese-stuffed zucchini with lentils and fruit
        (Mexico), v. II, 583-84
    chilled soup (Tanzania), v. II, 261-62
    dessert (Mozambique), v. II, 186
    fritters (Djibouti), v. II, 76
    fruit salad (Uganda), v. II, 283-84
    groundnut and vegetable soup (Djibouti),
        v. II, 72-73

index

bananas (cont'd)
    in aromatic sauce (Pakistan), v. I, 693-94
    in coconut milk (Thailand), v. II, 436
    ice cream (Tanzania), v. II, 264-65
    in pastry (Cape Verde), v. II, 44
    layered fruit salad (Cameroon), v. II, 34-35
    meatballs and fruit in curry sauce (Mozambique), v. II, 183-84
    omelet (São Tomé and Principe), v. II, 211
    papaya salad with curried island dressing (Pacific Islands – Vanuatu), v. II, 474
    pastry (Mauritania), v. II, 168
    phyllo tart (Central African Republics), v. II, 52
    pumpkin soup with coconut milk (Caribbean – Bahamas), v. II, 494
    salad, curried, with yam and hard-cooked egg (Pacific Islands), v. II, 475
    salad, green banana and vegetable (Costa Rica), v. II, 542-43
    salad, with rice (Kenya), v. II, 127
    slow cooker dried fruit curry (South Africa), v. II, 247-48
    soup, with *yucca* and coconut (Honduras), v. II, 573-74
    strudel (Namibia), v. II, 195-96
    tamarind dressing (Brunei), v. II, 308-309
    tropical fruit salad (Nigeria), v. II, 202
    vegetable and groundnut soup (Zambia), v. II, 292-93
    with cream, v. II, 289
    with mango and pineapple in mango-yogurt sauce (Oman), v. I, 537
    with uncooked coconut cream sauce (Pacific Islands – Cook Islands), v. II, 484-85
BANGLADESH, v. I, 644-54
barley
    and carrot pudding (Finland), v. I, 126-27
    and vegetable soup with sour cream (Poland), v. I, 322-23
    chilled soup with sour cream (Latvia), v. I, 233
    slow cooker vegetable soup with beans and barley (Croatia), v. I, 87-88
    sweet porridge (Mongolia), v. II, 406
    vegetable soup (Estonia), v. I, 112-13
    vegetable soup (Oman), v. I, 538
    with carrots (Belarus), v. I, 39
    with wild mushrooms and sage (Scotland), v. I, 452
basil, opal, information, v. II, 678 (note)
bay leaves, information, v. I, 334 (note)
beancurd, *see tofu*
beans, basic slow cooker preparation, v. II, 43-44
beans, black
    and sweetpotato appetizers (Caribbean), v. II, 491
    in tomato-garlic sauce (The Gambia), v. II, 103
    soup (The Netherlands), v. I, 300-301
    with green pepper (Native America), v. II, 667
    with rice and mango relish (Caribbean – Cuba), v. II, 499-500
beans, black, preserved/fermented
    lettuce wraps (Korea), v. II, 378
    stir-fried Chinese cabbage, peppers, and eggs (Malaysia), v. II, 394-95
    with roasted baby peppers (China), v. II, 334
beans, black-eyed peas, pigeon beans
    black-eyed peas (Namibia), v. II, 194-95
    and tomato soup (Liberia), v. II, 133
    beans in coconut milk (Chad), v. II, 56-57
    deep-fried with bananas (Niger), v. II, 199-200
    in coconut milk (Kenya), v. II, 127-28
    slow cooker *chili* (Uganda), v. II, 287-88
    with coconut and cocoa (Sierra Leone), v. II, 227
    with leeks and spinach in skillet (Iran), v. I, 479-80
beans, *borlotti*
    mixed legume soup (Morocco), v. II, 172-73
beans, chick peas (*garbanzos*)
    and *couscous* in vegetable soup (Angola), v. II, 11-12
    and Israeli *couscous* salad (Israel), v. I, 496
    and kale soup with peanut butter and tomatoes (Djibouti), v. II, 74
    and mushroom salad (Somalia), v. II, 235
    and potato salad (Armenia), v. I, 591
    and potato vegetable stew (Tunisia), v. II, 275-76
    and rice soup (Mongolia), v. II, 402-403
    and tomato soup with leeks (Uruguay), v. II, 623
    bread salad, with spinach, rice, and garlic-yogurt sauce with *tahini*, (Tunisia), v. II, 274-75
    couscous salad (Algeria), v. II, 4-5
    couscous salad (Mauritania), v. II, 162-63
    cream soup (Guatemala), v. II, 566-67
    curried (Nepal), v. I, 683-84
    dumplings in yogurt sauce (India), v. I, 667-68
    falafel (Jordan), v. I, 503
    hot yogurt soup with rice (Iran), v. I, 477-78
    hummus (Turkey), v. I, 567-68
    ground legume and spice mixture (Egypt), v. II, 78
    in tomato sauce (Guatemala), v. II, 569
    millet *couscous* with (Mauritania), v. II, 164-65
    mixed legume soup (Morocco), v. II, 172-73
    puréed cream soup with celeriac (Turkey), v. I, 569
    roasted beets and *hummus* (Israel), v. I, 494
    roasted, with nuts (Jordan), v. I, 503-504
    salad (Libya), v. II, 142
    sautéed with sage (Spain), v. I, 396-97
    soup, with rice (Peru), v. II, 612-13
    soup, with roasted red peppers and garlic (Greece), v. I, 165-66
    spicy, slow-cooked (Pakistan), v. I, 692-93
    sweet (Tunisia), v. II, 278
    tagliatelle with chick peas (Cyprus), v. I, 471
    three-bean salad with creamy dressing (Mongolia), v. II, 402
    tomato-black bean *vinaigrette* for *couscous* salad (Somalia), v. II, 234
    tomato bouillon with chick peas (Mauritania/Western Sahara), v. II, 164
    with fried spinach and grated cheese (Egypt), v. II, 81
    with groundnut butter in vegetable soup (Namibia), v. II, 192
    with *linguine*, red kidney beans, and seasoned soymeat (Afghanistan), v. I, 640
    with tomatoes and apricots (Yemen), v. I, 580-81

beans, cranberry
    bean salad with walnuts (Georgia), v. I, 615-16
    mixed legume soup (Morocco), v. II, 172-73
beans, fava, butter beans, or broad beans
    and scrambled eggs (Lebanon), v. I, 530
    artichoke skillet stew with eggs (Malta),
        v. I, 276-77
    bean stew with hominy and *chouriço* (Cape Verde),
        v. II, 42-43
    falafel (Jordan), v. I, 503
    patties (Sudan), v. II, 254-55
    salad (Malta), v. I, 275
beans, Great Northern, Navy, pea, and *cannellini*
    baked (Native America), v. II, 664
    bean and celery soup (Burundi), v. II, 27-28
    bean stew with hominy and *chouriço* (Cape Verde),
        v. II, 42-43
    Bosnian, v. I, 62
    chili bean soup, v. I, 283-84
    soup with pinched dumplings (Hungary),
        v. I, 176-77
    vegetable salad with white beans, root celery,
        kohlrabi, and potatoes (Czech), v. I, 96
    vegetable stew with beans and *chouriço* sausage
        (Angola), v. II, 13-14
    walnut and bean *paté* with vegetable filling
        (France), v. I, 132-33
    white beans in tomato sauce (Albania), v. I, 10
beans, green beans
    and garlic salad (Slovenia), v. I, 387
    and potato curry (Malaysia), v. II, 393-94
    bean salad (Caribbean - Haiti), v. II, 497
    curry (Sri Lanka), v. I, 701-702
    foot long beans with black mushrooms in brown
        garlic sauce (China), v. II, 331
    groundnut and vegetable soup (Djibouti),
        v. II, 72-73
    lentil *consommé* (Lichtenstein), v. I, 239
    lentil soup with vegetables (Burundi), v. II, 28-29
    meatballs and vegetables skillet (Niger),
        v. II, 198-99
    Milanese *minestrone* (Italy), v. I, 222-23
    millet *couscous* with vegetables (The Gambia),
        v. II, 103
    niçoise salad (France), v. I, 136
    soup, with potatoes (Slovakia), v. I, 373-74
    steamed vegetable salad with sweet black sesame
        dressing (Brunei), v. II, 308
    stir-fried long beans and mushrooms with garlic
        (Laos), v. II, 388
    stir-fried vegetables with coconut (Brunei),
        v. II, 311
    sweet and sour bean salad (Zimbabwe),
        v. II, 299-300
    three-bean salad with creamy dressing (Mongolia),
        v. II, 402
    vegetable and groundnut soup (Zambia),
        v. II, 292-93
    vegetable stew (Ethiopia), v. II, 94
    vegetable stew with beer (Belgium), v. I, 49-50
    vegetables in curried coconut milk (Thailand),
        v. II, 434-35

    with meatballs in yogurt sauce (Bosnia), v. I, 63
beans, lima beans
    and corn custard pudding (Brazil), v. II, 526
    and rice (Cape Verde), v. II, 41
    and tomato skillet (Peru), v. II, 616
    bean and celery soup (Burundi), v. II, 27-28
    beans, carrot, and creamed corn (Oman), v. I, 539
    slow cooker vegetable stew (Botswana), v. II, 19-20
    sweet and sour bean salad (Zimbabwe),
        v. II, 299-300
    vegetable stew (Bolivia), v. II, 515-16
    with tomatoes and eggs (Mexico), v. II, 585
beans, mung beans
    sauce with tomatoes and garlic (Uganda),
        v. II, 285-86
    sprouts, curried vegetables with *tofu* (Cambodia),
        v. II, 319
    sprouts, dumpling soup (Korea), v. II, 371-72
    sprouts, *wonton* appetizers (China), v. II, 323-24
    sprouts, stir-fried noodles and vegetables, (Brunei),
        v. II, 309-10
    stir-fried vegetables with coconut (Brunei),
        v. II, 311
beans peanuts, including peanut butter
    and rice pudding (Zambia), v. II, 297
    and tomato sauce with garlic (The Gambia),
        v. II, 104
    and tomato soup (Ghana), v. II, 111
    and winter squash soup (Senegal), v. II, 216-17
    and yogurt appetizer dip (Sudan), v. II, 252
    baby banana salad (The Philippines), v. II, 420-21
    butternut squash with greens (Botswana), v. II, 22
    cabbage and carrot slaw (Pakistan), v. I, 690-91
    cabbage and green mango salad (Myanmar/ Burma),
        v. II, 412
    chick pea and kale soup with tomatoes (Djibouti),
        v. II, 74
    citrus-shallot sauce for baked *tofu* (Pacific Islands
        – Polynesia), v. II, 481-82
    cream of peanut butter soup (Mexico), v. II, 581
    cucumber salad with peanut-lime dressing (Central
        African Republics), v. II, 48-49
    dressing for *pasta* and vegetable salad (Senegal),
        v. II, 221
    eggplant and brown rice (Indonesia), v. II, 355
    fruit and vegetable salad (Indonesia), v. II, 354
    ground legume and spice mixture (Egypt),
        v. II, 78
    groundnut and vegetable soup (Djibouti),
        v. II, 72-73
    groundnut biscuits (Zambia), v. II, 295-96
    groundnut ice cream (Senegal), v. II, 223
    peanut-apple crumble v. II, 469-70
    peanut candy (Angola), v. II, 16
    peanut-lime dressing (Central African Republics),
        v. II, 48-49
    peanut macaroons (Sudan), v. II, 257-58
    potatoes with peanut sauce (Peru), v. II, 617-18
    radish and garlic relish/salad (Myanmar/Burma),
        v. II, 413-14
    rice curry with bananas (Angola), v. II, 14

beans, peanuts (cont'd)
- rice pudding with peanut butter cream (Togo), v. II, 269
- salad dressing (Indonesia), v. II, 354-55
- sauce for potato cakes (Ecuador), v. II, 554
- sautéed squashes with peanuts (Chad), v. II, 57-58
- slow cooker dried fruit curry (South Africa), v. II, 247-48
- soup with greens and corn (Chad), v. II, 55
- spicy sauce with ginger (Togo), v. II, 268-69
- spinach stew (Central African Republics), v. II, 51
- summer squash with peanuts and garlic (Central African Republics), v. II, 49-50
- sweetpotato and greens in vegetable soup (Zimbabwe), v. II, 300
- sweetpotatoes with gingerroot (Vietnam), v. II, 441
- toasted millet salad (Mali) v. II, 155-56
- tomato and groundnut soup (Ghana), v. II, 111
- tomato and peanut sauce with cream (Brazil), v. II, 527-28
- tomato and peanut sauce (Zambia), v. II, 294
- vegetable and groundnut soup (Zambia), v. II, 292-93
- watermelon and cucumber salad (Vietnam), v. II, 439
- with chick peas in vegetable soup (Namibia), v. II, 192
- with greens (Tanzania), v. II, 264
- with lentils (Guinea), v. II, 118-19
- with pan-grilled plantains (Nigeria), v. II, 204-205

beans, pinto
- mixed legume soup (Morocco), v. II, 172-73
- spicy bean soup with coconut milk (Djibouti), v. II, 72

beans, red kidney
- and corn casserole (Tanzania), v. II, 263
- and red peppers (Latvia), v. I, 234
- and tomatoes with plantains (Colombia), v. II, 539
- and white eggplant salad (Ethiopia), v. II, 93
- bean and celery soup (Burundi), v. II, 27-28
- bean and hominy *chili* (Somalia), v. II, 238
- bean salad (Caribbean – Haiti), v. II, 497
- *chili*, v. II, 288
- chowder of vegetables and fine noodles (Montenegro), v. I, 294-95
- coconut-bean soup with rice (Nigeria), v. II, 203-204
- layered vegetable salad (Ghana), v. II, 111-12
- noodle soup (Central Asia), v. I, 625
- red pottage (Scotland), v. I, 449
- salad, with corn and mango (Burundi), v. II, 27
- salad with eggs (Slovenia), v. I, 388-89
- slow cooker vegetable soup with beans and barley (Croatia), v. I, 87-88
- soup, curried, with coconut and basmati rice (Tanzania), v. II, 260-61
- soup, with coconut and rice (Nigeria), v. II, 203-204
- sweet and sour bean salad (Zimbabwe), v. II, 299-300
- *tacos* or *tostados* with sautéed greens and goat cheese (Panama), v. II, 600-601
- three-bean salad with creamy dressing (Mongolia), v. II, 402
- with grated cheese (El Salvador), v. II, 562
- with *linguine*, chick peas, and seasoned soymeat (Afghanistan), v. I, 640

beans, Roman
- bean and corn salad (Liechtenstein), v. I, 239
- bean salad with walnuts (Georgia), v. I, 615-16
- mixed legume soup (Morocco), v. II, 172-73
- spicy bean soup with coconut milk (Djibouti), v. II, 72

beans, vegetarian baked beans
- curried beans with sausage (Madagascar), v. II, 149
- spicy beans (Malta), v. I, 277
- with pineapple (Pacific Islands – Hawaii), v. II, 480-81

beans, yellow wax beans, three-bean salad with creamy dressing (Mongolia), v. II, 402

beets
- and apple salad (Uruguay), v. II, 624
- and apple salad with sour cream (Lithuania), v. I, 247
- and garlic salad (Greece), v. I, 162-63
- and horseradish relish (Slovakia), v. I, 379-80
- and mushroom soup (Poland), v. I, 323-24
- and spinach salad with yogurt dressing (Georgia), v. I, 618-19
- and *tahini* salad with eggs (Syria), v. I, 564
- anise-scented (Algeria), v. II, 6
- Argentine-styled Russian salad, v. II, 508-509
- bean and corn salad (Liechtenstein), v. I, 239
- chilled *borsch* (Belarus), v. I, 37
- cooked, technique recommendations, v. I, 26 (note)
- curry (Sri Lanka), v. I, 703-704
- cutlets, breaded and fried (Norway), v. I, 312
- deviled potato, apple, and egg salad (Estonia), v. I, 111-12
- dip with roasted beets, garlic, and *hummus* (Israel), v. I, 494
- Harvard (Belarus), v. I, 38-39
- in cream (Honduras), v. II, 575-76
- oven preparation technique, v. I, 26, 312
- pickled (Denmark), v. I, 104
- pink potato salad (Panama), v. II, 598-99
- red pottage (Scotland), v. I, 449
- salad, shredded (Romania), v. I, 344
- salad with cheese (Austria), v. I, 26
- salad with eggs (Belarus), v. I, 35-36
- salad with *feta* cheese (Serbia), v. I, 366-67
- salad with garlic-mayonnaise dressing (Moldova), v. I, 285
- salad, with potato and carrot (Peru), v. II, 613-14
- salad, with yogurt and mint (Iran), v. I, 478
- shredded fresh (Russia), v. I, 355
- soup (Ukraine), v. I, 426-27
- vegetable salad with hearts of palm (Brazil), v. II, 525
- vicarage, with herbs (England), v. I, 439
- with chive oil (Armenia), v. I, 595
- with chopped egg (Iceland), v. I, 189-90
- with oil and lemon (Ethiopia), v. II, 96

index

beets (cont'd)
    with tart cherry sauce and fresh herbs (Georgia),
        v. I, 617-18
    Yale, v. I, 39 (note)
BELARUS, v. I, 32-42
BELGIUM, v. I, 43-57
berries, *see also* by name
    and honey over pancakes (Morocco), v. II, 176-77
beverages
    banana nectar beverage dessert (Ghana), v. II, 115
    chilled coffee milk with cardamom and cinnamon
        (Somalia), v. II, 240-41
    chocolate *demitasse* (Venezuela), v. II, 637
    creamy cocoa cordial (São Tomé and Principe),
        v. II, 213-14
    fresh fruit refresher (Mexico), v. II, 587-88
    fresh pineapple drink with fresh gingerroot
        (Liberia), v. II, 132
    fruit spiders (Australia), v. II, 458
    hot cocoa mix, v. I, 220
    iced mocha (Costa Rica), v. II, 546
    kiwifruit *frappé* appetizer (New Zealand),
        v. II, 461-62
    limoncello, v. II, 473-74
    mango smoothie (Pakistan), v. I, 697
    mochalata cordial (São Tomé and Principe),
        v. II, 213
    orange spiced tea (Russia), v. I, 361
    papaya juice (Eritrea), v. II, 84-85
    papaya punch (Pacific Islands – Hawaii), v. II, 472
    passion fruit appetizer (Caribbean), v. II, 490
    pomegranate refresher (Morocco), v. II, 170-71
    prickly pear-orange-apple- pineapple punch (Native
        America), v. II, 653-54
    spiced honey tea (Central Asia), v. I, 634
    strawberry-rhubarb juice (Finland), v. I, 121-22
    tea with rosebuds (China), v. II, 336
    watermelon punch (Turkmenistan), v. I, 634
    white wine and fruit juice cooler (Uruguay),
        v. II, 627
    yogurt drink (Senegal), v. II, 224
    yogurt drink (Uzbekistan), v. I, 633
BHUTAN, v. I, 655-62
blackberries
    cobbler (Ireland), v. I, 203
    sauce or dessert (Australia), v. II, 687
blueberries
    and strawberry summer pudding, v. I, 445-46
    hot-packed, v. II, 646
    pudding (Canada), v. II, 645-46
    salad, with peaches and cantaloupe and almond
        syrup and *moscato* wine sauce (Macedonia),
        v. I, 264
    sauce (Lithuania), v. I, 250
    tossed salad with hazelnuts (England), v. I, 436
    Yorkshire summer pudding (England), v. I, 444-45
bok choy, *see* cabbage
BOLIVIA, v. II, 514-18
BOSNIA and HERTZEGOVINA, v. I, 58-68
BOTSWANA, v. II, 17-24
BRAZIL, v. II, 519-29

breads
    adobe bread with amaranth (Native America),
        v. II, 660
    anise toast (Italy), v. I, 209
    baked corn *tortilla* chips (El Salvador), v. II, 560
    baking powder corn meal biscuits (Native America),
        v. II, 659
    banana biscuits (Pacific Islands – Fiji), v. II, 476-77
    banana custard cornbread (Caribbean), v. II, 501
    beer biscuits (Denmark), v. I, 105
    Belgian waffles (Belgium), v. I, 56-57
    brown buttermilk scones (Ireland), v. I, 196-97
    buttermilk cornbread, v. I, 368
    cashew appetizer toasts (Brazil), v. II, 522-23
    colonial-style, v. II, 523-24
    corn meal cake (Kenya), v. II, 128-29
    country corn (Portugal), v. I, 336-37
    crostini with oil, tomato, and capers (Malta),
        v. I, 272-73
    Dutch oven unkneaded bread, v. II, 191
    French-style *baquettes*, v. II, 101-102
    fried corn flatbreads (Sudan), v. II, 256
    fried loaves (Botswana), v. II, 23
    ginger buttermilk scones (Scotland), v. I, 450-51
    green onion sesame skillet bread (Tibet), v. II, 345
    groundnut biscuits (Zambia), v. II, 295-96
    hazelnut breads (Native America), v. II, 661
    honey barley (Estonia), v. I, 115-16
    injera for the western kitchen, v. II, 92
    leek wheaten scones (Ireland), v. I, 197-98
    maple multigrain, v. II, 106-107
    oat scones (Scotland), v. I, 449-50
    olive oil with *hummus* and mint (Cyprus), v. I, 473
    pancake, quick bread, and waffle mix, v. I, 304-305
    parmesan toasts (Italy), v. I, 226
    pumpernickel, with caraway seeds (Germany),
        v. I, 150 (note)
    raisin pumpernickel (Germany), v. I, 150
    skillet flatbread (Somalia), v. II, 232
    sultan's slices (Bulgaria), v. I, 80
    sweetpotato biscuits (Zimbabwe), v. II, 301
    thyme loaves (Algeria), v. II, 8
    tortilla skillet (Honduras), v. II, 574-75
    waffles, v. I, 304
    wheaten biscuit mix, v. II, 698
    whole grain (Finland), v. I, 122-23
    whole wheat baking powder biscuits with sage
        (Canada), v. II, 644-45
    whole wheat hot cross buns (England), v. I, 446-47
    wonton skins (China), v. II, 324-25
    za'atar toast (Lebanon), v. I, 523-24
broccoli
    and potato salad with Hollandaise sauce (Brazil),
        v. II, 521
    pasta and vegetable salad with peanut butter
        dressing (Senegal), v. II, 221
    steamed vegetable salad with sweet black sesame
        dressing (Brunei), v. II, 308
    with spaghetti and garlic (Botswana), v. II, 22-23
BRUNEI, v. II, 305-13
buerre manie, v. I, 559
BULGARIA, v. I, 69-80

index

bulgur wheat
    and lentils in cabbage rolls with dried fruits (Armenia), v. I, 592-93
    and red lentil soup (Turkey), v. I, 568-69
    and red lentil soup with apricots (Armenia), v. I, 589-90
    and tomato and spinach soup with mint (Armenia), v. I, 590-91
    salad (Jordan), v. I, 504-505
BURMA, see **MYANMAR**
BURUNDI, v. II, 25-30

Cabbage
cabbage, *bok choy*
    almond vegetables Mandarin *mu shu* (China), v. II, 329
    and *soba* noodles with *tukpa* broth (Tibet), v. II, 340-41
    curried vegetables with *tofu* (Cambodia), v. II, 319
    red grapefruit salad with soymeat and soy sprouts (Thailand), v. II, 433-34
    soup, with clear *cilantro* stock (The Philippines), v. II, 419-20
    steamed vegetable salad with sweet black sesame dressing (Brunei), v. II, 308
    steamed with sautéed mushrooms (China), v. II, 333
    tossed salad with noodles and onion *vinaigrette* (Mongolia), v. II, 401
cabbage, Chinese, including *napa* and celery cabbage
    cabbage pickle, *kimchi* (Korea), v. II, 376-77
    dumpling soup (Korea), v. II, 371-72
    stir-fried, with peppers and eggs (Malaysia), v. II, 394-95
cabbage, red
    and black currant slaw (Finland), v. I, 125
    Christmas slaw (Iceland), v. I, 188
    sweet and sour (The Netherlands), v. I, 302-303
    sweet and sour on vegetarian reubens (Pacific Islands – Cook Islands), v. II, 478-79
    sweet and sour with sour cream (Estonia), v. I, 115
cabbage, sauerkraut
    and potato *croquettes* (Luxembourg), v. I, 256-57
    slow cooker, with apples (Latvia), v. I, 235
    vegetarian reubens (Pacific Islands – Cook Islands), v. II, 478-79
cabbage, savoy
    and potatoes (Hungary), v. I, 180
    buttered (Ireland), v. I, 202
    sautéed with fennel leaves (Romania), v. I, 345-46
    slow cooker vegetable soup with beans and barley (Croatia), v. I, 87-88
    steamed with butter and chestnuts (Lithuania), v. I, 249
cabbage, white/green
    and carrot salad with yogurt dressing (Western Sahara), v. II, 163
    and carrot slaw with peanuts (Pakistan), v. I, 690-91
    and celery with sour cream (Canada), v. II, 641-42
    and green mango salad (Myanmar/Burma), v. II, 412
    and noodle skillet (Poland), v. I, 325
    and potato pie (Luxembourg), v. I, 255-56
    and potatoes in tomato sauce (Bangladesh), v. I, 648
    bean stew with hominy and *chouriço* (Cape Verde), v. II, 42-43
    beet soup (Ukraine), v. I, 426-27
    cabbage casserole with breadcrumbs (Serbia), v. I, 369
    cabbage pickles (Nepal), v. I, 687
    cabbage rolls stuffed with lentils, bulgur and dried fruits (Armenia), v. I, 592-93
    fried with tomatoes (Moldova), v. I, 288
    glass noodle and vegetable slaw (Tibet), v. II, 341
    groundnut and vegetable soup (Djibouti), v. II, 72-73
    lentil soup with vegetables (Burundi), v. II, 28-29
    Milanese *minestrone* (Italy), v. I, 222-23
    salad, with avocado and pickled red onion relish (Ecuador), v. II, 551
    salad, with pineapple (Liberia), v. II, 133-34
    salad, with shredded carrot (Cyprus), v. I, 468
    sautéed, with carrot and onion (Mozambique), v. II, 185
    sautéed, with fennel leaves (Romania), v. I, 345-46
    scalloped with cream (Montenegro), v. I, 297
    slaw (Slovenia), v. I, 389
    slaw of the *vuelta e 'Lola*, (Venezuela), v. II, 631
    slaw with carrot, onion, and apple (Ukraine), v. I, 426
    slaw with pineapple (Cameroon), v. II, 34
    slaw with corn and dillweed (Angola), v. II, 12-13
    soup (Russia), v. I, 352
    stir-fried vegetables with coconut (Brunei), v. II, 311
    stir-fried with carrots and red pepper (Tibet), v. II, 343
    sweet browned with sausage (Denmark), v. I, 102
    tossed vegetable salad with cheese (Sudan), v. II, 252-53
    vegetable and groundnut soup (Zambia), v. II, 292-93
    vegetable slaw (El Salvador), v. II, 560-61
    vegetable soup with barley (Estonia), v. I, 112-13
    vegetable soup with oatmeal or barley (Oman), v. I, 538
    vegetable stew (Uzbekistan), v. I, 628-29
    vegetable stew with beans and *chouriço* sausage (Angola), v. II, 13-14
    with tomatoes (Venezuela), v. II, 634
cakes
    almond (Iceland), v. I, 191
    brown sugar pound cake (Costa Rica), v. II, 545-46
    buttermilk (Moldova), v. I, 289
    carrot (Switzerland), v. I, 420
    chocolate almond *torte* (Hungary), v. I, 184
    chocolate "chemistry class" cake (Bosnia), v. I, 67
    coconut (Oman), v. I, 542
    coffee-spice "chemistry class" cake with honey (Paraguay), v. II, 608
    egg sponge cake with sugar syrup (Albania), v. I, 11-12
    flax-banana (The Gambia), v. II, 107-108
    gingerbread (England), v. I, 443
    ginger cake (Nigeria), v. II, 205-206

cakes (cont'd)
    gold [Lord Baltimore], v. I, 317-18
    milk cake (Ecuador), v. II, 557
    orange (Macedonia), v. I, 269
    orange *torte* (Portugal), v. I, 338
    peach with crumbled meringue (Uruguay), v. II, 625-26
    semolina with *tahini* (Lebanon), v. I, 533-34
    spiced pumpkin (Liberia), v. II, 135-36
    sweet egg sponge (Guatemala), v. II, 569-70
    toasted hazelnut *torte* (Hungary), v. I, 182-83
    walnut sponge (Russia), v. I, 358
    with lemon syrup (Bosnia), v. I, 66
    yogurt (Bulgaria), v. I, 80
CAMBODIA, v. II, 314-21
CAMEROON, v. II, 31-39
CANADA, v. II, 639-49
canning and preserving, *see also* vinegars
    applesauce, v. I, 185 (note)
    brown stock, v. II, 692-93 (note)
    cabbage pickle, *kimchi* (Korea), v. II, 376-77
    corn relish, v. II, 579-80
    daikon and red radish pickles (Tibet), v. II, 346
    lemon jelly infused with fresh herbs (Native America), v. II, 668-69
    papaya jam (Cameroon), v. II, 33-34
    peach jam, v. I, 619
    pickled baby beets (Denmark), v. I, 104
    pickled blue plums (Poland), v. I, 326-27
    pickled eggplant with dill (Turkmenistan), v. I, 626-27
    pickled mustard greens (Vietnam), v. II, 442-43
    pickled red onion relish with lime juice (Ecuador), v. II, 552
    pineapple jam, v. II, 564
    preserved lemon conserve (Morocco), v. II, 174
    preserved mango (Cape Verde), v. II, 42
    preserved sweet and sour eggs (The Philippines), v. II, 419
    tomato jam (Mozambique), v. II, 180
    vegetable stock from soup, v. II, 691-92 (note)
    vegetables stocks for soups, stews and sauces, v. II, 692-93 (note)
    white stock, v. II, 692-93 (note)
cannoli pastry (Italy/Sicilia) (Venezuela), v. II, 636-37
CAPE VERDE, v. II, 40-44
carambola **(starfruit)**
    and mango appetizer with *limoncello* (Pacific Islands – New Guinea), v. II, 472-73
    and orange dessert (Caribbean), v. II, 505
    fruit and vegetable salad (Indonesia), v. II, 354
    fruit salad with tamarind dressing (Brunei), v. II, 308-309
CARIBBEAN, THE, v. II, 488-505
carrots
    almond vegetables Mandarin *mu shu* (China), v. II, 329
    and barley pudding (Finland), v. I, 126-27
    and cabbage salad with yogurt dressing (Western Sahara), v. II, 163
    and cabbage slaw with peanuts (Pakistan), v. I, 690-91
    and *jicama* salad with mango (Colombia), v. II, 538-39
    and *kumara* puréed soup with gingerroot (New Zealand), v. II, 465-66
    and leeks with celery sauce (Scotland), v. I, 453
    Argentine-styled Russian salad, v. II, 508-509
    artichoke salad with leeks (Turkey), v. I, 570
    baby, in wild rice casserole with mushrooms (Canada), v. II, 642-43
    baked lentils with cheese (Germany), v. I, 147-48
    barley and vegetable soup with sour cream (Poland), v. I, 322-23
    bean soup with pinched dumplings (Hungary), v. I, 176-77
    beetroot curry (Sri Lanka), v. I, 703-704
    beet soup (Ukraine), v. I, 426-27
    black bean soup (The Netherlands), v. I, 300-301
    braised vegetables in olive oil with rice (Saudi Arabia), v. I, 556
    cake (Switzerland), v. I, 420
    chick pea and potato vegetable stew (Tunisia), v. II, 275-76
    chowder of vegetables and fine noodles (Montenegro), v. I, 294-95
    collard greens and kale with potatoes and carrots (Montenegro), v. I, 295-96
    cream of chick pea soup (El Salvador), v. II, 566-67
    cream soup with celeriac (Finland), v. I, 123-24
    creamy, puréed, vegetable soup (Venezuela), v. II, 632-33
    dark vegetable stock (Thailand), v. II, 431-32
    dumpling soup (Korea), v. II, 371-72
    Flemish (Belgium), v. I, 52-53
    glass noodle and vegetable slaw (Tibet), v. II, 341
    glazed with mint (Morocco), v. II, 176
    goulash (Hungary), v. I, 177-78
    groundnut and vegetable soup (Djibouti), v. II, 72-73
    Irish stew, v. I, 199-200
    kohlrabi and papaya salad with tamarind dressing (Laos), v. II, 385
    lentil soup with vegetables (Burundi), v. II, 28-29
    macaroni and vegetables (The Gambia), v. II, 104-105
    Milanese *minestrone* (Italy), v. I, 222-23
    millet *couscous* with vegetables (The Gambia), v. II, 103
    Moscow salad (Russia), v. I, 351
    noodle soup with kidney beans (Central Asia), v. I, 625
    omelet on omelet (Chile), v. II, 531
    oven-roasted root vegetables with cheese (Sweden), v. I, 402-403
    oven-roasted root vegetables with fresh herbs and mushrooms (Namibia), v. II, 193-94
    pancakes with vegetables (Mauritania), v. II, 161-62
    pasta and vegetable salad with peanut butter dressing (Senegal), v. II, 221
    pickled vegetables (Panama), v. II, 601-602
    pilaf (Kazakhstan), v. I, 630-31
    potato-meatball soup (Latvia), v. I, 232-33
    pudding (Saudi Arabia), v. I, 559

index

carrots (cont'd)
    pumpkin soup with coconut milk and banana (Caribbean - Bahamas), v. II, 494
    puréed chick pea and celeriac soup (Turkey), v. I, 569
    puréed *dhal* soup (Pacific Islands – Fiji), v. II, 476
    puréed lentil soup (Somalia), v. II, 232-33
    puréed potato and sweetpotato soup (Nigeria), v. II, 203
    puréed root vegetable soup (Saudi Arabia), v. I, 555
    quinoa and vegetable stew (Peru), v. II, 615
    root vegetables with yogurt-dill sauce (Bulgaria), v. I, 75-76
    salad, grated (Madagascar), v. II, 147
    salad, warm with leeks and celeriac (Norway), v. I, 310-11
    salad, whole with mayonnaise-mustard sauce with capers (Belgium) v. I, 47
    salad with beets and potato (Peru), v. II, 613-14
    salad with cabbage (Cyprus), v. I, 468
    samosa casserole (India), v. I, 666-67
    sautéed with cabbage and onion (Mozambique), v. II, 185
    sautéed with pomegranate glaze (Macedonia), v. I, 268-69
    shredded onion and vegetable salad (Denmark), v. I, 101
    shredded with sugar and lemon (Poland), v. I, 325-26
    slaw (Kazakhstan), v. I, 627
    slaw with cabbage, onion, and apple (Ukraine), v. I, 426
    slow cooker vegetable stew (Botswana), v. II, 19-20
    slow cooker vegetable soup with beans and barley (Croatia), v. I, 87-88
    steamed pudding with potatoes and raisins (Canada), v. II, 647-48
    stewed with barley (Belarus), v. I, 39
    stir-fried vegetables with coconut (Brunei), v. II, 311
    stir-fried, with cabbage and red pepper (Tibet), v. II, 343
    summer vegetable stew (Tunisia), v. II, 276-77
    tagine, with onions and prunes (Western Sahara), v. II, 165-66
    tomato-squash stew (Slovenia), v. I, 383-84
    tossed vegetable salad with cheese (Sudan), v. II, 252-53
    vegetable and cheese pies (Uruguay), v. II, 624-25
    vegetable and groundnut soup (Zambia), v. II, 292-93
    vegetable pasties (New Zealand), v. II, 467
    vegetable *ragoût* (Lebanon), v. I, 527-28
    vegetable relish (Tanzania), v. II, 262-63
    vegetable salad with white beans, root celery, kohlrabi, and potatoes (Czech), v. I, 96
    vegetable slaw (El Salvador), v. II, 560-61
    vegetable soup with barley (Estonia), v. I, 112-13
    vegetable soup with fine noodles (Malta), v. I, 274
    vegetable soup with oatmeal or barley (Oman), v. I, 538
    vegetable soup with sweetpotato, greens, and peanut butter (Zimbabwe), v. II, 300
    vegetable spaghetti with grainburger (Australia), v. II, 453-54
    vegetable stew (Ethiopia), v. II, 94
    vegetable stew (Uzbekistan), v. I, 628-29
    vegetable stew with beans and *chouriço* sausage (Angola), v. II, 13-14
    vegetable stew with beer (Belgium), v. I, 49-50
    winter squash and vegetable soup (Panama), v. II, 605-606
    with angel hair *pasta*, mushrooms, and *chorizo* in skillet (Spain), v. I, 395
    with beans and creamed corn (Oman), v. I, 539
    with ginger and dill (South Africa), v. II, 247
    with ginger, lemon, and dill (Germany), v. I, 149-50
    with pineapple (Pacific Islands - Samoa), v. II, 483
    with potatoes and leeks in cream sauce (Luxembourg), v. I, 257
    yellow pea soup (Sweden), v. I, 399-400
    yellow split pea soup with meatballs (Azerbaijan), v. I, 603-604
cashews, curried (Caribbean), v. II, 492
cassava, manioc, yucca (yuca) **root**, *see also*
    puddings, tapioca
        sweet fritters (Cameroon), v. II, 39
        fried, with garlicky lime mayonnaise (Peru), v. II, 611-12
        yuca root soup with banana and coconut (Honduras), v. II, 573-74
cauliflower
    almond vegetables Mandarin *mu shu* (China), v. II, 329
    and eggs (Myanmar/Burma), v. II, 409-10
    and noodle soup (Indonesia), v. II, 353
    and onion omelet (Georgia), v. I, 616
    breaded and fried florets (Bangladesh), v. I, 645-46
    casserole with sour cream (Croatia), v. I, 86-87
    gratin with spinach and fennel (Switzerland), v. I, 411-12
    pickled vegetables (Panama), v. II, 601-602
    pickle, with garlic (Iran), v. I, 482-83
    pudding (Portugal), v. I, 333-34
    spicy sautéed florets (Saudi Arabia), v. I, 557-58
    stir-fried, with straw mushrooms (Vietnam), v. II, 441-42
    summer vegetable stew (Tunisia), v. II, 276-77
    vegetables in curried coconut milk (Thailand), v. II, 434-35
    vegetable soup with fine noodles (Malta), v. I, 274
    whole with cheese and breadcrumbs (Estonia), v. I, 114-15
    with spicy tomato sauce (Pakistan), v. I, 695
celeriac, knob celery, celery root
    and apple soup (Australia), v. II, 450
    and leek soup (Croatia), v. I, 84-85
    and potato chowder (Switzerland), v. I, 409-10
    appetizer salad (Moldova), v. I, 282-83
    cream soup (Czech), v. I, 91-92
    cream soup with carrot (Finland), v. I, 123-24
    oven-roasted root vegetables with cheese (Sweden), v. I, 402-403

index

celeriac, knob celery, celery root (cont'd)
    oven-roasted root vegetables with fresh herbs and mushrooms (Namibia), v. II, 193-94
    puréed cream soup with chick peas (Turkey), v. I, 569
    salad (Hungary), v. I, 179
    salad, warm with leeks and carrots (Norway), v. I, 310-11
    salad with celery and radish, (Germany), v. I, 143
    vegetable salad with white beans, root celery, kohlrabi, and potatoes (Czech), v. I, 96
    vegetable soup with caraway (Romania), v. I, 342-43
    with creamy mustard sauce (France), v. I, 139-40

celery
    and apple salad (Slovakia), v. I, 375
    and bean soup with bananas (Burundi), v. II, 27-28
    and cabbage slaw with sour cream (Canada), v. II, 641-42
    apple and cheese salad (Switzerland), v. I, 410
    barley and vegetable soup with sour cream (Poland), v. I, 322-23
    bean salad (Caribbean – Haiti), v. II, 497
    black bean soup (The Netherlands), v. I, 300-301
    black-eyed pea and tomato soup (Liberia), v. II, 133
    cabbage salad with pineapple (Liberia), v. II, 133-34
    chick pea and potato vegetable stew (Tunisia), v. II, 275-76
    chili, v. II, 288
    cream soup with Stilton (England), v. I, 435
    eggplant relish (Australia), v. II, 455-56
    hunter's style sauce for vegetables and *pasta* (Italy), v. II, 684-85
    macaroni and vegetables (The Gambia), v. II, 104-105
    Milanese *minestrone* (Italy), v. I, 222-23
    Moscow salad (Russia), v. I, 351
    pickled with eggplant and dill (Turkmenistan), v. I, 626-27
    pink potato salad (Panama), v. II, 598-99
    pumpkin soup with coconut milk and banana (Caribbean – Bahamas), v. II, 494
    puréed *dhal* soup (Pacific Islands – Fiji), v. II, 476
    quinoa and vegetable stew (Peru), v. II, 615
    red lentil soup (Libya), v. II, 140-41
    red pottage (Scotland), v. I, 449
    salad, with apple (Slovakia), v. I, 375
    salt cod stew without the salt cod (Italy), v. I, 206-207
    sauce for sautéed leeks and carrots (Scotland), v. I, 453
    slow cooker black-eyed pea chili (Uganda), v. II, 287-88
    slow cooker vegetable soup with beans and barley (Croatia), v. I, 87-88
    slow cooker vegetable stew (Botswana), v. II, 19-20
    smoky lentils with vegetables (Panama), v. II, 599-600
    stewed carrots and barley (Belarus), v. I, 39
    stew with bananas and soymeat stew (Liberia), v. II, 134-35
    tofu "tuna"-stuffed cucumber boats (Côte d'Ivorie), v. II, 66-67
    tomato-squash soup (Algeria), v. II, 5
    vegetable *ragoût* (Lebanon), v. I, 527-28
    vegetable soup with fine noodles (Malta), v. I, 274
    vegetable stew with brown rice and soymeat (Serbia), v. I, 367-68
    vinegar (Canada), v. II, 642
    wild rice casserole with mushrooms and baby carrots (Canada), v. II, 642-43
    yellow pea soup (Sweden), v. I, 399-400
    yellow split pea soup with meatballs (Azerbaijan), v. I, 603-604

celery root, *see* celeriac

CENTRAL AFRICAN REPUBLIC (Central African Republics), v. II, 45-53

CHAD, v. II, 54-60

chayote, christophenes
    and pepper slaw (Panama), v. II, 598
    chayote, baked with onions (Caribbean – Martinique), v. II, 500-501
    pickled vegetables (Panama), v. II, 601-602

cheese and honey pastries (Malta), v. I, 279
cheese and pastry pies (Malta), v. I, 278-79

cheese, *Appenzeller*
    information, v. I, 408 (note)
    pan-fried sandwiches (Switzerland), v. I, 417
    stuffed mushroom appetizer (Switzerland), v. I, 407-408
    cheese dip with mayonnaise (Portugal), v. I, 330

cheese balls, baked in cream sauce (Tibet), v. II, 348-49

cheese, blues – Danish blue, Gorgonzola, Stilton
    cabbage slaw of the *vuelta e 'Lola* (Venezuela), v. II, 631
    cheese and *chili* sauce (Tibet), v. II, 347
    cheese toasts, deviled (Switzerland), v. I, 407
    chilies and cheese (Bhutan), v. I, 659-60
    cream of celery soup (England), v. I, 435
    onions with blue cheese sauce (Finland), v. I, 127
    potato slices in casserole (England), v. I, 438-39
    trahana with yogurt and cheese (Cyprus), v. I, 470

cheese, Brie
    compote with apples and raisins (South Africa), v. II, 243-44
    eggplant and tomato casserole (Slovakia), v. I, 377
    tossed salad with blueberries and hazelnuts (England), v. I, 436

cheese, *Caerphilly*
    glamorgan sausages (Wales), v. I, 460
    Welsh rabbit (rarebit) (Wales), v. I, 457-58

cheese, Cheddar
    baked lentils with cheese (German), v. I, 147-48
    baked oat appetizers with herbs (England), v. I, 434-35
    cheese and *chili* dip (Native America), v. II, 653
    cheese-stuffed zucchini with lentils and fruit (Mexico), v. II, 583-84
    corn chowder (Native America), v. II, 657-58
    fried, with eggs (Turkey), v. I, 570-71
    grits with cheese (Nicaragua), v. II, 591
    macaroni and cheese (England), v. I, 437-38

Cheese, Cheddar (cont'd)
    pan-fried sandwiches (England), v. I, 440
    potato and spinach *hunza* pie (New Zealand),
        v. II, 468
    puffed potato omelet (Ireland), v. I, 195-96
    shirred eggs in ramekins with cheese and onion
        sauce (Ireland), v. I, 193-94
    soup, cream (Canada), v. II, 640-41
    vegetable pasties (New Zealand), v. II, 467
    watercress omelet (Luxembourg), v. I, 253-54
    Welsh rabbit (rarebit) (Wales), v. I, 457-58
cheese *croissants* (Venezuela), v. II, 629-30
cheese, Edam
    braised onions with cheese (Portugal), v. I, 335
    marinated and seasoned (Norway), v. I, 310
    soup (The Netherlands), v. I, 301-302
cheese, *Emmentaler*
    apple and cheese salad (Switzerland), v. I, 410
    fondue Alice (Switzerland), v. I, 415-16
    fondue *Herren* (Switzerland), v. I, 416
    fried potato cakes (Switzerland), v. I, 413
    pan-fried sandwiches (Switzerland), v. I, 417
    vegetarian reubens (Pacific Islands – Cook Islands),
        v. II, 478-79
cheese, *feta*, including *queso fresco*
    and watermelon salad (South Africa), v. II, 244
    baby zucchini with *feta* and roasted red peppers
        (Armenia), v. I, 587-88
    baked acorn squash with rice- and cheese-stuffing
        (Bosnia), v. I, 64-65
    baked in foil (Bulgaria), v. I, 72
    baked macaroni casserole (Bolivia), v. II, 517
    baked with honey (Greece), v. I, 159-60
    beet salad (Serbia), v. I, 366-67
    cheese salad (Ethiopia), v. II, 92-93
    chilies and cheese (Bhutan), v. I, 659-60
    couscous with raisins and pine nuts (Saudi Arabia),
        v. I, 555-56
    cucumber salad (Bhutan), v. I, 657-58
    eggplant and tomato casserole (Slovakia), v. I, 377
    fried tomato and onion salad with brown rice
        (Bolivia), v. II, 516
    flatbread and cheese (Tajikistan), v. I, 631
    green onion pancakes (Mongolia), v. II, 400
    marinated appetizer (Greece), v. I, 158
    marinated *feta* and olive appetizer (Montenegro),
        v. I, 294
    mushroom casserole with sour cream (Ukraine),
        v. I, 428
    noodles with sour cream (Bosnia-Herzegovina),
        v. I, 64
    phyllo pastries (Turkey), v. I, 567
    potato and egg salad (Tunisia), v. II, 273
    potato and mushroom *momos* in *tukpa* broth
        (Bhutan), v. I, 656-57
    prickly pear salad with apricot-raspberry dressing
        (Mexico), v. II, 581
    scalloped potatoes (Peru), v. II, 616-17
    spread (Romania), v. I, 341
    spread (Slovakia), v. I, 373
    spread with garlic (Syria), v. I, 562
    stuffed frying peppers (Bulgaria), v. I, 73-74

    three-bean salad with creamy dressing (Mongolia),
        v. II, 402
    vegetable stew (Bolivia), v. II, 515-16
    village tossed salad (Greece), v. I, 161-62
    watermelon and tomato salad (Egypt), v. II, 79
cheese, fried appetizers (Lithuania), v. I, 245-46
cheese, goat (*fromage de chèvre*)
    and yogurt appetizer spread (Libya), v. II, 139-40
    red kidney bean *tacos* or *tostados* with sautéed
        greens (Panama), v. II, 600-601
    salad, with eggplant and tomato (São Tomé and
        Principe), v. II, 210-11
    St. John's Day fruit salad (Venezuela), v. II, 630-31
cheese, Gouda, braised onions with cheese (Portugal),
    v. I, 335
cheese, Gruyère
    apple and cheese salad (Switzerland), v. I, 410
    cheese toasts, deviled (Switzerland), v. I, 407
    fondue Alice (Switzerland), v. I, 415-16
    fondue *Herren* (Switzerland), v. I, 416
    fried potato cakes (Switzerland), v. I, 413
    fried, with eggs (Turkey), v. I, 570-71
    gratin with cauliflower, spinach, and fennel
        (Switzerland), v. I, 411-12
    open-faced sandwiches with mushrooms
        (Switzerland), v. I, 408-409
    pan-fried sandwiches (Switzerland), v. I, 417
    stuffed mushroom appetizers (Switzerland),
        v. I, 407-408
    watercress omelet (Luxembourg), v. I, 253-54
cheese, *Halloumi*
    and tomato *kebabs* (Cyprus), v. I, 471-72
    tomato salad with shredded *Halloumi* (Cyprus),
        v. I, 469
    pan-grilled, with *edamame*, peas, and red peppers
        (Australia), v. II, 453
cheese, *Havarti*
    breaded eggplant and cheese sandwiches (Armenia),
        v. I, 594-95
    macaroni and cheese (England), v. I, 437-38
cheese, homemade
    Indian *paneer* cheese (India), v. I, 676
    quark with pepper (Finland), v. I, 120-21
    ricotta, homemade (Italy), v. I, 220
    solstice cheese (Latvia), v. I, 231-32
    white soft cheese (Belgium), v. I, 45-46
cheese, Jarlsberg, sauce for vegetables (Norway),
    v. I, 314
cheese, *mascarpone*
    mousse (Kuwait), v. I, 519
    pineapple dessert with coconut and cream (Somalia),
        v. II, 239
**cheese, *mozzarella*, Monterey Jack, and white cheese
such as *queso blanco***
    avocado, egg, and cheese appetizer (El Salvador),
        v. II, 559-60
    cheese *croissants* (Venezuela), v. II, 629-30
    cheesy cornbread (Paraguay), v. II, 607
    corn and cheese salad (Peru), v. II, 613
    fresh, melon and peach salad (New Zealand),
        v. II, 463-64
    fried corn and cheese fritters (Ecuador), v. II, 550

index

cheese, *mozzarella* (cont'd)
    grits with cheese (Georgia), v. **I**, 617
    hearts of palm salad with cheese (Ecuador),
        v. **II**, 550-51
    lasagne (Italy/Sicilia), v. **I**, 216
    mashed potatoes with cheese and garlic (France),
        v. **I**, 138-39
    mozzarella, tomato, and basil salad (Venezuela),
        v. **II**, 632
    omelet on omelet (Chile), v. **II**, 531
    omelets with cheese (Albania), v. **I**, 5
    pan-grilled Portobello mushrooms with lentils,
        escarole, tomato, and olives (Italy/Calabria),
        v. **I**, 205-206
    potato and cheese soup (Ecuador), v. **II**, 552-53
    potato cakes with peanut sauce (Ecuador), v. **II**, 554
    potatoes in peanut sauce (Peru), v. **II**, 617-18
    rice with tomatoes and hearts of palm (Costa Rica),
        v. **II**, 544-45
    roasted winter squash with corn and eggs (Chile),
        v. **II**, 532-33
    scalloped potatoes (Peru), v. **II**, 616-17
    skillet *lasagne* with soymeat (Italy/Sicilia) v. **I**, 217
    slow cooker *polenta* (Montenegro), v. **I**, 296-97
    squash and cheese *quesadillas* (Mexico), v. **II**, 580
    steamed corn- and cheese-stuffed corn husks
        (Ecuador), v. **II**, 549
    sweet cheese pastry (Jordan), v. **I**, 510
    tomato salad with garlic and cheese (Belarus),
        v. **I**, 35
    tortilla skillet (Honduras), v. **II**, 574-75
    vegetable and cheese pies (Uruguay), v. **II**, 624-25
cheese, *paneer*
    and red peppers in spinach sauce (India),
        v. **I**, 674-75
    basic recipe (India), v. **I**, 676
    with peas (India), v. **I**, 675
cheese pudding (Greece), v. **I**, 160-61
cheese salad (Ethiopia), v. **II**, 92-93
cheese, Trappist, braised onions with cheese (Portugal),
    v. **I**, 335
cherimoya with orange sauce (Chile), v. **II**, 534
cherries, dried
    pears in spiced vanilla honey with chocolate and
        cherries (Poland), v. **I**, 327
    stewed fruit compote with walnuts (Armenia),
        v. **I**, 596
cherries, sour
    beets with tart cherry sauce (Georgia), v. **I**, 617-18
    in maple syrup (Native America), v. **II**, 671
cherries, sweet
    compote from the Ardennes (Belgium), v. **I**, 53-54
    cream of wheat pudding (Romania), v. **I**, 348
    in red wine (Italy), v. **I**, 213
    Israeli *couscous* and chick pea salad (Israel),
        v. **I**, 496-97
    juice in strawberry-blueberry summer pudding,
        v. **I**, 445-46
    Yorkshire summer pudding (England), v. **I**, 444-45
chervil, information, v. **I**, 51 (note)

chestnuts
    chestnut custard ice cream (Luxembourg),
        v. **I**, 258-59
    chestnut purée with whipped cream (Hungary),
        v. **I**, 185-86
    pilaf with fruits and nuts (Azerbaijan), v. **I**, 609
    steamed savoy cabbage (Lithuania), v. **I**, 249
CHILI, v. **II**, 530-35
CHINA, v. **II**, 322-36
chive oil (Armenia), v. **I**, 592
cinnamon variations, v. **II**, 379 (note)
citrus zest, dried, v. **I**, 482
clarified butter, v. **I**, 675-76
clarified butter, *ghee* (India), v. **I**, 675 (note)
clarified butter, spiced *kebbeh* (Ethiopia), v. **II**, 95
coconut
    corn starch pudding (Nicaragua), v. **II**, 595
    fruit salad (Central African Republics), v. **II**, 53
    individual custards (South Africa), v. **II**, 249
    preparation, v. **II**, 15 (note), 182-83, 593-94
    pudding (Nicaragua), v. **II**, 593-94
    soup, curried, with beans and basmati rice
        (Tanzania), v. **II**, 260-61
    soup, with beans and rice (Nigeria), v. **II**, 203-204
    with rice and tomatoes (Mozambique), v. **II**, 182-83
    yellow coconut pudding (Angola), v. **II**, 15
coffeecakes
    rhubarb *streusel* (Estonia), v. **I**, 117-18
    stollen, German Christmas bread, v. **I**, 153-54
colçots (Andorra), cultivation, v. **I**, 14
collard greens, *see* greens, cooked
COLOMBIA, v. **II**, 536-40
confections
    basic almond paste for confections (Tunisia),
        v. **II**, 279
    cinnamon candies (Somalia), v. **II**, 241
    coconut brittle (The Philippines), v. **II**, 427
    coconut tapioca sweet (Brazil), v. **II**, 529
    halva with almond butter (Estonia), v. **I**, 118
    honey-sweetened walnuts (Georgia), v. **I**, 620
    peanut candy (Angola), v. **II**, 16
cookies
    angel food (Bosnia), v. **I**, 68
    beaver tails (Canada), v. **II**, 648
    brown sugar cut-out cookies, v. **II**, 29-30
    Chinese almond cookies (China), v. **II**, 336
    oatmeal lace cookies (Scotland), v. **I**, 455
    peanut macaroons (Sudan), v. **II**, 257-58
    ranger (Moldova), v. **I**, 290-91
    refrigerator, caraway (Latvia), v. **I**, 236-37
    rolled sugar cookies, v. **II**, 697
coriander (*cilantro*) in yogurt (Palestine), v. **I**, 548
corn, including **hominy** and **hominy grits**
    and basil puréed cream soup with tomato (Chile),
        v. **II**, 532
    and bean casserole (Tanzania), v. **II**, 263
    and bean salad (Liechtenstein), v. **I**, 239
    and cheese pudding (Argentina), v. **II**, 510-11
    and cheese salad (Peru), v. **II**, 613
    and cheese stuffed corn husks (Ecuador), v. **II**, 549
    and lima custard pudding (Brazil), v. **II**, 526

corn (cont'd)
    and millet salad with avocado (Central African
        Republics), v. II, 47-48
    and papaya salad with citrus *vinaigrette* (Togo),
        v. II, 268
    and plantain soup (Cameroon), v. II, 35
    and sweetpotato soup (Thailand), v. II, 430-31
    appetizer dip with corn and walnuts (Mexico),
        v. II, 579
    baked corn *tortilla* chips (El Salvador), v. II, 560
    baking powder corn meal biscuits (Native America),
        v. II, 659
    banana custard cornbread (Caribbean), v. II, 501
    bean and hominy *chili* (Somalia), v. II, 238
    bean salad with corn and mango (Burundi), v. II, 27
    bean stew with hominy and *chouriço* (Cape Verde),
        v. II, 42-43
    buttermilk cornbread, v. I, 368
    cheesy cornbread (Paraguay), v. II, 607
    chowder (Native America), v. II, 657-58
    corn meal cake (Kenya), v. II, 128-29
    corn meal pudding with cheese (Romania),
        v. I, 344-45
    corn-on-the-cob, Cambodian style, v. II, 320
    corn-on-the-cob, Kenyan style, v. II, 129-30
    country corn bread (Portugal), v. I, 336-37
    creamed, soup, with egg whites (China), v. II, 328
    creamed, with beans and carrot (Oman), v. I, 539
    cream of potato soup (Columbia), v. II, 538
    curried corn chowder (South Africa), v. II, 245
    curry with garlic and onions (Pakistan), v. I, 694-95
    custard corn meal dessert (Zimbabwe), v. II, 302
    ersatz "maple syrup" (Native America), v. II, 662
    fried flatbreads (Sudan), v. II, 256
    fried fritters with cream (Ecuador), v. II, 550
    fufu with yam and potato (Cameroon), v. II, 36-37
    grilled (Iraq), v. I, 490
    grilled corn-on-the-cob (Native America),
        v. II, 665-66
    grits with cheese (Georgia), v. I, 617
    grits with cheese (Nicaragua), v. II, 591
    groundnut and vegetable soup (Djibouti),
        v. II, 72-73
    hazelnut breads (Native America), v. II, 661
    Indian pudding (Native America), v. II, 670-71
    layered vegetable salad (Ghana), v. II, 111-12
    meatball and vegetable pastry bundles (Mongolia),
        v. II, 405
    milk soup (Botswana), v. II, 18
    millet *couscous* with vegetables (The Gambia),
        v. II, 103
    oysters (Native America), v. II, 652-53
    polenta with herbs (Guinea), v. II, 119-20
    pudding with sage (Canada), v. II, 644
    relish, v. II, 579-80
    salad, with *couscous* and tomato-black bean
        vinaigrette (Somalia), v. II, 234
    sesame noodle salad (Mongolia), v. II, 400-401
    slow cooker *polenta* (Montenegro), v. I, 296-97
    slow cooker vegetable stew (Botswana), v. II, 19-20
    smothered (Native America), v. II, 664-65
    snow food, sweet popcorn clusters (Native
        America), v. II, 673
    soup (Kuwait), v. I, 514
    soup of greens and peanut butter (Chad), v. II, 55
    soup, puréed with sweet red peppers (Mexico),
        v. II, 582-83
    stewed, with coconut (Ghana), v. II, 113
    stove-top pudding (Native America), v. II, 666
    sweet corn meal pudding (São Tomé and Principe),
        v. II, 212
    sweet hominy dessert (Panama), v. II, 602
    tacos or *tostados* with sautéed greens and goat
        cheese (Panama), v. II, 600-601
    toasted millet salad (Mali), v. II, 155-56
    vegetable and groundnut soup (Zambia),
        v. II, 292-93
    vegetable stew (Bolivia), v. II, 515-16
    vegetable stew (Ethiopia), v. II, 94
    vegetarian vegetable soup (Ecuador), v. II, 553
    white, in St. John's Day fruit salad (Venezuela),
        v. II, 630-31
    with winter squash and eggs (Chile), v. II, 532-33
COSTA RICA, v. II, 541-46
CÔTE D'IVOIRE, v. II, 61-69
couscous
    and chick peas in vegetable soup (Angola),
        v. II, 11-12
    Israeli *couscous* and chick pea salad with cucumber,
        cherries, and dates (Israel), v. I, 496-97
    millet *couscous* with chick peas (Mauritania),
        v. II, 164-65
    millet *couscous* with vegetables (The Gambia),
        v. II, 103
    pumpkin porridge with (Kazakhstan), v. I, 632-33
    salad, with chick peas and tomatoes (Algeria),
        v. II, 4-5
    salad, with chick peas and tomatoes (Mauritania),
        v. II, 162-63
    salad, with roasted eggplant and red pepper
        (Morocco), v. II, 171-72
    salad, with tomato-black bean *vinaigrette* (Somalia),
        v. II, 234
    sweet pudding (The Gambia), v. II, 105
    sweet pudding with raisins and pineapple (Niger),
        v. II, 200
    with raisins, pine nuts, and *feta* cheese (Saudi
        Arabia), v. I, 555-56
cranberries
    and black walnut sauce/dessert (Native America),
        v. II, 672
    breaded and fried *semolina* pudding (Latvia),
        v. I, 378
    sauce with mustard (Lithuania), v. I, 248
    spiced whole cranberry relish (Native America),
        v. II, 668
    sweet and tart cranberry vinegar, v. II, 681
Cream of Rice cereal
    cardamom rice pudding (Pakistan), v. I, 696-97
    firni (India), v. I, 677 (note)
    sweet rice and millet pudding (Mali), v. II, 158-59
Cream of Wheat cereal, *see* farina
crème fraîche (Panama), v. II, 603

index

CROATIA, v. I, 81-88
cucumbers
    and olive salad (Azerbaijan), v. I, 602-603
    and red onion salad (Nepal), v. I, 682
    and shallot salad (Malaysia), v. II, 392-93
    and tomato salad (Hungary), v. I, 178-79
    and tomato salad with *chaat masala* (India), v. I, 669
    and tomato salad with grated cheese (Montenegro), v. I, 295
    and watermelon salad with *hoisin*-lime dressing (Vietnam), v. II, 439
    and yogurt salad (India), v. I, 671
    bean and corn salad (Liechtenstein), v. I, 239
    boats with *tofu* "tuna" (Côte d'Ivorie), v. II, 66-67
    bread and vegetable salad (Kuwait), v. I, 515-16
    cabbage pickle, *kimchi* (Korea), v. II, 376-77
    carved cucumber flower garnishes, v. II, 585-86
    chilled soup with yogurt (Bulgaria), v. I, 74-75
    cucumber pickles (Nepal), v. I, 687
    fruit and vegetable salad (Indonesia), v. II, 354
    fruit platter with lime *vinaigrette* (Caribbean), v. II, 496
    fruit salad with tamarind dressing (Brunei), v. II, 308-309
    Israeli couscous and chick pea salad (Israel), v. I, 496-97
    Kirby, salad (Korea), v. II, 377-78
    layered vegetable salad (Ghana), v. II, 111-12
    millet *tabbouleh* (Lebanon), v. I, 526-27
    mixed fruit salad with *chaat masala* (India), v. I, 670
    Moscow salad (Russia), v. I, 351
    rice noodle salad with mango and sweet *cilantro* dressing (Cambodia), v. II, 318
    salad (Slovakia), v. I, 375-76
    salad, sweet and sour (Japan), v. II, 363-64
    salad, with cheese (Bhutan), v. I, 657-58
    salad, with dill and garlic mayonnaise (Ukraine), v. I, 425
    salad, with peanut-lime dressing (Central African Republics), v. II, 48-49
    salad, with pomegranate *vinaigrette* (Iran), v. I, 479
    salad, shredded, with yogurt (Sudan), v. II, 253
    salad, wilted with honey (Belarus) v. I, 34-35
    sautéed in dill butter (Russia), v. I, 356
    soup, with mango (Saudi Arabia), v. I, 554
    toasted millet salad (Mali), v. II, 155-56
    tossed vegetable salad (Azerbaijan), v. I, 606
    vegetable bread soup (Spain), v. I, 393-94
    vegetable relish (Tanzania), v. II, 262-63
    vegetable salad (Macedonia), v. I, 265
    vegetable salad with hearts of palm (Brazil), v. II, 525
    village tossed salad (Greece), v. I, 161-62
currants
    lentil and bulgur cabbage rolls (Armenia), v. I, 592-93
    meat pies (Botswana), v. II, 21
    rice- and lentil-stuffed grape leaves (Lebanon), v. I, 525
    Yorkshire summer pudding (England), v. I, 444-45

CYPRUS, v. I, 465-74
CZECH REPUBLIC, v. I, 89-98

Dandelion
    and potato salad (Slovenia), v. I, 387-88
    wilted salad (Andorra), v. I, 16-17
dates
    and orange salad (Morocco), v. II, 174
    date balls with coconut (Yemen), v. I, 582
    Israeli *couscous* and chick pea salad (Israel), v. I, 496-97
    prickly pear salad with apples (Israel), v. I, 497
    rice pudding (Saudi Arabia), v. I, 558
    slow cooker dried fruit curry (South Africa), v. II, 247-48
    yogurt dessert with cream, v. I, 490-91
    pilaf with fruits and nuts (Azerbaijan), v. I, 609
    sweet, with onions (South Africa), v. II, 248
DEMOCRATIC REPUBLIC OF THE CONGO
    (Central African Republics), v. II, 45-53
DENMARK, v. I, 99-109
desserts, *see also* puddings, pies, cakes, and individual fruit entries
    almond ball sweet (Tunisia), v. II, 278-79
    almond pistachio sweet (Chad), v. II, 59-60
    autumn compote (Portugal), v. I, 331
    avocado cream (Venezuela), v. II, 635
    baked cheese balls in cream sauce (Tibet), v. II, 348-49
    baked cheese sweet (India), v. I, 676-77
    banana-lime whip (Pacific Islands – Cook Islands), v. II, 484
    banana, mango, and pineapple in mango-yogurt sauce (Oman), v. I, 537
    basic almond paste for confections (Tunisia), v. II, 279
    cannoli pastry (Italy/Sicily; Venezuela), v. II, 636-37
    cassava fritters (Cameroon), v. II, 39
    chick pea flour sweet (Tunisia), v. II, 278
    chocolate mousse *Kahlua*, (Switzerland), v. I, 421
    coffee ice dessert (Eritrea), v. II, 89
    cranberry and black walnut sauce/dessert (Native America), v. II, 672
    crème fraîche (Panama), v. II, 603
    croissants with jam (Uruguay), v. II, 627
    custard bread sweet (Turkey), v. I, 575
    date balls with coconut (Yemen), v. I, 582
    dried fruit compote (Tunisia), v. II, 277
    dulce de leche soufflé (Ecuador), v. II, 555-56
    fried dough balls (Nigeria), v. II, 208
    fried rice sweets (The Philippines), v. II, 425-26
    fried walnut pastries (Uzbekistan), v. I, 632
    fruit salad (Uganda), v. II, 283-84
    honey-sweetened walnuts (Georgia), v. I, 620
    mango whip (Cameroon), v. II, 37-38
    mascarpone mousse (Kuwait), v. I, 519
    Orthodox Easter *paskha* (Russia), v. I, 359-60
    palace honey bread (Egypt), v. II, 82
    "parson's" dessert (Finland), v. I, 129
    peanut-apple crumble v. II, 469-70
    pineapple pastry (El Salvador), v. II, 563

index

desserts *(cont'd)*
    puff pastry pillows with raspberry purée and
        peaches, v. II, 458
    puffed pastry with Argentine sweet milk
        (Argentina), v. II, 512
    raspberry swirl (Romania), v. I, 347
    shredded wheat in syrup (Greece), v. I, 169-70
    sour cream dessert (Nepal), v. I, 688
    squash or pumpkin in sweet syrup with walnuts
        (Turkey), v. I, 573-74
    stewed rhubarb with tapioca (New Zealand),
        v. II, 470
    sticky rice and banana sweet (Cambodia), v. II, 321
    sweet cheese pastry (Jordan), v. I, 510
    sweet coconut rice with mangoes (Cambodia),
        v. II, 321
    sweet egg dessert with papaya (Mozambique),
        v. II, 187
    sweet hominy (Panama), v. II, 602
    sweet *pasta* (Sudan), v. II, 257
    sweet *pasta* with almonds and raisins (Bangladesh),
        v. I, 652-53
    sweetpotato dessert fritters (Peru), v. II, 618-19
    sweet rice balls (Vietnam), v. II, 444
    sweet rice clusters (Nigeria), v. II, 207
    sweet saffron rice (Tibet), v. II, 349
    sweet scrambled eggs (Brazil), v. II, 528
    sweet wheat fritters (Ukraine), v. I, 431
    toasted semolina with honey (Algeria), v. II, 9
    vanilla meringues, v. II, 626
    yogurt with chopped dates and cream, v. I, 490-91
DJIBOUTI, v. II, 70-76
dulce de leche
    Argentine sweet milk (Argentina), v. II, 513
    preparation, v. II, 513 (Argentina); 556 (Ecuador)
    soufflé (Ecuador), v. II, 554-55
dumplings
    boiled (Switzerland), v. I, 414-15
    chick pea, in yogurt sauce (India), v. I, 667-68
    farina and cheese (Poland), v. I, 320-21
    pinched, in bean soup (Hungary), v. I, 176-77
    potato and mushroom *momos* in *tukpa* broth
        (Bhutan), v. I, 656-57
    potato-apricot (Slovenia), v. I, 386
    soup (Korea), v. II, 371-72
    with cheese and caramelized onions (Liechtenstein),
        v. I, 242

ECUADOR, v. II, 547-57

edamame
    with pan-grilled *Halloumi* cheese, peas, and red
        peppers (Australia), v. II, 453
    with *soba* noodles and vegetables in clear broth
        (Japan), v. II, 361-62
    salad with Armenian string cheese and chive oil
        (Armenia), v. I, 591-92
eggplant
    adobo (The Philippines), v. II, 422
    and brown rice (Indonesia), v. II, 355
    and cheese sandwiches (Armenia), v. I, 594-95
    and mushrooms with cream (Bosnia), v. I, 65-66
    and onions with yogurt (Azerbaijan), v. I, 602

    and pepper *caviar* (Serbia), v. I, 364-65
    and scallion salad (Korea), v. II, 375-76
    and tomato casserole (Slovakia), v. I, 377
    and tomato salad (Yemen), v. I, 579-80
    appetizer, with roasted red peppers (Saudi Arabia),
        v. I, 552-53
    baked slices (Mauritania/Western Sahara),
        v. II, 166-67
    baked with yogurt (Afghanistan), v. I, 642
    baked with yogurt (Iraq), v. I, 487-88
    baked with yogurt (Palestine), v. I, 547-48
    Byzantine (Greece), v. I, 167
    curry with tomatoes (Sri Lanka), v. I, 700-701
    greens and vegetables (Caribbean – Virgin Islands),
        v. II, 502
    kebabs (Greece), v. I, 166
    mixed grilled vegetables, Catalan-style (Andorra),
        v. I, 18
    pickled vegetables (Panama), v. II, 601-602
    pickled with dill (Turkmenistan), v. I, 626-27
    pie, roasted, in *phyllo* crust (Jordan), v. I, 506-507
    ratatouille, vegetable stew (France), v. I, 134-35
    ratatouille with puff pastry pillows (France),
        v. I, 135-36
    relish (Australia), v. II, 455-56
    roasted (Pacific Islands – Fiji), v. II, 481
    roasted appetizers (Lebanon), v. I, 523
    roasted appetizer spread with green peppers
        (Bulgaria), v. I, 71
    roasted *caviar* appetizer (Romania), v. I, 340-41
    roasted eggplant (India), v. I, 672-73
    roasted, in salad with onion dressing (Vietnam),
        v. II, 440
    roasted, with *couscous* and red pepper (Morocco),
        v. II, 171-72
    salad (China), v. II, 327-28
    salad, with herb dressing (Mongolia), v. II, 401-402
    salad, with tomato and goat cheese (São Tomé and
        Principe), v. II, 210-11
    spicy, with tomato and *chili* sauce (Brunei),
        v. II, 311-12
    steamed (Myanmar/Burma), v. II, 415
    stir-fried (Laos), v. II, 387-88
    tagine (Libya), v. II, 142-43
    vegetable *kebabs* with lemon (Kuwait), v. I, 518-19
    vegetable *mélange* (Malta), v. I, 275-76
    vegetable stew with brown rice and soymeat
        (Serbia), v. I, 367-68
    white eggplant and red kidney bean salad (Ethiopia),
        v. II, 93
    with tomato (Central African Republics),
        v. II, 50-51
    with yogurt (Palestine), v. I, 547-48
eggs
    allioli sauce with eggs (Andorra), v. I, 19
    almond cake (Iceland), v. I, 191
    and avocado salad (Colombia), v. II, 537
    and avocado salad (Israel), v. I, 498
    and cauliflower (Myanmar/Burma), v. II, 409-10
    and kidney bean salad (Slovenia), v. I, 388-89
    and lemon sauce (Macedonia), v. I, 267
    and lemon soup (Greece), v. I, 164-65

eggs (cont'd)
  and peas with curried tomato sauce (Tibet), v. II, 342-43
  and potato salad (Côte d'Ivoire), v. II, 65
  and potato salad with *feta* cheese (Tunisia), v. II, 273
  and radish salad (Tunisia), v. II, 274
  and rice (Italy), v. I, 212
  anise-scented sweet egg custard (Caribbean – Cuba), v. II, 504-505
  appetizer *guacamole* with avocado and cheese (El Salvador), v. II, 559-60
  asparagus salad with capers (Romania), v. I, 343
  baked (Belgium), v. I, 51-52
  baked honey-egg custard, v. II, 23-24
  baked macaroni casserole (Bolivia), v. II, 517
  baked pear and breadcrumb pudding (Canada), v. II, 646-47
  baked with cheese (Bulgaria), v. I, 78
  baked with rice and tomatoes (Malta), v. I, 278
  bean salad (Caribbean – Haiti), v. II, 497
  beet and *tahini* salad (Syria), v. I, 564
  beetroot and apple salad (Uruguay), v. II, 624
  beetroot salad (Belarus), v. I, 35-36
  blender Hollandaise sauce, v. II, 522
  broccoli and potato salad with Hollandaise sauce (Brazil), v. II, 521
  brown sugar pound cake (Costa Rica), v. II, 545-46
  buttermilk cake (Moldova), v. I, 289
  cake with lemon syrup (Bosnia), v. I, 66
  carrot cake (Switzerland), v. I, 420
  chocolate almond *torte* (Hungary), v. I, 184
  chocolate mousse *Kahlua* (Switzerland), v. I, 421
  coconut custard crustless pie (Colombia), v. II, 540
  coconut custards (South Africa), v. II, 249
  coffee eggs (Greece), v. I, 157-58
  coffee custards (France), v. I, 140
  corn and lima bean custard pudding (Brazil), v. II, 526
  corn oysters (Native America), v. II, 652-53
  corn pudding with sage (Canada), v. II, 644
  creamed corn soup with egg whites (China), v. II, 328
  crustless pineapple cheese pie (Ukraine), v. I, 430
  curried eggs and rice, v. I, 673-74
  curried, with green peas (Nepal), v. I, 683
  custard bread sweet (Turkey), v. I, 575
  custard pumpkin pie (Native America), v. II, 672-73
  custard sauce, v. II, 688
  dessert, with papaya (Mozambique), v. II, 187
  deviled (England), v. I, 437
  deviled beet, potato, apple, and egg salad (Estonia), v. I, 111-12
  dulce de leche soufflé (Ecuador), v. II, 555-56
  egg fried rice (China), v. II, 334-35
  eggnog bavarian (Germany), v. I, 151
  egg sponge cake with sugar syrup (Albania), v. I, 11-12
  fried cheese with (Turkey), v. I, 570-71
  fried on flatbread with garlic-yogurt sauce (Iran), v. I, 476-77
  gari with (Ghana), v. II, 113
  garlic soup (Portugal), v. I, 331-32
  individual omelets with cheese (Albania), v. I, 5
  layered vegetable salad (Ghana), v. II, 111-12
  lecsó omelet (Hungary), v. I, 175
  lemon curd (England), v. I, 443-44
  macaroni salad (Denmark), v. I, 107-108
  milk cake (Ecuador), v. II, 557
  mustard omelet (France), v. I, 133-34
  niçoise salad (France), v. I, 136
  omelet appetizers with potatoes (Belarus), v. I, 34
  omelet on omelet (Chile), v. II, 531
  omelets with parsley and scallions (Armenia), v. I, 587
  omelet with bananas (São Tomé and Principe), v. II, 211
  omelet with cauliflower and onion (Georgia), v. I, 616
  omelet with herbs (Azerbaijan), v. I, 606-607
  omelet with potato, mushroom, and onion (Belarus) v. I, 40-41
  omelet with potatoes and parsley (Algeria), v. II, 7
  omelet with roasted root vegetable filling (Sweden), v. I, 402
  omelet with sweetpotatoes (São Tomé and Principe), v. II, 211-12
  orange custards with honey and cinnamon (Portugal), v. I, 337
  orange *torte* (Portugal), v. I, 338
  peach cakes with crumbled meringue (Uruguay), v. II, 625-26
  peanut macaroons (Sudan), v. II, 257-58
  pickled (Indonesia), v. II, 352-53
  pink potato salad (Panama), v. II, 598-99
  poached with vegetarian gravy (Kenya), v. II, 124-25
  potatoes with peanut sauce (Peru), v. II, 617-18
  preserved sweet and sour (The Philippines), v. II, 419
  puffed potato-Cheddar omelet (Ireland), v. I, 195-96
  raspberry curd (Jordan), v. I, 509
  raspberry swirl dessert (Romania), v. I, 347
  rice soup with eggs and lemon (Albania), v. I, 6
  rice with onions and egg and lemon sauce (Macedonia), v. I, 266
  sauce, for asparagus and wonton noodles (Japan), v. II, 364-65
  shirred, with Cheddar and onion sauce in ramekins (Ireland), v. I, 193-94
  shirred, with vegetables (Libya), v. II, 143-44
  scrambled, v. I, 364
  scrambled with broad beans (Lebanon), v. I, 530
  scrambled with greens and mushrooms (Spain), v. I, 394
  scrambled with vegetables (Venezuela), v. II, 633
  shirred in yogurt (Lebanon), v. I, 530-31
  smørrebrød (Denmark), v. I, 106
  soufflé with grated cheese (Moldova), v. I, 287
  sour cream omelet (Romania), v. I, 342
  sour cream omelets (Russia), v. I, 355
  spicy (Saudi Arabia), v. I, 554
  spinach and beet salad with yogurt dressing (Georgia), v. I, 618-19

eggs (cont'd)
    steamed cheese pudding (Czech), v. **I**, 91
    stuffed (Latvia), v. **I**, 230-31
    sweet egg sponge cakes (El Salvador), v. **II**, 569-70
    sweet farina omelet (Czech), v. **I**, 98
    sweetpotato *soufflé* (Mali), v. **II**, 156-57
    sweet scrambled eggs (Brazil), v. **II**, 528
    sweet wheat fritters (Ukraine), v. **I**, 431
    toasted hazelnut *torte* (Hungary), v. **I**, 182-83
    tomato omelet (Cyprus), v. **I**, 467
    tomato omelet (Greece), v. **I**, 168-69
    vanilla meringues (Uruguay), v. **II**, 626
    walnut sponge cake (Russia), v. **I**, 358
    watercress omelet (Luxembourg), v. **I**, 253-54
    white sauce (or Kampan sturgeon) (The Netherlands), v. **I**, 300
    with angel hair spaghetti (Malta), v. **I**, 273
    with beets (Iceland), v. **I**, 189-90
    with buckwheat noodles (Bhutan), v. **I**, 658-59
    with curried tomato and onion (Bangladesh), v. **I**, 649-50
    with curried yam and banana salad (Pacific Islands – Saipan), v. **II**, 475
    with fava beans (Malta), v. **I**, 276-77
    with greens *vinaigrette* (Senegal), v. **II**, 218-19
    with lima beans and tomatoes (Mexico), v. **II**, 585
    with stir-fried Chinese cabbage and peppers (Malaysia), v. **II**, 394-95
    with winter squash and eggs (Chile), v. **II**, 532-33
    yellow coconut pudding (Angola), v. **II**, 15
EGYPT, v. **II**, 77-82
EL SALVADOR, v. **II**, 558-64
endive, cream soup (Belgium), v. **I**, 48
ENGLAND, *see* **UNITED KINGDOM, ENGLAND**
epazote, information, v. **II**, 583 (note)
EQUATORIAL GUINEA (Central African Republics), v. **II**, 45-53
ERITREA, v. **II**, 83-89
escarole
    crostini, toasted bread appetizers (Italy), v. **I**, 222
    portobellos with lentils, escarole, tomato, and olives (Italy), v. **I**, 205-206
ESTONIA, v. **I**, 110-18
ETHIOPIA, v. **II**, 90-97
evaporated milk (Pakistan), v. **I**, 696

Farina/Cream of Wheat cereal/semolina
    and cheese dumplings (Poland), v. **I**, 320-21
    breaded and fried *semolina* with cranberry garnish (Slovakia), v. **I**, 378
    cake with lemon syrup (Bosnia), v. **I**, 66
    coconut cake (Oman), v. **I**, 542
    cream dessert with cranberry sauce (Estonia), v. **I**, 116-17
    croquettes (Moldova), v. **I**, 287-88
    custard (Greece), v. **I**, 171
    dessert with bananas (Guinea), v. **II**, 121-22
    dessert with rose water (Oman), v. **I**, 541
    orange wheat pudding (Israel), v. **I**, 499-500
    potato pudding (Lithuania), v. **I**, 247-48
    pudding, with coconut and spices (Madagascar), v. **II**, 153
    pudding, with cherries (Romania), v. **I**, 348
    red wheat pudding (Norway), v. **I**, 317
    semolina dessert with walnuts (Bulgaria), v. **I**, 78-79
    stewed rhubarb with (Germany), v. **I**, 152
    sweet omelet (Czech), v. **I**, 98
    sweet wheat fritters (Ukraine), v. **I**, 431
    toasted semolina with honey (Algeria), v. **II**, 9
    wheat and coconut dessert with sweet syrup (Palestine), v. **I**, 549-50
    whipped dessert porridge (Finland), v. **I**, 128
fennel
    baked (Jordan), v. **I**, 508-509
    blood orange salad with fennel, *pecorino*, and pomegranate (Italy), v. **I**, 215
    gratin with cauliflower and spinach (Switzerland), v. **I**, 411-12
    salad with lemon and cheese (Angola), v. **II**, 12
    sautéed cabbage with fennel leaves (Romania), v. **I**, 345-46
feta cheese, *see* cheese, *feta*
figs
    pudding (Albania), v. **I**, 13
    sauce (Italy), v. **I**, 208-209
    stuffed, with chocolate and raspberry sauce (Italy), v. **I**, 207-208
    tarts (Albania), v. **I**, 12
FINLAND, v. **I**, 119-29
fish sauce substitute, v. **II**, 320
fondue dunkables, v. **I**, 416
fondues
    Alice (Switzerland), v. **I**, 415-16
    Herren (Switzerland), v. **I**, 416
FRANCE, v. **I**, 130-40
fritters
    banana (Djibouti), v. **II**, 76
    curried with *chilies* (Madagascar), v. **II**, 150
    fried corn and cheese (Ecuador), v. **II**, 550
    fried with yogurt (Herzegovina), v. **I**, 60
    mushroom (Andorra), v. **I**, 20
    sweet cassava (Cameroon), v. **II**, 39
    sweetpotato dessert (Peru), v. **II**, 618-19
    sweet wheat (Ukraine), v. **I**, 431
frostings
    maple buttercream (Canada), v. **II**, 649
    orange buttercream, v. **I**, 269-70
    vanilla buttercream, v. **I**, 183
fruits, *see* by name
fruits, dried, *see* by name

GABON (Central African Republics), v. **II**, 45-53
GAMBIA, THE, v. **II**, 98-108
garlic
    allioli sauce with eggs (Andorra), v. **I**, 19
    and greens (Cameroon), v. **II**, 36
    and radish salad/relish (Myanmar/Burma), v. **II**, 413-14
    and papaya soup (Caribbean), v. **II**, 492-93
    and parsley sauce (Nicaragua), v. **II**, 592
    and tomato sauce for black beans (The Gambia), v. **II**, 103
    and tomatoes in mung bean sauce (Uganda), v. **II**, 285-86

index

garlic (cont'd)
    and yogurt sauce with *tahini* (Tunisia), v. II, 272
    avocado soup (Côte d'Ivoire), v. II, 64
    baked eggplant with yogurt (Afghanistan), v. I, 642
    baked garlic and bread pudding with cheese (Guatemala), v. II, 568-69
    braised Chinese black mushrooms with (Indonesia), v. II, 356-57
    brown rice pilaf (Central Asia), v. I, 629-30
    "chicken" stew with tomato and (Sierra Leone), v. II, 227-28
    coriander sauce (Afghanistan), v. I, 641
    corn curry (Pakistan), v. I, 694-95
    curried tomato and onion with eggs (Bangladesh), v. I, 649-50
    dark vegetable stock (Thailand), v. II, 431-32
    dipping oil with yogurt (Eritrea), v. II, 85
    dip with roasted beets and *hummus* (Israel), v. I, 494
    dried mushroom condiment (Myanmar/Burma), v. II, 410
    eggplant and brown rice (Indonesia), v. II, 355
    eggplant and tomato salad (Yemen), v. I, 579-80
    eggplant relish (Australia), v. II, 455-56
    falafel (Jordan), v. I, 503
    fried, with fried rice (Brazil), v. II, 526-27
    fried potato cakes (Ghana), v. II, 112
    grilled vegetable salad (Kuwait), v. I, 516
    lime marinade for *tofu* (Caribbean – Cuba), v. II, 498
    marinara sauce (Italy), v. II, 682
    mushroom *wonton* appetizers (Laos), v. II, 382-83
    oil, v. II, 694
    oven-roasted root vegetables with fresh herbs and mushrooms (Namibia), v. II, 193-94
    peanut butter and tomato sauce (The Gambia), v. II, 104
    pickle, with cauliflower (Iran), v. I, 482-83
    pineapple fried rice (Laos), v. II, 386-87
    powder, homemade, v. II, 327 (note)
    puréed *dhal* soup (Pacific Islands – Fiji), v. II, 476
    red kidney bean *tacos* or *tostados* with sautéed greens and goat cheese (Panama), v. II, 600-601
    roasted eggplant appetizer (Lebanon), v. I, 523
    roasted potato soup (Tibet), v. II, 339
    sauce (Moldova/Romania), v. I, 286
    sautéed potatoes with sumac (Lebanon), v. I, 532
    shirred eggs in yogurt (Lebanon), v. I, 530-31
    soup (Portugal), v. I, 331-32
    spaghetti with broccoli (Botswana), v. II, 22-23
    stew with bananas and soymeat stew (Liberia), v. II, 134-35
    stir-fried long beans and mushrooms with garlic (Laos), v. II, 388
    summer vegetable stew (Tunisia), v. II, 276-77
    tomato and pepper appetizer salad (Israel), v. I, 495
    tomato-coriander sauce (Laos), v. II, 384
    tomato soup with basil (The Gambia), v. II, 100-101
    vegetable stew (Uzbekistan), v. I, 628-29
    vegetable stew with beans and *chouriço* sausage (Angola), v. II, 13-14
    vegetable-stuffed zucchini (Turkey), v. I, 571
    vegetarian *tukpa* broth (Tibet), v. II, 339-40
    winter squash soup (Mozambique), v. II, 180-81
    with lentils and tomatoes (Eritrea), v. II, 88
    with mashed *tofu* (Bangladesh), v. I, 649
    with potatoes and coriander in tomato sauce (Somalia), v. II, 236
    with sautéed cabbage, carrot, and onion (Mozambique), v. II, 185
    with thyme and bay in oil, v. II, 695
GEORGIA, v. I, 610-20
GERMANY, v. I, 141-54
GHANA, v. II, 109-15
ghee (India), v. I, 675 (note)
grainburger on vegetable spaghetti (Australia), v. II, 453-54
grapefruit, including *pomelo*
    and avocado salad (Somalia), v. II, 234-35
    dessert, with yogurt (Israel), v. I, 500
    fruit and vegetable salad (Indonesia), v. II, 354
    fruit salad (Central African Republics), v. II, 53
    fruit salad with citrus *vinaigrette* (Côte d'Ivorie), v. II, 66
    pomelo salad (Cambodia), v. II, 317
    salad, with papaya and avocado (Kenya), v. II, 126
    salad, with soymeat and soy sprouts (Thailand), v. II, 433-34
    St. John's Day fruit salad (Venezuela), v. II, 630-31
    with honey (Algeria), v. II, 9
    with honey (Nicaragua), v. II, 590
grape leaf appetizer with rice and lentils (Lebanon), v. I, 525
grapes, autumn compote (Portugal), v. I, 331
granola, v. II, 696
GREAT BRITAIN, see **UNITED KINGDOM**
gravy, "without the 'Sunday Roast,'" v. II, 124-25
GREECE, v. I, 155-71
greens, cooked, including **collards**, **escarole**, and **kale**; *see also* spinach, Swiss chard, turnips, i. e., greens
    and bamboo shoots (Uganda), v. II, 287
    and vegetables (Caribbean – Virgin Islands), v. II, 502
    chick pea and kale soup with peanut butter and tomatoes (Djibouti), v. II, 74
    collard and kale with potatoes and carrots (Montenegro), v. I, 295-96
    collards in black-eyed pea and tomato soup (Liberia), v. II, 133
    escarole on toasted bread appetizers with garlic and capers (Italy), v. I, 222
    fried, with "bacon" (Native America), v. II, 656
    greens *vinaigrette* (Senegal), v. II, 218-19
    kale with onion and spices (Ethiopia), v. II, 95-96
    lentils, escarole, tomato, and olives in pan-grilled portobello mushrooms (Italy), v. I, 205-206
    pickled mustard greens (Vietnam), v. II, 442-43
    sautéed kale with cream (Sweden), v. I, 404
    soup, with peanut butter (Chad), v. II, 55
    tacos or *tostados* with red kidney beans and goat cheese (Panama), v. II, 600-601
    with butternut squash (Botswana), v. II, 22
    with garlic (Cameroon), v. II, 36
    with peanuts (Tanzania), v. II, 264

greens, cooked (cont'd)
  with sweetpotato and peanut butter in vegetable
    soup (Zimbabwe), v. II, 300
grits, see corn
GUATAMALA, v. II, 565-70
guava cream tapioca pudding, v. II, 196
GUINEA. v. II, 116-22

Hazelnut butter, preparation, v. II, 667 (note)
hearts of palm
  and tomatoes in rice casserole (Costa Rica),
    v. II, 544-45
  broiled (Paraguay), v. II, 606-607
  curry (Sri Lanka), v. I, 702
  fruit platter with lime *vinaigrette* (Caribbean),
    v. II, 496
  salad (The Philippines), v. II, 421
  salad, with *jicama*, papaya, and lime *vinaigrette*
    (Pacific Islands), v. II, 474-75
  salad, with cheese (Ecuador), v. II, 550-51
  soup, cream of (Pacific Islands), v. II, 478
  vegetable salad (Brazil), v. II, 525
hominy, see corn
HONDURAS, v. II, 571-76
HUNGARY, v. I, 172-86

Ice creams
  avocado-ice cream dessert (Indonesia), v. II, 358
  banana (Tanzania), v. II, 264-65
  chestnut custard (Luxembourg), v. I, 258-59
  coconut (Honduras), v. II, 576
  creamsicle *sorbet*, v. II, 240
  French vanilla with star anise (Vietnam),
    v. II, 443-44
  ginger (Chad), v. II, 59
  green tea (Japan), v. II, 367
  groundnut (Senegal), v. II, 223
  mango (India), v. I, 678
  nutmeg (Caribbean), v. II, 502-503
  pineapple (Paraguay), v. II, 609
  plum and orange (Japan), v. II, 367-68
  vanilla with pear mincemeat (England), v. I, 440-41
ICELAND, v. I, 187-91
INDIA, v. I, 663-79
INDONESIA, v. II, 350-58
IRAN, v. I, 475-84
IRAQ, v. I, 485-91
IRELAND, v. I, 192-203
ISRAEL, v. I, 492-500
ITALY, v. I, 204-28

JAPAN, v. II, 359-68
Jarlsberg, see cheese, *Jarlsberg*
jicama
  and carrot salad with mango (Colombia),
    v. II, 538-39
  fruit and vegetable salad (Indonesia), v. II, 354
  fruit salad with tamarind dressing (Brunei),
    v. II, 308-309
  salad, with hearts of palm, papaya, and lime
    vinaigrette (Pacific Islands), v. II, 474-75

  salad, with sweetpotato and mango in citrus dressing
    (Caribbean), v. II, 494-95
JORDAN, v. I, 501-10

Kale, see greens, cooked *or* salads
KAZAKHSTAN (Central Asia), v. I, 622-34
kebabs, vegetable (Greece), v. I, 166
KENYA, v. II, 123-30
kiwifruit
  frappé appetizer (New Zealand), v. II, 461-62
  in mixed fruit salad with *chaat masala* (India),
    v. I, 670
  vinaigrette with honey (New Zealand), v. II, 465
knob celery, see celeriac
kohlrabi
  and papaya salad with tamarind dressing (Laos),
    v. II, 385
  slow cooker vegetable soup with beans and barley
    (Croatia), v. I, 87-88
  vegetable salad with white beans, root celery,
    kohlrabi, and potatoes (Czech), v. I, 96
  vegetable soup with *couscous* and chick peas
    (Angola), v. II, 11-12
  with butter and breadcrumbs (Czech), v. I, 95
KOREA, v. II, 369-80
KUWAIT, v. I, 511-20
KYRGYSTAN (Central Asia), v. I, 622-34

LAOS, v. II 381-90
LATVIA, v. I, 229-37
LEBANON, v. I, 521-34
lecsó in *phyllo* nest, v. I, 174
lecsó vegetable mélange (Hungary), v. I, 175-76
leeks
  and carrots with celery sauce (Scotland), v. I, 453
  and celeriac soup (Croatia), v. I, 84-85
  and potato gratin (Switzerland), v. I, 412-13
  and spinach soup with dill (Iraq), v. I, 488
  appetizer salad with celeriac (Moldova), v. I, 282-83
  artichoke salad with carrots (Turkey), v. I, 570
  baked (Albania), v. I, 8-9
  barley and vegetable soup with sour cream (Poland),
    v. I, 322-23
  black bean soup (The Netherlands), v. I, 300-301
  black lentil soup (Nepal), v. I, 681-82
  braised vegetables in olive oil with rice (Saudi
    Arabia), v. I, 556
  chick pea and tomato soup (Uruguay), v. II, 623
  cream of endive soup (Belgium), v. I, 48
  cream of sweetpotato soup (Côte d'Ivorie),
    v. II, 64-65
  creamy orange sauce (Wales), v. I, 461
  eggplant and brown rice (Indonesia), v. II, 355
  lentil soup (Macedonia), v. I, 263-64
  meatball and vegetable pastry bundles (Mongolia),
    v. II, 405
  mushroom casserole with sour cream (Ukraine),
    v. I, 428
  noodle and mushroom soup (Brunei), v. II, 307
  oven-roasted root vegetables with cheese (Sweden),
    v. I, 402-403

index

leeks (cont'd)
    oven-roasted root vegetables with fresh herbs and mushrooms (Namibia), v. II, 193-94
    pickled vegetables (Panama), v. II, 601-602
    potato and spinach pie (New Zealand), v. II, 468
    salad, warm with celeriac and carrots (Norway), v. I, 310-11
    slow cooker vegetable soup with beans and barley (Croatia), v. I, 87-88
    soup with leeks and potatoes (Luxembourg), v. I, 254-55
    stir-fried cauliflower and straw mushrooms (Vietnam), v. II, 441-42
    vegetable pasties (New Zealand), v. II, 467
    vegetable soup with caraway (Romania), v. I, 342-43
    vegetable spaghetti with grainburger (Australia), v. II, 453-54
    wheaten scones (Ireland), v. I, 197-98
    with black-eyed peas and spinach (Iran), v. I, 479-80
    with potatoes and carrots in cream sauce (Luxembourg), v. I, 257
lemon balm, information, v. I, 56 (note)
lemons
    and red onion salad (Myanmar/Burma), v. II, 413
    jelly infused with fresh herbs (Native America), v. II, 668-69
    lemon curd (England), v. I, 443-44
    limoncello, v. II, 473-74
    preserved, in conserve (Morocco), v. II, 174
    sauce, v. II, 689-90
    syrup, v. II, 690
    syrup (Bosnia), v. I, 66
    vegetable *kebabs* (Kuwait), v. I, 518-19
lentils
    and bulgur in cabbage rolls with dried fruits (Armenia), v. I, 592-93
    and fruit in cheese-stuffed zucchini (Mexico), v. II, 583-84
    and noodles (Syria), v. I, 563-64
    and *orzo* with caramelized onions (Cyprus), v. I, 469-70
    and *pasta* salad with nasturtium (Australia), v. II, 457
    and rice-stuffed grape leaves (Lebanon), v. I, 525
    and shallots in red wine and tomato sauce (France), v. I, 137-38
    and spinach salad (Libya), v. II, 141
    baked with cheese (Germany), v. I, 147-48
    black lentils and potatoes with lemon juice (Saudi Arabia), v. I, 553-54
    black lentil soup (Nepal), v. I, 681-82
    consommé (Liechtenstein), v. I, 239
    deep-fried *poppodum* chips with chutney dipping sauce (Bangladesh), v. I, 647-48
    mixed legume soup (Morocco), v. II, 172-73
    portobellos with lentil, escarole, tomato, and olives (Italy), v. I, 205-206
    puréed *dhal* soup (Pacific Islands – Fiji), v. II, 476
    puréed lentil soup (Somalia), v. II, 232-33
    red lentil and bulgur soup (Turkey), v. I, 568-69
    red lentil and bulgur soup with apricots (Armenia), v. I, 589-90
    red lentil and red onion cream soup (Ireland), v. I, 199
    red-lentil soup (Libya), v. II, 140-41
    red lentil stew with Bengali five-seed spice mixture (Bangladesh), v. I, 651
    salad (Iraq), v. I, 486-87
    slow cooker rice and (Egypt), v. II, 79-80
    smoky lentils with vegetables (Panama), v. II, 599-600
    soup (Macedonia), v. I, 263-64
    soup, puréed with potatoes (Kuwait), v. I, 513
    soup, with meatballs and rice (Cyprus), v. I, 467-68
    soup, with vegetables (Burundi), v. II, 28-29
    spiced orange lentils (South Africa), v. II, 246
    with gingerroot (Djibouti), v. II, 75
    with groundnut butter (Guinea), v. II, 119-120
    with tomato and garlic (Eritrea), v. II, 88
lettuce soup (Wales), v. I, 459
LIBERIA, v. II, 131-36
LIBYA, v. II, 137-44
LIECHTENSTEIN, v. I, 238-43
lime pickles (Sri Lanka), v. I, 706
lime pudding with sweetened condensed milk (Côte d'Ivoire), v. II, 68
lingonberries
    lingonberry cream dessert (Sweden), v. I, 404
    ruby pear salad (Sweden), v. I, 401
LITHUANIA, v. I, 244-51
lovage, information, v. I, 25 (note)
LUXEMBOURG, v. I, 252-60
lychees
    and *macapuna* balls in sweet cream (The Philippines), v. II, 425
    fruit compote with vanilla (Madagascar), v. II, 152
    in coconut milk (Myanmar/Burma), v. II, 415-16

MACEDONIA, v. I, 261-70

Macapuna balls and *lychees* in sweet cream (The Philippines), v. II, 425
MADAGASCAR, v. II, 145-53
MALAYSIA, v. II, 391-97
MALI, v. II, 154-59
MALTA, v. I, 271-79
mangoes
    and banana salad (The Gambia), v. II, 102
    and *carambola* appetizer with *limoncello* (Pacific Islands – New Guinea), v. II, 472-73
    and onion soup (Guinea), v. II, 117-18
    and papaya dessert with apricot sauce (Tanzania), v. II, 265
    and pineapple chutney (Uganda), v. II, 282-83
    and purple rice salad (Thailand), v. II, 432-33
    and rice noodle salad with sweet *cilantro* dressing (Cambodia), v. II, 318
    appetizer (Thailand), v. II, 429-30
    bean salad with corn (Burundi), v. II, 27
    black rice pudding (Brunei), v. II, 313
    fresh fruit refresher (Mexico), v. II, 587-88
    fruit and vegetable salad (Indonesia), v. II, 354

mangoes (cont'd)
 fruit platter with lime *vinaigrette* (Caribbean), v. II, 496
 fruit salad (Uganda), v. II, 283-84
 green, and cabbage salad (Myanmar/Burma), v. II, 412
 green, curried vegetables with *tofu* (Cambodia), v. II, 319
 ice cream (India), v. I, 678
 mango dice, preparation, v. II, 433 (note)
 mango powder (India), v. I, 667
 nectar, in passion fruit appetizer drink (Caribbean), v. II, 490
 pickled vegetables (Panama), v. II, 601-602
 preserved mango (Cape Verde), v. II, 42
 pudding (Caribbean), v. II, 503-504
 relish (Caribbean – Cuba), v. II, 499-500
 salad (Madagascar), v. II, 149-50
 salad, with avocado, orange and citrus dressing (Senegal), v. II, 219
 salad, with *jicama* and carrot (Colombia), v. II, 538-39
 salad, with pineapple and apricot (Niger), v. II, 198
 salad, with sweetpotato and *jicama* in citrus dressing (Caribbean), v. II, 494-95
 sauce, with yogurt (Oman), v. I, 537
 skewered fruits (Zambia), v. II, 295
 smoothie (Pakistan), v. I, 697
 soup, with cucumber (Saudi Arabia), v. I, 554
 stewed, with cloves (Liberia), v. II, 136
 St. John's Day fruit salad (Venezuela), v. II, 630-31
 whip (Cameroon), v. II, 37-38
 with banana and pineapple in mango yogurt sauce (Oman), v. I, 537
 with corn in bean salad (Burundi), v. II, 27
 with sweet coconut rice (Cambodia), v. II, 321
manioc, see cassava
marjoram, information, v. I, 25 (note)
MAURITANIA, v. II, 160-68
mayonnaise, blender, v. II, 675-76
mayonnaise, easy, light (Portugal), v. I, 330-31
melons, *see also* watermelon
 and soymeat skillet (Yemen), v. I, 581
 and walnut compote (Armenia), v. I, 598
 cantaloupe and watermelon in fresh fruit refresher (Mexico), v. II, 587-88
 cantaloupe, peach, and blueberry salad with almond syrup and *moscato* wine sauce (Macedonia), v. I, 264
 cantaloupe soup (Pacific Islands – Polynesia), v. II, 477
 cantaloupe with tomato and olive salad (Greece), v. I, 163-64
 honeydew and peach salad with fresh *mozzarella* (New Zealand), v. II, 463-64
 fruit platter with lime *vinaigrette* (Caribbean), v. II, 496
 melon soup with fresh mint (Oman), v. I, 537
 salsa, with strawberries and black pepper (Native America), v. II, 669-70
Mexican thickened cream, v. II, 581
MEXICO, v. II, 577-88

millet
 and corn salad with avocado (Central African Republics), v. II, 47-48
 and rice pudding (Mali), v. II, 158-59
 and yogurt pudding (Mauritania), v. II, 167
 couscous with chick peas (Mauritania), v. II, 164-65
 couscous with vegetables (The Gambia), v. II, 103
 croquettes with sour cream (Senegal), v. II, 220
 mushroom soup (Belarus), v. I, 36-37
 tabbouleh (Lebanon), v. I, 526-27
 toasted millet salad (Mali), v. II, 155-56
miso, information, v. I, 314 (note); v. II, 684 (note)
MOLDOVA, v. I, 280-91
MONGOLIA, v. II, 398-407
MONTENEGRO, v. I, 292-97
MOROCCO, v. II, 169-77
MOZAMBIQUE, v. II, 178-87
mushrooms
 and asparagus with oregano and fennel oil (Liechtenstein), v. I, 241
 and baby carrots in wild rice casserole (Canada), v. II, 642-43
 and barley soup with sour cream (Latvia), v. I, 233
 and beet soup (Poland), v. I, 323-24
 and chick pea salad (Somalia), v. II, 233
 and mango appetizer (Thailand), v. II, 429-30
 and meatballs in pastry bundles (Mongolia), v. II, 405
 and noodle soup with vegetables (Brunei), v. II, 307
 and potato *momos* in *tukpa* broth (Bhutan), v. I, 656-57
 and potato casserole (Czech), v. I, 94-95
 and shallots (Ireland), v. I, 201
 and wild rice casserole (Native America), v. II, 663
 barley and vegetable soup with sour cream (Poland), v. I, 322-23
 beancurd and mushrooms with Chinese brown sauce (China), v. II, 332-33
 breaded (Germany), v. I, 148-49
 Buddhist, with asparagus (China), v. II, 331-32
 casserole with sour cream (Ukraine), v. I, 428
 chili, v. II, 288
 Chinese black mushrooms braised with garlic (Indonesia), v. II, 356-57
 Chinese black mushrooms, information, v. I, 313 (note); II, 331
 Chinese black mushrooms with foot long beans in brown garlic sauce (China), v. II, 331
 cream soup (Germany), v. I, 144-45
 curried eggs and rice, v. I, 673-74
 deviled (Poland), v. I, 322
 dried, condiment (Myanmar/Burma), v. II, 410
 dried, in tomato sauce (Zambia), v. II, 294-95
 dried, stir-fried (Korea), v. II, 375
 dried, with *feta* cheese (Bulgaria), v. I, 76-77
 dumpling soup (Korea), v. II, 371-72
 eggplant and tomato casserole (Slovakia), v. I, 377
 enoki in curried vegetables with tofu (Cambodia), v. II, 319
 enoki, in stir-fried long beans and mushrooms with garlic (Laos), v. II, 388

mushrooms (cont'd)
    enoki mushroom wonton appetizers (Laos),
        v. **II**, 382-83
    fried egg noodles with (Ukraine), v. **I**, 428-29
    fritters (Andorra), v. **I**, 20
    hunter's style sauce for vegetables and *pasta* (Italy),
        v. **II**, 684-85
    kebabs (Greece), v. **I**, 166
    macaroni in spicy sauce with (Iraq), v. **I**, 489
    marinated (Greece), v. **I**, 159
    marinated salad (Romania), v. **I**, 346-47
    Moscow salad (Russia), v. **I**, 351
    omelet with potato, mushroom, and onion (Belarus),
        v. **I**, 40-41
    open-faced sandwiches (Switzerland), v. **I**, 408-409
    oven-roasted root vegetables with fresh herbs and
        mushrooms (Namibia), v. **II**, 193-94
    pâté (England), v. **I**, 433-34
    phyllo turnovers with mushroom and onion filling
        (Estonia), v. **I**, 113-14
    portobellos with lentils, escarole, tomato, and olives
        (Italy), v. **I**, 205-206
    ratatouille, vegetable stew (France), v. **I**, 134-35
    ratatouille with puff pastry pillows (France),
        v. **I**, 135-36
    rice with vegetables (Bhutan), v. **I**, 661-62
    roasted, in bread-cheese soup (Italy), v. **I**, 210-11
    salad (Finland), v. **I**, 124
    sauce (Norway), v. **I**, 313-14
    scrambled eggs with greens and (Spain), v. **I**, 394
    shiitake in clear soup with *soba* noodles and
        vegetables in (Japan), v. **II**, 361-62
    skillet with noodles and sausage (Spain), v. **I**, 395
    soup (Czech), v. **I**, 92-93
    soup with potatoes and mushrooms (Austria),
        v. **I**, 24-25
    soup with roasted millet (Belarus), v. **I**, 36-37
    stew (Bhutan), v. **I**, 660
    stewed (Russia), v. **I**, 356-57
    stir-fried with bamboo shoots (Tibet) v. **II**, 344
    straw, stir-fried with cauliflower (Vietnam),
        v. **II**, 441-42
    stuffed appetizers (Switzerland), v. **I**, 407-408
    tomato mushroom sauce (Italy), v. **II**, 686
    vegan "chopped liver", v. **I**, 493-94
    vegetables in curried coconut milk (Thailand),
        v. **II**, 434-35
    vegetable stew with beer (Belgium) v. **I**, 49-50
    vegetarian stock from *kombu* (Japan), v. **II**, 363
    warm spinach salad with mushrooms and garlic
        (Andorra), v. **I**, 15-16
    with steamed *bok choy* (China), v. **II**, 333
    wild mushroom stock, v. **II**, 694
    with barley and sage (Scotland), v. **I**, 452
    with eggplant in cream (Bosnia), v. **I**, 65-66
    with paprika (Hungary), v. **I**, 180-81
    with preserved lemons and snowpeas in broth
        (Cambodia), v. **II**, 316-17
    with steamed *bok choy* (China), v. **II**, 333
    with stir-fried spinach and *tofu* (Tibet), v. **II**, 341-42
    wonton appetizers (China), v. **II**, 323-24
mustard sauce, v. **II**, 685-86

mustard sauce, Scandinavian (Denmark), v. **I**, 102-103
mustard, uncooked (Sweden), v. **I**, 401
MYANMAR / BURMA. v. **II**, 408-16

NAMIBIA, v. **II**, 188-96
NATIVE AMERICA, v. **II**, 650-73
NEPAL, v. **I**, 680-88
NETHERLANDS, THE, v. **I**, 298-307
NEW ZEALAND (Oceania), v. **II**, 460-70
NICARAGUA, v. **II**, 589-95
NIGER, v. **II**, 197-200
NIGERIA, v. **II**, 201-208
noodles, *see also pasta*
    and cabbage skillet (Poland), v. **I**, 325
    and cauliflower soup (Indonesia), v. **II**, 353
    and cheese custard pudding (Slovakia), v. **I**, 376
    and lentils (Syria), v. **I**, 563-64
    and mushroom soup with vegetables (Brunei),
        v. **II**, 307
    and onion *vinaigrette* in tossed salad (Mongolia),
        v. **II**, 401
    buckwheat noodles (*soba*) with eggs and green
        onion (Bhutan), v. **I**, 658-59
    chowder of vegetables and fine noodles
        (Montenegro), v. **I**, 294-95
    clear soup with *soba* noodles and (Japan),
        v. **II**, 361-62
    cream of summer squash soup with (Lithuania),
        v. **I**, 246
    fried with mushrooms (Ukraine), v. **I**, 428-29
    glass noodle and vegetable slaw (Tibet), v. **II**, 341
    rice noodle and meatball soup (Laos), v. **II**, 386
    rice noodle salad with mango and sweet *cilantro*
        dressing (Cambodia), v. **II**, 318
    rolled noodle and spring onion salad (China),
        v. **II**, 326-27
    sautéed with spinach (Czech), v. **I**, 96-97
    sea broth with glass noodles (Myanmar/Burma),
        v. **II**, 411
    sesame noodle salad with corn (Mongolia),
        v. **II**, 400-401
    skillet, with cabbage (Poland), v. **I**, 325
    soba, and *bok choy* in *tukpa* broth (Tibet),
        v. **II**, 340-41
    soup, with kidney beans (Central Asia), v. **I**, 625
    stir-fried rice stick, with garlic and Thai basil
        (Thailand), v. **II**, 435
    stir-fried, with vegetables (Brunei), v. **II**, 309-10
    sweet with walnuts (Moldova), v. **I**, 290
    vegetable soup with fine noodles (Malta), v. **I**, 274
    with nuts and cheese (Austria), v. **I**, 26-27
    with onions (Pacific Islands – Solomon Islands),
        v. **II**, 483
    with sour cream and *feta* cheese (Bosnia-
        Herzegovina), v. **I**, 64
    with soymeat and yogurt-garlic sauce (Azerbaijan),
        v. **I**, 608
    wonton noodles and asparagus with egg sauce
        (Japan), v. **II**, 364-65
NORWAY, v. **I**, 308-18

Oatmeal/rolled oats
    and Cheddar baked appetizers with herbs (England), v. **I**, 434-35
    blue plum *streusel* tart (German), v. **I**, 152-53
    granola, v. **II**, 696
    maple multigrain bread, v. **II**, 106-107
    oatmeal lace cookies (Scotland), v. **I**, 455
    oat scones (Scotland), v. **I**, 449-50
    porridge with apple (Belarus), v. **I**, 41-42
    ranger cookies (Moldova), v. **I**, 290-91
    vegetable soup (Oman), v. **I**, 538
    yogurt *crème* with sweet oatmeal topping (Wales), v. **I**, 461-62

okra
    and tomato stew (Mali), v. **II**, 158
    breaded and deep-fried (The Gambia), v. **II**, 99-100
    breaded and deep-fried with tomato sauce (Cyprus), v. **I**, 472
    spicy fried (Bangladesh), v. **I**, 646-47
    with *vermicelli* and rice (Kuwait), v. **I**, 517

OMAN, v. **I**, 535-42

onions, including **scallions** and **chive buds**;
    see also leeks and shallots
    and artichokes in tomato sauce (Armenia), v. **I**, 593-94
    and cucumber salad (Nepal), v. **I**, 682
    and curried soymeat with coconut milk (Myanmar/ Burma), v. **II**, 414
    and eggplant with yogurt (Azerbaijan), v. **I**, 602
    and fried tomato salad with brown rice (Bolivia), v. **II**, 516
    and mango soup (Guinea), v. **II**, 117-18
    and scallions in cream of spinach and potato soup (New Zealand), v. **II**, 466-67
    and soymeat (El Salvador), v. **II**, 561-62
    and tomato salad (Syria), v. **I**, 562-63
    and tomato salad (Tanzania), v. **II**, 262
    and tomato sauce for fried plantains (Guinea), v. **II**, 120
    and tomato sauce for meatballs (Costa Rica), v. **II**, 543
    baked macaroni casserole (Bolivia), v. **II**, 517
    baked red, with raspberry *vinaigrette* (Australia), v. **II**, 454-55
    beancurd and Chinese chive bud soup (Vietnam), v. **II**, 438-39
    beetroot and apple salad (Uruguay), v. **II**, 624
    braised with cheese (Portugal), v. **I**, 335
    cabbage pickle, *kimchi* (Korea), v. **II**, 376-77
    "chicken" stew (Gabon), v. **II**, 49
    "chicken" stew with tomato and garlic (Sierra Leone), v. **II**, 227-28
    chili, v. **II**, 288
    corn and lima bean custard pudding (Brazil), v. **II**, 526
    corn curry (Pakistan), v. **I**, 694-95
    cream of artichoke hearts soup (Brazil), v. **II**, 524
    cream of chick pea soup (El Salvador), v. **II**, 566-67
    cucumber and red onion salad (Nepal), v. **I**, 682
    curried, with onions and eggs (Bangladesh), v. **I**, 649-50
    dark vegetable stock (Thailand), v. **II**, 431-32
    deviled (England), v. **I**, 439
    fried onion rings (Canada), v. **II**, 643-44
    fried potato cakes (Ghana), v. **II**, 112
    fried scallion turnovers (Afghanistan), v. **I**, 638-39
    fried yams with (Ghana), v. **II**, 114
    green onion sesame skillet bread (Tibet), v. **II**, 345
    greens and vegetables (Caribbean – Virgin Islands), v. **II**, 502
    grilled corn-on-the-cob (Cambodia), v. **II**, 320
    grilled vegetable salad (Kuwait), v. **I**, 516
    hearts of palm salad (The Philippines), v. **II**, 421
    hunter's style sauce for vegetables and *pasta* (Italy), v. **II**, 684-85
    Irish stew, v. **I**, 199-200
    kebabs (Greece), v. **I**, 166
    layered vegetable salad (Ghana), v. **II**, 111-12
    lentils and *orzo* with caramelized onions (Cyprus), v. **I**, 469-70
    lentils with gingerroot (Djibouti), v. **II**, 75
    meatballs and fruit in curry sauce (Mozambique), v. **II**, 183-84
    millet *couscous* with vegetables (The Gambia), v. **II**, 103
    orange and white radish salad with cumin (India), v. **I**, 670-71
    oven-roasted root vegetables with fresh herbs and mushrooms (Namibia), v. **II**, 193-94
    pancakes with green onions (Mongolia), v. **II**, 400
    peanut butter and tomato sauce with garlic (The Gambia), v. **II**, 104
    pearl in cream *au gratin* with *Gruyère* sauce (Belgium) v. **I**, 52
    pickled red onion relish with lime juice (Ecuador), v. **II**, 552
    pink potato salad (Panama), v. **II**, 598-99
    potato and tomato soup (Native America), v. **II**, 657
    potato cakes with peanut sauce (Ecuador), v. **II**, 554
    potatoes with peanut sauce (Peru), v. **II**, 617-18
    puréed *dhal* soup (Pacific Islands – Fiji), v. **II**, 476
    red, and lemon salad in lettuce rolls (Myanmar/ Burma), v. **II**, 413
    red kidney bean *tacos* or *tostados* with sautéed greens and goat cheese (Panama), v. **II**, 600-601
    roasted eggplant (India), v. **I**, 672-73
    salad (Czech), v. **I**, 94
    salad (Uzbekistan), v. **I**, 625-26
    salad with coconut milk (Sri Lanka), v. **I**, 703
    salsa, with garlic and *cilantro* (Peru), v. **II**, 614
    scallion and eggplant salad (Korea), v. **II**, 375-76
    scallions in celery and cabbage slaw with sour cream (Canada), v. **II**, 641-42
    scallions in egg and potato salad (Cote d'Ivoire), v. **II**, 65
    scallions in *hoisin* barbecue sauce (Mongolia), v. **II**, 404
    scallions in mango relish (Caribbean – Cuba), v. **II**, 499-500
    scallions in millet *tabbouleh* (Lebanon), v. **I**, 526-27
    scallions in mushroom *wonton* appetizers (Laos), v. **II**, 382-83

index

onions (cont'd)
    scallions in pickled mustard greens (Vietnam), v. II, 442-43
    scallions in pineapple fried rice (Laos), v. II, 386-87
    scallions in radish appetizer (China), v. II, 325-26
    scallions in rolled noodle salad (China), v. II, 326-27
    scallions in stir-fried bamboo shoots with sesame seeds (Laos), v. II, 388-89
    scallions in tomato-coriander sauce (Laos), v. II, 384
    scallions in *tortilla* skillet (Honduras), v. II, 574-75
    scallions, stir-fried with winter squash and red pepper (Australia), v. II, 448-49
    shirred eggs and vegetables (Libya), v. II, 143-44
    shredded salad with vegetables (Denmark), v. I, 101
    slow cooker black-eyed pea *chili* (Uganda), v. II, 287-88
    smoky lentils with vegetables (Panama), v. II, 599-600
    soup with cheese (Serbia), v. I, 365-66
    stew, with okra and tomato (Mali), v. II, 158
    stew, with onions (Sudan), v. II, 254
    stir-fried chive buds with beancurd in spicy sauce (Malaysia), v. II, 395
    stir-fried noodles and vegetables (Brunei), v. II, 309-10
    summer vegetable stew (Tunisia), v. II, 276-77
    sweet onions with dates (South Africa), v. II, 248
    sweet soy meatballs and caramelized onions (Slovenia), v. I, 385-86
    tagine, with carrots and prunes (Western Sahara), v. II, 165-66
    tagine, with Swiss chard and rice (Morocco), v. II, 175
    tart (Switzerland), v. I, 414
    tofu "tuna"-stuffed cucumber boats (Côte d'Ivoire), v. II, 66-67
    tomato and green onion salad (Zambia), v. II, 293
    tomato sauce (Bosnia-Herzegovina), v. I, 63
    tossed vegetable salad with cheese (Sudan), v. II, 252-53
    vegetable *kebabs* with lemon (Kuwait), v. I, 518-19
    vegetable *ragoût* (Lebanon), v. I, 527-28
    vegetable relish (Tanzania), v. II, 262-63
    vegetable soup with chick peas and groundnut butter (Namibia), v. II, 192
    vegetable stew with brown rice and soymeat (Serbia), v. I, 367-68
    vegetable stew (Uzbekistan), v. I, 628-29
    vegetarian vegetable (Ecuador), v. II, 553
    winter squash and vegetable soup (Paraguay), v. II, 605-606
    with baked *christophenes* (*chayote*) (Caribbean – Martinique), v. II, 300-301
    with blue cheese sauce (Finland), v. I, 127
    with noodles (Pacific Islands – Solomon Islands), v. II, 483
    with potatoes in aromatic cream sauce (India), v. I, 672
    with tomatoes (Bulgaria), v. I, 77
    yam salad with scallions (Chad), v. II, 56

    yucca soup (Guatemala), v. II, 567
oranges, including mandarin oranges
    and *carambola* dessert (Caribbean), v. II, 505
    and date salad (Morocco), v. II, 174
    and tomato salad (Kenya), v. II, 125-26
    blood orange salad with fennel, *pecorino*, and pomegranate (Italy), v. I, 215
    cantaloupe soup (Pacific Islands), v. II, 477
    creamsicle *sorbet*, v. II, 240
    custards with honey and cinnamon (Portugal), v. I, 337
    fruit compote with vanilla (Madagascar), v. II, 152
    fruit cream (Belgium), v. I, 55-56
    fruit salad (Uganda), v. II, 283-84
    in banana and mango salad (The Gambia), v. II, 102
    in cinnamon-orange syrup (Korea), v. II, 379
    mandarin oranges, in mixed fruit salad with *chaat masala* (India), v. I, 670
    mandarin oranges with caramelized sweetpotatoes (Pacific Islands - Hawaii), v. II, 479
    pear mincemeat with pecans (England), v. I, 441-42
    salad, with avocado, mango, and citrus dressing (Senegal), v. II, 219
    salad, with *calamarata* (Somalia), v. II, 235
    salad, with white radish and onion with cumin (India), v. I, 670-71
    Seville orange juice sauce for asparagus (Spain), v. I, 396
    St. John's Day fruit salad (Venezuela), v. II, 630-31
    sweet spiced orange vinegar, v. II, 680-81
    torte (Portugal), v. I, 338
    with orange flower water (Laos), v. II, 390
oregano and fennel oil (Liechtenstein), v. I, 241
oregano, information, v. II, 193 (note)

PACIFIC ISLANDS, v. II, 471-85
PAKISTAN, v. I, 689-97
PALESTINE, v. I, 543-50
PANAMA, v. II, 596-603
pancakes
    poppy seed filling for (Czech), v. I, 97
    custard dessert pancakes (Finland), v. I, 128-29
    dessert, with blueberry sauce (Lithuania), v. I, 250
    green onion pancakes with *feta* cheese (Mongolia), v. II, 400
    with berries and honey (Morocco), v. II, 176-77
    with vegetables (Mauritania), v. II, 161-62
papaya
    and garlic soup (Caribbean), v. II, 492-93
    and grilled pineapple *salsa* (Caribbean), v. II, 491-92
    and kohlrabi salad with tamarind dressing (Laos), v. II, 385
    and mango dessert with apricot sauce (Tanzania), v. II, 265
    and pineapple *salsa*, v. II, 491-92
    and tomato salad (Caribbean – Puerto Rico), v. II, 495-96
    fruit salad (Central African Republics), v. II, 53
    fruit salad with citrus *vinaigrette* (Côte d'Ivoire), v. II, 66

index

papaya (cont'd)
    fruit salad with tamarind dressing (Brunei), v. II, 308-309
    jam (Cameroon), v. II, 33-34
    juice (Eritrea), v. II, 84-85
    poached (Chile), v. II, 534-35
    punch (Pacific Islands – Hawaii), v. II, 472
    salad, and corn with citrus *vinaigrette* (Togo), v. II, 268
    salad, with avocado and grapefruit (Kenya), v. II, 126
    salad, with curried island dressing (Pacific Islands – Vanuatu), v. II, 474
    salad, with hearts of palm, *jicama*, and lime mayonnaise (Pacific Islands), v. II, 474-75
    steamed (Tanzania), v. II, 263-64
    sweet egg dessert (Mozambique), v. II, 187
    tropical fruit salad (Nigeria), v. II, 202
paprika cream (Hungary), v. I, 177-78
paprika, homemade, v. I, 186
PARAGUAY, v. II, 604-609
parsley
    and garlic sauce (Nicaragua), v. II, 592
    cream of celery soup with Stilton (England), v. I, 435
    cream of spinach and potato soup (New Zealand), v. II, 466-67
    curried *pasta* salad (Botswana), v. II, 19
    deep-fried (Switzerland), v. I, 418
    fried potato cakes (Ghana), v. II, 112
    marinara sauce (Italy), v. II, 682
    omelets with scallions (Armenia), v. I, 587
    potato omelet (Algeria), v. II, 7
    salad with *tahini* (Palestine), v. I, 548-49
    sauce (Ireland), v. I, 196
    tomato mushroom sauce (Italy), v. II, 686
    vegetable salad (Macedonia), v. I, 265
    vegetable soup (Moldova), v. I, 284
    vegetable soup with caraway (Romania), v. I, 342-43
    vegetable stew with beans and *chouriço* sausage (Angola), v. II, 13-14
parsnips
    bean soup and pinched dumplings (Hungary), v. I, 176-77
    oven-roasted root vegetables with fresh herbs and mushrooms (Namibia), v. II, 193-94
    root vegetables with yogurt-dill sauce (Bulgaria), v. I, 75-76
    steamed with honey-mustard glaze (The Netherlands), v. I, 303
    vegetable soup with caraway (Romania), v. I, 342-43
    vegetable spaghetti with grainburger (Australia), v. II, 453-54
passion fruit appetizer drink (Caribbean), v. II, 490
pasta, *see also* **couscous**
    and soymeat with *chimichuri* and herb dressing (Argentina), v. II, 509-10
    angel hair, mushrooms, and *chorizo* skillet, v. I, 395
    angel hair with caper and olive sauce (Croatia), v. I, 85-86
    angel hair with eggs (Malta), v. I, 273
    baked macaroni casserole (Bolivia), v. II, 517
    baked spaghetti with two sauces (Somalia), v. II, 236-37
    calamarata and orange salad (Somalia), v. II, 235
    egg and lemon soup (Greece), v. I, 164-65
    fettuccine with browned butter and fried sage leaves (Italy), v. I, 225
    fried *calamarata* with garlic mayonnaise (Spain), v. I, 392-93
    in spicy sauce with mushrooms (Iraq), v. I, 489
    lasagne (Italy), v. I, 216
    linguine, chick peas, and red kidney beans with seasoned soymeat (Afghanistan), v. I, 640
    macaroni and cheese (England), v. I, 437-38
    macaroni and "meat" casserole) Greece), v. I, 167-68
    macaroni and vegetables (The Gambia), v. II, 104-105
    macaroni salad (Denmark), v. I, 107-108
    macaroni salad (Madagascar), v. II, 147
    macaroni salad with *pesto* and *chouriço* (Uganda), v. II, 284-85
    noodle soup (Eritrea), v. II, 86-87
    orzo and lentils with caramelized onions (Cyprus), v. I, 469-70
    orzo with spinach and tomatoes (Oman), v. I, 538-39
    ravioli with spinach and sage butter (Italy), v. I, 224
    rolled noodle and spring onion salad (China), v. II, 326-27
    salad, curried (Botswana), v. II, 19
    salad, with vegetables and peanut butter dressing (Senegal), v. II, 221
    skillet *lasagne* (Italy), v. I, 217
    skillet *lasagne* with *ravioli*, (Italy), v. I, 217 (note)
    spaghettini and vegetable spaghetti with grainburger (Australia), v. II, 453-54
    spaghettini in "beef" soup (Paraguay), v. II, 606
    spaghetti with broccoli and garlic (Botswana), v. II, 22-23
    sweet *pasta* dessert (Sudan), v. II, 257
    sweet *pasta* dessert with almonds and raisins (Bangladesh), v. I, 652-53
    tagliatelle with chick peas (Cyprus), v. I, 471
    tiny shells and lentil salad with nasturtium (Australia), v. II, 457
    tomato soup with walnuts and *vermicelli* (Georgia), v. I, 614
    vermicelli and rice with vegetables (Kuwait), v. I, 517
    vermicelli with buttered breadcrumbs (Slovenia), v. I, 382-83
pâtés
    brie almond (France), v. I, 132
    mushroom (England), v. I, 433-34
    walnut and bean, with vegetable filling (France), v. I, 132-33
peaches
    and melon salad with fresh *mozzarella* (New Zealand), v. II, 463-64

peaches (cont'd)
    and raspberry purée over puff pastry pillows,
        v. II, 458
    cakes with crumbled meringue (Uruguay),
        v. II, 625-26
    dried, fruit salad (Uganda), v. II, 283-84
    jam, v. I, 619
    lemon-peach salad dressing (Mozambique),
        v. II, 181-82
    salad, with avocado and tomato (Mozambique),
        v. II, 181
    salad, with cantaloupe and blueberry with almond
        syrup and *moscato* wine sauce (Macedonia),
        v. I, 264
    sautéed with soymeat (Iran), v. I, 480-81
peanuts, *see* beans
pears, including **Asian pears**
    and anise-hyssop vinegar, v. II, 679-80
    Asian pear in fruit and vegetable salad (Indonesia),
        v. II, 354
    autumn compote (Portugal), v. I, 331
    baked Bosc pears (Belgium), v. I, 54
    baked, with breadcrumb pudding (Canada),
        v. II, 646-47
    fruit salad (Central African Republics), v. II, 53
    fruit salad with tamarind dressing (Brunei),
        v. II, 308-309
    in honey-lavender syrup (Morocco), v. II, 177
    meatballs and fruit in curry sauce (Mozambique),
        v. II, 183-84
    mincemeat with pecans, v. I, 441-42
    mixed fruit salad with *chaat masala* (India),
        v. I, 670
    poached Asian pears with black peppercorns
        (Korea), v. II, 379-80
    riced, with potatoes (Switzerland), v. I, 417-18
    salad with lingonberries (Sweden), v. I, 401
    sliced with ice cream and fresh strawberry sauce
        (Andorra), v. I, 21
    spiced vanilla honey with chocolate and cherries
        (Poland), v. I, 327
    vanilla pear dessert (Liechtenstein), v. I, 243
    with buttered crumbs (Lithuania), v. I, 249
    with sour cream sauce (Serbia), v. I, 369-70
peas, *dal*, *dal makhani*, **Beluga black lentils, red lentils**; *also see* lentils
    masur dal, puréed red lentil and bulgur soup
        (Turkey), v. I, 568-69
    masur dal, red lentil and bulgur soup with apricots
        (Armenia), v. I, 589-90
    masur dal, red lentil soup (Libya), v. II, 140-41
    masur dal, red lentil stew with Bengali five-seed
        spice mixture (Bangladesh), v. I, 651
peas, green
    and eggs in curried tomato sauce (Tibet),
        v. II, 342-43
    Argentine-styled Russian salad, v. II, 508-509
    artichoke and fava bean skillet with eggs (Malta),
        v. I, 276-77
    creamy, puréed, vegetable soup (Venezuela),
        v. II, 632-33
    egg curry (Nepal), v. I, 683

    glass noodle and vegetable slaw (Tibet), v. II, 341
    Irish stew, v. I, 199-200
    macaroni and vegetables (The Gambia),
        v. II, 104-105
    Moscow salad (Russia), v. I, 351
    samosa casserole (India), v. I, 666-67
    sautéed in the pod (Sweden), v. I, 403
    simmered in tomato sauce (Macedonia), v. I, 268
    tendrils, in rice with vegetables (Bhutan),
        v. I, 661-62
    tomato, onion, and pea salad (Portugal), v. I, 332-33
    tomato soup with (Palestine), v. I, 545-46
    vegetable pasties (New Zealand), v. II, 467
    vegetable salad (Brazil), v. II, 525
    vegetable stew (Bolivia), v. II, 515-16
    with basmati rice and dill (Kuwait), v. I, 514-15
    with cheese (India), v. I, 675
    with pan-grilled *Halloumi* cheese, *edamame*, and
        red peppers (Australia), v. II, 452
    with potatoes and cabbage in tomato sauce
        (Bangladesh), v. I, 648
    with stir-fried spinach, *tofu*, and mushrooms (Tibet),
        v. II, 341-42
    yucca soup (Guatemala), v. II, 567
peas, snowpeas
    almond vegetables Mandarin *mu shu* (China),
        v. II, 329
    noodle and mushroom soup with vegetables
        (Brunei), v. II, 307
    rice noodle salad with mango and sweet *cilantro*
        dressing (Cambodia), v. II, 318
    steamed vegetable salad with sweet black sesame
        dressing (Brunei), v. II, 308
    stir-fried noodles and vegetables (Brunei),
        v. II, 309-10
    stir-fry with sweetpotatoes (Bangladesh),
        v. I, 650-51
    with preserved lemons and *shiitake* mushrooms in
        broth (Cambodia), v. II, 316-17
    with *soba* noodles and vegetables in clear soup
        (Japan), v. II, 361-62
    with stir-fried spinach *tofu* and mushrooms (Tibet),
        v. II, 341-42
peas, split green, Milanese *minestrone* (Italy),
    v. I, 222-23
peas, split yellow
    soup (Sweden), v. I, 399-400
    soup with meatballs (Azerbaijan), v. I, 603-604
peppers
    and *chayote* slaw (Panama), v. II, 598
    and eggplant *caviar* (Serbia), v. I, 364-65
    and red kidney beans (Latvia), v. I, 234
    angel hair *pasta*, mushroom, and *chorizo* skillet
        (Spain), v. I, 395
    baby, roasted with black beans (China), v. II, 334
    baby zucchini with *feta* and roasted red peppers
        (Armenia), v. I, 587-88
    bean salad with corn and mango (Burundi), v. II, 27
    "beef" soup with noodles (Paraguay), v. II, 606
    beet soup (Ukraine), v. I, 426-27
    black beans with green pepper (Native America),
        v. II, 667

peppers (cont'd)
- black beans with rice and mango relish (Caribbean – Cuba), v. II, 499-500
- black-eyed peas in coconut milk (Kenya), v. II, 127-28
- cabbage salad with pineapple (Liberia), v. II, 133-34
- cabbage slaw with pineapple (Cameroon), v. II, 34
- cheese-stuffed frying peppers (Bulgaria), v. I, 73-74
- chili, v. II, 288
- *chilies* and cheese (Bhutan), v. I, 659-60
- *chilies*, in curried fritters (Madagascar), v. II, 150
- *chilies*, in peanut butter and tomato sauce (The Gambia), v. II, 104
- *chilies* with fried potatoes and yogurt (Malaysia), v. II, 393
- *chilies* with spinach, gingerroot, and coconut (The Philippines), v. II, 422-23
- chilled chick pea soup with roasted red peppers and garlic (Greece), v. I, 165-66
- coconut-bean soup with rice (Nigeria), v. II, 203-204
- corn and cheese salad (Peru), v. II, 613
- corn and lima bean custard pudding (Brazil), v. II, 526
- curried vegetables with *tofu* (Cambodia), v. II, 319
- frying peppers, roasted and marinated (Turkey), v. I, 572
- *goulash* (Hungary), v. I, 177-78
- grilled vegetable salad (Kuwait), v. I, 516
- *lecsó* omelet (Hungary), v. I, 175
- *lecsó*, vegetable mélange (Hungary), v. I, 175-76
- *lecsó* in *phyllo* nest (Hungary), v. I, 174
- lentil soup (Macedonia), v. I, 263-64
- macaroni in spicy sauce with mushrooms (Iraq), v. I, 489
- mango-pineapple chutney (Uganda), v. II, 282-83
- mango salad with vegetables (Pakistan), v. I, 691
- marinated and seasoned *Edam* cheese (Norway), v. I, 310
- meatball and vegetable pastry bundles (Mongolia), v. II, 405
- millet *couscous* with vegetables (The Gambia), v. II, 103
- onion, garlic, and *cilantro salsa* (Peru), v. II, 614
- pancakes with vegetables (Mauritania), v. II, 161-62
- paprika cream (Hungary), v. I, 177-78
- pickled vegetables (Panama), v. II, 601-602
- *quinoa* and vegetable stew (Peru), v. II, 615
- *polenta* with herbs (Guinea), v. II, 119-20
- potato and tomato soup (Native America), v. II, 657
- prickly pear salad with apples and dates (Israel), v. I, 497
- puréed cream of chick pea and celeriac soup (Turkey), v. I, 569
- red beans with grated cheese (El Salvador), v. II, 562
- red lentil soup (Libya), v. II, 140-41
- red pepper dip (Palestine), v. I, 544-45
- rice curry with peanut butter and bananas (Angola), v. II, 14
- rice with tomatoes and coconut milk (Mozambique), v. II, 182-83
- roasted red pepper and tomato appetizer salad (Israel), v. I, 495
- roasted pepper and tomato salad (Tunisia), v. II, 272-73
- roasted red pepper and eggplant appetizer (Saudi Arabia), v. I, 552-53
- roasted red peppers, freezing in oil, v. I, 553 (note)
- roasted red peppers, preparation, v. I, 165, 497, 553
- roasted, with pan-grilled *Halloumi* cheese, *edamame*, and peas (Australia), v. II, 453
- roasted, with yogurt and pecans (Israel), v. I, 498
- salad (Hungary), v. I, 182
- salad, with *couscous* and roasted eggplant (Morocco), v. II, 171-72
- salad, with onion and tomato and garlic sauce (Moldova), v. I, 285-86
- scrambled eggs with vegetables (Venezuela), v. II, 633
- shirred eggs and vegetables (Libya), v. II, 143-44
- skewered with soymeat (Mali), v. II, 157
- slow-cooker black-eyed pea *chili* Uganda), v. II, 287-88
- slow cooker vegetable soup with beans and barley (Croatia), v. I, 87-88
- smoky lentils with vegetables (Panama), v. II, 599-600
- soup, puréed, with corn (Mexico), v. II, 582-83
- spinach stew with peanut butter (Central African Republics), v. II, 51
- stir-fried with cabbage and carrots (Tibet), v. II, 343
- stir-fried with Chinese cabbage and eggs (Malaysia), v. II, 394-95
- stir-fried with winter squash and scallions (Australia), v. II, 448-49
- summer vegetable stew (Tunisia), v. II, 276-77
- toasted millet salad (Mali), v. II, 155-56
- tomato and cucumber salad with (Hungary), v. I, 178-79
- tomato and groundnut soup (Ghana), v. II, 111
- tomato soup (India), v. I, 668-69
- tossed vegetable salad (Azerbaijan), v. I, 606
- vegetable bread soup (Spain), v. I, 393-94
- vegetable *kebabs* with lemon (Kuwait), v. I, 518-19
- vegetable *mélange* (Malta), v. I, 275-76
- vegetable *ragoût* (Lebanon), v. I, 527-28
- vegetables in curried coconut milk (Thailand), v. II, 434-35
- vegetable soup with chick peas and ground nut butter (Namibia), v. II, 192
- vegetable spaghetti with grainburger (Australia), v. II, 453-54
- vegetable stew (Ethiopia), v. II, 94
- vegetable stew (Uzbekistan), v. I, 628-29
- vegetable stew with brown rice and soymeat (Serbia), v. I, 367-68
- with cheese in spinach sauce (India), v. I, 674-75
- with sautéed cabbage, carrot, and onion (Mozambique), v. II, 185
- *yucca* soup (Guatemala), v. II, 567

PERU, v. II, 610-20

index

PHILIPPINES, THE, v. II, 417-27
phyllo **pastry**
    Albanian spinach pie, v. I, 9-10
    banana tart (Central African Republics), v. II, 52
    cheese and pastry pies (Malta), v. I, 278-79
    fig tarts (Albania), v. I, 12
    lecsó in *phyllo* nest (Hungary), v. I, 174
    pastries with *feta* (Turkey), v. I, 567
    pastries with banana and chocolate (Côte d'Ivorie), v. II, 68-69
    pastries with *ricotta* and honey (Malta), v. I, 279
    pastries with rose water and honey (Saudi Arabia), v. I, 559-60
    pumpkin pie (Serbia), v. I, 370
    roasted eggplant pie (Jordan), v. I, 506-507
    sweet cheese pastry (Jordan), v. I, 510
    turnovers with mushroom and onion filling (Estonia), v. I, 113-14
pickled vegetables
    baby beets (Denmark), v. I, 104
    baby pepper salad (Bosnia), v. I, 61-62
    cabbage pickle (Nepal), v. I, 687
    cauliflower and garlic pickle (Iran), v. I, 482-83
    cucumber pickle (Nepal), v. I, 687
    daikon and red radish pickles (Tibet), v. II, 346
    onions (Austria), v. I, 28
    onion salad (Czech), v. I, 94
    pickled vegetables (Panama), v. II, 601-602
    potato with green *chilies* (Nepal), v. I, 686-87
    red onion relish (Ecuador), v. II, 552
    sweet and sour red cabbage with sour cream (Estonia), v. I, 115
pies and tarts
    apricot tart (Austria), v. I, 31
    banana *phyllo* tart (Central African Republics), v. II, 52
    blue plum *streusel* tart (Germany), v. I, 152-53
    cabbage and potato (Luxembourg), v. I, 255-56
    crustless coconut custard (Colombia), v. II, 540
    crustless pineapple cheese (Ukraine), v. I, 430
    custard pumpkin, v. II, 672-73
    fig tarts (Albania), v. I, 12
    fruit tart (Luxembourg), v. I, 259-60
    meat pies (Botswana), v. II, 21
    onion tart (Switzerland), v. I, 414
    potato and spinach (New Zealand), v. II, 468
    roasted eggplant in *phyllo* crust (Jordan), v. I, 506-507
    samosa (India), v. I, 666-67
    strawberry (Slovakia), v. I, 380
    vegetable and cheese (Uruguay), v. II, 624-25
    whole wheat pie crusts, v. II, 468-69
pineapple
    and avocado appetizer spread (Côte d'Ivorie), v. II, 62-63
    and avocado salad (Central African Republics), v. II, 47
    and mango chutney (Uganda), v. II, 282-83
    and mashed sweetpotatoes (Nicaragua), v. II, 593
    cabbage salad (Liberia), v. II, 133-34
    cabbage slaw (Cameroon), v. II, 34
    cheese-stuffed zucchini with lentils and fruit (Mexico), v. II, 583-84
    crustless pineapple cheese pie (Ukraine), v. I, 430
    curried island dressing (Pacific Islands – Vanuatu), v. II, 474
    dessert (Tanzania), v. II, 266
    drink with fresh gingerroot (Liberia), v. II, 132
    fresh fruit refresher (Mexico), v. II, 587-88
    fried rice (Laos), v. II, 386-87
    fried rice (Pacific Islands – Cook Islands), v. II, 480
    fruit and vegetable salad (Indonesia, v. II, 354
    fruit compote with vanilla (Madagascar), v. II, 152
    fruit cream (Belgium), v. I, 55-56
    fruit salad with citrus *vinaigrette* (Côte d'Ivorie), v. II, 66
    fruit salad with tamarind dressing (Brunei), v. II, 308-309
    grilled, and papaya *salsa* (Caribbean), v. II, 491-92
    grilled, with honey-lime glaze (Argentina), v. II, 513
    honey-pineapple *vinaigrette* (Burundi), v. II, 27
    ice cream (Paraguay), v. II, 609
    jam, v. II, 564
    layered fruit salad (Cameroon), v. II, 34-35
    meatballs and fruit in curry sauce (Mozambique), v. II, 183-84
    papaya punch (Pacific Islands - Hawaii), v. II, 472
    pineapple pastry (El Salvador), v. II, 563
    pineapple vinegar, v. II, 573
    pineapple vinegar, fermented (Honduras), v. II, 573
    salad, with mango and apricot (Niger), v. II, 198
    skewered fruits (Zambia), v. II, 295
    slices with cinnamon and ginger (Angola), v. II, 16
    sweet *couscous* pudding (Niger), v. II, 200
    sweet relish (Indonesia), v. II, 357
    tea-infused dried fruits with whipped cream (Chad), v. II, 58
    tropical fruit salad (Nigeria), v. II, 202
    with baked beans (Pacific Islands – Hawaii), v. II, 480-81
    with bananas and mango in mango-yogurt sauce (Oman), v. I, 537
    with carrots (Pacific Islands – Samoa), v. II, 483
    with coconut and cream (Somalia), v. II, 239
pine nut syndrome warning, v. I, 532 (note); v. II, 190 (note)
plantains
    and corn soup (Cameroon), v. II, 35
    baked, with cinnamon (Mexico), v. II, 586
    bean stew with hominy and *chouriço* (Cape Verde), v. II, 42-43
    fried (El Salvador), v. II, 562-63
    fufu with yam (Cameroon), v. II, 37
    mashed, with tomato and thyme (Caribbean – Dominican Republic), v. II, 499
    oven-baked dessert over ice cream (Peru), v. II, 620
    pan-grilled with peanuts (Nigeria), v. II, 204-205
    with beans and tomatoes (Colombia), v. II, 539
    with spicy tomato-onion sauce (Guinea), v. II, 120
plums and **prunes**
    and orange ice cream (Japan), v. II, 367-68
    autumn compote (Portugal), v. I, 331

prunes and **plums** (cont'd)
    blue plum *streusel* tart (Germany), v. I, 152-53
    carrot *pilaf* (Kazakhstan), v. I, 630-31
    cobbler (Switzerland), v. I, 419
    fruit tart (Luxembourg), v. I, 259-60
    ginger-steeped prunes (Australia), v. II, 459
    pickled (Poland), v. I, 326-27
    prunes with cardamom and almonds in red wine sauce (Ethiopia), v. II, 97
    sauce (Laos), v. II, 383-84
    slow cooker dried fruit curry (South Africa), v. II, 247-48
    stewed fruit compote with walnuts (Armenia), v. I, 596
    stewed prunes (Bulgaria), v. I, 79
    tagine with carrots and onion (Western Sahara), v. II, 165-66
    tea-infused dried fruits with whipped cream (Chad), v. II, 58

POLAND, v. I, 319-27

polenta, see corn

pomegranates
    blood orange salad with fennel, *pecorino*, and pomegranate (Italy), v. I, 215
    mixed fruit salad with *chaat masala* (India), v. I, 670
    molasses (Lebanon), v. I, 529
    pumpkin soup (Azerbaijan), v. I, 604
    refresher (Morocco), v. II, 170-71
    sautéed carrots with pomegranate glaze (Macedonia), v. I, 268-69
    sautéed soymeat and peaches (Iran), v. I, 480-81
    tossed vegetable salad (Azerbaijan), v. I, 606
    vinaigrette, for cucumber salad (Iran), v. I, 479

PORTUGAL, v. I, 328-38

potatoes
    and broccoli salad with Hollandaise sauce (Brazil), v. II, 521
    and cabbage in tomato sauce (Bangladesh), v. I, 648
    and celeriac chowder (Switzerland), v. I, 409-10
    and cheese casserole (Macedonia), v. I, 267-68
    and cheese soup (Ecuador), v. II, 552-53
    and Cheddar puffed omelet (Ireland), v. I, 195-96
    and chick pea salad (Armenia), v. I, 591
    and chick pea vegetable stew (Tunisia), v. II, 275-76
    and egg salad (Côte d'Ivorie), v. II, 65
    and green bean curry (Malaysia), v. II, 393-94
    and leek gratin (Switzerland), v. I, 412-13
    and meatballs in *tahini* sauce (Jordan), v. I, 508
    and mushroom *momos* in *tukpa* broth (Bhutan), v. I, 656-57
    and rutabaga casserole (Finland), v. I, 125-26
    and savoy cabbage (Hungary), v. I, 180
    and sauerkraut *croquettes* (Luxembourg), v. I, 256-57
    and spinach cream soup (New Zealand), v. II, 466-67
    and spinach pie (New Zealand), v. II, 468
    and tomato soup (Native America), v. II, 657
    and watercress soup (Ireland), v. I, 198
    and watercress soup with herbs (Wales), v. I, 458-59
    appetizer salad with celeriac (Moldova), v. I, 282-83
    Argentine-styled Russian salad, v. II, 508-509
    baked fries (Belgium), v. I, 45
    barley and vegetable soup with sour cream (Poland), v. I, 322-23
    beetroot and apple salad (Uruguay), v. II, 624
    beet soup (Ukraine), v. I, 426-27
    braised in aromatic cream sauce (India), v. I, 672
    cakes, fried (Ghana), v. II, 112
    cakes, fried (Switzerland), v. I, 413
    cakes with peanut sauce (Ecuador), v. II, 554
    casserole with potato slices and Stilton (England), v. I, 438-39
    casserole with shredded potato (Belarus), v. I, 38
    cheese soup (The Netherlands), v. I, 301-302
    chili bean soup, v. I, 283-84
    chowder of vegetables and fine noodles (Montenegro), v. I, 294-95
    collard greens and kale with potatoes and carrots (Montenegro), v. I, 295-96
    corn chowder (Native America), v. II, 657-58
    cream of asparagus soup (Germany), v. I, 143-44
    cream of summer squash soup with noodles (Lithuania), v. I, 246
    cream soup with corn (Colombia), v. II, 538
    creamy, puréed, vegetable soup (Venezuela), v. II, 632-33
    crushed (Nepal), v. I, 685-86
    curried corn chowder (South Africa), v. II, 245
    cutlets with cheese (Russia), v. I, 353-54
    deviled beets, potato, apple, and egg salad (Estonia), v. I, 111-12
    dumplings with apricots (Slovenia), v. I, 386
    egg roll appetizers (Belarus) v. I, 34
    fried, with yogurt and chilies (Malaysia), v. II, 393
    groundnut and vegetable soup (Djibouti), v. II, 72-73
    fufu with yam and corn (Cameroon), v. II, 36-37
    hot salad (Germany), v. I, 146
    Irish stew, v. I, 199-200
    kebabs made with mashed potatoes (Azerbaijan), v. I, 607-608
    layered vegetable salad (Ghana), v. II, 111-12
    lettuce soup (Wales), v. I, 459
    mashed with cheese and garlic (France), v. I, 138-39
    meatball and vegetable pastry bundles (Mongolia), v. II, 405
    meatballs and vegetables skillet (Niger), v. II, 198-99
    meat pies (Botswana), v. II, 21
    mixed grilled vegetables, Catalan-style (Andorra), v. I, 18
    Moscow salad (Russia), v. I, 351
    new, with chervil (Belgium), v. I, 50-51
    new, with parsley (Belgium), v. I, 51 (note)
    niçoise salad (France), v. I, 136
    noodle soup with kidney beans (Central Asia), v. I, 625
    omelet with potato and parsley (Algeria), v. II, 7
    omelet with potato, mushroom, and onion (Belarus), v. I, 40-41
    oven-browned potato wedges (Costa Rica), v. II, 544

index

potatoes (cont'd)
  oven-roasted root vegetables with cheese (Sweden), v. **I**, 402-403
  oven-roasted root vegetables with fresh herbs and mushrooms (Namibia), v. **II**, 193-94
  pancakes with vegetables (Mauritania), v. **II**, 161-62
  pickle with green *chilies* (Nepal), v. **I**, 686-87
  pie, with cabbage (Luxembourg), v. **I**, 255-56
  pink potato salad (Panama), v. **II**, 598-99
  potato and mushroom casserole (Czech), v. **I**, 94-95
  potato–meatball soup (Latvia), v. **I**, 232-33
  potato milk soup (Bosnia), v. **I**, 61
  pudding (Lithuania), v. **I**, 247-48
  pudding with cheese (Iceland), v. **I**, 189
  puréed lentil soup (Somalia), v. **II**, 232-33
  puréed root vegetable soup (Saudi Arabia), v. **I**, 555
  puréed, soup, with sweetpotatoes (Nigeria), v. **II**, 203
  riced with pears (Switzerland), v. **I**, 417-18
  rice with vegetables (Bhutan), v. **I**, 661-62
  roasted, soup (Tibet), v. **II**, 339
  root vegetables with yogurt-dill sauce (Bulgaria), v. **I**, 75-76
  salad (Albania), v. **I**, 7
  salad (Germany), v. **I**, 145-46
  salad (Madagascar), v. **II**, 148
  salad, with beets and carrots (Peru), v. **II**, 613-14
  salad, with dandelions (Slovenia), v. **I**, 387-88
  salad, with eggs and *feta* cheese (Tunisia), v. **II**, 273
  salad, with mayonnaise (Turkmenistan), v. **I**, 627-28
  salt cod stew without the salt cod (Italy), v. **I**, 206-207
  samosa casserole (India), v. **I**, 666-67
  sautéed with sumac (Lebanon), v. **I**, 532
  scalloped (Peru), v. **II**, 616-17
  shirred eggs and vegetables (Libya), v. **II**, 143-44
  skillet cakes (Algeria), v. **II**, 6-7
  slow cooker lentil soup (Palestine), v. **I**, 546
  slow cooker vegetable soup with beans and barley (Croatia), v. **I**, 87-88
  slow cooker vegetable stew (Botswana), v. **II**, 19-20
  sorrel-potato soup (Russia), v. **I**, 352-53
  soup, puréed with lentils (Kuwait), v. **I**, 513-14
  soup with cheese (Sweden), v. **I**, 400
  soup, with mushrooms (Slovakia), v. **I**, 374
  soup, with potatoes and leeks (Luxembourg), v. **I**, 254-55
  soup, with potatoes and mushrooms (Austria), v. **I**, 24-25
  sour soup, with green beans (Slovakia), v. **I**, 373-74
  spicy with spinach (Pakistan), v. **I**, 692
  skillet cakes (Algeria), v. **II**, 6-7
  spicy crisps (Zambia), v. **II**, 291-92
  squash *bisque* (Native America), v. **II**, 658-59
  steamed pudding with carrot and raisins (Canada), v. **II**, 647-48
  stew, with onion (Sudan), v. **II**, 254
  straw, deep-fried (Ukraine), v. **I**, 424
  sugar-browned (Denmark), v. **I**, 103
  summer vegetable stew (Tunisia), v. **II**, 276-77
  twice-baked (Palestine), v. **I**, 547
  vegetable and cheese pies (Uruguay), v. **II**, 624-25
  vegetable and groundnut soup (Zambia), v. **II**, 292-93
  vegetable pasties (New Zealand), v. **II**, 467
  vegetable salad with white beans, root celery, kohlrabi, and potatoes (Czech), v. **I**, 96
  vegetable soup with barley (Estonia), v. **I**, 112-13
  vegetable soup with cabbage (Albania), v. **I**, 5-6
  vegetable soup with chick peas and groundnut butter (Namibia), v. **II**, 192
  vegetable soup with sour cream (Moldova), v. **I**, 284
  vegetable stew (Bolivia), v. **II**, 515-16
  vegetable stew (Ethiopia), v. **II**, 94
  vegetable stew (Uzbekistan), v. **I**, 628-29
  vegetarian *tukpa* broth (Tibet), v. **II**, 339-40
  vegetarian vegetable soup (Ecuador), v. **II**, 553
  with bacon in lettuce salad (Burundi), v. **II**, 26
  with bay butter (Portugal), v. **I**, 334
  with black lentils (Saudi Arabia), v. **I**, 553-54
  with cheese and garlic (France), v. **I**, 138-39
  with garlic and coriander in tomato sauce (Somalia), v. **II**, 236
  with leeks and carrots in cream sauce (Luxembourg), v. **I**, 257
  with peanut sauce (Peru), v. **II**, 617-18
  with rice (Uganda), v. **II**, 286
  with spicy tomato sauce (Oman), v. **I**, 339-40
  with *vermicelli* and rice (Kuwait), v. **I**, 517
  with yogurt curds (Uganda), v. **II**, 285
  yellow split pea soup with meatballs (Azerbaijan), v. **I**, 603-604

prickly pear cactus
  prickly pear *vinaigrette* with *agave* nectar (Native America), v. **II**, 654-55
  punch, with orange, apple, and pineapple juices (Native America), v. **II**, 653-54
  salad, with apple and dates (Israel), v. **I**, 497
  salad, with apricot-raspberry dressing (Mexico), v. **II**, 581

puddings
  almond and coconut corn starch pudding (Afghanistan), v. **I**, 643
  almond junket (China), v. **II**, 335
  anise-scented sweet egg custard (Caribbean – Cuba), v. **II**, 504-505
  apple-oatmeal porridge (Belarus), v. **I**, 41-42
  apple with breadcrumbs (Denmark), v. **I**, 108-109
  apple with breadcrumbs (Russia), v. **I**, 359
  avocado (Western Sahara), v. **II**, 167-68
  baked honey-egg custard, v. **II**, 23-24
  baked pear and breadcrumb pudding (Canada), v. **II**, 646-47
  black rice, with mangoes (Brunei), v. **II**, 313
  blueberry (Canada), v. **II**, 645-46
  bread (Panama), v. **II**, 602-603
  bread and butter, with apricot topping (Ireland), v. **I**, 202-203
  bread and butter, with coconut (The Gambia), v. **II**, 106
  cardamom rice (Pakistan), v. **I**, 696-97
  cardamom wheat (India), v. **I**, 677-78
  carrot (Saudi Arabia), v. **I**, 559
  carrot-potato-raisin (Canada), v. **II**, 647-48

puddings (cont'd)
    chocolate (Venezuela), v. II, 634-35
    Christmas porridge with dried fruit and wheat berries (Armenia), v. I, 598-99
    Christmas, with pear mincemeat (England), v. I, 442
    coconut (Nicaragua), v. II, 593-94
    coconut corn starch pudding (Nicaragua), v. II, 595
    coconut custards (South Africa), v. II, 249
    coconut-rice porridge (Myanmar/Burma), v. II, 416
    coffee cream (Oman), v. I, 540
    coffee custards (France), v. I, 140
    coffee soft egg custard (Turkey), v. I, 574-75
    cooked cream (Italy), v. I, 226-27
    corn meal (São Tomé and Principe), v. II, 212
    cranberry (Latvia), v. I, 235-36
    creamed rice with cardamom (Tibet), v. II, 347-48
    cream of wheat with cherries (Romania), v. I, 348
    custard corn meal dessert (Zimbabwe), v. II, 302
    custard rice (Lithuania), v. I, 251
    custard with saffron and rose water (Kuwait), v. I, 520
    eggnog bavarian (Germany), v. I, 151
    farina with coconut milk and spices (Madagascar), v. II, 153
    farina cream dessert with cranberry sauce (Estonia), v. I, 116-17
    farina with rose water (Oman), v. I, 541
    farina custard (Greece), v. I, 171
    fig (Albania), v. I, 13
    fruit cream (Belgium), v. I, 55-56
    ginger cream (Thailand), v. II, 436
    guava-cream tapioca, v. II, 196
    Indian (Native America), v. II, 670-71
    lemon curd (England), v. I, 443-44
    lime, with sweetened condensed milk (Côte d'Ivorie), v. II, 68
    lingonberry cream dessert (Sweden), v. I, 404
    little rice puddings (Italy), v. I, 227-28
    mango (Caribbean), v. II, 503-504
    milk (Armenia), v. I, 597
    milk rice (Senegal), v. II, 222-23
    milk rice (Sri Lanka), v. I, 706
    millet and yogurt (Mauritania), v. II, 167
    orange custards with honey and cinnamon (Portugal), v. I, 337
    orange farina (Israel), v. I, 499-500
    pearl tapioca, creamed (The Philippines), v. II, 424
    pumpkin porridge with *couscous* (Kazakhstan), v. I, 632-33
    red wheat (Norway), v. I, 317
    rhubarb mousse (Iceland), v. I, 190
    rice and millet (Mali), v. II, 158-59
    rice and peanut butter (Zambia), v. II, 297
    rice flour pudding (Ghana), v. II, 114-15
    rice flour pudding with rose water (Iran), v. I, 483-84
    rice, vegan almond, v. I, 270
    rice, with dates (Saudi Arabia), v. I, 558
    rice, with honey (Belarus), v. I, 42
    rice, with peanut butter cream (Togo), v. II, 269
    rice, with saffron (Belgium), v. I, 55
    ricotta, with citron and chocolate (Italy), v. I, 219
    sago with coconut milk (Bhutan), v. I, 662
    semolina (Nepal), v. I, 688
    semolina with bananas (Guinea), v. II, 121-22
    semolina with walnuts (Bulgaria), v. I, 78-79
    stewed rhubarb with farina (Germany), v. I, 152
    summer, strawberry-blueberry, v. I, 445-46
    sweet barley porridge (Mongolia), v. II, 406
    sweet *couscous* (The Gambia), v. II, 105
    sweet *couscous* with raisins and pineapple (Niger), v. II, 200
    sweetpotato (Pacific Islands - Palua), v. II, 485
    sweetpotato and coconut (Sri Lanka), v. I, 707
    sweetpotato with coconut (Zambia), v. II, 296
    sweet yogurt dessert (Bangladesh), v. I, 653
    tapioca in coconut milk with fruit (Malaysia), v. II, 396-97
    tapioca with cloves (Nigeria), v. II, 206
    tapioca with sweetpotatoes (Laos), v. II, 389-90
    tapioca with warm spices (Oman), v. I, 541-42
    walnut rice cream (Spain), v. I, 397
    wheat and coconut dessert in sweet syrup (Palestine), v. I, 549-50
    whipped cranberry-raspberry with farina and strawberries (Finland), v. I, 128
    whole grain with raisins (Egypt), v. II, 81-82
    yellow coconut pudding (Angola), v. II, 15
    yogurt cream whip with ginger, v. II, 406-407
    yogurt cream whip with rhubarb (Norway), v. I, 316-17
    yogurt *crème* mousse (Russia), v. I, 357
    Yorkshire summer pudding (England), v. I, 444-45
puff pastry
    banana pastry (Mauritania), v. II, 168
    bananas in pastry (Cape Verde), v. II, 44
    banana *strudel* (Namibia), v. II, 195-96
    black olive purée and *hummus* appetizers (Bulgaria), v. I, 72-73
    cheese pastry pies (Malta), v. I, 278-79
    meatball and vegetable pastry bundles (Mongolia), v. II, 405
    nut roll with dried fruits and chocolate (Austria), v. I, 29-30
    pastries with *ricotta* and honey (Malta), v. I, 279
    pillows with raspberry purée and peaches, v. II, 458
    pineapple pastry (El Salvador), v. II, 563
    poppy seed pillows (Croatia), v. I, 88
    ratatouille with puff pastry pillows (France), v. I, 135-36
    vegetable and cheese pies (Uruguay), v. II, 624-25
    vegetable pasties (New Zealand), v. II, 467
    with Argentine sweet milk (Argentina), v. II, 512
pumpkin
    appetizer dip (Libya), v. II, 139
    cake (Liberia), v. II, 135-36
    custard pie, v. II, 672-73
    dark vegetable stock (Thailand), v. II, 431-32
    pie in *phyllo* roll (Serbia), v. I, 370
    porridge with *couscous* (Kazakhstan), v. I, 632-33
    soup (Malta), v. I, 274-75

pumpkin (cont'd)
    soup, with coconut milk and banana (Caribbean – Bahamas), v. II, 494
    soup, with pomegranate seeds (Azerbaijan), v. I, 604
    stove-top corn pudding (Native America), v. II, 666
    sweet soy-glazed (Korea), v. II, 373
    vegetable pasties (New Zealand), v. II, 467
    vegetable soup with chick peas and groundnut butter (Namibia), v. II, 192
    with cream (Slovakia), v. I, 379

purslane
    and tomato salad (Native America), v. II, 656-57
    bread and vegetable salad (Kuwait), v. I, 515-16

***Q**uesadillas*, squash and cheese (Mexico), v. II, 580

quinoa
    and vegetable stew (Peru), v. II, 615
    with cream (Ecuador), v. II, 555

Radishes
    and egg salad (Tunisia), v. II, 274
    appetizer (China), v. II, 325-26
    cabbage pickle *kimchi* (Korea), v. II, 376-77
    daikon and garlic relish/salad (Myanmar/Burma), v. II, 413-14
    daikon and red radish pickles (Tibet), v. II, 346
    daikon in clear vegetable stock (Thailand), v. II, 431
    daikon in dark vegetable stock (Thailand), v. II, 431-32
    daikon, in orange and onion salad with cumin (India), v. I, 670-71
    dumpling soup (Korea), v. II, 371-72
    green banana and vegetable salad (Costa Rica), v. II, 542-43
    salad with mint (Guatemala), v. II, 568
    salad with sour cream (Poland), v. I, 324

raspberries
    curd (Jordan), v. I, 509
    dessert (Romania), v. I, 347
    purée, and peaches over puff pastry pillows, v. II, 458
    sauce for stuffed figs (Italy), v. I, 207-208
    Yorkshire summer pudding (England), v. I, 444-45

relishes, including **chutneys** and *salsas*
    beet and horseradish (Slovakia), v. I, 379-80
    corn, v. II, 579-80
    eggplant (Australia), v. II, 455-56
    mango-pineapple chutney (Uganda), v. II, 282-83
    mango relish (Caribbean – Cuba), v. II, 499-500
    onion, garlic, and *cilantro salsa* (Peru), v. II, 614
    papaya and grilled pineapple salsa (Caribbean), v. II, 491-92
    pickled red onion with lime juice (Ecuador), v. II, 552
    radish and garlic relish/salad (Myanmar/Burma), v. II, 413-14
    spiced whole cranberry (Native America), v. II, 668
    strawberry, melon, and black pepper *salsa* (Native America), v. II, 669-70
    sweet and sour onion with olives (Andorra), v. I, 19
    sweet pineapple (Indonesia), v. II, 357
    tomato and onion *sambol* (Sri Lanka), v. I, 700
    tomato and pepper appetizer salad (Israel), v. I, 495
    vegetable (Tanzania), v. II, 262-63
    vegetable *mélange* (Malta), v. I, 275-76

REPUBLIC OF THE CONGO (Central African Republics), v. II, 45-53

rhubarb
    freezing, v. I, 152 (note)
    mousse (Iceland), v. I, 190
    strawberry-rhubarb juice (Estonia), v. I, 121-22
    stewed (England), v. I, 446
    stewed, with farina (Germany), v. I, 152
    stewed, with tapioca (New Zealand), v. II, 470
    streusel coffeecake (Estonia), v. I, 117-18
    yogurt cream whipped pudding (Norway), v. I, 316-17

rice
    and black beans with mango relish (Caribbean – Cuba), v. II, 499-500
    and cheese-stuffed acorn squashes, v. I, 64-65
    and chick pea soup (Mongolia), v. II, 402-403
    and chick pea soup (Peru), v. II, 612-13
    and coconut porridge (Myanmar/Burma), v. II, 416
    and eggs (Italy), v. I, 212
    and lentil-stuffed grape leaves (Lebanon), v. I, 525
    and lima beans (Cape Verde), v. II, 41
    and millet pudding (Mali), v. II, 158-59
    and spinach soup (Lebanon), v. I, 526
    and *vermicelli* with vegetables (Kuwait), v. I, 517
    and yogurt soup (Georgia), v. I, 613-14
    and zucchini in tomato sauce (Madagascar), v. II, 150-51
    baked with eggs and tomatoes (Malta), v. I, 278
    balls (Botswana), v. II, 20
    banana fritters (Djibouti), v. II, 76
    basmati, in bread salad with spinach, chick peas, and garlic-yogurt sauce with *tahini* (Tunisia), v. II, 274-75
    basmati, in soup with coconut and beans (Tanzania), v. II, 260-61
    basmati, with peas and dill (Kuwait), v. I, 514-15
    black rice pudding (Brunei), v II, 313
    brown rice and eggplant (Indonesia), v. II, 355
    brown rice and garlic *pilaf* (Central Asia), v. I, 629-30
    cardamom rice pudding (Pakistan), v. I, 696-97
    carrot *pilaf* (Kazakhstan), v. I, 630-31
    coconut, with mangoes (Cambodia), v. II, 321
    creamed, with cardamom (Tibet), v. II, 347-48
    croquettes (Albania), v. I, 11
    curried eggs and rice, v. I, 673-74
    curry with peanut butter and bananas (Angola), v. II, 14
    custard pudding (Lithuania), v. I, 251
    fried sweets (The Philippines), v. II, 425-26
    fried, with pineapple (Pacific Islands – Cook Islands), v. II, 480
    fried, with fried garlic (Brazil), v. II, 526-27
    fried, with shallots and garlic (The Philippines), v. II, 423
    hot yogurt soup with chick peas (Iran), v. I, 477-78
    in coconut milk (Sri Lanka), v. I, 706

index

rice (cont'd)
    lettuce wraps (Korea), v. **II**, 378
    little rice puddings (Italy), v. **I**, 227-28
    Milanese *minestrone* (Italy), v. **I**, 222-23
    milk pudding (Armenia), v. **I**, 597
    milk rice pudding (Senegal), v. **II**, 222-23
    pilaf with fruits and nuts (Azerbaijan), v. **I**, 609
    pilaf with garlic (Central Asia), v. **I**, 629-30
    pineapple fried rice (Laos), v. **II**, 386-87
    pudding, vegan rice with almond milk, v. **I**, 270
    pudding, with dates (Saudi Arabia), v. **I**, 558
    pudding, with honey (Belarus), v. **I**, 42
    pudding, with peanut butter (Zambia), v. **II**, 297
    pudding, with peanut butter cream (Togo), v. **II**, 269
    pudding, with saffron (Belgium), v. **I**, 55
    pumpkin soup with pomegranate seeds (Azerbaijan), v. **I**, 604
    purple rice and mango salad (Thailand), v. **II**, 432-33
    red and white (Bhutan), v. **I**, 661
    rice flour pudding (Ghana), v. **II**, 114-15
    salad, with banana (Kenya), v. **II**, 127
    salad, with brown rice and fried tomato (Bolivia), v. **II**, 516
    slow cooker lentils and (Egypt), v. **II**, 79-80
    soup, with coconut and beans (Nigeria), v. **II**, 203-204
    soup, with eggs and lemon (Albania), v. **I**, 6
    soup, with meatballs and lentils (Cyprus), v. **I**, 467-68
    soup, with walnuts (Azerbaijan), v. **I**, 605
    soup, with yogurt (Azerbaijan), v. **I**, 605-606
    spicy rice with tomatoes (Djibouti), v. **II**, 75-76
    sticky, and banana sweet (Cambodia), v. **II**, 321
    sweet, deep-fried clusters (Nigeria), v. **II**, 207
    sweet egg sponge cakes (Guatemala), v. **II**, 569-70
    sweet rice balls (Vietnam), v. **II**, 444
    sweet rice cakes (Cameroon), v. **II**, 38-39
    sweet rice flour balls (Sierra Leone), v. **II**, 229
    sweet saffron rice (Tibet), v. **II**, 349
    tagine, with Swiss chard (Morocco), v. **II**, 175
    tomato soup (Austria) v. **I**, 23-24
    vegetable stew with soymeat (Serbia), v. **I**, 367-68
    walnut rice cream (Spain), v. **I**, 397
    with braised vegetables in olive oil (Saudi Arabia), v. **I**, 556
    with butter (Sudan), v. **II**, 255-56
    with coconut milk (Indonesia), v. **II**, 352
    with onions and egg and lemon sauce (Macedonia), v. **I**, 266
    with potatoes (Uganda), v. **II**, 286
    with tomatoes (Caribbean), v. **II**, 498-99
    with tomatoes and coconut milk (Sierra Leone), v. **II**, 228-29
    with tomatoes and coconut milk (Mozambique), v. **II**, 182-83
    with tomatoes and hearts of palm (Costa Rica), v. **II**, 544-45
    with vegetables (Bhutan), v. **I**, 661-62
rice, powdered, v. **I**, 397 (note)
roasted red peppers, preparation, v. **I**, 165, 497, 552-53
ROMANIA, v. **I**, 339-48

rosemary, information, v. **II**, 194 (note)
rosemary powder, v. **I**, 283 (note)
RUSSIA, v. **I**, 349-61
rutabaga
    and potato casserole (Finland), v. **I**, 125-26
    oven-roasted root vegetables with fresh herbs and mushrooms (Namibia), v. **II**, 193-94
    vegetable soup with barley (Estonia), v. **I**, 112-13

Sage, information, v. **I**, 29 (note); v. **II**, 194 (note)
sage leaves, fried (Italy), v. **I**, 225
salad burnet, information, v. **II**, 512 (note)
salads, dressings
    apricot-raspberry (Native America), v. **II**, 654
    black sesame dressing (Brunei), v. **II**, 308
    blender mayonnaise, v. **II**, 675-76
    Bruneian tamarind dressing (Brunei), v. **II**, 308-309
    celery seed, v. **I**, 436
    Central African peanut-lime dressing (Central African Republics), v. **II**, 48-49
    citrus dressing (Caribbean), v. **II**, 494-95
    citrus dressing (Senegal), v. **II**, 219
    citrus *vinaigrette* (Côte d'Ivorie), v. **II**, 66
    classic French, v. **II**, 676-77
    creamy Italian, v. **II**, 677
    curried island dressing (Pacific Islands – Vanuatu), v. **II**, 474
    curried mayonnaise (Pacific Islands - Saipan), v. **II**, 475
    garlic-mayonnaise (Moldova), v. **I**, 285
    garlic mayonnaise (Spain), v. **I** 392-93
    garlic *vinaigrette* (Luxembourg), v. **I**, 255
    Greek oregano *vinaigrette* (Greece), v. **I**. 162
    herb dressing (Mongolia), v. **II**, 401-402
    honey-pineapple *vinaigrette* (Burundi), v. **II**, 27
    kiwifruit *vinaigrette* with honey (New Zealand), v. **II**, 465
    lemon-peach (Mozambique), v. **II**, 181-82
    lemon *vinaigrette* Dijon, v. **II**, 678
    lime mayonnaise with hot peppers and ginger (Côte d'Ivorie), v. **II**, 63
    lime *vinaigrette* (Caribbean), v. **II**, 496
    lime *vinaigrette* with cumin (Pacific Islands), v. **II**, 474-75
    nam jim (Thailand), v. **II**, 433-34
    onion salad dressing (Vietnam), v. **II**, 440
    onion *vinaigrette* (Mongolia), v. **II**, 401
    peanut butter (Indonesia), v. **II**, 354-55
    peanut butter (West Africa), v. **II**, 221
    pepper *vinaigrette* (Eritrea), v. **II**, 87
    pomegranate *vinaigrette* (Israel), v. **I**, 479
    prickly pear *vinaigrette* with *agave* nectar (Native America), v. **II**, 654-55
    raspberry *vinaigrette* (Australia), v. **II**, 452
    sesame dressing (Korea), v. **II**, 374
    sour cream (Czech), v. **I**, 93
    sour cream-dill (Lithuania), v. **I**, 247
    summer fruit dressing (Argentina), v. **II**, 511
    sweet *cilantro* dressing (Cambodia), v. **II**, 318
    tamarind dressing (Laos), v. **II**, 385
    tomato-black bean vinaigrette (Somalia), v. **II**, 234

index

salads, fruit
  and vegetable salad (Indonesia), v. II, 354
  apple and cheese (Switzerland), v. I, 410
  apple with onion and *feta* (Greece), v. I, 163
  avocado and egg (Israel), v. I, 498
  avocado and grapefruit salad (Somalia),
     v. II, 234-35
  avocado and mayonnaise (Ghana), v. II, 110
  avocado halves stuffed with tomato salad (New
     Zealand), v. II, 463
  avocado halves with spicy dressing (Guinea),
     v. II, 118
  avocado, mango, and orange (Senegal), v. II, 219
  avocado, peach, and tomato (Mozambique),
     v. II, 181
  baby banana with peanuts (The Philippines),
     v. II, 420-21
  banana and mango (The Gambia), v. II, 102
  banana and rice (Kenya), v. II, 127
  beet and apple with sour cream (Lithuania),
     v. I, 247
  beetroot and apple (Uruguay), v. II, 624
  blood oranges with fennel, *pecorino*, and
     pomegranate (Italy), v. I, 215
  cabbage and green mango salad (Myanmar/
     Burma), v. II, 412
  celery and apple (Slovakia), v. I, 375
  curried yam and banana with hard-cooked eggs
     (Pacific Islands - Saipan), v. II, 475
  egg and avocado (Colombia), v. II, 537
  fruit platter with lime *vinaigrette* (Caribbean),
     v. II, 496
  fruit salad (Central African Republics), v. II, 53
  fruit salad (Uganda), v. II, 283-84
  fruit salad with citrus *vinaigrette* (Côte d'Ivorie),
     v. II, 66
  fruit salad with tamarind dressing (Brunei),
     v. II, 308-309
  hearts of palm, *jicama*, and papaya salad with lime
     vinaigrette (Pacific Islands), v. II, 474-75
  green banana and vegetable (Costa Rica),
     v. II, 542-43
  kohlrabi and papaya with tamarind dressing (Laos),
     v. II, 385
  layered fruit salad (Cameroon), v. II, 34-35
  lemon and red onion in lettuce rolls (Myanmar/
     Burma), v. II, 413
  mango (Madagascar), v. II, 149-50
  mango salad with vegetables (Pakistan), v. I, 691
  mango with mango-lime dressing (Bhutan), v. I, 658
  mango, pineapple, and apricot (Niger), v. II, 198
  melon and peach with fresh *mozzarella* (New
     Zealand), v. II, 463-64
  melon, tomato, and olive (Greece), v. I, 163-64
  mixed fruit salad with *chaat masala* (India),
     v. I, 670
  nasturtium blossoms stuffed with avocado (Native
     America), v. II, 655
  orange and date (Morocco), v. II, 174
  orange and tomato (Kenya), v. II, 125-26
  orange with *calamarata* (Somalia), v. II, 235
  papaya and corn with citrus *vinaigrette* (Togo),
     v. II, 268
  papaya and tomato (Caribbean – Puerto Rico),
     v. II, 495-96
  papaya, avocado, and grapefruit (Kenya), v. II, 126
  papaya with curried island dressing (Pacific Islands
     – Vanuatu), v. II, 474
  peach, cantaloupe, and blueberry with almond syrup
     and *moscato* wine sauce (Macedonia), v. I, 264
  pineapple and avocado (Central African Republics),
     v. II, 47
  pomegranate *vinaigrette* (Iran), v. I, 479
  pomelo (Cambodia), v. II, 317
  prickly pear salad (Israel), v. I, 497
  purple rice and mango (Thailand), v. II, 432-33
  red grapefruit with soymeat and soy sprouts
     (Thailand), v. II, 433-34
  ruby pear salad with lingonberries (Sweden),
     v. I, 401
  St. John's Day fruit salad (Venezuela), v. II, 630-31
  tossed with blueberries and hazelnuts (England),
     v. I, 436
  tropical fruit salad (Nigeria), v. II, 202
  watermelon and cucumber with *hoisin*-lime dressing
     (Vietnam), v. II, 439
  watermelon and *feta* (South Africa), v. II, 244
  watermelon, tomato and *feta* (Egypt), v. II, 79
  wilted lettuce with strawberries and smoked
     Gouda cheese (Germany), v. I, 147
salads, vegetable
  and fruit salad (Indonesia), v. II, 354
  Argentine-styled Russian salad, v. II, 508-509
  artichoke hearts with preserved lemons and honey
     (Morocco), v. II, 173
  artichoke with leeks and carrots (Turkey), v. I, 570
  asparagus with capers (Romania), v. I, 343
  baby pepper (Bosnia), v. I, 61-62
  bean (Caribbean – Haiti), v. II, 497
  bean salad with corn and mango (Burundi), v. II, 27
  beans and corn (Liechtenstein), v. I, 239
  beans with walnuts (Georgia), v. I, 615-16
  beet and apple with sour cream (Lithuania), v. I, 247
  beet and cheese (Austria), v. I, 26
  beet and garlic (Greece), v. I, 162-63
  beet and *tahini* with eggs (Syria), v. I, 564
  beet, potato, and carrot salad (Peru), v. II, 613-14
  beetroot and apple (Uruguay), v. II, 624
  beetroot with eggs (Belarus), v. I, 35-36
  beet with *feta* cheese (Serbia), v. I, 366-67
  beet with garlic-mayonnaise dressing (Moldova),
     v. I, 285
  beet with yogurt and mint (Iran), v. I, 478
  Boston lettuce and onion with sour cream dressing
     (Czech), v. I, 93
  bread and vegetable (Kuwait), v. I, 515-16
  bread, with spinach, rice, chick peas, and garlic-
     yogurt sauce with *tahini* (Tunisia), v. II, 274-75
  broccoli and potato, with Hollandaise sauce (Brazil),
     v. II, 521
  bulgur wheat (Jordan), v. I, 504-505
  butter bean (Malta), v. I, 275

salads, vegetable (cont'd)
   cabbage and carrot slaw with onion and apple
     (Ukraine), v. **I**, 426
   cabbage and carrot slaw with peanuts (Pakistan),
     v. **I**, 690-91
   cabbage and carrot with yogurt dressing (Western
     Sahara), v. **II**, 163
   cabbage and green mango salad (Myanmar/ Burma),
     v. **II**, 412
   cabbage pickle, *kimchi* (Korea), v. **II**, 376-77
   cabbage slaw (Slovenia), v. **I**, 389
   cabbage slaw of the *vuelta e 'Lola* (Venezuela),
     v. **II**, 631
   cabbage slaw with corn and fresh dillweed
     (Angola), v. **II**, 12-13
   cabbage slaw with pineapple (Cameroon),
     v. **II**, 34
   cabbage with avocado and pickled red onion
     relish (Ecuador), v. **II**, 551
   cabbage with pineapple (Liberia), v. **II**, 133-34
   cabbage with shredded carrot (Cyprus), v. **I**, 468
   carrot slaw (Kazakhstan), v. **I**, 627
   cauliflower and garlic pickle (Iran), v. **I**, 482-83
   celeriac (Hungary), v. **I**, 179
   celeriac appetizer (Moldova), v. **I**, 282-83
   and apple salad (Slovakia), v. **I**, 375
   celery and apple salad (Slovakia), v. **I**, 375
   celery and cabbage slaw with sour cream
     (Canada), v. **II**, 641-42
   celery, celeriac, and radish (Germany), v. **I**, 143
   chayote and pepper slaw (Panama), v. **II**, 598
   chick pea (Libya), v. **II**, 142
   Christmas red cabbage slaw (Iceland), v. **I**, 188
   corn and cheese (Peru), v. **II**, 613
   couscous with chick peas (Algeria), v. **II**, 4-5
   couscous with chick peas and tomatoes
     (Mauritania), v. **II**, 162-63
   couscous with roasted eggplant and red pepper
     (Morocco), v. **II**, 171-72
   couscous with tomato-black bean *vinaigrette*
     (Somalia), v. **II**, 234
   cucumber (Slovakia), v. **I**, 375-76
   cucumber and olive (Azerbaijan), v. **I**, 602-603
   cucumber and red onion (Nepal), v. **I**, 682
   cucumber and shallot (Laos), v. **II**, 392-93
   cucumber and tomato with *chaat masala*, (India),
     v. **I**, 669
   cucumber and yogurt (India), v. **I**, 671
   cucumber with cheese (Bhutan), v. **I**, 657-58
   cucumber with dill and garlic mayonnaise (Ukraine),
     v. **I**. 425
   cucumber, with peanut-lime dressing (Central
     African Republics), v. **II**, 48-49
   cucumber with pomegranate *vinaigrette* (Iran),
     v. **I**, 479
   cucumber with yogurt (Sudan), v. **II**, 253
   curried *pasta* (Botswana), v. **II**, 19
   curried yam and banana with hard-cooked eggs
     (Pacific Islands – Saipan), v. **II**, 475
   deviled beet, potato, apple, and egg (Estonia),
     v. **I**, 111-12

   edamame with string cheese and chive oil
     (Armenia), v. **I**, 591-92
   egg and potato (Côte d'Ivorie), v. **II**, 65
   eggplant (China), v. **II**, 327-28
   eggplant and tomato (Yemen), v. **I**, 579-80
   eggplant and tomato with goat cheese (São Tomé
     and Principe), v. **II**, 210-11
   eggplant, with herb dressing (Mongolia),
     v. **II**, 401-402
   fennel with lemon and cheese (Angola), v. **II**, 12
   fried pepper, onion, and tomato with garlic sauce
     (Moldova), v. **I**, 285-86
   fried tomatoes and onions with brown rice
     (Bolivia), v. **II**, 516
   glass noodle and vegetable slaw (Tibet), v. **II**, 341
   grated carrot (Madagascar), v. **II**, 147
   green banana and vegetable (Costa Rica),
     v. **II**, 542-43
   green bean and garlic (Slovenia), v. **I**, 387
   greens *vinaigrette* (Senegal), v. **II**, 218-19
   grilled vegetable salad (Kuwait), v. **I**, 516
   hearts of palm (The Philippines), v. **II**, 421
   hearts of palm, *jicama*, and papaya salad with
     lime *vinaigrette* (Pacific Islands), v. **II**, 474-75
   hearts of palm with cheese (Ecuador),
     v. **II**, 550-51
   hot asparagus, with raspberry *vinaigrette*
     (Australia), v. **II**, 451
   hot potato (Germany), v. **I**, 146
   Israeli *couscous* and chick pea with cucumber,
     cherries, and dates (Israel), v. **I**, 496
   jicama and carrot with mango (Colombia),
     v. **II**, 538-39
   kidney beans with eggs (Slovenia), v. **I**, 388-89
   Kirby cucumber (Korea), v. **II**, 377-78
   kohlrabi and papaya with tamarind dressing (Laos),
     v. **II**, 385
   layered vegetable salad (Ghana), v. **II**, 111-12
   lentil and *pasta* salad with nasturtium (Australia),
     v. **II**, 457
   lentil and spinach (Libya), v. **II**, 141
   lettuce with potatoes and bacon (Burundi), v. **II**, 26
   macaroni (Denmark), v. **I**, 107-108
   macaroni (Madagascar), v. **II**, 147
   macaroni with *pesto* and *chouriço* (Uganda),
     v. **II**, 284-85
   marinated dried mushrooms with herbs (Romania),
     v. **I**, 346-47
   mesclún with shaved macadamia nuts (Australia),
     v. **II**, 451
   millet and corn salad with avocado (Central African
     Republics), v. **II**, 47-48
   mixed greens with sugar and lemon (Denmark),
     v. **I**, 101
   Moscow salad (Russia), v. **I**, 351
   mozzarella, tomato, and basil (Venezuela), v. **II**, 632
   millet *tabbouleh* (Lebanon), v. **I**, 526-27
   mushroom (Finland), v. **I**, 124
   mushroom and chick pea (Somalia), v. **II**, 233
   niçoise (France), v. **I**, 136
   onion salad (Czech), v. **I**, 94
   onion salad with coconut milk (Sri Lanka), v. **I**, 703

salads, vegetable (cont'd)
    parsley with *tahini* (Palestine), v. I, 548-49
    pasta and vegetable salad with peanut butter
        dressing (Senegal), v. II, 221
    pepper (Hungary), v. I, 182
    pink potato salad (Panama), v. II, 598-99
    potato (Albania), v. I, 7-8
    potato (Germany), v. I, 145-46
    potato (Madagascar), v. II, 148
    potato and chick pea (Armenia), v. I, 591
    potato with dandelions (Slovenia), v. I, 387-88
    potato and egg with *feta* cheese (Tunisia),
        v. II, 273
    potato with mayonnaise (Turkmenistan),
        v. I, 627-28
    prickly pear with apricot-raspberry dressing
        (Mexico), v. II, 581
    purslane and tomato (Native America), v. II, 656-57
    radish and egg (Tunisia), v. II, 274
    radish and garlic relish/salad (Myanmar/Burma),
        v. II, 413-14
    radish with mint (Guatemala), v. II, 568
    radish with sour cream (Poland), v. I, 324
    red cabbage and black currant slaw (Finland),
        v. I, 125
    red onion (Uzbekistan), v. I, 625-26
    rice noodle and spring onion (China), v. II, 326-27
    roasted eggplant with onion dressing (Vietnam),
        v. II, 440
    roasted frying peppers (Croatia), v. I, 83
    roasted sweetpotato with macadamia nuts (New
        Zealand), v. II, 464
    roasted tomato and roasted pepper (Tunisia),
        v. II, 272-73
    rolled noodle and spring onion (China), v. II, 326-27
    sesame noodle with corn (Mongolia), v. II, 400-401
    shredded beetroot (Romania), v. I, 344
    shredded onion and vegetable (Denmark), v. I, 101
    spinach and beet with yogurt dressing (Georgia),
        v. I, 618-19
    spinach and yogurt (Kuwait), v. I, 512-13
    spinach, warm with mushrooms and garlic
        (Andorra) v. I, 15-16
    steamed eggplant and scallion (Korea), v. II, 375-76
    steamed vegetable salad with sweet black sesame
        dressing (Brunei), v. II, 308
    sweet and sour bean (Zimbabwe), v. II, 299-300
    sweet and sour cucumber (Japan), v. II, 363-64
    sweetpotato, *jicama*, and mango in citrus dressing
        (Caribbean), v. II, 494-95
    three-bean salad with creamy dressing (Mongolia),
        v. II, 402
    toasted millet (Mali), v. II, 155-56
    tofu "tuna"-stuffed cucumber boats (Côte d'Ivoire),
        v. II, 66-67
    tomato and coriander (Yemen), v. I, 579
    tomato and cucumber with grated cheese
        (Montenegro), v. I, 295
    tomato and cucumber with peppers (Hungary),
        v. I, 178-79
    tomato and green onion salad (Zambia), v. II, 293
    tomato and onion (Syria), v. I, 562-63
    tomato and onion (Tanzania), v. II, 262
    tomato and onion *sambol* (Sri Lanka), v. I, 700
    tomato and pepper appetizer salad (Israel), v. I, 495
    tomato and shredded *Halloumi* (Cyprus), v. I, 469
    tomato, onion, and pea (Portugal), v. I, 332-33
    tomato, to stuff avocado halves (New Zealand),
        v. II, 463
    tomato, with basil (The Gambia), v. II, 100-101
    tomato, with garlic and cheese (Belarus), v. I, 35
    tossed (Azerbaijan), v. I, 606
    tossed vegetables with cheese (Sudan), v. II, 252-53
    tossed, with noodles and onion *vinaigrette*
        (Mongolia), v. II, 401
    vegetable (Albania), v. I, 7
    vegetable (Madagascar), v. II, 148
    vegetable bread soup (Spain), v. I, 393-94
    vegetable *mélange* (Malta), v. I, 275-76
    vegetable relish (Tanzania), v. II, 262-63
    vegetable slaw (El Salvador), v. II, 560-61
    vegetable, with hearts of palm (Brazil), v. II, 525
    vegetable, with white beans, root celery, kohlrabi,
        and potatoes (Czech), v. I, 96
    village tossed salad (Greece), v. I, 161-62
    warm leek celeriac and carrot (Norway), v. I, 310-11
    watercress with sesame dressing (Korea), v. II, 374
    white eggplant and red kidney bean (Ethiopia),
        v. II, 93
    whole carrots with mayonnaise-mustard sauce with
        capers (Belgium), v. I, 47
    wilted cucumber with honey (Belarus), v. I, 34
    wilted dandelion (Andorra), v. I, 16-17
    yam with scallions (Chad), v. II, 56
    zucchini *vinaigrette* (Israel), v. I, 499
sandwiches
    breaded eggplant and cheese (Armenia), v. I, 594-95
    pan-fried Cheddar (England), v. I, 440
    pan-fried cheese (Switzerland), v. I, 417
    open-faced onion sandwich with eggplant spread
        (Lebanon), v. I, 523 (note)
    open-faced with mushrooms (Switzerland),
        v. I, 408-409
    quesadillas, squash and cheese (Mexico), v. II, 580
    smørbrød, open-faced (Denmark), v. I, 106-107
    vegetables and sausage (Andorra), v. I, 20-21
    vegetarian reubens (Pacific Islands – Cook
        Islands), v. II, 478-79
    Welsh rabbit (rarebit) (Wales), v. I, 457-58
SÃO TOMÉ AND PRINCIPE, v. II, 209-14
sauces, savory, including **marinades**
    allioli, with eggs (Andorra), v. I, 19
    blender Hollandaise, v. II, 522
    brown garlic (China), v. II, 331
    brown onion (Norway), v. I, 315
    brown sauce (China), v. II, 332-33
    caper and olive, v. I, 85-86
    celery, for sautéed leeks and carrots (Scotland),
        v. I, 453
    cheese and *chili* sauce (Tibet), v. II, 347
    cheese, for vegetables (Norway), v. I, 314
    chili and garlic sauce (Malaysia), v. II, 396
    chili and ginger (Australia), v. II, 456-57

sauces, savory (cont'd)
   chili and tomato (Bolivia), v. II, 518
   citrus shallot (Pacific Islands – Polynesia), v. II, 481-82
   cold watercress (Belgium), v. I, 46-47
   coriander sauce (Afghanistan), v. I, 641
   cranberry with mustard (Lithuania), v. I, 248
   cream and mustard (Ireland), v. I, 200-201
   creamed sorrel (Ireland), v. I, 194-95
   cream, with roasted shallots and thyme (Australia), v. II, 456
   creamy cocktail (Iceland), v. I, 188
   egg and lemon (Macedonia), v. I, 267
   garlic (Moldova/Romania), v. I, 286
   garlic and parsley (Nicaragua), v. II, 592
   garlic-walnut (Macedonia), v. I, 263
   garlic-yogurt (Iran), v. I, 476-77
   ginger and sesame (China), v. II, 330
   gravy, "without the 'Sunday Roast,'" v. II, 124-25
   Greek marinade, v. I, 166
   hoisin barbecue (Mongolia), v. II, 404-405
   horseradish and sour cream, uncooked (Ukraine), v. I, 424-25
   hunter's style (Italy), v. II, 684-85
   lime marinade for *tofu* (Caribbean – Cuba), v. II, 498
   marinara sauce (Italy), v. II, 682
   mayonnaise-mustard with capers (Belgium), v. I, 47
   mushroom (Norway), v. I, 313-14
   mustard-sour cream (Bosnia-Herzegovina), v. I, 60
   paprika cream (Hungary), v. I, 177-78
   parsley (Ireland), v. I, 196
   peanut butter and tomato, with garlic (The Gambia), v. II, 104
   pesto (Italy), v. I, 223-24
   pesto, with macadamia nuts (New Zealand), v. II, 462
   pine nut, with *tahini* (Lebanon), v. I, 531-32
   plum (Laos), v. II, 383-84
   polonaise (Poland), v. I, 321
   remoulade with cornichons and capers (Switzerland), v. I, 411
   savory forest honey with herbs (Cyprus), v. I, 474
   sour cream and onion (Latvia), v. I, 234
   sour cream with horseradish (Belarus), v. I, 40
   sour cream with horseradish (Ukraine), v. I, 424-25
   sweet and sour glaze (Japan), v. II, 361
   sweet sesame marinade (Korea), v. II, 372
   sweet soy sauce (Brunei), v. II, 310
   tahini (Jordan), v. I, 508
   tart cherry sauce for beets (Georgia), v. I, 617-18
   tomato and cabbage (Russia), v. I, 352 (note)
   tomato and cream (Uruguay), v. II, 622-23
   tomato and onion, for meatballs (Costa Rica), v. II, 543
   tomato and peanut (Zambia), v. II, 294
   tomato and peanut, with cream (Brazil), v. II, 527-28
   tomato-coriander (Laos), v. II, 384
   tomato mushroom (Italy), v. II, 686
   tomato, with potatoes, garlic, and coriander (Somalia), v. II, 236
   vegan Worcestershire-style, v. II, 683-84
   walnut and garlic (Georgia), v. I, 612-13
   with ginger and peanut butter (Togo), v. II, 268-69
   yogurt and garlic (Georgia), v. I, 612-13
   yogurt condiment with fresh coriander, garlic, and *chilies* (Tibet), v. II, 346-47
   yogurt-dill (Bulgaria), v. I, 75-76
   yogurt-garlic (Azerbaijan), v. I, 608
   yogurt-mint (Armenia), v. I, 595-96
   yogurt sauce for chick pea dumplings (India), v. I, 667-68
   yogurt-sour cream (Russia), v. I, 354

sauces, sweet
   apple syrup (The Netherlands), v. I, 306
   basic chocolate syrup, v. II, 638
   blackberry sauce or dessert (Australia), v. II, 687
   blueberry (Lithuania), v. I, 250
   cinnamon-orange syrup (Korea), v. II, 379
   cinnamon syrup, v. II, 687
   citrus and honey (Scotland), v. I, 454-55
   cranberry (Estonia), v. I, 116-17
   cranberry and black walnut (Native America), v. II, 672
   creamy cinnamon (The Netherlands), v. I, 307
   custard sauce, v. II, 688
   English cream (Scotland), v. I, 451
   ersatz "maple syrup" (Native America), v. II, 662
   fig (Italy), v. I, 208-209
   fresh orange custard sauce, v. II, 689
   honey-lemon syrup (Bosnia), v. I, 68
   lemon sauce, v. II, 689-90
   lemon syrup, v. II, 690
   lemon verbena syrup, v. II, 690-91
   mango-yogurt (Oman), v. I, 537
   mocha-cinnamon (Mexico), v. II, 587
   pancake and waffle syrup, v. II, 688
   rose water syrup (Brunei), v. II, 312-13
   rum cream (Scotland), v. I, 454
   sour cream (Hungary), v. I, 184
   sour cream and honey (Kenya), v. II, 130
   sour cream for pears (Serbia), v. I, 369-70
   sweet coffee *coulis* (Caribbean), v. II, 503
   sweet ginger syrup (Australia), v. II, 459
   toasted hazelnut-rum hard sauce (Denmark), v. I, 109
   toffee (England), v. I, 444

SAUDI ARABIA, v. I, 551-60
sauerkraut, *see* cabbage
sausages, *glamorgan* (Wales), v. I, 460
SCOTLAND, see **UNITED KINGDOM, SCOTLAND**
seasoned salt (Caribbean – St. Croix), v. II, 497

seasoning mixtures
   Bengali five-seed spice mixture (Bangladesh), v. I, 652
   Chinese spicing mixture, v. II, 327
   curry powder, homemade (Cambodia), v. II, 320
   East African seasoning mixture (Djibouti), v. II, 73-74

seasoning mixtures (cont'd)
    Egyptian ground legume and spice mixture (Egypt), v. II, 78
    Ethiopian / Eritrean seasoning mixture, v. II, 86
    French country herb (*herbes de Provence*) (France), v. I, 136-37
    garam masala (India), v. I, 678-79
    garlic powder, homemade, v. II, 327 (note)
    Georgian herbed seasoning mixture (Georgia), v. I, 615
    Greek seasoning mix (Greece), v. I, 161
    hot pepper seasoning (Madagascar), v. II, 151-52
    Indian mango powder (India), v. I, 667
    Latin American spice mix (Chile), v. II, 533
    Kuwaiti spice mixture (Kuwait), v. I, 517-18
    Mediterranean dry marinade for vegetables (Lebanon), v. I, 529
    Nepali curry mixture (Nepal), v. I, 684
    Nigerian seasoning mixture (Nigeria), v. II, 205
    North African sumac seasoning mixture (Lebanon), v. I, 524
    paprika (Hungary), v. I, 186
    Persian spice mixture for *koresh* (Iran), v. I, 481
    rose petal spice mix (Tunisia), v. II, 280
    seasoned oil and butter for Lebanese cooking (Lebanon), v. I, 528
    seasoning mixture for dehydrated meat analogue, v. II, 698
    sesame salt (Japan), v. II, 366
    South African curry powder (South Africa), v. II, 245-46
    Sri Lankan curry powder (Sri Lankan), v. I, 705
    tandoori spice mixture, *chaat masala* (India), v. I, 679
    Tunisian coriander seasoning (Tunisia), v. II, 280
    Vietnamese spicing mixture (Vietnam), v. II, 442
    Yemeni fenugreek seasoning paste (Yemen), v. I, 577-78
    Yemeni seasoning mixture (Yemen), v. I, 581-82
SENEGAL, v. II, 215-24
SERBIA, v. I, 362-70
shallots
    and avocado in tomato soup (Australia), v. II, 449-50
    and cucumber salad (Malaysia), v. II, 392-93
    citrus-shallot sauce for baked *tofu* (Pacific Islands – Polynesia), v. II, 481-82
    curried vegetables with *tofu* (Cambodia), v. II, 319
    dried mushroom condiment (Myanmar/Burma), v. II, 410
    fried potatoes with yogurt and *chilies* (Malaysia), v. II, 393
    fried rice with garlic (The Philippines), v. II, 423
    lime marinade for *tofu* (Caribbean – Cuba), v. II, 498
    mushroom and chick pea salad (Somalia), v. II, 233
    oven-roasted root vegetables with fresh herbs and mushrooms (Namibia), v. II, 193-94
    roasted, in cream sauce (Australia), v. II, 456
    salad burnet and shallot vinegar with pepper, v. II, 511-12
    sauce for spicy eggplant (Brunei), v. II, 311-12
    tomato-coriander sauce (Laos), v. II, 384
    wild rice casserole with mushrooms and baby carrots (Canada), v. II, 642-43
    with roasted mushrooms (Ireland), v. I, 201
SIERRA LEONE, v. II, 225-29
SLOVAKIA, v. I, 371-80
SLOVENIA, v. I, 381-90
slow cooker
    baked acorn squash with chutney (Indonesia), v. II, 356 (note)
    basic slow cooker bean preparation, v. II, 43-44
    bean stew with hominy and *chouriço* (Cape Verde), v. II, 42-43
    black-eyed pea *chili* (Uganda), v. II, 287-88
    braised onions with cheese (Portugal), v. I, 335
    dried fruit curry (South Africa), v. II, 247-48
    lentils and rice (Egypt), v. II, 79-80
    lentil soup with potatoes and spinach (Palestine), v. I, 546
    mixed legume soup (Morocco), v. II, 172-73
    polenta (Montenegro), v. I, 296-97
    puréed carrot and *kumara* soup with gingerroot (New Zealand), v. II, 465-66
    spicy, slow-cooked chick peas (Pakistan), v. I, 692-93
    vegetable soup with beans and barley (Croatia), v. I, 87-88
    vegetable stew (Botswana), v. II, 19-20
soba buckwheat noodles, *see* noodles
SOMALIA, v. II, 230-41
sorrel
    sauce (Ireland), v. I, 194-95
    soup, with potatoes (Russia), v. I, 352-53
soups
    barley and vegetables with sour cream (Poland), v. I, 322-23
    bean and celery with bananas (Burundi), v. II, 27-28
    beancurd and Chinese chive bud (Vietnam), v. II, 438-39
    bean with pinched dumplings (Hungary), v. I, 176-77
    bean with pinched dumplings with vegetarian franks (Hungary), v. I, 177 (note)
    "beef" with noodles (Paraguay), v. II, 606
    beet (Ukraine), v. I, 426-27
    beet and mushroom (Poland), v. I, 323-24
    black bean (The Netherlands), v. I, 300-301
    black-eyed pea and tomato (Liberia), v. II, 133
    black lentil (Nepal), v. I, 681-82
    bread-cheese (Italy), v. I, 210-11
    broth with preserved lemons, snowpeas, and *shiitake* mushrooms (Cambodia), v. II, 316-17
    brown stock, v. II, 692-93
    butternut squash with soymeat (Israel), v. I, 495
    cabbage (Russia), v. I, 352
    cabbage with clear *cilantro* stock (The Philippines), v. II, 419-20
    cantaloupe (Pacific Islands – Polynesia), v. II, 477
    cauliflower and noodle (Indonesia), v. II, 353
    celeriac and apple (Australia), v. II, 450
    celeriac and leek (Croatia), v. I, 84-85
    cheese (The Netherlands), v. I, 301-302

index

soups (cont'd)
    cheesy cornbread (Paraguay), v. II, 607
    chick pea and kale soup with peanut butter and tomatoes (Djibouti), v. II, 74
    chick pea and rice (Mongolia), v. II, 402-403
    chick pea and tomato with leeks (Uruguay), v. II, 623
    chick pea, with rice (Peru), v. II, 612-13
    chick pea with roasted red peppers and garlic (Greece), v. I, 165-66
    chili bean, v. I, 283-84
    chilled avocado with garlic (Côte d'Ivoire), v. II, 64
    chilled banana (Tanzania), v. II, 261-62
    chilled barley with sour cream (Latvia), v. I, 233
    chilled *borsch* (Belarus), v. I, 37
    chilled cucumber and mango soup (Saudi Arabia), v. I, 554
    chilled cucumber and yogurt (Bulgaria), v. I, 74-75
    chowder of vegetables and fine noodles (Montenegro), v. I, 294-95
    clear *cilantro* stock with garlic (The Philippines), v. II, 420
    clear vegetable stock (Thailand), v. II, 431
    clear, with *soba* noodles and vegetables (Japan), v. II, 361-62
    coconut-bean soup with rice (Nigeria), v. II, 203-204
    corn (Kuwait), v. I, 514
    corn and sweetpotato (Thailand), v. II, 430-31
    corn chowder (Native America), v. II, 657-58
    creamed corn with egg whites (China), v. II, 328
    creamed tomato with yogurt (Afghanistan), v. I, 639
    cream of artichoke hearts (Brazil), v. II, 524
    cream of asparagus (Germany), v. I, 143-44
    cream of carrot and celeriac (Finland), v. I, 123-24
    cream of celery root soup (Czech), v. I, 91-92
    cream of celery with Stilton (England), v. I, 435
    cream of cheddar cheese (Canada), v. II, 640-41
    cream of chick pea (Guatemala), v. II, 566-67
    cream of corn and basil with tomato (Chile), v. II, 532
    cream of endive (Belgium), v. I, 48
    cream of hearts of palm (Pacific Islands), v. II, 478
    cream of mushroom (Germany), v. I, 144-45
    cream of peanut butter (Mexico), v. II, 582
    cream of potato with corn (Colombia), v. II, 538
    cream of spinach and potato (New Zealand), v. II, 466-67
    cream of summer squash with noodles (Lithuania), v. I, 246
    cream of sweetpotato (Côte d'Ivoire), v. II, 64-65
    cream of white asparagus (Belgium), v. I, 48-49
    creamy baked sweetpotato (Caribbean), v. II, 493
    creamy, puréed, vegetable soup (Venezuela), v. II, 632-33
    curried coconut-bean, with brown basmati rice (Tanzania), v. II, 260-61
    curried corn chowder (South Africa), v. II, 245
    dark vegetable stock (Thailand), v. II, 431-32
    dumpling (Korea), v. II, 371-72
    egg and lemon (Greece), v. I, 164-65
    garlic (Portugal), v. I, 331-32
    greens with corn and peanut butter (Chad), v. II, 55
    groundnut and vegetable soup (Djibouti), v. II, 72-73
    hot yogurt with rice and chick peas (Iran), v. I, 477-78
    leek and potato (Luxembourg), v. I, 254-55
    lentil (Macedonia), v. I, 263-64
    lentil *consommé* (Liechtenstein), v. I, 239
    lentil, puréed with potatoes (Kuwait), v. I, 513
    lentil with vegetables (Burundi), v. II, 28-29
    lettuce (Wales), v. I, 459
    mango and onion (Guinea), v. II, 117-18
    meatball with rice and lentils (Cyprus), v. I, 467-68
    melon and fresh mint (Oman), v. I, 537
    Milanese *minestrone* (Italy), v. I, 222-23
    milk with corn (Botswana), v. II, 18
    mixed legume (Morocco), v. II, 172-73
    mushroom (Czech), v. I, 92-93
    mushroom with roasted millet (Belarus), v. I, 36-37
    noodle (Eritrea), v. II, 86-87
    noodle and mushroom with vegetables (Brunei), v. II, 307
    noodle with kidney beans (Central Asia), v. I, 625
    onion, with cheese (Serbia), v. I, 365-66
    papaya and garlic (Caribbean), v. II, 492-93
    plantain and corn (Cameroon), v. II, 35
    potato and celeriac chowder (Switzerland), v. I, 409-10
    potato and cheese (Ecuador), v. II, 552-53
    potato and meatball (Latvia), v. I, 232-33
    potato and mushroom (Austria), v. I, 24-25
    potato and tomato soup (Native America), v. II, 657
    potato and watercress with herbs (Wales), v. I, 458-59
    potato milk (Bosnia), v. I, 61
    potato with cheese (Sweden), v. I, 400
    pumpkin (Malta), v. I, 274-75
    pumpkin with coconut milk and banana (Caribbean – Bahamas), v. II, 494
    pumpkin with pomegranate seeds (Azerbaijan), v. I, 604
    puréed banana, *yuca*, and coconut (Honduras), v. II, 573-74
    puréed carrot and *kumara* with gingerroot (New Zealand), v. II, 465-66
    puréed celeriac and leek (Croatia), v. I, 84-85
    puréed corn, with sweet red peppers (Mexico), v. II, 582-83
    puréed cream of chick pea and celeriac (Turkey), v. I, 569
    puréed cream of corn and basil soup with tomato (Chile), v. II, 532
    puréed *dhal* (Pacific Islands - Fiji), v. II, 476
    puréed lentil soup (Somalia), v. II, 232-33
    puréed potato and sweetpotato (Nigeria), v. II, 203
    puréed root vegetable (Saudi Arabia), v. I, 555
    red lentil (Libya), v. II, 140-41
    red lentil and bulgur (Turkey), v. I, 568-69
    red lentil and bulgur with apricots (Armenia), v. I, 589-90
    red lentil and red onion (Ireland), v. I, 199
    rice noodle and meatball soup (Laos), v. II, 386

index

soups (cont'd)
- red pottage (Scotland), v. I, 449
- rice with yogurt (Azerbaijan), v. I, 605-606
- roasted potato (Tibet), v. II, 339
- savory apple (Andorra), v. I, 17
- sea broth, v. II, 411
- sea broth with glass noodles (Myanmar/Burma), v. II, 411
- slow cooker lentil, with potatoes and spinach (Palestine), v. I, 546
- slow cooker vegetable with beans and barley (Croatia), v. I, 87-88
- sorrel-potato (Russia), v. I, 352-53
- sour green bean and potato (Slovakia), v. I, 373-74
- spicy bean soup with coconut milk (Djibouti), v. II, 72
- spinach and rice (Lebanon), v. I, 526
- spinach, with leeks and dill (Iraq), v. I, 488
- squash *bisque* (Native America), v. II, 658-59
- tomato (India), v. I, 668-69
- tomato and groundnut (Ghana), v. II, 111
- tomato and spinach with bulgur wheat and mint (Armenia), v. I, 590-91
- tomato and squash (Algeria), v. II, 5
- tomato bouillon with chick peas (Mauritania/Western Sahara), v. II, 164
- tomato with avocado and shallots (Australia), v. II, 449-50
- tomato with basil (The Gambia), v. II, 100-101
- tomato with brown rice (Austria), v. I, 23-24
- tomato with green peas (Palestine), v. I, 545-46
- tomato with walnuts and *vermicelli* (Georgia), v. I, 614
- *tukpa* vegetarian broth with soba noodles and *bok choy* (Tibet), v. II, 340-41
- vegetable and groundnut soup (Zambia), v. II, 292-93
- vegetable bread soup (Spain), v. I, 393-94
- vegetable stock from soup, v. II, 691-92
- vegetable stocks for soups, stews and sauces, v. II, 692-93
- vegetable *tukpa* broth (Tibet), v. II, 339-40
- vegetable, with barley (Estonia), v. I, 112-13
- vegetable, with cabbage (Albania), v. I, 5-6
- vegetable, with caraway (Romania), v. I, 342-43
- vegetable, with chick peas and groundnut butter (Namibia), v. II, 192
- vegetable, with *couscous* and chick peas (Angola), v. II, 11-12
- vegetable, with fine noodles (Malta), v. I, 274
- vegetable with oatmeal or barley (Oman), v. I, 538
- vegetable with peanut butter, sweetpotato, and greens (Zimbabwe), v. II, 300
- vegetable, with sour cream (Moldova), v. I, 284
- vegetarian stock from *kombu* (Japan), v. II, 363
- vegetarian *tukpa* broth (Tibet), v. II, 339-40
- vegetarian vegetable (Ecuador), v. II, 553
- walnut and rice (Azerbaijan), v. I, 605
- watercress and potato (Ireland), v. I, 198
- white stock, v. II, 692-93
- wild mushroom stock, v. II, 694
- winter squash and peanuts (Senegal), v. II, 216-17
- winter squash and vegetable (Paraguay), v. II, 605-606
- winter squash with garlic (Mozambique), v. II, 180-81
- yellow pea (Sweden), v. I, 399-400
- yellow split pea with meatballs (Azerbaijan), v. I, 603-604
- yogurt and bread (Yemen), v. I, 578-79
- yogurt with rice (Georgia), v. I, 613-14
- *yucca* (Guatemala), v. II, 567

SOUTH AFRICA, v. II, 242-49

soybean sprouts
- dumpling soup (Korea), v. II, 371-72
- fruit and vegetable salad (Indonesia), v. II, 354
- red grapefruit salad with soymeat and (Thailand), v. II, 433-34

soy meat analogue products, bacon
- beans and tomatoes with plantains (Colombia), v. II, 539
- bean stew with hominy and *chouriço* (Cape Verde), v. II, 42-43
- corn and sweetpotato soup (Thailand), v. II, 430-31
- fried greens with bacon (Native America), v. II, 656
- Irish stew, v. I, 199-200
- mushroom soup (Czech), v. I, 92-93
- slow cooker vegetable soup with beans and barley (Croatia), v. I, 87-88
- smoky lentils with vegetables (Panama), v. II, 599-600
- with potatoes in lettuce salad (Burundi), v. II, 26-27

soy meat analogue products, *chorizo* sausage (*chouriço*)
- bean stew with hominy and *chouriço* (Cape Verde), v. II, 42-43
- savory bread with vegetables and sausage (Andorra), v. I, 20-21
- skillet, with angel hair and mushrooms (Spain), v. I, 395
- with *pesto* in macaroni salad (Uganda), v. II, 284-85

soy meat analogue products, ground
- "beef" soup with noodles (Paraguay), v. II, 606
- fried meat (Guatemala), v. II, 572
- macaroni and meat casserole (Greece), v. I, 167-68
- meat pies (Botswana), v. II, 21
- noodles with soymeat and yogurt-garlic sauce (Azerbaijan), v. I, 608
- skillet *lasagne* (Italy), v. I, 217
- twice-baked potatoes (Palestine), v. I, 547
- vegetable stew (Uzbekistan), v. I, 628-29
- with *chimichuri* and herb seasoning over *pasta* (Argentina), v. II, 509-10
- with *linguine*, chick peas, and red kidney beans (Afghanistan), v. I, 640

soy meat analogue products, meatballs
- and caramelized onions (Slovenia), v. I, 385-86
- and fruit in curry sauce (Mozambique), v. II, 183-84
- and green beans in yogurt sauce (Bosnia), v. I, 63
- and vegetable pastry bundles (Mongolia), v. II, 405
- and rice noodle soup (Laos), v. II, 386
- and vegetables skillet (Niger), v. II, 198-99
- in *tahini* sauce with potatoes (Jordan), v. I, 508

index

soy meat analogue products, meatballs (cont'd)
    potato-meatball soup (Latvia), v. **I**, 232-33
    soup with rice and lentils (Cyprus), v. **I**, 467-68
    with garlic and yogurt curds (Albania) v. **I**, 8
    tomatoes, wheat berries, and yogurt (Armenia), v. **I**, 588-89
    with sweet and sour glaze (Japan), v. **II**, 361
    with tomato and onion sauce (Costa Rica), v. **II**, 543
    yellow split pea soup (Azerbaijan), v. **I**, 603-604

soy meat analogue products, sausages, breakfast links
    in sweet wine sauce (Slovenia), v. **I**, 384-85
    kidney bean salad with eggs (Slovenia), v. **I**, 388-89
    with curried beans (Madagascar), v. **II**, 149 with lemon (Greece), v. **I**, 157
    with sweet browned cabbage (Denmark), v. **I**, 102

soy meat analogue products, strips, nuggets, or **tempeh**
    and banana stew (Liberia), v. **II**, 134-35
    and melon skillet (Yemen), v. **I**, 581
    "chicken" stew (Gabon), v. **II**, 49
    broth with preserved lemons, snowpeas, and *shiitake* mushrooms (Brunei), v. **II**, 316-17
    butternut squash with soymeat (Israel), v. **I**, 495
    "chicken" stew with tomato and garlic (Sierra Leone), v. **II**, 227-28
    curried, with onions and coconut milk (Myanmar/Burma), v. **II**, 414
    deviled beet, potato, apple, and egg salad (Estonia), v. **I**, 111-12
    goulash (Hungary), v. **I**, 177-78
    grapefruit salad with soymeat and soy sprouts (Thailand), v. **II**, 433-34
    Irish stew, v. **I**, 199-200
    mushroom stew (Bhutan), v. **I**, 660
    pan-grilled soymeat brochettes (Cameroon), v. **II**, 32-33
    puréed butternut squash soup (Israel), v. **I**, 495-96
    sautéed with spices and peaches (Iran), v. **I**, 480-81
    skewered with peppers (Mali), v. **II**, 157
    vegetable *ragoût* (Lebanon), v. **I**, 527-28
    vegetable stew with beer (Belgium), v. **I**, 49-50
    vegetable stew with brown rice (Serbia), v. **I**, 367-68
    with coconut milk (Sri Lanka), v. **I**, 705
    with onions (El Salvador), v. **II**, 561-62

SPAIN, v. **I**, 391-97
spicebush, information, v. **II**, 667 (note)
spiced sugar, v. **II**, 505

spinach
    and beet salad with yogurt dressing (Georgia), v. **I**, 618-19
    and lentil salad (Libya), v. **II**, 141
    and potato cream soup (New Zealand), v. **II**, 466-67
    and potato pie (New Zealand), v. **II**, 468
    and rice soup (Lebanon), v. **I**, 526
    and spicy potatoes (Pakistan), v. **I**, 692
    and tomato soup with bulgur wheat and mint (Armenia), v. **I**, 590-91
    and tomatoes with *orzo* (Oman), v. **I**, 538-39
    and yogurt salad (Kuwait), v. **I**, 512-13
    avocado and mayonnaise salad (Ghana), v. **II**, 110
    bread salad, with rice, chick peas, and garlic-yogurt sauce with *tahini* (Tunisia), v. **II**, 274-75
    cheese and peppers in spinach sauce (India), v. **I**, 674-75
    dumpling soup (Korea), v. **II**, 371-72
    fried with chick peas and grated cheese (Egypt), v. **II**, 81
    garnish for stir-fried cauliflower and straw mushrooms (Vietnam), v. **II**, 441-42
    gratin with cauliflower and fennel (Switzerland), v. **I**, 411-12
    greens and vegetables (Caribbean – Virgin Islands), v. **II**, 502
    Israeli *couscous* and chick pea salad (Israel), v. **I**, 496-97
    macaroni salad (Denmark), v. **I**, 107-108
    noodle and mushroom soup with vegetables (Brunei), v. **II**, 307
    omelet with herbs (Azerbaijan), v. **I**, 606-607
    pie (Albania), v. **I**, 9-10
    ravioli with spinach and sage butter (Italy), v. **I**, 224
    rice noodle and meatball soup (Laos), v. **II**, 386
    salad, warm with mushrooms and garlic (Andorra), v. **I**, 15-16
    sesame (Korea), v. **II**, 373-74
    skewered with peppers (Mali), v. **II**, 157
    slow cooker lentil soup (Palestine), v. **I**, 546
    soup, with leeks and dill (Iraq), v. **I**, 488
    stew with peanut butter (Central African Republics), v. **II**, 51
    stir-fried, with *tofu* and mushrooms (Tibet), v. **II**, 341-42
    tossed salad with blueberries and hazelnuts (England), v. **I**, 436
    vegetables in curried coconut milk (Thailand), v. **II**, 434-35
    with black-eyed peas and leeks in skillet (Iran), v. **I**, 479-80
    with gingerroot and *chilies* in coconut milk (The Philippines), v. **II**, 422-23
    with sautéed noodles (Czech), v. **I**, 96-97
    wonton appetizers (China), v. **II**, 323-24

squashes, summer
    and cheese *quesadillas* (Mexico), v. **II**, 580
    and tomato stew (Slovenia), v. **II**, 383-84
    and tomatoes with pumpkin seeds (Nicaragua), v. **II**, 591-92
    baby zucchini with *feta* and roasted red peppers (Armenia), v. **I**, 587-88
    cheese-stuffed zucchini with lentils and fruit (Mexico), v. **II**, 583-84
    chick pea soup with rice (Peru), v. **II**, 612-13
    chowder of vegetables and fine noodles (Montenegro), v. **I**, 294-95
    cream soup with noodles (Lithuania), v. **I**, 246
    custard casserole (Saudi Arabia), v. **I**, 557
    green squash with warm *vinaigrette* (Kenya), v. **II**, 129
    in vegetable soup with *couscous* and chick peas (Angola), v. **II**, 11-12

squashes, summer (cont'd)
    kebabs (Greece), v. I, 166
    meatball and vegetable pastry bundles (Mongolia),
        v. II, 405
    Milanese *minestrone* (Italy), v. I, 222-23
    omelet on omelet (Chile), v. II, 531
    quinoa and vegetable stew (Peru), v. II, 615
    ratatouille, vegetable stew (France), v. I, 134-35
    ratatouille with puff pastry pillows (France),
        v. I, 135-36
    salad, with *couscous* and roasted eggplant and red
        pepper (Morocco), v. II, 171-72
    sautéed, with peanuts (Chad), v. II, 57-58
    summer squash with *crème* (Hungary), v. I, 181
    vegetable *kebabs* with lemon (Kuwait),
        v. I, 518-19
    vegetarian vegetable soup (Ecuador), v. II, 553
    with peanuts and garlic (Central African
        Republics), v. II, 49-50
    zucchini and rice in tomato sauce (Madagascar),
        v. II, 150-51
    zucchini *vinaigrette* (Israel), v. I, 499
    zucchini with vegetable stuffing (Turkey), v. I, 571
squashes, winter
    acorn, baked with chutney (Indonesia), v. II, 356
    acorn, baked with honey and hazelnut butter
        (Native America), v. II, 666-67
    acorn, baked with tomato stuffing (Norway),
        v. I, 311-12
    and tomato soup (Algeria), v. II, 5
    bean stew with hominy and *chouriço* (Cape Verde),
        v. II, 42-43
    butternut squash soup with soymeat (Israel),
        v. I, 495-96
    dark vegetable stock (Thailand), v. II, 431-32
    lentil soup (Macedonia), v. I, 263-64
    pumpkin pie in *phyllo* roll (Serbia), v. I, 370
    rice and cheese-stuffed acorn squashes (Bosnia),
        v. I, 64-65
    roasted, with corn and eggs (Chile), v. II, 532-33
    slow cooker vegetable stew (Botswana),
        v. II, 19-20
    squash *bisque* (Native America), v. II, 658-59
    squash or pumpkin dessert in sweet syrup with
        walnuts (Turkey), v. I, 573-74
    stir-fried with red pepper and scallions (Australia),
        v. II, 448-49
    sweet soy-glazed pumpkin or squash (Korea),
        v. II, 373
    vegetable pasties (New Zealand), v. II, 467
    vegetable soup with fine noodles (Malta),
        v. I, 274
    vegetable stew (Bolivia), v. II, 515-16
    winter squash and peanut soup (Senegal),
        v. II, 216-17
    winter squash and vegetable soup (Paraguay),
        v. II, 605-606
    winter squash in sweet vegetable stock (Japan),
        v. II, 362-63
    winter squash soup with garlic (Mozambique),
        v. II, 180-81
    with greens (Botswana), v. II, 22

strawberries
    and blueberry summer pudding, v. I, 445-46
    fresh fruit refresher (Mexico), v. II, 587-88
    fruit compote with vanilla (Madagascar), v. II, 152
    pears with ice cream and fresh strawberry sauce
        (Andorra), v. I, 21
    salsa, with melon and black pepper (Native
        America), v. II, 669-70
    strawberry-rhubarb juice (Finland), v. I, 121-22
    tart (Slovakia), v. I, 380
    whipped cranberry-raspberry with farina and
    wilted lettuce salad with smoked *Gouda* cheese
        (Germany), v. I, 147
    Yorkshire summer pudding (England), v. I, 444-45
SRI LANKA, v. I, 698-707
SUDAN, v. II, 250-58
SWEDEN, v. I, 398-404
sweetpotatoes and yams
    and black bean appetizers (Caribbean), v. II, 491
    and coconut pudding (Sri Lanka), v. I, 707
    and corn soup (Thailand), v. II, 430-31
    and snowpea stir-fry (Bangladesh), v. I, 650-51
    and tomato stew (Côte d'Ivoire), v. II, 67
    and vegetables (Caribbean – Virgin Islands),
        v. II, 502
    Argentine-styled Russian salad, v. II, 508-509
    bean stew with hominy and *chouriço* (Cape Verde),
        v. II, 42-43
    biscuits (Zimbabwe), v. II, 301
    broth with preserved lemons, snowpeas, and
        shiitake mushrooms (Brunei), v. II, 316-17
    caramelized with mandarin oranges (Pacific Islands
        – Hawaii), v. II, 479
    chick pea and tomato soup with leeks (Uruguay),
        v. II, 623
    cream of sweetpotato soup (Côte d'Ivoire),
        v. II, 64-65
    creamy soup (Caribbean), v. II, 493
    croquettes (Senegal), v. II, 221-22
    dessert fritters (Peru), v. II, 618-19
    fried (Guinea), v. II, 121
    fried, with onions (Ghana), v. II, 114
    fufu, with plantain (Cameroon), v. II, 37
    fufu, with white potato and corn (Cameroon),
        v. II, 36-37
    greens and vegetables (Caribbean – Virgin Islands),
        v. II, 502
    lentil soup with vegetables (Burundi), v. II, 28-29
    mashed, with pineapple (Nicaragua), v. II, 593
    omelet (São Tomé and Principe), v. II, 211-12
    pudding (Pacific Islands – Palua), v. II, 485
    pudding, with coconut (Zambia), v. II, 296
    puréed carrot and *kumara* (sweetpotato) soup with
        gingerroot (New Zealand), v. II, 465-66
    puréed, soup, with potato (Nigeria), v. II, 203
    roasted, salad, with macadamia nuts (New Zealand),
        v. II, 464
    salad. curried, with banana and hard-cooked egg
        (Pacific Islands – Saipan), v. II, 475
    salad, with *jicama* and mango in citrus dressing
        (Caribbean), v. II, 494-95
    salad, with scallions (Chad), v. II, 56

sweetpotatoes and yams (cont'd)
    soufflé (Mali), v. II, 156-57
    spicy with coconut milk (Sri Lanka), v. I, 704
    stir-fry with snowpeas (Bangladesh), v. I, 650-51
    tagine, with carrots and onion (Western Sahara),
        v. II, 165-66
    tapioca pudding with (Laos), v. II, 389-90
    vegetable soup with *couscous* and chick peas
        (Angola), v. II, 11-12
    with gingerroot (Vietnam), v. II, 441
    with greens and peanut butter in vegetable soup
        (Zimbabwe), v. II, 300
Swiss chard, *tagine*, with rice (Morocco), v. II, 175
SWITZERLAND, v. I, 405-21
SYRIA, v. I, 561-64

TAJIKISTAN (Central Asia), v. I, 622-34
tamarind liquid (Cambodia), v. II, 316
tangerine, dessert, with avocado (Mozambique),
    v. II, 185-86
TANZANIA, v. II, 259-66
tarragon, information, v. I, 408 (note)
tart crust and *streusel* topping (Germany), v. I, 152-53
tarts, *see* pies
THAILAND, v. II, 428-36
TIBET, v. II, 337-49
tofu **(soy beancurd)**
    and Chinese chive bud soup (Vietnam), v. II, 438-39
    and mushrooms with Chinese brown sauce (China),
        v. II, 332-33
    baked with citrus-shallot sauce (Pacific Islands –
        Polynesia), v. II, 481-82
    broiled, with sweet Korean sesame marinade
        (Korea), v. II, 372
    broiled, with two *miso* sauces (Japan), v. II, 365-66
    deep-fried, with *chili* and garlic sauce (Malaysia),
        v. II, 396
    deep-fried, with Chinese ginger and sesame sauce
        (China), v. II, 330
    fried *tofu* with dipping sauce (Brunei),
        v. II, 306-307
    mashed with garlic (Bangladesh), v. I, 649
    stir-fried (Nepal), v. I, 685
    tea-smoked with ginger (Mongolia), v. II, 403-404
    tofu "tuna"-stuffed cucumber boats (Côte d'Ivorie),
        v. II, 66-67
    with chive buds in spicy sauce (Malaysia), v. II, 395
    with curried vegetables (Cambodia), v. II, 319
    with stir-fried spinach and mushrooms (Tibet),
        v. II, 341-42
TOGO, v. II, 267-69
tomatoes
    and avocado dip (Zambia), v. II, 292
    and avocado dipping sauce (Venezuela), v. II, 630
    and beans with plantains (Colombia), v. II, 539
    and black-eyed pea soup (Liberia), v. II, 133
    and chick pea soup with leeks (Uruguay), v. II, 623
    and *chili* sauce for spicy eggplant (Brunei),
        v. II, 311-12
    and coriander salad (Yemen), v. I, 579
    and coriander sauce (Laos), v. II, 384
    and cream sauce (Uruguay), v. II, 622-23
    and cucumber salad with *chaat masala* (India),
        v. I, 669
    and cucumber salad with grated cheese
        (Montenegro), v. I, 295
    and cucumber salad with peppers (Hungary),
        v. I, 178-79
    and eggplant (Central African Republics),
        v. II, 50-51
    and eggplant casserole (Slovakia), v. I, 377
    and eggplant salad (Yemen), v. I, 579-80
    and garlic in mung bean sauce (Uganda),
        v. II, 285-86
    and garlic sauce for black beans (The Gambia),
        v. II, 103
    and green onion salad (Zambia), v. II, 293
    and groundnut soup (Ghana), v. II, 111
    and hearts of palm in rice casserole (Costa Rica),
        v. II, 544-45
    and lima beans (Peru), v. II, 616
    and mashed plantains (Caribbean – Dominican
        Republic), v. II, 499
    and mushroom sauce (Italy), v. II, 686
    and okra stew (Mali), v. II, 158
    and onion salad (Syria), v. I, 562-63
    and onion salad (Tanzania), v. II, 262
    and onion *sambol* (Sri Lanka), v. I, 700
    and onion sauce for fried plantains (Guinea),
        v. II, 120
    and onion sauce for meatballs (Costa Rica),
        v. II, 543
    and orange salad (Kenya), v. II, 125-26
    and papaya salad (Caribbean – Puerto Rico),
        v. II, 495-96
    and peanut butter sauce with garlic (The Gambia),
        v. II, 104
    and peanut sauce (Zambia), v. II, 294
    and peanut sauce with cream (Brazil), v. II, 527-28
    and potato soup (Native America), v. II, 657
    and purslane salad (Native America), v. II, 656-57
    and red pepper appetizer salad (Israel), v. I, 495
    and rice (Caribbean), v. II, 498-99
    and rice with coconut milk (Sierra Leone),
        v. II, 228-29
    and sautéed cabbage, carrot, and onion
        (Mozambique), v. II, 185
    and squash soup (Algeria), v. II, 5
    and squash stew (Slovenia), v. I, 383-84
    and spinach with bulgur wheat and meat (Armenia),
        v. I, 590-91
    and spinach with *orzo* (Oman), v. I, 538-39
    and summer squash with pumpkin seeds
        (Nicaragua), v. II, 591-92
    and sweetpotato stew (Côte d'Ivorie), v. II, 67
    and wheat berries, meatballs, and yogurt (Armenia),
        v. I, 588-89
    baby potatoes in spicy sauce (Oman), v. I, 539-40
    baked (Palestine), v. I, 549
    baked fennel (Jordan), v. I, 508-509
    baked spaghetti with two sauces (Somalia),
        v. II, 236-37
    baked with rice and eggs (Malta), v. I, 278
    bean and hominy *chili* (Somalia), v. II, 238

tomatoes (cont'd)
- bean stew with hominy and *chouriço* (Cape Verde), v. II, 42-43
- "beef" soup with noodles (Paraguay), v. II, 606
- bouillon with chick peas (Mauritania/Western Sahara), v. II, 164
- bread and vegetable salad (Kuwait), v. I, 515-16
- broccoli and potato salad with Hollandaise sauce (Brazil), v. II, 521
- butternut squash soup with soymeat (Israel), v. I, 495-96
- cabbage salad with pineapple (Liberia), v. II, 133-34
- cabbage slaw with pineapple (Cameroon), v. II, 34
- cabbage soup (Russia), v. I, 352
- caper and olive sauce (Croatia), v. I, 85-86
- cauliflower in spicy sauce (Pakistan), v. I, 695
- cheese and *chili* dip (Native America), v. II, 653
- cheese-stuffed appetizers (Moldova), v. I, 282
- cheese with peas (India). v. I, 675
- "chicken" stew with garlic and (Sierra Leone), v. II, 227-28
- chick pea and kale soup with peanut butter (Djibouti), v. II, 74
- chick pea and potato stew (Tunisia), v. II, 275-76
- *chili*, v. II, 288
- *chili* and ginger sauce (Australia), v. II, 156-57
- *chilies* and cheese (Bhutan), v. I, 659-60
- *chili* sauce (Bolivia), v. II, 518
- coconut-bean soup with rice (Nigeria), v. II, 203-204
- condiment (Madagascar), v. II, 151
- corn soup (Kuwait), v. I, 514
- *couscous* salad with chick peas and tomatoes (Mauritania), v. II, 162-63
- creamed tomato soup with yogurt (Afghanistan), v. I, 639
- cream of corn and basil soup (Chile), v. II, 532
- curried coconut-bean soup with basmati rice (Tanzania), v. II, 260-61
- curried sauce, with eggs and peas (Tibet), v. II, 342-43
- curried, with onions and eggs (Bangladesh), v. I, 649-50
- dark vegetable stock (Thailand), v. II, 431-32
- dipping sauce (The Gambia), v. II, 100
- dried mushrooms in tomato sauce (Zambia), v. II, 294-95
- eggplant and tomato salad (Yemen), v. I, 579-80
- eggplant curry (Sri Lanka), v. I, 700-701
- eggplant *tagine* (Libya), v. II, 142-43
- fenugreek and vegetable appetizer dip (Yemen), v. I, 578
- fried, with onions and brown rice (Bolivia), v. II, 516
- *gari* with eggs (Ghana), v. II, 113
- grape tomato, salad with green bananas and vegetables (Costa Rica), v. II, 542-43
- green tomato relish (Somalia), v. II, 238-39
- groundnut and vegetable soup (Djibouti), v. II, 72-73
- hearts of palm salad with cheese (Ecuador), v. II, 550-51
- hunter's style sauce for vegetables and *pasta* (Italy), v. II, 684-85
- jam (Mozambique), v. II, 180
- *kebabs* (Greece), v. I, 166
- *kebabs*, with *Halloumi* cheese (Cyprus), v. I, 471-72
- ketchup, homemade, v. II, 683
- layered fruit salad (Cameroon), v. II, 34-35
- layered vegetable salad (Ghana), v. II, 111-12
- macaroni and vegetables (The Gambia), v. II, 104-105
- macaroni in spicy sauce with mushrooms (Iraq), v. I, 489
- *marinara* sauce (Italy), v. II, 682
- meatballs and vegetables skillet (Niger), v. II, 198-99
- millet and corn salad with avocado (Central African Republics), v. II, 47-48
- millet *tabbouleh* (Lebanon), v. I, 526-27
- mixed legume soup (Morocco), v. II, 172-73
- omelet (Cyprus), v. I, 467
- oven-dried, v. II, 217-18
- pancakes with vegetables (Mauritania), v. II, 161-62
- papaya and corn salad with citrus *vinaigrette* (Togo), v. II, 268
- potatoes and cabbage in tomato sauce (Bangladesh), v. I, 648
- pumpkin appetizer dip (Libya), v. II, 139
- puréed lentil soup (Somalia), v. II, 232-33
- puréed potato and sweetpotato soup (Nigeria), v. II, 203
- *quinoa* and vegetable stew (Peru), v. II, 615
- red lentil and bulgur soup with apricots (Armenia), v. I, 589-90
- red lentil soup (Libya), v. II, 140-41
- red pottage (Scotland), v. I, 449
- rice and coconut milk (Mozambique), v. II, 182-83
- rice with potatoes (Uganda), v. II, 286
- roasted eggplant (India), v. I, 672-73
- roasted eggplant pie in *phyllo* crust, v. I, 506-507
- roasted, with roasted pepper salad (Tunisia), v. II, 272-73
- salad, grape tomato, with *mozzarella* and basil (Venezuela), v. II, 632
- salad stuffing for avocado halves (New Zealand), v. II, 463
- salad, with avocados and peaches (Mozambique), v. II, 181
- salad, with eggplant and goat cheese (São Tomé and Principe), v. II, 210-11
- salad, with garlic and cheese (Belarus), v. I, 35
- salad, with onions and peas (Portugal), v. I, 332-33
- salad, with shredded *Halloumi* (Cyprus), v. I, 469
- salad, with watermelon and *feta* (Egypt), v. II, 79
- sauce for breaded and deep-fried okra (Cyprus), v. I, 472
- sauce for zucchini and rice (Madagascar), v. II, 150-51
- sauce, with potatoes, garlic, and coriander (Somalia), v. II, 236
- scrambled eggs with vegetables (Venezuela), v. II, 633

tomatoes (cont'd)
    slow cooker black-eyed pea *chili* (Uganda), v. II, 287-88
    soup (India), v. I, 668-69
    soup, with avocado and shallots (Australia), v. II, 449-50
    soup, with basil (The Gambia), v. II, 100-101
    soup, with green peas (Palestine), v. I, 545-46
    soup, with walnuts and *vermicelli* (Georgia), v. I, 614
    spicy bean soup with coconut milk (Djibouti), v. II, 72
    spicy rice (Djibouti), v. II, 75-76 spicy sauce with ginger and peanut butter (Togo), v. II, 268-69
    spinach stew with peanut butter (Central African Republics), v. II, 51
    stewed tomatoes (Jordan), v. I, 506
    stew with bananas and soymeat (Liberia), v. II, 134-35
    stew with potatoes and onions (Sudan), v. II, 254
    summer vegetable stew (Tunisia), v. II, 276-77
    tagliatelle with chick peas (Cyprus), v. I, 471
    toasted millet salad (Mali), v. II, 155-56
    tortilla skillet (Honduras), v. II, 574-75
    tossed vegetable salad (Azerbaijan), v. I, 606
    tossed vegetable salad with cheese (Sudan), v. II, 252-53
    twice-baked potatoes (Palestine), v. I, 547
    vegetable and groundnut soup (Zambia), v. II, 292-93
    vegetable bread soup (Spain), v. I, 393-94
    vegetable relish (Tanzania), v. II, 262-63
    vegetable salad (Macedonia), v. I, 265
    vegetable soup with *couscous* and chick peas (Angola), v. II, 11-12
    vegetable soup with oatmeal or barley (Oman), v. I, 538
    vegetable soup with peanut butter, sweetpotato, and greens (Zimbabwe), v. II, 300
    vegetable stew (Bolivia), v. II, 515-16
    vegetable stew (Uzbekistan), v. I, 628-29
    vegetable stew with beans and *chouriço* sausage (Angola), v. II, 13-14
    vegetable stew with brown rice and soymeat (Serbia), v. I, 367-68
    vegetarian *tukpa* broth (Tibet), v. II, 339-40
    village tossed salad (Greece), v. I, 161-62
    with angel hair *pasta*, mushrooms, and *chorizo* in skillet (Spain), v. I, 395
    with artichokes and onions (Armenia), v. I, 593-94
    with cabbage (Venezuela), v. II, 634
    with chick peas and apricots (Yemen), v. I, 580-81
    with fried cabbage (Moldova), v. I, 288
    with lentils and garlic (Eritrea), v. II, 88
    with lima beans and eggs (Mexico), v. II, 585
    with *vermicelli* and rice (Kuwait), v. I, 517
    zucchini with vegetable stuffing (Turkey), v. I, 571
    yucca soup (Guatemala), v. II, 567
trahana with yogurt and *Gorgonzola* (Cyprus), v. I, 470
TUNISIA, v. II, 270-80
TURKEY, v. I, 565-75

TURKMENISTAN (Central Asia), v. I, 622-34
turnips, Canadian/rutabaga, *see* rutabaga
turnips, French
    cheese soup (The Netherlands), v. I, 301-302
    oven-roasted root vegetables with cheese (Sweden), v. I, 402-403
    puréed root vegetable soup (Saudi Arabia), v. I, 555
    slow cooker vegetable stew (Botswana), v. II, 19-20
    vegetable stew (Uzbekistan), v. I, 628-29

UGANDA, v. II, 281-89
UKRAINE, v. I, 422-31
UNITED KINGDOM, ENGLAND, v. I, 432-47
UNTED KINGDOM, SCOTLAND, v. I, 448-55
UNITED KINGDOM, WALES, v. I, 456-62
URUGUAY, v. II, 621-27
UZBEKISTAN (Central Asia), v. I, 622-34

Vanilla extract, homemade, v. II, 426
vanilla sugar (Belgium), v. I, 54
vanilla yogurt, v. I, 573 (note)
vegetables, frozen mixed, puréed vegetable soup with sour cream (Moldova), v. I, 284
VENEZUELA, v. II, 628-38
VIETNAM, v. II, 437-44
Vietnamese mint, information, v. II, 385 (note)
vinegars
    Canadian celery vinegar
        recipe, v. II, 642;
        applications, v. I, 311; v. II, 641
    Danish spiced vinegar
        recipe, v. II, 677-78;
        application, v. I, 310-11
    garlic – basil vinegar
        recipe, v. II, 678;
        applications, v. I, 7-8, 71, 83, 143, 162-63, 346-47, 373-74, 387, 389, 515-16, 591; v. II, 171-72, 210-11, 457, 499, 502, 537, 550-51, 598, 630-31
    lovage-chive vinegar
        recipe, v. I, 240;
        applications, v. I, 143, 239
    mixed flower vinegar with oregano
        recipe, v. II, 679;
        applications, v. I, 136, 162-63, 499, 518-19; v. II, 463-64
    oregano flower vinegar
        recipe, v. I, 265-66;
        applications, v. I, 161-62, 265; v. II, 598
    pear-anise hyssop vinegar
        recipe, v. II, 679-80;
        application, v. II, 463-64
    pineapple vinegar, v. II, 573
    pineapple vinegar, fermented (Honduras), v. II, 573
    raspberry vinegar
        recipe, v. II, 452;
        applications, v. II, 452, 454-55, 463-64, 465, 581, 654, 654-55, 675
    rosemary vinegar
        recipe, v. II, 680;
        application, v. I, 591

vinegars (cont'd)
    sage vinegar
        recipe, v. I, 28-29;
        applications, v. I, 28, 387-88, 388-89
    salad burnet and shallot vinegar with pepper
        recipe, v. II, 511-12;
        application, v. II, 511
    spicy nasturtium flower vinegar
        recipe, v. I, 240;
        applications, v. I, 239
    sweet and tart cranberry vinegar
        recipe, v. II, 681;
        applications, v. I, 188; v. II, 465
    sweet spiced orange vinegar
        recipe, v. II, 680-81;
        applications, v. II, 465

Waffles, v. I, 304
waffles (Belgium), v. I, 56-57
WALES, see **UNITED KINGDOM, WALES**
walnuts, honey-sweetened (Georgia), v. I, 620
watermelon
    and cucumber salad with *hoisin*-lime dressing (Vietnam), v. II, 439
    fresh fruit refresher (Mexico), v. II, 587-88
    punch (Turkmenistan), v. I, 634
    salad, with *feta* (South Africa), v. II, 244
    salad, with tomato and *feta* (Egypt), v. II, 79
watercress
    and potato soup (Ireland), v. I, 198
    and potato soup with herbs (Wales), v. I, 458-59
    broiled *tofu* with two *miso* sauces (Japan), v. II, 365-66
    cold sauce (Belgium), v. I, 46-47
    omelet (Luxembourg), v. I, 253-54
    roasted eggplant salad with onion dressing (Vietnam), v. II, 440
    salad, with sesame dressing (Korea), v. II, 374
WESTERN SAHARA, v. II, 160-68

wheat berries
    Christmas porridge (Armenia), v. I, 598-99
    with tomatoes and meatballs with yogurt (Armenia), v. I, 588-89
whey, buttermilk cornbread, v. I, 368
whey, information, v. I, 232 (note)
wild rice
    and mushroom casserole (Native America), v. II, 663
    casserole with mushrooms and baby carrots (Canada), v. II, 642-43
    pilaf with fruits and nuts (Azerbaijan), v. I, 609
winter savory, information, v. II, 194 (note)
Worcestershire-style sauce, v. II, 683-84

Yams, *see* sweetpotatoes
YEMEN, v. I, 576-82
yogurt, v. I, 572-73
yogurt *crème*, v. I, 654
    English cream (Scotland), v. I, 451
    herbed appetizer (Israel), v. I, 493
    sweet yogurt dessert (Bangladesh), v. I, 653
    with sweet oatmeal topping (Wales), v. I, 461-62
    yogurt sweet ("curds and treacle") (Sri Lanka), v. I, 707
    yogurt with green *chilies* (Palestine), v. I, 545
yogurt marinade (Afghanistan), v. I, 640-41
yuca (*yucca*) root, *see* cassava

ZAMBIA, v. II, 290-97
ZIMBABWE, v. II, 298-302

about the author

Born in Rochester New York, at the beginning of World War II, Mrs. Spinzia has seen a dramatic change in the eating habits of Americans extending from the days of rationing to the days of fast foods. Her travels have exposed her to the world beyond our shores and her journals have preserved her observations. From Rochester her family moved to Long Island where she did her undergraduate and graduate work, married, and taught biology at Adelphi University. It was at this point that the Spinzias chose to become vegetarians and the journals expanded to recipe research. After their daughter was grown, the Spinzias began to teach courses on Long Island history. They write and speak, jointly and separately, on a variety of Long Island-related subjects including the North Shore and South Shore estates, Louis Comfort Tiffany and the stained-glass windows of Tiffany Studios, the Vanderbilts of Long Island, Long Island's maritime heritage, women of Long Island, and Long Island's socialite spies. Together they have published seven books and numerous articles on Long Island-related subjects. Articles and sample pages from their books can be be found at the Spinzias' website, spinzialongislandestates.com.

Judith Spinzia now resides in central Pennsylvania with her husband of over fifty years and frequent co-author. They share their beautiful flower and herb gardens with three cats.